THE UNIVERSITY OF WINCHESTER

Martial Rose Library
Tel: 01962 827306

SEVEN DAY LOAN ITEM

To be returned on or before the day marked above, subject to recall.

The Routledge Companion to Accounting Education

Many enquiries into the state of accounting education/training, undertaken in several countries over the past 40 years, have warned that it must change if it is to be made more relevant to students, to the accounting profession, and to stakeholders in the wider community.

This book's over-riding aim is to provide a comprehensive and authoritative source of reference which defines the domain of accounting education/training, and which provides a critical overview of the state of this domain (including emerging and cutting edge issues) as a foundation for facilitating improved accounting education/training scholarship and research in order to enhance the educational base of accounting practice.

The Routledge Companion to Accounting Education highlights the key drivers of change – whether in the field of practice on the one hand (e.g. increased regulation, globalisation, risk, and complexity), or from developments in the academy on the other (e.g. pressures to embed technology within the classroom, and to meet accreditation criteria).

Thirty chapters, written by leading scholars from around the world, are grouped into seven themed sections which focus on different facets of their respective themes – including student, curriculum, pedagogic, and assessment considerations.

Richard M. S. Wilson is Professor of Business Administration & Financial Management (Emeritus) at Loughborough University, U.K. For more than 40 years he has actively engaged in accounting education/training policy-making in both domestic and international contexts. He is the founding editor of *Accounting Education: an international journal*, a member of the BAFA's Hall of Fame, an Academician of the Academy of Social Sciences, and holds a Lifetime Achievement Award specifically for his sustained contribution to accounting education/training.

ROUTLEDGE COMPANIONS IN BUSINESS, MANAGEMENT AND ACCOUNTING

Routledge Companions in Business, Management and Accounting are prestige reference works providing an overview of a whole subject area or sub-discipline. These books survey the state of the discipline including emerging and cutting edge areas. Providing a comprehensive, up to date, definitive work of reference, Routledge Companions can be cited as an authoritative source on the subject.

A key aspect of these Routledge Companions is their international scope and relevance. Edited by an array of highly regarded scholars, these volumes also benefit from teams of contributors which reflect an international range of perspectives.

Individually, Routledge Companions in Business, Management and Accounting provide an impactful one-stop-shop resource for each theme covered. Collectively, they represent a comprehensive learning and research resource for researchers, postgraduate students and practitioners.

Published titles in this series include:

The Routledge Companion to Fair Value and Financial Reporting
Edited by Peter Walton

The Routledge Companion to Nonprofit Marketing
Edited by Adrian Sargeant and Walter Wymer Jr

The Routledge Companion to Accounting History
Edited by John Richard Edwards, and Stephen P. Walker

The Routledge Companion to Creativity
Edited by Tudor Rickards, Mark A. Runco, and Susan Moger

The Routledge Companion to Strategic Human Resource Management
Edited by John Storey, Patrick M. Wright, and David Ulrich

The Routledge Companion to International Business Coaching
Edited by Michel Moral, and Geoffrey Abbott

The Routledge Companion to Organizational Change
Edited by David M. Boje, Bernard Burnes and John Hassard

The Routledge Companion to Cost Management
Edited by Falconer Mitchell, Hanne Nørreklit and Morten Jakobsen

The Routledge Companion to Digital Consumption
Edited by Russell W. Belk and Rosa Llamas

The Routledge Companion to Accounting Education

Edited by
Richard M. S. Wilson

Routledge
Taylor & Francis Group
LONDON AND NEW YORK

First published 2014
by Routledge
2 Park Square, Milton Park, Abingdon, Oxon OX14 4RN

and by Routledge
711 Third Avenue, New York, NY 10017

Routledge is an imprint of the Taylor & Francis Group, an informa business

British Library Cataloguing in Publication Data
A catalogue record for this book is available from the British Library

Library of Congress Cataloging in Publication Data
Wilson, R.M.S. (Richard Malcolm Sano)
    The Routledge companion to accounting education/Richard M.S. Wilson.
    — 1 Edition.
    pages cm — (Routledge companions in business, management and accounting)
    Includes bibliographical references and index.
    1. Accounting — Study and teaching. I. Title.
    HF5630.W557 2014
    657.071—dc23
    2013035357

ISBN: 978-0-415-69733-0 (hbk)
ISBN: 978-1-315-88980-1 (ebk)

Typeset in Bembo and Stone Sans
by Florence Production Ltd, Stoodleigh, Devon, UK

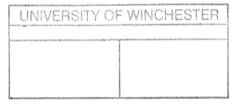

MIX
Paper from
responsible sources
FSC® C013604
www.fsc.org

Printed and bound by CPI Group (UK) Ltd, Croydon, CR0 4YY

This book is dedicated with gratitude and respect to three exemplary accounting educators:

Professor William Threipland Baxter (1906–2006), The London School of Economics and Political Science, U.K.

Professor Raymond John Chambers (1917–1999), The University of Sydney, Australia.

Professor Stephen A. Zeff (1933–), Rice University, U.S.A.

Their contributions have extended beyond their respective institutions and jurisdictions to influence developments in accounting education scholarship and practice on a global basis.

Tributes to each can be found in the Appendix.

Editorial team

The following established experts in the field of accounting education research and scholarship accepted invitations from the Editor to work with him in converting the publishing proposal for this book into the finished product:

Senior associate editors

Ralph W. Adler, University of Otago, New Zealand
Sue Pickard Ravenscroft, Iowa State University, U.S.A.
David E. Stout, Youngstown State University, U.S.A.

Associate editors

Paul A. de Lange, Curtin University, Australia
Angus Duff, University of the West of Scotland, U.K.
Barbara J. Eide, University of Wisconsin – La Crosse, U.S.A.
Barbara Flood, Dublin City University, Republic of Ireland
Hian Chye Koh, SIM University, Singapore
Ursula C. Lucas, University of the West of England, U.K.
Kim Watty, Deakin University, Australia

This distinguished group contains: five current/former Senior Associate Editors and four current/former Associate Editors of *Accounting Education: an international journal*; two former Editors of *Issues in Accounting Education*; and the current Editor of *Journal of Accounting Education*.

The role of each member of the Editorial Team involved reviewing a batch of:

* initial synopses (one for each chapter);
* revised synopses (which, once agreed, became the baseline for moving forward);
* initial drafts of each chapter; and
* revised drafts of each chapter.

At every stage three reviews were provided for each draft of every synopsis and chapter – one from the Editor and two from members of the Editorial Team. To facilitate revisions, the Editor provided feedback to authors after each phase of this process.

In addition, members of the Editorial Team were regularly consulted by the Editor to solicit their advice on a number of issues which arose from time to time during the project's gestation period of 30 months or so.

Contents

Contents

Contents

Exhibits

Figures

Tables

Foreword

This comprehensive anthology is a most welcome and timely contribution to the literature on accounting education. While scholarly inquiries into accounting education are of relatively recent vogue, perhaps most notably led by many of the authors who have contributed to this *Routledge Companion to Accounting Education,* rigorous and well-informed attention to the field is an imperative for both the accounting academy and the accounting profession. For in many jurisdictions around the world, there is an unprecedented interdependence between educational institutions in the tertiary education sector and professional accounting bodies in the provision of professional accounting education programmes. In some jurisdictions, however, interdependence has given way to competition. Irrespective of the education provider and the organizational requirements for professional certification, it is evident that there are ever-higher public expectations of the professional ethics, skills, competence, and judgement of professional accountants – most noticeably, perhaps, from the regulatory, investor, and auditing communities.

Within the academy, accounting competes with other business-related disciplines for intellectual standing and talented students – and all those disciplines compete against the more established intellectual traditions found in the humanities, social sciences, sciences, and professional fields such as engineering, law, and medicine. Unlike in those other professional fields, however, research in accounting appears to have had rather less impact upon education, policy, and practice. Yet, in the field of professional accounting education there is, arguably, mutual benefit for both the academic and practising arms of the profession in collaborative innovation and education that will attract the brightest students, enhance their interest in a career in accounting, and strengthen public confidence and trust in the practice of accounting. In the context of professional accounting education, research that informs understanding of 'best (educational) practice' and illustrative case studies of what constitutes educational innovation in major fields (such as financial reporting, auditing, and managerial accounting) would also be welcome additions to the literature.

Empowered by information and communication technologies, analytics, and mass transportation, there is an accelerating globalization of management education – and with it, of accounting education offered by business schools and professional accounting bodies. Driven by the strategic aspirations of education providers internationally, increasing mobility of labour, and the growing expectations of students for more convenient educational services, learning models and pedagogies have had to become increasingly adaptable across national borders and cultures, and responsive to different generational work-lifestyle choices. Conventional face-to-face teaching and learning models with their time–space constraints, are rapidly giving way to or being augmented by more service/student-oriented learning models that include blended learning, mixed-mode and online educational delivery strategies – increasingly in brand-enhancing and collaborative consortia and partnerships. These forces, together with the so-called MOOCs (massive open online courses) and the powerful institutional networked partnerships underpinning them, will progressively challenge the business models of tertiary institutions and professional accounting bodies.

As the boundaries around disciplines become increasingly blurred and expanded, the inter-disciplinary understanding of accounting students must increase. Students in business schools are increasingly challenged to think about 'business problems' as distinct from (say) accounting, finance, marketing, or regulatory problems. Students are expected to have sufficient under-standing of the wider intellectual, regulatory, and institutional contexts within which even 'technical accounting' problems arise when framing solutions to them – and the personal and communication skills to effectively tackle complex and unstructured problems in cross-disciplinary teams. The increasing cross-disciplinarity of accounting education and employers' demand for the development of so-called 'soft' skills further challenge programme and curriculum design, pedagogies, and teaching and learning models.

Many of the scenarios outlined above are crisply in focus in the 2012 Report of the Pathways Commission of the American Institute of Certified Public Accountants (AICPA) and American Accounting Association (AAA), as are threats to the adequacy of the future supply of highly-qualified academic accounting staff relative to the global demand for accounting education and the ageing demographic of accounting educators. They are at the epicentre of the higher purpose, mission, and work of the International Accounting Education Standards Board (IAESB). The Board exists, in the public interest, to raise the level of confidence and trust of stakeholders in the work of professional accountants. In the pursuit of that higher purpose, our mission is to serve the public interest by strengthening the worldwide accounting profession through the development and enhancement of education. The Board seeks to do this by promulgating a series of high-quality International Education Standards and other publications, reflecting good practice in the education, development, and assessment of professional accountants; by promoting the adoption and implementation of the International Education Standards; by developing education benchmarks for measuring the implementation of the International Education Standards; and by advancing international debate and thought leadership on emerging issues relating to the education of professional accountants, e.g. through research collaborations initiated with the International Association for Accounting Education and Research (IAAER).

It is within this dynamic and fascinating milieu of accounting education that this *Routledge Companion of Accounting Education* speaks. Of impressive scope and depth, this anthology comprises 30 chapters written by 67 scholars from 24 countries. It addresses seven critical 'considerations', including those deemed to be 'cornerstone', 'contextual', and 'institutional' to the field; and those pertaining to students, curriculum, pedagogy, and assessment. I warmly commend this meritorious work to all who are interested and involved in accounting education.

It is an honour to write the Foreword to this informative and thought-provoking work; and I congratulate Professor Richard Wilson and the international cast of associate editors and contributors whose vision, initiative, and scholarship have made it a reality. May it give impetus to a new wave of innovation and improvement in accounting education to the mutual benefit of current and future generations of professional accountants – and the stakeholder and public communities they serve.

Peter W. Wolnizer
Chairman, International Accounting Education Standards Board
Professor Emeritus, The University of Sydney

Acknowledgements

Acknowledgement is given for permission to use the following copyright material from other sources:

Taylor & Francis Ltd for Figure 3.3, taken from Wilson, R.M.S. & Gilligan, C. (2005) *Strategic Marketing Management*, 3rd edn, Oxford: Elsevier.

Emerald Group Publishing Limited for Figure 4.1, originally published in Cheetham, G. & Chivers, G. (1998) 'The reflective (and competent) practitioner: a model of professional competence which seeks to harmonise the reflective practitioner and competence-based approaches', *Journal of European Industrial Training*, 22(7), 267–276. © Emerald Group Publishing Limited, all rights reserved.

Taylor & Francis Ltd for Figure 17.2, originally published as Figure 3.6 on p. 70 in Jarvis, P. (ed.) (1995) *Adult and Continuing Education: Theory and Practice*, 2nd edn, London: Routledge. © Taylor & Francis Ltd, all rights reserved.

John Wiley & Sons, Ltd for Figure 19.1, originally published in Biggs, J., Kember, D., & Yeung, D.Y.P. (2010) *The Revised Two-Factor Study Process Questionnaire: R-SPQ-2F*. © John Wiley and Sons, all rights reserved.

Taylor & Francis Ltd and Professor J.T.E. Richardson for Figure 19.2, originally published in Richardson, J.T.E. (2005) 'Students' approaches to learning and teachers' approaches to teaching in higher education', *Educational Psychology*, 25(6), 673–680. © Taylor & Francis Ltd, all rights reserved. See www.tandfonline.com.

Elsevier Ltd for Table 19.1, originally published in Thomson, I. & Bebbington, J. (2013) 'Social and environmental reporting in the U.K.: A Pedagogic Evaluation', *Critical Perspectives on Accounting*, 16(5), 507–533. © John Wiley & Sons, all rights reserved.

Taylor & Francis Ltd for Figure 19.3, originally published in Coulson, A.B. & Thomson, I. (2006) 'Accounting and sustainability, encouraging a diological approach: integrating learning activities, delivery mechanisms and assessment strategies', *Accounting Education: an international journal*, 15(3), 261–273. © Taylor & Francis Ltd, all rights reserved. See www.tandfonline.com.

Taylor & Francis Ltd for Tables 25.4, 25.5, 25.6 and 25.7, originally published in Beard, D.F. (2007) 'Assessment of internship experiences and accounting core competences', *Accounting Education: an international journal*, 16(2), 207–220. © Taylor & Francis Ltd, all rights reserved. See www.tandfonline.com.

Tilburg University for Exhibit 26.2 and Figure 26.1, based on extracts from Karreman, G. (2013) *GAE 2012 Dynamics of Global Accountancy Education*, published and © by Tilburg University.

Taylor & Francis Ltd for Figure 30.1, originally published in Wilson, R.M.S. (2011) 'Alignment in accounting education and training', *Accounting Education: an international journal*, 20(1), 3–16. © Taylor & Francis Ltd, all rights reserved. See www.tandfonline.com.

The South African Institute of Chartered Accountants for Table 30.1.

The New Zealand Institute of Chartered Accountants for Table 30.2.

Taylor & Francis Ltd for Michael Gaffikin (2012) 'Professor Raymond J. Chambers: a personal reflection', *Accounting Education: an international journal*, 21(1), 25–39. © Taylor & Francis Ltd, all rights reserved. See www.tandfonline.com.

Taylor & Francis Ltd for Thomas R. Dyckman & Wil C. Uecker (2011) 'A tribute to Stephen A. Zeff', *Accounting Education: an international journal*, 20(1), 81–95. © Taylor & Francis Ltd, all rights reserved. See www.tandfonline.com.

Schedule of abbreviations

This schedule includes all the abbreviations used in *The Routledge Companion to Accounting Education*, in alphabetic sequence. In connection with organisations, where applicable, the city or country in which each organisation is based is specified, or its jurisdiction given in the case of an organisation's national or international remit. For concepts, models, techniques, etc., original sources are given where appropriate.

3-P Model	Presage, Process and Product Model (Biggs, 1993)
AAA	American Accounting Association (Sarasota, Florida, U.S.A.)
AACSB	International Association to Advance Collegiate Schools of Business (Tampa, Florida, U.S.A.)
AAHE	American Association for Higher Education (Washington, D.C.)
AASB	Australian Accounting Standards Board (Melbourne)
AAT	Association of Accounting Technicians (London)
AAUP	American Association of University Professors (Washington, D.C.)
ABAE	Advisory Board of Accountancy Education (London – now defunct)
AC	Abstract conceptualisation (See ELM)
ACA	Associate of the Institute of Chartered Accountants
ACAP	Advisory Committee on the Auditing Profession (U.S.A.)
ACBSP	Accreditation Council for Business Schools and Programs (Overland Park, Kansas, U.S.A., and Brussels, Belgium)
ACCA	Association of Chartered Certified Accountants (London)
ACS	Administrative Control System
ACT	American College Testing
AdFLAG	Adult Financial Literacy Advisory Group (U.K.)
ADI	Accountancy Development Index
AE	*Accounting Education: an international journal* (Abingdon, U.K.)
AE	Active experimentation (See ELM)
AECC	Accounting Education Change Commission (U.S.A.)
AES	Accounting Education Symposium
AFC	French Academic Accounting Association
AFQ	Australian Qualifications Framework
AHELO	Assessment of Higher Education Learning Outcomes (OECD, Paris)
AIA	American Institute of Accountants (Predecessor of AICPA)
AICPA	American Institute of Certified Public Accountants (New York)
AIS	Accounting Information System

ALEKS	Assessment and Learning in Knowledge Spaces (software)
ALTC	Australian Learning & Teaching Council (Sydney) (See OLT)
AMBA	Association of MBAs (London)
ANCOVA	Analysis of covariance
ANOVA	Analysis of variance
ANPCONT	Brazilian Association of Graduate Programs in Accounting
ANZ	Australia & New Zealand Banking Group (Sydney)
AQF	Australian Qualifications Framework
ARB	*Accounting Research Bulletin* (Issued by the Committee on Accounting Procedures of the AICPA)
ASI	Approaches to Studying Inventory (Entwistle & Ramsdem, 1983)
ASIC	Australian Securities and Investments Commission (Sydney)
ASOBAT	*A Statement of Basic Accounting Theory*
ASPE	Accounting Standards for Private Enterprises (Canada)
ASQ	Approaches to Study Questionnaire (Richardson, 1990)
ASSIST	Approaches and Study Skills Inventory for Students (Tait, Entwistle, & McCune, 1998)
BAAEC	Board of Accreditation of Accountancy Educational Courses (U.K.)
BAEC	Board of Accreditation of Educational Courses (U.K.)
BAFA	British Accounting & Finance Association
BGA	Business Graduates Association (London)
BICA	Botswana Institute of Chartered Accountants (Gaberone)
BP	British Petroleum plc (London)
BSA	Bachelor of Science in Accountancy
CA	Chartered accountant
CAAA	Canadian Academic Accounting Association
CAATs	Computer-Assisted Auditing Techniques
CACR	Chamber of Auditors of the Czech Republic (Prague)
CAE	Comparative accounting education
CAG	Controller and Auditor General (Dar-es-Salaam, Tanzania)
CAGS	Centre for Accounting, Governance and Sustainability (University of South Australia)
CAI	Chartered Accountants Ireland (Belfast and Dublin)
CAI	Computer-assisted instruction
CAL	Computer-assisted learning
CAO	Chief Academic Officer (U.S.A.)
CAPA	Confederation of Asian and Pacific Accountants
CATS	Credit Accumulation and Transfer System
CBA	College of Business Administration
CBA	Competence-based assessment
CBF	Commonwealth Bank Foundation (Sydney)
CBL	Computer-based learning
CCAB	Consultative Committee of Accountancy Bodies (British Isles)
CCI	Common Content Initiative
CDAS	Committee to Develop the Accountancy Sector (Singapore)
CE	Concrete experience (See ELM)
CEA	Commissie Eindtermen Accountantsopleiding (The Netherlands)
CEE	Council for Economic Education (U.S.A.)

CEO	Chief Executive Officer
CFC	Conselho Federal de Contabilidade (Brasilia)
CFEB	Consumer Financial Education Body (London)
CFF	Cash from Financing
CFI	Cash from Investing
CFO	Cash from Operations
CFO	Chief Financial Officer
CGA	Certified General Accountant (Canada)
CGAAC	Certified General Accountants Association of Canada (Burnaby, BC)
CGMA	Chartered Global Management Accountant (CIMA/AICPA)
CIA	Certified Internal Auditor (U.S.A.)
CICA	Canadian Institute of Chartered Accountants
CICPA	Chinese Institute of Certified Public Accountants
CIMA	Chartered Institute of Management Accountants (London)
CIPFA	Chartered Institute of Public Finance and Accountancy (London)
CIPP	Context, input, process and product
CIRP	Co-operative Institutional Research Program (New Zealand)
CLA	Collegiate Learning Assessment (Council for Aid to Education, New York)
CMA	Certified Management Accountant (U.S.A.)
CMB	Capital Markets Board of Turkey
CNCC	Compagnie National des Commissaires aux Comptes (Paris)
CODECE	Council of Deans of Economics of Argentina (Consejo de Decanos en Ciensias Económicas)
COPMM	Centre for Organisational Performance Measurement and Management (University of Otago, New Zealand)
CPA	Certified practising accountant (Australia)
CPA	Certified public accountant (U.S.A.)
CPA	Chartered professional accountant (Canada)
CPA Australia	Certified Practising Accountants of Australia (Melbourne)
CPA Canada	Chartered Professional Accountants of Canada
CPAAOB	Certified Public Accountants and Auditing Oversight Board (Japan)
CPAPNG	Certified Practising Accountants Papua New Guinea
CPC	Comtador Publico Certificado (certified public auditor, Mexico)
CPD	Continuing professional development
CPE	Continuing Professional Education
CPS	Centre for Policy Studies (London)
CS	Computer science
CSEAR	Centre for Social and Environmental Accounting Research (University of St Andrews, U.K.)
CSMAR	A data base
DC	District of Columbia (U.S.A.)
DCG	Diplôme Supérieur de Comptabilité et de Gestion (France)
DFD	Data flow diagram
DFES	Department for Education & Skills (U.K.)
DIT	Defining Issues Test (Rest, 1986)
EAA	European Accounting Association (Brussels)
EAAT	Expert Accountants' Association of Turkey (Istanbul)
EC	European Commission (Brussels)

EDP	Electronic data processing
EEOC	Equal Employment Opportunity Commission (U.S.A.)
EFL	English as a first language
EFMD	European Foundation for Management Development (Brussels)
EHEA	European Higher Education Area
ELAcc (1.3)	Expectations of Learning Accounting Inventory (Lucas & Meyer, 2005)
ELAcc (1.4)	Expectations of Learning Accounting Inventory (Lucas & Mladenovic, 2009b)
ELM	Experiential Learning Model (Kolb, 1984)
EPAS	EFMD Programme Accreditation System
EQUIS	European Quality Improvement System (Brussels)
ERP	Enterprise Resource Planning
ESL	English as a second language
ESTJ	Extrovert, sensing, thinking, judging (See MBTI)
EU	European Union
FASB	Financial Accounting Standards Board (Norwalk, CT, U.S.A.)
FBI	Federal Bureau of Investigations (Washington, DC)
FCA	Fellow of the Institute of Chartered Accountants
FCA	Financial Conduct Authority (U.K.)
FEE	Fédération des Experts-comptables Européens (Brussels)
FEI	Financial Executives Institute (Morristown, NJ, U.S.A.)
FIA	Fiji Institute of Accountants
FRC	Financial Reporting Council (London)
FSA	Federation of Schools of Accountancy (U.S.A.)
FSA	Financial Services Authority (U.K.)
FTE	Full-time equivalent
GAA	Global Accounting Alliance
GAAP	Generally accepted accounting principles
GAE	Global Accountancy Education (on-going research/publication)
GAO	Government Accountability Office (Washington, DC)
GAS	Generalized audit software
GDP	Gross domestic product
GE	General Electric (Fairfield, CT, U.S.A.)
GFC	Global Financial Crisis
GNS	Gross need strength
GPA	Grade point average
GRI	Global Reporting Initiative
HEA	Higher Education Academy (U.K.)
HEI	Higher Education Institution
HEP	Higher Education Provider (Australia)
HKICPA	Hong Kong Institute of Certified Public Accountants
IAAER	International Association for Accounting Education & Research
IAASB	International Auditing and Assurance Standards Board (New York)
IACBE	International Assembly for Collegiate Business Education (Lenexa, KS, U.S.A.)
IAESB	International Accounting Education Standards Board (New York)
IAS	International Standards on Auditing
IASB	International Accounting Standards Board (London)

ICAA	Institute of Chartered Accountants in Australia (Sydney)
ICAEW	Institute of Chartered Accountants in England & Wales (London)
ICAI	Institute of Chartered Accountants of India (Delhi)
ICAO	Institute of Chartered Accountants of Ontario (Toronto)
ICAP	Institute of Chartered Accountants of Pakistan (Karachi)
ICAS	Institute of Chartered Accountants of Scotland (Edinburgh)
ICPAI	Institute of Certified Public Accountants in Ireland (Dublin)
IEPS	International Education Practice Statements (IAESB)
IES	International Education Standard (IAESB)
IFAC	International Federation of Accountants (New York)
IFRS	International Financial Reporting Standards
IFRS Foundation	International Financial Reporting Standards Foundation (London)
IGFE	International Gateway for Financial Education (OECD, Paris)
IIA	Institute of Internal Auditors (Altamonte Springs, FL, U.S.A.)
ILO	Integrated learning objective
ILO	Intended learning outcome
ILP	Inventory of Learning Processes (Schmeck *et al.*, 1978, 1991)
ILS	Inventory of Learning Styles (Vermunt, 1992)
IMA	Institute of Management Accountants (Montvale, U.S.A.)
IMCP	Instituto Mexicana de Contadores Publicos (Mexico City)
INFE	International Network for Financial Education (OECD, Paris)
Intosei	International Organization of Supreme Auditing Institutions (Founded in Cuba, 1953)
IP	Information processing
IP	Instructional preference
IPCC	Integrated Professional Competence Course (India)
IPD	Initial professional development
IPSAS	International Public Sector Accounting Standards
IQAB	International Qualification Appraisal Board (Canada)
IRBA	Independent Regulatory Board for Auditors (South Africa)
IS	Information system
ISA	International Standard on Auditing
ISACA	Information Systems Audit and Control Association (Rolling Meadows, IL, U.S.A.)
ISSAI	International Standards of Supreme Audit Institutions (Mexico)
IT	Information technology
ITS	Intelligent tutoring systems
iXBRL	Inline XBRL
JBACC	Joint Board of Accountancy Colleges and Courses (U.K.)
JICPA	Japanese Institute of Certified Public Accountants (Tokyo)
KSA	Knowledge, skills, and attitudes (or abilities)
KTS	Keirsey Temperament Sorter (1978, 1998)
LEAP	National Leadership Council for Liberal Education and America's Promise (Washington, DC)
LIBOR	The London Inter-Bank Offered Rate (U.K.)
LS	Learning styles
LSE	London School of Economics & Political Science

LSI	Learning Styles Inventory (Kolb, 1984)
LSP	Learning style preference(s)
LSQ	Learning Style Questionnaire (Honey & Mumford, 2000)
LST	Learning Styles Inventory (Dunn *et al.*, 1989)
LTAS	Learning and Teaching Academic Standards (Australia)
MBA	Master of Business Administration
MBAd	Management & Business Administration degree (Spain)
MBTI	Myers-Briggs Type Indicator (1962)
MIS	Management information system
MOOCs	Massive open online courses
MOU	Memorandum of understanding
MPA	Master of Professional Accounting
MPQ	Motivation Profile Questionnaire (Arthur & Engels, 2000)
MRA	Mutual recognition agreement
MSA	Master of Science in Accountancy
MSCHE	Middle States Commission on Higher Education (U.S.A.)
MTax	Master of Taxation
NAFTA	North America Free Trade Agreement
NAO	National Audit Office (Dar-es-Salaam, Tanzania)
NAO	National Audit Office (London)
NASBA	National Association of State Boards of Accountancy (Nashville, TN, U.S.A.)
NBA	Nederlandse Beroepsorganisatie van Accountants (Amsterdam)
NBA	National Australia Bank (Melbourne)
NCACS	North Central Association of Colleges and Schools (U.S.A.)
NCEE	National Council on Economic Education (New York)
NEASC	New England Association of Schools and Colleges (U.S.A.)
NEO	Neuroticism, Extraversion, Openness personality inventory (revised) (Costa & McCrae, 1992)
NFLS	National Financial Literacy Strategy (Australia)
NHS	National Health Service (U.K.)
NZICA	New Zealand Institute of Chartered Accountants (Wellington)
OCEAN	Openness, conscientiousness, extraversion, agreeableness, neuroticism
OEC	Ordre des Experts-Comptables (Paris)
OECD	Organisation for Economic Co-operation & Development (Paris)
OERI	Office of Educational Research and Improvement (New Zealand)
OFSTED	Office for Standards in Education (U.K.)
OHS	Online homework system
OLT	Office of Learning and Teaching (Sydney)
ONS	Office for National Statistics (U.K.)
PAB	Professional accounting body
PAEP	Professional Accountant's Education Program (Russia)
PBL	Problem-based learning
PCAOB	Public Company Accounting Oversight Board (Washington, DC)
PcEEC	Pre-Certification Education Executive Committee (AICPA)
PDA	Personal digital assistant
PEPS	Productivity Environmental Preferences Scale (Dunn & Dunn, 1992)
PFEG	Personal Finance Education Group (U.K.)
PFRC	Personal Finance Research Group (U.K.)

PGD	Postgraduate diploma
PMAA	Performance Measurement Association of Australasia
PRA	Prudential Regulation Authority (U.K.)
PTS	Personal transferable skills
QAA	Quality Assurance Agency (U.K.)
QP	Qualification Programme (Hong Kong)
RA	*Registeraccountant* (The Netherlands)
RAE	Research Assessment Exercise (U.K.)
RASI	Revised Approaches to Studying Inventory (Tait, Entwistle & McCune, 1998)
REA	Resources-events-agents
REF	Research Excellence Framework (U.K.)
RIASEC	Realistic, investigative, artistic, social, enterprising, conventional (interests) (Holland: 1966, 1973; 1985; 1997)
RMBS	Residential mortgage-backed securities
RO	Reflective observation (See ELM)
RoLI	Reflections on Learning Inventory (Meyer, 2000, 2004)
ROSC	Report on the Observance of Standards and Codes (World Bank)
R-SPQ-2F	Revised Study Process Questionnaire Two Factor (Biggs, Kember & Leung, 2001)
RTE	Real-Time Economy
SACS	Southern Association of Colleges and Schools (U.S.A.)
SAICA	South African Institute of Chartered Accountants (Bruma Lake)
SAIPA	South African Institute of Professional Accountants (Kengray)
SAL	Students' approaches to learning
SAO	Superior Audit Office of Mexico (Mexico City)
SAP	A company, http://www.sap.com/index.epx
SAT	Scholastic Aptitude Test
SAT	Scholastic Assessment Test (College Board, NY, U.S.A.)
SATTA	*Statement of Accounting Theory and Theory Acceptance*
SCII	Strong Campbell Interest Inventory (1974)
SD	Systems diagrams
SEC	Securities & Exchange Commission (Washington, DC)
SEDI	Social and Enterprise Development Innovations (Canada)
SERU-S	Student Experience in the Research University Survey
SIG	Special Interest Group
SMAC	Society of Management Accountants of Canada (See also CPA Canada)
SMEs	Small and medium-sized enterprises
SMO	Statement of Membership Obligations (IFAC)
SOLO	Structure of the Observed Learning Outcome (Biggs & Collis, 1982)
SOX	Sarbanes-Oxley Act, 2002 (U.S.A.)
SPP	Supervised Professional Practice (Argentina)
SPQ	Study Process Questionnaire (Biggs, 1987) (See also R-SPQ-2F)
SUNY	State University of New York (U.S.A.)
TAFE	Technical and Further Education (Australia)
THE	*Times Higher Education* (U.K.)
TLO	Tertiary Learning Outcomes (New Zealand)
TPB	Theory of Planned Behaviour (Ajzen & Fishbein, 1975)

TPS	Test of Professional Skills (ICAS)
TQM	Total quality management
TRA	Theory of Reasoned Action (Ajzen, 1986)
TURMOB	Union of the Chambers of Certified Public Accountants of Turkey (Ankara)
UAS	Uniform Accounting System
U.K.	United Kingdom
UML	Unified modelling language
UNAM	National University of Mexico
UNCTAD	United Nations Conference on Trade and Development (Geneva)
UNESCO	United Nations Educational, Scientific and Cultural Organisation (Paris)
UNSW	University of New South Wales (Australia)
U.S.A.	United States of America
US–IQAB	United States' International Qualifications Appraisal Board
USSR	Union of Soviet Socialist Republics
VLE	Virtual learning environment
VPI	Vocational Preference Inventory (Holland, 1985)
WASC	Western Association of Schools and Colleges (U.S.A.)
WBLE	Web-based learning environments
WEF	World Economic Forum
WLF	World Literacy Foundation
XBRL	Extensible business reporting language
XML	Extensible markup language
Y2K	Year 2000

Editorial introduction

Richard M.S. Wilson

LOUGHBOROUGH UNIVERSITY, U.K.

The main aim

In embarking on this ambitious project, the over-riding aim has been to provide an authoritative reference work which defines the domain of accounting education, and which provides a critical overview of the state of this domain (including emerging and cutting-edge aspects) as a foundation for facilitating improved accounting education scholarship and research as a means of enhancing the educational base of accounting practice.

The rationale for the book

What is the justification for this book? Over the past 40 years numerous enquiries have been undertaken into accounting education and training in a number of countries, all resulting in reports containing recommendations for change, such as the Solomons Report in the U.K. (1974), the Bedford Committee Report (1986) and the Big 8 *White Paper* (1989) in the U.S.A., the Mathews Report in Australia (1990), the AAA-sponsored report by Albrecht & Sack in the U.S.A. (2000), those by Hancock *et al.* (2009), Evans *et al.* (2010), and Cappelletto (2010) relating to Australia, and – most recently – the Pathways Commission (2012) in the U.S.A. A common warning in all these reports has been that accounting education must change if it is to be relevant to students, to the accounting profession, and to stakeholders in the wider community (who rely in a variety of ways on the services rendered by accounting practitioners).

Of crucial significance in the calls for change in accounting education and training has been the array of changes taking place in the dynamic environment of accounting practice, including the following:

- the increasing pace of change in financial reporting;
- the increasing pace of change in financial markets;
- increasing uncertainty;
- increasing recognition of risk;
- increasing complexity;
- increasing regulatory activity;

- increasing globalisation;
- increasing interdisciplinary practices; and
- increasing technological change.

Within the academy, especially during the past two decades, there has been a massive increase in pressure upon educators to embed technology within their teaching and learning practice – both to increase efficiency and to increase students' engagement. This had led to the near universal adoption of virtual learning environments (VLEs), and greater use of a variety of social, communication, and learning technologies (such as Twitter, Facebook, YouTube, podcasts, and video-conferencing) to create virtual classrooms and other e-learning environments in order to provide students with learning opportunities at times that suit them. These are the technologies which have facilitated the recent interest in Massive Open On-line Courses (MOOCs) which are seen as being both a new opportunity for, and a threat to, the academy.

In addition to all the listed demands on the time and energy of the academy, one must add the increasing pressures on accounting educators from such stakeholders as government, funding agencies, and professional accounting bodies, brought about by research assessment exercises, teaching audits, and accreditation requirements.

There has been a need for accounting educators to respond to the demands for change by adapting traditional ways of addressing matters such as:

- students' motivation and approaches to learning;
- curriculum design and course content;
- pedagogy (including developments in educational technology);
- skills development (whether generic or technical);
- assessment (of students, programmes, and academic staff);
- contextual issues (including sustainability and ethics); and
- institutional issues (including the interface between academic education in accounting and professional training in accounting – whether initial or continuing).

At various times over the past 30 years or so, an increasing number of specialist publishing outlets have been created to deal with an increasing literature focussing on accounting education (in contrast, for example, to the modest space hitherto made available for an accounting education section in journals such as *The Accounting Review*, or the occasional paper on an accounting education theme appearing in a mainstream accounting journal). To some extent these specialist publications are affiliated to academic accounting associations (with *Accounting Education: an international journal* being affiliated to the International Association for Accounting Education and Research, and *Issues in Accounting Education* being affiliated to the American Accounting Association). But there are two electronic journals which are not affiliated in this way (*The Accounting Educator's Journal* and *Global Perspectives on Accounting Education*), and two hard copy journals (*Journal of Accounting Education* and the hard-back annual *Advances in Accounting Education*) which are independent of any academic association.

Special Interest Groups have been established by some academic associations (including the Accounting and Finance Association of Australia and New Zealand, the American Accounting Association, and the British Accounting and Finance Association – but conspicuously not the European Accounting Association) to cater for the growing number of academics with interests in accounting education scholarship and practice. This should not be seen as being surprising since, as has been noted elsewhere, whatever specialist expertise academic accountants may have (such as in regulatory matters, capital markets, or environmental reporting), the one thing which they all have in common is their role as educators. (See, for example, Wilson *et al.*, 2008.)

From the above, it is evident that there has been an increasing amount of interest in accounting education research and scholarship, along with an increasing volume of published research in this area. However, given the absence of any book that captures the current state of knowledge regarding the state of accounting education, or that offers a comprehensive guide to the contemporary debates and literature within the domain of accounting education, this seems an appropriate time to take stock – which explains the rationale behind the RCAE.

Key features of the book

The book's key features are:

- Thirty chapters, organised in groups on a thematic basis, have been written by recognised experts from a number of different countries who have proven track records of relevant research, publication, and pedagogic experience.
- It offers international coverage and contemporary relevance.
- It provides a balanced review of current knowledge and relevant debates, written in a way which is analytical, accessible, and engaging.
- It looks forward to reflect on where the current research agenda is likely to lead.
- It creates a single repository on the state of accounting education today.
- It presents perspectives of relevance to both academic and professional constituencies with an interest in accounting education research and scholarship as a basis for both education and training policy-making on the one hand, and improving practice in accounting education and training on the other, with a view to producing more effective accounting practitioners.

At the beginning of each chapter there is a Table of Contents to help readers navigate their way through the chapter. In addition, given the bewildering 'alphabet soup' of initials, acronyms, and contractions in the domain of accounting education, a Schedule of Abbreviations has been included.

The structure of the book

The book is structured into seven themed sections, each containing a group of chapters which focus on different facets of their respective theme. The themes can all be linked to the rationale outlined above.

Each chapter provides a balanced overview of current knowledge, identifying key issues, and offering informed coverage of relevant debates. The themes are as follows:

Section A	(Chapters 1–5)	Cornerstone Considerations
Section B	(Chapters 6–10)	Student-Related Considerations
Section C	(Chapters 11–15)	Curriculum Considerations
Section D	(Chapters 16–19)	Pedagogic Considerations
Section E	(Chapters 20–22)	Assessment Considerations
Section F	(Chapters 23–26)	Contextual Considerations
Section G	(Chapters 27–30)	Institutional Considerations

The target readership

The intended readership of the *Routledge Companion to Accounting Education* (RCAE) comprises those engaged in pedagogic practice and policy-making in various forms which focus on:

- academic education in accounting (primarily, but not exclusively, at tertiary level);
- professional training in accounting (whether the initial professional development (IPD) of aspiring accountants, or the continuing professional development (CPD) of professionally-qualified accounting practitioners);
- accounting education scholarship and research.

The book should be found not only in academic libraries, but also in the libraries of professional accounting bodies and major accounting firms.

The RCAE's international stance will ensure that there will be no restriction in its relevance with regard to different jurisdictions.

The contributors

The dozens of colleagues who have participated in this project (46 authors of the 30 chapters, seven writers of Prefaces, five authors of Tributes, one author of the Foreword, 10 members of the Editorial Team, and 21 contributors of short pieces to Chapter 15) – mostly with considerable enthusiasm and good humour – represent many of the world's leaders in accounting education research and scholarship, including past Presidents/Chairpersons of the American Accounting Association (AAA), the Accounting & Finance Association of Australia & New Zealand (AFAANZ), the Brazilian Association of Graduate Programs in Accounting (ANCPONT), the British Accounting & Finance Association (BAFA), the Canadian Academic Accounting Association (CAAA), the Chartered Institute of Management Accountants (CIMA), the Chinese Accounting Professors Association, the European Accounting Association (EAA), the Expert Accountants' Association of Turkey, the Irish Accounting & Finance Association (IAFA), the Mexican Association of Accounting & Business Faculty, the Southern African Accounting Association (SAAA), and the International Association for Accounting Education & Research (IAAER); plus several past Chairpersons of the BAFA's Special Interest Group on Accounting Education, and the AAA's Teaching, Learning & Curriculum Section. Moreover, this talented team also includes several current and past Editors of the leading journals in the field (*Accounting Education: an international journal*, *Issues in Accounting Education*, and *Journal of Accounting Education*) plus a former Joint Editor of both the annual *Advances in Accounting Education* and the short-lived *Accounting Education: a journal of theory, practice and research*.

While it may be deemed invidious to single out individual contributors, the authors range from:

- intellectual giants of accounting education scholarship and research – such as Tim Fogarty (Case Western Reserve University, U.S.A.), and Gordon Boyce (La Trobe University, Australia);
- providers of innovative practice-related research to facilitate informed accounting education/training policy-making – such as Gert Karreman (Leiden University, The Netherlands), Beverley Jackling (Victoria University, Melbourne, Australia), Don Wygal (Rider University, U.S.A.), Kim Watty (Deakin University, Australia), and Thomas Calderon (University of Akron, U.S.A.);

- scholars of encyclopaedic thoroughness – such as Barbara Flood (Dublin City University, Ireland), Angus Duff (University of the West of Scotland), Efrim Boritz (University of Waterloo, Canada), Greg Stoner (University of Glasgow, U.K.), and Hian Chye Koh (SIM University, Singapore);
- researchers who generate inspired insights – such as Ursula Lucas (University of the West of England), Rosina Mladenovic (The University of Sydney, Australia), Billie Cunningham (University of Missouri–Columbia, U.S.A.), and Elaine Evans (Macquarie University, Australia);
- academic ambassadors who provide constructive dialogue between the domains of accounting education research and the accounting profession – such as Bel Needles (DePaul University, U.S.A.), Trevor Hassall (Sheffield Hallam University, U.K.), and Elizabeth Gammie (The Robert Gordon University, Scotland); to
- long-established double acts – such as Marann Byrne and Pauline Willis (both of Dublin City University, Ireland); Joel Amernic (University of Toronto, Canada) and Russell Craig (Victoria University, Melbourne, Australia); and Catriona Paisey and Nick Paisey (University of Glasgow and Heriot-Watt University respectively, both in Scotland); and
- the leading international statesman of the accounting academy – Gary Sundem (University of Washington, U.S.A.).

It was most gracious of Peter Wolnizer (University of Sydney, Australia), Chair of the International Accounting Education Standards Board, to contribute the thoughtful Foreword. In addition, I appreciate the inputs from the seven eminent accounting educators from countries around the world who each agreed to write a short Preface, one for each of the RCAE's seven sections.

The hard work of the RCAE Editorial Team is acknowledged elsewhere, and I would also like to add a word of thanks to Geoffrey Whittington (University of Cambridge, U.K.) and Charles Oppenheim (Loughborough University, U.K.) for their specialist advice.

It has been a huge privilege to be in a position to work with all these talented colleagues from 'the college without walls'. I first came across a variation of this vivid expression some 30 years ago while browsing through the books on a shelf in a colleague's office at Macquarie University in Australia. During the latter half of the 1970s I had been in frequent correspondence with Stanley J. Shapiro (latterly Dean of the Faculty of Business Administration at Simon Fraser University, Canada), sharing research findings, and exchanging views on the interface between accounting and marketing – a shared and sustained passion (see, for example, Wilson, 1973, 1981, 1999, 2001; and Roslender & Wilson, 2012). One book in particular caught my attention (Shapiro & Kirpalani, 1984) and, in its Preface, Professor Shapiro referred to our collaboration as having taken place in 'the invisible college without walls' which I re-labelled as 'the college without walls'. This idea has inspired me ever since (the recognition that one can work constructively with colleagues in different institutions, located in different countries, perhaps meeting from time to time at international conferences, paths sometimes crossing as members of the same committees, or – in some instances – never meeting at all). And so it is with this book.

A book such as this requires a serious commitment from all participants, including colleagues from Routledge. I was honoured when Terry Clague (Publisher, Routledge Books – Business, Management, and Accounting), aided and abetted by Dan Trinder (Publisher, Taylor & Francis Journals – Economics and Business Management), invited me to compile the RCAE. I was given, in effect, *carte blanche*, to design and develop it as I saw fit, to invite whomever I wished to contribute to it, to set the timetable, and so on. Terry was always on hand, offering encouragement and advice when requested, but never interfering. Was any other Editor ever so fortunate?

At a more operational level at Routledge Books, the project has benefitted enormously from the initial support of Alex Krause (in dealing with contractual issues), and the subsequent patient care of Sinead Waldron in dealing with pre-publication production issues (including an array of copyright queries). Peter Lloyd saw the manuscript through the production process, and Susan Dunsmore dealt with the copy editing. The Author Index and Subject Index were compiled by Malcolm Henson. I thank them all!

And finally, while she did not contribute in any professional capacity, without the sustained support of my wife, Gillian, this project – as with so many of my other academic endeavours over the years – would not have come to fruition.

Dedication

The book is dedicated to perhaps the three most worthy of accounting educators, on whose shoulders their successors have stood.

Of each of them it can be said, to modify the words of Charles T. Horngren (as he said of his mentor, William J. Vatter):

> *For those who have known them, no words are necessary.*
> *For those who have not known them, no words will suffice.*

Having known Will Baxter, benefitting from occasional words of wisdom and support from him; having had guidance from Ray Chambers – in personal correspondence – as a young academic trying to find my way; and knowing Steve Zeff, I consider myself to be very fortunate. To give but a couple of examples: in 1991, when I was developing the proposal to set up *Accounting Education: an international journal*, I discussed this with Professor Zeff during a break at a conference. (I recall we were sitting by a staircase, but I forget where the conference was being held.) In the light of his experience as a distinguished former Editor of *The Accounting Review* (1978–83), he advised me not to simply wait to see what unsolicited submissions landed on my desk, but to be pro-active in soliciting inputs and exercising initiatives – which I took to heart, and pursued for 20 years as Editor of that journal. At another conference (held at the University of Glamorgan in Wales), on 4 July 2001 – an auspicious date for those from both the U.S.A. and the U.K. – I gave Professor Zeff a lift in my car from our hotel to the conference venue, so I can claim to have done something useful to show my gratitude in being (however briefly) his chauffeur!

I am grateful to Routledge Journals for allowing Tributes to Professors Chambers and Zeff, originally published in *Accounting Education: an international journal*, to be included in this book, and to Michael Bromwich and Richard Macve for responding so positively to my invitation to them to write a fitting Tribute to Professor Baxter – especially for this book. These three Tributes can be found in the Appendix.

Onwards and forwards – in the hope that some of the ideas in this book might encourage further research in the domain of accounting education, stimulate beneficial change in policy-making relating to the education and training of future generations of accountants, and lead to improvements in the pedagogic practice of accounting educators, all linked to the challenging task of enhancing the educational base of accounting practice.

Looking forward must be the right perspective since, while we can – and should – seek to learn from the past, in the sapient words of Charles F. Kettering:

> *I am interested in the future because that is where I intend to live.*

References

Albrecht, W.S. & Sack, R.J. (2000) *Accounting Education: Charting the Course through a Perilous Future* (Accounting Education Series, Vol. 16), Sarasota, FL: American Accounting Association.

American Accounting Association Committee on the Future Structure, Content and Scope of Accounting Education (The Bedford Committee) (1986) Future accounting education: preparing for the expanding profession, *Issues in Accounting Education*, 1(1), 168–195.

Big 8 (1989) *Perspectives on Education: Capabilities for Success in the Accounting Profession* (The Big 8 White Paper). Reprinted in Sundem, G.L. (1999) *The Accounting Education Change Commission: Its History and Impact* (Accounting Education Series, Vol. 15), Sarasota, FL: American Accounting Association. Available at: http://aaahq.org/aecc/big8/cover.htm.

Cappelletto, G. (2010) *Challenges Facing Accounting Education in Australia*, Sydney: AFAANZ, CPA Australia, AICA, NIA. Available at: http://afaanz.org.

de Lange, P.A. & Watty, K. (2011) AE briefing, *Accounting Education: an international journal*, 20(6), 625–630.

Evans, E., Burritt, R., & Guthrie, J. (eds) (2010) *Accounting Education at a Crossroads in 2010*, Sydney: Institute of Chartered Accountants in Australia, and Adelaide: Centre for Accounting, Governance and Sustainability, University of South Australia.

Hancock, P., Howieson, B., Kavanagh, M., Kent, J., Tempone, I., & Segal, N. (2009) *Accounting for the Future: More Than Numbers*, Sydney: Australian Learning and Teaching Council. Available at: www.altc.edu.au.

Mathews, R., Jackson, M., & Brown, P. (1990) *Accounting in Higher Education: Report of the Review of the Accounting Discipline in Higher Education*, Canberra: Australian Government Publishing Service, Department of Employment, Education and Training.

Pathways Commission (2012) *Charting a National Strategy for the Next Generation of Accountants*, Sarasota, FL: AAA, and New York: AICPA. Available at: www.pathwayscommission.org.

Roslender, R. & Wilson, R.M.S. (eds) (2012) *The Marketing/Accounting Interface*, Abingdon: Routledge.

Shapiro, S.J. & Kirpalani, V.H. (eds) (1984) *Marketing Effectiveness: Insights from Accounting and Finance*, Boston: Allyn and Bacon.

Solomons, D., with Berridge, T.M. (1974) *Prospectus for a Profession*, London: Advisory Board of Accountancy Education.

Wilson, R.M.S. (1973) *Management Controls in Marketing*, London: Heinemann (for the Institute of Marketing).

Wilson, R.M.S. (ed.) (1981) *Financial Dimensions of Marketing*, 2 vols, London: Macmillan (for CIMA).

Wilson, R.M.S. (1999) *Accounting for Marketing*, London: ITBP.

Wilson, R.M.S. (ed.) (2001) *Marketing Controllership*, Aldershot: Ashgate.

Wilson, R.M.S., Ravenscroft, S.P., Rebele, J.E., & St. Pierre, E.K. (2008) The case for accounting education research, *Accounting Education: an international journal*, 17(2), 103–111.

Section A

Cornerstone considerations

Preface

David E. Stout

YOUNGSTOWN STATE UNIVERSITY, U.S.A.

It is indeed an honour for me to provide this Preface for the first group of chapters of the RCAE.

Chapter 1, "Accounting education as field of intellectual inquiry", by Timothy Fogarty, traces the roots (or theoretical foundations) of accounting education research to three longer-established fields of inquiry: economics, psychology, and sociology. Professor Fogarty also offers in this chapter a critical evaluation of the current health of the accounting education sub-discipline.

In Chapter 2, "Modelling accounting education", Bel Needles provides an overview of different models which are found in different countries to produce qualified accountants, followed by an extended discussion of a comprehensive model of accounting education. The latter material should be of interest both to those involved in course and curriculum evaluation/change as well as those interested in conducting research into the learning process of accounting students. The availability of underlying models of the accounting education process helps to ensure the relevance, vibrancy, and value of investigative studies in the area.

Chapter 3, "The nature of financial literacy", by Richard Wilson, Anne Abraham, and Carolynne Mason, critically compares financial awareness and financial literacy, arguing for an expansive and elevated view of the latter as a cornerstone of accounting education. Beyond the more immediate arguments, the chapter serves as an excellent example of how conventional thinking in accounting education can be challenged. Such views can motivate substantive changes to both what we teach and how we teach, as well as future research in otherwise under-researched areas.

In Chapter 4, "The case for change in accounting education", Barbara Flood provides a comprehensive review (using stakeholder analysis) of the case for change in accounting education, covering perspectives from the U.S.A. and elsewhere. In addition, Professor Flood reviews educators' criticisms of accounting education based on what is viewed as being a narrow and ill-conceived focus on the transmission of knowledge concerning current accounting practice. This chapter will have particular appeal to those interested in expanding the boundaries and relevance of accounting education, both from a teaching and a research perspective.

Finally, in Chapter 5, "An agenda for improving accounting education", Kent St. Pierre and James Rebele advance the argument that, contrary to what might be considered conventional wisdom, focussing accounting education on the development of "soft skills" (rather than on technical knowledge) may be both ineffective and contrary to the best interest of our students. The corollary of their argument is the recommendation to return accounting education to a focus on the development of the technical competence of accounting students. This chapter will likely engender spirited debate based on the arguments and recommendations set forth by the authors.

Collectively, Section A comprises a set of chapters which provides a strong conceptual foundation (i.e., the "cornerstones") for the sections and chapters to follow. But these chapters do more! Specifically, they signal the importance of accounting education as a worthy field of intellectual inquiry and the importance of theory-based investigative efforts. A secondary theme of the chapters in Section A is that the *raison d'être* of accounting education research is to guide the development of learning experiences, models, and environments that will ensure future generations of accountants who are technically proficient, financially literate, and able to serve the public interest.

1

Accounting education as a field of intellectual enquiry

Timothy J. Fogarty

CASE WESTERN RESERVE UNIVERSITY, U.S.A.

CONTENTS

Abstract

As an applied field, accounting education draws upon economic, psychological, and sociological worldviews. This chapter traces these lines of influence. Economics has the deepest penetration, though psychology has selected areas of dominance, and sociology has strong potential. This chapter also explores the state of the accounting education literature. When compared against the void that existed not long ago, this area has done quite well. When compared against its potential, the area has not been a success. To some extent, this conclusion reflects systemic theoretical inadequacy. However, a larger share of blame should be apportioned to the social organization of the discipline. Work that is more explicitly theoretical and transcends the individual level of analysis has greater promise for the future of the area.

Keywords

economic analysis, level of analysis, psychological analysis, social organization of academic discipline, sociological analysis, theory

1.1 Introduction

Accounting, as a professional endeavour, must be constantly concerned with the calibre of its membership. The recognition that the discipline has nothing to sell but the capabilities and values of its practitioners has been consistently articulated (e.g. Melancon, 2002). This priority should therefore thrust accounting education into the limelight for all those with a stake in the success of the field.

A critical difference between accounting and the more established professions of law and medicine is that accounting has matured at a much later point in history. This timing has placed practice much closer in time to the emergence of an academic arm dedicated to the profession's contours and needs. Over time, academic accounting staff (i.e. faculty) have attained greater autonomy from practice than have their counterparts in law and medical schools. Positioned therefore as full-time educators, academic accounting staff could be expected to invest deeply in the educational process. As students and their employers become the main clients of academic accounting, knowledge about accounting education should naturally accumulate.

The accounting discipline can also be understood as an element of the education offered to those students interested in business management. This contextualization suggests comparisons between accounting and other business fields such as marketing, finance, and operations. Although those fields have dedicated academic staff and curricula, they lack professional recognition and a cohesive career path for their students. *Ceteris paribus*, we should expect that accounting's uniqueness should translate into a more sustained effort in understanding all aspects of its pedagogy.

To a large extent, these circumstances have contributed to a differentiated maturity for accounting education. By any reasonable metric, the attention devoted to the education of accountants exceeds that of any discipline outside of education itself. This situation provides much to celebrate and ample splendour to reflect upon. At the same time, we can also ask why we do not have more. Since no normatively correct extent of development exists, the proverbial glass is just as likely to be half-empty as half-full.

As an applied discipline, accounting education cannot be expected to have a unique conceptual framework that sets it apart from all disciplines. Although a raft of early efforts were attempted, and to some extent continue (see, for example, Needles, Chapter 2 – this volume), accounting education must look to the source disciplines of Western thought for its intellectual bearings. This journey brings us readily to economics, psychology, and sociology. These three areas collectively provide the structure of a brief review of the main lines of thought in the accounting education literature. This suggests that the intellectual foundations of accounting education can be understood as a function of how well it has applied, adapted, and furthered the source disciplines.

The aims of this chapter are:

- to develop the extent to which the great traditions of economics, psychology, and sociology have informed the study of accounting education as an intellectual exercise. Such influences can range from virtually exclusive with regard to a particular set of issues to virtually non-existent. In addition to recounting past inroads into thinking, the chapter also estimates the future potential of new influences as it relates to an organized area of concern (such as curriculum or students).
- to step back and to evaluate the extent to which accounting education as a field of inquiry has been a success. Part of this assessment could be fashioned as the subsidiary objective of heightening the reader's appreciation for the connection between field development and the social organization of the academy.
- to re-articulate the need for strong theory and a more robust treatment of our level of analysis. These are offered as positive ways forward for the literature.

Whereas the first aim of this chapter may have been enough ambition for the first chapter of this impressive work, it fails to place accounting education in the relative context of the accounting discipline as a whole. For these purposes, the second major objective of the chapter is to more directly assess progress within the accounting discipline. In short, this could be taken as an argument that accounting education research must successfully compete for the heart of those who are positioned to further it. In order to do that, some foundation requirements have to be established. Thus, this chapter not only reviews what the field uses, but also judges its adequacy.

These aims are sought over three subsequent sections. Section 1.2 offers an overview of what theoretical influences exist in accounting education. For these purposes, accounting education is organized as defined by the units of this book. This section also surveys the adequacy of this component of academic accounting. Section 1.3 offers two dimensions whereby the intellectual basis of accounting education research could be improved in a way that cuts across the major sources of intellectual influences. The chapter concludes with Section 1.4 which is a personal reflection and a summary of ideas, both offered as a means of contextualizing the contribution of other parts of this volume.

The entire chapter confesses a U.S.-centric perspective, and admits insufficient awareness of divergence sourced elsewhere in the world to appropriately variegate the assertions. Nevertheless, it offers food for thought to those who might like to consider its content in the context of their own jurisdictions. (For some perspectives from an array of other countries, see Sangster, Chapter 15, and Calhoun & Karreman, Chapter 26 – both in this volume.)

1.2 Economic, psychological, and sociological origins

This section attempts to evaluate the source from which the accounting education literature draws its intellectual power. Whereas one might argue that some other source discipline exists, the collective traditions of economics, psychology, and sociology cover a vast amount of intellectual terrain. Since this is not a literature review, not much effort will be made to document with great specificity the use of the source disciplines. Instead, the chapters in this volume will serve as examples of the use of these lines of thought.

The organization of the accounting education field could have been done in a variety of ways. For the purpose of providing the reader the maximum continuity, the chapter employs a variation of this book's organization. The application of each intellectual tradition will be discussed as it pertains to students, curriculum and pedagogy, assessment and measurement, and broader contexts.

1.2.1 Economic approaches

The legacy of the accounting discipline is most firmly grounded in economics. Disciplinary autonomy from economics progressed gradually and was not complete until well past the mid-point of the twentieth century (Previts & Merino, 1998). Although the failure to distinguish the two is now confined to novice students, accounting continues to draw upon the *Weltanschauung* of economics. Although this may be less true in accounting education than in other corners of the accounting literature, economics remains the strongest and most pervasive intellectual tradition that can be identified.

1.2.1.1 Students

The pervasive idea that students should be cost/benefit thinkers, or utility maximizers is rarely expressed directly, but still is not far from the surface in studies of accounting students. Accounting is an eminently practical course of study with the promise of relatively high income and low unemployment prospects in most markets. These attributes loom large in the minds of those who study the profession's efforts to attract 'the best and brightest' and the perceptions of those who should be entering into the field (see Laswad & Tan, Chapter 9 – this volume). A certain degree of righteous indignation seems to exist among researchers when the 'obvious' economic facts that underlie careers in accounting are not more broadly appreciated. Ironically, the costs of an accounting career, perhaps in foregone alternatives, are given no recognition (see Jackling, Chapter 10 – this volume).

1.2.1.2 Curriculum and pedagogy

The various proposals that have been offered over the years about what should constitute the proper courses for accounting students have incorporated economic notions of human capital formation. That the student should have had ample exposure to that which would make him/her immediately valuable in the service of organizational objectives has been mostly beyond debate. The battlefield of this literature has been the colonization of more generic skills for this task (see Watty, Chapter 13 – this volume). Here the literature has struggled with the extraction of real value from the liberal arts (see Amernic & Craig, Chapter 12 – this volume) as well as the identification of incremental and synergistic value from new curricular combinations and integrations (see Bloom, Chapter 14 – this volume). The belief that the set of experiences put before a student can be changed and reconfigured to derive more output constantly plagues the literature, serving as a Holy Grail of sorts.

Economic notions underlie the educational transformation process. Much has been written about new technologies and their impact upon accounting education (see Boritz & Stoner, Chapter 16 – this volume). New techniques and media are sometimes hailed for efficiency but, more recently, also purport effectiveness superiority in that they reach untapped tendencies of students. In a more traditional vein, the literature conceives of academic staff as being teaching resources (e.g. see Stevenson *et al.*, Chapter 19 – this volume) and worries that this factor's insufficiency, of a quantitative and qualitative nature, might impede student production (i.e. their conversion from students to graduates).

1.2.1.3 Assessment and measurement

Perhaps no corner of the accounting education literature is as marked by foundational economic thinking as that which can generally be called assessment. Student achievement reflects rather strict input–output causal expectations. The belief in place seems to be that extensions of human capital can be meaningfully reduced to small units of comprehension, abandoning ideas of a holistic education (see Koh, Chapter 20 – this volume). Although nobody in accounting has seriously advocated returns on educational investment calculations (elsewhere, however, books such as Bennett & Wilezol (2013) have created an intense ROI debate), the numerator for such appears to be forming. The notion that accounting programmes also must be evaluated is an idea of more recent origin. Here, the complex and esoteric elements of personal maturity and cognitive development are reduced to measurable, quantifiable targets and managed through the progressive accumulation of rubric categories (see Kidwell & Lowensohn, Chapter 21 – this volume). Economic logics, only vaguely constrained by more philosophic stances, also dominate the evaluation of entire educational offerings (see Calderon, Chapter 22, and Apostolou & Gammie, Chapter 29 – both in this volume). One soon forgets that it is education we are discussing! Gone are the days of *je ne sais quoi*, when the full weight of economic totalizing is brought to bear.

1.2.1.4 Broader contexts

Accounting education rarely stands alone, but instead is part of larger educational efforts and infrastructures. Furthermore, the very idea of education exists within a socio-economic framework the contours of which demand explicit recognition. To a considerable extent, these contexts have been drawn in economic terms.

Not surprisingly, the labour needs of the accounting profession create the most salient context for accounting education despite the insulation of students from the legal claims of potential employers. Although these needs are typically couched in opaque rhetoric designed to disguise economic motivations, they ultimately win out on several critical dimensions of the accounting student's experience. Recent shifts to less labour-intensive modes have led to many changes in the university experience, including longer periods of study and more routinized internship endeavours (see Beard & Humphrey, Chapter 25 – this volume). In the effort to render the nascent recruit most desired by accounting firms, accounting education is also expected to be synchronized with post-graduation firm training (see Evans, Chapter 28 – this volume). Surprisingly, tendencies also exist to reduce that which accounting students should know about ethics to the specific economic prohibitions accepted by the accounting profession in its code of ethics (see Boyce, Chapter 24 – this volume).

Many choices exist in selecting the dimensions of the socio-economic environment that affect accounting education. Perhaps the favourite of the literature has been general macro-economic conditions (e.g. Adler, Chapter 23 – this volume). Most obviously, boom times can be contrasted with recessionary ones in terms of employment prospects for students and public and private sector support for educational initiatives. (See Sangster, Chapter 15 – this volume.) Although less fluctuating, the role of government in accounting education is conventionally understood as being a source of funding that needs to be placated with increasing levels of accountability, much of which creates perverse incentives (see Paisey & Paisey, Chapter 30 – this volume). Thus, on balance, researchers are not indifferent to the broad economic impacts extended upon accounting education, but rarely fixate upon them.

1.2.1.5 Summary

Economic thinking pervades the nature of accounting education research. It does so by its ability to saturate the thinking of researchers in ways that may not always be conscious. Deeply held ideas of rationality and pecuniary salience tend to crowd out other intellectual traditions. Economic influences are advantaged by the relative depth of the training of most academic accounting staff in that subject. Accounting education, however, is not as exclusively or stridently economic in its scholarly orientation when compared to the discipline's mainstream research (Reiter & Williams, 2002). In part, the absence of complete domination reflects the ineludible multi-disciplinary nature of the educational undertaking.

1.2.2 Psychological approaches

The purpose of accounting education, like any form of education, is to prepare the minds of the young in specific ways. Combining both cognitive and motivational aspects, this agenda naturally brings us to a psychological worldview. Surveying the literature, such an authorial choice is common, but perhaps not as pervasive as the economic one. This selectively strong influence may reflect the somewhat *ad hoc* training of a considerable set of researchers in the field.

1.2.2.1 Students

How students differ from each other is a question of endless fascination for accounting education. Anyone who has taught appreciates the variation in innate ability for purposes of material mastery. Many studies approach this fact rather circumspectly in the differences that are selected for study. One of the most popular concepts over many years has been learning style differences, usually drafted to make the argument that some preferences are more generously facilitated and that more should be better accommodated (see Duff, Chapter 8 – this volume). Other psychological variables that have had some enduring presence in the literature are locus of control (e.g. Brownell, 1981) and introversion–extroversion (e.g. Booth & Winzar, 1993).

Perhaps due to the fact the few researchers are fully committed to this intellectual wellspring, the accounting literature has not kept up with the more recent explosion of research into human personality. We have not assembled a critical mass of work that is sufficiently normative so as to judge the relative probabilities of a more successful accounting education for some students and not others.

1.2.2.2 Curriculum and pedagogy

Although the implicit theories that underlie accounting curricular work might possess psychological elements, they have not been brought to the forefront by the literature in highly meaningful ways. Here, the critical mass that usually underlies any meaningful progress is missing.

If exceptions do exist, they do so in the study of decisions to major in accounting and related topics such as the design of the first university accounting course (see Wygal, Chapter 11 – this volume). In such contexts, certain personality types, such as those with more need for structure, are believed to be more drawn to the discipline (see Laswad & Tan, Chapter 9 – this volume), but at the cost of appealing to others.

Psychology should be at the heart of studies that explore the implementation of various pedagogies in the accounting classroom. If people have different cognitive approaches, they should be differently enabled to effectively produce critical thinking (see Cunningham, Chapter 18 – this volume) and differentially benefitted by experiential methods (see Hassall & Joyce, Chapter 17 – this volume). However, an excessive amount of effort has apparently been needed to convince academic staff of the appropriateness of such methods, and to describe their basic design. In the U.S.A., a certain reluctance exists to admit that pedagogies and techniques are not equally valuable for all. To some extent, the moral high ground attained by innovation seems to have dampened the need to empirically demonstrate actual educational superiority.

1.2.2.3 Assessment and measurement

The question of why some students perform better than others is an excellent illustration of the advantages of a social psychological perspective. Without question, students come to their accounting coursework with varying cognitions and motivations that can be treated as *a priori* by research designs. However, students also are the products of their past experiences, both academic and vocational (see Byrne & Willis, Chapter 7 – this volume). This recognition prevents us from any tendencies that might exist to render the question with a psychological reductionism reminiscent of economics.

Psychology has not entered into programme and school evaluation efforts. For now, we believe that neutral facts speak for themselves. Grappling with what the facts are, and why we have to confront them, necessarily precedes recognition of stylized subjectivity within the range.

1.2.2.4 Broader contexts

A large and convincing victory has been achieved by psychology in dominating our appreciation of the ethical environment of accounting education. The conventional approach of the literature has been the motif of staged cognitive development as the yardstick of achievement (see Boyce, Chapter 24 – this volume). The success of this conceptualization as the default research tool has resulted in the obfuscation of both situational contingencies and organizational responsibility.

The psychological realm has been less successful in research efforts to appreciate the critical practitioner interface of accounting education. Very little about practice and professionalism is known that does not devolve to monetary manners. That practitioners want what they want from accounting education seems to be enough of a conclusion for this literature. Along similar lines, psychology as an intellectual tradition has not been imported to the study of accrediting agents or governmental officials, despite the disproportionate influence they exert on accounting education (see Apostolou & Gammie, Chapter 29 – this volume). Unlike students, these individuals do not make themselves regularly available for what might be mentally intrusive study.

1.2.2.5 Summary

In contrast to economics, psychology is not a pervasive intellectual source for accounting education. However, its domination in selective areas renders its power quite visible. Psychology also integrates well with the other two sources. Particularly ambitious and clever authors strive to acknowledge the role of human agency in institutionally-structured experiences, as well as those marked by high monetary stakes.

1.2.3 Sociological approaches

The last of the major of intellectual traditions informing accounting education is the sociological. That groups of varying sizes and formality can influence the critical behaviour of students, academic staff, and administrators provides, if nothing else, an avenue of escape from the totalizing tendencies of economics and psychology. Sociology is the least well-developed source of influence. However, the case can be made that large future potential exists in more widespread and innovative utilizations.

1.2.3.1 Students

The core insight that sociology has about students is that they are immersed in a vast socialization effort. As they enter into their identities as accounting students, they have already been influenced by many groups – some of which are purposefully designed to shape them in specific ways. In this vein, the components of the literature that have depended upon the systemic collection of students' perceptions are tallying refracted socialization influence. This includes most distinctly that which we know about what novice students think about accounting careers (see Lucas & Mladenovic, Chapter 6 – this volume). Other related questions target more specific sources of personal influence such as prior work experience and mid-matriculation internships. (See Byrne & Willis, Chapter 7, and Beard & Humphrey, Chapter 25 – both in this volume.) Both positive and negative influences have been identified, with salience dependent upon the specific outcome that is contemplated.

1.2.3.2 Curriculum and pedagogy

Although the curriculum has remained virtually untouched as a field upon which social forces can be seen to be at work, applications can be readily imagined. The grandest choice between a liberal education and that suffused with technical content presents the sociology of knowledge dimensions. How accounting professionals come to know what they do, as well as to draw boundaries around useful knowledge, is poorly appreciated. Curricula narrow the choices that students are allowed to make across the marketplace of ideas. The recognition that knowledge is a social construct needs to make inroads if the normative debate on curriculum is to progress in meaningful ways. The notion held by many in the U.S.A. that curriculum is inexorably driven by professional certification examinations abdicates the responsibility of academic staff and suggests overly mechanical solutions to the knowledge problem.

How we should teach accounting has undergone serious scrutiny in recent decades. Perhaps the debate needs better recognition that learning requires structured social interaction, even if it is accomplished through technological intermediation. Some of the more impressive developments in the pedagogy of this discipline have occurred where students have actively engaged with others (see Hassall & Joyce, Chapter 17 – this volume), often by playing roles scripted by the professional world. Nonetheless, the social element is often obscured by the materials or the technology in play, vectors that systematically suppress human contingency or fixate on the process by which solutions are calculated. (See St. Pierre & Rebele, Chapter 5 – this volume.)

That the curriculum of accounting education is a dynamic construction and within the collective control of academic staff worldwide represents an invitation to a sociological praxis. The vast collection of case studies, teaching tips, and other ancillary materials that has been published by the accounting journals represents a pure form of a group undertaking a shared task. (See Stevenson *et al.*, Chapter 19 – this volume.) In essence, this development departs from the traditions of usual academic research (i.e. scientific method) and constitutes a clearer recognition that storytelling contributions within the kinship are the consequences of community belonging (see Wilson *et al.*, Chapter 3 – this volume). In most instances, these are not done for economic reward.

1.2.3.3 Assessment and measurement

The best illustration of the sociological imagination applied to the question of students' perform-ance is the large body of work exploring gender differences. Lacking biological explanations, the existence of group variations suggest the accumulations of social expectation and mirror-glass self. To a lesser extent, the studies that involve students' race and social class draw upon a similar logic. Less restrictively, the performance of all students is a function of peer-based norms and the dramaturgy of the modern student's role.

The programme assessment literature has not grappled with the sociological reality that the objectives and more generalized expectations of normal are reflections of past definitions and purposeful interpretations. The very idea that management of higher education is possible and that its progress can be reliably measured have strong self-fulfilling prophecy possibilities that need to be exposed. The premise that benchmarking creates a new factual stratum can be self-delusional, but only more theoretically informed work can expose it as such. (See Calhoun and Karreman, Chapter 26 – this volume.)

1.2.3.4 Broader contexts

Sociological analysis is inherently more capable of incorporating larger contexts than either economics or psychology. The tenor of the times enters into the analysis in several ways, including the increasing recognition of a post-modernity in cultural production (see Harvey, 1989; Jamison, 1991). Adler (see Chapter 23 – this volume) provides a much more specific variation of such an embedding. Sociology would prefer to begin with the contours of the *Zeitgeist*.

The very idea of a sustainable society is predicated upon broadly accepted understandings about acceptable behaviour. Finding the outlines of forbearance suggests that the ethics of professionalism has to transcend either economics or psychology. The so-called 'social contract' includes that the pursuit of a public interest must be at least displayed by professional organizations. However strongly bantered, the ethics of firm behaviour does not regularly enter into the typical accounting education. Such lacuna might contribute to the subsequent 'reality shock' of new graduates (see Dean *et al.* 1988).

Links between organizational constituents and higher education have become increasingly salient in recent times. Whereas demands for accountability by employers, independent accreditors, or the state are not very easily incorporated by the other intellectual sources, sociology strives to map the organizational field wherein such interests can be expressed. The extent to which higher education needs to conform to these external interests is usually not challenged. Studies often record practitioner curricular preferences, as if these demands should be accommodated. The literature also passively relays changes in accreditation standards as if there were no distributional consequences involved. A sociological analysis would tend to be more confrontational, perhaps through the systematic study of legitimacy claims. Where the coercive power of the state is involved (see Paisey & Paisey, Chapter 30 – this volume), social system requirements need to be considered.

If sociology shows us only one lesson, it might be that social esteem is unevenly distributed. When elements of a social system are unevenly valued, questions about appropriateness and system maintenance are necessary. Such an agenda should facilitate a deeper understanding about what and how practitioners really seek from accounting programmes, how the accreditation of unequal institutions is possible, and what values are implicit in state controls. Movements in these directions would help identify currently used leaps of faith.

1.2.3.5 Summary

Perhaps because accounting researchers tend to have no formal training in this area (especially in the U.S.A.), sociology has the smallest penetration as an intellectual source for accounting education. In most instances, the questions that it is capable of informing tend not even to be 'on the radar screens' of this sub-discipline. However, more realization that such questions are important and have a place would enhance accounting education.

1.2.4 A holistic assessment

In 1990, Boyer proclaimed the need to broaden that which we deem to be the suitable work of scholars. Dominated by scientific imagery and metaphor, the research that sought to discover how our world worked had crystallized the opposition of that work with the function of the scholar as an educator. Time spent thinking about students and attending to their experiences at the university had been relegated to a secondary status that many considered a regrettable use of time. Boyer (1990), leveraging a highly visible position in the academic community in the U.S.A., disputed this bifurcation by suggesting the need for a scholarship of pedagogy. Bringing the mindset of inquiry to education, along with the tools of systematic exploration, promised to usher in a 'scholarship of teaching' that would mitigate the schism in the academy. As a by-product of multiple forms of scholarship, the esteem with which researchers of all sorts would be provided would be levelled.

Few disciplines have responded with the vigour seen in academic accounting. Bolstered by practitioner commissions and occasional funding, a formidable literature of accounting education research has emerged. Journals explicitly devoted to this area were organized and conferences were held, allowing academic staff from around the globe to share their ideas and their enthusiasms. Careers could be built upon the premise that a scholarship of accounting education was sufficiently important.

Nearly a quarter century has elapsed since Boyer's declaration, but the promise of a broadly recognized scholarship of teaching remains mostly unfulfilled. Progress has been made when such is assessed on a cumulative basis, but achievement has been unevenly realized. We could say that we are in the midst of a sustained golden age, the apogee of which is yet to be realized, but the evidence for this would not be present. Albeit with individualized exceptions and national qualifications, we also have not seen the mitigation of prestige differences among researchers. Education research remains rather underdeveloped and only a secondary career for many of its proponents. Despite the multiple ways of seeing the world offered by economics, psychology, and sociology, we are right to wish for more.

1.2.5 The unfulfilled prospect of accounting education

1.2.5.1 The jurisdictional struggle

Abbott (1988) reset the sociology of the professions by asking us to imagine a world in which occupational groups are in constant struggle with each other for the right to service a clientele. Each group is necessarily involved in a never-ending jurisdictional tussle for recognition, privilege, and income. Extending this general idea, one can easily imagine battles within the business school by a set of disciplines for space in the curriculum, for academic staff positions, and over the allocation of discretionary monies. *A fortiori*, each discipline is itself not a tight homogeneous group but a set of sub-disciplines each trying to achieve supremacy in defining that collection to its environment. Accordingly, the progress of accounting education as a distinct scholarship has to be judged relative to the balance of the accounting academic literature. This contextualization prevents the tendency to list a set of accomplishments by the sub-field and have them taken, by definition, as progress. Viewing specific attainments within the context of victories by other groups allows a relative positioning to become clearer. In other words, sub-fields must always consider that which has not been achieved within a field of its possible success.

There are many markers that could be used to provide evidence of a sub-discipline's trajectory. While some are more conclusive than others, each offers some insight into social evaluation. Most of these dimensions are *ad populum* in their nature. Sub-disciplines thrive by attracting more human disciples and by garnering a larger slice of the available resources. Others are premised on relative success in securing the right to speak on behalf of the larger discipline. Success in non-numeric terms suggests that power does not necessarily parallel demographic representation.

In a perfect world, one could measure the heart of each academic accounting staff member's attachment to his/her field. With such a view, some sub-disciplines would stand out and others would be unmissed by their absence. Lacking this vantage, we assume that people 'vote with their feet' and participate with greater regularity in areas about which they feel most strongly. Here, accounting education should enjoy a distinct advantage. Since almost all academic accounting staff teach, proximity to the core of their sub-field exists for all in a way not true for any other segment of the discipline. All one has to imagine is that these people possess a modicum of enthusiasm, curiosity or excitement about what they are doing, to convert academic accounting staff into an audience and participators in the pursuit of deeper understandings only possible through research. Understanding academic staff in this way would make undergraduate programmes and students the centre of concern. It is in this translation that the current motto of the Teaching, Learning and Curriculum (TLC) section of the American Accounting Association (AAA) reads: '*Every accounting faculty member should be a member of the Teaching Learning and Curriculum section*' (e.g. Crumbley, 2007). Unfortunately, this logic only goes so far.

First, the elephant in the room in any discussion of the behaviour of an academic staff group bears identification. The vast majority of academic accounting staff in the U.S.A. are not scholars. Any interest they might have had above and beyond what exists in the textbooks that they use has long since left the building. Protected by tenure and coddled by the lack of meaningful post-tenure review, these white-collar workers cannot be said to 'vote with their feet' because they have no interest in the scholarship of any of accounting's sub-disciplines. That they might occasionally attend a meeting, join a section of the AAA, or even cast a vote should not be taken as signifying anything other than the expression of some personal agenda. While ignoring these people as socialization failures is convenient, their existence reminds us that the shortfalls of any sub-disciplinary area are a sub-set of the larger problem of inadequate total scholarship. This converts the TLC's motto to something like: '*If accounting faculty can be made to be interested in anything, they ought to be interested in education.*'

This would prove to be a hollow victory, except to the extent that more passive consumers for educational research would exist. To the extent that this is true, it compromises any *vox populi* measure of success. The health of the accounting education literature cannot be judged by the number of people who should be interested in its contents.

Every sub-discipline needs outlets that are receptive to its work. Journals that announce a specialized interest in a particular topic or methodology signal to academic staff that devotion to such can be the basis for the building of their careers within academic organizations, and a vehicle for their reputations within academic communities. Thus, that one might take the number (and perhaps thickness) of specialized journals as evidence of sub-disciplinary health seems reasonable.

This interpretation is somewhat weakened by shifts in the economics of journal production. The last 20 years have witnessed many relevant changes that have made the physical production process less expensive and more within the reach of small-scale operations. The advent of the new segment of electronic-only (web-based) publications is part of this trend. The emergence of colossal publishing corporations charging super-premium rates for library subscriptions has also introduced a profit motive that did not exist previously. All these changes clutter the meaning we can vest in outlet magnitude. Nonetheless, proponents of accounting education can take comfort in the fact that, thanks to the few who took on key editorial responsibilities, a strong demand exists for their work.

1.2.5.2 Intra-disciplinary honorifics

Given the existence of a readership and journal space that begs to be filled, all that is necessary is sufficient producer incentives to imagine, execute, and sell scholarly work. Here, however, the valence that associates with contributions of scholarly work to different journals has to be considered. If the emergence of a specialty journal justifies the exclusion of such work from more mainstream outlets, niche authors may be made worse off by the change if the value of publication in the mainstream journal remains greater. The new journal functions like a ghetto, the population of which allows the old journal to be 'gentrified'. Here the primary beneficiaries are those who continue to do work that can be published in the formerly all-purpose journal. As accounting education journals became part of the firmament, accounting education research was no longer welcome at places like *The Accounting Review* and *Accounting, Organizations and Society*. If publications are the currency of academic careers (Fogarty, 2009), sub-disciplines such as accounting education need to attend to the exchange rate before concluding that they have grown rich with a new form of wealth. (For a debate on this topic, set in the U.K., see issues 20(6), December 2011, and 21(1), February 2012, of *Accounting Education: an international journal*.)

Others point to the existence of honours earned by proponents of sub-disciplines as evidence of sub-disciplinary prominence. When a group such as the scholars of accounting education grows in size, recognition of differential, individual success within that segment is an appropriate response. However, the acid test is not those recognitions that are confined to the sub-group, but those deemed to be available on an at-large basis. Does such 'small pond' success create access to the bigger tables? That is a sterner test that would preclude such recognitions from being viewed as 'minor league' by others. Just as every small pond will have its large fish, every academic specialty will have its presidents and its prolific publishers. The extent to which people who have focussed their talents on accounting education questions can bootstrap such into entire discipline recognition would seem to be rather low.

Accounting education work does not seem to be represented in the annual contests for the *Notable Contributions to Accounting Literature* and *Seminal Contribution to Accounting Literature* awards given by the AAA. People who have made major contributions to accounting education scholarship have never won the AAA's *Accounting Educator of the Year* award. Am I the only one who finds this fact ironic? Likewise, people of that ilk tend to be systematically excluded from the resident faculty at events like the AAA Deloitte J. Michael Cook Doctoral Consortium, (Fogarty & Jonas, 2010). While the editors of journals such as *Issues in Accounting Education* are included on panels on how to get your work published, such venues are hardly opportunities to promote educational research. Until the people who do educational research can be held up as role models to the uninitiated, what they have done has really been validated as extraordinary outside the niche.

1.2.5.3 Supportive resources

Accounting education's main advantage is the degree of passion people feel for their sub-discipline. Whereas no organized collective is without its zealots, accounting education may reside close to the apex in this regard. The education of the young is an honourable calling, about which it is difficult to be too cynical. Facilitating the start of professional careers, especially for those whom we can imagine fighting the good fight, should call forth our best efforts to learn more about how students' experiences should be best organized. However, it may be that such enthusiasm also blinds us to the structural shortcomings of the area. Here we might be more willing to overlook those problems that cannot be fixed than we would be if we could be more dispassionate about the subject matter.

Accounting practitioner groups have consistently advocated for research on the practical problems that would benefit the success of the profession. On paper, this position would seem to align well with that which accounting education research seeks to deliver. (For example, the primary mission of this book is to enhance the educational base of accounting practice.) Relative to other sub-disciplines, accounting education makes reasonable assumptions and does not indulge in excessive methodological obfuscation. Most of the issues that accounting education confronts are those that would make direct or indirect contributions to the proper training of staff accountants. Notwithstanding such a natural alignment of interests, the practice community has not chosen to differentially support those who concentrate their investigative work in accounting education. The available evidence suggests that acquiring an affiliation with more prestigious universities is a stronger explanation of the pattern of funding by the large public accounting firms (Fogarty, 1995). This tendency works to the disadvantage of accounting education researchers who, as a group, tend to be more evenly distributed across the prestige strata of the academy.

Accounting firms possess a mountain of data that would be of great interest to those researching accounting education questions. These organizations continue the education of young professionals with intensive firm-specific training. They provide early career experiences that put the sufficiency of formal education to an acid test. Most importantly, people who are recruited either continue with the firm or do not. The firms have rarely allowed access to this information. Accordingly, their willingness to support inquiries into accounting careers should be seriously questioned.

1.2.5.4 Quality

In the final analysis, a sub-discipline must be judged by the quality and quantity of its research. Good and plentiful work should, even if only in the long run, garner respect and encourage more people to continue that which has been initiated. Academic accounting staff members should appreciate the application of the opportunity cost idea to their research. Time and effort placed into one project displace other ventures. *Ceteris paribus*, academic staff should want to have their names associated with problems that matter and with answers that are strong.

Whether the research in accounting education possesses high quality and approaches critical mass presents empirical questions that cannot be fully answered here. Quality poses difficult and potentially philosophic questions (Pirsig, 1974) that are usually deflected by resort to a self-referential impact terrain wherein citation counts can be made. Although we should not expect that sub-fields such as accounting education would have a major impact on the mainstream, we could perhaps observe a few breakthrough exceptions. Other than the commissions that have been useful in problematizing issues, little of this calibre seems to exist.

Although this is ultimately an untested empirical question, my impression is that the education literature is quite 'flat' in the sense that relatively few studies have had much impact on others. At times, we share the ambition that good ideas can be found outside accounting, for example, in the efforts of Marton & Säljö (1984), Kolb (1984), Rest (1986), Biggs (1987), and Ramsden (1992). These borrowings fail in part because we do not also learn from previous accounting borrowings. Visibility here is a short-lived prospect, in part because recent studies do not appear to be much better than those that came before them on that topic. This characteristic might be attributable to the tendency for studies to be based on data from single universities. I also suspect that empirical work in the area would find that work outside accounting education would be more influential than work inside the sub-discipline. I also suspect that not much consensus would be produced if resident experts were asked which articles truly made a difference. Although mostly of symbolic value, sub-disciplines need shining stars who could be the objects of near-universal aspiration.

The quantity of empirical studies in accounting education may also be diminished. Many may not have noticed that cases and other instructional material have a larger share of total available pages in some journals devoted to accounting education. These materials might have pedagogical value, but they should not be confused with research. Academics should share best practices and well-conceived tools, and journals have proven to be the main means of dissemination. However, the presence of teaching resources in research journals in magnitudes that rival more traditional studies, creates a mixed message to external parties. Case studies and teaching ideas tend to cheapen the currency of the realm, making it too easy for critics to evidence the second-class status of the education sub-discipline.

If a decline of real education research in accounting has occurred, the causes should be determined. The advance of authorities charged with human subject protection has increased the entry barriers for studies that want to gather empirical data on students. Many of the best studies done in the 1980s would not be approved today. We have reached the point where an educator cannot try one practice in one course section and not in the other. Apparently, pedagogy is so important that we cannot accept that some students will not get the best, even if we do not know *a priori* which is best.

While educational research might have become somewhat more difficult to conduct, the value of it to researchers might have disproportionately diminished. In the U.S.A. and the U.K., the management of the research undertaken by academic staff has grown quite fashionable. The escalated demands for a different type of accounting research have narrowed how today's academic staff define the scholarship component of their jobs. Whereas in the past, academic staff would carry a diverse portfolio of research projects, today they can ill afford to be so eclectic. This concentration on 'What counts' tends to drop the clever education project onto the cutting room floor. A niche that once thrived on the occasional participation of the many has now been left to the few who either work at more indulgent institutions, or are tone deaf to the demands that surround them.

1.2.5.5 Summary

In sum, it becomes necessary to consider the painful possibility that accounting education as a literature specialty is not in ascendancy. This result did not occur because of the lack of diligence or cultivation by its advocates. Here, the efforts of journal editors merit particular attention for building an infrastructure that has allowed this niche to emerge and, for a while, to thrive. However, the passion to know more about the students we teach and the institutions that engage us has not been sufficient to sustain growth. In the face of a somewhat trenchant mainstream discipline, educational issues have been removed to a secondary position in the firmament.

1.3 Two key dimensions

This section of the chapter probes for major explanations that would resolve the tension between the previous two sections of the chapter. To wit, how does a field capable of pulling together economic, psychological, and sociological influences not succeed to an enormous degree? Here, the research of the field, as opposed to all its publication activity, is addressed. Specifically, theory adequacy and level of analysis are explored.

1.3.1 Theory and its discontents

One of the largest revelations for any doctoral student is the need for theory. Theory accomplishes many useful functions for the scholar. For example:

(a) Theory signals to the world what our *ex ante* beliefs might be. We also learn the contours of our own perspective on the world through theory.

(b)   Theory provides a meta-level from which we learn to form expectations that are consistent. Only with theory is the world not chaotic and essentially *ad hoc*.

(c)   Theory enables us to make a contribution that is capable of transcending the four corners of that which we currently can see and manipulate. In other words, through theory we can escape the smallness of our projects and our humble data-sets. Theory is so important that it should serve as the first place we should look for problems when considering a shortcoming in the literature.

Perhaps the greatest hidden function of a good theory is that it provides scholars with common ground. Rather than having to reinvent the world with every paper, scholars can merely tap a common wellspring wherein high levels of interpersonal agreement exist about what is important and what cannot be done. A common theory tends to also offer a common vocabulary. Words in this language can be used without the need to defend against and worry over what idiosyncratic interpretations will be taken by readers.

Despite its many advantages, theory has not made a major impact on the accounting education literature. Again, I venture ideas with untested assertions of empirical regularities. However, I feel fairly confident in the proposition that accounting education work suffers from theory deficiencies.

Even relative to accounting itself, accounting education research is a relatively new field within the academy. The first specialty journal in the area did not begin to publish until 1983. Can we really be expected to have theory? We could be also somewhat persuasive that a hallmark of any good theory is that the test of time has been withstood. Along these lines, insufficient time has passed since people have had the freedom to pursue these matters on a full-time basis. Therefore, the best that accounting education can be expected to do is to borrow from the more established disciplines. As attested to by the review in Section 1.2 of this chapter, the first problem is that we had not borrowed well or deeply enough. The second problem is that we do not even see the need to borrow.

As a niche of the larger social collective we call academic accounting, we can learn much about accounting education as an intellectual exercise by the comparisons which the larger pool makes possible. This forces the question of the theoretical sufficiency of any accounting scholarship. If the lack of a theory is merely a reflection of the fact that accounting is such an applied field, its absence from education work is hardly a concern. However, if such is a distinct shortfall, the absence of theory might possess some importance.

I suspect that the truth lies somewhere between these two extremes. Accounting research certainly does not have material home-grown theory. The fruitlessness of the search for optimal accounting treatments for transactions has been recognized for some time. This realization has been instrumental in the ushering in of a post-modern economics as a *de facto* theory. When pressed about theory, most accounting researchers instinctively fall back upon agency theory. These ideas about informational asymmetries, signalling, and moral hazard offer an open architecture that borders on the vacuous. To an increasing extent, researchers do not even bother running the readers through these paces. The litany of actors' incentives to minimize so-called agency costs as the behavioural answer to any reporting or intra-organizational use of accounting tends now to be either bypassed or driven by in the blink of an eye. One could now say that accounting theory has become something with which to drill graduate students, and then largely ignore. Theory also serves as a cudgel with which reviewers beat manuscript authors, knowing full well that demands for such cannot be met. Nonetheless, the supposed existence of a theory provides accounting academics in mainstream areas with some implicit agreed-upon perspective, from which everyone derives mutually ascribed self-respect.

Those who toil in the fields of accounting education might also have an implicit theory that they incorporate into the design and execution of their research. However, they would be hard-pressed to identify what such a theory would be, and even more challenged to provide a reasonable consensus about it. The field of education does not provide a cohesive body of thought for these purposes. One could attempt to mine the educational philosophers, such as John Dewey, but hardly anyone believes that such action is necessary.

The best candidate for a theory might be a Skinnerian prospect whereby students can be seen as responding to the stimuli or potential rewards presented. Here, one is asked to imagine the classroom as a laboratory designed for human experimentation. For example, students who are shown a video about a notorious fraudster offer more ethical responses. However, these responses have been shown to have rapid deterioration. More generally, researchers collectively seem to have some ideas about the importance of motivation, but most of this continues to reside within the black box of students' brains. As a result, they do not easily lend themselves to research design. Recently, some have grabbed at the theory of planned behaviour (TPB). (See Laswad & Tan, Chapter 9 – this volume.) If one does not accept entropy as a suitable metaphor, that theory seems tautological on its face. To better approach why some students are better motivated, many other researchers resort to a grab bag of personality dimensions.

Others have taken more cognitive tact, especially to the question of how learning occurs. Some progress has been made on a descriptive level, in identifying different styles or dispositions. However, this work has not reached back to the causes of these differences, leaving us with an *a priori* stew. The research has not reached forward to consequences in any meaningful way. This situation leaves us with the empty conclusion that people are different.

The theory problem in accounting education might be grounded in relative distance. I suspect that the further a scholar is from the phenomenon, the more theory is thought to be needed and its absence deemed to be consequential. So when a person who normally teaches debits and credits to undergraduates wants to identify the subtle and hidden regularities in the reporting of global enterprises, he/she had better be armed with initial postulates. At the same time, doing education work might be just too close to where we are, and what we know best. Education is at our fingertips, rendering its problems intuitive to writers and obvious to readers. Theory would only obfuscate, some could easily think. Others would say that this familiarity has bred contempt.

If all problems do not gradually but surely come back to socialization, we are probably not thinking sufficiently deeply about them. Human beings have a very limited ability to re-invent themselves, a constraint that prevents practitioners from being academics and academics being much good in a 'real' world. In this application, we observe that accounting education is almost never 'Plan A' with regard to the life of scholarship that was set out for people during their doctoral training. I know of no person trained in the U.S.A. who did anything but accidently fall into the niche at some point long after taking their first faculty position. This diversion is not accidental, since doctoral programmes in this discipline in the U.S.A. would be more truthful if they admitted that students can study anything but education and history. Thus, having been well-trained to do something else, people 'discover' education at a time when they do not possess the freedom to drink deeply at the well. For many, pursuing accounting education as a topic of study begins as a part-time sideline. That it soon becomes much more for some, fails to gainsay the belief that low entry barriers exist. Being sufficiently trained to be able to bring theory to bear never enters into the equation for accidental adherents. As attested to by Section 1.2 of this chapter, we should be fortunate for the 'dog's breakfast' that we have.

If the accounting education literature were nothing but applied psychology, we would have a firmer theoretical footing. That many of its strongest proponents and producers would resist such a classification illustrates the theoretical vacuum that the field finds itself. Although 'letting a thousand flowers bloom' would seem like an enlightened approach, it creates the appearance of indecisiveness and incoherence once we get beyond the proverbial choir. The struggle would be more honest if it were either more visible or more complete. It remains *sub rosa* and partial, as theoretical elements are deployed on the fly and rarely twice in the same way.

In our current world, education is increasingly characterized as being an offshoot of the economy. Accounting as a field of study exists as the poster child for vocationalism to students. This positioning creates problems (self-selection) as well as advantages (more homogeneous career aspirations and placement) for the literature. Nonetheless, even such a strong context as this tends to be made invisible by most researchers who are all too willing to take such dimensions as a given state of nature. It seems ironic that those trained to identify wealth transfers in equity markets and supply chains, so readily ignore the distributive consequences of education.

Educational research also lacks humanistic or philosophical neutrality. Because, as most would agree, education has the ability to allow a person deeper participation in the best traditions of our civilization, it has utility not captured by economic value-added. However, with the possible exception of ethics, the accounting education literature has been rather resistant to the liberal arts. Instead, most would prefer to characterize it as pre-professional, an orientation that stresses its contribution to factual mastery and technical content. In other words, accounting researchers have tended to give lip service to the values that underlie a broad education. That which cannot be brought to bear into the service of an employing organization and its clients holds little interest for the literature. (See Amernic & Craig, Chapter 12 – this volume.)

In sum, the extensive borrowings described in Section 1.2 at first seemed like a celebratory cornucopia of possibilities. However, such eclecticism pales against a proprietary theory, or even a broader consensus that would facilitate the reasoned accumulation of scholarship.

1.3.2 Level of analysis

The stunted nature of theory in accounting education may also be related to how we define appropriate accounting education research. The close connection between that which we study with that which we do (i.e. teach) would seem to be a blessing. However, this merger poses the threat of the excessively practical. For some, this nexus encourages the belief that all we can know is what we can see. Research should be grounded in empirical observation, but should also engage the imagination by helping us see beyond our current setting. The practical in education exists as a dangerous allure since it offers us one interesting question after another.

A general regularity of the opportunity cost is our reluctance to identify research projects that transcend the individual level of analysis. Perhaps this tendency is a natural response to the availability of individual students, each of whom represents a separable set of behaviours and outcomes. The cost of this convenience is the fact that, as researchers offer us their classes, their university, and that which they bring pertaining to their subject, aggregation becomes quite problematic. Especially if innovation by educators is a critical design parameter, much research needs to be done before we can be comfortable in any generalization. That the experience of others may vary has become the unfortunate litany of just about every education paper.

Higher education, as we know it, is in the process of, if not revolutionary, then consequential change. Gradually losing the right to be the timeless repository of culture and civilization, we find ourselves whipsawed by the voraciousness of capitalism. Yet, we are still in the phase where we resent the demands of value for money and accountability for tangible results. With small exception, the education literature has not attended to the long march of history but has instead taken a business-as-usual stance. Just as we do not feel the rotation of the Earth, we do not see how we are slowly bringing about a world unrecognizable to us.

Most would admit that there is more to education than students reading books, attending classes, and taking examinations. Choices made as to what constitutes a proper curriculum, a well-rounded business school, and a complete university experience provide ample opportunity to conceive variations, both modest and bold. Those who work for these institutions, and in service of the objectives that these entities are designed to seek, should not accept as taken-for-granted that which has mere longevity.

Never before have we been asked to embrace the idea of the university as an extension of other parts of society as we are today. The various groups that employ accountants are no longer willing to sit back and accept what they are given by universities. Instead, various interested parties believe that they can impose their will upon these results, perhaps skewing outcomes into alignment with their immediate interests. Higher education, forced to do more on less and less public money, has never been more vulnerable. Not much time has been needed to transgress the distance from education as an end on its own terms to education as a means towards the ends of others. Add in those who aspire to define quality as a method of justifying stratifications (e.g. administrators, accreditors) and one has quite a contested terrain. Although I might not endorse Stalin's definition of education as dependent on who is pointing the gun at whom, to believe that we constitute one happy family, pursuing transparent objectives, is just as fanciful. In short, the individual level of analysis can be what you make of it. Without some recognition of inequality and irreconcilable ambition, it is a deception.

The accounting education literature has not offered much at this highest level of analysis. Although much of this non-involvement is again a result of just not seeing, it also tends to propagate the harmful myths that are part of the problem. In the U.S.A., where classlessness is the official religion, the distribution of resources (human and otherwise) usually goes unexamined. We rarely ask the *qui bono* question, perhaps because we would prefer not to know the answer.

The business school has been the vanguard of the movement toward group work by students. Justified by the idea that corporations and professional firms require work done in collaborative ways, schools have increasingly turned to designing academic work and evaluating it, as it is done by more than one person. (See Hassall & Joyce, Chapter 17 – this volume.) Sacrificing clarity of accountability, this transition premised the need for students' actual experiences in the process of working with others. Notwithstanding the debatable philosophic and psychological standing of this transition, very little work has been done that actually studies students working together – but see Millis & Cottell (1998), and Ravenscroft *et al.* (1999). Although most academic staff are aware of the dynamics of these teams (e.g. leadership, organization, free ridership), the literature hardly attests to their existence. Again, a certain degree of uncritical cheerleading has taken root.

Along similar (but more permanent) lines, individual members of academic staff do not work alone. They collaborate over the course of their careers with similarly situated others. Academic staff are grouped by their institutions into departments the collective purpose of which is to further the interests of their institution. Academic staff also co-author with people in their departments, in other departments, and at other universities. Again, however, these instances of a group level of analysis have not garnered any systematic attention. What we actually know about authorship teams, accounting departments, or the major academic organizations in the field is negligible. At the same time, the productivity of individuals continues to be the standard fascination, despite diminishing returns.

Levels of analysis are similar to spatial dimensions in that contentment within one makes others imperceptible. Just as the residents of Flatland (Abbott, 2010, originally published in 1884) were unable to imagine height, those who do a version of the educational literature, the contributions of which are limited to individual students and academic staff, cannot see the full world that surrounds them. In many instances, hostility may result since they cannot comprehend why such questions *should* be asked. As long as our journals content themselves with the individual level work, we are not nudging scholars into other realms. Even if the insights derived were plentiful and stunning, their sacrifice would be telling.

There are many important educational projects to do at the individual level of analysis. For many members of academic staff who have been around for some time, today's students are puzzling people who present us with an untold variety of empirical questions. In many ways we are presiding over the decline of an age, and the downsizing of another. Regarding the former, we need to retest that which used to be the conventional wisdom to measure how wrong we have become. The latter makes new connections available, often by virtue of the technology that has become readily available. We should not be shy about quantifying the hidden costs.

1.4 Ending issue

1.4.1 A personal reflection

The task of writing this chapter has the unfortunate consequence of projecting an author who appears to be above the fray. Nothing could be further from the truth. I have worked within the traditions of economics, psychology, and sociology, in both systematic and indiscriminate ways. Although I have tried to inform my work by theory, I have regularly failed and therefore have presented much work to the educational readership on a *res ipsa loquitur* basis. I have had theoretical attempts rebuffed by reviewers and therefore have been complicit in its non-appearance in the educational field. Whereas I have successfully developed work at higher levels of analysis, I also yield to the charms of studying students and trying to open the black box of their behaviour. I all too readily respond to the opportunities that are presented, even if they do not make the contributions that I know need to be made. In the final analysis, I am part of the problem.

Although I have to conclude that the accounting education literature is not the 'shining city upon a hill' that it may have had the promise to be, I respect others who might see it differently. Judged in absolute terms, the shortcomings of the field as an intellectual exercise are wide and apparent. Put into a relative context, the judgement is not as harsh, but still rather modestly unfavourable. Within the literature, the existence of many, many excellent works could have been sufficient reason for optimism about the future.

This chapter does not mean to diminish the efforts of the many scholars from across the world who have contributed to the accounting education literature. I could have written a chapter of praise and acknowledgement. However, I feel that a recounting of specific achievement either has been done well enough (e.g. St. Pierre *et al.* 2009) or that others are more predisposed toward the spirit with which such an effort should be accomplished. I come from a different philosophical front about these matters when I argue that we should have done better.

In many ways, those of us who have worked long and hard in this area have done as well as we could. However, we also should be attentive to those who actively or passively oppose the accounting education sub-field. Recognition and esteem tend to be zero-sum and therefore are not necessarily bestowed based on diligence, mental agility, or any other criteria of merit. Those who have prestige do not give it away for free.

I have taken what might have been for some an extreme interpretation of my subject. Perhaps this is because I do not accept the conventional definition of 'intellectual' as it is used in the title upon which I was asked to write. I attempted to prevent this word from becoming a rarified and absolute construction. For me, there is not much to this word that does not merge with the relativistic, social construction of the discipline. We are word-processing, statistics-generating warriors who do not battle ignorance as much as we battle other crusaders convinced that they have more of a right to do the same in very different ways.

1.5 Conclusion

This chapter has attempted to achieve three quite different objectives. The first was to attempt to trace the source of intellectual tradition into lines of accounting education work. What could be imagined is a three-columned spreadsheet (economic, psychological, sociological) wherein the rows constituted every cohesive topic of interest in the literature. What was attempted in that component of the chapter was a description that would at least colour the cell in a way that would indicate intense, modest, or scanty evidence of systematic application. The second objective provided a more judgemental and critical evaluation of the health of the accounting education sub-discipline. And the third addressed the need for strong theoretical foundations when undertaking accounting education research.

This chapter could have argued that accounting education would not be marginalized because it better sources the value proposition that subsumes academic accounting into the social contract between the profession and the public (see Pathways Commission, 2012). The case that the scholarship of accounting education merits more respect based solely on its own achievements has been made convincingly (Wilson *et al.*, 2008) and need not be repeated here.

This chapter, positioned as it is at the beginning of this book, needs to be understood as an introduction of sorts. This book offers an integrated view of accounting education, the likes of which can be found in no other single source. Bookended by a first section (Chapters 1–5) which provides a high-level 'where we are right now' set of treatments and the last section (Chapters 27–30) which places accounting education in a variety of contexts, the core involves who are our students (Chapters 6–10), what are we doing to them (Chapters 11–15 and Chapters 16–19), and how are we measuring the relative success of this journey (Chapters 20–22). In many ways, this chapter has attempted to find illustrations within the subsequent chapters.

The chapters of the book bring together many of the most prominent people who have contributed to the field, including several editors, former editors, and associate editors of the main journals. Reflecting the geographic distribution, four continents are represented – even if most of the authors hail from the U.K. or one of its former colonies. Apparently, the sun never sets on the accounting education literature, either. Capturing this talent dispersion, this book is well positioned to be a major contribution to the field.

References

Abbott, A. (1988) *The System of Professions*, Chicago: University of Chicago Press.
Abbott, E. (2010) *Flatland*, New York: Cambridge University Press.
Bennett, W. & Wilezol, D. (2013) *Is College Necessary?* Nashville, TN: Thomas Nelson, Inc.
Biggs, J.B. (1987) *Study Process Questionnaire Manual*, Melbourne: Australian Council for Educational Research.

Booth, P. & Winzar, H. (1993) Personality biases of accounting students: some implications for learning style preferences, *Accounting and Finance*, 33, 109–120.

Boyer, E. (1990) *Scholarship Reconsidered: Priorities of the Professorate*, Princeton, NJ: Carnegie Foundation.

Brownell, P. (1981) Participation in budgeting: locus of control and organizational effectiveness, *The Accounting Review*, 56, 844–860.

Crumbley, D.L. (2007) A message from the chair, *The Accounting Educator*, 17(1), 1–2.

Dean, R., Ferris, K., & Konstans, C. (1988) Occupational reality shock and organizational commitment: evidence from the accounting profession, *Accounting, Organizations and Society*, 14, 251–262.

Fogarty, T. (1995) Sponsored academic positions by large public accounting firms: an analysis of *quid pro quo*, *Advances in Public Interest Accounting*, 6, 133–162.

Fogarty, T. (2009) Show me the money, *Accounting Education: an international journal*, 18(1), 3–6.

Fogarty, T. & Jonas, G. (2010) The hand that rocks the cradle: disciplinary socialization at the AAA Doctoral Consortium, *Critical Perspectives on Accounting*, 21, 303–317.

Harvey, D. (1989) *The Condition of Postmodernity*, Malden, MA: Blackwell.

Jamison, F. (1991) *Postmodernism*, Durham, NC: Duke University Press.

Kolb, D.A. (1984) *Experiential Learning*, Englewood Cliffs, NJ: Prentice-Hall.

Marton, F. & Säljö, R. (1984) Approaches to learning, in Martin, F., Hounsell, D., & Entwistle, N. (eds) *The Experience of Learning*, Edinburgh: Scottish Academic Press, pp. 36–55.

Melancon, B. (2002) A new accounting culture, *Journal of Accountancy*, 194(4), 27–32.

Millis, B.J. & Cottell, P.G., Jr (1998) *Co-operative Learning for Higher Education Faculty*, Phoenix, AZ: American Council on Education.

Pathways Commission (2012) *The Pathways Commission: Charting a National Strategy for the Next Generation of Accountants*, Sarasota, FL: American Accounting Association.

Pirsig, R. (1974) *Zen and the Art of Motorcycle Maintenance: An Inquiry into Values*, New York: Quill, William Morrow.

Previts, G. & Merino, B. (1998) *A History of Accountancy in the United States*, Columbus, OH: Ohio State University Press.

Ramsden, P. (1992) *Learning to Teach in Higher Education*, London: Routledge.

Ravenscroft, S., Buckless, F.A., & Hassall, T. (1999) Co-operative learning: a literature guide, *Accounting Education: an international journal*, 8(2), 163–176.

Reiter, S. & Williams, P. (2002) The structure and progressivity of accounting research and the production of knowledge, *Accounting Organizations and Society*, 27(6), 575–607.

Rest, J. (1986) *Moral Development: Advances in Research and Theory*, New York: Praeger.

St. Pierre, E.K., Wilson, R.M.S., Ravenscroft, S.P., & Rebele, J.E. (2009) The role of accounting education research in our disciplines: an editorial, *Issues in Accounting Education*, 24, 123–130.

Wilson, R.M.S., Ravenscroft, S.P., Rebele, J.E., & St. Pierre, E.K. (2008) The case for accounting education research, *Accounting Education: an international journal*, 17(2), 103–112.

About the author

Timothy J. Fogarty is a Professor of Accounting at the Weatherhead School of Management, Case Western Reserve University, U.S.A. (tjf@case.edu). He has played many roles within the American Accounting Association, and also worked with the accounting practice community. He is currently an Associate Editor of *Journal of Accounting Education* and *Global Perspectives on Accounting Education*, and has also served as an Associate Editor of both *Accounting Education: an international journal* and *Issues in Accounting Education*. Although he has published on many topics, his heart belongs to accounting education, in part because of the steadfast support of Richard Wilson.

2

Modelling accounting education

Belverd E. Needles, Jr.

DEPAUL UNIVERSITY, U.S.A.

CONTENTS

Abstract

This chapter deals broadly with the modelling of accounting education beginning with a historical review. After summarizing the models of accounting education implied by the standards of the International Accounting Education Standards Board (IAESB), the integrated, linear, and parallel systems of qualifying to become professional accountants are compared. We present a comprehensive model of accounting education based on the model developed by Needles & Anderson (1994), which consists of: (1) teaching and learning cycles of educators and students; (2) integrated learning objectives; (3) technological support of teaching and learning cycles; (4) cognitive levels of learning; and (5) output skills development. Finally, we discuss and illustrate the general application of the comprehensive model.

Keywords

accounting qualification, cognitive levels of learning, elements of accounting education, integrated learning objectives, models of accounting education, output skills development, skills development, teaching and learning cycles, technological support

2.1 Introduction

The main aims of this chapter are:

- to briefly discuss the historical evolution of models of accounting education;
- to identify the elements of accounting education and show how these elements are structured in three common models of accounting education;
- to present a comprehensive model of accounting education;
- to enumerate the cognitive levels of learning in the comprehensive model; and
- to discuss considerations to take into account when applying the comprehensive model.

For decades, accounting education has been in a state of evolution. Changes in the way we do business, technological advances, and the need for thorough trustworthy reporting have affected what employers and the public expect of a professionally-qualified accountant. (See Flood, Chapter 4, and St. Pierre & Rebele, Chapter 5 – both in this volume.) From as far back as 1905 there have been attempts to move accounting education and the certification of professional accountants to align with other professional disciplines, such as law and medicine (Sterrett, 1905). This drive to align professional accounting with medicine and law has put an increased emphasis on in-class education integrated with professional experience. The coupling of classroom education with real-world experience is nothing new to accounting education, but how and when classroom instruction is delivered has differed greatly throughout the years and has varied depending on the country in which one is seeking certification. Today there is a heightened emphasis on output skills as opposed to traditional textbook and rules-based knowledge (see Watty, Chapter 13, and Kidwell & Lowensohn, Chapter 21 – both in this volume). This emphasis has changed how accounting education is delivered and approached (see Chapters 16–19 in this volume, making up Section D on Pedagogic Considerations). In this chapter we will give a brief context as to how accounting education has changed through the years (see also Fogarty, Chapter 1, and Flood, Chapter 4 – both in this volume), how education is modelled in different countries (see also Calhoun & Karreman, Chapter 26 – this volume), and how educational models can be applied to meet the ever-changing expectations that global employers and the public have for professionally-qualified accountants. Trying to keep abreast of the changing requirements for professional certification is reflected in the speed with which the contents of reference books such as Anyane-Ntow (1992) and Fay (1992) have ceased to be current.

2.2 Historical evolution

As mentioned above, as far back as the beginning of the twentieth century there have been approaches to accounting education which have sought to put it on a par with other professional training programmes such as those in medicine and law (Sterrett, 1905). Through the years there have been significant steps taken by accounting educators and employers alike. Taylor (1932) made a case for a fifth year of accounting education in the U.S.A. after the standard four years of university coursework which are undertaken for an undergraduate degree. He argued that the current four years of education should provide a broad overview of accounting and then, in the fifth or graduate year, allow for specialization and concentration. This call for post-graduate education was reinforced in the 1967 *Horizons for a Profession* report by the Beamer Committee (Roy & MacNeill, 1967). The Beamer Committee, also known as the American Institute of Certified Public Accountants (AICPA) Committee on Education and Experience Requirements, was sponsored by the Carnegie Corporation and the AICPA, and was tasked to define what it means to be considered a professional accountant, including the knowledge one must obtain upon entry to the profession. The recommendations of this committee were detailed in the *Horizons* Report. As a result of these recommendations, the AICPA made a Policy Statement that at least five years of college study would be required to cover the knowledge necessary to become an accountant. Today, in the U.S.A., candidates must complete 150 semester hours of university-level coursework to sit for the Certified Professional Accountant (CPA) Examination. (A typical course in the semester system involves three hours of classroom time each week for the duration of the semester.)

In the 1970s and 1980s, the discussion around accounting education began to expand from how much was being taught to the content of curricula and how that knowledge was being conveyed (see Chapters 11–15 in this volume making up Section C on Curriculum Considerations). In 1978, Manuel F. Cohen, former chairman of the Securities and Exchange Commission (SEC), released the Cohen Report, which investigated the roles and responsibilities of auditors and recommended standards by which auditors could be evaluated. One of the biggest discoveries of the report was the schism between academic and professional accountants. He found that, given the confidential nature of accounting, the professional community did not share information with academics to allow for relevant knowledge development and problem resolution, in contrast to what the legal and medical professions receive from their academic communities (Cohen *et al.*, 1978). (See also Bloom *et al.*, 1994.) This call for cooperation between the academic and professional accountants was supported by the 1989 Big 8 *White Paper*. The *White Paper* was a joint document developed by the managing partners of the top eight accounting firms in the U.S.A. and it called for a change in the ways in which accounting education was delivered (Arthur Andersen *et al*, 1989). The *White Paper* emphasized a need to teach students by doing rather than by rote memorization. The paper highlighted the need to develop core skills, such as writing and ethical awareness, throughout the curriculum (see Watty, Chapter 13, and Boyce, Chapter 24 – both in this volume) as opposed to isolated classes. The paper also acknowledged the information gap between academics and the profession, stressing the importance of students practising using real-world scenarios that they may face in the profession. The firms committed $4 million to the project, which was used to form the Accounting Education Change Commission (AECC, 1990). The objective of the AECC was to facilitate changes in accounting education (see Sundem, Chapter 27 – this volume). Educators were challenged to maintain the same competence demanded of professionals along with adapting to the changing needs of the accounting profession (Previts & Merino, 1998).

From the 1990s to today, one of the biggest topics which educators must address is ethics. Ethics in accounting is a critical component in functioning capital markets (Bean & Bernardi, 2007). With the financial collapse of both Enron and WorldCom in 2002, business ethics, and specifically accounting ethics, were brought onto the public stage. New legislation was developed to address the public concerns, an example of which was the Sarbanes–Oxley legislation in the U.S.A. that increased oversight into accounting practices (Young & Annisette, 2009). As yet, there are no new regulations as to how the teaching of ethics should be approached at the university level. There are many discussions on the table, such as requiring a mandatory amount of ethics education (ibid.), or modelling the approaches used by the medical and legal professions (Liu *et al.*, 2012). Regardless of the approach taken, it is apparent that educators will need to address ethics along with the business needs of the accounting profession to prepare students properly for entry into the profession.

2.3 Models of international accounting qualifications

Understanding the historical evolution and direction of accounting education is one component of understanding how to effectively educate today's accounting professionals. The next step is to understand the different models which countries use to produce professional accountants. Because of the differences in the legal, educational, social, economic, and commercial environments of the countries in which accounting and auditing are performed, the accounting profession and the education of accountants have tended to develop differently from country to country. As a consequence, the response of the accounting profession to meet the needs of society varies substantially from one country to another. In spite of these differences, several forces in the world economy provide incentives for increased uniformity or harmonization among accounting and auditing standards. Among the more important of these are the increases in international trade and investment, the growth of multinational corporations, and the larger trend toward globalization (Needles & Anderson, 1994). (See also Flood, Chapter 4; St. Pierre & Rebele, Chapter 5; and Calhoun & Karreman, Chapter 26 – all in this volume.)

Generally, progress in the harmonization of standards for the education of accountants has not been rapid, but efforts have been made to establish international standards for accounting education. The International Accounting Education Standards Board (IAESB), a part of the International Federation of Accountants (IFAC), has issued eight International Education Standards (IESs). These standards have been issued to further the IFAC's mission of:

> *contributing to the development, adoption and implementation of high-quality international standards and guidance; contributing to the development of strong professional accountancy organizations and*

accounting firms, and to high-quality practices by professional accountants; promoting the value of professional accountants worldwide; and speaking out on public interest issues where the accountancy profession's expertise is most relevant.

(IFAC, 2013)

The term *standards* is used advisedly here, because the IESs do not have the authority to override local educational standards in a particular country. To the extent that local regulations differ from, or conflict with IESs, IFAC's member bodies (i.e. professional accounting bodies in some 120 countries around the world) have agreed to work to meet the guidelines.

The eight existing IESs may be summarized as follows:

1   *Entry Requirements to a Programme of Professional Accounting Education* – lays down the entry requirements for an IFAC member body's programme of professional accounting education and practical experience, and provides a commentary on how to assess entry-level qualifications.
2   *Content of Professional Accounting Education Programmes* – prescribes the knowledge content of professional accounting education programmes which candidates need to acquire in order to qualify as professional accountants.
3   *Professional Skills and General Education* – prescribes the mix of skills that candidates require in order to qualify as professional accountants, and shows how a general education, which may be gained in a variety of ways and within different contexts, can contribute to the development of these skills.
4   *Professional Values, Ethics and Attitudes* – prescribes the professional values, ethics and attitudes which professional accountants should acquire during an education programme leading to qualification.
5   *Practical Experience Requirements* – prescribes the practical experience which IFAC member bodies should require their aspiring members (i.e. trainees) to obtain before qualification as professional accountants.
6   *Assessment of Professional Capabilities and Competence* – prescribes the requirements for a final assessment of a candidate's professional capabilities and competence before qualification.
7   *Continuing Professional Development* – sets standards for the successful development and operation of a programme of continuing professional education (CPE). (See Paisey & Paisey, Chapter 30 – this volume.)
8   *Competence Requirements for Audit Professionals* – prescribes competence requirements for audit professionals, including those working in specific environments and industries.[1] It should be noted that the IAESB's definition of competence – which involves being able to perform a work role to a defined standard, with reference to real working environments – precludes the assessment of competence within a classroom setting.

The standards themselves are currently undergoing redrafting for clarity by IAESB. The stated intention of the revision is:

> *[to] improve clarity, ensure consistency with concepts of their revised framework, and clarify issues resulting from changes in the environment of accounting education and the experience gained from implementation of the Standards by IFAC member bodies.*[2]

IES Nos 1 to 7 have been revised and published. IES No. 8 has been redrafted and publication is expected in the third quarter of 2014.[3]

Even with agreed-upon standards of education, countries will take different paths to certification. Each country's approach is rooted in its unique history, educational system, and accounting tradition. However, common elements may be found among the requirements which countries have for qualifying as a professional accountant. For the purpose of considering the broader issue of establishing international standards for accounting education, adequate comparisons must first identify the common elements of education that lead one to become a qualified accountant and then the ways in which these elements may interact in various environments. The elements of accounting education may be summarized as follows:

1   *Entry level* – the requirement to enter the educational process that will lead eventually to qualification as an accountant. Entry level usually occurs upon either completion of secondary education or graduation from a tertiary-level institution.
2   *General education* – the curricula in the areas of arts, sciences, and other topics that provide a foundation for professional study. General education may be obtained at both the secondary school level and the university level.
3   *Professional education* – the curriculum in accounting and auditing and in closely related professional topics that may be obtained in a variety of ways: at the university level, from professional associations, or through business schools or institutes.
4   *Practical experience* – the amount and type of on-the-job training required to become a qualified accountant.
5   *Test(s) of professional competence* – qualifying examination(s) taken prior to qualification to demonstrate a minimum level of knowledge and skill.

Although these elements are combined in many distinctive ways among various countries, the following discussion supports the proposition that, adjusting for these individual differences, the educational system of most countries can be matched to one of three different models. The educational systems of various countries are used as examples of these models to highlight some of the educational issues that have arisen, partly as a result of the types of educational models followed by the countries. The three models, based on a study of accounting education in 12 countries globally (Needles, 2013), labelled Model A, Model B, and Model C, are identified as the integrated system, the linear system, and the parallel system, respectively, and are illustrated in Figure 2.1.

Model A, the integrated model, is an educational system that has developed from the apprenticeship tradition, a practice common in the U.K. This model begins with a person entering practice and integrates professional education with practical experience. Under this model, the prospective accountant works full-time, or almost full-time, and receives professional education on a part-time basis. Although the Model B approach has traditionally been adopted in the U.S.A., increasingly students follow a form of the Model A approach by interrupting their formal coursework in the third or fourth year to participate in three- to six-month internships in order to gain some professional experience.

Model B is a linear system in which each element is taken in sequence, though the sequence may vary. To qualify as a professional accountant, students must obtain a general education and a professional education from a university and complete a period of professional practice; then they must take a qualifying test to determine professional competence. In some cases, the qualifying examination may be taken prior to obtaining practical experience. For example, the linear approach is used to become a qualified accountant in Russia. Candidates must complete what is called the Professional Accountant's Education Program (PAEP). The PAEP can be completed in one of three ways. The first course of action is to complete a degree at a higher

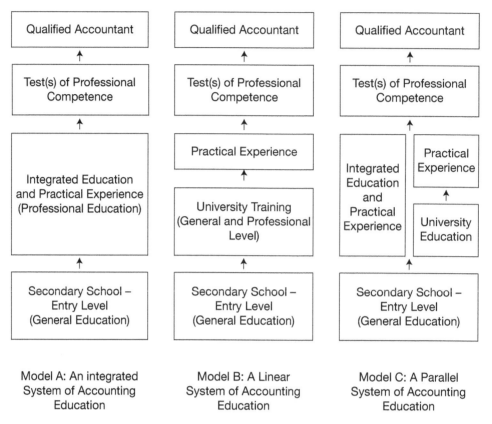

Figure 2.1 Models of accounting education

education institution (HEI) – such as a university – and complete three years of professional experience in one of the following occupations or fields: chief accountants; heads of finance; economics or law department professionals; the deputies of these positions; managerial positions which require the knowledge of accounting; auditors; lawyers; consultants; or university educators in accounting. If the candidate has not completed a degree at an HEI, or his/her degree is from a professional college in economics, the work experience requirement increases to five years in the above-mentioned fields. If the candidate's education is at a professional college but not in economics, he or she must undergo retraining in economics and must satisfy at least five years of work experience in one of the above-mentioned positions. Once the programme is completed, the candidate qualifies to take the two final examinations.

Model C presented in Figure 2.1 is the parallel system for becoming a qualified accountant. It is a combination of Models A and B and is characterized by parallel tracks with examinations given at various points in the process. The candidate may follow either track to become a qualified accountant. In one track, similar to Model B, the candidate may enter the profession through a linear track from the university to practical experience. In the parallel approach, a candidate may enter the profession through training in institutes and practical experience. An example of the parallel system can be found in The Netherlands. There a candidate may become a *registeraccountant* (RA) by attending the university or by taking the school-leaver's programme provided by Nyenrode University. Approximately 60 per cent of all candidates take the university route, which involves a four-year university education plus two years of post-graduate work in accounting on a part-time basis while they gain three years of practical experience. It takes approximately seven years to become a qualified accountant in The Netherlands through the university route. The education accumulated is equal to at least a Master's degree in the U.S.A. The minority, or the remaining 40 per cent of the candidates, take the Nyenrode route, which extends to approximately eight years. This approach to the education of qualified accountants is unique in that the total education is offered by the professional association. Under this system, while candidates work from Monday to Thursday, they take courses in the evenings and on Friday to obtain their education. The candidates take a series of 10 written and oral examinations over the seven- or eight-year period. This is one of the most extensive testing programmes in the world to become a professionally-qualified accountant.

The merits and flaws of each model can be discussed at length. For the purposes of this chapter it is important to note that, regardless of the country in which a candidate is studying, all countries share the need for general and professional education. As discussed earlier, how this education has been delivered has evolved and continues to change. At each level, whether general or professional, it is important to consider the candidates' readiness to take on additional subjects.

2.4 A comprehensive model of accounting education

A comprehensive model for accounting education, developed by Needles & Anderson (1994) and as presented in Figure 2.2, consists of the following components:

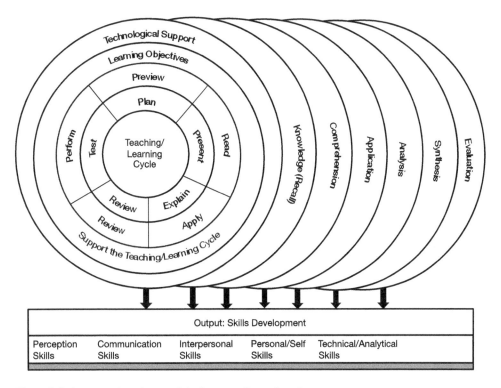

Figure 2.2 A comprehensive model of accounting education

- the teaching and learning cycles of educators and students;
- integrated learning objectives;
- technological support of teaching and learning cycles;
- cognitive levels of learning; and
- output skills development.

A feature of this model, as will be shown in a later section, is that it can be used to develop any course or group of courses in the accounting curriculum. At this point, however, each of these components will be discussed in turn.

2.4.1 Teaching and learning cycles

In the teaching and learning process, both educators and students follow natural cycles of activities. These cycles are illustrated by the two inner circles of the teaching/learning cycle in Figure 2.2. The innermost circle, the teaching cycle, consists of the activities and outcomes shown in Table 2.1.

Table 2.1 Teaching cycle activities and outcomes

Activity	Outcome
1. Plan	A syllabus or assignment
2. Present	A diverse set of presentation modes should be used
3. Explain	Answers to questions
4. Review	Summary and recapitulation of important concepts and techniques
5. Test or devise other form of evaluation	Evaluation of the results of the teaching/learning cycle

The second inner circle in Figure 2.2, the learning cycle, consists of the activities and outcomes from Table 2.2. These cycles take place simultaneously and, ideally, are coordinated with each other in successful educational encounters. For example, the teacher will carefully prepare a syllabus to which the students constantly refer as a course progresses. Because the syllabus communicates important objectives and tasks, the students will understand the nature of each task that must be carried out. When the teacher is ready to give a well-planned lecture or use another presentation mode, the students will be ready to receive it through having read the assigned material. When the teacher is ready to discuss and explain the application of the text material through questions, exercises, problems, or case studies, the students will be prepared to ask questions and participate in the discussion. Both teacher and students will be able to review key concepts and techniques at appropriate times. Finally, the teacher must prepare examinations or other evaluation assignments that will provide an objective and fair measure of the students' performance. This final step cannot be concluded successfully if the teacher and the students have not been working together throughout these cycles. Several reasons for the lack of coordination between the cycles may be found, including inadequate planning, presentation, explanation, review, or testing on the part of the teacher; poor follow-through or inadequate background on the part of the students; or personal problems and stresses faced by both teachers and students. Some problems cannot be overcome, but many can be avoided if the dynamics of the teaching and learning cycles are understood by both teachers and students.

Table 2.2 Learning cycle activities and outcomes

Activity	Outcome
1. Preview	An understanding of the task ahead
2. Read	An understanding of textual content
3. Apply	An ability to use the concepts and techniques presented
4. Review	Summary and practice of concepts and techniques that have been read and applied
5. Perform	Demonstration of competence

2.4.2 Integrated learning objectives

The teaching and learning cycles can be coordinated successfully through the use of integrated learning objectives (also known as intended learning outcomes – ILOs). This approach, first used in first-year accounting education in *Principles of Accounting* by Needles, Anderson, & Caldwell (1981) and refined through 12 editions (the latest published in 2013, (c) 2014, by Needles, Powers, & Crossen), involves the systematic and thorough application of action-oriented ILOs throughout the cycles. An ILO is a statement of the outcome or behaviour a student is expected to exhibit after completing a topical component in a programme of study. Simply put, an ILO indicates what the student should be able to do after completing the study of a subject. For this reason, an ILO should begin with an action verb that defines as precisely as possible the desired outcome or behaviour on the part of the student. For example, an ILO which states: 'record a journal entry' is more precise than one which states: 'illustrate a journal entry'. Precision is necessary for several reasons: it facilitates better communication of expectations; it provides more organized and directed plans, such as classroom presentations, in support of the programme of study; and it can lead to the development of more objective examinations, as well as other methods of evaluation. (See a detailed discussion of ILOs in Kidwell & Lowensohn, Chapter 21 – this volume.)

Also, as shown in Figure 2.2, integrated learning objectives are used to support the teaching and learning cycles in the ways described in Table 2.3.

This use of ILOs provides an effective means of organizing the teaching and learning cycles, communicating expectations to students, effectively delivering content to students, and objectively evaluating the results of the teaching and learning cycles.

Table 2.3 Roles of ILOs in the teaching learning cycle

Teaching activity	Learning activity	ILOs
Plan	Preview	ILOs stated at beginning of study communicate the task to be accomplished
Present	Read	ILOs referred to during reading and presentation
Explain	Apply	ILOs used with all assignment materials
Review	Review	Material is summarized by an ILO
Test or Other	Perform	Test or other form of evaluation directly relating to learning objectives

2.4.3 Technological support of the teaching and learning cycles

The traditional method of teaching and learning emphasizes the lecture/discussion/problem-solving/examination sequence. Technology has become the dominant tool used in the teaching and learning cycles. (See Boritz & Stoner, Chapter 16 – this volume.) Course management software (such as Blackboard and D2L) are now used at most universities. Teachers rely on electronic presentation software and videos instead of black/whiteboards and overhead projectors. More and more students are purchasing digital/e-textbooks. Technology has created online learning – teachers and students no longer have to be in the same building, city, or country. Technology enhances communication between teacher and students.

Figure 2.2 emphasizes that technology can be useful in supporting ILOs in the teaching cycle and cognitive responses in the learning cycle, when attention is focussed on realistically attainable goals.

The use of technology to support the teaching and the learning cycles comprehensively has many advantages. Among these are: improved management of the educational process; more efficient use of teachers' and students' time; shorter learning time frames; more frequent one-to-one tutoring; increased time for learning and mastering complex skills in real settings; and better motivation of students through realistic, visual training sessions. Ideally, online- and video-enhanced education will permit the lower levels of learning (for example, knowledge, comprehension, and application – see Section 2.5) to be achieved more often outside the classroom in order to allow more time for the study of higher levels of learning (analysis, synthesis, evaluation) inside the classroom.

2.5 Cognitive levels of learning in the comprehensive model

The cognitive levels of learning germane to this chapter, based on a taxonomy of educational goals and outcomes developed by Bloom (1956), are listed with cognitive examples in Table 2.4. In the cognitive domain, Bloom's educational objectives deal with the recall or recognition of knowledge, on the one hand, and the development of intellectual abilities and skills, on the other. This domain comprises the teaching/learning cycle in which knowledge is transmitted,

Table 2.4 Bloom's taxonomy of educational objectives – by levels with cognitive examples

Level 1: Knowledge (Recall)	Level 4: Analysis
Knowledge of specifics	Analysis of elements
Knowledge of ways and means of dealing with specifics	Analysis of relationships
Knowledge of the universals and abstractions in the field	Analysis of organizational principles
Level 2: Comprehension	**Level 5: Synthesis**
Translation	Production of a unique communication
Interpretation	Production of a plan, or proposed set of operations
Extrapolation	Derivation of a set of abstract relations
Level 3: Application	**Level 6: Evaluation**
The educational implications of objectives in the application category	Judgements in terms of internal evidence
	Judgements in terms of external criteria

received, and used. Its most integral parts are curriculum development, test development, and descriptions of anticipated behaviour. This taxonomy represents the shell of a total learning environment.

This taxonomy prescribed by Bloom has been subject to considerable analysis and critique over the years. Among the criticisms are changes in the order of the levels such as putting synthesis after evaluation, overlap and redundancy of levels because some learning outcome verbs address more than one level, the addition of levels, and the impracticality of implementing the levels due to the integrated nature of education (Moore, 1982; Bereiter & Scardamalia, 1998; Anderson *et al.*, 2001; Jui-Hung & Chien-Pen, 2005). Nevertheless, the basic structure as proposed by Bloom has proved to be an effective means of developing ILOs in accounting (Needles & Anderson, 1994; Clabaugh *et al.*, 1995; Kidwell *et al.*, 2011, 2013). (See also Section 21.3.2 of Kidwell & Lowensohn, Chapter 21 – this volume.)

2.5.1 Knowledge (recall)

According to Bloom, knowledge involves the recall of several elements: specific information and universal truths; methods and processes for doing something; and a specific pattern, structure, or setting. Measuring knowledge involves simply bringing to mind the relevant or necessary material. The knowledge objective primarily involves the processes of remembering and relating to assist the process of remembering. The recall of specific pieces of information, such as terminology and specific facts, takes place on the basic level of learning. Recalling definitions and reciting specific dates, rules, standards, events, persons, or places are examples of a knowledge of specifics. Although it represents a very low grade of abstraction, this material provides the foundation on which higher levels of learning are built.

This section of the taxonomy includes the knowledge of several elements, as follows:

- trends and sequences;
- classifications and categories;
- criteria; and
- methodology.

Knowledge of convention centres on the characteristic ways of treating and presenting ideas and phenomena. *Trends and sequences* deal with processes, directions, and movements of phenomena with respect to time. *Classifications and categories* include classes, sets, divisions, and arrangements regarded as being fundamental to a given subject field, purpose, argument, or problem. The *criteria* sub-set consists of testing and judging facts, principles, opinions, and conduct. The *methodology* area comprises methods of inquiry, techniques, and processes employed within a particular field, but not one's capacity to use these methods.

The focal point of this category of the taxonomy is the knowledge of principles, generalizations, theories, and structures. This area includes knowledge of major schemes and patterns by which phenomena and ideas are organized, and of accounting principles and the circumstances and conditions by which they are supported.

2.5.2 Intellectual abilities and skills

In Bloom's taxonomy, intellectual abilities and skills refer to organized models of operation and generalized techniques for dealing with materials and problems. In some cases, knowledge of a particular area will satisfy the issues raised by a situation. Other problems may require specialized or technical information at a higher level within the discipline. The abilities and skills objectives emphasize the processes of organizing and reorganizing information and material in order to achieve a particular purpose. Listed in ascending order, the intellectual abilities and skills covered by their objectives are comprehension, application, analysis, synthesis, and evaluation.

Comprehension represents the lowest level of understanding. Knowing the information that is being communicated and being able to use it in some way are the processes central to this objective. Sub-categories include translation, or the rendering or paraphrasing of one type of communication into another (i.e., translating a verbal message into a symbolic one); interpretation, the ability to explain the meaning of a message or proposal; and extrapolation, the ability to predict continuations of trends.

Application represents using information and ideas to solve a problem in a particular way. Under application, principles and theories of a discipline must be remembered and applied.

Analysis is the level of learning at which the characteristics and elements of a situation or problem are broken down, principles and techniques are applied, and the elements are reorganized for a stated purpose. Sub-sets of this objective include analysis of elements, or the ability to distinguish facts from hypotheses; analysis of relationships, the ability to check the consistency of a hypothesis using specific information and assumptions and to recognize interrelationships within a problem situation; and analysis of organizational principles, the ability to identify and use a known set of principles in understanding an approach or method to the solution of a problem.

At the *synthesis* level of learning, parts or elements are pieced together to form a whole. Sub-sets include production of a unique communication and of a plan or proposed set of operations, and the derivation of a set of abstract relations. Examples of a unique communication could range from a paper that uses an organized set of facts and statements to an effective oral account of a personal experience. Examples of the production of a plan or a set of instructions might include the development of a way of testing a hypothesis, the formation of a budget that will accomplish a corporate objective, or the preparation of a means of instructing someone on an issue or topic. The derivation of a set of abstract relations objectives would include the formulation of hypotheses and the discovery of new insights from existing facts and information.

Evaluation refers to making judgements about the importance and appropriateness of materials and methods for a given purpose, as when standards are used to appraise performance. Sub-sets of this objective include judgements in terms of internal evidence (evaluating the accuracy of a statement or message using knowledge of facts and other internal information) and judgements in terms of external criteria (judging a work by the use of external standards or the highest known standards in the field).

Cognitive levels of learning provide the foundation upon which the learning process is structured. The attainment of knowledge and the development of intellectual abilities and skills are the goals of formal education. Learning and teaching activities should be geared to specific learning levels as should testing and other student performance evaluation techniques. Based on the learning levels of knowledge (recall), comprehension, application, analysis, synthesis, and evaluation, the teaching and learning cycles of the model will be developed.

2.6 Skills development output of the comprehensive model

The output, or result, of the formal learning process should consist of a range of personal and professional skills. The use of learning levels and learning objectives may imply the development of certain of these skills, but inclusion of all skills in the learning process is unlikely to occur without explicit recognition. Emphasis must be placed on specific skill development within the

Table 2.5 Basic skill categories

Perception skills	*Personal/self skills*
• Problem recognition	• Initiative
• Awareness	• Independence
• Ability to critique	• Self-confidence
	• Decision-making ability
Communication skills	• Ethical principles
• Reading skills	• Motivation
• Writing skills	
• Speaking skills	*Technical/analytical skills*
• Ability to listen	• Knowledge in all areas of accounting
• Body language	• Thorough knowledge of business
• Negotiation skills	• Ability to analyze a data set
• Presentation skills	
Interpersonal skills	
• Interviewing skills	
• Leadership skills	
• Supervision skills	
• Empathy	

overall curriculum. Course requirements and class assignments must be tailored to accomplish this mission. Accounting courses can and should provide avenues to skills development, but skills development must also be the objective of the total formal learning process.

According to the *American Heritage Dictionary*, a skill is defined as: '*being able to do something because of proficiency, ability, or dexterity; expertness*'. Skills are developed through the learning process, are honed over time, and are never totally mastered. Skills are acquired by doing something that requires the application of some degree of mastery of that skill. Each time the application of that skill is necessary and is used, the degree of mastery increases. One may be born with a degree of aptitude toward a specific skill but everyone can and should strive continuously to improve his or her degree of skill mastery.

The five basic skill areas selected to illustrate specific skill needs in the accounting profession are perception skills, communication skills, interpersonal skills, personal/self skills, and technical/analytical skills. These skills, along with their sub-skill categories, are shown in Table 2.5. Approaches to their development within the accounting curriculum will be discussed in a subsequent section. Other skills areas and/or categories exist, but the five mentioned above are closely linked with the accounting professional. (See also Watty, Chapter 13, and Sundem, Chapter 27 – both in this volume.)

2.6.1 Perception skills

Through the use of perception skills, a professional should be able to obtain knowledge of a situation or develop an intuitive approach concerning a set of circumstances. The ability to perceive something may be gained through awareness, problem recognition, relevance recognition, or the critique of an approach or situation. Such skills are developed through tasks that require a person to be continuously alert to all types of information, and results, and other phenomena in the environment.

2.6.2 Communication skills

The ability to express oneself in a manner that is understood correctly by the recipient is the objective of communication skills, which can include writing skills, speaking skills, presentation skills or, in some circumstances, skills involving body language or other physical signals. Communication skills are developed through particular tasks and assignments and improved primarily through constructive criticism and suggestions for improvement. Reading skills, listening skills, and negotiation skills support the direct communication skills.

2.6.3 Interpersonal skills

Effective interaction between two or more people requires a solid foundation of interpersonal skills. The success of such interaction depends on empathy, or the ability to identify with and understand the problems, concerns, and motives of others. In addition to empathy, a professional should possess leadership, supervision, interviewing, and communication skills in order to interact effectively with people.

2.6.4 Personal/self skills

Personal/self skills provide the foundation for growth in the use of the other skill categories. To be successful, a professional must have self-confidence, be motivated, be able to take the initiative, be independent, have the ability to make sound decisions, and be ethical in all areas of his or her life. These skills are developed both inside and outside the classroom. Responses to questions, problems, and cases can identify skill weaknesses and help point out areas that need improvement. Personal/self skills should be enhanced significantly by the formal learning process, as peers and mentors can provide examples upon which students can build.

2.6.5 Technical/analytical skills

Obtaining the technical and analytical skills of one's discipline should be a major part of the learning process. Gaining a thorough knowledge of the global business environment and the accounting principles and techniques applicable to that environment should be the focal point of an accounting curriculum. However, technical skills range from the very general to the very specific, and much of the specifics should be learned in the field. Analytical skills are mastered as a result of applying the fourth cognitive levels of Bloom's taxonomy in the classroom environment. The formal learning process itself should emphasize the technical and analytical skills needed to provide the foundation for life-long learning.

2.7 General applications of the comprehensive model

The comprehensive model portrayed in Figure 2.2 and discussed above does not prescribe particular curricular structures or content, but is intended here to be a methodological framework for developing accounting curricula, but is useful in other disciplines as well. Based on a coordinated teaching/learning cycle, the model uses ILOs and cognitive levels of learning to give direction to the learning process. Technology provides support for both the teaching and the learning processes. Enhancement of the student's perception, communication, interpersonal, personal/self, and technical skills is the model's output.

The comprehensive model may be applied in many ways – even to a single accounting course. This section is an attempt to show at least some of the considerations that arise when applying the model to an accounting course. As will be demonstrated, application of the comprehensive model to an accounting course may lead to significant changes in the traditional approach to the subject.

2.7.1 The role of learning levels

Learning levels should play an important role in the planning and transmission of course content. The six levels of Bloom's taxonomy – knowledge (recall), comprehension, application, analysis, synthesis and evaluation – are geared to cope with progressively more difficult subject matter. Each learning level calls for increased cognitive learning skills to be employed by the student. Students just beginning the learning process should start primarily with knowledge or recall material. Graduate students, on the other hand, should deal almost exclusively with the synthesis and evaluation levels of learning.

At the university level, students should be exposed to all six levels of learning but in different overlapping configurations, depending on their year in the programme. As one progresses through a college career, higher levels of learning should be required and employed. Figure 2.3 depicts this shift to higher levels of learning in a four- or five-year curriculum as is common in the U.S.A. The same idea across years would apply to other models of accounting education such as those illustrated in Figure 2.1. In first-year courses, most of the content will focus on the use of the knowledge and comprehension learning levels. Although some material will continue to be presented at the higher levels, the use of these learning levels will decrease as the level of difficulty is increased. In the second year, therefore, less emphasis is placed on the knowledge and comprehension learning levels and more is made of the application, analysis, synthesis and evaluation levels.

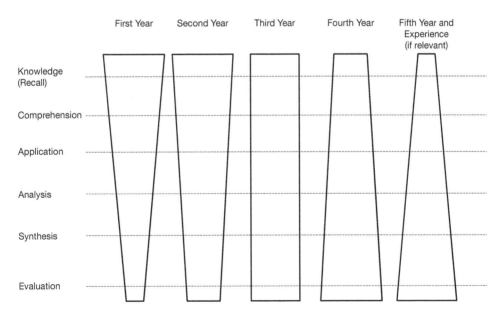

Figure 2.3 Example of learning level usage: four- or five-year programme

By the third year, all of the levels are being utilized with almost equal emphasis being placed on each level. The fourth year contains a major shift away from knowledge and comprehension levels and an increased reliance on the higher learning levels. At the fifth year, if applicable, knowledge, comprehension, and application levels have been replaced almost entirely by analysis, synthesis, and evaluation levels.

Figure 2.3 is based on average learning-level usage for each year shown. Although all levels are relevant to each year as a student progresses through the four- or five-year curriculum, there should be a continuous move from an emphasis on the knowledge learning level to higher levels of learning. Therefore, topics at the end of a one-year course should rely on higher overall learning levels than do those at the beginning of the year.

2.7.2 Using the teaching and learning cycles

Use of the comprehensive model in planning an accounting course may result in a different structure than that developed through the use of traditional planning methods. Table 2.6 shows the contrast between the traditional approach and one that uses a comprehensive model to apply ILOs and cognitive levels of learning to skills development in the context of the teaching and learning cycles.

Table 2.6 Planning models for accounting education

Model	Focus	Process	Output
Traditional Model	Content	Allocation of Time	Daily Class Assignments
Comprehensive Model	Skills Development	Learning Objectives and Cognitive Levels of Learning	Specification of Teaching and Learning Cycles

2.7.3 The traditional approach

The traditional approach to course development focusses on the content or subject matter of the course, emphasizing technical skills to the exclusion of other skills. The process of developing a course syllabus is an exercise primarily in allocating time periods to the subject matter, as when 14 chapters of a standard text are organized into a 16-week semester. Obviously, content and time become constraints that drive the planning process. Assuming that a total of 48 hours is available for both instruction and examinations, approximately three hours would be assigned per class for each chapter. Under this constraint, the preliminary output would be a course plan that consists of daily assignments and activities giving roughly equal attention to all chapters. This may be modified somewhat to take into account certain topics, case studies, out-of-class assignments, and other activities that may take more or less time, but the structure and content (i.e., chapters from the book) will govern the development of the course.

2.7.4 The comprehensive model approach

The central focus of the comprehensive model approach, by contrast, is on the output skills that are to be developed in the course. The teacher will determine what it is that the students should be able to do when they finish the course, specifying the ILOs and cognitive levels of learning which, if achieved, will provide students with the desired skills. This process leads, in turn, to a specification of the components of the teaching and learning cycles in order to accomplish the ILOs.

The use of this comprehensive model has several important implications for the *Introductory Accounting* course. (See also Wygal, Chapter 11 – this volume.) These implications include the following:

- The technical content of the introductory course may be reduced in order to accommodate the development of skills that heretofore have not been an objective of the course. For example, more attention paid to communication skills, and the time needed to develop them, may lead to reduced emphasis on technical skills.
- The order of topics may change, as when an emphasis on analytical skills over technical skills may dictate the coverage of certain analytical techniques earlier in the course.
- The way in which material is delivered may change; instead of focussing on the textbook, lecture, and discussion method, all methods of presentation, use of time and space, and technological support will be incorporated. (See Stevenson *et al.*, Chapter 19 – this volume.)
- The methods of testing and evaluation may change radically. Tests, as now constructed, typically measure the acquisition of technical skills by the students. (See Koh, Chapter 20 – this volume.) With the introduction of other kinds of skills as objectives, different methods of evaluation will be necessary.
- The traditional time frames for covering certain topics may change dramatically. Under the comprehensive model, the teacher determines at the outset what is necessary to achieve the desired skills without respect to time allocations. Consideration of classroom time can take place only after each segment of the teaching and learning cycles has been examined and a full range of alternatives for achieving the ILOs or skills has been selected. The overriding objective should be to determine which resources are necessary to enhance the desired skills.

In accomplishing the experience component of a student's preparation to become a professional accountant, there is always new terminology to learn and comprehend, but the emphasis should be on application, analysis, synthesis, and evaluation in professional situations.

2.7.5 ILOs and learning levels

ILOs are statements of action outcomes that begin with a verb in imperative form. As noted earlier, the verb should communicate as specifically as possible what the student should be able to do after completing a course of study. Certain verbs imply a specific cognitive level of learning. In informal surveys of educators, the author has found that certain action verbs are ambiguous whereas other verbs are perceived as being more closely associated with specific cognitive levels of learning. The verb *to illustrate*, for example, may be viewed as recall, comprehension, and application. The verb *to list*, on the other hand, is clearly a knowledge or recall verb. Table 2.7 shows the relationships between selected action verbs and the cognitive levels of learning as well as techniques and questions that may be used for achieving the ILOs and evaluating the results in the *Introductory Accounting* course.

For example, use of the action verb *to record* would imply the cognitive level of learning and may be accomplished through an exercise or problem. The student's performance may be evaluated by asking: 'How do you record the following transactions?' From the discussion above

Table 2.7 Cognitive levels of learning and ILOs

Cognitive level of learning	Example imperative verbs	Techniques for achieving objectives	Example questions for the evaluation of achieving
KNOWLEDGE (RECALL) Recite and recognize terms, facts, or procedures	Recognize State List Name Define Identify Describe	Review Question Frequent Repetition Patterns Acronyms Relationships	What is the name of . . .? List the five parts of . . .? State the sequence of . . .? Define the term . . .? Describe the preparation of . . .?
COMPREHENSION Make inferences, draw conclusions, or understand relationships	Differentiate Explain Relate Restate Compare Discuss Distinguish	Discussion Questions Explanations Limitations Examples Contrast	Why is . . .? What is the reason for . . .? What is the relationship between . . .? In your own words, explain . . .? Can you think of an example of . . .? Compare and contrast . . .? What do these statements mean . . .?
APPLICATION Apply a concept or principle to a straightforward presentation of facts	Allocate Amortize Calculate Compute Determine Perform Prepare Apply Record Journalize	Exercises Problems	How would you calculate . . .? How does this method apply . . .? Apply the principle of . . . to . . .? How do you record . . .?
ANALYSIS Deal with inter-relationships inherent in facts	Analyze Estimate	Decision Cases Interpreting Accounting Information "What if" Variations	Compare the use of . . . to . . .? Given these criteria, what decision should be made? What interpretation do you place on this set of data? If these variables change, what will be the impact?
SYNTHESIS and EVALUATION Forming a whole from elements and making judgements for a given purpose	Evaluate Recommend Assess	Comprehensive or cumulative cases Writing assignments Debates	Given your knowledge of the course to date, how would you assess . . .? Write a paper addressing the question of . . .?

of Figure 2.3, the development of an *Introductory Accounting* course at the second-year level would concentrate on those ILOs which are associated with the recall, comprehension, and application levels, with selected objectives at the analysis, synthesis, and evaluation levels. Whichever levels are chosen, they should relate directly to the desired output skills for this particular course, as discussed below.

2.7.6 Skills development examples

Skills development is the product or outcome of the educational process. In the *Introductory Accounting* course, numerous examples of skills development can be identified. Every classroom action or exercise should be driven by a skills enhancement objective. Table 2.8 illustrates five examples of skills development, with each of the five skill categories targeted for enhancement. The specific ILO is first identified; then the type of classroom assignment, the relevant learning levels, and the available technological support for each skills enhancement objective are highlighted.

ILO 1 in Table 2.8 directs the students to decide on a course of action to be taken by management and to defend the approach taken to arrive at the decision. Such an ILO can be found in almost any part of the *Introductory Accounting* course. Typically, some kind of case analysis would be employed. The comprehension, analysis, and evaluation learning levels would be used, and analysis would be facilitated by a computerized database. In carrying out this work, the students would have enhanced their perception skills by focussing on information relevant to the decision and by exercising awareness of all the facts and circumstances of the case.

The purpose of ILO 2 is preparation for the class debate. The students are asked to identify the pros and cons of the capitalization of a software costs issue and to prepare the materials for participation in a class debate. This exercise represents one approach to the class discussion scheduled weekly in the course. Learning levels that apply to this exercise include knowledge, comprehension, application, analysis, and synthesis. Reliance on technical support could involve a library search and the use of a word-processing package. The objective of the debate is to enhance the students' communication skills, focussing on presentation, writing, speaking, and listening. Because of its level of challenge to the students, the debate format is one of the most beneficial classroom exercises. The difficulty of the issue being debated would probably place this exercise in the middle of the second semester of the *Introductory Accounting* course.

In the third example, the ILO is to analyze a company's inventory system and recommend possible changes. The assignment is to participate in a group presentation, and the resulting exercise involves the analysis and evaluation learning levels. The technological support could include a computerized database and possibly a presentation-assistance software package. In addition to enhancing communication skills, this exercise would increase group leadership and supervision skills, as well as interpersonal skills.

ILO 4 in Table 2.8 directs the students to state the four categories of ethical standards for management accountants, and to prepare a written analysis of a case involving ethical issues. (See Boyce, Chapter 24 – this volume.) Because this assignment is offered for extra credit, the initiative of the students is also tested. The knowledge, analysis, and synthesis learning levels are required to complete the assignment. Technical support would come from the use of a word-processing software package. Again, communications skills would be used and personal/self skills would be enhanced.

The final ILO in Table 2.8 asks the students to calculate the net present value of a future stream of cash inflows. The traditional class problem assignment would be employed, as would the comprehension and application learning levels. This problem is ideal for use with a computer

Table 2.8 Skills development examples

	Learning objective	Type of assignment	Learning level(s)	Technological support	Targeted skill(s) development
LO. 1:	Decide on course of action to be taken by management and defend the approach to your decision	Case Analysis	Comprehension/ Analysis/ Evaluation	Database analysis	Perception skills (relevancy/awareness)
LO. 2:	Prepare to debate the pros and cons of the capitalization of software cost issue	Weekly Class Discussion	Knowledge/ Comprehension/ Application/ Analysis/ Synthesis	Library Search/ Word Processing package	Communication skills (presentation/writing/ speaking/listening)
LO. 3:	Analyze a company's inventory system and recommend possible changes	Group Presentation	Analysis/Evaluation	Database analysis	Interpersonal skills (leadership/supervision)
LO. 4:	State the four categories of ethical standards for management accountants and prepare written analysis of a case involving ethical issues	Extra Credit	Knowledge (recall)/ Analysis/ Synthesis	Word Processing package	Personal/Self skills (initiative/ethical principles)
LO. 5:	Calculate the net present value of a future stream of cash inflow	Class Problem	Comprehension/ Application	Spreadsheet application package	Technical/Analytical skills (time value of money)

spreadsheet application package. The result would be enhancement of technical accounting as well as analytical skills.

In summary, skills enhancement must become a leading objective of the teacher. Classroom support materials and sophisticated learning models can help to direct the teacher toward this objective, but skills enhancement also requires special assignments and classroom activities not found in the traditional approach to accounting classroom teaching. This is very important for the *Introductory Accounting* course, in which students' views of the accounting profession are shaped. (See Lucas & Mladenovic, Chapter 6 – this volume.) The teacher should purposely inject skills enhancement assignments into the class assignment schedule to give the course a more creative flavour while, at the same time, honing the students' skills.

2.7.7 Summary of application

In this section, the comprehensive model of Figure 2.2 has been applied to an *Introductory Accounting* course. Among the conclusions reached as a result of this application are the following:

- The accounting course should use a combination of the six levels of learning appropriate to the course in the curriculum.
- By addressing the objectives of the teaching and learning cycles to produce desirable skills in students, there should be rearrangements of and reductions in topics, changes in the delivery system, and different time frames employed than are found in the traditional course.
- Technology should be used to support teaching and learning rather than be only a means for students to perform accounting procedures.
- Learning objectives should be oriented to students' action outcomes and precisely related to specific cognitive levels of learning.

2.8 Conclusion

This chapter has examined the history of models of accounting education and shown that a change to emphasizing skills development in accounting education, as opposed to conveying technical subject matter, will likely have a significant impact on curriculum development. To demonstrate this impact, a comprehensive model for accounting education, consisting of cognitive levels of learning, teaching and learning cycles, integrated learning objectives, technological support, and skills development output, was presented and applied to the *Introductory Accounting* course. The impact on the *Introductory Accounting* course was significant, affecting the cognitive levels of learning emphasized; the amount, sequence, and duration of topics covered; the role and use of support technology; and the learning and skill enhancement objectives of the course. Finally, rather than specifying curriculum content or structure, this chapter has presented a methodology for developing courses and curricula that address the skills needs of accounting students.

Notes

1   IAESB (International Accounting Education Standards Board) (n.d.) 'International Education Standards Revision Project', online April 2012. Available at: www.ifac.org/Education.
2   IAESB (International Accounting Education Standards Board) (n.d.) 'International Education Standards Revision Project', online April 2012. Available at: www.ifac.org/Education.
3   IAESB (International Accounting Education Standards Board) (n.d.) 'Update-International Education Standards Revision Project', online January 2014. Available at: www.ifac.org/Education.

References

Accounting Education Change Commission (AECC) (1990) *Annual Report 1989–90*, Bainbridge Island, WA: AECC.

American Heritage Dictionary (2005) Boston: Houghton Mifflin Company.

Anderson, L.W., Krathwohl, D.R., Airasian, P.W., Cruikshank, K.A., Mayer, R.E., Pintrich, P.R., Raths, J., & Wittrock, M.C. (2001) *A Taxonomy for Learning, Teaching, and Assessing: A Revision of Bloom's Taxonomy of Educational Objectives*, New York: Longman.

Anyane-Ntow, K. (ed.) (1992) *International Handbook of Accounting Education and Certification*, Oxford: Pergamon Press.

Arthur Andersen & Co., Arthur Young, Coopers & Lybrand, Deloitte Haskins & Sells, Ernst & Whinney, Peat Marwick Main & Co., Price Waterhouse, & Touche Ross (1989) *Perspectives on Education: Capabilities for Success in the Accounting Profession* (The Big 8 White Paper), New York: Arthur Andersen & Co., Arthur Young, Coopers & Lybrand, Deloitte Haskins & Sells, Ernst & Whinney, Peat Marwick Mitchell, Price Waterhouse, & Touche Ross.

Bean, D. & Bernardi, R. (2007) A proposed structure for an accounting ethics course, *Journal of Business Ethics Education*, 4(1), 27–54.

Bereiter, C. & Scardamalia, M. (1998) Beyond Bloom's taxonomy: rethinking knowledge for the knowledge age, in Hargreaves, A., Lieberman, A., Fullen, M., & Hopkins, D. (eds) *International Handbook of Educational Change*, Boston: Kluwer Academic.

Bloom, B.S., Engelhart, M.D., Furst, E.J., Hill, W.H., & Krathwohl, D.R. (eds) (1956) *Taxonomy of Educational Objectives: The Classification of Educational Goals. Handbook 1: Cognitive Domain*, New York: David McKay.

Bloom, R., Heymann, H.G., Fuglister, J., & Collins, M. (1994) *The Schism in Accounting*, Westport, CT: Quorum Books.

Clabaugh, M.G., Jr, Forbes, J.L., & Clabaugh, J.P. (1995) Bloom's cognitive domain theory: a basis for developing higher levels of critical thinking skills in reconstruction of a professional selling course, *Journal of Marketing Education*, 17(3), 25–34.

Cohen, M. (Chairman of the Commission on Auditors' Responsibilities) (1978) *Report, Conclusions, and Recommendations of the Commission on Auditors' Responsibilities*, New York: AICPA.

Fay, J.R. (1992) *Accounting Certification, Educational, and Reciprocity Requirements: An International Guide*, Westport, CT: Quorum Books.

International Federation of Accountants (IFAC) (2013) *IFAC Organizational Overview: Our Mission.* Available at: www.ifac.org.

Jui-Hung, V. & Chien-Pen, C. (2005) The comparative study of information competencies using Bloom's taxonomy, *Journal of American Academy of Business*, 7(1), 136–143.

Kidwell, L., Fisher, D., Braun, R., & Swanson, D. (2011) Core knowledge learning objectives for accounting ethics education based on Bloom's taxonomy, in Swanson, D.L. & Fisher, D.G. (eds) *Toward Assessing Business Ethics Education*, Charlotte, NC: Information Age Publishing, pp. 307–334.

Kidwell, L., Fisher, D., Braun, R., & Swanson, D. (2013) Developing learning objectives for accounting ethics using Bloom's taxonomy, *Accounting Education: an international journal*, 22(1), 44–65.

Liu, C., Yao, L.J., & Hu, N. (2012) Improving ethics education in accounting: lessons from medicine and law, *Issues in Accounting Education*, 27(3), 671–690.

Moore, D.S. (1982) Reconsidering Bloom's taxonomy of educational objectives, *Educational Theory*, 32(1), 29–34.

Needles, Jr., B.E. (2013) Models of accounting education: a global assessment, working paper presented at the annual Meeting of the American Accounting Association, Anaheim, CA.

Needles, Jr., B.E. & Anderson, H.R. (1994) *A Comprehensive Model for Accounting Education*, Bainbridge Island, WA: AECC.

Needles, Jr., B.E., Anderson, H.R., & Caldwell, J. (1981) *Principles of Accounting*, Boston: Houghton Mifflin Company.

Needles, Jr., B.E., Powers, M., & Crossen, S. (2014) *Principles of Accounting*, 12th edn, Mason, OH: Southwestern/Cengage Learning.

Previts, G.J. & Merino, B.D. (1998) *A History of Accountancy in the United States: The Cultural Significance of Accounting*, Columbus, OH: Ohio State University Press.

Roy, R.H. & MacNeill, J.H. (1967) *Horizons for a Profession: The Common Body of Knowledge for Certified Public Accountants*, New York: AICPA.

Sterrett, J.E. (1905) Education and training of a certified public accountant, *Journal of Accountancy*, 1(1), 1–15.

Taylor, J.B. (1932) A program for graduate study of accounting, *The Accounting Review*, March, 42–47.

Young, J.J. & Annisette, M. (2009) Cultivating imagination: ethics, education and literature, *Critical Perspectives on Accounting* 20(1), 93–109.

About the author

Belverd E. Needles, Jr. is Ernst & Young Distinguished Professor of Accountancy at DePaul University, U.S.A. (bneedles@depaul.edu). He recently served two years as Vice-President (Education) of the American Accounting Association; is past Chair of the Board of Directors of the Illinois CPA Society; past president of the International Association for Accounting Education and Research (IAAER); and has published widely in the field of accounting education.

3

The nature of financial literacy

Richard M.S. Wilson*, Anne Abraham,**
and Carolynne L.J. Mason*

*LOUGHBOROUGH UNIVERSITY, U.K., **UNIVERSITY OF WESTERN SYDNEY, AUSTRALIA

CONTENTS

Abstract

The notion of *financial literacy* is not a new one. It is widely perceived as being important, hence something to be encouraged in those who are not financially literate, as exemplified by the existence of organisations dedicated to generating financial literacy in, for example, Australia, Canada, the U.K., and the U.S.A.

But what does the term *financial literacy* actually mean? What distinguishes a financially literate individual from one who is financially illiterate? This chapter investigates aspects of financial literacy in particular contexts (embracing households and formal organisations – whether profit-seeking enterprises or public sector bodies). As a prelude to defining what is meant by *financial literacy*, however, the basic idea of *literacy* itself (subsuming numeracy) is considered.

The fraught confusion over *financial awareness* and *financial literacy*, often viewed as being synonymous expressions, is addressed. This confusion arises (at least in part) from inadequate definitions of *financial literacy* (which clearly has implications for its operationalisation). These limitations are explored and a fuller definition of financial literacy is provided as a point of reference for accounting educators.

Keywords

financial awareness, financial literacy, literacy, meaning-making, numeracy

3.1 Introduction

The main aims of this chapter are:

- to discuss what is meant by literacy (subsuming numeracy);
- to consider the importance of literacy and the problem of illiteracy;
- to highlight the role of meaning-making in the context of being literate;
- to critically compare *financial awareness* and *financial literacy*; and
- to define financial literacy and assess its importance as a cornerstone of accounting education.

In Section 3.2 we begin by looking at the essence of being literate (and numerate), consider meaning-making (or sense-making) as being at the heart of what it means to be literate, and review the use of the term 'literacy' in a number of different contexts.

The discussion in Section 3.3 moves on to concerns which exist over an individual's ability to use financial information effectively, and some of the implications of this. Studies looking at particular aspects of financial awareness are examined, and questions are raised about the adequacy of this construct for both accounting educators and accounting practitioners. An argument is presented which suggests that financial *awareness* and financial *literacy* are not synonymous expressions.

Financial literacy is defined in Section 3.4 as being a complex phenomenon which needs to be defined in relation to meaning-making on the one hand, and purposive behaviour on the other.

Section 3.5 concludes the chapter by looking at the need for accounting educators to focus on financial literacy in the design, delivery, and assessment of their programmes.

Many of the examples given and literature cited reflect the authors' familiarity with the jurisdictions in which they are located. Nevertheless, their belief is that the issues raised are not restricted to Australia and the U.K., but have broader applicability.

Let us start by examining the notion of *literacy*.

3.2 What is literacy?

3.2.1 Some key ideas

In her book *Literacy*, Margaret Jackson attempts to respond to the question: What is literacy? She notes that the term literacy is '*very rarely carefully defined*' (1993, p. 1). That said, literacy is defined in the *Collins Dictionary* as '*the ability to read and write*' or '*the ability to use language effectively*'. The *Oxford English Dictionary* states that literacy is '*The quality or state of being literate; knowledge of letters; condition in respect to education, ability to read and write.*' These definitions probably encapsulate most people's initial thoughts about literacy. However, the discussion that follows shows that these definitions fail to grasp much of the complexity of what it means to be literate.

It is argued here that a literate individual is one who possesses a set of skills and abilities (including reading, writing, speaking, being numerate, and the ability to reflect) which allows him/her to locate and make use of resources in order to achieve objectives. The resources available to us in a complex society are extensive, with books being almost the tip of the iceberg. (See Stevenson *et al.*, Chapter 19 – this volume.) The objectives for those who are literate are also probably infinite. Jackson outlines a typical day where she begins by reading the shampoo bottle in the shower and moves through the day until she finishes by reading in bed. She states that, during the day, she has used print to '*inform, to remind, to persuade, to keep in touch, to amuse, to instruct and to disturb*' (1993, p. 90). It is literacy that allows her to successfully achieve these outcomes, and it is these skills that allow individuals to develop as individuals and contribute to the development of the society of which they are a part. The *functional* nature of literacy is therefore apparent. Functional literacy can be defined as:

> *A person is literate when he has acquired the essential knowledge and skills which enable him to engage in all those activities in which literacy is required for effective functioning in his group or community.*
>
> (UNESCO definition, 1962, cited in Oxenham, 1980, p. 87)

Burnet (1965) discussed the idea of functional literacy, emphasising that there is a difference between acquiring the skills to be able to read and write on the one hand, and becoming literate on the other. Functional literacy is viewed by Burnet as being:

> *the key that unlocks the door to the future, because the person who has achieved it has learned to learn for himself, and has thus gone a long way toward making his fundamental right to education a reality. He no longer has to be content with what other people choose to teach him; he can find out for himself what he wants to know. He can improve his occupational status and enrich his leisure. He has learned to reflect on what he reads, to make comparisons and draw his own conclusions.*
>
> (1965, p. 14)

Literacy, then, is not simply about reading, writing, and being numerate (though there is nothing simplistic about the acquisition of these skills). In these few sentences Burnet indicates that literacy is shown, at the very least, to be about:

- learning;
- achieving status;
- achieving human rights;
- knowing;

- making choices;
- improving occupational status and wealth;
- improving leisure pursuits;
- making comparisons;
- creating and confirming conclusions.

There appears to be little that we value in Western society that is not affected by literacy. But in what way does literacy allow all these individualistic and societal outcomes to happen? This takes us on to the crucial role of *meaning-making*.

3.2.2 Meaning-making

As an introduction to meaning-making (or sense-making), reference can be made to:

- the literature of sociology and social psychology (such as Berger & Luckmann, 1966; Weick, 1979, 1995; Weick *et al.*, 2005);
- that of organisational theory (such as Maitlis, 2005; Maitlis & Lawrence, 2007);
- that of accounting (such as Boland, 1980, 1984, 1987, 1993; Lavoie, 1987); and
- the social construction and socio-linguistics of literacy (see Cook-Gumperz, 1986; Gee, 1990).

An interesting (albeit brief) comment on making sense of the Global Financial Crisis (GFC) which began in 2008 relative to the crash of 1929 through the use of *narrative* (i.e. story telling – an important form of meaning-making) is given by Wagner (2011); and an insightful study of meaning-making using three different professional groups in Singapore (auditors, engineers, and architects) is reported by Cheuk (2002).

Jackson (1993) emphasises the *contextual nature* of literacy and highlights the view that the more complex the society, the more complex the notion of literacy becomes. In the Preface to her book, Jackson states: '*Literacy offers us access to information, ideas, opinions and by creating the potential for reflecting, provides opportunities for making and communicating meaning, and for learning.*' Literate individuals are able to make meaning as a basis for *learning* and this, we would argue, along with Jackson, is the key element of literacy. In order to operate effectively within the context of a complex society (or in one of its components, including households and more formal organisations), individuals need to be able to make sense of and understand the world in which they operate. In less complex societies, hunters need to respond to their environment in order to survive. In more complex societies, a great deal of the information required in order to make sense of the environment is contained within the symbolic representation systems of words and numbers. Individuals' chances of operating effectively are greatly enhanced by their being able to make sense of these word and number systems, and they do this by being both literate and numerate.

While recognising that literacy involves individuals being able to read and write, Jackson's definition above also emphasises that, on their own, these skills are not sufficient for an individual to become literate: individuals must also be able to *reflect* in order to make, and communicate, meaning and to learn.

The key questions here are:

- How do users of information (whether of a financial nature or not) extract meaning and make sense of it?
- What courses of action might this stimulate?

Each user is a distinct meaning-making individual, and each will make use of available information (words, numbers and other symbols) to construct a picture of the situation which he or she faces. Such constructions will vary from one person to another and, since they are made in a setting which includes interactions with other people, they are *social* constructions reflecting the unique perceptions of the social or organisational reality facing each person who is involved. For example, in difficult market conditions, a sales representative may have missed last month's sales quota by £50,000. Her view of this shortfall is likely to differ from that of her demanding boss on the one hand, and those of her envious peers on the other, yet the number in question (i.e. £50,000) is common to all parties. That which differs from one person to another, and from one situation to another, is how sense is being made of – or meaning being attributed to – the variance of £50,000 and what might be done about it.

Literate individuals have certain opportunities but, in order to utilise these effectively, they must be active and draw on a variety of personal skills (including their ability to read, write, speak, handle numbers, and reflect). This pro-active theme is expanded by the use of verbs such as reflecting, meaning-making, communicating, and learning. As we saw earlier, Burnet (1965) used similar verbs in her description of functional literacy. However, in his pioneering (1957) study, Hoggart showed that literacy is not always used to its best advantage and that, depending on the context, the changes which it brings are not necessarily positive ones.

The points raised so far can be represented diagrammatically as shown in Figure 3.1 which shows literacy to be a process whereby individuals use a combination of their skills plus available resources to make sense of – or understand – those resources in order to achieve objectives. The sub-section that follows examines *illiteracy* in order to further consider what being literate entails, and to examine why being literate and numerate is considered to be important.

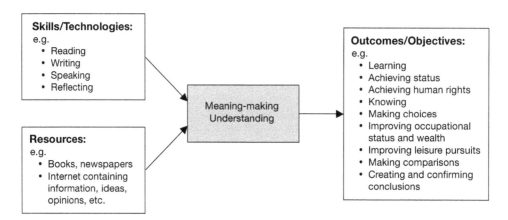

Figure 3.1 Literacy viewed as a meaning-making process

3.2.3 The problem of illiteracy

If being literate and numerate allows individuals to achieve desired objectives, then being illiterate and innumerate is problematic because it prohibits individuals from achieving desired objectives, and this necessarily presents problems at both individual and societal levels. Concerns over the prevailing standards of literacy and numeracy are rarely out of the newspaper headlines. Within the U.K., for example, there is a widely held concern that standards of literacy and numeracy have been falling dramatically, with negative consequences for both the individuals concerned and for society at large (see below). Improving literacy and numeracy have been high priorities for successive U.K. governments.

It is not only in the U.K. that literacy is on the agenda. For example, in the U.S.A., President Clinton stated (on International Literacy Day, in September 1994):

Literacy is not a luxury, it is a right and a responsibility. If our world is to meet the challenges of the twenty-first century we must harness the energy and creativity of all our citizens.

Illiteracy is conventionally portrayed as having negative consequences. As Sir Claus Moser noted (*The Sunday Times*, 1993, p. 9): '*The illiterate person is tragically handicapped. Without well-developed literacy skills an individual is an outsider [in his/her own] culture.*' In other words, 'Literacy is good, illiteracy is bad.' This is clearly a value judgement and, while it appeals intuitively, understanding why illiteracy is problematic contributes towards our understanding of the importance of literacy in general (and therefore of financial literacy in particular).

Before considering examples of illiteracy, it is important to highlight that, as noted above with regard to literacy (see Jackson, 1993), the problems associated with illiteracy are context-specific. Burnet (1965, p. 11) stated:

There has always been illiteracy, but it has not always been a problem – not everywhere, at least. In isolated, self-sufficient societies, where life followed a traditional pattern and nobody knew how to read and write, illiteracy was no problem. But there are few such societies left . . . As technical development moves faster and faster, and as populations increase, the problem of illiteracy becomes more and more acute.

Only as societies become more complex and technologically advanced does illiteracy become a problem. Individuals need to be well-equipped in order to respond to advances within the social and economic context. Literacy is important because it enables individuals to function more effectively in ever-changing contexts which become ever more complex. Burnet (1965, p. 8) cites the example of one textile mill owner in Guatemala who stated that '*we will not hire an illiterate man*'. The mill owners had established their own school to teach workers to read and write, not as a result of philanthropy, but because: '*Experience showed that literate workers absorbed training faster and worked more efficiently. Productivity increased, and this permitted higher wage rates along with greater profits.*'

According to this viewpoint, the benefits of literacy can be measured in human and economic terms, at both individual and societal levels. Literacy contributes to the well-being of the individual and also to the well-being of the society of which that individual is a part. Illiteracy is viewed as being negative because it prevents the rewards of advances being reaped by either individuals or society. Illiterate individuals cannot function as effectively as literate ones can in the context of complex societies.

Illiteracy, then, is potentially problematic both for individuals and for society. The cost of illiteracy within the U.K. as elsewhere is not only measured in lost earnings, but also in additional public expenditure on education, health, welfare, and the criminal justice system. (See *The Times*, 11 December 2006, p. 2, and *The Times*, 20 March 2008.) According to the European Commission, in terms of competitive performance, the U.K. is held back by having too many illiterate and innumerate adults with no qualifications. A report from the World Literacy Foundation (Cree *et al.*, 2012) noted that 20 per cent of adults in the U.K. are 'functionally illiterate', and it was reported by the Centre for Policy Studies (Gross, 2010) that there was an epidemic of illiteracy in London, with one million people being unable to read (cited in Atewill, 2010).

Given the continuing decline in low-skilled jobs, this is a serious problem. Almost 20 per cent of children in the U.K. leave school without the reading skills required to be productive members of society, with the equivalent figure for Shanghai being only 4 per cent (see Moynihan, 2012). And the U.K. is a member of the G8 and G20 groups of advanced nations.

Turning to numeracy, research undertaken by KPMG (see Frean, 2008) shows that there is a widespread problem with basic mathematical skills among the U.K.'s adult population (whether this involves simple mental arithmetic while shopping or helping children with their homework). (See also Woolcock, 2012.) The mathematical attainment of children in the U.K. lags well behind that of their counterparts in Hong Kong, Japan, Singapore and Taiwan at all ages. (See Buchanan, 2013; Bennett, 2008; Hurst, 2013.) This matters because it has the potential to impact negatively on the U.K.'s leadership in financial services. Furthermore, it is commonplace to find journalists setting a bad example by making numerical errors in their writing, such as failing to distinguish between a percentage change and a change in percentage (see Brooks, 2007).

There is a problem in both the U.K. and the U.S.A. with too many young people leaving school with inadequate numeracy skills. One estimate (Sugden, 2011) put the figure at 25 per cent of U.K. school leavers being 'functionally innumerate' (i.e. unable to use simple mathematics to solve everyday problems), whilst the figure mooted for school leavers in the U.S.A. has been estimated at 32 per cent (Walters, 2012).

Tracey Bleakley, Chief Executive of the Personal Finance Education Group (PFEG), noted:

> There is no question that maths skills need to improve. At present too many young people are leaving school without the basic maths they need to make a whole range of financial decisions, from setting a budget to planning borrowing and saving.
>
> (Cited in Budworth, 2012, p. 10)

This reinforces the view that: 'pupils need to become more comfortable with using numbers, including percentages and fractions used in the world of finance' (Sugden, 2011, p. 8). (See also Sugden, 2009, p. 17.) This problem applies beyond pupils at school to include university students who have to be given remedial classes in mathematics (e.g. see Frean, 2007). There is a good deal of evidence to show that schools in both the U.K. and the U.S.A. fail to prepare their pupils adequately with literacy and numeracy skills for higher education: see, for example, Blair et al. (2004); Birkhead (2006); Times Higher Education (2007); Frean et al. (2007); Anon (2008); Hanushek & Peterson (2011); Peterson et al. (2011).

There have been many reports in the U.K. of employers being either unable to fill vacancies due to applicants' poor literacy and numeracy skills (e.g. see Grimston, 2010b), or having to provide remedial training in mathematics and English to new recruits (e.g. see The Times, 14 October 2009, p. 9; Street-Porter, 2009; King, 2010). These limitations have inevitably impacted on the U.K.'s economic recovery from the GFC which began in 2008.

Having established that the importance of literacy and numeracy is reflected in the individualistic and societal benefits that arise from being literate and numerate, a discussion of the usage of the term literacy within other fields follows.

3.2.4 Literacy in different fields

While this chapter is primarily concerned with *financial* literacy, it is important to note that the term *literacy* is one that has been adopted by scholars and practitioners from a variety of backgrounds to indicate a level of proficiency within a given field. Some examples of using the term *literacy* in different fields are included here, along with a brief discussion of the implications for financial literacy.

A search of the literature identifies a host of studies that include *literacy* in their title. These include:

- academic literacy (Saunders, 2010; and a job advertisement in *Times Higher Education*, 10 January 2013, p. 56);
- biblical literacy (Beal, 2009);
- computer literacy (Day, 1987; Michaelson, 2004);
- cultural literacy (HEA, 2004);
- cyber literacy (Gurak, 2001);
- economic literacy (Whitehead & Halil, 1989);
- electronic literacy (Craver, 1997);
- graphicacy (Milner & Hill, 2008);
- health literacy (Cafferkey & Doyle, 2011; Sorensen *et al.*, 2012; Barrow, 2012);
- information literacy (Kulthau, 1991; Mutch, 1997; Jackson & Durkee, 2008; Hepworth & Walton, 2009);
- internet literacy (Martin, 1997);
- mental health literacy (Furnham, 2011);
- multi-media literacy (Hofsteter, 1995);
- musical literacy (Morrison, 2002);
- political literacy (Institute of Education, 1983);
- risk literacy (Henderson, 2009a);
- scientific and technological literacy (Layton, 1994);
- statistical literacy (Haack, 1979);
- sustainability literacy (Stibbe, 2009);
- symbolic literacy (Gardner, 1986);
- teleliteracy (Bianculli, 1992); and
- visual literacy (Wilde, 1991).

An examination of this literature shows that some of the characteristics of literacy highlighted earlier in this section are also to be found in these other uses of the term. However, the term *literacy* is often used with little or no care being paid to its definition. Definitions are sometimes not offered at all, and those that are offered are frequently found to be deficient.

It is also clear that much of the literature that examines literacies in other fields is written as a result of concerns over standards. These concerns could be expressed by educational practitioners who worry that their students are not performing well, or by managers anxious that, for example, the expected benefits of some new computer software have failed to materialise. Frequently, concerns over standards can be linked to concerns over a lack of understanding (or meaning-making) on the part of the individuals involved rather than being due to a lack of basic skills. In his book on statistical literacy, for example, Haack (1979, p. x) stated that the aim of the book was to get away from formulae when teaching statistics. Instead he stated: '*the purpose is to get students to understand the principles of hypothesis testing without trying to make them decide which of many tests is 'best''*. Without actually offering a definition of statistical literacy (other than by offering it as a mechanism to overcome *statistical doublespeak*), Haack deliberately moved away from the actual techniques used in statistical analysis and has, instead, viewed literacy as being about understanding. On p. 3, he states: '*Our emphasis is on understanding and interpreting the statistics.*'

More recent work on statistical literacy has been undertaken in the U.K. by MacInnes. (See MacInnes, 2013, http://www.sps.ed.ac.uk/ and http://www.rss.org.uk/.)

There is much to learn from examining *information literacy*, not least because this is one of the most frequently identified adoptions of the term *literacy*. There is a large amount of multi-disciplinary interest in the concept of information literacy. It is almost trite to observe that there has been a huge increase in the sheer volume of information in the last 50 years due to developments which include improvements in mass production printing techniques, the wide availability of personal computers and, more recently, the arrival of the internet. Schuman (1991, p. 4) stated:

> *A weekly edition of the* New York Times *contains more information than the average person was likely to come across in a lifetime in seventeenth-century England. The English language now contains 500,000 words, five times more than in Shakespeare's lifetime. The collection of the large research libraries has doubled in the last fourteen years. We readily throw out with our nightly garbage more print than past generations dreamed it was possible to own.*

The availability of all this information has led to concerns over how to manage it, and from this has stemmed much of the interest in information literacy. Individuals from two disciplines in particular, library studies and computing, have made information literacy a focus of their concerns. This inter-disciplinary interest has ensured that there is no single definition of, or approach to, information literacy.

The American Library Association's Presidential Committee on Information Literacy (1989, p. 1) defined information literacy in the following way:

> *To be information literate, a person must be able to recognise when information is needed and have the ability to locate, evaluate, and use effectively the needed information. Ultimately, information literate people are those who have learned how to learn. They know how to learn because they know how knowledge is organised, how to find information, and how to use information in such a way that others can learn from them. They are people prepared for lifelong learning, because they always find the information needed for any task or decision at hand.*

There are clearly parallels that can be drawn between this definition of information literacy and the earlier definition of literacy offered in this chapter (see Figure 3.1). The 1989 definition implies that information literacy is important because it enables individuals, *inter alia*:

- to learn how to learn;
- to be prepared for lifelong learning; and
- to find the information needed for any task or decision at hand.

A key theme in this definition is *learning*. The objective for information literate individuals is to learn. Learning was identified earlier as being one of the outcomes of being literate. Once again there is an emphasis on individuals needing certain skills and resources in order to achieve desired outcomes.

Further, it has been suggested that it is appropriate that information literacy not be '*taught as a separate course but [be] integrated with learning across the curriculum . . . and . . . developed around the basic need of every person to find meaning and understand his or her world*' (Kuhlthau, 1991, p. 9). This view of information literacy prioritises the process of meaning-making and the implication is that this relies on more than the development of a set of key skills within a classroom environment. The advent of computers was expected to be associated with improvements in the ways in which businesses and other organisations functioned as a result of the increased capacity for processing data which, it was anticipated, would lead to improved efficiency and better decision-making.

Mutch (1997, p. 377) suggested that these aspirations may not have been realised because '*computers are able to generate huge quantities of data which are either misused by or overwhelm those who are on the receiving end*'. Among the reasons which he suggested for this ineffective use of computers was that information itself is not well understood, and the relationship between data and knowledge is often not recognised. Concerns were directed at the process of acquiring, maintaining, and delivering data rather than understanding exactly why data was required, what use it would be, and in what way it would be used. This applies equally to financial data.

Mutch argued that information is better treated as a process rather than as a thing. While he recognised that there was considerable support for information being regarded as a thing, including the attempts by many to capitalise information as a business asset, Eaton & Bawden (1991) claimed that information is different from other assets in that it is not consumed in use, and is dynamic and unpredictable. (See also Oppenheim *et al.*, 2003a, 2003b, 2004; Wilson & Stenson 2008.) These qualities stem from the fact the information has meaning endowed by the user. Similarly, Boland (1987, p. 377) stated that:

> [*Information*] *is not a resource to be stockpiled as one more factor of production. It is meaning, and can only be achieved through dialogue in a human community. Information is not a commodity. It is a skilled human accomplishment.*

Again, the key element that is of interest here is *understanding* or *meaning*. Information is only of use if it is understood and used appropriately. In other words, the availability of resources, generically termed information, and the combination of hardware and skills to access these resources, are not sufficient to ensure positive outcomes, including good decision-making. A crucial part of the process has been omitted, namely meaning-making or understanding.

Thus it appears that the term *literacy* appears to be borrowed when a problem is in need of a solution and this is often when individuals are ineffective in being able to make meaning or sense-make in the context of increasingly challenging and complex environments. With statistical literacy, it was students' inability to understand the statistics they use, while for information literacy, the problems stem from the large volume of data and people's inability to use information effectively.

In summary, this section has indicated that being literate enables individuals in complex societies to achieve a range of objectives through engaging in meaning-making. In stark contrast, illiteracy was seen to be problematic in that it prevents both individuals and the societies in which they operate from achieving their full potential. Literacy was seen to be a term and a concept that have been adopted in a number of different fields, too often without adequate definitions being offered. It was noted that the adoption of the term *literacy* was often linked to concerns about a lack of competence or a lack of understanding. Problems present themselves, such as an inability to use a computer or an inability to make good financial decisions, and improving levels of literacy is commonly seen as being the answer. This can also be argued for financial literacy since this is also a term that has arisen as a result of the identification of a problem (e.g. when individuals have been shown to be ineffective in their use of financial information). The implications of a perceived lack of financial literacy can be far-reaching as the following two examples indicate.

In a macro-economic context, the credibility of the U.K.'s Office for National Statistics (ONS, a branch of government) was under question when numerical errors caused it to announce that economic growth in the building sector was 2.3 per cent in the second quarter of 2011. Seven hours later a corrected figure of 0.5 per cent was announced. This is not the ONS's first mistake, and such errors are serious because they affect the financial markets. (See Hopkins & Clark, 2011.)

Another example of this propensity for making errors occurred in 2012 when civil servants advising the U.K.'s then Secretary of State for Transport advised her to award the franchise for operating trains on the lucrative West Coast Main Line route from London to Scotland to First Group rather than to Sir Richard Branson's Virgin Trains. After the controversial decision was announced, Sir Richard sought a judicial review from which it emerged that the advisors had failed to allow for the impact of inflation in the figures on which they had provided their advice, thereby causing considerable political embarrassment to the government – and annoyance to Virgin Trains which had previously held the franchise, and which was continuing to operate West Coast Main Line services on an interim basis while the lengthy – and expensive – bidding process was repeated. (See Pank, 2012; and *The Times*, 16 January 2013, p. 2.)

This preliminary discussion has examined the nature of literacy, and its adoption in other guises. The section that follows examines another concept relevant to understanding the nature of financial *literacy* – that of financial *awareness*.

3.3 Financial awareness

3.3.1 Exploring the notion of financial awareness

While research dedicated to financial *literacy* has grown substantially in recent years, the earliest body of research in this field concerned financial *awareness*. This section concentrates mainly on a number of influential academic studies undertaken by researchers at Cardiff University in the U.K. where financial awareness was examined in a number of different contexts. But first, as a point of reference, it is informative to consider one of the few published non-academic empirical studies of managers' financial awareness. This was undertaken in 1992 by a market research agency (Taylor Nelson Financial) on behalf of a professional firm (KPMG Management Consulting), and we can set its findings against some more recent practitioner studies from the Association of Chartered Certified Accountants (ACCA) published in 2012, before returning to review the Cardiff studies.

The KPMG study was commissioned more as a practice development (i.e. marketing) exercise than as a rigorous inquiry seeking to generate real insights into the causes and consequences of managers' financial awareness, and it did achieve a good deal of media attention when the results were published. By means of a financial quiz (see Taylor Nelson Financial, 1992), it was found that non-financial managers in the U.K.'s top 1,000 companies (covering manufacturing, distribution, and service sectors) showed a lack of even the most basic levels of financial awareness. For example, there was little awareness of the effects of a lack of cash, the problems of rapid growth, the role of working capital, or the dangers of high gearing on a company's well-being, and little knowledge about how to undertake investment appraisal. This reflects an alarming state of affairs.

In a study of 500 investors, customers, suppliers and other stakeholders drawn from Canada, the U.K., and the U.S.A., the ACCA (2012a) found that 50 per cent of respondents rather surprisingly named the annual report as being their primary (or, in some cases, their only) source of information about a company, and that the majority of those respondents now read this more carefully than they did prior to the GFC. (See Adler, Chapter 23 – this volume.) In a second report, the ACCA (2012b) predicted that the accounting profession will continue to lose credibility if it fails to educate the public and its stakeholders about its value – but this view that there is a widespread lack of public understanding of the role that accountants play in driving the success of organisations in all sectors is compounded by the dramatic changes that impact on the context in which accountants must operate (stemming from, for example, increases in global competition, complexity, the rate of technological change, regulation, and decreases in product life cycles: see Flood, Chapter 4 – this volume). A third ACCA report (see Fast Futures Research, 2012) highlighted these changes, and noted that the importance of being financially aware is not reduced by their dynamic impact.

There is, as shown by these reports, a real problem concerning financial awareness. The work of the Cardiff researchers also raised questions about the ways in which financial information is understood by individuals, and this has implications for developing insights into financial awareness as a prelude to defining financial literacy.

Bartlett & Chandler (1997) replicated the earlier work of Lee & Tweedie (1975a, 1975b, 1976, 1977) in order to examine whether changes within the financial reporting environment (e.g. the introduction of a cash flow statement, a statement of recognised gains and losses, and an operating and financial review) had affected the ways in which financial reports were read by shareholders. They concluded that the annual report was not widely read despite 84 per cent of respondents stating that they made their own investment decisions. Bartlett & Chandler also found that the narrative sections of the annual report attracted the wider readership. This leads one to ask whether small shareholders were more confident in dealing with words rather than with numbers and, if so, whether this might be due to a lack of financial awareness.

Peel & Pendlebury (1998) focussed on financial awareness in their follow-up to a previous study (Peel et al., 1991) focussing on employee share ownership. They accepted that the term 'financial awareness' had many different meanings and could therefore be measured in a number of different ways, yet they did not offer a definition on which their measure was based.

One of the most interesting issues raised by Peel & Pendlebury was their suggestion that individuals with greater financial awareness were more likely to become members of a share ownership scheme than those who become members of such a share scheme achieving greater financial awareness as a consequence (1998, p. 45).

In addition, the employees in Peel & Pendlebury's study, like the shareholders in Bartlett & Chandler's work, preferred company news bulletins and magazines to annual reports, indicating a preference for narrative presentation rather than numeric. The narrative report may have allowed individuals lacking in financial expertise to feel confident that they understood the information presented when, in fact, they did not, because they may have merely recognised the words rather than understanding the concepts underpinning those words.

Both of these Cardiff studies found results which implied that annual reports were not well read or understood despite a considerable amount of effort aimed at achieving these outcomes. The findings highlighted the need to understand in far greater detail exactly how individuals gained the skills needed to be able to analyse and understand financial information and, having gained these skills, how they might be used. The results have contributed towards understanding more about financial awareness, but they also signal that financial awareness is a complex issue. (See Lucas & Mladenovic, Chapter 6 – this volume.) Another problem with both of these studies is that there was no discussion of either the causes or the consequences of a lack of financial awareness. Why were these individuals unable/unwilling to make full use of annual reports? What were the implications of not using the information with which they had been presented?

Two other Cardiff-based researchers, Marriott & Mellett, carried out a series of studies examining the financial awareness of managers in the U.K.'s National Health Service (NHS). The introduction of an internal market to the NHS meant that decisions with financial conse-quences within the NHS were often made by those with a clinical training rather than those with a financial background. Marriott & Mellett (1991, 1994, 1995, 1996) set out to assess the adequacy of managers in the NHS to make these decisions. They were concerned that, if the necessary financial skills were lacking, incorrect decisions that might have financial consequences could be made.

From their pilot study Marriott & Mellett (1991, p. 23) concluded that:

> *There exists a gap between managers' financial skills and those which will be needed to operate efficiently the novel procedures in the reformed NHS . . . The full extent of the need for financial training within the NHS has not been identified . . . Unless these steps are taken, the NHS will not operate to its potential as those taking decisions will not be in a position to make full or appropriate use of the information available.*

One of the main contributions of the Cardiff NHS studies is that they highlighted a lack of financial awareness on the part of managers within the NHS. Individuals were expected to make decisions requiring an understanding of their financial consequences without necessarily having the financial skills that enabled them to make those decisions in an effective manner. These findings were important both for the NHS and for other public sector organisations which have undergone similar reforms, whereby individuals may be expected to make decisions requiring an understanding of their financial consequences which they are ill-equipped to make.

In their attempt to assess the ability of NHS managers to make sound decisions requiring an understanding of their financial consequences, Marriott & Mellett used a 'financial skills index' as a proxy for financial awareness. However, while it is possible to state that the individuals in this study did have limited financial skill as measured by the instrument developed by Marriott & Mellett, this does not guarantee that the latter's conceptualisation of 'financial skill' is valid, or that the way in which it has been measured is necessarily sufficient. Indeed, there is no single external measure of financial awareness (Marriott & Mellett, 1996, p. 72).

Despite inadequate conceptualisation, financial awareness was measured using survey instruments by both Peel & Pendlebury (1998) and Marriott & Mellett (1996) with the latter study defining financial awareness as '*the manager's ability to understand and analyse financial information and act accordingly*' (1996, p. 64).

These authors measured the respondents' ability to define and calculate a restricted number of accounting measures, but being able to define and calculate is not necessarily synonymous with being able to understand and analyse. In this case, respondents may still have been financially aware using Marriott & Mellett's (1996) definition without being financially literate. Unlike the other studies at Cardiff, Marriott & Mellett were concerned with suggesting possible consequences of this lack of financial awareness. However, these consequences were merely hypothesised: there was no empirical evidence of the consequences offered by Marriott & Mellett.

Numerous other questions remain unanswered despite this research. For example:

- Did the users understand the budgets they received?
- Did the individuals who prepared the budgets feel that their recipients were using them effectively?
- Did the individuals in the sample really feel that the quality of their decisions was being affected by their lack of financial skills?
- Was there any evidence to suggest that 'bad' decisions were actually being made?

The researchers at Cardiff divorced their studies from the actions of the individuals (i.e. the intended readers of financial information). The reason that researchers were concerned with an individual's ability to understand and analyse financial information is that his/her actions were thought to depend on this ability. So, for example, a shareholder's ability to understand annual reports is thought to affect his/her investment decision-making. We now know that shareholders do not read annual reports thoroughly and yet we do not know what impact, if any, this has on their investment decision-making behaviour.

The Cardiff studies were premised on the underlying assumption that a lack of understanding of financial matters has negative consequences, but they did not actually demonstrate a link between financial awareness and an individual's ability to make sound decisions. Rather, the effect of financial information on decision-making behaviour has been ignored both as a theoretical possibility and as an empirical reality.

There also appears to be a widely held belief that more information (or clearer information) will lead to greater levels of financial awareness. Lee & Tweedie's work in the 1970s highlighted problems over shareholders not reading annual reports. In the years that followed, great emphasis was placed on 'improving' the annual reports and this was expected to result in improved usage of the reports by shareholders. A similar response has been offered to the identification of poor levels of consumers' financial understanding. An alternative approach is to focus on improving individuals' financial skills. What seems to be missing, however, is an attempt to understand why there is so much misunderstanding. Why are there poor levels of understanding? Why do shareholders not read the reports? How do these individuals compare with those who do understand reports? What does it mean to understand the reports? Thus, this early work at Cardiff showed that individuals did not make good use of financial information and that this may have been due, at least in part, to a lack of financial awareness.

3.3.2 Financial literacy and financial awareness

So what is the relationship between financial *literacy* and financial *awareness*? We suggest that financial literacy must be conceptualised as a complex phenomenon whereby individuals make sense of information in order to assess the financial consequences of their decisions made in order to achieve desired outcomes. To this end, financial awareness is a part of financial literacy because, in order to be financially literate, individuals must be financially aware. However, being financially aware is a necessary but not a sufficient condition for being financially literate: individuals may be financially aware without being financially literate. For example, the NHS managers in Marriott & Mellett's studies may have performed exceptionally well when assessed by the 'financial skills index' and yet still have failed to make effective decisions requiring an understanding of their financial consequences because they had not understood the factors relevant to their decision-making and can therefore be deemed to be financially illiterate. Alternatively, they may have performed badly on the test and still have been financially literate, as demonstrated by their being able to locate and understand the financial information relevant to their decision-making, and to predict the financial consequences of decisions made.

Financial awareness has been examined as a measure of people's understanding of terms that already exist (i.e. terms such as balance sheet, budget, and depreciation). However, the relationship between people's understanding of these terms and their ability to make effective decisions has not been empirically examined. Individuals may have a very good knowledge of certain financial terms, and therefore be financially aware, while still being unable to recognise the relevance of other information which prevents them from recognising the financial consequences of any decision which they may make. This may ultimately prevent them from achieving their desired outcomes so, in this instance, an individual would be financially aware but financially illiterate. See, for example, McDaniel *et al.* (2002) and Peecher (2002).

We now turn to developing a definition of financial literacy which accounting educators can use to underpin the design, delivery, and assessment of their programmes.

3.4 Defining financial literacy

3.4.1 Extending the notion of financial awareness

In line with the discussion in Section 3.2 above, it is proposed here that the term *literacy* is synonymous with understanding or meaning-making, and that this meaning-making is a prerequisite for the achievement of desired outcomes or objectives. With *financial* literacy, these outcomes have financial consequences.

Financial literacy is generally understood to represent knowledge and understanding of financial concepts or products (Kotlikoff & Bernheim, 2001; Hogarth *et al.*, 2003; Lusardi & Mitchell, 2011), with one of its most commonly accepted definitions being: '*the ability to make informed judgements and take effective decisions regarding the use and management of money*' (Noctor *et al.*, 1992). This restricted definition emphasises financial literacy as consisting of both objective knowledge on specific topics related to money, economics or financial matters, and also subjective measures of reported self-confidence (SEDI, 2005, p. 4).

In 2008, the American Institute of Certified Public Accountants (AICPA) defined financial literacy as being: '*the ability to effectively evaluate and manage one's finances in order to make prudent decisions toward reaching life goals and achieve financial wellbeing*' (AICPA, 2008, p. 5). While projecting beyond the immediacy of a particular decision, this definition is limited in focussing specifically: on *finances* (rather than information relating to resources more generally); on households; and on ignoring differing degrees of risk aversion on the part of different decision-makers by its emphasis on prudence.

It is argued here that financial literacy is more than these deficient definitions suggest: it is a process leading to a desired outcome and should be more appropriately defined as: '*an individual's ability to obtain, understand and evaluate the relevant information necessary to make decisions with an awareness of the likely financial consequences*' (Mason & Wilson, 2001, p. 31). In other words, financial literacy is not in itself the desired outcome from decision-making, but rather the process of making meaning from contextual knowledge with the use of financial skills.

There is clearly a similarity here between information literacy and financial literacy. This is not surprising since information that has financial implications is still information. The difference between the two terms arises because the outcomes are different, with the latter term being relevant where the outcomes have financial consequences.

The above definition attempts to recognise that information relevant to decision-making may not necessarily be financial information in its strictest sense. For example, a school may face a reduced intake of pupils. This in itself is not financial information – though there are financial implications where a school's funding is determined by the number of pupils. The ability to recognise the financial implications of non-financial information is fundamental to financial literacy.

Informed decision-making is recognised as being necessary for achieving desired outcomes. It seems likely that the majority of these outcomes will follow on from a decision being made which is then followed by a course of action. It is hard to think of an example in which financial literacy is relevant where a decision is not implicit. Even in cases where people use financial information to ensure that their current behaviour is appropriate, ultimately a decision will be required over whether or not to continue with their current actions. For example, an individual looking at his/her current savings or pension provision will need to make a decision over whether to continue with his/her current strategy or whether to make alternative arrangements. Similarly, an individual within an organisation will also need to be able to obtain and understand relevant information to ensure that current or proposed actions are appropriate (i.e. goal congruent).

It is important to note here that financial literacy can only ensure that individuals are informed to make decisions: it cannot ensure the 'right' decisions are actually made. This is because, *inter alia*, individuals do not always make decisions based purely on the basis of economic rationality. (See, for example, Wilson & Zhang, 1997.)

In this definition, financial literacy is seen as being distinct from the achievement of desired outcomes resulting from decision-making processes. Differentiating literacy from the outcomes it enables is not to say, however, that achieving the desired outcomes is incidental to literacy. The outcomes give literacy its importance. If there were no desired outcomes to be achieved, then literacy in general, and financial literacy in particular, would be unimportant. To illustrate the point in terms of the conventional use of the term literacy, people read books for a purpose, such as for pleasure or to acquire knowledge. In order to achieve either of these outcomes, a person needs to be literate (that is, he/she makes use of a range of skills to read the book in order to understand it). Without this understanding the chances of achieving the desired outcomes are dramatically reduced. Furthermore, it is proposed that it is functionality which establishes the importance of financial literacy, and it is the outcomes which determine the value of financial literacy.

Financial literacy as defined in this chapter is a meaning-making process which enables informed decisions to be made in order to achieve desired outcomes as shown in Figure 3.2. In this model it is proposed that individuals use a combination of skills and technologies, resources, and contextual knowledge to make sense of information in order to be sufficiently informed to make decisions requiring an understanding of their financial consequences. These terms have been deliberately adopted as general descriptive terms. In addition, Figure 3.2 demonstrates that decisions are not made for their own sake, but to facilitate the attainment of desired outcomes.

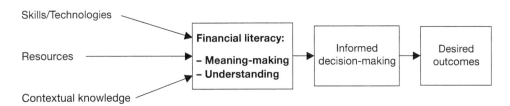

Figure 3.2 Financial literacy viewed as a meaning-making process

3.4.2 Financial literacy studies

Over the last decade and a half much has been written about the need to improve financial literacy, with studies having been carried out in a number of countries, but most especially in Australia, the U.K., and the U.S.A., in order to assess the general level of financial literacy in the community (e.g. Schagen & Lines, 1996; NCEE, 2012; ANZ, 2003, 2005, 2008, 2011; ASIC, 2011; SEDI, 2005), or among specific cohorts (Beal & Delpachitra, 2003; Bird, 2008; Chen & Volpe, 1998). These studies have resulted in online programmes being developed by government, corporate, and not-for-profit sectors, as well as the development of programmes to embed financial literacy skills into school curricula. This sub-section reviews the major financial literacy studies that have been conducted in Australia, the U.K., and the U.S.A. in recent years, and presents the results in tabular format. (See Tables 3.1, 3.2, and 3.3.) It also provides an overview of the recent OECD pilot study into financial literacy in fourteen countries, and comments briefly on the effectiveness of the programmes, noting that there has been much less

Table 3.1 Overview of major financial literacy studies in Australia

Study	Overview
ANZ (2011, 2008, 2005, 2003)	Aimed to capture the complexity of financial literacy through focussing on behaviours indicative of a person's financial literacy and examining the associations of those behaviours with people's demographic and other characteristics, including attitudes to finances
Commonwealth Bank Foundation (CBF) (2004a, 2004b)	The first survey on financial literacy that investigated the strength of any link between financial literacy and outcomes for individuals and the Australian economy
Citibank (Citi Australia, 2010)	Drew on the emerging field of behavioural economics to shed light on why people do not behave as rationally as economics textbooks would suggest
National Australia Bank (NAB) (Connolly *et al.*, 2011)	Building on NAB's ongoing interest in financial literacy since 2003, this study measured the extent of financial exclusion as a result of a lack of financial literacy, and the relationship this has with social and economic disadvantage

emphasis on financial literacy in an organisational setting as opposed to the setting of households and individuals.

Between late 2010 and 2011, the OECD's International Gateway for Financial Education (IGFE) conducted a pilot study in fourteen countries across four continents. Data was collected by each participating country undertaking a nationally representative survey using a core questionnaire and providing the results of interviews with at least 1,000 individuals, which were then weighted to reflect the population of each country. Data analysis focussed on variations in financial knowledge, behaviour, and attitudes across the participant countries, and also within countries, by using socio-demographic indicators.

Atkinson & Messy (2012) reported that the results highlighted a lack of financial awareness amongst a sizeable proportion of the population in each of the countries surveyed. The data also showed that attitudes to financial literacy varied widely. One particular concern was the relatively large proportion of people who could not calculate simple interest on a savings account over one year and then identify the impact of compounding over five years. Another was the lack of awareness of risk diversification benefits, with at least 33 per cent and in some countries more than 50 per cent of participants being unable to answer a question about this.

As might be expected, there was a consistently positive relationship between financial knowledge scores and financial behaviour scores, with participants having higher financial knowledge exhibiting more positive behaviours. The analysis on a socio-demographic basis indicated that, in all but one country, women had much lower levels of financial knowledge than men. For instance, in the U.K., a score of 6 or more for knowledge was obtained by 67 per cent of men but by only 40 per cent of women. The percentages were similar in Germany, being 67 per cent for men and 50 per cent for women. However, in most countries, women participants were more likely to have a more positive attitude towards the long-term perspective than their male peers. (For an international comparison among women, see *The Times of India*, 2011.)

Age and income provided other bases for variation in financial literacy. In most countries, the youngest and oldest respondents scored lower than those of middle age. Lower-income respondents were more likely to gain lower financial literacy scores than those in higher-income

Table 3.2 Overview of major financial literacy studies in the U.K.

Study	Overview
Schagen & Lines (1996)	A financial literacy survey of the general population with a particular focus on four groups: young people in work or training, students in higher education living away from home, single parents, and families living in subsidised housing. Results indicated that, in general, most participants were confident in their financial dealings. Notable exceptions were single parents who were less committed to saving, and students who were the least confident group in dealing with financial matters, with very few keeping any financial records.
Adult Financial Literacy Advisory Group (AdFLAG) (2000)	Concluded that the need for financial literacy would continue to grow because individuals are expected to become more self-reliant. Recommended that short-term financial literacy education should be built around education, employment, housing, financial services and communication, with a particular focus on needy population sectors (such as older people, young people, sole parents, ethnic minorities, people with disabilities, and people living in social housing).
Financial Services Authority (PFRC, 2005)	Considered the areas: 'managing money', 'planning ahead', 'choosing products', and 'staying informed'. Found that, while individuals may be particularly capable in one or more areas, they lacked skills or experiences in other areas. Recognised that it would take time for policies regarding financial education and the subsequent introduction of accounting education in this area to have an impact on the U.K. population.
Consumer Financial Education Body (Elliott *et al.*, 2010)	Concluded that there is enormous scope to alter the environment in a way that encourages greater levels of financial capability, hence providing an opening for using accounting education as one such means of increasing these levels.
Money Advice Service Board (CI Research, 2012)	Found that current opinion varies among academics and experts in the field regarding the extent to which financial interventions produce positive outcomes. Evidence suggested that young people must be engaged in financial education from an early age.

brackets. There was also a positive relationship between education and financial literacy, with those who were more highly educated being likely to demonstrate both positive behaviours and attitudes. The report's authors concluded that:

> *The data holds a great deal of potential. We will continue with our analysis in order to inform the work of the INFE, focussing particularly on variations in financial literacy by key socio-demographic groups, levels of financial inclusion and financial access, as well as exploring in more detail the relationship between various aspects of financial literacy.*
>
> (Atkinson & Messy, 2012, p. 12)

Furthermore, the results of the study will enable countries to identify needs and gaps in financial education provision in order to make progress in developing their own national policies or strategies.

Table 3.3 Overview of major financial literacy studies in the U.S.A.

Study	Overview
Mandell (1997), Huddleston-Casas *et al.* (1999), Williams-Harold (1999), the National Council on Economic Education (from 1998 to 2012) and the Jumpstart Coalition (from 1997 to 2008)	All studies investigated financial literacy levels among high school pupils and concluded that they showed a lack of both personal financial skills and knowledge
Council for Economic Education (CEE, 2012a, 2012b)	Concluded that the recent economic downturn following the GFC had brought nationwide attention to the dangers of a financially illiterate society, and that it was imperative to close the gap by providing educators with the knowledge, tools, and teaching skills they need to help individuals to develop essential real-world financial literacy skills
Securities and Exchange Commission (SEC) (2012)	Results indicated that retail investors in the U.S.A. lacked basic financial literacy. They demonstrated a weak grasp of elementary financial concepts and lacked critical knowledge of methods to identify and avoid investment fraud.

This sub-section has provided a summary of the major studies that have been undertaken in financial literacy both nationally and internationally. Rather than taking an organisational perspective, most of these studies have focussed on the financial literacy of individuals or socio-economic groups. In addressing the importance of financial literacy, the next sub-section provides an overview of various governmental and non-governmental financial literacy programmes that have been established across a wide range of countries.

3.4.3 Why is financial literacy important?

The authors' interest in financial literacy stems from a recognition that every individual in his/her domestic life, and every responsible manager, will be involved in decisions relating to the acquisition, allocation, and utilisation of resources, and that these processes inevitably have financial characteristics. In order to function in an effective manner, every citizen or manager needs to have a degree of financial literacy (whether as a user or a compiler of financial information). This is applicable in households, in (budget-constrained) public sector organisations, and in (profit-seeking) private sector organisations, whether large or small, service-rendering, or manufacturing. Managers across any organisation need to be able to consider things using the same language, and the most appropriate *lingua franca* to facilitate cross-functional communication is usually one couched in financial terms. (See Turner, 2008.) To give an example, suitable skills are needed on the part of carers to ensure that financial abuse of the elderly can be identified and resolved (Gilhooly, 2012, p. 9). As a consequence, social care, health, and banking professionals need to have appropriate training to become sufficiently financially literate to enable them to handle this problem.

Whether the focus is on the corporate sector or the personal sector, individuals can benefit from being financially literate by avoiding the need to defer to the specialist expertise of financial advisors. Henderson (2009b) referred to a study led by Gregory Berns at Emory University in the U.S.A. which suggested that financial advice can make people take leave of their senses because the brain sets rationality aside when it gets the benefit of supposedly expert opinion, thereby abdicating personal responsibility because of deference to the expert's authority.

Many examples of how this risk can be avoided are provided in both the corporate and personal sectors. With reference to the corporate sector, the Director of the *Finance for Executives* course at Oxford University's Said Business School, Alan Morrison, observed that:

> *Managers get to the stage where they are in charge of budgets, dealing with investors and deciding between conflicting uses of resources. They may not want to do the calculations themselves but they need to be able to have an informed discussion with [those] who do.*
>
> (Quoted in Lewis, 2008, p. 7)

An example of avoiding the risk in the personal sector occurred in 2007 when the Open University Business School in the U.K. offered for the first time its course entitled *You and Your Money: Personal Finance in Context.* This distance learning course aimed to help in developing practical financial skills as well as an understanding of the outside forces which affect personal finances and the jargon that surrounds them.

There is a noticeable lack of literature concerned with the financial literacy of managers within organisations, despite the proliferation of textbooks and short courses with titles such as *Finance for the Non-Financial Manager.* This widely-used label is itself misleading because 'finance' (which is concerned with the acquisition, allocation, and utilisation of funds) is quite distinct from 'accounting' (which is concerned with flows of information – largely but not exclusively of a financial nature – to help in planning, decision-making, and control). There is, however, a great deal of literature on the financial literacy of private individuals.

3.4.4 Attempts to address financial literacy

Much of the interest shown in financial literacy stems from a concern over people's *lack* of financial literacy. This is particularly true when individuals are viewed as consumers of financial products. Concern has been expressed over many years about the ability of these consumers to make effective decisions (e.g. Schagen & Lines, 1996; Jennings *et al.*, 1997). The evidence suggests that available information is used ineffectively, if at all, in consumer decision-making about financial products.

This concern, which is recognised internationally, is exemplified *at the personal and household levels* by the existence of bodies such as:

- the Financial Services Authority's national strategy on financial capability (which was launched in the U.K. in 2003 – see FSA 1998, 1999, 2006). (The FSA was replaced in 2013 by the Financial Conduct Authority, which is concerned with consumers' interests, and the Prudential Regulation Authority, which oversees the banking system.)
- the Financial Literacy Centre at the University of Warwick (U.K.);
- the Financial Literacy Foundation (Australia);
- the National Endowment for Financial Education (U.S.A.);
- the Financial Literacy Center (U.S.A.) (See U.S. Financial Literacy and Education Commission, 2006.)

It is also evidenced by the development of programmes such as:

- the Start Right Coalition for Financial Literacy (Canada);
- the Jump$tart Coalition for Personal Financial Literacy (U.S.A.);
- the OECD's International Gateway for Financial Education (see OECD, 2005, 2008, 2012);
- the Commonwealth Bank Foundation (Australia) which aims to encourage the development of financial education programmes primarily targeted on young people; and
- the U.K.'s Money Advice Service which, since 2011, has been involved in a number of projects aimed at raising the financial literacy/capability of consumers, which is the same target as most other government-sponsored programmes (including the Australian government's Money Management programme). A recent review of the Money Advice Service suggests that it is not achieving what was expected of it (see Hosking, 2013).

The Australian government established a Consumer and Financial Literacy Taskforce to develop the National Strategy for Consumer and Financial Literacy which aimed to develop a national strategy to reduce poverty, increase economic opportunity, support national savings, and create well-informed consumers. On an international basis, as briefly mentioned above, the OECD's International Gateway for Financial Education (IGFE) provides a policy forum for governments to exchange views and experiences around the issue of financial education. To this end, it has established an international online database, the IGFE, which '*serves as a global clearinghouse on financial education, providing access to a comprehensive range of information, data, resources, research and news on financial education issues and programmes around the globe*' (OECD, 2012).

One of the most recent attempts to address financial literacy by raising the level of financial capability in the U.K. was through the establishment of the Pathfinder Money Guidance service by the FSA in March 2009. Three channels were used to provide services in the two regions (North-West England and North-East England) in which Pathfinder was initially piloted. These channels consisted of a website, a telephone helpline, and a face-to-face information and guidance service. During its first year of operation, it was concluded that the programme '*largely achieved one of its key aims of reaching people who are potentially vulnerable to the consequences of poor financial decision making*' (Kempson *et al.*, 2010, p. 4). It is estimated to have delivered 570,000 Money Guidance sessions to 220,660 individuals. The website was the most used channel (with 192,250 individual users), followed by the face-to-face sessions (24,595), and then the telephone helpline (3,811). This was not what the designers had expected: they had anticipated that the website would be the most used medium, and expected that the telephone service would be more popular than the face-to-face medium. While no reason for this was suggested, it could be hypothesised that those with lower financial literacy levels may find that the face-to-face service allowed them to be able to see plans mapped out on paper rather than having to write information down for themselves from a telephone session, or maybe these face-to-face sessions facilitated their 'meaning-making' more effectively.

Similar programmes include:

- In Australia, the Federal Government provides an online website for its National Financial Literacy Strategy (NFLS) which identifies various programmes across a range of sectors: community, indigenous, government, workplace, and international (ASIC, 2012). These include interactive school education programmes, community forums providing investment and banking advice, a matched savings programme aiming to increase personal savings and the financial capability of people on low incomes, and workplace financial education programmes targeted at different demographic groups.

- The leading organisation that provides financial literacy education in the U.S.A. is the Council for Economic Education (CEE). It specifically focusses on the economic and financial education of pupils from kindergarten through to the end of secondary school with the aim of assisting children to grow into successful and productive adults who are capable of making informed and responsible decisions. To this end, it provides professional development for teachers, and develops teaching resources for use across the curriculum. Its programmes are delivered in face-to-face workshops, through partner organisations, and online (CEE, 2012a).

- In a similar way there have been pressures over many years for financial literacy to be taught in U.K. schools to counteract what has been described as financial illiteracy on the part of both younger children (see Sugden, 2009; Grimston, 2010a) and teenagers (see Bennett, 2008). For example, an initiative in 2006 by the Institute of Chartered Accountants in England & Wales (ICAEW) and others to establish a data-base of experts who could help schools in providing a practical understanding of financial matters – including how to make informed financial decisions – was to be based on the experts tutoring the teachers, with the latter then dealing with the pupils. (See *Accountancy Age*, 17 August 2006, p. 10, and http://www.barclaysmoneyskills.com.)

- In New Zealand, the Financial Education and Research Centre was founded by Massey University and Westpac New Zealand to improve New Zealanders' knowledge, attitudes, and behaviour towards money matters by addressing the quality of and access to education on personal finance, and identifying knowledge gaps and how these can be bridged. Key projects include a 20-year longitudinal study that will follow up to 300 New Zealanders to understand their needs for financial knowledge at different life stages, a multi-level certification programme for personal financial educators, and the New Zealand Retirement Expenditure Survey – a joint initiative between the Centre and the savings industry body Workplace Savings NZ – which aims to establish guidelines for 'modest' and 'comfortable' retirement. (See Strangl & Matthews, 2012.)

- In Australia, the Money Smart Teaching website (www.teaching.moneysmart.gov.au) provides resources to help in integrating financial literacy into schools.

- Across the European Union there are online resources to assist teachers with delivering financial literacy classes (as part of the Dolceta programme: see www.dolceta.eu); and the OECD's International Gateway for Financial Education does a similar thing on a world-wide basis.

- In the U.S.A., the Financial Literacy Center (which was established in October 2009 by the RAND Corporation, the Wharton School of the University of Pennsylvania, and Dartmouth College) has developed educational tools and programmes to improve financial literacy and promote informed financial decision-making (www.rand.org/labor/centers/financial-literacy).

Once again, the focus of all the above initiatives tends to be on financial literacy for personal rather than organisational decision-making. However, a novel variation is the International Certificate in Financial English set up by the University of Cambridge and the ACCA. This aims to cater for those working in international finance on a global basis by providing high levels of English language (rather than financial) skills which are relevant to this fast-moving field in order to boost the international mobility of young accountants.

Another variation on the theme comes from the Chartered Institute of Management Accountants (CIMA) which now offers certificates and a diploma in Islamic Finance '*to provide*

the skills and knowledge needed to exploit the global shortage of qualified Islamic finance professionals'.
(See *Financial Management*, December 2012, p. 40.)

In 2007, the then U.K. government announced that, from 2008, a new subject (Economic Well-Being and Financial Capability) would be introduced into the curriculum of secondary schools, aiming to help school leavers cope better with life after school (see Bennett, 2007; Purves, 2007; Grimston, 2010a). However, critics objected to its inclusion in the Mathematics curriculum, thereby detracting from mathematics without having the substance to ensure financially-informed decision-making (see Woolcock, 2008). It is a powerful argument that young people's primary and secondary education should ensure that they emerge from school with adequate literacy and numeracy skills to *subsequently* become financially literate, since those who are only semi-literate or innumerate when they leave school are unlikely – as adults – to remedy the deficiencies in their education or, as a consequence, to become financially literate.

Despite all the above initiatives, it is significant – and disappointing – that such academic assessments of financial education as have been undertaken do not offer evidence of measurable success in improving participants' financial well-being. See, for example, Cole & Shastry (2008), and Willis (2009).

Despite the level of activity revolving around financial literacy, there does not appear to be any published material attempting to characterise a financially literate person. Advice is offered to those who are considered financially illiterate, yet what makes one person financially literate and the next person not? Centres dedicated to financial literacy aim to improve individuals' financial literacy because there is evidence that many individuals make poor use of financial information and this is blamed on financial illiteracy – which brings us back to questions such as:

- What does this actually mean?
- In what way are these individuals failing to use available information effectively?
- What do they not understand?
- Why do they not understand it?
- Do they not understand it or do they simply not make good use of it?
- Is the information presented in a way which is unhelpful?
- Do the individuals lack the necessary skills to analyse and interpret the information?
- Do they use other sources of information (e.g. the advice of friends and family) in lieu of making their own reasoned decisions?

These questions and many others remain unanswered.

3.5 Implications and conclusion

In this chapter it has been argued that financial literacy can be seen to have considerable importance – whether in the context of households or in the setting of more formal organisations. To some degree this 'self-evident' importance has resulted in surprisingly little attention being devoted to developing an adequate definition of financial literacy, with the focus instead being given to encouraging individuals to become financially aware (i.e. focussing on skills rather than on meaning-making). This is not the same as being financially literate, so the situation is clearly problematic, and applies as much in the domain of accounting education as elsewhere.

In discussing literacy and numeracy more generally, along with the non-trivial problems of illiteracy and innumeracy, the important roles of meaning-making and learning were introduced as being vital aspects of gaining an understanding of what is going on in one's field of activity.

When this was extended to financial awareness, we argued that the level of understanding of financial matters needed in order for an individual to be deemed financially aware does not render an individual financially literate. The latter presupposes the former, plus insights into the ways in which financial awareness can be used in the decision-making process to achieve desired outcomes with an understanding of their likely financial consequences.

At several points in the chapter there has been an emphasis on *context*, and a number of ways in which accounting educators might use financial literacy as a cornerstone of their programmes can be suggested, based on a concern for context. We could teach accounting techniques from dawn to dusk, but this would be of limited value if devoid of context. Accounting numbers are surrogates which represent events, activities and outcomes – but meaning can only be attributed to them when one knows the context to which the numbers refer. We will look at two possible ways of using financial literacy as a point of reference for accounting educators. These focus on the *derived nature of financial literacy*, on the one hand, and on *key managerial questions*, on the other.

Taking the first of these, one can argue with some conviction that the outputs from accounting systems help facilitate planning, decision-making, and control – whether in relation, say, to an individual's affairs, those of a small charity, those of a university, or those of a multi-national corporation. However, this is not to suggest that accounting information is desired for its own sake. The demand for such information, from a financial literacy perspective, is to help individuals to make meaning and to develop a narrative in order to understand what is happening around them, and then using this understanding to make purposive decisions with a reasonable insight into the likely financial consequences of those decisions. In other words, the demand for accounting information is of a *derived* nature.

This is clearly illustrated in Figure 3.2. The sequence, with its first-order and second-order effects, was also evident in a novel definition of managerial accounting offered by Wilson & Chua (1993, p. 16), which extended previous definitions by emphasising the derived nature of information generated by managerial accounting systems (MAS):

> *Managerial accounting encompasses techniques and processes that are intended to provide financial and non-financial information to people within an organization [to enable them] to make better decisions and thereby achieve organizational control and enhance organizational effectiveness.*

This can be illustrated as shown (Wilson & Chua, 1993, p. 424):

Managerial accounting	LEADS TO	Satisfaction of people's need for information for decision-making	LEADS TO	Organizational control and effectiveness

A crucial element in this definition is the notion of organisational control, which focusses on the process of ensuring that an organisation pursues courses of action which seek to achieve its aims. The organisation can be deemed to be effective to the extent that it is successful in this endeavour. To this end, those who design, implement, and operate MAS need to recognise the social processes by which people attach meaning to managerial accounting information in order to make sense of the context in which they are seeking to make effective decisions. In other words, both compilers and users of accounting information need to be financially literate – and accounting educators need to be mindful of this when designing curricula, pedagogic approaches for delivery, and assessment strategies for their programmes.

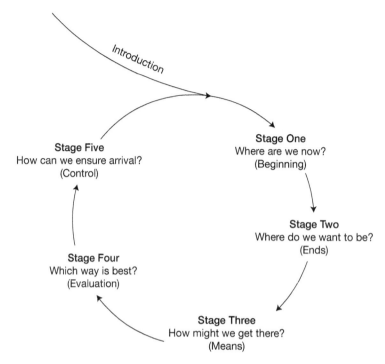

Figure 3.3 Key managerial questions

The second contextual possibility relates to *key managerial questions*, which are illustrated in Figure 3.3 (Wilson & Gilligan, 2005, p. 8). This logical sequence of questions, which requires re-iteration on a continuous basis to reflect the dynamics of a changing world, represent planning (Q 1 and Q 2), decision-making (Q 3 and Q 4), and control (Q 5). The questions are:

1   *Where are we now?* This raises the question of where the organisation is now in terms of such factors as its competitive position, financial performance, and product range. Published financial reports can provide some insights (subject to their inherent limitations), as can activity-based costing reports showing where resources were consumed in the recent past (e.g. by product, process, market segment, distribution channel, etc.), and with what consequences (e.g. by segmental profit statements and productivity reports).

2   *Where do we want to be?* This refers to the specification of aims (or desired outcomes), which may not be explicitly framed in financial terms, but the attainment of which will inevitably entail the consumption of resources which have a cost, and usually the requirement to generate revenue and either a profit or a surplus.

3   *How might we get there?* This is concerned with the identification of possible means by which desired ends might be achieved, together with their likely financial characteristics.

4   *Which way is best?* Having to choose among the competing alternatives identified in stage 3 while being faced with resource constraints is central to decision-making, and requires attention to be paid to aspects of risk and the time-frame (i.e. short-term or long-term) in judging the relative attractiveness of competing alternatives. An array of accounting techniques is available for addressing this question, but the right one has to be chosen to fit the circumstances.

5   *How can we ensure arrival?* This relates to the effective implementation of the chosen course(s) of action from stage 4. Monitoring performance is necessary in order that corrective action (as necessary) may be taken, and again there is an array of accounting techniques which can help in this challenge.

While the above questions are unambiguously managerial, there are characteristics of each which require that those individuals involved in addressing them are financially literate. Financial literacy leads to informed decision-making, and informed decision-making is more likely to result in desired outcomes.

The key messages for accounting educators from this chapter are that they should:

•   Be precise in distinguishing between financial *awareness* (i.e. what do you know?) and financial *literacy* (i.e. how can what you know be used to bring about desired outcomes?).
•   Present financial reports (of whatever type) as inputs into a broader process involving a need for understanding (via meaning-making) on the part of both compilers and users within a particular context (whether domestic, corporate, or other).
•   Recognise that technical accounting skills are necessary but not sufficient for accounting students/trainees/practitioners to be deemed financially literate.
•   Accept that meaning-making (which is so central to understanding) is an individual matter, within differing social and cultural settings.

The development of narratives based on the meaning which one makes gives a basis for learning, and learning is of critical importance since it embraces:

•   using one's understanding to explain what is going on in the present;
•   using one's understanding of the present to make more accurate predictions of the future;
•   basing one's decisions on the predictions derived from understanding;
•   using one's understanding to control the outcomes from those decisions; and
•   learning in order that one might do things better next time.

In sum, accounting educators need to ensure that the Accounting curriculum is designed, delivered, and assessed in ways which show Accounting in its personal, organisational, and societal contexts (e.g. relating to processes such as planning, decision-making, and control) if future users and compilers of financial information are to exhibit financial literacy.

References

Adult Financial Literacy Advisory Group (AdFLAG) (2000) *Report to the Secretary of State for Education and Employment*, Department of Education and Skills, London. Available at: http://www.dfes.gov.uk/adflag/ (accessed 10 September 2005).

American Institute of Certified Public Accountants (AICPA) (2008) Financial literacy: knowing what you need to know to achieve your financial goals. Available: http://aicpa.org/download/financialliteracy/ financial_literacy_toolkit/financial_literacy_power_point_10-8-8.ppt (accessed 30 May 2009).

American Library Association's Presidential Committee on Information Literacy (1989) *Final Report: 1989*, Chicago: American Library Association.

Anonymous (2008) The kids aren't all right: functionally illiterate and frankly not bothered, *Times Higher Education*, 21, February, pp. 26–27.

ANZ (2003) *National Survey of Adult Financial Literacy*, Melbourne: ANZ and Roy Morgan Research, May.

ANZ (2005) *ANZ Survey of Adult Financial Literacy in Australia*, Melbourne: ANZ and AC Nielson, November.

ANZ (2008) *ANZ Survey of Adult Financial Literacy in Australia*, Melbourne: ANZ and The Social Research Centre, October.

ANZ (2011) *Adult Financial Literacy in Australia*, Melbourne: ANZ and The Social Research Centre, November.

ASIC (2011) *Financial Literacy and Behavioural Change*, Canberra: Australian Government, March.

ASIC (2012) *National Financial Literacy Strategy*, available at: http://www.financialliteracy.gov.au/other-programs-and-resources (accessed 20 October 2012).

Association of Chartered Certified Accountants (2012a) *Reassessing the Value of Corporate Reporting*, London: ACCA.

Association of Chartered Certified Accountants (2012b) *Closing the Value Gap: Understanding the Accountancy Profession in the 21st Century*, London: ACCA.

Atewill, F. (2010) One million Londoners cannot read, *Metro*, 19 July, p. 12.

Atkinson, A. & Messy, F. (2012) Measuring financial literacy: results of the OECD/International Network on Financial Education (INFE) Pilot Study, OECD Working Papers on Finance, Insurance and Private Pensions, No. 15, OECD Publishing. doi: 10.1787/5k9csfs90fr4-en.

Barrow, M. (2012) Doctors' orders too complicated for most patients, *The Times*, 7 December, p. 23.

Bartlett, S.A. & Chandler, R.A. (1997) The corporate report and the private shareholder: Lee and Tweedie twenty years on, *British Accounting Review*, 29, 245–261.

Beal, D.J. & Delpachitra, S.B. (2003) Financial literacy among Australian university students, *Economic Papers*, 22(1), 65–78.

Beal, T. (2009) *Biblical Literacy*, London: HarperOne.

Bennett, R. (2007) Children to get lessons in money – and debt, *The Times*, 9 July, pp. 1–2.

Bennett, R. (2008) Clueless generation need to do the maths, *The Times*, 10 March, p. 29.

Berger, P.L. & Luckmann, T. (1966) *The Social Construction of Reality*, Garden City, NJ: Doubleday.

Bianculli, D. (1992) *Teleliteracy*, New York: Continuum.

Bird, S. (2008) Financial literacy among university students: an Australian case study, unpublished Master's dissertation, University of Wollongong, Australia.

Birkhead, T. (2006) Riting good is a tuff choar, innit? *Times Higher Education*, 9 June, p. 62.

Blair, A., Coulombeau, S., & Brown, O. (2004) University students not as clever as they used to be, *The Times*, 10 August, p. 7.

Boland, R.J. (1980) Organizational sense making and alternative accounting systems: a case analysis, paper presented at the Annual Meeting of the Academy of Management, Detroit, 11–13 August.

Boland, R.J. (1984) Sense-making of accounting data as a technique of organizational diagnosis, *Management Science*, 30(7), 868–882.

Boland, R.J. (1987) The in-formation of information systems, in Boland, R. & Hirscheim, R. (eds) *Critical Issues in Information Systems Research*, Chichester: Wiley, pp. 363–381.

Boland, R.J. (1993) Accounting and the interpretive act, *Accounting, Organizations and Society*, 18(2/3), 125–146.

Brooks, M. (2007) Heroes and zeros, *Financial Management*, October, p. 12.

Buchanan, R. (2013) Cleverest maths pupils 'fall behind children in Far East', *The Times*, 22 February, p. 20.

Budworth, D. (2012) The maths skills that everyone should have, *The Times*, 10 November, p. 60.

Burnet, M. (1965) *Abc of Literacy*, Paris: United Nations.

Cafferkey, K. & Doyle, G. (2011) Health literacy and economic costs, paper presented at the Irish Accounting & Finance Association Annual Conference, 2011.

Chen, H. & Volpe, R.P. (1998) An analysis of personal financial literacy among college students, *Financial Services Review*, 7(2), 107–128.

Cheuk, B. (2002) *Using Sense-Making to Study Information Seeking and Use in the Workplace*. Available at: http://communication.sbs.ohio-state.edu/sense-making/inst/instcheuk02workplace.html (accessed 11 December 2012).

CI Research (2012) *Impact Review of Financial Education for Young People: A Summary Report for the Money Advice Service*, Wilmslow, Cheshire: author.

Citi Australia (2010) *Evidence Versus Emotion: How Do We Really Make Financial Decisions?* Canberra: Citi Australia and The Australia Institute.

Cole, S. & Shastry, G.K. (2008) If you are so smart, why aren't you rich? The effects of education, financial literacy and cognitive ability on financial market participation, Harvard Business School Working Paper 09-071. Available at http://www.afi.es/EO/FinancialLiteracy.pdf (accessed 12 December 2012).

Commonwealth Bank Foundation (CBF) (2004a) *Australians and Financial Literacy*, Sydney: Commonwealth Bank Foundation.

Commonwealth Bank Foundation (CBF) (2004b) *Improving Financial Literacy in Australia: Benefits for the Individual and the Nation*, Research Report, Sydney: Commonwealth Bank Foundation.

Connolly, C., Georgouras, M., Hems, L., & Wolfson, L. (2011) *Measuring Financial Exclusion in Australia*, Sydney: Centre for Social Impact (CSI) – University of New South Wales for National Australia Bank.

Cook-Gumperz, J. (ed.) (1986) *The Social Construction of Literacy*, Cambridge: Cambridge University Press.

Council for Economic Education (CEE) (2012a) All resources. Available at: http://www.councilforeconed.org/resources/ (accessed 20 October 2012).

Council for Economic Education (CEE) (2012b) Council for Economic Education's survey of the states reveals slow progress in economic and personal finance education implementation, Press Release, 12 March, New York. Available at: http://www.councilforeconed.org/news-information/survey-of-the-states/ (accessed 20 October 2012).

Craver, K.W. (1997) *Teaching Electronic Literacy: A Concepts-Based Approach for Library Media Specialists*, Westport, CT: Greenwood Press.

Cree, A., Kay, A., & Steward, J. (2012) *The Economic and Social Costs of Illiteracy: A Snapshot in a Global Context*, Melbourne: World Literacy Foundation.

Day, J.M. (1987) *Computer Literacy and Library and Information Studies: A Literature Review*, British Library Research Paper No. 18, London: British Library.

Eaton, J. & Bawden, D. (1991) What kind of resource is information? *International Journal of Information Management*, 11, 156–165.

Elliott, A., Dolan, P., Vlaev, I., Adriaenssens, C., & Metcalfe, R. (2010) *Transforming Financial Behaviour: Developing Interventions That Build Financial Capability*, Consumer Research Report CR01, London: Consumer Financial Education Body (CFEB).

Fast Futures Research (2012) *100 Drivers of Change for the Global Accountancy Profession*, London: ACCA's Accountancy Futures Academy.

Financial Services Authority (1998) Promoting public understanding of financial services: a strategy for consumer education, November, Consultation Paper No. 15, London: FSA.

Financial Services Authority (1999) *Consumer Education: A Strategy for Promoting Public Understanding of the Financial System*, London: FSA.

Financial Services Authority (2006) *Financial Capability in the UK: Delivering Change*, London: FSA. Available at: http://www.fsa.gov.uk/pubs/other/fincap_delivering.pdf (accessed 12 December 2012).

Frean, A. (2007) Students have to learn basic maths at university, *The Times*, 25 April, p. 27.

Frean, A. (2008) Adults struggling with the sum total of life, *The Times*, 3 March, p. 25.

Frean, A., Yobbo, Y., & Duncan, I. (2007) A-level students unable to write essays, *The Times*, 15 August, p. 9.

Furnham, A. (2011) In some parts of business psychopaths are the norm, *The Sunday Times*, 8 May, p. 72.

Gardner, H. (1986) The development of symbolic literacy, in Wrolstad, M. & Fisher, D. (1986) *Toward a Greater Understanding of Literacy*, New York: Praeger; and in Posner, R. (ed.) (1985) *Zeitschrift fuer Semiotik* (Vol. 4), pp. 319–333.

Gee, J. (1990) *Socio Linguistics and Literacies*, Basingstoke: Falmer Press.

Gilhooly, M. (2012) Financially safeguarding the elderly, *Society Now*, Issue 14, Autumn, p. 9.

Grimston, J. (2010a) Pupils to be given lessons on debt, *The Sunday Times*, 3 January, p. 6.

Grimston, J. (2010b) Top firms forced to reject 'barely literate' graduates, *The Times*, 1 August, p. 6.

Gross, M. (2010) *So Why Can't They Read?* London: Centre for Policy Studies.

Gurak, L.J. (2001) *Cyberliteracy: Navigating the Internet with Awareness*, New Haven, CT: Yale University Press.

Haack, D.G. (1979) *Statistical Literacy: A Guide to Interpretation*, North Scituate, MA: Duxberry Press.

Hanushek, E.A. & Peterson, P.E. (2011) Why can't American students compete with the rest of the world? *Newsweek*, 5 September, 158(10), 42–45.

Henderson, M. (2009a) Probability lessons may teach children how to weigh life's odds and be winners, *The Times*, 5 January, pp. 14–15.

Henderson, M. (2009b) Brain's critical opt-out makes us suckers for a hard sell, *The Times*, 24 March, p. 17.

Hepworth, M. & Walton, G. (2009) *Teaching Information Literacy for Inquiry-Based Learning*, London: Chandos Publishing.

Higher Education Academy's Subject Center for Philosophical and Religious Studies (HEA PRS) (2004) Cultural literacy, *The Times*, 15 October, p. iv.

Hofsteter, F.T. (1995) *Multi-media Literacy*, New York: McGraw-Hill.

Hogarth, J., Beverly, S.G., & Hilgert, M. (2003) Patterns of financial behaviors: implications for community educators and policymakers, paper presented at Federal Reserve System Community Affairs Research Conference, February, pp. 1–22.

Hoggart, R. (1957) *The Uses of Literacy*, London: Chatto & Windus.

Hopkins, K. & Clark, A. (2011) Concern over statisticians who keep getting numbers wrong, *The Times*, 15 August, p. 36.

Hosking, P. (2013) Debt advice service a waste of money, say furious MPs, *The Times*, 3 December, p. 45.

Huddleston-Casas, C.A., Danes, S.M., & Boyce, L.M. (1999) Impact evaluation of a financial literacy program: evidence for needed educational policy changes, *Consumer Interests Annual*, Vol. 45, pp. 109–114.

Hurst, G. (2013) Anxious UK pupils lag behind in maths, *The Times*, 4 December, p. 12.

Institute of Education (1983) *Teaching Political Literacy: Implications for Teacher Training and Curriculum Planning*, London: University of London, Institute of Education, Paper 16.

Jackson, M. (1993) *Literacy*, London: David Fulton Publishers.

Jackson, S. & Durkee, D. (2008) Incorporating information literacy into the accounting curriculum, *Accounting Education: an international journal*, 17(1), 83–97.

Jennings, M., Nelson, E., & Boucher, A. (1997) Financial literacy: the cost of ignorance, *RSA Journal*, March, 31–35.

Kempson, E., Collard, S., Finney, A., Atkinson, A., Davies, S., & Hayes, D. (2010) *Money Guidance Pathfinder: A Report to the FSA*, Evaluation Report ER01, Bristol: Personal Finance Research Centre, University of Bristol.

King, J. (2010) Thunderer, *The Times*, 22 February, p. 24.

Kotlikoff, L.J. & Bernheim, B. (2001) Household financial planning and financial literacy, in Kotlikoff, L.J. (ed.) *Essays on Saving, Bequests, Altruism, and Lifecycle Planning*, Cambridge, MA: MIT Press.

Kulthau, C.C. (1991) Introduction, in Varlejs, J. (ed.) *Information Literacy: Learning How to Learn, Proceedings of the Twenty-eighth Annual Symposium of the Graduate Alumni and Faculty of the Rutgers School of Communication, Information and Library Studies, 6 April 1990*, Jefferson, NC: McFarland & Company.

Lavoie, D. (1987) The accounting of interpretations and the interpretation of accounts: the communicative function of 'the language of business', *Accounting, Organizations and Society*, 12(6), 579–604.

Layton, D. (1994) *Scientific and Technological Literacy: Meanings and Rationales: An Annotated Bibliography*, Leeds: Centre for Studies in Science and Mathematics Education, University of Leeds in association with UNESCO.

Lee, T.A. & Tweedie, D.P. (1975a) Accounting information: an investigation of private shareholder usage, *Accounting and Business Research*, 20, Autumn, 280–291.

Lee, T.A. & Tweedie, D.P. (1975b) Accounting information: an investigation of private shareholder understanding, *Accounting and Business Research*, 21, Winter, 3–17.

Lee, T.A. & Tweedie, D.P. (1976) The private shareholder: his sources of financial information and his understanding of reporting practices, *Accounting and Business Research*, 24, Autumn, 304–314.

Lee, T.A. & Tweedie, D.P. (1977) *The Private Shareholder and the Corporate Report*, London: ICAEW.

Lewis, C. (2008) Master the money and the rest falls into place, *The Times*, 21 February, p. 7.

Lusardi, A. & Mitchell, O.S. (2011) Financial literacy around the world: an overview, *Journal of Pension Economics and Finance*, 10(4), 497–508.

McDaniel, L., Martin, R.D., & Maines, L.A. (2002) Evaluating financial reporting quality: the effects of financial expertise vs. financial literacy, *The Accounting Review*, 77 (Supplement), 139–167.

MacInnes, J. (2013) Sexy statistics? *Society Now*, Autumn, pp. 16–17.

Maitlis, S. (2005) The social processes of organizational sense-making, *Academy of Management Journal*, 48(1), 21–49.

Maitlis, S. & Lawrence, T. (2007) Triggers and enablers of sense-giving in organizations, *Academy of Management Journal*, 50(1), 57–84.

Mandell, L. (1997) *Personal Financial Survey of High School Seniors*, Jump Start Coalition for Personal Financial Literacy, March/April. Washington, DC.

Marriott, D.N. & Mellett, H.J. (1991) *The Financial Awareness of Managers in the Reformed NHS*, Occasional Research Paper No. 10, London: ACCA.

Marriott, D.N. & Mellett, H.J. (1994) *Resources, Responsibility and Understanding in the NHS*, Research Report No. 37, London: ACCA.

Marriott, D.N. & Mellett, H.J. (1995) The level of financial skills of National Health Service managers, *Financial Accountability & Management*, 11(3), 271–282.

Marriott, D.N. & Mellett, H.J. (1996) Health care managers' financial skills: measurement, analysis and implications, *Accounting Education: An international journal*, 5(1), 61–74.

Martin, L.H.M. (ed.) (1997) *The Challenge of Internet Literacy: The Instruction-Web Convergence*, New York: Haworth Press.

Mason, C.L.J. & Wilson, R.M.S. (2001) Conceptualising financial literacy, paper presented at the Annual Conference of the British Accounting Association, University of Nottingham, 26–28 March.

Michaelson, R. (2004) Computer literacy in the information age, Paper presented at the BAA-SIG Education Conference, Dublin Institute of Technology, May.

Milner, M.M. & Wan Ying Hill (2008) Support for graphicacy: a review of textbooks available to accounting students, *Accounting Education: an international journal*, 17(2), 173–185.

Morrison, J. (2002) Classical stars rail at musical 'illiteracy', *The Independent on Sunday*, 1 December, p. 15.

Moynihan, J. (2012) $135–$12 = the pay gap the West can't bridge, *The Times*, 15 August, p. 17.

Mutch, A. (1997) Information literacy: an exploration, *International Journal of Information Management*, 17(5), 377–386.

National Council on Economic Education (NCEE) (2012) *Survey of the States: Economic and Personal Finance Education in Our Nation's Schools in 2011*, New York: National Council on Economic Education.

Noctor, M., Stoney, S., & Stradling, R. (1992) *Financial Literacy: A Discussion of Concepts and Competences of Financial Literacy and Opportunities for its Introduction into Young People's Learning*, report prepared for the National Westminster Bank, National Foundation for Education Research, London.

Oppenheim, C., Stenson, J.A., & Wilson, R.M.S. (2003a) Studies in information as an asset – I, *Journal of Information Science*, 29(3), 159–166.

Oppenheim, C., Stenson, J.A., & Wilson, R.M.S. (2003b) Studies in information as an asset – II, *Journal of Information Science*, 29(5), 419–432.

Oppenheim, C., Stenson, J.A., & Wilson, R.M.S. (2004) Studies in information as an asset – III, *Journal of Information Science*, 30(2), 181–190.

Organisation for Economic Co-operation & Development (OECD) (2005) *Improving Financial Literacy: Analysis of Issues and Policies*, Paris: OECD.

Organisation for Economic Co-operation and Development (OECD) (2008) *International Gateway for Financial Education*, Paris: OECD. Available at: http://www.financial-education.org (accessed 12 December 2012).

Organisation for Economic Co-operation & Development (OECD) (2012) *International Gateway for Financial Education*. Available at: http://www.financial-education.org/home.html (accessed 20 October 2012).

Oxenham, J. (1980) *Literacy: Writing, Reading and Social Organisation*, London: Routledge & Kegan Paul.

Pank, P. (2012) West Coast franchise inquest exposes a 'first-class fiasco', *The Times*, 7 December, pp. 14–15.

Peecher, M.E. (2002) Discussion of 'Evaluating financial reporting quality: the effects of financial expertise vs. financial literacy', *The Accounting Review*, 77 (Supplement), 169–173.

Peel, M.J. & Pendlebury, M. (1998) *Employee Share Ownership and Financial Awareness: Some Further Evidence*, ACCA Research Report No. 24, London: ACCA.

Peel, M.J., Pendlebury, M.W., & Groves, R.E.V. (1991) *Employee Share Ownership, 'Financial Awareness' and the Reporting of Financial Information to Employees*, ACCA Research Report No. 22. London: ACCA.

Personal Finance Research Centre (PFRC) (2005) *Measuring Financial Capability: An Exploratory Study*, report prepared for the Financial Services Authority (FSA) by Personal Finance Research Centre, University of Bristol.

Peterson, P.E., Woessmann, L., Hanushek, E.A., & Lastra-Anadón, C.X. (2011) Are U.S. students ready to compete? The latest on each state's international standing, *Education Next*, 11(4), 51–59.

Purves, L. (2007) What we want is facts. Financial facts, *The Times*, 10 July, p. 15.

Saunders, J. (2010) Foreigners flock to academic-literacy lessons, *Times Higher Education*, 18 February, p. 11.

Schagen, S. & Lines, A. (1996) *Financial Literacy in Adult Life: A Report to the NatWest Group Charitable Trust*, Slough, Berkshire: National Foundation for Educational Research.

Schuman, P.G. (1991) Introduction, in Varlejs, J. (ed.) *Information Literacy: Learning How to Learn, Proceedings of the Twenty-eighth Annual Symposium of the Graduate Alumni and Faculty of the Rutgers School of Communication, Information and Library Studies, 6 April 1990*, Jefferson, NC: McFarland & Company.

Securities and Exchange Commission (SEC) (2012) *Study Regarding Financial Literacy Among Investors*, New York: U.S. Securities and Exchange Commission.

SEDI (2005) *Why Financial Capability Matters, Synthesis Report on Canadians and Their Money: A National Symposium on Financial Capability*, Ottawa: Canadian Government.

Sorensen, K., Van Den Brouke, S., Fullam, J., Doyle, G., Pelikan, J., Slonska, Z., & Brown, H. (2012) Health literacy and public health: a systematic review and integration of definitions and models, *BMC Public Health*, 12.80. doi: 10.1186/1471-2458-12-80.

Stibbe, A. (ed.) (2009) *Handbook of Sustainability Literacy: Skills for a Changing World*, Totnes: Green Books.

Strangl, J. & Matthews, C. (2012) *How Young New Zealanders Learn About Personal Finance: A Longitudinal Study*, Financial Education and Research Centre, November, Wellington, NZ: Massey University.

Street-Porter, J. (2009) If kids can't read or count, how do they get a job? *The Independent on Sunday*, 29 November, p. 21.

Sugden, J. (2009) Schools call in bankers to teach maths to the credit crunch class, *The Times*, 14 September, p. 17.

Sugden, J. (2011) Make maths compulsory for all until 18, *The Times*, 8 August, p. 8.

Taylor Nelson Financial (1992) *Financial Quiz Summary Report*, London: Taylor Nelson.

The Sunday Times (1993) *Wordpower: Part 1 Literacy*, London: The Sunday Times.

The Times of India (2011) Indian women surpass Chinese in financial literacy, 1 March. Available at: http://timesofindia.indiatimes.com/india/Indian-women-surpass-Chinese-in-financial literacy/articleshow/7602651.cms (accessed 12 December 2012).

Times Higher Education (2007) We must tackle the literacy crisis, *THE*, 30 March, p. 10.

Turner, J. (2008) Give me credit – I admit I'm financially illiterate, *The Times*, 20 September, p. 21.

U.S. Financial Literacy and Education Commission (2006) *Taking Ownership of the Future: The National Strategy for Financial Literacy*. Available at: http://www.mymoney.gov/sites/default/files/downloads/ownership.pdf (accessed 12 December 2012).

Wagner, E. (2011) Weekly column in *The Times* (Saturday Review), 13 August, p. 15.

Walters, W. (2012) U.S. students can't compete without math proficiency, *Lubbock Avalanche-Journal*, 27 February. Available at: http://lubbockonline.com/editorial-columnists/2012-02-27/williams-us-students-cant-compete-without-math-proficiency#.UXKcicq6-X8 (accessed 15 April 2013).

Weick, K.E. (1979) *The Social Psychology of Organizing*, 2nd edn, Reading, MA: Addison-Wesley.

Weick, K.E. (1995) *Sense-making in Organizations*, Thousand Oaks, CA: Sage.

Weick, K.E., Sutcliffe, K.M., & Obstfeld, D. (2005) Organizing and the process of sense-making, *Organization Science*, 16: 409–421.

Whitehead, D.J. & Halil, T. (1989) *The Test of Economic Literacy: Standardization in the U.K.*, Research Papers in Economics Education, London: Institute of Education, University of London.

Wilde, J. (1991) *Visual Literacy: A Conceptual Approach to Graphic Problem-Solving*, New York: Watson-Guptill.

Williams-Harold, B. (1999) Saving is fundamental, *Black Enterprise*, 29, 30.

Willis, L.E. (2009) Evidence and ideology in the assessment of financial literacy, *San Diego Law Review*, 46, 415. Available at: http://www.papers.ssrn.com/sol3/papers.cfm?abstract_id=1098270 (accessed 12 December 2012).

Wilson, R.M.S. & Chua, W.F. (1993) *Managerial Accounting: Method and Meaning*, 2nd edn, London: Chapman & Hall.

Wilson, R.M.S. & Gilligan, C.T. (2005) *Strategic Marketing Management: Planning, Implementation & Control*, 3rd edn, Oxford: Butterworth-Heinemann.

Wilson, R.M.S. & Stenson, J.A. (2008) Valuation of information assets on the balance sheet, *Business Information Review*, 25(3), 167–182.

Wilson, R.M.S. & Zhang, Q. (1997) Entrapment and escalating commitment in investment decision-making: a review, *British Accounting Review*, 29, 277–305.

Woolcock, N. (2008) Maths may be wrong lesson to learn personal finance, *The Times*, 25 August, p. 5.

Woolcock, N. (2012) Half of adults have maths skills of a primary pupil, *The Times*, 2 March, p. 5.

About the authors

Richard M.S. Wilson is Emeritus Professor of Business Administration & Financial Management at Loughborough University, U.K. (rms.wilson@btinternet.com), founding Editor of *Accounting Education: an international journal*, a member of the British Accounting & Finance Association's Hall of Fame, and holds a Lifetime Achievement Award for his contribution to accounting education scholarship and research.

Anne Abraham is Associate Professor in Accounting in the School of Business at the University of Western Sydney, Australia (a.abraham@uws.edu.au). Her major research interests include financial literacy, peer review, scaffolded assessment, and blended learning. Professor Abraham's contributions to accounting education have been recognised by teaching awards, educational consultancies, research grants, and publications.

Carolynne L.J. Mason is a Senior Research Associate at Loughborough University, U.K. (c.l.j.mason@lboro.ac.uk) where she completed her PhD on 'Conceptualising Financial Literacy: An Ethnographic Study of School Governors', under Professor Wilson's supervision. Since 2006 she has been an Associate Lecturer with the Open University, U.K., teaching the course 'You and Your Money: Personal Finance in Context'.

4

The case for change in accounting education

Barbara Flood

DUBLIN CITY UNIVERSITY, IRELAND

CONTENTS

Abstract

The accounting education change debate is not new. For as long as accounting programmes have been offered by higher education institutions, or by professional accounting bodies, their relevance and appropriateness have been questioned. The purpose of this chapter is to examine the case for change by reviewing, first, the common criticisms of accounting education put forward over the past 30 years and, second, the factors which are driving the change agenda and which are likely to shape accounting education in the future. The views of the accounting profession, which are influenced by the demands placed on accountants in the workplace, are examined and the perspectives of many educators, who seek to place the study of accounting in a broader context, are also considered.

Keywords

critical thinking, criticisms of accounting education, knowledge obsolescence, professional competence, skills

4.1 Introduction

The overall objective of this chapter is to provide a comprehensive review of the case for change in accounting education. More specifically, the main aims are:

- to examine the principal criticisms of accounting education reviews published in the U.S.A. over the past 30 years;
- to report on accounting education reviews undertaken in a number of other countries;
- to consider the criticisms of accounting education put forward by accounting educators and researchers;
- to explore the nature of professional competence and consider how the competence demands on professional accountants may drive change in accounting education;
- to evaluate the arguments for the study of accounting in a broader context; and
- to examine how these arguments may shape change in accounting education.

The previous chapters of this book have already considered the challenging topics of 'accounting education as a field of intellectual enquiry' (Chapter 1), 'modelling accounting education' (Chapter 2), and 'the nature of financial literacy' (Chapter 3) and, in so doing, have either explicitly outlined or implicitly alluded to the complexity and density of accounting education as a focus of attention. Before addressing the specific aims of this chapter, it seems appropriate, first of all, to acknowledge the broad scope of accounting education and, second, to indicate the specific sub-set which is considered in this chapter.

'Accounting education' is a multi-dimensional umbrella term applied to a wide variety of programmes or activities that seek to educate students in the field of accounting. For example, the term is considered appropriate to describe the pre-qualification education (i.e. initial professional development, or IPD) of prospective members of professional accounting bodies (PABs), such as the programmes provided by PABs in Ireland, the U.K. and elsewhere, in preparation for the examinations of those bodies. The label is widely used in the higher education setting to refer both to the education of those pursuing specialised degree programmes in accounting (or majoring in accounting) and also to general *Introductory Accounting* modules that are taught to a wide variety of non-specialist students. 'Accounting education' can also refer to the study of accounting within the secondary school system, vocational education, or workplace-based education settings. (See Byrne & Willis, Chapter 7 – this volume.) Furthermore, not only does the term embrace provision at different educational levels, it also is readily applied to a wide variety of content or subject matter. This arises because there is no universally accepted definition of the scope of the field of accounting. Consequently, 'accounting education' is associated with a wide range of areas commonly practised by professional accountants (for example, financial reporting, management accounting, auditing, taxation, corporate finance, and corporate governance). Furthermore, the practice of accounting occurs in a wide array of organisations (e.g. profit-oriented and not-for-profit organisations). As the focus of this chapter is on examining the case for change in accounting education generally, it is not subject-matter or organisation-type specific. However, in terms of educational level, and in keeping with much of the prior accounting education research, it is primarily restricted to the consideration of accounting education within the setting of higher education and also to the IPD associated with membership of PABs.

4.2 Criticisms of accounting education

The debate surrounding the state of accounting education is longstanding (Black, 2012), but the nature and scale of the debate intensified in the 1980s, which was likely due to the continued expansion of accounting education within higher education and the increasing demand for those with accounting knowledge and skills in the workplace (Sundem, 1992; Wilson, 1992). At that time, the large accounting firms, PABs, and academic accounting associations were prominent in discussions regarding the relevance of accounting education to the contemporary practice of accounting and to the demands on professional accountants in ever-changing work environments. Section 4.2.1 examines many of the reviews and reports published in the U.S.A., and Section 4.2.2 considers some of the reviews concerning accounting education which have been published in other countries. Section 4.2.3 then explores a sample of the long-held criticisms of accounting education as articulated by accounting educators and researchers.

4.2.1 Reviews of accounting education undertaken in the U.S.A.[1,2]

The accounting education change debate was amplified in the U.S.A. in the 1980s with the publication of two major reports, which gained considerable attention from accounting educators in both the U.S.A. and beyond. First, the Bedford Committee Report (American Accounting Association (AAA), 1986, p.172) identified the critical problem of accounting education as being its failure to keep pace with the changes encountered in the accounting profession, contending that '*[a] growing gap exists between what accountants do and what accounting educators teach*'. It acknowledged that the emergence of such a gap between education and practice was not unique to the accounting profession and was evident at different times (and may continue today) in different professions.[3] The second significant report in the U.S.A. in this period was the *Perspectives on Education: Capabilities for Success in the Accounting Profession* White Paper issued by the then Big 8 accounting firms (Arthur Andersen *et al.*, 1989). This also focussed on the inadequate preparation for the workplace provided by accounting education. Taken together, the two reports highlighted that the role of the accountant had been altered significantly due to changes in the nature and complexity of organisational activities, increasing globalisation, the contribution of information technology (IT), and increasing regulation and scrutiny of accounting practice. It was explicated that, despite the changing demands facing accountants, accounting education in the U.S.A. had altered little over the past decades and it was thus deemed to be failing the profession.

Both the Bedford Committee Report and the *Perspectives on Education* White Paper identified a number of problems with accounting education programmes. First, programmes traditionally had a content orientation, focussing on imparting large amounts of technical knowledge to students using 'chalk-and-talk' lectures. The reports recognised that, given the rate of change in accounting regulation and practice, and the dynamic environment in which accounting operated, no accounting programme could provide a student with all the technical and general knowledge that he/she would need throughout his/her professional life. The obsolescence of discipline-specific knowledge and the development of new knowledge are seen as being a major challenge for professions in general (Taylor, 1997). Sundem & Williams (1992, p. 56) contended that the expanding knowledge base of accounting has a compounding negative impact on the effectiveness of accounting education, as students are forced to take more technical accounting courses at the expense of wider business and general education courses as they conclude: '*we have the worst of all worlds: more narrowly focussed graduates who still know a smaller and smaller percentage of the specialized accounting knowledge-base*'.

The second principal problem associated with accounting programmes was their failure to prioritise the development of the wide variety of skills required to survive in the dynamic professional work environment.

In the light of the identified problems, the reports recommended wide-sweeping changes in the structure, form, and content of programmes in order to regain the relevance of accounting education. In particular, the reports recommended that accounting education needed to emphasise empowering students with the skills necessary to deal with the changes which they will inevitably encounter during their careers. This focus involves developing a wide range of skills and attributes that will enable them to learn independently as they progress in their professional lives. It was recognised also that programmes needed to move from a content orientation to focussing on the process of students' learning and the encouragement of learning approaches that foster independent and lifelong learning. It was acknowledged that these new objectives required changes in teaching orientation and classroom activity.

At this point it is interesting to ask why the change debate was so intense in the U.S.A. in the late 1980s, and why the profession, particularly the big firms, were so dominant in the debate. In considering this issue it seems that a chronic shortage in supply of appropriately educated graduates (in terms of knowledge and skills) were at the heart of the concern of employers, such that employers were motivated to drive change in accounting programmes offered by universities (Sundem, 1992). It must be remembered that the pre-qualification education of professional accountants in the U.S.A. occurs almost exclusively in the university sector. While those seeking professional accounting accreditation have to sit a qualifying examination (e.g. the Uniform CPA examination[4] of the American Institute of Certified Public Accountants (AICPA)), PABs in the U.S.A. typically do not offer preparation courses for this examination and, indeed, many prospective members sit this examination in their final year at university, or shortly after graduation.

Recognising the importance of taking action in response to the criticisms which had been identified, the AAA, with the support of the largest accounting firms, established the Accounting Education Change Commission (AECC) in 1989 to act as a catalyst for change. Membership of the 18-person AECC was drawn from a wide range of stakeholders (Williams, 1993). In establishing a roadmap for change, the AECC stated that the objective of accounting programmes is: '*[to] prepare students to become professional accountants not to be professional accountants at the time of entry to profession*' (AECC, 1990, p. 307; AECC, 1996, p. 1. Emphasis in original). This objective acknowledges that it is implausible for accounting programmes to equip new entrants to the profession with all the knowledge and skills that they would need during their professional careers. Rather, programmes should prepare students by developing the foundations for lifelong learning, based on a multi-disciplinary knowledge base, a wide set of skills and competencies, and an understanding of the nature of professionalism. The AECC provided further guidance to educators concerning such issues as instructional methods, and it funded a grant system to universities to aid improvements (Sundem & Williams, 1992). It was acknowledged that the work of the AECC to change accounting education was not happening in isolation as there were concurrent developments to re-orientate the focus of higher education in the U.S.A. from a knowledge to a process orientation (e.g. reports by the Carnegie Foundation for the Advancement of Teaching, National Institute of Education, Association of American Colleges) (Sundem, 1992).

Looking back, it is clear that the AECC initiative drove some change in accounting education in the U.S.A. in the early 1990s, as several universities received grants and re-engineered their accounting programmes to reflect the AECC's objectives (see Williams, 1993; Flaherty, 1997; Sundem, 1999). Furthermore, the AECC initially encountered support from much of the professional and academic communities (Mathews, 1994). However, it must be noted that, even in the early days, there was some criticism of the AECC and this grew as the years went on. Previts (1991) argued that, rather than a temporary change commission, the accounting discipline needed a permanent organisation to drive research and developments in accounting education. Barefield (1991, p. 306) contended that concluding that the AECC had been successful in its early years was *'a dangerous view'* since, while projects may have started, their outcomes were still uncertain. Furthermore, he disagreed with some of the actions of the AECC. He considered that the AECC did not adequately consult with the full academic community in framing the change agenda (he felt it was too influenced by the *Perspectives* White Paper issued by the Big 8 accounting firms) and could be perceived to have engaged in *'research bashing'* (ibid., p. 307). He also felt that there was a rush to find solutions and that the grant programme was instigated too quickly. He argued that time was needed to truly evaluate the criticisms and to determine future pathways in a more considered way. In a survey of academic accounting staff, May *et al.* (1995) reported that, while a majority of academics acknowledged the need for change in accounting education, there was considerable disagreement regarding the extent and form that the change should take. Similarly, Davis & Sherman (1996) argued that, while there was agreement that accounting education was not working, the AECC simply rushed ahead – thoughtlessly pushing for change. Doost (1999) echoes the sentiment that the change agents seemed focussed on change for change's sake and were satisfied to identify quick fixes, thereby failing to examine major issues pertaining to accounting education. As the years went on, many more became openly critical of the contribution of the AECC, as Tinker (1998, p. 17) commented: *'with few exceptions, this effort has been a spectacular disaster'*.

Not surprisingly, given the mixed reaction to the AECC's efforts, the change debate within the profession in the U.S.A. rumbled on into the late 1990s and the twenty-first century. For example, the Institute of Management Accountants (IMA) (1994, 1996, 1999) considered the knowledge and skills needed by industry, and identified a mismatch between those needs and what accounting programmes delivered. In 2000, a collaborative project between the AAA, AICPA, IMA and the then 'Big 5' accounting firms resulted in the publication of another influential review concerning the future of accounting education (the Albrecht & Sack monograph). Albrecht & Sack (2000, p. 1) stated that the problems with accounting education *'cannot get much worse'*. They outlined that the numbers of students choosing accounting were still falling, and accounting practitioners described the model of accounting education as being broken and obsolete since it was failing to provide students with the knowledge and skills that were relevant to contemporary accounting careers. These criticisms echoed those of the various reports over the years and indicated that the lessons had not yet been reflected in accounting programmes, indeed, the monograph reported that 'the gap between education and practice had been widening' (ibid., p. 3). Thus, while some changes may have occurred in accounting education over the years, the changes were not sufficiently pervasive and there was also the possibility that, even where change had occurred, a process of continued change had not been maintained. Albrecht & Sack argued that, if the criticisms were not heeded, the future for accounting education was bleak. Subsequently, the scandal of Enron, the demise of Arthur

Andersen, and more recent financial crises have intensified the public scrutiny of the accounting profession. (See Chapter 23 – this volume, in which Adler presents a full discussion of the impact of financial crises on accounting education.) Yet again there have been many calls for accounting education to focus more heavily on developing students' knowledge and skills, and particularly to foster an understanding of the ethical responsibilities associated with accounting careers (i.e. PricewaterhouseCoopers, 2003). (See also Boyce, Chapter 24 – this volume.)

The most recent report is that of the Pathways Commission on Accounting Higher Education, which was formed by AAA and AICPA in 2010 to study the future structure of higher education for the accounting profession (Behn *et al.*, 2012).[5] The Commission's recommendations call for, *inter alia*:

- a greater interaction between teaching, research and practice;
- the provision of flexible modes of entry to doctoral education;
- enhancing the recognition and rewards afforded to high quality teaching in accounting; and
- changing the curricula models in accounting.

A fundamental premise of the endeavours of the Pathways Commission was that: '*the educational preparation of accountants should rest on a comprehensive and well-articulated vision of the role of accounting in wider society*' (ibid., p. 596).

Further, the Commission was aware that many of the challenges, impediments and recommendations contained in its report had been identified in earlier reports, thus it has placed considerable emphasis on determining processes and structures which will enable changes to be implemented and for ongoing review and renewal to occur. Given the recentness of the Commission's report, it has been the subject of little critical review to date and it will be interesting to see in the years ahead whether real change is delivered.

4.2.2 Reviews of accounting education undertaken in other countries

The intensity and visibility of the accounting education change debate in the U.S.A. since the mid-1980s have permeated the discussions within the profession in other countries, as similar problems with accounting education were noted. Indeed, Sundem & Williams (1992, p. 56) contend that the objectives for change outlined by the AECC '*seem equally applicable to accounting education throughout the world*'. It is not possible within a single chapter to cover the debates occurring in all countries, so what is presented here are some brief examples of discussions and changes in countries where major reviews were conducted and the reports are accessible.[6]

In Australia, the Mathews Report (Mathews *et al.*, 1990) on *Accounting in Higher Education*, emphasised the need to support and revitalise the accounting discipline within higher education as it had suffered a long period of chronic neglect. There have also been many reports outlining the generic skills requirements for accounting graduates entering the workplace (e.g. Birrell, 2006). More recently, a project funded by the Australian Learning and Teaching Council explored the changing skills requirements for professional accounting graduates (Hancock *et al.*, 2009). It identifies that non-technical skills (e.g. communication, team work, problem-solving initiative, etc.) are highly sought after, are discriminating factors at the point of recruitment, and also are related to career advancement. In addition, the report also provides examples of best practice in the development of generic skills, though it was acknowledged that accounting departments faced reduced funding which may impair their ability to adopt new strategies for the development of skills (Hancock *et al.*, 2009). (See also Watty, Chapter 13, and Jackling, Chapter 10 – both in this volume.)

The Institute of Chartered Accountants in Australia (ICAA), in conjunction with the University of South Australia, organised a forum to discuss the future of accounting education which culminated in the publication *Accounting Education at a Crossroad in 2010* (Evans *et al.*, 2010). In critiquing the *Crossroad* publication, De Lange & Watty (2011) note its failure to examine the role of accounting education research in framing new pedagogical approaches to address many of the problems. Another recent report (Cappelletto, 2010), commissioned by the three main PABs in Australia, also focussed on the challenges facing accounting education. Reporting many of the same issues, De Lange & Watty (2011, p. 629) contend that the strength of the Cappelletto report lies in its empirical base and '*its ability to illuminate both real and current issues facing the sector*'. Ultimately, these publications in Australia highlight the fact that many of the systemic problems in accounting education which had been reported by Mathews *et al.* (1990) '*still exist and, in some cases, they have been exacerbated*' (De Lange & Watty, 2011, p. 626).

In the U.K., many PABs have similarly grappled with the challenge of preparing the accountants of the future and have made changes to their systems of pre-qualification education.[7] In reviewing its education process and making recommendations for syllabus changes, the Institute of Chartered Accountants in England and Wales (ICAEW) emphasised the need to reshape students' current modes of learning and to encourage them to develop understanding and to view their learning as a long-term activity (ICAEW, 1998). While much of the education debate within the ICAEW in the 1990s was dominated by fierce arguments over whether the professional examinations' syllabus should move to a 'core and options' model (Paisey & Paisey, 2006, see also Chapter 30 – this volume), its qualification system today is clearly focussed on providing IPD that fosters the knowledge, skills and experience that will enable the prospective member 'to successfully handle a variety of different situations' that he/she may encounter during his/her professional career (ICAEW, 2012, p. 8). Research by Hassall *et al.* (2005) reported that U.K. employers found that Chartered Institute of Management Accountant (CIMA) trainees commenced employment with knowledge and skills that did not match the demands of the workplace, hence changes to syllabus and examinations were made. In Ireland, Chartered Accountants Ireland[8] recognised the need to adapt the education and training of prospective members away from a content-focussed, technical orientation. In 2007, Chartered Accountants Ireland adopted a competence model of education and training which emphasises both a broader, business-focussed knowledge base and a wide range of personal and professional competencies (Chartered Accountants Ireland, 2012).

In Canada, concern over the supply of labour to the accounting profession was a significant feature of the accounting education change debate for over 30 years (e.g. Rosen, 1978). Cognisant of the AECC's efforts in the U.S.A., the Canadian Academic Accounting Association (CAAA) commissioned a research project to explore dimensions of university accounting education in Canada. The outcome of the project was a set of papers published in a special issue of *Contemporary Accounting Research*, in 1994 which provided a rich description of features of accounting education in Canada with regard to student profile, accounting academics, content and delivery of courses, and institutional pressures. In summarising the project, Etherington & Richardson (1994) encouraged policy-makers to review the outcomes of the project, and they also sought to stimulate educational-based research in the discipline of accounting. Over the years, the Canadian Institute of Chartered Accountants (CICA) has fundamentally reviewed and re-shaped the demands of pre-qualification education of its prospective members. Recently, in conjunction with the University of Toronto, it led a symposium on the theme of 'Leveraging Change – The New Pillars of Accounting Education' at which academics and delegates discussed the future directions (Wiecek & Deal, 2011).

4.2.3 Criticisms of accounting education by accounting educators and researchers

Calls for changes in accounting education have been made repeatedly by accounting educators and researchers. As will be seen below, this stakeholder group has focussed on different dimensions of the problem, but the conclusion of the body of work is that accounting education (whether in higher education or within the profession itself) is failing students in two ways:

- It does not adequately prepare students for the workplace. (See Hassall & Joyce, Chapter 17, and Beard & Humphrey, Chapter 25 – both in this volume.)
- At the same time, it is failing to develop the type of critical thinking and intellectual development that might reasonably be expected of higher education and professional education. (See Cunningham, Chapter 18 – this volume.)

There is a wide body of academic literature asserting the failure of accounting education to develop the broad range of knowledge, skills, and attributes deemed necessary to enable graduates to thrive in changing, dynamic workplaces. Needles & Powers (1990), in chronicling the development of accounting education models by professional bodies in the U.S.A. between the years 1967 and 1990, contend that the imparting of technical and rule-based material was clearly prioritised over the development of skills. Indeed, the emphasis in much of the academic research in the area has been on issues related to the development of non-technical, generic skills, such as communication skills, team-working, and information technology (IT) competence. (See Boritz & Stoner, Chapter 16 – this volume.) For example, having surveyed employers in the U.K. and Spain, Hassall *et al.* (2005) report that non-technical skills are a prerequisite for management accountants to perform in the modern workplace and they felt that these skills should be developed in the education setting. The need for generic skills among graduates generally and specifically for prospective professional accountants is covered in detail by Watty in Chapter 13 in this volume, so at this point it is only necessary to provide an illustration of the criticisms rather than comprehensively review the issues. These types of concerns are well expressed by Deppe *et al.* (1991, p. 258): '*Training in accounting that was sufficient for the industrial era is no longer adequate. Competencies for accountants must be expanded beyond the technical knowledge and skills currently emphasized.*' (For an alternative view, see St. Pierre & Rebele, Chapter 5 – this volume.)

In considering the mismatch between the skills needed and the output of accounting programmes, Frederickson & Pratt (1995) warn fellow educators that the call for the development of a broader skills set among accounting students cannot be ignored. They argue that, if accounting programmes fail to develop desirable accounting graduates, then accounting employers will simply look elsewhere for suitable recruits and this would impact on the standing of accounting departments within higher education institutions (HEIs) and on the profession as a whole. Tinker & Koutsoumandi (1997) similarly highlight the threat of accounting employers recruiting from outside their traditional source of supply if accounting programmes do not change to deliver graduates with the desired skills to suit the marketplace. Indeed, Tinker has been an outspoken critic of accounting education over the years. While he has criticised the failure of accounting programmes to develop a broad range of skills, he has criticised accounting education more vehemently for failing to foster accounting students' intellectual curiosity and critical thinking, leaving them bereft of the abilities to question and interrogate accounting rules and practice:

Today's students and tomorrow's practitioners are saturated with a litany of rules and procedures that are supported by little other than expedient reasoning, ad hoc explanations and piecemeal rationalizations. Professional accounting education is certainly not a talkshop for exploring the meaning of social existence: rather it resembles a rote-learning process in which students are inculcated with the profession's party line by pedantic and legalistic methods. The role of accounting in major social controversies is never articulated in accounting education because the intellectual apparatus necessary for conducting a comprehensive appraisal is withheld.

(Tinker, 1985, pp. xx–xxi)

The importance placed on technical knowledge in accounting education and its failure to consider either the context in which regulation emerged or alternative perspectives, are heavily criticised by many academics. Ultimately, technical, rule-focussed accounting education provides '*a narrow, functionalist view of the discipline*' (Boyce, 2004, p. 569) and, as Parker (2007, p. 46) comments: '*limits the possibility of producing accountants of insight, imagination, creativity and ethical leadership*'. Chambers (1999, pp. 250–251) described the fact-based nature of what is taught to accounting students (particularly the emphasis given to Generally Accepted Accounting Principles (GAAP)) as leading to a '*poverty of discourse*' and is an '*educational scandal*'. This '*poverty*' arises from a failure to strenuously interact with core concepts in accounting, such as measurement. In analysing and extending the work of Chambers, Amernic & Craig (2004, p. 358) argue that '*a poverty of accounting discourse will arise from condemning students to an exclusive diet of conventional accounting technique – one that is lacking in the vital trace elements of critique*'.

Sikka (1987, p. 293) contends that, while the accounting profession '*purports to attach considerable importance to the theoretical as well as the practical knowledge and is interested in the intellectual development of future accountants*', the reality falls far short of the assertions. Puxty *et al.* (1994, p. 86) argued that traditional accounting education makes little effort to locate accounting in any social or organisational context. Instead, it supports a process of transmitting factual information: '*"Fact"-based learning is dominant; but there is no indication of how "facts" are formulated or that their construction is always contingent upon particular trajectories of histories, politics and nexus of power relations.*' Thus, accounting education has been heavily criticised for fostering conformity and failing to nurture those who might question current practice (Hanlon, 1994, p. 115).

The limitations of the technically-orientated, rote-learning emphasis of accounting education were also articulated by Kinney (1990), when reflecting on his own experiences of professional education in the 1960s. He describes how his accounting courses did little to develop his understanding of accounting as a social, legal, or political phenomenon, or of the dynamics of accounting regulation and practice. Similarly, in ethnographic research, Power (1991, p. 350) describes his experiences of professional education as a student member of ICAEW in the 1980s and concludes that '*discursive values are displaced by those of technique and strategy*'.

The spate of corporate scandals that were exposed in the early 2000s prompted an unprecedented level of scrutiny of the role of professional accountants (Amernic & Craig, 2004). Williams (2004) argues that educators must take some responsibility for failing to encourage a discourse that would prevent scandals like Enron occurring, and he concludes that, until the scandals are viewed as a moral problem as opposed to a technical problem which has a quick fix, transformation of the discipline will not be possible. Diamond (2005, pp. 353–354) contends that the scandals should act as a '*wake-up call for accounting educators*'. He argues that much thought is needed to reform accounting education so that it will give students the range of intellectual and other skills '*[to] make wise decisions in the face of change and helps them to continue their professional development throughout their careers*'. He suggests that, while the debate about change has been '*endless*', the reality is that the process has been stuck in '*neutral*' for decades (ibid., p. 355). More recently, this view has been echoed by Boyce *et al.* (2012, p. 48) who contend that traditional perspectives and approaches to accounting education still dominate and there has been '*little in the way of systemic change*'.

Before progressing to the next section of this chapter, which will examine the drivers of change, it is useful to summarise the criticisms of accounting education. In essence, these are:

- failure of accounting education to keep pace with the changes occurring in the practice of accounting (*gap between what is taught and what is practised*), which is characterised by

  — failure to address the expanding knowledge base and the issue of knowledge obsolescence;
  — failure to develop generic skills that are needed in the workplace;
  — failure to foster the skills and attitudes necessary for lifelong learning.
- failure of accounting education to achieve the aims of higher and professional education regarding the development of critical thinking and intellectual development (*the poverty of accounting discourse*).

4.3 Drivers of change in accounting education

Professional accountants today work in organisations that engage in complex activities which are changing constantly. While in the past the role of the professional accountant was dominated by gathering and recording data and conveying information to management, many of these traditional activities are now performed by IT. As a result, accountants are now being asked to contribute to organisations by converting information into knowledge and by adding value to the decision-making process. (See the definition of financial literacy by Wilson *et al.*, Chapter 3 – this volume.) In examining changing roles, Burns & Baldvinsdottir (2005, p. 726) contend that accountants spend less time on traditional activities and, instead, occupy roles that '*encompass a business-orientation that stretches considerably beyond routine and technical accounting*'.

The dissonance between accountants' traditional and emerging roles is blurring the boundaries of the domain of the accounting profession and is causing a crisis of identity to the extent that some PABs today describe their members as 'business advisors' or 'business professionals' rather than as accountants. In this regard, cognisance should be taken of a recent report from the Institute of Management Accountants (IMA) and the Association of Chartered Certified Accountants (ACCA) which highlights the need for chief financial officers (CFOs) to be capable of adapting in the face of greater economic uncertainty, cost pressures, and a more demanding regulatory environment. Nine key priorities are identified as being characteristic of the challenges for which CFOs should be prepared (ACCA, 2013). These are:

- regulation;
- globalisation;
- technology (especially IT);
- risk management;
- transformation (e.g. re-engineering to reduce costs or improve efficiency);
- stakeholder management;
- validation of corporate strategy;
- changes in financial reporting (e.g. to accommodate IFRS and embrace social and environmental metrics); and
- finding the right staff with the right skills.

To this list we might add a tenth priority, which is to balance the other nine. (See also Cunningham, Section 18.2 of Chapter 18 – this volume.)

As was outlined in the previous section, one of the major criticisms of accounting education is that it is failing to prepare prospective professional accountants for the realities and complexities of professional work as indicated above (in addition to issues concerning knowledge obsolescence and appropriate skills). Accordingly, this section considers:

- how the concept of professional competence, which embraces a holistic perspective on knowledge and skills, offers a way of framing change in accounting education;
- an evaluation of the suggestions put forward by accounting educators and researchers to drive change by locating the study of accounting in a broader context, thereby fostering critical thinking among accounting students.

The section concludes by briefly considering whether the professional and 'critical' agendas are mutually exclusive, or whether they may complement one another.

4.3.1 The nature of professional competence

Professional competence is not clearly defined in the literature. However, there appears to be a general understanding that professional competence implies that an individual is able to fulfil his professional and occupational responsibilities satisfactorily. Jarvis (1983, p. 34) suggests that competence is embodied by good practice based on sound theory, and therefore, '*this demands that the practitioner should have both the knowledge and the skill to undertake the demands of the job, proficiency in one but not the other area is less than competency.*'

The use of appropriate *knowledge* and *skills* in the conduct of one's professional activities is at the heart of the concept of professional competence and as professional activities are subject to constant change, competence must be recognised to be a dynamic concept.

Jarvis (ibid., p. 74) describes professional knowledge as '*that selection from the overall body of knowledge considered by members of the profession to be the foundation of their practice*', but there is a need to delve deeper to get to the heart of the nature of that knowledge. The categorisation of knowledge forms as 'knowledge that' and 'knowledge how'[9] is very useful in the context of professions. 'Knowing that' commonly refers to an individual's factual knowledge (for a professional accountant this would include, for example, knowledge of accounting standards or tax regulations), whereas 'knowing how' captures knowledge of application and transforms theoretical knowledge into professional practice (e.g. knowledge of how to make judgements regarding the application of accounting standards and regulations). Jarvis (ibid., pp. 76–77) describes professional skills as being special abilities that commonly emerge from training. He contends that, in professional contexts, skills are more than just the psychomotor ability to complete a task (i.e. ability to make a presentation or write a report): they require the interaction with the different types of knowledge.

Wilensky (1964) proposes that aspects of professional knowledge are tacit as opposed to explicit and involve accumulated un-codified knowledge, and Eraut (1992, p. 101) states that many professionals '*cannot explain the nature of their own expertise*'.

Eraut (1985) describes professional competence in terms of three types of knowledge: propositional, process and personal knowledge.

- *Propositional knowledge* is multi-dimensional and reflects the core theories and concepts that underpin a discipline, the practical principles applied in professional action, and also specific knowledge about particular scenarios. (In accounting, this knowledge type might include underlying theories of neo-classical economics or concepts such as income measurement, as well as practice knowledge regarding regulations and their application in particular circumstances.) He suggests that the theoretical underpinnings of a discipline can often get forgotten and knowledge from practice often dominates, leading to a theory–practice gap within professions.

- *Process knowledge* as defined by Eraut (1992, p. 105) is '*knowing how to conduct the various processes that contribute to professional action*' and includes: acquiring information, skilled behaviour, deliberative processes, giving information, and controlling one's own behaviour. (For the professional accountant, this knowledge type relates to identifying and applying appropriate propositional knowledge and engaging in this regard with colleagues, clients or other stakeholders in a professional manner.) In other words, process knowledge facilitates the transformation of propositional knowledge into professional action.
- *Personal knowledge*, the third component of Eraut's depiction of professional competence, captures the stock of knowledge that the individual acquires through experience; it can often be tacit and held at the impression level, and is generally poorly understood. (For the professional accountant this may not only include his/her personal sense of professional values and ethics, but also the personal learning which has occurred regarding professional action.) Taylor (1997, p. 19) argues that the challenge of professional education is to bring personal knowledge to the surface so that it can be examined in the light of the other knowledge types and then its influence on professional action can be explored.

Eraut (2000) suggests that professional knowledge can also be described as embracing both codified/public knowledge and personal knowledge. Codified knowledge consists of propositional knowledge, which is subject to quality control by regulators, the research community, and professional debate. On the other hand, personal knowledge is encapsulated as the cognitive resource that an individual brings to a situation which allows him/her to think and perform. It embraces personal interpretations of codified knowledge, in addition to procedural, process, and experiential knowledge. While codified knowledge is explicit, much personal knowledge is tacit.

A seminal piece of work concerning professional competence was the development of the idea of the '*reflective practitioner*' by Schön (1983). He challenges the 'technical rationality' epistemology of professional practice which views practice as being the systematic application of previously determined theories, concepts, and methods to practical situations. Schön contends that such an epistemology separates theory and practice and assumes a steady, predefined operating environment, which he argues is divergent from the reality. He suggests that a significant component of professional practice revolves around dealing with ambiguous, unfamiliar problems, which are not easily solved by the simple application of previously developed theories and concepts. Instead, he argues that the practice of professionals hinges on reflection on, and in, action. This reflection first comes from the tacit knowing in-action which the professional develops through practice. The professional then seeks to make sense of action and thinks about the understanding that is implicit in his/her practice. He/she brings this understanding to the surface, critically evaluates it, and embodies it into future action. Schön proposes that this reflection in-action is central to the 'art' that enables professionals to deal with ill-defined situations.

The conceptualisation of professional practice as knowing and reflecting in action is very different to the many conceptualisations of competence that focus on knowledge types. However, the perspectives are not necessarily mutually exclusive. Schön's approach places emphasis on the creation of knowledge through reflection which then enables practice. The work of Jarvis, Eraut and others focusses more on the forms of explicit knowledge and skills which can be articulated and classified and which foster competence. These approaches recognise that tacit and personal knowledge contribute to competent practice, but they do not conceptualise and explicate them in the way that the reflective practitioner epistemology does.

Cheetham & Chivers (1996, 1998) bring together the reflective practitioner and competencies approaches to professional education. As illustrated in Figure 4.1, their model presents four core components of competence: knowledge/cognitive competence, functional competence, personal/behavioural competence, and values/ethical competence. Each of these core components consists of a number of constituent parts. Furthermore, overarching the core components are meta-competencies (such as reflection, communication, self-development, creativity, analysis, and problem-solving) which develop, enhance, and mediate all of the other competencies in the model. All of the elements of the model interact to produce outcomes and to contribute to the iterative development of professional competence and practice.

The appropriateness of combining the competence approach and the reflective practitioner approach is confirmed by research examining how professionals in six professions actually work (Cheetham & Chivers, 2000). This study found that neither the reflective practitioner nor technical rationality epistemologies individually capture the reality of professional action. It was found that, while reflection is very important in professional practice, reliance on technical specialised knowledge is greater than anticipated by Schön (1983). Thus, Cheetham & Chivers (2000) argue that an epistemology of professional practice needs to combine professional knowledge (different types) with work-based competence, reflective thinking, and flexible, innovative practice.

Given the demand by the accounting profession for accounting education to provide prospective professional accountants with knowledge and skills appropriate for the challenges of professional work, it is not surprising that many change initiatives in professional accounting education are framed by the objective of developing professional competence. As far back as 1990, the AECC set out the objective of accounting education as being the development of appropriate knowledge, skills, and values (AECC, 1990), and PABs in different countries have adopted competency-based objectives in IPD. The dominance of the competency approach is perhaps best illustrated by the *Framework for International Education Standards (IESs) for Professional Accountants* outlined by the International Accounting Education Standards Board (IAESB). The framework states that '*the overall goal of accounting education is to develop competent professional accountants*' (IFAC, 2010, para. 11). Further, it states that:

> Competence is defined as the ability to perform a work role to a defined standard with reference to working environments. To demonstrate competence in a role, a professional accountant must possess the necessary (a) professional knowledge, (b) professional skills, and (c) professional values, ethics, and attitudes.
>
> (ibid., para. 12)

IESs apply to over 160 PABs worldwide which are members of the International Federation of Accountants (IFAC). For example, in Ireland, Chartered Accountants Ireland (which is a member body of IFAC) describes the objective of its IPD programme for prospective members as the development of a set of functional competencies (disciplinary knowledge), business competencies (broader business knowledge and skills), and core professional values and competencies (knowledge of ethics and professionalism, and self-awareness regarding knowledge, values, and limitations) (Chartered Accountants Ireland, 2012).

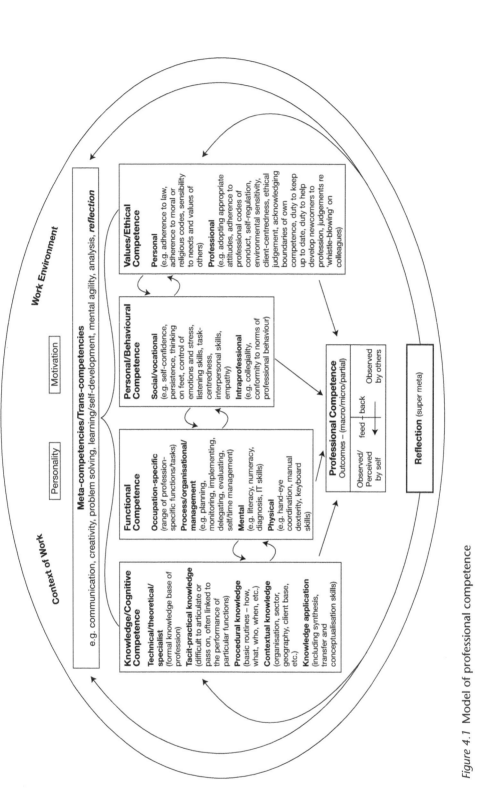

Figure 4.1 Model of professional competence

Thus, in terms of shaping a new agenda for accounting education, it appears that the competence model has merit and it also has traction among PABs as a way of responding to criticisms concerning the relevance of accounting education and training. It is also clear that a competence-focussed approach may offer a framework for the development of the broader education encouraged for accounting programmes in higher education. However, as will be outlined in Section 4.3.2, many accounting educators argue that there is no agreement regarding what a broader education entails.

4.3.2 Accounting in a broader context

As already outlined in Section 4.2.3, many accounting educators and researchers have criticised accounting education for the narrow view provided of the discipline. One of the main reasons why a limited perspective on the discipline can arise is that GAAP dominates the syllabus in order to meet the (stated or presumed) demands of the profession.[10] The profession may argue that GAAP (and related material concerning current practice) are providing the appropriate types of knowledge as outlined in the models of professional competence. However, critics contend that just teaching what is currently practised perpetuates that practice and stifles innovation such that research and new ideas find no outlet (e.g. Arnold, 1989). Furthermore, Ravenscroft & Williams (2005, p. 364) state that 'GAAP is neither a set of principles nor generally accepted' and, in the following words, Chambers (1999, p. 249) associated GAAP with the failure to enrich accounting discourse:

> In the last sixty years, instead of the richness and rigour of thought that arises from the cross-fertilisation of ideas, accountants have insulated themselves from the world of affairs by a cocoon of their own making. It is called 'generally accepted accounting principles'.

Williams (2004:, p. 996) similarly argues that the accounting profession itself is responsible for the limited knowledge base of the discipline, and its efforts to create a more 'scientific' image of accounting has led to the accounting function now being 'a purely technical one, which has no robust technical foundations'. Today, the complexity and detail of International Financial Reporting Standards (IFRS), which are becoming increasingly important in global business, exacerbate the challenges for accounting educators (Adler, 2011). By teaching accounting standards (IFRS or local standards), and other basic accounting tools and techniques, in an unquestioning way, accounting educators are perpetuating the problem of a narrow view of accounting, and they are failing to give students the opportunity or capacity to question the rationale of current accounting practices. (See Wilson & Adler, 2012.)

So what would an expanded knowledge base of accounting look like? Ultimately, the expanded knowledge base would place accounting in context, consider accounting issues from multiple perspectives, would facilitate an understanding of how accounting practice has developed, and would explore alternatives to existing practice. As a starting point, it necessitates that students are exposed to 'a wide range of materials and perspectives' (Humphrey, 2005, p. 348). Diamond (2005) argues that the appropriate study of accounting needs to be built on a truly liberal arts foundation. He contends that a liberal arts undergraduate experience, covering only limited accounting material, would provide students with the capabilities and the lifelong learning skills to subsequently pursue postgraduate or professional education. (See Sangster & Wilson, 2013.)

Amernic & Craig (2004, p. 343) passionately and convincingly argue the need for accounting education to encourage students to understand 'the idiosyncratic, political, rhetorical, ideological and *non-objective nature of accounting'*. They contend that accounting students and society at large need to appreciate that accounting is not a precise, objective measurement system and, instead, the abstract dimension of accounting needs to be conveyed. They encourage educators to nourish students intellectually and to encourage students to think critically and question extant practice. Moreover, they suggest that *'accounting educators should promote a scholarly environment in which freedom to be sceptical and critical of conventional wisdom is tolerated and actively encouraged'* (ibid., p. 360).

To enable reform of accounting education, Amernic & Craig put forward three sets of recommendations for educators to adopt:

1   They suggest that themes such as embeddedness and complexity should permeate the accounting curriculum.
2   Efforts must be made to enhance the intellectual discourse in the study of accounting by interrogating the underlying fundamentals of accounting theory, and by encouraging scepticism and questioning of conventional practice.
3   Finally, they argue for the need to encourage students to pierce the *'technical surface of accounting to expose its underlying ideology'* (ibid., p. 368).

In Chapter 12 of this volume, Amernic & Craig provide in-depth consideration of liberalising the accounting curriculum.

In the literature there is a sense that the resistance or barriers to adopting a more liberal, critical accounting education in universities is at its height in the U.S.A., whereas it is perceived that there is a greater willingness to adopt such an approach in Europe and elsewhere (Diamond, 2005). While there are a number of examples of initiatives already introduced (see, for example, McPhail, 2004; Boyce *et al.*, 2012), the challenge for educators lies in designing and implementing those changes. Furthermore, educators must grapple with how to add a more critical orientation to programmes while also acknowledging the need for programmes to deliver the technical and professional elements for those who intend to pursue a professional accounting qualification on graduation. (See Jackling, Chapter 10 – this volume.) Indeed, a recent study of the motives and expectations of a sample of students commencing the study of accounting in universities in the U.K., Ireland, Spain, and Greece found that students expect their degree programmes both to enhance their career prospects and enable intellectual growth (Byrne *et al.*, 2012). Amernic & Craig (2004, p. 360) identify the need to strike a balance, *'[being] mindful of the need for a rapprochement between the "academic-scholarly" and "practice-oriented" cultures that influence curriculum design'*.

4.3.3 Accounting education for non-specialists

It is important to remember that many students study accounting at university but do not proceed to pursue professional accounting careers. Indeed, as is often said, 'the first course in accounting may also be the last course in accounting'. In many ways, the debate about the drivers of change in accounting education is as relevant for these students as for specialist students. In some universities, specialist and non-specialist students take the same *Introductory Accounting* course, which often focusses on techniques and practices. In other universities, while a separate introductory course may be offered to non-specialist students, which excludes detailed coverage of double-entry book-keeping, it is still commonly techniques-driven. As Lucas (2000) illustrates, these introductory courses often result in cementing many students' perceptions that accounting is mathematical and precise (see Lucas & Mladenovic, Chapter 6 – this volume, for a full discussion of students' perceptions of accounting). Thus, there is a need to consider the knowledge and skills appropriate for such non-specialist accounting courses, recognising that it is likely that students taking these courses will be users rather than preparers of financial information at some stage in their careers. It would seem sensible that these courses should enable students to understand the nature, role, and context of accounting, and thus the suggestions for accounting educators to place accounting in a broader context as outlined above have resonance in this form of accounting education also. (See Wygal, Chapter 11 – this volume.)

4.4 Conclusion

This chapter has examined the longstanding debate concerning the need for change in accounting education. Two particular dimensions to this debate were explored with regard both to the traditional criticisms of accounting education and to the drivers for change. First, the perspective of the accounting profession was considered which highlighted the failure of accounting education to appropriately prepare students for challenging and dynamic professional work. In terms of reshaping accounting education, the emphasis of the profession is on the need to develop professional competence, which captures a wide range of knowledge, skills, values and attributes.[11] The second perspective on change is that put forward by accounting educators and researchers, who criticise accounting education for focussing on the transmission of knowledge concerning current accounting practice. Further, they argue that it fails both to expose students to multiple perspectives of accounting and to develop their intellectual capabilities to critique current practice and develop innovative ideas. Thus, there is a drive to redress these limitations in reforming accounting education.

In exploring these two dimensions to the case for change in accounting education, it seems that there is scope to cater for both the vocational, work-based demands of the profession and also the arguments by educators for a more rounded, critical approach to accounting. While there will always be differences between the two approaches, they are not mutually exclusive. However, it must be reiterated that the debate to change accounting education has existed for decades and, while we can articulate the problems and examine ways to frame change in accounting education, the complexity and depth of accounting knowledge and practice and the challenging nature of the relationships between education and training are likely to see the perpetuation of this debate for many years to come.

Notes

1 Black (2012) provides a comprehensive review of the major reports on accounting education in the U.S.A. since the early twentieth century. This chapter will not replicate that review, rather it emphasises some key reports in the past 30 years which have triggered major debate in the U.S.A. and beyond.

2 Sundem (in Chapter 27 in this volume) provides a more detailed review than is presented here of the various reports and changes emanating in the U.S.A. over the past 50 years. That chapter particularly examines the role of various institutions, including professional associations, in accounting education change.

3 Fuelled by the publication of a review by the Carnegie Foundation (Sullivan et al., 2007), there is considerable debate currently in the U.S.A. concerning the appropriateness of legal education offered by universities. The Carnegie Foundation review particularly criticises the case-dialogue pedagogy of law schools for failing to prepare students for the practice of law. The review contends that new practice-oriented or clinical pedagogies are needed to provide students with, among other things, different forms of knowledge and 'lawyering' skills that will enable them to make appropriate decisions and judgements in the practice of law. As a cursory review of legal education research will indicate, there is a wide variety of opinion on the issues raised in the Carnegie Foundation's review but an exploration

of this debate is beyond the scope of this chapter. Nonetheless, the debate surrounding legal education highlights that the accounting profession is not alone in grappling with developing appropriate forms, content, and approaches to pre-qualification education. For those interested in the debate in legal education, the Carnegie Foundation review (ibid.) is thought-provoking, as are critiques of the work, such as that provided by Alfieri (2009). Furthermore, the Carnegie Foundation has not only focussed on legal education, it has an ongoing programme of research focussed on professional education generally, and recent reports have also addressed engineering education, clergy education, medical and nursing education (see http://www.carnegiefoundation.org/previous-work/professional-graduate-education). In the U.K., Paisey & Paisey (2004) highlight how the accounting, medical, and legal professions face similar dilemmas regarding the development of professional knowledge and skills.

4 It should be noted that CPA licensure is granted by State Boards of Accountancy in individual states in the U.S.A. and those seeking a CPA licence must meet the requirements of the particular state in addition to passing the Uniform CPA examination.

5 The full report of the Pathways Commission is available at http://commons.aaahq.org/groups/2d690969a3/summary.

6 Chapter 26 of this volume is a useful reference point on models of accounting education in different countries.

7 Interestingly, in the 1970s, the Solomons Report (1974), commissioned in the U.K. by the short-lived Advisory Board on Accounting Education, suggested radical reform of accounting education. However, the recommendations were never implemented.

8 The body was previously known as the Institute of Chartered Accountants in Ireland (ICAI).

9 The distinction between 'knowing that' and 'knowing how' was first made by Ryle (1949) (Eraut, 1992, p. 105).

10 In the U.S.A., the concern is to prepare students to take the Uniform CPA examination. In other countries, such as the U.K., Ireland, and Australia, attention to the demands of the profession for GAAP coverage is driven by the need for programmes to be given exemption from certain professional examinations.

11 In contrast, Chapter 5 of this book by St. Pierre & Rebele makes an interesting and compelling argument that accounting programmes could best service the profession and other stakeholders by going back to basics and focussing on developing students' technical knowledge and skills as opposed to vocationally-oriented, 'soft-skills'.

References

Accounting Education Change Commission (AECC) (1990) Objectives of education for accountants: Position Statement No.1, *Issues in Accounting Education*, 5(2), 307–312.

Accounting Education Change Commission (AECC) (1996) *Position and Issues Statements of the Accounting Education Change Commission*, (Accounting Education Series, Vol. 13), Sarasota, FL: American Accounting Association.

Adler, R. (2011) Editorial, *Accounting Education: an international journal*, 20(4), 299–301.

Albrecht, W.S. & Sack, R.J. (2000) *Accounting Education: Charting the Course through a Perilous Future*, Sarasota, FL: American Accounting Association.

Alfieri, A. (2009) Against practice, *Michigan Law Review*, 107, 1073–1092.

American Accounting Association (AAA) Committee on the Future Structure, Content and Scope of Accounting Education (The Bedford Committee) (1986) Future accounting education: preparing for the expanded profession, *Issues in Accounting Education*, 1(1), 168–195.

Amernic, J. & Craig, R. (2004) Reform of accounting education in the post-Enron era: moving accounting 'out of the shadows', *Abacus*, 40(3), 342–378.

Arnold, J. (1989) Accounting education and research: the role of universities, in MacDonald, G. & Rutherford, B. (eds) *Accounting, Auditing and Accountability*, London: Van Nostrand Reinhold and ICAEW, pp. 1–24.

Arthur Andersen & Co., Arthur Young, Coopers & Lybrand, Deloitte Haskins & Sells, Ernst & Whinney, Peat Marwick Mitchell, Price Waterhouse, & Touche Ross (1989) *Perspectives on Education: Capabilities for Success in the Accounting Profession*, New York: the authors.

Association of Chartered Certified Accountants (2013) *The Changing Role of the CFO: Why Breadth and Depth of Finance Capability Matter in Today's Finance Function*, London: ACCA. Available at: www.accaglobal.com/transformation (accessed 8 August, 2013).

Barefield, R.M. (1991) A critical review of the AECC and the converging forces for change, *Issues in Accounting Education*, 6(2), 305–312.

Behn, B.K. (Chair), Ezzell, W.F., Murphy, L.A., Rayburn, J.D., Stith, M.T., & Strawser, J.R. (2012) The Pathways Commission on accounting higher education: charting a national strategy for the next generation of accountants (executive summary), *Issues in Accounting Education*, 27(3), 595–600.

Birrell, B. (2006) *The Changing Face of the Accounting Profession in Australia*, Melbourne: CPA Australia.

Black, W.H. (2012) The activities of the Pathways Commission and the historical context for changes in accounting education, *Issues in Accounting Education*, 27(3), 601–625.

Boyce, G. (2004) Critical accounting education: teaching and learning outside the circle, *Critical Perspectives on Accounting*, 15(4/5), 565–586.

Boyce, G., Greer, S, Blair, B., & Davids, C. (2012) Expanding the horizons of accounting education: incorporating social and critical perspectives, *Accounting Education: an international journal*, 21(1), 47–74.

Burns, J. & Baldvinsdottir, G. (2005) An institutional perspective of accountants' new roles: the interplay of contradictions and praxis, *European Accounting Review*, 14(4), 725–757.

Byrne, M., Flood, B., Hassall, T., Joyce, J., Arquero, J., Gonzalez, J., & Tourna-Germanou, E. (2012) Motivations, expectations and preparedness for higher education: a study of accounting students in Ireland, the UK, Spain and Greece, *Accounting Forum*, 36(2), 134–144.

Cappelletto, G. (2010) *Challenges Facing Accounting Education in Australia*, Melbourne: AFAANZ.

Chambers, R.J. (1999) The poverty of accounting discourse, *Abacus*, 35(3), 241–251.

Chartered Accountants Ireland (CAI) (2012) *CAP2 Competency Statement 2012/13*, Dublin: CAI.

Cheetham, G. & Chivers, G. (1996) Towards a holistic model of professional competence, *Journal of European Industrial Training*, 20(5), 20–30.

Cheetham, G. & Chivers, G. (1998) The reflective (and competent) practitioner: a model of professional competence which seeks to harmonise the reflective practitioner and competence-based approaches, *Journal of European Industrial Training*, 22(7), 267–276.

Cheetham, G. & Chivers, G. (2000) A new look at competent professional practice, *Journal of European Industrial Training*, 24(7), 374–383.

Davis, S.W. & Sherman, W.R. (1996) The Accounting Education Change Commission: a critical perspective, *Critical Perspectives on Accounting*, 7(1), 159–189.

De Lange, P. & Watty, K. (2011) AE briefing: accounting education at a crossroad in 2010 and challenges facing accounting education in Australia, *Accounting Education: an international journal*, 20(6), 625–630.

Deppe, L., Sonderegger, E., Stice, J., Clark, D., & Streuling, G. (1991) Emerging competencies for the practice of accountancy, *Journal of Accounting Education*, 9, 257–290.

Diamond, M. (2005) Accounting education, research and practice: after Enron, where do we go? *European Accounting Review*, 14(2), 353–362.

Doost, R. (1999) The missing links in accounting education, *Managerial Auditing Journal*, 14(3), 93–114.

Eraut, M. (1985) Knowledge creation and knowledge use in professional contexts, *Studies in Higher Education*, 10(2), 117–133.

Eraut, M. (1992) Developing the knowledge base: a process perspective on professional education, in Barnett, R. (ed.) *Learning to Effect*, Buckingham: SHRE and Open University Press, pp. 98–118.

Eraut, M. (2000) Non-formal learning and tacit knowledge in professional work, *British Journal of Educational Psychology*, 70, 113–136.

Etherington, L.D. & Richardson, A.J. (1994) The university context of accounting education in Canada, *Contemporary Accounting Research*, Special Issue, 3–14.

Evans, E., Burritt, R., & Guthrie, J. (eds) (2010) *Accounting Education at a Crossroad in 2010*, Sydney: Institute of Chartered Accountants in Australia and University of South Australia. Available at (accessed on 19 July 2012). Available at: http://www.charteredaccountants.com.au/Students/News-and-updates/Teachers/New-publication-Accounting-Education-at-a-Crossroad-in-2010.aspx.

Flaherty, R.E. (ed.) (1997) *The Accounting Education Change Commission Grant Experience: A Summary* (Accounting Education Series, Vol. 14) Sarasota, FL: American Accounting Association.

Frederickson, J.R., & Pratt, J. (1995) A model of the accounting education process, *Issues in Accounting Education*, 10(2), 229–246.

Hancock, P., Howieson, B., Kavanagh, M., Kent, J., Tempone, I., & Segal, N. (2009) *Accounting for the Future: More Than Numbers*, Sydney: Australian Learning and Teaching Council.

Hanlon, G. (1994) *The Commercialisation of Accountancy*, New York: St Martin's Press.

Hassall, T., Joyce, J., Arquero Montano, J.L., & Donoso Anes, J.A. (2005) Priorities for the development of vocational skills in management accountants: a European perspective, *Accounting Forum*, 29(4), 379–394.

Humphrey, C. (2005) In the aftermath of crisis: reflections on the principles, values and significance of academic inquiry in accounting: introduction. *European Accounting Review*, 14(2), 341–351.

Institute of Chartered Accountants in England and Wales (ICAEW) (1998) *Creating the Added-Business Advisor*, Milton Keynes: ICAEW.

Institute of Chartered Accountants in England and Wales (ICAEW) (2012) *How to Become an ICAEW Chartered Accountant*, London: ICAEW. Available at: http://careers.icaew.com/~/media/Files/Graduate%20brochure.ashx (accessed 4 April 2013).

Institute of Management Accountants (IMA) (1994) *What Corporate America Wants in Entry-Level Accountants – Executive Summary*, Montvale, NJ: IMA.

Institute of Management Accountants (IMA) (1996) *The Practice Analysis of Management Accounting: Results of Research*, Montvale, NJ: IMA.

Institute of Management Accountants (IMA) (1999) *Counting More, Counting Less: Transformations in the Management Accounting Profession*, Montvale, NJ: IMA.

International Federation of Accountants (IFAC) (2010) Framework for International Education Standards for Professional Accountants, in *Handbook of International Education Pronouncements 2010 Edition*, New York: IFAC. Available at: http://www.ifac.org/publications-resources/handbook-international-education-pronouncements-2010-edition (accessed 30 August 2012).

Jarvis, P. (1983) *Professional Education*, London: Croom Helm.

Kinney, W. (1990) Some reflections on a professional education: it should have been more positive, *Issues in Accounting Education*, 5(2), 296–301.

Lucas, U. (2000) Worlds apart: students' experiences of learning introductory accounting, *Critical Perspectives on Accounting*, 11(4), 479–504.

Mathews, R., Jackson, M., & Brown, P. (1990) *Accounting in Higher Education: Report of the Review of the Accounting Discipline in Higher Education*, Canberra: ACT Australian Government.

Mathews, M.R. (1994) An examination of the work of the Accounting Education Change Commission 1989–1992, *Accounting Education: an international journal*, 3(3), 193–204.

May, G., Windal, F., & Sylvestre, J. (1995) The need for change in accounting education: an educator survey, *Journal of Accounting Education*, 13(1), 21–43.

McPhail, K. (2004) An emotional response to the state of accounting education: developing accounting students' emotional intelligence, *Critical Perspectives on Accounting*, 15(4/5), 629–648.

Needles, B. & Powers, M. (1990) A comparative study of models for accounting education, *Issues in Accounting Education*, 5(2), 250–267.

Paisey, C. & Paisey, N. (2004) Professional education and skills: liberalising higher education for the professions in the United Kingdom, *Research in Post-Compulsory Education*, 9(2), 161–181.

Paisey, C. & Paisey, N. (2006) Cutting to the core? A reflection upon recent education policy debates within the Institute of Chartered Accountants in England and Wales, *British Accounting Review*, 38(1), 31–61.

Parker, L. (2007) Professionalisation and UK accounting education: academic and professional complicity: a commentary on 'Professionalizing claims and the state of UK professional accounting education: some evidence', *Accounting Education: an international journal*, 16(1), 43–46.

Power, M. K. (1991) Educating accountants: towards a critical ethnography, *Accounting Organizations and Society*, 16(4), 333–353.

Previts, G.J. (1991) Accounting education: the next horizon, *Journal of Accountancy*, 172(4), 35–36.

PricewaterhouseCoopers (2003) *Educating for the Public Trust*, New York: PwC.

Puxty, A., Sikka, P., & Willmott, H. (1994) (Re)forming the circle: education, ethics and accountancy practices, *Accounting Education: an international journal*, 3(1), 77–92.

Ravenscroft, S. & Williams, P.F. (2005) Rules, rogues and risk assessors: academic responses to Enron and other accounting scandals, *European Accounting Review*, 14(2), 363–372.

Rosen, L.S. (1978) Accounting education: a grim report card, *CA Magazine*, 111(June), 30–35.

Ryle, G. (1949) *The Concept of Mind*, London: Hutchinson.

Sangster, A. & Wilson, R.M.S. (eds) (2013) *Liberalising the Accounting Curriculum in University Education*, Abingdon: Routledge.

Schön, D. (1983) *The Reflective Practitioner: How Professionals Think in Action*, New York: Basic Books.

Sikka, P. (1987) Professional education and auditing books: a review article, *British Accounting Review*, 19, 291–304.

Solomons, D. ,with Berridge, T. (1974) *Prospectus for a Profession: The Report of the Long Range Enquiry into Education and Training for the Accounting Profession (The Solomons Report)*, London: Advisory Board of Accounting Education.

Sullivan, W.M., Colby, A., Welsh Wenger, J., Bond, L., & Shulman, L.S. (2007) *Educating Lawyers: Preparation for the Profession of Law*, San Francisco: Jossey-Bass.

Sundem, G.L. (1992) Changes in accounting education in the United States: the impact of the Accounting Education Change Commission, in Anyane-Ntow, K. (ed.) *International Handbook of Accounting Education and Certification*, Oxford: Pergamon Press, pp. 305–318.

Sundem, G.L. (1999) *The Accounting Education Change Commission: Its History and Impact* (Accounting Education Series, Vol. 15), Sarasota, FL: American Accounting Association.

Sundem, G.L., & Williams, D.Z. (1992) Changes in accounting education: preparing for the twenty-first century, *Accounting Education: an international journal*, 1(1), 55–61.

Taylor, I. (1997) *Developing Learning in Professional Education: Partnerships for Practice*, Buckingham: The Society for Research into Higher Education and Open University Press.

Tinker, T. (1985) *Paper Prophets: A Social Critique of Accounting*, New York: Praeger Publishers.

Tinker, T. (1998) The second millennium bomb: education malaise and technological change, *Accounting & Business*, 1(7/8), 16–18.

Tinker, T. & Koutsoumandi, A. (1997) A mind is a wonderful thing to waste: 'think like a commodity', become a CPA, *Accounting, Auditing, & Accountability Journal*, 10(3), 454–467.

Wiecek, I.M. & Deal, G. (eds) (2011) *Leveraging Change: The New Pillars of Accounting Education*, Toronto: Canadian Institute of Chartered Accountants. Available at: http://www.cica.ca/becoming-a-ca/supporting-ca-academics/item62031.pdf (accessed 19 July 2012).

Wilensky, H.L. (1964) The professionalization of everyone?, *The American Journal of Sociology*, 70(2), 137–158.

Williams, D.Z. (1993) Reforming accounting education, *Journal of Accountancy*, 176(2), 76–82.

Williams, P.F. (2004) You reap what you sow: the ethical discourse of professional accounting, *Critical Perspectives on Accounting*, 15(6/7), 995–1001.

Wilson, R.M.S. (1992) Accounting education: a statement of intent and a tentative agenda, *Accounting Education: an international journal*, 1(1), 3–11.

Wilson, R.M.S. & Adler, R.W. (eds) (2012) *Teaching IFRS*, Abingdon: Routledge.

About the author

Barbara Flood is Professor of Accounting at Dublin City University, Ireland, where she is also Deputy Dean of DCU Business School. (barbara.flood@dcu.ie). Her PhD was undertaken in the field of accounting education (under the supervision of Richard M.S. Wilson), and her principal research currently explores accounting students' learning experiences in higher education and in professional accounting education. She is a Senior Associate Editor of *Accounting Education: an international journal*.

5

An agenda for improving accounting education

E. Kent St. Pierre*and James E. Rebele**

*SAINT JOSEPH'S UNIVERSITY, U.S.A. **ROBERT MORRIS UNIVERSITY, U.S.A.

CONTENTS

Abstract

Position statements on accounting education have generally called for an increased emphasis on developing students' so-called 'soft skills', including critical thinking, communication skills, and ethics. This chapter provides a critical review of past agendas for improving accounting education, and argues that efforts to develop soft skills have not produced the intended results and, more importantly, have taken attention away from developing students' technical accounting competence. Specific attention is given to why efforts to develop accounting students' critical thinking ability and ethical awareness are not likely to be effective. In contrast to past accounting agendas, this chapter argues that accounting education programmes should return to the basics, which is to teach accounting to our students. Developing accounting students' technical competence should be the primary objective of accounting education programmes, and only when this objective is met should attention be given to developing other competencies.

Keywords

soft-skill competencies, teaching accounting competence, teaching limitations

5.1 Introduction

The main aims of this chapter are:

- to understand why continuing to emphasize the development of accounting students' soft skills is likely to be ineffective and not in the students' best interests; and
- to understand why accounting education programmes should return to emphasizing the development of students' technical competence.

Although the authors acknowledge that their expertise lies in the educational system of the U.S.A., they trust that their suggestions will be applicable to an international audience.

The chapter sets forth an agenda for improving accounting education and, consequently, for producing graduates who are better prepared to succeed as accounting professionals. We are concerned with the long-term development of accounting professionals in all areas of accounting, including the often ignored private sector. Setting an agenda for improving accounting education is not a new undertaking and existing monographs and articles (e.g. American Accounting Association (AAA) (1986); Accounting Education Change Commission (AECC) (1990); Albrecht & Sack (2000); Arquero *et al.* (2001); Hassall *et al.* (2003); and the Pathways Commission (2012)) have offered advice and suggestions designed to improve the educational experience for our students. If recommended changes were successfully implemented, presumably accounting education programmes would provide the profession with graduates who are technically competent, ethical, critical thinkers, clear communicators, independent learners, effective team members, and polished business persons who can competently advise clients, all while still in their early twenties! The ability of college students to actually achieve the objectives set forth in these studies is often minimized, or ignored, which may explain why the call for developing these attributes have continued over the years with apparently limited success.

Accounting staff and programme administrators took some of the past criticisms of accounting education seriously and primarily made changes to incorporate the above-noted 'soft skills' in courses and curricula to improve how accounting students are educated (Siegel *et al.* 2010). Such changes required investments of time and money, and involved opportunity costs since, for example, devoting time to developing students' soft skills often came at the expense of covering additional technical accounting material and non-accounting material. Very little evidence exists to document the success or effectiveness of past calls for changes to accounting education, especially in the soft skills area. Most accounting staff who teach undergraduate accounting students would likely agree, though, that today's accounting graduates are not better communicators, do not think more critically, are not more ethical, and do not function better as team members compared to students who graduated 20 years ago (ibid.). Unless 'Googling' is considered independent learning, today's students do not appear to be more competent life-long learners than were students from past generations.

We argue in this chapter that efforts to develop accounting students' so-called soft skills, as recommended by past accounting agendas, have wasted significant time and money without producing noticeable improvement in graduates' preparedness for careers as accountants. We present our case that removing demands placed on class time to develop soft skills and getting back to our core objective, which is to teach accounting with the required technical focus, will improve the educational experience for our students and prepare them to be more accomplished and valuable accounting professionals. The basic message of this chapter might appropriately be summarized as 'the best way to deal with increasing complexity is to keep things simple'. We base our arguments on what we consider to be two important considerations:

- Can the soft skills be taught?
- If so, are academic accounting staff the proper individuals to teach these skills?

The next section of this chapter takes a closer look at several past attempts to develop and advance agendas for improving accounting education. Our understanding as to why past agenda-setting efforts have not apparently yielded significant change or improvements in accounting education will also be provided. A detailed description of our proposed agenda for improving accounting education will then be presented, along with arguments supporting the specifics of the agenda. Our proposed agenda calls for academic accounting staff to return to emphasizing the development of accounting students' technical competence, an expansion of non-accounting technical skills, and a de-emphasis on attempts to develop soft skills as part of the students' undergraduate educational experience. (For other views, see Flood, Chapter 4; Amernic & Craig, Chapter 12; Watty, Chapter 13; Sangster, Chapter 15; and Cunningham, Chapter 18 – all in this volume.)

5.2 Previous agenda efforts

Previous 'agenda' efforts to improve accounting education have included specific efforts sponsored by third parties in studies undertaken in the U.S.A., such as:

- the Bedford Committee Report (American Accounting Association, 1986);
- Big Eight White Paper (Arthur Andersen et al., 1989);
- Accounting Education Change Commission (AECC) (1990–1993);
- Albrecht & Sack (2000);
- Pathways Commission (2012).

And in Australia:

- The Mathews Committee Report (Mathews et al., 1990);
- Hancock et al. (2009); and
- Cappelletto (2010).

In addition, there have been numerous research articles on setting agendas that were not sponsored by outside parties such as the excellent work undertaken by Milner & Hill in Scotland (2008) and in the U.K. more broadly (2010), and the 'under'-reported efforts by parties around the world on the needs of those entering management accounting such as Siegel et al. (2010), Tan et al. (2004), and Arquero et al. (2001). All have called for more education, a higher quality education, or a different education in order to better prepare students for accounting careers. Most reports were issued in response to an apparent crisis in the accounting profession, with a common complaint being that academicians were not teaching students what was needed to perform well as 'professionals'. As Baril *et al.* (1997) have noted, it is not clear from the public practice side of the profession that practitioners really know what they want in our graduates, even though the attributes noted earlier are constantly alleged as being missing in our students. The profession's response, as noted in the agenda reports, was to charge academicians with changing and improving what and how students are taught.

Although these prior reports calling for change in accounting education were not without problems, there was a surprising lack of critique by academicians when each report was issued. Instead, academic accounting staff and administrators seemed to simply accept each report's basic message (e.g. your future is perilous and you may not survive unless you change now) without questioning the merit of what was being proposed, or even whether it could be accomplished. Accounting academicians' acquiescence to public accounting practitioners' opinions and directives about education resulted in lost time, money, and opportunities to actually improve accounting education. The remainder of this section summarizes several of the more noteworthy agendas for improving accounting education (or more appropriately, accounting education for public practice) and potential problems with their conclusions. We will address the problem with the focus of most of these studies on the public accounting sector rather than the significant population of private (corporate, not-for-profit, and governmental) accountants. Since we provide an agenda for what we think should occur in the future, we provide only summary comments on past efforts in this section. (In Chapter 4 of this volume, Flood provides another critical review of the major reports on accounting education. Interested readers should therefore consult Chapter 4 for additional comments about prior agendas for accounting education. In Chapter 2 of this volume, Needles presents a model of accounting education that is focussed on 'qualified' accountants, or accountants who have met the requirements to be a member of a professional accounting body (PAB). The education of management and government accountants is only considered to the extent that it overlaps with the education of public accountants.)

The Bedford Committee (AAA, 1986) called for an undergraduate curriculum consisting of more liberal arts classes with most technical accounting coverage occurring at the graduate level. Ideas on more participatory teaching methods, a change in emphasis to reward teaching rather than research, and a move away from preparing students to take professional examinations were suggested by this group. The Big Eight White Paper (Arthur Andersen *et al.*, 1989) was similar to the Bedford Committee report in that it also called for graduates who possess a wide array of skills and knowledge. Less emphasis on technical competence and more emphasis on general knowledge was a theme in the White Paper, though evidence supporting this recommended shift in educational focus was not provided.

The AECC (1990) followed the general approach of earlier groups and called for a complete overhaul of the academic side of the profession, focussing on the reward structure which emphasizes research over teaching, and the standard accounting curriculum which prepares students for professional examinations. Recommended educational changes offered by the AECC included:

- a shift from memorization to the development of analytical and conceptual thinking;
- an emphasis on having students learn on their own; and
- having students become active learners who are capable of thinking critically instead of being passive recipients of information provided by a teacher.

The AECC provided financial grants to several universities to support changes in their accounting education programmes (see Mathews, 1994; Flaherty, 1998; Sundem, 1999.) Unfortunately, the institutions receiving AECC grants were not representative of the cross-section of institutions/ programmes in the U.S.A. or internationally. Small institutions were not selected to receive AECC grants, and all the grant-recipient institutions had Assembly to Advance Collegiate Schools of Business (AACSB) accreditation, with most having separate accounting accreditation. (For more on accreditation, see Calderon, Chapter 22, and Apostolou & Gammie, Chapter 29 – both in this volume.) In addition, 55 per cent of the institutions receiving grants had doctoral programmes and just one school offered only a bachelor's degree. It would seem that, if the AECC wanted to be able to generalize any results from changes to the education process, they would have been careful to select institutions which truly represented a cross-section of accounting education programmes. Since this was not the case, it is not surprising that the results were not widely adopted as predicted when the AECC was established.

The influence of the then Big Eight on these early attempts to set an accounting education agenda is well documented by Davis & Sherman (1996). For example, the AECC was created by request of the Big Eight and their influence was apparent through the funding process for the AECC, Big Eight-sponsored professorships at commission members' institutions, and the importance of Big Eight recruiting efforts at the institutions receiving grants. In addition, the fact that only certain institutions were included in the large firm recruiting process to begin with creates a situation where control by the Big Eight was evident and the results were predictable: the suggested agenda focussed on the needs of public accounting and was driven by the small percentage of students who work in that segment versus the larger corporate and not-for-profit sectors of our profession.

Mathews *et al.* (1990) authored a well-publicized Australian report that addressed major issues with the state of accounting education in Australia. Rather than an agenda for specific curriculum changes, this report emphasized concerns with government funding of accounting and business programmes, large class sizes, diversion of resources from accounting and business to other disciplines, and the general neglect of the accounting major.

The monograph by Albrecht & Sack (2000) is the most widely-discussed position statement from the U.S.A. on accounting education issued in the past two decades. In their choice of its title (*Accounting Education: Charting the Course through a Perilous Future*), and the title of Chapter 1('Why Accounting Education May Not Survive in the Future'), Albrecht & Sack sounded the ominous warning that accounting education, as we knew it, was in danger of disappearing as an academic discipline. The fact that Albrecht & Sack completely misinterpreted the effects of the market for accounting majors, and the rapid growth in this market because of the decrease in the number of systems majors and the lack of employment opportunities in other competing majors, has not apparently diminished the credibility of this monograph. Accounting education as we know it has clearly not disappeared, nor is it in danger of losing its importance in the professional environment. We do believe, however, that Albrecht & Sack's call for additional systems classes for accounting majors was very insightful and is included in our agenda discussed later in the chapter.

Albrecht & Sack argued that accounting education programmes needed to provide what the business world wanted, which was a good business person, not necessarily a technically-competent accountant. Consistent with past accounting education position statements, they also called for more focus on developing soft skills, such as critical thinking and analysis (see Cunningham, Chapter 18 – this volume) and ethics (see Boyce, Chapter 24 – this volume). Albrecht & Sack viewed the accounting curriculum as achieving a new and different set of educational objectives. Their suggested curriculum would focus on analyzing and using account-ing information, research, and decision-making, with less emphasis on developing students' technical competence.

Hancock *et al.* (2009) added to the body of literature by addressing where accounting education in Australia should be heading in the future. Their concerns built upon the earlier Mathews *et al.* study (1990) with a more direct discussion of curriculum and specifics on what should be included in the education of accounting majors. As with the Cappelletto study noted later, the concerns at the time of this report included very large class sizes with a very diverse student population, lack of communication skills due to the international student dominance in the classroom, and the lack of higher-level English-speaking skills, staff shortages, the aging of academic accounting staff, and problems with alternative pathways into the profession. The soft skills most often mentioned as being important to the needs of the students were (in order of frequency):

*   communication and presentation (again the result of the number of international students with limited English language skills);
*   teamwork and interpersonal skills;
*   self-management, initiative and enterprise;
*   problem-solving ability;
*   technological competence; and
*   planning/organization skills.

The area of professional communication skills was the most cited deficiency by employers both within and outside the country. The major change from this report and the earlier Mathews Report was that generic skills had evolved into softer skills (such as critical analysis and strategic thinking) on the part of the graduate. Surprisingly, critical thinking and problem-solving were not listed as highly as in the agenda reports in the U.S.A. The importance of technology was noted in this study as in the Albrecht & Sack report, with a range of information technology (IT) skills and the ability to apply these skills as being critical. (See Boritz & Stoner, Chapter 16 – this volume.) Unfortunately, as in the previous studies noted, the Hancock *et al.* study included very little discussion about the difficulty of teaching the desired skills, or whether the skills could be taught. (See Watty, Chapter 13 – this volume.)

Cappelletto (2010) continued on the same theme as Hancock *et al.*, and both were included in the *Accounting Education at a Crossroad in 2010* discussion in Australia. In both this report and in Hancock *et al.*'s study, it was noted that very little improvement in the state of accounting education in Australia had occurred since the Mathews Report 20 years earlier. Cappelletto reinforces this conclusion by again emphasizing the problems created by the lack of funding and the need to recruit large numbers of international students to increase financial support (with similar issues arising in the U.S.A. – see the China Conundrum, 2011). This in turn has created significant issues in professional communications of the accounting graduates since the international students confront English as a second language. The oft-noted lack of adequate funding and the aging of academic accounting staff are also discussed – as in the earlier reports. The efforts of the authors were supposed to lay the groundwork for discussion of the issues and, at some point, open the door to potential solutions. In addition, the question was raised as to what makes a well-rounded graduate, what skills are required, and where are the skills obtained?

The Pathways Commission (2012) represents the latest effort in the U.S.A. to reform accounting education. In its report, the Commission acknowledges that its recommendations are similar to those made in past position statements, with the focus still on developing an expanded skills set. The Pathways Commission Report has a major focus on impediments to change, including the silo effect by which courses are viewed as being independent (see Bloom, Chapter 14 – this volume), the reward structure for academic staff working on curricular issues, and administrators' unwillingness to make needed changes. The Commission's goal is to identify implementation strategies that will make future accounting education change efforts more successful than those of past efforts. Since the Commission's Report offers no evidence that its recommended suggestions will be more effective than past attempts at reforming accounting education, there is ample reason to question whether this latest change initiative will be any more effective than past efforts.

The emphasis on a broader education by past accounting education change efforts appears to follow the general strategy when there are concerns with a profession. A call for more liberal arts education (see Amernic & Craig, Chapter 12 – this volume, and Sangster & Wilson, 2013), and the idea that this may solve the problems with the deficiencies of our graduates has been called 'knee jerk formalism' by Rossides (1991) and others. As Rossides (ibid.) notes:

> Are there failures in our economy, professions, politics? Blame the schools, restore discipline, require more mathematics and natural science, have children pray, deflate grades, tighten up on tenure, invoke the authority of the classics, and so on.

Barefield (1991) also questions the approach by which more liberal arts classes would remedy alleged deficiencies in business majors and asks if a change to a liberal arts emphasis is warranted. Addressing the concerns raised by the groups issuing the previous agenda studies may require solutions not currently offered in the accounting education literature.

It is not apparent that groups proposing new agendas for accounting education addressed the fact that technical accounting courses make up approximately 25 per cent of the curriculum in accounting programmes, with the other 75 per cent being other business classes or liberal arts classes. Those proposing more liberal arts as part of an accounting student's education ignore the legitimate question concerning what is currently being done in the liberal arts side of the education model. Instead of asking why the softer skills are not being addressed in the significant number of required liberal arts classes, the profession often seems to accept the idea that more liberal arts is better, even though the technical side is already a relatively small part of the college curriculum. Except for the constant call for students who have the abilities of a more mature individual with years of experience by the public accounting side of our profession, where is the empirical evidence to support the points made as to what is wrong with the existing educational models? In addition, where is the support as to the potential success of the remedies offered? In fact, it is interesting that, with the problems apparent in our graduates, or at least alleged to be present in our graduates, the market for our students is so strong and that they have more employment opportunities than other business and non-business majors on our campuses. Perhaps the alleged problems and deficiencies in our accounting graduates are issues that are apparent in many majors and simply a result of the age, maturity, or cognitive development of the typical college student. (See Duff, Chapter 8 – this volume.)

We question whether a greater emphasis on non-technical issues is the proper approach, and whether the move has been successful in the past or will be successful in the future. For example, the popular idea that we should emphasize ethics, team-building and teamwork, communication skills, interpersonal skills, and critical thinking were evident in the conclusions in the prior reports discussed in this chapter. Yet one must question a profession that puts the 'softer' issues as a higher priority than technical skills, and whether a profession such as accounting can afford to place technical issues in a secondary role. Given what we do as accountants, and the importance of knowing the technical standards and rules in the accounting, audit, and tax areas, can we afford to relegate these to anything but the most important objectives of what we do in the classroom? If we examine the requirements for success in the corporate sector, is a move to a greater emphasis on soft skills the proper approach? In an increasingly litigious environment, the ability to meet the technical standards is a key to minimizing legal exposure. Although fraud is apparent in some of the more significant corporate and audit failures, many more of the legal issues for the accounting profession are based on questionable auditing approaches or lack of understanding of very complex accounting issues (St. Pierre & Anderson, 1984). Technical skills are vital to the success of the accounting practitioner and even more so in the smaller public accounting firms where the practitioner must be proficient in all areas to meet clients' demands. Perhaps partners feel that the softer skills are critical, but as Sack & Burton (1991) pointed out years ago:

> [T]he local office recruiters did not share the vision of their managing partners . . . it is one thing to ask that the firm's future partners, hired from the local university, have judgment and perspective and a commitment to continued education. It is quite another thing to put those high minded people to work as soon as they come on board.

In other words, the attributes needed later in one's career are not necessarily the attributes that allow one to progress in the firm and reach the position where the softer skills may be more important.

5.3 Can the desired traits be taught and who will teach them?

The reports discussed in Section 5.2 completely ignored whether college-age students could develop the identified skills, and whether these skills can actually be taught. This question has been noticeably absent in not only the 'agenda' reports, but in many of the education articles published in our field. It would seem to be a given that, before recommending that the academic side of the profession take responsibility for teaching certain skills/attributes, the parties issuing the reports would have determined if the skills/attributes are those acquired in the home environment, over time in the process of maturing, on the job while obtaining real-world experience, or in a classroom.

Several additional issues need to be addressed before suggesting that accounting academics should assume primary responsibility for the development of these traits in our students. Given the growth in time allotted to liberal arts classes and other required business courses, accounting staff have a limited number of courses in which to cover the required technical topics – which are increasing every day in a global environment – let alone the coverage of an increasing number of softer skills. Do we really believe that, in a class meeting several hours a week, we can cover the technical issues and also teach/develop the soft skills in our students? Is there evidence that students can develop these skills in a class without a coordinated effort throughout the entire university curriculum to reinforce the efforts by a particular teacher?

Perhaps the more critical issue concerns the ability of most accounting educators to teach or develop students' soft skills. One must ask where the required expertise to develop skills, such as critical thinking or proper ethical behaviour, has been obtained by the accounting teacher and, in an environment where fewer accounting academics have a background in the real working world of accounting, whether there is reliable knowledge about what is actually needed in the practice environment. Academic staff trained primarily in accounting and other business disciplines, with a heavy emphasis on quantitative methods, may not have the expertise to address ethical behaviour, critical thinking, or the other soft skills in the manner needed by our students. Are our egos so great that we think we have the knowledge and expertise to help students develop the softer skills? If academic staff psychology or philosophy departments were to teach accounting, we would raise major concerns and question the wisdom of such a scenario, yet we feel competent to cover issues best left to experts in the fields where the soft skills are researched and discussed as part of their normal curriculum. In addition, with an ever-increasing presence of international members of staff in accounting departments, are we certain that their training and expertise allows them to perform in a similar manner, and is their educational background adequate to develop students' soft skills?

We will expand on our concerns about teaching the soft skills by addressing two often discussed traits that are constantly mentioned as being items which should be taught in the accounting classroom. Ethics and critical thinking have been the subject of numerous education papers in our profession and the call for our students to be taught these traits is common. (See Cunningham, Chapter 18, and Boyce, Chapter 24 – both in this volume.) For example, the call for additional emphasis on ethics education follows every scandal in our field and has been the subject of numerous papers, presentations, committees, and organizational studies. There is evidence that accounting students are more exposed to ethics education than at any other time in the past (Mastracchio, 2005). At least 77 per cent of accounting staff integrate ethics education into their accounting curriculum and 69 per cent indicate a need for more (McNair & Milam, 1993). Yet, has there been progress in addressing the ethical issues presented in our profession? A new scandal seems to appear every week, again raising the question about the lack of ethical behaviour in the business sectors, both in the U.S.A. and around the world.

At the macro level, Transparency International states that corruption and unethical behaviour are facts of life and that, in their world poll, eight out of ten people say political parties are corrupt, one out of four people report paying bribes in the past year, and 50 per cent of those polled feel that their governments' anti-corruption efforts are ineffective. In addition, 60 per cent of those polled feel that corruption has increased in the last three years. In Europe, 75 per cent of those polled believed that corruption had increased. Unfortunately, the numbers are higher than the previous year in all aspects of the survey (Gordon, 2012). A survey by Edelman, a public relations firm, finds that only 18 per cent of people trust business leaders to tell the truth; for political leaders the number is 13 per cent (*The Week*, 26 January 2013). The daily headlines show that unethical behaviour is not limited by geographic boundaries and that the problem is an international one. For example:

- the Royal Bank of Scotland must pay $610 million over the rate-rigging scandal on LIBOR;
- Barclays Bank set aside $1.6 billion for the scandal concerning the selling of financial products to clients who did not need them or could not use them;
- Citigroup paid $730 million to settle allegations that it misled investors about its exposure to toxic subprime mortgages;
- SAC Capital paid the Securities and Exchange Commission (SEC) a $616 million fine to settle a probe into insider trading;
- KPMG estimates the value of fraud cases in the first six months of the year will be £19.5 million in Scotland;
- the U.S.A.'s Federal Bureau of Investigation (FBI) in 2011 obtained $2.4 billion in restitution and $16.1 million in fines on fraud cases; and
- KPMG categorized 57 cases of management fraud in the U.K. in 2011 with a value of £729 million (Goodley, 2012).

At the individual level, the lack of ethics is also noteworthy. The Minister of Education and Research for Germany was stripped of her doctoral qualification due to plagiarism in her dissertation, and the *Ethics Newsline* discloses that the majority of retracted scientific papers are pulled due to misconduct (fraud) and plagiarism and that the problem is global in nature (*Ethics Newsline*, 2012). At the same time that these scandals – along with the dishonest dealings that helped turn the sub-prime crisis into a Global Financial Crisis (GFC) – were occurring, a recent poll of 500 financial workers in the U.S.A. and in the U.K. disclosed that 24 per cent of the respondents stated that they believe unethical or illegal behaviour could help people in their industry be successful. Sixteen per cent said they would commit insider trading if they knew they could get away with it (*The Week*, 20 July 2012). John Delaney (*Wall Street Journal*, 6 February 2012) states that business schools have been giving students some education in ethics for at least 25 to 30 years and the business sector still has problems with unethical behaviour at the highest level of business. Surveys by the Aspen Institute show that about 60 per cent of new MBA students view the maximization of shareholder value to be the primary responsibility of a company, and that number rises to 69 per cent by the time the students reach the mid-point of their programmes (Browning, 2003).

At the undergraduate level, the picture is as depressing as noted in the 'real-world' business sector. The *New York Times* ('the China Conundrum') reported on 3 November 2011 that an entire industry has developed in China with the main function being to take the Scholastic Aptitude (SAT) examinations for students, write the required essays for those who can pay, and actually add awards and honours to résumés, all with the purpose of obtaining admittance to desired universities in selected countries such as the U.S.A., the U.K., or Australia. Whitley (1998) noted that, in 46 studies from 1970–1996, the frequency of cheating among college students was at a disturbing 70 per cent level. Hard *et al.* (2006) noted that studies after this time period continued to find high levels of cheating behaviour. Other conclusions stated that students cheated more in large and crowded classrooms and when the classes were taught by part-time staff or graduate assistants – in other words, when they thought they could get away with the unethical behaviour. Lowery & Beadles (2009) concluded that, while actual ethics instruction may have some immediate effect on this behaviour, the long-term effects may be minimal or non-existent. In a survey of 1,100 students on 27 college campuses in the U.S.A., Merritt (2002) found that, though the majority were disturbed by corporate scandals and thought CEOs should be held personally responsible for their actions, those same students admitted to cheating in an examination. Merritt also noted that this disconnect has long-term effects since students who engage in dishonest acts in college are more likely to engage in dishonest acts in the real world. She also concluded that academic staff underestimate the incidence of academic dishonesty. According to McCabe (2001), a significant percentage of middle school pupils cheat and carry that behaviour on to the college environment.

Outside the business sector, one could not find a greater emphasis on the teaching of ethics and moral behaviour than in the training of Catholic priests, yet the behaviour of an unknown number of priests and the resultant effects on many individuals directly and indirectly involved leads one to seriously question whether the subject can ever be taught. A recent allegation of the theft of $5.1 million by an Italian priest from a hospital in Rome just increases the questions concerning the lack of ethical behaviour in what is considered to be the most ethical of all professions (Winfield, 2013).

Many would argue that the moral and ethical 'compass' is formed early in life and developed in the home with very little change occurring at later ages, and definitely not in an accounting classroom for a short time each week when the student is already a young adult. In addition, as noted earlier, even if one could teach ethics, do accounting educators have the knowledge, background, and ability to do so? It is not clear that this expertise is currently provided in the normal training for PhD students in accounting and, more importantly, there has been no conclusive research as to the ability to teach this and the other soft skills called for by the public accounting sector. Accounting academics continue to add ethics courses or topics with little concern as to whether their efforts result in a change to the student or result in anything beneficial from an ethical perspective (McNair & Milam, 1993).

The attempt to develop critical thinking in our students parallels the attempts at teaching ethics. Unfortunately, like ethical behaviour, critical thinking is a term with no universally accepted definition – even among those who are experts in the field. The lack of a clear definition is magnified when one studies the research on the definition and meaning of soft skills – including critical thinking – to the group that has been a leader in the call for the development of these skills. The work by Baril et al. (1998) in the U.S.A. and Milner & Hill (2008, 2010) in both Scotland specifically and in the U.K. more generally with practitioners, exemplifies a major problem with critical thinking in our profession. In these studies, public accountants use the term 'critical thinking' to represent all types of competencies, such as good communication skills, curiosity, confidence, initiative, the ability to plan and anticipate, and other personal skills and characteristics not normally associated with critical thinking. This calls into question whether the profession truly knows what it is asking for when stating that our students need to be better at critical thinking, or is it one of many popular terms used when criticizing alleged deficiencies in current graduates? Another issue that arises with the discussion on critical thinking focusses on the idea that the skill can be taught or discussed separately from an extensive knowledge of a particular discipline. Kurfiss (1988) states that the problem with specific courses in critical thinking is that the questions asked determine the value of the inquiry, and without extensive knowledge of the subject it is difficult to ask intelligent questions. McPeck (1981) was one of the first to make this point when he stated that critical thinking in isolation from a particular subject is both conceptually and practically empty. To state that one teaches critical thinking is vacuous because there is no generalized skill properly called critical thinking. Critical thinking always manifests itself in connection with some identifiable subject area. Willingham (2007) supported this belief when he stated that knowing that one should think critically is not the same as being able to do so. To do so requires domain knowledge and practice. It is simply imperative that one have extensive knowledge of the subject matter to be able to think critically about the subject itself. The extensive knowledge of the subject matter required to critically think about the subject supports our argument in this chapter for the increased emphasis on technical issues. To assume that our students can be taught to critically think, to assume that accounting educators have the expertise to teach this skill, and to assume that our students could critically think about accounting without extensive training in the subject of accounting, are ideas that should be seriously questioned.

It is legitimate to ask whether we should make changes to our educational system and our technical versus non-technical emphasis in the classroom in order to address these soft skills and, in addition to the points noted above, whether they can be taught in the limited time during which we actually have access to our students in our curriculum. As Wolcott et al. (2002) stated in their paper on critical thinking research, though there are many ideas on how to address critical thinking in our profession, there remains a significant lack of empirical evidence that any specific instructional method can enhance the critical thinking skills of students. In fact, according to a 2010 article by the *Wall Street Journal*, incoming college students lack critical thinking skills and, unfortunately, college graduates scored just as poorly. In addition, even a number of corporate executives ranked abysmally low on critical thinking skills. Adding further complexity to the discussion is the question about what critical thinking skills are needed early in one's career versus those that may be developed over time and used in later stages. As noted, perhaps the profession continues to call for this skill in our graduates simply because it has become a standard complaint/criticism without any knowledge as to whether it can be taught and exactly what we mean when we discuss the concept.

The final concern with the concept of teaching critical thinking focusses on the ability of academic staff to teach this soft skill. Paul *et al.* (1997) concluded that academic staff lack a substantive concept of critical thinking. Studying the question about the extent to which academic staff are teaching critical thinking, they found that academic staff claimed they permeated their instruction with an emphasis on critical thinking. Unfortunately, their results did not support this contention. Though the overwhelming majority of academic staff claimed critical thinking to be a primary objective of their instruction (89 per cent), only a small number could give a clear explanation of what critical thinking entailed (19 per cent). While 50 per cent of those interviewed said that they explicitly distinguished critical thinking skills from traits, only 8 per cent were able to provide a clear conception of the critical thinking skills they thought were most important. Although the majority (67 per cent) said that their concept of critical thinking is largely explicit in their thinking, only 19 per cent could elaborate on their concept of thinking. Although the vast majority (89 per cent) stated that critical thinking was of primary importance to their instruction, 77 per cent had little or no conception of how to reconcile content coverage with the fostering of critical thinking.

To summarize, there are several major concerns with the constant call for enhancing the softer skills of our students. These are:

1   Can these skills be taught given the level of cognitive development of our students during their college years, the minimal time we have with these students in our accounting classes, the fact that many of these skills may be a function of genetic and home/environmental histories, and the apparent lack of success in our previous attempts to develop students' soft skills? The calls for enhancing non-technical skills have been made for many years by the profession and our attempts have apparently not worked since the problems and the calls for addressing them continue to be made.

2   Where is the evidence that the accounting educator has the necessary background and expertise to develop these skills, where was this expertise developed, and why have the liberal arts requirements that dominate our curriculum not enhanced the required skills?

3   In addition, does the ever-increasing numbers of international academic staff who are teaching accounting at universities in the U.S.A. create another variable that must be addressed?

4   Finally, should the fact that the required knowledge base for the accounting profession continues to expand at an ever-increasing pace cause us to question the allocation of class time to the softer skills versus technical knowledge?

Authors of several chapters in this volume continue to call for the development of accounting students' soft skills. For example, Flood (Chapter 4) calls for developing expanded competencies, including ethical awareness and appropriate personal values. In Chapter 13, Watty supports developing soft skills as part of accounting education programmes. She offers the opinion that employers are looking for graduates who are able to demonstrate courage, resilience, and empathy. Because past efforts to develop soft skills may have been less effective than desired, Watty offers an alternative way of considering and conceptualizing the development of soft skills. Cunningham, in Chapter 18, reviews relevant literature and presents a case for developing critical thinking in accounting education programmes. Our position on developing soft skills in undergraduate accounting education programmes differs from the positions taken by these other authors, which will hopefully lead to some debate as to whether accounting education programmes should attempt to develop expanded competencies, and how best to do this.

5.4 A return to basics

Our discussion in this chapter goes against the current popular thought in our field and argues against recommendations from past accounting agendas and what is found in the accounting education literature. We call for a move back to teaching the basics of accounting and to an approach where we teach in our area of expertise and prepare our students for the increased demands for technical expertise. Although this may seem to be sacrilegious, the views we propose were evident during the time of the reports analyzed earlier, but the biases of the different committees caused them to ignore or overlook differing opinions. For example, Novin, *et al.* (1990) found that certified management accountants in the U.S.A. believed that the accounting curriculum should be more heavily weighted toward accounting courses rather than the softer skills presented and supported by the American Institute of Certified Public Accountants (AICPA) and the large public accounting firms. This is especially significant since the number of accountants practising outside of public accounting (corporations, government, and private sector) far exceeds those in public accounting – though one would never know this based upon previous agendas. As Siegel *et al.* (2010) noted, almost two-thirds of accounting graduates begin their careers in industry and other non-public accounting positions, most of these having only an undergraduate degree, yet the education side of our profession never questions whether the accounting curriculum is appropriate for this majority segment of our graduates. The power and prestige of the large firms, especially with their chaired professorships and hiring power in the initial phase of graduates' careers, may have clouded our thinking in accounting education and caused us to miss the needs of a major segment of our profession.

None of the major agenda efforts reported any evidence of students' input, or that students' input was even solicited. This mirrors the lack of input from small colleges and universities, small or medium-sized public accounting firms, the private sector, and governmental bodies that make up the bulk of the jobs in the profession. It is interesting that universities which emphasize and specialize in undergraduate education with academic staff who dominate the education literature are not represented in the majority of these studies. The influence of the large firms and the doctoral granting universities in the education side of our profession has been criticized extensively, although with minimal effect. We believe that their influence will continue when discussing the agenda we propose in this chapter.

As noted earlier, we believe that the primary objective of accounting education should be to develop students' technical competence. Without being technically competent in accounting, students cannot think critically about their discipline, nor can they communicate effectively about technical accounting issues. Rather than prioritizing 'soft skills' or 'expanded competencies', as recommended by past accounting education agendas, accounting education programmes should focus on producing graduates who understand and can apply technical accounting material. We are not arguing that ethics, critical thinking, or communication skills are not important to a successful graduate. We are arguing, though, that it is not clear that these competencies can be taught, or whether accounting educators have the expertise to teach the non-technical skills. Our responsibility and comparative advantage, as accounting educators, are to teach students technical accounting material.

Even developing the required technical competence has proved to be difficult for today's generation of undergraduate accounting students. Perhaps this generation of students has a different work ethic than most accounting staff and past generations of undergraduate accounting students, and their expectations for grades, professional opportunities, and financial compensation are inconsistent with the effort that many make, or are willing to make, to achieve success and reap the accompanying rewards. Perhaps undergraduate students have not been taught how to study, and spending time reading a textbook and working on accounting problems is difficult because it requires an extended period of concentration, which many have not been required to do up to this point in their lives. We can only hypothesize about our students' attributes, but we raise these points so that readers will understand that, when we emphasize the teaching of technical skills and technical material, it is still a difficult task made more difficult by the ever-increasing body of accounting and related business information. The major attribute that accounting staff have in their favour when teaching technical material is that they have expertise in the area and know that the subject can be taught – which is not the case with soft skills.

Although some might argue against a 'customer focus' to education, we must consider why students enter accounting education programmes. (See Laswad & Tan, Chapter 9 – this volume.) Do students choose to enrol in our programmes with the expectation that they will learn accounting and related business subjects and obtain a well-respected position after graduation? Students want to learn technical accounting material in order to obtain positions after graduation, pass any certifying examinations, and lay the groundwork for long-term careers. Technical accounting proficiency is what both students and their parents expect, and it is the primary competency that we should develop. It is interesting to note that past graduates from accounting programmes who are now serving as partners in public accounting firms, managers in corporate accounting departments, and accounting educators, learned accounting by reading textbooks, professional pronouncements, and working on numerous problems on technical topics. 'Time-on-task' was a key to learning technical accounting material and doing well in the examinations, often the sole measurement method for course success. All of this was accomplished with minimal activities focussing on the soft skills; nevertheless, the graduates became successful practitioners and accounting educators. Yet these are the same individuals now calling for a higher priority for non-technical soft skills in order to do well after graduation. Perhaps the variables that helped to shape the ethics, critical thinking, and communication abilities of the past generations of accounting graduates are still in play and shaping the same attributes in current graduates, regardless of our attempts to teach these skills.

5.4.1 Curriculum and pedagogy

The amount of technical accounting material that needs to be covered has, no doubt, expanded greatly in the past 30 years, but the time devoted to covering this material has not expanded accordingly. Adhering to a one-size-fits-all model presents accounting educators with difficult decisions on which topics to omit and which topics to cover. (See Sangster, Chapter 15 – this volume.) The technical knowledge gained from an accounting curriculum should be viewed as the students' primary preparation for a job and future career in the accounting profession. (See Needles, Chapter 2 – this volume.) Since not all accounting jobs and careers are the same, accounting curricula across universities, or even within the same university, need not be the same or even similar. In the past, textbook content largely drove the accounting curriculum because academic staff were constrained in which topics they could cover given the chosen course textbook. (See Stevenson *et al.*, Chapter 19 – this volume.) Technology has, though, made it possible to customize textbooks, which should lead to more flexibility in curriculum design. (See Boritz & Stoner, Chapter 16 – this volume.) It is possible to construct course textbooks that are tailored to a particular institution's student make-up and job opportunities. Those universities producing graduates for the large accounting firms should not have the same curriculum, or course materials, as do universities producing graduates for smaller firms, corporations, or the not-for-profit sector. The capability to adjust course content to match students' needs exists; we just have to use it more effectively.

To expand on this idea, Siegel *et al.* (2010) discussed potential topics for the significant number of students who do not initially enter or remain in public accounting but choose to enter the corporate or not-for-profit segments of our profession. (See Jackling, Chapter 10 – this volume.) For example, in the non-accounting area it is suggested that students take classes that allow them to develop greater skills in business and finance along with the increasing need to be proficient in IT. This allows the corporate and not-for-profit accountants not only to produce needed financial reports, but also to understand the nature of the problem being addressed and the information most relevant to solving the problem. Specifically, the non-accounting skills developed should provide knowledge of long-term strategic planning, financial and economic analysis, customer and product profitability, computer systems and operations, and process improvement. The accounting side of the equation needs to increase the coverage of planning, budgeting, and forecasting; management reporting; transaction processing; enterprise-wide risk management; and regulatory compliance. A call for the rebalancing of the curriculum would emphasize a four-year programme with a greater focus on financial reporting, management accounting, corporate taxation, and internal auditing. The curriculum for the private sector would enable accounting majors to achieve extensive working knowledge in finance, operations management, IT, marketing, supply chain management, statistics, and quantitative methods.

5.4.2 Accounting and management information systems

Accounting practitioners and accounting educators would be hard pressed to name an accounting-related position that does not require an understanding of systems. Knowledge of systems adds to the opportunities available to our students and is an integral part of our profession. There are programmes that have wedded their accounting curriculum to a heavy exposure of systems courses and these programmes have been very successful in the placement and opportunities presented to their graduates. It is not possible to determine how many accounting programmes include an extensive coverage of information systems, resulting in our calling for a significant presence of systems coverage within our accounting curriculum. Albrecht & Sack (2000) included a similar recommendation in their study in the U.S.A., as did Hancock *et al.* (2009) in their Australian study.

However, it is not enough to simply add a systems class to the curriculum to pay homage to the growth of this field and the importance of systems knowledge to accounting graduates. Information systems must be considered as being part of the accounting core, and handled as we currently handle taxes and auditing topics. Interestingly, more of our students will be confronted with IT issues and problems than with tax or auditing issues, since most of our students will spend their careers working in the government or corporate sectors. For the group working in public accounting, a major part of their career will be spent dealing with control systems that are technology driven, or as consultants in the systems area.

Whether the offerings are packaged as a major, minor, or added required courses, there are numerous papers describing what would be a beneficial set of systems courses for accounting majors to take to enhance their knowledge base and increase their employment opportunities. The technology topics can be taught by academic staff with expertise in the area and, unlike the softer skills, the subjects can be mastered in the classroom and used by our students throughout their careers. We recommend a study with an international focus by Boritz (1999) to provide an example of the potential topics that could be covered in systems classes for our accounting majors. Boritz notes that, in many business schools, IT is not considered to be a core knowledge area. To move forward in the systems area, Boritz believes the topic should be defined as part of the core accounting programme. He also believes that programmes receiving accreditation from the different accrediting bodies should be required to incorporate systems into their curriculum, and systems should be part of any certifying examinations in accounting. At a minimum, the accounting curriculum should include the following five general areas of information systems:

- IT Concepts for Business Systems;
- Internal Control in Computer-Based Business Systems;
- Development Standards and Practices for Business Systems;
- Management of IT Adoption, Implementation, and Use; and
- Evaluation of Computer-Based Business Systems.

The suggested topics can be enhanced by including Electronic Commerce, Enterprise Resource Planning Systems, Knowledge Management, and any new Assurance Services.

How the offerings are packaged will be determined by the academic staff involved in the particular programme, but acknowledging an increasing need to be competent in the information systems area is an important first step. Boritz & Stoner (see Chapter 16 – this volume) review the role and place of IT in accounting education. Their chapter provides a more comprehensive discussion of the interrelationships among systems-oriented courses and accounting programmes. Chapter 16 also identifies IT skills and competencies needed by accounting students.

5.4.3 Internships and hands-on learning

The use of internships by public accounting firms, corporations, and not-for-profit organizations as a primary recruiting tool emphasizes one aspect of the benefits of hands-on experiences. (See Beard & Humphrey, Chapter 25 – this volume.) We believe that this form of learning and experiencing the real world of accounting will increase across accounting firms and businesses of all sizes, in addition to not-for-profit organizations and governmental agencies. Although internships have been a normal situation with the larger public accounting firms, we predict that the value of these experiences to the student, and the benefits of observing the potential employee in a work environment before making a hiring decision, will increase their use to a growing number of employers. The potential value of an internship from a learning perspective is excellent, and based upon our dealings with students completing internships, it is one of the most valuable experiences in the accounting curriculum. (See also Jackling, Chapter 10 – this volume.)

This value added is also present in many service learning situations like the tax support programmes for low-income individuals or the short-term leadership programmes offered by accounting firms. If we truly want our students to understand the accounting profession before entering the work world, and add an experience that will bring their coursework 'to life', then the internship or other hands-on experiences should become a part of the normal curriculum for all students in our programmes.

5.5 Conclusion

We state in this chapter that an agenda for accounting education should be very simple and straightforward with the idea that we need to get back to the basics. Encouraging and supporting reform directed at developing accounting students' so-called soft skills has been misguided as it has asked students and academic accounting staff to do the impossible and directed them away from developing what accountants need most, which is knowledge of technical accounting material.

We believe that:

- The accounting profession is not really clear on what soft skills they desire.
- The profession is not clear as to what the terms mean when they ask for these skills in our students.
- It is open to question as to whether the skills can be taught.
- It is questionable whether students are at a level of cognitive development which would allow them to understand and incorporate these skills into their daily lives.

And we wonder:

- whether accounting educators have the expertise to teach these skills; and
- whether the ability to learn and incorporate these skills can ever be done in a specific course or courses – especially without extensive knowledge of the subject area where these skills are to be used.

This means that the student needs to thoroughly understand the subject area before he/she can, for example, ever think critically about the subject. The major concern with these skills, however, is that their development may be a function of other environmental factors that are developed long before we see the student in our classes for a few hours each week. In addition, while we are supposed to be addressing these soft skills, we must still teach an ever-increasing body of knowledge in accounting that also requires knowledge of related areas such as systems, finance, and quantitative methods. We believe that accounting educators should focus on what they do best, and on the subject that they have mastered, rather than attempt to address subjects that are not in their area of expertise and may be impossible to teach in the normal sense of teaching as we know it.

The promise of classroom technology improving education has not been met, and greater emphasis needs to be put on adapting instructional resources to fit today's students' learning styles. (See Duff, Chapter 8 – this volume.) This is not a problem which is unique to accounting education, but a technology-centred profession such as accounting should be a leader in developing technology applications that effectively engage students and promote learning. Only by focussing on developing students' technical accounting competence and adapting course materials and teaching to fit new learning styles will accounting education improve and provide the type of education that students want and which the market demands.

The inclusion of accounting and management information systems courses in our accounting curriculum will improve the ability of our graduates to perform in the accounting profession. Integration of these topics throughout the curriculum, offering a minor in the subject area, or support for a double major in accounting and systems, are different approaches to addressing this opportunity. Regardless of the approach, the systems field should be a part of the training of future accounting majors.

Finally, an increased emphasis on hands-on learning experiences will support the move back to basics and bring the real world into the classroom, making the technical aspects of the courses more relevant and enhance the entire learning process.

References

Accounting Education Change Commission (AECC) (1990) *Objectives of Education for Accountants,* Position Statement Number One, reprinted in *Position and Issues Statements of the Accounting Education Change Commission* (Accounting Education Series, Vol. 13), Sarasota, FL: American Accounting Association.

Accounting Education Change Commission (AECC) (1996) *Position and Issues Statements of the Accounting Education Change Commission* (Accounting Education Series, Vol. 13), Sarasota, FL: American Accounting Association.

Albrecht, W.S. & Sack, R.J. (2000) *Accounting Education: Charting the Course through a Perilous Future* (Accounting Education Series, Vol. 16), Sarasota, FL: American Accounting Association.

American Accounting Association, Committee on the Future Structure, Content and Scope of Accounting Education (1986) Future accounting education: preparing for the expanding profession (the Bedford Report), *Issues in Accounting Education*, 1(1), 168–175.

Arquero, J., Donoso, J., Hassall, T., & Joyce, J. (2001) Vocational skills in the accounting professional profile: the Chartered Institute of Management Accountants (CIMA) employers' opinions, *Accounting Education: an international journal*, 10(3), 299–313.

Arthur Andersen & Co., Arthur Young, Coopers & Lybrand, Deloitte Haskins & Sells, Ernst and Whinney, Peat Marwick Main & Co., PriceWaterhouse & Touche Ross (1989) *Perspectives on Education: Capabilities for Success in the Accounting Profession*, (the Big Eight White Paper). New York: authors.

Barefield, R.M. (1991) A critical view of the AECC and the converging forces of change, *Issues in Accounting Education*, 6(2), 305–312.

Baril, C., Chain, M., Cunningham, B., Fordham, D., Gardner, R., St. Pierre, K., & Wolcott, S., (1997) *Critical Thinking Competencies Essential to Success in Public Accounting*, Report of the Federation of Schools of Accountancy 1997 Educational Research Committee. St. Louis: Federation of Schools of Accountancy.

Baril, C., Chain, M., Cunningham, B., Fordham, D., Gardner, R., St. Pierre, K., & Wolcott, S., (1998) Critical thinking in the public accounting profession: aptitudes and attitudes, *Journal of Accounting Education* 16(3/4), 381–406.

Boritz, J. (1999) The accounting curriculum and IT. Available at: www.ifac.org, September.

Browning, L. (2003) *New York Times*, May 20.

Cappelletto, G. (2010) *Challenges Facing Accounting Education in Australia*, Melbourne: AFAANZ.

Carr, N. (2008) Is Google making us stupid? What the Internet is doing to our brains, *The Atlantic*, July/August.

Davis, S.W. & Sherman, W.R. (1996) The Accounting Education Change Commission: a critical perspective, *Critical Perspectives in Accounting*, 7, 159–189.

Ethics Newsline (2012) 8 October. Available at: http://www.globalethics.org/newsline/2012/10/page/2/.

Flaherty, R.E. (ed.) (1998) *The Accounting Education Change Commission Grant Experience: A Summary* (Accounting Education Series, Vol. 14), Sarasota, FL: American Accounting Association.

Goodley, S. (2012) *The Guardian*, 29 January.

Gordon, T. (2012) Transparency International Corruption Perception Index, *Global Ethics Newsline*, October.

Hancock, P., Howieson, B., Kavanagh, M., Kent, J., Tempone, I., & Segal, N., (2009) *Accounting for the Future: More than Numbers. A Collaborative Investigation into the Changing Skill Set for Professional Accounting Graduates over the Next Ten Years and Strategies for Embedding Such Skills into Professional Accounting Programs*, Sydney: Australian Learning and Teaching Council.

Hard, S., Conway, J., & Moran, A. (2006) Faculty and college students' beliefs about the frequency of student academic misconduct, *The Journal of Higher Education*, 77(6).

Hassall, T., Joyce, J., Arquero, J., & Donoso Anes, J. (2003) The vocational skills gap for management accountants: the stakeholders' perspectives, *Innovations in Education and Teaching International*, 40(1), 78–88.

Kurfiss, J. (1988) *Critical Thinking: Theory, Research, Practice, and Possibilities*, Washington, DC:ASHE-ERIC Higher Education Report No. 2.

Lowery, C. & Beadles, N. (2009) Assessing the impact of business ethics instruction: a review of the empirical evidence, *Journal of the Academy of Business Education*, 10(Fall).

Mastracchio, N. (2005) Teaching CPAs about serving the public interest, *The CPA Journal*, 75(1).

Mathews, R., Jackson, M., & Brown, P. (1990) *Accounting in Higher Education: Report of the Review of the Accounting Discipline in Higher Education*, Vol. 1, Canberra: ACT, Australian Government.

Mathews, R.M. (1994) An examination of the work of the Accounting Education Change Commission 1989–1992, *Accounting Education: an international journal*, 3(3), 193–204.

McCabe, D. (2001) Cheating: why students do it and how we can help them stop, *American Educator*, Winter.

McNair, F. & Milam, E. (1993) Ethics in accounting education: what is really being done, *Journal of Business Ethics*, 12(10).

McPeck, J. (1981) *Critical Thinking and Education*, New York: St. Martin's Press.

Merritt, J. (2002) You mean cheating is wrong?, *Business Week*, 3811.

Milner, M. & Hill, W. (2008) Examining the skills debate in Scotland, *International Journal of Management Education*, 6(3), 13–20.

Milner, M. & Hill, W. (2010) Setting the skills agenda: the views of UK accounting academics, unpublished working paper.

Novin, A.M., Pearson, M.A., & Stephen, V.S. (1990) Improving the curriculum for aspiring management accountants: the practitioner's point of view, *Journal of Accounting Education*, 8(2), 207–224.

Paul, R., Elder, L., & Batell, T. (1997) *California Teacher Preparation for Instruction in Critical Thinking*, Sacramento, CA: California Commission on Teacher Credentialing.

Rossides, D.W. (1991) Knee-jerk formalism: the higher education reports, *Journal of Accounting Education*, 9(2), 233–256.

Sack, R.J. & Burton, J.C. (1991) Changes in accounting education and changes in practice, *Accounting Horizons*, September.

Sangster, A. & Wilson, R.M.S. (eds) (2013) *Liberalising the Accounting Curriculum in University Education*, Abingdon: Routledge.

Siegel, G., Sorensen, J., Klammer, T., & Richtermeyer, S. (2010) The ongoing preparation gap in management accounting education: a guide for change, *Management Accounting Quarterly*, 11(3), 41–53.

St. Pierre, K. & Anderson, J. (1984) An analysis of the factors associated with lawsuits against public accountants, *The Accounting Review*, 59(2), 242–263.

Sundem, G.L. (1999) *The Accounting Education Change Commission: Its History and Impact* (Accounting Education Series, Vol. 15), Sarasota, FL: American Accounting Association.

Tan, L., Fowler, M., & Hawkes, L. (2004) Management accounting curricula: striking a balance between the views of educators and practitioners, *Accounting Education: an international journal*, 13(1), 51–67.

The China Conundrum, *New York Times*, 3 November 2011.

The Pathways Commission (2012) *Charting a National Strategy for the Next Generation of Accountants*, Sarasota, FL: AAA, and New York: AICPA.

The Week, 20 July 2012.

The Week, 26 January 2013, p. 63.

Wall Street Journal, 19 July 2010.

Wall Street Journal, 6 February 2013.

Whitley, B. (1998) Factors associated with cheating among college students, *Research in Higher Education*, 39(3).

Willingham, D. (2007) Critical thinking – why is it so hard to teach?, *American Educator*, Summer, 8–19.

Winfield, N. (2013) Italian priest stole $5.1 million from hospital, Associated Press.

Wolcott, S., Baril, C., Cunningham, B., Fordham, D., & St. Pierre, K. (2002) Critical thought on critical thinking research, *Journal of Accounting Education*, 20, 85–103.

About the authors

Kent St. Pierre is Sutula Professor of Accounting, Saint Joseph's University, U.S.A. (estpierr@sju.edu) His primary interests/achievements include serving as Editor, *Journal of Accounting Education* (1983–1998), and as Editor, *Issues in Accounting Education* (2007–2010). He has published in *The Accounting Review*, *Journal of Accounting, Auditing and Finance*, *Accounting*

Horizons, Journal of Accountancy, Research in Accounting Regulation, Journal of Accounting Education, Accounting Education: an international journal, and *Journal of Management Development.*

James E. Rebele is Professor of Accounting, Robert Morris University, U.S.A. (rebele @rmu.edu) His primary interests/achievements include serving as Editor-in-Chief, *Journal of Accounting Education* (1999–2010). He has published in *Issues in Accounting Education, Journal of Accounting Education,* and *Accounting Education: an international journal.*

Section B

Student-related considerations

Preface

Judy S.L. Tsui

THE HONG KONG POLYTECHNIC UNIVERSITY

The five chapters in Section B of this *Routledge Companion to Accounting Education* have put students in the centre stage of tertiary education and, more specifically, education in accounting. This sets the scene for the *Companion*'s enquiry into Accounting Education by identifying a major stakeholder in tertiary education: our students.

A unifying framework on which one can rely in order to understand the importance of these five chapters is:

Input   →   Process   →   Output

Input includes a consideration of the contexts (such as students' prior accounting knowledge, working experience, and cultural background), which can all affect students' perceptions of what accounting should be or is. Evidence from the developed countries has revealed that students tend to have negative perceptions of accounting, leading to misguided views on appropriate learning approaches, ultimately affecting their learning outcomes.

Students' perceptions could be influenced by a multitude of factors, including the perceptions of their parents and family, the image of accountants in their society and their work, their personal interests, and their views on employment prospects, career development, and the financial rewards of an accounting career. These are the factors identified as being instrumental in affecting their choice of an accounting major.

In order for students' learning to be effective, educators should be aware of the contexts in which students learn – namely, how the above factors affect students' learning style preferences, motivation to learn, and approaches to learning. By tapping into research on factors influencing students' learning in different individual and cultural contexts, educators can design better learning strategies to achieve more effective learning. Ultimately, this will translate into accounting education with a focus on one of the most important of the key stakeholders, our students, to make a positive difference in the global world of business.

6

Perceptions of accounting

Ursula Lucas* and Rosina Mladenovic**

*THE UNIVERSITY OF THE WEST OF ENGLAND, U.K.
**THE UNIVERSITY OF SYDNEY, AUSTRALIA

CONTENTS

Ursula Lucas and Rosina Mladenovic

Abstract

Perceptions of accounting can have a powerful impact on how students learn and on the outcomes of their learning. This impact is often negative. Students may enter their studies with stereotypical views of accounting as being dull, boring, and associated with mathematics and rigid techniques which suggest a process of rote-learning and poor understanding. A constructivist view of learning acknowledges the importance of these perceptions. Learning is seen to be an active process of 'meaning-making' whereby what one already 'knows' about accounting has to be worked with to come to new understandings. This process involves a focus on the subjectivity inherent within accounting and the need for critical thinking and moral reasoning. This chapter investigates the nature of students' perceptions of accounting, the difficulties inherent in changing what are often deeply-held beliefs, and how perceptions may be changed through changes in learning environments and from further research.

Keywords

approaches to learning, constructivist model of learning, socio-cultural context, students' perceptions of accounting, teaching interventions

6.1 Introduction

The main aims of this chapter are:

- to explain the importance of perceptions within a constructivist model of learning;
- to define the term 'perceptions' and review the literature on students' perceptions of accounting;
- to explore the relationship between students' perceptions of accounting, approaches to learning, and learning outcomes;
- to critique the impact of various teaching interventions on changing students' negative perceptions of accounting; and
- to identify ways forward for research and teaching.

In this chapter we shall explain why an understanding of students' perceptions is central to the effective support of students' learning. This will involve an explanation of the constructivist model, or view, of learning. This model underpins a large area of research within higher education (e.g. Biggs & Tang, 2007; Prosser & Trigwell, 1999; Ramsden, 2003), and comprises an important field of intellectual enquiry (see Fogarty, Chapter 1 – this volume). An understanding of its assumptions highlights the importance of 'what a student already knows' as a key part of the learning process. We shall then provide an overview, from research conducted in this field, of students' perceptions of accounting. Finally, we shall conclude with an identification of ways forward for both research and teaching.

6.1.1 The importance of perceptions of a subject within a constructivist model of learning

> [T]he most important single factor influencing learning is what the student already knows. Ascertain this and teach him [sic] accordingly.
>
> (Ausubel, 1968, p. 36)

Most academic staff will recognize that students bring into the classroom a variety of perceptions of accounting. For students who do not intend to specialize in accounting (non-specialists), but who face accounting as a compulsory subject, accounting is often seen as being dull and boring, and associated with numbers and mathematics, and this can lead to worries about learning accounting. Alternatively, some students, hopefully those who will specialize in it, may view accounting more favourably, relishing its systematic and logical techniques. They experience the satisfaction of 'balancing the books'. However, such students may feel negatively challenged when the subjectivity inherent in structured techniques gradually becomes apparent. All of these perceptions, whether negative or positive, comprise an important part of '*what a student already knows*' and they powerfully affect the way in which a student learns, and the outcomes of that learning.

Ausubel's assertion (above) that, in learning, we build on what we already know, rests on a constructivist model of learning. Within this model, learning is seen as a process of 'making meaning'. This contrasts with many taken-for-granted views of learning which involve learning new facts and techniques which are inscribed upon a *tabula rasa* (or blank slate). Within constructivism, it is assumed that a student either takes new knowledge and fits it into her existing knowledge frameworks (assimilation), or she may amend those frameworks where the new knowledge does not appear to 'fit' (accommodation) (Inhelder & Piaget, 1958). Depending on the nature of existing knowledge frameworks, assimilation may be relatively straightforward, but accommodation may prove problematic and challenging for the student. This constructivist view of learning underpins an approach to financial literacy that sees it as being a process of 'sense-making' (see Wilson *et al.*, Chapter 3 – this volume).

This model of learning underlies a large body of research into students' approaches to learning (SAL) within higher education. Probably the best known constructivist model is the 3-P model (Presage, Process and Product) (Biggs, 1993). These three elements form the foundation of other models, such as Ramsden's model of student learning (Ramsden, 2003), which then seek to elaborate or emphasize particular aspects of the basic model. In this chapter we shall refer to Duff & McKinstry's (2007) model (amended). It draws on both of these models and is illustrated in Figure 6.1.

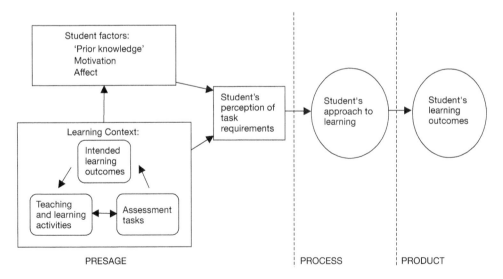

Figure 6.1 Duff & McKinstry's (2007) 3P-SLC model (amended)

From Figure 6.1 it can be seen that:

- *Presage* represents the stage before learning takes place (i.e. what the student 'brings with her').
- *Process* represents what happens during learning (usually referred to as the student's approach to learning).
- *Product* refers to the outcome of learning.

Presage factors are many. Figure 6.1 uses only three headings, but they include a complex range of inter-related aspects. 'Prior knowledge' includes a wide range of knowledge, some of which may be explicit (such as knowledge from prior courses of study) and some of which may be tacit (such as unacknowledged perceptions of accounting, learning and knowledge in general). Motivation is concerned with the student's overall goal and this will be related to specific intentions which arise in relation to a course of study. Motivation may be *intrinsic*, involving enjoyment or interest in the task itself, or *extrinsic* involving a focus on the outcome of the task. *Affect* refers to the emotion or feeling that a student brings to a learning situation. This may be a powerful aspect of presage. Emotions such as fear of failure (Fransson, 1977) or interest and enjoyment (Entwistle, 1987) may inhibit or enhance learning respectively. In practice, as will be seen from the discussion in this chapter, it can be quite difficult to separate these three aspects of presage as they interact and may mutually reinforce one another.

Insofar as process is concerned, the central finding of the wide range of research conducted is that students broadly adopt one of two contrasting approaches to learning: surface or deep. Research has also identified a third – an achieving approach to learning, though findings as to whether this comprises a separately identifiable approach are mixed. (A discussion of this issue is available in Lucas & Mladenovic, 2004, p. 404.) The adoption of a 'surface' approach is typically characterized by an extrinsic motivation to pass an assessment task and an intention to do so through a process of rote-learning. The adoption of a 'deep' approach is characterized by an intrinsic interest in the task and an intention to understand and to make personal sense of what is being studied. Approaches to learning are strongly related to the quality of a student's learning outcome. A review of the research supporting this assertion is provided in Prosser & Trigwell, (1999, p. 15). It is important to note, however, that this is a slightly contentious area as the position may not be as straightforward as Prosser & Trigwell (1999) imply. Coffield, Moseley, Hall & Ecclestone (2004, p. 98) refer to Entwistle (2002), who argues that the absence of standardized criteria in higher education makes predictive validity difficult to demonstrate.

The constructivist model is based on an assumption that learning is a response to a particular context. An approach to learning is not an invariant 'learning style' adopted by a student (though a student may bring a preferred way of learning to a particular context[1]). Rather, it varies according to a student's perception of a specific learning encounter and environment, regardless of what might be described as the objective intentions of the educator (alternative models of learning, that are assumed to be less context-dependent, are discussed by Duff, Chapter 8 – this volume). For example, Prosser (1993) provides a fascinating example of two students' accounts of the *same* lecture: one student describes an episode in discovery learning whereas the second student describes an hour of taking down notes geared at passing the examination. Crawford, Gordon, Nicholas & Prosser (1998, p. 81–82) effectively sum up the situation faced by an educator:

> *university teachers, in designing learning and teaching contexts and in engaging in the teaching, need to be continually aware that each student is situated differently within that context and will perceive his or her situation differently.*

(as quoted by Tight, 2003, p. 73)

It follows that a central focus of what is often termed the 'approaches to learning' field of research has focussed on the identification of *variation* within the student cohort: whether at the presage, process, or product stage. Understanding the nature of variation and the related differential adoption of approaches to learning and outcomes is a central objective. Research within other subject settings, such as mathematics and economics (Crawford *et al.*, 1998; Meyer & Eley, 1999; Meyer & Shanahan, 2001), has identified significant variation in students' perceptions of the subject, motivations for learning, and their relationship to surface and deep approaches to learning. Clearly, it is well worth reviewing what is known about students' perceptions of accounting and of learning accounting.

6.2 What do we know about perceptions of learning accounting?

6.2.1 What do we mean by 'perceptions' and how can they be identified?

The word 'perceptions' is widely used within research on learning and teaching, but often understood in different ways. Within a constructivist model of learning, the term *perception* involves the identification of what may be deeply-held, or taken-for-granted, beliefs or ways of looking at the world. These may be about the subject, learning in relation to that subject, and motivations to learn that subject. Tapping into such beliefs, or ways of looking at the world, is not straightforward. Consequently, the most common research methods focus on a deep enquiry into a student's lifeworld. The first method is phenomenography, which can be defined as '*the empirical study of the limited number of qualitatively different ways in which various phenomena in, and aspects of, the world around us are experienced, conceptualized, understood, perceived and apprehended*' (Marton, 1994, p. 4424). It usually takes the form of interview-based research or, alternatively, uses written accounts by students. It comprises a '*production task*' (Baxter Magolda, 1999, p. 353) in which learners are given an opportunity, either in writing or verbally, to describe their own experiences. The focus is the nature of the experience as identified by the learner, rather than the identification of categories supplied by the researcher.

The second research method uses an inventory (i.e. questionnaire). This comprises a '*recognition task*' (ibid., p. 353), in which learners indicate the strength of their agreement or disagreement with statements that describe beliefs, motivations, and learning processes which might apply to them in particular contexts. Statements used in inventories are often direct quotations from phenomenographic research. Within the SAL research field, many inventories are used. These include:

- the Approaches to Studying Inventory (ASI) (Entwistle & Ramsden, 1983);
- the Study Processes Questionnaire (SPQ) (Biggs, 1987; Biggs *et al.*, 2001);
- the Approaches to Study Questionnaire (ASQ) (Richardson, 1990);
- the Revised ASI (RASI) (Tait & Entwistle, 1996);
- the Approaches and Study Skills Inventory for Students (ASSIST) (Tait *et al.*, 1998); and
- the Reflections on Learning Inventory (RoLI) (Meyer, 2000, 2004).

The use of an inventory is a practical way of accessing the experience of a large number of students through the use of a self-report. Such inventories have to be designed and validated with care. Their validity is dependent on the extent to which the inventory statements provide an adequate and authentic operationalisation of constructs previously identified in phenomenographic research.

These two research methods should be regarded as being complementary, rather than competing (Lucas & Meyer, 2005). Phenomenography provides an opportunity to access a rich description of a student's lifeworld, and provides an analysis of *qualitative* variation. Inventory research provides quantitative findings and may confirm (or disconfirm) variation across a population sample. In addition, its results may provide further data about relationships between presage and process, and so raise questions that may only be answered by a further immersion in phenomenographic research.

The inventories referred to above cover both presage and process factors and are generic in nature. However, the constructivist model assumes that a student's approach to learning is a response to a specific context. Accordingly, it is not surprising that there has been speculation amongst researchers that presage and process factors may differ between disciplines (Entwistle, 1984; Ramsden, 1984; Meyer *et al.*, 1990; Meyer & Watson, 1991; Eley, 1992). In particular, Meyer & Eley (1999, p. 198) argue that: '*individual students might well adopt differentiated patterns of learning behaviours that are attributable to the learning contexts shaped by different subjects*'. Indeed, there is evidence that perceptions and experiences of learning contexts are shaped by the *epistemology* and *practice* of a discipline, and they might therefore vary considerably between disciplines (Ramsden & Entwistle, 1981; Watkins & Hattie, 1981). As a result, one might question how effectively these differences are accounted for within a *generic* inventory and if there is a need for more research that is specific to disciplines.

6.2.2 A review of prior research on perceptions of accounting

No educator is likely to be surprised by the findings of several studies in the 1990s that *Introductory Accounting* students come to their study of accounting (sometimes via prior accounting education and/or work experience, as discussed by Byrne & Willis, Chapter 7 – this volume) with many 'negative' stereotypical perceptions of accounting (Cory, 1992; Cohen & Hanno, 1993; Fisher & Murphy, 1995; Friedlan, 1995; Saudagaran, 1996). The focus on *Introductory Accounting* recognizes the large number of students who enrol in these programmes and its significance within accounting education (see Wygal, Chapter 11 – this volume). In this context, 'negative' perceptions refer to perceptions that are either inappropriate or unrealistic from the point of view of the educator, such as the perception that accounting is, in the main, mechanical and repetitive 'number-crunching'. Along with the growth in higher education research within a constructivist framework, studies started to delve deeper into the nature of such perceptions and of how these perceptions differed from those held by academic staff.

Mladenovic (2000) administered a questionnaire to first year students in an Australian university. The questionnaire design was informed by students' negative perceptions discovered over many years of teaching accounting, as well as negative perceptions reported in the literature (e.g. Ramsden, 1992; Cohen & Hanno, 1993). In addition, the questionnaire captured many of the metaphors suggested by Morgan (1988) in his discussion of the inherently complex, multi-dimensional and paradoxical nature of accounting as a social phenomenon. Metaphors included accounting as:

- history
- economics
- information
- language
- rhetoric
- politics
- mythology

- magic
- disciplined control
- ideology
- exploitation and domination, and
- as an objective numerical view of reality.

In order to determine whether students' initial perceptions of accounting were realistic or negative, teachers' perceptions were used as a benchmark. Consistent with prior research, results confirmed that students initially held many negative stereotypical perceptions of accounting when compared with teachers' perceptions. In contrast to teachers, a greater proportion of students perceived accounting as being primarily *numerical*, *objective*, and *noncontroversial*, and were less able to perceive the importance of *creative judgment* and *communication skills* for accountants. Students were also more inclined to perceive accounting as having an affinity with *mathematics* and *statistics* than were teachers, and less able to perceive that accounting had an affinity with areas such as *history*, *philosophy*, *literature*, and *politics*.

Concurrent with the Mladenovic study, a phenomenographic study within the U.K. (Lucas, 2001) also investigated the nature of students' perceptions (involving five accounting and five business studies students). This research identified similar perceptions. Understandably, since these were long interviews rather than responses to a questionnaire, the findings revealed some complexity in perceptions. It was difficult to sum up the variety of students' perceptions in just a few headings. It was not that a student held just one particular perception or another. Rather, a student's view of accounting appeared to be a mixture of different perceptions. A key perception was that accounting was about numbers and mathematics. Students either saw the positive or negative side of numbers. Some accounting students chose accounting because they liked courses with numbers. The business studies students, on the other hand, had a negative attitude to numbers. Furthermore, even though these students reported that they found the course to be less numbers-based than they had expected, their negative perceptions about accounting survived intact. Fundamentally, this connection of accounting with mathematics and numbers was linked to the issue of accounting as an objective science. (See Laswad & Tan, Chapter 9 – this volume, for coverage of students' choice of Accounting as a discipline to study.)

This phenomenographic research led to the development of an inventory which allowed these qualitative findings to be tested in a statistical sense within several student cohorts (Lucas & Meyer, 2005). *The Expectations of Learning Accounting Inventory* (ELAcc 1.3) was used to survey more than 1,200 *Introductory Accounting* students across five universities in the U.K. Not surprisingly, perceptions of accounting as *objective* (and links with mathematics, numbers, technique, and formulae) were confirmed: so too, was the issue of *enjoyment* and *worry* (differing forms of satisfaction to be derived from learning accounting). The large sample also identified the relationship between *intention* (to relate to the subject or to pass an examination on the subject) and *relevance* (in a personal, work-related, and business sense). The findings show that there were variations in perception and approach to learning between students who specialize in accounting and those who do not, and between male and female accounting students.

Further research extended the ELAcc inventory (version 1.4) (Lucas & Mladenovic, 2009b). Relevance was now split into two parts:

- Does the student have the intention to understand the *reality/meaning* behind accounting?
- Does the student have a view of knowledge that recognizes that accounting provides a framework through which we construct a *view of society or the economy*?

Two further perceptions were added:

- Does the student have a view of knowledge that it is important to question the basis on which accounting techniques are founded (*questioning*)?
- Does the student have a perception of accounting indicating that it represents a subject in which he or she has a strong motivation to succeed (*achieving*)?

One additional perception was included to complement the perception that accounting is about numbers: namely, that accounting is an *objective* subject involving little uncertainty or subjectivity.

The findings, following the administration of the combined inventory (ELAcc and RoLI) to 1,600 students at two Australian universities, indicated that the additional sub-scales within the inventory were effective in identifying significant variation in the student cohort. Of particular interest was that the findings were strongly indicative of perceptions of accounting which varied across three students groups: by gender (male/female), language (English as a first or second language (EFL/ESL), and major (specialist/non-specialist).

More recent research continues to support these findings on perceptions of accounting. Through an analysis of phenomenographic data collected from six student cohorts over a three-year period, McGuigan & Weil (2011) examined students' experiences in a New Zealand first year accounting course and found that students' perceptions fell into the following categories: enjoyment, technical language, numerical and objective discipline, boredom, fear, and difficulty.

6.2.3 What is the relationship between perceptions of accounting, approaches to learning, and learning outcomes?

There is a range of research within higher education which indicates that perceptions of a subject are related to the way in which students approach their learning. For example, in economics (Meyer & Shanahan, 2001, 2003) and in mathematics (Meyer & Eley, 1999; Eley & Meyer, 2004). This is confirmed by two studies in accounting. Lucas & Meyer (2005) linked the ELAcc 1.3 with the RoLI to identify those discipline-specific perceptions and motivations that may be related to surface or deep learning approaches. The findings show that there are variations in perception and approach to learning between students who specialize in accounting and those who do not, and between male and female accounting students. Moreover, these perceptions were differentially linked with surface, deep, and pathological approaches to learning in a conceptually consistent manner. (The term 'pathological' refers to learning approaches that are so inappropriate that they inhibit learning in contrast with the surface approach which supports a limited range of learning.) For both male and female accounting students, enjoyment and relevance are linked with deep approaches to learning. For business studies students only, relevance is linked with the deep approach to learning. There is also a link between examination focus, lack of interest, worry, and a pathological learning approach. Further work with the ELAcc 1.4, combined with the RoLI in Australia (Lucas & Mladenovic, 2009b) found similar relationships.

There is little evidence concerning the relationship of perceptions of accounting with learning outcomes. Ferreira & Santoso (2008), in a study of 380 management accounting students in Australia, found that students' performance is negatively affected by the negative perceptions of accounting that students bring to the subject. The negative perceptions were those of accounting as bean-counting, number-crunching, and bookkeeping. In contrast, the positive perceptions of accounting (interesting, stimulating and exciting, motivating) that students had at the start of the semester were found to affect performance only indirectly through positive perceptions of accounting at the end of the semester. The study found that, though positive perceptions of accounting at the end of the semester translate into improved students' performance, its impact is much smaller than that of negative perceptions of accounting. Once the negative perceptions of accounting had been formed, there is limited scope to modify such views with positive reinforcement. Lucas & Mladenovic (2009b) also looked at the relationship between perceptions of accounting, SAL, and learning outcome (in the form of final grade). The results showed that the surface approach to learning had a negative loading on final grade.

6.2.4 Have teaching or other interventions supported change in perceptions of accounting?

Understandably, the following question then arises:

> What can academic staff do to support changes in perceptions in accounting – and mitigate any negative impact upon approaches to learning and learning outcomes?

There are relatively few studies that have addressed this issue. Friedlan (1995), in the U.S.A., compared the effect of two types of *Introductory Accounting* course on perceptions. A traditional lecture-based, technically-focussed course was compared with a non-traditional, case-based course, with less emphasis placed on technical material and more emphasis on critical thinking and discussion. Students were surveyed at the beginning and again at the end of semester. For 17 of the 25 (i.e. 68 per cent) statements in the survey, desirable significant differences were reported for students in the non-traditional course. These students tended to have perceptions that were more consistent with those of accountants when compared with the perceptions of students in the traditional course. The perceptions of students in the traditional course were either unaffected or adversely affected.

Similarly, a study based on an innovative *Introductory Accounting* course – aimed at dispelling American students' perceptions that accounting and bookkeeping are synonymous – reported that 74 per cent of students in the redesigned course, when surveyed at the end of term, indicated that the course had improved their perceptions of accounting (Saudagaran, 1996). Caldwell, Weishar, & Glezen (1996) found that American students commenced their study of *Introductory Accounting* with positive perceptions of accounting. Students who used cooperative learning techniques were more likely to maintain their initial positive perceptions of accounting than students receiving a traditional lecture format (Caldwell *et al.* 1996), though the results were mixed. (See also Wygal, Chapter 11 – this volume, for a discussion of the first course in accounting.)

Reviewing these three studies, Mladenovic (2000, p. 138) concluded that the limited success of prior research raised questions as to why only some perceptions of accounting changed when non-traditional teaching methods were employed, while others were either not affected or adversely affected. Accordingly, she set out to explore the effects of a constructively-aligned teaching environment (Biggs, 1996) versus only changing teaching methods on students' negative perceptions of accounting. In a constructively-aligned teaching environment, the emphasis is on what the student is intended to learn through carefully designed learning activities that take into account 'what the student already knows'. Such an environment would focus specifically on the nature of beginning perceptions and the extent to which these might hinder, rather than support, learning. The studies of Friedlan (1995) and Caldwell *et al.* (1996) served as quasi-control groups (changes to teaching methods), against which Mladenovic evaluated the impact of an aligned teaching environment. At the beginning of the course, students (n = 924) and teachers (n = 8) completed a questionnaire about their perceptions of accounting[2] (as described in Section 6.2.2). The students then studied the constructively-aligned accounting course and participated in two direct interventions designed to support changes in perceptions of accounting. These involved the explicit discussion of students' perceptions. At the end of the semester, a survey of students (n = 408) revealed significant positive changes in 14 of the 15 perceptions of accounting.

Overall, Mladenovic (2000, p. 148) found that:

> an alignment of teaching methods, curriculum and assessments, and directly challenging students' perceptions, appears to be more effective in changing students' negative perceptions than changing teaching methods as the main intervention, as demonstrated in prior research (Friedlan, 1995, and Caldwell et al., 1996).

Follow-up student focus groups and surveys showed that, while students found the two discussions about their perceptions of accounting to be somewhat useful, it was only by engaging with the course and the course materials that they developed more realistic perceptions of accounting. This confirms the importance of students being actively involved in constructing their own knowledge, which is central to the constructivist view of learning.

For this reason, it can be valuable to encourage and support students to reflect upon their own learning. In New Zealand, McGuigan & Weil (2011) analysed students' reflective work and found transformative shifts over time in how students perceived accounting (e.g. from accounting being objective and factually accurate to being subjective and opinion-based, and from accounting being boring to being interesting and relevant). Even so, the authors found that not all students underwent these changes, but continued to struggle with some of the course concepts and ways of learning. They concluded that students' perceptions of the accounting discipline form a major threshold in their learning and may not be that easy to change. Accordingly, in the next section, we shall discuss whether the constructivist framework that has, to date, been used to frame research into perceptions of accounting and approaches to learning accounting is sufficient to inform our understanding of students' learning.

6.3 Widening the constructivist framework to engage with the socio-cultural context

As might be expected, the dominance of SAL research within higher education since the 1980s has led to a growing critique of its sufficiency as an explanatory framework. Haggis (2003, p. 89), extending the discussion by Webb (1997), suggests that, while this 'model may be successful in creating a generalized description of the "elite" goals and values of academic culture, it says surprisingly little about the majority of students in a mass system'.

In particular, she notes that changing students' approaches is extremely difficult and that this indicates that something rather more complex may underpin, and affect, students' learning. She points out that, although the constructivist view of learning acknowledges the central importance of context, too many educators have neglected the need to acknowledge disciplinary and cultural specificities. While Marshall & Case (2005, p. 263) agree with Haggis that there needs to be more critical engagement with the conceptual basis of the approaches to learning framework, they argue that:

> [I]t is nevertheless a powerful framework with which to make sense of aspects of student learning situations. Rather than discarding the theory altogether, we would argue that other perspectives have the potential to enrich and extend it.

One perspective that should inform research into perceptions focusses on the beliefs that students hold about the nature of knowledge. We have already discussed the way in which many students are predisposed to consider the subject of accounting as being inherently technical and objective in nature. This is of concern, given the large role that professional judgement and ethics plays within accounting, and the role that accounting plays within society. There is a growing body of evidence that students' beliefs about knowledge are related to their learning (Hofer, 2004). (See also the discussion of different types of knowledge in Section 4.3.1 of Chapter 4 – this volume.)

Baxter Magolda's work (1992) has shown how a student's epistemological beliefs or 'ways of knowing' are related to approaches to learning. Recall that within a constructivist model of learning, the term 'perception' involves the identification of what may be deeply-held, or taken-for-granted beliefs, or ways of looking at the world. Beliefs that knowledge is essentially factual are associated with a surface approach to learning, whereas relativistic or contextual beliefs about knowledge are associated with deep approaches to learning. Within accounting, epistemological beliefs have been found to be related to study strategies and performance (Phillips, 2001). In particular, Lucas & Meyer (2005) showed that accounting students who reported a belief that knowledge is discrete and factual also reported a surface approach to learning, and those students who reported a more relativistic and committed way of knowing also reported a deep approach to learning. Building on this finding, Lucas & Tan (2013) conducted 32 interviews with 17 accounting and business studies placement students in a university in the U.K. and found that, even towards the end of their studies, they believed that knowledge is essentially factual in nature.

We need to know more about students' beliefs about knowledge because this is linked to a students' ability to engage in the abstract reasoning required for accounting (and is highly relevant to the development of moral reasoning and critical thinking as discussed by Boyce, Chapter 24, and Cunningham, Chapter 18 respectively – both in this volume). Accounting is an abstract subject representing an attempt to model phenomena of great complexity (such as the financial status, impact, and worth of an organization). The recognition of accounting as being a modelling technique involves an understanding of the role of such models within professional life generally, and within accounting in particular. There is a need for students to be able to engage in formal (abstract) reasoning as opposed to concrete reasoning (Inhelder & Piaget, 1958). Yet there is relatively little evidence concerning the capacity of accounting students to engage in formal (hypothetical and deductive) reasoning. Shute (1979), in a study carried out in the U.S.A., used three modes of representation: concrete, transitional and formal. He found that, over five years within a freshman to graduate sample of 179 students, the mean cognitive level for each sub-population was transitional. The percentage of students within the formal mode in the senior year was 37 per cent, rising to 50 per cent in graduate students. Shute also found that students functioning at the concrete level could not do problems which required formal reasoning (ibid., p. 36). Another accounting study (Ramburuth & Mladenovic, 2004) used the *Structure of the Observed Learning Outcome* (SOLO) taxonomy (Biggs & Collis, 1982) to measure first year undergraduate students' responses to a comprehension task involving the reading of an article about leadership. They found that only 25 per cent of the students evidenced formal reasoning. They also found that this was related to subsequent academic performance. A study by Lucas & Mladenovic (2009a) extended this analytical approach to two accounting tasks completed by first year undergraduate students. For each task, only 32 per cent and 14 per cent of students respectively evidenced formal reasoning. We are not aware of any more recent studies within the area of accounting education, but these three studies indicate that, while we might expect students to operate at a formal level, only a minority may do so.

There is a substantial literature on the difficulty inherent in changing beliefs about knowledge. In part, this arises because such beliefs are intimately bound up with issues of identity and voice. To move towards a belief in knowledge as being relativistic or contextual involves an acceptance of uncertainty and subjectivity, a willingness to challenge the authority of academic staff and experts, and a commitment to evaluate evidence in context. It involves the transformation of beliefs, attitudes, opinions, and emotional reactions that constitute students' ways of looking at the world. The change in belief systems involved may be so fundamental that the students see themselves as being different people. Interestingly, this would involve a perception of learning that involves changing as a person, as one changes one's relationship with the world (and accounting), rather than learning by rote just to pass an examination (Marton *et al.*, 1993).

Students may well find the higher education culture, with its expectations of engagement with more abstract reasoning and the abandonment of the certainty of accounting techniques, to be somewhat alien. Lucas (2000), in her phenomenographic interviews with 10 accounting and business studies students, looked beyond the identification of individual perceptions of accounting to reveal two contrasting worlds (or views) of accounting: a world of detachment, and a world of engagement. The different aspects of the detached world of *Introductory Accounting* reinforce each other such that, for most students, learning accounting is about learning a technique and accounting is seen to be a technique. Students are primarily motivated to pass the examination. They express no doubts about what is required to achieve this: they must work through the learning materials and learn the techniques. This perception of what is required fits in clearly with their perceptions about accounting: that it is about numbers and structured techniques. Moreover, in the absence of any immediate relevance of accounting to them, it becomes a mere article of faith that accounting will eventually be relevant in their future careers. For some students, this lack of relevance is overcome as they immerse themselves in what is for them the more appealing aspect of accounting: its logic and the fact that there is a 'right' answer. By way of contrast, the world of engagement shows that some students are able to engage with accounting and relate it to their own personal relevancies. For them, the course is one in which they can develop their understanding of accounting and of the world.

Interesting new light is thrown on these two worlds by a study carried out by Sin, Reid & Jones (2012). They conducted a phenomenographic interview study with 18 accounting students who were in different stages of completion of their undergraduate degree at a university in Australia. Sin *et al.* identified three perceptions of accounting work within that student group:

- The first was that accounting is seen as comprising routine work, with a focus on the recording and reporting of financial information. It is seen as being a repetitive process and potentially boring.
- The second sees accounting as comprising meaningful work with links to compliance and accountability. This involves a need for credibility of information and a need for effective two-way communication between accountant and client/stakeholder.
- The third sees accounting as being moral work with a focus on the complexity of ethics and the subjectivity of accounting.

One can see that there are conceptually coherent linkages across these three perceptions and the differing beliefs about the nature of accounting and knowledge in general.

6.4 Ways forward for research and teaching

We acknowledge that the ways forward for research and teaching are inextricably linked. For convenience, our suggestions are discussed in separate sections below, highlighting the unique contribution which each strand can make in improving the quality of the students' learning experience in accounting.

6.4.1 For research

We began this chapter with a quotation from Ausubel (1968) who claimed that the most important factor influencing learning is what the student already knows, and that this 'knowing' should inform teaching practices. Our exploration has revealed that students come to their study of accounting with unrealistic negative perceptions of accounting and misguided perceptions of what learning is in accounting (Mladenovic, 2000; Friedman & Lyne, 2001; Lucas, 2001; Lucas & Meyer, 2005; Lucas & Mladenovic, 2009b; McGuigan & Weil, 2011). Evidence suggests that these perceptions impact on students' motivation to learn, their approaches to learning and, consequently, the quality of their learning outcomes. Furthermore, research shows that students' perceptions are deeply held and are often taken-for-granted beliefs which are difficult to uncover and to change (Mladenovic, 2000; McGuigan & Weil, 2011).

In recommending ways to further research in this area, our discussion comes full circle as we suggest there is a need to extend our understanding of students' existing 'knowing' and the context in which they know. Research in this area has tended to focus on accounting education within the U.S.A., the U.K., Australia, and New Zealand. But is it reasonable to generalize from these findings? We need to know more about accounting education within other cultural contexts (such as Latin America, the Middle East, the Far East, and South-East Asia). We can then use this understanding to develop learning environments to enable students to uncover their perceptions, understand how they impact upon their learning and, where appropriate, to challenge their unrealistic perceptions. This process can be supported by engaging in research that further develops the existing theoretical and conceptual frameworks which inform and underpin our current understandings. These theories and frameworks will, in turn, support empirical research endeavours using both qualitative and quantitative research methods (e.g. phenomenographic and inventory-based research). Hence research and teaching activities are inextricably linked.

Theoretical and conceptual development could begin with the approaches to learning paradigm. While this paradigm has – and continues to offer – a fruitful framework for research, Webb (1997), Haggis (2003) and Marshall & Case (2005) challenge researchers to widen the framework so that it encompasses the socio-cultural context in which we live. In this way, the approaches to learning framework could be enriched and extended to enhance our understanding of accounting education practice.

For example, research exploring students' perceptions needs to take into account the diversity in the cohorts of students studying accounting. The work of Lucas & Mladenovic (2009b) indicated that students' perceptions of accounting varied between different groups of students by gender (male/female), language (English as a first or second language (EFL/ESL)), and major (specialist/non-specialist). Research that expands accounting educators' understanding of these differences, their impact on SAL, and outcomes are valuable areas for improving future pedagogic practice. In addition, we should also consider the diverse contexts within which students study accounting. Existing research has focussed on the undergraduate curriculum, but there is little research amongst students on professional training courses. A number of researchers

(Entwistle, 1984; Ramsden, 1984; Meyer *et al.*, 1990; Meyer & Watson, 1991; Eley, 1992) have suggested that presage and process factors may differ between disciplines. Therefore, in addition to students' differences, models of students' learning and future research studies need to consider the impact of disciplinary differences on students' learning.

Furthermore, given that accounting is a complex and abstract subject in which financial information is used to model business complexity, it is of concern that Ramburuth & Mladenovic (2004) and Lucas & Mladenovic (2009a) found very few accounting students displaying formal reasoning (i.e. the ability to reason abstractly). Research that explores students' beliefs about the nature of knowledge may shed light on these findings. It may also shed light on how accounting educators can engage students to adopt a deep approach to learning. The latter will support students in developing:

- an understanding of the diverse and complex roles which accounting plays within society;
- their professional judgement;
- an ability to work with ethical conflict resolution processes: and, most importantly,
- preparing students so they can make a positive impact on society as leaders in business, government, and community.

This is not solely a concern in the design, delivery, and assessment of the undergraduate curriculum. It is of key relevance to the accounting profession and the way in which students are educated to achieve professional qualifications.

Finally, prior research in accounting shows that students report negative emotions (boredom, worry, and fear) and positive emotions (enjoyment, satisfaction, and interest) about accounting and their studies of accounting (Mladenovic, 2000; Lucas, 2001; Lucas & Meyer, 2005; Lucas & Mladenovic, 2009b; McGuigan & Weil 2011). Whether negative or positive, students' emotions (represented as the 'affective' domain in the presage section of Figure 6.1) comprise an important part of 'what a student already knows' and powerfully affect the way in which a student learns and the outcomes of that learning. Further research on the affective domain will support the development of teaching environments that can reduce students' negative emotions which are related to poorer performance (Fransson, 1977), and support positive emotions which are positively related to performance (Entwistle, 1987).

For the many reasons outlined above, uncovering and challenging students' unrealistic and negative perceptions of accounting is a valuable area for future research. Nevertheless, we must bear in mind that existing research highlights that this is a difficult process, with studies reporting varying levels of success (Mladenovic, 2000; McGuigan & Weil, 2011). A powerful way forward is to include students in the research process in which they discover, evaluate, and construct their own perceptions within a constructive-developmental pedagogy as described below.

6.4.2 For teaching

The 3P model is a particularly valuable way of conceptualizing our teaching and learning, because it emphasizes the need to achieve constructive alignment (Biggs, 2003). First, this term acknowledges the constructive assumption underpinning the model. Second, it stresses the need to align the three aspects of the model: presage, process, and product. Having identified the learning outcomes for a course (see Needles, Chapter 2, and Kidwell & Lowensohn, Chapter 21 – both in this volume), one would expect these to be aligned with learning activities designed to support the achievement of those learning outcomes (as featured in Figure 6.1). Further, the design of learning activities would take account of the presage factors within that particular teaching context such that, if students were entering a course with negative or unrealistic perceptions that might adversely affect their approaches to learning, then learning activities might be designed to support a change in those perceptions (Mladenovic, 2000).

It may be helpful to consider the principles that should underlie such an approach. This is particularly important when we consider the difficulties that may be involved in supporting students in changing tacit, and possibly deeply-held, beliefs and emotions. Baxter Magolda (1999) argues for a constructive-developmental pedagogy involving three mutually supportive and interacting principles:

1 Validating students as knowers by acknowledging their capacity to hold a point of view, recognizing their current understandings, supporting them in explaining their current views, listening to students' thinking, and promoting dialogue amongst learners. This process makes apparent students' beliefs about knowledge.
2 Situating learning in students' own experience, by using their experience, lives, and current knowledge as a starting point for learning. Students can thereby readily understand and connect to their ways of making meaning.
3 Defining learning as being the mutual construction of meaning. This makes both teachers and students active players in learning.

So far as validating students as knowers is concerned, an accounting educator should seek to acknowledge and engage with the students' own worlds of accounting. As Lucas (2000, p. 498) points out:

> *Anecdotally, we may assemble a catalogue of complaints about some students: they are lazy, do not work hard enough, cannot be bothered to read around the subject and only look for a figure that will allow the balance sheet to balance. We could, alternatively, ask ourselves: 'is it possible that a student sees accounting in such a way that such behaviour is perfectly reasonable?' That is, that the student sees accounting as primarily a technique, a subject to be passed, lacking relevance and is immune to our appeals to conceptual understanding.*

The findings of studies discussed above reveal some of the ways in which students view accounting.

Yet, as certain studies acknowledge (for example, Mladenovic, 2000; McGuigan & Weil, 2011), the most effective way to validate students as knowers is to promote dialogue and ask students to identify their ways of viewing accounting. This is not necessarily straightforward since students may not recognize tacitly held views, and they may be resistant to this form of archaeology. As McGuigan & Weil (2011) point out, students' preconceived ideas or perceptions of accounting are often ill-conceived, formed in the context of a lack of exposure to practical experience or to reliable information. Instead, they are born from public and social media sources, parental influences, and commonly held stereotypes, which often give rise to misconceptions. Hence the principle of validating students as knowers must work in conjunction with the other two principles discussed below.

Validating students as knowers, in part, requires that educators become more aware of the way in which students experience the world. However, this is a necessary but not a sufficient condition. Learning has to be situated within the student's own experience. Students themselves have to become *aware* of their own meaning-making structures before they can come to question them. Stimulating this moment of awareness becomes an important issue within teaching. Lucas

(2008) provided a reflection on the nature of such learning activities within auditing. The nature of the activities involved was such that they halted students in their tracks and propelled them into questioning taken-for-granted assumptions about themselves and the subject. Notably, none of these activities explicitly related to the subject of auditing:

- They were activities that attached themselves to the everyday life of the student.
- Each one was capable of being related to whatever meaningful experience with which the student chose to connect it (hence supporting relevance for the student).
- The nature of each activity was such that it was 'playful' – challenging in a non-threatening way.
- None were linked to assessment, so fear of failure was reduced.
- Finally, they provided students with a way of contrasting their own ways of thinking with those of others.

In addition, academic staff can support students in identifying perceptions of accounting as an explicit activity in its own right. Inventories such as ELAcc, or questionnaires such as that used by Mladenovic (2000), can be used formally, or informally, as a way of supporting students in understanding the nature of their own perceptions compared with those of others. Equally, students might be encouraged to interview others (e.g. members of the public, students from other courses) about their perceptions of accounting. When it comes to addressing students' powers of reasoning and ability to abstract, classroom questions (and exemplar responses) such as those used by Lucas (2000, 2001) and Lucas & Mladenovic (2009a) can provide a focus for classroom discussion, or even assessment.

It can be enlightening for students to realize that there are other ways of viewing financial statements, and that other students experience the learning of accounting in different ways. When students provide comments or explanations about how they approach their learning or understand the subject, the educator can be on the alert that this is an opportunity to make visible unacknowledged ways of seeing learning or the subject. The educator may acknowledge (but not dismiss) a variety of perceptions wherever they emerge within the classroom and open them up for further reflection and discussion. Extracts from published phenomenographic interviews may be used to highlight the different ways in which students view aspects of accounting.

Assessment methods may be revised to encourage students to address issues surrounding perceptions of accounting and their relevance. For example, learning activities and assessments might expect students to enquire into, and discuss, the nature of perceptions about accounting held by themselves and others, and the ways in which this may affect the role of accounting in businesses and society.

Finally, if learning is to be regarded as a process which involves the mutual construction of meaning, then this has to be a foundation on which the curriculum is designed. Thus it is not surprising to find, as the Mladenovic (2000) study illustrates, that a process of constructive alignment places the study of perceptions of accounting at the heart of the curriculum. The perceptions of academic staff can be contrasted with those of students, and the discussion of differing perceptions can become a central focus of learning and teaching.

Throughout this chapter we have highlighted the key role that students' perceptions play in their motivation to learn, their approach to learning and, ultimately, the quality of students' learning outcomes. We wish to encourage students to consider accounting as both educational and a career choice (as discussed by Laswad & Tan, Chapter 9, and Jackling, Chapter 10 – both in this volume). By actively engaging in research and teaching practices that enable accounting educators to understand students' perceptions, we open up a view into the students' world. Employing a constructivist model, teachers can develop learning environments which allow students to engage in ways that uncover and challenge their unrealistic negative perceptions of accounting and support the development of more realistic perceptions. From this perspective, higher education becomes not only a ground from which students can develop as individuals, but it enables accounting educators to have a significant impact: as the graduates of tomorrow make a positive difference in the world of business and society as a whole.

Notes

1　Ramsden (2003, p. 51) explains the concept of an 'orientation to study' as follows:

> [A]lthough it is abundantly clear that the same student uses different approaches on different occasions it is also true that general tendencies to adopt particular approaches, related to the different demands of course and previous educational experiences, do exist. Variability in approaches thus coexists with consistency.

2　The importance of addressing instructors' perceptions is highlighted by Geiger & Ogilby (2000) who found significant differences between individual instructors in terms of how they might support changes in students' perceptions of accounting.

References

Ausubel, D.P. (1968) *Educational Psychology: A Cognitive View*, New York: Holt, Rinehart & Winston.

Baxter Magolda, M.B. (1992) *Knowing and Reasoning in College: Gender Related Patterns in Students' Intellectual Development*, San Francisco: Jossey-Bass.

Baxter Magolda, M.B. (1999) *Creating Contexts for Learning and Self-Authorship: Constructive Developmental Pedagogy*, San Francisco: Jossey-Bass.

Biggs, J.B. (1987) *Study Processes Questionnaire Manual*, Melbourne: Australian Council for Educational Research.

Biggs, J.B. (1993) From theory to practice: a cognitive systems approach, *Higher Education Research and Development*, 12(1), 73–85.

Biggs, J.B. (1996) Enhancing teaching through constructive alignment, *Higher Education*, 32, 347–64.

Biggs, J.B. (2003) *Teaching for Quality Learning at University*, 2nd edn, Buckingham: Society for Research into Higher Education and Open University Press.

Biggs, J.B. & Collis, K. (1982) *Evaluating the Quality of Learning: The SOLO Taxonomy (Structure of the Observed Learning Outcome)*, New York: Academic Press.

Biggs, J.B., Kember, D., & Leung, D.Y.P. (2001) The revised two-factor Study Process Questionnaire: R-SPQ-2F, *British Journal of Educational Psychology*, 71, 133–149.

Biggs, J.B. & Tang, C. (2007) *Teaching for Quality Learning at University*, Buckingham: Society for Research in Higher Education/Open University Press.

Caldwell, M.B., Weishar, J., & Glezen, G.W. (1996) The effect of cooperative learning on student perceptions of accounting in the principles courses, *Journal of Accounting Education*, 14(1), 17–36.

Coffield, F., Moseley, D., Hall, E., & Ecclestone, K. (2004) *Learning Styles and Pedagogy in Post-16 Learning: A Systematic and Critical Review*, London: Learning and Skills Research Centre.

Cohen, J. & Hanno, D. (1993) An analysis of underlying constructs affecting the choice of accounting as a major, *Issues in Accounting Education*, 8(2), 219–238.

Cory, S. (1992) Quality and quantity of accounting students and the stereotypical accountant: is there a relationship? *Journal of Accounting Education*, 10, 1–24.

Crawford, K., Gordon, S., Nicholas, J., & Prosser, M. (1998) Qualitatively different experiences of learning mathematics at university, *Learning and Instruction*, 8(5), 455–468.

Duff, A. & McKinstry, S. (2007) Students' approaches to learning, *Issues in Accounting Education*, 22(2), 183–214.

Eley, M.G. (1992) Differential adoption of study approaches within individual students, *Higher Education*, 23, 231–254.

Eley, M.G. & Meyer, J.H.F. (2004) Modelling the influences on learning outcomes of study processes in university mathematics, *Higher Education*, 47, 437–454.

Entwistle, N.J. (1984) Contrasting perspectives on learning, in Marton, F., Hounsell, D.J., & Entwistle, N.J. (eds) *The Experience of Learning*, Edinburgh: Scottish Academic Press, pp. 1–18.

Entwistle, N.J. (1987) A model of the teaching learning process, in Richardson, J.T.E., Eyesenck, M.W., & Warren Piper, D. (eds) *Student Learning Research in Education and Cognitive Psychology*, London: S.R.H.E./Open University Press.

Entwistle, N.J. (2002) Response to LSRC draft report on learning styles. Personal communication.

Entwistle, N.J. & Ramsden, P. (1983) *Understanding Student Learning*, London: Croom Helm.

Ferreira, A. & Santoso, A. (2008) Do students' perceptions matter? A study of the effect of students' perceptions on academic performance, *Accounting and Finance*, 48, 209–231.

Fisher, R. & Murphy, V. (1995) A pariah profession? Some student perceptions of accounting and accountancy, *Studies in Higher Education*, 20(1), 45–58.

Fransson, A. (1977) On qualitative differences in learning, IV: effect of motivation and test anxiety on process and outcome, *British Journal of Educational Psychology*, 47, 244–257.

Friedlan, J.M. (1995) The effect of different teaching approaches on students' perceptions of the skills needed for success in accounting courses and by practicing accountants, *Issues in Accounting Education*, 10(1), 47–63.

Friedman, A.L. & Lyne, S.R. (2001) The beancounter stereotype: towards a general model of stereotype generation, *Critical Perspectives on Accounting*, 12, 423–451.

Geiger, M.A. & Ogilby, S.M. (2000) The first course in accounting: students' perceptions and their effect on the decision to major in accounting, *Journal of Accounting Education*, 18, 63–78.

Haggis, T. (2003) Constructing images of ourselves? A critical investigation into 'approaches to learning' research in higher education, *British Educational Research Journal*, 29(1), 89–104.

Hofer, B.K. (2004) Introduction: paradigmatic approaches to personal epistemology, *Educational Psychologist*, 39, 1–4.

Inhelder, B. & Piaget, J. (1958) *The Growth of Logical Thinking from Childhood to Adolescence*, London: Routledge & Kegan Paul.

Lucas, U. (2000) Worlds apart: students' experiences of learning introductory accounting, *Critical Perspectives on Accounting*, 11, 479–504.

Lucas, U. (2001) Deep and surface approaches to learning within introductory accounting: a phenomenographic study, *Accounting Education: an international journal*, 10(2), 161–184.

Lucas, U. (2008) Being 'pulled up short': creating moments of surprise and possibility in accounting education, *Critical Perspectives on Accounting*, 19(3), 383–403.

Lucas, U. & Meyer, J.H.F. (2005) 'Towards a mapping of the student world': the identification of variation in students' conceptions of, and motivations to learn, introductory accounting, *The British Accounting Review*, 37, 177–204.

Lucas, U. & Mladenovic, R. (2004) Approaches to learning in accounting education, *Accounting Education: an international journal*, 13(4), 399–408.

Lucas, U. & Mladenovic, R. (2009a) The identification of variation in students' understandings of disciplinary concepts: the application of the SOLO taxonomy within introductory accounting, *Higher Education*, 58(2), 257–283.

Lucas, U. & Mladenovic, R. (2009b) The identification of students at academic risk: the development of a discipline-specific inventory to support teaching interventions, paper presented to the 17th Improving Student Learning Symposium, 6–9 September, Imperial College, London.

Lucas, U. & Tan, P. L. (2013) Developing a capacity to engage in critical reflection: students' 'ways of knowing' within an undergraduate business and accounting programme, *Studies in Higher Education*, 38(1), 104–123.

McGuigan, N. & Weil, S. (2011) Addressing a 'preconceptual threshold': a transformation in student preconceptions of introductory accounting, *ACCESS Critical Perspectives on Communication, Cultural and Policy Studies*, 30(2), 15–33.

Marshall, D. & Case, J. (2005) 'Approaches to learning' research in higher education: a response to Haggis, *British Educational Research Journal*, 31(2), 257–267.

Marton, F. (1994) Phenomenography, in Huson, T. & Postlethwaite, T.N. (eds) *The International Encyclopedia of Education*, 2nd edn, Oxford: Pergamon Press, pp. 4424–4429.

Marton, F., Dall'Alba, G., & Beaty, E. (1993) Conceptions of learning, *International Journal of Educational Research*, 19(3), 277–300.

Meyer, J.H.F. (2000) An overview of the development and application of the Reflections on Learning Inventory (RoLI), RoLI Symposium, Imperial College, London.

Meyer, J.H.F. (2004) An introduction to the RoLI, *Innovations in Education and Teaching International*, 41(4), 491–497.

Meyer, J.H.F. & Eley, M.G. (1999) The development of affective subscales to reflect variation in students' experiences of studying mathematics in higher education, *Higher Education*, 37, 197–216.

Meyer, J.H.F., Parsons, P., & Dunne, T.T. (1990) Individual study orchestrations and their association with learning outcomes, *Higher Education*, 20, 67–89.

Meyer, J.H.F. & Shanahan, M. (2001) A triangulated approach to the modelling of learning outcomes in first year economics, *Higher Education Research Development* 20(2), 127–145.

Meyer, J.H.F. & Shanahan, M. (2003) Dissonant forms of memorising and repetition, *Studies in Higher Education*, 28(1), 5–20.

Meyer, J.H.F. & Watson, R.M. (1991) Evaluating the Quality of Student Learning, II: study orchestration and the curriculum, *Studies in Higher Education*, 16(3), 251–275.

Mladenovic, R. (2000) An investigation into ways of challenging introductory accounting students' negative perceptions of accounting, *Accounting Education: an international journal*, 9(2), 135–155.

Morgan, G. (1988) Accounting as reality construction: towards a new epistemology for accounting, *Accounting, Organizations and Society*, 13(5), 477–485.

Phillips, F. (2001) A research note on accounting students' epistemological beliefs, study strategies, and unstructured problem-solving performance, *Issues in Accounting Education*, 16, 21–39.

Prosser, M. (1993) Phenomenography and the principles and practices of learning, *Higher Education Research and Development*, 12(1), 21–31.

Prosser, M. & Trigwell, K. (1999) *Understanding Learning and Teaching: The Experience in Higher Education*, Buckingham, The Society for Research into Higher Education and Open University Press.

Ramburuth, P. & Mladenovic, R. (2004) Exploring the relationship between students' orientations to learning, the structure of students' learning outcomes and subsequent academic performance, *Accounting Education: an international journal*, 13(4), 507–527.

Ramsden, P. (1984) The context of learning, in Marton, F., Hounsell, D.J., & Entwistle, N.J. (eds) *The Experience of Learning*, Edinburgh: Scottish Academic Press, pp. 124–143.

Ramsden, P. (1992) *Learning to Teach in Higher Education*, London: London: Routledge.

Ramsden, P. (2003) *Learning to Teach in Higher Education*, 2nd edn, London: Routledge.

Ramsden, P. & Entwistle, N.J. (1981) Effects of academic departments on students' approaches to studying, *British Journal of Educational Psychology*, 51, 368–383.

Richardson, J.T.E. (1990) Reliability and replicability of the approaches to studying questionnaire, *Studies in Higher Education*, 15(2), 155–168.

Saudagaran, S.M. (1996) The first course in accounting: an innovative approach, *Issues in Accounting Education*, 11(1), 83–94.

Shute, G.E. (1979) *Accounting Students and Abstract Reasoning: An Exploratory Study*, Sarasota, FL: American Accounting Association.

Sin, S., Reid, A., & Jones, A. (2012) An exploration of students' conceptions of accounting work, *Accounting Education: an international journal*, 21(4), 323–340.

Tait, H., Entwistle, N.J., & McCune, V. (1998) ASSIST: a reconceptualisation of the approaches to studying inventory, in Rust, C. (ed.) *Improving Student Learning: Improving Students as Learners*, Oxford: Oxford Centre for Staff and Learning Development, pp. 262–271.

Tight, M. (2003) *Researching Higher Education*, Maidenhead: Open University and SRHE.

Watkins, D. & Hattie, J. (1981) The learning processes of Australian university students: investigations of contextual and personological factors, *British Journal of Educational Psychology*, 15, 384–93.

Webb, G. (1997) Deconstructing deep and surface: towards a critique of phenomenography, *Higher Education*, 33, 195–212.

About the authors

Ursula Lucas is Emerita Professor of Accounting Education at the University of the West of England, U.K. (Ursula.Lucas@uwe.ac.uk). Her research interests include: students' approaches to learning within accounting, students' perceptions of key skills, and the development of reflective practice within the business and accounting curriculum. She has served as a Senior Associate Editor of *Accounting Education: an international journal* (for which she received an *AE*/IAAER Distinguished Service Award), as Chair of the Assessment Committee of the ICAEW, and is an HEFCE National Teaching Fellow.

Rosina Mladenovic is an Associate Professor at the University of Sydney Business School, Australia (Rosina.Mladenovic@sydney.edu.au). She has received five teaching awards (two national awards and one international) and five international 'best paper' awards for her research in accounting education. Her main areas of research include: students' approaches to learning, curriculum design, and threshold concepts.

7

The role of prior accounting education and work experience

Marann Byrne and Pauline Willis

DUBLIN CITY UNIVERSITY, IRELAND

CONTENTS

Abstract

This chapter adopts a constructivist stance which identifies prior knowledge as being a significant factor which influences students' achievements. For many incoming tertiary accounting students, their initial knowledge of accounting is acquired through studying the subject in school and/or by gaining experience in the accounting workplace. The chapter documents and evaluates previous research which has focussed on prior accounting education and work experience, and the influence of these factors on performance, career choice, and perceptions of accounting. The absence of significant research exploring the content and style of school accounting courses is highlighted. Additionally, the inconsistent findings regarding the impact of prior study on subsequent performance are also discussed. Finally, the chapter concludes by outlining several avenues for further research which would provide educators and the accounting profession with enhanced insights into their students' first experiences of accounting.

Keywords

prior accounting education, prior knowledge, prior work experience, school accounting

7.1 Introduction

The main aims of this chapter are:

- to review studies which evaluated the accounting curriculum experienced by pupils in school;[1]
- to evaluate research which investigated the role of prior accounting education and/or work experience[2] in influencing or predicting students' performance in their tertiary[3] accounting courses;
- to examine research into the influence of prior accounting education and/or work experience on students' choice of discipline and/or career;
- to assess studies which explored the impact of prior accounting education and/or work experience on students' perceptions of accounting; and
- to identify avenues for future research relating to prior accounting education and work experience.

The constructivist view of learning sees learning as being a cognitive process in which learners construct knowledge by interpreting new information in the light of what they already know and understand. Researchers sharing this perspective have demonstrated that prior knowledge has a powerful impact on students' learning and performance (e.g. Tobias, 1994; Dochy, 1994, 1996), with studies in educational psychology identifying prior knowledge as being the most important single factor influencing learning (e.g. Ausubel, 1968; Dochy, 1994, 1996; Shapiro, 2004). Following a review of research on prior knowledge, Dochy, De Ridjt & Dyck (2002) concluded that between 30–60 per cent of the variation in students' learning outcomes can be explained by prior knowledge. Furthermore, there is evidence showing that prior knowledge impacts on study behaviour and learning strategies (e.g. Biggs, 1987; Hegarty-Hazel & Prosser, 1991a, 1991b; Dochy *et al.*, 1996; Ramsden, 2003), and that good quality prior knowledge leads to better knowledge acquisition and the application of higher order cognitive skills (Dochy *et al.*, 2002; Hailikari *et al.*, 2008).

Given the significance of prior knowledge on learning, educational psychologists have stressed the importance of educators taking into consideration and utilising students' prior knowledge and experiences in order to help their students develop a clear understanding of the concepts being currently taught (Ginsburg & Opper, 1979; Myhill & Brackley, 2004). In the context of accounting, tertiary students' prior accounting knowledge is frequently acquired through the study of the subject in school and/or through working in accounting prior to the commencement of their tertiary accounting courses. In light of the foregoing, this chapter documents and evaluates research in accounting which has focussed on prior accounting education and work experience.

7.2 Evaluation of students' prior accounting education

The first course in accounting has been identified in the accounting literature as being an area of key importance to accounting educators (Accounting Education Change Commission, 1992; Cohen & Hanno, 1993; Albrecht & Sack, 2000; Geiger & Ogilby, 2000; Hunt et al., 2004). Its importance stems from its ability:

- to impact on students' performance in subsequent accounting courses;
- to shape their perceptions of the accounting profession;
- to influence their decision to pursue a career in accounting; and
- to affect their beliefs about the aptitudes and skills needed to be a successful accountant.

Consequently, there have been numerous studies which have focussed on the first course in accounting (see Wygal, Chapter 11 – this volume). These studies typically considered the first tertiary accounting course taken by students. However, for many incoming higher education accounting students their first experience of learning the subject was in school. Indeed, the strong link between the study of accounting in school and the selection of tertiary accounting courses is evident in many different countries. To illustrate, Table 7.1 presents a list of studies, carried out since 2000 in several countries, which give details of the percentage of incoming tertiary accounting students with prior accounting education. While there is great variation across the different studies, in general, the percentage of students with prior accounting education is significant.

Surprisingly, although a significant number of tertiary accounting students have studied accounting in school, there has been very little research into the accounting education experienced by pupils in schools. Indeed, Ireland is the only country in which accounting education researchers have explored the topic in depth. In a series of empirical studies, Byrne & Willis (1997, 2001, 2003, 2008) evaluated the accounting course on offer as part of the Leaving Certificate programme[4] in Irish schools. Their initial study reported that the majority of teachers did not cover the full syllabus and that many pupils omitted further topics when revising for their final examination in the subject (Byrne & Willis, 1997). Worryingly, this narrowing of the syllabus did not have an adverse effect on pupils' performance due to the predictability of the examination. In fact, the analysis revealed that the pupils considered the accounting examination paper to be more predictable than the examination papers in other subjects, and a detailed review of past papers supported their view. In a second study, following a revision to the syllabus, Byrne & Willis (2001) found improved course coverage with a greater range of topics being examined. They also reported that, while the pupils' ability to predict the examination paper had diminished, nevertheless many of them still believed the examination was highly predictable. The study also found that there was little variation in the content of questions for many of the topics that were common to the old and new syllabi, again lending support to the predictability of the examination paper.

Table 7.1 Percentage of incoming tertiary accounting students with prior accounting education

Study	Year	Country	Percentage
Byrne & Willis	2001	Ireland	88
Gracia & Jenkins	2003	Wales	36
Rankin, Silvester, Vallely & Wyatt	2003	Australia	55
Tickell & Smyrnios	2005	Australia	83
Nelson, Vendrzyk, Quirin & Kovar	2008	U.S.A.	31
Tan & Laswad	2008	New Zealand	54
Guney	2009	England	24
McPhail, Paisey & Paisey	2010	Scotland	49
Jones & Wright	2011	Canada	39
Xiang & Gruber	2012	U.S.A.	47

Building on their research with pupils, Byrne & Willis (2003) elicited teachers' views of the school accounting course. This research found that over two-thirds of teachers believed they had insufficient time to cover the course material and the majority considered the standard of the examination was too high and that the examination paper could not be completed in the allotted time. There was also evidence that teachers were overly focussed on past examination papers. Furthermore, many of them expressed concerns over the difficulty of teaching pupils of mixed ability in a single class. The findings of this study were confirmed by Clarke & Hession (2004) in another Irish study which surveyed a limited number of teachers.

To gain further insights into students' prior accounting education, Byrne & Willis (2004) used the Course Experience Questionnaire (Ramsden, 1991) to explore tertiary accounting students' perception of the quality of their school accounting course. This study found that the majority of students had a positive perception of their course and, on the whole, they had enjoyed it. They believed the workload and assessment were appropriate, that the goals and standards of the course were clear, and they were happy with the standard of teaching. However, they believed that the course was not very successful in developing generic skills. In their final study on students' prior experiences of accounting, Byrne & Willis (2008) gathered data from incoming tertiary accounting students on their approaches to learning accounting in school. The analysis showed that, in general, the students favoured a strategic approach to learning and there was a highly significant difference in their scores on this scale compared to their scores on both the deep and surface scales. Interestingly, the surface approach was the students' least favoured approach with their scores on this scale being significantly lower than their scores on either of the other two scales. However, in the light of their other findings, the authors issued a cautionary warning when interpreting the findings on the students' approaches to learning. They stressed that their study measured the students' perceptions of their approaches to learning and not necessarily their actual approach to learning. (Detailed coverage of students' approaches to learning (SAL), with strategic, deep and surface dimensions, is provided by Lucas & Mladenovic, Chapter 6, and Duff, Chapter 8 – both in this volume.)

Considering the findings from all of the foregoing studies, there is evidence that students' prior experiences of learning accounting in Irish schools may be less than optimal. In particular, the predictability of examination papers together with concerns over the time available to cover the syllabus and a tendency to overly focus on examination papers may be fostering a learning environment that promotes rote learning. In such circumstances students are likely to acquire a sketchy and a confused understanding of the course content which will be an impediment to their learning of the subject in their subsequent studies. To more accurately determine if this is the case, research which evaluates the quality of students' prior knowledge is warranted.

Unfortunately, research exploring the accounting course on offer in schools in other countries is very limited. In an early study from the U.S.A., Schroeder (1985) elicited the views of tertiary students on their school accounting course. He found that the majority believed that their school accounting course was beneficial to them in their study of accounting in higher education. Furthermore, he noted that course dropout rates were significantly lower among those students with prior accounting education. In another study from the U.S.A., which focussed on the links between school and college accounting, Norton (1977) outlined some of the positive aspects of studying accounting in school. He felt students come away from the school accounting course with '*study habits, knowledge, attitude, and analytical ability that can be applied to many college courses including college accounting*' (ibid., p. 24).

Using a qualitative approach, Malthus & Fowler (2009) conducted research in New Zealand which gathered evidence from school pupils, their accounting teachers, and career advisers on their perceptions of the school accounting course. One of the issues which emerged from the analysis was that both teachers and pupils criticised the school accounting curriculum as being too repetitive and monotonous, and they concluded that this was turning pupils off studying accounting at tertiary level. In another New Zealand study, Agnew (2010) investigated trends in school accounting participation and achievement following revisions to the assessment regime in New Zealand schools. While he found that there was an increase in the number of pupils studying accounting, they were taking fewer courses and, generally, there had been a decline in their performance. This pattern led him to conclude that those who studied accounting in school now have a weaker grasp of the subject content which is likely to have a negative impact on their study of accounting in higher education.

In a study undertaken in the U.K., Fee, Greenan, & Wall (2009) compared the assessment that incoming business and accounting tertiary students had experienced in a range of A-level subjects,[5] including accounting, to the assessments they would encounter in their first year at university, in order to examine how well prepared they were for their university learning environment. While the authors did not identify any specific issues relating to accounting, they concluded that there was a considerable gap between school and university assessment, resulting in many incoming tertiary students struggling with the demands of higher education assessments.

To date, there has only been one published study which has tried to assess the quality of incoming tertiary students' prior accounting knowledge. Sangster & McCombie (1993) used a case study to assess whether students who had studied accounting in Scottish schools had a better understanding of a set of financial statements than students with no prior accounting knowledge. Their analysis revealed that prior study of accounting acquainted students with the terminology and basic mechanics of accounting, but it did not instil any interpretative awareness in them. There was also evidence that students with prior accounting education were over-confident in their ability and, as a result, they under-estimated the work effort required to do well in their tertiary accounting courses.

7.3 Prior accounting education and academic performance

There is a vast array of research which seeks to determine what influences the performance of students in tertiary education, with school results consistently found to be the most significant predictive variable of tertiary success. A sub-set of this literature focusses on the impact of prior study of particular subjects. Over the last 40 years a large body of literature has developed within the accounting education domain which investigates whether the study of accounting in school confers an advantage for tertiary studies. This research has provided contradictory results and hence continues to be of interest to accounting education researchers.

7.3.1 Studies focussing on prior accounting education

Amongst the most frequently cited studies in the area are two unpublished PhD theses from the U.S.A.: Smith (1968) and Jacoby (1975). Smith (1968), albeit with a very small sample size, reported that high school exposure to bookkeeping had a positive influence on performance in college elementary accounting. In contrast, Jacoby (1975) concluded that there was no difference in performance in the first tertiary course between those who had taken school accounting and those who had not. He reported that school accounting gave the students an advantage in early assessments but that the advantage disappeared in later assessments in which those with no previous exposure to accounting produced better results. Baldwin & Howe (1982) and Bergin (1983) reported similar findings to Jacoby (1975) in their studies, also undertaken in the U.S.A. As an extension to the previous studies, Bergin (1983) looked at performance in both conceptual and computational elements of the assessments and reported the same findings for both elements. Mitchell (1985) conducted a similar study in Scotland, where he suggested that findings from the earlier studies carried out in the U.S.A. might not be applicable due to cultural variations in the educational environments and differences in the content, scope, and assessment of the courses. In contrast to Bergin (1983), he found that students who had school accounting qualifications outperformed those who had none in a computational examination, but that there was no difference in the end-of-course qualitative examination.

The studies discussed above all grouped students depending on whether they had taken an accounting course in school or not. Mitchell (1988) extended his earlier work by exploring whether the grade obtained in accounting at school impacted on the results achieved in the first-level university course. The study also examined a greater range of assessments. Consistent with his earlier findings, Mitchell reported that those with school accounting scored higher than those without it in the quantitative assessments throughout the year. However, there was no statistical difference in performance on the essay-based assessments or the final weighted grade. Unsurprisingly, he found that those with better school accounting grades achieved higher aggregate results, though there was no difference in some of the qualitative elements of the assessment.

The early studies from the U.S.A. also combined all students who studied accounting in school together, regardless of the length of course undertaken. Schroeder (1986) addressed this by grouping students based on whether they had no school accounting, one year or less, or more than one year. No differences were noted on performance between those who had not studied accounting previously and those who had studied it for one year or less. Those who had more than a year of school accounting achieved higher results than their peers in the first university course.

As already noted, findings from one educational environment may not be relevant in another, hence a number of subsequent studies were conducted in a range of countries and educational contexts. As well as replicating the early studies, many sought to investigate additional features of the courses undertaken. The first of these was a group of three studies conducted in New Zealand. Keef (1988) differentiated between different levels of accounting in school and found that the level of previous study in accounting had no effect on the final grade achieved in the first university course or on performance in any of the individual sections of *Financial Accounting*, *Management Accounting*, or *Financial Management*. In contrast, Keef & Hooper (1991) found that studying accounting at lower levels in school was of no benefit, but that the study of accounting at the highest level in school was beneficial. They attributed the contradiction between these two studies to differences between the university courses in each of the studies. In the third New Zealand study, Keef (1992) sought to investigate whether Schroeder's (1986) findings regarding the number of years of prior study applied in a different educational setting. His findings (that the study of accounting for either one year or two consecutive years in school did not provide any advantage over the absence of such study) were in contrast to those of Schroeder (1986). This supports the contention that findings in this arena may be context specific and not generalizable to other educational settings.

Lynn, Shehata, & White (1994) reported that performance in the first-level *Financial Accounting* course in a Canadian university was highly correlated with prior study of the subject, and those who studied accounting for three years performed significantly better than those who studied it for one or two years. In an Australian study, Rohde & Kavanagh (1996) found that the first year tertiary accounting result was between one and two grades higher for those students who had studied accounting in school compared to those who had not. They also concluded that the advantage of prior study of accounting was greater for students of lower academic ability.

Lee (1999) noted that the studies at that time had all been conducted in Western countries and she sought to extend the research to a non-Western cultural and educational system. She observed that '*most researchers attributed the variance across studies to disparities in the education systems and methodologies used*' (ibid., p. 302). She considered that the results achieved by students in their prior accounting courses could also account for some of the variability in the findings. However, her findings showed that, while the level of study of accounting undertaken in school was a significant variable in explaining performance in the first level tertiary accounting course, the grade achieved or the duration of the course was not. This contrasts with the findings of Mitchell (1988), the only other study which considered results.

Xiang & Gruber (2012) noted that much of the literature in this area is dated and hence re-examined the issue recently in the U.S.A. They found a positive relationship between taking an accounting course in school and overall performance in the first tertiary course. However, in common with the early studies of Baldwin & Howe (1982) and Bergin (1983), they found that the influence of prior study declined as students progressed through this first course.

7.3.2 Multivariate studies

While a number of the studies discussed above also explored the impact of other variables, their main focus was on the relationship between school accounting and performance at tertiary level. There is a parallel literature which seeks to predict tertiary performance in accounting utilising multivariate models. This literature is considered by Koh in Chapter 20 – this volume. However, as one of the common variables included in that research is the study of accounting in school, some of the studies are mentioned briefly here. In common with the studies focussing on school accounting, the findings from this literature are inconsistent. Eskew & Faley (1988) and Doran, Bouillon, & Smith (1991), in two studies from the U.S.A., found the prior study of accounting to be a predictor of performance in first year tertiary accounting courses. Gul & Fong (1993), Tho (1994), and Naser & Peel (1998) report similar findings for Hong Kong, Malaysia, and the Occupied West Bank respectively. Three more recent studies in Australia and New Zealand, Rankin *et al.* (2003), Tickell & Smyrnios (2005), and Tan & Laswad (2008), also found that whether a student had taken accounting in school or not was a significant variable in their prediction models.

In contrast, other studies report that the study of accounting in school is not a significant variable in explaining tertiary performance. Included among these studies are those by Bartlett, Peel, & Pendlebury (1993), Gammie, Jones, & Robertson-Millar (2003), Gracia & Jenkins (2003), and Guney (2009), all of which were conducted in the U.K. Koh & Koh (1999) also reported that prior accounting knowledge was not an explanatory variable when examining the first year performance of students undertaking an accounting degree in Singapore. However, it was a significant variable in the regression models exploring performance in second and third years, with those who had not studied accounting in school outperforming those who had. Doran *et al.* (1991) also reported a negative relationship between school accounting and performance in the second tertiary accounting course.

In addition to the contrasting results between different studies, inconsistencies have also been reported within studies. Byrne & Flood (2008) found prior accounting knowledge to be positively associated with students' overall performance in the first year of an accounting degree programme at an Irish university, but found no relationship between prior accounting knowledge and performance in either the *Financial Accounting* or *Management Accounting* modules. Kalbers & Weinstein (1999) conducted their study with three different samples of students attending a university in the U.S.A. While the study of accounting in school was a significant variable explaining performance for one sample, it was not for the other two. They conclude that:

> [the] inconsistent pattern of the influence of high school accounting in this and other studies suggests that something about high school accounting may influence results, but that the nature of it has not been sufficiently captured in measures to date.

> (Kalbers & Weinstein, 1999: 13)

7.3.3 Alternative focussed studies

A range of studies with other motivations also explored the impact of school accounting on tertiary performance. The first four of these were conducted in Australia and the latter in New Zealand. Loveday (1993) sought to investigate the appropriateness of a policy that offered students who had achieved an A grade in their state external accounting examinations an optional exemption from the first semester of their tertiary accounting studies at an Australian university. No statistical difference was found in the performance of the exempt and non-exempt students in the second semester accounting module. Hence, she concluded that the first semester module was redundant for those who had achieved high grades in school accounting and suggested that students who intend to study accounting at tertiary level should not study it in school, as the material is taught again in university. Alternatively, she suggested that achieving an A grade in school accounting could be a condition of entry to an accounting degree, thereby reducing the material which needs to be taught in university.

Auyeung & Sands (1994) sought to predict tertiary first year accounting performance using a gender-based learning analysis at an Australian university. They found the prior study of accounting to be a strong predictor of performance of male students. They also classified components of their assessment as evaluating either deep or surface learning. The prior study of accounting was a significant predictor of overall performance in surface elements of the assessment, but there was no relationship between the study of the subject in school and deep elements of the assessment.

Two other studies focussed on the different backgrounds of students. The effect of different entry paths on performance in a second year *Management Accounting* module at an Australian university was explored by Jackling & Anderson (1998) who found the study of accounting in school to have no significant effect on performance. In a study which investigated the relationship between students' origin and performance, Hartnett, Romcke, & Yap (2004) found school accounting to be significant in explaining first year performance at another Australian university, but to have no significance in later years.

Finally, in a report from New Zealand on whether particular subjects are associated with better performance in university, Engler (2010) reported that how well students performed was more closely related to their overall school results than to the specific subjects studied. However, there were some school subjects which were found to have a link to university performance. For students on tertiary accounting programmes, those who had studied accounting in school outperformed those who had not and it was '*the strongest association for any school subject/university course combination*' (ibid., p. 26).

7.3.4 Impact of prior study on later years

It is not surprising that many of the studies cited above, particularly the initial ones, confined their focus to the influence that the study of accounting in school has on the first tertiary course in accounting, as this is where the greatest impact might be expected. Nevertheless, it is also important to investigate whether the effect extends beyond the initial tertiary course. A number of the studies discussed above explored performance in the later years, but again the findings are inconsistent. Lee (1999) found no relationship between the prior study of accounting and performance in the second accounting course, which was predominately Management Accounting. Bartlett *et al.* (1993), Gammie *et al.* (2003), and Gracia & Jenkins (2003) reported that the study of accounting in school did not have an impact on final year results. In contrast, Tickell & Smyrnios (2005) found that it did have an enduring effect, while Doran *et al.* (1991), Van Rensburg, Penn, & Haiden (1998) and Koh & Koh (1999) reported that those who did not study accounting in school outperformed those who did in later courses.

Many reasons have been put forward for the inconsistent results from this body of research. A number of researchers, including Mitchell (1988) and Tickell & Smyrnios (2005), suggest that the different educational contexts in which the studies have been conducted may offer an explanation. Another reason for the conflict in results may be that insufficient attention was paid to the content of the courses in the prior studies, and to the overlap between the school course undertaken and the tertiary curriculum. Keef & Hooper (1991, p. 88) concluded that '*the benefit of prior study was primarily a function of the type of material covered in the school and university courses rather than just a function of exposure to the material*'. While it is probable that context and course overlap differences are responsible for the inconsistent findings, this cannot be concluded categorically. Insufficient detail is provided in the studies to enable comparison of the contexts in which they were conducted. Similarly, little information is provided regarding the content of the courses included in the studies, particularly the school courses. As outlined earlier, there is a dearth of research on school curricula, which adds to the difficulty in reaching firm conclusions in this area.

Baldwin & Howe (1982) and Koh & Koh (1999) are among those who posit that differences in the design of the studies explain the inconsistent results. Eskew & Faley (1988) noted that previous studies neglected to control for the influence of many of the other factors which are known to be related to academic performance. The failure to discriminate with regard to the duration of prior study or the level of achievement attained by students in the school accounting assessments offers a further explanation for the conflicting results. Many studies simply looked at the difference between those who had studied accounting in school and those who had not. Results from studies which grouped students based on the duration of their prior study, such as Schroeder (1986) and Lynn *et al.* (1994), suggest that course length has an impact. Somewhat surprisingly, few researchers grouped students based on results achieved in school even though Mitchell (1988) and Tickell & Smyrnios (2005) found that the grade achieved in school accounting was a significant factor in explaining tertiary performance.

Despite the inconsistencies in the findings from the prior research, the evidence indicates that, in many instances, the study of accounting in school influences performance in tertiary courses. The impact is likely to depend on the type of course undertaken, the degree of overlap in the content covered, the number and duration of courses undertaken, and the results achieved. The effect is likely to lessen as students progress through their tertiary studies with the experiences of the early tertiary courses superseding those of school.

7.4 Prior accounting work experience and academic performance

A small number of empirical studies have investigated the relationship between prior work experience in accounting and performance in order to acquire a better understanding of the drivers of academic achievement. This research typically found evidence that previous employment in accounting had a positive effect on students' performance. However, most of this research was conducted with students in the later years of their undergraduate degree, or with incoming postgraduate students, and in many instances it is not clear if the students' work experience had occurred prior to their tertiary studies or concurrently (e.g. Burdick & Schwartz, 1982; Moses, 1987; Krausz *et al.*, 1999; Ballantine & McCourt Larres, 2004; Guney, 2009). In contrast with the general findings, Ballantine & McCourt Larres (2004) reported no significant differences in the perceived benefits of using case studies in an *Advanced Management Accounting* module between students in Northern Ireland with relevant work experience and those without.

There are only a few studies which have investigated the influence of prior work experience on students' first year performance. Naser & Peel (1998) focussed on the performance of first year students, at a university situated in the Occupied West Bank. They identified prior study or work experience in accounting as having a positive impact on students' results in their accounting module. However, as this was measured as a single variable, it is not possible to conclude whether the impact was caused by the prior study, the prior work experience, or both. Koh & Koh (1999) showed that students, studying in Singapore, with previous accounting work experience performed significantly better in the first year of their accounting programme than those without work experience. Finally, in an Australian study, which compared the accounting performance of resident and international students, Hartnett *et al.* (2004) found a positive association between prior work experience and first year performance in accounting.

In its focus on *prior* accounting education and work experience, the coverage of Chapter 7 is complementary to that of Beard & Humphrey (Chapter 25 – this volume), which concentrates on work experience *within* a degree programme.

7.5 Prior accounting education and accounting work experience and students' discipline/career choice

Studies on occupational choices have identified a multitude of factors that influence students' decisions to major in or pursue a career in accounting and this research is the primary focus of Laswad & Tan in Chapter 9, and Jackling in Chapter 10 – both in this volume. Included in this list of factors are the study of accounting in school and prior work experience in accounting, and the findings relating to these factors are considered in this chapter.

Empirical evidence regarding the influence of school accounting on students' discipline/career choice is mixed. Felton, Buhr, & Northey (1994), in a Canadian study, and Chen, Jones, & McIntyre (2005), in a study from the U.S.A., found that students who selected a career in accounting were more likely to have studied accounting in school than were students selecting other business careers. Likewise, Malthus & Fowler (2009) claimed that, if New Zealand students decide not to study accounting in school, then it is highly unlikely that they will pursue a career in accounting. In contrast, additional research carried out in New Zealand (Ahmed *et al.*, 1997), and Hong Kong (Law & Yuen, 2012), found that exposure to accounting in school had no significant impact on students' decisions to major in or pursue a career in accounting. Interestingly, Jones & Wright (2011), in their Canadian study, reported that, while the study of accounting in school was positively associated with students' initial decision to major in accounting, it did not affect their eventual choice of discipline.

Research exploring the influence of prior work experience on students' occupational choices has generally found that previous employment is not a determinant of students' career choices. In an Australian study, Gul, Andrew, Leong, & Ismail (1989) examined whether prior work experience was an important career choice factor for first year students interested in studying either accounting, law, medicine, or engineering. Their analysis revealed that previous work experience did not have a significant influence on students' choice of discipline. Using a similar approach, Lowe & Simons (1997), in a study from the U.S.A., reported that students' decision to major in accounting was not influenced by prior work experience. Likewise, in a study with South African students, Myburgh (2005) found that previous work experience did not influence students' decisions to pursue a career in accounting, although the students' performance in their school accounting course had a positive influence on their decision to become an accountant. However, a serious limitation of all of the foregoing studies is the fact that none of them actually determined if any of their sample had prior work experience, and so it is impossible to draw any firm conclusions on the influence of this factor on students' discipline/career choices.

7.6 Prior accounting education and accounting work experience and perceptions of accounting

Research into students' perceptions of accounting has been widespread and is considered in detail by Lucas & Mladenovic in Chapter 6 – this volume. However, falling within the scope of this chapter is the extent to which prior accounting education and work experience influence students' perceptions of accounting.

Byrne & Willis (2005) in Ireland, Jackling & Calero (2006) in Australia, and Malthus & Fowler (2009) in New Zealand found that students who studied accounting in school had a better understanding of what accountants did and a more positive image of the profession than students with no prior accounting education. Furthermore, Irish school pupils believed that society holds the accounting profession in high esteem (albeit lower than five other professional groups), and this belief was strongest amongst those pupils studying accounting in school (Byrne & Willis, 2005). Conversely, Wessels & Steenkamp (2009), in a South African study, found very little difference in the perceptions of students who had been exposed to accounting in school and those who had not. Interestingly, Wells, Kearins, & Hooper (2008) reported that, while accounting pupils in schools in New Zealand had a better understanding of accounting, they had a more negative perception of it than non-accounting school pupils. In a criticism of the school accounting curriculum in the U.S.A., Albrecht & Sack (2000) suggest that misconceptions about the activities and roles of accountants are caused, in part, by an emphasis on bookkeeping in the school curriculum.

7.7 Future research

While the above research strands are important in providing accounting educators with an enhanced understanding of their students, there is still plenty of scope for further research into these areas. In the case of prior accounting education, the research undertaken to date has tended to focus mainly on whether the experience of studying accounting in school had an impact on other factors (such as subsequent examination performance, perceptions of accounting, and career choices). However, contemporary learning theories have highlighted the importance of gaining a deeper insight into students' prior knowledge. Thus, if educators are to facilitate their students' learning, they must first acquire an understanding of the quality of their students' prior knowledge. This is particularly important in a subject area such as accounting, where the material is sequential, with each higher-level course building upon the successful completion of the preceding course (Beavers, 1975). Unfortunately, this is an area of research that has received very little attention from accounting educators.

The initial step in evaluating the quality of students' prior knowledge is to decide on what type of knowledge should be assessed. In this regard, research in educational psychology (see e.g. Hailikari et al., 2007) offers some very useful guidance to accounting academics. This research shows that there are different components or dimensions of prior knowledge (Rankin et al., 2003). Consequently, care must be taken in identifying the most appropriate method for assessing prior knowledge as different methods measure different forms and, as a result, produce different types of information about students' prior knowledge (Dochy et al., 1999; Hailikari et al., 2007). In the light of this, Valencia, Stallman, Commeyras, Pearson, & Hartman (1991) suggest that multiple forms of assessment should be used in order to fully capture the extent of a student's prior knowledge. Furthermore, decisions must be made about whether prior knowledge should be assessed at a general level or at a detailed level. In this respect, research into prior knowledge supports the view that a more detailed assessment of prior knowledge provides more useful information for identifying the areas which need attention and instructional support, and therefore it is of more practical value to the educator and the student (Portier & Wagemans, 1995; Dochy, 1996).

Once accounting educators have properly evaluated their students' prior knowledge, they will be better positioned to develop teaching interventions which help support and develop their students' learning (Ausubel et al., 1978; Glaser, 1976). In particular, such interventions should address any misconceptions of key concepts, since inaccurate subject-specific prior knowledge can have a negative effect on learning, and seriously impair students' understanding (Lipson, 1983; Thompson & Zamboanga, 2003).

This chapter also highlights the need for future studies to provide a more detailed account of the educational context in which their research is situated. As noted earlier, very few studies describe the school accounting curriculum experienced by students, thereby making it very difficult to interpret or compare the findings from different countries. Additionally, research which evaluates the accounting education experienced by school pupils is warranted. Given the influence of the first course in accounting on students' perceptions of accounting and career choices, it is important that both tertiary accounting educators and the accounting profession develop a better appreciation of the accounting courses on offer in schools. The profession should consider taking a more active role in influencing school curricula, ensuring that these reflect an up-to-date portrayal of the work being undertaken by accountants and do not focus on bookkeeping to the exclusion of other areas of interest.

The body of work exploring the influence of prior accounting education and work experience on performance has concentrated on students' achievements in higher education accounting courses. No studies were uncovered which investigated these variables in the context of the performance of school leavers in professional accounting examinations, despite the fact that many of the professional accounting bodies (e.g. Association of Chartered Certified Accountants, Institute of Chartered Accountants in England & Wales, Chartered Institute of Management Accountants, Japanese Institute of Certified Public Accountants) provide a direct entry route into the profession for school leavers. (See Calhoun & Karreman, Chapter 26 – this volume, for other international comparisons.) This lack of research provides an opportunity for researchers interested in identifying the determinants of success in professional examinations. Furthermore, no research was identified which explored the impact of prior accounting education and/or work experience on school pupils' ability to perform the work of a trainee accountant. Again, this provides scope for future research projects.

In reviewing the research which has been conducted with tertiary students on the influence of prior work experience in accounting, it is evident that this is an area which has received limited considered attention. Indeed, as pointed out earlier, though some studies included prior work experience in their analysis, all failed to establish whether any of their samples had, in fact, experienced relevant work, hence their findings could not be relied upon in evaluating the relevance of this factor. In future studies it is critical that researchers first determine if their students have had the opportunity to gain prior work experience in accounting. Only then will it be possible to assess the influence of this experience on factors such as:

- students' motivation to study accounting;
- their performance in their first course in accounting;
- their perceptions of accounting; and
- the extent to which this experience provides them with a sound understanding of the fundamental concepts of accounting.

7.8 Conclusion

The constructivist's view of learning highlights the critical influence of prior knowledge on students' subsequent learning achievements. Accordingly, this chapter discusses studies which have focussed on prior accounting education and prior work experience. Most of this research has explored the influence of prior accounting education on students' performance in tertiary accounting courses. While the findings from this line of enquiry have been mixed, nevertheless there is considerable evidence which suggests that the influence is likely to depend on the type of course undertaken, the degree of overlap between the school and tertiary accounting curricula, and the number and duration of the school accounting courses studied. Researchers have also reported a positive association between prior work experience and students' achievements in higher education accounting courses. Prior accounting education has also been identified as a significant factor which impacts on students' discipline/career choices and their perceptions of accounting. All this evidence suggests that prior accounting education and prior work experience are important factors which should not be ignored by either accounting educators or the accounting profession. Indeed, further research is needed to gain a more thorough understanding of the influence of these factors from both the perspectives of tertiary accounting education and the accounting profession. Crucially, failure to acquire this insight may well result in students learning something opposed to the educator's intentions – no matter how well those intentions are executed (Roschelle, 1995).

Notes

1   The term 'school' is used in this chapter to capture the period of full-time secondary education typically completed by pupils between the ages of 12 and 18.
2   Prior accounting education and work experience are interpreted as being that which takes place in advance of students' enrolment on tertiary education programmes.
3   Tertiary education is synonymous with higher education, and is that which occurs after school at either college or university.
4   In Ireland, in their final two years of school education, pupils complete a two-year programme referred to as the Leaving Certificate programme. At the end of this, the majority of pupils will sit state public examinations in seven subjects, which may include accounting.
5   The public examinations taken for university entry by pupils at secondary schools in England, Northern Ireland, and Wales (but not in Scotland) are known as A-levels (where A = advanced).

References

Accounting Education Change Commission (1992) The first course in accounting: position statement no. 2, *Issues in Accounting Education*, 7(2), 249–251.

Agnew, S. (2010) Accounting for the NCEA: has the transition to standards-based assessment achieved its objectives? *Australasian Accounting Business and Finance Journal*, 4(4), 87–102.

Ahmed, K., Alam, K., & Alam, M. (1997) An empirical study of factors affecting accounting students' career choice in New Zealand, *Accounting Education: an international journal*, 6(4), 325–335.

Albrecht, W.S. & Sack, R.J. (2000) *Accounting Education: Charting the Course through a Perilous Future* (Accounting Education Series, Vol. 16), Sarasota, FL: American Accounting Association.

Ausubel, D. (1968) *Educational Psychology: A Cognitive View*, New York: Holt, Rinehart & Winston.

Ausubel, D., Novak, J., & Hanesian, H. (1978) *Educational Psychology: A Cognitive View*, New York: Holt, Rinehart & Winston.

Auyeung, P.K. & Sands, D.F. (1994) Predicting success in first-year university accounting using gender-based learning analysis, *Accounting Education: an international journal*, 3(3), 259–272.

Baldwin, B.A. & Howe, K.R. (1982) Secondary-level study of accounting and subsequent performance in the first college course, *The Accounting Review*, 57(3), 619–626.

Ballantine, J. & McCourt Larres, P. (2004) A critical analysis of students' perceptions of the usefulness of the case study method in an advanced management accounting module: the impact of relevant work experience, *Accounting Education: an international journal*, 13(2), 171–189.

Bartlett, S., Peel, M.J., & Pendlebury, M. (1993) From fresher to finalist, *Accounting Education: an international journal*, 2(2), 111–122.

Beavers, L. (1975) Elementary accounting achievement of junior college transfer students in Oklahoma, *Delta Pi Epsilon Journal*, 17(4), 38–47.

Bergin, J.L. (1983) The effect of previous accounting study on student performance in the first college-level financial accounting course, *Issues in Accounting Education*, 1(1), 19–28.

Biggs, J. (1987) *Student Approaches to Learning and Studying*, Hawthorne: Victoria: Australian Council for Education Research.

Burdick, R. & Schwartz, B. (1982) Predicting grade performance for intermediate accounting, *Delta Pi Epsilon Journal*, 24(3), 117–127.

Byrne, M. & Flood, B. (2008) Examining the relationships among background variables and academic performance of first year accounting students at an Irish university, *Journal of Accounting Education*, 26(4), 202–212.

Byrne, M. & Willis, P. (1997) An analysis of accounting at second level, *Irish Accounting Review*, 4(1), 1–26.

Byrne, M. & Willis, P. (2001) The revised second level accounting syllabus: a new beginning or old habits retained?, *Irish Accounting Review*, 8(2), 1–22.

Byrne, M. & Willis, P. (2003) Second level accounting: the view from the blackboard, *Irish Accounting Review*, 10(2), 1–12.

Byrne, M. & Willis, P. (2004) Leaving certificate accounting: measuring students' perceptions with the course experience questionnaire, *Irish Educational Studies*, 23(1), 49–64.

Byrne, M. & Willis, P. (2005) Irish secondary school students' perceptions of the work of an accountant and the accounting profession, *Accounting Education: an international journal*, 14(4), 367–381.

Byrne, M. & Willis, P. (2008) An exploration of tertiary accounting students' prior approaches to learning accounting, *International Journal of Management Education*, 7(3), 35–46.

Chen, C., Jones, K., & McIntyre, D. (2005) A re examination of the factors important to selection of accounting as a major, *Accounting and Public Interest*, 5, 14–31.

Clarke, P. & Hession, A. (2004) An examination of the leaving certificate accounting syllabus, *Irish Journal of Management*, 25(2), 139–154.

Cohen, J. & Hanno, D. (1993) An analysis of the underlying constructs affecting the choice of accounting as a major, *Issues in Accounting Education*, 8(2), 219–238.

Dochy, F. (1994) Prior knowledge and learning, in Husen, T. & Postlethwaite, N. (eds) *International Encyclopedia of Education*, 2nd edn, London: Pergamon.

Dochy, F. (1996) Assessment of domain-specific and domain-transcending prior knowledge: enter assessment and the use of profile analysis, in Birenbaum, M. & Dochy, F. (eds) *Alternatives in Assessment of Achievements, Learning Processes and Prior Knowledge*, Boston: Kluwer.

Dochy, F., De Ridjt, C., & Dyck, W. (2002) Cognitive prerequisites and learning. How far have we progressed since Bloom? Implications for educational practice and teaching, *Active Learning in Higher Education*, 3(3), 265–284.

Dochy, F., Moerkerke, G., & Martens, R. (1996) Integrating assessment, learning and instruction: assessment of domain-specific and domain-transcending prior knowledge and progress, *Studies in Educational Evaluation*, 22(4), 309–339.

Dochy, F., Segers, M., & Buehl, M. (1999) The relation between assessment practices and outcomes of studies: the case of research on prior knowledge, *Review of Educational Research*, 69(2), 145–186.

Doran, B., Bouillon, M., & Smith, C. (1991) Determinants of student performance in accounting principles I and II, *Issues in Accounting Education*, 6(1), 74–84.

Engler, R. (2010) *Are Particular School Subjects Associated with Better Performance at University?*, Wellington: Ministry of Education.

Eskew, R. & Faley, R. (1988) Some determinants of student performance in the first college-level financial accounting course, *Accounting Review*, 63(1), 137–147.

Fee, H., Greenan, K., & Wall, A. (2009) An investigation into secondary school exit standards: implications for university lecturers, *International Journal of Management Education*, 8(2), 43–52.

Felton, S., Buhr, N., & Northey, M. (1994) Factors influencing the business students' choice of a career in chartered accountancy, *Issues in Accounting Education*, 9(1), 131–141.

Gammie, E., Jones, P., & Robertson-Millar, C. (2003) Accountancy undergraduate performance: a statistical model, *Accounting Education: an international journal*, 12(1), 63–78.

Geiger, M. & Ogilby, S. (2000) The first course in accounting: students' perceptions and their decision to major in accounting, *Journal of Accounting Education*, 18(2), 63–78.

Ginsburg, H. & Opper, S. (1979) *Piaget's Theory of Intellectual Development*, Englewood Cliffs, NJ: Prentice-Hall.

Glaser, R. (1976) Components of a psychology of instruction: toward a science of design, *Review of Educational Research*, 46(1), 1–24.

Gracia, L. & Jenkins, E. (2003) A quantitative exploration of student performance on an undergraduate accounting programme of study, *Accounting Education: an international journal*, 12(1), 15–32.

Gul, F.A., Andrew, B., Leong, S., & Ismail, Z. (1989) Factors influencing choice of discipline of study – accountancy, engineering, law and medicine, *Accounting and Finance*, 29(2), 98–101.

Gul, F.A. & Fong, S. (1993) Predicting success for introductory accounting students: some further Hong Kong evidence, *Accounting Education: an international journal*, 2(1), 33–42.

Guney, Y. (2009) Exogenous and endogenous factors influencing students' performance in undergraduate accounting modules, *Accounting Education: an international journal*, 18(1), 51–73.

Hailikari, T., Katajavuori, N., & Lindblom-Ylanne, S. (2008) The relevance of prior knowledge in learning and instructional design, *American Journal of Pharmaceutical Education*, 72(5), 113–122.

Hailikari, T., Nevgi, A., & Lindblom-Ylanne, S. (2007) Exploring alternative ways of assessing prior knowledge, its components and their relation to student achievement: a mathematics-based case study, *Studies in Educational Evaluation*, 33(3–4), 320–327.

Hartnett, N., Romcke, J., & Yap, C. (2004) Student performance in tertiary-level accounting: an international student focus, *Accounting and Finance*, 44(2), 163–185.

Hegarty-Hazel, E. & Prosser, M. (1991a) Relationship between students' conceptual knowledge and study strategies – part 1: student learning in physics, *International Journal of Science Education*, 13(3), 303–312.

Hegarty-Hazel, E. & Prosser, M. (1991b) Relationship between students' conceptual knowledge and study strategies – part 2: student learning in biology, *International Journal of Science Education*, 13(4), 421–429.

Hunt, S., Falgiani, A., & Intrieri, R. (2004) The nature and origins of students' perceptions of accountants, *Journal of Education for Business*, 79(3), 142–148.

Jackling, B. & Anderson, A. (1998) Study mode, general ability and performance in accounting: a research note, *Accounting Education: an international journal*, 7(1), 65–78.

Jackling, B. & Calero, C. (2006) Influences on undergraduate students' intentions to become qualified accountants: evidence from Australia, *Accounting Education: an international journal*, 15(4), 419–438.

Jacoby, C.R. (1975) The effects of teaching methods and experiences in achievement of business studies in the first college level accounting course, unpublished doctoral dissertation, Pennsylvania State University.

Jones, S. & Wright, M. (2011) Effect of cognitive style on performance in introductory financial accounting and the decision to major in accounting, *Global Perspectives on Accounting Education*, 8, 7–26.

Kalbers, L.P. & Weinstein, G.P. (1999) Student performance in introductory accounting: a multi-sample, multi-model analysis, *Accounting Educators Journal*, XI, 1–28.

Keef, S.P. (1988) Preparation for a first level university accounting course: the experience in New Zealand, *Journal of Accounting Education*, 6(2), 293–307.

Keef, S.P. (1992) The effects of prior accounting education: some evidence from New Zealand, *Accounting Education: an international journal*, 1(1), 63–68.

Keef, S.P. & Hooper, K.C. (1991) Prior accounting education and the performance in a first level university course in New Zealand, *Accounting and Finance*, 31(1), 85–91.

Koh, M. & Koh, H. (1999) The determinants of performance in an accountancy degree programme, *Accounting Education: an international journal*, 8(1), 13–29.

Krausz, J., Schiff, A., Schiff, J., & VanHise, J. (1999) The effects of prior accounting work experience and education on performance in the initial graduate-level accounting course, *Issues in Accounting Education*, 14(1), 1–9.

Law, P. & Yuen, D. (2012) A multilevel study of students' motivations of studying accounting: implications for employers, *Education and Training*, 54(1), 50–64.

Lee, D.S-Y. (1999) Strength of high school accounting qualification and student performance in university-level introductory accounting courses in Hong Kong, *Journal of Education for Business*, 74(5), 301–306.

Lipson, M. (1983) The influence of religious affiliation on children's memory for text information, *Reading Research Quarterly*, 18(4), 448–457.

Loveday, P.M. (1993) Exemptions from first semester accounting and performance in the second semester course: an empirical study, *Accounting Education: an international journal*, 2(2), 143–150.

Lowe, D. & Simons, K. (1997) Factors influencing choice of business major – some additional evidence: a research note, *Accounting Education: an international Journal*, 6(1), 39–45.

Lynn, B., Shehata, M., & White, L. (1994) The effects of secondary school accounting education on university accounting performance: a Canadian experience, *Contemporary Accounting Research*, 10(2), 737–758.

Malthus, S. & Fowler, C. (2009) Perceptions of accounting: a qualitative New Zealand study, *Pacific Accounting Review*, 21(1), 26–47.

McPhail, K., Paisey, C., & Paisey, N. (2010) Class, social deprivation and accounting education in Scottish schools: implications for the reproduction of the accounting profession and practice, *Critical Perspectives on Accounting*, 21(1), 31–50.

Mitchell, F. (1985) School accounting qualifications and student performance in first level university accounting examinations, *Accounting and Business Research*, 15(58), 81–86.

Mitchell, F. (1988) High school accounting and student performance in the first level university accounting course: a UK study, *Journal of Accounting Education*, 6(2), 279–291.

Moses, D. (1987) Factors explaining performance in graduate level accounting, *Issues in Accounting Education*, 2(2), 281–291.

Myburgh, J.E. (2005) An empirical analysis of career choice factors that influence first-year accounting students at the University of Pretoria: a cross-racial study, *Meditari Accountancy Research*, 13(2), 35–48.

Myhill, D. & Brackley, M. (2004) Making connections: teachers' use of children's prior knowledge in whole class discourse, *British Journal of Educational Studies*, 52(3), 263–275.

Naser, K. & Peel, M. (1998) An exploratory study of the impact of intervening variables on student performance in a principles of accounting course, *Accounting Education: an international journal*, 7(3), 209–223.

Nelson, I., Vendrzyk, V., Quirin, J., & Kovar, S. (2008) Trends in accounting student characteristics: results from a 15-year longitudinal study at FSA schools, *Issues in Accounting Education*, 23(3), 373–389.

Norton, C. (1977) The link between high school and college accounting, *Business Education Forum*, February, 23–24.

Portier, S. & Wagemans, J. (1995) The assessment of prior knowledge and its relevance to student achievement in introduction to psychology, *Teaching of Psychology*, 96(4), 778–784.

Ramsden, P. (1991) A performance indicator of teaching quality in higher education: the course experience questionnaire, *Studies in Higher Education*, 16(2), 129–150.

Ramsden, P. (2003) *Learning to Teach in Higher Education*, 2nd edn, London: Routledge.

Rankin, M., Silvester, M., Vallely, M., & Wyatt, A. (2003) An analysis of the implications of diversity for students' first level accounting performance, *Accounting and Finance*, 43(3), 365–393.

Rohde, F.H. & Kavanagh, M. (1996) Performance in first year university accounting: quantifying the advantage of secondary school accounting, *Accounting and Finance*, 36(2), 275–285.

Roschelle, J. (1995) Learning in interactive environments: prior knowledge and new experience, in Falk, J.H. & Dierking, L.D. (eds) *Public Institutions for Personal Learning: Establishing a Research Agenda*, Washington, DC: American Association of Museums.

Sangster, A. & McCombie, I. (1993) How well do accountancy students understand a set of accounts? *Accounting Educational: an international journal*, 2(1), 53–70.

Schroeder, N.W. (1985) The effects of pre-college accounting on the college accounting student, *Journal of Business Education*, 60(5), 207–211.

Schroeder, N.W. (1986) Previous accounting education and college level accounting exam performance, *Issues in Accounting Education*, 4(1), 37–47.

Shapiro, A. (2004) How including prior knowledge as a subject variable may change the outcomes of learning research, *American Educational Research Journal*, 41(1), 159–189.

Smith, J.W. (1968) Articulation of high school bookkeeping and college elementary accounting, unpublished doctoral dissertation, University of Oklahoma.

Tan, L. & Laswad, F. (2008) Impact of prior content and meta-cognitive knowledge on students' performance in the introductory accounting course, *Pacific Accounting Review*, 20(1), 63–74.

Tho, L. (1994) Some evidence on the determinants of student performance in the University of Malaya introductory accounting course, *Accounting Education: an international journal*, 3(4), 331–340.

Thompson, R. & Zamboanga, B. (2003) Prior knowledge and its relevance to student achievement in introduction to psychology, *Teaching of Psychology*, 30(2), 96–101.

Tickell, G. & Smyrnios, K. (2005) Predictors of tertiary accounting students' academic performance: a comparison of year 12 to university students with TAFE to university students, *Journal of Higher Education Policy and Management*, 27(2), 239–259.

Tobias, S. (1994) Interest, prior knowledge and learning, *Review of Educational Research*, 64(1), 37–54.

Valencia, S., Stallman, A., Commeyras, M., Pearson, P., & Hartman, D. (1991) Four measures of topical knowledge: a study of construct validity, *Reading Research Quarterly*, 26(3), 204–233.

Van Rensburg, P., Penn, G., & Haiden, M. (1998) A note on the effect of secondary school accounting study on university accounting performance, *South African Journal of Accounting Research*, 12(1), 93–98.

Wells, P., Kearins, K., & Hooper, K. (2008) High school student perceptions of accounting and accountants: a stereotypical analysis, paper presented at AFAANZ Conference, Sydney, Australia.

Wessels, P. & Steenkamp, L. (2009) An investigation into students' perceptions of accountants, *Meditari Accountancy Research*, 17(1), 117–132.

Xiang, M. & Gruber, R. (2012) Student performance in their first postsecondary accounting course: does high school accounting matter?, in Feldmann, D. & Rupert, T.J. (eds) *Advances in Accounting Education: Teaching and Curriculum Innovations*, Vol. 13, ebooks: Emerald Group Publishing Limited.

About the authors

Marann Byrne is an Associate Professor of Accounting at Dublin City University, Ireland, where she is Head of the Accounting Group (marann.byrne@dcu.ie). She has published in the areas of students' learning in higher education, the school accounting curriculum, perceptions of accounting, academic burnout and job satisfaction.

Pauline Willis is a lecturer and Director of the B.A. in Accounting and Finance at Dublin City University, Ireland (pauline.willis@dcu.ie). She has published in the area of students' prior experiences of accounting, accounting students' approaches to learning, students' perceptions of accounting, and academic burnout.

8

Learning styles and approaches in accounting education

Angus Duff

UNIVERSITY OF THE WEST OF SCOTLAND, U.K.

CONTENTS

Abstract

An interest in students' learning, alongside more pragmatic concerns such as the need to teach ever-increasing numbers of accounting students efficiently and effectively, has motivated a long-standing interest by accounting educators in learning styles and students' approaches to learning. This chapter provides an overview of the main models of learning applied by accounting education researchers, summarizes the extant empirical evidence, offers a critique to this body of work, and identifies fecund areas for future research.

Keywords

learning styles, students' approaches to learning

8.1 Introduction

The main aims of this chapter are:

- to provide an overview of learning styles and students' approaches to learning;
- to provide an overview of how different models of learning relate to each other;
- to produce evidence of how learning styles and approaches have been used by accounting educators; and
- to provide a critique of accounting educators' use of learning styles and approaches.

How can we teach students if we do not know how they learn?

(Coffield *et al.*, 2004, p. 1)

The learning styles (LS), students' approaches to learning (SAL), instructional preferences (IP), and trait theory literatures are highly developed and the product of vigorous efforts by researchers in the psychology of education. Much of this interest is motivated by the belief that, by understanding the different ways in which students learn, the efficacy of educators' efforts can be enhanced. The past three decades have seen rapid expansion in higher education on an international scale. However, this growth has not been accompanied by a corresponding increase in teaching resources, and educational policy has encouraged the notions of producing independent learners, making greater use of technology, and increased class sizes meaning less reliance on – or availability of – academic staff. Perhaps reflecting the pivotal role which accounting plays in the financial contribution to university budgets, accounting educators were enthusiastic adopters of research into learning, and have made a significant contribution to the higher education literature in their own right. This chapter reviews accounting education scholars' applied use of these ideas, and reveals a fascinating smorgasbord of research efforts in the field of LS and SAL. In particular, this chapter links to other chapters in this volume, notably: Needles, Chapter 2, with Bloom's (1956) seminal taxonomy; Lucas & Mladenovic, Chapter 6, addressing perceptions; Laswad & Tan, Chapter 9, considering choice of discipline; Jackling, Chapter 10, concerning career choices; the detailed coverage of experiential learning by Hassall & Joyce in Chapter 17; and, finally, the critical role which assessment plays, as described by Koh in Chapter 20 and by Kidwell & Lowensohn in Chapter 21.

In accounting, research considering individual differences in learning originated during the early 1980s, and is a vigorous area of research today. There have been three broad research questions posed by those investigating individual differences in accounting education:

- how to improve learning;
- how to identify variation in students' learning repertoires; and
- how to relate individual differences to a choice of career or academic discipline.

In seeking to describe the main learning styles and approaches that have been employed by accounting education researchers, this chapter aims to offer a comprehensive review of the literature as adopted by accounting educators. However, Coffield *et al.* (2004) provide a structured account of the use of learning styles and associated pedagogy in the wider field of educational research. In terms of structure, the chapter focusses on three levels (or layers) of research: (1) personality-related measures; (2) learning styles and approaches; and (3) learner preferences. Personality measures are widely used by occupational and industrial psychologists, particularly when the investigator wishes to gain a quick and reliable assessment of an individual's constellation of traits. Kolb's (1976) conceptualization of learning styles has been widely applied by management development professionals in industrial and commercial settings, while the SAL paradigm has become ingrained in higher educational development programmes – especially for those new to lecturing in universities.

8.2 Learning styles and approaches to learning

To organize the baffling array of educational work available in the area, Curry's (1987) onion model is employed. The 'onion' model is a three-layered classification which provides some insight into how competing conceptions of individual difference and associated measurement instruments fit together. These three levels are:

1   cognitive personality elements;
2   information processing style; and
3   instructional preferences.

The three levels are organized into levels or 'onion' layers. Curry's (1987) onion metaphor organizes individual difference models based on the stability of the models, as measured by the test–retest reliability of scores produced by their measurement instruments. For the purposes of this chapter, rather than make extensive reference to psychometric evidence regarding specific inventories, I refer to the theoretic stability of the constructs under review. That is, at the two polar extremes, is a person's behaviour likely to be stable over time (i.e., a stable trait) or is it likely to be highly variable given the context, environment, and demands of the learning environment (i.e., a transient state)? Essentially, the onion model is a means of presenting a continuum of learning approaches/styles/strategies, many of which overlap considerably. A style is seen here as being trait-like and possessing a relatively enduring quality, while an approach is seen as being something malleable, contextual, and open to change.

Curry's organization (see Figure 8.1) suggests that learning is controlled by core personality dimensions. These then are formed using middle layer information processing dimensions. Learning is then influenced by contextual matters encountered in the outer strata. The inner onion layer is the most stable and reflects a trait. A personality trait can be thought of as '*a way in which an individual differs from another*' (Cohen *et al.*, 1996, p. 385). The outer layer, by contrast, conveys a personality state or '*the transitory exhibition of some personality trait*' (ibid., p. 386).

The inner core of the onion taxonomy is labelled 'cognitive personality elements'. These elements are viewed as an individual's approach to organizing information, which relates to an underlying personality trait, which is expressed indirectly and is only observable across many learning situations (Riding & Cheema, 1991). Examples of instruments which are said to assess this type of individual differences include the Myers-Briggs Type Indicator (MBTI) (Myers & Briggs, 1976) and the Neuroticism, Extraversion, Openness personality inventory (revised (NEO)) (Costa & McCrae, 1992).

The second, middle layer of the onion metaphor is 'information processing style'. This layer describes how an individual assimilates information. As this assimilation does not directly involve the environment, 'information processing style' measures are considered to be more stable than 'instructional preferences' (Riding & Cheema, 1991). However, measures of this style are still believed to be modifiable by learning strategies. Measures categorized in this middle layer of the onion taxonomy include Kolb's (1976) Learning Style Inventory (LSI) and Honey & Mumford's ([1992] 1986) Learning Style Questionnaire (LSQ). Both these measures deal with information processing styles that reflect personality differences and contextual learner preferences.

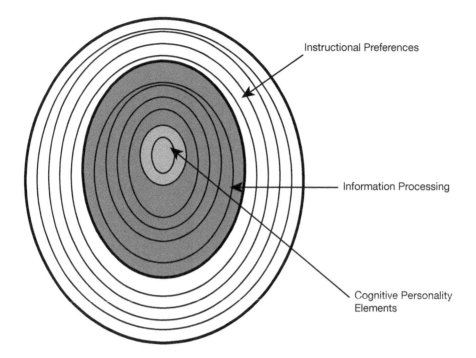

Figure 8.1 The onion taxonomy
Source: Adapted from Curry (1987).

The outer layer of the onion (and the most observable element) represents 'instructional prefer-ence'. This describes an individual's preferred learning environment. The 'instructional preference' is the most malleable element of the onion taxonomy. This reflects the fact that this layer is closest to the environment and expectations of learner and teacher (Riding & Cheema, 1991).

Finally, between the 'information processing' and 'instructional preference' layers, lies the burgeoning SAL literature and the proliferation of contextual measures of learning in tertiary education.

8.2.1 Cognitive personality elements

As noted above, the first and innermost layer of Curry's onion taxonomy relates to 'cognitive personality elements'. Such a notion of style is said to be 'an underlying and relatively permanent personality dimension' (Riding, 1997, p. 42). Cognitive personality elements are apparent when behaviour can be frequently observed (Riding & Cheema, 1991) and directs much learning behaviour (Curry, 1987). Although there is no one definition of personality, it can be viewed as '*an individual's constellation of psychological traits*' (Cohen *et al.*, 1996, p. 383). Measures I consider to be within this category include the MBTI (Myers & Briggs, 1976), the NEO (Costa & McCrae, 1992), and related instruments.

8.2.1.1 Myers-Briggs Type Indicator (Myers-Briggs, 1976)

The MBTI was inspired by the typology of Carl Jung ([1921] 1971) and has been widely applied to topics such as a selection of college major to marriage guidance counselling (Cohen *et al.*, 1996). As indicated in Figure 8.2, the MBTI assesses four bipolar dimensions of personality:

- introversion–extroversion;
- perceiving–judging;
- sensing–intuition; and
- thinking–feeling.

Essentially each of these four bipolar dimensions describes four fundamental human foci: energy; perception; making choices; and action. According to Jung, individuals may be categorized at the two extremes of each of these four bipolar dimensions. This creates $2^4 = 16$ categories of personality. Each is given a four-letter label (e.g. INFJ or ESTP) – see Figure 8.3. (See also Section 9.3.2 in Laswad & Tan, Chapter 9 – this volume.)

Focus	MBTI dichotomy	
Energy	**Introversion (I)** energy directed by an inner world of thoughts, ideas, and interests	**Extraversion (E)** energy directed by an external world of activity, people, and events
Perception	**Sensing (P)** thinking is routed in the present and the past	**Intuition (N)** thought is focused on developing an overall 'big' picture and anticipating future possibilities
Making decisions	**Thinking (T)** is detached, analytic and objective	**Feeling (F)** is attached and related to emotion
Action	**Judging (J)** a desire to plan and organise one's own environment and be prepared	**Perceiving (P)** desire to take life in its stride, be happy-go-lucky, and respond to new opportunities

Figure 8.2 The Myers-Briggs Type Indicator model

| Extravert (E) | Sensing (S) | Thinking (T) | Judging (J) |
| Introvert (I) | Intuition (N) | Feeling (F) | Perceiving (P) |

Figure 8.3 The four dichotomies of the MBTI

8.2.1.2 NEO (Costa & McCrae, 1992) and the Five-factor (OCEAN) Model of Personality

The five-factor model represents a near-consensual structure of personality constructs (Costa & McCrae, 1992). Importantly, five factors have been identified from correlational work involving most personality inventories. The Big Five traits are broad personality constructs that are indicated by a number of more specific traits. The five-factor model is sometimes referred to as the OCEAN model representing an acronym of the first letter of each of the factors:

- *Openness* to experience (or intellect) is a tendency to be open to new ideas, experiences, and ways of working.
- *Conscientiousness* is a tendency to seek achievement and to be reliable and dependable.
- *Extraversion* is an expression of how outgoing and active an individual is.
- *Agreeableness* represents a tendency to be warm, kind, and accepting.
- *Neuroticism* is a predilection to demonstrate low emotional stability which manifests itself in symptoms such as anxiety and stress.

In their review of the links between personality, learning, and education, De Raad & Schouwenburg (1996, p. 327) suggest that:

> *[A]ll the Big Five factors or facets appear to have a say in learning and education, but they differ in the extent to which they play a role and there are differences in the way their role is played. Conscientiousness is the most prominent, also in combination from facets from Extraversion, Emotional Stability, and Intellect.*

McCrae (1987) identified the factors of conscientiousness and openness to experience as being the two factors of most interest to educational researchers. Individuals who score highly on openness to experience consider themselves to be more intelligent than others (McCrae & Costa, 1987). Conscientiousness has been found to be consistently positively related to university performance (see De Raad & Schouwenburg, 1996).

8.2.1.3 Accounting educators' use of cognitive personality elements research

A number of researchers have successfully applied the MBTI in an accounting context (see Wheeler, 2001, for a detailed review). The stereotypical profile for students (Geary & Rooney, 1993; Abdolmohammadi *et al.*, 2003, 2009) and practising accountants (Jacoby, 1981; Otte, 1984; Descouzis, 1989; Booth & Winzar, 1993; Scarborough, 1993; Vaassen *et al.*, 1993; Schloemer & Schloemer, 1997; Wolk & Nikolai, 1997; Kovar *et al.*, 2003; Briggs *et al.*, 2007) has been identified as an ISTJ (introverted-sensing-thinking-judging) type.

Nourayi & Cherry (1993) related students' personality preferences, as measured by MBTI, to their performance in seven accounting classes at a university in the U.S.A. Sensing (S) students performed significantly better than intuitive (N) students in three of the seven modules.

Oswick & Barber (1998), using a sample of business undergraduates (n = 344) in the U.K., examined the relationship between students' MBTI profiles and academic performance on an *Introductory Accounting* module. The authors reported that personality type had no bearing upon the level of achievement. It was concluded that there was little relationship between the prevalent STJ type and performance. This finding suggests that STJs do not necessarily make the best accounting students, simply that their over-representation indicates the tendency of this type to gravitate towards the accounting profession.

In an applied study of 132 Australian undergraduate accounting students, Ramsay *et al.* (2000) investigated the association between cognitive personality traits, as measured by the MBTI, and students' preferences for cooperative learning. They reported that preference for cooperative learning is significantly associated with the extroversion/introversion dimension of the MBTI.

Brown (2002, 2003, 2004) reported the results of a programme of research examining the meta-programmes of accounting and business students in the U.K., which assess 'up to fifty-one thinking preferences, not all of which are opposite in nature' (2004, p. 233). Brown (2002,

2003) used Arthur & Engel's (2000) Motivation Profile Questionnaire (MPQ) to establish the meta-programmes of accounting educators (Brown, 2002) and compare teachers to students (Brown, 2002, 2003). Meta programmes are rooted in neuro-linguistic programming. He concluded that meta programmes can affect the (in)ability of individual students to negotiate higher education. Further work developed and validated the MPQ when applied to samples of accounting students (n = 62) and accounting teachers (n = 20) (Brown, 2003).

Abdolmohammadi *et al.* (2009), studying staff and students (n = 168) in the U.S.A., found that the predominant accounting cognitive style (ST/SF) is empirically associated with lower ethical reasoning scores as assessed by Rest's (1986) Defining Issues Test (DIT).

Bealing *et al.* (2009) sampled 95 students at one institution in the U.S.A. and administered the Keirsey Temperament Sorter (KTS), as a measure of personality, and related scores to *Introductory Financial Accounting* performance. Six questions on the KTS, which categorize individuals as being either sensing or intuitive types, were found to be significantly related to performance on the module. Notably, sensing types were found to be advantaged over intuitive types, providing some evidence for the predominance of sensing types in the accounting profession.

Despite a growing consensus in the area of personality measurement supporting the five-factor OCEAN model, no researchers have used the model in applied research to consider the learning, academic, or job performance of accounting students or practitioners.

8.2.2 Information processing style

Information processing style is an expression of an individual's approach to assimilating information. Such measures are believed to be more stable than 'instructional preference', but still capable of modification by the use of different learning strategies (Riding & Cheema, 1991). Kolb's Experiential Learning Model (ELM) (1976) is an example of an 'information processing' model.

Kolb's ELM is a process model rather than an outcome model. It posits that learning has four stages:

1   concrete experience (CE);
2   observation and reflection (RO);
3   creation of abstract concepts and generalizations (AC); and
4   the testing of these concepts in new situations (AE). These in turn lead to further concrete experiences – see Figure 8.4.

The learning cycle can be entered at any stage. However, learning operates in the sequence proposed by Kolb. Different learners may adapt better to, or prefer, some elements of the learning cycle relative to others. Each stage reflects a level of ability (i.e., the model learner can work equally well with all four stages of the ELM). However, most individuals will have a preference for one or more stages in the cycle.

The cycle has also been further developed as two orthogonal dimensions, based on empirical work using the LSI (Kolb, 1976). The two dimensions are labelled 'prehension' (CE-AC) and 'transformation' (RO-AE). Prehension is the acquisition of information via direct experience emphasizing intuition, while transformation is the transformation of internal information by contemplative reflection followed by testing this new information in the environment.

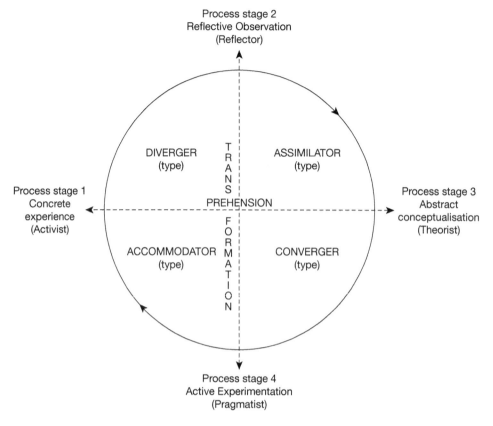

Figure 8.4 Kolb's ELM: the relationships among four process stages, two orthogonal bipolar
dimensions, and four types

Note: Kolb's bipolar dimensions are indicated by the two orthogonal broken lines labelled 'Prehension' and
'Transformation'. Honey and Mumford's (1992) LSQ labels for each of the four learning styles are shown in parentheses.

At least three measures exist which attempt to identify an individual's preferred style of learning.
The most popular include:

- the Learning Style Inventory (LSI) (Kolb, 1976);
- a later revision of the LSI (LSI-1985) (Kolb, 1985); and
- the Learning Styles Questionnaire (LSQ) (Honey & Mumford, [1986], 1992).

All three instruments were developed for use with adult learners, with the LSQ being developed
specifically for *management trainees*. In the U.K. and Europe, Honey & Mumford's Learning
Style Questionnaire (LSQ) is a common method of assessing LS in both educational and commercial training environments (Swailes & Senior, 2000). The LSQ measures four dimensions,
which correspond approximately to those suggested by Kolb: Activist (cf. AE); Reflector
(cf. RO); Pragmatist (cf. CE); and Theorist (cf. AC).

8.2.2.1 Accounting educators' use of information processing style

Accounting educators soon recognized the utility of Kolb's (1976) ELM. Nearly 30 years ago,
Baldwin & Reckers (1984) examined students' preferred LS in an accounting education context

in the U.S.A. using the LSI-1976. Considerable further research was undertaken by a number of authors, mainly in the U.S.A., using the LSI-1976. However, further research queried the measurement properties of scores produced by the LSI (Stout & Ruble, 1991a, 1991b, 1994; Ruble & Stout, 1993). Perhaps reflecting concerns about the measurement qualities of the LSI, research using the inventory fell out of fashion. More recently, Adler *et al.* (2004), at a university in New Zealand, assessed the effect of case studies in a *Management Accounting* course on learning styles, matching pre-test to post-test learning style profiles. Post-test scores analysed a move from accommodators (AE/CE) and divergers (CE/RO) towards assimilators (RO/AC).

In an extension to Adler *et al.*'s (2004) work, Wynn-Williams *et al.* (2008), also in New Zealand, considered the use of multiple case-studies in an *Intermediate Accounting* course, using a pre-test to post-test design, finding that engagement in the case studies had the consequence of creating a more balanced learning style. Duff *et al.* (2008) critiqued the canon of literature concerning the LSI and evaluated Wynn-Williams *et al.*'s (2008) findings. Adler *et al.* (2008) provided a response to Duff *et al.*'s (2008) comments and offered a robust defence of their conclusions, while acknowledging some of the limitations of the use of the LSI.

Sugahara & Boland (2010) undertook a comparative empirical study of students in Australia and Japan using the LSI and Hofstede's Cultural Values. They identified two key findings:

- Australian students exhibited a preference for individualism over their Japanese counterparts.
- Australian students were more likely to be assimilators (RO/AC) than their Japanese contemporaries, who were more likely to be divergers (CE/RO).

They concluded that the less individualistic Japanese students preferred to 'attend class simply to absorb knowledge from watching what their teachers show them' (ibid., p. 252), suggesting active approaches to learning require careful implementation with students from non-Australian backgrounds.

Fewer accounting education scholars have adopted the LSQ. Duff (1997a), in an investigation of 142 accounting students in the U.K., reported that the instrument yielded scores of unsatisfactory internal consistency reliability, construct validity, and predictive validity. Sangster (1996) sampled accounting students in the U.K. and related scores on the LSQ to their preference for assessment using computer-based objective testing. However, Duff (1998), drawing on his experience of the LSQ, and the results of validity studies in other disciplines, criticized Sangster's (1996) application of the LSQ as being premature. Work in disciplines other than accounting has indicated that the LSQ produces scores with inadequate measurement properties and is unsuitable for use in correlational studies (Swailes & Senior, 2000; Duff & Duffy, 2002).

In summary, in accounting education, Kolb's theory of LS's has been a popular avenue for individual difference research. Psychometric research has identified that Kolbian measures (LSI-1976, LSI-1985, and LSQ) are of questionable validity. However, accounting educators should not be too quick to dismiss research in this area as the ELM alone provides a useful means of introducing important ideas of individual learning to students, and has significant utility in helping students to develop a greater awareness of their own learning.

8.2.3 Students' approaches to learning (SAL)

SAL is generally conceived as lying between the information processing and instructional preferences layers of the onion taxonomy. The now extensive SAL literature has been complemented by an array of studies in the field of accounting. Accounting educators were quick to see SAL's potential as the concept is rooted in the context and environment of education, the classrooms, lecture halls, and personal study patterns of the students. SAL is generally concerned with learning in higher education in contrast to Kolb's ELM where the focus has more often been management learning (see Reynolds, 1997; Haggis, 2009). Significantly, SAL research is associated with a constructivist view of learning which is characterized by four features:

- learners construct their own meanings;
- learners make use of prior knowledge;
- social interaction enhances learning; and
- by using authentic tasks and materials, learning moves from experience to knowledge rather than the traditional knowledge to experience (Cooperstein & Kocevar-Weidinger, 2004, p. 114).

The seminal work conducted by Marton & Säljö (1976) identified two approaches among Scandinavian students in reading academic work:

- A *deep approach* where the student looks for meaning in the matter being studied and tries to relate it to other experiences and ideas (i.e. the student engages in criticality. See Cunningham, Chapter 18 – this volume).
- A *surface approach* which describes rote-learning and memorization in isolation of other ideas.

A deep approach is said to be consistent with the philosophy of higher education (Hayes *et al.*, 1997), and is also a product of relevance to: students' interests (Fransson, 1977); the demonstrable interest, support, and enthusiasm of the educator (Ramsden, 1979); and a means whereby students can self-regulate (i.e., manage) their own learning (Ramsden & Entwistle, 1981).

A third approach was identified by Ramsden (1979), which he labelled a *strategic approach*. This approach is characterized by a concern to achieve high marks, and the particular activities undertaken by the student are influenced by this motivation.

Table 8.1 summarizes the key features of these three approaches to learning.

The three most widely applied instruments to evaluate students' approaches to learning are:

- Entwistle *et al.*'s (1979) Approaches to Studying Inventory (ASI), developed in the U.K.; Biggs' (1987) Study Processes Questionnaire (SPQ) created in Australia, and popular in Australasia and the Far East; and
- Vermunt's (1992) Inventory of Learning Styles (ILS), developed in the Netherlands.

Reviewing the development of SAL inventories is beyond the scope of this chapter, but detailed reviews can be found in Duff & McKinstry (2007) and Richardson (2000).

8.2.3.1 Accounting educators' use of SAL

My literature search reveals 29 published empirical studies of accounting students' approaches to learning and five literature reviews (Beattie *et al.*, 1997; Lucas & Mladenovic, 2004, 2006; Duff, 2004a; Duff & McKinstry, 2007), making SAL the predominant paradigm for the assessment of learning differences. The quantitative investigations utilize six instruments:

- Biggs' (1987) SPQ (Eley, 1992; Gow *et al.*, 1994; Booth *et al.*, 1999; Abhayawansa *et al.*, 2012);
- Biggs *et al.*'s (2001) Revised SPQ (R-SPQ-2F) (de Lange & Mavondo, 2004);
- Schmeck *et al.*'s (1977) ILP (Tan & Choo, 1990; Duff, 1997a);

Table 8.1 Defining features of students' approaches to learning (SAL)

A SURFACE APPROACH can be identified by:

- Intention to complete task requirements
- Memorizing information needed for assessments
- Failing to distinguish principles from examples
- Treating task as an external imposition
- Focussing on discrete elements without integration
- Lack of reflection on purpose or strategies

A DEEP APPROACH can be identified by:

- Intention to understand
- Vigorous interaction with content
- Relating new ideas to previous knowledge
- Relating concepts to everyday experience
- Relating evidence to conclusions
- Examining the logic of the argument

A STRATEGIC APPROACH can be identified by:

- Intention to obtain highest possible grades
- Organizing time and distributing effort to greatest effect
- Ensuring conditions and materials for studying are appropriate
- Using previous examination papers to predict questions
- Being alert to cues about assessment criteria/marking schemes

Source: Adapted from Entwistle (1987).

- Tait & Entwistle's (1996) Revised Approaches to Studying Inventory (RASI) (Duff, 1999; Hassall & Joyce, 2001);
- Entwistle *et al.*'s (2000) Approaches and Study Skills Inventory (ASSIST) (Byrne *et al.*, 2002, 2004; Ballantine *et al.*, 2008; Flood & Wilson, 2008); and
- Meyer's (2000) Reflections on Learning Inventory (RoLI) (Lucas & Meyer, 2005).

8.2.3.2 Exploratory approaches

Exploratory investigations into SAL undertaken by accounting education scholars can be broadly categorized into two types. First, considerations of students' attitudes and approaches towards learning (Sharma, 1997; Lucas, 2000, 2001, 2011; Jackling, 2005; Abhayawansa & Fonseca, 2010; Watty *et al.*, 2010). Second, investigations into educators' conceptions of learning (Lucas, 2002, 2011; Leveson, 2004). The collective results of these studies are shown in Table 8.2.

Many of these qualitative studies were undertaken in a phenomenographic tradition, i.e. seeking '*to identify the qualitatively different ways in which individuals experience such aspects of their world as teaching, learning, or the meaning of disciplinary concepts*' (Ashworth & Lucas, 2000, p. 295).

The first study of this genre (Sharma, 1997) undertook a phenomenographic examination of second-year undergraduate accounting students in Australia, and required 101 students to respond to one open-ended question: *What do you mean by learning?* A taxonomic exercise was undertaken to classify students' conceptions into Säljö's (1979) five conceptions of learning categories. A total of 75 per cent of students' responses were categorized into levels 2 and 3, suggesting these students see learning as being about acquiring knowledge and application of

Table 8.2 Summary of qualitative investigations undertaken by accounting education researchers

Author(s)	Participants	Research question and findings
1. Sharma (1997)	101 second-year undergraduate accounting students in Australia	'What do you mean by learning?' What is 'learning accounting'? Majority of students classified as seeing learning as 'acquiring knowledge' and 'application'.
2. Lucas (2000)	10 first-year undergraduate students studying Introductory Accounting in the U.K.	What are students' conceptions of learning? Two alternative 'worlds' of accounting: (i) a world of detachment where accounting is a 'technique' and 'lacks relevance'; (ii) a world of engagement, where accounting is relevant and possesses inherent meaning.
3. Lucas (2001)	10 first-year undergraduate students studying Introductory Accounting in the U.K.	Identify key aspects of what constitutes 'learning accounting' for students. Identify students' conceptions of accounting. Identifies features which are characteristic of deep and surface approaches to learning accounting. Also identifies contextual features surrounding accounting SAL which are central to understanding them.
4. Lucas (2002)	10 educators from U.K. universities, teaching Introductory Accounting	Analyze teachers' conception of teaching Introductory Accounting using Fox's (1983) framework; Assess the descriptive validity of Fox's (1983) model. Fox's model is identified as relevant, but identifies key contradictions and uncertainties within conceptions of teaching accounting; reflecting a tension between the stated aim of conceptual understanding and an emphasis on mastering techniques.
5. Leveson (2004)	24 accounting academics from seven universities in Australia	Conceptualization of: Student learning in accounting; teachers' teaching role; educators' teaching approach. Four different ways of conceptualizing teaching and five approaches to learning and teaching identified. Broadly, these fall under two orientations: teacher-centred/content and student-centred/learning orientation.
6. Jackling (2005)	12 second-year undergraduate accounting students in Australia	Conceptualization of: students' conceptions of accounting learning processes; and their views on what they had learned. Students who view teaching quality favourably tended to have deep motives when learning accounting. Students perceived memory as being important in the context of learning Financial Accounting.
7. Abhayawansa & Fonseca (2010)	10 Sri Lankan accounting students studying in Australia	Conceptions of learning and SAL. Students had lower-order conceptions of learning as a consequence of their vocational perceptions of accounting as a discipline. Students can adopt deeper level approaches in classroom discussion and where research- and practice-based approaches are used.
8. Watty et al. (2010)	14 focus groups in Australia, Hong Kong, and Singapore	What is the role of assessment on SAL? English competency has the greatest effect, how an assessment is written has a significant impact on students' performance, students' approaches to assessment are not homogeneous.

Source: Adapted from Duff & McKinstry (2007: 195).

knowledge. However, only 6 per cent were categorized into level 5, *seeing something in a different way*, compared to van Rossum & Schenk's (1984) classification of 19 per cent of first-year psychology students into this category. Sharma (1997, p. 135) speculates that this finding may be due to psychology being 'less technical and computationally oriented and more open-ended than accounting'.

Sharma's (1997) investigation was replicated by Lord & Robertson (2006) in Australia, based on third-year accounting students' conceptions of learning. They provided an extension to Sharma by comparing conceptions to contextual experiences of learning in class. Almost half the 77 students viewed learning as being a process involving the acquisition of knowledge which could be readily reproduced for the purposes of assessment. Students with a more instrumental conception of learning tended to see learning as being the teacher's responsibility, whereas those with higher conceptions of learning saw responsibility shifting towards the student, or a joint process between teacher, student and peers.

Lucas (2000, 2001) considered the experiences of 10 first-year accounting undergraduate students at universities in the U.K., used a phenomenographic analysis of responses provided at interview to two accounting questions relating to elements of the balance sheet and profit & loss account. Her findings identified two contrasting worlds of accounting (Lucas, 2000):

- for most, it is a world of detachment; and
- for only a few, it is a world of engagement.

Extending this analysis, Lucas (2001) uses students' responses to identify the characteristics of deep and surface approaches within the context of accounting, and identified those elements that are key to understanding SAL in accounting.

Jackling (2005) used interviews with 12 second-year accounting undergraduate students in Australia to establish which approach to learning motives and strategies were used, and related this to the outcomes of learning. Positive perceptions of the learning context were associated with deep and achieving approaches to learning, yet surface approaches (e.g. memorization) were also important in learning accounting as a consequence of the learning tasks in accounting, rather than a characteristic of the learner. Her finding that lower-level accounting necessitates rote learning and paraphrasing before students can make use of knowledge and engage in criticality echoed findings by Hall *et al.* (2004).

Abhayawansa & Fonseca (2010) explore conceptions of learning and approaches to learning (SAL) of a group of 10 Sri Lankan students studying accounting in an Australian university. The focus is on how cultural background and home country learning experiences shape the conceptions of learning and SAL of these students. Their findings are that the students interviewed have lower-order conceptions of learning, displaying characteristics of surface learning. However, they can adopt deeper-level learning when engaged in classroom discussions, student presentations, and assessments that are research-oriented or practice-based. Conceptions of learning and SAL reflect the interviewees' presumptions of accounting as being a vocational discipline, rooted in practice, and the baggage of secondary education.

Just two studies have considered accounting educators' conceptions of learning. If student learning is context- and discipline-dependent, then their teachers' conceptions of teaching should also be similarly subject-specific (e.g. Prosser *et al.*, 1994). The first investigation (Lucas, 2002), interviewed 10 teachers of *Introductory Accounting* at universities in the U.K. Her work utilized Fox's (1983) four conceptions of teaching, labelled: shaping, travelling, growing, and building. The *shaping conception*, as the most populated category, describes a teacher who wanted to shape the student into a person who has mastered a technique and produced a set of accounts.

By contrast, the *travelling conception* involves seeing education as a journey, with the educator as the guide. Those adopting the travel metaphor tend to reject shaping students as it may deter them from exploring. The *growing conception* associates learning with personal growth, with the students and their relation to accounting at the forefront. The *building conception* was identified in all participants, with building metaphors relating to the provision of a foundation for future study. (See also Section 19.3 in Stevenson *et al.*, Chapter 19 – this volume.) Interestingly, Lucas (2002) reported that the building conception failed to be fully actualized in participants' reflections on teaching, as there tended to be either inherent contradictions in interviewees' accounts of the conceptual understanding required, or uncertainties about the relationship between conceptual understanding, techniques, and the efficacy of assessment.

Watty *et al.* (2010) identified that the role of assessment and SAL remains under-researched and conducted 14 focus groups in Australia, Hong Kong, and Singapore. They reported that:

- English language competency has the greatest impact on students' assessment and, consequently, SAL.
- How an assessment is developed and communicated and how, in particular, the assessor conveys his/her expectations, were highly significant to students' performance.
- Students' approaches to assessment were not culturally homogeneous.

Lucas (2011) neatly stitched the perspectives of teachers and students together. She conceptualizes an *outer world* of students' learning, and a vocationally-dominated curriculum, alongside her own personal reflexivity, an *inner world*, encouraging others to create their own personal auto-ethnographic accounts and support a community of scholarship of teaching and learning in accounting.

8.2.3.3 Measurement approaches

The quantitative studies can be broadly categorized into three areas:

- The first group assess accounting students' predilections for different approaches to learning, using questionnaire methods. Deep and strategic approaches are generally held to be positively associated with success in studying accounting (Byrne *et al.*, 1999, 2002; Davidson, 2002; Duff, 2004b). Similarly, surface approaches are associated with poorer performance in accounting (Booth *et al.*, 1999; Byrne *et al.*, 2002; Duff, 2004b; Ramburuth & Mladenovic, 2004; Tan & Choo, 1991). However, it is important to understand that different assessment instruments will measure different learning outcomes. Therefore, as many accounting educators have identified (e.g. Davidson, 2002; English *et al.*, 2004; Ramburuth & Mladenovic, 2004), it is important not to aggregate assessments measuring different outcomes. Likewise, some of these studies consider gender differences in SAL, reporting differences that are of low magnitude (Byrne *et al.*, 1999; Duff, 1999; de Lange & Mavondo, 2004), which is similar to meta-analytic findings across all disciplines (Severiens & ten Dam, 1994, 1998). We also know that mature students are more likely to adopt a deep approach (Duff, 1999), as studies in other areas suggest (Richardson, 1994, 2000; Sadler-Smith, 1996; Sadler-Smith & Tsang, 1998).
- A second branch of enquiry into SAL considers the measurement characteristics of scores produced by the associated measuring instruments (see Duff, 2001). Duff (1997a) was one of the first of these studies to question the validity of cores yielded by Schmeck and colleagues' (1977) ILP when administered to accounting students in the U.K. A similar study (Duff, 1997b) found more positive support for the measurement qualities of the Entwistle and colleagues'

RASI when applied to accounting and business students in the U.K. Byrne *et al.* (2004) administered ASSIST to samples of business undergraduate students in the U.S.A. and Ireland, reporting results that are broadly equivalent across the two samples. However, alpha coefficients estimated for seven (of 13) scales are below 0.6 for the sample from the U.S.A., indicating that accounting education researchers should consider re-wording some of the items within these scales before using ASSIST in applied research with students in the U.S.A.

- The third category of quantitative investigations into accounting SAL are longitudinal studies. The first example of this research is provided by Gow *et al.*'s (1994) longitudinal study in Hong Kong, which reported that accounting students tend to exhibit less desirable SAL scores (increased surface approach and decreased deep approach) as they progress through their studies. They speculated that their findings were attributable to students encountering excessive workload, assessment methods that reward reproduction, and didactic teaching methods, all of which are problems that were well-documented by various commentators in the 1980s and 1990s – as discussed earlier in this chapter.

English *et al.* (2004) undertook a comparison of two Australian higher education institutions (HEIs) teaching *Introductory Accounting*. One institution was implementing an intervention to develop students' writing skills, while the other acted as a control group. Although both HEIs recorded similar pre-test SPQ scores, the HEI implementing the writing skills programme produced higher scores on deep approach and lower scores on surface approach.

Hall *et al.* (2004) report the results of a longitudinal study undertaken in Australia that reports the effect of changes in the learning environment to promote the use of deep learning. That is, they adopt constructivist principles to create a powerful learning environment. The paper is novel in that it uses a within-subjects design[1] and finds that students exhibit an increase in deep approach scores and a decrease in surface approach scores as a consequence of the introduction of the changes in instructional methods.

Lucas & Meyer (2005) constructed an accounting discipline-specific inventory, the *Expectations of Learning Accounting Inventory* (ELAcc) with Meyer's (2000) RoLI. ELAcc assesses students' motivations, intentions, and epistemological beliefs about studying accounting. It is therefore similar to elements of the strategic approach of both Entwistle's and co-workers' ASI, RASI, and ASSIST, and Biggs' SPQ. Where ELAcc is markedly different, it includes students' epistemological beliefs about the nature of studying, which are, of course, discipline-specific. Lucas & Meyer's (2005) work is novel in an accounting context as it uses the constructivist idea that meaning is constructed by the individual. This was demonstrated by the presence of three types of students: deep learners, surface learners, and a third group who possess a *dissonant* pattern of learning: a pattern which cannot be readily interpreted (for example, a student scoring high on both deep and surface).

Ballantine *et al.* (2008) undertook a longitudinal study of students in Ireland of self-reported SAL in a *Management Accounting* course that was intended to promote deep learning. However, the changes identified were relatively slender, with an increase in strategic and surface approaches to learning being identified, suggesting that SAL become less malleable over time spent at university. The increase in surface approaches was contrary to expectations.

In the one study of professional students (i.e., accounting trainees) in Ireland, Flood & Wilson (2008) administered the ASSIST. The authors reported:

- no statistically significant differences in approaches to learning between those failing a professional examination and the group that passed it; and
- that strategic approaches dominated the constellation of SAL scores.

Table 8.3 Summary of quantitative investigations undertaken by accounting education researchers

Authors	Participants, inventory	Results
Cross-sectional, inter-group differences		
1. Tan & Choo (1990)	Undergraduate accounting students in Australia (n = 89), ILP	Students obtaining high scores on deep and elaborative processing scales statistically significantly outperform in assessments those with low scores on these two scales.
2. Sharma (1997)	Second-year undergraduate accounting students in Australia (n = 124), ASI	Variables associated with good teaching positively associated with deep approach scales.
3. Booth *et al.* (1999)	Undergraduates in Australia (n = 95 and n = 279), SPQ	Comparison of accounting students' scores versus previously reported norms. Accounting students have relatively high scores on surface approach and low scores on deep approach. High surface approach scores related to poor academic performance.
4. Duff (1999)	U.K. accounting undergraduate students (n = 316), RASI	Comparison of second- and third-year accounting/business students' approach to learning vs. entry qualifications, age and gender. No differences by entry qualifications. However statistically significant gender and age effects.
5. Hassall & Joyce (2001)	U.K. professional accounting students (n = 547), RASI	Four cross-sectional panels of students by examination stage. Surface approach scores decline over the four stages of the CIMA qualification, while deep approach scores remain stable.
6. Byrne *et al.* (2002)	Accounting undergraduates in Ireland (n = 95), ASSIST	Deep and strategic approaches to learning positively associated with academic performance, instrumental approach negatively related to academic performance.
7. Davidson (2002)	Business undergraduates in Canada, studying an accounting module (n = 211), SPQ	Deep approach scores positively related to performance on 'complex' examination questions, but not on 'less complex' examination questions or mean scores. Surface approach scores not related to any aspect of academic performance.
8. Abhayawansa *et al.* (2012)	Accounting students with and without a background in a technical and further education college (TAFE) SPQ (n = 190)	Contrary to expectations, students from a TAFE background, frequently labelled as an inferior education, are more likely to adopt deep and achieving approaches to learning than those who came to university from school.

Table 8.3 Summary of quantitative investigations undertaken by accounting education researchers—*continued*

Authors	Sample	Results
Cross-sectional, inter-group differences		
9. de Lange & Mavondo (2004)	Undergraduate business students in Australia studying by open-learning (n = 246), R-SPQ-2F	Learning strategies are engendered. In particular, males' pattern of responses differ from expectations.
10. Duff (2004b)	Accounting and business economics first-year undergraduate students in the U.K. (n = 60), RASI	Two clusters identified: 'effective learner' characterized by high scores on deep approach have 75% progression rate, while 'ineffective learner' characterized by high scores on surface approach only a 12% rate of progression. However, prior academic achievement is still the best predictor of academic performance.
11. Ramburuth & Mladenovic (2004)	Accounting undergraduate students in Australia (n = 966), SPQ	Relationship between students' levels of cognitive engagement in a comprehension task, SAL and academic achievement. Level of cognitive engagement on entry positively associated with future academic performance. Scores on surface approach negatively correlated with academic performance.
Measurement qualities of SAL inventories when applied to samples of accounting students		
12. Duff (1997a)	240 U.K. business undergraduate students, RASI	High internal consistency reliability (alpha coefficients ranging from .80 to .82 for three scales); high construct validity indicated by exploratory factor analysis.
13. Duff (1997b)	Accounting (n = 80) and business (n = 62) undergraduate students in the U.K., ILP	Replication study of Tan & Choo (1997). Finds results not replicable due to poor measurement qualities of ILP when administered to U.K. accounting students.
14. Duff (1999)	316 U.K. accounting undergraduate students, RASI	High internal consistency reliability (alpha coefficients ranging from .79 to .82 for three scales); high construct validity indicated by exploratory factor analysis.
15. Byrne *et al.* (2004)	Business undergraduates in the U.S.A. (n = 298) and Ireland (n = 437), ASSIST	The data for both samples broadly fits the ASSIST model. However, 7 (of 13) alpha coefficients are below .6 for the U.S. sample suggesting U.S. researchers wishing to apply the inventory should consider rephrasing some of the items.

Table 8.3 Summary of quantitative investigations undertaken by accounting education researchers—*continued*

Authors	Sample	Instrument Version/Results
Studies considering contextual factors and/or longitudinal studies		
16. Gow et al. (1994)	Accounting and business students in Hong Kong (n = 793), SPQ	Longitudinal study. As accounting and business students progress through their programme of study, they are more likely to adopt a surface approach and less likely to adopt a deep approach. Findings are said to be attributable to excessive workload, assessment methods which reward reproduction, didactic teaching methods, and high staff to student ratios.
17. English et al. (2004)	Business undergraduate students in Australia to two universities (n = 354, 706), SPQ	Longitudinal study compares students in two universities: one where an intervention was developed to improve students' writing skills, the other institution acted as a control group. Both samples had similar pre-test scores. Statistically significant differences in approach scores were identified between the two samples as hypothesized.
18. Hall et al. (2004)	Accounting undergraduate students in Australia (n = 158), SPQ	Longitudinal study records a small increase in deep approach and small decrease in surface approach scores in response to changes in the learning environment.
19. Lucas & Meyer (2005)	Undergraduate business (n = 706) and accounting students in the U.K. (n = 505), RoLI	Differences exist between accounting and business students' SAL and their conceptions of learning accounting.
20. Ballantine et al. (2008)	Final year undergraduate accounting students in Ireland (n = 276), ASSIST	Longitudinal study finds statistically significant increase in strategic and surface approach scores, gender and degree programme have no significant effects.
21. Flood & Wilson (2008)	Professional accounting students in Ireland (n = 942), ASSIST	Strategic approaches to learning dominate in professional accounting students.

Source: Adapted from Duff & McKinstry (2007: 197–9).

Abhayawansa *et al.* (2012) undertook an empirical comparison of accounting students from further education backgrounds (direct entrants) versus those who entered university from school in Australia, in part replicating earlier work by Duff (1999) sampling U.K. accounting students. Administering the SPQ, Abhayawansa *et al.* (2012), using a univariate design, finds direct entrants are more likely to adopt deep and achieving approaches than are traditional university students recruited from school. Duff (1999), by contrast, used a multivariate design and reported that there are few differences between direct and non-direct entrants in their approaches to learning. These collective findings are shown in Table 8.3.

8.2.4 Instructional preferences

Instructional preferences may be thought of as an individual's tendency to report a liking for a specific instructional technique or suite of techniques. Instructional preferences, for example, are advocated by Dunn *et al.* (1989) – the Dunn & Dunn model identifies the learner's response to five forms of key stimuli, identified by 21 elements:

- environmental (sound, light, heat, design);
- emotional (structure, persistence, motivation, responsibility);
- sociological (peers, pair, adults, self, team, varied);
- physiological (perceptual, intake, time, mobility);
- psychological (global-analytic, impulsive-reflective, hemisphericity) – see Figure 8.5.

Although the Dunn & Dunn model consists of multiple elements, individuals tend to be affected by between 6–14 of the 21 elements. Only those 6–14 elements are said to represent each individual's preferred style of learning (Dunn *et al.*, 1989).

As Rayner & Riding (1997) identify, Dunn and her colleagues' notion of individual difference can be more accurately described as 'a learning repertoire rather than a style' (i.e., a repertoire made up of learning preferences). This concept is operationalized by the Learning Styles Inventory (LST) (Dunn *et al.*, 1989). Although the majority of research applying this instrument has been applied to school-aged children, another version, the Productivity Environmental Preference Survey (PEPS) has been specifically developed for use with adults.

8.2.4.1 Use of instructional preferences models within Accounting Education

No evidence of the use of 'instructional preferences' instruments can be found in the accounting literature.

8.3 Conclusion

> *What we know about student learning depends where we look, and is always a reflection of specific purposes and interests, which are tied to particularities of temporal and spatial contexts.*
>
> (Haggis, 2009, p. 388)

In the field of accounting education, then, individual differences research has a rich heritage. The specific purposes and interests we have examined are typically relatively instrumental: differences in career choice or major; or predictive value in assessing performance. This perhaps reflects accounting's ties as a vocational subject, and its affiliations with accounting employers, professional accounting bodies, and institutional pressures to teach ever-growing numbers of students as a consequence of accounting's function as a university cash cow. Often our burgeoning literature

Stimuli	Elements			
Environmental	Sound	Light	Temperature	Design
Emotional	Motivation	Persistence	Responsibility	Structure
Sociological	Self	Pair	Peers	Adult
Physiological	Perceptual	Intake	Time	Team	Mobility	Varied
Psychological	Global v. Analytic	Hemisphericity (left brain, right brain)		Impulsive-reflective

Figure 8.5 The PEPS model

Source: Adapted from Dunn & Dunn (1989).

makes little reference to trends in higher education research or wider agendas within higher education. I suggest that our horizons are too limited in the following ways:

- To a significant degree, individual differences research in accounting education is subject to fads. In the 1980s and early 1990s, Kolb's ELM and associated LSs dominated. From the mid-1990s, SAL took over. SAL research is still an active interest in accounting education, but recently has adopted a more critical and interpretative stance. I would argue that this is a positive trend. However, earlier research efforts by accounting education scholars on individual differences still have much to teach us. For example, Kolb's LSs chime with the principles of constructivist learning:

  — experience before knowledge;
  — learners construct their own meanings;
  — learners use prior knowledge; and
  — authenticity enhances learning (see also Salomon, 1998).

- Relatively little work tries to link the paradigms of individual differences in learning research. Are the traits associated with the Big Five personality factors really so different from predilections to adopt study strategies? Or are students a blank canvas and willing to change their approach to learning? We assume a deep approach is 'good' and a surface one 'bad' – even when we recognize that early learning in accounting requires a surface approach. Frequently, our curriculum does not move much beyond elementary learning, with senior courses often promoting rote learning of more advanced techniques (Duff & Marriott, 2012). This also prompts questions concerning the ethics of using learning styles. Learning in a university context is heavily associated with cultural capital. What does it mean? What are the effects of labelling someone a pragmatist in an environment which celebrates the theorist? Similarly, who would wish to be accused of surface learning (or promoting surface learning) when deep approaches are so heavily favoured by educational theorists?

- Relatively little work in accounting education research chooses to involve itself in the context of accounting learning. The growing number of qualitative studies identified in this review do, to some extent, as does Lucas & Meyer's (2005) development of ELAcc. Generic models and inventories have much utility for us, but how can they be improved or adapted to encompass students' experiences of learning accounting?

- Relatively little effort has been made to integrate technology into learning styles/approaches research or applied teaching. This is perhaps surprising given the extensive development work that occurs when developing a new model of learning and its associated inventory. An exception to this is Entwistle et al.'s (2000) ASSIST which owes its value to a computer-package created as part of a government-funding initiative which allowed students to self-diagnose their learning (Tait et al., 1998). By increasing their awareness of their own strengths and weaknesses in learning, it was hoped that this would improve their learning effectiveness.

- Although it is assumed that research into learning is motivated by an interest in informing pedagogy, accounting educators have made fewer efforts to relate their investigations of students' learning to academic practice. The reasons for this are unclear, although perhaps they reflect researchers' fascination with re-ploughing familiar furrows (e.g. psychometric (re-)examination of measuring instruments and the quest for replicability) rather than the application of knowledge.

- Finally, we often seem to neglect the role of ourselves as academics and the institutional environment in individual difference research. Globally, accounting departments are subject to an ever-growing burden of accreditations, are consumed within the machinations of business schools or wider structures, and have decreasing links with the accounting profession. This is despite policy-makers' calls for our research to be 'relevant' and our students to be 'employable'. Our academic identity is then threatened, or at least subject to constant change (Haggis, 2009). Academic identities (cf. Becher, 1989; Becher & Trowler, 2001), perhaps then provide the key to why so little synthesis work has been undertaken in accounting education: researchers identify with one of the key paradigms of individual differences research (e.g. trait theory, LSs, or SAL) because attempting to build bridges between theories is either fraught with problems or threatens their very identity.

Note

1   That is, it uses matched pairs of students to consider changes in individual students' SAL rather than comparing aggregate cohort scores at different points in time.

References

Abdolmohammadi, M.J., Fedorowicz, J., & Davis, O. (2009) Accountants' cognitive style and ethical reasoning: a comparison across 15 years, *Journal of Accounting Education*, 27(4), 185–196.

Abdolmohammadi, M.J., Read, W.J., & Scarborough, D.P. (2003) Does selection-socialization help to explain accountants' weak ethical reasoning?, *Journal of Business Ethics*, 42(January), 71–81.

Abhayawansa, S. & Fonseca, L. (2010) Conceptions of learning and approaches to learning: a phenomenographic study of a group of overseas accounting students from Sri Lanka, *Accounting Education: an international journal*, 19(5), 527–550.

Abhayawansa, S., Tempone, I., & Pillay, S. (2012) Impact of entry mode on students' approaches to learning: a study of accounting students, *Accounting Education: an international journal*, 21(4), 341–361.

Adler, R.W., Whiting, R.H., & Wynn-Williams, K. (2004) Student-led and teacher-led case presentations: empirical evidence about learning styles in an accounting course, *Accounting Education: an international journal*, 13(2), 213–229.

Adler, R.W., Whiting, R.H., & Wynn-Williams, K. (2008) On approaches to learning versus learning styles: a reply to Duff *et al.*'s comment, *Accounting Education: an international journal*, 17(2), 145–149.

Arthur, J. & Engel, G. (2000) *The Motivation Profile Questionnaire*, Denver, CO: Lifestar.

Ashworth, P. & Lucas, U. (2000) Achieving empathy and engagement: a practical approach to the design, conduct and reporting of phenomenographic research, *Studies in Higher Education*, 25(3), 295–308.

Baldwin, B.A. & Reckers, P.M.J. (1984) Exploring the role of learning style research in accounting education policy, *Journal of Accounting Education*, 2(2), 63–76.

Ballantine, J.A., Duff, A., & McCourt Larres, P. (2008) Accounting and business students' approaches to learning: a longitudinal study, *Journal of Accounting Education*, 26(4), 188–201.

Beattie, V., Collins, B., & McInnes, B. (1997) Deep and surface learning: a simple or simplistic dichotomy? *Accounting Education: an international journal*, 6(1), 1–12.

Bealing, Jr., W.E., Staley, A.B., & Baker, R.L. (2009) An exploratory examination of the relationship between a short form of the Keirsey Temperament Sorter and success in an introductory accounting course: a research note, *Accounting Education: an international journal*, 18(3), 331–339.

Becher, T. (1989) *Academic Tribes and Territories: Intellectual Enquiry and the Cultures of Discipline*, Buckingham: SRHE and Open University Press.

Becher, T. & Trowler, P.R. (2001) *Academic Tribes and Territories*, 2nd edn, Buckingham: SRHE and Open University Press.

Biggs, J.B. (1987) *Study Process Questionnaire Manual*, Hawthorn, Victoria: Australian Council for Educational Research.

Biggs, J.B., Kember, D., & Leung, D.Y.P. (2001) The revised two-factor Study Process Questionnaire: R-SPQ-2F, *British Journal of Educational Psychology*, 71(2), 133–149.

Bloom, B.S., Engelhart, M.D., Furst, E.J., Hill, W.H., & Krathwohl, D. (1956) *Taxonomy of Educational Objectives: Handbook I: Cognitive Domain*, New York: David McKay.

Booth, P., Luckett, P., & Mladenovic, R. (1999) The quality of learning in accounting education: the impact of approaches to learning on academic performance, *Accounting Education: an international journal*, 8(4), 277–300.

Booth, P. & Winzar, H. (1993) Personality biases of accounting students: some implications for learning style preferences, *Accounting and Finance*, November, 109–120.

Briggs, S.P., Copeland, S., & Haynes, D. (2007) Accountants for the 21st century, where are you? A five-year study of accounting students' personality preferences, *Critical Perspectives on Accounting*, 18, 511–537.

Brown, N. (2002) Meta programme patterns in accounting educators at a UK business school, *Accounting Education: an international journal*, 11(1), 1–13.

Brown, N. (2003) A comparison of the dominant meta programme patterns in accounting undergraduate students and accounting teachers at a UK business school, *Accounting Education: an international journal*, 12(2), 159–175.

Brown, N. (2004) What makes a good educator? The relevance of meta programmes, *Assessment and Evaluation in Higher Education* 29(5), 515–533.

Byrne, M., Flood, B., & Willis, P. (1999) Approaches to learning of Irish accounting students, *Irish Accounting Review*, 6(2), 1–29.

Byrne, M., Flood, B., & Willis, P. (2002) The relationship between learning approaches and learning outcomes: a study of Irish accounting students, *Accounting Education: an international journal*, 11(1), 27–42.

Byrne, M., Flood, B., & Willis, P. (2004) Validation of the approaches and study skills inventory for students (ASSIST) using accounting students in the USA and Ireland: A research note, *Accounting Education: an international journal*, 13(4), 449–459.

Coffield, F., Moseley, D., Hall, E., & Ecclestone, K. (2004) *Learning Styles and Pedagogy in Post-16 Learning: A Systematic and Critical Review*, Oxford: Learning and Skills Research Centre.

Cohen, R.J., Swerdlik, M.E., & Philips, S.M. (1996) *Psychological Testing and Assessment*, 3rd edn, Mountain View, CA: Mayfield Publishing.

Cooperstein, S.E. & Kocevar-Weidinger, P. (2004) Beyond active learning: a constructivist approach to learning, *Reference Services Review*, 32(2), 141–148.

Costa, P.T. & McCrae, R.R. (1992) Four ways five factors are basic, *Personality and Individual Differences*, 13, 861–865.

Curry, L. (1987) *Integrating Concepts of Cognitive or Learning Style: A Review with Attention to Psychometric Standards*, Ottawa: Canadian College of Health Service Executives.

Davidson, R.A. (2002) Relationship of study approach and exam performance, *Journal of Accounting Education*, 20(1), 29–44.

Descouzis, D. (1989) Psychological types of tax preparers, *Journal of Psychological Type*, 17, 36–38.

De Lange, P. & Mavondo, F. (2004) Gender and motivational differences in approaches to learning by a cohort of open learning students, *Accounting Education: an international journal*, 13(4), 431–448.

De Raad, B. & Schouwenburg, H.C. (1996) Personality traits in learning and education, *European Journal of Personality*, 10, 185–200.

Duff, A. (1997a) A note on the reliability and validity of a 30-item version of Entwistle and Tait's Revised Approaches to Studying Inventory, *British Journal of Educational Psychology*, 67(4), 529–539.

Duff, A. (1997b) Validating the Learning Styles Questionnaire and the Inventory of Learning Processes in accounting: a research note, *Accounting Education: an international journal*, 6(3), 263–272.

Duff, A. (1998) Objective tests, learning to learn, and learning styles: a comment, *Accounting Education: an international journal*, 7(4), 335–345.

Duff, A. (1999) Access policy and approaches to learning, *Accounting Education: an international journal*, 8(3), 99–110.

Duff, A. (2001) Psychometric measurement in accounting education: a review and some comments, *Accounting Education: an international journal*, 10(4), 383–401.

Duff, A. (2004a) The role of cognitive learning styles in accounting education: developing learning competencies, *Journal of Accounting Education*, 22(1), 29–52.

Duff, A. (2004b) Understanding academic performance and progression of first-year accounting and business economics students: the role of approaches to learning and prior academic achievement, *Accounting Education: an international journal*, 13(4), 409–430.

Duff, A., Boyle, E.A., Dunleavy, K.A., & Ferguson, J. (2004) The relationship between personality, approach to learning and academic performance, *Personality and Individual Differences*, 36(8), 1907–1920.

Duff, A., Dobie, A., & Guo, X. (2008) The influence of business case studies and learning styles in an accounting course: a comment, *Accounting Education: an international journal*, 17(2), 129–144.

Duff, A. & Duffy, T. (2002) Psychometric properties of Honey and Mumford's Learning Styles Questionnaire (LSQ), *Personality and Individual Differences*, 33(1), 147–163.

Duff, A. & Marriott, N. (2012) *Teaching and Research: Partners or Competitors?*, Edinburgh: ICAS.

Duff, A. & McKinstry, S. (2007) Students' approaches to learning, *Issues in Accounting Education*, 22(2), 183–214.

Dunn, R., Dunn, K., & Price, G.E. (1989) *Learning Styles Inventory (LST): An Inventory for the Identification of How Individuals in Grades 3 Through 12 Prefer to Learn*, Lawrence, KS: Price Systems Inc.

Eley, M.G. (1992) Differential adoption of study approaches within individual students, *Higher Education*, 23(3), 231–254.

English, L., Luckett, P., & Mladenovic, R. (2004) Encouraging a deep approach to learning through curriculum design, *Accounting Education: an international journal*, 13(4), 461–488.

Entwistle, N.J. (1987) A model of the teaching-learning process, in Richardson, J.T.E., Eysenck, M.W., & Piper, D.W. (eds) *Student Learning: Research in Education and Cognitive Psychology*, Milton Keynes: The Society for Research into Higher Education/Open University Press, pp. 13–27.

Entwistle, N.J., Hanley, M., & Hounsell, D. (1979) Identifying distinctive approaches to studying, *Higher Education*, 8, 365–380.

Entwistle, N.J., Hanley, M., & McCune, V. (2000) Patterns of response to an approach to studying inventory across contrasting groups and contexts, *European Journal of Psychology of Education*, XV(1), 33–48.

Entwistle, N.J. & Waterston, S. (1988) Approaches to studying and levels of processing in university students, *British Journal of Educational Psychology*, 58, 258–265.

Flood, B. & Wilson, R.M.S. (2008) An exploration of the learning approaches of prospective professional accountants in Ireland, *Accounting Forum*, 32(3), 225–239.

Fox, D. (1983) Personal theories of teaching, *Studies in Higher Education*, 8(2), 151–163.

Fransson, A. (1977) On qualitative differences in learning, IV: Effects of intrinsic motivation and extrinsic test anxiety on process and outcome, *British Journal of Educational Psychology*, 47, 244–257.

Geary, W.T. & Rooney, C.J. (1993) Designing accounting education to achieve balanced intellectual development, *Issues in Accounting Education*, 8, 60–70.

Gow, L., Kember, D., & Cooper, B. (1994) The teaching context and approaches to study of accounting students, *Issues in Accounting Education*, 9(Spring), 118–130.

Haggis, T. (2009) What have we been thinking of? A critical overview of 40 years of student learning research in higher education, *Studies in Higher Education*, 34(4), 377–390.

Hall, M., Ramsay, A., & Raven, J. (2004) Changing the learning environment to promote deep learning approaches in first-year accounting students, *Accounting Education: an international journal*, 13(4), 489–506.

Hassall, T. & Joyce, J. (2001) Approaches to learning of management accounting students, *Education and Training*, 43(3), 145–152.

Hayes, K., King, E., & Richardson, J.T.E. (1997) Mature students in higher education: III. Approaches to studying in access students, *Studies in Higher Education*, 22(1), 19–31.

Honey, P. & Mumford, A. ([1986] 1992) *The Manual of Learning Styles*, Maidenhead: Peter Honey.

Jackling, B. (2005) Perceptions of the learning context and learning approaches: implications for quality learning outcomes in accounting, *Accounting Education: an international journal*, 14(3), 271–291.

Jacoby, P.F. (1981) Psychological types and career success in the accounting profession, *Research in Psychological Type*, 4, 24–37.

Jung, C.G. ([1921] 1971) *Psychological Types*, Princeton, NJ: Princeton University Press.

Kolb, D.A. (1976) *Learning Style Inventory: Technical Manual*, Boston, MA: McBer & Company.

Kolb, D.A. (1985) *Learning Style Inventory*, Boston, MA: McBer & Company.

Kovar, S.E., Ott, R.L., & Fisher, D.G. (2003) Personality preferences of accounting students: a longitudinal case study, *Journal of Accounting Education*, 21(1), 75–94.

Leveson, L. (2004) Encouraging better learning through better teaching: a study of approaches to teaching in accounting, *Accounting Education: an international journal*, 5(1), 87–98.

Lord, B.R. & Robertson, J. (2006) Students' experiences of learning in a third-year management accounting class: evidence from Australia, *Accounting Education: an international journal*, 15(1), 41–59.

Lucas, U. (2000) Worlds apart: students' experiences of learning introductory accounting, *Critical Perspectives on Accounting*, 11(4), 479–504.

Lucas, U. (2001) Deep and surface approaches to learning within introductory accounting: a phenomeno-graphic study, *Accounting Education: an international journal*, 10(2), 161–184.

Lucas, U. (2002) Contradictions and uncertainties: lecturers' conceptions of teaching introductory accounting, *British Accounting Review*, 34(3), 183–204.

Lucas, U. (2011) Towards a scholarship of teaching and learning: the individual and the communal journey, *Accounting Education: an international journal*, 20(3), 239–243.

Lucas, U. & Meyer, J.H.F. (2005) Towards a mapping of the student world: the identification of variation in students' conceptions of, and motivations to learn, introductory accounting, *British Accounting Review*, 37(2), 177–204.

Lucas, U. & Mladenovic, R. (2004) Approaches to learning in accounting education, *Accounting Education: an international journal*, 13(4), 399–407.

Marton, F., Hounsell, D., & Entwistle, N.J. (eds) (1984) *The Experience of Learning*, Edinburgh: Scottish University Press.

Marton, F. & Säljö, R. (1976) On qualitative differences in learning I: outcomes and processes, *British Journal of Educational Psychology*, 46, 4–11.

McCrae, R.R. (1987) Creativity, divergent thinking, and openness to experience, *Journal of Personality and Social Psychology*, 52(6), 12–58.

McCrae, R.R. & Costa, P.T. (1987) Validation of the five-factor model of personality across instruments and observers, *Journal of Personality and Social Psychology*, 52(1), 81–90.

Meyer, J.H.F. (2000) The modelling of 'dissonant' study orchestration in higher education, *European Journal of the Psychology of Education*, 15, 49–60.

Myers, I.B. & Briggs, K.C. (1976) *Myers-Briggs Type Indicator*, Palo Alto, CA: Consulting Psychologists Press Inc.

Nourayi, M.M. & Cherry, A.A. (1993) Accounting students' performance and personality types, *Journal of Education for Business*, 69(2), 111–115.

Oswick, C. & Barber, P. (1998) Personality type and performance in an introductory accounting course: a research note, *Accounting Education: an international journal*, 7(3), 249–254.

Otte, P. (1984) Do CPAs have a unique personality?: Are certain personality types found more frequently in our profession?, *The Michigan CPA*, 42(1), 29–36.

Prosser, M., Trigwell, K., & Taylor, P. (1994) A phenomenographic study of academics' conceptions of science learning and teaching, *Learning and Instruction*, 4, 217–231.

Ramburuth, P. & Mladenovic, R. (2004) Exploring the relationship between students' orientations to learning, the structure of students' learning outcomes and subsequent academic performance, *Accounting Education: an international journal*, 13(4), 507–527.

Ramsay, A., Hanlon, D., & Smith, D. (2000) The association between cognitive style and accounting students' preference for cooperative learning: an empirical investigation, *Journal of Accounting Education*, 18, 215–228.

Ramsden, P. (1979) Student learning and perceptions of the academic environment, *Higher Education*, 8, 411–427.

Ramsden, P. & Entwistle, N.J. (1981) Effects of academic departments on students' approaches to studying, *British Journal of Educational Psychology*, 51, 368–383.

Rest, J.R. (1986) *Ethical Development: Advances in Research and Theory*, New York: Praeger.

Reynolds, M. (1997) Learning styles: a critique, *Management Learning*, 28(2), 115–133.

Richardson, J.T.E. (1994) Mature students in higher education: academic performance and intellectual ability, *Higher Education*, 28, 373–386.

Richardson, J.T.E. (2000) *Researching Student Learning: Approaches to Studying in Campus-based and Distance Learning*, Buckingham: SRHE and Open University Press.

Riding, R.J. (1997) The nature of cognitive style, *Educational Psychology*, 17(1, 2), 29–49.

Riding, R.J. & Cheema, I. (1991) Cognitive styles: an overview and integration, *Educational Psychology*, 11(3–4), 193–215.

Ruble, T.L. & Stout, D.E. (1993) Comments on the use of the LSI in research on student performance in accounting education, *Accounting Educators' Journal*, 5(2), 35–45.

Sadler-Smith, E. (1996) Approaches to studying: age, gender and academic performance, *Educational Studies*, 22, 367–379.

Sadler-Smith, E. & Tsang, S. (1998) A comparative study of approaches to studying in Hong Kong and the United Kingdom, *British Journal of Educational Psychology*, 68(1), 81–93.

Säljö, R. (1979) *Learning in the Learner's Perspective. I: Some Commonsense Conceptions*, Goteborg: Reports from the Institute of Education, University of Goteborg, 76.

Salomon, G. (1998) Novel constructivist learning environments and novel technologies: some issues to be concerned with, *Learning and Instruction*, 1, 3–12.

Sangster, A. (1996) Objective tests, learning to learn and learning styles, *Accounting Education: an international journal*, 5(2), 131–146.

Scarborough, D.P. (1993) Cognitive styles and job satisfaction of accountants, *Journal of Psychological Type*, 25(1), 3–10.

Schloemer, P.G. & Schloemer, M.S. (1997) The cognitive styles and preferences of CPA firm professionals: an analysis of changes in the profession, *Accounting Horizons*, 11(4), 24–39.

Schmeck, R., Ribich, F.D., & Ramaniah, N. (1977) Development of a self-report inventory for assessing individual differences in learning processes, *Applied Psychological Measurement*, 1, 413–431.

Severiens, S.E. & ten Dam, G.T.M. (1994) Gender differences in learning styles: a narrative review and quantitative meta-analysis, *Higher Education*, 27, 647–682.

Severiens, S.E. & ten Dam, G.T.M. (1998) A multilevel meta-analysis of gender differences in learning orientations, *British Journal of Educational Psychology*, 68, 595–608.

Sharma, D. (1997) Accounting students' learning conceptions, approaches to learning, and the influence of the learning-teaching context on approaches to learning, *Accounting Education: an international journal*, 6(2), 125–146.

Stout, D.E. & Ruble, T.L. (1991a) The LSI and accounting education research: a cautionary view and suggestions for future research, *Issues in Accounting Education*, 6(1), 41–52.

Stout, D.E. & Ruble, T.L. (1991b) A reexamination of accounting students' learning styles, *Journal of Accounting Education*, 9(2), 341–354.

Stout, D.E. & Ruble, T.L. (1994) A reassessment of the Learning Style Inventory (LSI-1985) in accounting education research, *Journal of Accounting Education*, 12(2), 89–104.

Sugahara, S. & Boland, G. (2010) The role of cultural factors in the learning style preferences of accounting students: a comparative study between Japan and Australia, *Accounting Education: an international journal*, 19(3), 235–255.

Swailes, S. & Senior, B. (2000) The dimensionality of Honey and Mumford's Learning Styles Questionnaire, *International Journal of Selection and Assessment*, 7(1), 1–11.

Tait, H. & Entwistle, N.J. (1996) Identifying students at risk through ineffective study strategies, *Higher Education*, 31(1), 97–116.

Tait, H., Entwistle N.J., & McCune, V. (1998) ASSIST: a reconceptualisation of the approaches to studying inventory, in Rust, C. (ed.) *Improving Student Learning: Improving Students as Learners*, Oxford: The Oxford Centre for Staff Development.

Tan, K. & Choo, F. (1990) A note on the academic performance of deep-elaborative versus shallow-reiterative information processing students, *Accounting and Finance*, May, 67–81.

Vaassen, E.H.J., Baker, C.R., & Hayes, R.S. (1993) Cognitive styles of experienced accountants in the Netherlands, *British Accounting Review*, 25, 367–382.

van Rossum, E.J. & Schenk, S.M. (1984) The relationship between learning conception, study strategy and learning outcome, *British Journal of Educational Psychology*, 54, 73–83.

Vermunt, J.D.H.M. (1992) *Leerstijlen en sturen van leerprocessen in het hoger onderwijs – Naar procesgerichte in zelfstandig denken* [Learning styles and regulation of learning in higher education: towards process-oriented instruction in autonomous thinking], Amsterdam: Swets and Zeitlinger.

Watty, K., Jackson, M., & Yu, X. (2010) Students' approaches to assessment in accounting education: the unique student perspective, *Accounting Education: an international journal*, 19(3), 219–234.

Wheeler, P. (2001) The Myers-Briggs Type Indicator and its application to accounting education and research, *Issues in Accounting Education*, 16(1), 125–150.

Wolk, C. & Nikolai, L.A. (1997) Personality types of accounting students and faculty: comparisons and implications, *Journal of Accounting Education*, 15(1), 1–17.

Wynn-Williams, K., Whiting, R.H., & Adler, R.W. (2008) The influence of business case studies on learning styles: an empirical investigation, *Accounting Education: an international journal*, 17(2), 113–128.

About the author

Angus Duff is Professor in the School of Business at the University of the West of Scotland, U.K. (angus.duff@uws.ac.uk). His current research, teaching, and consulting interests are in the accounting profession, education and educational research, and credit rating agencies. He is at present Research Advisor to the Institute of Chartered Accountants of Scotland, and has served as an Associate Editor of *Accounting Education: an international journal*.

9

The choice of accounting as a study discipline

Fawzi Laswad and Lin Mei Tan

MASSEY UNIVERSITY, NEW ZEALAND

CONTENTS

Abstract

Concerns over a perceived decline in interest in studying accounting, and the shortage of quality accounting graduates, raise the question of what can be done to motivate students to consider and choose accounting as their study major. This chapter provides an overview of the growing literature that addresses students' choice of accounting as a study major, and identifies various factors that influence this choice. Some studies have theoretical underpinnings and others merely build on prior studies and/or through the use of focus groups. Significant factors include first year experience, personal characteristics and interests, employment and career opportunities and financial rewards, perception of accountants, accounting study and accounting work, prior learning, and parental and others' influence. Based on these insights, we suggest what can be done to motivate students to enrol in accounting programmes and what future research could focus on to fill the gap in the literature.

Keywords

accounting discipline, students' major choice, study major, Theory of Planned Behaviour

9.1 Introduction

The main aims of this chapter are:

- to outline the theoretical models that attempt to explain discipline choice;
- to discuss the factors that influence students in choosing accounting as a study major;
- to address the implications of the findings; and
- to suggest areas for future research.

The current chapter, focussing on factors influencing the choice of accounting *as a major*, complements Chapter 10, which specifically addresses the influences on the choice of accounting as *a career*. While there is inevitably some commonality, the aims of the two chapters are clearly differentiated.

We begin the chapter by providing some insights into the concerns over attracting students, if not always the best and brightest, into the accounting discipline at universities. This concern has prompted a number of researchers to carry out studies on factors that influence students' choice of major. This is followed by a brief review of studies that have adopted theoretical frameworks in examining students' behaviour regarding study major choice and decision-making. In Section 9.3, we examine the impact of various factors that influence study major choice and their relative importance. The final section provides the conclusions and implications of the insights gained from the extant literature, with suggestions for future research.

9.2 Concerns over choice of major

Business has become the most popular academic subject within the expanding area of tertiary education. In the U.S.A., the proportion of bachelor degrees awarded in business increased from 14 per cent in 1971 to 20 per cent in 2009, while the number of bachelor graduates increased by 90 per cent during the same period.[1] However, it appears that interest in accounting as a study discipline is in decline, and fewer top business students are choosing accounting as their study major. Albrecht & Sack (2000) reported a decline in the number of accounting graduates in the U.S.A. by 20 per cent between 1996 and 1998. The decline in students majoring in accounting is also noted in other countries, such as Australia (Jackling & Calero, 2006), the U.K. (Marriott, 2002), Ireland (Byrne & Willis, 2005), Japan (Sugahara *et al.*, 2006), and New Zealand (Heaton, 1999).

Students vary as to when they select their accounting major; some may choose prior to commencing university study (Karnes *et al.*, 1997; Jackman & Hollingworth, 2005), while others may decide during or at the end of their first (Mauldin *et al.*, 2000) or second year of university (Hermanson *et al.*, 1995). Some students may even change their major in later years, or add another major to their degree (Nelson *et al.*, 2008). As business education is expanding while interest in accounting as a study discipline appears to be declining, it is important to comprehend not only when students choose their study majors but also to understand what motivates, influences, or dissuades students from choosing accounting studies when they are faced with a wide range of specialisations. The accounting discipline competes with other disciplines in attracting students and this competition is likely to intensify as new study specialisations emerge and business education fragments. This chapter examines the various factors that attract and deter students from pursuing accounting as a study discipline.

Drawing on the literature, Figure 9.1 outlines six key drivers that have the potential to influence the choice of accounting major:

- first year experience;
- prior education;
- personal characteristics and interests;
- influence of parents and others;
- perceptions of employment and career opportunities including perceptions of pecuniary and non-pecuniary rewards; and
- perceptions of the nature of accounting studies and the accounting profession.

The empirical literature is summarised in Table 9.1.[2] We first discuss those studies with theoretical underpinnings where the researchers set out to either test the key factors that predict students' choice of accounting major, or identify the personality types of accounting students.

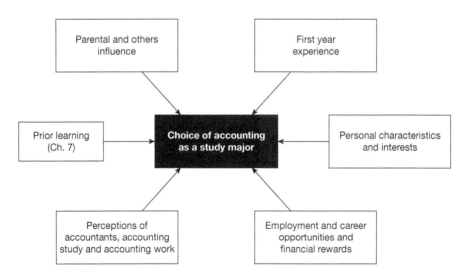

Figure 9.1 Factors that influence the choice of accounting as a study major

Table 9.1 Research on students' choice of academic majors

Author	Research method/theory	Subject and sample size	Key variables/factors	Primary results
Law & Yuen (2012)	Semi-structured interviews followed by questionnaire survey/Theory of Reasoned Action (TRA)	422 first year accounting students and 60 master's students of four Hong Kong larger campus universities; Accounting major = 140, others = 282	First accounting course, high school accounting, intrinsic interest, parental influence, financial rewards, gender.	Significant factors: parental influence and intrinsic interest. Females more likely than males to major in accounting.
Law (2010)	Survey/TRA	214 final year accounting students from three universities in Hong Kong; General accounting career choice = 92, CPA career choice = 87, others = 35	Intrinsic factors, parental influence, flexibility of career options, high school accounting, financial rewards, gender	Significant factors: Intrinsic factors (attitude toward the behaviour) and parental influence (subjective norm). Flexibility of career options most influential of all variables. Females dominate males in choosing CPA career.
Pringle, DuBose, & Yankey (2010)	Survey	899 sophomore business students in a medium-sized public university in U.S.A.; Accounting major = 150, others = 749	Personality characteristics: achievement motivation, conformity, creativity, conscientiousness, extroversion. Used various scale, e.g. Kirton Adaption-Innovation Inventory, Entrepreneurial Attitude Orientation Scale, etc.	Students choose major compatible with their personalities based upon commonly held stereotypes. Accounting majors are highest in conformity.
Chen, Jones, & McIntyre (2008)	Survey	556 business students at different stages in their academic career in a university in south-eastern U.S.A.; Accounting major = 185, others = 371	Perceived benefits and costs of pursuing accounting	Experience in the first university accounting course is differentially associated with benefits and cost perceptions, and nature of association depends on whether students took accounting in secondary school. Perceptions also differ between students at early and late stages of their respective academic programmes, and accounting vs. non-accounting majors.
Jackling & Keneley (2009)	Survey/TRA	428 accounting major students at Victoria University in Australia; Local students = 124, overseas = 303	Enjoy accounting topics, interested in accounting problems, accounting will assist with other studies, wanted to get better idea, expect high grades, good job opportunities, high salary potential, improve career advancement, high status jobs, recommendations of friends	Influential factors: intrinsic interest (enjoyment of topics and interest in accounting problems), market and extrinsic factors (good job opportunities and potential high salary). Referent groups important for international students.

Study	Method/Theory	Variables	Sample	Findings
Sugahara & Boland (2009)	Survey	or relatives, similarity to parents' occupation, parental encouragement, increase points for permanent residency, recommendation of university staff Parents, peers, business people, chance to make a contribution, nature of job, element of variety and adventure, flexibility in career option, interaction with others, good long-term earnings, good initial salary, advancement opportunities, a structured career path, social prestige, security of employment, job availability, length of work hours, sufficient time for personal life, good physical working conditions	373 Japanese tertiary business graduate and undergraduate students of eight universities in Japan; Accounting students (intention of becoming a CPA) = 99, Others = 274	Major influence affecting vocational choice for accounting students was intrinsic values (chance to make a contribution and nature of job). Non-accounting students indicated career prospects (structured career path, social prestige, advancement opportun ties) were major contributing factors when choosing a career.
Tan & Laswad (2009)	Survey/Theory of Planned Behaviour (TPB) Longitudinal analysis, extended study by Tan & Laswad (2006)	Used same variables as Tan & Laswad (2006)	Traced 304 third and final year accounting students who participated in Tan & Laswad (2006) study (i.e. when they were in first year) in one multi-campus NZ university	Students' choices of major are consistent with their intentions at start of university study. Some attitudes and beliefs may change over time but major choice tends to remain relatively stable.
Sugahara, Boland, & Cilloni (2008)	Survey	Students' creativity, vocational expectation factors (intrinsic value, career status, work environment, job market condition) and perceptions of accounting profession	114 undergraduate and graduate students in two large Australian universities; Accounting major = 61, others = 53, Domestic = 114, International = 68	Domestic students with higher creativity unlikely to major in accounting whereas Chinese students with lower creativity level were more likely to major in accounting.
Heiat, Brown, & Johnson (2007)	Survey	Genuine interest in subject, availability of employment, instructors, ability to interact with people, starting pay, personal liability, prestige, ability to maintain high GPA, expected ease of earning a degree	345 business students in one U.S.A. university; Accounting major = 69, others = 276	Significant factors: genuine interest in subject matter, availability of employment, starting pay, ability to interact with people.
Bealing, Baker, & Russo (2006)	Survey/Jung's theory	Used Keirsey Temperament Sorter instrument to examine personality type of accounting majors and business majors	56 freshmen accounting majors and 54 non-accounting majors at one university in the U.S.A.	Accounting majors are extraverts, sensors, thinkers, and judgers (ESTJ)

Table 9.1 Research on students' choice of academic majors—continued

Author	Research method/theory	Subject and sample size	Key variables/factors	Primary results
Briggs (2006)	Survey	651 first year students undergraduates across 6 universities in Scotland; Accounting students = 399, engineering students = 252	22 factors	Academic reputation, distance from home and location were top three factors.
Tan & Laswad (2006)	Survey/TPB	1009 introductory accounting students in a multicampus university in NZ; Accounting major = 215, others = 794	Personal perceptions, perceptions of referents, perceived control	Personal, referents, and control are determinants of students' intention to major in accounting or other business disciplines. Parents have a stronger influence on students' intentions to major in accounting. Accounting majors hold positive perceptions of some of the qualities of study of accounting and the accounting profession. Significant differences were also found in the control perception between accounting and non-accounting major students.
Byrne & Flood (2005)	Survey	129 first year students in accounting and finance at one university in Ireland	Motives for entering higher education, rationale for selecting accounting programme, preparedness for further study and their expectations	Career aspirations and desire to develop intellectually motivates choice of accounting degree.
Chen, Jones, & McIntyre (2005)	Survey	450 business senior, junior and sophomore students from a large south-eastern university in U.S.A.; Accounting majors = 182, others = 268	Intrinsic values, long-term earning, initial earnings, job market factors, ratio of benefits to costs	Students' overall experience in Introductory Accounting class most important factor in distinguishing major choice between accounting and non-accounting students. Accounting majors place less importance on intrinsic factors and report a higher ratio of perceived benefits to costs of choosing accounting rather than non-accounting majors. But initial earnings, long-term earnings and job market considerations rank low in discrimination between accounting and non- accounting majors.

Study	Method	Sample	Topic	Findings
Allen (2004)	Survey/TPB	410 business majors in *Introductory Accounting* at one college and two universities in U.S.A.; Accounting major = 66, others = 344	150 hour requirement, image of accounting	Factors shown to influence students' choice of major prior to the 150-hour requirement continue to influence students' choice of major in the presence of the 150-hour requirement. Regarding the image of accounting in the presence of the 150-hour requirement, the results suggest that merely extending the length of the accounting programme has not signalled that the nature of accounting is interesting and appealing.
Hunt, Falgiani, & Intrieri (2004)	Survey	474 business students at one university in the U.S.A.; Accounting majors = 71, others = 403	Impressions of accountants.	Non-accounting majors' overall impression of accountants lower than accounting majors. Accountants seen as professional but not particularly personable.
Nelson, Vendrzyk, Quirin, & Allen (2002)	Survey; comparison of 2000 results to 1995 results.	Graduate and senior accounting majors and graduate students at 22 Federation of Schools of Accountancy (FSA) universities in the U.S.A.; 1995 = 1,352 students, 2000 = 1,475 students	Factors influencing students' decisions to choose accounting as a major and the timing of such decisions	Decline in percentage of accounting majors who seriously considered majoring in accounting while in high school (45% vs. 40%). Relatively fewer students actually decided to major in accounting while in high school (26% versus 32% in 1995); sophomore year represents the most common year for actually selecting the major. Reasons for choosing accounting as a major are changing: "availability of jobs" is still the most important reason; however, "money/good salaries" and "interesting or exciting profession" also relatively important.
Strasser, Ozgur, & Schroeder (2002)	Survey	63 sophomore and 49 senior business majors from one college in the U.S.A.	Choice-of-major is a function of: Interest, Influence, and Career. Career is a function of money, job availability and growth, and job requirements. Job requirements are a function of computer usage and interpersonal skills	Students value the interest they have in the major as far more important than the career benefits of a major or someone else's influence on them to choose a particular major. Within career, most important were money/compensation and job availability/growth. Students will choose a career that fits

Table 9.1 Research on students' choice of academic majors—continued

Author	Research method/theory	Subject and sample size	Key variables/factors	Primary results
				their interpersonal skills rather than a career based on the amount of computer usage they believe will be required on the job. Decision inconsistency much more prevalent for sophomore, as compared to senior students.
Geiger & Ogilby (2000)	Survey	331 students in *Introductory Accounting* courses (taught by eight different instructors) from two different institutions (mostly first-semester sophomores) in U.S.A.; Accounting major = 53, others = 278	Students' perceptions of first accounting course and the relationship between these perceptions, final grades, and instructors on the decision to major in accounting	Changes in students' perceptions during the first accounting course, as well as the decision to major in accounting, are instructor-related. End-of-term selection of accounting as a major depends also on beginning-of-semester intentions to major in accounting and on performance in the first course and individual instructors.
Mauldin, Crain, & Mounce (2000)	Survey	166 students in first and second *Introductory Accounting* courses and *Intermediate Accounting* from three universities in U.S.A.; Accounting major = 60, others = 106	Influence of *Principles of Accounting* instructor on decision to major in accounting; timing of the decision to choose a particular major	Factors influencing major decision: career opportunities, interest in subject, teacher, money, parents. Of these, the *Principles of Accounting* instructor viewed as the most influential. Decision to major in accounting often made in first accounting course.
Taylor (2000)	Focus-group meetings; telephone interviews	2,174 telephone interviews (1,000 with high school students, the balance with college students in four locations in U.S.A.); College student planning on accounting major = 1%, high school students planning on accounting major= 2%; 9 focus groups (40 high school students, 427 college students)	Students' perceptions and systemic barriers (to accounting career); attributes making a career attractive to students	Students often make career decisions in high school and have misinformation (e.g., "accountants do boring, tedious, and monotonous number-crunching by themselves") about accountants. Students impacted by role models, quality of instructor, quality of *Introductory Accounting* courses, and perceptions of CPAs. Seven attributes important to students: lucrative, rewarding, limitless, creative, multidisciplinary, travel and group work. Students looking for personally rewarding careers, careers where you are able

Study	Method	Sample	Variables	Findings
				to work with people, and careers that make a contribution to society and maintain a balance of home and work. They don't see accounting as providing these rewards. The licensing exam, 150-hour requirement, and CPE are not viewed as barriers to students.
Saemann & Crooker (1999)	Survey	196 introductory accounting students in one university in the U.S.A.; Accounting major = 51, others = 145	Relationship between students' inherent creativity and perceptions of the accounting profession ("structure," "precision," "solitary," and "interest") on the decision to major in accounting; extent to which experience in a lecture-based introductory accounting course changes students' perceptions and choices in major.	Students were much more likely to choose an accounting major when they considered accounting to be interesting. Students are more likely to find the accounting profession interesting when they do not perceive it to be highly structured, rule-oriented, or solitary.
Ahmed, Alam, & Alam (1997)	Survey	295 third year accounting students of five NZ universities; Accounting major = 241, others = 54	Intrinsic, financial, parental, peer influence, work experience, benefit-cost ratio of becoming an accountant, completion high school accounting	Students choosing an accounting career give significantly higher priority to financial factors and the benefit-cost ratio of becoming an accountant than the students not choosing an accounting career.
AuYeung & Sands (1997)	Survey	632 first and second year undergraduate accounting major students from Australia, China and Taiwan; Australian = 303, Chinese Hong Kong =172, Taiwanese = 157	Significant others (parent, teacher, peer influence, association with others), materials (availability of employment, prestige and social status, earning potential, cost of education, years of required formal education), belief (job satisfaction, aptitude, previous work experience)	Chinese and Taiwanese students' choice of accounting is more affected by the influence of teachers, parents, and peers, and by the students' association with others in the field. Alternatively, aptitude for the subject matter has a greater influence on Australian students. Material factors (e.g. income, prestige, and employment availability) are more influential with Chinese and Taiwanese students.
Bebbington, Thomson & Wall (1997)	Survey	227 first year accounting students (of whom 96 who completed first year accounting) at two universities in Scotland; Accounting first choice = 82%, others = 18%	Interest, passport to many other careers, maths ability, career advisor or family/friend suggestion, impression of accounting profession	Career opportunities and financial rewards motivated students' choice to study accounting. Accounting students have a distinctive masculine gender.

Table 9.1 Research on students' choice of academic majors—continued

Author	Research method/theory	Subject and sample size	Key variables/factors	Primary results
Karnes, King & Hahn (1997)	Survey	469 high school students in grades 9–12 at seven high schools and 38 freshmen at one public university in U.S.A.; Chose accounting career = 26, others = 481	High potential or not based on GPA or American College Testing (ACT) scores	High potential students were more likely to have chosen a career in the traditional professions (e.g. law, medicine, engineering, accounting); and students choosing accounting as a career were more likely to be female and less likely to have college-educated parents.
Lowe & Simons (1997)	Survey	551 sophomore business students (accounting, finance, management, and marketing majors) at a private college in U.S.A.; Accounting major = 232, others = 319	Future earnings, career options, initial earnings, ability or aptitude, intellectual challenge, interesting subject, self-employ, prestige, parents' advice, high school teacher, work experience, friends, parents' professions	Accounting majors distinctive in placing most emphasis on future earnings and career options. Marketing majors placed more emphasis on nature of the subject matter, management majors influenced by self-employment opportunities, and finance majors most like accounting majors.
Stice & Swain (1997)	Survey	389 Introductory Accounting students, at a private university in U.S.A., with a minimum GPA (two large sections taught each semester over a two term period by each of two instructors); (162 "unqualified" based on average performance on two mid-term exams in the Introductory Accounting course, and 227 "qualified" using the same criterion)	Performance in Introductory Accounting course and intention to major in accounting	For the set of pre-screened students (i.e., those meeting a minimum GPA) better classroom performance in Introductory Accounting courses did not influence students' decisions to major in accounting. Qualified students may conclude that a demonstrated mastery of the mechanics is not sufficient and rely on other factors in the decision to major in accounting.
Wolk & Nikolai (1997)	Survey/Jung's theory	94 accounting graduate students, 98 accounting staff members and 152 undergraduate accounting students at two universities in the U.S.A.	Examines Myers-Briggs Type Indicator personality types of undergraduate and graduate accounting majors as well as accounting staff.	Accounting students are predominantly extraverts, sensors, thinkers, and judgers (ESTJ). They are more likely to prefer sensing and thinking when compared to graduate students.
Felton, Dimnik, & Northey (1995)	Survey/TRA	Graduating business students from seven Canadian institutions; 431 CA students, 63 non-CA students, 145 finance students, 251 non-finance students.	Career selection (CA versus non-CA) as a function of: beliefs regarding CA-career outcomes (e.g., good long-term earnings) and importance of these outcomes in choosing a career; ratio of	CA and non-CA students indicated little difference in the importance of 10 career outcomes but significant difference in the likelihood of a career in CA providing those outcomes.

Study	Method	Sample	Variables	Findings
Lowe, Lowe, & Simons (1994)	Survey	608 Sophomore business students at a specialty business college in U.S.A.; Accounting major = 232, others = 406	Choice of business major as a function of gender and 13 selection criteria.	Accounting majors placed more weight on financial factors in selecting majors. Female accounting majors placed relatively higher value on the inherent nature of the subject matter being challenging and interesting.
Adams, Pryor, & Adams (1994)	Survey, archival data analysis; longitudinal analysis	194 *Introductory Accounting* students from a large residential state university in U.S.A. (eight sections taught by one instructor); Accounting major = 20, others = 174	AICPA Aptitude Test scores; good job opportunities, high earnings potential, similar to parents' occupations, recommendations of friends and relatives or counsellors, high status of job in this area, expected ease of earning a degree, ability to maintain a high GPA, faculty reputation, parental pressure, genuine interest in the field.	Good job opportunities, high earnings potential, and genuine interest in the field are the most important major-selection factors. High aptitude non-accounting majors placed most significance on genuine interest in the area and less influence on monetary and/or job availability. Students are not selecting majors based on perceived difficulty of the curriculum.
Felton, Buhr, & Northey (1994)	Survey	897 fourth year business students at seven Ontario institutions; CA career choice = 431, others = 396	Career choice (decision to choose a career as a CA) and: (1) importance of intrinsic rewards, financial rewards, and job market; (2) perception of accounting profession; and (3) exposure to high school accounting.	Students choosing CA, compared to other business majors: (1) place less importance on intrinsic factors and initial earnings; (2) more heavily emphasize long-term earnings and both short-term (e.g., immediate job availability) and long-term (e.g., job security, career flexibility) job market condition.; (3) perceive a higher benefit/cost ratio to being a CA; and (4) have had more exposure to high school accounting. The most important factor was perceptions regarding the benefit/cost ratio to being a CA.
Cohen & Hanno (1993)	Survey/TPB	287 sophomores and seniors from five separate institutions in U.S.A.; Accounting major = 111, others = 170	Three constructs: differential attitude, differential subjective norm; and, differential perceived control.	Students not choosing accounting believe that accounting is too number-oriented and boring. Their choice is also affected by perceptions of important referents. Success in accounting courses, skills and background in maths, and the workload in accounting courses also facilitated/hindered choice of accounting as a major.

beliefs regarding benefits and costs of CA career option.

Table 9.1 Research on students' choice of academic majors—continued

Author	Research method/theory	Subject and sample size	Key variables/factors	Primary results
Graves, Nelson, & Deines (1993)	Survey	1622 graduate and senior accounting majors from 26 FSA schools in U.S.A.; Accounting career for seniors = 69%, Accounting career for graduates = 60%	How and when students decide to major in accounting.	Little change from 1991 survey results: 42% seriously considered a career in accounting while in high school; 30% actually decided on an accounting career while in high school; of individuals, after "self" (39%) parents/other relative (22%) played most important role in career choice; top two factors affecting accounting career choice = availability of jobs, and money/good salaries.
Chacko (1991)	Survey/Holland's theory of vocational choice	97 undergraduate business students from an urban university in U.S.A. Accounting majors = 45, Hospitality management majors = 52	Used Strong Campbell Interest Inventory Scores to classify students into their majors	Accounting students are more conventional (i.e. students having a certain image of accounting profession seemed to have matched their interest with that image).
Gul, Andrew, Leong, & Ismail (1989)	Survey	367 first-year students in medicine, law, engineering and accounting at two Australian Universities Accountancy students = 87, others = 280	Earnings potential, association with others in field, parental influence, social status, job satisfaction, years of formal education, aptitude for subject, teachers' influence, previous work experience, availability of employment	Accounting students have different and more distinctive profile than medicine, engineering, and law students. Earnings, aptitude, employment, and years of education most important to accounting students. Job satisfaction important to all.
Inman, Wenzler, & Wickert (1989)	Survey, archival data analysis; longitudinal analysis	Used 3 data sources of accounting students: AICPA, the Cooperative Institutional Research Program (CIRP), and the Office of Education Research and Improvement (OERI) in U.S.A., and a focus group.	Analysed college enrolment data, accounting graduate supply and demand statistics, self-reported student characteristics	Interest in accounting is declining. Process of accounting education and image of public accounting professions cited as contributing factors.
Paolillo & Estes (1982)	Survey	694 Professionals: 121 doctors, 185 lawyers, 219 accountants, 169 engineers in the U.S.A.; n = 694 (28%)	Career choice as a function of 12 influencing factors: earnings potential, association with others in field, parents, cost of education, social status, job satisfaction, years of education, aptitude, teachers, peers, work experience, and job availability.	The most important factors influencing the selection of accounting as the chosen profession were: aptitude for the subject matter, job satisfaction level, and earnings potential. They also found teacher influence to be more important than parental influence or peer influence.

9.3 Theoretical underpinnings

9.3.1 Theory of Reasoned Action/Theory of Planned Behaviour

Choosing a major can involve a complex decision-making process. To capture the complex nature of the decision process and explain the interrelations between the various factors, some researchers adopted a conceptual framework derived from social psychology in their studies on accounting major choice. For instance, the studies carried out by Felton *et al.*, (1994), Jackling & Keneley (2009), Law (2010), and Law & Yuen (2012) draw on the cognitive-based Theory of Reasoned Action (TRA) (Ajzen, 1988) while the studies carried out by Cohen & Hanno (1993), Allen (2004), Tan & Laswad (2006), and Tan & Laswad (2009), draw on the Theory of Planned Behaviour (TPB), an extension of the TRA which incorporates 'control' as a third variable (Fishbein & Ajzen, 1975).

Figure 9.2 outlines the TRA and the TPB and identifies the factors that influence intentions and behaviour. The theories posit that people act in accordance with their intentions and perceptions of control over the behaviour, while intentions in turn are influenced by attitudes towards the behaviour (formed by perceptions and beliefs about salary, job opportunity, image, workload, etc.), subjective norms (e.g. parents' and friends' influence), and perceptions of behavioural control (i.e. how easy or difficult it is to perform the behaviour) (Ajzen, 2001, p. 43). The literature indicates that students hold diverse attitudes towards accounting as a major and some are influenced by important referent groups. Students may also perceive that they do not have the ability or control to complete an accounting programme successfully due to, perhaps, study workload, or the skills and aptitude required of the accounting course. The TRA or TPB, therefore, provides a suitable framework for examining the factors that explain and predict students' academic major decisions.

The findings of studies that used this theoretical framework were consistent (i.e. attitudes and norms influenced major choice decisions). Researchers (Cohen & Hanno, 1993; Allen, 2004; Tan & Laswad, 2006) who added 'perceived control' to the TPB model also found this was a significant factor in predicting career choice. As students may change their intentions expressed

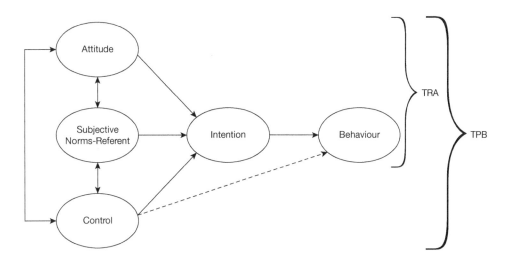

Figure 9.2 Ajzen's (1988) Theory of Reasoned Action and Fishbein & Ajzen's (1975) Theory of Planned Behaviour

in the first year of studying accounting, Tan & Laswad (2009) extended their 2006 study by targeting the same students who have progressed to the senior (third) year of study. Their longitudinal study provides evidence that, overall, there were very few changes in students' personal attitudes and perceived control between their first and third years of study. The variables which differentiate the underlying attitudes and beliefs of accounting and non-accounting major students are discussed in Section 9.4 of this chapter.

9.3.2 Theory of vocational choice/theory of psychological type

Deciding on a study major is not always an easy task for many students. One way in which students may go about their major choice decisions is to choose one that matches their interests, likes, and dislikes (Holland, 1985). Holland's vocational choice theory argued that students often choose occupations with environments that match their personalities. The six personality-interest types and corresponding environments are depicted in Figure 9.3: they are Realistic, Investigative, Artistic, Social, Enterprising, and Conventional. Each type is characterised by a particular set of interests, traits, values, competence, and perceptions. According to Holland, those who fall under the conventional type prefer structured, verbal and numerical activities, and value material possessions and status. These descriptions fit well with the public's traditional image of the stereotypical accountant. Thus, students may decide to major in accounting because they perceive that the work environment and lifestyle of the professional accountant matches their own abilities and interests. This interesting aspect of vocational choice has prompted Chacko (1991) to examine the efficacy of Holland's theory of vocational choice in business education, and to test the accuracy of predicting undergraduate students' choices of two major fields of study: accounting and hospitality management. The Hanson's (1984) Strong Campbell Interest Inventory (SCII) which is organised according to Holland's theory, is used to categorise personality types. Chacko's results show that accounting students scored higher than hospitality management students in the conventional type as described in Holland's theory.

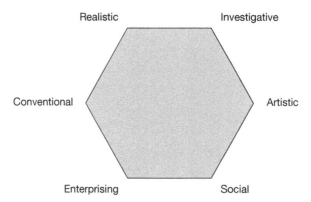

Figure 9.3 Holland's (1985) personality types
Source: Holland (1985).

Wolk & Nikolai (1997) examine the personality types of accounting students by drawing on Jung's theory which postulates that individuals have an orientation toward their outer worlds. Jung was an analytical psychologist who developed a *theory of psychological types* designed to group people in various personality patterns. Based on this theory, eight functions affect how students behave:

- sensing (prefer uncomplicated tasks);
- intuition (prefer complex tasks);
- thinking (objective, logical and well-organised student);
- feeling (subjective, prefer learning through group/team work);
- extravert (prefer working in groups, talking and discussing);
- introvert (prefer working alone, verbal reasoning and reading);
- judgement (decisive, work in steady orderly manner, see things in black and white); and
- perception (like flexibility, informal unstructured problem-solving, curious) (Wolk & Nikolai, 1997: 11–12).

Wolk & Nikolai used the Myers-Briggs Type Indicator (MBTI) to link personality type and career choice. The MBTI[3] is designed to access an individual's personality preferences in four primary areas: introvert/extravert, sensing/intuitive, thinking/feeling, and judging/perceiving (Bealing *et al.*, 2006). Accounting students were typically found to be Extraverts, Sensors, Thinkers and Judgers (ESTJ) which is consistent with the findings of Lawrence & Taylor (2000).[4] However, this finding is inconsistent with earlier studies by Wolk & Cates (1994), and Gul & Fong (1993), whose studies suggest that accounting students are introverts who prefer to work in an environment where there is an emphasis on individual rather than group effort.

A more recent study of business students by Bealing *et al.* (2006) raised two questions:

- Do incoming majors have a predisposition to be a particular personality type?
- Do the personality types of accounting majors differ from those of other business majors?

They used the Keirsey Temperament Sorter (KTS), which corresponds to the MBTI, to examine personality type. Consistent with Wolk & Nikolai (1997), the dominant type for an undergraduate accounting major student was also ESTJ. Interestingly, non-accounting business majors were also mainly of ESTJ personality.

Although these theoretical-based studies provide valuable insights into how students match their personalities with their perception of commonly held stereotypes of particular occupations, there are other drivers or influences that may also contribute to their choice of study discipline.

9.4 Key drivers of study choice

The key variables or factors that influence students' choice of major can be classified in various ways or discussed in different contexts.[5] In this chapter we focus on the influences/drivers of students' choice of the accounting as a study discipline. The factors considered in both theory-based and non-theory-based studies are grouped into six categories and are discussed below.

9.4.1 First year experience

The accounting major competes with a wide range of study majors and often students form their impressions of disciplines during the experience of their first year's study. First-year impressions can, therefore, exert considerable influence on their choice of academic majors. In particular, the first accounting course, often compulsory for all business students, is important as it shapes students' perceptions of the profession, the aptitudes and skills needed for a successful career in accounting, and the nature of career opportunities in accounting[6] (Cherry & Reckers, 1983; Cohen & Hanno, 1993; Adams *et al.*, 1994; Stice & Swain, 1997). Chen *et al.*'s (2005) study lends support to this assertion as they found that overall experience in the *Introductory*

Accounting class to be the most important factor in distinguishing study major choices between accounting and non-accounting students.

Students' experience in their first year of study is viewed in terms of the course content, the workload, the teacher, and their grades (Cohen & Hanno, 1993). Generally, students prefer courses that are well-organised, interesting, and intellectually stimulating, but not courses with heavy course workloads. Teachers also play an important role in students' perceptions of the course. Students' evaluations of teachers show that they like effective teachers – those who are enthusiastic and passionate about teaching, and those who actively engage students in their learning (Albrecht & Sack, 2000). Good teachers certainly can inspire students to want to learn more about the subject area. In deciding whether to major in accounting, students may also reflect on the grades which they achieved in the *Introductory Accounting* course in comparison with other subjects. Students tend to perceive success in the *Introductory Accounting* as reflecting an aptitude for the subject (Geiger & Ogilby, 2000). Poor performance, on the other hand, may be perceived by students as being a signal that they may not have the required aptitude for accounting and, therefore, should pursue a non-accounting major (Cohen & Hanno, 1993).

The importance of the qualities of the first accounting course in influencing students' study major choice is evident in some studies carried out with accounting students. For instance, Saemann & Crooker's (1999) findings show that students in the U.S.A. are more likely to choose an accounting major if their experience during the *Introductory Accounting* course is interesting and enjoyable. Uninteresting accounting coursework focussed on rote learning of accounting rules may discourage the best students from pursuing an accounting major (Inman *et al.*, 1989). Mauldin *et al.*'s (2000) survey of undergraduate accounting students indicates that the teacher of *Accounting Principles* is very influential in students' decisions to major in accounting. Students' choice of an accounting major is further affected by their perceptions of course workload – a heavy workload in the *Introductory Accounting* course discourages students from majoring in accounting (Cohen & Hanno, 1993; Saemann & Crooker, 1999; Allen, 2004). Workload, when viewed in terms of number of required formal years of education, can also be influential in students' decisions when choosing study majors (Paolillo & Estes, 1982; Gul *et al.*, 1989; Auyeung & Sands, 1997; Mauldin *et al.*, 2000; Allen, 2004).

The findings of studies which examined students' performance in the *Introductory Accounting* course were mixed. Some did not find that students' decisions to major in accounting depended on course performance (e.g. Adams *et al.*, 1994; Stice & Swain, 1997; Tan & Laswad, 2006). For instance, Stice & Swain (1997) found high-performing students to be less concerned about their performance in *Introductory Accounting* than low-performing students when deciding whether to major in accounting. Other researchers (e.g. Geiger & Ogilby, 2000; Cohen & Hanno, 1993; Tan & Laswad, 2006) show that course performance is a significant factor in students' choice of major. Some interesting insights were obtained from the study carried out by Geiger & Ogilby (2000) who examined students' perceptions of the first accounting course and its impact on selection of accounting as a major:

- Students' final grades in accounting and their teachers are significant predictors of students' choice of major.
- Students' positive perceptions about the *Introductory Accounting* course at the beginning of the course diminished at the end of the course.
- Students appeared more bored with the course at the end of the semester. Finding accounting 'boring' appears to be a common perception of non-accounting majors (Cohen & Hanno, 1993; Allen, 2004; Tan & Laswad, 2006).

Overall, these studies indicate the importance of curricula, teacher, workload, and performance in attracting students to the accounting major. These are major challenges for educators as *Introductory Accounting* courses often include greater readings, higher workload, and lower performance than other introductory courses. Further, the demands of teaching large *Introductory Accounting* classes may discourage good teachers from being involved.

9.4.2 Prior education

Those who choose to study accounting at secondary school could do so out of interest or curiosity and will, therefore, have some idea of what accounting entails, hence their choice of major at university could be affected by their experience of the course at school. Interestingly, various studies have examined the influence of prior high school accounting education on students' choice of major and/or career, and have found mixed results (Felton *et al.*, 1994; Ahmed *et al.*, 1997; Nelson *et al.*, 2002). This influence is examined in more detail by Byrne & Willis in Chapter 7 – this volume, and by Jackling in Chapter 10 – this volume.

9.4.3 Personal characteristics and interests

The literature further suggests a link between students' personal attributes (such as aptitudes, interests, and personalities) and their study major choice decisions. Numerous studies have confirmed the influence of this factor on business and accounting students' choice of major. Students tend to choose study majors which they perceive as being compatible with their own aptitude for the subject (e.g. Paolillo & Estes, 1982; Gul *et al.*, 1989; Auyeung & Sands, 1997; Jackling & Keneley, 2009). In addition, genuine interest in the subject is an important selection factor (Adams *et al.*, 1994; Mauldin *et al.*, 2000). If students' perceptions of accounting indicate that it requires numerical skills, those who are weak in mathematics may not select accounting as their study major. Cohen & Hanno (1993) and Tan & Laswad (2006, 2009) provided evidence that students' perceptions of their skills and background in mathematics could facilitate or hinder their decision to major in accounting. However, the link between numeracy skills and mathematics is erroneous. This on-going misperception needs to be corrected: success in accounting study and an accounting career requires numeracy skills, and not necessarily mathematical skills. (Numeracy, rather than mathematical expertise, is considered by Wilson *et al.*, as being a key element of financial literacy in Chapter 3 – this volume.)

Students also tend to choose study majors which they perceive as being compatible with their personality style or characteristics (see e.g. Gul, 1986; Chacko, 1991; Wolk & Cates, 1994; Saemann & Crooker, 1999; Pringle *et al.*, 2010). It is interesting to note that Herbert Simon, the 1978 Nobel Laureate in Economics, reflected on his experiences as an undergraduate student at the University of Chicago as follows:

> *Henry Simons, on price theory, teetering on two legs of his chair, gave me a glimpse of the applications of rigor and mathematics to economics. I resolved to major in economics, until I learned that it required an accounting course. I switched to political science, which had no such requirement.*
>
> (Simon, 1991, p. 39)

Certainly he had a particular perception of the accounting subject at that stage – and one that was not to his liking. Nevertheless, he led a team which made a seminal contribution to accounting in the first study which recognised the influence of accounting on organisational behaviour (Simon *et al.*, 1954).

Compared to other factors, the influence of personality is an area that is least explored in research on the choice of accounting major. As mentioned earlier, studies carried out by Bealing *et al.* (2006), Wolk & Nikolai (1997), and Chacko (1991) found that students who choose to major in accounting are those with an extrovert, sensing, thinking and judging (ESTJ) personality type – meaning that they tend to be practical, matter-of-fact, and well-organised. It appears that students who have a particular image of the accounting profession matched their interests, competencies, and preferences with the perceived environment of the accounting profession. This 'person–environment fit' insight suggests that it is pertinent to dispel the stereotypical image of an accountant as being 'boring' and a 'number-cruncher'.

9.4.4 Influence of parents and others

In making career choices, students can be influenced by other people such as their school counsellors, accounting teachers, parents, relatives, friends, and other role models. For instance, a secondary school career counsellor or adviser can shape pupils' perceptions of accounting and the profession by providing information, views and opinions about the discipline, as well as encouragement and support in choosing a major. However, the findings of several studies carried out on accounting and business students are inconclusive. The studies by Inman *et al.* (1989) and Mauldin *et al.* (2000) show that parents, followed by teachers, have a strong influence on a student's choice of major. Other studies (e.g. Paolillo & Estes, 1982; Hermanson *et al.*, 1995; Geiger & Ogilby, 2000; Mauldin *et al.*, 2000) suggest that individual teachers have a profound influence on a student's decision to major in accounting.

There are also studies that suggest that teachers do not play a significant role in a student's choice of major (Cangelosi *et al.*, 1985; Gul *et al.*, 1989). Cangelosi *et al.* (1985) show that friends are not influential in swaying a student's decision toward or away from an accounting career. Gul *et al.* (1989) note that parental influence is not a significant factor in students' choice of discipline decisions – which is inconsistent with other studies (e.g. Tan & Laswad, 2006, 2009; Law, 2010). Similarly, studies by Paolillo & Estes (1982), Hermanson *et al.* (1995), and Lowe & Simons (1997) indicate that friends, parents, and secondary school teachers are less influential factors in students' major choices.

Perhaps cultural factors partly explain the inconsistencies: this is evident in Auyeung & Sands' (1997) and Jackling & Keneley's (2009) studies, undertaken in Australia, where referents were found to have a greater influence on Asian students (e.g. Hong Kong and Taiwanese students) and international students (e.g. China, Hong Kong, etc.) respectively, than on Australian students. In an Asian culture, a person's identity is often linked to his/her in-group network which is bound by values such as obedience, duty, and loyalty. Therefore, in such cultures, parents' views in particular are well respected and have significant influence over the behaviour and attitudes of their children. In contrast, Western societies are often characterised as having an individualistic culture tending to orientate towards the individual self rather than towards significant others (Auyeung & Sands, 1997).

9.4.5 Employment and career opportunities

Students' choice of study discipline can be influenced by the earnings potential and job opportunities once they graduate. In terms of earnings potential, students may consider both initial and future earnings. In choosing their majors, students are also keen to know how easy it is to get a job when they graduate, and the opportunities for advancement in their careers.

In periods of economic recession, this factor perhaps could be even more important to students in their selection of a study major.

If salary and job opportunities are the most compelling deciding factors for students, then the accounting major could be a popular choice. This is because accounting graduates in many countries consistently earn above-average salaries compared to graduates in other business disciplines, and in humanities and social sciences.[7] Apart from the attractive salary, the accounting profession provides accounting graduates with career structures that lead to job security and senior positions, which are not usually available to other non-accounting graduates.

There is ample evidence which indicates that students select accounting as their study major because they perceive it as having high earnings potential and good job market conditions or opportunities (Paolillo & Estes, 1982; Gul et al., 1989; Inman et al., 1989; Cohen & Hanno, 1993; Adams et al., 1994; Felton et al., 1994; Auyeung & Sands, 1997; Lowe & Simons, 1997; Mauldin et al., 2000; Byrne & Flood, 2005; Tan & Laswad, 2006; Nelson et al., 2008). Ahmed et al. (1997) and Lowe & Simons (1997) found that students who major in accounting place greater importance on future earnings. This should not be surprising. As indicated earlier, the accounting profession has provided stable and financial rewarding careers for many graduates. Students who choose to major in accounting because they see earnings potential and job opportunities as being paramount in their choice of major are, perhaps, more aware that there are greater employment opportunities in accounting than in most non-accounting disciplines. In Chapter 25 – this volume, Beard & Humphrey discuss the attraction of internships as an element of an accounting degree programme in attracting students to major in accounting.

The intrinsic appeal of the job itself (such as job satisfaction, opportunity to be creative, autonomy, intellect, and a challenging and dynamic working environment) may further influence students' academic major choice. However, a number of studies indicate that job satisfaction, though important in accounting students' discipline choice (Paolillo & Estes, 1982; Gul et al., 1989; Auyeung & Sands, 1997), is not as important as many other factors (Paolillo & Estes, 1982; Felton et al., 1994; Sugahara & Boland, 2009).

9.4.6 Perceptions of accounting work and the accounting profession

Positive or negative perceptions of what accountants do may influence students' choice of major. A poor image of the accounting profession may influence students in selecting other majors. Images in the media of doctors, lawyers, police officers, and fire fighters are often positive. In comparison, the public image of accountants generally is less than positive. Images of accountants are rarely presented in the media and, when they do appear, they are often portrayed as being dull and dishonest. Further, publicised incidents involving dishonest accountants have tarnished the image of the profession, and might have discouraged students from considering accounting as a career.

As indicated in many studies, the unfavourable public perception of a stereotypical accountant as being dreary, cautious, and a boring number-cruncher is one of the main disincentives to majoring in accounting (see e.g. Horowitz & Riley, 1990; Fisher & Murphy, 1995; Hermanson et al., 1995; Byrne & Willis, 2005; McDowall et al., 2011).

Social image, prestige and status all play a role in students' choice of major. Furthermore, accountants' work is perceived by students to be excessively time-consuming, repetitive, and not stimulating (Mauldin et al., 2000), or as being narrow, lacking diversity, audit-focussed and restricted to 'core' accounting (Marshall, 2003). In comparing accounting and non-accounting majors' perceptions, Hermanson et al. (1995) found that accounting majors had more positive views of the nature of accounting work, the ability to interact with people, and the prestige or social status of the profession than did the non-accounting majors. These findings suggest the need to promote accounting work and the accounting profession as being interesting and stimulating, offering career opportunities, involving interaction with people, and having respect from the public. [8]

9.5 Conclusions, implications, and future research

9.5.1 Conclusions

A recurring theme that connects the insights gained from the extant literature is the influence of more than one factor on students' choice of accounting major. Economic factors (such as availability of employment or career opportunities and earnings) are important factors in students' choice of accounting as their study major. As we have seen, other factors that are instrumental in the choice of major include aptitude, interest in the subject area, the image of the accounting profession, and students' first year experience in *Introductory Accounting*. The influence of teachers, advisers or parents is inconclusive; they appeared important in some studies but not in others. Where they appeared as a significant factor, parents usually stand out amongst other referents as being the most influential, particularly for those who choose to major in accounting and for international students.

9.5.2 Implications

What are the implications? First, students commencing their university study basically fall into two groups: those who have already decided on their study major, and those who have not. Those who have selected their major choice might have already considered various factors, and the choices they have made might depend on how they weighed each of the factors – some being more important than others from their perspectives. Others might have decided on a major by taking a less rigorous approach such as through experience and discovery 'heuristics'. For instance, a student might eliminate a particular major if he/she has developed some negative and preconceived views about certain aspects of study majors, such as 'I don't like boring subjects' or 'I don't like dealing with numbers' and therefore 'I will not major in accounting' (Beggs *et al.*, 2008). However, even though these students may have made their major choices when they entered university, they may still change their minds after their first year of study. Whichever group students fall into, it is important that they have the opportunity to make informed choices and to remedy the misperceptions or misinformation about studying accounting and accounting as a career.

As a significant number of students decide on their majors at high school, the university accounting staff and the accounting profession should take the opportunity to disseminate information about accounting study and career opportunities to pupils at high school. Closer links with secondary school teachers and advisors need to be established as they are the direct link to pupils at school. Jackling & Calero (2006, p. 434) aptly highlighted the need for the accounting profession to promote itself to students '*in such a way that it is represented as a career choice of challenging opportunities, with a technical emphasis on decision-making roles, analysis and problem-solving, in addition to well-developed generic skills*'.

With the image of accountants and accounting still stereotyped as being 'boring' and 'number crunching', the accounting profession needs to dispel this misperception by projecting a positive image of accountants making a valuable contribution to business and in the wider community, being people-focussed and involved in all facets of business – including planning and strategy decisions. Evidence to support this view was provided in 2012 by the Association of Chartered Certified Accountants (ACCA, 2012) in a report which predicted that the accounting profession would lose credibility if it fails to educate the public and other stakeholders about its value in driving the success of organisations in all sectors.

Highlighting successful models in the profession could also appeal to students - especially the 'best and brightest'. This would help students to make their choices based on their abilities and interests in the major. Dissemination of such information would certainly assist students in making informed decisions. Bearing in mind that some students are sensitive to parental and others' influence in choosing study majors, the profession as well as university accounting academics need to promote the positive aspects of an accounting career, not only to pre-university students but also to the general public.

Students' experience in the *Introductory Accounting* course is another important factor in attracting and retaining students in the major accounting. As indicated in Tan & Laswad's (2009) longitudinal study, students' attitudes develop early in their university careers, are generally stable, and tend to last. Attempts to influence these attitudes therefore need to be made early, hence generating students' interest in a subject area during their first year is an important determinant. If students are dissatisfied with the course, which could be due to the course content, workload, or even the teacher, it could affect their decision to major in accounting. If students view the course as being dynamic, relevant and intellectually stimulating, it could attract them (including the 'best and brightest' students) to the accounting major. On the other hand, if the course is perceived as being boring and uninteresting, it may lead to the loss of the more academically capable students (Adams *et al.*, 1994). It is worthwhile engaging the best teachers in teaching *Introductory Accounting* as they have better skills in making the course interesting and challenging, particularly for those students who are undecided on their major – it is crucial that they have positive experiences in the first accounting course to be motivated to choose accounting as their major. Their choice could be influenced by the teacher and what they do in the classes – a good teacher can stimulate interest in the accounting discipline and foster a positive impression of the accounting profession. The important role played by teachers in influencing those who are initially undecided in their major is also alluded to by Geiger & Ogilby (2000).

9.5.3 Future research

Although it is clear that there are multiple factors which influence the choice of study majors, students' decision-making processes can fall anywhere along a simple to complex, or structured to unstructured continuum. Choosing an appropriate major is an important decision for students. However, some may spend more time than others in exploring and seeking information on different disciplines, weighing the pros and cons of different majors, and self-reflecting on their capabilities to take up a particular major, before they finally decide on what their major should be. Beggs *et al.* (2008, p. 381) point out that some students: '*employ strategies of indecision as opposed to strategies of cognitive decision-making in that they "back into" a major rather than actively choose a major, often by employing heuristics*'. It follows that the understanding of students' decision-making processes requires an understanding of their decision strategies, the weightings they place on various positive and negative factors associated with study and career, and their personalities. The 'What' question (i.e. What are the factors that have the potential to influence students' choice of major?) is well-researched but the 'How' question (i.e. How do students go about choosing their major?) is less well-researched by comparison. Are there different decision-making styles and, if so, do they affect the ways in which students conceptualise the decision to choose a major? More qualitative and quantitative studies are required to fill this gap in knowledge to help in demystifying how students go about deciding on their study majors. Perhaps future researchers could draw on decision-making theories to help explain choices among alternative study disciplines.

There are also research opportunities in identifying which successful messages about accounting study and careers would appeal to new generations of young people seeking tertiary study. This research objective could be pursued, for example, through experimental designs. Future studies could further focus on students who change their study majors either from accounting to non-accounting or vice versa. For instance, is the change due to confusion or doubt about the discipline, or was the course misrepresented to students? There is still much to learn about why students change their majors. Findings from such research would be useful as they would provide practical ideas for improving academic advice and retaining students in the accounting major.

Lastly, research on the role which personality plays in students' choice of major is scarce in the accounting education literature. Researchers in other disciplines who used Holland's (1985) theory of vocational choice found that the Holland's personality scales are strong predictors of students' choice of major. Accounting researchers could contribute to the body of knowledge by drawing on social cognitive career theories (such as Holland's) to examine not only the importance of the 'person-environment fit' in relation to students' choice of major, but also their perception of the stereotypical accountant. Holland (1959, pp. 40–41) pointed out that '*people with more information about occupational environment make more adequate choices than do persons with less information*'.

Further empirical support of the 'person–environment fit' in relation to accounting major choice suggests that, to draw the appropriate type of students to the accounting discipline, it is of the utmost importance that students need to have accurate perceptions of the accounting discipline and work environment.

Notes

1 National Center for Educational Statistics (2011), *Digest of Education Statistics 2010*, Table 282. Bachelor's degrees conferred by degree-granting institutions, by field of study: selected years, 1970–71 through 2008–09. Available at: http://nces.ed.gov/fastfacts/display.asp?id=37.

2 The summary of studies published up to 2002 was adapted from Simons, Lowe & Stout's (2004) literature review. We may not have captured all studies in Table 9.1. However, we have conducted a comprehensive search for studies relating to choice of accounting majors, particularly in the three main accounting education journals: *Accounting Education: an international journal, Issues in Accounting Education*, and *Journal of Accounting Education*.

3 Jung's theory and the MBTI are also briefly described by Duff in Chapter 8 – this volume, which considers personality styles in the context of students' learning.

4 See Chapter 8 for more discussion on the link between personality preferences and students' learning and performance.

5 For instance, Jackling (see Chapter 10 – this volume) considers four factors (i.e. the influence of students' gender, referents, prior accounting study, and extrinsic and intrinsic motivation) in pursuing a career in accounting. In Chapter 6 – this volume, Lucas & Mladenovic look at students' perception of accounting and how they affect students' learning and learning outcomes. Wygal, in Chapter 11 – this volume, discusses the first course in accounting in the context of the accounting curriculum. In Chapter 25 – this volume, Beard & Humphrey consider the impact of internships as an attraction for choosing to major in accounting.

6 See also Wygal (Chapter 11 – this volume) who considers curriculum design and delivery of the first course in accounting.

7 For example, in New Zealand, according to a New Zealand Government database on graduate earnings (www.careers.govt.nz), after five years from graduation, accounting graduates' average earning is 12 per cent and 23 per cent higher than average earnings of business and humanities graduates, respectively.

8 See also the coverage by Jackling (in Chapter 10 – this volume) on accounting as a profession.

References

Adams, S., Pryor, L., & Adams, S. (1994) Attraction and retention of high-aptitude students in accounting: an exploratory longitudinal study, *Issues in Accounting Education*, 9, 45–58.

Ahmed, K., Alam, K., & Alam, M. (1997) An empirical study of factors affecting accounting students' career choice in New Zealand, *Accounting Education: an international journal*, 6, 325–335.

Ajzen, I. (1988) *Attitudes, Personality and Behavior*, Chicago: The Dorsey Press.

Ajzen, I. (2001) Nature and operation of attitudes, *Annual Review of Psychology*, 52, 27–58.

Albrecht, S. & Sack, J. (2000) *Accounting Education: Charting the Course Through a Perilous Future* (Accounting Education Series, Vol. 16), Sarasota, FL: American Accounting Association.

Allen, C. (2004) Business students' perception of the image of accounting, *Managerial Auditing Journal*, 19, 235–258.

Association of Chartered Certified Accountants (2012) *Closing the Value Gap: Understanding the Accountancy Profession in the 21st Century*, London: ACCA.

Auyeung, P. & Sands, J. (1997) Factors influencing accounting students' career choice: a cross cultural validation study, *Accounting Education: an international journal*, 6, 13–23.

Bealing, W., Baker, R., & Russo, C. (2006) Personality: what it takes to be an accountant, *The Accounting Educators' Journal*, XVI, 119–128.

Bebbington, J., Thomson, I., & Wall, D. (1997) Accounting students and constructed gender: an exploration of gender in the context of accounting degree choices at two Scottish universities, *Journal of Accounting Education*, 15, 241–267.

Beggs, J., Bantham, J., & Taylor, S. (2008) Distinguishing the factors influencing college students' choice of major, *College Student Journal*, 42, 381–394.

Briggs, S. (2006) An exploratory study of the factors influencing undergraduate student choice: the case of higher education in Scotland, *Studies in Higher Education*, 31, 705–722.

Byrne, M. & Flood, B. (2005) A study of accounting students' motives, expectations and preparedness for higher education, *Journal of Further and Higher Education*, 29, 111–124.

Byrne, M. & Willis, P. (2005) Irish secondary students' perceptions of the work of an accountant and the accounting profession, *Accounting Education: an international journal*, 14, 367–381.

Cangelosi, J., Condi, F., & Luthy, D. (1985) The influence of introductory accounting courses on career choices, *Delta Pi Epsilon Journal*, 27, 60–68.

Chacko, H. (1991) Can you pick out the accountant? Students' interests and career choices, *Journal of Education*, 66(3), 151–154.

Chen, C., Jones, K., & McIntyre, D. (2005) A reexamination of the factors important to selection of accounting as a major, *Accounting and the Public Interest*, 5, 14–31.

Chen, C., Jones, K., & McIntyre, D. (2008) Analyzing the factors relevant to students' estimations of the benefits and costs of pursuing an accounting career, *Accounting Education: an international journal*, 17, 313–326.

Cherry, A. & Reckers, P. (1983) The introductory financial accounting course: its role in the curriculum for accounting majors, *Journal of Accounting Education*, 1, 71–82.

Cohen, J. & Hanno, D. (1993) An analysis of underlying constructs affecting the choice of accounting as a major, *Issues in Accounting Education*, 8, 219–238.

Felton, S., Buhr, N., & Northey, M. (1994) Factors influencing the business student's choice of a career in chartered accountancy, *Issues in Accounting Education*, 9, 131–141.

Felton, S., Dimnik, T., & Northey, M. (1995) A theory of reasoned action model of the Chartered Accountant career choice, *Journal of Accounting Education*, 13, 1–19.

Fishbein, M. & Ajzen, I. (1975) *Belief, Attitude, Intention and Behavior: An Introduction to Theory and Research*, Reading, MA: Addison-Wesley.

Fisher, R. & Murphy, V. (1995) A pariah profession? Some student perceptions of accounting and accountancy, *Studies in Higher Education*, 20, 45–58.

Geiger, M. & Ogilby, S. (2000) The first course in accounting: students' perceptions and their effect on the decision to major in accounting, *Journal of Accounting Education*, 18, 63–78.

Graves, O.F., Nelson, I., & Deines, D. (1993) Accounting student characteristics: results of the 1992 Federation of Schools of Accountancy (FSA) survey, *Journal of Accounting Education*, 11, 211–225.

Gul, F. (1986) Adaption – innovation as a factor in Australian accounting undergraduates' subject interests and career preferences, *Journal of Accounting Education*, 4, 203–209.

Gul, F., Andrew, B., Leong, S. & Ismail, Z. (1989) Factors influencing choice of discipline of study: accountancy, engineering, law and medicine, *Accounting and Finance*, 29, 93–101.

Gul, F. & Fong, C. (1993) Predicting success for introductory accounting students: some further Hong Kong evidence, *Accounting Education: an international journal*, 2, 33.

Hanson, J. (1984) *User's Guide for the SVIB-SCII*, Stanford, CA: Stanford University Press.

Heaton, G. (1999) Developing customer focus in accounting education, *Chartered Accountants Journal*, 78, 22–25.

Heiat, A., Brown, D., & Johnson, D. (2007) An empirical analysis of underlying factors affecting the choice of accounting major, *Journal of College Teaching and Learning*, 4, 83–98.

Hermanson, D., Hermanson, R., & Ivancevich, S. (1995) Are America's top businesses students steering clear of accounting?, *Ohio CPA Journal*, 54, 26–30.

Holland, J. (1959) A theory of vocational choice, *Journal of Counseling Psychology*, 6, 35–45.

Holland, J. (1985) *Making Vocational Choices: A Theory of Vocational Personalities and Work Environments*, Englewood Cliffs, NJ: Prentice Hall.

Horowitz, K. & Riley, T. (1990) How do accountancy students see us?, *Accountancy*, 106, 75–77.

Hunt, S., Falgiani, A., & Intrieri, R. (2004) The nature and origins of students' perceptions of accountants, *Journal of Education for Business*, 79, 142–148.

Inman, B., Wenzler, A., & Wickert, P. (1989) Square pegs in round holes: are accounting students well-suited to today's accounting profession?, *Issues in Accounting Education*, 4, 29–47.

Jackling, B. & Calero, C. (2006) Influences on undergraduate students' intention to become qualified accountants: evidence from Australia, *Accounting Education: an international journal*, 15, 419–438.

Jackling, B. & Keneley, M. (2009) Influences on the supply of accounting graduates in Australia: a focus on international students, *Accounting and Finance*, 49, 141–159.

Jackman, S. & Hollingworth, A. (2005) Factors influencing the career choice of accounting students: a New Zealand study, *New Zealand Journal of Applied Business Research*, 4, 69–83.

Karnes, A., King, J., & Hahn, R. (1997) Is the accounting profession losing high potential recruits in high school by default?, *Accounting Educators' Journal*, 9, 28–43.

Law, P. (2010) A theory of reasoned action model of accounting students' career choice in public accounting practices in the post-Enron environment, *Journal of Applied Accounting Research*, 11, 58–73.

Law, P. & Yuen, D. (2012) A multilevel study of students' motivations of studying accounting: implications for employers, *Education and Training*, 54, 50–64.

Lawrence, R. & Taylor, L. (2000) Student personality type versus grading procedures in intermediate accounting courses, *Journal of Education for Business*, 76, 28–35.

Lowe, D., Lowe, L., & Simons, K. (1994) Criteria for selection of an academic major: accounting and gender differences, *Psychological Reports*, 75, 1169–1170.

Lowe, D. & Simons, K. (1997) Factors influencing choice of business majors: some additional evidence: a research note, *Accounting Education: an international journal*, 6, 39–45.

Marriott, P. (2002) A longitudinal study of undergraduate accounting students' learning style preferences at two UK universities, *Accounting Education: an international journal*, 11, 43–63.

Marshall, R. (2003) Calling on tomorrow's professionals, *Chartered Accountants Journal*, 82, 4–9.

Mauldin, S., Crain, J., & Mounce, P. (2000) The accounting principles instructor's influence on students' decision to major in accounting, *Journal of Education for Business*, 75, 142–148.

McDowall, T., Jackling, B., & Natoli, R. (2011) Are we there yet? Changing perceptions of accounting as a career preference, *International Journal of Learning*, 18, 335–352.

Myers, I. & Myers, P. (1993) *Gifts Differing: Understanding Personality Type*, Palo Alto, CA: Consulting Psychologists Press.

Nelson, I., Vendrzyk, V., Quirin, J., & Allen, R. (2002) No, the sky is not falling: evidence of accounting student characteristics at FSA schools, 1995–2000, *Issues in Accounting Education*, 17, 269–287.

Nelson, I., Vendrzyk, V., Quirin, J., & Kovar, S. (2008) Trends in accounting student characteristics: results from a 15-year longitudinal study at FSA schools, *Issues in Accounting Education*, 23, 373–389.

Paolillo, J. & Estes, R. (1982) An empirical analysis of career choice factors among accountants, attorneys, engineers and physicians, *The Accounting Review*, LVII, 785–793.

Pringle, C., DuBose, P., & Yankey, M. (2010) Personality characteristics and choice of academic major: are traditional stereotypes obsolete?, *College Student Journal*, 44, 131–142.

Saemann, G. & Crooker, K. (1999) Student perceptions of the profession and its effect on decisions to major in accounting, *Journal of Accounting Education*, 17, 1–22.

Simon, H.A. (1991) *Models of My Life*, New York: Basic Books.

Simon, H.A., Kozmetsky, G., Guetzkow, H., & Tyndall, G. (1954) *Centralization vs. Decentralization in Organizing the Controller's Department*, New York: The Controllership Foundation. (Reprinted in 1978 by Scholars Book Co., Houston, TX, with special permission of the Financial Executives Research Foundation.)

Simons, K., Lowe, D., & Stout, D. (2004) Comprehensive literature review: factors influencing choice of accounting as a major, *Journal of Academy of Business Education*, 5, 97–110.

Stice, J. & Swain, M. (1997) The effect of performance on the decision to major in accounting, *Journal of Education for Business*, 73, 54–69.

Strasser, S., Ozgur, C., & Schroeder, D. (2002) Selecting a business college major: an analysis of criteria and choice using the analytical hierarchy process, *Mid-American Journal of Business*, 17, 47–56.

Sugahara, S. & Boland, G. (2009) The accounting profession as a career choice for tertiary business students in Japan: a factor analysis, *Accounting Education: an international journal*, 18, 255–272.

Sugahara, S., Boland, G., & Cilloni, A. (2008) Factors influencing students' choice of an accounting major in Australia, *Accounting Education: an international journal*, 17, 37–54.

Sugahara, S., Kurihara, O., & Boland, G. (2006) Japanese secondary school teachers' perceptions of the accounting profession, *Accounting Education: an international journal*, 15, 405–418.

Tan, L. & Laswad, F. (2006) Students' beliefs, attitudes and intentions to major in accounting, *Accounting Education: an international journal*, 15, 167–187.

Tan, L. & Laswad, F. (2009) Understanding students' choice of academic majors: a longitudinal analysis, *Accounting Education: an international journal*, 18, 233–253.

Taylor Research and Consulting Group, Inc. (2000) *AICPA Student and Academic Research Study: Final Quantitative Report*, July, pp. 1–28.

Wolk, C. & Cates, T. (1994) Problem-solving styles of accounting students: are expectations of innovation reasonable?, *Journal of Accounting Education*, 12, 269–281.

Wolk, C. & Nikolai, L. (1997) Personality types of accounting students and faculty: comparisons and implications, *Journal of Accounting Education*, 15, 1–17.

About the authors

Fawzi Laswad is Professor and Head of the School of Accountancy at Massey University, New Zealand (f.laswad@massey.ac.nz). His main research interests are in financial reporting and accounting education. He is the Deputy Chair of the Joint Education Board of the New Zealand Institute of Chartered Accountants (NZICA) and the Institute of Chartered Accountants in Australia (ICAA).

Lin Mei Tan is Senior Lecturer in the School of Accountancy, Massey University, New Zealand (l.m.tan@massey.ac.nz). Some of her research interests lie in the domain of students' learning and choice of major, and her work in these areas has been published in several refereed journals, including *Accounting Education: an international journal* and *Pacific Accounting Review*.

10

The choice of accounting as a career

Beverley Jackling

VICTORIA UNIVERSITY, MELBOURNE, AUSTRALIA

CONTENTS

Abstract

This chapter examines the choice of accounting as a career to provide perspectives about the future of the profession in a global environment. Background literature on choice of accounting that outlines the influences on the supply of accountants for the profession is provided. The chapter also reviews Holland's model of occupational choice in relation to career decision-making. Furthermore, it examines the role of professional accounting bodies in promoting accounting as a career choice, and addresses the need for accounting educators to provide a realistic vision of the work of accountants via curriculum design. Recommendations are provided for reshaping the curriculum together with recognition of the need for a greater emphasis on the professional development of accounting educators to improve the 'currency' of accounting education. An appropriate image portrayed of the accounting profession, as well as the work of accountants, requires efforts from a range of sources, including career counsellors, educators and professional accounting bodies.

Keywords

accounting profession, career choice, perceptions of the accounting profession, vocational interests

10.1 Introduction

The main aims of this chapter are:

- to outline the global demand for accountants;
- to consider the factors that influence the supply of accountants, including choice of accounting as a career, and comparison with other professions;
- to review Holland's model of occupational choice that endeavours to match interests with career choice, in particular its potential to have an adverse impact on recruitment;
- to consider the role of recruiters and professional accounting bodies in attracting the 'best and brightest' to the profession; and
- to project/speculate as to the role of the accountant in the future in terms of matching aspirations of individuals with the opportunities afforded by the role of professional accountant and 'up-skilling' accounting educators to meet a changed educational landscape.

The current chapter, focussing on factors influencing the choice of accounting *as a career*, complements Chapter 9, which specifically addresses the influences on the choice of accounting *as a major*. While there is inevitably some commonality, this chapter more broadly addresses a range of societal and educational influences on the supply of accountants for the profession in the future. The argument posited is that not only is there a need for educators and the profession to work towards changing attitudes towards the profession, but there is also a need for the accounting curriculum to reflect an increasingly global business environment, accompanied by 'up-skilling' of educators. These measures are considered important in attracting students to choose accounting as a career.

The chapter commences with an overview of the global demand for employment for accountants. It is followed by a brief review of prior literature on the supply of accountants for the profession by examining reasons for the selection of accounting as a career both by pupils at secondary level and students at tertiary level. The literature review addresses motivational aspects and perceptions of the profession. Section 10.3 focusses on matching vocational interests with the career choice of accounting, and this is followed by a discussion on the role of the accounting profession in projecting an image of accountants which promotes accounting as a career choice. The chapter concludes with the challenges for educators in curriculum design to enable a matching of aspirations of individuals with the opportunities afforded by the role of the professional accountant in a global environment.

10.2 Global demand for accountants and influences on the supply of accountants

10.2.1 The global demand for accountants

In attempting to identify the global demand for accountants, the Manpower Group (which examines talent shortages based on feedback from employers in the world's leading economies) note that, in 2012, employers overwhelmingly reported difficulties in filling accounting positions. This data continues a trend over time which illustrates that world economies have consistently experienced a shortage of accountants. In particular, in 2012, employers reported that there was a lack of suitable candidates with the right technical expertise and employability skills (Manpower Group, 2012, p. 2). Of interest is that the talent shortage in accounting has been reported as being acute in the Asia-Pacific region (ibid., p. 7). Countries within the Asia-Pacific region which have particularly acute shortages of accountants include China, where the 140,000 certified accountants have not been able to meet the demands of the economy over an extended period of time (Ryan, 2008). Similarly, evidence from Australia indicates that a skill shortage in accounting persists. In 2012, in Australia, as a result of increased interest in the performance of companies following the Global Financial Crisis (GFC, which is covered by Adler in Chapter 23 – this volume), demand increased in various areas of the financial market, particularly auditing, as part of the process of increasing vigilance on financial performance and compliance requirements (Clarius Group, 2012).

In other parts of the world, for example the U.S.A., employment opportunites typically abound for graduate accountants (Warrick et al., 2010). It has been forecast in the U.S.A. that the demand for accountants will continue to grow over time. Evidence provided from a survey undertaken by the American Institute of Certified Public Accountants (AICPA) indicates that the demand for accounting graduates has recovered significantly from the economic downturn experienced with the GFC (AICPA, 2011). In the 15-year longitudinal study in the U.S.A., sponsored by the Federation of Schools of Accountancy (FSA), it was reported by Nelson, Vendrzyk, Quirin, & Kovar (2008) that, by 2006, job availability had become the single most important factor that influenced students' decisions to pursue an accounting career. As the need for accounting graduates increases, the perceptions of the accounting graduates themselves about future opportunities is of importance. The next section of this chapter examines the prior literature in accounting that has addressed students' intentions to seek accounting as a career choice, thus addressing the supply side of the equation in terms of accounting career choice.

10.2.2 Influences on the supply of accountants

In undertaking career planning, regardless of discipline area, students and their parents often look for a 'gap' in the employment market (potential for demand to exceed supply) in an endeavour to maximise employment opportunities on qualification. Consideration is also given to the extent to which the student's academic performance/capacity matches the required academic pathway to qualify in the employment area. Closely allied with this approach to career choice, a second group may take a more aspirational approach, contemplating a career that represents for the family – and specifically the student – an elevation in socio-economic status (Ostrove *et al.*, 2011). Others take a more pragmatic approach to career choice by pursuing a pathway to qualification based on interest in the discipline area. The literature on background characteristics that influence the choice of accounting as a career addresses some of these factors. In the accounting education literature, some of the influences considered to be important in the choice of accounting as a career include: the gender of the students, the influence of reference groups, prior studies of accounting (including secondary school studies), motivational factors, and cultural background. These will each be discussed in turn.

10.2.2.1 Gender

In terms of gender, accounting as a profession has traditionally been viewed as being male-dominated, with very few females qualifying for entry to professional accounting bodies (PABs). However, in the past two decades the proportion of females in the accounting profession has now overtaken that of males, particularly in some Western societies. The percentage of female members of professional accounting bodies in the U.K. has risen from 30 per cent in 2006 to 34 per cent in 2011 (Professional Oversight Board, 2012). In Australia, the proportion of females has grown more dramatically. For example, 57 per cent of new entrants into the CPA program in Australia for 2010 were women. Overall, women accounted for 43 per cent of CPA Australia's 129,000-strong membership in 2010 (CPA Australia, 2010). Despite this trend, evidence suggests that women are more likely than men to depart public accounting (Greenhaus *et al.*, 1997). The early departure of women from the profession has been attributed to them having less desire than men to be promoted to partner, rather than the impact of greater family pressures (Wallace, 2009). Despite this negative aspect of career progression, in a study undertaken in the U.S.A., Nelson & Vendryzk (1996) have shown that female students have more favourable attitudes towards accounting as a career choice than do male students.

10.2.2.2 Influence of reference groups on choice of accounting as a career

Research in education has typically explored the potential influence of reference groups – such as parents, teachers, and peers – in terms of their influence on career choice. The theoretical support for the importance of reference groups is found in social cognitive theory which hypothesises that 'significant others' strongly influence career choices (Middleton & Loughead, 1993).

In terms of parental influence, research has indicated that socio-economic status and parental educational background influence students' selection of career (Pearson & Dellman-Jenkins, 1997; Dandy & Nettelbeck, 2002). However, prior research suggests that the most significant influence on choice of career appears to be parental encouragement and various family structure variables such as working status of mother and residential status of father (Pearson & Dellman-Jenkins, 1997).

In accounting, a number of studies across a range of countries have shown that parental influence has been significant in impacting on secondary school pupils' decisions to pursue accounting as a career (for example, in the U.S.A., Cohen & Hanno, 1993; in Ireland, Byrne & Flood, 2005; in Japan, Sugahara & Boland, 2005; and in Australia, McDowall *et al.*, 2012). Furthermore, Jackling & Keneley's (2009) study shows that advice given by parents and relatives has been particularly important for students studying overseas. This finding was supported by the earlier work of Auyeung & Sands (1997) and, more recently, by Jackling, de Lange, Phillips, & Sewell (2012). One question that arises from these findings is whether reference groups (particularly parents) are sufficiently well informed to provide specific career guidance for a career in accounting. Evidence suggests that parental groups may exercise influence over career decision-making based on potential extrinsic rewards (e.g. potential salary, prestige and, in some instances, opportunities for migration) rather than encouraging career direction linked to intrinsic interest, which may not necessarily have the same extrinsic rewards (Jackling & Keneley, 2009).

In terms of other reference groups (such as friends, career counsellors, and teachers), in overall terms, the empirical evidence shows mixed results. For example, Gul, Andrew, Leong, & Ismail (1989) found that teachers did not have a significant role in students' choice of majors studied at university. In contrast, Geiger & Ogilby (2000) and Mauldin, Crain, & Mounce (2000) suggest that teachers have an important influence on students' decisions to pursue an accounting qualification. (For a fuller discussion of the choice of accounting as a discipline, see Laswad & Tan, Chapter 9 – this volume.)

Overall prior research suggests that reference groups have a limited role in choice of accounting as a career (Paolillo & Estes, 1982; Hermanson & Hermanson, 1995; Lowe & Simons, 1997; Mauldin et al., 2000; Strasser et al., 2002; Jackling & Calero, 2006). These studies have highlighted a range of additional factors influencing intentions to pursue accounting as a career, some of which are outlined below.

10.2.2.3 Prior study of accounting, including at secondary school and university

One of the principal factors found to influence students' perceptions of accounting as a career has related to the study of the subject in school and at university. In particular, the need to recruit students who are interested in accounting as a profession has led researchers to gather evidence from high school pupils in relation to their accounting studies. In Byrne & Willis' (2005) study, pupils studying accounting at secondary school in Ireland had a less negative image of accounting than those not studying accounting. However, those studying accounting still held a traditional view of the profession and of the work of the accountant. Byrne & Willis (2005) found that the nature of the accounting pedagogy reinforced pre-existing negative perceptions. The study provided evidence that secondary schools emphasised mechanical bookkeeping and assessment. This approach to accounting is likely to confirm rather than challenge pupils' traditional stereotypical view of the work of an accountant and the profession. Similarly, in a study of Australian secondary school pupils, McDowall et al. (2012) found that, although pupils studying accounting had fewer negative perceptions of accounting than non-accounting pupils, they still held views that were typical of a traditional view of the profession and the work of an accountant. The results suggested that the accounting curriculum at secondary school level in Australia continues to perpetuate the mechanistic approach linked to bookkeeping. From a New Zealand perspective, the evidence also suggests that students studying accounting tend to have more positive perceptions of the work of accountants than do non-accounting students (Malthus & Fowler, 2009). This theme is discussed at length by Byrne & Willis in Chapter 7 – this volume.

According to a report published some years ago in the U.S.A., accounting is viewed by university students who choose accounting as their major and their potential career choice as requiring hard work and a good career opportunity for lovers of mathematics (Albrecht & Sack, 2000). Mladenovic (2000) found that Australian university students tend to perceive accounting as being primarily numerical, objective, and non-controversial, hence suited to those with an affinity towards mathematics and statistics. (Numeracy is discussed by Wilson et al. in Chapter 3 – this volume, and perceptions of accounting are covered in detail by Lucas & Mladenovic in Chapter 6 – this volume.) Prior studies have also suggested that accounting is not portrayed as being a creative profession, nor is it portrayed as being a profession in which you work with other people, in an advisory role, to solve problems (Albrecht & Sack, 2000, p. 30).

Negative perceptions derived from the study of accounting at secondary school and university clearly indicate that accounting education has the potential to send the wrong message to those seeking a career in accounting. Additionally, students who initially may not intend to major in accounting may be deterred from studying accounting and pursuing a career in accounting as their studies at introductory levels reinforce the perception that accounting is procedural and dealing with a lot of numbers (Marriott & Marriott, 2003). However, the broadening of the professional accountant's role in areas such as assurance and management services, as well as financial planning, has meant that the role of an accountant has changed considerably beyond routine tasks (Howieson, 2003; Jackling & Calero, 2006). Thus it is important for accounting educators to recognise the importance which the accounting curriculum has in potentially influencing students' career choice. The need for change in accounting education in terms of its impact on choice of accounting as a career cannot be underestimated. The importance of accounting education is dealt with more fully in Section 10.5.1.

10.2.2.4 Extrinsic and intrinsic motivation

Extrinsic factors refer to the perceived outcomes and rewards which students believe accrue from pursuing a career in a particular profession. Research into extrinsic influences has found that financial remuneration, perception of job availability, job security and opportunities for advancement are important factors in the choice of a career in accounting (Paolillo & Estes, 1982; Shivaswamy & Hanks, 1985; Gul et al., 1989; Felton et al., 1994; Ahmed et al., 1997; Jackling & Calero, 2006). Paolillo & Estes (1982) found that extrinsic rewards were a stronger incentive for accounting students in the U.S.A. than for other professions (such as medicine, law, and engineering). Evidence suggests that university students in a range of countries, including the U.S.A., Ireland, and Japan, have also been attracted by career prospects and social status and prestige (Francisco et al., 2003; Byrne & Flood, 2005; Sugahara & Boland, 2005).

Although job rewards and prestige are viewed favourably by many, several studies report that extrinsic motivation is less effective than intrinsic motivation in terms of the sustainability of career choice, progression, and success. There is a wealth of research which suggests that students who are intrinsically motivated are likely to display confidence and interest, resulting in enhanced performance, persistence, and creativity (e.g. Ryan & Deci, 2000; Deci et al., 1999) as well as high self-esteem (Deci & Ryan, 2008). In particular, intrinsic motivation has been shown to have a strong effect upon performance and career success (Deci & Ryan, 1985). Thus, intrinsic motivation would appear to be a highly desired attribute for both students and graduates to possess for pursuing a career in accounting.

Prior studies have also highlighted the relationship between level of interest, the quality of learning, and learning outcomes of university students (e.g. Entwistle & Ramsden, 1983; Ramsden, 2003). This research derives more generally from the higher education literature which indicates that students with high intrinsic interests (i.e. those who engage in interest-orientated learning, with satisfaction derived from the intellectual challenge of the curriculum) are able to recognise and solve problems at a more complex level than are students motivated by extrinsic interest (i.e. those who are motivated by the potential to earn high salaries or achieve high job status).

10.2.2.5 Cultural background

Research suggests that the formation of beliefs and perceptions are partly determined by exposure to cultural influences (Clikeman et al., 2001). Hofstede (1980) makes the distinction between individualistic and collectivist outlooks in explaining cultural influences. For example, countries of Western cultural background have more individualistic societies when compared with other cultural groups, such as people of Chinese heritage, who tend to be more collectivist (Auyeung & Sands, 1997). In the career choice decision-making process, Auyeung & Sands (1997) found that Australian accounting students tended to be more influenced by aptitude for the subject than were international students studying in Australia. They also found that the international student cohort, when compared with Australian students, placed a higher value on 'material entity' factors including earning potential, social status, employment prospects, and education. However, limited research has been conducted on the intrinsic motivation of different cultures. In a recent study, Jackling & Keneley (2009) found that, in an Australian context, international students were more likely than local (i.e. domestic) students to focus on extrinsic motivational factors in choosing accounting as a career. This finding was attributed in part to the motivation for international students to gain permanent residence status on completion of their accounting studies in Australia, given the migration policy that prevailed at that time (Jackling, 2007).

10.2.3 Accounting as a profession

Attitudes towards the accounting profession have, in part, been influenced by students' perceptions of what Marriott and Marriott (2003) term, 'pre-entry attitudes' or expectations based on societal stereotyping, childhood experiences, and the imagery portrayed by the profession. The negative perceptions of accounting as a profession held by the public have persisted over time. Typically, accountants have been referred to as number-crunchers, focussed on numerical accuracy, routine recording, and calculation methods (Parker, 2000). Prior studies have shown that the perceptions and stereotypes that people hold are important factors which influence their career decisions (Holland, 1973). The next part of this section examines the underlying factors that impact on students' perceptions of the accounting profession, including the work activities of accountants and the prestige of the profession.

10.2.3.1 Work activities of an accountant

The stereotype of the accountant – usually portrayed as male, introverted, cautious, methodical, systematic, anti-social and, above all, boring (Bougen, 1994; Cory, 1992) – has been linked to the historical development of the profession. For example, the stereotype has been attributed to the nature of accounting work in the eighteenth and nineteenth centuries (Edwards, 1989; Fisher & Murphy, 1995; Parker, 2000). The evidence indicates that early bookkeeping and auditing work emphasised numerical accuracy, personal honesty, commitment to secrecy, and rote memory learning of bookkeeping and auditing methods. These aspects of the development of the profession appear to have been a major cause in perpetuating an out-dated image of the accountant (Jackling, 2002).

Accountants have also been portrayed as unflattering individuals via various sources, including the media and in films (DeCoster & Rhode, 1971; Cory, 1992; Murphy, 2000). For example, in films, accountants have been portrayed as being financial experts who are inept, dysfunctional misfits, with anti-social tendencies and a dowdy nerdishness (Beard, 1994; Bougen, 1994; Smith & Briggs, 1999; Parker, 2001). This is an image that has persisted over time. Some researchers have attributed this ongoing negative perception of the work of accountants to misinformation or lack of information about what accounting is and the nature of the duties performed by accountants (Cory, 1992; Garner & Dombrowski, 1997; Albrecht & Sack, 2000).

Albrecht & Sack (2000) suggest that one reason why accounting graduate numbers were declining in the U.S.A. was because of misinformation about what accounting is and the work of accountants.

10.2.3.2 Status of accounting compared with other professions

It is possible that the image of accounting and accounting as a profession is also influenced by the perception of the profession when compared with other career choices. Students are more likely to aspire to a career which is held in high esteem by society. A study of Irish high school pupils ranked accountants behind doctors, lawyers, dentists, and architects as professionals (Byrne & Willis, 2005). Additionally, differences in rankings were identified between accounting students (who ranked accountants fifth) and non-accounting students (who ranked accountants seventh) of 10 professional categories. Gul *et al.* (1989) found that accounting students appeared most concerned with job satisfaction, earnings potential, availability of employment, aptitude for the subject, and years of formal education, and to have a different, and more distinctive, profile than students studying engineering, law, and medicine. A New Zealand study incorporating the views of high school teachers showed that the accounting profession was of lower ranked social status relative to the professions of law, medicine, and engineering (Wells & Fieger, 2005). This was also the view of high school teachers in the U.S.A. (Hardin *et al.*, 2000) and Japan (Sugahara *et al.*, 2006).

10.3 Interests and career choices

The accounting profession has been viewed in a negative way for a variety of reasons, as outlined so far in this chapter. Although there have traditionally been negative perceptions of the work of accountants, accounting as a career has more recently been considered to have extrinsic rewards, such as job potential and prestige relative to some other occupations. However, there are many theories that have been developed more intensively in the psychological and education literature to explain career choice decision-making (e.g. Bordin, 1984; Holland, 1985; Roe, 1984; Super, 1984). Holland's (1985) theory of vocational choice has been particularly attractive to career counsellors (Brown, 1987). According to Holland, adolescents are influenced to choose an occupation that has an environment that will match their interests. Thus students may choose to undertake a major in accounting as a prelude to an accounting career because the perceived work environment and lifestyle of the professional accountant match their own abilities and interests (Chacko, 1991).

10.3.1 Holland's model of occupational choice: 'matching men with work'

As briefly discussed in Section 9.3.2 of Chapter 9 – this volume, in the development of his Vocational Preference Inventory (VPI), Holland (1973, 1985, 1992) viewed vocational preferences as consisting of a six-category typology of persons and their work environments. He categorised interests into six groups (RIASEC):

- Realistic
- Investigative
- Artistic
- Social
- Enterprising, and
- Conventional.

Although these interest groups may be described as personality types, the extent to which a person resembles each of the types constitutes an *interest profile*. An individual need not be assigned exclusively to one of the six types but, according to Holland, he/she can be described as having a pattern of vocational interest consisting of a predominance of two or three of the types. Holland's (1973, 1985) typology of person–environment interactions relates to the notion that particular work environments attract persons with similar vocational interests. The matching of persons and environments as part of Holland's 'matching men with work' is professed to lead to job satisfaction and higher standards of work performance. This concept of congruence is shown diagrammatically in Figure 10.1, in which a match between individual vocational interests related to specific fields of work and a particular occupational environment provides a congruent environment that results in job satisfaction (Jackling, 2001).

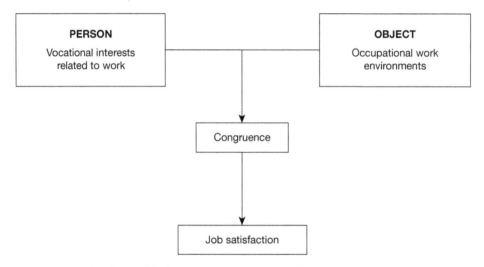

Figure 10.1 Holland's model of congruence and job satisfaction

There has been strong support for models linking Holland's six interest themes with interpretative maps of work. For example, the World-of-work maps (Prediger *et al.*, 1993) and maps of College Majors (Lamb & Prediger, 1981) have identified relationships between interest scores and occupational categories. In particular, some of these studies have shown strong associations between conventional interests and business associated occupations and tasks. The early work by Lamb & Prediger (1981) and Prediger (1982) adapted Holland's six interest themes to two bipolar work task dimensions:

- *working with data* (e.g. facts, records) versus ideas (e.g. theories, insights); and
- *working with things* (e.g. materials, machines) versus people (e.g. care services).

Of particular interest to this chapter is the research of Prediger, Swaney, & Mau (1993) which showed that students with career aspirations in accounting were placed high in the hexagon in the working with data dimension, between Holland's Enterprising and Conventional interest categories (see Figure 9.3). Occupational categories within the Conventional interests/*working with data* classification have typically been linked with jobs related to business operations and financial transactions.

10.3.2 Criticisms of Holland's model of occupational choice

Although the work of Prediger *et al.* (1993) showed some worthwhile extensions of linking Holland's work with interpretative maps of work, there have been a number of criticisms of these endeavours which provide further insights into the work of Holland and its adaptation by Prediger *et al.* (1993). For example, an in-depth analysis of Holland's model of occupational choice, by Chen, Jones, Scarlata, & Stone (2012) focussed on the relevance of the definition of the Conventional interest type, linked with people who prefer activities such as record-keeping. According to Holland, people with Conventional interests like environments which stimulate them to '*engage in recording and organising data or records*' where they are encouraged to see themselves as having '*clerical competencies*' (Holland, 1992). Chen *et al.* (2012) indicate that the persistence of classification of the stereotypical accountant in what they term a '*Beancounter Bookkeeper*' potentially impedes efforts to recruit accountants who will serve the public interest. Chen *et al.* profess that the Conventional interest category fails to champion the cause of accountants to achieve broad economic and social well-being, utilising skills that require strong investigative and leadership skills (ibid., p. 371).

The focus on the Holland model of occupation choice by career counsellors has, according to Chen *et al.* (2012), bolstered and sustained the '*Beancounter Bookkeeper*' stereotype of professional accountants among potential entrants to professional accounting. In challenging Holland's work on occupation choice and, in particular, the determination of the Conventional Interests category of RIASEC, Chen *et al.* have argued that the use of this model of occupational choice has potentially done much to deter suitable entrants to the accounting profession, and thereby impeded the profession's ability to serve the public interest. They conclude that much research needs to be done to discover alternatives to the Holland model of occupational choice – especially as it is used extensively by career counsellors in directing students towards particular career choices.

10.4 Changing the perceptions of accounting as a career choice

10.4.1 Recruitment practices: the changing value system

As previously outlined, the '*Beancounter Bookkeeper*' image has repercussions for the accounting profession, and implications for the recruitment of accounting graduates. For instance, Friedman & Lyne (2001) outline that the narrow-minded stereotype has an effect on the management of organisations and, more importantly for the long term, a negative effect on future professional recruitment: '*For young people, the reputation of a profession as dull and boring is just about the most serious disincentive, particularly for the "best and brightest"*' (2001, p. 424).

In recognition of the established negative image of accountants, in recent times recruiters and PABs have endeavoured to swing the pendulum in the opposite direction, by promoting the profession as engaged, young in spirit, and playful. A study by Jeacle (2008) investigated the recruitment literature of the Big 4 firms and the six chartered PABs in the U.K. in an attempt to identify how recruitment practices endeavour to dispel the stigma of the accounting stereotype. She provides evidence of the attempts to reconfigure the traditional *persona* of the accountant. The reconfiguration of the image of accounting is first conveyed by recruiters via the workplace which is part of the 'young generation'. The recruitment practices of accounting firms have also seen the 'team player' as being a highly-ranked attribute of graduates. Similarly, the emphasis on social activities portrayed in promotional material of Big 4 firms leads Jeacle (2008) to conclude that the attributes sought in the recruitment process provide a stark contrast to the stereotypical image of the bespectacled beancounter poring over the latest spreadsheet.

See also Beard & Humphrey, Chapter 25 – this volume, who discuss the role of internships as part of an accounting degree programme which can give students real work experience in an accounting environment to help them gain insights regarding their perceived suitability for an accounting career as well as giving recruiters opportunities to assess the students in a work-place setting. In addition, of course, internships give potential employers of accounting graduates valuable opportunities to see students as they function in the workplace, which can influence whether jobs are offered to those students once they have graduated.

10.4.2 The role of professional accounting bodies

To date, efforts by PABs and professional accounting firms to change the negative and inaccurate perceptions of accounting and accountants have been limited in their success (Jackling & Calero, 2006; Jeacle, 2008). However, as Jeacle (2008) reports, the 'fun loving' image of accounting is found in the promotional material of PABs. Jeacle (2008) makes reference to website postings of six PABs:

- from the U.S.A., the AICPA;
- from Australia, the Institute of Chartered Accountants in Australia (ICAA);
- from Wales, the Institute of Chartered Accountants in England & Wales (ICAEW);
- from Ireland, Chartered Accountants Ireland – formerly known as the Institute of Chartered Accountants in Ireland (ICAI);
- from Scotland, the Institute of Chartered Accountants of Scotland (ICAS); and
- the London-based but globally-active Chartered Institute of Management Accountants (CIMA).

The evidence suggests that, collectively, the PABs, in a similar vein to the accounting firms, use an array of techniques to construct an exciting and colourful characterisation of the accounting profession. The results show that, through text and image, there is a campaign of impression management to construct an image of the trendy and fun-loving accountant that casts aside the boring bookkeeper characterisation.

The campaigns by recruiters and PABs to dispel the stereotypical image of the accountant have not been widely scrutinised in terms of a substantive body of academic research. Earlier work by Jackling & Calero (2006) in a study of Australian accounting students indicated that advertising by PABs was not important in students' decisions to pursue a career in accounting. However, there is scope for more research to test the impact of campaigns by professional service firms and PABs, that target changes to the negative stereotypes. (As emphasised by St. Pierre & Rebele in Chapter 5 – this volume, we should not lose sight of the fact that the majority of professional accountants do not work in public practice.)

10.5 Projections for the future of accounting as a career choice

10.5.1 Changing the accounting curriculum to enhance accounting as a career choice

Prior research shows that, at secondary and tertiary levels of study, the curriculum reinforces images of accountants as undertaking procedural tasks (see, for example, Laswad & Tan, Chapter 9 – this volume). From an accounting educator's perspective, there needs to be a change in the curriculum, as the role of the accountant has changed. While it is difficult to forecast 20 to 50 years in advance as to what the role of an accountant might be, efforts need to be made to at least move with the times. The way we do business is subject to constant, widespread, and significant change. The major drivers of change include growth and flexibility of communications and business technology, resulting in a more globalised business environment with a focus on knowledge capital and the growing importance of intellectual property (Howieson, 2003). (See also Flood, Chapter 4 – this volume.) As stated by the Institute of Chartered Accountants in Australia (ICAA, 2002a), the greater access to information (and the resulting '*information overload*') will increase the demand for '*effective methods of sorting and screening information*' (ibid., p. 21). The importance of knowledge capital is likely to continue the trend away from a focus on profit towards the maximisation of shareholder value with more attention being paid to non-financial measures of performance (ibid., p. 5).

Due to globalisation and, more specifically, as illustrated by the adoption of International Financial Reporting Standards (IFRS) by more than 120 countries in the past seven years globally, there is a change in the way in which business is conducted. The move from local Generally Accepted Accounting Principles (GAAP) to IFRS also illustrates that there is a need to re-educate existing accounting practitioners, investors, and other users of financial information. As a consequence, there also needs to be a change in the approach to teaching from a rules-based approach to a principles-based approach to reflect the underlying features of IFRS (see, for example, Wells, 2011; Wilson & Adler, 2012). As outlined by Jackling *et al.* (2012), the promotion of framework-based teaching of IFRS provides the impetus for accounting educators to enhance their teaching practices so that a globally-relevant curriculum can be employed.

More generally, as the role of the accountant has changed and will continue to change, there is a need to constantly monitor the accounting education curriculum so that individuals choosing to study accounting have prospects of a viable career in the profession. Additionally, there is a sense of responsibility that accounting educators at all levels, whether pre-qualification (i.e. initial professional development or IPD) at the university level, or post-qualification (i.e. via continuing professional development or CPD), need to ensure that the profession is capable of serving the public interest in regulation, oversight, and resource allocation decisions.

In 2000, Albrecht & Sack published their monograph *Accounting Education: Charting a Course through a Perilous Future*, which, in the specific context of the U.S.A., provided warnings about the future viability of accounting education, yet their bold statements about the threats for the future of accounting have largely gone unheeded. They claimed that, in too many respects, accounting education was being delivered in 2000 in the same way as it was 20 or 30 years beforehand (ibid., p. 2). One could argue that, as we move well into the second decade of the twenty-first century, not much has changed. While it is acknowledged that some accounting educators have made significant changes to provide a curriculum that is relevant and inspiring for students (see the chapters making up Section C of this volume), these changes have not been significant or pervasive enough and the words of Albrecht & Sack (2000) retain some currency today (see for example, Craig & Amernic, 2002; Howieson, 2003; Boyce, 2004; Wong *et al.*, 2013). (See also Flood, Chapter 4 – this volume, who outlines how traditional accounting has not been 'fit for purpose'.)

Accounting courses have been criticised for too often being focussed on mechanics and therefore failing to give students a glimpse of the benefits of a more exciting and comprehensive accounting curriculum. Not only is a mechanical approach seen as being dull, it turns off the more creative students and both encourages and rewards those students who find comfort in the mechanical processing of transactions. As Albrecht & Sack (2000) state, if accounting is perceived as being both demanding and mechanical, it is no wonder that our classes are less attractive to prospective students. Teaching to a set of detailed rules may bring with it certainty for the teacher and the student, but it also entails significant drawbacks. Among these is a concern that talented people will not be attracted to the accounting profession (Barth, 2008; Sunder, 2010) and that a memory-based approach to teaching the accounting curriculum is unworthy of both a university education and a profession (Sunder, 2010).

As noted in Section 10.4.1, the influence on career choice of internships as part of an accounting degree programme is discussed by Beard & Humphrey, Chapter 25 – this volume.

10.5.2 The way forward

This chapter has provided an overview of some of the factors that influence the choice of accounting as a career. There has also been a case put forward to indicate that the work of accountants is changing rapidly and, therefore, accounting educators need to change their ways to better prepare accounting students for a career in accounting. In concluding the chapter, there are two important messages to be conveyed.

The first message relates to attracting students suited to the study of accounting. The challenge for the accounting profession is to attract students to study accounting who are genuinely interested in accounting, given that intrinsic interest is linked with the quality of learning outcomes (Entwistle & Ramsden, 1983; Ramsden, 2003). Identifying intrinsic interest is important in assisting in the identification of those most suited to a career in accounting. The impetus to attract and retain the best, well-suited students to accounting careers has important economic implications, given the significant worldwide shortage of professional accountants. An appropriate image portrayed of the profession as well as the work of accountants, requires efforts from a range of sources including career counsellors, educators, and PABs.

Various measures of vocational interest have been developed which assist in career choice. For example, as previously outlined, Holland's model of occupational choice has been widely used by career counsellors in guiding students' vocational career choices. However, more recently, researchers have suggested that this type of instrument be used with caution due to its questionable classification of accountants (Chen *et al.*, 2012). The use of models of matching personality with vocational choice needs to be carefully re-examined to ensure that unrealistic stereotypes of the professional accountant are not perpetuated as part of career counselling.

PABs have a role to play in promoting the profession to both students and, more widely, to those likely to influence students' decisions to seek accounting as a career choice. The projection of the image of the profession by PABs, to a wide international community via advertising and promotional activities that portray an accurate image of the accounting profession, has the potential to inform parents and other reference groups, as well as to encourage students with intrinsic interest to select accounting as a career choice. Additionally, there is scope in many countries for PABs to work more closely with educators and career advisors to encourage students with personalities matched with accounting to contemplate accounting as a career choice.

Once students have embarked on studies of accounting, it is important that accounting educators do not 'turn them off', so *the second message for the future in terms of promoting accounting as a career choice is to improve the quality of accounting education.* The first step in this process is to invest in the professional development of accounting educators, whether it is the secondary school teacher of accounting or the professor teaching a postgraduate accounting course. Educational providers cannot expect academics without professional development opportunities to make the kinds of changes needed to enhance the quality of education that encourages students to pursue a career in accounting. Many accounting educators were educated in ways that are no longer relevant. As Albrecht & Sack (2000) indicated, it is critical that accounting educators be given the resources to maintain the *'currency of their skills'*, which means that they must develop technologically, globally, and have current and broad business and accounting knowledge. This view is reinforced more recently by the recommendations of the Pathways Commission (2012) in addressing the future of higher education for the accounting profession in the U.S.A.

To ensure that the accounting curriculum has *'currency'*, there needs to be CPD for accounting educators. The International Accounting Education Standards Board (IAESB), an independent standard-setting board within the International Federation of Accountants (IFAC), develops standards and guidance on pre-qualification education and training (i.e. IPD) and CPD for all member bodies. (For a fuller discussion of the role of the IAESB and its International Education Standards see Needles, Chapter 2, and Sundem, Chapter 27 – both in this volume.) An examination of the IAESB's International Education Standards (IES) shows that they do not address the professional development of accounting educators. PABs, such as CPA Australia, in their professional accreditation guidelines for higher education providers (e.g. CPA Australia, 2012), outline the qualifications and professional development expected of educators. These are, as the name suggests, 'guidelines'. The details relating to the professional development of educators are relatively 'broad brush' including CPD activities related to: research, reviewing academic research articles, 'active' membership of relevant academic or professional boards or committees. To maximise the quality and currency of accounting education, there is an opportunity for the IAESB to address CPD requirements for educators as part of accreditation requirements for accounting courses. For a more comprehensive coverage of the accreditation process as a mechanism for assuring the learning component within accounting degrees, see Apostolou & Gammie, Chapter 29 – this volume.

In the light of the changes which impact on accounting practice, particularly in the international arena as illustrated by the role of accounting educators in teaching a principles-based approach to IFRS, there is an increasing need for educators to be involved in 'up-skilling' which involves structured CPD activities. One approach would be to make accounting educators more aware of the need for curriculum revisions via a range of CPD activities. Measures of peer assessment and benchmarking activities across universities also represent ways of working towards improvement in the curriculum content. Initiatives such as the Business Disciplines (including Accounting) setting and assessing standards in Australia has been developed to address quality assurance including assessments by external peer reviewers (Australian Learning and Teaching Council (ALTC), 2010). There is scope for this type of peer assessment to be extended to curriculum content and teaching approaches in accounting. The provision of a vibrant curriculum is necessary to ensure that students seeking accounting as a career choice are suitably prepared and, as best possible, are not 'turned off' accounting by the preparation that they receive from accounting educators. The provision of high quality CPD that improves the skills of accounting educators ought to be more systematically employed to improve the quality of teaching and, ultimately, the provision of high quality graduates for the profession. (See Calderon, Chapter 22 – this volume.)

In conclusion, accounting education researchers have, over an extended period of time, endeavoured to track the characteristics of students to assist in determining how to attract the best and brightest students to the study of accounting and ultimately to a career in the accounting profession. This chapter has focussed on influences on the choice of accounting as a career. If accounting educators can address the pedagogical criticisms, this is one important aspect in enhancing the quality of graduates for the profession. Addressing these concerns (in conjunction with PABs) provides a further opportunity to impact more broadly on the perceptions of the profession held by society which have, in the past, adversely impacted on attracting quality students to the profession.

References

Ahmed, K., Alam, K.F., & Alam, M. (1997) An empirical study of factors affecting accounting students' career choice in New Zealand, *Accounting Education: an international journal*, 6(4), 325–335.

AICPA (2011) Trends in the supply of accounting graduates and the demand for public accounting recruits, available at: http://www.aicpa.org/Press/PressReleases/2011/Pages/StrongHiringDemand ForecastforAccountingGraduates.aspx?action=print.

Albrecht, W.S. & Sack, R.J. (2000) *Accounting Education: Charting the Course through a Perilous Future* (Accounting Education Series, Vol. 16), Sarasota, FL: American Accounting Association.

Allen, C.L. (2004) Business students' perceptions of the image of accounting, *Managerial Auditing Journal*, 19(2), 235–258. doi:10.1108/02686900410517849.

Australian Learning & Teaching Council (ALTC) (2010) *Accounting Standards: Learning and Teaching Academics Standards Statement for Accounting*, Sydney: ALTC.

Andon, P., Chong, K.M., & Roebuck, P. (2010) Personality preferences of accounting and non-accounting graduates seeking to enter the accounting profession, *Critical Perspectives on Accounting*, 21, 253–265.

Auyeung, P. & Sands, J. (1997) A cross-cultural study of the learning style of accounting students, *Accounting and Finance*, 36, 261–275.

Barth, M.E. (2008) Global financial reporting: implications for U.S. academics, *The Accounting Review*, 83(5), 1159–79.

Beard, V. (1994) Popular culture and professional identity: accountants in the movies, *Accounting, Organizations and Society*, 19(3), 308–318.

Bordin, E.S. (1984) Psychodynamic model of career choice and satisfaction, in Brown, D. & Brooks, L. (eds) *Career Choice and Development*, San Francisco: Jossey-Bass, pp. 94–136.

Bougen, P.D. (1994) Joking apart: the serious side to the accountant stereotype, *Accounting, Organizations and Society*, 19(3), 319–335.

Boyce, G. (2004) Critical accounting education: teaching and learning outside the circle, *Critical Perspectives on Accounting*, 4–5, 565–586.

Briggs, S.P., Copeland, S., & Haynes, D. (2007) Accountants for the 21st century, where are you? A five-year study of accounting students' personality preferences, *Critical Perspectives on Accounting*, 18(5), 511–537.

Brown, D. (1987) The status of Holland's theory of vocational choice, *Career Development Quarterly*, 36(1), 13–24.

Byrne, M. & Flood, B. (2005) A study of accounting students' motives, expectations and preparedness for higher education, *Journal of Further and Higher Education*, 29(2), 111–124.

Byrne, M. & Willis, P. (2005) Irish secondary students' perceptions of the work of an accountant and the accounting profession, *Accounting Education: an international journal*, 14(4), 367–381.

Byrne, M. & Willis, P. (2001) The revised second level accounting syllabus: a new beginning or old habits retained? *Irish Accounting Review*, 8(2), 1–22.

Chacko, H. (1991) Can you pick out the accountant? Students' interests and career choices, *Journal of Education for Business*, 66(3), 151–154.

Chen, C., Jones, K., Scarlata, A.N., & Stone, D. N. (2012) Does the Holland model of occupation choice (HMOC) perpetuate the Beancounter-Bookkeeper (BB) stereotype of accountants?, *Critical Perspectives on Accounting*, 23, 370–389.

Clarius Group (2012) *Clarius Skills Index*, Sydney, NSW: Clarius Group. Available at: http://www. clarius.com.au/news_centre/clarius_skills_index.aspx (accessed 28 September 2012).

Clikeman, P.M., Geiger, M.A., & O'Connell, B. T. (2001) Student perceptions of earnings management: the effects of national origin and gender, *Teaching Business Ethics*, 5, 389–410.

Cohen, J. & Hanno, D.M. (1993) An analysis choice of accounting as a major, *Issues in Accounting Education*, 8(2), 219–238.

Cory, S.N. (1992) Quality and quantity of accounting students and the stereotypical accountant: is there a relationship? *Journal of Accounting Education*, 10(1), 1.

CPA (2012) Professional Accreditation Guidelines for Australian Accounting Degrees, available at: http://www.cpaaustralia.com.au/cps/rde/xbcr/cpa-site/australian-accreditation-guidelines.pdf.

CPA Australia (2010) Figures show more women choose accounting, available at: http://www.cpaaustralia. com.au/cps/rde/xchg/cpa-site/hs.xsl/8177.html (accessed 28 September 2012).

Craig, R. & Amernic, J. (2002) Accountability of accounting educators and the rhythm of the university: resistance strategies for post modern blues, *Accounting Education: an international journal*, 11(2), 121–171.

Dandy, J. & Nettelbeck, T. (2002) Research note: a cross-cultural study of parents' academic standards and educational aspirations for their children, *Educational Psychology*, 22(5), 621–627.

Deci, E.L., Koestner, R., & Ryan, R.M. (1999) A meta-analytic review of experiments examining the effects of extrinsic rewards on intrinsic motivation, *Psychological Bulletin*, 125(6), 627–668.

Deci, E.L. & Ryan, R.M. (1985) *Intrinsic Motivation and Self-Determination in Human Behaviour*, New York: Plenum Press.

Deci, E.L. & Ryan, R.M. (2008) Self-determination theory: a macro theory of human motivation, development, and health, *Canadian Psychology/Psychologie canadienne*, 49(3), 182–185.

DeCoster, D.T. & Rhode, J.G. (1971) The accounting stereotype, *The Accounting Review*, 9, 651–64.

Edwards, J.R. (1989) *A History of Financial Accounting*, London, Routledge.

Entwistle, N.J. & Ramsden, P. (1983) *Understanding Student Learning*, London: Croom Helm.

Felton, S., Buhr, N., & Northey, M. (1994) Factors influencing the business student's choice of a career in chartered accountancy, *Issues in Accounting Education*, 9(1), 131–141.

Fisher, R. & Murphy, V. (1995) A pariah profession? Some student perceptions of accounting and accountancy, *Studies in Higher Education*, 20(1), 45–58.

Francisco, B., Parham, A.G., & Kelly, A. (2003) Skills development in accounting education: members in education, New York: American Institute of Certified Public Accountants, April. Available at: www.aicpa.org/members/div/career/edu/index.html (accessed 28 September 2012).

Friedman, A.L. & Lyne, S.R.(2001) The bean counter stereotype: towards a general model of stereotype generation, *Critical Perspectives on Accounting*, 12(4), 423–451.

Garner, R.M. & Dombrowski, R.F. (1997) Recruiting the best and brightest: the role of university accounting programs and state CPA societies, *Issues in Accounting Education*, 12(2), 299.

Geiger, M.A. & Ogilby, S.M. (2000) The first course in accounting: students' perceptions and their effect on the decision to major in accounting, *Journal of Accounting Education*, 18, 63–78.

Greenhaus, J.H., Collins, K.M., Singh, R., & Parasuraman, S. (1997) Work and family influences on departure from public accounting, *Journal of Vocational Behavior*, 50, 249–270.

Gul, F., Andrew, B., Leong, S., & Ismail, Z. (1989) Factors influencing choice of discipline of study – accountancy, engineering, law and medicine, *Accounting and Finance*, 29(2), 93–101.

Hardin, J.R., O'Bryan, D., & Quirin, J.J. (2000) Accounting versus engineering, law, and medicine: perceptions of influential high school teachers, in P.M.J. Reckers (ed.) *Advances in Accounting*, 17, 205–220.

Hermanson, D.R. & Hermanson, R.H. (1995) Are America's top business students steering clear of accounting? *Ohio CPA Journal*, 54(2), 26–30.

Hofstede, G. (1980) *Culture's Consequences: International Differences in Work-related Values*, Thousand Oaks, CA: Sage Publications.

Holland, J.L. (1973) *The Psychology of Vocational Choice*, Englewood Cliffs, NJ: Prentice Hall.

Holland, J.L. (1985) *Making Vocational Choices: A Theory of Vocational Personalities and Work Environments*, 2nd edn, Englewood Cliffs, NJ: Prentice-Hall.

Holland, J.L. (1992) *Making Vocational Choices: A Theory of Vocational Personalities and Work Environments*, 3rd edn, New York: Psychological Assessment Resources Inc.

Howieson, B. (2003) Accounting practice in the new millennium: is accounting education ready to meet the challenge? *The British Accounting Review*, 35(2), 69–103.

Institute of Chartered Accountants in Australia (2002a) CA Student and Entry Program: Overview. Available at: http://www.icaa.org.au/enty/index.cfm?menu = 183andid = A104651268.

Institute of Chartered Accountants in Australia (2002b) *CA Foundations: Candidate Learning Pack*, Sydney: ICAA.

Jackling, B. (2001) Learning approaches of tertiary accounting students, unpublished PhD thesis, University of Melbourne.

Jackling, B. (2002) Are negative perceptions of the accounting profession perpetuated by the introductory accounting course? An Australian study, *Asian Review of Accounting*, 10(2), 52–80.

Jackling, B. (2007) The lure of permanent residency and aspirations of international students studying accounting in Australia, *People and Place*, 15(3), 31–41.

Jackling, B. & Calero, C. (2006) Influences on undergraduate students' intentions to become qualified accountants: evidence from Australia, *Accounting Education: an international journal*, 15(4), 419–437.

Jackling, B., de Lange, P., Phillips, J., & Sewell, J. (2012) Attitudes towards accounting: differences between Australian and international students, *Accounting Research Journal*, 25(2), 113–130.

Jackling, B., Howieson, B., & Natoli, R. (2012) Some implications of IFRS adoption for accounting education, *Australian Accounting Review*, 22(4), 331–340.

229

Jackling, B. & Keneley, M. (2009) Influences on the supply of accounting graduates in Australia: a focus on international students. *Accounting and Finance*, 49(1), 141–160.

Jeacle, I. (2008) Beyond the boring gray: the construction of the colorful accountant, *Critical Perspectives on Accounting*, 19(8), 1296–1320.

Lamb, R.R. & Prediger, K.J. (1981) Technical report for the Unisec Edition of the ACT Interest Inventory (UNIACT), Iowa City, IA: American College Testing.

Lowe, D. & Simons, K. (1997) Factors influencing choice of business major – some additional evidence: a research note, *Accounting Education: an international journal*, 6(1), 39–45.

Malthus, S. & Fowler, C. (2009) Perceptions of accounting: a qualitative New Zealand Study, *Pacific Accounting Review*, 21(1), 26–47.

Manpower Group (2012) *2012 Talent Shortage Survey: Research Results*, Milwaukee, WI: (Manpower Group). Available at: http://www.manpowergroup.com/research/research.cfm (accessed 28 September 2012).

Marriott, P. & Marriott, N. (2003) Are we turning them off?:A longitudinal study of undergraduate accounting students' attitudes towards accounting as a profession, *Accounting Education: an international journal*, 12(2), 113–133.

Mauldin, S., Crain, J., & Mounce, P. (2000) The accounting principles instructor's influence on students' decision to major in accounting, *Journal of Education for Business*, 75, 142–148.

McDowall, T., Jackling, B., & Natoli, R. (2012) Are we there yet? Changing perceptions of accounting as a career preference, *The International Journal of Learning*, 18(4), 335–348.

Middleton, E.B. & Loughead, T.A. (1993) Parental influence on career development: an integrative framework for adolescent career counselling, *Journal of Career Development*, 19(3), 161–173.

Mladenovic, R. (2000) An investigation into the ways of challenging introductory accounting students' attitudes towards accounting as a profession, *Accounting Education: an international journal*, 12(2), 113–133.

Murphy, K.J. (2000) Performance standards in incentive contracts, *Journal of Accounting and Economics*, 30(3), 245–278.

Nelson, I.T. & Vendryzk, V.P. (1996) Trends in accounting student characteristics, *Journal of Accounting Education*, 14(4): 453–475.

Nelson, I.T., Vendrzyk, V.P., Quirin, J.J., & Kovar, S.E. (2008) Trends in accounting student characteristics: results from a 15-year longitudinal study at FSA schools. *Issues in Accounting Education*, 23(3), 373–389.

Ostrove, J.M., Stewart, A.J., & Curtin, N.L. (2011) Social class and belonging: implications for graduate students' career aspirations, *The Journal of Higher Education* 82(6) 748–774.

Paolillo, J. & Estes, R. (1982) An empirical analysis of career choice factors among accountants, attorneys, engineers and physicians, *The Accounting Review*, 57(4), 785–793.

Parker, L.D. (2000) Goodbye, number cruncher, *Australian CPA*, March, 50–52.

Parker, L.D. (2001) Back to the future: the broadening accounting trajectory, *British Accounting Review*, 33(4), 421–453.

Pathways Commission (2012) *Charting a National Strategy for the Next Generation of Accountants*, Sarasota, FL: American Accounting Association.

Pearson, C. & Dellman-Jenkins, M. (1997) Parental influence on a student's selection of a college major, *College Student Journal*, 31(3), 301–314.

Prediger, D.J. (1982) Dimensions underlying Holland's hexagon: missing link between interests and occupations?, *Journal of Vocational Behavior*, 21(3), 259–287.

Prediger, K., Swaney, K., & Mau, W. (1993) Extending Holland's hexagon: procedures, counseling applications and research, *Journal of Counseling and Development*, 71, 422–428.

Professional Oversight Board (2012) *Key Facts and Trends in the Accountancy Profession*. Available at: www.frc.org.uk/getattachment/. . ./Key-Facts-and-Trends-2012.aspx.

Ramsden, P. (2003) *Learning to Teach in Higher Education*, 2nd edn, London: Routledge.

Roe, A. (1984) Personality development and career choice, in Brown, D. & Brooks, L. (eds) *Career Choice and Development*, San Francisco: Jossey-Bass, pp. 31–53.

Ryan, J. (2008) Talent crunch: Mainland's shortage of trained accountants has standard setters scrambling to help, *A Plus*, Hong Kong: Hong Kong Institute of Certified Public Accountants.

Ryan, R.M. & Deci, E.L. (2000) Intrinsic and extrinsic motivation: classic definitions and new directions, *Contemporary Educational Psychology*, 25(1), 54–67.

Shivaswamy, M.K. & Hanks, G.F. (1985) What do accounting students look for in a job?, *Management Accounting*, 66, 60–61.

Smith, M. & Briggs, S. (1999) From bean counter to action hero, *Management Accounting*, 77(1), 28–30.

Strasser, S., Ceyhun Ozgur, E., & Schroeder, D.L. (2002) Selecting a business college major: an analysis of criteria and choice using the analytical hierarchy process, *Mid-American Journal of Business*, 17(2), 17 56.

Sugahara, S. & Boland, G. (2005) Perceptions of the certified public accountants by accounting and non-accounting tertiary students in Japan, *Asian Review of Accounting*, 14(1/2), 149–167.

Sugahara, S., Kurihara, O., & Boland, G. (2006) Japanese secondary school teachers' perceptions of the accounting profession, *Accounting Education: an international journal*, 15(4), 405–418.

Sunder, S. (2010) Adverse effects of uniform written reporting standards on accounting practice, education, and research, *Journal of Accounting and Public Policy*, 29(2), 99–114.

Super, D.E. (1984) Career and life development, in Brown, D. and Brooks, L. (eds) *Career Choice and Development*, San Francisco: Jossey-Bass, pp. 192–234.

Wallace, P. (2009) Reasons women chartered accountants leave public accounting firms prior to achieving partnership status: a qualitative analysis, *Canadian Journal of Administrative Sciences*, 26(3), 179–196.

Warrick, C.S., Daniels, B., & Scott, C. (2010) Accounting students' perceptions on employment opportunities, *Research in Higher Education Journal*, 7, 1–10.

Wells, M.J.C. (2011) Framework-based approach to teaching principle-based accounting standards, *Accounting Education: an international journal*, 20(4), 303–316.

Wells, P. & Fieger, P. (2005) High school teachers' perceptions of accounting: an international study, paper presented at the AFAANZ conference, Melbourne, Australia.

Wilson, R.M.S. & Adler, R.W. (eds) (2012) *Teaching IFRS*, Abingdon: Routledge.

Wong, G., Cooper, B.J., & Dellaportas, S. (2013) A classroom experience: perceptions of Mainland Chinese students in Australian universities, paper presented at the AFAANZ conference, Perth, Western Australia.

About the author

Beverley Jackling is Professor and Director of the Financial Education Research Unit at Victoria University, Melbourne, Australia (beverley.jackling@vu.edu.au). She has served as an Associate Editor of *Issues in Accounting Education*. Her research publications are primarily in the field of accounting education and she has educational research affiliations with a number of professional and employer bodies, nationally and internationally, as well as with government.

Section C

Curriculum considerations

Preface

Fred Phillips

UNIVERSITY OF SASKATCHEWAN, CANADA

A curriculum serves as a map to identify possible routes that learners may travel to reach potential learning outcomes. In some situations, the routes, methods of transportation, and outcomes are well-defined and generally agreed upon because they provide a clear, efficient, and consistent means of moving from point A to point B. In other cases, a multitude of routes and vehicles exist, yielding different experiences and destinations.

Accounting curricula are interesting in that they exhibit such dual purposes, striving to achieve certain goals while demonstrating the desire to explore alternatives. The chapters in this section can help readers understand where we currently stand, the opportunities to explore, and the possible paths that can be taken, whether traversing the world or enriching our own backyards.

In Chapter 11, 'The first course in accounting', Don Wygal begins our journey through accounting curricula by discussing the first course in accounting. This chapter not only depicts the current lay of the land, but also narrates a rich history to help readers understand how we have arrived at our current position. In Chapter 12, 'Liberalising accounting curricula using "angles of vision"', Joel Amernic and Russell Craig invite readers to consider ways of perceiving accounting not only for what it does but also for what it is and what it represents. Kim Watty then reminds readers in Chapter 13, 'Generic skills within the accounting curriculum', that success in accounting depends as much on generic skills as on discipline-specific competencies. Robert Bloom follows in Chapter 14, 'Integrating the accounting curriculum', with specific examples of course pairings that aim to integrate topics as they exist in the world around us. Finally, in Chapter 15, 'Emerging areas within the accounting curriculum', Alan Sangster fittingly concludes with an around-the-world tour of accounting curricula developments.

Taken together, these chapters provide the signposts that will help readers navigate the curricula that underlie accounting education and which guide students toward their professional careers in accounting.

11

The first course in accounting

Donald E. Wygal

RIDER UNIVERSITY, U.S.A.

CONTENTS

Abstract

The 'first course' has been designed and defined in a variety of ways to meet programme and stakeholders' needs worldwide. In this chapter many viewpoints on the roles played and to be played by the first course in accounting are explored. The first course has been an avenue of research enquiry by educators for many decades, and is the focal area of consideration in several calls for accounting education reform.

The chapter's narrative follows a model that views accounting knowledge to be a pathway to facilitate global commerce. Accounting education provides a variety of pathways for students to become professionals. The first course can play an important role as an entry point to students in their study of accounting and as a gateway on their journey to becoming professionals.

Keywords

accounting education reform, course design, first course, pathways, professionalism

11.1 Introduction

The main aims of the chapter are:

- to provide historical perspectives on the nature and roles of the first course in accounting;
- to identify stakeholders' perspectives on the role of the first course as an entry point to academic accounting studies;
- to identify stakeholders' perspectives on the role of the first course as a gateway to later curriculum delivery and to the profession; and
- to explore the potential for ongoing and innovative approaches to first course design and delivery to enhance pathways to the profession.

Any complete discussion and consideration of 'the first course in accounting' is well served to encompass perspectives from each of the individual chapters in this volume. Thus, while the following narrative is identified as 'Chapter 11', the approach followed here will be to call attention as appropriate to integrative themes to be found throughout the volume. This will include a review of current and antecedent debate on the definition, purpose, and place of 'the first course'. Such coverage will relate perspectives from academics and accounting practice professionals across many national settings and over an extended period of time. The narrative identifies both commonalities and differences in viewpoints and themes over time. A concluding focus on the present suggests opportunities for future research and actionable policy-making.

Current knowledge and debate address issue areas that have been raised over several decades. These include initial proposals to enrich the first course beyond coverage of purely technical/procedural dimensions (but see St. Pierre & Rebele, Chapter 5 – this volume), to apply innovative instructional resources (including technology applications – see Stevenson *et al.*, Chapter 19 – this volume), and to design delivery approaches to meet multiple stakeholders' needs (including student enrolments of majors and non-majors: see Laswad & Tan, Chapter 9 – this volume). More recent works have dealt with similar dimensions and others that reflect the dynamic practice environment. In addition, current considerations in many instances reflect enhanced access to and application of information technology (IT). (See Boritz & Stoner, Chapter 16 – this volume.)

Thus, current research across the globe may be measured in terms of antecedent works produced over the previous half-century. Given the need for brevity (and the extensive coverage of related themes to be found elsewhere in this volume), a specific focus will be placed on considerations of works from recent decades and, in particular, those that apply more directly to 'first course in accounting' perspectives. Thus, the chapter will use as a starting point for reviewing insights and proposals that were put forth in a fairly contemporaneous fashion over 30 years ago. This includes relevant points from the Solomons Report (1974) in the U.K., the work of Mathews (1990) in Australia, and related initiatives from the U.S.A. The latter include the Bedford Committee Report (AAA, 1986) and Big 8 White Paper (1989), followed by recommendations of the Accounting Education Change Commission (AECC) in the 1990s. As reflected throughout this volume, much of the attention accorded to accounting education change across the globe reflects more fundamental and similar calls to address perceived needs generally in higher education. (See Needles, Chapter 2, and Flood, Chapter 4 – both in this volume.)

Many scholarly papers on course-specific and programmatic efforts have been reported. Perceptible themes associated with 'the first course in accounting' in these published works include most or all of the elements contained in each section of this volume, including perspectives on ethical imperatives (see Boyce, Chapter 24), skills development (see Watty, Chapter 13), and the evolving (or dynamic) role of technology in practice and in higher education (see Boritz & Stoner, Chapter 16). The literature is rich with perspectives on the place and purpose of the first course. Focal areas include pedagogy (see Section D, comprising Chapters 16–19), assessment of students' learning (see Koh, Chapter 20), and the articulation of desired objectives of the first course with those of the overall curriculum (see Bloom, Chapter 14).

This chapter sits 'first' in a section devoted to curricular issues, a place which reflects the inter-connected importance of the first course in accounting to curriculum design and delivery. The reader is encouraged, therefore, to include consideration of first course perspectives as an important object of attention itself and also with regard to most or all other chapter coverage in this volume. Moving forward, there will be a need to identify how practical considerations discussed more fully elsewhere in the volume may impact upon both a research agenda and proposed policies for a future first course model. Budget constraints, enrolment trends, and supply of qualified accounting educators have played important roles in the debate to date. Any discussion of the future of the first course must consider these factors.

In the 1980s, Hopwood (1989) noted the significance and influence of accounting in facilitating pathways for economic enterprise on a global basis. The narrative to follow underscores a view that the usefulness of accounting knowledge to the flow of commerce is equally compelling in the twenty-first century. Indeed, it can be argued that the pervasive influence of accounting to global enterprise has only gained in importance in recent decades. As the pathways *of* accounting influences have grown, so too have the pathways *to* accounting become increasingly more important to accounting educators, practice professionals, and related stakeholders.

The chapter proceeds with an overview of historical milestones, followed by a consideration of emerging and on-going research themes. A concluding section suggests perspectives moving forward with regard to stakeholders' roles and policy/research initiatives on the first course as a pathway to the profession.

11.2 A brief review of historic milestones

While the literature pertaining to first course in accounting perspectives extends to earlier periods, it is useful to refer to initiatives and reports associated with the decades of the 1980s and 1990s to frame issues surrounding the current debate. In all such instances, a focus on the first course in accounting reflects extensions and applications of broader perspectives pertaining to the accounting profession, and to perceived conditions in accounting education. For clarity and brevity, a focus will be placed on overview perspectives generated from the U.K., Australia, and the U.S.A. More detailed coverage of reports worldwide calling for accounting education change are to be found in earlier chapters of this volume. (See, in particular, Flood, Chapter 4.) Therefore, the discussion to follow is crafted with specific reference to recommendations or proposals pertaining to the 'first course in accounting'. Because such a specific focus during the time period to be discussed is to be found mainly in calls to action that emanated from the U.S.A., coverage in this section will be relatively more extensive on such specific recommendations. Subsequent extensions and applications of baseline points conveyed in this section as they apply specifically to 'the first course' will be considered in the sections of the chapter to follow.

Prior to the 1980s in the U.K., David Solomons served as director of the *Long Range Enquiry into Education and Training for the Accountancy Profession* (Solomons, with Berridge, 1974). This work was commissioned by the short-lived Advisory Board of Accountancy Education, and identified proposed characteristics of the professional accountant. Of particular interest here is an emphasis on the need for accountants to be viewed as members of a true 'profession'. The report conveys the importance of a formal education for entrants to the profession as being a key ingredient of quality while also allowing for the value of field experience and training. Little reference is made to perspectives on the first course, except to suggest (ibid., pp. 142–143) that a proposed curriculum would begin with a half-year of study of *Introduction to Financial Accounting* followed by another half-year course devoted to an *Introduction to Managerial Accounting*.

Of related interest, the report underscores the value of required coverage within the curriculum of mathematics, statistics, economics, behavioural science, and other allied disciplinary perspectives. In addition, the report presents the view that any conception of appropriate qualities for an educated professional cannot remain static. The dynamics of the professional environment will place ongoing pressures on stakeholders to maintain and monitor emerging demands. Perhaps reflecting its visionary status, the report asserts (ibid., p. 14): 'A Long Range Enquiry once a decade would have much to commend it.'

In Australia, the *Report of the Review of the Accounting Discipline in Higher Education* (commonly referred to as the Mathews Report) was published in 1990. The report itself had a gestation period of several years, reflecting concerns raised by practitioners and academics regarding a perceived decline in the quality of accounting education. Key elements of concern pertained to perceptions that inadequate academic salaries and deteriorating working conditions were major impediments to assuring high quality accounting education. As a result, a large part of the report identified problem areas and suggested recommendations for action pertaining to changes in funding strategies to better support accounting educators.

While specific reference to the nature or purpose of a first course in accounting was not conveyed, the report did call upon higher education institutions in Australia to move away from a traditional vocational view of accounting education. Also recommended was a movement away from a traditional structure for a 3-year degree for accounting majors (oriented toward attainment of certification/chartered status) and toward a broad-based education that could foster future careers in management. A corollary view was that professional accounting qualifications could be provided for via a fourth year of undergraduate study. Such recommendations suggested the possibility for students to pursue double majors as a part of their first three years of study. Therefore, while no recommendations were conveyed as to whether and how the first course in accounting should be changed, the specific points conveyed provided much to consider for educators and policy-makers in Australia moving forward.

In the same time frame, in 1984, the American Accounting Association (AAA) created a committee consisting of academics, business executives, and members from public accounting practice to study emerging and expanding professional roles, and to make recommendations pertaining to implications for accounting education. In 1988, *Future Accounting Education: Preparing for the Expanding Profession* (commonly referred to as the Bedford Report) was published. The report identified a typical undergraduate accounting programme in the U.S.A. as consisting of 120 semester hours, of which 30 hours are devoted to accounting coverage. (Credit for a course is tied to contact hours of instruction in a semester. Thus, for example a '3 credit hour course' is one that meets 3 hours per week for the duration of a semester.) The 30 hours of coverage in the major were said to include 'elementary' accounting as a first course, followed by intermediate accounting, cost accounting, auditing, tax, and (more recently in the 1980s) information systems.

The report identifies the existence of an increasing number of graduate programmes in accounting, as well as an emerging recognition in the practice environment of the value of a 150 credit-hour requirement (i.e. five years of study at university) for candidates to become Certified Public Accountants (CPAs). Nonetheless, the report conveys a fundamental message that, despite the apparent ability of higher education institutions (HEIs) in the U.S.A. to provide for sufficient credit hour requirements, there were major perceived deficiencies in the nature, content, and scope of how accounting education was delivered. The report conveyed a total of 28 recommendations for change which, for purposes here, may be said to reflect the need for accounting education to redirect its focus from a traditional emphasis on the purely technical to one which captures the richness of the accounting professional in an expanded decision-making context. (For an alternative view, see St. Pierre & Rebele, Chapter 5 – this volume.) Noted prominently in the report are the benefits of addressing the development of multiple skill sets and of fostering students' ability to recognize the value of 'lifelong learning' perspectives.

None of the 28 recommendations addressed the nature, scope, or content of the 'first course' specifically. However, strong support is conveyed throughout the report for educators, administrators, accrediting bodies, and practice professionals to promote and reward innovative approaches. In particular, the report identifies the value of enhanced coverage of ethical perspectives and, in general, of curricular innovations designed to draw upon disciplinary perspectives from the humanities, arts, and sciences to foster students' analytical, problem-solving, communications, and other skills. (See Amernic & Craig, Chapter 12 – this volume, and Sangster & Wilson, 2013.) In addition, the report recommends that specialized accounting coursework, reflective of a growing number of practice specialty areas, be added to curriculum content, preferably in a 'fifth year' of graduate study. Thus, while the report did not attempt to prescribe how a first course may be redesigned or created from whole cloth, the totality of the recommendations provided a great deal of food for thought regarding the curriculum as a whole for a wide variety of stakeholders – including accounting educators and administrators. In addition, the report identified a possible timetable for future implementation of its recommendations moving forward to the year 2000 and called upon the AAA to be an active facilitator of educators' responses.

Within months of the Bedford Report came the release of *Perspectives on Education: Capabilities for Success in the Accounting Profession* (commonly referred to as *The Big 8 White Paper*, 1989). Signed by the chief executives of the eight largest public accounting firms in the U.S.A. at the time, the report was distributed to accounting staff and administrators, business school deans, accrediting bodies, accountancy boards, state CPA societies, and U.S. Senators and Members of Congress. In addition to noting imperatives and themes conveyed in the Bedford Report, the *Big 8 White Paper* provides a call for active stakeholder initiatives to study and address perceived needs for accounting education change. Specifically noted were the relative dynamism of changes in the practice environment in recent years, during which time accounting education was characterized as remaining relatively stagnant. Also noted specifically was a growing demand from accounting practice for new hires at a time when the number and quality of accounting graduates were on the decline.

The centre-piece of the report is a focus on newly-issued proposals from the American Institute of Certified Public Accountants (AICPA) on expectations for emerging entry requirements for students to meet the needs of practice. These expectations echo many themes in the Bedford Report, including the development of multiple skill sets in addition to increasing general and specialized knowledge capabilities. No specific mention was accorded to the first course in accounting. However, the report asserts that improvements in educational delivery at the undergraduate level are needed, and that implementation of 150 credit-hour requirements planned for by the year 2000 would suggest the potential for additional curriculum change.

To make such a call even more compelling, the signatories to the report pledged a total of $4 million over a 5-year period in the form of grants to academic units to promote innovative curricular responses. Also envisioned was the formation of a coordinating committee consisting of major identifiable stakeholders to implement the funding and oversight process. The American Accounting Association (AAA) was encouraged to take a leadership role in establishing the coordinating mechanism, and practice professionals were asked to support the AAA and its members in their efforts to promote accounting education change.

Within a year, the Accounting Education Change Commission (AECC) was created. (See Sundem, Chapter 27 – this volume.) In 1990, the AECC published Issues Statement No. 1 (AECC, 1990a), *AECC Urges Priority for Teaching in Higher Education*. This is a very brief but powerful statement to accounting educators and related stakeholders calling for innovative approaches to meet the demands of dynamic changes in society and the accounting profession. (The possible dangers of undue corporate/practice influence on accounting education policy should not be overlooked, as will be considered in Section 11.5 of this chapter.) Specific reference is made to developments resulting from the advent of the 'information age' (ibid., p. 1) and rapidly changing technology. The Commission states (ibid., p. 1): '*Our ability to retain a competitive and viable society depends on our ability to educate. Accordingly, the importance of effective teaching and innovative curriculum and course development cannot be over-emphasized*' (emphasis added).

The statement concludes (ibid., p. 1) by encouraging '*all who are interested in the future of the higher education to become involved in helping academia reorder its priorities and place renewed emphasis on teaching and curriculum and course development*'.

Very soon thereafter, the Commission published Position Statement Number One (AECC, 1990b), *Objectives of Education for Accountants*. This statement provides a broad definition of the accounting professional to include entry into and future career paths in public accounting firms of varying sizes, as well as multiple decision-oriented roles in business, government, and other forms of economic endeavour. The AECC states that accounting education (ibid., p. 1): '*should prepare students to become professional accountants, not to be professional accountants at the time of entry to the profession*' (emphasis in original).

The AECC identifies four components of professional accounting education:

- general education;
- general business education;
- general accounting education; and
- specialized accounting education.

A specific foreshadowing of the AECC's views on the first course in accounting is notable in this Position statement. With regard to the curriculum as a whole, the statement asserts (ibid., p. 2): '*The overriding objective in developing course content should be to create a base upon which continued learning can be built.*'

Furthermore, specific attention is then conveyed on the importance of the first course in accounting as a component of the 'general business' component of an accounting student's education:

> *[The first accounting course] must serve the interests of students who are not going to enter the profession as well as those who are. The broad approach recommended in these objectives serves the interests and needs of both groups. The course should teach, reinforce, and reward the skills, abilities, and attitudes*

that are necessary for success in the accounting profession. This will give students accurate knowledge about the nature of accounting careers, which will help them make a well informed choice about entering the profession.

(ibid., p. 3)

The perceived importance of the first course in accounting is further underscored by the AECC in their Position Statement Number Two: *The First Course in Accounting* (AECC, 1992). This statement draws upon and extends points conveyed in its first position statement. In this second position statement, the commissioners specifically address the nature and role of 'the first course.' Accordingly, '*The concepts in this Statement apply directly to the first course in accounting at the undergraduate level. However, they are also applicable to courses in introductory accounting at the graduate level*' (ibid., p. 2).

In addition, a point is made that, in the U.S.A., the term 'first course in accounting' actually refers to a two-course 'introductory' accounting sequence, usually taught over two terms.

The AECC underscores here the importance of the first course not only to students who seek to pursue careers as accountants, but also to others who will work in businesses, governmental units, or other entities, all of which employ accounting information in decision contexts. However, in amplifying points conveyed in its first position statement, the AECC further asserts here that (ibid., p. 2):

The first course has even more significance for those considering a career in accounting and those otherwise open to the option of majoring in accounting. The course shapes their perceptions of (1) the profession, (2) the aptitudes and skills needed for successful careers in accounting, and (3) the nature of career opportunities in accounting. These perceptions affect whether the supply of talent will be sufficient for the profession to thrive. For those who decide to major in accounting or other aspects of business, the course is an important building block for success in future academic work.

Many specific, yet multi-purpose, objectives are suggested for the first course including the ability to engender students' analytical and other skills development, as well as recognition of the vital role that accounting information plays in economic decision-making. Attention is accorded to the value of a student's knowledge of accounting's place in society, including foundational coverage of ethics, professional responsibilities, and international dimensions. Many other specific points are conveyed, and the interested reader is encouraged to access the statement for additional detail. For the purposes here, one additional specific citation is useful to inform the later considerations in this chapter:

In general, the first course in accounting should be an introduction to accounting rather than introductory accounting. It should be a rigorous course focussing on the relevance of accounting information to decision-making (use) as well as its source (preparation).

(ibid., p. 3; emphasis added)

While additional AECC position and issue statements were conveyed, only one other will be given specific attention here, Issue statement no. 6: *Transfer of Academic Credit for the First Course in Accounting Between Two-Year and Four-Year Colleges* (AECC, 1995). This statement reflects the importance to many students in the U.S.A. of having access to education at two-year institutions, often due to advantages of location and cost savings. A basic thrust of this statement is that academics and administrators at both two-year and four-year institutions should be aware of the imperatives conveyed by the AECC regarding the need for innovative approaches. For an ongoing flow of students from one institution to the other to be facilitated, students must be able to achieve credit for coursework at the two-year level that will be acceptable and transferable to the four-year academic setting. This requires close coordination between such institutions and an expectation that the 'first course' credits (wherever acquired) will be reflective of the parameters suggested in previous AECC documents. The importance of two-year schools to higher education and to accounting education in the U.S.A. is conveyed in a separate AECC statement. This importance continues today. The importance of articulation agreements in this regard applies specifically to higher education in the U.S.A. However, extensions of these points will be explored more fully in Section 11.5 with regard to the flow of international students today and moving forward. (On the evaluation of accounting programmes, see Calderon, Chapter 22 and, on accreditation, see Apostolou & Gammie, Chapter 29 – both in this volume.)

11.3 Educators' research on the first course: the 1980s and 1990s

Many educators recognized the importance of the first course prior to the calls for action described above. Much of the research in the 1990s can be seen to extend earlier findings while adding considerations raised by the AECC and others. In addition, because of the specific attention accorded the first course in policy statements in the U.S.A., many useful works of the 1990s address the implications of first course characteristics within overall curricular change efforts. The discussion that follows centres around works, the specific focus of which is on the first course. Coverage begins with a depiction of overall major themes pertaining to characteristics of first course delivery, followed by a consideration of published reports of educators' redesign efforts in response to calls for reform.

11.3.1 Research focus on first course characteristics

Many of the themes explored more fully in separate chapters of this volume were the focus of educators' research on the first course during this period of time. This includes consideration of cognitive style (see Duff, Chapter 8), choice of major (see Laswad & Tan, Chapter 9), career choice (see Jackling, Chapter 10), generic skills development (see Watty, Chapter 13), assessment (see Koh, Chapter 20), and ethics (see Boyce, Chapter 24). The focus of many educators was on the nature of the first course setting as an entry point to the academic study of accounting. During the same time frame, other researchers examined similar themes with a focus on the role of the first course as a gateway to the overall objectives of the curriculum. As the following discussion demonstrates, such themes were examined in a variety of programme contexts worldwide.

Several studies explored possible predictors of students' success, including relationships between a student's secondary school preparation and performance in the first accounting course. Baldwin & Howe (1982) examined relationships between previous secondary school coursework and students' performance in the first college accounting course. They report that students who had taken an accounting course in secondary school appeared to do no better than those who had not. Keef (1988) reported similar results in extending Baldwin & Howe's work to the context of first course delivery in New Zealand. However, Eskew & Faley (1988) report that previous secondary school coursework had at least some explanatory power, and point to measures of aptitude and effort to explain much more of the variance. Mitchell (1988) examined the relationship of secondary school and university first course students' performance in Scotland.

These works point to the need for additional study, noting that such research is at the same time important and complex. (See Byrne & Willis, Chapter 7 – this volume.)

A study by Auyeung & Sands (1994) extends previous works to address questions of gender effects, previous secondary school accounting experience, and entry test scores as predictors of success in the first-year college accounting course in Australia. Also of interest is their extension of focus to deep versus surface measures of students' learning. Tho (1994) examined possible predictors of students' performance in Malaya, including urban/rural status, gender and secondary school coursework.

Gul & Fong (1992) examined first course delivery in Hong Kong, suggesting the importance of previous secondary education coursework and of proficiency in English and mathematics. In addition, their findings suggest the possibility of measures of student personality type as predictors of students' performance at the college level. Wong & Chia (1996) also examined first-year students' performance in Hong Kong. Their findings suggest an association between a student's proficiency in mathematics and performance in a *Financial Accounting* course. Oswick & Barber (1998) explored a possible link between students' first course performance and indicators of personality type in a U.K. setting, and reported no significant relationships. Naser & Peel (1998) explored performance characteristics for first-year accounting students in the Occupied West Bank. Their findings suggest the value of additional study of class size, educators' attributes, a student's effort, and overall course rigour as being indicators of performance. (See Koh, Chapter 20 – this volume.)

Additional studies of the first course examined skills development and assessment. Webb, English, & Bonanno (1995) explored connections between students' skills development and assessment in a first accounting course context in Australia. They report the value of interim assessment techniques and early diagnostics to enhance students' skills development and to alert for the possible need for remedial actions. Hand, Sanderson, & O'Neill (1996) studied the use of assessment techniques for *Introductory Accounting* students in the U.K. They assert the potential for well-considered approaches to assessment to also enhance students' performance and promote active learning.

As noted above, several studies focussed on the role of the first course as a gateway to the accounting curriculum. Cherry & Reckers (1983) report a study of how the approach to the first course in accounting may be related to students' performance in later accounting courses. They provide preliminary evidence of the importance of a more conceptual (and less procedural) approach in the first course and underscore the importance of ongoing educator research in first course characteristics.

The potential of the first course for harm or for good with regard to attracting students was studied in New Zealand by Taylor & Dixon (1979). Their findings showed that students who chose not to major in accounting exhibited a very negative impression of the accounting profession. In the U.S.A., Paolillo & Estes (1982) identified a link between students' experiences in the first course and in their first two years of college with the decision to major in accounting. Further, their subjects reported that they were very much influenced in their choice of major by the influence and example of their teachers. (See Laswad & Tan, Chapter 9 – this volume.)

Carland, Carland, & Dye (1994) explore applications of learning style theory to accounting education. An implication for first course research is the assertion that a typical second-year student taking a first course in accounting exhibits learning style preferences (LSP) that are contrary to a traditional lecture delivery mode. (For further discussion on LSP, see Duff, Chapter 8 – this volume.) The authors suggest the application of cooperative learning approaches to enhance students' performance. Much subsequent attention has been placed on a variety of cooperative learning approaches to first course delivery both in the 1990s and to the present (as discussed in Section 11.4 of this chapter).

Adler & Milne (1995) explore the potential for educators in a New Zealand context to expand from more traditional lecture approaches to enhance students' awareness of the value of learning to learn. Specific applications in a managerial course context are identified. In addition, Adler & Milne (1997a) point to possible conflicts between educators' objectives to foster students' learning and a perceived failure of professional admissions standards in New Zealand to promote such approaches. Adler & Milne (1997b) provide educators who teach the first and later courses with suggested strategies to develop active learning approaches.

McClure (1988) reports on efforts at a university in the U.S.A. to infuse coverage of international perspectives throughout an *Introductory Financial Accounting* course. He asserts that the infusion of such materials (in a course normally devoted to financial accounting standards in the U.S.A.) enabled students to better understand both domestic and international topical considerations. Leung & Cooper (1994) report on the implementation of a required ethics course at Hong Kong Polytechnic. While their focus was not with specific regard to first course delivery, the authors address issues pertaining to whether and how ethical perspectives may be addressed within the overall curriculum. Of related relevance is their discussion of such issues in the context of evolving professional accreditation standards. Reported experiences of course and curriculum redesign have relevance to first course delivery and are discussed below.

11.3.2 Innovative first course redesign issues

The following identifies research reported during the 1990s which address 'redesign' needs conveyed in the previous calls to action. Such works place a particular focus on ways to design/redesign course content and delivery to articulate entry point delivery with integrative needs of the overall curriculum.

Norgaard & Hussein (1990) surveyed a large number of academic institutions in the U.S.A., including community colleges, to provide a profile of the typical components of the 'elementary' accounting two-course sequence, with a specific focus on 'managerial' elements. They report that academic units largely employ a principles (procedural) approach to financial accounting as opposed to a conceptual, user-oriented emphasis. Further, they assert the need for educators to recognize the importance of adequately addressing managerial imperatives and not simply those pertaining to financial accounting in future first course sequence redesign.

Adams, Lea, & Harston (1999) report on the use of a 'serial case' in an *Introductory Managerial Accounting* course. Motivation to do so comes from persistent negative feedback from students regarding the traditional 'principles' approach. Their findings suggest that the case approach enhances students' perceptions of the richness of the accounting professional environment as they consider a possible future career path.

Abdolmohammadi, Brown, Feldman, Gujarathi, & Haselkorn (1998) report on a revised two-course sequence which included a focus on financial accounting and managerial accounting, and also included an integration of tax, information systems, and auditing. The revised sequence was designed to pursue objectives to enhance decision contexts, ethical perspectives, and international dimensions of accounting. Citing data collected over the four-year implementation period, the authors assert that the revised approach enhances students' learning.

Innovative redesign of *Introductory Accounting* courses at Kansas State University (KSU) is the focus of Ainsworth (1994). Responding to recommendations for action as conveyed in the Bedford Report, the Big 8 White Paper, and AECC statements, KSU redesigned its introductory two-course sequence. Emphasis was placed on developing/assessing students' skills (primarily oral, written, and interpersonal communication). In addition, the redesign emphasized the development of an integrated approach to coverage of financial accounting and managerial accounting topics. Evidence over several semesters of implementation suggests the potential exists for transferability of the revised approach to other institutions.

Hardy & Deppe (1995) report on the redesign efforts at Brigham Young University, resulting from an AECC grant. Redesign covered all aspects of their curriculum, including the first course. Emphasis was placed on skills development and integrative coverage employing a focus on business cycles. Also noted is an increased systems emphasis. The authors suggest the value of the revised approach to students' learning and note the potential for the transfer of applications to other institutions, both in the U.S.A. and abroad.

Saudagaran (1996) reports on a redesigned *Introduction to Accounting* sequence in the early 1990s at Santa Clara University in California. A change in focus includes an emphasis on written and oral communication and the use of cases to model the decision contexts in practice that exhibit the need to exercise judgement. Also introduced is the integration of coverage of auditing, accounting policy, managerial considerations, and international dimensions. Evidence collected over several semesters suggests several benefits, including students' enhanced perceptions of the richness of the accounting profession as a possible career path.

AECC grant experience includes awards with reference to first course initiatives. Flaherty (1998) reports on redesign and implementation efforts at Arizona State University (ASU) and at Mesa (Arizona) Community College. The approach at ASU includes the redesign of its *Introduction to Accounting* two-course sequence to a decision-oriented, user approach. In addition, the accounting staff designed and implemented a third course to address important IT perspectives. Also of note is a report (Flaherty, 1998, p. 9) of unexpected benefits to academic staff and students which accrued over the process of visioning and implementing change. Specifically identified were transfer gains from the first course environment to later courses in the application of cooperative learning techniques and new and useful approaches to assessment. Further, the efforts expended by accounting staff resulted in a demonstrable enhancement of the department's reputation throughout the university. In turn, their efforts and accomplishments resulted in regional and national recognition for the department and university.

Mesa Community College transformed the former first course preparer focus to a two-course *Introduction to Accounting* sequence following a user approach (ibid., p. 51.) Specific attention was paid to AECC recommendations pertaining to the transfer of first course credits and involved frequent communication with the academic accounting staff at ASU. The revised sequence (ibid., pp. 52–53) marked a move from lecture delivery to cooperative learning techniques and a skill-building emphasis.

A common theme among these reports is that planning for redesign drew upon the insights of multiple stakeholders, and resulted in a diversity of approaches to meet identifiable needs. In a real sense, calls for reform and ongoing educators' inquiry have created opportunities for creativity and course/curriculum redesign. This aspect is explored more fully in Section 11.5 of this chapter.

By the end of the twentieth century, the diversity and richness of research on the first course had grown demonstrably. In many ways, the diversity of intellectual pursuits to study first course issues may be seen as a measure of fulfilment of the promise of the scholarship of teaching and learning as suggested by Ernest Boyer (1990). Ongoing exploration of earlier themes, and the addition of a growing and diverse number of works to support teaching and learning in the first course, are discussed in Section 11.4.

11.4 First course perspectives in the twenty-first century

As the twentieth century came to a close, Albrecht & Sack (2000) issued a study calling for further change efforts in accounting education in the U.S.A. Perhaps not coincidentally, Hancock issued a report almost a decade later in Australia (Hancock *et al.*, 2009). Its major theme is the need for ongoing attention to necessary and evolving students' skill sets, and a renewed call for educators to address such needs. While specific criticisms with regard to first course delivery are not identified in either report, each underscores the need for accounting educators and related stakeholders to remain ever-vigilant with regard to evolving (sometimes dynamic) changes in the practice environment. An ongoing characteristic of such calls for reform is recognition of the need to develop curricula that will serve to capture the richness of a dynamic professional environment. For accounting educators, inter-connected themes of the twenty-first century relate to ways to leverage technology to better model the richness of the practice environment in coursework, and to gain deeper understanding of students' learning needs. In turn, advances in IT enable a fairly pervasive dissemination of results and insights that may facilitate approaches to add value to the teaching and learning environment.

With regard to the dynamics of practice, a focus continues on skills development, ethics, and other themes identifiable from previous works. These build upon insights gained in earlier years and explore issues of emerging importance. Topics in the latter category include (among many) sustainability and international standards development.

In addition, educators' attention has been directed to the creation and sharing of teaching/learning resources, many of which are intended for application in the first course. Their efforts are designed to provide interested readers with additional course learning modules, cases, and other approaches as derived from experience to fit individual course needs and contexts. Reported works include applications devoted to skills development (Stoner & Milner, 2010), computer simulation (Wynder, 2004), introductory course-level case materials (Dikolli & Sedatole, 2003), learning portfolios (Samkin & Francis, 2008), and service learning in an *Introductory Managerial Accounting* setting (Chiang, 2008). These are only several examples of the growing interest of educators in adding value to first course delivery via the creation and sharing of teaching/learning resources. A further indication of the growth in diversity of approaches with regard to the role and delivery of the first course may be found in Cunningham (2011). Given the widespread use of large lecture class settings for the first course, Cunningham suggests the value of designing course delivery by applying lessons learned from theatrical stage productions. In the interest of brevity, discussion here must continue with an additional overview of major themes of research in recent years on the first course.

Coverage of international financial reporting standards (IFRS) in the curriculum provides an interesting example presently. Zhu, Rich, Michenzie, & Cherubini (2011) report on an extensive survey of academic staff with regard to the extent of IFRS coverage in *Introductory Accounting* courses in the U.S.A. They note that relatively little time is spent on IFRS by the vast majority of respondents. While noting the likely future importance of IFRS coverage to students, respondents note the uncertainty of implementation presently (2009 at the time of the survey) as an important reason why little time is devoted to such considerations in the first course. However, Coetzee & Schmulian (2012) convey a quite different perspective in their first course setting in South Africa where IFRS standards are the norm. Given the perceived importance of IFRS coverage, the authors examine possible effects of alternative pedagogical approaches on students' technical competence. Thus, while there are many common issue areas attracting attention around the world, the dynamics and context of perceived practice needs remain an important factor in the nature and type of inquiry being conducted. (See Wilson & Adler, 2012.)

A great deal of ongoing attention has been accorded to the study of cooperative learning, skills development, and the use of assessment techniques. Many recent studies have examined the potential for IT gains as applied to each or all of these topical areas. For purposes of this chapter, the following discussion is necessarily brief and is intended to suggest broad themes of the past decade. Jones & Fields (2001) study the results of supplemental instruction techniques (for example, online tutorials) for a large sample of students in multiple sections of *Principles of Accounting* courses. They report many gains with regard to critical thinking skills development and students' overall performance. Kealey, Holland, & Watson (2005) report on the application of a holistic measurement approach to assess students' critical thinking skills. They assert the power of students' critical thinking measures in explaining students' overall performance in the course. Findings underscore the importance of an educator focus on both the development and assessment of students' critical thinking skills. (See also Cunningham, Chapter 18 – this volume.)

For first year students in the U.K., Aisbitt & Sangster (2005) report positive findings between the use of online assessment measures and final examination performance, and provide guidance for future educators' use and research. Marriott & Lau (2008) report gains in students' learning, motivation, and overall course satisfaction through the use of online assessment methods in a first course setting in the U.K. Baxter & Thibodeau (2011) apply intelligent learning assessment software in an *Introductory Accounting* course in the U.S.A. They report gains in students' competency measures and overall course performance, as well as efficiencies with regard to teachers' time demands.

Learning theory applications in first course delivery in Australia are examined by Mladenovic (2000), and show promise of promoting students' learning and enhancing positive perceptions of the accounting profession. Lucas (2001) explores characteristics of deep versus surface learning for *Introductory Accounting* students in the U.K. and identifies approaches to teaching and assessment that show promise for transfer gains to multiple contexts. Byrne, Flood, & Willis (2002) examine associations between reported diagnostic measures of approaches to learning for first year students in Ireland, and their subsequent learning outcomes in the course, as measured by assessment techniques. They report a positive association with high academic performance for students exhibiting deep or strategic learning approaches. Some evidence of gender effects is reported as well. Marriott (2002) reports on a longitudinal study of students' learning styles at two universities in the U.K. Of particular interest here is a finding that a large sample of accounting students did exhibit differing learning styles and that, for many, the preferences changed over time. (See also Duff, Chapter 8 – this volume.)

Multiple gains through the use of a business simulation in an *Introductory Accounting* course in the U.S.A. are reported by Springer & Borthick (2004). These include enhanced higher-order thinking skills and improvement in students' reported satisfaction with the course. Springer Sargent, Borthick, & Lederberg (2011) showed short online video tutorials to *Principles of Accounting* students. They report improved students' examination performance, reduced class dropout rates, and increases in students' satisfaction with the course.

Kern (2002) examined active learning and lecture classroom approaches in a first course setting in the U.S.A., taking note of students' learning preferences. Results suggest the value of an active learning approach to enhance students' problem-solving performance. Murdoch & Guy (2002) investigated the effects of large class size in an active learning context in an *Introductory Accounting* course. They report students' performance in a small class setting was significantly better than for those who experienced active learning treatments in a large class environment. Opdecam & Everaert (2012) report favourable results in a Belgian context for an active learning versus lecture approach in a large class context, both in terms of students' performance and with regard to satisfaction with the course.

Premuroso, Tong, & Beed (2011) employ a controlled environment to examine the use and non-use of audience response system (clicker) technology in multiple sections of an *Introductory Accounting* course. They report enhanced classroom participation by students, and overall course performance gains for students in sections employing clicker applications.

A common thread in the narrative of many of these works is the ability of the educator/ researcher to employ techniques in the first course that previously had been applied only in upper-level courses in the curriculum. In a real sense, such approaches enrich the role of the first course, both as an entry point for students and as a gateway to enhanced future learning in later courses.

This brief overview discussion of current themes suggests that, moving forward, accounting education research will continue to focus on the needs of stakeholders while also addressing ways to enhance the teaching and learning environment. Research of the past decade reflects the growth in the importance of the scholarship of teaching and learning to accounting educators, and to an increasing number of interested stakeholders. These points are explored more fully in Section 11.5.

11.5 Conclusion: first course as pathway to and of accounting

The foregoing discussion underscores the point that the usefulness of accounting knowledge to the flow of commerce has continued to grow as 'doing business' globally has become more commonplace. In turn, increased demand for accounting graduates (with proper reference to peaks and valleys over time) is demonstrable worldwide. Therefore, in a very real sense, accounting educators can now identify a multitude of potential pathways for students 'to become' accountants. History suggests that the value of developing and applying the knowledge and skill sets of accounting is demonstrable in a growing number of decision contexts across the globe. This establishes the potential for rich and innovative approaches in the future for stakeholders to seize upon such opportunities.

Educators presently may pursue the development of pathways to accounting that meet the needs of students who recognize early on that their career will define them as being 'accountants'. Other future accounting students will recognize the value of such a career path only at some later time, perhaps after having already achieved another type of degree. For these students, the pathway to the profession may seem to them to 'begin' with graduate or professional study. Within this mix will be those who may find that their pathway to the profession will begin or continue only through study abroad options. (See also Jackling, Chapter 10 – this volume.)

The diversity of potential pathways to the profession is addressed by the International Federation of Accountants (IFAC). This point is underscored by the International Accounting Education Standards Board (IAESB) in its recent (February 2013) International Education Standard 1 (Revised): *Entry Requirements to Professional Accounting Education Programs*. IES 1 (2013, p. 4) notes the benefit of 'allowing flexible access to professional accounting education programs' and the possibility of 'different pathways' in this pursuit. The diversity of such potential pathways is underscored in IES 1 (Explanatory Material A1, p. 5):

> *Professional accounting education programs are designed to support aspiring professional accountants to develop the appropriate professional competence by the end of Initial Professional Development (IPD). They may consist of formal education delivered through degrees and courses offered by universities, other higher education providers, IFAC member bodies, and employers, as well as workplace training.*

The design of professional accounting education programs during IPD may therefore involve substantive input from stakeholders other than IFAC member bodies.

For any and all such pathways, the 'first course in accounting' will be particularly relevant. As the foregoing narrative has established, the nature and content of the first course do not fit the description 'one size fits all'. Indeed, the first course has been conceived and delivered across the world in a variety of ways for many years (and very commonly as, at least, a two-course sequence). Much time and effort has been addressed to the nature, content, and positioning of this sequence. Recent attention also has been placed upon possible gains of articulation with related courses in communications skills and IT (to name only two examples).

Therefore, consideration of the 'first course' promises to be vitally important to educators, practice professionals, and related stakeholders moving forward. One indicator of this ongoing importance may be found in the work of the Pathways Commission (2012) which includes specific recommendations pertaining to the role of the first course.

This commission was created in the U.S.A. in 2010 under the sponsorship of the AAA and the AICPA. Its many working groups consist of accounting educators, practice professionals, and a broad array of related stakeholders. Their stated objective (Pathways Commission, 2012, p. 9) is:

> to study the future structure of higher education for the accounting profession and develop recommendations for education pathways to engage and retain the strongest possible community of students, academics, practitioners and other knowledgeable leaders in the practice and study of accounting.

Many of its recommendations echo themes of earlier works regarding the need for reform in accounting education to enhance innovative approaches, and to underscore the importance of teaching in higher education. In conveying its recommendations, the Commission takes note of both 'opportunities' and 'impediments'.

The Commission places a particular focus on the role of the first course as an entry point, with a specific recommendation (ibid., p. 39) '*[to] improve the ability to attract high potential, diverse entrants into the profession*'. A potential objective or opportunity in this regard is the ability (ibid., p. 40) to '*transform the first course in accounting*'.

A recognized pathway to the profession that has grown in importance in the U.S.A. pertains to opportunities for non-accounting majors at the 'fifth-year' level. The Commission identifies traditional approaches to the first course in such curricula as an impediment (ibid., p. 41): '*The inability to efficiently satisfy business and accounting prerequisite coursework often dissuades non-accounting undergraduates from considering these programs as a pathway to the accounting profession.*' Such an impediment will be a barrier to entry if left unaddressed. However, there is intuitive appeal in the suggestion that a creative (and perhaps collaborative) redesign of a first course sequence by educators and related stakeholders can create new and viable pathways to the profession.

The view taken here to conclude the chapter is one of optimism with regard to issues identified in this report. Much productive, interesting and thought-provoking research has been generated to date. Perhaps as importantly, the many calls to action cited here have focussed the collective attention of an increasing number of stakeholders on the needs for reform, and to specific considerations of the role of the first course to the mission and context of individual academic units. There is clear potential, therefore, for additional work to be applied to perceived ongoing problem areas that can then be converted to opportunities for mutual gain moving forward. A brief examination of proposed Pathways Commission's 'action items' for the first course provides useful examples.

These action items (ibid., pp. 87–88) underscore the value of building on previous research on the design and delivery of the first course. Of corollary value is the proposed development of a library of teaching and learning materials related to the first course. This firmly suggests the potential for developing learning communities in the future where dialogue can be promoted, and gains from experience may be shared. In this regard, such an enhanced sense of community can be seen to extend the promise of scholarly endeavour suggested by Ernest Boyer over two decades ago.

The potential for shared future gain may also be seen for other suggested action areas, including the development and use of engaging integrative materials and enhanced abilities to leverage technology. The role of accounting practice in sharing insights and resources via technology appears to be quite promising. Many firms have made resources available on their websites which address a wide range of topics of common interest to practice and to educators. These address issues and approaches relating to ethics, international accounting information technology, and sustainability, to name only several. As educators work to develop and evolve their curricula and to consider/reconsider the role of first course sequencing in such future visions, an open dialogue between academics and the practice community will be greatly facilitated through the enhanced connective capabilities provided by technology. (See Bloom, Chapter 14; Boritz & Stoner, Chapter 16; and Stevenson *et al.*, Chapter 19 – all in this volume.)

However, at the same time, it is not appropriate to suggest that all stakeholders in higher education will or should speak with one voice. Nor is it necessarily the case that trust can be/has been easily earned across all stakeholder groups. Our brief survey of historical antecedents shows that, in many contexts, there can be clear 'winners' or 'losers' where stakeholders' interests apply. This includes the potential for funding decisions in a university setting to be adversely affected by the perceptions of administrators and others with regard to the legitimacy of accounting as a true profession, or as an academic discipline. Similarly, it is possible for accounting educators to be wary, or perhaps viscerally opposed, to perceived 'mandates' from the profession. Not everything in the practice world or in higher education is to be valued or perceived equally.

In this sense, it is not suggested here that educators should simply 'respond' to the perceived needs of practice. Educators as stakeholders have the freedom, even the duty, to be aware of stakeholders' emerging needs, including those of parents, students, practice professionals, and others. For example, the definition of what constitutes 'high potential, diverse entrants to the profession' (Pathways Commission, 2012) will likely be quite different over a variety of contexts and stakeholders' interests. This suggests the ongoing opportunity for educators and stakeholders in given settings to develop creative approaches to address their specific needs, objectives, and sensibilities. Thus, educators as stakeholders can and should work with one another (and with other stakeholders) to develop curricular approaches which are appropriate to educational objectives as they see them, perhaps even as a counter-point to the perceived demands of the practice environment. (This theme is explored more fully by Sangster in Chapter 15, and Evans in Chapter 28 – both in this volume.)

The optimistic tone conveyed presently derives from a premise that stakeholders (even those who may seem not to be in 'our camp') can work together for mutual benefit as each sees the light to do so. This view is expressed by Wygal (2011, p. 236):

> *[I]ndividuals and groups who may be viewed as separate from one another, in fact, can work meaningfully and well together. Thus, so long as potentially-beneficial individuals or groups remain separate, how can we expect them to understand or value or trust one another?*

Collectively, the present chapter underscores a point that valuable insights have been gained on the role and place of the first course in the pathway to the accounting profession. The profession has called upon educators to enhance a student's ability to *become an accounting professional*. At the same time, educators have placed a focus on the role and place of the first course as a gateway for students as they learn to *become a student*. Therefore, while future calls for change and reform are likely to be forthcoming, many valuable contributions have been made to date that can help to guide future pursuits of each of these worthwhile objectives.

The potential for gain from future research in the first course is quite large. Experiences to date reflect both the increasing importance of, and stakeholders' attention to, the value of the first course. Pathways to additional scholarly enquiry on the design and articulation of innovative 'first course' approaches and the potential for mutual gain may be limited only by our collective imaginations and energies.

References

Abdolmohammadi, M., Brown, C., Feldman, D., Gujarathi, M., & Haselkorn, M. (1998) Designing and implementing an AECC complying introductory accounting course: a four-year perspective, *Advances in Accounting Education*, 6(2), 147–162.

Accounting Education Change Commission (AECC) (1990a) *AECC Urges Priority For Teaching in Higher Education*, Issues statement no. 1, Torrence, CA: AECC. Available at: http://aaahq.org/aecc/Positions andIssues/issues1.htm.

Accounting Education Change Commission (AECC) (1990b) *Objectives of Education for Accountants: Position Statement Number One*, Torrence, CA: AECC.

Accounting Education Change Commission (AECC) (1992) *The First Course in Accounting*: Position statement number two, Torrence, CA: AECC. Available at: http://aaahq.org/aecc/PositionsandIssues/pos2.htm.

Accounting Education Change Commission (AECC) (1993) *Evaluating and Rewarding Effective Teaching*: Issues statement no. 5, Torrence, CA: AECC. Available at: http://aaahq.org/aecc/PositionsandIssues/issues5.htm.

Accounting Education Change Commission (AECC) (1995) *Transfer of Academic Credit for the First Course in Accounting Between Two-Year and Four-Year Colleges*, Issue statement no. 6, Torrence, CA: AECC.

Adams, S.J., Lea, R.B., & Harston, M.E. (1999) Implementation of a serial-case pedagogy in the introductory managerial accounting course, *Issues in Accounting Education*, 14(4), 641–656.

Adler, R. & Milne, M. (1995) Increasing learner control and reflection: towards learning-to-learn in an undergraduate management accounting course, *Accounting Education: an international journal*, 4(2), 105–119.

Adler, R. & Milne, M. (1997a) Translating ideals into practice: an examination of international accounting bodies' calls for curriculum changes and New Zealand tertiary institution' assessment methods, *Accounting Education: an international journal*, 6(2), 109–124.

Adler, R. & Milne, M. (1997b) Improving the quality of accounting students' learning through action-oriented tasks, *Accounting Education: an international journal*, 6(3), 191–215.

Ainsworth, P. (1994) Restructuring the introductory accounting courses: the Kansas State University experience, *Journal of Accounting Education*, 12(4), 305–323.

Aisbitt, S. & Sangster, A. (2005) Using internet-based on-line assessment: a case study, *Accounting Education: an international journal*, 14(4), 383–394.

Albrecht, W.S. & Sack, R.J. (2000) *Accounting Education: Charting the Course through a Perilous Future* (Accounting Education Series, Vol. 16), Sarasota, FL: American Accounting Association.

American Accounting Association Committee on the Future Structure, Content and Scope of Accounting Education (The Bedford Committee) (1986) Future accounting education: preparing for the expanding profession, *Issues in Accounting Education*, 1(1), 168–195.

Auyeung, P. & Sands, D. (1994) Predicting success in first-year university accounting using gender-based learning analysis, *Accounting Education: an international journal*, 3(3), 259–275.

Auyeung, P. & Sands, D. (1997) Factors influencing accounting students' career choice: a cross-cultural validation study, *Accounting Education: an international journal*, 6(1), 13–23.

Baldwin, B.A. (1993) Teaching introductory financial accounting in mass-lecture sections: longitudinal evidence, *Issues in Accounting Education*, 8(1), 97–111.

Baldwin, B.A. & Howe, K.R. (1982) Secondary level study of accounting and subsequent performance in the first college course, *The Accounting Review*, 57(3), 619–626.

Baxter, R. & Thibodeau, J. (2011) Does the use of intelligent learning and assessment software enhance the acquisition of financial accounting knowledge? *Issues in Accounting Education*, 26(4), 647–656.

Big 8 (1989) *Perspectives on Education: Capabilities for Success in the Accounting Profession*, (The Big 8 White Paper). Reprinted in Sundem, G.L. (1999) *The Accounting Education Change Commission: Its History and Impact* (Accounting Education Series, Vol. 15), Sarasota, FL: American Accounting Association.

Boyce, G., Greer, S., & Davids, C. (2012) Expanding the horizons of accounting education: incorporating social and critical perspectives, *Accounting Education: an international journal*, 21(1), 47–74.

Boyer, E.L. (1990) *Scholarship Reconsidered: Priorities of the Professoriate*, Princeton, NJ: The Carnegie Foundation for the Advancement of Teaching.

Byrne, M., Flood, B., & Willis, P. (2002) The relationship between learning approaches and learning outcomes: a study of Irish accounting students, *Accounting Education: an international journal*, 11(1), 27–42.

Carland, J., Carland, J.C., & Dye, J. (1994) Accounting education: a cooperative learning strategy, *Accounting Education: an international journal*, 3(3), 223–236.

Cherry, A. & Reckers, P. (1983) The introductory financial accounting course: its role in the curriculum for accounting majors, *Journal of Accounting Education*, 1(1), 71–82.

Chiang, B. (2008) Integrating a service learning project into Management Accounting coursework: a sharing of implementation experience and lessons learned, *Accounting Education: an international journal*, 17(4), 431–445.

Coetzee, S. & Schmulian, A. (2012) Critical analysis of the pedagogical approach employed in an introductory course to IFRS, *Issues in Accounting Education*, 27(1), 83–100.

Cunningham, B. (2011) Introductory accounting as theater: a look behind the scenes of large-lecture production, *Issues in Accounting Education*, 26(4), 815–834.

Dikolli, S. & Sedatole, K. (2003) Schlotzky's gourmet franchise store, *Accounting Education: an international journal*, 12(4), 427–435.

Duff, A. (2004) Understanding academic performance and progression of first-year accounting and business economics undergraduates: the role of approaches to learning and prior academic achievement, *Accounting Education: an international journal*, 13(4), 409–430.

Englis, L., Luckett, P., & Mladenovic, R. (2004) Encouraging a deep approach to learning through curriculum design, *Accounting Education: an international journal*, 13(4), 461–488.

Eskew, R.K. & Faley, R.H. (1988) Some determinants of student performance in the first college-level financial accounting course, *The Accounting Review*, 63(1), 137–147.

Flaherty, R.J. (ed.) (1998) *The Accounting Education Change Commission Grant Experience: A Summary*, Sarasota, FL: Accounting Education Change Commission and American Accounting Association.

Gul, F. & Fong, S. (1992) Predicting success for introductory accounting students: some further Hong Kong evidence, *Accounting Education: an international journal*, 2(1), 33–42.

Hall, M., Ramsay, A., & Raven, J. (2004) Changing the learning environment to promote deep learning approaches in first-year accounting students, *Accounting Education: an international journal*, 13(4), 489–505.

Hancock, P., Howieson, B., Kavanagh, M., Kent, J., Tempone, I., & Segal, N. (2009) *Accounting for the Future: More Than Numbers*, Sydney: Australian Learning and Teaching Council.

Hand, L., Sanderson, P., & O'Neill, M. (1996) Fostering deep and active learning through assessment, *Accounting Education: an international journal*, 5(2), 103–119.

Hardy, J. & Deppe, L. (1995) A competency-based, integrated approach to accounting education, *Accounting Education: an international journal*, 4(1), 55–75.

Hazelton, J., Haigh, M., Staley, A.B., & Baker, R. (2010) Incorporating sustainability into accounting curricula: lessons learnt from an action research study, *Accounting Education: an international journal*, 19(1–2), 159–178.

Hopwood, A. (ed.) (1989) *International Pressures for Accounting Change*, London: The Institute of Chartered Accountants in England and Wales.

International Accounting Education Standards Board (2013) *International Education Standard 1 (Revised): Entry Requirements to Professional Accounting Education Programs*. Available at: www.Ifac.org.

Johnson, B., Phillips, F., & Chase, L. (2009) An intelligent tutoring system for the accounting cycle: enhancing textbook homework with artificial intelligence, *Journal of Accounting Education*, 27(1), 30–39.

Jones, J. & Fields, K. (2001) The role of supplemental instruction in the first accounting course. *Issues in Accounting Education*, 16(4), 531–545.

Kealey, B., Holland, J., & Watson, M. (2005) Preliminary evidence on the association between critical thinking and performance in principles of accounting, *Issues in Accounting Education*, 20(1), 33–49.

Keef, S.P. (1988) Preparation for a first level university accounting course: the experience in New Zealand, *Journal of Accounting Education*, 6(2), 293–307.

Kelly, M. & Pratt, M. (1994) Management accounting texts in New Zealand: the need for a paradigm shift, *Accounting Education: an international journal*, 3(4), 313–329.

Kern, B. (2002) Enhancing students' problem-solving skills: the use of a hands-on conceptual model in an active learning environment, *Accounting Education: an international journal*, 11(3), 235–256.

Leung, P. & Cooper, B.J. (1994) Ethics in accountancy: a classroom experience, *Accounting Education: an international journal*, 3(1), 19–33.

Lucas, L. (2001) Deep and surface approaches to learning within introductory accounting: a phenomenographic study, *Accounting Education: an international journal*, 10(2), 161–184.

Lyons, J. (2006) An exploration into factors that impact upon the learning of students from non-traditional backgrounds, *Accounting Education: an international journal*, 15(3), 325–334.

Marriott, P. (2002) A longitudinal study of undergraduate accounting students; learning style preferences at two U.K. universities, *Accounting Education: an international journal*, 11(1), 43–62.

Marriott, P. & Lau, A. (2008) The use of on-line summative assessment in an undergraduate financial accounting course, *Journal of Accounting Education*, 26(1), 43–62.

Mathews, R. (Chairman) (1990) *Accounting in Higher Education: Report of the Review of the Accounting Discipline in Higher Education*, Canberra: Australian Government Publishing Service, Department of Employment, Education and Training.

McClure, M.M. (1988) Internationalization of the introductory financial accounting course, *Journal of Accounting Education*, 6(1), 159–181.

Mladenovic, R. (2000) An investigation into ways of challenging introductory students' negative perceptions of accounting, *Accounting Education: an international journal*, 9(2), 135–155.

Murdoch, B. & Guy, P. (2002) Active learning in small and large classes, *Accounting Education: an international journal*, 11(3), 271–282.

Naser, K. & Peel, M. (1998) An exploratory study of the impact of intervening variables on student performance in a Principles of Accounting course, *Accounting Education: an international journal*, 7(3), 209–223.

Ng, J., Lloyd, P., Kober, R., & Robinson, P. (1999) Developing writing skills: a large class experience: a teaching note. *Accounting Education: an international journal*, 8(1), 47–55.

Norgaard, C. & Hussein, M. (1990) The managerial accounting component of elementary accounting, *Journal of Accounting Education*, 8(1), 77–92.

Opdecam, E. & Everaert, P. (2012) Improving student satisfaction in a first-year undergraduate accounting course by team learning, *Issues in Accounting Education*, 27(1), 53–82.

Oswick, C. & Barber, P. (1998) Personality type and performance in an introductory level accounting course: a research note, *Accounting Education: an international journal*, 7(3), 249–254.

Paolillo, J.G.P. & Estes, R.W. (1982) An empirical analysis of career choice factors among accountants, attorneys, engineers and physicians, *The Accounting Review*, October, 785–793.

Pathways Commission (2012) *Charting a National Strategy for the Next Generation of Accountants*, Sarasota, FL: AAA, and New York: AICPA. Available at: www.pathwayscommission.org.

Premuroso, R., Tong, L., & Beed, T. (2011) Does using clickers in the classroom matter to student performance and satisfaction when taking the introductory financial accounting course? *Issues in Accounting Education*, 26(4), 701–723.

Prinsloo, P., Muller, H., & Du Plessis, A. (2010) Raising awareness of the risk of failure in first year accounting students, *Accounting Education: an international journal*, 19(1–2), 203–218.

Samkin, G. & Francis, G. (2008) Introducing a learning portfolio in an undergraduate financial accounting course, *Accounting Education: an international journal*, 17(3), 233–271.

Sangster, A. & Wilson, R.M.S. (eds) (2013) *Liberalising the Accounting Curriculum in University Education*, Abingdon: Routledge.

Saudagaran, S. (1996) The first course in accounting: an innovative approach, *Issues in Accounting Education*, 11(1), 83–94.

Solomons, D., with Berridge, T.M. (1974) *Prospectus for a Profession*, London: Advisory Board of Accountancy Education.

Springer, C. & Borthick, A.F. (2004) Business simulation to stage critical thinking in introductory accounting: rationale, design, and implementation, *Issues in Accounting Education*, 19(3), 277–303.

Springer Sargent, C., Borthick, A.F., & Lederberg, A. 2011. Improving retention for principles of accounting students: ultra-short online tutorials for motivating effort and improving performance, *Issues in Accounting Education*, 26(4), 657–679.

Stoner, G. & Milner, M. (2010) Embedding generic employability skills in an accounting degree: development and impediments, *Accounting Education: an international journal*, 19(1–2), 123–138.

Tan, L.M. & Laswad, F. (2006) Students' beliefs, attitudes and intentions to major in accounting, *Accounting Education: an international journal*, 15(2), 167–187.

Taylor, D.B. & Dixon, B.R. (1979) Accountants and accounting: a student perspective, *Accounting and Finance*, November, 51–62.

Tho, L. (1994) Some evidence on the determinants of student performance in the University of Malaysia introductory accounting course, *Accounting Education: an international journal*, 3(4), 331–340.

Van den Brink, H., Kokke, K., Loo, I., Nederlof, P., & Verstegen, B. (2003) Teaching management accounting in a competencies-based fashion, *Accounting Education: an international journal*, 12(3), 245–259.

Webb, C., English, L., & Bonanno, H. (1995) Collaboration in subject design: integration of the teaching and assessment of literacy skills into a first-year accounting course, *Accounting Education: an international journal*, 4(4), 335–350.

Wilson, R.M.S., & Adler, R.W. (eds) (2012) *Teaching IFRS*, London: Routledge.

Wygal, D. (2011) Teaching, scholarship and sharing: perspectives on community, *Accounting Education: an international journal*, 20(3), 227–237.

Wynder, M. (2004) Facilitating creativity in management accounting: a computerized simulation. *Accounting Education: an international journal*, 13(2), 231–250.

Young, M. & Warren, D. L. (2011) Encouraging the development of critical thinking skills in the introductory accounting courses using the challenge problem approach, *Issues in Accounting Education*, 26(4), 859–881.

Zhu, H., Rich, K., Michenzi, A., & Cherubini, M. (2011) User-oriented IFRS education in introductory accounting at U.S. academic institutions: current status and influencing factors, *Issues in Accounting Education*, 26(4), 725–750.

About the author

Donald E. Wygal teaches financial accounting and the integrative professional capstone course at Rider University in Lawrenceville, N.J., U.S.A. (wygal@rider.edu). Professor Wygal has chaired the AAA's Teaching & Curriculum (now Teaching, Learning & Curriculum) Section; chaired the AAA's Innovation in Accounting Education Committee in 2011; served on the AICPA's Education Executive Committee; and was inducted into the TLC Hall of Honor in 2008. His research interests include course design, scholarship of teaching and learning, and emerging applications of technology in academic settings.

12

Liberalising accounting curricula using 'angles of vision'

Joel H. Amernic* and Russell J. Craig**

*UNIVERSITY OF TORONTO, CANADA **VICTORIA UNIVERSITY, AUSTRALIA

CONTENTS

Joel H. Amernic and Russell J. Craig

Abstract

We acknowledge the ambiguous nature of the term 'liberalising' and briefly review some pertinent literature. Our argument is that liberalised accounting curricula will expose students beneficially to a broader set of perceptions of accounting and help them to develop better understandings of accounting. We adopt a novel perspective. Rather than push explicitly for mandatory infusions of broadening subject matter (such as history, philosophy, and English literature) into already constrained accounting curricula, we advocate a pedagogic pathway involving liberal approaches to learning through which liberal *non*-accounting subject matter will emerge serendipitously. The pathway which we recommend and illustrate encourages students to explore accounting by using one or more of the nine 'angles of vision' or 'lenses' proposed by Peshkin (2001), plus two additional lenses. We explain these 'angles of vision' and illustrate how they can be used effectively by accounting educators. Thus, what we propose is a more spontaneous, informal, teacher-led liberalising of accounting curricula.

Keywords

accounting, angles of vision, curricula, liberal, pedagogy, Peshkin

12.1 Introduction

The main aims of this chapter are:

- to introduce the idea that accounting educators should structure courses as applications of liberal learning;
- to discuss what is meant by 'liberalising accounting curricula';
- to (briefly) position the chapter within the literature;
- to introduce and discuss 11 'angles of vision,' or 'lenses', by which accounting educators and their students may, by intention, broaden their perceptions of accounting and its effects; and
- to (briefly) mention, in a final discussion section, some further considerations in liberalising accounting curricula.

In this chapter we focus mainly on the undergraduate accounting curriculum in universities. We acknowledge the ambiguous nature of the term 'liberalising', and briefly review literature on liberalising the undergraduate curriculum. We argue that accounting curriculum proposals which endorse the inclusion of specified 'literary classics' (Lister, 2010) and approaches that require the inclusion of 'new' versions of 'liberal arts courses' (Willits, 2010) are perhaps misguided (see also Craig, 2010). Rather, we agree with Willits' contention that: '*it falls on accounting educators to structure courses in ways that will make them exercises in liberal learning*' (2010, p. 13). Such a contention is consistent with the recent Carnegie Foundation for the Advancement of Teaching research study which – while referring to undergraduate business education in general – recommended the following:

> *Borrowing from the famous DNA model developed by Watson and Crick, we propose the double helix as a metaphor for an undergraduate business curriculum that explicitly and continually links*

students' learning of business to their use of various arts-and-sciences disciplines that provide a larger, complementary view of the world.

(Colby *et al.*, 2011a, in summarising their Carnegie-funded
work in Colby *et al.*, 2011b)

We argue that accounting students would benefit from a liberalised accounting curriculum because this would expose them to a broader set of perceptions of accounting, and would thereby help them to develop a better understanding of how accounting should serve, and be perceived by, the wider community. Technology is almost always a wild card in curriculum prescription, as the impact of the rise and emergent maturity of the Internet has shown vividly (Amernic, 1998; Amernic & Craig, 1999). (See also Boritz & Stoner, Chapter 16 – this volume.) Although we do not consider the roles of technology (such as, for example, social media) in liberalising the accounting curriculum, we are stimulated by the possibilities, and intrigued by initiatives to integrate online virtual world websites (such as Second Life) into the accounting curricula of various universities (see, for example, Buckless, Krawczyk, & Showalter, 2012).

In developing proposals for curriculum reform, we draw upon the nine 'angles of vision' that Peshkin (2001) proposes as ways of liberating (including broadening) perceptions of phenomena and assisting how we know and learn.[1] Also, we add tenth and eleventh 'angles of vision'.

Our suggestions to liberalise accounting curricula are presented as follows:

- We discuss the benefits of applying each of Peshkin's perceptual lenses of: *patterns*; *time*; *emic*; *positionality*; *themes*; *ideology*; *metaphor*; *irony*; and *silences* in the education of accounting students.
- Then, we introduce two additional lenses: *framing* and *culture*.

Our use of all 11 lenses might be perceived as limiting as well as liberating since, like physical lenses, our attention is focussed (metaphorically and literally) in one direction at a time. However, the scope and diversity of directions on offer, and their inter-connectedness, move substantively towards liberating our perspectives as accounting educators and the perspectives of our students. Thus, a more diverse, sensitive, and ethical accounting pedagogy is enabled – consistent with the conclusions of Colby *et al.* (2011a, 2011b) and the enduring perspective of Alfred North Whitehead ([1929] 1957); see also Craig & Amernic (2002). Our discussion of how each 'lens' can be applied to liberalise accounting curriculum is illustrated by examples from accounting education.

In our view, the broad aim of a university education is: '*to produce graduates who will serve a useful purpose in society and be better [citizens] than they otherwise would be*' (Craig & Amernic, 2002, p. 125). So, if accounting graduates are to help construct a civil society as part of a vibrant democracy, they should be able to question deeply, pursue alternative perspectives, challenge ideology, and bring context to bear when they engage with accounting issues. They should be 'reflective practitioners' who contribute to the public good (Waddock, 2005). They should be sensitive to alternative cognitive worldviews (Underhill, 2011).

In other words (and following Colby *et al.*, 2011a, 2011b), a liberal arts curriculum and an accounting curriculum are not disjoint sets. (For an alternative view, see St. Pierre and Rebele, Chapter 5 – this volume.)

A liberalised accounting curriculum will assist students to better fulfil their innate human potential as citizens. However, rather than push explicitly for mandatory infusions of broadening subject matter (such as history, anthropology, philosophy, foreign languages, politics, and

English literature) in already constrained accounting curricula, we adopt a fresh perspective. We advocate a pedagogic pathway to liberalising curricula in accounting – one in which liberal approaches to learning, and the study of liberal *non*-accounting subject matter, will emerge serendipitously, and perhaps inevitably. This is a pedagogic approach in which the design of curricula encourages students to explore accounting by using one or more of the nine 'angles of vision' proposed by Peshkin (2001) along with the two additional 'angles' we propose – *framing* and *culture*.

Much of this chapter is devoted to explaining these 11 'angles of vision' and to illustrating how they can be used to good effect by accounting educators. What we advocate is a more spontaneous, informal, teacher-led liberalising of accounting curricula – rather than one that is imposed formally through administrative fiat, changes in university degree rules, or formal responses to the accreditation requirements of professional accounting bodies (PABs). (See Calderon, Chapter 22, and Apostolou & Gammie, Chapter 29 – both in this volume.)

The Carnegie Foundation's research report, *Rethinking Undergraduate Business Education: Liberal Learning for the Profession* identifies the four 'central dimensions' of liberal learning as:

- analytical thinking;
- multiple framing;
- reflective exploration of meaning; and
- practical reasoning (Colby *et al.*, 2011b, p. 60).

As we explain below, each of these dimensions is likely to be captured if a teacher applies the various angles of vision discussed herein. For example, Colby *et al.* (2011b, p. 60) describe 'multiple framing' as '*the ability to work intellectually with fundamentally different, sometimes mutually incompatible, analytical perspectives. It involves conscious awareness that any particular scheme of Analytical Thinking or intellectual discipline frames experience in particular ways.*' Each of Peshkin's nine angles of vision, plus the two additional angles we add, has the potential to sensitise students to the importance of multiple framing, and to provide thinking tools to engage in that activity.

Accounting educators should avoid allowing students to be imprisoned in a deficient mindset. The angles of vision seem likely to be helpful in this regard. They frame ways of liberating and broadening perceptions of phenomena and assisting users to appreciate how they know and how they learn. As we show below, various 'angles of vision' provide amenable design criteria for liberalising accounting curricula. Accounting educators should encourage students to be mindful of ethical relationships, to challenge received doctrine, and to examine the implications of implicit assumptions and other ways of thinking. While none of the various angles of vision are unique individually, as a set they have strong potential to motivate accounting students and educators to draw from a wider palette of curriculum materials and processes.

We now position this chapter in the literature (Section 12.2) before then considering in Section 12.3 the ambiguous nature of the term 'liberalising', and then briefly reviewing some pertinent literature. Thereafter, we outline (with examples) in Section 12.4 how the various perceptual angles of vision can be applied to liberalise accounting curricula.

12.2 Positioning within the literature

Over the past several years, there have been many institutional and academic attempts to stimulate reform in accounting education. These have encompassed numerous papers and reports, including: in the U.S.A., the Accounting Education Change Commission (1990), the American Accounting Association (1986), and Pathways Commission (2012); in Australia, Mathews,

Jackson, & Brown (1990) and Cappelletto (2010); in the U.K., Solomons (1974); and others internationally, as well as the work of the International Accounting Education Standards Board (IAESB). Accounting educators have contributed significantly to accounting education reform, in journals such as: *Journal of Accounting Education*; *Issues in Accounting Education*; *Accounting Education: an international journal*; and *Critical Perspectives on Accounting*. In 2010, *Accounting Education: an international journal* published a themed issue on 'Liberalising the Accounting Curriculum' (19(4) August 2010; see also the *Bloom & Webinger Forum* in the same journal, 20(5), October 2011).

There has been much activity and creative thinking about accounting education reform, including the rather complex and multi-faceted conception of liberalising the accounting curriculum. Indeed, the prominence of this conception is made more vivid with the publication of Routledge's recently-released book *Liberalising the Accounting Curriculum in University Education* (Sangster & Wilson, 2013), based on the 2010 themed issue in *Accounting Education: an international journal*, mentioned above. The publication of the present companion volume, although positioned to address accounting education more generally, is part of this intellectual foment.

This chapter complements, rather than repeats, the wealth of work (some of it contradictory) on liberalising the accounting curriculum mentioned above. But, let us be clear about what we do, and not do, in this chapter. What we present is an 'idea' or a novel approach which, if adopted by accounting teachers, would help develop 'liberalised' accounting subject matter. We do not present a definitive review of all that has been said and written previously on the subject of 'liberalising the accounting curriculum'. Nor do we review all prior reports that have advocated reform of accounting education. (These are covered extensively in other chapters of this volume.) Rather, we are evangelists for a novel pedagogic approach – one which we contend will help to liberalise accounting curricula. We do not seek to provide an historically complete catalogue or critical literature review of 'liberalising the accounting curriculum'. We do not chronicle many of the laudable attempts, using unconventional pedagogical approaches, which have been adopted by accounting scholars internationally to liberalise accounting curricula. Readers wanting to familiarise themselves with the broader literature, reform suggestions, and unconventional pedagogic approaches, should consult Sangster & Wilson (2013).

The present chapter has explicit and implicit links to other chapters in this volume, including potentially, and most productively, the following:

Chapter 3   The nature of financial literacy
Chapter 6   Perceptions of accounting
Chapter 8   Learning styles and approaches in accounting education
Chapter 11   The first course in accounting
Chapter 14   Integrating the accounting curriculum
Chapter 18   Developing critical thinking in accounting education
Chapter 24   Ethics and accounting education

These links emphasise the highly integrated nature of the various aspects of education generally.

12.3 What does 'liberalising accounting curricula' mean?

We do not conceive 'liberalising' narrowly to mean the study of liberal arts subjects. Rather, we subscribe to the view, endorsed in a report in 2007 by The National Leadership Council for Liberal Education and America's Promise (hereafter LEAP) that liberal education can be achieved through ways other than studies in arts and science disciplines. The LEAP report included

---

Exhibit 12.1 Four essential learning outcomes

Beginning in school, and continuing at successively higher levels across their college studies, students should prepare for twenty-first-century challenges by gaining:

Knowledge of human cultures and the physical and natural world

- Through studies in the sciences and mathematics, social sciences, humanities, histories, languages, and the arts.

Focussed by engagement with big questions, both contemporary and enduring.

Intellectual and practical skills, including
- Inquiry and analysis
- Critical and creative thinking
- Written and oral communication
- Quantitative literacy
- Information literacy
- Teamwork and problem-solving

Practised extensively, across the curriculum, in the context of progressively more challenging problems, projects, and standards for performance.

Personal and social responsibility, including

- Civic knowledge and engagement – local and global
- Intercultural knowledge and competence
- Ethical reasoning and action
- Foundations and skills for lifelong learning

Anchored through active involvement with diverse communities and real-world challenges.

Integrative learning, including

- Synthesis and advanced accomplishment across general and specialized studies

Demonstrated through the application of knowledge, skills and responsibilities to new settings and complex problems.

Source: LEAP Report (2007, p. 3).

---

a non-partisan definition of 'liberal education' as '*[a] description of the kinds of learning needed to sustain a free society and to enable the full development of human talent*' (2007, p. 11). The LEAP report described four essential learning outcomes '*for a globally engaged democracy and for a dynamic, innovation-fueled economy*' (ibid., p. 3). See Exhibit 12.1.

Generally, these learning outcomes are consistent with the view of leaders in management education, such as Martin (2007). Indeed, Martin's work on integrative thinking is highly relevant in the present context. It was reviewed favourably in the 2011 Carnegie Foundation report, mentioned previously, as follows:

> From a study of exceptionally successful business leaders, Martin has distilled the qualities of thinking employed by these leaders ... More routine-focussed managers tend to shun messy situations and seek to apply one-track solutions to problems, which often locks them into unproductive tradeoffs among competitive strategies. By contrast, Martin's integrative thinkers are able to keep a large, complex problem in mind while investigating its several parts. This is because these leaders can see patterns, connections, and relationships among different aspects of the problems confronting their company. Unlike purely linear thinkers who only see one-way causation, integrative thinkers have developed the ability to hold conflicting strategies and imperatives together at the same time. **The capacity to find integrative solutions created by the messy conjunction of conflicting opposites is a cardinal feature of a high-quality liberal education.** Martin's discovery is that this is precisely the capacity that identifies the most innovative and successful business professionals.
>
> (Colby *et al.*, 2011b, pp. 30–31; emphasis added)

Attempts by university accounting educators to liberalise curricula imply two tacit obligations. These are:

- to commit to a goal of rendering accounting curricula consistent with the university's role in assisting students to become responsible, questioning, and creative citizens in an open, democratic society; and
- to acknowledge that the practice of accounting is embedded unavoidably in the social world, so that accounting curricula should be designed with essential thinking requirements and analysis tools uppermost in mind.

This implies that students can have university-level experiences with 'liberal arts' (in courses such as history, languages, and philosophy). But, it also implies that the content and process of courses in accounting, and in related extra-curricular experiences, should be designed with the desired learning outcomes advocated in the LEAP report (see Exhibit 12.1) uppermost in mind.

Consequently, history, language analysis (including the crucial importance of understanding metaphor), critical thinking (including particularly about that which is more ideologically-focussed, such as in Amernic (1998)) should be embedded in all accounting courses. In this way, perhaps Zeff's (1989, p. 206) oft-cited plaintive query: 'Does accounting belong in the university curriculum?' would become redundant. Zeff (ibid., p. 206) concluded that: '*it is desirable in any field of liberal learning that students be equipped with a critical faculty for evaluating alternatives and making decisions.*' In a clear reference to accounting, he continued by saying that: '*A curriculum that dwells on current practice, without instilling a critical faculty, is more suited to the preparation of technicians than professionals.*'

12.4 Liberalising accounting curricula by deploying angles of vision as design stimuli

Peshkin (2001, p. 242) recommended the use of nine possible angles of vision or 'lenses through which to perceive'. This goal of opening up and thereby facilitating the broadening of *perception* of accounting students seems fundamental to the design of liberalised accounting curricula. Such angles of vision help develop an awareness that there is almost always more than one substantive way in which an accounting phenomenon can be looked at, and reflected upon. Although Peshkin contended that angles of vision would be especially useful in qualitative research and inquiry, the idea of multiple, overlapping, angles of vision seems equally fruitful as a way of stimulating the design and content of accounting courses. How Peshkin's nine angles of vision, and the two additional ones we suggest, can assist in liberalising accounting curricula, is now explained and illustrated.

12.4.1 Patterns

Most elementary school students are encouraged to seek out patterns in subjects such as mathematics, as a prelude to a more general understanding of phenomena such as an arithmetic series. This 'lens' of pattern recognition and the subsequent ensuing inferences and deductions, form the first of Peshkin's nine lenses. As Peshkin writes:

> [W]e naturally look for what recurs, taking note of what we are perceiving that we have perceived before in more or less the same way, under more or less the same circumstances. There are, for example, individual, group, and institutional responses that are generally constant, in the sense that if X does A, then Y usually does B. One way to understand a . . . problem is through those actions and outcomes that, by their regularity, give form and content to what we perceive.
>
> (2001, p. 243)

As one way of perceiving, we should focus attention on identifying what occurs regularly. We can learn from knowing what patterns exist in a situation, and when those patterns are breached. Analysing patterns, and breaches in patterns, can contribute to the idea that financial reporting and managerial accountability do not involve a simple, straightforward delivery of the financial facts, but that they are strategic and social communication endeavours.

The concept of patterns is a powerful, yet flexible, way of stimulating cognition. Suppose, as an illustration, that we use the financial accounting topic of cash flow statement analysis. Accepted accounting standards require that reporting companies disclose three categories of cash flows:

- cash flow from operations (CFO)
- cash flow from investing (CFI) and
- cash flow from financing (CFF).

Ignoring zeroes (and thus restricting each of CFO, CFI, and CFF to a positive or negative algebraic sign), there are then eight patterns of cash flow for any given company, for any given reporting period (Dugan *et al.*, 1991). Students can be encouraged to write short scenarios explaining their expectations regarding each pattern. For example, the pattern CFO < 0, CFI < 0, and CFF > 0 might plausibly be found in the cash flow statement of a start-up company which is raising equity and/or debt capital, is investing in capital assets, but is unable to generate positive operating cash flow. Students might then apply their expectations to real company data to see whether their expectations have been fulfilled and, if not, why not?

Even if a company's cash flow pattern is as expected, students should still ask 'Why?' For example, Enron 'manufactured' a cash flow pattern for 2000 which showed CFO > 0 by inaptly classifying US$4.2 billion in CFF as CFO. In other words, desirable patterns may be created by management to tell a financial accounting story as an attractive myth. Forensic examination of patterns reinforces a student's ability to develop a sceptical and realistic attitude towards financial reporting and accounting generally.

Other examples of employing the lens of 'patterns' in the accounting curriculum would include observing the 'normal' sequence of topics in a company's CEO Letter to Shareholders which is included as part of the annual report, and then looking for deviations from this pattern and linking such deviation to important changes in the company and in its environment; and observing patterns in cost accounting variances that may suggest underlying process issues.

12.4.2 Time

Peshkin writes:

> *I suggest history as a lens because knowing what happened earlier is critical for grasping the meaning of what currently is going on. By gaining a historical understanding, we avoid the arrogance of presentism, whereby we focus on what is current as if there never had been another time that is the basis for the state of the present . . . How long something lasts, the duration of an event relative to other events, and variations in duration of the same event over time are all ways of obtaining a measure of salience.*
>
> (2001, p. 243)

By shunning 'the arrogance of presentism', accounting educators can ask students to explore almost any topic in the broader discipline of accounting through the lens of history to 'grasp meaning' and 'uncover honor, respect, concern and importance' (ibid., pp. 243–244). As an example, Craig & Greinke (1994, p. 117) developed historically-based accounting curriculum materials that enabled students to engage:

> *[i]n adversarial roleplay recreat[ing] a Wage Stabilization Board hearing in Washington, D.C. which, in 1952, led to President Truman's seizure of the American steel industry and ultimately to a constitutional crisis. The roleplay centered on the accounting issues debated by that Board in response to a highly provocative submission by W.A. Paton on behalf of the steel industry.*

This setting represented a liberalising of the curriculum by requiring students to understand the American economic and socio-political setting, 1945–1955, including knowledge of McCarthyism, the effects of American involvement in the Korean War, and the biographical profile and constitutional authority of President Truman.

We can obtain a better appreciation of the reasons for present-day corporate failures and the nature of regulatory responses from a study of prior corporate collapses. For example, students' understanding of the reasons for the Global Financial Crisis (GFC) of 2008–09 would be informed considerably by their reading, albeit (by necessity) briefly, of literature relating to the Great Depression of the 1930s and the South Sea Bubble of 1720. (See Adler, Chapter 23 – this volume.)

12.4.3 Emic

Peshkin uses the word 'emic', drawn from the anthropology literature, to refer to the perspective of those inside an organisation or other culture. He writes:

> *We display respect to . . . others by taking seriously what they say, what they think they are doing, what they make of things. In this way, we communicate that we have not come with preconceived notions of the type that preclude careful, serious listening. The much-discussed native's point of view*

. . . is a necessary part of every effective qualitative research endeavor. It is no substitute for the researcher's interpretation, but it is foundational for characterizing what the actors understand about what they have done and are doing and about the consequences of what is going on.

(2001, p. 244)

Peshkin contrasts an 'inside' or *emic* view with one from 'outside' the particular phenomenon being examined – the so-called *etic* view. An interesting accounting example of this 'inside versus outside' perspective appeared in the anthropology literature: an *emic* view was taken by Acheson (1972) an anthropologist, in studying how accounting systems affected business decisions in a Tarascan Indian village in Mexico. He concluded that the local, *emic* (or insider) view of profit, *ganancia*, is a truncated cash flow concept, and led local businesses to make decisions markedly inferior to what might have eventuated had they used outsider, or *etic*, accounting measures (e.g. those based on accrual accounting). Thus, to understand poor decision-making, Acheson assumed the *emic* perspective, from which the 'poor' decisions seemed quite reasonable.

Sensitivity to *emic* and *etic* perspectives has a variety of implications for liberalising accounting curricula. For example, in studying the classic *Birch Paper Company* case in management control, students who accept the rationality of only *etic*-type mathematical solutions would ignore the rich *emic* perspectives that raise awareness of Birch managers' life-world, their ego, their humanity, etc. It seems superficial to set this case without requiring students to examine the interior life world of a pivotal manager at Birch Paper, James Brunner (i.e. to adopt an *emic* perspective). What implications for management control and leadership reside in the language he has chosen, including the metaphors he has deployed? Is there room for fairness in the company's management control system? Brunner raises the idea of fairness in connection with overhead costs, but is there a more fundamental sense in which fairness is important in the sustainability of the company's management control system, even if the 'numbers' tend to ignore such considerations? There are numerous issues from an *emic* point of view (e.g. gender) that deserve airing in a discussion of this case.

Thus, the use of cases and role-plays (keeping in mind the strengths and weaknesses of an *emic* perspective) offers strong potential to frame accounting subject matter: that is, to ask students what they would do in the case situation and what values and strategic actions would influence them. Schön (1987, p. 324) sees effective use of cases as being: *'linked to disciplines like organizational theory, social psychology, psychology of motivation, or theories of internal and external market behavior'*, so that *'students gain a different way of looking at offerings of the discipline'*.

12.4.4 Positionality

The 'lens' of *positionality* extends the above *emic–etic* discussion to the particular individual human perspective. Peshkin describes this lens thus:

Each of these attributes [age, religion, profession, social class, and the like] is the basis for a position, a way of seeing and comprehending. Positionality as a source of lenses assumes that we are not unalterably fixed within these givens . . .

For example, what can we learn when our lens, our perceptual stance – of places, events, processes, actors, outcomes – is as a poor or rich student, a young or old teacher, a male or female administrator, a state legislator, parent, or housewife?. . . Do we feel that we have exhausted the promise of perception from within our own positionality and need a fresh perspective? Try on someone else's.

(2001, pp. 244–245)

The positionality lens is similar to the *emic* lens. However, it stresses the possibility of multiple (human) perspectives. Some such perspectives might not be apparent readily as an educator goes about the task of accounting curriculum design. Students asked to assume the role of a person in a case are likely to develop empathy and emotional resonance with that character, leading to better awareness of the integrative nature of the accounting and management phenomena involved.

Positionality can be assumed at a more fundamental and insightful level to help reveal the contestable nature of accounting concepts. Kelly (2003, p. 77) draws attention to the possibility of asking students to assume an alternative world in which:

> *employees and stockholders change places: where labour rights are primary and explicit, and where employees are spoken of as THE corporation, make up boards of directors, nominate new members on such boards and have a fiduciary responsibility to maximize.*

In a similar vein, accounting educators could design courses that were not corporate-centric, but 'society-centric or even nature-centric' so that they operate from post-conventional levels of moral reasoning that: '*allow them to view situations from a variety of perspectives that include all stakeholders and society as a whole*' (Waddock, 2005, p. 150).

12.4.5 Ideology

According to Peshkin, this '*lens*' has the following implications:

> *Incorporated in several contemporary schools of thought about the proper conduct of research are ideological stances that frame their advocate's perspectives on the foundational matters of what research ought to accomplish and what the researcher's role ought to be. Clearly, these advocates provide researchers with lenses for perception, leaving no doubt about their preferred foci of attention . . . The lenses of ideology are a powerful means of perception.*

> (2001, pp. 245–246)

One (contestable) view of ideology is that it is: '*[a] shared, relatively coherent interrelated set of emotionally charged beliefs, values, and norms that bind some people together and help them to make sense of their worlds*' (Weick, 1995, p. 113; but see Eagleton, 1991, for a more capacious view of the word).

Usually, the world of which accounting students are asked to make sense operates according to a guiding economic ideology of capitalism (itself a contested term). Accounting educators should encourage students to be sceptical and to not accept any ideology as a taken-for-granted truth. Liberalising the curriculum will help to resolve the common 'submission of students to prevailing ideology' and help them contest the established social order (Chabrak & Craig, 2013, p. 92; see also other papers in the thematic issue of the journal *Critical Perspectives on Accounting* of which this paper is the focus).

We need to be alert to the fact that the sense-making of the authors of any text is an ideological discourse. Understandings can be enhanced if students are asked to read closely and tease out the ideological character of a text. This is important because the ideology inherent in any text is something otherwise 'apt to be hidden from view' (Postman, 1993, p. 124). Accounting curricula can be improved by enabling students to discover what aspects of ideology underlie and/or are reinforced by various metaphors for accounting techniques, practices, and processes. For example, when students read about measures of fair value, they should be aware that the 'free market' is a metaphor masking an ideology (Carrier, 1997); and that the theory and practical processes of generating the numbers supporting fair value estimates are highly contestable. Even ostensibly non-ideological, apparently just mechanical aspects of accounting, such as the journal entry, are replete with ideology and metaphor (Aho, 1985).

We should acknowledge too that managers choose words to establish an ideological theme to assist them in exercising control over companies and individuals, and mediate relations with other key institutions, including government (Amernic & Craig, 2006). As such, the words of CEOs (and people generally) are an instrumental part of a complex communicative act possessing symbolic, emotional, cultural, and political overtones. In reading text to discover ideology, students could be encouraged to adopt an interrogatory approach: '*What are the assumptions in the text about what is natural, just and right?*' (Lye, 1997). This question is important because '*exactly the same piece of language may be ideological in one context and not in another*' (Eagleton, 1991, p. 9).

12.4.6 Themes

The lens of *themes*, though related to the lens of *patterns*, has important distinctive features. As Peshkin explains:

> [We can]. . . perceive [a] . . . setting through one or another theme and thereby expect to arrive at seeing more sharply . . . for example, binary themes, such as conflict and cooperation, order and confusion, success and failure, resistance and compliance, and the critical theorist's themes of race, class, gender, and ethnicity, all of which are in fact joined, making any separation a knowingly artificial and ad hoc move that we take to enhance perception. . .
>
> Thematic possibilities proliferate. Adaptation, transition, and change also come to mind. As do events. We can invent our own themes and seek events as themes . . . putting our imagination to the challenge of finding the most fruitful forms of perception.
>
> (2001, pp. 246–247)

Amernic and Robb (2003, p. 1) illustrate how the idea of '*[the] quality of earnings can serve as a productive framing device and a unifying theme in curriculum design*' especially in *Intermediate Financial Accounting* courses. They chose quality of earnings as a theme because of the role which they allege this theme plays in shaping accounting standard setting (ibid., p. 13). They emphasise how the '*quality of earnings*' theme leads them to develop in students the ideas that accounting is '*a social system and process [with] links to finance . . . [and with] potential strategic and political roles*' (ibid., p. 2); and that it is '*a variegated information system and language*' (ibid., p. 5).

More broadly, the theme of 'power' may be employed in accounting curriculum materials for management control. For example, Heffernan (2012) contends that a plausible explanation for global energy company BP's repeated safety culture crises – resulting in tragedies such as the *Deepwater Horizon* disaster in the Gulf of Mexico – was the pervasiveness of '*the hierarchical power structure within BP*' (ibid., p. 5), by which the CEO '*sat atop a structure where he had vast powers of reward and no appetite or process for debate*' (ibid., p. 5).

Thus, the theme of power – examined deeply within an organisation's management control system – may have potential for educational understanding of (at least some) corporate crises. These crises can be seen as being less likely to be due to personal ethical lapses than to management control systems (MCS) structure and culture being socially-constructed inaptly on the basis of a theme of power. Many other themes may be deployed in all areas of accounting curriculum design.

12.4.7 Metaphor

The literature on *metaphor* is extremely broad, rich, controversial in places, and multidisciplinary. Amernic (2013) gives a brief overview of the use of metaphor in accounting communication, including comments on accounting education. Peshkin's description of the importance of metaphor as a lens is as follows:

> For Lakoff and Johnson (1980) . . . it is imperative to search out metaphors to use because, as they affirm, 'if we are right in suggesting that our conceptual system is largely metaphorical, then the way we think, what we experience, and what we do every day is very much a matter of metaphor' (p. 3). Their book Metaphors We Live By is a primer for grasping this perspective. The first example they present— 'argument is war'— illustrates their point:
>
> > It is important to see that we don't just talk about arguments in terms of war. We can actually win or lose arguments. We see the person we are arguing with as an opponent. We attack his positions and defend our own. We gain and lose ground. We plan and use strategies (p. 4)
> > . . .
>
> . . . metaphors point our attention somewhere and thereby enable our perception . . . metaphor is a way of seeing that which other lenses direct us to.
>
> (2001, p. 247)

There is a close reinforcing relationship between the *emic* and *positionality* angles of vision and the pervasiveness of metaphor as worldview-making (Underhill, 2011; Nünning *et al.*, 2009). Indeed, we should acknowledge that a master metaphor plausibly describes accounting: ACCOUNTING IS AN INSTRUMENT (Amernic & Craig, 2009).

Referring specifically to education, Postman (1996, p. 174) describes a metaphor as 'an organ of perception'. A serviceable understanding of metaphor in designing accounting curricula would benefit accounting educators and their students. Amernic (2013) briefly refers to the importance of metaphor in aspects of accounting education. Ivie (1996, p. 59) writes that: '*Metaphor offers us a reflective tool which can be used to analyze basic assumptions . . . selectively evaluating metaphors [habitually] is an important step in developing a reflective mind.*'

Ivie's view is consistent with Waddock's (2005) call for university accounting graduates to be '*reflective practitioners*'; and with Postman's (1996, p. 174) emphasis on the practical curriculum design importance of metaphor: '*a student cannot understand what a subject is about without some understanding of the metaphors that are its foundation.*'

There are many fronts along which metaphor is important in the design of accounting curricula. Gregory (1987) and Postman (1996) urge educators to examine critically those metaphors which they implicitly accept (see also Craig & Amernic, 2002; Amernic & Craig, 2004). Curriculum materials ranging from the standards published by the Financial Accounting Standards Board (FASB) and the International Accounting Standards Board (IASB) comment letters on proposed new accounting standards, and almost all accounting learning teaching/materials (from highly-directed so-called technical problems to the most convoluted and extensive case) resonate unavoidably with subtle, and at times not-so-subtle, metaphors. Their use is astonishingly wide, from the simple to more complex root metaphors, to some that create so-called text-worlds (Werth, 1994).

12.4.8 Irony

In his oft-cited reference work, Lanham (1991, p. 189) defines *irony* as '*implying a meaning opposite to the literal meaning*'. Peshkin elaborates further on the utility of *irony* as a perceptual lens:

> '*Irony is a metaphor of opposites*' writes [sociologist] *Brown (1989) and by seeing something from the 'viewpoint of its antithesis . . . we become more aware of what that thing is*' (p. 172). Sociologists point to irony in the work of Merton (1957) who drew . . . attention to unintended consequences . . . and of Vidich and Bensman (1958) who saw in the small town they studied the contradictions between prevailing beliefs and the realities of mass society . . . What seems to be uniformly accepted is that irony is an enabling perspective for enhancing perception, of making it more acute, of noting what could otherwise pass by unnoticed . . . to appreciate complexity is to come naturally to irony.
>
> (2001, pp. 248–249)

This angle of vision enables us to enhance the perception and understanding of accounting phenomena by drawing attention to the irony inherent in paradoxes, incongruities, and contradictions. Yuthas & Tinker (1994, p. 295), for example, point to the irony of '*Academe's heavy commitment to empirical enquiry [yet] its inability to prove or (refute) anything significant with empirical evidence.*' They draw attention to the effect of such irony on forming conclusions: '*about the efficacy of activity-based costing [and] total quality management*' (ibid., p. 295).

Irony seems particularly well-suited to studying the roles and performance of public company auditors, especially if there is '*[a] legitimacy paradox surrounding the financial audit function*' (Guénin-Paracini & Gendron, 2010, p. 152). The paradox is that, despite '*a continuous flow of audit failure episodes the auditing profession keeps on being seen as technically fit and morally legitimate*' (ibid., p. 134).

Adoption of irony as an angle of vision seems likely to motivate students to explore questions of morality and legitimacy. But, additionally, exploring irony would involve students in understanding two notions that '*are assumed to play a key role in the creation and maintenance of legitimacy paradoxes*' (ibid., p. 153): *mimesis* (from philosophy) and *mythification* (from classics).

Lee, Clarke, & Dean (2008, p. 677) also emphasise the paradox '*of a corporate auditor denying or limiting responsibility to detect material accounting misstatement facilitated by dominant senior managers, while relying on the honesty of [representations made to auditors by] senior managers*'. Framing the matter as a paradox provides a good opportunity to explore with students matters of credibility, ethicality, morality, and theories of dominance and [mis]representation.

12.4.9 Silence

In many instances, omission is as potent as commission. The ninth and final of Peshkin's 'lenses', the lens of *silence*, focusses on the potential salience of such omission. Peshkin's description is as follows:

> *Having addressed above a variety of means to perceive what is there before us, it seems appropriate to conclude with what conversely is not. . . The lens of silence requires an uncommonly imagining eye and ear directed to what is not occurring within our . . . setting that, we conclude, could or should occur there. Its application requires stepping back from the concreteness of what is there before us and drawing on a sense of things that we may acquire from earlier data collection. We use this lens to visualize what, for example, students are not hearing [or reading].*
>
> (2001, pp. 249–250)

We tend to over-expose our students to disclosure studies which report, often in excruciating detail, what IS disclosed in annual financial reports. All too rarely does such analysis extend to exploring what IS NOT disclosed: that is, to explore the disclosure 'silences'. Chwastiak and Young (2003, p. 533) illustrate how annual reports are silent about injustices in order '*to make profit appear to be an unproblematic measure of success*'.

They argue that:

> *the earth's role in sustaining life, our kinship with animals, the horrors of war and starving children, the emptiness of consumption, the drudgery of work, all must be silenced in order for annual reports to read as success stories.*

(ibid., p. 549)

They emphasise the need to break the silence and to pose counter-narratives that promote a better world. By invoking such a frame, students can be led through readings on capitalism and alternative modes of economic organisation, equity, injustice, and social domination, and we can, thereby, develop a more compassionate and egalitarian society.

There was an important silence, for example, in Microsoft's webpage disclosures of financial and related information in respect to the implications of a major anti-trust case for future revenue, income, and viability of Microsoft as a going concern, '*[the] omission [being] clearly inappropriate considering the profound impact that [any] ruling to "break up" Microsoft would have on shareholders' wealth*' (Amernic & Craig, 2006, p. 50).

The *silence* angle of vision is amenable also to the study of contemporary auditing practices. Sikka (2009), for example, draws attention to the silence of auditors in the prelude to financial crises such as the GFC of 2008–09. He alleges that '*fee dependency impairs claims of [auditor] independence and has the capacity to silence auditors*' (ibid., p. 872).

The idea of 'silence' thereby provides a good lens through which to assess '*the value of company audits, auditor independence and quality of audit work, economic incentives for good audits and the knowledge base of auditors*' (ibid., p. 868). For instance, are there contextual features of specific audit arrangements between an external auditor and the 'client', such as personal and/or monetary influences, that subvert the auditor's role as being truly independent?

Having reviewed Peshkin's nine 'angles of vision', and illustrated their applicability in the context of the accounting curriculum, we now propose to add two more possibilities: *framing* and *culture*.

12.4.10 Framing

Entman (1993, p. 52, emphasis in original) describes framing through the following comments:

> *Framing essentially involves* selection *and salience. To frame is to* select some aspects of a perceived reality and make them more salient in a communicating text, in such a way as to promote a particular problem definition, causal interpretation, moral evaluation, and/or treatment recommendation *for the item described . . . Frames, then,* define problems *– determine what a causal agent is doing with what costs and benefits, usually measured in terms of common cultural values;* diagnose causes *– identify the forces creating the problem;* make moral judgments *– evaluate causal agents and their effects; and* suggest remedies *– offer and justify treatments for the problems and predict their likely effects. A single sentence may perform more than one of these four framing functions, although many sentences in a text may perform none of them. And a frame in any particular text may not necessarily include all four functions.*

Not only can words and text serve as frames, but other means of communication, such as photographs, can do so too.

In accounting education, *framing* can be intentional or unintentional, and can either facilitate or hamper efforts to liberalise the curriculum. For example, if a compulsory *Introductory Financial Accounting* course commences by focussing almost exclusively on double-entry bookkeeping, with an emphasis on 'correct' and 'incorrect' answers, then this curriculum introduction will tend to frame neophyte students' perception of accounting as being a rigid and mechanistic discipline. The result may be that potentially good, creative, students are 'turned off' and do not pursue accounting courses beyond those that are compulsory for them. (For more on this theme, see Laswad & Tan, Chapter 9, and Wygal, Chapter 11 – both in this volume.) As an aside, this example is not intended to disparage the importance of double-entry bookkeeping in the accounting curriculum, but rather its potential for inapt framing effects if presented inappropriately in the curriculum.

12.4.11 Culture

Cultural anthropologists Pant and Alberti (1997, p. 4, emphasis in original) write about culture and organisations as follows:

> Behaviour and organizations are shaped by the interplay of interpersonal interactions, biophysical endowments, material situation, social factors and interior dynamism such as values and conscience. All that is **culture**. Culture is not a product but an ongoing, open-ended process. It is not just one more variable among many others. It is all-pervading, invisible and influential. It is the totality of external and internal impulses arranged as a huge blueprint for the individual and collective behavior.

There are many views of *culture*. Pant and Alberti's view is not universal, but it is serviceable for our purposes. In the management control literature, Malmi and Brown (2008, pp. 288–295) elaborate five types of controls that '*conceptually constitute an MCS [management control system] package*'. These are:

- planning (or *ex ante*) controls;
- cybernetic controls (including budgets and the Balanced Scorecard);
- reward and compensation controls;
- administrative controls (including organisational design and structure, company governance structures, and procedures and policies); and
- cultural controls ('culture is . . . a control system when it is used to regulate behavior' (ibid., p. 294)).

Thus, culture is an important, crucial, and pervasive lens through which to view an organisation, both inside and outside. For the accounting education curriculum in management control, for example, we might encourage students to consider culture both within and without the organisation. This can help students to understand failures in MCS, such as the Tokyo Electric Power Company's Fukushima nuclear tragedy of 2011, in respect of which the chairman of the Fukushima Nuclear Accident Independent Investigation Commission concluded:

> What must be admitted – very painfully – is that this was a disaster 'Made in Japan.' Its fundamental causes are to be found in the ingrained conventions of Japanese culture: our reflexive obedience; our

reluctance to question authority; our devotion to 'sticking with the program'; our groupism; and our insularity.

(National Diet of Japan, The Fukushima Nuclear Accident Independent Investigation Commission, 2012, p. 9)

From a curriculum perspective, the important learning issue is how to design and implement structures and processes of management control to counteract dysfunctional social and organisational culture – and how to do this while still being respectful of attributes such as 'face-saving' in many Eastern cultures. Indeed, safety and such cultural traits may conflict inherently. Here is where inside versus outside, *emic* versus *etic*, perspectives might be useful.

The *culture* lens seems likely to be beneficial in all areas of accounting education. For example, in financial accounting, Amernic, Craig, & Tourish (2012) argue that BP's apparently inapt safety culture *before* the 20 April 2010 explosion of the *Deepwater Horizon* in the Gulf of Mexico could have justified accruing a provision for disaster in prior years.

12.5 Discussion

Peshkin's nine angles of vision, as well as the two additional ones – *framing* and *culture* – which we propose, can possibly assist in 'liberating or freeing the mind to its fullest potential' (see Note 1). The scope and diversity of directions which these angles offer, and their inter-connectedness, have the effect of liberating otherwise narrower perspectives. Thus, accounting educators who adopt the various angles of vision are enabled to contemplate a more diverse, sensitive, and ethical accounting pedagogy. Such an outcome is consistent with recent conclusions of Colby *et al.* (2011a, 2011b) the enduring perspective of Alfred North Whitehead ([1929] 1957) and the views of Craig & Amernic (2002).

We should not overlook the reinforcing and integrative complementarity of the individual angles of vision that Peshkin recommends. Each angle of vision has strong potential to strengthen, complement, and extend one or more other angles of vision. (e.g. *ideology* and *metaphor; positionality* and *emic; time* and *patterns*). The *patterns* angle of vision, for example, might be used to show how financial accounting reports of another era can be viewed through the *time* lens to enable students in a *Financial Accounting* course to understand how accounting has changed over the years, and to identify possible causes of change, such as apparent management self-interest (Amernic & Elitzur, 1992).

A pedagogic approach to liberalise accounting curricula, involving application of the 11 angles of vision, has strong potential to help achieve the essential learning outcomes specified in the LEAP report. For example, by adopting an *emic* or *positionality* lens, we can improve knowledge of human cultures and the physical and natural world, and our civic knowledge; and by using *irony, metaphors,* and *themes,* our intellectual and practical skills in inquiry and analysis, and in written communication, can be enhanced.

We need to design curricula that will tolerate scepticism, offer critique of the existing social order and accounting landscape, and re-connect accounting to the ambient social world. We can do so through encouraging the use of 'linguistic means, imaginings and literary devices' (Chabrak & Craig, 2013). For example, we can liberalise how we set assessment tasks, as illustrated vividly by Chabrak & Craig (2013). They describe an assessment task that required students to assess the collapse of Enron in 2001. The students self-select literary and artistic devices (e.g. irony, parody, caricature, and photography) and various historical incidents (e.g. collapse of Enron, death of Robert Maxwell, Panama Canal crisis of the 1880s, and the grounding of the *Erika* in the Bay of Biscay in 1999) to illustrate their answers.

The route to liberalised undergraduate accounting curricula should strongly emphasise the incorporation of written exposition and critical analysis of writing. This seems sensible if we are to make full use of angles of vision involving *patterns, ideology, themes*, and *metaphor*. If writing is akin to thinking (Oatley & Djikic, 2008), then enabling accounting students to benefit from liberalised curricula will work much better if writing is embedded in a substantive way.

Like all human beings, accounting educators have limited cognitive capacity and limited energy; and they are also subject at times to perverse university-administered performance measurement systems (Burrows, 2012; Craig *et al.*, 2014). Accordingly, accounting educators require some means of enabling normative curricula designs. It is far too easy to just 'teach the textbook' and/or the curriculum mandated by various professional accounting accreditation bodies. (See Apostolou & Gammie, Chapter 29 – this volume.)

If our contention regarding the broad aim of a university (see earlier) seems sensible, then scripts such as Peshkin's nine lenses may help us overcome, at least to some extent, barriers to liberalising accounting curricula. Furthermore, since it falls largely on doctorally-qualified accounting educators to conceive, design, and implement the undergraduate accounting curriculum, an important issue regarding liberalising the (undergraduate) accounting curriculum is to explore the implications for the design of accounting PhD programmes: that is, to explore how accounting educators should be educated – and to liberalise that curriculum too.

Note

1 Indeed, the idea of 'liberating' as a curriculum goal is well expressed on Yale University's website, thus:

> Yale is committed to the idea of a liberal arts education through which students think and learn across disciplines, *literally liberating or freeing the mind to its fullest potential*. The essence of such an education is not what you study but the result – gaining the ability to think critically and independently and to write, reason, and communicate clearly – the foundation for all professions.
>
> (http://admissions.yale.edu/liberal-arts-education;
> last visited 11 April 2013; emphasis added)

References

Accounting Education Change Commission (1990) *Position Statement Number One: Objectives of Education for Accountants*, Sarasota, FL: American Accounting Association.

Acheson, J.M. (1972) Accounting concepts and economic opportunities in a Tarascan village: emic and etic views, *Human Organization*, 31(1), 83–91.

Aho, J. (1985) Rhetoric and the invention of double entry bookkeeping, *Rhetorica*, 3(1), 21–43.

Albrecht, S. & Sack, R. (2000) *Accounting Education: Charting the Course through a Perilous Future* (Accounting Education Series, Vol. 16), Sarasota, FL: American Accounting Association.

American Accounting Association (AAA) (1986) *Committee on the Future Structure, Content, and Scope of Accounting Education* (The Bedford Committee), Future accounting education: preparing for the expanding profession, *Issues in Accounting Education*, (Spring), 168–195.

Amernic, J. (1992) A case study in corporate financial reporting: Massey-Ferguson's visible accounting decisions 1970–1987, *Critical Perspectives on Accounting*, 3(1), 1–43.

Amernic, J. (1998) 'Close readings' of internet corporate financial reporting: towards a more critical pedagogy on the information highway, *The Internet and Higher Education*, 1(2), 87–112.

Amernic, J. (2013) Perspectives on the role of metaphor, in Jack, L., Davison, J., & Craig, R. (eds) *The Routledge Companion to Accounting Communication*, London: Routledge, pp. 76–93.

Amernic, J. & Craig, R. (1999) The internet in undergraduate management education: a concern for neophytes among metaphors, *Prometheus*, 17(4), 437–450.

Amernic, J. & Craig, R. (2004) Reform of accounting education in the post-Enron era: moving accounting 'out of the shadows', *Abacus*, 40(3), 342–378.

Amernic, J. & Craig, R. (2006) *CEO-Speak: The Language of Corporate Leadership*, Montreal: McGill-Queen's University Press.

Amernic, J. & Craig, R. (2009) Understanding accounting through conceptual metaphor: ACCOUNTING IS AN INSTRUMENT? *Critical Perspectives on Accounting*, 20, 875–883.

Amernic, J., Craig, R., & Tourish, D. (2012) Reflecting a company's safety culture in 'fairly presented' financial statements: the case of BP, *CPA Journal*, April, 6, 8–10.

Amernic, J. & Elitzur, R. (1992) Using historical annual reports in teaching: letting the past benefit the present, *The Accounting Historians Journal*, 19(1), 29–50.

Amernic, J. & Enns, R. (1979) Levels of cognitive complexity and the design of accounting curriculum, *The Accounting Review*, 54(1), 133–146.

Amernic, J, & Robb, S. (2003) 'Quality of earnings' as a framing device and unifying theme in intermediate financial accounting, *Issues in Accounting Education*, 18(1), 1–20.

Bloom, R., & Webinger, M. (2011) Contextualising the intermediate financial accounting courses in the global financial crisis, *Accounting Education: an international journal*, 20(5), 469–494.

Buckless, F., Krawczyk, K., & Showalter, S. (2012) Accounting education in the Second Life world, *The CPA Journal*, March, 65–71.

Burrows, R. (2012) Living with the H-index? Metric assemblages in the contemporary academy, *The Sociological Review*, 60(2), 355–372.

Carrier, J.G. (1997) *Meanings of the Market: The Free Market in Western Culture*, New York: Berg.

Cappelletto, G. (2010) *Challenges Facing Accounting Education in Australia*, Melbourne: AFAANZ. Available at http://twentytwentyone.com.au/afaanz2/images/stories/pdfs/general_pdf/challeges%20facing%20accounting%20education%20report%20-%202010.pdf (accessed 25 April 2013).

Chabrak, N. & Craig, R. (2013) Student imaginings, cognitive dissonance and critical thinking, *Critical Perspectives on Accounting*, 24, 91–104.

Chwastiak, M. & Young, J.J. (2003) Silences in annual reports, *Critical Perspectives on Accounting*, 14, 533–552.

Colby, A., Ehrlich, T., Sullivan, W.M., & Dolle, J.R. (2011a) Blueprint for a better business curriculum, *The Chronicle of Higher Education*, June 5. Available at: http://chronicle.com/article/Blueprint-for-a-Better/127764/ (accessed March 25 2012).

Colby, A., Ehrlich, T., Sullivan, W.M., & Dolle, J.R. (2011b) *Rethinking Undergraduate Business Education: Liberal Learning for the Profession*, San Francisco: Carnegie/Jossey-Bass.

Craig, R. (2010) Will compelled study of literary classics engender enrichment, creativity, curiosity and romance in accounting students? *Accounting Education: an international journal*, 19(4), 347–350.

Craig, R. & Amernic, J. (2002) Accountability of accounting educators and the rhythm of the university: resistance strategies for postmodern blues, *Accounting Education: an international journal*, 11(2), 121–171.

Craig R., Amernic, J., & Tourish, D. (2014) Perverse audit culture and accountability of the modern public university, *Financial Accountability and Management*, 30(1), 1–24.

Craig, R.J. & Greinke, A.J. (1994) Accounting history and governmental inquiries: an experiment in adversarial roleplay, *The Accounting Historians Journal*, 21(2), 117–134.

Dugan, M.T., Gup, B.E., & Samson, W.D. (1991) Teaching the statement of cash flows, *Journal of Accounting Education*, 9, 33–52.

Eagleton, T. (1991) *Ideology: An Introduction*, London: Verso.

Entman, R. (1993) Framing: towards clarification of a fractured paradigm, *Journal of Communication*, 43(4), 51–58.

Gregory, M. (1987) If education is a feast, why do we restrict the menu? A critique of pedagogical metaphors, *College Teaching*, 35(3), 101–106.

Guénin-Paracini, H. & Gendron, Y. (2010) Auditors as modern pharmakoi: legitimacy and the production of economic order, *Critical Perspectives on Accounting*, 21, 134–158.

Heffernan, M. (2012) Opening talk by Margaret Heffernan, Trust and Integrity in the Global Economy, Tuesday, 17 July 2012, International CAUX Conferences 2012. Available at: www.caux.iofc.org/sites/all/files/Margaret Heffernan.pdf (accessed September 23, 2012).

Ivie, S.D. (1996) Metaphors: tools for critical thinking, *McGill Journal of Education*, 31(1), 57–68.

Kelly, M. (2003) *The Divine Right of Capital*, New York: Berrett Koehler Press.

Lanham, R.A. (1991) *A Handlist of Rhetorical Terms*, Berkeley, CA: University of California Press.

Lee, T.A., Clarke, F., & Dean, G. (2008) The dominant senior manager and the reasonably careful, skilful, and cautious auditor, *Critical Perspectives on Accounting*, 19, 677–711.

Lister, R.J. (2010) A role for the compulsory study of literature in accounting education, *Accounting Education: an international journal*, 19(4), 329–344.

Lye, J. (1997) Ideology: a brief guide. Available at: http://www.brocku.ca/ english/jlye/ideology.html.

Malmi, T. & Brown, D. (2008) Management control systems as a package: opportunities, challenges and research directions, *Management Accounting Research*, 19, 287–300.

Martin, R.L. (2007) *The Opposable Mind: How Successful Leaders Win Through Integrative Thinking*, Boston: Harvard Business School Press.

Mathews, R., Jackson, M., & Brown, P. (1990) *Accounting in Higher Education: Report of the Review of the Accounting Discipline in Higher Education*, Vol. 1, Canberra, ACT: Australian Government.

National Diet of Japan (2012) *The Fukushima Nuclear Accident Independent Investigation Commission, Executive Summary*, Tokyo.

National Leadership Council for Liberal Education and America's Promise (2007) *College Learning for the New Global Century*, Washington, DC: Association of American Colleges and Universities.

Nünning, A., Grabes, H., & Baumbach, S. (2009) Metaphor as a way of worldmaking, or where metaphors and culture meet, in Grabes, H., Nünning, A., & Baumbach, S. (eds) *Yearbook of Research in English and American Literature 25: Metaphors Shaping Culture and Theory*, Tübingen: Gunter Narr Verlag, pp. xi–xxviii.

Oatley, K. & Djikic, M. (2008) Writing as thinking, *Review of General Psychology*, 12(1), 9–27.

Pant, D.R., & Alberti, F. (1997) Anthropology and business: reflections on the business applications of cultural anthropology, Liu Papers no. 42, *Serie Economia e Impressa*, 11, 1–25.

Pathways Commission (2012) *Charting a National Strategy for the Next Generation of Accountants*, Sarasota, FL: AAA, and New York: AICPA. Available at: www.pathwayscommission.org.

Peshkin, A. (2001) Angles of vision: enhancing perception in qualitative research, *Qualitative Inquiry*, 7, 238–253.

Postman, N. (1993) *Technopoly*, New York: Basic Books.

Postman, N. (1996) *The End of Education*, New York: Vintage Books.

Sangster, A. & Wilson, R.M.S. (eds) (2013) *Liberalising the Accounting Curriculum in University Education*, London: Routledge.

Schön, D.A. (1987) *Educating the Reflective Practitioner*, San Francisco: Jossey-Bass.

Sikka, P. (2009) Financial crisis and the silence of the auditors, *Accounting, Organizations and Society*, 34, 868–873.

Solomons, D., with Berridge, T.M. (1974) *Prospectus for a Profession: The Report of the Long Range Enquiry into Education and Training for the Accountancy Profession*, Advisory Board of Accountancy Education: Distributed by Gee and Co.: London.

Underhill, J.W. (2011) *Creating Worldviews: Metaphor, Ideology and Language*, Edinburgh: Edinburgh University Press.

Waddock, S. (2005) Hollow men and women at the helm . . . hollow accounting ethics? *Issues in Accounting Education*, 20(2), 145–150.

Weick, K.E. (1995) *Sensemaking in Organizations*. Thousand Oaks, CA: Sage.

Werth, P. (1994) Extended metaphor: a text world account, *Language and Literature*, 3(2), 79–103.

Whitehead, A.N. ([1929] 1957) *The Aims of Education and Other Essays*, New York: The Free Press.

Willits, S.D. (2010) Will more liberal arts courses fix the accounting curriculum? *Journal of Accounting Education*, 28, 13–25.

Young, J.J. & Annisette, M. (2009) Cultivating imagination: ethics, education and literature, *Critical Perspectives on Accounting*, 20(1), 93–109.

Yuthas, K. & Tinker, T. (1994) Paradise regained? Myth, Milton and management accounting, *Critical Perspectives on Accounting*, 5, 295–310.

Zeff, S.A. (1989) Does accounting belong in the university curriculum? *Issues in Accounting Education*, 4(1), 203–209.

About the authors

Joel Amernic is Professor of Accounting at the Joseph L. Rotman School of Management, University of Toronto, Canada (amernic@rotman.utoronto.ca). He has served as editor of the Education Department of *CA Magazine*, made a number of contributions to the literature, and is the recipient of several teaching and 'best paper' awards.

Russell Craig is Professor of Accounting at Victoria University, Melbourne, Australia (Russell.Craig@vu.edu.au). His main research interests include financial reporting, international accounting, management education, and the accountability discourse of executives. He is the author of over 150 research papers, research monographs, and book chapters on a wide variety of topics in accounting and cognate fields, many of which have won awards.

13

Generic skills within the accounting curriculum

Kim Watty

DEAKIN UNIVERSITY, AUSTRALIA

CONTENTS

Abstract

There has been no shortage of published papers in higher education generally, and accounting education specifically, related to the development and assessment of generic skills in the curriculum. Every stakeholder it appears has a view to share, including graduate employers, academic staff, graduates, students, and governments. This chapter's focus on generic skills is discussed, along with the changes that have occurred in accounting curricula across the globe. Further, readers will find useful resources as Appendices to the chapter that are designed to assist with the development and assessment of generic skills in accounting education.

Finally, fresh approaches that utilise digital technologies and which recognise the prior learning of students are presented as potential 'game changers' in this discussion.

Keywords

generic skills, stakeholders' perceptions, technology

13.1 Introduction

The main aims of this chapter are:

- to review calls for the development of generic skills in accounting education globally, and how the discipline is responding;
- to provide a practical resource for readers who are interested in designing assessment strategies which address generic skills in accounting; and
- to consider alternatives to current course designs which adopt a more constructivist approach to students' learning and which involve greater consideration of the use of appropriate technologies to develop personalised pathways to learning.

The generic skills discourse in accounting education is not dissimilar to that in other areas of higher education. Numerous reports in the arts, sciences, and humanities have called for academics to provide opportunities for the development of personal transferable skills (PTS) designed to enhance graduates' employability and capacity for lifelong learning. These reports, and subsequent responses from the academic community, have been explicit in two areas:

- linking higher education to employment; and
- linking the development of skills, other than those defined as technical, to employability.

Despite these reports, and an increasing volume of literature in the area, accounting education continues to be primarily content-driven.

The integration of generic skill development into unit/subject design continues to be the focus of those who champion the cause of developing generic skills in accounting education. While the literature calls for a holistic approach to the integration of generic skills, the existing evidence points to changes on a unit/subject basis, rather than across a whole programme. In addition, the current focus has a one-size-fits-all approach to generic skills development, thus ignoring the underlying principles of a constructivist approach to teaching and learning in higher education. Perhaps now the time is right for a reconsideration of this focus on embedding the development of generic skills in subject content. Is there another way?

In this chapter we will discuss various approaches to the identification and development of generic skills in accounting curricula from across the globe, and a different way of considering and conceptualising the development of generic skills in accounting education – with a nod to the past, acknowledgement of the present, and an eye on the future. In addition, this chapter includes an Appendix that may be used by readers as a resource to assist with the assessment of generic skills in an accounting curriculum. The chapter concludes with some thoughts about how we might reconceptualise the development of generic skills in an accounting curriculum, moving away from the current focus on a fully-embedded approach, to one which recognises the skills and expertise required of academics to develop any suite of generic skills for graduates.

13.2 Literature overview

This review begins with an overview of the calls for a stronger focus on generic skills generally, and then the calls for the focus in accounting education specifically. However, first there is a need to acknowledge the various meanings attached to the term *generic skills* which may also be used as a synonym for, *inter alia*, graduate attributes, personal transferable skills, employability skills, competencies, and soft skills (Clanchy & Ballard, 1995; Hardern, 1995; De La Harpe *et al.*, 2000).

Calls for a stronger focus on the development of generic skills for graduates have occurred at multiple levels, and over several decades. For example, at the global level, see:

- UNESCO's World Declaration on Higher Education for the Twenty-first Century (1998); and
- the European Higher Education Area: the official Bologna Website 2010–2012 (EHEA) (www.ehea.info).

At the national level, see, for example:

- in the U.K., the Dearing Commission for the National Committee of Inquiry in Higher Education (Dearing Commission, 1997);
- in the U.S.A., The Secretary's Commission on Achieving Necessary Skills (2000); and
- in Australia, *Our Universities: Backing Australia's Future, Assuring Quality* (Commonwealth of Australia, 2003).

As these calls intensified over the decades, calls for change cascaded down to discipline level. In the accounting discipline, many readers will be aware of the work in this area presented by the Bedford Committee (AAA, 1986); Albrecht & Sack (2000); Arthur Andersen *et al.* (1989); the International Accounting Education Standards Board's (IAESB), International Education Standard (IES) 4, *Professional Values, Ethics and Attitudes*; and Birkett (1993). These references are not exhaustive and are provided as evidence of the calls for improved generic skill development at the global, national, and accounting-specific level.

As with many key definitions in higher education (HE), for example, 'quality', 'standards', and 'benchmarks', tensions exist over the accepted definition of generic skills and graduate attributes. The latter is the umbrella term often used at university level, in mission or vision statements:

> *Broadly speaking, in Australia 'generic graduate attributes' have come to be accepted as being the skills, knowledge and abilities of university graduates, beyond disciplinary content knowledge, which are applicable to the range of contexts.*

(Barrie, 2006, p. 217)

Within a Faculty (i.e. a group of related departments – such as is found in a Business School), where disciplines operate at a programme level, graduate attributes have been deconstructed into discipline-specific, technical skills and knowledge, plus generic skills, deemed as being necessary for the application of technical skills and knowledge in the workplace. In this chapter, *generic skills* is the chosen label for this skills set. In accounting, these skills include judgement, critical thinking, problem-solving, and communications. This listing is indicative and the specific generic skills in accounting education are presented later in this chapter. However, before turning our attention to generic skills in the accounting curriculum, it is worth noting the debate in the literature around whether these skills are discipline-specific or general. Davies (2011) refers to this debate as being between *generalists* and *specifists*.

Broadly speaking, *generalists* consider the development of certain generic skills, critical thinking for example (see Cunningham, Chapter 18 – this volume), as being general to all discipline areas, and the development of the skills as not necessarily discipline-specific. Not surprisingly, *specifists* see certain generic skills as being discipline-specific and, in so doing, believe that in the development of the skill, the language and culture of the discipline is relevant (Jones, 2010). Davies (2011) provides an insightful and comprehensive analysis of this debate in his introductory discussion of critical thinking in *Higher Education Research and Development*, published in a themed issue devoted to this complex issue in 2011.

In a qualitative study using in-depth interviews across two Australian universities, Jones (2010) investigated the relationship between disciplinary culture and generic attributes. The three generic skills included were:

- critical thinking;
- communication; and
- problem-solving.

These were chosen because they are considered important in HE as well as by employer groups. Her findings revealed that the way in which academics conceptualise these three generic skills is influenced by the culture of the discipline in which they are taught. Jones (2010) contends that, while the skills may be generalised, they must be conceptualised in their specific social and cultural context.

In the preceding literature there has been scant acknowledgement of how constructive learning potentially impacts on the effectiveness of one-size-fits-all approaches to developing generic skills (be they framed around a *generalist* or a *specifist* perspective). While there are a multitude of views (see Honebein *et al.*, 1993; Simons, 1993; Duffy & Cunningham 1996) as to what constructivism in the learning environment encapsulates, underpinning these views is a shared emphasis on: '*the role of the teacher, the student, and the cultural embeddedness of learning*' (Nanjappa & Grant, 2003, p. 40).

Constructivism potentially addresses the all-important twin pedagogical goals of learning effectiveness and motivation (Mott *et al.*, 1999). Mott *et al.* explain that constructivism is seen as being beneficial to learning effectiveness because it emphasises knowledge construction as opposed to mere rote learning. As Piaget (1954) explains, constructivism promotes active learning and results in a learner playing an active role in his/her own learning. In relation to accounting curricula, Yonghai & Guoying (2010) suggest that students are able to construct their own knowledge and learning by cooperative learning and independent study. The role of the educator then becomes one of facilitator, coordinator, and mediator of a more personalised learning experience for the student. In a paper that is focussed on accounting education, Lucas (2008, p. 389) suggests that: '*Validating students as knowers, in part, requires that educators become aware of the ways in which students experience the world.*'

Given the nature of generic skills (that is, many are skills that most students will have observed, experienced, or been exposed to in some form prior to entering university), constructive learning is of relevance as we consider how we might design courses that recognise the 'prior knowing' of our students. This aspect is taken up later in this chapter.

In the accounting literature, there has been general agreement that the generic skills necessary for the employability of accounting graduates are specific to the profession. This is evidenced by published papers in accounting education that are based on a skill set determined by employers of accounting graduates, including national and international business organisations, and professional accounting bodies (PABs). This reflects the strong vocational nature of the accounting discipline, where employers and PABs are key stakeholders in the design of accounting programmes (Watty *et al.*, 2012a. See also Sundem, Chapter 27 – this volume, and

Apostolou & Gammie, Chapter 29 – this volume). However, there is also some concern that employers and/or PABs have captured the generic skills agenda. Some authors question the development of accounting curricula that reflect a strong reliance on the views of these two stakeholder groups, often at the exclusion of the views of academics who hold a different view (Sin & Reid, 2005). Further, some suggest that generic skills are best developed and applied in the workforce (Purcell, 2001); and not developed and assessed by teachers in a university environment (Brown & McCartney, 1995). Simply put, employers have expectations that graduates will be work-ready, while many academics have a stronger focus on the development of intellectual capability and ability (Bui & Porter, 2012).

Where PABs identify specific generic skills for development (for example, in Australia, the PABs detail generic skills that include communication, teamwork, and judgement), the skills identified are those best suited to the unique business environment in which professional accountants operate.

There is recognition that each skill, or grouping of skills, has a multi-layered complexity, thus reference to the discipline is important. For example, *written communication skills* require understanding by both those demonstrating the skill and the audience receiving the information. Demonstrating written communication skills may involve arguing, interpreting, challenging, and contrasting, all of which are valued by the accounting profession, and are expected to be developed in the accounting curriculum (Jackson *et al.*, 2006a).

Within some higher education institutions (HEIs), there is always potential for change to be slowed, as inordinate amounts of time and effort are spent focussing on definitions. However, the development of a curriculum that explicitly embraces (and most importantly assesses) generic skills is required (see Sangster, Chapter 15 – this volume, for a more detailed discussion). We can continue debating specific definitions but what we cannot ignore is the need for generic skills to be developed as part of the accounting curriculum in HEIs. But see St. Pierre and Rebele, Chapter 5 – this volume, for an opposing view.

13.3 Changes in the accounting curriculum: examples from across the globe

In this section several examples of how accounting academics are developing curricula that recognise the importance of generic skills as key to graduate employability are provided. Many of these examples are sourced from Watty *et al.* (2012a).

In a paper that discusses a whole-of-programme approach to generic skills development in accounting in Australia, Willcoxson *et al.* (2012) provide evidence of a mapping process which is designed to build academic capacity in relation to a better understanding and the embedding of generic skills development leading, ultimately, to an improved curriculum which enhances students' learning outcomes. In a layered approach that often underpins programme mapping, academics (with, where appropriate, their subject teams) first map their subjects, ensuring alignment between objectives, generic skills, and assessment. The individual maps form the basis for the whole-of-programme mapping process, where comparisons between subjects can be made and gaps and overlaps exposed. The overall map provides the basis for discussions between academics to enhance a shared understanding of generic skills in the programmes, and the potential for change and improvement in course design. Importantly, the beneficiaries of this process are the students, who have the opportunity to develop important skills to enhance their employability. The authors share their experiences of 'heated discussions' between academics as a part of this process - an aspect of continuous improvement in accounting education to which many accounting academics will relate.

For many readers the process outlined will, to a large extent, mirror the underlying principles of Assurance of Learning – a process designed to provide evidence of students' achievement of specified students' intended learning outcomes (ILOs). Willcoxson *et al.* (2012) usefully provide readers with templates of the mapping documentation used in their project.

With a focus on postgraduate students, Fortin & Legault (2012) share their experience and insights developed by implementing a mixed teaching approach to assist in developing generic and professional skills in a Canadian graduate accounting programme. The graduate programme reported includes a 15-month segment during which students spend 10 weeks working for a mock firm that simulates the environment of a Chartered Accounting (CA) firm. The mock firm is called VTA (*Vire, Tuelle and Associates*). Students operate as the young professionals, and educators take the role of partners. The authors use a mixed-method approach which includes simulation as an alternate pedagogy to the traditional lecture design, seeking to develop 32 generic competencies drawn from the *CA Candidates' Competency Map* (Canadian Institute of Chartered Accountants, 2005) and the literature. As the authors suggest: '*This experience is intended to prepare students to become chartered accountants and develop their generic and professional skills by emphasising the integration of knowledge rather than its acquisition*' (Fortin & Legault, 2012, p. 99). A survey undertaken by the authors that specifically focussed on the VTA simulations revealed that the approach was useful in developing all 32 competencies. (See also Byrne & Willis, Chapter 7 – this volume; Hassall & Joyce, Chapter 17 – this volume; and Beard & Humphrey, Chapter 25 – this volume.)

Within the New Zealand context, Bui & Porter (2012) propose, test, and evaluate an expectations–performance gap, designed to test a hypothesised structure of the gap between the competencies which accounting graduates are, on the one hand, *expected*, and, on the other, *perceived* to possess, by employers of accounting graduates. Their work underlines the importance of recognising the view of graduate employers in the discussions of generic skills and the accounting curriculum. This importance is recognised in much of the work undertaken and published on generic skills in accounting education (e.g. Kavanagh & Drennan, 2008; Awayiga *et al.*, 2012; Sin *et al.*, 2011; Jackling & Watty, 2010).

The primary components of the gap are developed by Bui & Porter (2012) from prior literature, and include:

- Differences between the expectation of accounting graduate employers and educators about competencies (the 'expectation gap').
- Differences between the perceptions of educators about competencies reasonably expected, and those desired by them. Constraints on the effectiveness of accounting education (the 'constraints gap').
- Differences between the perceptions of academics about the competencies developed in the university and which those employers perceive graduates to possess when entering employment (ibid., p. 30).

The findings from extensive interviews and analyses of semi-structured interviews with partners from accounting firms, recent graduates, accounting educators, and final year students (intending to work in public accounting upon graduation) revealed support for the proposed framework. Most importantly, strategies for ways in which the identified gaps may be narrowed were also determined. In particular, and with respect to the 'expectation gap', greater interaction between 'town and gown' (i.e. graduate employers and academics) is suggested, with the potential for collaboration between both parties in curriculum design.

Finally, a study by Abayadeera & Watty (2011) reports on the development of generic skills in an accounting programme in Sri Lanka. Embedded within the accounting programme outlined in the paper are pedagogies based on the use of case-studies, team assignments, dedicated rooms for technology skills development, and a language laboratory – the Skills Development Centre – dedicated to improving the English language skills of students. The use of a 'music room' (a designated space that is set-up for student activity) encourages students to engage in cultural activities outside of the classroom, and this has resulted in many performances and activities (see http://www.sjp.ac.lk/2011). Similar to the findings of Awayiga *et al.* (2012), who examined the perceptions of graduate employers on the adequacy of generic skills developed in Ghana, the listing of generic skills used in the Abayadeera & Watty (2011) study were also similar to those used in other studies in many different countries across the world. Appendix 1 to this chapter provides details of a collection of generic skills lists used in accounting education research across various countries. The listings of the suite of generic skills relevant in accounting education are generally consistent, regardless of country. (See also Exhibit 27.1 – this volume.)

The accounting profession and, by extension, accounting education, are global. (See Calhoun & Karreman, Chapter 26 – this volume.) Thus, global mobility and the portability of accounting qualifications are pressing issues for all accounting education stakeholders. Evidence from Appendix 1 indicates that efforts are being made to develop a consistent suite of generic skills, regardless of the country. Appendix 1 highlights similarities in how researchers and the IAESB consider generic skills. This is welcomed by the global accounting profession and, in particular, the IAESB, given that its primary objectives are to serve the public interest by:

- establishing a series of high-quality standards and other publications which reflect good practice in the education, development, and assessment of professional accountants;
- promoting the adoption and implementation of the IESs;
- developing education benchmarks for measuring the implementation of the IESs; and
- advancing international debate on emerging issues relating to the education, development and assessment of professional accountants. (IAESB, 2012; http://www.ifac.org/education/about-iaesb/terms-reference, accessed September 2012).

While embedding the development of generic skills in the accounting curriculum is important, the ability to evidence assessment of those skills, framed as students' ILOs, is equally important.

In a major Australian study, Jackson *et al.* (2006b) developed *A Manual for Improving Assessment in Accounting Education*, aimed at providing academics teaching in an undergraduate accounting programme with information about assessment design specifically focussed on the development of generic skills. The Manual is based on a major, nationally-funded project, completed by the same authors entitled: *Assessing Students Unfamiliar with Assessment Practices in Australian Universities.*

Developed on the basis of feedback from accounting students, academics, and graduate employers, the Manual is a resource for accounting educators in the assessment of generic skills in accounting education, and includes five sections, entitled:

- *Linking Assessment Design and Generic Skills*
- *A Strategic Approach to Assessing Generic Skills in an Undergraduate Accounting Program*
- *Designing Assessment that Improves Learning for All*
- *Assisting Staff to Develop Assessment that Improves Learning for All*, and
- *References to Existing Good Practice.*

In Australia, for over two decades, there has been an explicit expectation by key PABs that accounting students will acquire a set of generic skills. In addition, the PABs require details of where the generic skills are explicitly planned for in curriculum design (CPA/ICAA, 2012, p.13).

This requirement goes some way to explain why a good deal of research in this area has emanated from Australia, over a sustained period of time. The *Model for Mapping Generic Skills and Assessment* is also part of Appendix 2 of this chapter which is provided as a source of guidance for readers. (It should be noted at this point that, insofar as generic skills are deemed to be equivalent to competences, the IAESB defines competence as involving an ability to perform a work role to a defined standard, with reference to real working environments. This indicates that it is not the case that they can be assessed in the setting of a classroom or an examination hall.)

13.4 The future: how might we do things differently?

While Appendix 1 details the generic skills considered in past literature, the conversation around generic skills in the accounting curriculum continues in the literature, and additional generic skills are constantly being identified. Daff *et al.* (2012) explore the need for accountants to have a combination of emotional intelligence and generic skills, suggesting that emotional intelligence can be embedded in the curriculum through readings, role-play, and vignettes based on workplace scenarios. Haigh & Clifford (2011) suggest that education, generally, should address personal, social, and environmental responsibility. These are areas that others have presented in the literature, however, Haigh & Clifford (ibid., p. 581) extend the position by suggesting that: '*graduate attributes need to address levels of concern that rise through the self and the social toward the welfare of the whole planet*'. Further, they conclude: '*the question needs to be asked: what do we want our graduates to be like and who or what should they serve: themselves, their employer, their society, their world, and the future?*' (ibid.).

Regardless of the number of generic skills listed, there is still very little evidence that accounting education has changed to accommodate the demands of key stakeholders (namely, graduate employers and PABs). There are, however, pockets of change, often based on individual 'champions' in the area of generic skills development. Winchester-Seeto & Bosanquet (2009, p. 327) suggest: '*To date there is little evidence of the impact of graduate attributes on student learning.*' Here the authors define attributes around four broad conceptions of purpose:

- employability;
- life-long learning;
- uncertain futures; and
- acting for the social good (2009, p. 326).

Similarly, there is little evidence from employers (or feedback from PABs) that the level of generic skills development (and subsequent on-the-job performance) has improved over the past two decades, regardless of the focus in the literature. Given the increasing literature in the area, the explicit global focus on evidence-based learning outcomes, and the increasingly competitive, public and private business/accounting education sector, this seems surprising. So, what might be different? How could we reconsider the development of generic skills in the accounting curriculum?

The current approach to embedding generic skills in accounting education assumes two things:

- that academics/teachers are expert in developing these non-technical skills; and
- that a one-size-fits-all approach is appropriate.

In other words, each student is expected to develop the same suite and level of generic skills, regardless of his or her previous educational, professional, and social experiences. This approach ignores, to a large extent, the principles of constructive learning (see Lucas & Mladenovic,

Chapter 6 – this volume, for a more detailed discussion). Constructivism promotes active learning, and the learners play an active role in generating their own understandings, influenced by the teacher and their own individual environments. In this way, the learner constructs knowledge, with reference to personal filters that may include experiences, goals, and beliefs, all of which vary greatly between students. If we accept these notions of constructivism, perhaps we can accept the benefit of students undertaking diagnostic testing in relation to generic skills (or sets of generic skills), that is, identify their current levels of development. If students are able to determine their own benchmarks as a result of a diagnostically-styled test, then a tailored programme of learning may be 'selected' by the student (for example, from a suite of basic, intermediate, and advanced learning resources). In this context, the generic skills may be developed in a separate suite of compulsory subjects (for example, interpersonal skills, intrapersonal skills, leadership, and social enterprise), and assessment of these generic skills can be embedded within the assessment of the core technical units, where application of knowledge-utilising generic skills should be assessed.

As accounting educators, technology provides us with a myriad of new opportunities for reimagining our subject design for a new generation of 'connected students' with new cognitive capacities and learning styles (Margaryan et al., 2011). (See also Duff, Chapter 8, and Boritz & Stoner, Chapter 16 – both in this volume.) Increasingly, open access is available to a diverse array of credible learning resources providing opportunities for students to develop unique and individualised learning pathways for generic skills development. Technologies will increasingly challenge academics to consider how digital education can enhance learning (MacGregor, 2013). In this environment, academics and students become collaborators in learning, and students are able to take an active role in constructing their learning pathway for the development of generic skills. The process of learning itself becomes a significant development opportunity.

Students come to universities with varying skills and knowledge levels. Technologies can assist us to better determine those levels. Further, we can work in partnership with students to assist them in locating those activities (some designed in-house, yet many available as open-access educational resources) that will best support them to achieve agreed levels of achievement, evidenced in suitably designed assessment.

13.5 Conclusion

Generic skills in the accounting curriculum are a matter of immense interest and importance to a variety of stakeholders, including: graduate employers, PABs, national governments, academics, and students. For several decades the links between employability and generic skills development have been made. As a result, a stronger focus on the role and responsibility of academics designing and teaching in accounting degree programmes has intensified. To date, credible examples of embedding generic skills in specific subjects are available, as are approaches that acknowledge the need for a holistic approach to generic skills development across a whole programme. However, this work has not diminished the calls from graduate employers and PABs for graduates with stronger generic skills development. As a result, there is room to consider the development of generic skills in the accounting curriculum from a different perspective. This perspective reflects an approach that develops the generic skills of individual students using diagnostic testing to determine base levels, and a selection of learning resources and activities to add value to the learning outcomes for individual students. Application of generic skills is assessed in core knowledge units, thus making an explicit link between the technical knowledge skills and the non-technical generic skills. Digital technologies have a major role to play in this expansive view of generic skills development and assessment in the accounting curriculum.

Appendix 1

Table 13.1 Generic skill categories of accounting graduates

Skill List	Watty et al. (1998)	Albrecht & Sack (2000)	Kavanagh & Drennan (2008)	Jackling & De Lange (2009)	Hancock et al. (2009)	IES 3	Skills from Sri Lankan Job Advertisements	Skills Considered for this Study
1. Intellectual Skills								
Analytical	✓	✓	✓			✓	✓	✓
Creativity	✓		✓			✓		✓
Critical thinking		✓	✓			✓		✓
Decision modelling		✓	✓		✓	✓		✓
Independent thought	✓		✓			✓	✓	✓
Informed decision-maker	✓							
Logical argument			✓			✓		
Problem-solving			✓		✓	✓	✓	✓
Research		✓	✓			✓		✓
Risk propensity			✓					
Able to deal with complexity					✓	✓	✓	✓
Uncertainty					✓			
Enthusiastic					✓		✓	✓
Achieve given targets by the management							✓	✓
2. Technical and Functional Skills								
Professional accounting qualifications							✓	✓
Academic accounting qualifications							✓	✓
Accounting software			✓			✓	✓	✓
Computer technology competence	✓	✓	✓	✓	✓	✓	✓	✓
Key accounting/Bookkeeping			✓	✓	✓	✓	✓	✓
Measurement		✓	✓			✓		
Reporting						✓		
Auditing					✓			
Business recovery								
Risk analysis		✓	✓			✓	✓	
Compliance with legislative and regulatory requirements						✓		
Literacy/Numeracy					✓			

Table 13.1 Generic skill categories of accounting graduates—continued

Skill List	Watty et al. (1998)	Albrecht & Sack (2000)	Kavanagh & Drennan (2008)	Jackling & De Lange (2009)	Hancock et al. (2009)	IES 3	Skills from Sri Lankan Job Advertisements	Skills Considered for this Study
3. Personal Skills								
Work long hours/willing to work extra hours							✓	✓
Right personality							✓	✓
Smart appearance							✓	✓
Adaptable	✓					✓		
Flexible			✓		✓			✓
Commitment to professional development				✓	✓	✓		✓
Continuous learning		✓	✓		✓			
Cope with stress	✓				✓			
Personal discipline	✓						✓	✓
Practical	✓				✓			
Professional attitude/behaviour		✓	✓		✓		✓	✓
Meeting tight deadlines					✓	✓	✓	✓
Self-promotion			✓					
Self-motivated	✓		✓			✓	✓	✓
Self-management					✓	✓		
Initiative, influence and self-learning					✓	✓		
Professional scepticism						✓		
Work ethics	✓		✓		✓	✓		
Positive attitudes values			✓		✓	✓	✓	✓
Ambition					✓			
Hardworking, dedicated					✓		✓	✓
Well-rounded, mature, confident persons					✓			
4. Interpersonal and Communication Skills								
Fluency in English language							✓	✓

Skill							
Oral communication	✓	✓		✓	✓	✓	✓
Written communication	✓	✓		✓	✓	✓	✓
Critical comment	✓			✓		✓	✓
Listening				✓	✓	✓	✓
Reading with understanding	✓	✓		✓	✓		✓
Negotiation	✓	✓		✓	✓	✓	✓
Interpersonal team work	✓	✓		✓	✓	✓	✓
Value-adding team member	✓			✓		✓	✓
Cross-cultural	✓	✓		✓	✓		✓
Customer orientation					✓		
Salesmanship	✓						

5. Organizational and Business Management Skills

Skill							
Change management	✓	✓		✓		✓	✓
Resource management	✓	✓		✓		✓	✓
Decision-making	✓	✓		✓		✓	✓
Inter-disciplinary	✓	✓		✓		✓	✓
Leadership	✓	✓		✓	✓	✓	✓
Project management	✓	✓		✓	✓	✓	✓
Strategic management	✓			✓			✓
Organise and delegate tasks to motivate and develop people						✓	
Professional judgement and discernment						✓	
Entrepreneurship		✓		✓			
Management skills							✓
Planning and organising				✓		✓	✓
Community involvement and social responsibility				✓		✓	

6. Other

Skill							
Socially, environmentally aware	✓					✓	
Workplace experience	✓					✓	✓

Source: Abayadeera & Watty (2011).

Appendix 2

This Appendix is taken from *A Manual for Improving Assessment in Accounting Education*. Report to the Carrick Institute (Jackson *et al.*, 2006).[1]

As part of the research underpinning this Manual, several attempts were made to link the specific generic skills identified by the professional accounting bodies (PABs) with specific assessment tasks. This *direct* linking, or mapping, as part of a modelling process has been problematic at best, because:

• the skills identified by the PABs were not defined with a view to accommodating direct mapping;
• the skills overlap; and
• whether a specific skill or set of skills is developed is *less dependent on the assessment task* (essay, report, case-study) and *more dependent on the context of the task*. The latter includes reference to the framing of the questions, whether the task is completed individually or as a group, and whether assessment of the task is undertaken by the academic, self, and/or peers.

The example that follows shows how the conduct and assessor of a specific task can influence the set of generic skills developed and assessed.

Assessment task: written report

Varying the combination of the conduct and assessor of the same assessment task leads to the development of a different suite of generic skills. (See Figure 13.1 and Table 13.2.)

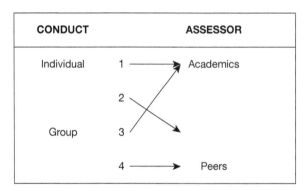

Figure 13.1 Report writing: Conduct and Assessor

Table 13.2 Report writing: combinations of conduct and assessor

Combination 1	The report is an individual assessment task assessed by the academic
Combination 2	The report is an individual assessment task assessed by peers (and perhaps the academic)
Combination 3	A group report is prepared and assessed by the academic
Combination 4	A group report is prepared and assessed by peers

In addition, the framing of questions and the expectations of the academic when designing the assessment will also determine the generic skills that are the focus of the assessment. In short, the design of any assessment task involves multiple perspectives and variables which potentially influence the type of generic skills being assessed.

With these limitations in mind, any attempt to directly link the generic skills with assessment tasks only is, to a large extent, subjective and dependent on the ability of the academic to clearly articulate the skills that the task is seeking to assess. Any process to make direct links is artificial and forced.

That is not to say that these links are not possible. Indeed, as part of ensuring teaching quality, there is value in clearly establishing such links. The real value in establishing the links is more about the academic ensuring that he/she is confident about the aims of the assessment task and that he/she can clearly articulate the links between the task and the students' learning outcomes identified for the specific course.

A Model for Mapping Generic Skills and Assessment

The two illustrations that follow may assist in clarifying the discussion above. To reiterate, the model reflects an individual academic's approach to an assessment task that reflects the context of the assessment and the aims of the course.

In the first example, an industry-based assignment is a task which students have the option of completing individually or in groups. The report is both self-assessed and assessed by the academic. The output is a written report.

In the model (see Figure 13.2), the assessment *task* is considered in terms of a process that involves the conduct of the task (individual or group) and the assessor of the task (academic, peer, self). Traditionally, in accounting education, assessment has been designed primarily as an individual task although, increasingly, group work assessment is being used. Whether the primary motive for this increase in group work requirements is based around the development of unique generic skills, or the assessment (marking) demands on academics, remains unclear. What is clear is that different generic skills are developed when the assessment process varies in terms of 'conduct' and the 'assessor'.

Comments regarding the model

In designing this assessment task, the academic has identified the generic skills that can be assessed, dependent on whether students choose to conduct the task in groups or individually. In addition, by including self-assessment in the process, some additional generic skills (such as engaging in lifelong learning, and recognising one's own strengths and weaknesses), are specifically addressed. Further details of the assessment design that links to the model above are provided in Section Three of the Manual, under 3.3.1 Assessment Packages.

This process of considering and documenting specific links to generic skills is invaluable in clarifying the focus of the assessment on generic skills. However, it is only possible when all the variables associated with the design of the assessment are taken into account. This knowledge rests with the academic or academic team designing the task and the process.

A second example is detailed below using a traditional form of assessment – with an examination as the assessment task. (See Figure 13.3.)

By comparing the two models above, the type of generic skills development will vary greatly, depending upon the assessment task, the conduct of the task and the assessor. While a written business-based report undertaken in groups and self-assessed has the potential to develop

CONDUCT

ASSESSOR – ACADEMIC

INDIVIDUAL
Additional Skills

Computer Literacy
Identify, find, evaluate,
organise and manage
information and evidence
Initiate and conduct research
Receive, evaluate and react to
new ideas
Make judgements derived
from one's own value framework
Know what question to ask
Apply disciplinary and
multidisciplinary perspectives

GROUP
Additional Skills

**ASSESSOR –
SELF AND PEER**
Additional Skills

Listen effectively
Present, discuss and defend views
Transfer and receive knowledge
Negotiate with people from different
backgrounds and with different
value systems
Understand group dynamics
Collaborate with colleagues

Engage in lifelong learning
Recognise own strengths
and limitations

Figure 13.2 Generic skills development (Business Report): Example 1

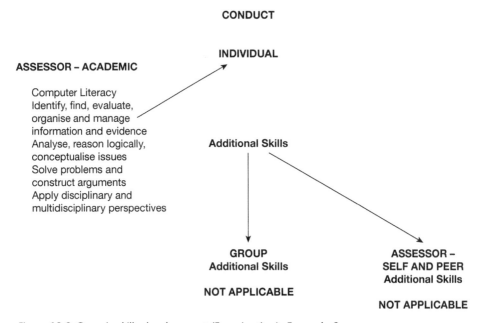

CONDUCT

ASSESSOR – ACADEMIC

INDIVIDUAL

Computer Literacy
Identify, find, evaluate,
organise and manage
information and evidence
Analyse, reason logically,
conceptualise issues
Solve problems and
construct arguments
Apply disciplinary and
multidisciplinary perspectives

Additional Skills

GROUP
Additional Skills

NOT APPLICABLE

**ASSESSOR –
SELF AND PEER**
Additional Skills

NOT APPLICABLE

Figure 13.3 Generic skills development (Examination): Example 2

a suite of specific generic skills, the more traditional, examination assessment is limited in the number of generic skills that can be developed and assessed.

Modelling the links between assessment and generic skill development clarifies and highlights, both for students and staff, the focus and aim of the assessment being considered.

Note

1   The materials provided in this Appendix are from the Manual that is focussed on practical assistance to academics. The details are based on empirical research reported in the main report entitled *Assessing Students Unfamiliar with Assessment Practices in Australian Universities*, see http://www.olt.gov.au/project-assessing-students-unfamiliar-rmit-2005 (accessed 20 April 2013).

References

Abayadeera, N. & Watty, K. (2011) Quality of accounting graduates in an emerging and developing country: evidence from Sri Lanka. Accounting Education Special Interest Group (SIG). Paper presented at 2011 AFAANZ Conference, Darwin.

Albrecht, W.S. & Sack, R. (2000) *Accounting Education: Charting the Course through a Perilous Future* (Accounting Education Series Vol. 16), Sarasota, FL: American Accounting Association.

American Accounting Association (AAA) (1986) Committee on the future structure, content and scope of accounting education (The Bedford Committee), Future accounting education: preparing for the expending profession (the Bedford Report), *Issues in Accounting Education,* 1(1), 168–195.

Arthur Andersen and Co., Arthur Young, Coopers and Lybrand, Deloitte Haskins and Sells, Ernst and Whinney, Peat Marwick Main and Co., Price Waterhouse, and Touche Ross (1989) *Perspectives on Education for Success in the Accounting Profession* (Big 8 White Paper), New York: the authors.

Awayiga, J.Y., Onumah, J.M., & Tsamenyi, M. (2012) Knowledge and skills development of accounting graduates: the perceptions of graduates and employers in Ghana, in Watty, K., Jackling, B., & Wilson, R.M.S. (eds) *Personal Transferable Skills in Accounting Education*, New York: Routledge, pp. 137–156.

Barrie, S. (2006) Understanding what we mean by the generic attributes of graduates, *Higher Education*, 51, 215–241.

Birkett, W. (1993) *Competency Based Standards for Professional Accountants in Australia and New Zealand*, Sydney: Australian Society of Certified Practising Accountants, The Institute of Chartered Accountants in Australia, and the New Zealand Society of Accountants.

Brown, R.B. & McCartney, S. (1995) Competence is not enough: meta-competence and accounting education, *Accounting Education: an international journal*, 4(1), 43–53.

Bui, B. & Porter, B. (2012) The expectation-performance gap in accounting education: an exploratory study, in Watty, K., Jackling, B., & Wilson, R.M.S. (eds) *Personal Transferable Skills in Accounting Education*, New York: Routledge, pp. 22–49.

Canadian Institute of Chartered Accountants (2005) *The CA Candidates' Competency Map: Understanding the Professional Competencies of CAs*, Toronto: Canadian Institute of Chartered Accountants.

Clanchy, J. & Ballard, B. (1995) Generic skills in the context of higher education, *Higher Education Research and Development*, 14(2), 155–166.

Commonwealth of Australia (2003) *Our Universities: Backing Australia's Future, Assuring Quality.* Canberra: Australian Government Publishing Service.

CPA/ICAA (2012) *Professional Accreditation Guidelines for Australian Accounting Degree*, Melbourne: CPA Australia and the Institute of Chartered Accountants in Australia, June.

Daff, L., De Lange, P., & Jackling, B. (2012) A comparison of generic skills and emotional intelligence in accounting education, *Issues in Accounting Education*, 27(3), 627–645.

Davies, M. (2011) Introduction to the special issue on critical thinking in higher education, *Higher Education Research and Development*, 30(3), 255–260.

Dearing Commission (1997) *Higher Education in the Learning Society*, Report to National Committee of Inquiry into Higher Education, London: HMSO.

De La Harpe, B., Radloff, A., & Wyber, J. (2000) Quality and generic (professional) skills, *Quality in Higher Education*, 6(3), 231–243.

Duffy, T.M. & Cunningham, D.J. (1996) Constructivism: implications for the design and delivery of instruction, in Jonassen, D.H. (ed.) *Educational Communications and Technology*, New York: Simon & Schuster, pp. 170–199.

Fortin, A. & Legault, M. (2012) Development of generic competencies: impact of a mixed teaching approach on students' perceptions, in Watty, K., Jackling, B., & Wilson, R.M.S. (eds) *Personal Transferable Skills in Accounting Education*, New York: Routledge, pp. 91–120.

Gracia, L. (2012) Accounting students' expectations and transition experiences of supervised work experience, in Watty, K., Jackling, B., & Wilson, R.M.S. (eds) *Personal Transferable Skills in Accounting Education*, New York: Routledge, pp. 50–64.

Haigh, M. & Clifford, V.A. (2011) Integral vision: a multi-perspective approach to the recognition of graduate attributes, *Higher Education Research and Development*, 30(5), 573–584.

Hancock, P., Howieson, B., Kavanagh, M., Kent, J., Tempone, I. & Segal, N. (2009) Accounting for the future: more than numbers, *Australian Learning and Teaching Council*, 1, 1–80.

Hardern, G. (1995) The development of standards of competence in accounting, *Accounting Education: an international journal*, 4(1), 17–27.

Honebein, P.C., Duffy, T.M. & Fishman, B.J. (1993) Constructivism and the design of learning environments: context and authentic activities for learning, in Duffy, T.M., Lowyck, J., & Jonassen, D.H. (eds) *Designing Environments for Constructive Learning*, Berlin: Springer-Verlag, pp. 87–108.

IAESB, IES 4, Professional Values, Ethics and Attitudes, http://www.ifac.org/news-events/2012-07/iaesb-proposed-revised-standard-professional-values-ethics-and-attitudes (accessed September 2012).

IAESB http://www.ifac.org/education/about-iaesb/terms-reference (accessed September 2012).

International Accounting Education Standards Board (2011) *IES 3, Professional Skills and General Education Contents*, New York: IAEC.

Jackling, B. & De Lange, P. (2009) Do accounting graduates' skills meet the expectations of employers? A matter of convergence or divergence, *Accounting Education: an international journal*, 18(4/5), 369–385.

Jackling, B. & Watty, K. (2010) Generic skills, *Accounting Education: an international journal*, 19(1–2), 1–3.

Jackson, M., Watty, K., Yu, L., & Lowe, L. (2006a) *Assessing Students Unfamiliar with Assessment Practices in Australian Universities*, Sydney: Report to the Carrick Institute.

Jackson, M., Watty, K., Yu, L. & Lowe, L. (2006b) *A Manual for Improving Assessment in Accounting Education*, Sydney: Report to the Carrick Institute.

Jones, A. (2010) Generic attributes in accounting: the significance of the disciplinary context, *Accounting Education: an international journal*, 19(1–2), 5–21.

Kavanagh, M.H. & Drennan, L. (2008) What skills and attributes does an accounting graduate need? Evidence from student perceptions and employer expectations, *Accounting and Finance*, 48(2), 279–300.

Lucas, U. (2008) Being "pulled up short": creating moments of surprise and possibility in accounting education, *Critical Perspectives on Accounting*, 19(3), 383–403.

MacGregor, K. (2013) A higher education avalanche is coming, says new report, *University World News*, 263. Available at: www.universityworldnews.com/article.php?story=20130316093956321. (accessed 21 March 2013).

Margaryan, A., Littlejohn, A., & Vojt, G. (2011) Are digital natives a myth or reality? University students' use of digital technologies, *Computers and Education*, 56(2), 429–440.

Mott, B.W., Callaway, C.B., Zettlemoyer, L.S., Lee, S.Y., & Lester, J.C. (1999) Towards narrative-centered learning environments, in Mateas, M. & Sengers, P. (eds) *Narrative Intelligence: Papers from the 1999 Fall Symposium*, Menlo Park, CA: American Association for Artificial Intelligence, pp. 78–82.

Nanjappa, A. & Grant, M.M. (2003) Constructing on constructivism: the role of technology, *Electronic Journal for the Integration of Technology in Education*, 2(1). Available at: http://ejite.isu.edu/Volume2No1/nanjappa.htm (accessed 30 June 2013).

Piaget, J. ([1954] 1970) Piaget's theory, in Mussen, P.H. (ed.) *Carmichael's Manual of Child Psychology*, 3rd edn, Vol. 1, New York: Wiley, pp. 703–732.

Purcell, J. (2001) National vocational qualifications and competence-based assessment for technicians: from sound principles to dogma, *Education and Training*, 43(1), 30–39.

Simons, P.R.J. (1993) Constructive learning: the role of the learner, in Duffy, T.M., Lowyck, J. & Jonassen, D.H. (eds) *Designing Environments for Constructive Learning*, New York: Springer-Verlag, pp. 291–313.

Sin, S. & Reid, A. (2005) Developing generic skills in accounting: resourcing and reflecting on trans-disciplinary research and insights, paper at Australian Association for Research in Education (AARE) Conference, Sydney, 28 November–1 December.

Sin, S., Reid, A., & Dahlgren, L.O. (2011) The conceptions of work in the accounting profession in the twenty-first century from the experiences of practitioners, *Studies in Continuing Education*, 33(2), 139–156.

The Secretary's Commission on Achieving Necessary Skills (2000) *Skills and Tasks for Jobs: A SCANS Report for America*, Washington, DC: US Department of Labor.

UNESCO (1998) Higher education in the twenty-first century: vision and action, paper presented at the World Conference on Higher Education, Paris, October.

Watty, K., Cahill, D., & Cooper, B. (1998) Graduate attributes: perceptions of accounting academics, *Asian Review of Accounting*, Special Edition Education Issue, 6(1), 68–83.

Watty, K., Jackling, B., & Wilson, R.M.S. (eds) (2012a) *Personal Transferable Skills in Accounting Education*, London: Routledge.

Watty, K., Jackling, B., & Wilson, R.M.S. (eds) (2012b) Introduction, in *Personal Transferable Skills in Accounting Education*, London: Routledge, pp. 1–4.

Willcoxson, L., Wynder, M., & Laing, G.K. (2012) A whole-of-program approach to the development of generic and professional skills in a university accounting program, in Watty, K., Jackling, B., & Wilson, R.M.S. (eds) *Personal Transferable Skills in Accounting Education*, New York: Routledge, pp. 64–90.

Winchester-Seeto, T. & Bosanquet, A. (2009) Will students notice the difference? Embedding graduate capabilities in the curriculum, paper at 32nd HERDSA Annual International Conference, Darwin, July.

Yonghai, W. & Guoying, L. (2010) China accounting education change in the knowledge society: the constructivism education, *Education Technology and Computer Science (ETCS)*, 3, 542–545.

About the author

Kim Watty is a Professor of Accounting and Associate Dean (Teaching and Learning Scholarship) in the Faculty of Business and Law at Deakin University, Melbourne, Australia (kim.watty@deakin.edu.au). She has published widely on several themes within the domain of accounting education, has led several major nationally-funded and internationally-funded projects, and is a Senior Associate Editor of *Accounting Education: an international journal*.

14

Integrating the accounting curriculum

Robert Bloom

JOHN CARROLL UNIVERSITY, U.S.A.

CONTENTS

Abstract

This chapter considers alternative approaches to integrating the accounting curriculum. The concept of integration in this context is to relate accounting to allied business disciplines in a decision-making context. Also included in this concept of integration is the ability of students to communicate orally and in writing, as well as their overall employability.

Emphasis is placed on bringing collaborative endeavours to the course work at hand, including team preparation and team teaching across disciplines. The specific proposals set forth

294

pertain to integrating accounting and finance (A & F) education and incorporating a sustainability module within an *International Financial Accounting and Reporting* course. While the ideas discussed here have broad applicability to many jurisdictions, particular attention is paid to the U.S.A., the U.K., and Australia. Consideration is given to authoritative reports on accounting education in these three countries.

Keywords

accounting & finance, curriculum reform, integrative education, inter-disciplinary curriculum, sustainability, team teaching

14.1 Introduction

The main aims of this chapter are:

- to offer a cross-disciplinary approach to providing accounting instruction, overcoming the insularity inherent in the traditional approach to presenting this discipline as being self-contained;
- to provide food for thought to encourage accounting educational reform via ideas for designing new coursework; and
- to encourage academic staff to think about modifying existing courses to make them more challenging to accounting majors and to attract additional majors.

14.2 Overview

This chapter examines several alternative approaches to integrating the accounting curriculum. Accounting education involves more than rote learning; it also involves the development of professional judgement. To use an example, studying an accounting standard could conceivably entail learning about the history of this topic, the alternatives considered, the rationale for the standard *per se*. (See Paisey & Paisey, Chapter 30 – this volume.)

The proposals discussed in this chapter conform to this notion of accounting education. 'Integration' refers to connecting accounting to business practice, and linking it to other subject areas taught in business schools, with an emphasis on finance, and sustainability. The basic premiss is that students cannot achieve an adequate command of accounting if they are taught this discipline as an isolated subject. Integration of accounting with each of the other business disciplines (including economics, finance, and organizational behaviour) can be compared to a jig-saw puzzle in which all the pieces interconnect. '[O]ne can think of the knobbly bits as introducing ideas from one course into adjacent courses in order to create an integrated whole' (this analogy was made by the Editor, Richard M. S. Wilson).

The intent of this integration is to enhance the analytical and decision-making skills of the students to better prepare them for long-term careers in the broad realm of professional A & F. Academic staff may view this perspective as being beyond their comfort zone, particularly since textbooks tend to emphasize a solo approach to accounting instruction. Real integration (as opposed to just covering each discipline in separate courses) is a synergistic endeavour with the intended learning outcomes (ILOs), including critical thinking and decision-making involving multi-disciplinary issues, being greater than the sum of the parts. That aim conceivably would involve team teaching and joint syllabi preparation with academic staff from both disciplines, which could be problematic in terms of meshing different teaching styles and generating a loss of individual authority on the part of different groups of academic staff.

This chapter capitalizes on ideas set forth by Amernic & Craig in Chapter 12, and Watty in Chapter 13 – both in this volume. (See also Sangster & Wilson, 2012, and Watty *et al.*, 2012.) Chapter 12 focusses on a pedagogic approach to liberalizing the accounting curriculum, enabling students to: integrate their university studies, challenge conventional wisdom, analyse implicit assumptions and their implications, reflect upon the ethical aspects in decision-making, and reason practically.

Chapter 13, on generic skills, covers communication and other employability skills that should be taught in accounting courses. In so doing, Chapter 13 stresses a wider role for accounting in society, dealing with non-technical aspects of accounting in the curriculum to better prepare students for the business world. Chapter 14 will attempt to apply those ideas specifically to accounting education in terms of integrating:

- Accounting with Finance courses, and
- Sustainability

within an undergraduate/graduate accounting course – *International Financial Accounting and Reporting*. The contents of this chapter should be relevant to an international readership, recognizing different cultural characteristics, primarily in the U.S.A., the U.K., and Australia.

14.2.1 Integrative teaching ideas from non-accounting education literature

In the science education literature, McComas offers a comprehensive model for different degrees of course integration (McComas, 2009).

- Level 1 would involve minimal integration, covering the solitary discipline, but sprinkling in aspects of related disciplines without specific attention. This level applied to accounting could view this discipline as part of overall management in an organization in terms of scorekeeping in planning, control, and performance evaluation.
- The next level (Level 2) of integration would make clear-cut references to other disciplines in the instructional process, emphasizing that accounting relates to the other business disciplines, bringing in examples of applications of accounting in business decision-making. Also it should be stressed that one cannot understand accounting as a separate field of endeavour in view of its interrelationships with the other disciplines.
- McComas' Level 3 would actually involve a non-business discipline in the teaching process – perhaps through textbooks and articles. Other disciplines could be logic, taught by the philosophy academic staff (or, in some cases, by the mathematics academic staff).
- Level 4 would entail team teaching in close co-ordination with non-business academic staff.
- Finally, Level 5 would no longer emphasize accounting as the core discipline, but instead provide the courses with an inter-disciplinary, decision-oriented theme such as sustainability, thereby embracing several fields.

The foregoing approach could be applied to accounting, which is usually taught by itself as a solo or could be integrated with other business disciplines, especially finance. However, it would be quite extraordinary to see accounting integrated across the liberal arts, if not the sciences, in a thematic course (Lister, 2010, pp. 329–344).

Amadei & Sandekian (2010, pp. 84–92) are essentially concerned with infusing sustainability into engineering education, especially to meet the challenges of developing countries in regard to water, sanitation, food, health, and energy in order to convey to the students a global perspective. What they discuss could also be readily applied to contemporary business education. I will be using this approach to integrating sustainability into an undergraduate/graduate *International Financial Accounting and Reporting* course later in this chapter.

Carruthers and Peterson call for integrating social justice into economics education, emphasizing assumptions behind economic theory. What they provide is a perspective on social justice, so that students can understand the conflict between market effects and social welfare (Carruthers & Peterson, 2010, pp. 415–436). At John Carroll University (JCU) in the U.S.A., where I teach, there is a required first-year seminar course for all undergraduates, which applies social justice as an overriding theme, with separate learning communities such as poverty, education, and business.

From humanities and engineering departments respectively, Ford & Riley (2003) explore ways of integrating communications in engineering education, including writing across the curriculum and online resources (see Watty, Chapter 13; Boritz & Stoner, Chapter 16; and Stevenson *et al.*, Chapter 19 – all in this volume). What they cover can serve to integrate communications into the accounting curriculum (Ford & Riley, 2003, pp. 325–328).

McCarthy & McCarthy (2006) argue that experiential learning should be integrated into business education, so that students can see for themselves how a business functions. (See also Hassall & Joyce, Chapter 17 – this volume.) The authors explore the integration of job-shadowing into a business programme. Experiential learning is more beneficial than case method analysis – presumably in the light of its hands-on nature (McCarthy & McCarthy, 2006, pp. 201–204).

Barrett (2013) reports on a study of double major students at nine prestigious universities in the U.S.A. For those students who double-majored in the same area (such as sciences, humanities, social sciences), the researchers found the students to be most skilful at integrating knowledge, and that students doing a particular assignment in one course could often rework it for another course in a second related discipline. For students double-majoring in two unrelated disciplines, the researchers found that students could approach their assignments thinking creatively. At the conclusion of their study, the researchers advise academic staff to assist double-majors by jointly serving on committees to supervise their capstone projects and theses.

14.2.2 Ideas on integration from authoritative accounting education reports

Before I examine two specific efforts to integrate the accounting curriculum, let us consider authoritative education reports from the U.S.A., the U.K., and Australia:

- From the U.S.A., Bedford (American Accounting Association 1986), Accounting Education Change Commission (AECC) (1990), Albrecht & Sack (2000), and the Pathways Commission (2012) reports warrant consideration.
- From the U.K., there are no such recent reports, only the Solomons Report (1974) to consider.
- From Australia, there are several reports which could be considered (and which are addressed in other chapters of this volume), but attention in the present chapter will focus on the Mathews Report (1990) and the Cappelletto Report (2010).

The Bedford Report observes: '*Accountants who remain narrowly educated will find it more difficult to compete in an expanding profession*' (AAA, 1986, p. 95). The profession is changing, calling for broader backgrounds on the part of our students. Bedford (1986, p.99) recommends more emphasis in accounting instruction on the ability of the student to apply accounting knowledge, to use cases, promoting a more active role for students in the classroom for them to think creatively. Bedford further asserts (ibid., pp. 107–108): '*The more interdisciplinary applications that are included in the classroom, the greater the likelihood that students will be able to place accounting in a broad perspective.*' While the Bedford Report is from 1986, its principal recommendations are still relevant in today's accounting environment.

Similar to the Bedford Report, the AECC Position Statement No. 1, *Objectives of Education for Accountants* (1990), recommends the development of analytical and conceptual skills in accounting students. Accordingly, students should acquire:

> *(1) the ability to identify goals, problems, and opportunities, (2) the ability to identify, gather, measure, summarize, verify, analyze, and interpret financial and nonfinancial data . . ., and (3) the ability to use data, exercise judgments, evaluate risks, and solve real-world problems.*

(See Duff, Chapter 8 and Cunningham, Chapter 18 – both in this volume.) Thus, the AECC views the accountant as being not simply a recorder and provider of information but, more importantly, as a key business decision-maker.

In the same vein as the previous authoritative reports, the Albrecht & Sack study criticizes the over-emphasis in accounting education on recording transactions as opposed to analyzing information for decision-making. This study finds that accounting education is too silo-oriented, failing to integrate the other areas of business. As part of this study, a survey of academics and practitioners was undertaken, one finding of which is that 58.6 per cent of practitioners, in contrast to 41.2 per cent of academics, favour combining A & F education. Given what practitioners have observed in the course of their work, they appear to be more inclined than do academics to perceive the need for accounting students to study finance in depth.

The recently published Pathways Commission Report (2012) makes several key recommendations to improve the integrative nature of accounting education, including:

- linking accounting education to practice and research;
- putting more incentives and hence emphasis on teaching in evaluating the performance of academic staff. (See Kidwell & Lowensohn, Chapter 21, and Calderon, Chapter 22 on Assessment; and Apostolou & Gammie, Chapter 29, on accreditation – all in this volume.)
- updating and revising the accounting curriculum, starting with the introductory course (see Wygal, Chapter 11 – this volume); and
- giving university credit for rigorous accounting courses taken by pupils in secondary schools. (See Byrne & Willis, Chapter 7 – this volume.)

In the U.K., Solomons was critical of professional accounting bodies (PABs) for not providing specific training in financial management to its members, most of whom function in industry after a short time in auditing or taxation, and he called for three years of university or polytechnic education in addition to three years of practical training prior to certification as a professional accountant. Overall, Solomons recommends a better integration of study and practice in preparation for professional accounting work. His recommendations were not implemented, and there has been no recent authoritative accounting education report in the U.K. since the Solomons Report (1974), which is now 40 years old. (See Solomons, with Berridge, 1974.)

In Australia, the Mathews Report (1990) found that accounting education was a publicly neglected area, discriminated against due to its vocational orientation and hence grossly underfunded. Student to staff ratios in universities were too high, and working conditions unsatisfactory. This report recommends that accreditation agencies: '*look for evidence of a broad general education and the integration of communication and computing skills into the teaching and learning process*' (ibid., p. xxiv). (See also Watty, Chapter 13, and Boritz & Stoner, Chapter 16 – both in this volume.)

In addition, this report calls for undergraduate accounting programmes: '*[t]o integrate the different disciplinary units, so that students may gain an understanding of how the disciplines interact in the business environment and the economy*' (ibid., p. xxxi). (See also Amernic & Craig, Chapter 12 – this volume.)

Overall, the Mathews Report and its successor, the Cappelletto Report (2010), both point to mostly large-scale public universities in Australia, which are bureaucratic and inflexible in their policies and practices (Cappelletto Report, 2010). Like the Mathews Report, the Cappelletto Report has nothing positive to say about Australian accounting education. Cappelletto presents a litany of negatives, most prominent of which are:

- heavy staff workloads;
- reduced classroom standards;
- a cash-cow orientation;
- elevated expectations for an ageing academic staff;
- a decline in student quality, especially weak international students (whose tuition is fully funded by the government); and
- poor student communication skills. (See also Watty, Chapter 13 – this volume.)

Additionally, academic staff lack the autonomy to give failing grades to all the students who deserve them. Furthermore, research is far more highly regarded than is teaching. In 2010, minimum standards were set for all Australian bachelor's and master's degree programmes, including accounting, as a basis for government funding and expansion plans (*Drivers of Policy Change*, 2010).

14.3 The body of the chapter

The balance of this chapter analyzes two specific examples of integration:

- Accounting with finance courses based on what has been done in various universities in different jurisdictions, and what could be done.
- Sustainability as a theme in an undergraduate/graduate course on *International Financial Accounting and Reporting*, which is based on what has been done and what could be done by the author of this chapter at JCU.

Academic staff could do a much better job of connecting the dots between A & F, two disciplines closely intertwined in enterprise decision-making and in managing an organization. In stressing the supporting role of accounting in terms of furnishing a vast array of information for operating and financial management, emphasis should be placed on the interdisciplinary nature of these fields of endeavour, particularly on how accounting data are used. Case studies, group work, and team teaching would all be applied in the instructional delivery process within this programme.

Accordingly, this chapter examines this curriculum reform with a view to improving the instructional process in order to better position the students for their long-term careers in the wide realm of the accounting profession. Hence, this programme, which offers an integrative learning experience in a multi-disciplinary framework, is geared to future preparers, auditors, and analysts of accounting information. The degree of integration could vary. Some students may wish to emphasize accounting or finance and then pursue the other field. Other students may wish to take a full track of A & F courses. Still others may desire to pursue just specialty courses in either accounting or finance, while majoring in one field.

Sustainability integration could be brought to bear upon a combined undergraduate/graduate course in *International Financial Accounting and Reporting*, as the author of this chapter has done. The traditional objectives of this course have been for students to achieve an understanding of differences in financial accounting principles and practices from country to country. Students should be able to contrast and explain differences between the accounting principles of a particular country and International Financial Reporting Standards (IFRS). (See Wilson & Adler, 2012.) This module involves a comparative consideration of corporate sustainability reporting, examining how different cultures can affect social accountability reporting. This level of integration would accord with McComas' Level 2, with accounting being the core discipline underlying this course.

14.3.1 Integrating accounting and finance (A & F)

This initiative, which is in the exploratory phase at JCU and which may also be suitable for adoption at other universities in other jurisdictions, could enable our students to be well-qualified for leadership positions in the ever-expanding and complex field of accounting. As such, this course-of-study is intended to provide students with specialization in A & F, two closely related areas in business enterprise, over a five-year period. The programme would prepare students for long-term careers in public and managerial accounting, controllership, and financial management. While a number of students have expressed an interest in inter-disciplinary study, there is no such formal programme offered at JCU at this time. Instituting this programme would capitalize on our talent as educators in both areas and provide JCU with a special niche to attract high-calibre students from a larger geographic region. Beyond that, this programme is consistent with JCU's mission to promote critical thinking (see Cunningham, Chapter 18 – this volume), and analysis in order to develop responsible leaders in the business, government, and not-for-profit sectors.

The proposed programme would expose students to a comprehensive course-of-study, in both accounting and finance, giving students a user's perspective in financial and management information reporting, not just a preparer's or auditor's perspective as is currently the case in most undergraduate and graduate accounting programmes, including those at JCU. Students would benefit from studying accounting in an inter-disciplinary manner – whether pursuing this full-fledged programme or, if that is not possible, just taking additional course work – especially with respect to finance since neither subject is an isolated discipline. Auditors and managerial accountants need to understand a broader range of subjects than those provided in traditional accounting courses, including the valuation of enterprises and financial instruments such as derivatives. With this integration, students could better understand such interdisciplinary topics as present value analysis, capital budgeting, ratio analysis, and the cash flow statement (Leauby & Wentzel, 2012). Additionally, since the recent global financial crisis (GFC), other common themes have emerged in A & F courses, including:

- the moral hazard of short- versus long-term bonus arrangements;
- the nature of risk management; and
- how derivatives can be used and accounted for.

Reinforcement of the foregoing concepts in A & F courses should help the student remember and be able to apply them.

The students in the proposed programme at JCU would pursue the regular track of accounting courses as indicated in Table 14.1. Team or jointly taught courses, which can bring at least two different perspectives into the instructional framework, would include our existing course *Problems in Business Finance and Accounting*, the required capstone course in the finance major, which is case-driven and emphasizes financial statement analysis. This course could also stress valuation of the firm. Not enough emphasis is placed in finance courses, and virtually none in accounting courses, on valuing an enterprise in terms of sensitized accounting data and the role of intangibles in that valuation. The course could also place more emphasis than it currently does on the use of financial statement ratios in decision-making, as well as the impact of accounting changes on the financial statements.

Table 14.1 Curricular requirements

Sample Course Schedule (each course 3 hours a week for 15 weeks, including final examination)		
Junior Year (third year in a four year undergraduate programme)	Intermediate Accounting I Accounting Information Systems Business Finance	Intermediate Accounting II Cost Accounting Money and Banking Interdisciplinary Internship

Senior Year (fourth year)	Tax I
	Advanced Accounting
	Investments
	Intermediate Macroeconomics
	Intermediate Corporate
	   Finance
		Tax II
		Auditing
		Problems in Business Finance
		   and Accounting
		   (new course)
		Financial Statement Analysis &
		   Valuation (an existing finance
		   course, which can be retro-
		   fitted as a joint capstone
		   course)

Graduate Year (possible fifth year)	Government/Not-for-Profit
	   Accounting
	International Accounting
	   (an existing course-capstone)
	Portfolio Management
	Managing Financial Risk with
	   Derivatives (Finance,
	   Accounting, and Taxation)
		Controllership
		Fraud Examination
		Choice from:
		• International Finance,
		• Risk Management,
		• Real Estate Finance,
		• Sustainability Management
		   (the last being a new course)

Other possible new courses for undergraduate or graduate study	Behavioural Finance and
	   Accounting
	Capital Budgeting
	Corporate fraud
	Project Management
		Financial and Accounting
		   History
		Accounting, Finance, and
		   Income Taxation for Private
		   Companies

Controllership is a joint undergraduate and graduate elective course which also lends itself to team teaching and capstone status. The misuse of accounting data, especially the management of earnings (e.g. how deferred tax assets could be managed) is a principal theme of the course, which has required students to analyze rigorous business school cases on this subject. The students lack a clear conception of what controllers, chief financial officers (CFOs), and boards of directors do. Nor do they have a solid grasp of governmental regulations concerning financial reporting. This course could serve to fill in those gaps.

Another team-taught course could be the current course *Managing Financial Risk with Derivatives*. Currently this course covers the various types of derivatives and how they are used in hedging risk, including different models and metrics for determining the appropriate numbers. Case studies in which derivatives are applied in real-world business situations are analysed. This course could also include derivatives accounting.

A new team-taught capstone course in the A & F programme could be on *Sustainability*, involving several business disciplines and covering the comprehensive strategic impact that a firm would have by introducing a sustainability reporting framework such as the Global Research Initiative (GRI) and the UN Sustainability Framework. The course would cover the benefits and costs of adopting specific metrics in the realm of economics, the environment, and society, and may have a university listing, involving the arts and sciences academic staff and students as well as their business school counterparts. (For one perspective on a collaborative group sustainability project in a graduate accounting course, see Coulson & Thomson, 2006, pp. 261–273.)

It is envisioned that the A & F academic staff would eventually link up to develop at least one of the capstone courses in these disciplines, and perhaps engage in team-teaching. JCU would continue to pursue the traditional programme, which has produced many accomplished alumni in public and management accounting. The proposed programme would be geared to a sub-set of students who demonstrate the motivation, discipline, and talent to succeed in the double major or the major and concentration as undergraduate and graduate students. This programme should attract students to JCU who might not otherwise apply, but may be intrigued by the programme from recruiting advertisements.

As for potential drawbacks, this would be a very challenging course of study, beyond the capability of a number of JCU's current students. This programme would start out with a limited number of students. Additionally, this programme would entail additional work for academic accounting staff, given that it is inter-disciplinary in nature, including gaining the seamless cooperation of the academic finance staff for joint curriculum development and possible team teaching. Moreover, a number of academic staff feel overburdened as it is, and might be reluctant to consent to this proposed programme without guaranteed additional funding and staffing as well as released time to prepare the necessary teaching materials, plus graduate students to assist the academic staff involved. The key question is:

> *In an era of highly constrained resources, would this programme be a suitable means of deploying those resources?*

In the U.K., the University of Warwick, Cardiff University, and the University of Manchester all participate in an *Undergraduates Partnership Programme* with the Institute of Chartered Accountants in England & Wales (ICAEW), whereby students pursue a joint undergraduate degree in A & F and can undertake a year of accounting experience in an accounting firm or other company (*Undergraduate Partnership Programme*).

The University of Manchester offers foundation courses in accounting and finance during the first year. The student has the ability to specialize in particular subject areas in the remaining years of the programme. This is a flexible course of study which includes a significant array of courses in its joint A & F undergraduate programme.

The University of Manchester has an integrated A & F programme, in which the two groups of academic staff belong to a joint department. The programme includes courses in *Financial Statement Analysis, Auditing*, and *Corporate Governance*, all of which deal with risk analysis. Additionally, students can undertake a special accounting project course in their last undergraduate year, which can be interdisciplinary, for example, analyzing companies for possible inclusion in investment portfolios (Humphrey, pers. comm., 2013).

The London School of Economics (LSE) offers the following courses in its joint accounting/finance undergraduate degree programme:

- Introductory courses: economics, statistics and mathematics, principles of accounting, principles of banking and finance.
- Advanced courses: managerial economics, micro-economics, financial reporting, auditing, management accounting, financial management, and corporate finance (BSc Accounting and Finance).
- AC 100: *Accounting and Finance* is a required course at LSE consisting mostly of accounting topics with one small module in finance. All teaching and evaluation in the other courses are conducted by the separate departments (Baker, pers. comm., 2013).
- In the BSc Accounting and Finance programme, students actually take courses in both areas, but the accounting and finance staff all belong to one joint department.

In the U.K., '*[m]ost accredited programs are specialist undergraduate accounting degrees, sometimes joint honors degrees with other subjects often including finance (capital markets and business finance)*' (see Stoner & Sangster, 2013, p. 297).

In Australia, the minimum accounting standards for university courses are already somewhat integrated with finance (see Freeman & Hancock, 2009, p. 269). Furthermore, the three principal PABs in Australia promote a broad-based curriculum, so the combination of A & F would conform to their perspectives (see Jackling *et al.*, 2013, pp. 268–269). It should be noted that, in Australia, three years of supervised work experience in finance, accounting, or business is required in addition to an undergraduate degree to qualify for the CPA or CA designation. (See Calhoun & Karreman, Chapter 26 – this volume.) Accordingly, the specific recommendations delineated above for a proposed JCU A & F programme would be especially suitable for adoption in both the U.K. and Australia.

14.3.2 Sustainability integration in a single course

The second attempt to integrate the accounting curriculum incorporates a Sustainability Integration in a combined undergraduate and graduate course in *International Financial Accounting and Reporting*. The integration involves a comparative consideration of corporate sustainability reporting, examining how different cultures can affect financial and social accountability reporting. While sustainability can be considered to be a separate topic, it can also be viewed as an integrative feature in this course.

Sustainability involves the following goals:

- Protection and conservation of the environment.
- Enhancement of the capabilities of employees in the organization.

- Improvement in safety conditions in the workplace.
- Promotion of social and economic improvements in the community, including hiring and maintaining a diverse workforce and fostering human rights (Belkaoui, 1984; Belkaoui & Karpik, 1989, pp. 1–11; Gray, 1993, pp. 1–15; Riahi-Belkaoui, 1999; Fleischman & Schuele, 2006, pp. 35–36).

Since we live in a global village, multinational companies introduce and share socially responsible practices in their operating divisions in many countries, despite fundamental differences in cultures.

The integration includes assigned readings, case studies, and papers along with mostly interactive classroom instruction. Students taking this course come to realize that over-emphasis on short-run income, emphasizing the investor as the stakeholder while ignoring social considerations and other stakeholders, can be counter-productive, leading to lower long-run earnings. The students also achieve an understanding of the multi-dimensional aspects of corporate sustainability – not only maintaining the environment and conserving human resources, but also engaging in fair trade practices, promoting civil rights, and encouraging diversity.

I teach this integration as a 'guided seminar', presenting the material in an open discussion format. Subsequent to class discussion, the students break out into groups, each consisting of two to three members, to review their responses to the questions which they receive in advance as part of their homework assignment based on the readings. Thereafter, the entire class engages in discussion. Assignments include cases on sustainability. Besides the specific questions in each case, the students, again in groups, prepare a short paper analyzing the options available to the decision-maker in question. Their analysis is in terms of benefits and costs, justifying an option to pursue. Furthermore, each group of students selects a company from a different region in the world and evaluates its social accountability disclosures. Using the well-known Hofstede and Gray models, along with the Anglo-Saxon, Continental, Latin American, Mixed Market, and Islamic frameworks as described below (which were a principal aspect of this course even before the sustainability module was included), students analyze the culture of the country in which the firm is located and attempt to relate the culture to the nature of disclosures. For example, a number of students are surprised to find that issues on human rights, diversity, and labour management relations are included in supplemental social reports from companies in different countries. The students previously thought that sustainability only dealt with the physical environment, safety issues in the workplace, and human resource conservation.

The basic premiss underlying this integrative theme is that culture, which encompasses the traditional values in a society – its customs, economic, political, legal, and religious heritage – should be related to sustainability. Caring about the environment, conserving human resources, showing concern for workplace safety, paying attention to human rights, and diversity are all a function of societal values, which vary dramatically from country to country.

Hofstede, the Dutch management scholar, derived several cultural dimensions based on a survey study of employees at 50 centres within a multinational company – IBM (Hofstede, 1980). These are:

(a) individualism versus collectivism;
(b) large versus small power distance;
(c) strong versus weak uncertainty avoidance;
(d) masculinity versus femininity; and
(e) Confucian dynamism (which was not one of the original dimensions).

In contrast to the characteristics of Hofstede's model, the characteristics of Gray's model represent a hypothesized accounting cultural model, although there has been limited empirical research to confirm it (Gray, 1988, pp. 1–15). (See also Doupnik & Tsakumis, 2004, pp. 1–30.)

Gray set forth the following accounting cultural characteristics:

(a) statutory control versus professionalism;
(b) uniformity versus flexibility;
(c) conservatism versus optimism; and
(d) secrecy versus transparency.

It should be emphasized that neither Hofstede nor Gray has asserted that their respective societal values constitute a complete set. Like all models, Hofstede's and Gray's frameworks constitute attempts to simplify complex realities.

I request the students to integrate the Hofstede and Gray models in a specific exercise. Accordingly, the students attempt to link the two frameworks and explain the apparent relationships. The students debate the following issues inconclusively:

•   Does uniformity relate to anti-individualism?
•   Does uniformity reflect intolerance for accounting alternatives?
•   Does power distance pose a threat to 'outsiders'?
•   Does power distance lead to uniformity?
•   Is professionalism linked to individualism?
•   Does professionalism reflect a high threshold for uncertainty?
•   Does a short-term orientation reflect a high threshold for uncertainty?
•   Does a long-term orientation go hand-in-hand with conservatism, secrecy, and income smoothing practices?
•   Does professionalism reflect flexibility in professional judgement?

Some students have asserted that Hofstede's femininity and Gray's transparency are suitable proxies for sustainability reporting in a country. Several students have contended that long-term orientation and transparency go hand-in-hand with sustainability.

Next I attempt to relate the Hofstede and Gray models to the international accounting models covered in this course, which are:

(a) Anglo-Saxon
(b) Continental
(c) Latin American
(d) Mixed market
(e) Islamic.

The students and I analyze and compare the models in terms of their principal characteristics. (See Calhoun & Karreman, Chapter 26 – this volume.)

The Anglo-Saxon model, applicable primarily to English-speaking countries, is distinctive in its emphasis on preparing financial statements for decision-making. The main users represent a vast array of investors and creditors. The key source of financing is the stock market. The legal system is common law, in which settlements of court cases provide the foundation of the law. Because accounting principles and income tax regulations are essentially separate, traditionally there has been a strong accounting profession in most of the countries belonging to this model. Income smoothing occurs despite the emphasis on short-run rather than long-run earnings. While known for its innovativeness in financial reporting, this model has taken a back-seat until recently in sustainability reporting, which could be due to its traditional short-run orientation.

The Continental model views stewardship and accountability as being the main purpose of financial statements. The principal users are creditors, governments, investors, employees, and suppliers. By contrast with the Anglo-Saxon model, investors are not the main users in the Continental model because financing is primarily accomplished with bank loans and government grants in these countries. Disclosures in this model are typically limited, since the main users of financial statements have been primarily large banks and government agencies, having ready access to the companies. Other characteristics of accounting in this model include an emphasis on conservatism in financial reporting because that is what bankers prefer. Also, in the light of the socialistic countries among its members, this model is known for innovativeness in sustainability reports accompanying, if not incorporated into, financial reports. Several European countries, in fact, require green disclosures. In some European countries, employees play a considerable role in enterprise governance, given the influence which trades unions have.

The Latin American model closely resembles its Continental counterpart since Spain and Portugal, two Continental countries, colonized Latin America. However, two prominent differences between the Continental and Latin American models are that the main users in the latter include wealthy land owners, and the Latin American model is known for innovativeness in accounting for inflation. In contrast to the Continental model, there is little concern for business sustainability and a lack of transparency in financial reporting (e.g. pertaining to environmental pollution) in Latin America. There is rampant corruption in business and environmental degradation in those countries, as ethics takes a back seat to wealth generation (Arruda, 1997, pp. 1529–1538).

The Mixed Market model includes China, Russia and other former member countries of the USSR, as well as former Warsaw Pact countries. Traditionally, the government was the sole user of financial statements of enterprises in these countries. That is no longer the case. In recent years, some countries (e.g. China), have received significant funding from the World Bank and the International Monetary Fund (IMF) to develop International Accounting Standards Board (IASB) standards. The extent and nature of disclosures have expanded. There seems to be little concern for corporate sustainability in this model compared to its Latin American counterpart. Limited disclosures appear in the financial statements and accompanying notes. Nevertheless, the ideas of Confucius have traditionally influenced ethics in China and Japan, among other countries in the Pacific Rim (Bloom & Solotko, 2003, pp. 27–40).

The Islamic model emphasizes religion, which permeates all aspects of society. Accounting, as in the Continental and Mixed Market models, is clearly conservative. Each business enterprise is required to contribute to charities. The government (which regulates accounting) and banks are the principal sources of funds for enterprise development. Hence, there is no need for extensive disclosures in the financial reports. The accounting profession is weak as accounting and tax requirements are similar. In Islamic countries, there is an emphasis on trust and honesty in business transactions (Wilson, 2006, p. 9), and an emphasis on charitable giving since the rich are viewed as being trustees for the public rather than owners of the wealth which they have amassed (Uddin, 2003, pp. 23–32).

I taught this course most recently in the Summer of 2013. Half the students taking it were undergraduate accounting majors, who needed it to fulfil an advanced elective requirement in the accounting programme prior to graduation. During this term, I emphasized for the first time in this course the global reporting initiative (GRI) template in covering the sustainability of international companies. In 2000, the GRI issued a framework for reporting voluntarily on sustainability, which it modified in 2006, and has done so again in 2013, to facilitate comparability in reporting on this subject matter. While more and more major global companies are using this template, most companies are keeping their GRI reports separate from their annual reports. Additionally, many companies producing GRI reports are pursuing third-party reviews of their reports from consulting or accounting firms in terms of compliance with the GRI.

To evaluate the Sustainability component in the *International Financial Reporting and Accounting* course in the Summer of 2007, 2008, and 2010, I used a pre-course and post-course question-naire. In this manner, we could test whether students had any pre-conceived notions about Sustainability. Overall, the 25 students believed it was important to include information on this subject in annual reports, so that shareholders and other users could properly analyze the total performance of the companies. The students also took a broader view of the role of Sustainability after I covered the subject matter in class than before in terms of recognizing its significance as an important business strategy, not simply for public relations purposes. Most students felt that failure to reflect Sustainability information in annual reports would be detrimental to the company's image and long-term profitability.

During the Summer of 2013, I had 10 students in the international course, and I covered the GRI as planned, which calls for significant disclosures of Sustainability measures in the economic, environmental, and social realms. However, a few of the students felt that the GRI did not highlight the negative aspects of company performance in each of those realms. Further-more, some of the students were disappointed that American-based companies were generating Sustainability reports which were inferior to their European counterparts in terms of depth and breadth of coverage.

14.3.3 Applying sustainability and integration in general in the U.K. and Australia

Sustainability and ethics are two disciplines gaining considerable importance in professional education syllabi in the U.K. as promoted by three principal PABs: the Association of Chartered Certified Accountants (ACCA), the ICAEW, and the Institute of Chartered Accountants of Scotland (ICAS).

As in the U.S.A., there appears to be a significant gulf between academic and professional preparation for a career in accounting in the U.K. Ethics (see Boyce, Chapter 24 – this volume) is not given the emphasis it should have in accounting programmes in the U.K. (Agrizzi *et al.*, n.d.). There is also scant attention paid to the application of technology in accounting instruction (see Boritz & Stoner, Chapter 16 – this volume). Overall, the relationship between the six PABs and university accounting programmes is not clearly defined in terms of the specific roles of each party. However, the PABs play a role in the accreditation of U.K. accounting programmes in terms of approving programmes for their general curricula unlike their American counterparts which play no role at all in this process. Each PAB has its own examination and professional training programme. (See Stoner & Sangster, 2013, pp. 295–297; Evans, Chapter 28 – in this volume; Evans *et al.*, 2012; Wilson, 2009, pp. 467–469.)

Furthermore, there have been no recent academic or practice commissions such as the Solomons Report (1974) on the state of accounting education in the U.K. (See Calhoun & Karreman, Chapter 26 – this volume.) Since most professionally-qualified accountants in the U.K. have not studied accounting as undergraduates, they may be better prepared in terms of diverse backgrounds for the broad accounting discipline than those who did. PABs in the U.K. (and especially the ICAEW) encourage individuals without relevant degrees to pursue accounting careers. That is hardly the case in the U.S.A. (Pathways Commission, 2012, pp. 40–41).

Additionally, undergraduate accounting education in U.K. universities does not involve direct preparation for professional examinations (as is the case in the U.S.A. in relation to the CPA examination) since an accounting degree is not required to sit for professional examinations in the U.K. However, there are reductions (i.e. exemptions – see Apostolou & Gammie, Chapter 29 – this volume) in the total examination requirements offered by the different PABs (such as ACCA, ICAEW, ACCA and ICAS). ICAEW has been encouraging universities to use its ACA learning syllabi and professional stage examinations as part of their accounting degree programmes in what it calls a *Partner in Learning Scheme* ('HEW Higher Education Partnerships', 2008).

While internships are not usually a part of educational programmes, a training period of at least three years either in public or corporate accounting is required for a candidate to complete his/her certification eligibility (see Hassall & Joyce, Chapter 17; Beard & Humphrey, Chapter 25; and Evans, Chapter 28 – all in this volume). To qualify as a professional accountant, apart from the on-the-job training, the student is required to pursue a rigorous set of courses geared to the professional examinations which are taken in the years following their university studies. This examination encompasses two stages: professional and advanced. Quite desirably, the advanced stage requires a multi-disciplinary approach to accounting in terms of integrating taxation, audit, financial reporting, management, and finance in a case context (see Calhoun & Karreman, Chapter 26 – this volume).

Despite the issues associated with accounting education in Australia, innovative instruction along the lines presented in this chapter conceivably makes sense. Doing something different (such as team teaching) across subject areas might motivate both the academic staff and students to enhance the scope and quality of accounting education. This could be an antidote to the international students' request for rote learning as observed in the Cappelletto Report (2010). That minimum standards have been set for Australian education programmes provides an incentive for accounting programmes to stand out, so as to be better funded and expanded. (See *Emerging Pathways for the Next Generation of Accountants*.)

As might be expected from the Cappelletto Report, the *Introductory Accounting* course at Australian universities (with particular regard to its objectives, content, teaching strategies, and assessments) reflects little evidence of innovation (Palm & Bisman, 2012). In Australia, it may be advisable to introduce visiting academic staff (perhaps from other countries) with innovative teaching ideas who understand Australian culture to spark interest in redesigning accounting curricula. Using the accounting/finance and sustainability integration as recommended in this chapter might encourage capable students in Australia to major in accounting rather than pursue other degrees first and then gravitate into professional accounting. It appears that such creative students shy away from accounting as they perceive this discipline to be too procedural for their tastes (see Sugahara *et al.*, 2008).

The minimum academic standards that have been set for Australian bachelor and master's degrees in accounting in 2010 are based on the new demand-driven funding of public educational institutions (Freeman & Hancock, 2011, pp. 265–273). In 2011, a pilot project was launched, including one-quarter of the country's universities offering accounting education, to evaluate the actual outcomes of graduating students against national standards. Five threshold learning outcomes that were set for accounting are:

- judgement
- knowledge
- application skills
- communication and teamwork, and
- self-management.

Bachelor graduates in Accounting will be able to exercise judgment under supervision to solve routine accounting problems in straightforward contexts using social, ethical, economic, regulatory and global perspectives.

(Freeman & Hancock, 2009, p. 269)

Routine accounting problems include the recording and analysis of transactions, application of accounting standards in financial reporting, business operations analysis, and financial projections. These problems are further decomposed into, for example, for financial projection: '*analysis of historical trends for budgeting, analysis of financial ratios for investing decisions, assessing solvency, or raising funds, analysis of cash flow from operations, and analysis of financial risks*' (ibid.). In the light of those expectations, accounting courses in Australia would seem to be somewhat integrated already with finance. Additionally, the three primary PABs – known as the Joint Accounting Bodies, in similar fashion to their counterparts in the U.K. – play an oversight role in the accreditation process. To attract a diversity of graduates to their memberships, they seek a broad-based curriculum with a solid core rather than dictating the specific content of each course in the programmes. (See Jackling *et al.*, 2013, pp. 268–269.)

14.4 Conclusion

Many issues in the study of business are multi-disciplinary, transcending traditional departmental boundary lines, including examples such as health care, sustainability, mergers and acquisitions, and climate change. Hence, the need exists for integrative courses to avoid the insularity of single disciplinary curricula. That is why this chapter has focussed on two areas as illustrations of accounting course integration: a joint A & F programme and the infusion of Sustainability in to the *International Financial Accounting and Reporting* course.

The integration framework delineated in this chapter involves clearly setting forth the aims of the courses in question, each of which should fulfil a specific need. The topics and concepts to be covered should follow the ILOs of each course. Particular subjects – such as cost-volume-profit analysis, present valuation, and internal rate of return, fair valuation approaches, budgeting, ratio analysis, performance evaluation, firm valuation, dividend policy, and capital structure – straddle the border between A & F courses, and are often taught in both sets of courses.

In designing curricula, the point is to ensure coverage, but to avoid unnecessary redundancy, repeating the same coverage in different courses across departments. Ethics and sustainability, as examples, should be taught from different perspectives in A & F courses. So it is desirable for accounting and finance academic staff to link up to decide how to present those subjects without superfluous overlap. The Business School Dean may have to step in to encourage two different groups of academic staff such as these to collaborate on this matter. In those universities in which A & F are in the same department, intervention by the Dean will generally not be necessary. In any case, academic accounting staff may decide to introduce those concepts while academic finance staff could provide particular applications in short or long case studies for the students to analyze and resolve.

As for general guidance on course design, I recommend starting with specific ILOs for each course and then going to particular course requirements followed by the specification of textbooks, reading, and other resources. (See Stevenson *et al.*, Chapter 19 – this volume.) Upper-level courses in A & F, as far as ILOs go, may be geared to helping students transition from academic work to employment. Skills to be developed in those courses might include: researching, decision-making, and reporting.

In the final analysis, there are several factors which are conducive to integrative curriculum reform, including a supportive administration, financial incentives, harmony among academic staff, and an eagerness on the part of the academic staff to foster promising changes. Unfortunately, departmentalization in universities, illustrated by separating Accounting from Finance, promotes curricular insularity, treating each discipline as being solitary. Achieving integration is problematic since it entails closer rapport among the academic staff in different departments in terms of preparing teaching materials and team teaching. Many accounting and other business educators would be uncomfortable in the integration process, lengthening their course preparation time and distracting them from research endeavours. Academic staff would worry about losing their independence and control of their courses. (See Exhibit 14.1 for general guidance on developing, launching, and assessing an integrated curriculum.)

Exhibit 14.1 Steps in developing and launching an integrated curriculum

1　A chairperson or senior member of the academic staff should take the lead in this endeavour, requesting interested representatives from the academic staff in different disciplines to meet to discuss course integration. Appropriate administrators (e.g. the School of Business Dean) should also be invited in order to secure their approval – in terms of offering possible financial incentives and released time from teaching and student-advising to pursue the integration.

2　The 'integration' group has to decide whether the proposed idea can go forward and, if so, how the group will function, who is expected to do what (the responsibility of each member of the group), when, and how often it will meet as a whole and/or in sub-groups. The group should set a timetable for the planning, implementation, and assessments of the integration project.

3　The group should formulate the ILOs of the integrative curriculum, and then proceed from there to decide on the specific courses that are needed to fulfil the ILOs. Academic staff from more than one discipline should volunteer to develop the individual courses collaboratively, starting with specific ILOs for each course and moving on to specifying the specific textbooks and assignments, which should conform to the overall ILOs of the programme and be approved by the group as a whole.

4　The group should: make periodic progress reports on planning, implementation, and assessment to the participating departments; attend department meetings; and report progress to the appropriate administrators.

5　The group should be candid with academic colleagues and administrators who are not involved in this project regarding problems and issues that occur in all aspects of this endeavour, and about what can be done to resolve those difficulties.

6　Prior to full implementation of the integration, it is desirable to pilot the integration perhaps in a few courses with just a few academic staff from the group to evaluate how the project is faring relative to plans, and to make the necessary changes in a timely fashion.

This chapter has provided two specific examples of integrating the accounting curriculum – one on a joint A & F programme, and the other on incorporating Sustainability into an *International Financial Accounting and Reporting* course. Moreover, the chapter has outlined a broad-brush framework for developing and implementing an integrative curriculum.

References

Accounting Education Change Commission (1990) *Objectives of Education for Accountants. Position Statement No. 1*, Sarasota, FL: American Accounting Association.

Academics/Ethics at Babson (2010) Available at: http://www3.babson.edu/, academics/ethics.cfm.

Agrizzi, D., Sikka, P., Haslam, C., & Kuriacou, O. *The State of UK Professional Accountancy Education: Professionalism Claims*. Available at: http://eprints.soton.ac.uk/37022/1/CRAAG-05-09.pdf.

Albrecht, S. & Sack, R. (2000) *Accounting Education: Charting a Course through a Perilous Future*, Sarasota, FL: American Accounting Association.

Al-Khatib, C., Robertson, A., D'Auria, S., & Vitell, S. (2002) Business ethics in the Arab Gulf States: a three-country study, *International Business Review*, 11(1), 97–111.

Amadei, B. & Sandekian, R. (2010) Model of integrating humanitarian development into engineering education, *Journal of Professional Issues in Engineering Education & Practice*, 136 (2), 84–92.

American Accounting Association; Bedford Committee on the Future Structure, Context, and Scope of Accounting Education (1986) Future accounting education: preparing for the expanded profession, *Issues in Accounting Education*, 1(1), 168–195.

Arruda, M.C. (1997) Business ethics in Latin America, *Journal of Business Ethics*, 16(14), 1529–1538.

Baker, R.J. (2013) Email to the author on LSE BSc accounting and finance programme, (accessed 23 January 2013).

Baldwin, J.N. & Chesser, D.L. (2003) An approach to integrating accounting courses, *Journal of Accounting Education*, 21(2), 101–126.

Barrett, D. (2013) Double majors produce dynamic thinkers, study finds, *The Chronicle of Higher Education*, (accessed 15 March).

Bartelmus, P. & Seifert, E. (eds) (2003) *Green Accounting*, Hants: Ashgate.

Beattie, V. & Smith, S.J. (2012) *Today's Ph.D. Students: Is There a Future Generation of Accounting Academics or Are They a Dying Breed? A UK Perspective*, Edinburgh: ICAS.

Beekun, R. & Badawi, J. (2005) Balancing ethical responsibility among multiple organizational stakeholders: the Islamic perspective, *Journal of Business Ethics*, 60(2), 131–145.

Belkaoui, A. (1984) *Socio-Economic Accounting*, Westport, CT: Quorum Books.

Belkaoui, A. & Karpik, P. (1989) Determinants of the corporate decision to disclose social information. *Accounting, Auditing and Accountability Journal*, 2(1), 1–11.

Berleant, A. (1982) Multinationals, local practice, and the problem of ethical consistency, *Journal of Business Ethics*, 1(3), 185–193.

Bloom, R. & Solotko, J. (2003) The foundation of Confucianism in Chinese and Japanese accounting, *Accounting, Business & Financial History*, 13(1), 27–40.

Bloom, R. & Webinger, M. (2011a) Contextualizing the financial crisis in the intermediate accounting courses, *Accounting Education: an international journal*, 20(5), 469–494.

Bloom, R. & Webinger, M. (2011b) Rejoinder to 'Contextualizing the Financial Crisis in the Intermediate Accounting Courses', *Accounting Education: an international journal*, 20(5), 529–537.

Broberg, M. (1996) Corporate social responsibility in the European Communities: the Scandinavian viewpoint, *Journal of Business Ethics*, 15(6), 615-622.

BSc Accounting and Finance (2013) Undergraduate. Available at: http://www2.lse.ac.uk/study/undergraduate/degreeProgrammes2013/accounting AndFinance/NN34_BSc_accfin.aspx.

Cappelletto, G. (2010) *Challenges Facing Accounting Education in Australia*, Sydney: AFAANZ, CPA Australia, AICA, NIA. Available at: http://afaanz.org.

Cardiff University, *Degree Programmes*. Available at: http://business.cardiff.ac.uk/degree-programmes (accessed 31 March 2013).

Carruthers, D.F. & Peterson, D. (2010) Integrating a social justice perspective in economics education: creating a distinctly Catholic education, *Catholic Education: A Journal of Inquiry & Practice*, 13(4), 415–436.

Chatterjee, S.R. & Pearson, C. (2003) Ethical perceptions of Asian managers: evidence of trends in six divergent national contexts, *Business Ethics: A European Review*, 12(2), 203–211.

Chen, H. & Volpe, R.P. (2004) Integrating finance in certified public accounting education: a comparative analysis of CPA practice and education in the US and China, *Academy of Education Leadership Journal*, 8(2), 87–134.

Coulson, A. & Thomson, I. (2006) Accounting and sustainability, encouraging a dialogical approach; integrating learning activities, delivery mechanisms and assessment strategies. *Accounting Education*, 15(3), 261–273.

Dewing, I. & Russell, P. (2012) Accounting education and research: Zeff's warnings reconsidered, *British Accounting Review*, 30(3), 203–212.

Doupnik, T. & Tsakumis, G. (2004) A critical review of the tests of Gray's theory of cultural relevance and suggestions for future research, *Journal of Accounting Literature*, 23, 1–30.

Drivers of Policy Change (2010) *The Accountability for Quality Agenda in Higher Education*, 2010. 22. Available at: http://www.go8.edu.au/__documents/go8-policy- analysis/2010/accountability-for-quality-agenda/2_drivers.pdf (accessed 3 January 2013).

Emerging Pathways for the Next Generation of Accountants, Available at: http://www.unisa.edu.au/Global/business/centres/cags/docs/Emerging%20pathways%20for%20the%20next%20generation%20of% 20accountants.pdf (accessed 22 January 2013).

Evans, E., Juchau, R., & Wilson, R.M.S. (Eds.) (2012) *The Interface of Accounting Education and Professional Training*, Abingdon: Routledge.

Fleischman, R. & Schuele, K. (2006) Green accounting: a primer, *Journal of Accounting Education*, 24(1), 35–66.

Ford, J.D. & Riley, L.A. (2003) Integrating communication and engineering education: a look at curricula, courses, and support systems. *Journal of Engineering Education*, 92(4), 325–328.

Freeman, M. & Hancock, P. (2009) Future of accounting education, *Australian Accounting Review*, 19(3), 249–260.

Freeman, M. & Hancock, P. (2011) A brave new world: Australian learning outcomes in accounting education, *Accounting Education: an international journal*, 20(3), 265–273.

Global Research Initiative available at: www.globalreporting.org (accessed 31 March 2013).

Gray, R., Bebbington, J. & Walters, D. (1993) *Accounting for the Environment*, Princeton, NJ: Markus Wiener Publishers.

Gray, S. J. (1988) Towards a theory of cultural influence on the development of accounting systems internationally, *Abacus*, 24(1), 1–15.

Hazelton, J. & Haigh, M. (2010) Incorporating sustainability into accounting curricula: lessons learned from an action research studying, *Accounting Education: an international journal*, 19(1–2), 159–178.

Hancock, P., Nowieson, B., Kavanagh, M., Kent, J., Tempone, I., Segal, N., & Freeman, M. (2009) The roles of some key stakeholders in the future of accounting education in Australia, *Australian Accounting Review*, 50(19), 249–260.

Hofstede, G. (1980) *Culture's Consequences*, London: Sage.

Humphrey, C. (2013) Email to the author, 24 January.

Jackling, B., deLange, P., & Natoli, R. (2013) Transitioning to IFRS in Australian classrooms: impact on teaching approaches, *Issues in Accounting Education*, 28(2), 263–275.

Kumar, K. & Thibodeaux, M. (1998) Differences in value systems of Anglo-American and Far Eastern students: effects of American business education, *Journal of Business Ethics*, 17(3), 253–262.

Leauby, B. & Wentzel, K. (2012) Linking management accounting and finance: assessing student perceptions, *Management Accounting Quarterly*, 13(2), 14–20.

Linowes, D. (1968) Development of socio-economic accounting, *Journal of Accountancy*, November, 62–65.

Lister, R.J. (2010) A role for the compulsory study of literature in accounting education, *Accounting Education: an international journal*, 19(4), 329–344.

Mathews, R., Jackson, M., & Brown, P. (1990) *Accounting in Higher Education: Report of the Review of the Accounting Discipline in Higher Education*, Canberra: Australian Government Publishing Service, Department of Employment, Education and Training.

McCarthy, P.A. & McCarthy, H.M. (2006) When case studies are not enough: integrating experiential learning into business curricula, *Journal of Education for Business*, 81(4), 201–204.

McComas, W.F. (2009) Thinking, teaching and learning: science outside the boxes, *Science Teacher*, 76(2), 24–28.

New Higher Education Partnerships (2008) *Accounting Magazine* (AU), October, p. 87.

Palm, C.Y. & Bisman, J. (2012) Benchmarking introductory accounting curricula: experience from Australia, *Accounting Education: an international journal*, 19(1–2), 179–201.

Parker, R.H. (1995) David Solomons and British accounting, *Accounting and Business Research*, 25, 311–314.

Pathways Commission (2012) *Charting a National Strategy for the Next Generation of Accountants*, Sarasota, FL: AAA, and New York: AICPA.

Riahi-Belkaoui, A. (1999) *Corporate Social Awareness and Financial Outcomes*, Westport, CT: Greenwood Publishing Group.

Sangster, A. & Wilson, R.M.S. (eds) (2012) *Liberalising the Accounting Curriculum in University Education*, Abingdon: Routledge.

Solomons, D., with Berridge, T. (1974) Prospectus for a profession: the report of the long ranges enquiry into education and training for the accountancy profession, *Advisory Board of Accountancy Education*, London: Gee and Co.

Stoner, G. & Sangster, A. (2013) Teaching IFRS in the U.K.: contrasting experiences from both sides of the university divide, *Issues in Accounting Education*, 28(2), 291–307.

Sugahara, S., Boland, S., & Cilloni, A. (2008) Factors influencing students' choice of an accounting major in Australia, *Accounting Education: an international journal*, 17 (Supplement 1), 537–554.

The Association of Chartered Accountants, available at: http://www.acaus.org/.

The Institute of Chartered Accountants in England and Wales, available at: http://www.icaew.com/ (accessed 22 January 2013).

The Institute of Chartered Accountants of Scotland, available at: http://icas.org.uk/default.aspx (accessed 22 January 2013).

Turner, L.E. (2006) Learning from accounting history: will we get it right this time? *Issues in Accounting Education*, 14(3), 383–407.

Uddin, S.J. (2003) Understanding the framework of business in Islam in an era of globalization: a review, *Business Ethics: A European Review*, 12(1), 23–32.

Undergraduate Partnership Programme (UPP) Undergraduate Partnership Programme. Available at: http://careers.icaew.com/school-students-leavers/Entry-routes/University-and-higher-education/ Undergraduate-Partnership-Programme (accessed 31 January 2013).

University of Manchester, available at: www.manchester.ac.uk/undergraduate/coursessearch2012atoz/ course/ ?code=051518pg=all (accessed 31 January 2013).

University of Warwick, available at: www2.warwick.ac.uk/study/undergraduate/courses/deptaZZ/ ubs/nn34 (accessed 31 January 2013).

Watty, K., Jackling, B., & Wilson, R.M.S. (eds) (2012) *Personal Transferable Skills in Accounting Education*, Abingdon: Routledge.

Wiese, N.M. & Sherman, D.J. (2011) Integrating marketing and environmental studies through an interdisciplinary, experiential, service-learning approach. *Journal of Marketing Education*, 33(1), 41–56.

Wilson, R. (2006) Islam and business. *Thunderbird International Business Review*, 48(1), 109.

Wilson, R.M.S. (2009) Editorial. *Accounting Education: an international journal*, 18(4–5), 467–469.

Wilson, R.M.S. & Adler, R.W. (eds) (2012) *Teaching IFRS*, Abingdon: Routledge.

About the author

Robert Bloom is the KPMG Professor of Accountancy at the Boler School of Business, John Carroll University, Ohio, U.S.A. (rbloom@jcu.edu). He has also taught at a number of other universities in the U.S.A., Canada, the U.K., China, and Croatia. The author/editor of nine books, he has contributed extensively in the international academic and professional accounting literature. His current research interests pertain to accounting education – with emphasis on the global financial crisis and sustainability.

15

Emerging areas within the accounting curriculum

Alan Sangster

GRIFFITH UNIVERSITY, AUSTRALIA

CONTENTS

Abstract

This chapter investigates changes that are occurring in the accounting curriculum and the factors that are driving these changes. It does so by taking a snapshot of accounting education in 21 different countries from around the world. The result of this analysis is an image of change driven in many instances by changes in accounting regulation, by the requirements of the accounting profession, and by changes in the environment in which accounting operates. A sense of a common driving force is found in many cases, although national efficiency drivers are noticeable factors in some cases.

Keywords

curriculum, curriculum trends, drivers of change in the curriculum, future curriculum, international comparisons

15.1 Introduction

The main aims of this chapter[1] are to identify:

* current trends in the accounting curriculum on a global basis;
* the direction in which the curriculum is moving; and
* the drivers of change in the accounting curriculum.

It is generally acknowledged that the roots of modern accounting can be traced to thirteenth-century merchants in Northern Italy and, in particular, to Florence, Genoa, and Venice (De Roover, 1945; Lee, 1977). Classroom education in accounting, while commonplace today, was rare at that time, though some classroom instruction in accounting for debtors and creditors was evident in Pisa in the early thirteenth century (Zervas, 1975). Around the mid-fifteenth century, double-entry bookkeeping, while mainly learnt in the workplace, was also increasingly taught in the classroom (Arlinghaus, 2004), with the first known school text on the topic dating from 1475.

At that time, accounting was a craft skill, a technical subject which served as the means to monitor debtors, creditors, and cash. There were no equivalents of accounting standards, nor even a uniform approach to how accounting was performed. This all began to change with the printing in 1494 of Luca Pacioli's Venetian didactic treatise on double-entry bookkeeping. The method he described was widely copied and became the *de facto* standard for how to maintain accounts. With the availability of this and other printed classroom texts, over the following centuries, classroom education in accounting became increasingly available in the mercantile centres of Europe. As in its beginning, it was then and always has been focussed upon preparing students of accounting to *be* accountants, not to *become* accountants – accounting educators in general focus upon providing students of accounting with specific technical skills that they will use in the role of accountants.

Even when accounting was added to university curricula in the U.S.A. in the mid-nineteenth century, this did not change. A call issued by the American Accounting Association's *Accounting Education Change Commission* (AECC) in 1990, which encouraged accounting educators to change their focus towards educating their students to *become* accountants, while given much attention, did little to alter academic practice. The focus continued and continues to range from preparation of a trial balance to preparation of financial statements, to processing accruals and applying the rules as laid down in accounting standards in arriving at the amounts to include in financial statements.

Shifting to the present, there is today much emphasis upon technical matters, such as International Financial Reporting Standards (IFRS), and arguably too little emphasis upon fostering the growth of transferable skills and a capacity for life-long learning among our graduates. (But see St.Pierre & Rebele, Chapter 5 – this volume, for an alternative perspective.) Many perceive that the profession drives our curriculum innovations and, in countries such as the U.K., Australia, and New Zealand, where the accreditation of degree programmes is a means for graduates to shorten and/or minimise further study during the post-graduation route to becoming qualified members of a professional accounting body (PAB), this is particularly dominant in any discussion of curriculum change but, to date, no research has been undertaken into the global picture. (See Apostolou & Gammie, Chapter 29 – this volume, for a discussion of the impact of accreditation on accounting education.)

This chapter seeks to address this information gap by soliciting the views on the future of the accounting curriculum of 21 experienced accounting educators from across the world. In the following pages, the background, present position, and future direction of accounting education is identified across three countries from each of seven geographic regions (as shown in the Contents).

It is a rich view, and one that has some sobering implications. As to where to begin, classroom teaching of double-entry bookkeeping dates from the fifteenth century, but it was not the only accounting method in use at that time. In India, the Bahi-Khata system has been claimed to be much older (Lall Nigam, 1986) and, in Turkey, the Stairs Method and its instruction certainly predates the Italian system we all now use today, with instructional texts surviving from the fourteenth century (Elitaş *et al.*, 2008). However, many Egyptian accounting fragments have survived, dating from the eleventh century (Scorgie, 1994), suggesting some education in accounting was likely to have been taking place there at that time. For this reason, we start our review of emerging areas within the accounting curriculum in the Middle East.

References

Accounting Education Change Commission (1990) Objectives of education for accountants: position statement number one, *Issues in Accounting Education*, 5(2), 307–312.

Arlinghaus, F.-J. (2004) Bookkeeping, double-entry bookkeeping, in Kleinhenz, C. (ed.) *Medieval Italy: An Encyclopedia*, Vol. 1, New York: Routledge, pp. 147–150.

De Roover, R. (1945) New perspectives on the history of accounting, *The Accounting Review*, 30(3), 405–420.

Elitaş, C., Aydemir, O., Özcan, U., Güvemli, O., Erkan, M., & Oğuz, M. (2008) *Accounting Method used by Ottomans for 500 Years: Stairs (Merdiban) Method*, Ankara: Turkish Republic Ministry of Finance Strategy Development Unit.

Lee, G.A. (1977) The coming of age of double entry: the Giovanni Farolfi ledger of 1299–1300, *Abacus*, 4(2), 79–95.

Lall Nigam, B.M. (1986) Bahi-Khata: the pre-Pacioli double-entry system of bookkeeping, *Abacus*, 22(2), 148–161.

Pacioli, L. (1494) *Summa de Arithmetica Geometria Proportioni et Proportionalita*, Venice: Paganino de Paganini.

Scorgie, M.E. (1994) Accounting fragments stored in the Old Cairo Genizah, *Accounting Business and Financial History*, 4(1), 29–41.

Zervas, D.F. (1975) The Trattato dell' Abbaco and Andrea Pisano's design for the Florentine Baptistery door, *Renaissance Quarterly*, 28(4), 483–503.

15.2 The Middle East

15.2.1 Current issues in Egyptian accounting education

Ibrahim O. Shahin

HELWAN UNIVERSITY, EGYPT (IOSHAHIN@YAHOO.COM)

15.2.1.1 Introduction

The Egyptian accounting education system is perhaps the oldest in the world, and the following topics have – or are currently having – significant impacts on the content of many accounting research theses and on the curricula of relevant under-graduate and post-graduate courses.

15.2.1.2 The Uniform Accounting System

This topic drove the syllabus of accounting programmes for many years. It arose when, to meet the requirements of a policy of national central planning, a Uniform Accounting System (UAS) for the government-owned (business) sector was adopted in 1966. The UAS consists mainly of a uniform chart of accounts and financial statements redesigned in a manner that could serve both financial accounting, budgeting, and central planning requirements (State Audit Organisation, 1966). Thereafter, *Financial Accounting* and *Management Accounting* courses started including various relevant aspects of the study of UAS; and several PhD and MA theses have also focussed on the study of UAS. However, a new open-door policy (adopted in the mid-1970s) resulted in a decrease in the size of the public sector and, consequently, a decrease in the importance of UAS. In the early-1990s, a new policy of privatization (i.e. selling-off the public sector gradually to non-governmental individuals and/or organizations) has resulted finally in reducing the UAS. It is currently being taught in some courses on a limited scale – mainly as accounting history.

15.2.1.3 International Accounting and Auditing Standards

In 1997, Egypt adopted both the International Financial Reporting Standards (IFRS) and the International Standards on Auditing (ISA). This has resulted in increased interest in both types of standards in both *Financial Accounting* and Auditing courses. They had been studied with great interest before, and included in relevant curricula. However, after 1997, the interest increased and researchers started investigating various issues relating to these standards.

Each new revision has caused a good deal of academic and professional interest, and a relevant revision to the curriculum.

15.2.1.4 The Global Financial Crises

Two financial issues have caused a shock wave of events throughout the world. Both had significant impacts on the Accounting and Auditing disciplines in Egypt:

- The Sarbanes-Oxley Act (SOX) (2002) was covered in detail in many textbooks and included in all relevant *Auditing* courses (Shahin, 2005, pp. 322–328). It has also been the subject of many research studies. Furthermore, some new regulations similar to SOX regulations were issued.
- A surge of interest has emerged regarding what is being referred to as 'Creative Accounting' (Abozir, 2010). This interest is reflected in the Financial Accounting and Auditing areas in both course curricula and research topics.

These topics will feature more in the Egyptian curriculum over the coming years.

References

Abozir, A.I. (2010) The impact of creative accounting practices on the quality of financial statement information, *Journal of Accounting Thought*, 2(1), 31–45.

Shahin, I.O. (2005) *Auditing Studies and Case Studies: A Behavioural Approach* 7th edn, Cairo: Helwan University, Egypt.

State Audit Organisation (1966) *The Uniform Accounting System (UAS)*, Cairo.

15.2.2 Collaborative accounting education: the case of Kuwait

Wael I. Al-Rashed

KUWAIT UNIVERSITY (PROFALRASHED@GMAIL.COM)

Accounting education in Kuwait is offered by the only state university in the country, and commenced in 1966, provided by the College of Business Administration (CBA) as a full-time degree programme over four years. Since the late-1990s, the accounting programme is set and periodically reviewed by the CBA within an accreditation process, and academic excellence has been seen as a priority. For the first time since the inception of the accounting programme, in 2009, the CBA introduced an exit examination process. Results reveal some areas of concern that require more attention, such as:

- the shallow technical knowledge of graduates in accounting;
- poor use of advanced accounting systems and software; and
- poor inter-disciplinary research among students of different fields of study.

There is also poor competency in English across the CBA's intakes. Demographically, there is a shifting gender balance with a large and ever-growing proportion of female students. Yet the most remarkable trend in accounting education in Kuwait is an increasing tendency among students towards more quantitative subjects as a result of their questionable ability at verbal expression. This is clearly in evidence in *Financial Accounting* and *Corporate Accounting* courses where grades tend to be, in relative terms, on the high side. Managerial and theoretical issues in accounting are less evident in students' work.

The current target is an improvement in graduate competency so that they are in a position to contribute to the emerging Kuwaiti economy. Solutions include introducing IT into the Accounting programme on more than one level by splitting the course curriculum into two or three courses distributed through the 2nd year to the 4th year. During the 2nd year, students are introduced to basic IT Accounting principles and practices. In the 3rd year, Accounting would contain more advanced issues in *Accounting Information Systems*, such as adopting collaboration software and automation accounting, while 4th year courses would contain projects on IT-based Accounting (such as billing systems, payroll, and auditing systems). Advanced versions of these courses are currently taught on the master's programme as a core course or as a term project.

As a result, more pressure is on Accounting staff to produce fully-automated course materials, resulting in locally-branded accounting tools and subsequent cases. In fact, the CBA has celebrated its first publication of a local cases handbook, which covers more than 123 companies from different sectors, with a supporting data warehouse.

The goal of enhancing the competency of Accounting students is gaining momentum as the whole region is getting into globalized trading and international financial reporting. This entails considering all variables in restructuring the Accounting Department's strategic plan. In pursuit of this goal, CBA staff are working closely with their colleagues in the IT Department to strengthen Accounting students' exposure to IT applications.

For accounting policy-makers, all efforts are being made to strengthen the public awareness of IT accounting education in Kuwait, which would certainly improve students' competencies. Contracted research for concerned agencies (such as the Stock Exchange and the Capital Market Authority) would also expedite the fulfilment of the mission.

15.2.3 Recent developments in the accounting curriculum in Turkey

Recep Pekdemir
UNIVERSITY OF ISTANBUL, TURKEY (PEKDEMIR@ISTANBUL.EDU.TR)

There has been a huge need for accounting educators to respond to the demands for change due to the internationalization of financial reporting and auditing in Turkey. As a result of major amendments made in mid-2012 in the Turkish Trade Code, the mandatory implementation of International Financial Reporting Standards (IFRS) is now required – not only for listed companies and financial institutions operating in the country, but also for large-scale entities. As a result, preparers, auditors, and regulators do need up-to-date knowledge to put those standards into practice.

On the other hand, financial statements which comply with IFRS must also be audited by the audit professionals. The current capacity is not sufficient to deal with the expansion of IFRS implementation. As a legal/code law country for accounting, Turkey has established internationally accepted benchmarks for the competence of audit professionals. Historical financial information audit has been one of the areas of specializations in Turkish accounting. Therefore the audit professionals in Turkey are expected to have sufficient advanced knowledge in related fields. By the beginning of 2013, the professional capabilities and competence of prospective candidates seeking to become licensed auditors are being assessed by the Capital Markets Board of Turkey (CMB) through a comprehensive examination.

Taking over the authority, the *Public Oversight, Accounting and Auditing Standards Board of Turkey*, established in December 2011, started a transitional programme in order to meet the current needs for the financial statement audit environment. Currently, certified public accountants and sworn-in certified public accountants can be candidates to become licensed auditors, provided they have at least 15 years' experience in public practice. They must then take the 150-hour-courses in the subjects of the *International Financial Reporting Standards*, the *International Standards of Auditing and Assurance*, the *Principles of Corporate Governance*, and some other courses relating to the banking, insurance, and capital markets legislation. Some universities have started to provide these transitional training programmes in different cities in Turkey.

However, a crucial question still on the table should be considered: Whose knowledge is right in teaching international accounting and auditing standards in an emerging country? Julius Paulus (Roman jurist, third century AD) stated: '*what is right is not derived from the rule, but the rule arises from our knowledge of what is right*'. The key indicator in his statement is 'our knowledge'. Both in practice and in the training programmes, there are certain debates among preparers, auditors, educators, trainers, and sometimes regulators. I have investigated the revealed data and published documents from quality control activities carried out by the CMB on listed companies. The documents relate to the implementations of international accounting and auditing standards for the period 2008–2011. I found that some auditing firms/auditors who did not conduct audit engagements in accordance with the international accounting and auditing standards were punished by cancellation of their accreditation, by having to pay administrative fines, or being given warnings. In the light of these events, Turkey has been putting more effort into adopting international accounting standards. Thus, some advances are needed in the accounting curriculum in the country.

(See also Section 26.2 of Chapter 26 – this volume.)

15.3 Africa

15.3.1 Emerging issues in the accounting curriculum in Botswana

O.O. Othata

UNIVERSITY OF BOTSWANA (OTHATAOO@MOPIPI.UB.BW)

Developments and changes in the accounting curriculum in Botswana are largely traceable to the 2006 World Bank *Report on the Observance of Standards and Codes* (ROSC). This report identified several weaknesses in the observance and application of International Financial Reporting Standards (IFRS) issued by the International Accounting Standards Board (IASB) and International Standards on Auditing (ISA) issued by the International Federation of Accountants (IFAC). As a result of the identified weaknesses, several recommendations were made and these included the upgrading of accounting education and training in Botswana. Providers of accounting educators (such as the University of Botswana) which offer degree-level education were recommended to emphasize standards for practical application: '*[t]he University of Botswana's accounting degree curricula should be harmonized with professional requirements at the national level*' (World Bank, 2006, p. 26).

In addition, there was a recommendation calling for professional awareness seminars and courses for practising accountants and, perhaps most significantly, the establishment of a National Professional Accountancy qualification and the development of simplified reporting requirements for small and medium-sized enterprises (SMEs). These recommendations are largely responsible for the current developments in the accounting curriculum in Botswana.

The process of revising the university curriculum was formally completed in 2010. The new curriculum focusses especially on standards that were identified as presenting challenges to practitioners, the most significant of which are reporting standards on:

- related party disclosure;
- employee benefits;
- contingent liabilities;
- property plant and equipment;
- segmented reporting; and
- disclosure in financial statements.

The curriculum now incorporates these standards as well as exposure drafts issued by the international bodies. On 1 April 2011, a National Chartered Accountancy Qualification was launched under a twinning arrangement between the Botswana Institute of Chartered Accountants (BICA) and the Institute of Chartered Accountants in England & Wales (ICAEW). The curriculum for this qualification includes a new practical component aimed at improving students' ability to properly apply standards, and to function effectively as professional accountants. In order for university accounting graduates to qualify for exemptions on some papers in the Chartered Accountancy Qualification programmes, further changes were incorporated into the curriculum in the area of taxation. Finally, BICA has a near complete (as at March 2013) draft document on simplified reporting requirements for SMEs. This is perhaps the most anticipated document in accounting education in Botswana because, once approved, the requirements will have to be incorporated into the accounting curriculum. A quick look at the draft requirements reveals that they follow a Generally Accepted Accounting Principles (GAAP) as opposed to a Fair Value Framework.

In summary, changes and developments in the accounting curriculum in Botswana are largely being led by changes in professional requirements, with the latter being led by the Botswana Institute of Chartered Accountants.

15.3.2 Developments in the accounting curriculum in South Africa

Lesley J. Stainbank

UNIVERSITY OF KWAZULU-NATAL, SOUTH AFRICA (STAINBANKL@UKZN.AC.ZA)

South Africa has 23 universities divided into three categories:

- traditional universities;
- comprehensive universities; and
- universities of technology.

The traditional and comprehensive universities have, in the main, aligned their academic curricula to that required by the South African Institute of Chartered Accountants (SAICA) and, to a lesser extent, to those of the Association of Chartered Certified Accountants (ACCA) and the Chartered Institute of Management Accountants (CIMA).

The Johannesburg Stock Exchange, through its Listings Requirements, has made it compulsory for all listed companies to apply King III (*King Code of Governance for South Africa*) and produce an integrated report for their financial years starting on and after 1 March 2010, or to explain why they are not applying the King III recommendations. Through the Listing

Requirements, integrated reporting, which includes sustainability reporting, is embedded in the CA curriculum in SAICA-accredited universities. The demands of aligning university curricula to the CA curriculum of SAICA have resulted in only three universities introducing new accounting qualifications around the emerging topics of *Integrated Reporting, Forensic Accounting*, and *Forensic Auditing*, at both undergraduate and postgraduate levels, with some emphasis on the public sector. These are expanded upon below.

The Albert Luthuli Centre for the Responsible Leadership (at the University of Pretoria) offers a multidisciplinary Postgraduate Diploma (PGD) in Integrated Reporting which includes *Integrated Reporting Assurance* and the latest developments within XBRL (Extensible Business Reporting Language). This university also offers a PGD in Investigative and Forensic Accounting. The key objectives of this latter programme are to develop knowledge and expertise to prevent, detect, and investigate fraud, and to recover funds derived from criminal activities and financial awards resulting from civil disputes.

North-West University offers a specialized three-year degree in Forensic Accounting. Students study two modules in *Forensic Accounting* at the first year level, a second-year module on *Forensic Specific Crimes*, and three modules entitled *Forensic Accounting and Investigation* (two at second-year level and one at third-year level). (These modules would be in addition to other modules which comprise the degree.) Honours and master's study in Forensic Accounting is also offered.

Nelson Mandela Metropolitan University offers a PGD in Internal Auditing which includes a module on *Forensic Auditing*. This module has as its purpose the integration of theoretical and practical principles and components of fraud and fraud detection. The PGD also includes a module in *Public Service Accountability*. The purpose of this module is to integrate theoretical and practical components of the public sector environment and the public sector accounting framework in the design of internal engagement plans. This university has also indicated that it is considering incorporating a public sector perspective into certain of its non-CA programmes.

The introduction of a public sector perspective is important for South Africa where there is a lack of accounting and auditing skills, and a dearth of specialized public sector programmes in Financial Management. Universities are being encouraged to engage more with the public sector and to offer programmes which focus on the public sector (as opposed to the private sector).

(See also Section 26.2 of Chapter 26 – this volume.)

15.3.3 Emerging issues in the accounting curriculum in Tanzania

Ernest G. Kitindi

UNIVERSITY OF DAR-ES-SALAAM, TANZANIA (EKITINDI@YAHOO.COM)

The pending/emerging/future issues relating to the accounting curriculum in Tanzania are:

15.3.3.1 Public sector accounting

Public sector reforms in Tanzania demanded that central government use the International Public Sector Accounting Standards (IPSASs) modified cash-basis of accounting, and that Local Government Authorities use IPSAS's accrual-basis, which is a change from the cash-basis of accounting. It has proved challenging for central government to use the modified cash-basis, and more so for agencies expected to operate on a pseudo-commercial basis. This challenge could be addressed by accounting institutions designing programmes which enable central government staff to acquire accrual-based accounting skills.

Reforms of the local government sector are on-going. Accounting institutions could, in the meantime, address the problem of facilitating the adoption of accrual accounting by local government accounting personnel. The curricula of accounting training institutions in Tanzania must be revamped to place more emphasis on Public Sector Accounting.

15.3.3.2 Government audit

The National Audit Office (NAO), headed by the Controller and Auditor General (CAG), is the Supreme Audit Institution in Tanzania. The CAG controls government spending and audits central and local government accounts, plus those of the judiciary, the national assembly, and parastatals. The CAG is empowered to use private audit firms to complement the NAO's work. It is still unclear how the constitutional requirement of ensuring authorization, use as intended, and the ensuing audit is done. Occasionally, government funds have been released for non-normal government expenditure. Cases in point include the stimulus package of 2009 and the empowerment funds that were released in the period immediately after the elections of 2005. It is not clear whether, in conducting its audits, NAO 'follows' the funds to where they have been taken to (even if the recipient is a non-government entity) in order to verify how they were spent, or whether it confines its audit to transactions involving government only. This is an issue that needs to be understood for the role of the CAG to properly be put in perspective.

15.3.3.3 Accounting for gas and mineral resources

During the past decade, several gold mines became operational in Tanzania. Recently, substantial natural gas deposits have also been discovered, and there are plans to start commercial exploitation. Undoubtedly, this is a phenomenon that is likely to create accounting challenges. Such challenges include the valuation and disclosure of gas and mineral deposits. This is an area in which accounting educators and practitioners alike can spearhead the development of relevant and appropriate standards to address the challenges. The accounting curricula need to now move beyond *Accounting for Royalties* to include the whole spectrum from prospecting to exploitation, storage, and discharge/disposal.

15.3.3.4 Environmental accounting

Related to gas and minerals, *Accounting for the Environment* is another area that needs to be developed. There is widespread concern over environmental destruction caused by mining activities. The financial impact on the economy needs to be recognized and properly accounted for. Economic entities in Tanzania do not report on the environment. The provision of high quality environmental reports is required. Accounting educators could lead the process by enriching the accounting curricula to include environmental accounting so as to provide such reports.

15.4 The Far East

15.4.1 The diversity development of accounting curricula in China (with the typical characteristics of a transitional economy)

Xiaohui Qu
XIAMEN UNIVERSITY, CHINA (XHQU@XMU.EDN.CN)

In China, the Ministry of Education (MOE) accredits programmes and sets mandatory requirements on the curricula for general education (such as mathematics and foreign languages), leaving the remainder for subject-based curricula and additional subjects relating to the major.

Depending upon the knowledge and expertise of academic staff, if an accounting programme is authorized to award bachelor degrees, it may adopt specialist tracks such as CPA or Auditing.

15.4.1.1 The transitional economy

Accounting curricula have been driven by China's economic reform and development. From late 1978, following the economic reform, accounting and the curricula converted from being planned economy-based to a market orientation. The curriculum reform was mainly informed by American curricula, leading to the introduction of new courses. Meanwhile, a reform of accounting standards in 1993 led to the reform of the accounting curriculum from ownership-based courses to industry-based courses, such as manufacturing accounting. Following the development of the economy and in the structure of firms, advanced accounting was introduced into the curriculum in the 1990s.

15.4.1.2 Internationalization

The opening up policy dating from late 1978 led to some new accounting course offerings, such as:

- accounting for joint ventures;
- international accounting;
- international reporting and multinational enterprises; and
- financial statement analysis for multinational enterprises.

The shift to substantially converged GAAP with IFRS in 2006 resulted in IAS/IFRS and IFRS-based courses. With the eagerly pursued target of accreditation from professional accounting bodies, such as the Association of Chartered Certified Accountants (ACCA) and Certified General Accountants Association of Canada (CGAAC), some universities aligned their core courses closely with the body which they preferred. An example is the international track in the accounting programme at Xiamen University, which is aligned with ACCA. In addition, with competitive support from the MOE for internationally-oriented programmes, a specially designed curriculum was established at Zhongnan University of Economics and Law.

15.4.1.3 Capital market and job market influences

A number of other issues have impacted on the curriculum. To encourage students to become CPAs, the Chinese Institute of Certified Public Accountants (CICPA) awarded financial grants to universities to offer a CPA specialist track to meet the education requirement of the CICPA. An example is the accounting programme at Shanghai University of Finance and Economics. Demands for increased awareness of corporate governance have resulted in an increase in courses on risk management and on internal control. The widespread adoption by organizations of ERP software such as SAP and Oracle has led to a growth in XBRL-related courses.

The more popular jobs sought by accounting graduates are in the investment or security industry, banks, and giant state-owned enterprises. As a result, courses in the following subjects are becoming increasingly popular:

- accounting for financial instruments;
- mergers and acquisitions;
- investment;
- valuation; and
- financial management.

At the same time, the development of the Chinese capital market and an increase in graduate programme enrolment have led to the emergence of courses on research methodology and database-related courses, such as CSMAR and Compustat. Following the development of the capital market, illegal and fraudulent behaviour is occurring, leading to an increased demand from police, the profession, and courts of justice for specialist abilities, which has led to courses being offered in, for example, *Accounting for Legal Affairs*, *Auditing for Fraud*, and *Accounting for Illegal Evidences*.

15.4.1.4 The future

In the foreseeable future, the accounting curriculum is expected to continue to reflect the demands and requests arising from economic development and the capital market, while progressing gradually in line with the ongoing Chinese economic transition.

15.4.2 Emerging topics in the accounting curriculum in Japan

Akihiro Noguchi
NAGOYA UNIVERSITY, JAPAN (A.NOGUCH@SOEC.NAGOYA-U.AC.JP)

In Japan, not only elementary and secondary education, but also the major part of tertiary education, is conducted in Japanese. English technical terms in accounting have been translated into Japanese since the beginning of modern accounting education which was introduced at the end of the nineteenth century. Especially after the *Financial Accounting Standards for Business Enterprises* was issued in 1949, accounting education in Japan has been focussed on explanation and the training of accounting treatments based on Japanese GAAP.

However, the amendments to Japanese accounting standards since the 1990s have removed the material differences between Japanese GAAP and IFRS. Designated listed companies have been allowed to register their consolidated financial statements based on IFRSs since 2010 (*Ordinance on Terminology, Forms and Preparation Methods of Consolidated Financial Statements*, Article 1-2). Slowly but steadily, the number of Japanese companies choosing IFRS when preparing consolidated financial statements is increasing.

Affected by the changes in the accounting environment, it became necessary to modify the contents to be taught in accounting courses in Japan. Professional graduate schools for accounting (Accounting Schools) were established in order to improve accounting education for CPA candidates, so the courses implemented there fulfil the requirements of the International Accounting Education Standards (IESs). Not only traditional courses such as *Financial Accounting*, *Management Accounting*, and *Auditing*, but also courses related to *Information Technology*, *Business Law*, *International Communication Skills*, and *Ethics*, are included in the Accounting Schools' curriculum. New textbooks have been published and new subjects, such as *Accounting Ethics*, *Public Sector Accounting*, and *Accounting English*, are taught in Accounting Schools.

However, according to the Certified Public Accountants and Auditing Oversight Board (CPAAOB) (2013), among the 1,347 who passed the Japanese CPA examination in 2012, only 89 (6.6 per cent) were Accounting School graduates, and 298 (22.1 per cent) were undergraduate students, which means that many talented students pass the Japanese CPA examination before finishing their undergraduate course. The majority of the CPA candidates (763, or 56.6 per cent) who passed the CPA examination were university graduates but not Accounting School graduates. High quality education at Japanese Accounting Schools is not yet being fully utilized because the Japanese CPA examination do not require a master's degree.

As for large listed corporations, knowledge about IFRS and English have become very important, but for small and medium-sized enterprises (SMEs), Domestic Tax Accounting dominates. As two-thirds of employees are employed by SMEs, the importance of education for Domestic Tax Accounting and Japanese GAAP cannot be overlooked.

(See also Section 26.2 of Chapter 26 – this volume.)

References

Certified Public Accountants and Auditing Oversight Board (2013). HEISEI24NENDO KOUNIN KAIKEISHI SHIKEN GOUKAKUSHA SHIRABE. Available at: www.fsa.go.jp/cpaaob/kouninkaikeishi-shiken/ronbungoukaku_24h.pdf (accessed 8 March 2013).

Nishikawa, K. (1956) The early history of double-entry book-keeping in Japan, in Littleton, A.C. & Yamey, B.S. (eds) *Studies in the History of Accounting*. London: Sweet & Maxwell, pp. 380–387.

Small and Medium Enterprise Agency (2012) *White Paper on Small and Medium Enterprises in Japan*, available at: www.chusho.meti.go.jp/pamflet/hakusyo/H24/download/2012hakusho_eng.pdf (accessed 8 March 2013).

Tokyo Stock Exchange (2013) *List of Companies Applying or Planning to Apply IFRS*, available at: www.tse.or.jp/rules/ifrs/info.html (accessed 8 March 2013).

15.4.3 Emerging areas within the accounting curriculum in Singapore

Themin Suwardy
SINGAPORE MANAGEMENT UNIVERSITY (TSUWARDY@SMU.EDU.SG)

15.4.3.1 Introduction

Accounting curricula in Singapore universities, and in many other countries in the South East Asian region, are greatly influenced by the level of development of the local accounting profession. In the absence of a post-university qualifying examination, the responsibility for producing technically-competent professional accountants for Singapore rests largely with academe. Local regulators, with oversight duties relating to the registration of public accountants, may also prescribe what should go into an Accounting programme's curriculum.

Thus, in this region, a typical Accounting programme adopts a very traditional perspective, one that emphasizes the functional aspects of Accounting (in particular, *Financial Reporting*, *Tax*, and *Assurance* courses) which aim to produce graduates who would, theoretically, become competent public accountants. Given such a focus, Accounting curricula in universities are known to be demanding, rigid, and offer very few degrees of freedom in terms of innovative content.

This is beginning to change. In 2008, the Singapore government set up the Committee to Develop the Accountancy Sector (CDAS), to undertake a holistic review of the sector, including the education of aspiring accountants. In its final report, CDAS suggested that an accounting education should be broad-based and equip its graduates with versatile skills to embark on a range of career opportunities in many sectors of the broader economy. It also encouraged universities to enhance their curricula beyond a traditional focus on external audit and to consider developments in other areas. With this encouragement, we are seeing more breadth in the Accounting curriculum.

15.4.3.2 Breadth in accounting courses

Important new frontier areas that have been neglected for a long while will begin to feature as electives in accounting programmes. For example, one Singapore university now offers its Accounting students the choice of four Accounting electives while still meeting all the prescriptive technical requirements of an Accounting programme. It is launching electives in other courses that are traditionally not available to undergraduate Accounting students, and in the following areas:

- *Internal Audit*
- *Valuation for Accounting*
- *Corporate Financial Management*
- *Enterprise Accounting Systems*
- *Risk Management.*

15.4.3.3 Breadth in non-discipline courses

All three universities offering Accounting programmes in Singapore now also require students to study courses outside the traditional Accounting/Business disciplines. This requirement ranges from four to seven courses. For example, one Singapore university now requires students to take one course each from the areas of:

- *Arts, Humanities & Social Sciences;*
- *Science, Technology & Society; and*
- *Liberal Studies.*

15.4.3.4 Breadth in second majors

We are also seeing an increase in the popularity of a 'second major' in an area complementary to Accounting. Students complete additional courses beyond their basic degree in order to qualify for a second major. For example, about 75 per cent of Accounting graduates from a Singapore university have a second major in Business-related areas, with a second major in Finance being the most popular (85 per cent of the 75 per cent). (See also Bloom, Chapter 14 – this volume.)

These attempts at broadening university Accounting curricula aim to produce graduates who are not only technically competent, but also well-rounded and broad-minded – hailing a new 'pedigree' of Accounting graduates for the future.

15.5 Australasia

15.5.1 Recent developments in the provision of accounting curriculum at the professional level across the Melanesian Independent Countries

Alistair Brown
CURTIN UNIVERSITY, AUSTRALIA (ALISTAIR.BROWN@CBS.CURTIN.EDU.AU)

In recent years there has been rapid growth in professional accounting courses within the relatively small formal sector of 'the Melanesian family of nations' of Fiji, Papua New Guinea (PNG), the Solomon Islands, and Vanuatu (Pacific Institute of Public Policy, 2011; CAPA, 2013), which have had a profound impact on accounting curricula offered in the Melanesian region. One emerging topic and relatively new development in Fiji has been the promulgation of International Financial Reporting Standards (IFRS) by the South Fiji Institute of Accountants (FIA, 2011, 2012), University of the South Pacific (USP, 2013), University of Fiji (2013), and Fiji National University (2013). IFRS also dominate the accounting curricula offered by the Certified Practising Accountants Papua New Guinea (CPAPNG, 2013), and PNG's five tertiary institutions (University of Papua New Guinea, Divine World University, University of Goroka, Pacific Adventist University, and PNG University of Natural Resources & Environment).

Another emerging trend in the accounting curriculum of the Melanesian region is that carried out by the Solomon Islands with its general shift from cash accounting to accrual accounting, possibly at the urging of the Australian-led Regional Assistance Mission to Solomon Islands (Goldsmith & Dinnen, 2007; Hameiri, 2009), the Institute of Solomon Islands Accountants (CPAPNG), CPA Australia (Anonymous, 2012), and Solomon Islands National University.

Vanuatu appears to have taken into account the diversity of its space and circumstances by developing emerging topics in livestock management accounting (Vanuatu Agricultural College), record-keeping for the fishing and boat sector (Vanuatu Maritime College, 2013), and offering the more familiar accounting curricula of business studies, financial management, and accounting to a wide-ranging workforce. By paying more attention to internal points of reference rather than to outside standards, a possible development in the Melanesian accounting curriculum which may gain traction from organizations such as the Melanesian Spearhead Group is for the accounting curriculum to pay deference to communal customs and oral traditions.

References

Anonymous (2012) Institute of Accountants seek to improve standards, *Solomon Times*, 19 November. Available at: http://www.solomontimes.com/news/institute-of-accountants-seek-to-improve-standards/7399.

CAPA (2013) The Confederation of Asian and Pacific Accountants. Available at: http://www.capa.com.my/.

CPAPNG (2013) Continuing Professional Education. Available at: nhttp://www.cpapng.org.pg/admission-and-education/continuing-professional-development/cpes.

FIA (2011) *Fiji Institute of Accountants Annual Report 2010*, Suva, Fiji Islands.

FIA (2012) *Fiji Institute of Accountants Annual Report 2011*, Suva, Fiji Islands.

Fiji National University (2013) *Finance for Non-Finance Directors and Senior Managers*, School of Accounting, Fiji National University. Available at: http://www.fnu.ac.fj/newsite/images/stories/NTPC/2012/finance.pdf.

Goldsmith, A. & Dinnen, S. (2007) Transnational Police building: critical lessons from Timor-Liste and Solomon Islands, *Third World Quarterly*, 28(6), 1091–1109.

Hameiri, S. (2009) State building or crisis management? A critical analysis of the social and political implications of the Regional Assistance Mission to Solomon Islands, *Third World Quarterly*, 30(1), 35–52.

Pacific Institute of Public Policy (2011) *Melanesia Poll Results*, The Pacific Institute of Public Policy, Port Vila, Vanuatu. Available at: http://masalai.files.wordpress.com/2011/03/p01-msg-1103.pdf.

The University of Fiji (2013) Postgraduate Diploma in Professional Accounting (PGDPA). Available at: http://www.unifiji.ac.fj/postgraduate-study/postgraduate-study-field/pg-accounting/postgraduate-diploma-in-professional-accounting-pgdpa/?template=psf.

USP (2013) Professional Development, School of Accounting and Finance, University of South Pacific Available at: http://www.afm.fbe.usp.ac.fj/index.php?id=9270.

Vanuatu Maritime College (2013) Rural Fisheries Training, Available at: www.vanuatumaritimecollege.com.vu/nautical.htm.

15.5.2 Developments in the accounting curriculum in Australia

Bryan Howieson[2]

UNIVERSITY OF ADELAIDE, AUSTRALIA (BRYAN.HOWIESON@ADELAIDE.EDU.AU)

In recent years the Government of the Commonwealth of Australia has instituted important reforms in higher education (HE), including the creation of a new quality assurance agency (*Tertiary Education Quality and Standards Agency Act, 2011*) and the development of discipline-specific Learning and Teaching Academic Standards (LTAS) for Higher Education Providers (HEPs) (*Higher Education Standards Framework (Threshold Standards) 2011*).

National generic standards for HE are set out in the Australian Qualifications Framework (AQF) (AQFC, 2013), and some disciplines have sought to translate these into LTAS. Each HEP must be able to demonstrate that graduates have achieved the minimum level of their discipline's LTAS. LTAS in Accounting were developed in 2010 in a nationwide collaborative project involving professional accounting bodies, members of the business community, and accounting academics.[3] Five standards were identified pertaining to outcomes for:

- judgement
- knowledge
- application skills
- communication and teamwork, and
- self-management (Hancock *et al.*, 2010, p. 10).

Typically, accounting studies have concentrated almost exclusively on knowledge-based skills with little attention being given to other LTAS outcomes (Howieson, 2003). In future, HEPs will *have* to show evidence of graduate achievement of the relevant AQF threshold standards, and that the LTAS are a reliable translation of the accounting community's consensus of what is threshold. Accounting educators will be obliged to adjust the curriculum of their accounting programmes to explicitly teach and provide opportunities for students to practise and demonstrate achievement of the LTAS. Curricula will need to be recast to embed the technical material in the context of the other non-knowledge-based LTAS. In the past, accounting educators have tended to resist calls to incorporate non-knowledge-based skills into their courses, citing issues such as a lack of space in the programme due to the amount of technical knowledge to be covered, or that they do not possess the qualifications to educate students in teamwork, communications, etc. However, apart from the regulatory imperative, such arguments need to be tempered by recognizing that the LTAS were developed in close co-operation with accounting practitioners, and reflect their desire for more 'well-rounded' graduates who are strong in 'people skills' and not just technical knowledge. Also, some accounting academics around the country are now working more closely with their HEP's student support staff to include in their curricula explicit opportunities for students to learn from qualified experts the non-knowledge LTAS in an accounting context. The introduction of the LTAS offers the promise that Australian accounting education will develop graduates more closely aligned with the requirements of the profession. (See Watty, Chapter 13 – this volume.)

(See also Section 26.2 of Chapter 26 – this volume.)

References

Australian Qualifications Framework Council (2013) *Australian Qualifications Framework*, 2nd edn, South Australia: AQFC.

Hancock, P., Freeman, M. and Associates (2010) *Learning and Teaching Academic Standards Statement for Accounting*, Strawberry Hills, NSW: ALTC.

Howieson, B.A. (2003) Accounting practice in the next millennium: is accounting education ready to meet the challenge?, *British Accounting Review*, 35(2), 69–103.

15.5.3 New developments in the accounting curriculum in New Zealand

Keith Dixon

UNIVERSITY OF CANTERBURY, NEW ZEALAND (KEITH.DIXON@CANTERBURY.AC.NZ)

Accounting education in New Zealand (NZ) has long been professionalized. Concomitantly, it has been dominated by *accountant* education, largely didactic, focussed on *technical* content, and assessed using orthodox examinations. The factors presently shaping this curriculum have changed, but not radically. They derive from the other, larger, mostly English-speaking countries and are manifested in various ways. For example:

- how the profession is organized;
- how qualifications, study programmes, and courses are specified;
- how research is conducted;
- how academics are developed; and
- how learning is assured using graduate profiles.

The New Zealand Institute of Chartered Accountants (NZICA) now has a more commercial mission and faces competitors, notably the Australian Society of Certified Practising Account-ants (CPAA). It has reduced its tertiary education study requirements for aspiring members to only a 360 Credit Accumulation and Transfer System (CATS) bachelor degree, and then not necessarily in Accounting, although students still require courses that cover its 2011 *tertiary learning outcomes* (TLOs). This will bring these requirements in line with those of the Institute of Chartered Accountants in Australia (ICAA), with which it is planning to merge, and be as attractive as CPAA's. Among the curriculum consequences of these changes are the decimation of bachelor's honours degree programmes, and a reduction in separate courses from those that cover the TLOs.

The TLOs are specified as being about Financial Accounting and Management Accounting, Finance, Auditing, and Taxation in (implicitly) the private corporate sector. They are underpinned by functional orthodoxy and accounting being technical, albeit that there is some recognition that aspiring accountants should develop interpersonal skills. However, while they are significant in the courses that cover them, hence in the curriculum as a whole, this influence is not always overwhelming. It is countered by the disposition of educators being greatly affected by their steadily increasing research activities over the past 25 years. Those activities too are under threat from reactionary elements.

Although driven partly by the exhilaration of doing research, attending conferences, and getting published, a factor which is probably of increasingly greater effect since 1997 has been a research performance and funding mechanism that the NZ Government has imposed in collaboration with university managers. It is arguable that the time which educators are increasingly incentivized to spend on generating research outputs has made them less inclined to exploit linkages of learning and research to bring about research-based and student-centred courses. Instead, their courses are at best only research-led, and more commonly orthodox (foreign) textbook-driven, with an emphasis on the technical and analytical deriving from the 'important countries', and little that is socio-political, environmental, cultural and critical, or peculiar to NZ. This and other impediments (classed as professional, institutional, teaching, peer-academic, student) identified from accounting education research conducted in NZ continue to face educators seeking to transform the accounting curriculum.

An extenuated response to NZICA by universities is to begin offering programmes for graduates of other disciplines. They will be able to join the profession having covered the same TLOs and be admitted to taught degrees designated as Master of Professional Accounting (MPA). The quality of these degrees in terms of research and alternative accountings is yet to be seen.

(See also Section 26.2 of Chapter 26 – this volume.)

15.6 Latin America

15.6.1 Recent developments in the accounting curriculum in Argentina

Martin Quadro

NATIONAL UNIVERSITY OF CÓRDOBA, ARGENTINA (QUADRO@ECO.UNC.EDU.AR)

15.6.1.1 Introduction

In Argentina, there are different governing bodies that regulate the subject in question. The Ministry of Education, Science and Technology establishes the minimum training requirements to acquire a university degree in Accounting. The professional incumbencies are defined in Law No. 20.488. Moreover, the Higher Education Act gives universities the power to govern themselves in a macro full autonomy. In this context, and until the 1990s, the Argentine's universities designed their curricula in an endogenous and autonomous way, attending fundamentally to local order factors. While respecting the minimum requirements established in the regulation of the Ministry, the curricula differed across jurisdictions, giving rise to differences in training and also to serious problems in establishing an equivalence between universities in order to promote student exchanges.

15.6.1.2 Facing diversity of university accounting education

In 2006, an inter-university organization, *the Council of Deans of Economics of Argentina* (CODECE), initiated the revision of the university curriculum, encouraging each university to reform its curriculum content based on an agreed minimum content. In that sense, mention can be made of the substantial events that have marked the development of the Accounting curriculum in recent years:

- *Harmonization*: The curricula of the universities must contain a minimum of 2,730 hours (2,315 hours to apply to the areas of training, and the remaining 415 may be freely assigned by the academic units under the graduate profile that has been proposed). There are established specific contents training areas (accounting and tax, economy, law, arts, etc.).
- *Final integration content*: Each university should implement a final level of integration, called supervised professional practice (SPP), in which the students face situations similar to those which they might encounter in their future professional careers. Through internships, temporary jobs in accounting firms, large firms or integrative seminars, the students must demonstrate practical training that reflects the transition from theory to practice.
- *Globalization of Accounting*: Considering the internationalization of accounting and its regulation, the curriculum must include the teaching of IFRS issued by the IASB. Since Argentina is in the process of introducing these standards, it is essentially a comparative study with local regulation.
- *Pedagogical-didactic approach*: One of the weaknesses noted in accounting education is related to the fact that students prioritize and attach importance to the procedures and rules set out in accounting standards (national or international) above the principles and conceptual foundations that support them. Therefore, an *Accounting Theory* course was introduced prior to the study of accounting standards, to encourage the development of critical thinking and a broader view in the disciplinary field.

15.6.1.3 Conclusion

Ten years into the discussion about what should be taught in universities, the CODECE effort has been evident in the reformed processes of curriculum development at different universities in the country, constituting a significant advance for the accounting profession.

15.6.2 Emerging topics and new developments in the accounting curriculum in Brazil

Edgard B. Cornacchione, Jr.

UNIVERSITY OF SÃO PAULO, BRAZIL (EDGARDBC@USP.BR)

Three factors have recently affected the accounting curriculum in Brazil:

- a national professional examination (2010);
- IFRS adoption (2007); and
- new curriculum guidelines (2004).

Implemented in 2010 by the professional body, the *Federal Council of Accounting* (CFC), the national professional examination (for graduates in Accounting) represents the entry route to the profession, aiming at quality and covering several topics: *Financial Accounting, Cost Accounting, Public Sector Accounting, Managerial Accounting, Accounting Theory, Ethics, Accounting Standards, Auditing, Forensic Accounting, Law, Business Mathematics, Statistics,* and *Portuguese.* In addition, all the 1,291 authorized undergraduate Accounting programmes have had to cope with massive curriculum developments due to IFRS adoption in 2007. Many players have been engaged in redefining the curriculum, training academic staff, and revising or creating instructional materials, while observing the real-world consequences of IFRS adoption. As an example, the Inter-American Development Bank partnered with the *Brazilian Institute of Independent Auditors* and the *Accounting, Actuary and Finance Research Foundation* to support the development of instructional materials (online included) with a train-the-trainer approach. Finally, the new curriculum guidelines (bachelor's degree in Accounting), issued by the Ministry of Education in 2004, indicate a minimum of four years and 3,000 hours of education (combining contact hours and up to 20 per cent of extra activities). These guidelines (connected to IFAC and IAESB) refer to contents in three dimensions:

- foundation (Economics, Law, Mathematics, Statistics, Business);
- professional (Accounting, Actuary, Finance, Auditing, Forensic, Managerial, for public and private sectors); and
- theory–practice (internship, extra activities, independent study, elective subjects, computing and software laboratories).

Since 1999, continuing professional education (CPE) has played a stronger role in Brazil, especially among independent auditors. The CFC has been issuing regulations since 2002 on this topic. However, in 2012, the CFC introduced various types of programmes, formats, minimum annual credit-hour requirements, and contents. This advanced model recognizes credits in various forms (including courses taken, teaching, participation in professional or academic committees, and publications).

Currently, with 20 master's and six doctoral programmes, accounting graduate education in Brazil has experienced a strong expansion. Programmes operate under strict oversight of the

Coordination for Improvement of Higher Education branch of the Ministry of Education. Typically, programmes respect the traditional model of coursework, followed by proposal defence (qualification examination) and final oral examination, once the research is complete and the report is finished (30 months for master's and 48 months for doctoral programmes). Internationalization (increasing links with IAAER, EAA, AAA, ACCA, AICPA) with substantial advances in research quality standards and publication environment has been remarkable. The consolidation of the *Brazilian Association for Graduate Programs in Accounting* (ANPCONT) represents the maturity of the field.

Emerging topics in Brazilian accounting education can be identified in four major areas:

1   Financial Accounting (IFRS and CPC, the local normative authority);
2   Managerial Accounting (accounting for sustainability, controllership, elements of institutional theory, accounting artifacts and behavioural models, in addition to GECON (*Gestão Econômica*, or Economic Management), a creative contribution to managerial accounting, based on transactions and opportunity costs);
3   Capital and Credit Markets (targeting the expansion of the Brazilian financial system); and
4   Accounting Education (teaching and learning process, instructional strategies, generations, gender factor, educational technology, and evaluation). Several comparative studies (involving data from other nations) have been essential for new developments in the Brazilian accounting curriculum.

(See also Section 26.2 of Chapter 26 – this volume.)

15.6.3 Colombia: emerging areas within the accounting curriculum

Mary A. Vera-Colina
NATIONAL UNIVERSITY OF COLOMBIA (MAAVERACO@UNAL.EDU.CO)

According to the Minister of Education, Colombia has more than 100 institutions offering Accounting programmes at the undergraduate level. Nevertheless, only 20 per cent of these have been accredited with a high quality degree, representing the leading schools of the academic and professional branch (only three of which have recently initiated graduate courses).

The accounting curriculum in these institutions is designed following 'core problems', or 'competences based' approaches. In either case, the main topics for courses are related to *Financial Accounting, Managerial Accounting, Accounting Theory, Taxation, Finance, Auditing and Assuring, Ethics, Economics, Mathematics, Statistics, Information Systems, Regulation, Management, Humanities,* and *Foreign Languages* (see, for example, Rueda Delgado, 2009). It is usual for universities to have an interdisciplinary curriculum for students of Accounting, Economics, and Business programmes, which also include a range of elective courses in other disciplines. Professional practice and internship are also an important component in these programmes.

Most curricula consider the relevance of research formation at undergraduate and graduate levels. Frequently, students have the opportunity to share experiences with researchers and they are encouraged to write and publish their first papers.

Recent teaching and research proposals for Accounting in Colombia, as emerging issues, are connected to current global accounting discussions, especially to those affecting Latin American countries. Some areas where teaching and research efforts are related to are:

•   *Critical approaches to Accounting Theory*: this could be considered a prolific research area for Colombian academics. Most of them are concentrated on the revision of international literature from a critical view, and their relationship with the accounting profession, regulation, and practice in the country.

- *Accounting Regulation (Financial Accounting)*: in the past, this area was basically related to the study of models and laws affecting accounting practice, from a local viewpoint. Currently, both academics and practitioners are focussing on the process of harmonization with international standards, such as IFRS and International Public Sector Reporting Standards (IPSAS), discussing their advantages/disadvantages, alternative models, and potential impacts on Colombian entities. This discussion is increasing in importance every day, considering that the government harmonized IPSAS in 2007, and has plans to adopt IFRS in 2015–2016.
- *Social Responsibility and Accountability*: this is a major issue, especially for researchers, including topics such as environmental accounting, ethics, and social reporting.
- *Accounting education*: there is an increasing concern about educational models that can be applied to Accounting curricula and courses, covering undergraduate, graduate, and professional development programmes.

Other important emerging areas are:

- Auditing, Assurance and Control.
- Finance Modelling and Measurement.
- Accounting and Finance in SMEs.

As stated earlier, these emerging topics follow similar trends to those in other Latin American countries, focussing on the Colombian context. On the other hand, we can identify some areas that are equally important for the profession, but which have not yet been sufficiently studied. That would be the special case for Taxation and Managerial Accounting.

Reference
Rueda Delgado, G. (ed.) (2009) *Enfoque y estructura curricular. Convenio de cooperación académica entre programas de contaduría pública*, Bogotá: Universidad Javeriana.

15.7 North America

15.7.1 Innovations in teaching governmental auditing in Mexico

Salvador Ruiz-De-Chavez
MEXICAN ASSOCIATION OF ACCOUNTING AND BUSINESS FACULTY
(GENERALGMCE@PRODIGY.NET.MX)

Since 2010, the Superior Audit Office of Mexico (SAO) has established links with different academic organizations, such as:

- The National University of Mexico (UNAM) to set up an undergraduate elective senior course.
- The Queretaro State University to start a continuing professional education (CPE) programme.
- The Durango State University to upgrade the curriculum of its under-graduate Accounting programme.
- The National Association of Accounting and Business Faculty to offer CPE courses to educators.

All these activities have been developed in order to promote the teaching of the topics relating to Governmental Auditing, as noted below.

Since its inception in 1867, the main functions of SAO were set down as those of examining and commenting on the federal budget's accounting submitted by the Federal Ministry of Finance. The SAO was created as a technical body attached to the Lower Chamber.

The Federal Superior Auditing Act of 2000 marked the start of the modern conception of superior auditing, providing the institution with updated procedures to conduct the audits, visits, and inspections entrusted to it by the law.

When dealing with federal resources, the SAO carries out its external auditing function of the three branches of Government:

- the constitutionally autonomous entities;
- Mexico's states and municipalities; and
- individuals.

The aim is to assess the financial management outcomes, checking compliance with the provisions of the Federal Budget and the corresponding Revenues Act, and to verify the manner in which, and the extent to which, the goals and objectives of the Government's programmes have been fulfilled (Performance Audit).

SAO's findings foster effectiveness, productivity, and integrity in the use of federal funds; and promote transparency and accountability, whenever federal resources are used.

The 2011–2017 SAO's Strategic Plan defines an approach to action based on several strategic lines such as:

- to foster efficiency and efficacy in the public sector;
- to promote the adoption of better governmental practices;
- to support the establishment of the National Governmental Auditing System;
- to encourage internal control systems; and
- to foster transparency and accountability based on Governmental Accounting harmonization.

One of SAO's most important projects is the adoption of the International Standards of Supreme Audit Institutions (ISSAI) developed by the International Organization of Supreme Auditing Institutions (Intosai). Mexico has been a country member of Intosai since its creation in 1953. Intosai operates as an umbrella organization for the external government audit community. It has provided a solid framework for supreme audit institutions to promote the development and transfer of knowledge, improve government auditing worldwide, and enhance professional capacities. It is an organization with special consultative status with the Economic and Social Council of the United Nations.

The SAO has a robust training programme for its auditors and the auditors of the State Supreme Audit Institutions. This programme is focussed on the ISSAI, and its online courses are also open mainly to students and staff of the Accounting programmes in Mexico.

(See also Section 26.2 of Chapter 26 – this volume.)

References

http://www.intosai.org/en/about-us/issai.html (accessed 12 March 2013).
http://www.asf.gob.mx (accessed 13 March 2013).

15.7.2 Canada: everything is new again

Irene M. Gordon
SIMON FRASER UNIVERSITY, CANADA (GORDON@SFU.CA)

Emerging topics in Canadian accounting education that will affect the curriculum reflect themes which have been repeated over the past three decades, and which represent topics and challenges that are also present in other countries. Such shared curriculum topics/challenges include:

- incorporating ethical and social issues in *Financial Accounting* courses (e.g., ethical reporting to a broad set of stakeholders) and *Managerial Accounting* courses (e.g., how the management compensation plan performs as an evaluation tool to promote ethical and socially responsible conduct);
- addressing the 'online' generation's learning needs (such as shorter attention spans and perceptions that the material can be learned without the benefit of classroom experiences and interactions);
- balancing educators' needs to be current in both changing accounting standards and academic research;
- including academic topics to ensure that students have a liberal educational background or are exposed to topics beyond standards (e.g., strategic management accounting necessary for planning and evaluation) which have longer-term value for their careers; and
- keeping classroom materials updated by using global companies' current financial statements, real-world examples and cases.

Other curriculum topics/challenges are essentially Canadian. The most pressing of these are:

- the merging of accounting bodies; and
- the co-existence of International Financial Reporting Standards (IFRS) and Canadian Accounting Standards for Private Enterprises (ASPE).

Canada's three professional accounting bodies (PABs), the Canadian Institute of Chartered Accountants (CICA), the Certified General Accountants Association of Canada (CGAAC), and the Society of Management Accountants of Canada (SMAC), have co-existed for more than half a century. Merger activities are complete (e.g., in Quebec, all three groups have merged) or continuing at the national and provincial levels. Uncertainty surrounds the merger outcome and this affects the curriculum through the educational background required of students entering the accounting profession. The knowledge and skills which an early career accountant needs relate directly to the PABs' competency maps. Until 2012, each of the three PABs had its own competency map. While competencies are clearly best measured in the accountant's work environment, accounting education assists in preparing accounting students for their future careers through the accounting curriculum (e.g., specific accounting topics), and by providing opportunities for students to practise some of the 'soft' skills (e.g., team work, presentations, written assignments' content and tone). Accounting educators and programmes heed competency maps since students require adequate preparation for their future accounting careers. Until the merger situation is resolved and there is clarity as to the emphasis of any resulting combined competency maps, curriculum uncertainty will continue.

The second Canadian accounting curriculum challenge is the co-existence of IFRS and ASPE. This situation demands decisions by educators regarding what material to cover in a limited time-frame. Students, preparing for public accounting careers, must learn IFRS requirements to pass professional examinations. However, many future accountants will normally only work within smaller, private enterprises. This second challenge forces educators to attempt to balance how and when to address the differences between IFRS and ASPE.

(See also Section 26.2 of Chapter 26 – this volume.)

15.7.3 Evolving accounting curricula in a dynamic environment – the case of the U.S.A.

Philip Reckers
ARIZONA STATE UNIVERSITY, U.S.A. (PHILIP.RECKERS@ASU.EDU)

Choices regarding curriculum content and pedagogy are among the most important responsibilities entrusted to educators. Nonetheless, the myriad of recent environmental changes in education and business will continue to restrict educators' choices in substantive ways, with the outcome being very hard to predict.

In the U.S.A., the most far-reaching change in the education environment over the last decade (even greater than technology) has been the sharp acceleration of the 'privatization of public education'. State universities, from which the preponderance of young accountants graduate, have witnessed the portion of their budgets supported by tax revenues fall precipitously. The costs of education increasingly are borne by students, not taxpayers. Core contributors to this change include troubled economic conditions. But, also contributing, are factors that may not ease or reverse in the near future, namely a general decline in appetite among citizens for taxes, and increasing demands for limited state dollars for other government services. As a result, the level of student debt has shot up markedly, leading prospective students and their parents to re-evaluate the costs and benefits of higher education.

To accommodate the new environment, state universities are increasingly found to 'operate as for-profit businesses', weighing carefully the revenues versus costs of educational 'products'. In an attempt to cut costs, class sizes too often have been pushed to non-prudent levels, very large online courses have been developed (irrespective of whether that pedagogy fits the course content or students' ability), and lower-cost but less well-trained instructors, teaching more course sections, have displaced doctorally-trained academic staff. To increase revenues, institutions are pressed to recruit whoever can pay the price: accepting more marginal students without providing commensurate provision for counseling, and tutoring services, etc., and aggressively target-marketing 'out-of-state' and international students who pay substantially higher tuition and fees. The composite effect of these changes on the American Collegiate Model has been truly profound, and clearly eclipses any curriculum content changes over the last decade.

Nonetheless, prospectively, universities are expected to do more with less. The public accounting profession has and is aggressively pressuring universities to include more content related to:

- Auditing Internal Controls' Design Adequacy and Compliance
- International Financial Reporting Standards (IFRS)
- Fair Value Accounting
- Sustainability (Green) Accounting.

Several of these content areas simply cannot be provided in 'small bites'. For example, competence with respect to fair value accounting would require a substantial curriculum change (likely two or more courses), with a much greater focus on Mathematics and Economic Prediction Modelling. Similarly, embracing Sustainability Accounting would neither be a trivial effort nor possible without significant retraining of academic staff.

In the face of these pressures for curriculum changes, an introspective re-examination of the objectives of university education is occurring. Adding significant new content to curricula means that something else must come out. Only so much can be achieved from efforts to synergistically blend in continuing attention to critical and creative thinking, communications, and team work skills, and solid student value-grounding in ethics, diversity and global issues with new vocational skills. Real trade-offs are required. It has been 50 years since the future of university accounting education in the U.S.A. has been so much in question.

(See also Section 26.2 of Chapter 26 – this volume.)

15.8 Europe

15.8.1 Accounting education in Belgium: emerging areas within the accounting curriculum

Patricia Everaert
GHENT UNIVERSITY, BELGIUM (PATRICIA.EVERAERT@UGENT.BE)

15.8.1.1 General background on education at university level

In Belgium, there are eight universities offering a variety of bachelor's and master's programmes. Tuition fees are about € 600 per year. There are no entrance examinations (except for the study of Medicine). The only requirement is that the student has successfully finished secondary school. It is common knowledge that certain majors in secondary school have higher success rates for particular bachelor's degree programmes, but the general rule is that students can apply for the programme of study that they want.

As a result of this lenient policy, about half of first year undergraduate students fail. In order to increase success rates, universities expend effort on informing students before they begin their studies about the content and expectations of the different programmes (through information sessions, sitting-in on classes, and visiting days on campus). Additionally, major efforts are devoted to guiding students in the first undergraduate year with voluntary sessions on difficult topics of the courses and office hours (one-to-one meetings) for the main courses.

15.8.1.2 The Accounting curriculum

For students of Business Economics, *Financial Accounting* is taught in the first undergraduate year. In the second year, courses such as *Financial Statement Analysis* and *Cost Accounting* follow, while *Management Accounting*, *Tax*, and *Finance* are typically taught in the third year. There are no minors or majors at the undergraduate level within Business Economics, and 99 per cent of the students subsequently follow the master's programme in Business Economics.

In the late 1990s, universities started offering majors at the master's level, such as Accounting, Finance, Marketing, and Human Resources. Courses such as *IFRS*, *Management Control*, and *Audit* are taught at this level, as shown in Figure 15.1.

Two emerging areas over the past five years are seen in the curriculum for students majoring in Accounting: *more research-orientation*, and *more practice-orientation*. On the one hand, some programmes include in their master's year a dedicated course on *Research Methods in Accounting* (or *Research Methods in Finance*), where research papers are discussed with the students. This

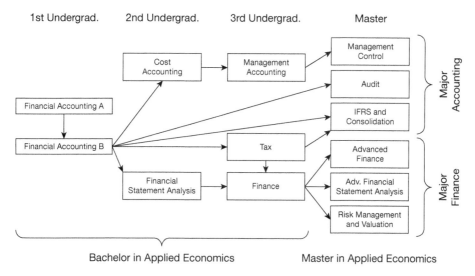

Figure 15.1 Flow of the Accounting courses in the curriculum of Master of Science in Business Economics

helps students in the preparation of their own master's theses. On the other hand, universities try to enforce the link between the profession and the curriculum by including guest speakers (financial professionals) on specific topics, by using problem-based learning (to develop the soft skills of the students as future accountants or auditors), and by discussing case studies relating to Belgian companies.

For some students, these practical initiatives were not enough. Therefore, very recently, some universities have offered an internship for all students at the master's level, while universities offer the possibility to do an *internship* during the summer holidays. Students receive credits for the internship (and a grade). The experience of working on a specific project in a company is considered to be very valuable by the students. (See also Beard & Humphrey, Chapter 25 – this volume.)

15.8.2 Emerging topics and recent developments in the accounting curriculum in Denmark

John Christensen
UNIVERSITY OF SOUTHERN DENMARK (JCN@SAM.SDU.DK)

Accounting education is concentrated in four universities in Denmark: the Copenhagen Business School, Aarhus University, University of Southern Denmark, and Aalborg University. All these universities offer a five-year master's programme in Auditing. In addition, the master's degree in Business Economics features a specialization in Accounting in the four universities. It is impossible to review all developments in the Danish universities, but two major trends or developments can be seen:

*   to develop the fields of financial statement analysis; and
*   to incorporate the economic foundation of accounting into the accounting curriculum.

Accounting courses with an emphasis on the economic foundations of accounting have been developed at Aarhus University and at the University of Southern Denmark. Because accounting is viewed as being a source of information, these courses are based in information economics. Accounting control can be viewed as a response to moral hazard between shareholders and management. The control issue is even more complicated since management has to report their private information to shareholders. Auditing is applied to the reporting process in response to the adverse selection problem, and items are excluded from the financial statements if they are impossible to audit. Consequently, the moral hazard problem of the firm limits the information content of the accounting system. Furthermore, auditing delays the publication of accounting information and favours a historical basis, and yet accounting information is valuable. This is due to the fact that accounting information is hard to manipulate and is used to discipline other more timely information sources.

Courses in *Financial Statement Analysis* have been developed at the Copenhagen Business School and at Aarhus University. The development of the *Financial Statement Analysis* course at Aarhus University follows the path of information economics. The course provides a comprehensive analysis of the relation between financial information and the valuation in the markets. This is followed by a fundamental analysis of the differences between accounting valuation (as defined by accounting principles) and market valuation. The purpose of this analysis is to build models to predict the future value of the firm based upon financial information as well as other information sources. The primary focus of the *Financial Statement Analysis* course at the Copenhagen Business School is to develop a wider user perspective. Consequently, the course includes valuation, credit risk, and accounting-based bonus plans for executives.

The common denominator in the reported trends in accounting education in Denmark is a strengthening of the relationship between accounting and economics. Accounting is supposed to provide a true-and-fair view of the economics of the firm, and this is reflected in the accounting curriculum. Accounting principles do not suffice as a basis for a professional life as an accountant: accounting must be studied in relation to the economics of the firm. This development is seen as the response to current trends in accounting education as it allows an in-depth understanding of fair value accounting, impairment testing, and non-financial performance indicators as integrated components of the accounting curriculum.

15.8.3 Accounting education in Spain: (un)fortunately following the course

José L. Arquero
UNIVERSITY OF SEVILLE, SPAIN (ARQUERO@US.ES)

15.8.3.1 Introduction
Two circumstances have had a strong influence on recent changes in accounting education in Spain:

- the integration into the European Higher Education Area (EHEA); and
- the harmonization of Spanish Accounting Standards in 2007.

Prior to 2008–2009, no specific degrees existed in Accounting. This area was covered by Management and Business Administration (MBAd) degrees, with a strong emphasis on Accounting. Although Accounting was the main choice of career for those graduates,[4] there was a lack of provision of specialized Accounting courses, limited to a narrow range of electives in a rigidly-designed curriculum.

Spain's integration into the EHEA allowed universities to propose a new range of degrees, with an unprecedented level of freedom. The reasons put forward to justify the need for a specific Accounting & Finance degree were:

- complexity of the new accounting standards, designed to harmonize with the IFRS;
- the demands from the job market; and
- the existence of this degree in most other advanced countries.

In the case of the University of Seville, which is typical of the sector, the total credits required for graduation decreased from 334 (a five-year degree in Management and Business Administration) to 240 (a four-year programme) to be applied to any of the new accounting and finance or management and business administration degrees. The new curriculum map implied a stronger specialization: accounting subjects cover between 22.5–32.5 per cent of the curriculum compared with 10–17 per cent of the curriculum in the old MBAd degrees.

Not only did the relative weights increase, but a major shift to a competence-based approach was expected. The number of innovations relating to pedagogy, assessment, etc., also increased. Unfortunately, most universities keep enrolling students in large numbers making innovations unsustainable, and the trend already reported in other countries (e.g. in the U.K. and the U.S.A.) quickly developed: accounting and finance degrees do not appear to attract the most suitable students (Arquero & Tejero, 2011).

15.8.3.2 Expected future trends

Experience with these new accounting curricula is currently almost non-existent. The first cohort of graduates in accounting will have completed their studies at the end of the 2012–2013 academic year. Therefore, at the time of writing, there is no information on how the different syllabuses designed by universities for this degree will develop. However, changes are expected. Due to financial restrictions, rumours of a change to a three-year degree grow stronger, day-by-day, leaving the last level of the current degree to postgraduate education, which is more expensive for students and not financed by the government. This reduction will change the existing weights among the subject areas. Quite probably, non-core subjects, or those not considered to add value in terms of employability, will be eliminated, regardless of their contribution to general education.

References

Arquero, J.L., Donoso, J.A., Jiménez, S., & González, J.M. (2009) Exploratory analysis of the demanded professional profile on Business Administration Degree: implications for the Accounting Area, *Spanish Accounting Review*, 12(1), 43–66.

Arquero, J.L. & Tejero, C. (2011) How well adapted are accounting students for Bologna? A comparative analysis of learning styles of Spanish social sciences students, *EDUCADE*, 3, 145–156.

Escobar, B. & Jiménez, S.M. (2009) The implementation of an accounting degree in the context of the EHEA, *Revista Española de Financiación y Contabilidad*, 142, 293–310.

15.9 Overview

These 21 contributions reveal a picture of accounting education change being heavily informed by a combination of IFRS and pressure from or influence of professional accounting bodies (PABs). Fourteen of the 21 contributors refer to the ongoing impact of IFRS on the curriculum, and 11 describe the restrictive influence which PABs have upon curriculum content and change.

(See also Apostolou & Gammie, Chapter 29 – this volume.) In all these cases, this influence is very strong, prompting comments such as:

[t]he public accounting profession has and is aggressively pressuring universities to include more content related to. . .

(Philip Reckers, U.S.A.)

[t]he traditional and comprehensive universities have, in the main, aligned their academic curriculum to that required by the South African Institute of Chartered Accountants (SAICA) and, to a lesser extent, [ACCA and CIMA].

(Lesley Stainbank, South Africa)

Accounting curricula . . . are greatly influenced by the level of development of the local accounting profession . . . [and offer] very few degrees of freedom.

(Themin Suwardy, Singapore)

Australian accounting education will develop graduates more closely aligned with the requirements of the profession.

(Bryan Howieson, Australia).

To the descriptions of emerging topics and topics likely to receive greater coverage provided by the contributors can be added increasing coverage in the U.K. of IFRS, accounting theory, forensic accounting, and internship. Overall, increasing coverage of the following topics is indicated:

- IFRS (9 times);
- corporate social reporting/environmental accounting (6);
- auditing (5) (international auditing standards (3), internal audit (1), auditing (1));
- public sector accounting (4);
- accounting theory (3);
- ethics (3);
- forensic accounting (4);
- AIS/Enterprise Reporting Systems (ERP) (3);
- internships (2); and
- tax (2).

In developing regions, the emphasis on curriculum development, while more focussed upon local needs, such as accounting for exploration (Tanzania), and livestock management accounting, fishing accounting, and boat accounting (Melanesia), also looks to coverage of international regulation, such as International Public Sector Accounting Standards (Tanzania) and IFRS. Changes in delivery modes were also highlighted by contributors, with greater use of IT, to the exclusion of traditional delivery; and a greater concern for improving communication skills of accounting graduates was highlighted as an area of concern in Egypt, as it is currently in Australia.

There can be little doubt that change is occurring – but how will space be found for it in the curriculum? Will it be accommodated by adding a year to accounting education at university (as is happening currently in Australia, and as happened over the past two decades in the U.S.A.), or will it be accommodated by removing subjects currently covered (as has happened to double-entry bookkeeping in the U.K. over the past decade)? As Philip Reckers (U.S.A.) concludes: *'real trade offs are required'*

Perhaps if we stopped kow-towing to the wish of the accounting profession that we prepare students to *be* accountants and, instead, revert to preparing them to *become* accountants (AECC, 1990), we would find we had vast opportunities for improving the prospects of our accounting graduates by modernizing our curriculum and our modes of delivery and learning, which would enhance the educational base of accounting practice.

Reference

AECC [Accounting Education Change Commission] (1990) Objectives of education for accountants: position statement number one, *Issues in Accounting Education*, 5(2), 307–312.

Notes

1   The design of this chapter, the choice of countries (comprising three from each of seven geographic regions around the world), the identification of potential contributors from those countries, the solicitation of contributions, and the negotiation of the content of those contributions were undertaken by Professor Richard M.S. Wilson.
2   Thanks to Mark Freeman, University of Sydney, for his helpful comments.
3   For more details on this process, see Hancock *et al.* (2010, pp. 5–6).
4   Some 70 per cent of MBAd alumni reported relevant professional experience in accounting – auditing (Arquero *et al.*, 2009); 60 per cent of the job offers for MBAd graduates have this profile (Escobar & Jiménez, 2009).

About the author

Alan Sangster is Professor of Accounting Education at Griffith University, Australia. (a.j.a.sangster@btinternet.com). His research interests lie in accounting systems, accounting education, and accounting history (in which his focus is upon accounting and business practice from 1200 to 1900 and, in particular, the work of Luca Pacioli). He has published more than 50 articles and book chapters. In 2012 he became Editor of *Accounting Education: an international journal*.

Section D

Pedagogic considerations

Preface

Christine V. Helliar

UNIVERSITY OF SOUTH AUSTRALIA, AUSTRALIA

As accounting educators we need to consider pedagogy. Are we teachers, or facilitators of learning? Are we passive transmissive lecturers where we expect students to learn by rote, or do we help our students to learn how to learn and transform them to start on a road to life-long learning? What we do in the classroom or, indeed, outside the classroom, has a fundamental effect on whether the accountants of the future will meet the requirements of business and society in the years to come. Not only will our students have to be IT literate (Boritz & Stoner, Chapter 16), but they will also need social media skills as well as a detailed understanding of the nuts and bolts of hardware and software packages.

Our students need to learn by doing – and not by just listening. For example, we can listen to a swimming instructor on how to learn to swim, and we can watch people swimming, but we need to be thrown in (hopefully in the shallow end) and actually try to swim in order to swim ourselves. As educators, we can tell our students about accounting, but we need to throw them in – at the shallow end – and let them learn for themselves. Increasingly, they will begin to move into deeper water until, finally, they become competent accountants.

As educators, we need to use experiential learning and situated learning (Hassall & Joyce, Chapter 17), develop critical thinking (Cunningham, Chapter 18), and use role play, interactive case studies, field visits and other innovative teaching methods to enable our students to learn to learn. PowerPoint and textbooks (Stevenson, Ferguson, & Power, Chapter 19) are the ubiquitous methods of teaching accounting, but we need to help our students to acquire skills, values, ethics and attitudes rather than just technical knowledge.

We, the educators, need to ramp up our game. We need to change our philosophy on how students learn, and ensure that students develop their cognitive skills and begin to internalise the values and requirements of their chosen profession. Pedagogy matters.

16

Technology in accounting education

J. Efrim Boritz* and Gregory N. Stoner**

*UNIVERSITY OF WATERLOO, CANADA **UNIVERSITY OF GLASGOW, U.K.

CONTENTS

Abstract

An uneasy relationship has existed between the field of accounting and information technology (IT) for decades. This is despite the fact that accountants are masters at producing information for internal and external consumers and were among the earliest users of computers, especially applications devoted to recording streams of transactions and converting them into reports containing information useful for monitoring operations and making business decisions. This chapter discusses and evaluates the role and place of IT within accounting education. As the practice of accounting is heavily intertwined with the utilization of IT, awareness of its role in practice as well as the development of the skills necessary to use and manage IT are an essential part of accounting in theory and practice, and therefore should be an integral part of accounting education.

Keywords

accounting education, business information technology, educational technology, information technology, IT competencies

16.1 Introduction

The main aims of this chapter are:

- to discuss and evaluate the role and place of information technology (IT) within accounting education and to evaluate the key pedagogy and curriculum issues associated with promoting IT knowledge, understanding, and awareness in the accounting curriculum;
- to discuss the IT and Information Systems (IS) knowledge, understanding, and awareness that accounting students require to understand the possibilities and evolution of the discipline;
- to discuss the IT and information systems (IS) knowledge, understanding and awareness that accounting students require for future careers in the accounting profession;

- to identify and discuss the key IT skills (competencies) that students graduating from accounting programmes should possess in order to provide them with the foundations of the discipline and a career in accounting; and
- to identify and discuss significant IT-based learning technologies that are used within, and have potential to facilitate, accounting education.

An uneasy relationship has existed between the field of accounting and IT for decades. This is despite the fact that accountants are masters at producing information for internal and external consumers. In fact, accountants were among the earliest users of computers, especially applications devoted to recording streams of transactions and converting them into reports containing information useful for monitoring operations and making business decisions. Today, in many pockets of the accounting profession and academe, intense use is made of information technologies of one kind or another (for example, accounting packages, tax preparation software, computer-assisted auditing software, the ubiquitous spreadsheet and financial databases, and statistical analysis software). Most recently, Extensible Business Reporting Language (XBRL), a reporting technology for enhancing the transfer of information over the Internet, has captivated the imaginations of policy-makers and standard setters. Nevertheless, when it comes to the accounting curriculum, the IT and IS component (including the resource allocation to topics, support systems, and personnel) is often fighting for its life and its legitimacy.[1]

As noted above, the primary aim of this chapter is to discuss and evaluate the role and place of IT[2] within accounting education. As the practice of accounting is heavily intertwined with the utilization of IT, awareness of its role in practice as well as the development of the skills necessary to use and manage IT should be an integral part of accounting education. We focus on 'modern' information technologies that include software applications, computers and other devices such as tablets and networks, and therefore exclude older/original learning technologies, such as writing, the printed book, the black/whiteboard and other information technologies that are, of course, still widely used in accounting education. Although we review some materials produced by professional accounting bodies (PABs), the main focus of this chapter is on IT in an academic accounting education setting. We have attempted to identify all English-language publications relevant to our chapter by using e-journals at our respective institutions as well as other online search facilities.[3] We cover present practices as well as some thoughts about the future, and how we might improve accounting education in the future: an area covered more fully by Flood (see Chapter 4 – this volume) and by St. Pierre & Rebele (see Chapter 5 – this volume). Since practices evolve at different rates and are implemented at different times in various jurisdictions, some practices that are current in some jurisdictions represent an agenda for the future in others. Thus, if every academic unit was in a position to include the best pedagogic practices described in this chapter within its accounting curriculum, this would be a huge step forward for IT in accounting education. As technology took on ever greater importance in the processing of transactions, the preparation of financial reports and business analysis has evolved from the accounting of the 1960s. There have been corresponding changes in the accounting curriculum, including the introduction of word-processing, spreadsheets, databases, and accounting packages. However, research on the effects of including these tools in the accounting curriculum did not necessarily find a significant impact on the learning of accounting concepts per se (Bromson et al., 1994). Today's Millennial Generation (people born after 1982), which makes up almost the entire undergraduate population, is considered 'tech savvy' and social (i.e. enjoy working in a team setting) but is still challenged to translate these characteristics into better understanding of how the technology works or might be applied to accounting (Fogarty, 2008). Thus, there remains a need for discussion of and research on how to integrate technology into the accounting curriculum (Rebele *et al.*, 1998; David *et al.*, 2003). A complication for accounting programmes and educators is their need to balance the goals of promoting high quality learning and learning for the future ('learning to learn') with students' and some other stakeholders' vocational expectations: the desire for content aimed at helping students to succeed in professional examinations. In some jurisdictions this has led to de-emphasizing of coverage of IT topics, in part by the integration of IT topics throughout the curriculum (Wessels, 2010). Despite this, in practice in this model, coverage of IT elements is at risk of being crowded out by the demands of topics seen as being more examinable and more core to the discipline.[4] Our view is that accounting is an information discipline; therefore, it must include, and keep evergreen, curriculum components devoted to building knowledge of and experience with the information technologies that are central to an understanding of the theory and practice of accounting. A useful starting point for identifying desirable curriculum components is the IT knowledge and skills required by the various roles occupied by professional accountants in the various sectors in which they are employed. In addition, accounting educators must keep abreast of instructional technologies being used and developed both within and outside business schools, and adopt those that are appropriate across the accounting curriculum without undue delay.

In the next three sections, we explore the key pedagogy and curriculum issues associated with promoting IT knowledge, understanding and awareness (Section 16.2); specific IT knowledge and skills that should be part of the accounting curriculum (Section 16.3); and technology-based tools that can be used to help develop these competencies (Section 16.4). This is followed by a brief concluding section.

16.2 IT & IS knowledge, understanding and awareness: pedagogy and curriculum issues

The IT and IS knowledge, understanding, and awareness which students in accounting programmes require both to understand the possibilities and evolution of the discipline and for future careers in the accounting profession, whether in business or the public sector, consist of both general knowledge of topics related to information production and specific knowledge that depends on the different domains of accounting and the roles of accountants within them. For example, each of the following roles has different implications for required IT understanding:

*   *Accountant as user of IT* – preparing external reports, handling routine transactions, interpreting data from IS, designing appropriate reports, presentations, or other ways of informing stakeholders and clients with the data. In an auditing context, this would include preparing working papers and documenting audit/assurance procedures.
*   *Accountant as manager of IT* – management of IT, working with the senior information officer/director, interpreting reports that are prepared for a wide range of users.
*   *Accountant as designer of IT* – development of information and processes to create and communicate information, working with business process managers and system analysts, creating reports and reporting systems for a wide range of internal and external users, ensuring the systems meet accounting and audit needs, especially in relation to control.
*   *Accountant as IT consultant* – providing advice and support in various industries, systems and tasks such as security analysis, cyber forensics, project management.
*   *Accountant as auditor/evaluator of IT-based accounting systems* – external auditors, internal auditors, IT auditors, other evaluative and assurance roles.

- *Accountant as provider of accounting and tax services* – provide specialized services using IT to internal and external users related to compliance, filing of returns and planning tax strategies.
- *Accountant as educator* – facilitating students to learn how to choose appropriate data from that available, designing appropriate reports and presentation and complete the other roles noted above, choose appropriate IT to include in the curriculum and know how to evaluate and implement IT-based solutions in the classroom and extended learning environment.

IAESB's[5] (2010b) International Education Standard 2 (IES 2) explicitly notes the need for accounting programmes to include IT-related knowledge and competencies[6] related to the above roles and tasks including, particularly, assessing IT risks and IT controls, being aware of the role of IT in business systems, and being able to apply appropriate IT tools.[7] In addition International Education Practice Statement (IEPS) 2, *Information Technology for Professional Accountants* (IAESB, 2010b) provides more detail in relation to IT knowledge and the skills which educators should provide to accounting students to prepare them for qualification as professional accountants. This is a very useful approach both in higher education and in continuing professional development (CPD), which is also discussed in Section G of this volume. In this context it is also important to recognize the significant overlap between some of the IT topics that are integral to many aspects of business product and service delivery, accounting, information services and assurance within business and non-commercial organizations, including issues such as:

- interrelationship between Information Systems (IS, MIS, AIS, etc.) and accounting programmes;
- business systems – IT governance; e-commerce; enterprise systems; business intelligence; cloud-outsourcing; social networks and social media; mobile systems;
- accounting systems – file systems; reporting systems; REA (resources–events–agents); XBRL (eXtensible Business Reporting Language);
- information life-cycle; information and data integrity;
- system development life-cycle and project management; outsourcing;
- risks associated with all of the above.
- internal control frameworks/IT control frameworks designed to respond to the risks; security, availability, integrity, confidentiality, privacy;
- electronic evidence; business contracts; audit.

In organizations, data integration is very important, at least in part because the technology used by organizations is designed to be ubiquitous, inexpensive, and easy to use. This can also be difficult to achieve (Dechow *et al.*, 2007). Given this, and the wide range of IT systems in use, students should be exposed to different types of technology systems, including the nature of the hardware and software elements (for example, General Ledger systems, ERP systems, data warehousing, best of breed applications, and XML/XBRL). Students should understand the people–process–technology trio that all systems require, and the relationships between information, IT, IS, and management controls. The attitude of accounting educators and the way in which IT is integrated into the curriculum seem to affect students' overall perceptions of using IT, with positive approaches creating greater interest (Marriott *et al.*, 2003). However, there is often a gap either in understanding between practitioners and educators, or in the educators serving of the needs of practice. A study by Hastings & Solomon (2005) found that accounting educators and practitioners in the U.S.A. have different perceptions about the type and amount of coverage of technology and systems concepts that should be embedded in the accounting curriculum, with particularly high deficiencies in the more complex business and database systems, and this is in a country where accounting and business information systems courses are fairly common. Unsurprisingly, Chang & Hwang (2003), based on Australian and US data, found that junior auditors report receiving more IT education in their college degrees compared to their senior counterparts, several years earlier, which suggests that universities/colleges are adapting their curriculum to provide stronger IT education than was the case in the past. Internal control and information security were identified as being the most important areas and the study found that the respondents rated their IT training at the accounting firm higher than the university/college training. This may reflect audit firms' stronger incentives and greater resources, compared with HEIs. However, Thambar (2012) has observed (in the Australian context) that there is an increasing need for accountants, and accounting students, to be aware of and use more advanced IT systems: a view also reflected in the recommendations of the recent American Accounting Association's Pathways Commission report (AAA, 2012).

The message from the literature is far from clear on what is required at what specific levels of detail in order for graduates of accounting programmes to fully appreciate the development of accounting and to understand accounting from an IS perspective, or to provide the skills and background demanded by potential employers, let alone the demands of wider groups of stakeholders. Nonetheless, it is clear that there is demand and need for accounting graduates to have a sound grounding in these areas. The next section looks at some of the more specific IT-related knowledge and skills (termed competencies in many publications: see Watty, Chapter 13 – this volume) that are important elements of the accounting curriculum.[8]

16.3 IT & IS knowledge and skills (competencies) in and for the accounting curriculum

In this section, we identify the key IT knowledge and skills (competencies) that students graduating from accounting programmes should possess in order to provide them with a good basis for future careers in the accounting profession, accounting roles in business or the public sector, or to be in effect an integral part of the discipline. We concentrate on the most important issues which are unlikely to be covered elsewhere in students' learning profiles. As noted in the previous section, IAESB's (2010a) IEPS 2 on *Information Technology for Professional Accountants* covers the IT knowledge and skills that educators should address in order to prepare accounting students for qualification as professional accountants in the above roles, and tasks such as assessing IT risks and IT controls. Within this IEPS the general knowledge IT topics are categorized under six headings, summarized in Table 16.1 and, on this foundation, a layer of internal control and IT knowledge and skill requirements are built, summarized in Table 16.2. Internal control is an area of particular concern of accountants in all areas of practice and therefore is considered to be part of the foundation for all professional accountants. The IT user competencies,

Table 16.1 General knowledge of IT topics

•   IT Strategy
•   IT Architecture
•   IT as a Business Process Enabler
•   Systems Acquisition and Development Process
•   Management of IT
•   Communication and IT

Source: summarized from IEPS 2, Table 1, IAESB (2010, pp. 131–132).

Table 16.2 Internal control IT topics

• Understanding of business and accounting systems
• The application of appropriate IT systems and tools to business/accounting problems
• Suitable control criteria for analyzing and evaluating IT controls in business and accounting systems, including IT general controls and automated application controls
• The IT internal control environment
• Selected IT objectives
• Identified IT events
• IT risk assessment
• Selected IT risk responses
• IT control activities
• Information and communication in relation to IT
• The monitoring process and actions taken in relation to IT
• The application of controls to personal systems

Source: Summarized from IEPS 2, IAESB (2010, pp. 132–133).

Table 16.3 IT user competencies

• Apply appropriate IT systems and tools to business and accounting problems
• Demonstrate an understanding of business and accounting systems
• Apply controls to personal IT systems.

Source: Summarized from IEPS 2, IAESB (2010, p. 134).

summarized in Table 16.3 and included in this Standard, are also relevant in this section as these are seen, particularly in practice, as being an integral part of the discipline.

Table 16.4 summarizes role-based competencies expected of accountants involved in designer, manager, auditor, evaluator, and academic roles. The latter of these is not discussed in IEPS 2: the group to which it would apply is comparatively small and beyond the scope of the statements. The items added highlight that there are identifiable competencies in applying IT to accounting education. IEPS 2 also provides for mixed roles and post-qualification competencies for these and other more specialized roles.

These skills and competencies are considered in some respects as being part of the generic skills debate which is discussed by Watty in Chapter 13 – this volume. There has been a host of research on skills from the perspectives of employers, students, and academic accounting staff, much of which covers the IT-related areas, and some of which specializes in this domain (e.g. Marriott *et al.*, 2003; Stoner, 2009; Ahadiat, 2008, in relation to educators' personal use).

From a different perspective, and in a very different country, Bawaneh (2011) surveyed financial institutions in Jordan, finding that employers showed a high recognition of the importance of IT and the advantages of using technology in their business and of employing highly-qualified university accounting graduates who understood the vital role of technology in the creation of information from accounting data. Interestingly, the results also identified the need for more coordination between universities and employers in this area in order to improve students' university education.

Aspects of the skills debate are intertwined with the IT issues central to the themes of this chapter. In this context we now provide a brief discussion of a selection of specific IT skills and competencies that are particularly important within the practice and discipline of accounting, and which therefore should be considered as being important elements of the accounting

Table 16.4 Role-based competencies

Designer of IS Role

- Analyzing and evaluating the role of information in an entity's business processes and organization
- Applying project management methods
- Applying systems investigation and project initiation methods
- Applying user requirements determination and initial design methods
- Applying detailed systems design and acquisition/development methods
- Applying systems implementation methods
- Applying systems maintenance and change management methods

Manager of IS Role

- Managing an entity's IT strategy
- Managing an IT organization
- Managing IT operations' effectiveness and efficiency
- Maintaining financial control over IT
- Managing IT controls
- Managing systems acquisition, development and implementation
- Managing systems change and related problem management

Evaluator of IS Role

- Planning systems evaluation
- Understanding the impact of IS/IT on business strategies and tactics
- Evaluating systems
- Communicating results of evaluations and following-up

Financial Auditor Role

- Evaluating an entity's overall IT control environment
- Planning financial accounting and reporting systems evaluation
- Evaluating financial accounting and reporting systems including understanding and assessing the design and operating effectiveness of control activities in automated business processes
- Communicating results of evaluations and following-up

Academic Role

- Principles of curriculum design and pedagogy
- Concepts and tools relevant to the use of technology in education
- Concepts, topics and tools relevant to all accounting areas (e.g., accounting information systems)
- Concepts, topics and tools relevant to particular accounting areas (e.g., tax package, audit software)

Source: Summarized from IEPS 2, IAESB (2010, pp. 135–137), except the last panel.

curriculum. Many of the competencies that are discussed here can only be developed to a modest extent and at a more conceptual rather than practical level by academic accounting programmes. More advanced and more practical levels need to be addressed in the work environment. Nevertheless, including coverage of the topics listed in Tables 16.1–16.4 at suitable intellectual and applied levels within the academic curriculum will both prepare accounting students to better integrate these competencies after graduation, when they are in the process of becoming professional accountants, and to better understand theoretical aspects of accounting and its role in organizations.

16.3.1 Spreadsheet: design, development, use, and control

Spreadsheets have been a favoured IT tool of accountants from the beginning of the micro-computer revolution of the 1980s (if not earlier, Mattessich & Galassi, 2000), and continue to be one of the most often cited required skills of accounting professionals (Hastings & Solomon, 2005). Further, their use in practice has raised some serious cause for concern[9] and continues to do so due to the high incidence of errors in spreadsheet models used in practice (Powell *et al.*, 2008, 2009) including errors of qualitative as well as calculative and quantitative natures (Panko & Aurigemma, 2010). There appears to be a degree of belief within the academy that new students, of the 'millennial generation', will have skills in this area since this is seen as being an area of generic IT skill, however, this confidence seems to be misplaced (Stoner, 1999, 2009). Consequently, it is important that the curriculum addresses the skills required in this area: skills that go beyond the technical use of packages and the complex, as well as simple, functions within them, but also includes good modelling and control skills as well as the generic modelling and decision skills required in order to decide when spreadsheet modelling approaches are or are not appropriate.

There has been research in these areas, including, for example, Marriott (2004) on these skills in a simulation context, and spreadsheet use is reported within the context of other learning discussions and modelling (Stoner & Milner, 2010; Spraakman, 2011). Cases and instructional resources are sometimes published, for example, Loraas & Key (2010) which is an instructional resource which aims to develop a combination of accounting, tax, and spreadsheet development skills. There is considerable need for further research with respect to several facets of the domain. Under-researched areas here include:

- the types and levels of skills required;
- how they might best be learned;
- the interrelationship with decision theory and psychology;
- the extent to which this might best be learned in the academy or in practice (as CPD); and
- the relationships with the development of an understanding of accounting principles and theory.

16.3.2 Database: design, use, and control

In a study of required IT skills (Hastings & Solomon, 2005), database management software skills[10] were identified as being the second most important IT skill required by accountants in terms of desired level of training. To those who understand the importance of databases in practice and the strengths of database approaches, compared to, say, spreadsheets, this is probably not a surprise. However, experience suggests that this is not a view held by significant numbers of accounting academicians (many of whom see this as an IT technology that is divorced from the theory, operation, and understanding of accounting). Yet in practice, database management systems are the core of almost all accounting systems, and in many cases would provide a more controllable environment for the storage of data than the ubiquitous spreadsheet.

In the North American accounting education environment, where AIS (Accounting Information Systems) is included in the accounting curriculum in most higher education institutions (HEIs), the importance of database-related skills and knowledge is recognized (at least by academic staff in those areas) not least due to the importance of the REA (resources–events–agents) model in the teaching of accounting transaction structures, commitment, and business policy specifications (McCarthy, 2003; Geerts, 2008). The REA framework can be used to teach concepts and skills such as value chains, cost-benefit analysis, business process specifications, and database design and implementation, which is one reason why many AIS instructors in the U.S.A. include this topic in their AIS course. In contrast, in many other parts of the world (for example, in the U.K. and Australia), the position of AIS in the accounting curriculum is less prominent, and database-related skills are largely neglected.[11] Accounting educators without comprehension of the way in which visualizing data in such forms has the potential to alter the modes and models of informing (especially perhaps non-practice-exposed accounting staff) are likely to see database concepts and skills as being divorced from many aspects of the theory of accounting and accountability. In consequence, this area of IT and IT skills is probably one of the most neglected areas within the accounting curriculum, and is an area worthy of significant further research (as observed by Stoner, 1999, 2009).

16.3.3 Accounting and business systems: implementation, use, and control

Accounting (nominal/general) ledger systems were introduced into accounting programmes in a wide variety of ways across time and national regimes, both as theoretical ideas and as practical implementations, this being one of the first IT-related interfaces of accounting practice with electronic data processing (EDP). It is not uncommon for these, including basic hands-on use, to be introduced in mainline accounting courses as an example of double-entry accounting in practice, especially in regimes where specialist AIS courses are not offered. Where AIS courses are part of the programme, these types of systems, including the transaction processing and support systems, are the mainstay of many of those courses. The level of detail to which general aspects of business systems, and systems controls are considered varies greatly, depending on the nature of the programmes. This is an area in which research has been conducted but often within the IS rather than AIS discipline and it is worthy of more attention within accounting education.

16.3.4 ERP (Enterprise Resource Planning) systems: implementation, use, and control

Though often thought of by significant parts of the accounting academy as being beyond the scope of the discipline, the centrality of ERP systems and other forms of enterprise systems[12] within real-world business systems means there is a growing need for awareness of and, arguably, practical experience of, ERP systems as core within the discipline. During the late 1990s, when ERP systems were being implemented to replace legacy systems and thereby forestall the anticipated Y2K crisis, many accounting academics were attracted to SAP's University Alliance Program.[13] Although the program provided funding to universities that incorporated coverage of SAP into the accounting curriculum, the program proved to be unsustainable, due to the heavy investment of time required to master the technology on the part of academics who also had research and other commitments to fulfil. The initiative was a lesson to those academics and others to be wary in the future of jumping into similar technology initiatives due to the time commitment required. Nevertheless, some coverage of ERP systems is necessary for financial reporting and audit professionals due to the need to design and audit the flexible and complex reporting and costing structures. In relation to the management reporting side of the profession in particular, Grabski, Leech, & Sangster (2009) discuss the implementations of ERP systems in organizations. Based on case data, they show that the involvement of accountants both improves success and enhances the role of the accountant. In particular, it increases the need for the accountant to understand the business processes of the organization and improves post-implementation decision-making. These findings, supported by the high demands of skills training in these areas (Hastings & Solomon, 2005), provide the rationale for covering this topic in the accounting curriculum, and Bradford (2011) provides a case-based instructional resource in this area.

16.3.5 E-commerce system implementation and control

E-commerce has become a critical component of the economy and, therefore, of an accounting student's knowledge base. In their nationwide survey of academic accounting staff and practising accountants in the U.S.A., Rezaee, Elam, & Cassidy (2005) found that an overwhelming proportion of practitioners (92 per cent) and academicians (88 per cent) saw a need for a course in E-Commerce. Kotb & Roberts (2011) find that, while there is a similar environment and assumed similar needs, E-Business courses are less frequently offered in U.K. and Ireland than in the U.S.A. Again, in the context of the U.S.A., Rezaee, Lambert, & Harmon (2006) looked at the nature and structure of a selection of worldwide E-commerce courses, identifying 79 courses (mainly in the U.S.A., but 20 per cent elsewhere), finding a mixed pattern of delivery at graduate (54 per cent), undergraduate (28 per cent), or mixed (18 per cent) levels. Less than a fifth of these courses included hands-on-project or web-site design elements. The authors suggest that the point of including this material in the course is not the technology itself, but to meet professional knowledge and skill needs. In this regard, some of the key topics that should be covered in such a course include: e-commerce business models, strategies and value propositions; e-commerce website effectiveness criteria; revenue models, order processing and payment collection; e-procurement, trading exchanges and supply chain management; e-marketing, customer relationship management; business analytics; and security, availability, processing integrity, confidentiality and privacy controls.

16.3.6 Real Time Economy (RTE)

The Real Time Economy (RTE) is causing changes in business, internal and external financial reporting, and the audit industry, as RTE focusses on reducing the delay between processes, including the related recording, reporting, and auditing of transactions. Vasarhelyi, Teeter, & Krahel (2010) address educational media that may be incorporated into the auditing curriculum as a way of developing skills required for a changing auditing environment. In particular, they focus on the processes of continuous auditing, monitoring and data assurance, together with a focus on how auditors need to be prepared for the RTE and continuous auditing: a methodology that focusses on current transactions and data instead of the firm's history of records. Vasarhelyi & Alles (2008) take a broader view, raising similar questions to a wider area of the accounting domain for research with educational implications.

16.3.7 XBRL (eXtensible Business Reporting Language) implementation, control, and assurance

XBRL is the tagging of information in computer-readable documents with codes according to an agreed taxonomy[14] in order to produce computer-readable, interpretable and transferable financial reports. As such, XBRL is an important technological advance facilitating the re-use and transfer of data with important implications for all information professionals, especially accountants. The mandatory adoption of XBRL for SEC filings for public companies in the U.S.A. starting in 2009, and similar mandatory filing requirements elsewhere,[15] has now made this topic essential knowledge for accounting and auditing students (Taylor & Dzuranin, 2010;

Elam *et al.*, 2012). Debreceny & Farewell (2010) discuss the need for coverage of XBRL to be integrated into the current accounting curriculum as opposed to redesigning it. They suggest that dispersing it through different courses (ranging from introductory to managerial to intermediate financial accounting) will enable its integration, but this will be a challenge for many accounting academics due to the perceived technology barrier to their understanding of XBRL. Thus, this promises to become an increasingly interesting area for future education research, as adoption spreads and the implications become more important, both nationally and internationally.

16.3.8 Tax preparation and planning software: use and control

With online tax compliance procedures becoming important in many (if not most advanced) national regimes, IT skills at a basic level are vital to tax accounting. Further, the nature of the tax environment, with complex interlocking rules combined with the need to project future economic outcomes, makes this a natural environment for specialist modelling software for tax planning purposes, including interest in intelligent (knowledge-based) systems elements (Baldwin-Morgan, 1995; Lymer, 1995). Though skills with specific software may not be high on the list of employers' demands (ranked 8th of 14 in a U.K. context (Miller & Woods, 2000) and 7th of 8 in Malaysia (Ling & Nawawi, 2010)), studies show that employers do consider these skills to be moderately important. With the increasing effect of electronic filing, however, it is expected that the importance of these (Ling & Nawawi, 2010) and other IT-related skills such as those in the XBRL arena will increase over time.

16.3.9 Information integrity/data quality

The first word in Information Technology is information. In spite of the fact that accounting is an information discipline, there are many aspects of information that are not routinely addressed in the accounting curriculum, particularly the characteristics and attributes of high quality information and the impact of impairments of that information on decision-making. Berger & Boritz (2012) investigate how accounting students incorporate information integrity impairments into performance evaluation judgements and judgement confidence, focussing on four information integrity attributes (completeness, currency, accuracy, and authorization). Their results show that, as the severity of the integrity impairments increased, accounting students assigned more weight to information integrity impairments in judging the performance of division managers, as if they were rewarding and penalizing division managers for the level of information integrity as well as their managerial performance. Also, as information integrity impairments increased, students wished to postpone their judgements and seek additional information. Given the importance of information integrity in the accounting profession, it is critical that accounting students develop the ability to appropriately consider information integrity impairments when making judgements: Berger & Boritz (2012) suggest ways for accounting educators to help accounting students develop this ability.

16.3.10 System documentation techniques

Accounting students should be inculcated with system documentation skills that include techniques for obtaining an understanding of a system or process; documenting that understanding effectively and efficiently; and leveraging that documentation to perform risk and control assessments. Courses in AIS and auditing routinely cover system documentation techniques, at least in the context of the U.S.A. Bradford, Richtermeyer, & Roberts (2007) focus on system diagrams (SD) in the classroom and in practice, including: data flow diagram (DFD), resources–events–agents (REA) models, process maps, and Unified Modelling Language (UML). The study concludes that SDs are important due to the ever-increasing regulatory environment; the results showed gaps between practice and pedagogy where accounting textbooks can be improved. Regrettably, these findings are based on opinions rather than on convincing evidence that diagrammatic representation leads to improved performance. Boritz, Borthick, & Presslee (2012) use an experiment that compares students' performance on a business process risk and control assessment task using two informationally equivalent methods that are commonly taught in the classroom to document business processes: textual narrative and diagrammatic representation (Business Process Modelling Notation). They find that, while the method of representation has no effect on students' accuracy, those receiving the textual representation were more efficient and had a greater weighted-average (accuracy plus efficiency) performance than those receiving the diagrammatic representation. Both self-efficacy and academic achievement interact with the type of representation to affect students' performance. The implications of this study depend on the objective of including coverage of documentation techniques in the curriculum. If the SDs are intended to influence practice, then they may add little value. However, if they are intended to enhance pedagogy, then the jury is still out, as that aspect of the use of SDs has not yet been studied.

16.3.11 Intelligent systems implementation and use

Interest in knowledge processing systems within accounting education (also called expert system, intelligent knowledge-based systems, and artificial intelligence systems) seems to have waned, despite the fact that such systems are widely used in business and accounting. For example, most audit planning systems incorporate rule-based subsystems within them to process complex chains of planning rules. Older research in this area (Baldwin-Morgan, 1995; Lymer, 1995)[16] did find benefits of teaching expert systems to accounting students including breaking down complex knowledge in spheres such as tax, and the interpretation of accounting standards.

16.3.12 CAATs (Computer Assisted Auditing Techniques): implementation, use, and control

The potential benefits of including CAAT systems, such as GAS (Generalized Audit Software), in the accounting curriculum go well beyond learning how to use the software (in itself a useful skill set in professional services firms) and expanding on the theory typically learned in classrooms. Experience with CAATs can enhance students' understanding of other related topics (such as AIS, data quality and auditing concepts). For example, Richardson & Louwers (2010) discuss the use of GAS to teach statistical sampling concepts in auditing. Boritz & Datardina (2013) discuss the use of CAAT-oriented cases in the classroom and note the positive reception to implementing CAATs/GAS in a classroom setting, with 72 per cent of students agreeing that the use of GAS helped supplement their understanding of audit procedures, and 82 per cent recommending the continued use of CAATs in the course.

16.3.13 Other related areas of IT & IS knowledge and skill

Other IT & IS-related knowledge and skill (competencies) areas that are important to accounting in theory and practice[17] include topics such as:

- the cloud;
- systems analysis and design (particularly related to the role of accountants in the process as creator of data, user of information, manager, and designer of business processes, including both automated and manual elements necessary to achieve business objectives);
- project management systems and software;
- data analytics (filtering and organizing mass data to provide informing insights);
- data visualization systems (systems to enhance the informing power of data through innovative graphical presentation);
- web portal systems (to bring together and enhance data from/into intranets and extranets), use of on-line search and financial tools;
- the control and protection of personal technologies (e.g. mobiles, personal digital assistants (PDAs), and tablet devices) used in business systems and the data accessed via them (particularly when they are not business-supplied systems); and
- social networks used in a business context.

All these technologies constitute important elements of many accounting systems and have the potential to have broad effects on the practice of accounting. Therefore, students ought to be made aware of them and their potential. Badua, Sharifi, & Watkins (2011) survey AIS educators in the U.S.A. and analyse texts, syllabuses, and the literature and make recommendations for the design of AIS provision within the accounting curriculum in the context of the U.S.A. Although the study is limited and potentially biased in favour of AIS, they conclude that the size and dynamic nature of the IT and IS area are such that there is a need for more space in the U.S.A. accounting curriculum, possibly for a second course, and for flexible approaches to delivery. In other areas of the world where AIS provision is less likely, there is a potential need for far greater provision. For some of these areas, there is literature and research published within the specialist IS and IS education literature (including *Accounting Education: an international journal*, the *International Journal of Accounting Information Systems*, and the journals of the AAA: *Issues in Accounting Education*, *Journal of Information Systems*, and the *Journal of Emerging Technologies in Accounting*, and possibly the journal of the AIS Educator Association, the *AIS Educator Journal*). There is considerable scope for translating that work into forms that would be useful to the more mainline accounting academy, particularly for those regimes within which there is not a strong tradition of AIS as a separate discipline: a task beyond the scope of this chapter.

16.4 Integration and use of IT-based learning technologies to facilitate education

This is an area which has attracted a good deal of attention for over two decades in general education fields as well as within the sphere of accounting education. The purpose of this section is not to recount or to summarize the wide variety of literature in this area, which would be beyond the scope of this chapter. Instead, after a short introduction to the general area and to a selection of work that has looked at a range of learning technologies in the accounting field, we discuss a selection of areas of particular interest to accounting, including some of the interesting emerging learning technologies that seem likely to be of particular interest among accounting educators.

In part, this section is about e-learning, of either the online or blended learning variety – both of which are concerned with synchronous and asynchronous learning using electronic communications (Garrison, 2011) and, in part, the section is concerned with the use of technology in the physical learning environment. The e-learning aspect is an important element of this mix, especially as increasingly the boundaries are fuzzy. For example, many of the newer classroom technologies use electronic communications, from interactive whiteboards to the use of mobile phones in the classroom. In effect, most if not all accounting education now takes place in either online or blended learning environments: online for distance education, blended for the rest, including campus-based provision where online and face-to-face elements of the environment are integrated. In the online environment, the academy also needs to rise to the new challenges and opportunities offered by the recent interest in Massive Open On-line Courses (MOOCs). The approach discussed by Garrison (2011), which is based on constructivist principles, stresses the importance of e-learning not just to provide access to information, but also to introduce (reintroduce or maintain) reflective and collaborative discourse, particularly in the face of tightening financial and resource constraints. In many ways this is an approach not unlike that of Laurillard (1993) who discussed the importance of the dialogue of learning between the participants (learners and teachers/facilitators) within the learning space.

Within the accounting sphere the literature suggests that a wide variety of learning technologies are used (or at least experimented with) and, as is illustrated by the discussions below, there is a variety of publications that look at the use, benefits, and problems of using individual technologies in individual courses, or across a small range of environments. Widespread surveys (across locations or types technology) are relatively rare. One exception is Bryant & Hunton (2000), who set out a framework for the discussion and evaluation of the use of educational technologies in the field, and review the existing literature. They conclude that there is a need for more research in the area, that more notice should be taken of the theoretical background, and that, while the newer technologies may have potential, there is a real need to choose educational technologies which are appropriate and that educators and researchers '*should not jump on the latest technology bandwagon simply because it is rolling nearby*' (ibid., p. 157).

Ahadiat (2008), in the U.S.A., took a different approach, looking at the IT used by accounting educators (not just within their teaching). His results indicate that the most prevalent uses of technology were:

- email communication with colleagues (90.2 per cent);
- retrieving information from the Internet (89.9 per cent);
- word processing-based student assignments (88.1 per cent);
- use of spreadsheets for administration (grades and other records) (86.0 per cent); and
- spreadsheet-based student assignments (84.3 per cent).

Just as these uses are unsurprising, so is the finding that younger educators tended to use more technology.

In recent years, the use of technology in education has exploded and there are many useful websites with information on educational technologies, assessment of their benefits and costs, and implementation guidance. For example, Johnson, Adams, & Cummins (2012) report on the key international trends that are currently affecting teaching and learning in higher education, and identify educational technologies that are expected to have near-term (mobile apps, tablet computing), medium-term (game-based learning, learning analytics), and long-term impacts (gesture-based computing, the internet of things) on higher education. The American Accounting Association's (AAA) Commons website[18] contains a blog on *Teaching with Technology* and serves as a repository for articles, presentations, conference materials, cases, multi-media content, links to other relevant sites, and various other materials on educational technologies available to AAA members. Table 16.5 summarizes educational technologies which are widely used in secondary and tertiary education under five main headings.

Table 16.5 General technologies for teaching

Presentations and Multi-Media Technologies	Discussion and Collaboration Technologies
• Comics	• Blogs
• Digital Story Telling	• Chats/Discussion Forums
• Discovery Ed Teaching	• Collaborative Writing
• Ebooks	• Google Docs
• Games	• Social Bookmarking
• Infographics	• Social Networks
• Interactive Whiteboards/Smartboards	• WebQuests
• Maps	• Wikis
• Multi-media Presentations	• Video Chat
• Online Charts and Graphics	*Research and Writing Technologies*
• Personal Response Systems ('Clickers')	• Citation Generators
• Podcasts	• Creative Commons
• Posters	• Mindmapping/Concept Mapping
• Presentation Systems	• Note Taking and Archiving
• Publishing Images	• Social Bookmarking
• Scrapbooks	• Students' Newspapers
• Screencasts/Webcasts	• Word Clouds
• Speaking Avatars	• Publishing Papers
• Timelines	• Plagiarism Checkers
• Video	*Assessment and Rubrics*
• Virtual Tours	• Assessment Criteria
• Voice Threads	• Online Assessment/Testing Tools
• Web Pages	• Rubrics
	Mobile Devices
	• Tablets, Smartphones and Laptops
	• Apps

Sources: Adapted from data at http://www.thwt.org/; http://commons.aaahq.org and http://www.theideacenter.org (both accessed 13 October 2012).

In this brief section, it is impossible to cover all the educational technologies that are being used and developed both within and outside the accounting domain. The sources noted in Table 16.5 are useful, describing these technologies and their potential uses, as is the discussion of teaching resources covered by Stevenson *et al.*, in Chapter 19 – this volume, several of which are IT-related. Based on the technologies that are being used and discussed by accounting educators in accounting education journals, at conferences, and on related websites, we have identified the following areas for further consideration here:

- In-class technologies – presentation software; personal response systems or 'clickers'; interactive whiteboards
- Computer-based learning systems; hypertext; simulations; online tutorials
- On-line course management systems and distance education
- Social networks, social media, and collaboration tools – blogs, wikis, discussion forums, etc.
- Performance, learning assessment software
- Mobile devices – laptops; tablets; smartphones
- Plagiarism checkers.

One caution is in order: students can be sceptical about the value of some educational technologies. Pimpa (2010) focussed on online engagement by accounting, finance, and international business undergraduate students (in Australia). Interview-based results highlighted that there are a lot of different resources and tools online, but they are generally poor in design and guidance. Also, the lack of proper training of new students in the use of educational technologies (such as discussion boards) can lessen their value. Somewhat sceptically, students also believed that teachers added online components because they were forced to and not for the value of their education.

16.4.1 In-class technologies – presentation software, personal response systems or 'Clickers', and interactive whiteboards

Many of the educational technologies listed in Table 16.5 are meant for online use outside the classroom. However, several educational technologies are widely used in the classroom.

- *Presentation software and multi-media technologies*: Perhaps the most widely used in-class technology is presentation software such as PowerPoint. PowerPoint is both loved and hated by educators and students alike. While providing powerful facilities for organizing and communicating, PowerPoint can also create mind-numbing lists of points which inhibit free discussion in the classroom. Rankin & Hoass (2001) investigated the effect of PowerPoint presentations on students' performance in a small accounting class experiment and found no significant effects, though the study (based in the U.S.A.) is very limited. Other presentation and multi-media technologies such as podcasts and webcasts are listed in Table 16.5, and the *Teaching History with Technology* website[19] provides useful information about these tools, their benefits, sources for obtaining them, and learning more about them. In the U.K., Marriott & Teoh (2012) report that students reported positive reactions to the use of screencasts to provide feedback on assessment performance, but caution that this could be time-consuming for staff.

- *Personal Response Systems*: A technology that has gained a following among many educators is the use of Student Response Systems also called Audience Response Systems (aka Clickers). These systems use handheld keypads which transmit signals to a teacher's laptop in response to a question posed to the class. Since each device is individually identified and recorded, all students' responses and non-responses can be collated and feedback can be provided instantly to the class. Such systems are thought to promote active learning and interaction as well as immediate individual feedback to students. However, results are mixed. Carnaghan & Webb (2007), who implemented a student response system in a *Managerial Accounting* class in Canada, found that there was a decline in students' engagement and, though students believed that the system helped them academically, they only performed marginally better when the questions on examinations were similar to ones that were asked in class using clickers. Conversely, in an *Introductory Accounting* course in the U.S.A., Premuroso, Tong, & Beed (2011) found that students performed better with the use of clickers, thought that using clickers increased their understanding of course material, and did not find them to be a hindrance. The authors hypothesized that the clickers boosted their interactions with students.[20] Cost, administration, and inconvenience are seen as being barriers to the wider adoption of these systems, but technology is moving towards similar systems based on mobile technologies that are almost ubiquitous among students in many environments (i.e. the mobile phone using either texts or mobile web applications or apps).

- *Interactive whiteboards:* This is a technology for making the use of whiteboards more interactive. For example, functions such as screen shade, cloning, move and reveal enable the teacher to facilitate learning of how to solve accounting problems. An obstacle to the use of this technology for some institutions is its cost, as staff are unlikely to use them unless their provision is widespread across the campus, or at least those parts of campus where they might be expected to teach.

16.4.2 Computer-based learning systems, simulations, and online tutorials

Known under various labels, computer-based learning (CBL) systems represent an instructional technology that has been used for professional development and distance education as well as in university/college education for decades. Kaye & Nicholson (1992) point out that early use of CBL in accounting education fell into three categories: for teaching Computer Science (CS); as computational tools (CCT); and in Computer-assisted Instruction (CAI). Today, CBL has been expanded into several additional areas, including:

- Research (Datastream, MicroEXSTAT, etc. – real data for analysis);
- Teaching accounting in a computerized environment (SAGE, PEGASUS – gives insight to integrated accounting packages);
- Administration (Question Mark – system used for course management and examinations);
- Management of learning (giving control of learning to students);
- Learning source (using Computer-Assisted Learning technologies [CAL]).

- *Computer-Assisted Learning (CAL)*: CAL systems and resources take many forms but they are mainly a mixture of multi-media-based texts and other learning resources with imbedded interactive learning elements. Stoner (2003) reports on the use of two contrasting CAL systems[21] in a first level *Management Accounting* course in supplantive and supportive modes in a U.K. university. Using multiple data sources, the integration of the learning technology resources was seen as being broadly successful, based both on students' reactions to the systems and the feedback which they provided, and course results. McDowall & Jackling's (2006) conclusion focusses on students' perceptions of the usefulness of CAL packages and how this had an impact on learning accounting concepts. In the study of second-year Australian students in an accounting course, the teacher used CAL packages, such as Accounting Equation, General Ledger, together with commercial accounting software QuickBooks Pro, with computer laboratory sessions replacing tutorials to allow students to complete CAL-related case studies. Students had a positive reaction to the use of the CAL programmes and believed they would positively impact academic performance. Suwardy *et al.* (2013) report on the use of an innovative CAL application (in Singapore) based on digital storytelling, and conclude that it had a positive effect on students' engagement in learning, particularly by contextualising the role of accounting in management decision-making.
- *Use of accounting software:* The use of commercial style software to teach or illustrate the practicalities of accounting at introductory level or in AIS courses is widespread. In a *Management Accounting* context in Australia, Tan & Ferreira (2012) report that the use of commercial activity-based costing software in a well-integrated and aligned way within a course can improve students' understanding of concepts and willingness to learn, and that the students' satisfaction with the software is pivotal in this enhanced learning.

- *Hypertext learning:* Hypertext learning aids embed links within educational content which enable the designer and the learner to create associations between content 'nodes' to facilitate active learning. Such systems can encourage exploration, enquiry and discovery and thereby promote learning. Jones & Wright (2010) investigated the use of hypertext learning aids in an *Advanced Accounting* course in Canada, and report disturbing results which suggest the need for caution in using such aids as they can actually decrease students' performance.
- *Simulations:* Computer-based simulations can help students compensate for a vital missing component in their backgrounds – experience. Accounting students often lack concrete experience so Marriott (2004) recommends the use of computer simulations to provide students with simulated concrete experience in an educational setting to help them develop algorithmic thinking, spreadsheet modelling, and enhanced cognition. Students (in the U.K.) provided positive feedback about the business simulation, and believed it aided them in their learning process. Stanley & Edwards (2005) discuss the design and development of a CD ROM containing real-life scenarios in contexts designed to assist students' learning of AIS cycles within an Australian university. The CD ROM was seen to provide:

  — authentic contexts;
  — learning activities;
  — access to expert performances, and the modelling of processes;
  — multiple roles and perspectives;
  — reflection to enable abstractions to be formed;
  — coaching by teachers at appropriate times; and
  — authentic assessment of learning.

- Surveys of students who used the software found that there is value associated with the use of such multi-media technologies in terms of providing effective learning experiences, especially in large learning environments. Using a somewhat different application in the U.S.A. – Second Life, an immersive virtual world – but with similar goals, Hornik & Thornburg (2010) found that both students' perceived level of engagement and performance in examinations improved. The paper addresses how Second Life can make an impact on education (having discussion boards, lectures with the software, etc.).
- *Online tutorials:* Tutorials are widely used in accounting education to help students develop knowledge and understanding of technical subject matter and related problem-solving skills. Conventional tutorials are limited by the availability of resources such as capable tutors and the need to schedule workable meeting times and physical space for the tutorial. Online homework systems and tutorials reduce or eliminate these constraints. They can be responsive to the individual needs and capabilities of students, and have the added advantage that students can repeat them as often as necessary to master the material being presented. Gafney, Ryan, & Wurst (2010) and Johnson, Phillips, & Chase (2009) show, in the U.S.A. and Canada respectively, that online homework system (OHS) and intelligent tutoring systems (ITS) outperform conventional accounting homework assignments. Phillips & Johnson (2011) compare OHS and ITS in a Canadian university and report that students using ITS outperform those using OHS in a sophomore-level *Financial Accounting* course.

16.4.3 Online course management systems and distance education

Distance education is playing a bigger role in both developed and developing countries, to enable students to have more equal opportunities to receive education (Ozkul *et al.*, 2011, in Turkey).

Accounting has had a tradition of offering access to education programmes through distance education. Discussion boards are one of the educational technologies that can enhance distance education. Although discussion boards and several other of the educational technologies listed in Table 16.5 can be used independently in a distance education programme, web-based course management systems bring many of the most popular features together under one umbrella management system.

- *Web-Based Learning Environments (WBLEs)*: WBLEs, also known as Virtual Learning Environments (VLEs), enable the management and delivery of course content, and provide access to a variety of educational technologies to students and administrative tools to academic staff over the web. By facilitating anytime, anywhere self-service access to learning, they are changing interactions between academic staff and students, and are often a core part of the delivery of blended learning. Prompted by the notion that active participation is an important element of students' learning, Basioudis & De Lange (2009) in the U.K., and Halabi & De Lange (2011) in Australia, Singapore, and Hong Kong, surveyed students after the use of two different WBLEs in an *Introductory Accounting* course. They found that the provision of lecture notes and model answers to tutorials were important parts of students' satisfaction, but that active elements such as online discussion boards and online assessment were also appreciated by students. It was also observed that 'novelty' seems to be an important element in students' engagement, and that the results of this study in the U.K. were comparable to other tests on students in Australia and New Zealand (for example, Wells *et al.*, 2008, and Basioudis *et al.*, 2012, which provides an international comparison of the 2001–2005 data used in the earlier studies). Using the WBLE as a support tool seems to have been endorsed by the students as enhancing their learning outcomes. However, Chen, Jones, & Moreland (2013), in the U.S.A., report that the perceived effectiveness of learning environments and knowledge development depend upon the course level. The delivery method affects course outcomes for courses at the advanced undergraduate course level, but not at the *Principles* level. Among the conclusions of Osgerby (2013) are indications that students in the U.K. see a mix of advantages and disadvantages of VLEs and, in particular, that they are likely to choose to use less formal social networking platforms than the official VLE for peer communication and support.

A downside of widely-used course management systems (such as Blackboard, WebCT, Angel and Desire2Learn) is their cost. However, open source systems (such as Moodle) are making it possible for academic programmes with resource constraints to avail themselves of these systems for managing distance education offerings and allowing more flexible implementations.

16.4.4 Social networks, discussion boards, social media, and collaboration tools

Accounting students have a reputation for preferring to work in isolation rather than teams. Thus, it is not a given that social networks and collaborative tools would appeal to them, though the use of social networks and social media could be appealing to students with a cultural affinity for collectivism.

- *Discussion boards:* One of the earliest online facilities designed to enhance collaboration is the use of discussion boards or chat rooms, which enable classroom-like discussions to be incorporated into otherwise solitary learning at a distance, either within distance education or blended learning environments. Weila, McGuigan, & Kernb (2011) focus on online discussion boards in a case-based *Intermediate Accounting* course in New Zealand. The introduction of case studies alongside educational technologies such as discussion boards, were new to the course and, as such, surveys were conducted at the end of the course to gauge feedback pertaining to the implementation. The use of a case study in this environment is seen to benefit students as it enhances their ability to identify the relevant data in the case, ability to think critically about issues, and the ability to summarize the available information, an issue addressed by Hassall & Joyce in Chapter 17, and Cunningham in Chapter 18 – both in this volume. Students agreed that both the use of case studies and online discussion forum were very valuable learning methods. Weila *et al.* (2011) also correlate the impact of the online discussion forums on non-native English speakers and encourage more studies to be done on that topic specifically.

- *Social media:* The Khan Academy is famous for its use of social media (e.g. YouTube) to spread knowledge, primarily in the sciences. This is a useful source of speeches, lectures and other materials which can be used to inform, challenge, and motivate students in accounting as well. For example, Mark Holzblatt and Norbert Tschakert were honoured by the AAA in 2011 for their creative use of technology to teach IFRS.[22] They developed and implemented a pilot 12 weeks, 36 contact hours, IFRS accounting course entitled *Global Accounting*. They also started the IFRS Student Video Competition among universities. The Pilot Program showcased a series of High Definition IFRS student-produced videos which involved interviews with IFRS experts located in six different countries. The student videos can be viewed at http://www.vimeo.com/ifrs (accessed 13 October 2012). Other social media tools that can be incorporated into accounting courses are blogs, wikis, document-sharing tools such as Google drive, Dropbox, and other tools listed in Table 16.5.

16.4.5 Performance, learning assessment software

The issue of assessment of students' learning is covered extensively in Section E (see, for example, Koh, Chapter 20 – this volume), and this is an arena in which technology has a significant impact, and one that might become more important in the future. One recent U.S. study of interest, Baxter & Thibodeau (2012), examines the effectiveness of online learning and assessment software in an *Introduction to Accounting* course. The study compared one class that used the online software versus two classes from a previous term that did not use the software. The same individual taught all the classes and the examinations were the same. The study uses the ALEKS software (Assessment and Learning in Knowledge Spaces), which is a web-based, artificially intelligent assessment and learning system that can be used in any location in which a student can access the internet, and thus the student can receive timely feedback. Knowledge Spaces are a collection of all the knowledge states that might be feasibly observed in a population. The system can identify an individual student's Knowledge Space after 25–35 questions based on its algorithms. The results of the study indicate that, for students in the group who used the software, the average grades for the first mid-term and the final examinations were marginally higher (86.4 per cent versus 84.0 per cent and 77.1 per cent versus 73.4 per cent, respectively).

16.4.6 Mobile devices

Kalbers & Rosner (2003) looked at the frequency of laptop initiatives at sample universities in the U.S.A. and concluded that accounting undergraduates required laptops. They believed that possessing a laptop is a valuable component in quality accounting education and conclude that the ubiquitous nature of IT in today's business and accounting environment makes it crucial for students to gain familiarity and competence with mobile devices such as laptops.

Of course, laptops are not always available or affordable and are being supplanted by other mobile devices (such as tablets and smartphones). Davis (2010) identifies mobile/cell-phones as a means to deliver education to children in Africa. More than a quarter of Africans now have a mobile phone service, but many are unaware that their cellular phones have access to the internet. The introduction of educational games available for computers and mobile phones has also begun, targeting areas such as problem-solving. In other, more desolate areas, radios are an effective tool for teaching, where volunteers teach students with the help of a solar-powered radio.

The appearance of smartphones and tablets on campuses has sparked much discussion about what protocols are most suitable for controlling (or encouraging) their use in the classroom. Some teachers find these mobile devices very disturbing, whereas others are finding ways to encourage their use. For example, as noted above, it is becoming possible to use texting or web-based mobile applications to avoid the costs of implementing proprietary, clicker-based student response systems. Disturbing uses include clicking away at the keyboard while a teacher is lecturing, browsing, and staring at the screen during class discussion, playing YouTube videos during class discussion, and visiting inappropriate sites and causing a commotion. These types of behaviours have caused some teachers to ban laptops and tablets from the classroom, only to find the students using smartphones for similar purposes.

16.4.7 Plagiarism checkers

The *Webster's Dictionary* definition of plagiarism is '*the unauthorized use of the language and thoughts of another author and the representation of them as one's own*'. However, Ercegovac & Richardson Jr. (2004) note discrepancies in the definition and scope of plagiarism used by various educational bodies. Research shows that one particular form of academic misconduct among secondary school pupils – letting someone else copy one's work – had risen from 58 per cent of pupils in 1969 to 97 per cent in 1989. Nearly 90 per cent of college students agree that it is wrong to hand in someone else's writing as one's own, yet 92 per cent of students sampled at a mid-sized four year university in the U.S.A. reported to be engaged in such academic misconduct, primarily attributable to the use of the internet, e-mail, and other digital communication services. Many colleges and universities now require the use of cyber-cheating prevention software such as TurnItIn. Some universities also have honour codes that result in fewer repeat offenders.

Guo (2011) in the U.K. identifies factors associated with plagiarism by students in accounting education and suggests ways of reducing plagiarism, in particular, that accounting educators should be more supportive in promoting and motivating students to act in an ethical manner, in lieu of the robust prevention approach recommended by HEIs. Some recommendations include understanding cultural differences, including ethics-related modules in a course, integrating students into academic life, and considering the impact of new technology on plagiarism. There are further studies in the special issue of *Accounting Education: an international journal* on Academic Dishonesty (21(3), June 2012). There is also a host of web-based material and discussion, including the informative and extensive treatment on Bob Jensen's website (http://www.trinity.edu/rjensen/plagiarism.htm: 13 October 2012).

16.5 Discussion and conclusion

In this chapter we have covered the key pedagogy and curriculum issues associated with promoting IT knowledge, understanding, and awareness in the accounting curriculum, and specific IT knowledge and skills that should be part of the accounting curriculum, especially if it seeks to prepare students for professional accreditation/certification. In addition, we have considered the technology-based tools that can be used to help develop these and many other competencies. There are some knowledge and skill areas that are foundational and relevant to all accounting students, and others that differ according to the roles for which students are being prepared following graduation. Also, there are specialist areas of knowledge and skill that could be considered in professional development programmes, though we have not covered most of these specialist areas in this review.

Some issues that were touched on, but which need further exploration by accounting educators and researchers, are how the knowledge, skills, and educational technology tools ought to be integrated in 'mainline' subjects in the accounting curriculum as opposed to specific information systems and technology-oriented courses such as *Introduction to Business Systems, Accounting Information Systems, Computer Audit*, and *E-Commerce*. If IT and IS are so integral to accounting that relevant knowledge and skills ought to be fully integrated in courses throughout the curriculum, how will teachers with limited experience and education, and little enthusiasm in these areas fulfil such important integrative objectives?

We are aware that some of the IS and IT skills discussed in this chapter may be viewed by some educators as being overly practical or too vocational to be covered in a university curriculum. However, we view this perspective to be extreme and unrealistic. Most of the literature that we reviewed indicates that there is value in including practical hands-on instructional resources to enhance students' understanding of the broader issues being addressed within the accounting curriculum. Further, given that IT and IS concepts are at the core of information science, and that accounting is concerned with the provision and use of information (albeit primarily financial), the concepts and skills in these areas are a fundamental part of the discipline. A balance needs to be struck between over-using practical exercises beyond their value added so that they become seen by students as pointless 'busy work', and under-using them and losing the opportunity to develop deeper understanding of IS and IT-related topics. A problem with using and developing practical exercises is that:

- they can consume academic staff time without certainty of pay-off to the students or the teacher;
- they can have limited reusability potential due to the ever-changing nature of technology; and
- they may require resources in terms of technical support, software and hardware that are not readily available.

Another important point is that business and accounting programmes around the world and in various institutions are at very different stages of development. They do not have the same levels of autonomy or the same levels of material support. Thus, it may be a challenge for some programmes to avail themselves of the educational technologies identified in this chapter, and provide the coverage of knowledge and skills that are expected of students seeking professional accreditation/certification in accordance with relevant IAESB Education Standards and Guidelines. Fortunately, there are many resources available on the web and in open source format, and we have identified some of these in this chapter. Echoing the views of Laurillard

(1993) and Garrison (2011), the challenge is going to be not so much how the technology should be used to do more of the same, but how the technology can be implemented to help us introduce, keep, or put back the discussion and dialogue into teaching within the discipline, particularly as class sizes increase and unit resources for teaching stagnate or decrease.

Overall, it appears that there is a lot to be achieved if IT knowledge, skills, and the use of IT-based learning technologies reach the levels indicated as being desirable within this review, which is supported in principle by the recent accounting education curriculum 'pathway' reviews in both the U.S.A. (AAA, 2012) and Australia (Evans *et al.*, 2012). Implicit here is the notion that there are (or at least have been) barriers that have hindered moves towards this direction. It is our view that this is the case and, although the barriers are different across many dimensions (international, organizational, and personal), Senik & Broad (2008, 2011) in the U.K. suggest three broad sets of barriers in relation to the IT skills discussed here:

- academic staff-based barriers;
- environment-based barriers; and
- student-based barriers.

Additional research is clearly required in these arenas.

Looking to the future, a lot needs to be done, both in the classroom and in the research community, and a lot of this work requires looking beyond the traditional academic boundaries of the accounting discipline. We need to look in at least three directions: (1) to the cognate disciplines of information systems and information technology; (2) to the educational discipline, particularly in relation to pedagogical issues with implications for IT and IS knowledge, skills, and competencies; and (3) to the world of accounting in practice: the profession of accounting and the varied roles of accounting professionals. Without these broadened perspectives, the (academic) accounting discipline risks an isolated redundancy.

Notes

1 A literature review by Spraakman (2011) focusses on the role of IS/IT in management accounting curricula, concluding that IS/IT is under-utilized in management accounting education. Our perception is that, in many respects, this is equally the case in financial accounting and other areas of accounting education.

2 Although IT is different from IS, in this chapter IT should be read as including IS.

3 We rely on the peer review process of the journals in which the cited works have been published to provide a quality screen for them. We do not cite works if they have significant limitations. Where we have been able to identify limitations of cited studies, we identify them or draw attention to works with alternative findings.

4 An issue which is probably more likely to arise in those areas (of accounting and/or geographically) is where the teaching staff have little, or little recent, exposure to accounting in practice, and are therefore less aware of the increasing importance of IT within the domain of accounting practice and the supply of information in organizations.

5 The International Accounting Education Standards Board (IAESB) is the independent standard-setting board that operates under the auspices of the International Federation of Accountants (IFAC).

6 Paragraphs 3, and 28–33 in the 2010 Standard which, at the time of writing, is under review, with revised standards planned for 2013/14.

7 The Exposure Draft for a proposed revision of IES 2 (IAESB, 2012a, Table A, panel h) lists required competencies in IT including components of ISs, controls for effective AIS and other applications and continuity plans. This is supplemented by the required competency to 'Apply appropriate technology to work tasks' in the Exposure Draft for a proposed revision of IES 3 (IAESB, 2012b, Table A, panel d).

8 For a comprehensive critical review of the literature on competencies for the accounting profession, see Boritz & Carnaghan (2003).

9 Interest in and concern within the profession about the use of spreadsheets, for example, are illustrated by the interest in and levels of activity on the ItCounts discussion board of the Institute of Chartered Accountants in England & Wales (ICAEW) (http://www.ion.icaew.com/itcountshome, accessed 8 October 2012) and the now separated Excel Community (members only) site of that body (http://www.ion.icaew.com/excelcommunity, accessed 8 October 2012) created due to the high levels of interest in this area.

10 In the form of MS Access.

11 Ironically, this occurs even in relation to databases of research data, where the data is often collated, stored and manipulated within spreadsheet (or other flat table format) environments, despite the potential flexibility and control advantages of relational databases.

12 Including, for example, knowledge management systems, customer relationship management systems, supply chain management systems and data warehousing.

13 See http://business.fullerton.edu/accounting/pfoote/aispaper.html (accessed 15 October 2012).

14 With, for example, different (but related) taxonomies to represent accounts in US GAAP compared to IFRS format reports.

15 For example, tax filings in iXBRL format are now compulsory in the U.K. in many circumstances, where the iXBRL (Inline XBRL) format is a modified form of document that is both human- and computer-readable, with XBRL tags hidden from view in the document.

16 Both of which were published in the special/themed issue of *Accounting Education, an international journal*, 4(3), September 1995, on the subject *The Integration of Expert Systems within the Accounting Curriculum* (guest edited by Alan Sangster).

17 Evidenced by, for example, their inclusion in the syllabus/educational requirements of the PABs, referred to by IFAC, or typically included in AIS courses.

18 At http://commons.aaahq.org/pages/home (accessed 13 August 2012).

19 Available at: http://www.thwt.org/index.php/presentations-multimedia (accessed 13 August 2012).

20 More information can be obtained on the *Teaching History with Technology* website on this topic at http://www.thwt.org/index.php/presentations-multimedia/polls-surveys (accessed 13 August 2012).

21 Byzantium, a pseudo-intelligent, problem-based, human tutor emulation system, and EQL (BPP) *Understand Management Accounting*, a more traditional interactive computer based text with progress tests.

22 See http://facultyprofile.csuohio.edu/csufacultyprofile/detail.cfm?FacultyID=M_HOLTZBLATT (accessed 13 August 2013).

References

Ahadiat, N. (2008) Technologies used in accounting education: a study of frequency of use among faculty, *Journal of Education for Business*, 83(3), 125–133.

American Accounting Association (2012) *The Pathways Commission: Charting a National Strategy for the Next Generation of Accountants*, Sarasota, FL: AAA, and New York: AICPA.

Badua, F.A., Sharifi, M., & Watkins, A.L. (2011) The topics, they are a-changing: the state of the accounting information systems curriculum and the case for a second course, *The Accounting Educators' Journal*, 21, 89–106.

Baldwin-Morgan, A.A. (1995) Integrating artificial intelligence into the accounting curriculum, *Accounting Education: an international journal*, 4(3), 217–229.

Basioudis, I.G. & De Lange, P.A. (2009) An assessment of the learning benefits of using a Web-based Learning Environment when teaching accounting, *Advances in Accounting*, incorporating *Advances in International Accounting*, 25(1), 13–19.

Basioudis, I.G., De Lange, P., Suwardy, T., & Wells, P. (2012) Accounting students' perceptions of a learning management system: an international comparison, *Accounting Research Journal*, 25(2), 72–86.

Bawaneh, S.S. (2011) Information technology, accounting information system and their effects on the quality of accounting university education: an empirical research applied on Jordanian financial institutions, *Interdisciplinary Journal of Contemporary Research in Business*, 3(2), 1815–1840.

Baxter, R.J. & Thibodeau, J.C. (2012) Does the use of intelligent learning and assessment software enhance the acquisition of financial accounting knowledge? *Issues in Accounting Education*, 26(4), 647–656.

Berger, L. & Boritz, J.E. (2012) Accounting students' sensitivity to attributes of information integrity, *Issues in Accounting Education*, 27(4), 867–893.

Boritz, J.E., Borthick, F., & Presslee, A. (2012) The effects of business process representation type on the assessment of business and control risk: diagrams versus narratives, *Issues in Accounting Education*, 27(4), 895–915.

Boritz, J.E. & Carnaghan, C.A. (2003) Competency-based education and assessment for the accounting profession: a critical review, *Canadian Accounting Perspectives*, 2(1), 7–42.

Boritz, J.E. & Datardina, M. (2013) CAATs in the Classroom, Working Paper, University of Waterloo available at: http://accounting.uwaterloo.ca/uwcisa/resources/CAATs%20in%20the%20Classroom/CAATs_in_the_Classroom_rev%2013.pdf.

Bradford, M. (2011) North Carolina State University: Implementing ERP Student Modules. *Issues in Accounting Education*, 26:3, 507–520.

Bradford, M., Richtermeyer, S. B. & Roberts, D. F. (2007) System Diagramming Techniques: An Analysis of Methods Used in Accounting Education, *Journal of Information Systems*, 21:1, 173–212.

Bromson, G., Kaidonis, M.A. & Poh, P. (1994) Accounting information systems and learning theory: an integrated approach to teaching, *Accounting Education: an international journal*, 3:2, 101–114.

Bryant, S.M. & Hunton, J.E. (2000) The Use of Technology in the Delivery of Instruction: Implications for Accounting Educators and Education Researchers, *Issues in Accounting Education*, 15:1, 129–162.

Carnaghan, C. & Webb, A. (2007) Investigating the Effects of Group Response Systems on Student Satisfaction, Learning, and Engagement, *Issues in Accounting Education*, 22:3, 391–409.

Chang, C.J. & Hwang, N.R. (2003) Accounting education, firm training and information technology: a research note, *Accounting Education: an international journal*, 12 (4), 441–450.

Chen, C.C., Jones, K.T., & Moreland, K.A. (2013) Online accounting education versus in-class delivery: does course level matter? *Issues in Accounting Education*, 28(1), 1–16.

David, J.S., MacCracken, H., & Reckers, P.M.J. (2003) Integrating technology and business process analysis into introductory accounting courses, *Issues in Accounting Education*, 18(4), 417–425.

Davis, M.R. (2010) Mobile devices deliver learning in Africa: educators are finding innovative ways to bring education to students in remote areas using cellphones, laptops, and MP3 players, *Education Week*, 29, 26–32.

Debreceny, R. & Farewell, S. (2010) XBRL in the accounting curriculum, *Issues in Accounting Education*, 25(3), 359–364.

Dechow, N., Granlund, M., & Mouritsen, J. (2007) Management control of the complex organization: relationships between management accounting and information technology, in Chapman, C.S., Hopwood, A.G., & Shields, M.D. (eds) *Handbook of Management Accounting Research*, Vol. 2, Oxford: Elsevier, pp. 625–640.

Ercegovac, Z. & Richardson Jr., J. (2004) Academic dishonesty, plagiarism included, in the digital age: a literature review, *College & Research Libraries*, 65(4), 301–318.

Elam, R., Wenger, M.R., & Williams, K.L. (2012) XBRL tagging of financial statement data using XMLSpy: the small company case, *Issues in Accounting Education*, 27(3), 761–781.

Evans, E., Burritt, R., & Guthrie, J. (eds) (2012) *Emerging Pathways for the Next Generation of Accountants*, The Institute of Chartered Accountants in Australia: Sydney and the Centre for Accounting, Governance and Sustainability, University of South Australia: Adelaide.

Fogarty, T.J. (2008) The millennial lie, *Issues in Accounting Education*, 23(3), 369–371.

Gaffney, M.A., Ryan, D., & Wurst, C. (2010) Do on-line homework systems improve student performance? *Advances in Accounting Education*, 11, 49–68.

Garrison, R. (2011) *E-Learning in the 21st Century: A Framework for Research and Practice*, 2nd edn, New York: Routledge.

Geerts, G.L. (2008) Introduction to REA 25th Anniversary Special Section, *Journal of Information Systems*, 22(2), 215–217.

Grabski, S., Leech, S., & Sangster, A. (2009) *Management Accounting in Enterprise Resource Planning Systems*, Oxford: CIMA/Elsevier.

Guo, X. (2011) Understanding student plagiarism: an empirical study in accounting education, *Accounting Education: an international journal*, 20(1), 17–37.

Halabi, A.K. & De Lange, P. (2011) The usefulness and interactions of WebCT from an accounting student's perspective, in Catanach, A.H. & Feldmann, D. (eds) *Advances in Accounting Education: Teaching and Curriculum Innovations* (Advances in Accounting Education, Vol. 12), Emerald Group Publishing Limited, pp. 77–95.

Hastings, C.I. & Solomon, L. (2005) Technology and the accounting curriculum: where it is and where it needs to be, *Advances in Accounting*, 21, 275–296.

Hornik, S. & Thornburg, S. (2010) Really engaging accounting: Second Life(tm) as a learning platform, *Issues in Accounting Education*, 25(3).

IAESB (2010a) *International education Practice Statement 2 (IEPS2): Information Technology for Professional Accountants*, New York: IFAC. Available at: http://www.ifac.org/publications-resources/handbook-international-education-pronouncements-2010-edition) (accessed 8 October 2012).

IAESB (2010b) *International Education Statement 2 (IES2): Content of Professional Accounting Education Programs*, New York: IFAC. Available at: http://www.ifac.org/publications-resources/handbook-international-education-pronouncements-2010-edition (accessed 8 October 2012).

IAESB (2012a) *Exposure Draft: Proposed International Education Standard (IES) 2: Initial Professional Development—Technical Competence (Revised) July 2012*, New York: IFAC. Available at: https://www.ifac.org/publications-resources/ies-2-initial-professional-development-technical-competence. (accessed 27 April 2013).

IAESB (2012b) *Exposure Draft: Proposed International Education Standard (IES) 3: Initial Professional Development—Professional Skills (Revised), July 2012*, New York: IFAC. Available at: https://www.ifac.org/publications-resources/ies-3-initial-professional-development-professional-skills (accessed 27 April 2013).

Johnson, B.G., Phillips, F., & Chase, L.G. (2009) An intelligent tutoring system for the accounting cycle: enhancing textbook homework with artificial intelligence, *Journal of Accounting Education*, 27(1), 30–39.

Johnson, L., Adams, S., & Cummins, M. (2012) *The NMC Horizon Report: 2012 Higher Education Edition*, Austin, TX: The New Media Consortium.

Jones, S.H. & Wright, M.E. (2010) The effects of a hypertext learning aid and cognitive style on performance in advanced financial accounting, *Issues in Accounting Education*, 25(1), 35–58.

Kalbers, L.P. & Rosner, R.L. (2003) An investigation of the emerging trend towards a laptop requirement for accounting majors in the USA, *Accounting Education: an international journal*, 12(4), 341–372.

Kaye, G.R. & Nicholson, A.H.S. (1992) An educational framework for information technology in accounting and management education, *Computers & Education*, 9(1/2), 105–112.

Kotb, A. & Roberts, C. (2011) E-business in accounting education: a review of undergraduate accounting degrees in the UK and Ireland, *Accounting Education: an international journal*, 20(1), 63–78.

Laurillard, D. (1993) *Rethinking University Teaching*, London: Routledge.

Ling, L.M. & Nawawi, N.H.A. (2010) Integrating ICT skills and tax software in tax education: a survey of Malaysian tax practitioners' perspectives, *Campus-Wide Information Systems*, 27(5), 303–317.

Loraas, T.M. & Key, K.G. (2010) Integrating AIS and accounting for income taxes: from calculation to disclosure, *Issues in Accounting Education*, 25(3), 583–597.

Lymer, A. (1995) The integration of expert systems into the teaching of accountancy: a third-year option course approach, *Accounting Education: an international journal*, 4(3), 249–258.

Madigan, D. (2006) The technology literate professoriate: are we there yet? IDEA Paper #43. Available at: http://www.theideacenter.org/sites/default/files/Idea_Paper_43.pdf (accessed 13 October 2012).

Marriott, N. (2004) Using computerized business simulations and spreadsheet models in accounting education: a case study, *Accounting Education: an international journal*, 13(suppl.), 55–70.

Marriott, N., Marriott, P., & Selwyn, N. (2003) *Information and Communications Technology in UK Accounting Education*, Occasional Research Paper no. 34, London: ACCA.

Marriott, P. & Teoh, L.K. (2012) Using screencasts to enhance assessment feedback: students' perceptions and preferences, *Accounting Education: an international journal*, 21(6), 583–598.

Mattessich, R. & Galassi, G. (2000) History of the spreadsheet: from matrix accounting to budget simulation and computerization, in AECA (ed.) *Accounting and History: Selected Papers from the 8th Congress of Accounting Historians*. Madrid: Asociación Española de Contabilidad y Administración, pp. 203–232 (Spanish translation as: Historia de la hoja de cálculo, in *Revista Internacional Legis de Contabilidad & Auditoria*, 18, April–July, 2004: 41–86).

McCarthy, W.E. (2003) The REA modelling approach to teaching accounting information systems, *Issues in Accounting Education*, 18(4), 427–441.

McDowall, T. & Jackling, B. (2006) The impact of computer-assisted learning on academic grades: an assessment of students' perceptions, *Accounting Education: an international journal*, 15(4), 377–389.

McVay, G.J., Murphy, P.R., & Yoon, S.W. (2008) Good practices in accounting education: classroom configuration and technological tools for enhancing the learning environment, *Accounting Education: an international journal*, 17(1), 41–63.

Miller, A.M. & Woods, C.M. (2000) Undergraduate tax education: a comparison of educators' and employers' perceptions in the UK, *Accounting Education: an international journal*, 9(3), 223–241.

Osgerby, P. (2013) Students' perceptions of the introduction of a blended learning environment: an exploratory case study, *Accounting Education: an international journal*, 22(1), 85–99.

Ozkul, F.U., Pektekin, P., & Rena, B.E. (2011) Impact of the E-Education on the Equal Opportunities in Education and Research on E-Accounting Course, *The Journal of American Academy of Business*, 16:2, 209–215.

Panko, R.R. & Aurigemma, S. (2010) Revising the Panko–Halverson taxonomy of spreadsheet errors, *Decision Support Systems*, 49, 235–244.

Phillips, F. & Johnson, B.G. (2011) Online homework versus intelligent tutoring systems: pedagogical support for transaction analysis and recording, *Issues in Accounting Education*, 26(1), 87–97.

Pimpa, N. (2010) E-business education: a phenomenographic study of online engagement among accounting, finance and international business students, *iBusiness*, 2, 311–316.

Powell, S.G., Baker, K.R. & Lawson, B. (2008) A critical review of the literature on spreadsheet errors, *Decision Support Systems*, 46, 128–138.

Powell, S.G., Baker, K.R. & Lawson, B. (2009) Impact of errors in operational spreadsheets, *Decision Support Systems*, 47, 126–132.

Premuroso, R.F., Tong, L., & Beed, T.K. (2011) Does using clickers in the classroom matter to student performance and satisfaction when taking the introductory financial accounting course? *Issues in Accounting Education*, 26(4), 701–723.

Rankin, E.L. & Hoaas, D.J. (2001) Teaching note: does the use of computer-generated slide presentations in the classroom affect student performance and interest?, *Eastern Economic Journal*, 27(3), 355–366.

Rebele, J.E., Apostolou, B.A., Buckless, F.A., Hassell, J.M., Paquette, L.R., & Stout, D.E. (1998) Accounting education literature review (1991–1997), Part II: students, educational technology, assessment, and faculty issues, *Journal of Accounting Education*, 16(2), 179–245.

Rezaee, Z., Elam, R., & Cassidy, J.H. (2005) Electronic-commerce education: insights from academicians and practitioners, *Advances in Accounting*, 21, 233–258.

Rezaee, Z., Lambert, K.R. & Harmon, W.K. (2006) Electronic commerce education: analysis of existing courses, *Accounting Education: an international journal*, 15(1), 73–88.

Richardson, R.C. & Louwers, T.J. (2010) Using computerized audit software to learn statistical sampling: an instructional resource, *Issues in Accounting Education*, 25(3), 553–567.

Sangster, A. (1995) The integration of expert systems within the accounting curriculum, *Accounting Education: an international journal*, 4(3), 211–216.

Senik, R. & Broad, M.J. (2008) Perceived factors influencing information technology (IT) skills development in undergraduate accounting programme, *International Journal of Economics and Management*, 2(2), 302–322.

Senik, R. & Broad, M.J. (2011) Information technology skills development for accounting graduates: intervening conditions. *International Education Studies*, 4(2), 105–110.

Spraakman, G. (2011) Crisis in management accounting curricula: the unclear role of information systems and information technology (13 January 2011). CAAA Annual Conference 2011. Available at: SSRN: http://ssrn.com/abstract=1740142 or http://dx.doi.org/10.2139/ssrn.1740142.

Stanley, T. & Edwards, P. (2005) Interactive multimedia teaching of Accounting Information System (AIS) cycles: student perceptions and views, *Journal of Accounting Education*, 23, 21–46.

Stoner, G. (1999) It is part of youth culture, but are accounting graduates confident in IT?, *Accounting Education: an international journal*, 8(3), 217–237.

Stoner, G. (2003) Using learning technology resources in teaching management accounting, in Kaye, R. & Hawkridge, D. (eds) *Learning & Teaching for Business: Case Studies of Successful Innovation*, London: Kogan Page for BEST (Business Education Support Team: the Learning and Teaching Support Network for Business, Management and Accountancy), pp. 138–152.

Stoner, G. (2009) Accounting students' IT application skills over a 10 year period, *Accounting Education: an international journal*, 18(10), 7–31.

Stoner, G. & Milner, M. (2010) Embedding generic employability skills in an accounting degree: development and impediments, *Accounting Education: an international journal*, 19(1–2), 123–138.

Suwardy, T., Pan, G., & Seow, P. (2013) Using digital storytelling to engage student learning, *Accounting Education: an international journal*, 22(2), 109–124.

Tan, A. & Ferreira, A. (2012) The effects of the use of activity-based costing software in the learning process: an empirical analysis, *Accounting Education: an international journal*, 21(4), 407–411.

Taylor, E.Z. & Dzuranin, A.C. (2010) Interactive financial reporting: an introduction to eXtensible Business Reporting Language (XBRL). *Issues in Accounting Education*, 25:1, 71–83.

Thambar, P. (2012) The Transforming Finance Function: Implications for the Education and Training of Accountants, Chapter 7 in Evans, E., Burritt, R. & Guthrie, J. (editors) (2012) *Emerging Pathways for the Next Generation of Accountants*, The Institute of Chartered Accountants in Australia: Sydney and the Centre for Accounting, Governance and Sustainability, University of South Australia: Adelaide, 65–72.

Todorova, N. & Bjorn-Andersen, N. (2011) University learning in times of crisis: the role of IT, *Accounting Education: an international journal*, 20(6), 597–599.

Vasarhelyi, M.A. & Alles, M.G. (2008) The 'now' economy and the traditional accounting reporting model: opportunities and challenges for AIS research, *International Journal of Accounting Information Systems*, 9, 227–239.

Vasarhelyi, M.A., Teeter, R.A., & Krahel, J.P. (2010) Audit education and the real-time economy, *Issues in Accounting Education*, 25(3).

Weila, S., McGuigan, B.N. & Kern, B.T. (2011) The usage of an online discussion forum for the facilitation of case-based learning in an intermediate accounting course: a New Zealand case, *Open Learning*, 26(3), 237–251.

Wells, P., De Lange, P. & Fieger, P. (2008) Integrating a virtual learning environment into a second-year accounting course: determinants of overall student perception, *Accounting & Finance*, 48, 503–518.

Wessels, P. L. (2010) A critical learning outcome approach in designing, delivering and assessing the IT knowledge syllabus, *Accounting Education: an international journal*, 19(5), 439–456.

About the authors

Efrim Boritz is the Ontario CPA's Chair in Accounting and Head of the Assurance and IS areas in the School of Accounting & Finance at the University of Waterloo, Canada (jeboritz@uwaterloo.ca). Dr Boritz is the author of numerous publications and has served on boards, task forces and committees of the AAA, AICPA, CAAA, CICA, CPA Canada, ICAO, IIA and ISACA.

Greg Stoner is a Senior Lecturer in Accounting and Information Systems in the Adam Smith Business School of the University of Glasgow, Scotland, U.K. (greg.stoner@glasgow.ac.uk). Dr Stoner's research interests are in accounting education, particularly student skills and the use of technology in teaching, and aspects of accounting history concerned with Fra Luca Pacioli and his textbook and teaching innovations of the fifteenth century. He is an Associate Editor of *Accounting Education: an international journal*, and has previously served as an Associate Editor of *Issues in Accounting Education*.

17

The use of experiential learning in accounting education

Trevor Hassall and John Joyce

SHEFFIELD HALLAM UNIVERSITY, U.K.

CONTENTS

Abstract

Criticism of accounting education has focussed on pedagogic approaches which are seen as being formulaic, relying on traditional lecture/seminar content-based approaches. These concentrate on technical content, primarily aimed at professional accreditation, and not preparing students for 'reality'.

The concepts and development of experiential learning, and the appropriateness of such an approach as a catalyst for change in accounting education, will be reviewed. Potential approaches to the implementation of experiential learning in teaching and learning from an empirical perspective will then be identified and evaluated. Allied concepts (such as action learning and situated learning) will also be reviewed. It will be shown that experiential learning has developed and expanded to include the learning environment, learning activities, experience and emotions, experience and intelligence, and learning and change.

Keywords

action learning, experiential learning, pedagogy, problem-based learning, situated learning

17.1 Introduction

The main aims of this chapter are:

- to identify the perceived problems of accounting education pedagogy;
- to explore the development of experiential learning;
- to highlight the major models of experiential learning; and
- to critically evaluate the potential for experiential learning to be used to improve pedagogy.

Emerging from substantive criticisms of accounting education by employers, professional accounting bodies (PABs), and academics is a 'wish list' of the changes which they perceive as being necessary to ensure continued vocational relevance. (See Flood, Chapter 4 – this volume.) Specifically mentioned in this list is pedagogy. Current pedagogic approaches have been criticized as lacking creativity. They are seen as being formulaic, relying on traditional lecture/seminar-based approaches, primarily aimed at professional accreditation, and not preparing students for the reality of the ambiguous business world. (See Apostolou & Gammie, Chapter 29 – this volume.) A major criticism is the focus on technical content rather than the development of the vocational and personal skills that are of increasing importance for the changed role of the accountant. But see St. Pierre & Rebele (Chapter 5 – this volume) for an alternative perspective.

Accounting education originated as primarily a workplace activity. Subsequent economic events have in some instances led to calls for a return to this situation. This leads to a fundamental question concerning the relationship between work and learning, and the issue of knowledge and its transfer.

The overall aim of this chapter is to evaluate the potential for the use of experiential learning as a solution to the pedagogic problems identified above. This will be approached in two distinct stages. The first stage will be a review of the concept of experiential learning and the appropriateness of the overall pedagogic approach to initiate potential change in accounting education. The second stage will be to identify and evaluate potential approaches to the implementation of experiential learning in accounting education from an empirical perspective.

17.2 The problem

As indicated above, accounting is often taught using traditional pedagogic approaches (chalk, or the modern equivalent, and talk) in lectures and seminars. It is important to understand why this approach may not meet the requirements of employers and PABs, and to evaluate the potential for experiential learning to do so. In their study undertaken in the U.S.A., Albrecht & Sack (2000) identify three key areas in which traditional approaches fail:

1 They do not develop critical skills. This is supported by Wolcott *et al.* (2002) who suggest there is little empirical evidence that traditional pedagogic methods can enhance the critical thinking skills of accounting students.
2 They do not prepare students for the ambiguous business world that they will soon encounter (see also Blundell & Booth, 1988; Kelly *et al.*, 1999; Adler *et al.*, 2004).
3 Finally, the often used content-based approaches encourage memorization and promote the idea that there is a right answer to every problem.

Albrecht & Sack (2000) also stress that a key skill, the ability to 'learn how to learn', is not developed. This was also identified by the Accounting Education Change Commission (AECC) in its Position Statement Number One, *Objectives of Education for Accountants* (1990, p. 1), which stated:

> [G]raduates cannot be expected to have the range of knowledge and skills of experienced professional accountants. To attain and maintain the status of professional accountant requires continual learning. Therefore pre-entry education should lay the base on which lifelong learning can be built. In other words, graduates should be taught how to learn.

The subsequent focus by the accounting profession on continuing professional development (CPD) further emphasizes the importance of this. Specifically, Albrecht & Sack (2000) point to the following as being key problems with pedagogy:

• too much emphasis on memorization;
• too much reliance on text books as course drivers;
• a reluctance to develop creative types of learning;
• a reluctance to use 'out of classroom' experiences.

Their critical appraisal of accounting education pedagogy provides the framework through which we will examine the extent to which experiential learning could add the needed vocational relevance to accounting education.

17.3 The foundations of experiential learning

The concept of experiential learning is encapsulated in the aphorism:

> I hear and I forget, I see and I remember, I do and I understand.

There are claims that this can be traced to Eastern, Confucian philosophy. This may have laid the very early foundations for subsequent Western interpretations, and many writers have contributed to the debate about the notion of learning from experience, or learning from doing. Brah & Hoy (1989) point out that experiential learning has become something of an ideology in education and that it stems from a number of traditions. Dewey (1938), Piaget (1977), Revans (1982), and Kolb (1984) have all published perspectives or theories based on the notion of an individual interacting with the external environment, sensing and perceiving stimuli, and making sense of and personally experiencing the world.

Quay (2003) explores the relationship between experiential learning and other theories of learning. He initially locates experiential learning within constructivism and evidences this through Davis *et al.* (2000) in that the learner's basis of meaning is found by experiencing a dynamic and responsive world. Experiential learning is located in constructivism through its encompassing of learning as active adaptation. Quay broadens this by placing experiential learning as a social constructionism (see Wilson *et al.*, Chapter 3, and Lucas & Mladenovic, Chapter 6 – both in this volume – for more details of 'social constructions'). This is primarily an extension to acknowledge that learning can occur through social interaction and, as such, highlights the importance of the social world in learning rather than learning being confined to a detached individual. Central to this line of argument is the work of Vygotsky (1978) and his *zone of proximal development* which explores the gap between what an individual can learn in isolation and what he/she can learn as a member of a collaborative group. Quay (2003) extends this further to consider the role of cultural discourses and suggests that knowledge is centred in, and defined by, a culture. As with other writers, Quay identifies fellow travellers and notes the overlaps between experiential learning and other theories (such as situated learning, action learning, problem-based learning and transformative learning). These will be further discussed later in this chapter.

Experiential learning can therefore be seen as a meta-model that incorporates and is incorporated by many other theories of learning. Central to experiential learning is the relationship between experience and learning. Kant (1993, p. 30) states in the opening of his *Critique of Pure Reason* that '*all our knowledge begins with experience*'. Dewey (1916), one of the first proponents of the importance of experience, explained experience as a lens through which he could link thought and action. This establishes two important concepts in the analysis of experience: thought and action. Cuffaro (1995) counselled that they should be seen as factors which informed each other rather than as being discrete. Rogers (1996) and Boud *et al.* (1993) take this stage further by stating that, in their view, experience forms the basis of all learning. It should also be noted that these writers reflect a wide spectrum of experiential learning as their work covers contexts ranging from early schooling through to professional development programmes. Kolb (1984, p. 41) draws together the work of the early theorists in a series of propositions:

- Learning is best conceived as a process rather than in terms of outcomes.
- Learning is a continuous process grounded in experience.
- The process of learning requires the resolution of conflicts between dialectically opposed modes of adaptation to the world.
- Learning is a holistic process of adaptation to the world.
- Learning involves transactions between the individual and the world.
- Learning is the process of creating knowledge.

A later summary by Miller & Boud (1996, pp. 8–10) also offers insight into the basic tenets of experiential learning:

- Experience is the foundation of, and stimulus for, learning.
- Learners actively construct their own experience.
- Learning is holistic.
- Learning is socially and culturally constructed.
- Learning is influenced by the socio-economic context within which it occurs.

We can therefore see that the underlying principle of experiential learning is that ideas and knowledge are personal and are constantly being formed and reformed by experience. This led Boud *et al.* (1993) to conclude that the benefits accruing from learning that occurs in isolation from, and is unrelated to, the student's personal experience are limited.

17.4 Two initial models of experiential learning

The experiential learning cycle of Kolb (1984), which combines the previous models of Dewey's learning process (1938) and Lewin's feedback process (1951), is perhaps the most recognizable model in this area. (See also Duff, Chapter 8 – this volume.)

Kolb (1984) identified four major elements of experiential learning to explain how individuals process and respond in a learning situation (see Figure 17.1). (See also Figure 8.4.) The four elements of the learning cycle are:

1   Concrete Experience (CE): learning from intuitive feelings and responses related to the specific experience.
2   Reflective Observation (RO): learning by watching and listening.
3   Abstract Conceptualization (AC): learning by logical thinking and a willingness to patiently consider many alternatives.
4   Active Experimentation (AE): learning by doing and pragmatically testing previously generated concepts.

The experiential learning model (ELM) shows that, in order to learn, an individual must recognize that he/she has had an 'experience'. The initial experience provides the basis for observation and reflection which are then assimilated into an idea, image, or theory from which implications

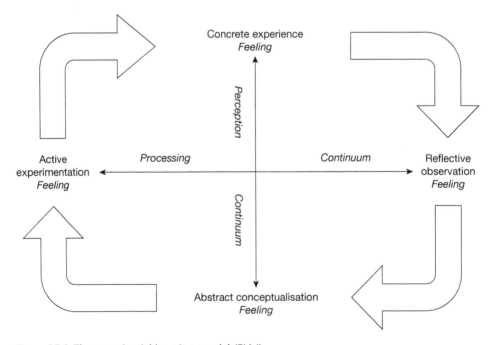

Figure 17.1 The experiential learning model (ELM)

for future action may be derived and tested. Learning occurs when the individual has the ability to actively engage in new experiences (CE), to reflect on these experiences (RO), to integrate these reflections and observations into abstract concepts or theories (AC), and to use these theories to guide decision-making and experimental action to solve problems (AE).

A further development enabled the approach to be used to identify individual learning styles. The four elements of the ELM are the polar points of the two learning dimensions: the concrete-abstract and the active-reflective dimensions. The first dimension (concrete-abstract continuum) indicates how people perceive experience and information. It represents how people gather information from their environment ranging from a preference for involvement to a preference for detached analysis. The second dimension (reflective-active continuum) indicates how a person processes experience and information ranging from those who take an observational role in their learning to those who prefer active participation. The two dimensions of perceiving experience (concrete-abstract continuum) combined with the two methods of transforming experience (reflective-active continuum) result in four different forms of learning styles that Kolb (1984) assigned in each quadrant of the ELM:

- *convergent* AC + AE (unemotional, task-orientated, and practical application of ideas);
- *divergent* CE + RO (imaginative emotional and views experiences from many perspectives);
- *assimilative* RO + AC (generates theories and models); and
- *accommodative* AE + CE (conducts experiments and executes plans).

An excellent introduction to the accounting literature on learning styles is provided by Wilson & Hill (1994). Empirical evidence indicates that accountants and accounting students have a predilection to display the 'convergent' approach to learning which becomes more deeply ingrained in the latter stages of their formal education and, in particular, the professional qualification process (Baldwin & Reckers, 1984; Baker *et al.*, 1987; Brown & Burke, 1987; Adler *et al.*, 2004). The 'converger' seeks to apply acquired knowledge to specific problems for the purpose of problem-solving and decision-making. The reliance on the 'converger' learning style (which centres on a single correct answer or solution to a problem) means that students are less inclined to use and develop deep learning approaches (Adler *et al.*, 2004).

Baker *et al.* (1987) conducted a cross-sectional study of accounting students in the U.S.A. Even though this study indicated a predominance of the 'converger' approach in accounting students, it also reported a wide dispersion of learning style preferences (LSPs) within individual classrooms. The research indicated that the LSPs of accounting majors are closer to those of business students than to those of students from any other disciplines. A longitudinal study of accounting students in the U.K. by Marriott (2002) indicated that the LSPs of students can change over time. Marriott usefully points out the importance of further research into the assumed link between LSP and academic performance, and the need to determine the LSPs of teaching staff and internal examiners, to discover if any correlation exists between teachers/examiners and students' LSPs, and whether this has any impact on students' performance.

In a comparative study of American and Norwegian accounting students, McKee *et al.* (1992) found that there were significant differences in their LSPs. In contrast to previous research on American students, Norwegian students' LSP was 'assimilator'. The study found that 'experience' influenced the emergent LSP and that it had the effect of spreading students more evenly across the four learning styles. The role of cultural factors was investigated by Sugahara & Boland (2010) using a comparative study of Japanese and Australian accounting students. They too identified significant differences: the LSP for Australian accounting students was found to be that of 'assimilator' while, for Japanese students, it was found to be 'diverger'. The study showed that the preference of students to learn by doing or watching was driven by their individualism, and it questioned the reliability of culture as a critical factor in explaining LSP. This suggests that it is not impossible to overcome cultural differences.

The ELM has received much criticism. A primary criticism by Boud *et al.* (1985) was that insufficient attention was paid to the process of reflection and, subsequently, they refined the model to include factors such as feelings and emotions. Jarvis (1987) and Tennant (1997) were both of the opinion that the claims made for the four different LSPs were extravagant. They claim that, though Kolb's learning styles neatly fit with the different dimensions of the experiential learning model, they are not validated by it. Even though individuals will have a LSP, it may change in certain contexts. It is useful for teachers or trainers to recognize LSPs and similarly for learners to be aware of their LSP. Anderson (1988) adds to the criticisms by stating that the model takes very little account of different cultural experiences and that there is a need to take account of differences in cognitive and communication styles that are culturally-based. Having previously criticized this approach, Stout & Ruble (1994) found no empirical support for the validity of the learning styles inventory (LSI) which Kolb developed to gauge LSPs, and recommended the suspension of its use in accounting education research.

The idea of stages or steps does not sit well with the reality of an individual's thought process. As Jarvis (1987) points out, the relationship between learning processes and knowledge is problematic: Kolb does not really explore the nature of knowledge in any depth, or confront the debate on the nature of knowledge that raged over the centuries within philosophy and social theory. Jarvis (1987) asserts that empirical support for the model is weak, and claims that the initial research base was small, and there have only been a limited number of studies that have sought to test or explore the model. However, as Tennant (1997: 92) points out: '*the model provides an excellent framework for planning teaching and learning activities and it can be usefully employed as a guide for understanding learning difficulties, vocational counselling, academic advising and so on*'.

A learning styles questionnaire (LSQ) was developed by Honey & Mumford (1982) to identify an individual's LSP by exploring general behavioural tendencies. It was built on the premise that individuals, because of their attitudes and abilities, will react differently to the same learning opportunity. In this model it is accepted that individuals may start at different points in the learning cycle. However, they are all expected to complete the learning cycle. If they fail to move through a full cycle, the learning process will be incomplete and the failure will compromise future actions. Honey & Mumford's model recognized four styles of learners and posited that individuals move around the styles to suit the specific context they face at any one time:

- *Activists*: prefer to become openly involved in an experience and assess the implications subsequently.
- *Reflectors*: prefer to gather information and carefully consider it before reaching a conclusion. Being thoughtful and cautious, they reserve judgement until they feel they have a measure of reliability.
- *Theorists*: prefer to gather information and to develop a theoretical framework about their experience.
- *Pragmatists*: prefer to apply theories and techniques to test them. Their aim is to improve operational effectiveness.

The accounting education literature in this area provides a major contribution. Having found no significant relationship in his studies between the academic performance of students and the scores recorded on the two sub-scales of the instrument, Duff (1997, 2001) questions the reliability of this approach and, in particular, the construct validity of the LSQ. (Construct validity is the extent to which the instrument used to measure a construct actually measures the presence of the intended construct.) Duff cautions against the use of this approach when selecting instructional methods and in the monitoring and measuring of improvements in the student's learning process; his study indicates that the LSQ is based on a model that is not sufficiently sophisticated to describe the learning that takes place within accounting education.

In their report on learning styles, Coffield *et al.* (2004) note the potential benefits that have been created by the use of psychometrically-sound and ecologically-valid models. They do, however, present several criticisms. One of the most relevant for this chapter is the lack of communication between different research perspectives on pedagogy. The approaches developed separately by psychologists and sociologists rarely interact with each other. Such a divide and lack of communication cannot be seen to be in the national policy interest. They characterize research into learning styles as being small-scale, non-cumulative, uncritical and inward-looking, and attribute this largely to the lack of interdisciplinary research in this area. This results in the major criticism that clear implications for pedagogy do not emerge from this stream of research.

In relation to students' approaches to learning (SAL), which is discussed by Lucas & Mladenovic in Chapter 6 – this volume, they point to the lack of any clear pedagogic innovations to emerge to redress the balance towards deep learning. They importantly note the work of Desmedt *et al.* (2003) stressing the importance of assessment in determining a strategic approach adopted by students who favour surface learning.

Jarvis (1987, 1995) developed a model to show that there are a number of responses to any potential learning situation. He used Kolb's model with a number of different adult groups and asked them to explore it based on their own experience of learning. He was then able to develop a model of learning which allowed different routes. (See Figure 17.2.)

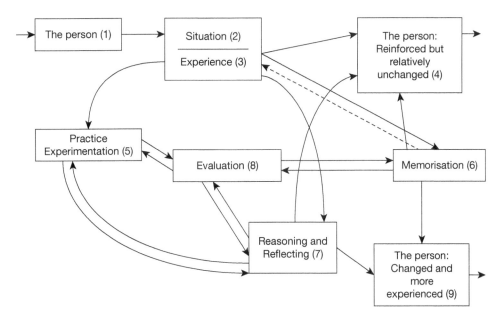

Figure 17.2 A model of the learning process

The aim of the model is to show how individuals enter a situation and construct their experience. Jarvis (1987, 1995) and Barnett (1994) stress the need to distinguish between biography and past experiences. The former includes the hidden and unconscious, while the latter only includes experiences of which an individual is conscious. The importance of individuals entering situations and constructing experiences is stressed: in this sense the situation is the context within which the experience occurs, not the experience itself. Jarvis also notes the importance of understanding the nature of the experience.

17.5 The nature of experience

Having established that individuals can learn from certain experiences, why does it seem that individuals appear not to learn from all experiences? The outcome of an experience can be either conformity or change. This potential change in an individual's mental schema is consistent with Ramsden's (1992) definition of learning as being a change in the way an individual understands experiences or conceptualizes the world around him/her. However, while experience may underpin learning, it appears that this does not always result in learning.

Wilson & Beard (2003) note the importance of perception. As individuals, we are overloaded with experiences in everyday life. Why do we perceive some of them and apparently not perceive others? If an experience confirms existing knowledge or beliefs, then little attention will be paid to it. Our brains select what they perceive to be meaningful experiences and ignore others. Jarvis (1987, 1995) analyses this further into three responses to experience:

- non-learning;
- non-reflective learning; and
- reflective learning.

Each of these is then further analysed in terms of his model (see Figure 17.2). Non-learning may occur because of presumption, and information overload leads to the necessity that, in certain areas, there will be no change and stimuli can be ignored. Non-consideration may be caused by distraction, fear or lack of understanding (in Jarvis's model both of these follow route 1–4). Rejection may be a matter of principle which may serve to confirm existing beliefs which may be a societally-conditioned response (in which case the route is 1–3–7, then to 4 or 9). Learning that does not involve reflection can be preconscious; this learning is often referred to as incidental learning. It often occurs through secondary rather than primary experiences (a typical route would be 1–3–6–4). Where an individual is developing skills, learning is often through observing a demonstration (route 1–3–5–8–6, then to 4 or 9). The key question here is whether what has been achieved is understanding or memorization. Memorization is a very common form of learning (Route 1–3–6, possibly 6–8–6, then either 4 or 9). At the simplest level it is the way that children 'learn' by chanting mathematical tables (1 times 3 is 3, 2 times 3 is 6 . . .).

Jarvis identifies three types of reflective learning. In *contemplation learning* the key factor is the ability to think about an experience and reach conclusions without the restrictions of a wider social reality. This has parallels with critical thinking (route 1–3–7–8–6–9). (See Cunningham, Chapter 18 – this volume.) *Reflective skills learning* has parallels with Schön's (1983) reflection in action. It involves not only learning a skill but also understanding the concepts that underpin the skill (route 1–3–5–7–8, then looping between 5–8–6–9). *Experimental learning* (route 1–3–5–7–8, then looping between 7–8–6–9) is where theory is tested in practice which then results in new knowledge.

There are many dimensions to 'experience': it could be behavioural, action-based, cognitive, or social. We can also think about experience chronologically (past and/or present). Experience can be real or artificial. This analysis indicates the importance of reflection and its centrality to experiential learning. It further emphasizes the need to place reflection as a key element in curriculum design and pedagogic practice.

17.6 Reflection

Schön (1983, 1987) was principally concerned with the development of professional practice. He describes two types of reflection (reflection *in* action and reflection *on* action) in order to identify how individuals used their experience to identify and analyse problems, and subsequently propose action and evaluate their actions. Reflection *in* action (also called concurrent learning) is characterized by the consideration of the action while the individual is still in the process. Reflection *on* action is retrospective learning and involves thinking about previous experiences and developing personal theories by analysis. Reflection *in* action is normally spontaneous and is an active process that is organized by the learner and takes place at the time the event is happening.

Reflection *on* action is normally a planned intervention which occurs at a specific time at a place where the event may not have occurred and is after the occurrence of the event(s), and may or may not be supported by a facilitator. The link between the two is explained as follows: '*We reflect on action, thinking back on what we have done in order to discover how our knowing-in-action may have contributed to an unexpected outcome*' (Schön, 1983, p. 26).

Knowing-in-action is often the tacit information that we know about doing something which is often left unexplained or unmentioned when we describe what we do. It is revealed in skilful performance. Schön also notes the importance of learning environments which he refers to as the *reflective practicum*. This is where students learn by doing with the help of coaching. The importance of learning environments is discussed later in this chapter. (Flood, in Chapter 4 – this volume, discusses the ideas of Schön.)

Transformative learning, as defined by Mezirow (1981), separates childhood learning and adult learning. Children accept learning from sources of authority as part of the process of socialization. Adults, however, need to acquire 'meaning' perspectives. Mezirow introduced the approach of transformative learning as being a critical theory of adult education. He distinguishes two kinds of learning identified by Habermas (1972, 1984) which could evolve into transformative learning.

- *Instrumental learning* is learning that is gained by being involved in controlling or manipulating the environment, in improving performance or prediction.
- *Communicative learning* stems from trying to understand what someone means when he/she communicates with you.
- *Transformative (or emancipatory) learning* involves identifying and challenging distorted meaning perspectives through a process of critical reflection (Mezirow, 1991, p. 87). Here the educator's role is to assist learners in becoming aware of assumptions so that transformative learning may occur when critical reflection takes place.

Techniques for developing critical thinking skills in accounting students have been considered by Bonk & Smith (1998), Cunningham (1996, and Chapter 18 – this volume), and Kimmel (1995). Of particular interest is the study by Lucas (2008) which investigated critical reflections on her approach to teaching an *Auditing* course to accounting students in the U.K. The paper, which is about a teacher reflecting on her practice (the practice focussing in part on how to get students to reflect), is both theoretical and practical, and includes pedagogic examples. The notion of incidents of being 'pulled up short' and 'dawning awareness' add a new dimension.

The introduction of a learning portfolio in an undergraduate *Financial Accounting* course in New Zealand is reported by Samkin & Francis (2008). The use of learning portfolios in accounting courses is in itself an interesting development, the only previous examples being an Australian study by Day *et al.* (2003), and a further Australian study by Howieson (2004). Additionally, in this example, students were also required to maintain a personal or reflective section aimed at personalizing and deepening the quality of their learning. Samkin & Francis (2008) justify this by noting that reflection assists students to develop a questioning attitude as well as the ability to update their knowledge and skills continually. They conclude that, from the entries in their personal journals and summary and reflection essays, it appeared that some students did indeed start to develop a deep approach to learning. They used the Kember *et al.* (1999) coding framework to test the extent and depth of a sample of students' reflections contained in their summary and reflection essays, and comment that this proved useful in that it provided confirmation of reflective thought by some students, as well as measuring the depth of reflective thinking. The limitation of the study, as seen by the authors, was the extent to which their methods were capable of identifying reflective thought and measuring the depth of reflective thinking.

17.7 Fellow travellers

Earlier in this chapter the overlap between experiential learning and several other theories of learning was noted. Each of these areas will now be briefly examined to investigate the potential for their use in combination with experiential learning in accounting education.

17.7.1 Situated learning

The concept of situated learning has parallels with that of experiential learning. Situated learning was originally proposed by Lave (1988), and subsequently developed into a model of learning by Brown *et al.* (1989). It is based on 'experience' but the focus is jointly on the context (or a situation), and knowledge now deemed to be constructed rather than developed through purposeful interaction with the environment. Goel *et al.* (2010) argue that all learning occurs in a situation-dependent context and, according to this view, there is not a 'non-situated' form of learning (i.e. learning cannot occur outside of a context). Situated learning differs from traditional learning whereby an individual acquires general information from a decontextualized body of knowledge in a classroom and when learning is focussed on the acquisition of facts (Kirshner & Whitson, 1997). Choi & Hannafin (1995) assert that situated learning develops higher-order thinking processes. This leads to the development of the potential for behavioural change which results from the reflective observations of experience (Lankard, 1995).

According to Anderson *et al.* (1996) and Wilson (1993), there are four key elements in situated learning:

- learning is grounded in the actions of everyday situations;
- knowledge is acquired situationally and transfers only to similar situations;
- learning is the result of a social process encompassing ways of thinking, perceiving, problem-solving, and interacting in addition to declarative and procedural knowledge; and

- learning is not separated from the world of action but exists in robust, complex, social environments made up of actors, actions, and situations.

This fourth element marks a fundamental change from traditional learning environments. The emphasis is now placed on the realism, or approximate realism, of the learning environment. This is emphasized by Heeter (2005) who states that the *authenticity* of the learning environment depends on a number of factors which include:

- the extent of the environment's parallels with real-world situations;
- the extent of the emphasis on the context; and
- the application of knowledge rather than memorization.

In this sense the university environment and traditional classroom activities lack authenticity because they are removed from the culture of the environments in which real-world activities take place (Andersen *et al.*, 1996), whereas a situated learning environment provides an authentic context that reflects the way in which the knowledge will be used in real life.

Accounting education was originally developed through an apprenticeship that was conducted in the workplace (Langenderfer, 1987). Subsequently, higher education courses replaced part of this but the requirement to complete a professional qualification to become a 'qualified' accountant inevitably involves a period of practical experience. Therefore two distinct forms of learning are being used: theory to practice, on the one hand, and practice to theory, on the other. What situated learning may question in the case of accounting education is the approach to pedagogy used in the higher education phase. Do the students see the relevance of their learning to practical situations of which, in many cases, they have little or no experience? Could pedagogic approaches be incorporated which would bring more reality to their learning and thus develop higher order skills?

17.7.2 Problem-based learning

Problem-based learning (PBL) is a classroom-based approach to situating learning. It has been used in several disciplines and is extensively applied in medical schools. It aims to maximize the extent to which the classroom can reflect the situation of the real world of work where the knowledge and skills being developed would be actually applied. Boud & Feletti (1991: 14) define PBL as '*constructing and teaching courses using problems as the stimulus and focus of student activity*'. They advocate not only using problems as part of the teaching in a traditional curriculum, but also building a curriculum around key problems that would be encountered in professional practice. Engel (1991), who argues that PBL must be thought of as an approach to learning using a problem-based curriculum, identifies four key elements:

- learning is seen as being cumulative;
- learning is integrated;
- learning is progressive; and
- learning is consistent. This final element implies that summative assessment should be used sparingly and should test the application of knowledge rather than recall.

The proponents of PBL state that this type of assessment would enable students to acquire knowledge and skills and, in order to facilitate this, students should be presented with a staged sequence of problems which are context focussed. This should be supplemented by relevant learning materials and support from teachers. This implies that, in many instances, students will work collaboratively and therefore be replicating the workplace: the group investigates the problem and proposes a solution using the learning materials supplied and the support of the tutor(s). This involves key changes. Collaborative work has many problems, of which assessment is a major one.

The problem-based approach implies that students should engage with problems from a very open standpoint. The learning materials used will need to be fundamentally different to those used in a traditional approach to teaching and learning. The problems presented to the students should not be defined, and should be 'open-ended' in terms of possible solutions. The problems may also be multi-disciplinary and will therefore develop knowledge and skills across several traditional academic discipline boundaries. (See Bloom, Chapter 14 – this volume.) This approach involves a fundamental change in the role of the educator from teacher to facilitator/ mentor. PBL emphasizes context (i.e. situation); students are encouraged to apply knowledge in a relevant context through defining and solving problems, and are therefore applying experiential learning approaches.

PBL has recently been defined by Savin-Baden (2000) with reference to problem-solving learning. The latter is characterized by students attending a lecture and then being given a set of questions to solve which are then used as the basis of discussion in a seminar. This is an approach that has been, and still is, frequently used in accounting education. The problems used are structured, tend not to cross disciplinary boundaries, and are linked to specific curriculum content. The extent to which students are trained in problem-solving techniques varies considerably. As such, this does not reflect, and is not a preparation for, the ambiguous business world that accounting students will encounter, and the unstructured and inter-disciplinary nature of the problems it will pose. Vitally, Savin-Baden sees PBL as focussing on students engaging with the complex situations presented to them, and deciding what information they need to learn and what skills they need to gain in order to manage the situation effectively. Most importantly, the students are not expected to arrive at a predetermined series of 'right answers'. Under this approach, PBL is seen as being an approach to curriculum design rather than as a pedagogic approach.

An interesting example in the context of Canadian accounting education is provided by Breton (1999): an accounting theory course was taught to one group using a traditional lecture/seminar approach, and to a second group using a PBL approach. The group taught using PBL showed significantly higher marks in assessments, and indicated a perception of having acquired better and longer lasting knowledge.

(For a further discussion of PBL, see Section 23.2.1 of Chapter 23 – this volume.)

17.7.3 Action learning

Action learning is initiated when learners realize what they don't know, rather than what they do know, and feel obliged to remedy the deficit. Unlike previously mentioned theories of learning which attempt to bring the workplace into the classroom, action learning attempts to take educational processes into the workplace. It was designed as a management learning process by Revans (1982). Fundamentally, it involves groups of managers, or action learning sets, supporting each other in their action learning. Action learning is initiated in order to explore solutions to real problems and decide on the action to be taken. The stages in this process are as follows:

- describing the problem;
- receiving contributions from others in the form of questions;

- reflecting on the discussion and deciding what action to take;
- reporting back on what happened when action was taken; and
- reflecting on the problem-solving process and how well it worked.

Taking action is the critical factor, and the only real learning comes from doing something and then reflecting on the outcome. The central concept, the spiral of learning, views learning as being a continuous process of action and reflection. Learning is the product of knowledge (i.e. taught learning) plus questioning and reflecting. There are clear overlaps with other approaches to learning in terms of the incorporation of problems, reflection, its being situated in the workplace, and its being an experiential process.

17.8 Further models

Wilson & Beard (2003) developed an experiential learning model based on the perception process model of Gibson *et al.* (1985) and Massaro & Cowan's (1993) information processing model as shown in Figure 17.3.

The model shows how a response to a stimulus is achieved. The recognition and inclusion of the 'affective response' are an important addition as it is the affective response which determines the development of attitudes and beliefs (Krathwohl *et al.*, 1964). The affective response can occur before or after a cognitive response, with cognitive activity being initiated by affect, and affect being subsequently modified by the cognitive process (Lerner & Keltner, 2000). An affective and cognitive response which leads to a self-discovery of new knowledge will develop a world-view that may change actual practice. The behavioural response is normally the final and least frequent response to the perceived stimuli.

Experiential learning, as perceived by Beard & Wilson (2006), concerns the sense-making process of active engagement between the inner world of the person and the outer world of the environment. These two domains form the basis of the 'Learning Combination Lock' (ibid.). This is a development from their earlier model of experiential learning. The Learning Combination Lock focusses on the learning cycle and the stimuli that initiate learning. The outer world of experiences is represented by the learning environment (where), and learning activities (what). The connection between the outer world and the inner world is made by the senses of the individual learner (how), and this is the beginning of the process of interpreting and responding to the stimuli presented in the outside world. In the inner world, there are three domains:

- emotions in learning;
- reasoning and intelligence; and
- learning and change.

The way in which the stimuli are presented and subsequently interpreted and responded to is a process that interlocks in a coordinated way. If, as previously stated, learning creates a change in understanding, then this will occur in the final phase.

The learning environment has, in recent years, become the focus of increased attention. In accounting education there has been an emphasis on traditional environments: lecture theatres and seminar rooms. Lecture theatres generally have fixed seating and, as such, are relatively inflexible learning environments which were designed to facilitate the one-way communication of technical content to large groups of students. Seminar rooms offer more flexibility and more

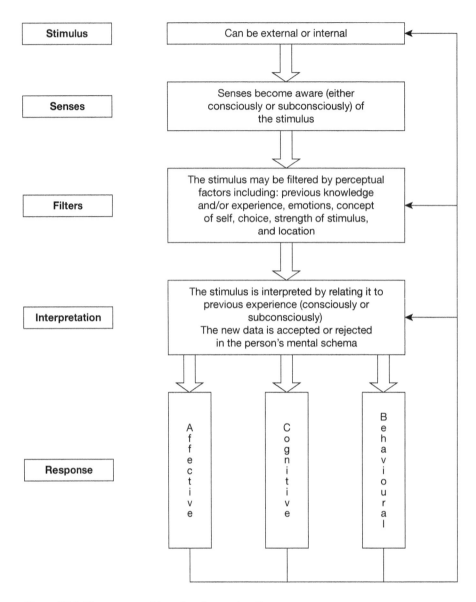

Figure 17.3 The process of learning from stimuli

Source: Based on Wilson & Beard (2003).

opportunity for two-way communications in smaller groups. In order to change accounting education we may need to change the way we think about learning environments. Many educational institutions are rethinking their approach to learning environments. There is a shift from classrooms to learning spaces. The current thinking is emphasizing the link between the nature of learning activities and the learning environment in which they take place. The U.K. Design Council (2005), following a review of learning environments, reported that the existing learning environments:

- reduce the range of teaching and learning styles possible;
- affect the interaction between teacher and student;
- hinder creativity;
- do not meet individual needs;
- are inefficient in terms of time, effort, and cost.

Traditional lecture and seminar rooms may not facilitate the development of the vocational and personal skills that are needed to meet the needs of current and future accounting professionals. The need to facilitate presentations and group work should be considered when designing and developing learning spaces.

Savin-Baden (2007) identifies learning spaces fundamentally as being spaces, both mental and metaphorical, where individuals, both academics and students, have opportunities to reflect and critique their own unique learning position. She offers the view that:

1 Learning spaces are increasingly absent in academic life.
2 The creation and re-creation of learning spaces are vital for the survival of the academic community.
3 The absence of learning spaces is resulting in increasing dissolution and fragmentation of academic identities.
4 Learning spaces need to be valued and possibly redefined in order to regain and maintain the intellectual health of academe.

Albrecht & Sack (2000) argue that current approaches to accounting education lack creativity and contact with real business situations. They emphasize the need to use, where possible, out-of-classroom experiences. Many universities encourage their students to have a 'placement year' in order to expose students to the world of work. Internships also provide such benefits (see Beard & Humphrey, Chapter 25 – this volume). Service-learning, involving supervised work experience, is one example in which students learn and benefit from real-world experiences (McCoskey & Warren, 2003). According to Surridge (2009), this has a positive and significant influence on the academic performance of accounting students in the U.K. A further example is provided by Dellaportas & Hassall (2013) where accounting students went on visits to Australian prisons, in the course of which they met inmates who were former professional accountants. They note the affective response of the students to the prison environment which, combined with cognitive responses, meant that:

> [S]tudents appeared to learn a number of lessons including the nature of conflicts faced by professional accountants, factors contributing to fraudulent conduct, and strategies on how they might deal with such conflicts in their professional careers.
>
> (Dellaportas & Hassall, 2013, p. 1)

A relevant adaptation of the 'Cone of Experience' (Dale, 1946) illustrates how students engaging with different forms of learning opportunities can be analysed in terms of the level of abstraction. This is illustrated in Figure 17.4.

The degree of abstraction is low at the base of the cone and high at the top. Learning from a text is seen as being highly abstract and it is suggested that this is useful for information transfer. (See Stevenson et al., Chapter 19 – this volume.) At the base of the cone is direct purposeful learning such as service-learning, and this is seen as being capable of cognitive, skills, and attitude learning. The more abstract the learning is, the less rich the learning in terms of the potential

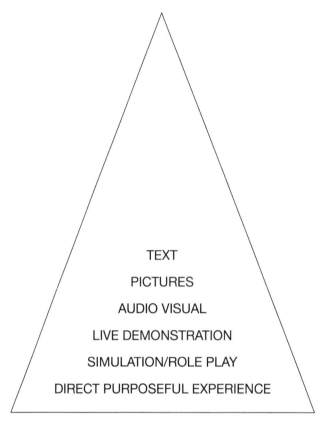

Figure 17.4 The cone of experience
Source: Based on Dale (1946).

for experiential learning. There is also a parallel here with situational learning: when the degree of abstraction is lower, the more the learning is situated in the workplace.

Developments in accounting education pedagogy have followed the trend to reduce the level of abstraction and to situate the learning in a realistic workplace scenario. An initial attempt to do this was by using 'guest' speakers. In a study undertaken in the U.S.A., Metrejean *et al.* (2002) invited accounting professionals into the classroom for them to relate their early and current career experiences to students. The students reported that they enjoyed and benefitted from the speakers in terms of improving their understanding of the real world, their motivation, and their appreciation of the differing career choices available to them. (See Jackling, Chapter 10 – this volume.) This was extended by Webb *et al.* (2009) who took groups of Australian students on a planned international study tour, making site visits to world class global organizations where the students were addressed by senior personnel of the organizations. Six key benefits were perceived by the students:

- Enhanced appreciation of accounting's structures and impacts on society.
- Increased self-confidence.
- Greater awareness of global issues.
- Exposure to practical aspects of accounting and business – the 'real world'.

- Enhanced employability and being 'work-ready'.
- Experiences from the international study tour will help in other studies.

An interesting extension of this is provided by Killian *et al.* (2012). Students taking an *Introductory Financial Accounting* course at a university in the U.S.A. were encouraged to conduct an interview with a professional about the uses and limitations of financial statements, and then reflect on the experience. Their findings indicated that students:

- discover 'real-world' uses and limitations of accounting information;
- connect information from the interview to material from the course;
- reflect on their study habits or attitudes toward learning;
- develop respect for the accounting profession;
- reflect on the skills required for success in accounting and related professions;
- reflect on the contributions of accountants and related business professionals;
- identify accounting-related career choices;
- reflect on the challenges, rewards, and opportunities of accounting-related careers;
- reflect on the suitability of accounting-related careers for self.

The use of case studies by accounting educators is increasing. There are now textbooks that are based on case studies and all of the major academic journals related to accounting education regularly publish accounting case studies. An overall introduction to the use of case studies is provided by Hassall *et al.* (1998). The ability to present unstructured problems that develop intellectual and vocational skills in a situated environment is identified. However, there are limitations identified in terms of whether the case studies are effectively achieving the intended learning outcomes (ILOs). In a recent development, Drake (2011) introduces the idea of the 'living case' to students at a university in the U.K. in order to foster critical understanding of audit practice. A living case is a framework for analysis of a reported media story, such as a financial event or crisis.

The adoption by PABs of case studies and scenarios as part of their assessment systems can be seen as being an influential and encouraging change. In recent years many PABs have used case studies as the 'ultimate' assessment method in their final qualifying examinations. This may have prompted the International Federation of Accountants (IFAC) to recommend the introduction of a final test of 'professional competence' into the assessment methods used by PABs. This has typically been interpreted to mean a case study. IFAC views competence as relating to the ability to carry out a real work task to an acceptable standard in a real work environment. This is obviously impossible for individual universities and colleges to implement, and even more so for PABs, given the constraints imposed by the logistics of ensuring validity and reliability across a global spread of students. Currently, case studies appear to be the chosen viable substitute.

A further step is the use of simulations (the imitation of the operation of a real-world process or system). A general introduction to this area is provided by Marriott (2004). Specific examples involve the use in universities in the U.S.A. of an asset market involving derivatives (Berg *et al.*, 1995), and the board game Monopoly™ (Knechel, 1989; Tanner & Lindquist, 1998). Greenberg & Schneider (2010) use a simulation of job order costing and report high levels of satisfaction on the part of students in the U.S.A. in terms of the experience being seen as relevant and meaningful. An interesting use is identified by Fawcett (1996) who explores the use of a simulation to improve the financial literacy of non-finance managers. (On this theme, see Wilson *et al.*, Chapter 3 – this volume.)

The ultimate learning opportunity, as identified by Dale (1946), consists of direct purposeful experience. In accounting education, the opportunity for internships and placement periods during higher education are examples of this. All of the major PABs insist that a period of monitored work/practical experience is completed before they will confer membership.

17.9 Conclusion

Making changes to higher education and pedagogic practices always involves the careful consideration of achieving the correct balance between benefits and costs. The most noticeable influences on accounting education in recent years have come from:

- the calls from employers resulting from an expectations gap in the area of vocational or employability skills;
- the Global Financial Crisis (GFC) created an environment which resulted in many instances of student numbers increasing while resources are decreasing in real terms and, in an attempt to counteract this, some countries have increased the level of students' fees; and
- a potential change in the relationship between academics and students whereby 'students' become 'customers'.

The criticisms of the pedagogic approaches used in accounting education aroused an interest in the potential of experiential learning. The initial research into experiential learning was concerned with identifying students' LSPs. While this was used to identify the LSPs of accounting students, it has been largely subsumed by the emerging paradigms in this area, for example, students' approaches to learning (SAL) (Marton & Säljö, 1984). (See also Lucas & Mladenovic, Chapter 6 – this volume.)

Further experiential learning research identifies the importance of learning environments and learning opportunities. There are documented examples of attempts to change pedagogic approaches in these areas in accounting education. These examples have attempted to create learning opportunities and to situate them in real-world contexts.

As accountants, we are also aware of the potential costs of some of these proposed changes. In a higher education environment, where student numbers are increasing while at the same time financial resources are in the main decreasing, any potential changes must be carefully evaluated and justified. For example, the availability of funds to change existing learning environments will be extremely limited. Given such budgetary constraints, a major challenge for future accounting education researchers is to find appropriate methods of evaluating the effectiveness and efficiency of proposed changes to pedagogic methodology.

Accounting education was originally established as a workplace activity. In order to gain professional respectability, it has become a higher education discipline. However, it can be considered unusual in the sense that, unlike in other occupations, the award of a degree is not considered to be the end of the formal education requirements. Accountants are required to undertake further formal education and training, along with related assessments. They are also required to evidence a period of practical or workplace experience which, in most cases, is time-defined. The overall period of pre-qualification education (or initial professional development – IPD) therefore contains elements of formal learning and work-based experiential learning. The relationship between this formal learning and the required practical experience is unclear. The extent to which the required practical experience does or does not support more formal learning needs to be the subject of further research. As a response to the GFC, there has been exploration of the idea of a return to apprenticeships for accountants. This may well have its basis in cost considerations, but it does raise interesting questions about the relationship between work and learning, and the need for a wider debate on the future curriculum and pedagogy to be used in the education of tomorrow's accountants.

References

Accounting Education Change Commission (AECC) (1990) Objectives of education for accountants: position statement no. 1, *Issues in Accounting Education*, 5(2), 307–312.

Adler, R.W., Whiting, R.H., & Wynn-Williams, K. (2004) Student-led and teacher-led case presentations: empirical evidence about learning styles in an accounting course, *Accounting Education: an international journal*, 13(2), 213–229.

Albrecht, W.S. & Sack, R.J. (2000) *Accounting Education: Charting the Course through a Perilous Future* (American Accounting Association Accounting Education Series, Vol. 16), Sarasota, FL: American Accounting Association.

Andersen, J.R., Reder, L.M., & Simon, H.A. (1996) Situated learning and education, *Educational Researcher*, 25(4), 5–11.

Anderson, J.A. (1988) Cognitive styles and multicultural populations, *Journal of Teacher Education*, 39(1), 2–9.

Baker, R. Simon, J.R., & Bazeli, F.P. (1987) Selecting instructional design for introductory accounting based on the experiential learning model, *Journal of Accounting Education*, 5, 207–226.

Baldwin, B.A., & Reckers, P.M.J. (1984) Exploring the role of learning style research in accounting education policy, *Journal of Accounting Education*, 2(2), 63–76.

Barnett, R. (1994) *The Limits of Competence: Knowledge, Higher Education and Society*, Buckingham: Research into Higher Education and the Open University Press.

Beard, C. & Wilson, J.P. (2006) *Experiential Learning: A Best Practice Handbook for Educators and Trainers*, London: Kogan Page.

Berg, J., Dickhaut, J., Hughes, J., Maccabe, J. & Rayburn, J. (1995) Capital market experience for financial accounting students, *Contemporary Accounting Research*, 11(2), 941–958.

Blundell, L. & Booth, P. (1988) Teaching innovative accounting topics: student reaction to a course in social accounting, *Accounting and Finance*, 28, 75–85.

Bonk, C.J. & Smith, G.S. (1998) Alternative instructional strategies for creative and critical thinking in the accounting curriculum, *Journal of Accounting Education*, 16(2), 261–293.

Boud, D., Cohen, R., & Walker, D. (1993) *Using Experience for Learning*, Buckingham: Open University Press.

Boud, D. & Feletti, G. (eds) (1991) *The Challenge of Problem Based Learning*, London: Kogan Page.

Boud, D., Keogh, R., & Walker, D. (1985) *Reflection: Turning Experience into Learning*, London: Kogan Page.

Brah, A. & Hoy, J. (1989) Experiential learning, a new orthodoxy, in Weil, S. & McGill, I. (eds) *Making Sense of Experiential Learning*, Buckingham: Society for Research into Higher Education and the Open University Press.

Breton, G. (1999) Some empirical evidence on the superiority of the problem based learning (PBL) method, *Accounting Education: an international journal*, 8(1), 1–12.

Brown, D.H. & Burke, R.C. (1987) Accounting education: a learning-styles study of professional-technical and future adaptation issues, *Journal of Accounting Education*, 5, 187–206.

Brown, J.S., Collins, A. & Duguid, P. (1989) Situated cognition and the culture of learning, *Educational Researcher*, 18(1), 32–42.

Choi, J. & Hannafin, M. (1995) Situated cognition and learning environments: roles, structures and implications for design, *Educational Technology Research and Development*, 43(2), 53–69.

Coffield, F., Moseley, D., Hall, E., & Ecclestone, K. (2004) *Learning Styles and Pedagogy in Post 16 Learning: A Systematic and Critical Review*, London: Learning and Skills Development Agency.

Cuffaro, H.K. (1995) *Experimenting with the World: John Dewey and the Early Childhood Classroom*, New York: Teachers College Press.

Cunningham, B.M. (1996) How to restructure an accounting course to enhance creative and critical thinking, *Accounting Education: A Journal of Theory, Practice and Research*, 1(1), 49–66.

Dale, E. (1946) *Audio-visual Methods in Teaching*, New York: The Dryden Press.

Davis, B., Sumara, D., & Luce-Kapler, R. (2000) *Engaging Minds: Learning and Teaching in a Complex World*, Mahwah, NJ: Lawrence Earlbaum Associates.

Day, M.M., Kaidonis, M.A., & Perrin, R.W. (2003) Reflexivity in learning critical accounting: implications for teaching and its research nexus, *Critical Perspectives on Accounting*, 14(5), 597–614.

Dellaportas, S. & Hassall, T. (2013) Experiential learning in accounting education: a prison visit, *British Accounting Review*, 45(1), 24–36.

Design Council (2005) *Kit for Purpose: Design to Deliver Creative Learning, Report of the Design Council*, London: Design Council.

Desmedt, E., Valcke, M., Carrette, L., & Derese, A. (2003) Comparing the learning styles of medicine and pedagogical sciences students, in Armstrong, S., Graff, M., Lashley, C., Peterson, E., Raynor, S., Sadler-Smith, E., Schiering, M., & Spicer, D. (eds) Bridging theory and practice, in *Proceedings of the Eighth Annual European Learning Styles Information Network Conference, University of Hull*, Hull: University of Hull, pp. 133–138.

Dewey, J. (1916) *Democracy and Education*, New York: Macmillan.

Dewey, J. (1933) *How We Think*, New York: Heath.

Dewey, J. (1938) *Experience and Education: The Kappa Delta Pi Lecture Series*, New York: Macmillan.

Drake, J. (2011) Adding value to audit education through 'living' cases, *Accounting Education*, 20(2), 203–222.

Duff, A. (1997) Validating the learning styles questionnaire and inventory of learning processes in accounting: a research note, *Accounting Education: an international journal*, 6(3), 263–272.

Duff, A. (2001) A note on the psychometric properties of the Learning Styles Questionnaire (LSQ), *Accounting Education: an international journal*, 10(2), 185–197.

Engel, C.E. (1991) Not just a method but a way of learning, in Boud, D. & Feletti, G. (eds) *The Challenge of Problem Based Learning*, London: Kogan Page.

Fawcett, S.L. (1996) Fear of accounts: improving managers' competence and confidence through simulation exercises, *Journal of European Industrial Training*, 20(2), 17–24.

Gibson, J.L., Ivancevich, J.M., & Donnelly, J.H. (1985) *Organisations: Behavior, Structure, Process*, Plano, TX: Business Publications Inc.

Goel, L., Johnson, N., Junglas, I., & Ives, B. (2010) Situated learning: conceptualization and measurement, *Decision Sciences Journal of Innovative Education*, 8(1), 215–240.

Greenberg, R.K. & Schneider, A. (2010) Job order costing: a simulation and vehicle for conceptual discussion, *Academy of Educational Leadership Journal*, 14(3), 39–57.

Habermas, J. (1972) *Knowledge and Human Interest*, London: Heinemann.

Habermas, J. (1984) *The Theory of Communicative Action*, Vol. 1, Cambridge: Polity Press.

Hassall, T., Lewis, S., & Broadbent, J.M. (1998) The use and potential abuse of case studies in accounting education, *Accounting Education: an international journal*, 7(suppl.), 37–47.

Heeter, C. (2005) Situated learning for designers: social, cognitive and situative framework. Available at: http://teachvu.vu.msu.edu/public/designers/social_interactions/index.php?page_num=4 (accessed 26 February 2008).

Honey, P. & Mumford, A. (1982) *Manual of Learning Styles*, Maidenhead: Honey Publications.

Howieson, B. (2004) The use of self-reflective study journals in a postgraduate accounting theory course: a case study, paper presented to the 2004 IAAER/Southern African Accounting Association Conference, Durban, 30 June–2 July.

Jarvis, P. (1987) *Adult Learning in the Social Context*, London: Croom Helm.

Jarvis, P. (1995) *Adult and Continuing Education, Theory and Practice*, 2nd edn, London: Routledge.

Kant, I. (1993) *Critique of Pure Reason*, London: J. M. Dent.

Kelly, M., Davey, H., & Haigh, N. (1999) Contemporary accounting education and society, *Accounting Education: an international journal*, 8(4), 321–340.

Kember, D., Jones, A., Loke, A., McKay, J., Sinclair, K., Tse, H., Webb, C., Wong, F., Wong, M., & Yeung, E. (1999) Determining the level of reflective thinking from students' written journals using a coding scheme based on the work of Mezirow, *International Journal of Lifelong Education*, 18(1), 18–30.

Killian, L.J., Huber, M.M., & Brandon, C.D. (2012) The financial statement interview: intentional learning in the first accounting course, *Issues in Accounting Education*, 27(1), 337–360.

Kimmel, P. (1995) A framework for incorporating critical thinking into accounting education, *Journal of Accounting Education*, 13(3), 299–318.

Kirshner, D. & Whitson, J. (eds) (1997) *Situated Cognition*, Mahwah, NJ: Lawrence Erlbaum Associates.

Knechel, R.K. (1989) Using a business simulation game as a substitute for a practice set, *Issues in Accounting Education*, 4(2), 411–424.

Kolb, D.A. (1984) *Experiential Learning*, Englewood Cliffs, NJ: Prentice Hall.

Krathwohl, D.R., Bloom, B.S., & Masia, B.B. (1964) *Taxonomy of Educational Objectives: Handbook II*, New York: David McKay Co.

Langenderfer, H.Q. (1987) Accounting education's history: a 100 year search for identity, *Journal of Accountancy*, 163(5), 302–331.

Lankard, B. (1995) *New Ways of Learning in the Workplace*, Eric Digest No 161, Columbus, OH: Eric Clearinghouse on Adult, Career and Vocational Education.

Lave, J. (1988) *Cognition in Practice: Mind, Mathematics, and Culture in Everyday Life*, Cambridge: Cambridge University Press.

Lerner, J.S. & Keltner, D. (2000) Beyond valence, toward a model of emotion specific influences on judgement and choice, *Cognition and Emotion*, 14(4), 473–493.

Lewin, K. (1951) *Field Theory in the Social Sciences*, New York: Harper and Row.

Lucas, U. (2008) Being 'pulled up short': creating moments of surprise and possibility in accounting education, *Critical Perspectives on Accounting*, 19, 383–403.

Marriott, N. (2004) Using computerized business simulations and spreadsheet models in accounting education: a case study, *Accounting Education: an international journal*, 13(Supplement 1), 55–70.

Marriott, P. (2002) A longitudinal study of undergraduate accounting students' learning style preferences at two UK universities, *Accounting Education: an international journal*, 11(1), 43–62.

Marton, F. & Säljö, R. (1984) Approaches to learning, in Marton, F. *et al.* (eds) *The Experience of Learning*, Edinburgh: Scottish Academic Press.

Massaro, D.W. & Cowan, N. (1993) Information processing models: microscopes of the mind, *Annual Review of Psychology*, 44, 383–425.

McCoskey, M. & Warren, D.L. (2003) Service-learning: an innovative approach to teaching accounting: a teaching note, *Accounting Education: an international journal*, 12(4), 405–413.

McKee, T.E., Mock, T.J., & Flemming Ruud, T. (1992) A comparison of Norwegian and United States accounting students' learning styles preferences, *Accounting Education: an international journal*, 1(4), 321–341.

Metrejean, C., Pittman, J. & Zareski, M.T. (2002) Guest speakers: reflections on the role of accountants in the classroom, *Accounting Education: an international journal*, 11(4), 347–364.

Mezirow, J. (1981) A critical theory of adult learning and education, *Adult Education*, 32, 3–23.

Mezirow, J. (1991) *Transformative Dimensions of Adult Learning*, San Francisco: Jossey-Bass.

Miller, N. & Boud, D. (1996) Animating learning from experience, in Boud, D. & Miller, N. (eds) *Working with Experience*, London: Routledge.

Piaget, J.P. (1977) *Science of Education and Psychology of the Child*, Harmondsworth: Penguin.

Quay, J. (2003) Experience and participation: relating the theories of learning, *The Journal of Experiential Education*, 26(2), 105–116.

Ramsden, P. (1992) *Learning to Teach in Higher Education*, London: Routledge.

Revans, R.W. (1982) *The Origin and Growth of Action Learning*, London: Chartwell Bratt.

Rogers, A. (1996) *Teaching Adults*, Buckingham: Open University Press.

Samkin, G. & Francis, G. (2008) Introducing a learning portfolio in an undergraduate financial accounting course, *Accounting Education: an international journal*, 17(3), 233–271.

Savin-Baden, M. (2000) *Problem-Based Learning in Higher Education: Untold Stories*, Buckingham: The Society for Research into Higher Education and Open University Press.

Savin-Baden, M. (2007) *Learning Spaces: Creating Opportunities for Knowledge Creation in Academic Life*, Buckingham: The Society for Research into Higher Education and Open University Press.

Schön, D.A. (1983) *The Reflective Practitioner*, New York: Basic Books.

Schön, D.A. (1987) *Educating the Reflective Practitioner*, San Francisco, CA: Jossey-Bass.

Stout, D.E. & Ruble, T.L. (1994) A reassessment of the role of the learning styles inventory (LSI-1985) in accounting education research, *Journal of Accounting Education*, 12(2), 89–104.

Sugahara, S. & Boland, G. (2010) The role of cultural factors in the learning style preferences of accounting students: a comparative study between Japan and Australia, *Accounting Education: an international journal*, 19(3), 235–255.

Surridge, I. (2009) Accounting and finance degrees: is the academic performance of placement students better? *Accounting Education: an international journal*, 18(4/5), 471–485.

Tanner, M.M. & Lindquist, T.M. (1998) Using Monopoly and team-games-tournaments in accounting education: a cooperative learning teaching resource, *Accounting Education: an international journal*, 7(2), 139–162.

Tennant, M. (1997) *Psychology and Adult Learning*, 2nd edn, London: Routledge.

Vygotsky, L. (1978) *Mind in Society: The Development of Higher Psychological Processes*, Cambridge, MA: Harvard University Press.

Webb, L., De Lange, P., & O'Connell, B. (2009) A programme to expose students to senior executives in the world of accounting: an innovative learning method, *Accounting Education: an international journal*, 18(2), 183–205.

Wilson, A. (1993) The promise of situated cognition, in Merriam, S.B. (ed.) *An Update on Adult Learning Theory*, San Francisco: Jossey-Bass, pp. 71–79.

Wilson, J.P. & Beard, C. (2003) The learning combination lock: an experiential approach to learning design, *Journal of European Industrial Training*, 27(2), 88–97.

Wilson, R.M.S. & Hill, A.P. (1994) Learning styles: a literature guide, *Accounting Education: an international journal*, 3(4), 349–358.

Wolcott, S.K., Baril, C.P., Cunningham, B.M., Fordham, D.R., & St. Pierre, K. (2002) Critical thought on critical thinking research, *Journal of Accounting Education*, 20(2), 85–103.

About the authors

Trevor Hassall is Professor of Accounting Education at Sheffield Hallam University, U.K. (t.hassall@shu.ac.uk). His primary interests are in the areas of the barriers to the vocational skills development of accounting students, and the introduction of new pedagogic approaches to accounting education.

John Joyce is Professor of Management Accounting Education at Sheffield Hallam University, U.K. (j.joyce@shu.ac.uk). His interests are in the development of vocational skills of accounting students, and the introduction of new pedagogic approaches to accounting education.

18

Developing critical thinking in accounting education

Billie M. Cunningham

UNIVERSITY OF MISSOURI, U.S.A.

CONTENTS

Abstract

The idea of *critical* thinking as a moving target, towards which one's 'life of the mind' should progress, has been around for quite a long time. Most definitions cluster around common traits and attitudes, but vary depending on their contexts, purposes, and the disciplines in which they are practised.

What does critical thinking mean for accounting educators? As the accounting profession has expressed a need for accountants to think critically in carrying out their professional responsibilities, how can educators help aspiring accountants and those immersed in their careers improve their critical thinking skills? What are associated potential benefits, perceived roadblocks, and practical issues of doing so? This chapter explores attempts to answer these questions, including research, proposed ideas, and examples relating to this challenge. It also offers a glimpse of where these efforts might head in the future, and serves as a reference for accounting educators.

Keywords

continuing professional development, critical education, critical thinking, ethics, initial professional development, intellectual development

18.1 Introduction

The main aims of this chapter are:

- to provide a brief history of the interest in and development of critical thinking as a component of accounting education, including various definitions of critical thinking;
- to discuss the relationships between level of intellectual development, maturity, and identity and improvement in critical thinking skills;
- to offer an overview of the current thinking and debates regarding the development of critical thinking in accounting education;
- to describe how the nature of critical thinking development can impact on continuing professional development (CPD); and
- to look at where the current critical thinking research agenda in accounting education is likely to lead.

Although this chapter has an implicit U.S. orientation (because of the author's background), the development of critical thinking in accounting education has relevance in other jurisdictions.

> *In professional education, it is insufficient to learn for the sake of knowledge and understanding alone: one learns in order to engage in practice.*

> (Shulman, 2005, p. 18)

If one looked at a list of typical university accounting courses, one might conclude that an accounting education includes learning some combination of accounting principles and concepts, tax laws, regulations, managerial and cost accounting, systems, auditing, ethics, forensic accounting, and other essential topics that will prepare accounting students to contribute to skilled professional accounting practice. But, accountants don't merely practise; they make judgements and perform with a sense of personal and social (public) responsibility. For accountants, practice must not only be skilled and theoretically grounded; it must be characterized by judgement, integrity, and by a commitment to ethical, responsible service.

To draw again on Shulman, from his description of liberal education for professionals, one could say that accounting education must be about '*developing pedagogies to link ideas, practices, and values under conditions of inherent uncertainty that necessitate not only judgment in order to act, but also cognizance of the consequences of one's action*' (ibid., p. 19).

18.2 The interest in and development of critical thinking as a component of accounting education

As described in Section A of this volume, recent sentiments of accountants, standard setting and accrediting bodies, and accounting educators from Australia, the U.K., and the U.S.A., for example, suggest that the domain of accounting education should include the discipline, principles, values, and practices of accounting, but also nurture students' abilities to use the critical thinking skills that will help them act with integrity, make responsible judgements under uncertainty, and learn from experience – all of which will be relevant in the rapidly changing business environment in which accounting is practised (American Accounting Association (AAA), 1986; Arthur Andersen *et al.*, 1989; Mathews, 1990; Birkett, 1993; Siegel & Sorenson, 1999; the American Institute of Certified Public Accountants (AICPA), 1999; Albrecht & Sack, 2000; the Quality Assurance Agency (QAA), 2000; International Federation of Accountants (IFAC), 2002, 2008a, 2008b; the Institute of Chartered Accountants in England & Wales (ICAEW), 1996; Hancock *et al.*, 2009; Evans *et al.*, 2010; Pathways Commission, 2012), but see St. Pierre & Rebele, Chapter 5 – this volume, for an alternative perspective.

While the business environment is experiencing energetic and exciting transformation, the resulting complex, ambiguous, dynamic, and difficult to interpret economic events and transactions provide accountants with opportunities to support the public interest through growth and added value in the services that they provide. But these same events and transactions also can raise the level of risk which accountants must navigate, and cause challenges for which no guidelines, or only sketchy guidelines, exist. These challenges include more complex ways of conducting business, information overload and gaps in information, technological advances, globalization, and escalating regulations. (See also Flood, Chapter 4 – this volume.)

18.2.1 More complex ways of conducting business

Companies, not-for-profit organizations, and governmental agencies are finding new and more flexible ways to accomplish their objectives, such as partnering with other organizations, forming joint venture partnerships for the duration of specific projects, or developing special purpose entities to 'outsource' specific aspects of their activities. Additionally, these organizations are financing their activities more creatively, finding new, complex outlets for investing their excess cash, using a larger variety of alternatives for compensating their employees, and manoeuvring more complicated tax laws. These complexities create more challenges for understanding and interpreting these activities, accounting for them, and auditing them.

18.2.2 Information overload and gaps in information

The growing volume and accessibility of information have exceeded the capacity to use it, let alone understand it all. (See Wilson *et al.*, Chapter 3 – this volume, for a discussion of information literacy and financial literacy.) Furthermore, new forms of business and transactions quickly can make old information invalid or irrelevant. As a result, information overload, invalid information, and gaps in information create more challenges for evaluating, filtering, and recognizing gaps in available information as accountants select what is relevant and timely for all the various responsibilities and decisions that comprise accounting.

18.2.3 Technological advances

The pace of technological change affects not only the amount and timeliness of available information, but also the products and services we use, the ways in which products are manufactured, and the speed and method by which business is conducted. The speed of technological advances also affects the security and dependability of information, as well as the pace of information flow, reporting, and decision-making by organizations and accountants. (See Boritz & Stoner, Chapter 16 – this volume.) As technology advances, companies and organizations must adapt their internal controls to address new weaknesses which result. To keep up, auditors must have a continual presence at some companies and organizations and make quick judgments.

18.2.4 Globalization

The *globalization* of business activities and economies provides more opportunities for both companies and accountants by creating a larger, more diverse marketplace. But it also complicates the ways in which companies and, therefore, accountants conduct business. Not only must accountants cross the hurdle of language barriers, but they also must translate transactions involving foreign currencies, learn to negotiate other cultures, economies, laws, and ways of conducting business, and adapt to evolving international accounting standards which affect the ways in which international companies and their accountants report their activities.

18.2.5 Escalating regulations

Both companies and accountants are facing an increasing number of regulations. This development is recently illustrated in the U.S.A., for example, by the 2002 Sarbanes–Oxley Act and the consequential changes that resulted from the act. For instance, while the U.S. Securities and Exchange Commission (SEC) is tightening up regulations over public company reporting, the U.S. Public Company Accounting Oversight Board (PCAOB) is regulating the auditing of companies' external accounting reports and managements' assertions about the effectiveness of the internal controls surrounding the companies' accounting systems. At the same time, in order to comply with PCAOB regulations, companies' internal accountants are scrambling to update and assess the effectiveness of the companies' internal controls.

In a complex business environment such as this, accountants must be able to anticipate and adapt to these changes. In order to do this, they must be willing and able to be open to the viewpoints of others, to respect and appreciate differences among people, to take educated and thoughtful risks, to anticipate environmental trends and identify the potential problems and opportunities associated with these trends, and to willingly abandon old assumptions and conclusions if new information or technology make them less valid. In this environment, accountants are not operating in a 'textbook world' where there are clear cut, right and wrong answers, and where the relevant facts for making decisions are neatly laid out. Instead, the environment is messy and open-ended. Problems may have numerous acceptable solutions, some of which are better than others. Together, the complementary skills of creative and critical thinking can help accountants to be more effective in making the judgments necessary to choose among solutions, and in navigating this environment.

18.3 What is critical thinking?

It is difficult to discuss critical thinking without acknowledging the relationship between creative and critical thinking. In the context of accounting (and particularly in the wake of some of the recent corporate accounting scandals), some may think of creativity, 'cooking the books', and financial statement 'special effects' as being different names for the same activity. However, creative *thinking* in the conduct of accounting services and practice is more positive, and can be described as a process of finding or generating inventive alternatives or solutions to complex accounting and reporting problems. These alternatives or solutions usually result from a free flow of thoughts which give rise to new ideas.

Creative alternatives or solutions are just a beginning in grappling with the challenges present in today's post-global financial crisis (GFC) economic circumstances, and the potential challenges of future economic events. *Critical* thinking, when paired with creative thinking, can help accountants identify the *best* alternatives or solutions and make optimal decisions about them. Ruggiero (1988) suggests that educators (including accounting educators) should help students develop appropriate attitudes, habits, and skills to improve both their creative thinking and their critical thinking.

Educators from the U.K. and the U.S.A., for example, have defined critical thinking in various ways (Nickerson *et al.*, 1985; Kurfiss, 1988; Ruggiero, 1988; Paul, 1990; Huffman *et al.*, 1991; Moon, 2008; Chaffee, 2011). At a basic level, Chaffee (2011, p. 4) defines *thinking* as the process that we use '*to make sense of the world*'. He describes *critical* thinking as '*thinking for ourselves by carefully examining the way that we make sense of the world . . . thinking about [our] thinking so that [we] can clarify and improve it*'.

Our understanding of critical thinking primarily derives from psychology and philosophy (Ruggiero, 1988). Psychology contributes to our understanding of intellectual development and how people think. Philosophy emphasizes 'critical' thinking – that is, the process of '*(recognizing and/or constructing) sound arguments, applying the principles of formal and informal logic and avoiding fallacies in . . . reasoning*' (ibid., p. 2). Critical thinking helps one evaluate ideas and solutions resulting from creative thinking against predetermined criteria to see whether any of them will work, what types of problems are associated with them, whether they can be improved, and which ideas are better than others.

Unfortunately, critical thinking '*is a term with no universally-accepted definition*' (Baril *et al.*, 1997, p. 1). Nonetheless, the various definitions in the literature contain common ideas. Underlying each definition is the ability a person has to rationally organize, interpret, and use information – even when the information may be incomplete, or when the decision context or the environment in which the information is to be used may be new or unfamiliar. Kurfiss (1988, p. 2) provides a description of critical thinking that is relevant for accountants:

> *Critical thinking is a rational response to questions that cannot be answered definitively and for which all the relevant information may not be available. It is defined here as an investigation whose purpose is to explore a . . . problem to arrive at a . . . conclusion about it that integrates all available information and that can therefore be convincingly justified.*

This ability usually involves both mental and behavioural processes. Examples of mental processes identified with critical thinking include using inductive and deductive reasoning, synthesizing information, seeing connections between concepts, and making judgements backed by evidence. Behavioural processes identified with critical thinking include:

- thinking independently;
- valuing truth above self-interest;
- persevering intellectually;
- suspending judgement while gathering information; and
- maintaining intellectual curiosity.

Differences in the definitions of critical thinking usually arise from the variety of ways in which researchers describe and classify these mental and behavioural processes. For example, Table 18.1 illustrates the similarities and differences in definitions of critical thinking between two

Table 18.1 Academic models of critical thinking

Dimensions and traits of critical thinking (Adapted from Paul 1993)

Qualities of perfect thought	*Elements of thought*	*Traits of critical thinking*
• Clarity • Precision • Specificity • Accuracy • Relevance • Consistency • Logicalness • Depth • Completeness • Significance • Fairness • Adequacy (for purpose)	• The problem or question at issue • The purpose or goal of the thinking • The frame of reference or points of view involved • Principles or theories used • Evidence, data, or reasons advanced • Interpretations and claims made • Inferences, reasoning, and lines of formulated thought • Implications and consequences which follow	• Intellectual humility • Intellectual courage • Intellectual empathy • Intellectual good faith (integrity) • Intellectual perseverance • Faith in reason • Intellectual sense of justice

Elements of critical thinking (Adapted from Huffman et al., 1991)

Affective components	*Cognitive components*	*Behavioural components*
• Valuing truth above self-interest • Accepting change • Empathizing • Welcoming divergent views • Tolerating ambiguity • Recognizing personal biases	• Thinking independently • Defining problems accurately • Analyzing data for value and content • Employing a variety of thought processes in problem-solving • Synthesizing • Resisting over-generalization • Employing metacognition (reflective thinking)	• Delaying judgment until adequate data is available • Employing precise terms • Gathering data • Distinguishing fact from opinion • Encouraging critical dialogue • Listening actively • Modifying judgments in light of new information • Applying knowledge to new situations

Table 18.2 Mental traits of critical thinking in the public accounting profession: cognitive attributes and characteristics

Public accounting profession's 'definition' of critical thinking

- **Recognizes problem areas**

  Auditors without this skill accept assertions/information/evidence given without considering its congruence with other available evidence. May miss conflicting pieces of evidence or when a piece of evidence conflicts with an assumption of 'no problem'.

  Tax practitioners without this skill may not be able to 'read meaning into the numbers' and recognize problems on their own. Good critical thinkers create expectations of what evidence should be, and then recognize when data is incompatible with those expectations.

- **Recognizes when additional information is needed**

  Auditors without this skill waste time searching for missing data, when the data would have little impact on the final outcome or solution.

  Tax practitioners without this skill may not be able to make a logical assumption or substitute for missing data.

- **Fits details into the overall environment; sees the 'Big Picture'**

  Auditors without this skill can flawlessly perform substantive testing procedures, but are unable to see exactly where or how their work fits into the overall objectives of the audit.

  Tax practitioners without this skill may be experts at filling out returns, and even making determinations about reporting and classifications, but are unable to relate these tasks to the broader business operations of their clients.

  Systems experts without this skill may be outstanding programmers, or proficient in developing technical specifications, but may be unable to recognize how their work affects other components of a project or of their client's business.

- **Transfers knowledge from one situation to another**

  Auditors without this skill tend to blindly follow last year's working papers when conducting this year's audit, or follow a textbook approach to an audit, rather than stopping to analyse the situation to see if different procedures are warranted.

  Tax practitioners without this skill may simply copy numbers from financial reports onto tax returns without considering the client's overall picture in light of new statutory, judicial, or regulatory law in an attempt to identify new opportunities for tax savings.

  Systems experts without this skill may not take into consideration non-accounting information when solving accounting problems, such as training, support, payment terms, cash flow, and maintenance details.

- **Anticipates, thinks ahead, plans**

  Without this skill, any accountant may not be able to construct an overall picture of circumstances, and then anticipate what the outcome of those circumstances will be, or be able to analyse alternatives and anticipate the outcomes of those alternatives.

Source: Adapted from Baril *et al.* (1998, p. 392).

well-known critical thinking researchers from the U.S.A., and also provides more detailed lists of the mental and behavioural processes that make up critical thinking. A quick glance through these lists reveals that the majority of these mental and behavioural processes parallel those of accountants (Baril et al., 1997, 1998; Wolcott et al., 2002).

Baril et al. (1997, 1998) interviewed various levels of practising public accountants in the U.S.A. to identify the critical thinking competencies valued by that sub-set of the accounting profession. The accountants identified mental and behavioural traits that match those of academic models of creative and critical thinking, and also identified other related traits not viewed as 'pure' critical thinking in academic models, but related to the traits of critical thinking. Table 18.2 presents these mental traits, along with examples of how the lack of these traits can hinder accountants from performing efficiently.

Table 18.3 lists the behavioural traits identified by accounting professionals that match the academic models of critical thinking, and includes the other related traits identified by accounting professionals.

Table 18.3 Behavioural traits of critical thinking in the public accounting profession: non-cognitive attitudes and behaviours

Public accounting profession's 'definition' of critical thinking
• Exhibits initiative
• Exhibits curiosity
• Exhibits confidence
• Communicates clearly and articulately
Other competencies mentioned occasionally by interviewees
• Displays creativity
• Accepts ambiguity
• Recognizes when there is more than one acceptable solution
• Makes qualitative judgements
• Displays rapid thought process
• Displays healthy scepticism; asks 'why?' or 'why not?'
• Challenges the status quo
• Determines the extent of what is reasonable; defines the limits of acceptability
• Recognizes personal limitations
• Exposed to diverse cultures, knowledge and backgrounds
• Recognizes presence of biases

Source: Adapted from Baril et al. (1998, p. 392).

18.4 The relationship between level of intellectual development and improvement in critical thinking skills

Research on intellectual development, conducted in the U.K. and the U.S.A., suggests that learning to think critically is an ongoing process: people pass through non-linear levels, or stages, of intellectual development that make them more or less receptive to learning certain aspects of critical thinking (Perry, 1970; Belenky et al., 1986; Kurfiss, 1988; Francis et al., 1995; O'Donovan, 2010; Lucas & Tan, 2011). Additionally, intellectual development is tied to both education and maturity. It takes several years for college students to move through the first stage of intellectual development into the next stage and, for most people, it takes a lifetime (or more) to master the last stage. Additionally, studies undertaken in the U.S.A. found that it is not uncommon for students to mix their intellectual stages from topic to topic, sometimes regressing to previous intellectual stages as topics become more complicated (Cunningham, 1992, 1996). Baxter Magolda (1992) and Belenky *et al.* (1986) suggest that moving between levels of intellectual development is difficult, and that teaching critical thinking is not clear-cut because intellectual development is bound up with identity and gender.

Perry (1970), Belenky *et al.* (1986), and Kurfiss (1988), in studies conducted in the U.S.A., identified four general stages of intellectual development related to critical thinking in college students and beyond:

- dualism
- multiplicity
- contextual relativism, and
- commitment (or responsible knowing).

Their research suggests that most students in undergraduate accounting classes are in the first or second stage of development (i.e. dualism or multiplicity). Recognizing the existing range of students' intellectual development can help educators identify which aspects of critical thinking students are most receptive to learning, and then use that information to focus teaching efforts on helping them begin to move into the next level of intellectual development – from dualism into multiplicity, or from multiplicity into contextual relativism (Cunningham, 1992, 1996).

Typically, students in the dualism stage tend to see issues as being 'black or white', right or wrong. For these students, there are only absolutes – no shades of grey. Issues and problems are unambiguous. From their point of view, authorities (e.g. parents, educators, newspapers, textbooks) convey the rules and facts that make up 'knowledge'. Where two authorities differ from each other, these students believe that there are two possible explanations for the difference – either:

- one authority must have made a mistake; or
- one must be more experienced than the other, in which case the one with more experience must be 'correct'.

Many of these students believe that accounting is similar to mathematics (but, in a business context), where information is precise and where the accounting process results in accurate answers.

In the multiplicity stage of intellectual development, students are able to identify an ambiguous issue or area of uncertainty, and often recognize that multiple options or solutions can exist. However, they are unable to select a 'best' alternative by using criteria, standards, or evidence. When there is no authority on the subject, or when multiple authorities exist with opposing views, these students value opinion unsupported by evidence. Each authority's opinion is valid for that authority. In fact, each *student's* opinion is valid for that student ('You're entitled to your opinion, and I'm entitled to mine'). Students in the multiplicity stage tend to make intuitive or arbitrary choices rather than well-reasoned choices.

Very few undergraduate students reach the contextual relativism stage or the commitment stage of intellectual development. Students in the contextual relativism stage move from accepting opinion unreservedly to understanding the criteria, standards, and evidence used within a discipline, such as accounting, to select preferable theories and alternatives despite meaningful uncertainty. However, while students *understand* the criteria used to select preferable ideas, they struggle with *applying* these criteria until they reach the commitment stage of intellectual development. Kitchener (1986) suggests that people cannot begin the commitment stage until their mid- to late-twenties, at the earliest, and that education must be combined with age and maturity for a person to have the ability to think relatively consistently in this stage (while continuing to improve). In the commitment stage, students (usually graduate students) and professionals know there are diverse frameworks from which they can approach problems. They can delineate the advantages and disadvantages of these frameworks, address trade-offs among frameworks, and describe why they support a particular approach.

Baxter Magolda (1992), in the U.S.A., builds on the work of Perry, Belincky *et al.*, and Kitchener, and further explains why learning to think critically is non-linear and why these skills develop slowly. She intertwines students' intellectual development with the transformation of their 'ways of knowing', or epistemological beliefs. This transformation requires self-reflection about the assumptions underlying one's deeply-held beliefs, attitudes, emotions, and opinions, resulting in changes to one's identity. This evolvement of self is non-linear and complicates the movement through the levels of intellectual development. A U.K. study by Lucas (2008) provides specific examples of a pedagogic approach that can help transformative learning occur.

A study by Wolcott *et al.* (2002, p. 92) in the U.S.A., found commonalities in the different developmental models proposed by various researchers which have implications for improving critical thinking skills over an extended time:

- Critical thinking skills can be arrayed on a continuum from less complex to more complex.
- Students must develop less complex skills before they can develop more complex skills.
- Most college students operate at cognitive levels that are too low for adequate critical thinking performance.
- Critical thinking skills develop slowly (if they do develop).
- Cross-curricular educational efforts, and educational efforts over time, are needed to give students sufficient time and practice for development of critical thinking skills.

18.5 Current thinking regarding the development of critical thinking in accounting education

At this point, several questions arise:

- Is the development of critical thinking skills part of the domain of *accounting* education?
- In the university environment, wouldn't these skills be taught better or more efficiently elsewhere in the university curriculum, such as in the liberal arts and the sciences?
- And, within those areas of the university, aren't there special courses that address critical thinking skills?
- How can educators add another component to their already-crowded courses?

However, on the other hand, while there is value in exposing students to critical thinking across the curriculum, can accounting educators afford to leave the teaching of these skills exclusively to the general education courses, electives, and other courses that students take outside their major courses? Wouldn't accounting students be better prepared for their careers if they also learned these skills within the context of accounting?

There are practical reasons why critical thinking should be taught outside of the accounting curriculum. For example, specialized courses in critical thinking (perhaps taught in the liberal arts) can focus on a deep understanding of critical thinking and provide in-depth critical thinking training that can be useful across disciplines. Teaching critical thinking across the curriculum can reinforce students' understanding and application of critical thinking in multiple disciplines and scenarios, opening the door for students to see the social relevance of accounting (Boyce, 2004).

But there are several compelling reasons why critical thinking also should be part of the domain of accounting education:

- value to the discipline (accountants value critical thinking competencies differently from people in other disciplines);
- pedagogical value (students will gain a deeper understanding of – and retain more about accounting – if critical thinking is part of the domain in which they learn accounting);
- the relationship between critical thinking and ethics (ethical situations often are ambiguous and messy, and must be resolved in the presence of incomplete information);
- practical value (students will be more prepared for their careers by learning how to think critically within the discipline of accounting – how accountants think, what are uncertainties, issues, debates); and
- attractiveness to potential accounting majors and a better match between qualities and characteristics of accounting majors and the qualities and characteristics required for a career in accounting.

18.5.1 What is different about the ways in which accountants and educators in other disciplines value critical thinking?

Helping students develop critical thinking skills means teaching them a way of thinking, or a thinking process. But that thinking process may be unique from discipline to discipline. Powers & Enright (1987), after interviewing educators in six different disciplines from the U.S.A., learned that the higher-level thinking skills which these educators valued the most for success in their disciplines only partially overlapped. Differences in critical thinking skills valued among various disciplines are inherent in the assumptions that each discipline makes about the nature of its reality, the foundational knowledge of each discipline, and the unique definitions that form the framework of each discipline. For example, scientists use and value a fairly traditional method-ology for analysis – the 'scientific method' – and draw inferences from their observations. English educators, on the other hand, place more value on the ability to elaborate on arguments, or recognize the central thesis in a work. In accounting, 'reality' is based, for example, on assumptions specific to accrual accounting and definitions that can appear to contradict the common usage of the terms they define (e.g. depreciation), or the tax law and how transactions can be structured to minimize taxes and be in compliance with the tax law, or on various business and transaction structures. This 'reality', and the role of accounting in society and the business environ-ment, influence the critical thinking skills which are valued by accountants.

Two studies, one in the U.S.A. and the other in Botswana, found that, if one looks at the competencies recommended by the AICPA (1999), the Institute of Management Accountants (IMA,1994), the IFAC (2002, 2008a, 2008b), the Institute of Chartered Accountants in Australia (ICAA,1998a,b), ICAEW (1996), Canadian Institute of Chartered Accountants (CICA, 2001, 2005), as well as the competencies identified by a cross-section of public accountants (Baril *et al.*, 1998; Mgaya & Kitindi, 2009), it is clear that accountants value a sub-set of critical thinking skills which does not precisely match those valued by other disciplines. And while accounting programmes in universities have traditionally given students a strong 'nuts and bolts' knowledge base in accounting, it is important that accounting students also learn the processes that accountants use to think about business and accounting information, and the critical thinking skills that they use to filter and interpret that information. Students need to develop the ability to use critical thinking skills in the context of both the accounting and business environment, and in the context of what their responsibilities will be within that environment. (See St. Pierre & Rebele, Chapter 5 – this volume, for a challenging alternative perspective.)

18.5.2 How can critical thinking within accounting education help students learn more about accounting?

In their discussion of critical thinking traits suggested by the models discussed earlier, Pascarella & Terenzini (1991, pp. 114, 115) relate the traits to students trying to learn. Those thinking traits allow students to do the following:

- process and utilize new information;
- reason objectively and draw objective conclusions from various types of data;
- evaluate new ideas and techniques efficiently;
- evaluate arguments and claims critically; and
- make reasonable decisions in the face of imperfect information.

It is by using these processes, rather than rote learning, that students can truly learn accounting and begin to think like accountants.

The Accounting Education Change Commission (AECC, 1990) asserts that an accounting student's formal education should be the basis on which life-long learning of accounting can be built. In other words, students should learn how to learn. To learn, students must be able to locate, order, and structure data and facts, all of which require critical thinking. As discussed by Hassall & Joyce in Chapter 17 – this volume, research in educational psychology indicates that students learn more, and retain their knowledge longer when they actively grapple with problems and issues than they do from reading or from listening to a lecture. In fact, the results of classic research that has evaluated what students learn and retain from lectures indicate that educators should use the lecture only in certain, very limited cases (Verner & Dickinson, 1967; McKeachie, 1967; Bligh, 1972; Costin, 1972; Eble, 1983). This suggests that structuring problems or issues to involve the students, and allowing them to use accounting facts and principles to solve less structured problems that more closely resemble what they will encounter when they practise accounting, will help students improve their higher level thinking skills as well as gaining a deeper understanding of accounting.

By practising thinking within the discipline – thinking the way professional accountants must think, and by using higher-level thinking skills within the subject matter of business and accounting – students will develop habits of the mind and be able to better apply these higher-level skills when they begin their careers. They already will have practised 'thinking like an accountant' in situations that resemble those in the business environment.

18.5.3 The relationship between critical thinking and ethics

In the midst of the fast-evolving, complex, high-tech world economy, accountants still strive to protect the public interest as they serve the needs of their employers or individual clients.

How well they do this affects the credibility of the profession and contributes to the public's *'confidence and trust in the functioning of markets and the economy in general'* (IFAC, 2012a, A13). As discussed by Boyce in Chapter 21 – this volume, ethical behaviour, accompanied by strong critical thinking skills, can guide accountants through the maze of ethical dilemmas and decisions which they must navigate, and result in decisions that better protect the public trust and the credibility of the profession. In the U.S.A., both research (Libby & Thorne, 2003; Bernardi *et al.*, 2002) and cognitive development theory suggest that an emphasis on the 'self-in-the-making' (Young & Annisette, 2009), and critical thinking in accounting education (McNeel, 1994; Apostolou & Apostolou, 1997; Libby & Thorne, 2003), will help students to develop more sophisticated moral reasoning.

IES 4 (Exposure Draft, IFAC, 2012a, p. 21) includes ethics in its description of proficiency levels for professional skills, and includes intended learning outcomes (ILOs) similar to those that describe critical thinking:

- assessing, researching, and resolving complex problems while applying professional ethics;
- making judgements on appropriate courses of action drawing on professional ethics;
- integrating technical competence and professional skills, along with professional values, ethics, and attitudes to resolve complex problems.

It also suggests that the development of ethical judgement occurs over a long period of time through structured learning programmes and practical experience, combined with maturity and a sense of identity, as evidenced by intellectual development, at least through the contextual relativism stage – similar to the development of critical thinking skills. Because professional ethics and critical thinking are so intertwined, and permeate everything that professional accountants undertake in their professional capacity, by integrating ethical issues and dilemmas with critical thinking, students can practise thinking about ethical issues at the same time they use critical thinking skills.

18.5.4 How will critical thinking in accounting education attract a better match of students?

In spite of the need for accountants with critical thinking skills, anecdotal evidence indicates that students who choose to major in accounting do so because they are 'good at mathematics', 'like to work in structured situations', or feel more comfortable in subject areas where there are 'correct and incorrect' answers. More creative students, and those who are comfortable in ambiguous situations, tend to choose other majors where they think they can better use those characteristics. (See Laswad & Tan, Chapter 9 – this volume, for a discussion of choosing accounting as a major.) Hunton (2002), in the U.S.A., argues that many traditional accounting tasks can be reliably automated, supporting claims that an accountant's worth is now increasingly reflected in higher-order skills such as critical thinking, problem-solving, and analytical skills. A change in the domain of accounting education to include the development of critical thinking skills will attract students with a more realistic expectation about their major and their chosen profession, and will provide them with a skill set that better matches the skills they will need. (See Jackling, Chapter 10 – this volume, for a discussion of choosing accounting as a career.)

18.5.5 Practical issues for developing students' critical thinking skills

As described by Hassall & Joyce in Chapter 17 – this volume, many accounting educators have responded to the numerous calls to improve accounting students' critical thinking skills by using experiential learning. Other educators, such as Wolcott (a leading authority on critical thinking development and assessment in accounting education), have taken a critical approach to improving students' critical thinking skills. In addition, they responded by trying a variety of course assignments or activities, specific courses, programmatic designs, and teaching styles or practices (Wolcott *et al.*, 2002, p. 86), such as:

- In Finland, Canada, and the U.S.A., course assignments or activities, such as student-developed problems (Krumwiede & Bline, 1997), critical reading and reflective dialogue (Manninen, 1997), collaborative writing-to-learn assignments (Catanach & Rhoades, 1997), experimental markets (Frischmann, 1996), double-entry journal writing (Scofield, 1994), conflict-resolution/role-play/case study (Craig & Amernic, 1994), writing assignments (Scofield & Combes, 1993), journal writing (Cunningham, 1991), cases (Libby, 1991; Campbell & Lewis, 1991), business simulation (Springer & Borthick, 2004), use of clickers (Cunningham, 2008), designing assignments at different curriculum levels (Wolcott, 2000), and focus on questions about ambiguity in introductory courses (Wolcott, 1998). Boritz & Stoner in Chapter 16 – this volume, illustrate how the use of technology facilitates these course assignments and activities.
- In the U.S.A., specific courses, such as *Financial Statement Analysis* (Koehn & Hallam, 1999), *Introductory Accounting* (Springer & Borthick, 2004; Kealey *et al.*, 2005).
- In the U.S.A., programmatic designs such as those implemented at Brigham Young University (Albrecht *et al.*, 2000) and Kansas State University (Ainsworth & Plumlee, 1993).
- In the U.S.A., frameworks for incorporating critical thinking into accounting education (Kimmel, 1995).
- In Australia and the U.K., critical (or transformative) accounting curricula and education (Boyce, 2004; Kaidonis, 2004; Lucas, 2008).
- In the U.S.A., teaching styles or practices, such as teaching methods that promote active learning (Cunningham, 1996; Bonner, 1999), and consultative teaching style (Roush & Smith, 1997).

While these interventions seem promising, researchers continue to provide little empirical evidence that any specific method enhances the critical thinking skills of students (Wolcott *et al.*, 2002, p. 86). Rather, most empirical research on critical thinking in accounting education is descriptive or relational, offering documentation of students' cognitive levels, or studying the relationships between these cognitive levels and performance on various types of examination questions. While useful in describing the relationships between specific characteristics of students and their critical thinking performance, these studies were not designed to measure the effect of educational design on the development of critical thinking skills.

Several practical issues have made it difficult to know how to improve students' critical thinking skills, or whether any particular intervention is effective in improving their critical thinking skills (Wolcott *et al.*, 2002). For example:

- Little is known about why critical thinking skills improve during college (therefore, it is difficult to identify or design appropriate educational activities and measure the effects of those activities).
- There is no universally-accepted definition of critical thinking, and researchers may not explicitly state which definition they are using (Baril *et al.*, 1997, 1998).

- Public accountants' definition of critical thinking includes a set of competencies which includes traits outside of the academic definition of critical thinking.
- Critical thinking does not develop over short spans of time (making it difficult to observe improvements in critical thinking in a single course – even if specific interventions are effective). Measuring over longer periods of time makes it difficult to know *which* interventions may have been effective.
- There are pros and cons in using available measures of critical thinking, such as examination questions, performance of skills, outside reviews of students' performance (e.g. internships, scores on professional examinations), and feedback from students, alumni, and employers. Palomba & Banta (1999), Erwin (1991), Doney *et al.* (1993), DeMong *et al.* (1994), and Gainen & Locatelli (1995), in the U.S.A., offer help understanding these pros and cons. Wolcott *et al.* (2002, pp. 97, 98) summarize these measures.
- There are pros and cons to using normed, objective tests, such as the Watson-Glaser Critical Thinking Appraisal, the California Critical Thinking Skills Test, and the California Critical Thinking Dispositions Inventory, as well as to using measures where the subjects construct their own responses, such as the Reflective Judgment Interview. King & Kitchener (1994), Eyler & Giles (1999) Erwin (1991), and Wolcott & Lynch (1997), all in the U.S.A., offer help in understanding the trade-offs involved with using these appraisal methods. Wolcott *et al.* (2002, pp. 97, 98) summarize these methods.

18.6 How the nature of critical thinking development can impact on continuing professional development

Just as accounting graduates come into the profession of accounting prepared to *become* accountants, so do those who have received professional training and experience where an accounting degree is not a prerequisite for entry to the accounting profession. Both arrive having achieved a certain range of intellectual development, and ready to *become* improved critical thinkers. Just as we plan continuing professional development (CPD) to help professional accountants develop their technical skills as they take on new roles in their careers, we also should plan CPD to help them develop their critical thinking skills as they mature, become more experienced, and take on new roles and a changed business environment that requires higher-level thinking skills. Because intellectual development and learning to think critically are an ongoing process, and are tied to education, maturity, and identity, the intellectual development achieved during the initial professional development (IPD) and training, or a college education must be renewed, modified, and developed further during CPD throughout an accountant's career.

> *An aspiring professional accountant is an individual who has commenced a professional accounting education program as part of IPD. The inclusion of professional skills in IPD lays the base for the ongoing development and application of professional skills throughout the professional accountant's career. Not all professional skills may be fully developed by the end of IPD. Some may be the focus of Continuing Professional Development (CPD).*
>
> (IFAC, IES 7, 2012b)

Because of the tie between critical thinking and ethics, CPD should integrate ethics materials with critical thinking materials and, ideally, use actual workplace examples, situations, and dilemmas as part of the discussion. However, assessment of the development of critical thinking skills in CPD may be even more challenging than in an IPD environment. The means for assessing the development of professional values, ethics, and attitudes in the workplace may include discussion and facilitated resolution of dilemmas as they arise in the workplace. Along with reviews of decision-making combined with performance reviews and appraisals (IFAC, IES4, 2012a).

18.7 Where the current critical thinking research agenda in accounting education is likely to lead

Although some researchers are attempting to generate empirical evidence to show that specific interventions enhance critical thinking skills, there is still much need for more evidence. Without it, accounting educators' efforts toward enhancing students' and professionals' critical thinking skills may slow down, in spite of the persistent call for improved critical thinking skills in both accounting education and professional accounting literature. Wolcott *et al.* (2002) suggest that the scarcity of empirical evidence exists, in large part, because of the difficulty of designing and conducting sufficiently powerful tests. Using models of cognitive development that allow researchers to isolate incremental critical thinking development can offset this problem. To accomplish this, future research on enhancing critical thinking skills through IPD and CPD can add empirical evidence to the existing knowledge by doing the following (ibid., p. 100):

- defining educational objectives narrowly to facilitate isolating changes in students' performance;
- linking educational interventions directly to narrowly-defined educational objectives;
- ensuring that critical thinking measures are valid and reliable for the specific competencies to be examined;
- if validity and reliability can be reasonably assured, using more naturalistic measures of critical thinking (rubrics for evaluating case analyses, oral presentations, and so forth) along with normed and well-validated measures.

Wolcott & Lynch (1997) describe two rubrics that can accomplish this:

- shifting the research focus to experimental and quasi-experimental designs to study the impact of specific educational interventions on critical thinking; and
- using sufficiently powerful interventions to expect improvements in critical thinking performance over the time-frame of the study, where the time-frame is short enough to rule out uncontrollable causes of changes in critical thinking.

The trend toward competency-based education by the AICPA (1999), IMA (1994), IFAC (2002, 2008a, 2008b), ICAA (1998a, 1998b), ICAEW (1996), CICA (2001, 2005), is a positive development that can help researchers implement, and begin to test the efficacy of, various interventions meant to improve accounting students' critical thinking skills.

18.8 Conclusion

In a global business environment where changes and uncertainty are accelerating, accountants have to continue to adapt to these changes, and to the resulting changes in the practice of accounting. As Roger Smith (Johnston *et al.*, 1986, p. 26), the former CEO of General Motors Company pointed out, liberal arts may ultimately prove to be the most relevant learning model: '*People trained in the Liberal Arts learn to tolerate ambiguity and to bring order out of apparent confusion.*'

In a changing environment, it is specifically the critical thinking skills, rooted in the liberal arts (psychology and philosophy), that our accounting students begin to develop when they are in college that will insert a core of stability and rationality. As Raymond T. Schuler, president of the New York State Business Council, stated so well:

> *Business will always prefer people who have broad-based skills – people who can think critically, who can adapt well to new situations, and who can teach themselves. A person who is taught today's skills may have obsolete skills by the time he or she reaches the workforce. But a person who is taught to think well will always be able to adapt.*

> (Schuler, 1983, cited in Ruggiero, 1988, pp. 7, 8)

On the theme of liberalizing the accounting curriculum, see Amernic & Craig, Chapter 12 – this volume, and Sangster & Wilson (2013).

In this environment, it is clear that accounting educators cannot afford to leave the teaching of critical thinking skills exclusively to general education courses, electives, and other courses that students take outside their majors. The pressure continues for accounting educators (both for IPD and CPD) to 'take on' the elements of critical thinking that accountants value as being important and make them an integral part of the domain of accounting education. Providing students with the opportunity to learn the 'nuts and bolts' of accounting, as well as the thought processes that accountants use to think about business information and ethics, also provides students with the opportunity to develop skills that will allow them to succeed in their careers in accounting. (See also Watty, Chapter 13 – this volume.)

Alan Schoenfeld, the distinguished mathematics educator, made the following comment about the vast difference between what mathematics educators *think* their students are learning and what their students actually are learning. Substituting 'accounting' for 'mathematics' in his statement, one can assume that he was describing the need to develop accounting students' and practitioners' critical thinking skills:

> *All too often we focus on a narrow collection of well defined tasks and train students to execute those tasks in a routine, if not algorithmic fashion. Then we test the students on tasks that are very close to the ones they have been taught. If they succeed on those problems, we and they congratulate each other on the fact that they have learned some powerful [accounting] techniques. In fact, they may be able to use such techniques mechanically while lacking some rudimentary thinking skills. To allow them, and ourselves, to believe that they 'understand' [accounting] is deceptive and fraudulent.*

> (Schoenfeld, 1988, p. 30)

This sobering comment implies that, if we truly want our students to learn and *understand* accounting, and if we want to feel confident that they really *have* learned and really *do* understand the accounting we have taught them, we must change certain aspects of the accounting courses and curricula to integrate the development of higher level-thinking skills for decision-making and problem-solving with accounting. The work of the AECC (1990), AICPA (1999), and IMA (1994) in the U.S.A., the IFAC (2002, 2008a, 2008b), the ICAA (1998a,1998b) in Australia, the ICAEW (1996) in the U.K., and the CICA (2001, 2005) in Canada suggest that, in order to do this, we must rethink all aspects of these courses and curricula, including content, teaching strategies, assessment, and classroom atmosphere.

References

Accounting Education Change Commission (1990) Objectives of education for accountants: position statement number one, *Issues in Accounting Education* 5(2), 307–312.

Ainsworth, P.L. & Plumlee, R.D. (1993) Restructuring the accounting curriculum content sequence: the KSU experience, *Issues in Accounting Education*, 8(1),112–127.

Albrecht, W.S., & Sack, R.J. (2000) *Accounting Education: Charting the Course through a Perilous Future*. Sarasota, FL: American Accounting Association.

American Accounting Association, Committee on the Future Structure, Content, and Scope of Accounting Education (The Bedford Committee) (1986) Future accounting education: preparing for the expanding profession, *Issues in Accounting Education* (Spring): 168–195.

American Institute of Certified Public Accountants (1999) *AICPA Core Competency Framework for Entry into the Accounting Profession*, New York: AICPA. Available at: http://www.aicpa.org.

Apostolou, B. & Apostolou, N. (1997) Heroes as a context for teaching ethics, *Journal of Education for Business*, 73(2), 121–125.

Arthur Andersen & Co., Arthur Young, Coopers & Lybrand, Deloitte Haskins & Sells, Ernst & Whinney, Peat Marwick Main & Co., Price Waterhouse, and Touch Ross (1989) *Perspectives on Education: Capabilities for Success in the Accounting Profession*, available at: http://aaahq.org/AECC/history/cover.htm.

Baril, C.P., Chain, M.M., Cunningham, B.M., Fordham, D.R., Gardner, R.L., St. Pierre, K., & Wolcott, S.K. (1997) Critical thinking competencies essential to success in public accounting, *Report of the Federation of Schools of Accountancy 1997 Educational Research Committee*, St. Louis: Federation of Schools of Accountancy.

Baril, C.P., Cunningham, B.M., Fordham, D.R., Gardner, R.L., & Wolcott, S.K. (1998) Critical thinking in the public accounting profession: aptitudes and attitudes, *Journal of Accounting Education*, 16(3/4), 381–406.

Baxter Magolda, M.B. (1992) *Knowing and Reasoning in College: Gender-Related Patterns in Students' Intellectual Development*, San Francisco: Jossey-Bass.

Belenky, M.F., Clinchy, B.M., Goldberger, N.R., & Tarule, J.M. (1986) *Women's Ways of Knowing*, New York: Basic Books.

Bernardi, R.A., Massey, D.W., Thorne, L., & Downey, A. (2002) Critical thinking and moral reasoning of intermediate accounting students, *Research on Accounting Ethics*, 8, 73–102.

Birkett, W.P. (1993) *Competency Based Standards for Professional Accountants in Australia and New Zealand*, Sydney, NSW: Institute of Chartered Accountants in Australia and the New Zealand Society of Accountants.

Bligh, D.A. (1972) *What's the Use of Lectures?* Harmondsworth: Penguin.

Bonner, S.E. (1999) Choosing teaching methods based on learning objectives: an integrative framework, *Issues in Accounting Education*, 14(1), 11–39.

Boyce, G. (2004) Critical accounting education: teaching and learning outside the circle, *Critical Perspectives on Accounting*, 15(4–5), 565–586.

Campbell, J.E. & Lewis, W. F. (1991) Using cases in accounting classes, *Issues in Accounting Education*, 6(2), 276–283.

Canadian Institute of Chartered Accountants (CICA) (2001) *The Canadian CA Competency Map*, Toronto: CICA.

Canadian Institute of Chartered Accountants (CICA) (2005) *The CA Candidate's Competency Map: Understanding the Professional Competencies of CAs*, Toronto: CICA.

Catanach, Jr., A.H., & Rhoades, S.C. (1997) A practical guide to collaborative writing assignments in financial accounting courses, *Issues in Accounting Education*, 12(2), 521–536.

Chaffee, J. (2011) *Thinking Critically*, Independence, KY: Cengage Learning.

Costin, F. (1972) Lecturing versus other methods of teaching: a review of research, *British Journal of Educational Technology*, 3(1), 4–30.

Craig, R. & Amernic, J. (1994) Roleplaying in a conflict resolution setting: description and some implications for accounting, *Issues in Accounting Education*, 9(1), 28–44.

Cunningham, B.M. (1991) Classroom research and experiential learning: three successful experiences – The impact of student writing in learning accounting, *Community/Junior College Quarterly of Research and Practice*, 5(3), 317–325.

Cunningham, B.M. (1996) How to restructure an accounting course to enhance creative and critical thinking, *Accounting Education: A Journal of Theory, Practice and Research*, 1(1), 49–66.

Cunningham, B.M. (2008) Using action research to improve learning and the classroom learning environment, *Issues in Accounting Education*, 23(1), 1–30.

DeMong, R.F., Lindgren, Jr., J.H., & Perry, S.E. (1994) Designing an assessment program for accounting, *Issues in Accounting Education*, 9(1), 11–27.

Doney, L.D., Lephardt, N.E., & Trebby, J.P. (1993) Developing critical thinking skills in accounting students, *Journal of Education for Business*, 68(5), 297–300.

Eble, K. (1983) *The Aims of College Teaching*, San Francisco: Jossey-Bass.

Erwin, T.D. (1991) *Assessing Student Learning and Development: A Guide to the Principles, Goals, and Methods of Determining College Outcomes*, San Francisco: Jossey-Bass.

Evans, E., Burritt, R. & Guthrie, J. (eds), with Institute of Chartered Accountants in Australia (ICAA) (2010), *Accounting Education at a Crossroad in 2010*, Sydney: Centre for Accounting, Governance and Sustainability, University of South Australia, Institute of Chartered Accountants in Australia. Available at: http://www.charteredaccountants.com.au/Students/News-and-updates/Teachers/New-publication-Accounting-Education-at-a-Crossroad-in-2010.aspx (accessed 30 September 2012).

Eyler, J. & Giles Jr., D.E. (1999) *Where's the Learning in Service Learning?* San Francisco: Jossey-Bass Publishers.

Francis, M.C., Mulder, T.C., & Stark, J.S. (1995) *Intentional Learning: A Process for Learning to Learn in the Accounting Curriculum*, Sarasota, FL: Accounting Education Change Commission and American Accounting Association.

Frischmann, P.J. (1996) Real time classroom tax planning using experimental markets, *Issues in Accounting Education*, 11(2), 281–296.

Gainen, J. & Locatelli, P. (1995) *Assessment for the New Curriculum: A Guide for Professional Accounting Programs* (Accounting Education Series, Vol. 11), Sarasota, FL: Accounting Education Change Commission and American Accounting Association.

Hancock, P., Howieson, B., Kavanagh, M., Kent, J., Tempone, I., & Segal, N. (2009) *Accounting for the Future: More Than Numbers*, Sydney: Australian Learning and Teaching Council.

Huffman, K., Vernoy, M., Williams, B., & Vernoy, J. (1991) *Psychology in Action*, New York: John Wiley & Sons.

Hunton, J.E., (2002) Blending information and communication technology with accounting research, *Accounting Horizons*, 16(1), 56–67.

Institute of Chartered Accountants in Australia (ICAA) (1998a) *The Future for Business*, prepared by Chan Link & Associates, Sydney: ICAA.

Institute of Chartered Accountants in Australia (ICAA) (1998b) *The CFO of the Future*, prepared by M. Simister, P. Roest, & J. Sheldon of KPMG for the Chartered Accountants in Business Committee, Sydney: ICAA.

Institute of Chartered Accountants in Australia (ICAA) (2001) *The CFO of the Future: Finance Functions in the Twenty-first Century*, prepared by M. Simister for KPMG Consulting for the ICAA, Sydney: ICAA.

Institute of Chartered Accountants of England & Wales (ICAEW), Education and Training Committee (1996) *Added Value Professionals: Chartered Accountants in 2005*, London: ICAEW.

Institute of Management Accountants (IMA) (1994) *What Corporate America Wants in Entry-Level Accountants*, Executive summary (with the Financial Executives Institute), Montvale, NJ: IMA.

International Federation of Accountants (IFAC) (2002) *International Education Standard on Professional Skills and General Education*, New York: IFAC.

International Federation of Accountants (IFAC) (2008a) *International Education Standards 3. Initial Professional Development – Professional Skills*, New York: IFAC.

International Federation of Accountants (IFAC) (2008b) *International Education Standards 8. Competence Requirements for Audit Professionals*, New York: IFAC.

International Federation of Accountants (IFAC) (2012a) *International Education Standard 4. Initial Professional Development – Professional Values, Ethics, and Attitudes (Revised)*, New York: IFAC.

International Federation of Accountants (IFAC) (2012b) *Proposed International Education Standard (IES) 7. Continuing Professional Development*, New York: IFAC.

Johnston, J.S., Burns, S.T., Butler, D.W., Hirsch, M.S., Jones, T.B., Kantrow, A.M., Mohrman, K., Smith, R.B., & Useem, M. (1987) The liberal arts and the art of management, in *Educating Managers: Executive Effectiveness through Liberal Learning*, San Francisco: Jossey-Bass, pp. 21–33.

Kaidonis, M.A. (2004) Teaching and learning critical accounting using media texts as reflexive devices: conditions for transformative action or reinforcing the status quo?, *Critical Perspectives on Accounting*, 15 (4–5), 667–673.

Kealey, B.T., Holland, J., & Watson, M. (2005) Preliminary evidence on the association between critical thinking and performance in principles of accounting, *Issues in Accounting Education*, 20(1), 33–49.

Kimmel, P. (1995) A framework for incorporating critical thinking into accounting education, *Journal of Accounting Education*, 12(3), 299–318.

King, P.M. & Kitchener, K.S. (1994) *Developing Reflective Judgment: Understanding and Promoting Intellectual Growth and Critical Thinking in Adolescents and Adults*, San Francisco, CA: Jossey-Bass.

King, P.M., Kitchener, K.S., & Wood, P.K. (1985) The development of intellect and character: a longitudinal study of intellectual and moral development in young adults, *Moral Education Forum*, 10(1), 1–13.

Kitchener, K.S. (1986) The reflective judgment model: characteristics, evidence and measurement, in Mines, R.A. & Kitchener, K.S. (eds) *Adult Cognitive Development: Methods and Models*, New York: Praeger, pp. 76–91.

Koehn, J.L. & Hallam, J.J. (1999) A course survey of financial statement analysis, *Issues in Accounting Education*, 14(3), 413–421.

Krumwiede, T. & Bline, D. (1997) Encouraging active learning through the use of student developed problems, *The Accounting Educators' Journal*, 9(2), 116–129.

Kurfiss, J.G. (1988) *Critical Thinking: Theory, Research, Practice, and Possibilities*, ASHE-ERIC Higher Education Report Number 2, Association for the Study of Higher Education.

Libby, P.A. (1991) Barriers to using cases in accounting education, *Issues in Accounting Education*, 6(2), 193–213.

Libby, T. & Thorne, L. (2003) Virtuous auditors, *CA Magazine*, 136(9), 45–48.

Lucas, U. (2008) Being 'pulled up short': creating moments of surprise and possibility in accounting education, *Critical Perspectives on Accounting*, 19(3), 383–403.

Lucas, U. & Tan, P. (2011) Developing a capacity to engage in critical reflection: students' 'ways of knowing' within an undergraduate business and accounting program, *Studies in Higher Education*. DOI:10.1080/03075079.2011.56906.

Manninen, A. (1997) Critical reading in accounting, *Accounting Education: an international journal*, 6(4), 281–294.

Mathews, R. (Chairman) (1990) *Accounting in Higher Education: Report of the Review of the Accounting Discipline in Higher Education*, Canberra: Australian Government Publishing Service, Department of Employment, Education and Training.

McKeachie, W.J. (1967) Research in teaching: the gap between theory and practice, in Lee, C. (ed.) *Improving College Teaching*, Washington, DC: American Council on Education.

McNeel, S.P. (1994) College teaching and student moral development, in Rest, J.R. & Narvaez, D. (eds) *Moral Development in the Professions: Psychology and Applied Ethics*, Hillsdale, NJ: Lawrence Erlbaum Associates.

Mgaya, K.V. & Kitindi, E.G. (2009) Essential skills needed by accounting graduates in a developing country: the views of practising accountants and accounting educators in Botswana, *International Journal of Accounting, Auditing and Performance Evaluation*, 5(3), 329–351.

Moon, J. (2008) *Critical Thinking: An Exploration of Theory and Practice*, London: Routledge.

Nickerson, R.S., Perkins, D.N., & Smith, E.E. (1985) *The Teaching of Thinking*, Hillsdale, NJ: Lawrence Erlbaum Associates, Inc.

O'Donovan, B. (2010) Filling a pail or lighting a fire? The intellectual development of management undergraduates, *International Journal of Management Education*, 9(1), 1–10.

Palomba, C.A. & Banta, T.W. (1999) *Assessment Essentials: Planning, Implementing, and Improving Assessment in Higher Education*, San Francisco: Jossey-Bass.

Pascarella, E.T., & Terenzini, P.T. (1991) *How College Affects Students: Findings and Insights from Twenty Years of Research*, San Francisco: Jossey-Bass.

Pathways Commission on Accounting Higher Education (2012) *Pathways to a Profession: Charting a National Strategy for the Next Generation of Accountants*, Washington, DC: American Accounting Association (AAA) and the American Institute of Certified Public Accountants (AICPA).

Paul, R. (1990) *Critical Thinking*, ed. A.J.A. Binker, Rohnert Park, CA: Center for Critical Thinking and Moral Critique, Sonoma State University.

Paul, R. (1993) *Critical Thinking: What Every Person Needs to Survive in a Rapidly Changing World*, ed. A.J.A. Binker, Rohnert Park, CA: Center for Critical Thinking and Moral Critique, Sonoma State University.

Perry, Jr., W.G. (1970) *Forms of Intellectual and Ethical Development in the College Years*, New York: Holt, Rinehart and Winston.

Powers, D.E., & Enright, M.K. (1987) Analytical reasoning skills in graduate study: perceptions of faculty in six fields, *Journal of Higher Education*, 58(6), 658–682.

Quality Assurance Agency for Higher Education (QAA) (2000) *Accounting Benchmarks*, Gloucester: QAA.

Roush, M.L. & Smith, G.S. (1997) Consultative teaching: international examples, *Issues in Accounting Education*, 12(1, Spring), 199–213.

Ruggiero, V.R. (1988) *Teaching Thinking Across the Curriculum*, New York: Harper & Row.

Sangster, A. & Wilson, R.M.S. (eds) (2013) *Liberalizing the Accounting Curriculum*, Abingdon: Routledge.

Schoenfeld, A.H. (1988) When good teaching leads to bad results: the disasters of 'well taught' mathematics classes, *Educational Psychologist*, 23(2), 145–166.

Scofield, B.W. (1994) Double entry journals: writer-based prose in the intermediate accounting curriculum, *Issues in Accounting Education*, 9(2), 330–352.

Scofield, B.W. & Combes, L. (1993) Designing and managing meaningful writing assignments, *Issues in Accounting Education*, 8(1), 71–85.

Shulman, L.S. (2005) Pedagogies of uncertainty, *Liberal Education*, Spring(2), 18–25.

Siegel, G. & Sorenson, J.E. (1999) *Counting More, Counting Less: Transformations in the Management Accounting Profession*, Montvale, NJ: Institute of Management Accountants.

Johnston, J.S., Burns, S.T., Butler, D.W., Hirsch, M.S., Jones, T.B., Kantrow, A.M., Mohrman, K., Smith, R.B., & Useem, M. (1987) The liberal arts and the art of management, in *Educating Managers: Executive Effectiveness through Liberal Learning*, San Francisco: Jossey-Bass, pp. 21–33.

Springer, C.W. & Borthick, A.F. (2004) Business simulation to stage critical thinking in introductory accounting: rationale, design and implementation, *Issues in Accounting Education*, 19(2), 277–303.

Verner, C., & Dickinson, G. (1967) The lecture: an analysis and review of research, *Adult Education*, 17, 85–100.

Wolcott, S.K. (1998) Critical thinking development in the accounting curriculum: focussing on ambiguity in introductory accounting courses, in Fetyko, D.F. (ed.) *Changes in Accounting Education: Implementation in Specific Accounting Courses and Subject Areas*, St. Louis, MO: Federation of Schools of Accountancy, pp. 1–16.

Wolcott, S.K. (2000) Designing assignments and classroom discussions to foster critical thinking at different levels in the curriculum, in Borghans, L., Gijselaers, W.H., Milter, R.G., & Stinson, J.E. (eds) *Educational Innovations in Education and Business*, Dordrecht: Kluwer Academic Publishers, pp. 231–251.

Wolcott, S.K., Baril, C.R., Cunningham, B.M., Fordham, D.R., & St. Pierre, K. (2002) Critical thought on critical thinking research, *Journal of Accounting Education*, 20(2), 85–103.

Wolcott, S.K. & Lynch, C.L. (1997) Critical thinking in the accounting classroom: a reflective judgment developmental process perspective, *Accounting Education: A Journal of Theory, Practice and Research*, 2(1), 59–78.

Young, J.J. & Annisette, M. (2009) Cultivating imagination: ethics education and literature, *Critical perspectives on Accounting*, 20(1), 93–109.

About the author

Billie Cunningham is a Teaching Professor at the University of Missouri, U.S.A. (Cunningham @missouri.edu). She has chaired the AAA's Teaching, Learning & Curriculum Section (and has been inducted into its Hall of Honor) and the AICPA's Core Competency Best Practices Task Force, as well as serving as AAA Vice-President and a member of the AAA's Accounting Education Advisory Committee. Her primary interests are critical thinking, pedagogies and teaching strategies, and assessment, particularly using action research. She has co-authored several accounting textbooks, published articles, conducted workshops, and made numerous presentations addressing various aspects of teaching and learning.

19

The use of teaching resources in accounting education

Lorna A. Stevenson*, John Ferguson,** and David M. Power***

*UNIVERSITY OF ST ANDREWS, U.K. **UNIVERSITY OF STRATHCLYDE, U.K.
***UNIVERSITY OF DUNDEE, U.K.

CONTENTS

Abstract

There has been little research in the domain of accounting education on the use of teaching resources, though some journals do provide case studies and teaching notes for educators. This chapter presents a review of current knowledge, key issues, and pertinent debates in the arena of resource use in education provided for both accounting specialist and non–specialist students, and is relevant to undergraduate, postgraduate and, to some lesser extent, professional training.

General, and then accounting-specific, discussions of teaching resources and their role in learning are provided, in the context of conceptions of teaching. In addition, the chapter provides the results of the first systematic investigation in 20 years into the use of different teaching and assessment resources by U.K. and Irish accounting academics, and an insight into those educators' conceptions of teaching through building on prior studies in economics and finance.

Keywords

conceptions of teaching, resources in learning, teaching resources use

19.1 Introduction

The main aims of this chapter are:

- to present an introduction to some of the debate on normative issues in accounting education;
- to address a 20-year gap in the accounting literature by reporting the results of a survey of accounting and finance academics in the U.K. and Ireland of their use of teaching resources and their conceptions of teaching; and
- to thereby provide an indication of where future research effort might usefully be focussed.

An examination of the accounting education literature suggests that research on the use of teaching resources is somewhat limited. For example, while sections of some journals provide case studies and teaching notes as resources for accounting educators, there is scant attention paid to how, or the extent to which, case studies are actually used in accounting education (but see Adler *et al.*, 2004; Hassall & Milne, 2004; Healy & McCutcheon, 2010). Similarly, while there exists a literature on various aspects of accounting textbooks (for example, Davidson, 2005; Ferguson *et al.*, 2005; 2006), there are very few studies which explore how, or the extent to which, textbooks are used in accounting education (however, see James, 2000; Phillips & Phillips, 2007). Indeed, there has not been, as far as the present authors are aware, a systematic investigation into the extent to which different teaching resources or 'modes of instruction' are used in accounting for almost 20 years (see Brown & Guilding, 1993, p. 212). This gap in the accounting literature is somewhat at odds with the education literature in economics and finance, where survey-based studies can regularly be found on the use of teaching resources and assessment in these disciplines. For example, in economics, a national quinquennial survey of academic economists in the U.S.A. has been undertaken in 1995, 2000, 2005 and 2010 to establish how undergraduate economics is taught and assessed, and what modes of instruction are used (Becker & Watts 1996, 2001a, 2001b; Watts & Becker, 2008; Watts & Schaur, 2011). Employing a similar survey instrument, Iqbal *et al.* (2006) provide evidence on the modes of instruction and assessment in finance in Canada, the U.S.A., and the British Isles (i.e. the U.K. and the Republic of Ireland).

This chapter aims to provide a critical overview of the use of teaching resources in accounting education and to address the existing gap in the accounting literature by reporting the results of a survey of accounting and finance academics in the U.K. and Ireland. In this sense, the present chapter provides both an overview of the current use of teaching resources in accounting education as well as providing a forward-looking agenda on where research in this area could develop. The survey reported here builds upon prior studies in economics and finance by incorporating respondents' 'conceptions of teaching' into the analysis (Gow & Kember, 1993; Kell & Jones, 2007; Norton *et al.*, 2005). In addition, a review of current knowledge, key issues, and pertinent debates in the arena of resource use in accounting education is provided.

A scan of the article sub-headings in Apostolou *et al.*'s (2011) accounting education literature review between 2006 and 2009 provides an overview of research elements explored by accounting education researchers in that period across the six main accounting education journals:

- curriculum;
- assurance of learning;
- instruction;
- educational technology;
- staff issues in teaching (including teaching skills, and textbooks); and
- student matters (including skills, characteristics, learning styles, and learning approaches).

These issues are dealt with in other chapters of this volume, and such an overview can also helpfully be used as a way of thinking about the teaching resources available to accounting educators, and thus it provides a useful conception of the potential content of this chapter. Nonetheless, some specific elements will be discussed in more detail than others, and the gaps may provide an indication of where future research effort might usefully be focussed.

It should also be noted that this chapter focusses on current and future aspects of education provided for both accounting specialist and non-specialist students, and is relevant to undergraduate, postgraduate and, to some lesser extent, professional training. The specific dimensions of accounting education in primary and secondary schools, and professional training are therefore not explicitly addressed.[1] In addition, while we provide an introduction to some of the debates on normative issues in accounting education, we focus our discussion on describing the arena, and leave readers to arrive at their own view on how accounting education should develop. This introductory section is followed, in Section 19.2, by a discussion of teaching resources and learning generally. Section 19.3 then discusses conceptions of teaching while Section 19.4 addresses teaching resources and accounting specifically. The research method and results for the questionnaire administered for this chapter are described in Sections 19.5 and 19.6, and concluding comments are offered in Section 19.7.

19.2 Teaching resources and learning

A rather loose definition of 'teaching resources' might be any resource used to facilitate or enhance the teaching and learning experience. This, of course, might encompass an abundance of things. For example, this would most likely include traditional resources such as the recommended course textbook, recommended journal articles, case studies, and perhaps magazine and newspaper cuttings. It could also include other web-based resources such as the textbook/ publisher's website, specific websites (for example, company websites), and virtual learning environments (VLEs) such as WebCT or Blackboard. It might also include a range of media, such as DVDs, podcasts, audio lectures, social networking, and instructional tools such as games (see Boritz & Stoner, Chapter 16 – this volume). Further, an assessment of the situations which maximise or impede the efficacy of resources, and of the characteristics of the staff and students involved, may also comprise a discussion of 'teaching resources' (see Hassall & Joyce, Chapter 17, and Cunningham, Chapter 18 – both in this volume).

A dominant and systems view of learning within higher education, supported by not insignificant amounts of current evidence, is Biggs' (2003) constructivist '3P' model (see Figure 19.1), which stresses the context of learning and teaching, and emphasises learner-focussed activities rather than teaching activities *per se*. Biggs' model seeks to align student factors and

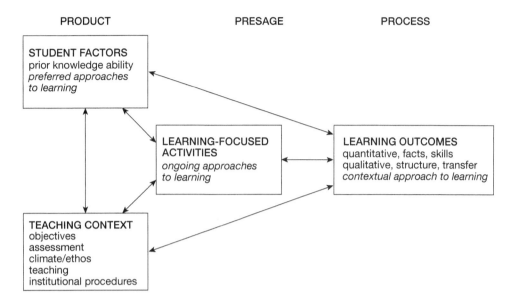

Figure 19.1 The '3P' model of learning and teaching

Source: Reprinted with permission from Biggs *et al.* (2001). © John Wiley and Sons.

teaching context with students' approaches to learning (SAL) and teaching in ways which acknowledge their respective impacts on the final learning outcome. Such a view is helpful in focussing attention on the educator's provision of a teaching context, itself a helpful location of the role of teaching resources in the overall learning situation. Similarly, in his review of 25 years of research into learning and teaching in higher education, Richardson (2005) presents an integrated model of teachers' approaches to teaching, conceptions of teaching, perceptions of the teaching environment, disciplinary characteristics, and what he called situational factors (see Figure 19.2).

Another perspective often adopted in this literature is Freire's (1996) 'Dialogic' model which contrasts '*Banking*' education where '*motionless, static, compartmentalised and predictable*' knowledge

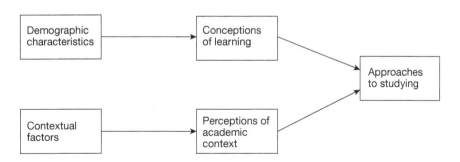

Figure 19.2 An integrated model of students' approaches to studying, conceptions of learning, and perceptions of their academic context

Source: Reprinted with permission from Professor J.T.E. Richardson, and Taylor & Francis Ltd. © 2005, all rights reserved.

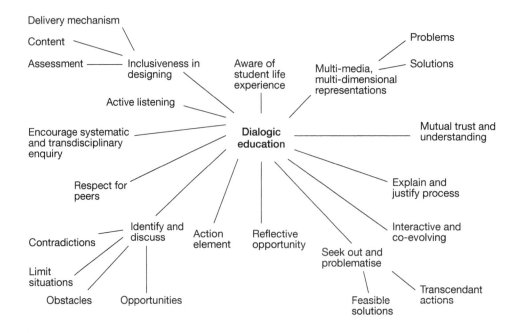

Figure 19.3 Attributes of a dialogical education

Source: Reprinted with permission from Coulson, A.B. & Thomson, I. (2006, p. 263). © Taylor & Francis Ltd

Table 19.1 Attitudes and practices of a banking education

(a)	The teacher teaches and the students are taught
(b)	The teacher knows everything and the students know nothing
(c)	The teacher thinks and the students are thought about
(d)	The teacher talks and the students listen – meekly
(e)	The teacher disciplines and the students are disciplined
(f)	The teacher chooses and enforces his choice, and the students comply
(g)	The teacher acts and the students have the illusion of acting through the actions of the teacher
(h)	The teacher chooses the program content and the students (who were not consulted) adapt to it
(i)	The teacher confuses the authority of knowledge with his or her own professional authority which she or he sets in opposition to the freedom of the students
(j)	The teacher is the subject of the learning process while the pupils are mere objects

Source: Thomson & Bebbington (2005, p. 513). © Elsevier Ltd.: used with permission.

is conveyed to students who are assumed to be '*passive, patient, listening receptacles*' with '*Problem Posing*' education which provides '*the means by which men and women deal critically and creatively with reality and discover how to participate in the transformation of their world*' (Freire, 1996, p. 16). (See Figure 19.3 and Table 19.1.)

In these senses the 'learning and teaching resources' of this chapter's theme can be seen to be the educator's own perspective of his/her role and of education *per se*, as well as the tools and materials available for the teaching experience. For example, Van Driel *et al.* (1997) noted that teachers' conceptions of teaching underpin their whole approach to education, including views about assessment, their role and their identification, and use of teaching resources. Further, Magolda & Terenzini (1999) wrote that, among other things, educators embody:

- prior experience as a learner and/or educator (see also Dunkin, 2002);
- multiple ways of knowing, learning styles, learning abilities, and intelligences;
- assumptions about knowledge, learning, and teaching;
- goals and priorities for education practice.

All of these mediate educational practice. Indeed, some commentators (see, for example, Boyce *et al.*, 2012; Coulson & Thomson, 2006; Thomson & Bebbington, 2004) note that the educator's approach is possibly more important than the classroom or institutional resources in creating the educational experience. Such a view is echoed by Leveson when she states that '*attempts to improve teaching strategies may be better served if they are viewed as part of an integrated system of relationships that constitute the teaching experience as a whole*' (2004, p. 530).

Nonetheless, elements of the current chapter do focus on resources as more commonly understood; the questionnaire reported on here was administered to all accounting academics listed in the *British Accounting Review Research Register* in 2010, and used a range of questions to interrogate academics' teaching conceptions and practices. One question, derived from Leveson's (2004) work, utilised a variety of dimensions of two key alternatives for conceptualising teaching and teaching approaches: a teacher-centred/content-oriented view, and a student-centred/learning orientation perspective (see also Kember, 1997). This was employed in the light of Kell & Jones' (2007) noting of Entwistle's view (2000) that teachers with a learning facilitation orientation in the classroom tended to use a range of teaching methods and assessments, while educators operating in a knowledge transmission mode were more likely to adopt teacher-focussed approaches.

To this list of learning and teaching resources upon which accounting educators may draw we might also add awareness of, and insights from, many of the section headings of this Routledge Companion text, such as considerations of student-related, curriculum, pedagogic, assessment, institutional, contextual, and cornerstone issues. Nonetheless, the discussion now turns to an explicit consideration of conceptions of teaching which contextualises identification, and use, of teaching resources.

19.3 Conceptions of teaching

One of the earlier, and now widely-cited, articles on conceptions of teaching is Fox's (1983) 'Personal Theories of Teaching' which presented a conceptual model for thinking about the process of teaching. Fox based his model on teachers' responses to the question 'What do you mean by teaching?' and he identified four 'basic theories of teaching':

1 *the transfer theory* – which treats knowledge as a commodity to be transferred from one vessel to another;
2 *the shaping theory* – which treats teaching as a process of shaping or moulding students to a predetermined pattern;
3 *the travelling theory* – which treats a subject as a terrain to be explored with the teacher, the travelling companion or expert guide; and
4 *the growing theory* – which focusses more attention on the intellectual and emotional development of the learner (Fox, 1983, p. 151). (See also Section 8.2.3 of Chapter 8 – this volume.)

Subsequent work (such as Leveson, 2004, and Kember, 1997) can be seen as developments of these categorisations which Fox suggested:

- reflect a teacher's way of thinking about his (*sic*) teaching;
- affect his approach(es) to the teaching task; and
- determine the task(s) he attempts (1983, p. 162).

For example, a recent phenomenographic study of computing academics' understanding of teaching by Lister *et al.* (2007, p. 105) produced interview responses that were '*reasonably consonant*' with Fox's theories, despite interviewees' lack of familiarity with them. Indeed, as highlighted by Norton *et al.* (2010, p. 345), a substantial body of research work has examined '*the way that university teachers' beliefs link with their actual teaching practices or intentions*', though little of it is specific to accounting education.

For example, Eskola's (2011) phenomenographic study of Finnish higher education students in accounting identified students' and teachers' attributes and teaching methods as being important mediators in successful learning. Important teaching methods were noted as being collaborative methods supplemented with self-study instruments (such as exercises and work experience), and the author revealed the importance of the conception of learning on the relative positions of the student and teacher in the learning process. However, contrasting findings were reported in an examination of German accounting teachers' '*pedagogical beliefs, domain-specific beliefs and conceptions of teaching and learning*' which '*established significant relationships between teachers' beliefs, . . . self reports on the organisation of classroom activities and teaching patterns*' (Seifried, 2012, p. 1). Markely *et al.* (2009) observed that educators often state that their teaching is student-centred, but classroom observations indicate a dominance of teacher-centred, didactic transfer of information content practices. Nonetheless, Seifried concluded that a teacher-centred, instructional approach is dominant in accounting education in German commercial schools with little implementation of more student-centred practices. Postareff's (2007, p. vii) series of four studies

> indicated that pedagogical training organised for university teachers is needed in order to enhance the development of their teaching. The results implied that the shift from content-focussed . . . profiles towards . . . learning-focussed profiles is a slow process and that teachers' conceptions of teaching have to be addressed first in order to promote learning-focussed teaching.

As noted above, Entwistle observed that a wider range of teaching resources is employed by educators with a less teacher-focussed approach, and so the discussion now turns to specific teaching resources available in accounting education.

19.4 Teaching resources and accounting

In a survey of teaching methods employed on university accounting courses, Brown & Guilding (1993) compared 10 modes of instruction used by accounting and non-accounting teachers (see Table 19.2). The findings indicate that, for both accounting and non-accounting departments, the top three teaching methods employed were: lectures, seminar/tutorial, and prescribed textbooks respectively. However, it was noted that accounting departments placed considerably more emphasis on both lectures and prescribed textbooks than their non-accounting contemporaries. According to Brown & Guilding (1993, p. 211), this is because:

Table 19.2 Survey of teaching methods

Pedagogical method
1. Lectures
2. Seminar/Tutorials
3. Prescribed Textbooks
4. Case-study discussion
5. Debate/discussion
6. Practical workshops
7. Instructional films or videos
8. Computer simulations
9. Role play
10. Industrial Visits

Source: Adapted from Brown & Guilding (1993).

> *accounting focusses on widely accepted practices, then much of the teaching can be achieved through textbooks and prescriptive lectures . . . If, however, attempts are made . . . to develop analytical and professional judgement skills. . . then different teaching methods are needed.*

In this respect, the lower emphasis accorded to tutorials in accounting departments might be suggestive of a less dialogical approach to teaching (Thomson & Bebbington, 2005), an emphasis on teacher-orientated activities (Biggs, 2003; Entwistle, 2000), and a conception of learning which emphasises a knowledge transmission mode and the adoption of teacher-focussed approaches.

Studies which consider the use of accounting textbooks are limited, although a few studies have examined how educators use textbooks (James, 2000; Ferguson *et al.*, 2007), how and where students read textbooks (Phillips & Phillips, 2007), and the 'critical' reading of accounting textbooks (Manninen, 1997). In assessing the efficacy of a single textbook approach to teaching in comparison with an approach which requires students to read more widely, James (2000) employed both approaches in two parallel courses on the principles of taxation. The findings of this U.K. study were based on students' performance on each course and on students' feedback, and suggest that a single textbook approach yields better results. However, the study acknowledged that students tended to prefer a single textbook approach because it saved time, and made '*life easier*', while noting that a single textbook approach was probably too narrow and only offered one interpretation (James, 2000, p. 287).

Phillips & Phillips (2007) argue that, despite the emphasis which institutions place on textbooks in *Introductory Accounting* courses, there is little research that actually describes how students interact with textbooks. Their study, undertaken in the U.S.A., reports on the accounts of 172 undergraduate students regarding '*their experiences with 13 chapters of an introductory financial accounting textbook*' (ibid., p. 21). The purpose of their research was to '*determine whether students' reading behaviors are likely to prevent textbooks from achieving their intended goals*' (ibid., p. 22).

The results indicated that students used the textbook in a variety of settings: '*only 15% of students read the textbook in the library as opposed to 78% who read at home*' (ibid., p. 30). Students who read the textbook outside the library stated that they read '*while watching TV, babysitting, working at a job, working out, visiting friends and family, waiting at a hair salon, travelling in a car, attending church, or sitting in another class*' (ibid., p. 30).

427

In addition, various other distractions to reading were noted by students, including illness, hangovers, and relationship problems, with the biggest obstacle being a heavy workload from other courses.

Two reading strategies were typically employed by students – '*sinking*' or '*skimming*':

- Sinking entailed carefully reading the textbook, taking notes and highlighting important topics so that the information content would '*sink in*'.
- Skimming involved reading quickly over a chapter (often skipping the learning objectives) just to get through the assigned reading.

Phillips & Phillips (ibid., p. 31) reported that students' approaches to reading the recommended textbook had a bearing on their course performance. For example:

> [O]f those who read the learning objectives, 39% were in the top quartile and 27% were in the second quartile. In contrast, most students who skipped the learning objectives were in the third and fourth quartiles (33% and 30% respectively).

However, Phillips & Phillips did not report any association between students' performances and the sink or skim approaches to reading, since students reported that they typically used both strategies depending on their situation. It was also noted that 85 per cent of students skipped the self-study questions, while 68 per cent omitted the end of chapter problem-based questions.

In their conclusions, Phillips & Phillips discuss the merits of talking to students about the sinking versus skimming approaches to reading in an attempt to encourage good reading habits. They cautioned that:

> [T]here is no need to scare students by emphasizing how difficult the material is in an attempt to spur students to put more effort into reading. . . students already fear the textbook and expect topics to be confusing.

> (ibid., p. 38)

In this sense, according to Phillips & Phillips (ibid., p. 38), it is better to encourage good reading habits, '*especially in the first few days of the course*'.

In an interview study concerned with educators' perceptions of the emphasis given to different stakeholders in *Introductory Accounting* textbooks, Ferguson *et al.* (2007) consider the extent to which teachers in the U.K. supplement their textbooks to provide students with '*alternative perspectives*'. Findings suggest that all but one of the interviewees held the view that students should be presented with '*alternative perspectives*' which emphasised the user needs of stakeholder groups other than the shareholder or owner. Participants in this research indicated that such perspectives may be introduced during the lectures and tutorials, or by recommending supplementary reading material.

Other commentaries on textbooks contend that accounting students are entitled to learn how to read '*persuasive accounting texts critically*' (Manninen, 1997, p. 281). The impetus for this view, based on an analysis of an article in the journal *Management Accountant*, stems from the post-modern notion that textbooks can engender a world of their own and can thus maintain a social reality. Manninen warns us that an unreflective reader may accept: '*the problems and solutions that the text creates as the problems and solutions of accounting*' (ibid., p. 282).

We maintain that Manninen's (1997) view holds today when he points out that all texts are written with some purpose in mind and are therefore representative of some vision of the world. The importance for students to engage in the critical reading of texts is apparent when one considers the suggestion that textbooks contain '*certain silenced assumptions*' and are '*built on many choices and concealments*' (ibid., p. 287).

Periodic reviews of the accounting literature have produced guides for accounting educators to teaching cases published in relevant journals. For example, Apostolou *et al.* (2001) provided an overview of the accounting literature published in the five main accounting education journals between 1997 and 1999 (*Journal of Accounting Education, Issues in Accounting Education, Accounting Education: an international journal, The Accounting Educators' Journal,* and *Advances in Accounting Education*). They noted over 60 case studies available in the studied journals over the period, and they detailed primary topic areas (Managerial Accounting, Non-profit Organisations, Cost Accounting, Financial Accounting, Systems, Auditing, International, Ethics, Governmental, and Tax) and journal location for interested educators. Watson *et al.* (2003) presented a literature review of accounting education appearing between 2000 and 2002 primarily in *Journal of Accounting Education, Accounting Education: an international journal, Advances in Accounting Education,* and *Issues in Accounting Education.* In addition, the authors note 53 case studies (2003, p. 312) in these journals over the same period, each of which provides teaching notes and a suggested solution. The range of topic areas addressed by these case studies included accounting information systems, auditing, management accounting, financial accounting, not-for-profit organisations, and taxation. Watson *et al.* (2007) repeated this review exercise for 2003–2005 and provided an overview of 58 case studies addressing audit, managerial accounting, ethics, financial accounting, and taxation matters. Apostolou *et al.* (2011) performed a similar review of the literature between 2006 and 2009 across six journals: *Journal of Accounting Education, Accounting Education: an international journal, Advances in Accounting Education, Global Perspectives on Accounting Education, Issues in Accounting Education,* and *The Accounting Educators' Journal.* In this article, 89 case studies were classified across audit, financial accounting & reporting, corporate governance, managerial accounting, and taxation categories.

Other writers have focussed specifically on providing searchable databases which may be of use to accounting educators. For example, Brasel & Hentz (2006) created and described a database[2] of articles, case studies, and instructional resources from the short-lived *Accounting Education: A Journal of Theory, Research and Practice,* plus *Accounting Education: an international journal, The Accounting Educators' Journal, Issues in Accounting Education,* and *Journal of Accounting Education.* In addition, Lipe (2006) described the categories and topics addressed by teaching cases published in *Issues in Accounting Education* from its inception until November 2006; and Weinstein (2005) explained how to access and use a computerised database of accounting case studies for teaching.

Despite the prevalence of case studies and accompanying resources in accounting education journals, Healy & McCutcheon (2010, p. 556) note that:

> *a greater understanding of and insight into accounting lecturers' experiences of teaching with case studies is needed to inform on-going debates surrounding their potential, at departmental and institutional levels, as well as across the academic accounting community generally.*

While it is widely assumed that the use of case studies has the benefit of '*expos[ing] students to real-world complexity, particularly with respect to decision-making*' (Weil *et al.*, 2001, p. 138), others have noted that '*it is how the case studies are used and the level of student involvement that is of vital importance*' (Adler *et al.*, 2004, p. 213; see also Hassall & Milne, 2004).

Drawing on their analysis of the use of case studies by teachers on accounting courses at a university in Ireland, Healy & McCutcheon (2010) suggest that the users of case studies could be classified into three categories:

1   controllers
2   facilitators
3   partners.

Those who adopted a controlling approach tended to view the case study as a means of training students to read or interpret accounting information in a specific way – and thus could be described as '*the imparting knowledge to a largely passive student body*' (Healy & McCutcheon, ibid., p. 564). Those who took a facilitating approach to the case study tended to '*use cases with the objective of engaging students with the subject area*', whereby the teacher provides the '*structure to allow students to personalize and internalize concepts*' (ibid., p. 564). The partner approach treats students as equal learning partners where both the teacher and student are viewed as 'travellers on a common journey' and hence, both teacher and student find the process enriching (ibid., p. 564).[3] In many respects, the partner approach shares the characteristics of Freire's (1996) dialogic model.

A focus on education and learning has long been one of the defining characteristics of the Centre for Social and Environmental Accounting Research network (CSEAR), now based at the University of St Andrews in Scotland. CSEAR members and affiliates have been generous in sharing a range of teaching resources which, at the time of writing, can be accessed via the CSEAR website. The resources include:

- case studies and tutorials;
- examination questions;
- other assessments;
- movies;
- details and links to the research literature on social and environmental accounting research and educational research in general;
- textbooks;
- helpful teaching tips on designing social and environmental accounting classes, and integrating social and environmental accounting into mainstream classes;
- classroom exercises; and
- class outlines.

Although this chapter is tasked with providing an international perspective, we acknowledge that a limitation in this regard relates to the dominance of English language resources discussed. In this context, the following quotation from Wilson (2002, p. 299) in his review of the first 10 years of *Accounting Education: an international journal* which was launched with the explicit aim of providing material of interest to '*an international readership*' should be noted:

> At least 70% of inputs [to the journal] are from the same four countries namely the U.K., the U.S.A., Australia and New Zealand – although there have been inputs from a total of 21 countries.

We turn now to the specific results of the educational survey conducted with higher education accounting academics in the U.K. and Ireland.

19.5 Research method

The data presented in this chapter is drawn from the results of a questionnaire survey which was emailed to all the academic staff listed in the *British Accounting Review Research Register 2010* (Helliar *et al.*, 2010). The questionnaire was based on an instrument used by Iqbal *et al.* (2006) in their analysis of the teaching methods and modes of assessment used by finance academics in the U.K., Canada, and the U.S.A.[4] The questionnaire used by Iqbal *et al.* shares many of the characteristics used in prior studies into the teaching of economics in the U.S.A. – most notably, the scale in which respondents indicate the extent to which a teaching resource is used is the same as Becker & Watts (1996, 2001), Watts & Becker (2008), and Watts & Schaur (2011). More specifically, the questionnaire asked respondents to indicate whether a particular method was used never (0), rarely (1), occasionally (2), frequently (3), or always (4), which was defined on the survey as a non-linear range for each of the response options (0 = 0 per cent of the time, 1 = 1–10 per cent of the time, 2 = 11–33 per cent of the time, 3 = 34–65 per cent of the time, and 4 = 66–100 per cent of the time).[5] In addition to the exclusive focus on teaching and assessment methods in the extant economics and finance surveys, the results of the survey documented in this chapter also report on teachers' perceptions of teaching, drawing on the U.K.-based studies of Gow & Kember (1993) and Kell & Jones (2007).[6] The use of the questionnaire instrument employed in the international study by Iqbal *et al.* (2006), while drawing on the perceptions of teachers in prior studies undertaken in the U.K. should facilitate an international comparison of academic views on teaching resources.

The survey reported in this chapter contained 14 questions which related to:

1   the background and institutional characteristics of the respondent;
2   the use of in-class teaching resources;
3   the use of out-of-class teaching resources;
4   assessment methods; and
5   teaching beliefs and intentions.

All responses were completely confidential and responses were not attributable to any identifiable individuals. When completing the survey, respondents were asked to consider the *full suite* of courses on which they teach.[7, 8]

The *British Accounting Review Research Register 2010* contains the correspondence details of 1,708 academic staff in accounting and finance based in universities in the British Isles (i.e. the U.K. and the Republic of Ireland). The questionnaire was distributed to all the individuals listed in the *Register* by email using the questionnaire software package Qualtrics. The software recognises which email addresses are no longer operational (either because staff have moved to another institution or have retired) and filters these out. The filtering process meant that 1,665 emails were sent with links to the survey. The survey was first sent on 12 October 2012, with a reminder being sent on 25 October 2012, and the survey closed on 1 November 2012. Overall, 148 valid questionnaires were completed, representing a response rate of 8.9 per cent.[9] While the response rate is quite low, Watts & Becker (2008) note that, over the course of their quinquennial survey of academic economists, response rates have fallen from 20.6 per cent in 1995 to 13 per cent in 2005. They note that they can offer no explanation for this trend and suggest that their '*intuition [is] that economists with greater interest in teaching were more likely to complete the questionnaires*', implying a possible selection bias (ibid., p. 274).

19.6 Results

19.6.1 Respondents' demographics

An inspection of Table 19.3 shows that the percentage of female respondents is slightly lower than the percentage of male respondents (44 per cent and 56 per cent respectively). It is worth noting that this gender profile is considerably different from that for similar surveys in economics, for example, in describing the gender profile over the period of their quinquennial survey, Watts & Becker (2008, p. 282) report that '*males made up 76% of respondents in 2005, 81% in 2000, and 83% in 1995*'. In finance, Iqbal *et al.* (2006) documented that males made up 71 per cent of British, 80 per cent of American, and 25 per cent of Canadian respondents. These figures would suggest that there may be a greater gender balance among academic accountants or among our survey respondents than the mix present in other related disciplines.

The majority of respondents to the current survey held the post of Senior Lecturer (41 per cent), while Lecturers and Professors were fairly evenly represented among the remainder of those completing the questionnaire.[10] The preponderance of senior academics (Senior Lecturers, Readers, and Professors) among the respondents suggests that the views expressed represent the opinions of 'leaders' within the departments surveyed. In addition, it will be interesting to compare the results of the current study with the findings from the U.K. of Iqbal *et al.* (2006) in which the percentage of less-senior staff was much higher.

The highest qualification held by the majority of respondents was a PhD (57 per cent), with 29 per cent holding a Master's degree, and 5 per cent no more than an undergraduate degree. These figures are broadly similar to those reported by Iqbal *et al.* (2006) in relation to U.K.-based finance academics (54 per cent PhD, 38 per cent Master's), while more academics in the U.S.A. and Canada tended to have a PhD (92 per cent and 88 per cent respectively). Finally, the typical respondent to the current survey had a professional qualification and over 16 years of teaching experience in the area of accounting.

19.6.2 Teaching methods

Table 19.4 reports the results of the survey findings on in-class teaching methods. In particular, the mean and standard deviation of the respondents' scores about usage of different methods within class time is reported from a 5-point Likert scale (where 0 = never and 4 = always). In addition, the ranking of the various methods on the basis of the mean scores is supplied. The final six columns of Table 19.4 report the mean score and ranking from Iqbal *et al.*'s (2006) survey of academics in the U.K., the U.S.A., and Canada.

An inspection of Table 19.4 shows that the predominant mode of in-class teaching for accounting and finance students in the British Isles was a PowerPoint lecture (Mean = 3.56).[11] This is in contrast to Iqbal *et al.*'s (2006) earlier findings which documented that the most popular approach to the classroom teaching of finance was the delivery of a lecture using an overhead projector (Mean = 3.3). The use of PowerPoint slides was only ranked second in Iqbal *et al.*'s investigation (Mean = 2.6). In the present study, a lecture involving an overhead projector only had a mean of 1.04, suggesting that there has perhaps been a pronounced decline in this mode of delivery since Iqbal *et al.*'s (2006) survey was completed. The PowerPoint approach has become somewhat ubiquitous, presumably as educational technology has spread. Indeed, the high mean score awarded to lectures involving PowerPoint slides was associated with the fourth smallest standard deviation among the 18 different options highlighted in Table 19.4,

Table 19.3 Respondents' demographics

		Stevenson et al. (2014) (%)	Iqbal et al. (2006)		
			U.K. (%)	U.S.A. (%)	Canada (%)
Gender	Male	56	71	80	85
	Female	44	29	20	15
Age	Under 25	0	N/A	N/A	N/A
	25–34	6	N/A	N/A	N/A
	35–44	27	N/A	N/A	N/A
	45–54	35	N/A	N/A	N/A
	55–64	30	N/A	N/A	N/A
	65 or over	2	N/A	N/A	N/A
Rank	Teaching Fellow	7	2	4	9
	Lecturer	24	45	24	27
	Senior Lecturer	41	29	20	15
	Reader	2	N/A	N/A	N/A
	Professor	20	19	34	27
	Other	5	N/A	N/A	N/A
Qualification	Undergraduate	5	N/A	N/A	N/A
	Master's	29	38	8	12
	PhD	57	54	92	88
	Other	9	N/A	N/A	N/A
Professional	Yes	59	46	N/A	27
Qualification	No	41	54	N/A	73
Years teaching	0–5	8	N/A	N/A	N/A
	6–10	15	N/A	N/A	N/A
	11–15	17	N/A	N/A	N/A
	16–20	16	N/A	N/A	N/A
	Over 20	44	N/A	N/A	N/A

Notes: This table provides background details about respondents to the current survey. In particular, data on Gender, Age, title (Rank – see footnote 10) and highest degree qualification (Qualification) are given. In addition, information about whether respondents had a professional qualification (Professional Qualification) and their number of years of experience of teaching in higher education (Years Teaching) are also included. Details about the British, American, and Canadian respondents to Iqbal *et al.* (2006) are supplied for comparison purposes.

N/A = 'not available'.

thus a sizable number of respondents rated this mode of in-class teaching as being one of the methods almost always used.

A comparison of the mean scores awarded by respondents to the different options suggests that there is emphasis on direct instruction as opposed to student-centred learning. For example, the top seven methods of in-class teaching include 'Teacher-led problem-solving' and 'Teacher-led case study'. More student-centred approaches such as 'Individual student computer work' and 'Individual student presentations' were ranked in the bottom half of all the methods employed. Perhaps a growth in class sizes and downward pressure on teaching resources available have contributed to the relatively small mean scores awarded by the respondents to the more costly

Table 19.4 In-class teaching methods

| | Stevenson et al. (2014) | | Iqbal et al. (2006) | | | | | |
| | | | U.K. | | U.S.A. | | Canada | |
	Mean (SD)	Rank	Mean	Rank	Mean	Rank	Mean	Rank
Computer PowerPoint lecture	3.56 (0.95)	1	2.6	2	1.5	5	1.8	4
Teacher-led problem solving	2.20 (1.24)	2	2.2	4	2.6	2	2.4	3
Small group activities	2.11 (1.06)	3	1.6	6=	0.8	9	0.9	8=
Journal article discussion	2.05 (1.14)	4	1.7	5	0.6	10=	0.7	13=
Group student presentations	1.85 (1.08)	5	1.4	9=	0.6	10=	0.9	8=
Newspaper/magazine article discussion	1.67 (1.09)	6	1.3	11	1.6	4	1.4	5=
Teacher-led case study	1.55 (1.17)	7	1.4	9=	0.9	8	1.4	5=
Writing on board lecture	1.51 (1.27)	8	2.4	3	3.0	1	2.8	1
Guest lectures	1.32 (0.83)	9	1.0	13=	0.6	10=	0.7	13=
Individual student computer work	1.29 (1.25)	10	1.1	12	1.1	7	0.9	8=
Student debates	1.27 (1.14)	11	1.0	13=	0.3	16	0.6	15
Overhead projector lecture	1.08 (1.41)	12	3.3	1	2.0	3	2.6	2
Group student computer work	1.04 (1.08)	13	0.9	15	0.6	10=	0.9	8=
Individual student presentations	0.92 (1.01)	14	1.5	8	0.6	10=	0.8	12
Television/DVD	0.81 (0.93)	15	0.6	16	0.6	10=	0.4	16
Other	0.77 (1.02)	16	N/A	N/A	N/A	N/A	N/A	N/A
Teacher computer demonstration	0.70 (0.89)	17	1.6	6=	1.2	6	1.1	7
Transparency slides lecture	0.34 (0.75)	18	N/A	N/A	N/A	N/A	N/A	N/A

Note: This table reports results on the respondents' usage of different methods in their in-class teaching. Specifically, the average score (Mean) from a 5-point Likert scale (where 0 = never and 4 = always) is given along with the standard deviation (SD) of responses. Rank refers to the ranking of the different in-class methods within a country. Details about the British, American, and Canadian respondents to Iqbal *et al.* (2006) are supplied for comparison purposes. N/A = 'not available'.

methods associated with student-centred learning. An alternative interpretation might be that responding accounting educators are simply more inclined to employing teacher- or content-oriented approaches: if so, this could be due to the teaching beliefs of the staff who were surveyed (Fox, 1983).

A direct comparison of the mean scores awarded to the different teaching methods in the current study with those reported for U.K.-based finance academics in Iqbal *et al.* (2006) suggest that there have been a number of changes to in-class teaching approaches. For example, 'Small group activities', 'Group student presentations', 'Newspaper/magazine article discussion' and 'Guest lectures' have all improved their ranking by three or more places. In fact, the Spearman correlation coefficient between the rankings of in-class methods in the current study with their counterparts in the U.K. in Iqbal *et al.* (2006) at 0.444, was not significantly different from zero at the 5 per cent level ($p = 0.09$). The current rankings of in-class teaching methods in the British Isles are also different from the results from the U.S.A. and Canada reported in Iqbal *et al.* (2006). 'Writing on board lectures' and 'Overhead projector lectures' are ranked less highly in this survey, while 'Small group activities' and 'Journal article discussion' are rated more highly.

Inspection of Table 19.5 suggests that there has been a lot less change in the out-of-class teaching methods used by the respondents to the current survey when compared with the results reported by Iqbal *et al.* (2006). For example, 'Textbook reading' is still ranked first while 'Television/DVD' and 'Group take-home tests' are rated towards the bottom of the list with 52.8 per cent and 87.1 per cent respectively of respondents indicating that they never used these approaches in the current study. In this instance, there is a significant relationship between the rankings of the current study and the rankings on out-of-class teaching methods reported by Iqbal *et al.* (2006) for academics based in the U.K., the U.S.A., and Canada since the Spearman correlation coefficients were large and positive (at 0.781, 0.679 and 0.525) and significantly different from zero at the 5 per cent level (the *p*-values were 0.00, 0.01 and 0.04 respectively).

Despite the overall similarity in the ranking accorded to some of the various out-of-class teaching methods, a number of differences are apparent in Table 19.5. Not surprisingly, technology is being used more frequently according to respondents to the current survey. Thus 'WebCT, Blackboard or other platform' is now rated second – up from tenth in Iqbal *et al.*'s (2006) questionnaire to U.K.-based finance academics. By contrast, 'Work-book assignments' are a relatively less popular method of out-of-class teaching, having dropped in the rankings from second to eleventh. Despite this decline in relative usage, 'Work-book assignments' still had a mean score of 1.19 and were 'occasionally', 'frequently', or 'always' used by a majority of the respondents.

19.6.3 Assessment methods

Responses to a question about the use of different assessment methods are reported in Table 19.6. A number of points emerge from an analysis of Table 19.6, namely:

- 'Individual examinations' were ranked first with a very high mean score of 3.55 and a relatively low standard deviation value of 0.86. In fact, 69.9 per cent of the respondents rated this form of assessment as 4 (Always used) while a further 21.0 per cent gave it a score of 3 (Frequently used). Indeed, the mean score for 'Individual examinations' was 1.28 higher than the average score for the next highest rated assessment method ('Individual essays', Mean = 2.29).

Table 19.5 Out-of-class teaching methods

| | Stevenson et al. (2014) | | Iqbal et al. (2006) | | | | | |
| | | | U.K. | | U.S.A. | | Canada | |
	Mean (SD)	Rank	Mean	Rank	Mean	Rank	Mean	Rank
Textbook reading	2.85 (1.07)	1	2.4	1	3.5	1	2.9	1
WebCT, blackboard or other platform	2.78 (1.46)	2	1.0	10	N/A	N/A	N/A	N/A
Journal article reading	2.59 (1.10)	3	1.6	2=	0.4	9=	0.5	10=
Individual essays	2.20 (1.12)	4	1.6	2=	1.0	4=	0.8	8=
Case studies	1.96 (1.05)	5	1.3	6	0.8	6	1.1	3=
Newspaper/magazine article reading	1.92 (1.11)	6	1.2	7	1.1	3	0.8	8=
Group homework	1.77 (1.21)	7	1.1	8=	0.5	7=	1.0	5=
Textbook websites/ publishers websites	1.56 (1.22)	8	1.1	8=	N/A	N/A	N/A	N/A
Small group activities	1.45 (1.17)	9	0.9	11	0.4	9=	0.5	10=
Individual student computer work	1.19 (1.13)	10	1.4	5	1.5	2	1.2	2
Workbook assignments	1.19 (1.29)	11	1.6	2=	1.0	4=	1.1	3=
Group essays	1.06 (1.15)	12	0.7	13=	0.4	9=	1.0	5=
Guest lectures	0.84 (0.92)	13	0.3	15	0.2	13	0.1	14
Individual take-home tests	0.79 (1.16)	14	0.9	11=	0.3	12	0.4	12
Group student computer work	0.77 (1.07)	15	0.7	13=	0.5	7=	0.9	7
Television/DVD	0.62 (0.77)	16	0.2	16=	0.1	14=	0.0	15
Other	0.51 (0.93)	17	N/A	N/A	N/A	N/A	N/A	N/A
Group take-home tests	0.32 (0.75)	18	0.2	16=	0.1	14=	0.2	13

Note: This table reports results on the respondents' usage of different methods in their out-of-class teaching. Specifically, the average score (Mean) from a 5-point Likert scale (where 0 = Never and 4 = Always) is given along with the standard deviation (SD) of responses. Rank refers to the ranking of the different out-of-class methods within a country. Details about the British, American, and Canadian respondents to Iqbal *et al.* (2006) are supplied for comparison purposes. N/A = 'not available'.

- Three further assessment methods had average scores that were greater than 1.00 ('Individual in-class-tests', 'Group presentations' and 'Individual homework'). At the other end of the ranking, 'Group in-class tests', 'Individual take-home tests', and 'Group take home tests' all had mean scores of less than 0.50, suggesting that they were 'never' or 'rarely' used by our respondents. Again, there was a good deal of uniformity among the respondents in the use of these latter three assessment methods since the standard deviation values were low.

- Not a lot of change was evident in the ranking of the different assessment methods by academics based in the British Isles since Iqbal *et al.* conducted their survey in 2005 – though the average scores increased for nine of the 12 options that were common across both surveys. In fact, the Spearman correlations coefficient between the rankings in the current study and the U.K. rankings in Iqbal *et al.* (2006) was 0.77. Thus, although there seems to be a greater diversity in the assessment methods now employed by accounting academics in the British Isles relative to their finance counterparts in the U.K. in 2005 (as evidenced by the higher mean scores), the relative ranking of the different assessment methods has not changed dramatically. Indeed, the evidence from the ranking only suggests that 'Group homework' has grown in importance relative to 'Individual homework'. Further investigation is needed to see whether this change is the result of staff taking advantage of new social media which facilitates group discussion outside of class time, or the impact of resources constraints on staff who do not have the time to mark individual homework assignments.

19.6.4 Perceptions of teaching

The final section of the questionnaire sought respondents' perceptions about the aims of their teaching, how their teaching approach facilitated learning, and what knowledge dimensions they tried to transmit via their teaching approach. The results from these questions are reported in Panel A, Panel B and Panel C of Table 19.7 respectively; specifically, the average score (Mean) from a 5-point Likert scale (where 1 = Strongly Disagree and 5 = Strongly Agree) is given along with the standard deviation (SD) of responses. The final two columns report a t-test of the null hypothesis that the mean score is statistically different from the neutral score of 3.00; the *p*-value for the t-test is provided in the final column.

An analysis of the results in Panel A of Table 19.7 reveals that the respondents agreed with all five statements about the aims of their teaching. Thus, the evidence suggests that all of the *'basic theories of learning'* outlined by Fox (1983) were employed by educators who responded to this survey. The mean scores varied from a low of 3.80 for 'Imparting information' to a high of 4.70 for 'Facilitating understanding on the part of the student'. All of the means were greater than the neutral score of 3.00 since the *p*-values for the t-tests were all less than 0.05. Although all of the means were statistically different from 3.00 at the 95 per cent confidence interval, there was a clear ranking of the five alternatives listed. The top three rated statements about perceptions of teaching were student-centred and suggested that respondents' teaching aims were to facilitate the student's understanding, encourage the student's intellectual development, and encourage interaction with the student. All of these top three statements suggest a student-centred/learning orientation as opposed to a teacher- centred/content orientation. By contrast, the final two statements with the lowest means seemed to view the learning process as a one-way channel of communication from the teacher to the student.

A similar picture emerges from Panel B of Table 19.7. The top three statements suggest that, if the teacher's goal was to facilitate learning, then participation by the student was rated highly:

Table 19.6 Assessment methods

	Stevenson et al. (2014)		Iqbal et al. (2006)					
			U.K.		U.S.A.		Canada	
	Mean (SD)	Rank	Mean	Rank	Mean	Rank	Mean	Rank
Individual examinations	3.55 (0.86)	1	3.8	1	3.5	1	3.4	1
Individual essays	2.27 (1.33)	2	1.0	2=	0.6	3=	0.4	6
Individual in-class tests	1.46 (1.48)	3	0.7	4	N/A	N/A	N/A	N/A
Group presentations	1.44 (1.21)	4	0.4	6=	0.2	6=	0.3	7
Individual homework	1.34 (1.47)	5	1.0	2=	0.8	2	0.7	2
Group essays	0.94 (1.20)	6	0.6	5	0.3	5	0.6	3=
Group homework	0.86 (1.10)	7	0.2	10=	0.1	9=	0.6	3=
Participation	0.80 (1.10)	8	0.2	10=	0.6	3=	0.5	5
Individual presentations	0.79 (0.99)	9	0.4	6=	0.2	6=	0.2	8=
Group in-class test	0.39 (0.93)	10	0.2	10=	0.1	9=	0.1	11=
Other	0.37 (0.80)	11	N/A	N/A	N/A	N/A	N/A	N/A
Individual take-home tests	0.21 (0.61)	12	0.3	8=	0.2	6=	0.2	8=
Group take-home tests	0.17 (0.51)	13	0.3	8=	0.1	9=	0.1	11=

Note: This table reports results on the respondents' usage of different assessment methods in their teaching. Specifically, the average score (Mean) from a 5-point Likert scale (where 0 = Never and 4 = Always) is given along with the standard deviation (SD) of responses. Rank refers to the ranking of the different in-class methods within a country. Details about the British, American, and Canadian respondents to Iqbal *et al.* (2006) are supplied for comparison purposes. N/A = 'not available'.

the three statements with the highest means related to 'Motivating students', 'Interactive teaching', and 'Facilitative teaching'. However, the final two statements were also given mean scores which were statistically greater than the neutral value of 3.00 suggesting that, even when a respondent's approach to teaching was characterised as facilitating learning, a teaching approach which utilised methods such as problem–solving were also seen as being important. Rather than falling neatly into Fox's (1983) four discrete groupings of '*approaches to learning*', the respondents to this survey seemed to adopt multiple-perspective teaching approaches.

Table 19.7 Views on teaching, learning, and knowledge transmission

	Mean	SD	t-test	p-value
Panel A: Perception of Teaching				
Facilitating understanding on the part of the student	4.70	0.52	39.52	0.00
Bringing on the intellectual development of the student	4.62	0.57	34.48	0.00
An interaction between the teacher and the student	4.34	0.71	22.78	0.00
Transmitting structured knowledge	4.00	0.84	14.31	0.00
Imparting information	3.80	0.99	9.73	0.00
Panel B: Learning Facilitation				
Motivating students	4.32	0.74	21.27	0.00
Interactive teaching	4.10	0.78	17.03	0.00
Facilitative teaching	4.07	0.71	17.94	0.00
Problem-solving	4.04	0.79	15.85	0.02
Pastoral interest	3.22	1.05	2.47	0.00
Panel C: Knowledge Transmission				
Knowledge of subject	4.25	0.74	20.23	0.00
Imparting information	3.80	0.86	11.89	0.00
Training for specific jobs	2.88	1.10	−1.30	0.20
Use of media	2.74	1.02	−3.08	0.00

Note: This table reports responses to questions about educators' teaching aims (Panel A), how their teaching approach facilitates students' learning (Panel B), and the knowledge aspects which their teaching approach seeks to convey (Panel C), using a 5 point Likert scale where 1 = Strongly Disagree and 5 = Strongly Agree. Mean responses and the standard deviations of the means are shown, as well as the results of a t-test (and the corresponding p-value) of the null hypothesis that the mean score is statistically different from the neutral score of 3.00.

The final Panel of Table 19.7 reports views where respondents classified their teaching in accounting as being about transmitting specific aspects of knowledge. While those who answered this question strongly agreed that they were interested in conveying knowledge of the subject and imparting information (the '*transfer theory of teaching*' in Fox's (1983) typology), they were neutral about the statement that their approach to teaching provided training for a specific job (Mean = 2.88, $p = 0.20$). In addition, they strongly disagreed with the view that their approach involved knowledge about the use of media in terms of audio-visuals and new technology. In this instance, the average score was less than the neutral value of 3.00 by a statistically significant amount (Mean = 2.74, $p = 0.00$).

The answers of those responding to the final statement[12] in Panel A of Table 19.7 were split into two groups depending on whether they disagreed or strongly disagreed with the view their teaching was 'imparting information' (19 respondents) or not (106 respondents). Those who were neutral on this statement were omitted from this part of the analysis. The replies to questions about the use of different methods for in-class teaching, out-of-class teaching, and assessment were then split according to the new grouping, and mean responses were compared via a two-sample t-test. In particular, it was expected that the 19 respondents in the first group might be more innovative in their teaching and assessment methods because of the lower emphasis given to 'imparting information'. An analysis of the statistical results (not reported here) reveals that a number of differences emerged. For example, those in the first group (i.e. who did not see themselves as primarily imparting information) used 'Small group activities' more in their in-class teaching (Mean difference = 0.556, p = 0.03), employed 'Group take-home tests' more in their out-of-class teaching (Mean difference = 0.628, p = 0.04), used 'Television/DVDs' more in their out-of-class teaching (Mean difference = 0.453, p = 0.04), and employed 'Participation' more as an assessment method for determining a student's final grade (Mean difference = 0.664, p = 0.09). The final difference was significant only at the 10 per cent level.

19.6.5 Sub-group findings

Statistical interrogation of respondents' demographics and questionnaire responses revealed four groups of significant correlations:

1 In four of the questions, the answers of male respondents were statistically different from those of their female counterparts. In this context it is worth noting that, in their discussion of conceptions of teaching and consequent teaching intentions, Norton *et al.* (2010, p. 564) note '*women were more orientated towards learning facilitation than men*'. Specifically in our survey, male respondents were less likely to use a 'Computer PowerPoint lecture', a 'Guest lecture', and to determine a final grade using the 'Participation method of assessment'. In contrast, they were more likely than the female respondents to use an Individual essay as an out-of-class teaching method. In each case, the F-statistic for a one-way ANOVA was higher than its critical value at the 5 per cent level.

2 The responses of the survey participants also varied to a significant extent across the five age categories employed for four of the questions asked: the use of a 'Computer PowerPoint lecture' and 'Group student computer work' were used much less by those aged 45–54. Surprisingly, an 'Overhead projector lecture' and 'Group homework' were used most by those aged 55–64. Perhaps those teaching resources which involved relatively new technology were used less frequently by older lecturing staff who had trained with overhead projectors. In seven questions, responses varied according to the position of the respondent. Specifically, answers about:

    (i)   the use of 'Teacher-led case studies', 'Teacher-led problem-solving' and 'Journal article discussions' as in-class teaching methods,
    (ii) the use of 'Case studies', 'Individual essays', 'Web CT', and 'Workbook assignments' as out-of-class teaching resources differed depending on the respondents' positions. Senior Lecturers tended to be more innovative in terms of the in-class and out-of-class teaching resources used. For example, they used 'Case studies', 'Individual essays', and 'Workbook assignments' more than respondents with other job titles. For four questions, answers differed according to the qualification of the respondent: those with a PhD tended not to use 'Small group activities in class', the use of 'Individual take-home tests', or 'Other out-of-class teaching resources'. Instead, they relied more heavily on 'Individual examinations' than those with different qualifications. Perhaps those with a PhD devoted relatively more of their time to research and did not employ teaching resources which they perceived might be more time-consuming.

3 Survey respondents with a professional qualification were more likely to use 'Instructor computer demonstrations' (F statistic = 5.54, p = 0.02) and 'Journal article discussions' (F statistic = 6.41, p = 0.01), but less likely to employ 'Small group activities' (F statistic = 4.53, p = 0.04), or 'Teacher-led case studies' (F statistic = 6.40, p = 0.01) as in-class

teaching methods. These respondents were also less likely to use 'Case studies' as an out-of-class teaching resource (F statistic = 13.10, p = 0.00). This unwillingness to use case studies (either in-class or out-of-class) may have something to do with their professional training where other types of teaching resources tend to be employed (Ferguson *et al.*, 2011).

4   Replies to five questions varied according to the number of years of teaching experience of the respondent: one of these related to an in-class teaching method ('Individual student computer work') while four referred to out-of-class teaching resources ('Case studies', 'Individual student computer work', 'Individual take-home tests', and 'Newspaper/magazine article reading'). In most cases, those respondents in the second most experienced category (with 16–20 years of teaching experience) had the lowest mean score, indicating that they did not use these teaching resources. Again, this unwillingness to use time-intensive teaching methods may have been linked with a desire to preserve research time or a lecture-centred approach to teaching. Further work is needed on this issue.

19.7 Conclusion

This review of the use of teaching resources has indicated a range of ways of conceiving of what is meant by the term 'teaching resources', which inevitably has consequential influences on which accounting education materials are brought into view, and how they are subsequently used. One gap in the accounting literature of the use (by U.K.-based and Irish accounting academics) of teaching resources and their conceptions of accounting education has been addressed: it revealed some differences from earlier studies of finance academics in the U.S.A., Canada, and the U.K. and Ireland. Notwithstanding the geographical differences, many of these changes appear to be the result of the passage of time and the more ubiquitous use of technology and software. However, not all differences appear to be explained by this. For example, findings reported in this chapter suggest that PowerPoint is more prevalent than the 'chalk and talk' approach favoured in economics (Becker & Watts, 1996; Watts & Becker, 2008), or the use of the overhead projector in finance (Iqbal *et al.*, 2006). We would suggest that the use of PowerPoint is most likely to be the result of the growing prevalence of this technology in higher education, although we would also point out that the continued prevalence of 'chalk and talk' in economics and its relative emphasis in finance might suggest that where instruction requires the use of mathematical formulae and calculations, then perhaps the chalkboard is a more suitable medium. In terms of out-of-class resources, the textbook is the favoured approach in both this study and across the three countries reported in Iqbal *et al.* (2006). However, we have noted that the use of WebCT and Blackboard are more prevalent in our study which, again, might be the result of the passage of time and the growing use of these technologies.

The present chapter extends upon previous research into the use of teaching resources by eliciting accounting educators' views regarding their conceptions of teaching. This was deemed important in the light of Entwistle's (2000) comments that teachers with a learning facilitation orientation in the classroom tended to use a range of teaching methods and assessments, while educators operating in a knowledge transmission mode were more likely to adopt teacher-focussed approaches. It is perhaps noteworthy that responses to the survey reported in this chapter suggest that accounting academics in the U.K. and Ireland tend to exhibit a preference for more student-oriented approaches to teaching. For example, the top three rated statements about perceptions of teaching suggested that respondents' teaching aims were to facilitate the student's understanding, encourage the student's intellectual development, and encourage interaction with the student. By contrast, the final two statements with the lowest means seemed to view the learning process as being a one-way channel of communication from the teacher to the student.

In some respects, it could be argued that our responses in relation to educators' perceptions of teaching are somewhat at odds with the teaching resources used by respondents. More specifically, one might expect, given the positive ranking of student-centred conceptions of teaching, that greater use of student-centred teaching resources would be employed by accounting educators. In this respect, one is reminded of Markely *et al*.'s (2009) observation that, while educators often state that their teaching is student-centred, classroom observations suggest a dominance of a teacher-centred approach. However, it is noteworthy that, when the sample was split according to whether respondents agreed or disagreed with the statement that teaching was about 'imparting information', respondents who disagreed tended to use more student-centred approaches (such as small-group activities, group tests and DVDs).

The results of the study reported here provide a snapshot of the prevalent teaching resources employed in accounting academia in the U.K. and Ireland, as well as providing information on accounting academics' perceptions of teaching. These results provide a broad overview of the teaching resources used in accounting that had hitherto remained relatively unexplored compared to the related subjects of economics and finance. In this respect, the results of this study provide a basis for further research into the use of specific resources in accounting education. As alluded to earlier in this chapter, there is generally a dearth of literature which explores the use of specific resources in accounting education (with a few notable exceptions in relation to textbooks and case studies). Further exploration into the use of specific resources is important for a number of reasons:

- While our study provides a broad overview, our findings do not shed light on the prevalence of teaching resources used on either specific subjects or at different levels of study. For example, some feedback on our questionnaire and anecdotal evidence would suggest that a lecture/PowerPoint format is more prevalent on introductory courses where student numbers tend to be larger, with perhaps less scope for an interactive approach. Similarly, it has been suggested that interactive approaches are more likely to be employed on the final years of undergraduate programmes where the student numbers tend to be smaller and where professional accreditation requirements are less applicable, giving more flexibility in terms of what the teacher can cover (Ferguson *et al.*, 2006). (See also Apostolou & Gammie, Chapter 29 – this volume.)
- As Coulson & Thomson (2006) and Thomson & Bebbington (2004) suggest, the educator's approach is possibly more important than the classroom or institutional resources in creating the educational experience. More qualitative research could be employed to consider the context in which teaching resources are used and their relative importance in relation to educators' approaches or their conceptions of teaching.

Notes

1 See Ferguson *et al.* (2008) for a discussion of the predominant use of training manuals in professional accounting education, and see Byrne & Willis, Chapter 7 – this volume, for coverage of accounting in secondary schools.
2 At the time of writing, this was maintained by Iowa State University personnel.
3 The distinction between a controlling approach, on the one hand, and a facilitator or partner approach, on the other, is consistent with Hassall & Milne's (2004) description of 'inactive' and 'active' uses of case studies. According to Hassall & Milne (ibid., p. 135), an inactive approach is where the educator '*dominates the problem definition, analysis, solution set and recommendation phases*', while in an active approach '*learners are given or even have to find the case study material and then have a class session in which to present and discuss the material with their peers*'.
4 We are, therefore, analysing responses from a sample of U.K.-based academics and comparing answers to replies from a survey of academics in cognate but different disciplines. To an extent, this problem

is common to all survey investigations – especially where findings are being compared with previous survey results. In addition, it is worth noting that the respondents to the current questionnaire include both accounting and finance academics; thus, the comparison with results from Iqbal *et al.* (2006) is not completely unreasonable.

5 While Becker & Watts (2001) transform the 0–4 responses to the mid-points in the ranges, Iqbal *et al.* (2006) report the mean for each. The results of the present study will be reported in line with the Iqbal *et al.* study for the purposes of comparison.

6 We acknowledge that a potential limitation of our survey is that it is informed by prior research which was undertaken in different time periods and across different locations. Therefore, any differences in our results from previous findings may be attributable to the contextual location of the research. Further, the responses in the various surveys may be time-period specific, though such a limitation applies to all research which adopts a longitudinal perspective. Finally, it is worth noting that differences in the results may be due to the samples of academics surveyed. Nevertheless, the findings presented in the current chapter are based on responses from relatively experienced academics currently using teaching resources within accounting education. As such, we believe that they are worthy of consideration.

7 A copy of the survey is available on request to any of the authors.

8 While, ideally, it would have been preferable to collect data in relation to the range of teaching and assessment methods which accounting and finance academics employ in different subject areas and at different levels, this would have required respondents to complete the survey multiple times for each of the courses on which they teach. Such an approach was considered impractical. Moreover, the aim of the survey was to establish, more broadly, the teaching and assessment methods used generally by accounting and finance academics. As noted previously, such an overview is lacking in the extant accounting education literature.

9 We are, therefore, analysing responses from a non-randomly drawn sample of U.K.-based academics and comparing answers to replies from another survey of non-randomly drawn samples at different dates. However, it is worth pointing out that respondents in the current survey are not very different in response rate or profile terms from those who replied to an on-line survey of U.K.-based academics in Lowe & Locke (2005). This increases our confidence in the generalisability of our findings – at least within the U.K.

10 As the survey was undertaken in the U.K. and Ireland, traditional academic titles from these two countries were used. The equivalent titles in other jurisdictions are as follows: Lecturer = Assistant Professor; Senior Lecturer = Associate Professor; Reader/Professor = Full Professor.

11 While we do not discuss here the relative merits or demerits of each teaching resource, it is worth noting that Boritz & Stoner (Chapter 16 – this volume) allude to the potential limitations of PowerPoint as a teaching resource (see also Rankin & Hoass, 2001).

12 It was not possible to split the sample on the basis of the other statements in Panel A of Table 19.7 because most of the respondents gave them a rating of either 3 (neutral), 4 (agree), or 5 (strongly agree).

References

Adler, R., Whiting, R.H., & Wynn-Williams, K. (2004) Student-led and teacher-led case presentations: empirical evidence about learning styles in an accounting course, *Accounting Education: an international journal*, 13(2), 213–229.

Apostolou, B., Hassell, J.M., Rebele, J.F. & Watson, S.F. (2011) Accounting education literature review (2006–2009), *Journal of Accounting Education*, 28(2), 145–197.

Apostolou, B., Watson, S.F., Hassell, J.M., & Webber, S.A. (2001) Accounting education literature review (1997–1999), *Journal of Accounting Education*, 19(1), 1–61.

Becker, W.E. (1997) Teaching economics to undergraduates, *Journal of Economic Literature*, 35(September), 1347–1373.

Becker, W.E. & Watts, M. (1996) Chalk and talk: a national survey of teaching undergraduate economics, *American Economic Review*, 86(May), 448–454.

Becker, W.E. & Watts, M. (2001a) Teaching economics at the start of the 21st century: still chalk and talk, *American Economic Review*, 91(May), 446–451.

Becker, W.E. & Watts, M. (2001b) Teaching methods in U.S. undergraduate economics courses, *Journal of Economic Education*, 32(Summer), 269–279.

Becker, W.E. & Watts, M. (2004) Good-bye old, hello new in teaching economics, *Australasian Journal of Economics Education*, 1(1), 5–17.

Benzing, C. & Christ, P. (1997) A survey of teaching methods among economics faculty, *Journal of Economic Education*, 28(Fall), 350–368.

Biggs, J. (2003) *Teaching for Quality Learning at University*, Buckingham: Society for Research into Higher Education and Open University Press.

Biggs, J., Kember, D., & Leung, D. (2001) The revised two-factor Study Process Questionnaire: R-SPQ-2F, *British Journal of Educational Psychology*, 71 (2), 133–149.

Boyce, G., Greer, S., Blair, B., & Davids, C. (2012) Expanding the horizons of accounting education: incorporating social and critical perspectives, *Accounting Education: an international journal*, 21(1), 47–74.

Brasel, K. & Hentz, B. (2006) Increasing accessibility to academic publications in accounting education: database for research and teaching, *Issues in Accounting Education*, 21(4), 411–416.

Brown, R.B. & Guilding, C. (1993) A survey of teaching methods employed in university business school accounting courses, *Accounting Education: an international journal*, 2(3), 211–218.

Coulson, A. & Thomson, I. (2006) Accounting and sustainability, encouraging a dialogical approach; integrating learning activities, delivery mechanisms and assessment strategies, *Accounting Education: an international journal*, 15(3), 261–273.

Davidson, R.A. (2005) Analysis of the complexity of writing used in accounting textbooks over the past 100 years, *Accounting Education: an international journal*, 14(1), 53–74.

Dunkin, M.J. (2002) Novice and award-winning teachers' concepts and beliefs about teaching in higher education, in Hativa, N. & Goodyear, P. (eds) *Teacher Thinking, Beliefs and Knowledge in Higher Education*, Dordrecht: Kluwer, pp. 41–57.

Entwistle, N.J. (2000) Approaches to studying and levels of understanding, in Smart J. (ed.) *Higher Education: Handbook of Theory and Research*, 15, New York: Agathon Press, pp. 156–218.

Eskola, A. (2011) Good learning in accounting: phenomenographic study on experiences of Finnish higher education students, dissertation, the School of Business and Economics of the University of Jyväskylä, Finland.

Ferguson, J., Collison, D.J., Power, D.M., & Stevenson, L.A. (2005) What are recommended accounting textbooks teaching students about corporate stakeholders? *British Accounting Review*, 37(1), 23–46.

Ferguson, J., Collison, D.J., Power, D.M., & Stevenson, L.A. (2006) Accounting textbooks: exploring a cultural and political artifact, *Accounting Education: an international journal*, 15(2), 162–245.

Ferguson, J., Collison, D.J., Power, D.M., & Stevenson, L.A. (2007) Exploring accounting educators' perceptions of the emphasis given to different stakeholders in introductory textbooks, *Accounting Forum*, 31(2), 113–216.

Ferguson, J., Collison, D.J., Power, D.M., & Stevenson, L.A. (2008) *An Analysis of the Role of the Textbook in the Construction of Accounting Knowledge*, Edinburgh: ICAS.

Ferguson, J., Collison, D.J., Power, D.M., & Stevenson, L.A. (2011) Accounting education, socialization and the ethics of business, *Business Ethics: A European Review*, 20(1), 12–21.

Fox, D. (1983) Personal theories of teaching, *Studies in Higher Education*, 8(2), 151–163.

Freire, P. (1996) *Pedagogy of the Oppressed*, London: Pelican.

Gow, L. & Kember, D. (1993) Conceptions of teaching and their relationship to student learning, *British Journal of Educational Psychology*, 63(1), 20–33.

Hassall, T., Lewis, S., & Broadbent, J.M. (1998) The use and potential abuse of case studies in accounting education. *Accounting Education: an international journal*, 7(supplement), 37–47.

Hassall, T. & Milne, M.J. (2004) Using case studies in accounting education, *Accounting Education: an international journal*, 13(2), 135–138.

Healy, M. & McCutcheon, M. (2010) Teaching with case studies: an empirical investigation of accounting lecturers' experience, *Accounting Education: an international journal*, 19(6), 555–567.

Helliar, C., Monk, E.A., & Hannah, G. (2010) *British Accounting Review Research Register (2010)*, London: Academic Press for the British Accounting Association in association with the Institute of Chartered Accountants in England and Wales.

Iqbal, A., Farooqi, N., & Saunders, K. (2006) Teaching methods and assessment techniques used for the introductory level undergraduate finance course in British and Irish universities, *Journal of Economics and Finance Education*, 5(1), 47–61.

James, S. (2000) Teaching tax principles and policy: comparing the single textbook and wider reading approaches, *Accounting Education: an international journal*, 9(3), 281–289.

Kell, C. & Jones, L. (2007) Mapping placement educators' conceptions of teaching, *Physiotherapy*, 93, 273–282.

Kember, D. (1997) A reconceptualisation of the research into university academics' conceptions of teaching, *Learning and Instruction*, 7, 255–275.

Leveson, L. (2004) Encouraging better learning through better teaching: a study of approaches to teaching in accounting, *Accounting Education: an international journal*, 13(4), 529–548.

Lipe, M.G. (2006) Using cases published in *Issues in Accounting Education*: categories and topics at a glance, *Issues in Accounting Education*, 21(4), 417–430.

Lister, L., Berglund, A., Box, I., Cope, C., Pears, A., Avram, C., *et al.* (2007) Differing ways that computing academics understand teaching, *Proceedings of Ninth Australasian Computing Education Conference*, 66, 97–106.

Lowe, A. & Locke, J. (2005) Perceptions of journal quality and research paradigm: results of a web-based survey of British accounting academics, *Accounting, Organizations and Society*, 30(1), 81–98.

Magolda, B.M. & Terenzini, P. T. (1999) Learning and teaching in the 21st century: trends and implications for practice. Available at: http://www.acpa.nche.edu/srsch/magolda_terenzini.html.

Manninen, A. (1997) Critical reading in accounting, *Accounting Education: an international journal*, 6(4), 281–294.

Markley, C.T., Miller, H., Kneeshaw, T., & Herbert, B.E. (2009) The relationship between instructors' conceptions of geoscience learning and classroom practice at a research university, *Journal of Geoscience Education*, 54(4), 264–274.

Norton, L., Aiyegbayo, O., Harrington, K., Elander, J., & Reddy, P. (2010) New lecturers' beliefs about learning, teaching and assessment in higher education: the role of the PGCLTHE programme, *Innovations in Education and Teaching International*, 47(4), 345–356.

Norton, L., Richardson, J.T.E., Hartley, J., Newstead, S., & Mayes, J. (2005) Teachers' beliefs and intentions concerning teaching in higher education, *Higher Education*, 50, 537–571.

Phillips, B.J. & Phillips, F. (2007) Sink or skim: textbook reading behaviors of introductory accounting students, *Issues in Accounting Education*, 22(1), 21–45.

Postareff, L. (2007) Teaching in higher education: from content-focussed to learning-focussed approaches to teaching, Research Report 214, University of Helsinki, Department of Education.

Rankin, E.L. & Hoaas, D.J. (2001) Teaching note: does the use of computer-generated slide presentations in the classroom affect student performance and interest?, *Eastern Economic Journal*, 27(3), 355–366.

Richardson, J.T.E. (2005) Students' approaches to learning and teachers' approaches to teaching in higher education, *Educational Psychology*, 25(6), 673–680.

Seifried, J. (2012) Teachers' pedagogical beliefs at commercial schools: an empirical study in Germany, *Accounting Education: an international journal*, 21(5), 489–514.

Thomson, I. & Bebbington, J. (2004) It doesn't matter what you teach? *Critical Perspectives on Accounting*, 15(4), 609–628.

Thomson, I. & Bebbington, J. (2005) Social and environmental reporting in the UK: a pedagogic evaluation, *Critical Perspectives on Accounting*, 16(5), 507–533.

Van Driel, J.H., Verloop, N., Van Werven, H.I., & Dekkers, H. (1997) Teachers' craft knowledge and curriculum innovation in higher engineering education, *Higher Education*, 34, 105–122.

Watson, S.F., Apostolou, B., Hassell, J.M., & Webber, S.A. (2003) Accounting education literature review (2000–2002), *Journal of Accounting Education*, 21, 267–325.

Watson, S.F., Apostolou, B., Hassell, J.M., & Webber, S.A. (2007) Accounting education literature review (2003–2005), *Journal of Accounting Education*, 25, 1–58.

Watts, M. & Becker, W.E. (2008) A little more than chalk and talk: results from a third national survey of teaching methods in undergraduate economics courses, *The Journal of Economic Education*, 39(3).

Watts, M. & Schaur, G. (2011) Teaching and assessment methods in undergraduate economics: a fourth national quinquennial survey, *The Journal of Economic Education*, 42(3), 294–309.

Weil, S., Oyelere, P., Yeoh, J., & Firer, C. (2001) A study of student perceptions of the usefulness of case studies for the development of finance and accounting-related skills and knowledge, *Accounting Education: an international journal*, 10(2), 123–146.

Weinstein, G.P. (2005) A tool for accessing accounting cases, *Journal of Accounting Education*, 23(3), 204–214.

Wilson, R.M.S. (2002) Accounting education research: a retrospective over ten years with some pointers to the future, *Accounting Education: an international journal*, 11(4), 295–310.

About the authors

Lorna A. Stevenson is Professor in Accounting at the University of St Andrews, Scotland, U.K. (lorna.stevenson@st-andrews.ac.uk). Her research interests include the implications for business education of the social, environmental, and economic consequences of accounting, and she has published on these themes with, *inter alia*, John Ferguson and David Power.

John Ferguson is Reader in Accounting at the University of Strathclyde, Scotland, U.K. (john.ferguson@strath.ac.uk). He has published research in the areas of accounting education, corporate governance and ethics, and is on the editorial boards of a number of journals including *Issues in Accounting Education*.

David M. Power is Professor of Business Finance in the School of Business at the University of Dundee, Scotland, U.K. (d.m.power@dundee.ac.uk). His research interests are in the areas of accounting education, emerging markets, and behavioural finance. He is on the editorial board of several journals and the author of numerous published articles.

Section E

Assessment considerations

Preface

Sue Pickard Ravenscroft

IOWA STATE UNIVERSITY, U.S.A.

'What you measure is what you get' is a business cliché. In this section of the RCAE the authors address measurement in higher education inputs and outcomes and find the relationship is not so clear or direct.

In Chapter 20, Koh summarizes research on the characteristics which students bring as they embark upon their accounting courses: those characteristics range from the fixed (e.g. eye colour) to those which are more easily changed (e.g. previous accounting courses taken). Perhaps this diversity among the 'inputs' gives rise to the lack of uniform results regarding their impact on learning. Koh suggests that much of the research in the field of student assessment is atheoretical but, given the diversity of students and their backgrounds, as well as the variety of pedagogies and curricula on offer, a broad theory of specific 'inputs' leading to predictable outcomes seems unlikely.

Kidwell & Lowensohn (Chapter 21) summarize findings on assessing learning, and observe that researchers have not coalesced around a single theory. In part, this is because what is susceptible to assessment does not always align with the learning objectives which educators find useful as they design and structure their coursework.

In the final chapter of Section E (Chapter 22), Calderon addresses the more global assessment of accounting programmes within a framework of an administrative control system, based on accountability and the interest of stakeholders. Calderon echoes Kidwell & Lowensohn in noting the tension between administrative controls and the more embedded, ongoing assessment which responsible educators carry out as they routinely try to improve students' learning.

Despite the oft-repeated cliché about measurement, in higher education we are not sure of how to best measure inputs, process, or even outputs. Much interesting and challenging work remains to be done.

20

Determinants of students' performance in accounting programmes

Hian Chye Koh

SIM UNIVERSITY, SINGAPORE

CONTENTS

Abstract

The increasing demand for accounting education and the need to use university resources optimally have led to an increasing interest in the determinants of students' performance in accounting programmes (Byrne & Flood, 2008). Understanding these determinants also has implications for teaching performance and modifications in teaching styles (Guney, 2009). In addition, information on the determinants of academic success is useful to potential students in deciding their tertiary education and career choices (Tickell & Smyrnios, 2005). Consistent with the call for more research into the determinants of students' performance in accounting programmes (Bonaci *et al.*, 2010), this chapter provides a critical review of the literature and suggests possible directions for future research in the area.

Keywords

academic performance, accounting education, accounting performance, accounting programmes, determinants of academic success

20.1 Introduction

The main aims of this chapter are:

- to summarise prior studies on the determinants of students' performance in accounting programmes;
- to review the sample data analysed and data analyses performed;
- to explore the potential reasons for the different findings;
- to highlight limitations in the literature; and
- to suggest possible directions for future research.

This chapter deals with academic accounting programmes. (Professional accounting education and training are discussed by Evans in Chapter 28 and by Paisey & Paisey in Chapter 30 – both in this volume.)

In evaluating students' performance, the primary focus is on assessments in academic programmes, whether they be at a programme level (e.g. Gammie *et al.* 2003), year level (e.g. Byrne & Flood, 2008), or course level (e.g. Fogarty & Goldwater, 2010). However, the findings and conclusions are expected to be relevant to the professional context as well. Determinants that drive performance in academic assessments (such as attitudes, skills, motivation, effort, and learning approach) are also likely to drive performance in assessments conducted by professional bodies (e.g. professional qualifying examinations).

This chapter is organised as follows. The literature review in Section 20.2 summarises prior studies in the area, classified into major categories of determinants. The variables investigated, the accounting courses examined, and the findings reported are included in this section. Section 20.3, the research methodology/methods section, examines the sample data analysed and data analyses performed in prior studies. The former looks at the data sources and variables, while the latter investigates dimensions such as qualitative versus quantitative, univariate/bivariate versus multivariate, and descriptive versus statistical.

Section 20.4 explores the potential reasons for the different findings in the literature. In particular, it discusses the lack of a theoretical framework as well as variations across prior studies and their implications for the findings. Finally, Section 20.5 highlights the limitations of prior studies and suggests directions for future research.

The last two decades have seen an increasing interest in the determinants of students' performance in accounting programmes. One important reason for this is the increasing demand for accounting education (Tan & Laswad, 2008). With limited university resources, their optimal use makes it necessary that accounting programmes admit only students with a reasonable chance of academic success (Byrne & Flood, 2008). This, in turn, requires universities to set appropriate selection criteria and admission qualifications as well as facilitate the learning of accounting students when they are enrolled. Understanding the determinants of students' performance in accounting programmes can help universities do this (Kirk & Spector, 2006).

Academic failure can have serious consequences, including financial and emotional issues for students, and resource and performance implications for higher education institutions (HEIs) (Gracia & Jenkins, 2002). Hence, the reasons behind it should be understood so that appropriate remedial actions can be implemented (Al-Twaijry, 2010). Kealey et al. (2005) have suggested that students' failure may be due to insufficient preparation, and Kirk & Spector (2006) have urged that academic staff and advisors facilitate students' learning and achievement. In this respect, understanding the determinants of accounting academic performance in accounting can have implications for teaching performance and teaching styles (Guney, 2009), including managing classroom diversity, addressing differing student needs, identifying students at risk, ensuring successful disciplinary and institutional outcomes, and facilitating good teaching and quality learning (Ramburuth & Mladenovic, 2004).

Information on the determinants of academic success can also help potential students in their tertiary education and career choices. (See Jackling, Chapter 10 – this volume.) It can further help students prepare themselves better to succeed in accounting programmes (Tickell & Smyrnios, 2005). In addition, academic success in universities can contribute to professional success when the accounting graduates join the profession and industry. Hence, firms do attach importance to academic performance in their selection process (Gammie et al., 2003). Fogarty & Goldwater (2010) have suggested that accounting educators should be concerned with students' performance, as this influences the calibre of the next generation of accounting professionals.

Finally, there is the realisation that accounting education research can impact on teaching and practice (Byrne & Flood, 2008). The more that is known about what can affect accounting students' performance or predict academic success, the better accounting educators and university policy-makers can make informed decisions on curriculum, selection criteria, and admission qualifications.

Given the above, the call for more research into the determinants of students' performance in accounting programmes has remained strong (Bonaci et al., 2010). This chapter is in line with this call.

20.2 Literature review

There exists a substantial body of literature on the determinants of academic performance in accounting. This section focusses on recent research (done since 2000), with a few exceptions to provide a more comprehensive review. The existing literature comprises mainly studies involving lower-level accounting courses and undergraduate degree programmes. Some notable exceptions include Schleifer & Dull (2009), Rotenstein et al. (2009), and Bonaci et al. (2010).

The determinants can be classified into the following major categories:

- demographic characteristics;
- educational experience and background;

- attitudes and skills;
- course and class features; and
- other factors.

We will now look at each in turn.

20.2.1 Demographic characteristics

The most common demographic characteristics studied as potential determinants of academic accounting performance include academic aptitude (i.e. prior academic performance or achievement), age, and gender. To a much lesser extent, disability has also been examined. Ethnicity is discussed under international student status (see under 'Other factors' below) as the focus is usually on international students rather than race *per se*.

20.2.1.1 Academic aptitude (or prior academic performance/achievement)

Academic aptitude is the most consistent determinant of accounting academic performance found to date, and the most frequently examined. Prior academic performance or achievement may indicate a student's commitment, diligence, and intelligence (Guney, 2009). This determinant is often measured by a student's grade point average (GPA).

Kirk & Spector (2006), in a study undertaken in the U.S.A., have reported that a student's GPA is significantly related to success in *Cost Accounting*, after controlling for different grading schemes across teachers. Similarly, Al-Twaijry (2010) found that students in a Saudi Arabian university who performed better in pre-university do significantly better in their *Managerial Accounting* course as well as in their first term at university. In addition, students' overall GPA at university is significantly correlated with their performance in *Managerial Accounting, Cost Accounting,* and *Advanced Managerial Accounting.*

Byrne & Flood (2008) examined academic performance in the first year of an accounting programme at an Irish university, and concluded that it is significantly and positively related to prior academic achievement. The same finding is also found for performance in *Financial Accounting* and *Management Accounting.* (See also Byrne & Willis, Chapter 7 – this volume.)

20.2.1.2 Age

Among other things, age may reflect a student's maturity as well as motivation. Pokorny & Pokorny (2005) have suggested that mature students in England have greater exposure to life and work experience and are more likely to want to understand and hence adopt a 'deeper' approach to learning. Maturity, motivation, life/work exposure, and deep learning are expected to positively influence academic performance. To date, however, the significance of age as a determinant of accounting academic performance is not conclusive.

While Koh & Koh (1999) and Tickell & Smyrnios (2005) have found that younger accounting students perform better than older accounting students in Singapore and Australia, respectively, Lane & Porch (2002) and Guney (2009) have found that older students at a Welsh and an English university respectively, perform better. On the other hand, age is not a significant determinant of academic performance in accounting in several studies, including Duff (2004) in Scotland, Kirk & Spector (2006) in the U.S.A., Tan & Laswad (2008) in New Zealand, and Keller *et al.* (2009) in the U.S.A. In examining the honours classification of accounting and finance graduates at a university in Scotland, Gammie *et al.* (2003) found age to be insignificant.

20.2.1.3 Gender

With the increasing participation rate of females in tertiary education and in the workplace, gender issues have taken greater prominence in recent decades. While gender may not have a direct impact on academic performance in accounting, it may be associated with factors that may affect academic performance – such as motivation, cognitive abilities, and learning strategies (see Sizoo et al., 2003, de Lange & Mavondo, 2004, and Elias, 2005, who conducted their studies in the U.S.A., Australia, and the U.S.A. respectively).

As in the case of age, findings on the significance of gender as a determinant of academic performance in accounting have been mixed. For example, while Koh & Koh (1999) and Huh et al. (2009) (the latter in the U.S.A.) found that male accounting students outperform their female counterparts, Schleifer & Dull (2009) (in the U.S.A.) and Mustata et al. (2010) (in Romania) reported the converse.

In several studies, gender is found to be insignificant: Crawford et al. (2003); Duff (2004); Kealey et al. (2005); Potter & Johnston (2006); Byrne & Flood (2008); and Keller et al. (2009). Fogarty & Goldwater (2010) found that females at a university in the U.S.A. where they conducted their study do exert a greater amount of effort, though this does not translate into better grades.

20.2.1.4 Disability

For students with disability (e.g. dyslexia), additional effort and time may be necessary in order to be able to learn. Hence, disadvantaged students may not perform as well as other students, keeping all things constant. This is consistent with the finding of Wooten (1998) in the U.S.A., but not with that of Guney (2009).

20.2.2 Educational experience and background

Educational experience and background look at students' performance in other courses, type of pre-university educational institutions, accounting background, mathematics background, English background, university workload, and whether the students are accounting majors.

20.2.2.1 Performance in other courses

The intellectual abilities and skills required for students to do well in accounting courses may also be relevant to other non-accounting (but especially accounting-related) courses. Hence, the academic performance in other courses may be associated with that in accounting courses.

According to Kirk & Spector (2006), performance in *Managerial Accounting Principles* and performance in *Statistics* are significantly related to success in *Cost Accounting*, after controlling for different grading schemes across teachers. They have also reported that students do better in *Cost Accounting* if they complete *Intermediate Accounting* first. Al-Twaijry (2010) found that performance in *Financial Accounting* is significantly and positively related to performance in *Managerial Accounting* and *Advanced Managerial Accounting*. Performance in *Managerial Accounting* is also significantly associated with performance in *Cost Accounting* and *Advanced Managerial Accounting*. Similarly, Potter & Johnston (2006) have reported that performance in a prerequisite accounting course is associated with the performance of a subsequent *Cost Management* course at an Australian university.

20.2.2.2 Type of pre-university educational institutions

Apparently, different types of pre-university education institutions prepare students differently for accounting at university. Bonaci et al. (2010) have suggested that students from economic high schools in Romania perform better in *Financial Accounting* at a university level. Also, Tickell & Smyrnios (2005) have found that students from government secondary schools (versus private secondary schools) perform better in an accounting programme. However, Al-Twaijry (2010) has reported that whether or not students come from scientific or other pre-university educational institutions has no impact on university academic performance. Likewise, Gammie *et al.* (2003) report that the type of secondary school is not a significant factor in the honours classification of accounting and finance graduates.

20.2.2.3 Prior accounting education/knowledge

It seems logical that prior accounting education can benefit students when they study accounting at universities since these students would already have a foundation (see also Byrne & Willis, Chapter 7 – this volume). According to Archer *et al.* (1999), prior accounting education in Australia provides the content knowledge that students need in order to develop the necessary cognitive and self-regulatory strategies for learning, and know when and how to deploy them. However, the benefits actually realised depend on the extent of similarity between the prior accounting education/knowledge and the university accounting courses (Tan & Laswad, 2008).

Along these lines, Al-Twaijry (2010) has reported better performance in *Advanced Managerial Accounting* for students who have a pre-university accounting background. Tickell & Smyrnios (2005) reported that better performance in an earlier year of an accounting programme is significantly associated with better performance in a later year of an accounting programme. Guney (2009), however, found no significant relationship between prior accounting education and performance in accounting courses at a British university.

20.2.2.4 Mathematics background

It has been argued that, given the numerate nature of accounting, students with mathematics background should perform better in accounting programmes/courses than those without. Consistent with this, Al-Twaijry (2010) found that a better mathematics background is significantly associated with better performance in *Managerial Accounting* (but not in *Cost Accounting* or *Advanced Managerial Accounting*). Kealey *et al.* (2005) found the same for *Principles of Accounting* and Guney (2009) for several accounting courses.

This finding, however, is not consistent with that of Kirk & Spector (2006), who have reported that performance in a mathematics course is not associated with performance in *Managerial Accounting*. (Numeracy is discussed as one aspect of financial literacy by Wilson *et al.* in Chapter 3 – this volume.)

20.2.2.5 English background

Generally, a strong language background facilitates university studies, whether in accounting or otherwise. This is especially so for international students who study in English-speaking countries but whose native language is not English. Such international students are likely to have more difficulties in learning and communication. Kealey *et al.* (2005), in a study undertaken in the U.S.A., have found a significant correlation between the English sub-score in ACT (American College Testing) with performance in *Principles of Accounting*.

20.2.2.6 University workload

Al-Twaijry (2010) has found that students with a heavier university workload have performed better in *Managerial Accounting* (as well as university GPA), which seems counter-intuitive since a heavier university workload implies less time to study. However, it can also be argued that better students are the ones who are confident in taking more courses.

20.2.2.7 Accounting major

The choice of an undergraduate major may depend on career perspectives, expectation of job opportunities and earnings, stability of the career, and personal interest and skills set (Mo & Waples, 2011). The selection of an accounting major, therefore, is expected to reflect the motivation to do well in accounting programmes/courses (Guney, 2009). However, some authors (e.g. Chen *et al.*, 2008, in the U.S.A.) have suggested a reverse sequence in that performance in *Introductory Accounting* courses is an important factor influencing students' major selection. (See Laswad & Tan, Chapter 9 – this volume.)

Al-Twaijry (2010) found that students who are accounting majors outperform those who are non-accounting majors in accounting courses (such as *Managerial Accounting* and *Cost Accounting*) as well as in non-accounting courses. This finding is consistent with that of Kealey *et al.* (2005), Bonaci *et al.* (2010) in Romania, and Mo & Waples (2011) in the U.S.A., all of whom looked at performance in one or more accounting courses.

Tickell & Smyrnios (2005) discovered that students who major in accounting because of their teachers' advice in their secondary schools perform less well in their university accounting programme. They suggest that perhaps extrinsic motivation is not as powerful as intrinsic motivation as a determinant of academic performance in accounting. Also, students who decide to major in accounting while in secondary school do better than their counterparts who make the decision later. (More discussion on the choice of accounting as a discipline and as a career can be found in Laswad & Tan, Chapter 9 and Jackling, Chapter 10, respectively – both in this volume.)

20.2.3 Attitudes and skills

The attitudes and skills of students that have been examined with respect to their association with academic performance in accounting programmes include critical thinking skills, motives and motivation, expectations/preparedness for tertiary education, students' approaches to learning, and other perceptions.

20.2.3.1 Critical thinking skills

There is general agreement that critical thinking skills are important to the success of professional accountants. To the extent that critical thinking skills are part of tertiary education (whether or not specific to accounting), such skills are expected to be associated with the academic success of accounting students. It has also been suggested that accounting coursework requires students to learn and demonstrate critical thinking skills (Kealey *et al.*, 2005). In fact, critical thinking has been identified as being one of the objectives of accounting education (AECC, 1990). (See also Cunningham, Chapter 18 – this volume.)

Kealey *et al.* (2005) found that, even after controlling for academic aptitude, critical thinking skills contribute significantly to explaining cross-sectional variations in students' performance in an *Accounting Principles* course. The significant finding remains the same even after controlling for teacher differences. In a more elaborate study undertaken in the U.S.A., Coate *et al.* (2005) discovered that higher-level critical thinking is most positively and significantly associated with the performance of decision-based problems in a *Managerial Principles* course, and lower level critical thinking with that of procedurally-based problems.

20.2.3.2 Motives and motivation

It can be argued that motivation drives performance – that better motivated students perform better. According to Jonassen & Grabowski (1993), motivated students are more likely to acquire and use effective learning strategies.

Davidson (2002) found that Canadian students who are more motivated (by an accounting career) perform better in an *Introductory Financial Accounting* course. Similarly, Bonaci *et al.* (2010) report that students who perceive accounting to be useful, as well as those who intend to pursue an accounting career, perform better in *Financial Accounting*. In another study, Byrne & Flood (2008) found that students who believe that an accounting degree will enable them to get a good job perform significantly better in *Financial Accounting*, while those who believe that tertiary education will develop their intellectual abilities perform significantly better in *Management Accounting*. Even for non-accounting students, Guney (2009) states that those who believe that accounting can help them in their future career perform better in accounting courses than do their counterparts.

20.2.3.3 Expectations/preparedness for tertiary education

Similar to motives and motivation, it can be argued that students who have higher expectations and who are better prepared for tertiary education perform academically better. Byrne & Flood (2008) provide some evidence of this. They found that students who are confident of their skills and abilities perform significantly better in the first year of their accounting programme as well as in *Financial Accounting* and *Management Accounting*. Surprisingly, those who are willing to ask teachers for help perform significantly less well in *Financial Accounting*. It can perhaps be argued that it is the weaker students who have a greater need to ask. Conversely, the U.K.'s National Audit Office (NAO) has identified the lack of preparedness for higher education as being one of the main reasons for student drop-out (NAO, 2002).

20.2.3.4 Students' approach to learning

According to Svensson (1977), students' approach to learning (SAL) affects both the knowledge acquired and how the knowledge can be used. A *surface approach* is associated with memorising facts that are contained in structures, while a *deep approach* results in knowledge that can be used in other contexts. Consequently, there is a relationship between students' approach to learning and both text comprehension and examination performance. (See Lucas & Mladenovic, Chapter 6, and Duff, Chapter 8 – both in this volume.)

Accordingly, Davidson (2002) found that a deep approach to learning is associated with better grades received on complex accounting examination questions. A similar finding was reported by Duff (2004), who examined first-year academic performance and progression at a Scottish university. Ramburuth & Mladenovic (2004), on the other hand, have found no significant relationship between a deep approach and academic performance but a significant negative correlation between a surface approach and lower academic performance in two *Introductory Accounting* courses at an Australian university. They also found that students with more complex learning skills do better.

20.2.3.5 Other perceptions

Guney (2009) has argued that, in investigating the determinants of academic performance in accounting, the inclusion of exogenous factors is essential to gain a complete picture. For example, it is important to know the students' perceptions with respect to the quality of teaching, the commitment of their academic staff, the teaching environment, etc. In his study, Guney applied factor analysis to reduce 13 perception statements to three factors, namely 'lecturers and assessment', 'teaching material', and 'teaching environment'. He found that students with favourable perceptions of 'lecturers and assessment' and 'teaching material' outperform those with less favourable perceptions. In addition, Mustata *et al.* (2010) report that Romanian students with positive perceptions of computers and accounting perform better in a *Financial Accounting* course than those who do not.

20.2.4 Course and class features

It can be expected that certain course and class features are more conducive to learning, and hence are positively associated with students' performance. These features include course or class format (some incorporating interactive online learning features), course/class attendance, and class size.

20.2.4.1 Course/class format

Traditionally, the teaching and learning of accounting take place in the physical classroom (e.g. lectures, tutorials, and seminars). The advent of affordable and accessible computers and mobile devices, coupled with the development and availability of learning management systems, e-learning technology, and publishers' online materials, have made teaching and learning possible in cyberspace (i.e. in an online or web-based environment). Also, interactive online features are becoming an important supplementary component of traditional teaching and learning. (See Boritz & Stoner, Chapter 16 – this volume.)

Besides being totally online, courses can also be blended (i.e. they have a mixture of face-to-face classes and online learning). Potter & Johnston (2006) have suggested that interactive online features can contribute to students' learning, and hence to academic performance. Among other things, online learning empowers students to take greater control of their own learning outside the classroom. It also encourages self-directed learning and a deep approach to learning which increases conceptual understanding and the likelihood of enhanced learning outcomes. Further, interactive online features are frequently accompanied by the provision of timely and detailed feedback, which aids learning.

In the study conducted by Keller *et al.* (2009) in the U.S.A., no significant association between course/class format and academic performance in a *Principles of Managerial Accounting* course is found, after controlling for other factors. Instead, control factors such as performance in the Scholastic Aptitude Test (SAT) and a prerequisite accounting course (i.e. educational background) are found to be significantly associated with academic performance in *Managerial Accounting*.

In contrast, Potter & Johnston (2006), who examined the use of an interactive online learning system and the performance of students in a second-year undergraduate accounting course, found a positive association of such use and students' examination and internal assessment performance.

20.2.4.2 Course/class attendance

It can be expected that students with better course/class attendance perform better than those with poorer attendance. Among other things, attendance may be a surrogate for greater seriousness and interest in study or in accounting, as well as greater motivation and effort. Also, students benefit from attending classes as they can receive direct knowledge transfer from their teachers, learn from peers and class activities, and clarify their doubts in class. Gracia & Jenkins (2002), Crawford *et al.* (2003), Guney (2009) and Mustata *et al.* (2010) reported that better course/class attendance is associated with better academic performance.

20.2.4.3 Class size

Logically, a smaller class size facilitates learning as it enables the class to have more opportunities for interaction (between the teacher and students, as well as among students). A smaller class size also facilitates class activities and participation. Hence, a smaller class size is expected to lead to better academic performance. This is consistent with the univariate results from Guney (2009).

20.2.5 Other factors

Other factors have been investigated as potential determinants of academic performance in accounting programmes. These include transfer status; international student status; procrastination; effort/time spent on study; personal problems; accounting (and other) work experience; and others.

20.2.5.1 Transfer status

In some universities, transfer students (i.e. those who have moved from other education institutions to the universities) comprise a significant proportion of their student enrolments. Tickell & Smyrnios (2005) say that students who are transferred from technical institutions do not perform as well as other students. However, Keller *et al.* (2009) report no significant difference between transfer and non-transfer students in the performance on a *Principles of Managerial Accounting* course.

20.2.5.2 International student status

Recent years have seen a significant increase in international students in accounting programmes (Tan & Laswad, 2008). Several reasons why these students may not perform as well as their local counterparts have been suggested, including:

- a poor command of the language of instruction (primarily English);
- 'cultural shock' in terms of a very different education system and learning styles/requirements in the host country as compared to those of the home country;
- a need to adjust to the local environment and culture;
- the lack of a support social network; and
- attachment to family and friends in the home country (Hartnett *et al.*, 2004).

Ramburuth & Mladenovic (2004) also found international students to be at the lower end of the learning complexity scale. Consistent with the above, Guney (2009) claims that local students perform better than their international counterparts, after controlling for previous academic performance and perceptions.

Tickell & Smyrnios (2005) investigated the country of birth of the accounting students at an Australian university as well as that of their parents. They found that students whose mothers are born locally outperform other students. Further, in New Zealand, Tan & Laswad (2008) found that students in an *Introductory Accounting* course whose first language is English outperform those whose first language is not.

20.2.5.3 Procrastination

Generally, it can be expected that procrastination can adversely affect academic performance because of inadequate effort due to insufficient time, unexpected delays resulting in the inability to get the work done, the stress of an impending deadline, and the greater risk of leaving tasks to the last minute. Rotenstein *et al.* (2009) state that procrastination has a significant negative effect on academic performance, after controlling for the quality of graduate students in the U.S.A.

20.2.5.4 Effort/time spent on study

It can be expected that greater effort or more time spent on study translates into better grades; it also reflects a student's motivation and interest. This is supported by Bonaci *et al.* (2010) for *Financial Accounting* performance. Contrary to expectations, however, Guney (2009) claims that study effort is negatively related to performance. He suggests that less academically inclined students may need to study more. Also, Fogarty & Goldwater (2010) discovered that a greater effort does not necessarily translate to better grades, at least for the female students enrolled in the *Management Accounting* course in their study.

From a slightly different perspective, Crawford *et al.* (2003) found in a study in the U.S.A. that students who expected a better grade do in fact achieve a better grade. However, this expectation may arise from a combination of factors, including the effort/time spent on study, motivation to do well, and interest in the accounting courses.

20.2.5.5 Personal problems

Academic performance may be affected not only by students' intellectual ability, but also by other non-intellectual factors. In particular, personal problems may affect academic success, as stated by Guney (2009). In a qualitative study in Mexico, Sosa *et al.* (2010) report that students who perform less well are also affected by economic problems (e.g. unemployment and work–study conflicts), emotional problems (e.g. divorce and stress), family problems (e.g. lack of communication with relatives and domestic violence), and health problems (e.g. depression and illness).

20.2.5.6 Accounting (and other) work experience

Similar to prior accounting education/knowledge, prior accounting work experience is expected to benefit students studying accounting as it enhances students' understanding of accounting and helps them relate academic accounting to professional practice. The results of Bonaci *et al.* (2010) support this, but not the results of Guney (2009). In addition, Koh & Koh (1999) found work experience (not necessarily accounting work experience) to be associated with better academic performance in an accounting programme.

Some studies have also examined part-time work (during studying). It may have an adverse effect on academic performance if it distracts students from their study. This has been substantiated by Guney (2009) and Sosa *et al.* (2010), but not by Huh *et al.* (2009) or Katsikas & Panagiotidis (2011) in Greece. (See also Byrne & Willis, Chapter 7, and Beard & Humphrey, Chapter 25 – both in this volume.)

20.2.5.7 Others

Some studies have included quite unique potential determinants. For example, Schleifer & Dull (2009) in their study undertaken in the U.S.A. reveal that metarecognitive knowledge (i.e. knowledge about one's skills, intellectual resources and abilities as a learner, and knowledge about when, how and why to implement learning procedures/strategies) is positively and significantly associated with performance in accounting courses. Higher levels of metarecognitive knowledge go with better performance.

Further, they also found that a higher level of metarecognitive regulation (i.e. planning, information management, monitoring, debugging, and evaluating) is negatively and significantly associated with performance in accounting courses. This finding probably relates to students who are overly active or zealous in regulating study, which undermine their efforts to do well. (See also Duff, Chapter 8 – this volume.)

20.3 Research methodology/methods employed in prior studies

This section summarises the research methodology/methods used in these prior studies by focussing on the sample data and methods of data analysis. The potential reasons for the variations in prior findings are explored in a later section.

20.3.1 Sample data

In the literature, students' academic performance is the variable of interest or the dependent variable. The determinants investigated are the independent variables. Prior studies have used different measures of academic performance. They also collected data from very varied sources.

20.3.1.1 Measures of the dependent variable

Academic performance has been measured by students' performance with reference to an accounting programme, or one or more accounting courses in an accounting programme. For example, while Gammie et al. (2003) looked at performance at a programme level, Byrne & Flood (2008) looked at performance in the first year of an accounting programme, and Sosa et al. (2010) looked at performance at various years/levels of an accounting programme.

At a course (or courses) level, measures have included performance in *Business/Introductory Accounting* (e.g. Tan & Laswad, 2008), *Business Control* (e.g. Guney, 2009), *Business Financial Statements* (e.g. Lane & Porch, 2002), *Cost Accounting* (e.g. Al-Twaijry, 2010), *Management/Managerial Accounting* (e.g. Keller et al., 2009), *Advanced Managerial Accounting* (e.g. Fogarty & Goldwater, 2010), *Financial Accounting* (e.g. Mustata et al., 2010), and combinations of the above (e.g. Schleifer & Dull, 2009).

Some studies have examined perceptions of performance (e.g. Bonaci et al., 2010) instead of objective, empirical performance (such as examination results). Others have studied honours classification (e.g. Gammie et al., 2003), accounting programme failure (e.g. Gracia & Jenkins, 2002), academic progression (e.g. Duff, 2004), accounting assignments instead of accounting examinations (e.g. Rotenstein et al., 2009), and accounting assignments in addition to accounting examinations (e.g. Potter & Johnston, 2006).

Within an accounting course, assessments can take the form of essays, tests, projects, case tudies, quizzes, worksheet exercises, and examinations. However, performance in the individual components has not been used to measure academic performance in accounting, except for Potter & Johnston (2006) in Australia and Rotenstein et al. (2009) in the U.S.A. Invariably, performance at the course, year, or programme level (or a combination of these) has been used as the dependent variable.

20.3.1.2 Data sources

Data sources for the different prior studies vary greatly, depending mainly on the affiliation/location of the researchers/authors. These have ranged across different countries, universities, and student populations. In particular, prior studies have been conducted on first-year undergraduate students (e.g. Byrne & Flood, 2008), second-year undergraduate students (e.g. Gracia & Jenkins, 2002), third-year undergraduate students (e.g. Bonaci et al., 2010), honours-year undergraduate students (e.g. Gammie et al., 2003), undergraduate students enrolled in various accounting courses (e.g. Al-Twaijry, 2010), and graduate students (e.g. Rotenstein et al., 2009). Most of the studies have focussed on or included accounting students (e.g. Al-Twaijry, 2010), although a few have focussed on only non-accounting students (e.g. Guney, 2009).

The range of countries covered by prior studies is also large. Many of the studies were conducted in the U.K. (e.g. Guney, 2009), the U.S.A. (e.g. Fogarty & Goldwater, 2010), and Australia (e.g. Potter & Johnston, 2006). To a lesser extent, studies on the determinants of students' performance in accounting programmes have also been conducted in other countries such as Canada (e.g. Davidson, 2002), Hong Kong (e.g. Lee, 1999), Malaysia (e.g. Tho, 1994), Mexico (e.g. Sosa et al., 2010), New Zealand (e.g. Tan & Laswad, 2008), Romania (e.g. Bonaci, 2010), Saudi Arabia (e.g. Al-Twaijry, 2010), Scotland (e.g. Gammie et al., 2003), and Singapore (e.g. Koh & Koh, 1999).

Finally, almost all studies are based on cross-sectional data. One exception is Lane & Porch (2002), who used longitudinal data in their study at a university in Wales.

20.3.2 Methods of data analysis

Prior studies have deployed different methods to analyse the sample data. However, given the interval nature of the dependent variables in most of the studies, the range of methods used for data analysis is relatively restricted. Almost all of the studies have reported some form of univariate statistics (such as means, standard deviations, and frequency distributions) to provide background information on the variables investigated.

Bivariate analyses to assess the effects of the potential determinants on academic performance in accounting have included t-tests/mean comparisons and Pearson correlations (see, for example, Guney, 2009; Al-Twaijry, 2010; Fogarty & Goldwater, 2010). In addition, and as a slight variation, Rotenstein *et al.* (2009) used partial-correlation analysis.

The most common multivariate analysis that has been employed in prior studies is the 'ordinary least squares' multiple regression (see, for example, Byrne & Flood, 2008; Keller *et al.*, 2009). Bonaci *et al.* (2010) and Tickell & Smyrnios (2005), however, respectively have used ordinal regression analysis and hierarchical regression analysis to analyse academic performance. Also, Gammie *et al.* (2003) have used logistic regression to analyse honours classification, and Duff (2004) has similarly used logistic regression to analyse academic progression. Further, Ramburuth & Mladenovic (2004), and Schleifer & Dull (2009) have used ANOVA (analysis of variance), while Kirk and Spector (2006) have used ANCOVA (analysis of covariance) in addition to ANOVA.

Non-parametric statistical methods have also been chosen by Gammie *et al.* (2003) (Mann-Whitney tests and Chi-square tests), Kealey *et al.* (2005) (Spearman correlations), Kirk & Spector (2006) (Chi-square tests), and Huh *et al.* (2009) (Wilcoxon z-tests). In addition, some researchers/ authors have used more unique statistical methods to perform further analysis on the data. Coate *et al.* (2005), for instance, used factor analysis to reduce the classification of examination problems to four categories (i.e. formula-procedural, format-procedural, analytical-decision, and relevance-decision). Performance measures of these categories are then used as dependent variables in several regression models to relate to critical thinking scores. In another study, Guney (2009) used factor analysis to reduce 13 students' perception items to three factors – namely, as noted earlier: 'teaching environment', 'lecturers and assessment', and 'teaching material'. These factors are, in turn, used as inputs in several regression models.

Mustata *et al.* (2010) used cluster analysis (a very simplified version) to group students based on their academic performance and a list of potential determinants. The clustering results show the association between academic performance and its determinants.

One notable exception to statistical analysis is Gracia & Jenkins (2002), who used in-depth semi-structured interviews at a university in Wales to generate the sample data, and an exploratory/qualitative approach to analyse the data. Similarly, Sosa *et al.* (2010) did not use any statistical tests but primarily a tabulation of responses to analyse data from their questionnaire survey.

20.4 Potential reasons for differences in findings

In reviewing the literature on the determinants of students' performance in accounting programmes, one conclusion that stands out is that the findings to date have largely been mixed and inconclusive. Perhaps the only exception is the consistent, significant, and positive association between academic aptitude (or prior academic performance/achievement) and academic performance. Some potential reasons for the differences in findings include the lack of a theoretical framework, model differences, and sampling/contextual and measurement differences.

20.4.1 Lack of a theoretical framework

Rankin *et al.* (2003) attributed the mixed and inconclusive findings in the literature to the lack of a theoretical framework to support the research. This view has been reinforced by Tan & Laswad (2008). (See also Fogarty, Chapter 1 – this volume, who expresses a more general concern over the limited use of theory in accounting education research.)

Almost invariably, the potential determinants investigated in prior studies have been generated from the hypotheses developed and findings obtained in other (earlier) prior studies. Incrementally, the later studies have built upon the results of earlier studies (e.g. Mo & Waples, 2011). Several studies have also attempted to incorporate the literature from other disciplines/areas, such as orientations to learning and structure of learning outcomes (Ramburuth & Mladenovic, 2004), critical thinking (Kealey *et al.*, 2005), online learning (Keller *et al.*, 2009), exogenous factors (Guney, 2009), and effort (Fogarty & Goldwater, 2010).

Another set of important sources for potential determinants is observations, anecdotal evidence, logic, and expectations. Some studies have attempted to examine potential determinants not yet investigated in the literature at that time. For example, based on individual in-depth interviews, Gracia & Jenkins (2002) analysed the impact of affect, patterns of participation, expectation gap, and locus of control over learning as determinants of students' failure in an undergraduate accounting programme. Also, Sosa *et al.* (2010) introduced the following as potential determinants of academic performance: family, economic, emotional, health, social, and cultural factors.

Notable exceptions to the lack of a theoretical framework include Duff (2004), Tan & Laswad (2008), and Bonaci *et al.* (2010). Duff (2004), for example, motivated his study by invoking Biggs' (1985) model, which consists of the presage, process, and product stages (3Ps) and which:

> *suggests that the quality of student learning (the product) is influenced by their approach to learning. Their approach to learning (the process of learning) is affected by students' perceptions of the requirements of the learning task which are, in turn, influenced by: first, their perceptions of the context of learning, that is teaching methods, the curriculum and assessment methods; and second, their general orientation to learning. Their orientation to learning (presage stage) is determined by their prior educational experience and the learning context.*
>
> (Duff, 2004, pp. 411, 412)

Based on this model, variables and measures are generated, research questions formulated, and data collected and analysed.

Similar to Duff (2004), Bonaci *et al.* (2010) organised the determinants of academic performance into the 3Ps model comprising the following three levels:

> *Presage level (where prior education experience and current learning context influence both the student's learning orientation and the student's perception of the task requirements), SAL level (Students' approaches to learning level which is influenced by the presage level) which determines the Learning outcome (on the third level).*
>
> (Bonaci *et al.*, 2010, p. 560)

From a further analysis of the Presage level, the determinants are re-organised into three dimensions, namely students, teaching/learning environment, and teachers. While a theoretical framework imposes a structure (or boundary) on the research, and hence can be expected to result in more consistent findings, this positive impact is often negated by other cross-sectional differences among studies.

Tan & Laswad (2008) also attempted to introduce a theoretical framework of academic performance by conceptualising prior content knowledge and metacognitive knowledge. The former is further broken down into declarative and procedural knowledge, and the latter into self/person, task, and strategy knowledge. (For a discussion on categories of knowledge, see Flood, Chapter 4 – this volume.) The potential determinants examined are then discussed under these theoretical constructs.

20.4.2 Model differences

One consequence of relying on the existing literature (instead of a theoretical framework) to identify potential determinants of academic performance for study is the availability of a very large set of such potential determinants for selection. As shown in the literature review (see Section 20.2), candidates can include any combination of the following: demographic characteristics; educational experience and background; attitudes and skills; course and class features; and other factors (e.g. effort/time spent on study and accounting (and other) work experience).

When different sets of variables are included in a model for analysis, different results can occur. The dependent variable in prior studies has ranged from academic performance in an individual course or a combination of courses (which vary across studies) to academic performance in different years of an accounting programme or the entire accounting programme.

Further, there is great variation in the sets of independent variables used in prior studies. Even if the dependent variable remains the same, the results on different sets of independent variables can be expected to vary. The reason is that, in a multivariate analysis (e.g. multiple regression), the model coefficients are partial coefficients. That is, the model coefficient for a particular independent variable indicates the effect of that independent variable on the dependent variable keeping the other independent variables 'constant'. In other words, the effect assessment result of a particular variable in a determinants model depends also on the other independent variables included (or not included) in the model. Hence, model differences at least partially explain the mixed and inconclusive findings in the literature.

The discussion above can also be used to explain differences in findings that result from differences in analytical methods employed. For example, correlation analysis examines only two variables at a time (i.e. it is bivariate in nature). Hence the correlation between, say, age and academic performance shows the association between these two variables. If age is now included as one of several independent variables in a multiple regression model (which is multivariate in nature as all the independent variables in the model are simultaneously analysed), the multiple regression finding on age may not be similar to the correlation finding on age.

20.4.3 Sampling/contextual and measurement differences

The results obtained from the analysis of data depend greatly on the data analysed. Hence, even if the same variables are used, differences in data (i.e. sampling and contextual differences) can lead to differences in the findings. The main cause of sampling/contextual differences is the source of the sample data. Prior studies have collected and analysed data across different countries, universities, and student populations. To the extent that the context of a study is different from those of other studies, differences in findings can be expected. For example, prior studies have been conducted on accounting undergraduates in different years of an accounting programme (e.g. first-year undergraduates in Byrne & Flood, 2008, versus third-year under-graduates in Bonaci et al., 2010), and on students enrolled in different accounting courses or different combinations of accounting courses (e.g. *Financial Accounting* at the graduate level in Rotenstein et al., 2009; versus *Managerial Accounting, Cost Accounting,* and *Advanced Managerial Accounting* in Al-Twaijry, 2010). Again, these sampling and contextual differences can lead to differences in the findings of prior studies. (A discussion on comparative accounting education by Calhoun & Karreman can be found in Chapter 26 – this volume.)

Another potential reason for differences in findings is measurement differences. For example, academic aptitude (or prior academic performance/achievement) has been measured in various ways, such as by:

- the previous year's result before enrolling in the university (Tickell & Smyrnios, 2005);
- the ACT score (Coate et al., 2005);
- the national secondary school leaving examination grades converted into a point measure (Byrne & Flood, 2008);
- GPA (Huh et al., 2009);
- the SAT score (Keller et al., 2009); and
- pre-university academic ability (Al-Twaijry, 2010).

When a potential determinant is measured differently in different studies, differences in findings can arise. Also, the use of different statistical methods may dictate the measurement of the variables and vice versa (e.g. while multiple regression analysis works well with both metric and non-metric independent variables, ANOVA works only with non-metric independent variables). The same independent variable measured with a different scale of measurement can give a different statistical result.

20.5 Conclusion

In this concluding section, it is appropriate to highlight the limitations of prior studies and suggest directions for future research. Some closing remarks are also given.

20.5.1 Limitations of prior studies

One limitation that has been frequently highlighted in prior studies is the lack of external validity (or generalisability). Several researchers and authors have cautioned that their findings may be limited to their studies only (see, for example, Byrne & Flood, 2008; Guney, 2009; Fogarty & Goldwater, 2010). This is not surprising given the modelling, sampling, contextual, and measurement differences across studies, as discussed earlier. Such differences increase the chance of each study being unique in its characteristics, thereby limiting the generalisability of its findings.

Several researchers and authors have also highlighted data biases that are specific to their studies. In this respect, Guney (2009) has pointed out that the students in his study completed the questionnaires only after they had completed the examinations and had been informed of their marks. This may result in biased perceptions and evaluations. In Keller et al.'s (2009) study, the students are not randomly assigned to treatment (hybrid learning) and control (traditional learning) groups. Consequently, there may be a self-selection bias and there may not be an equivalence of groups which permits valid comparison and testing. Further, Bonaci et al. (2010) also highlighted that the students' self-reported academic performance measures as used in their study may not be true and fair; in fact, they are likely to be over-rated and hence biased.

Another limitation that has been raised in prior studies is the incomplete specification of the research model. That is, there may be important variables that may have been omitted from the list of determinants examined. Potential determinants that could/should have been added include other forms of learning outcomes that are not necessarily captured in formal assessment instruments, and a wider range of cultural variables (Potter & Johnston, 2006), the different skills that students possess, their study approaches or learning strategies, and their critical thinking skills (Tan & Laswad, 2008), and other forms of assessment, and the total effort related to the class (Fogarty & Goldwater, 2010). Along similar lines, a few researchers and authors have expressed the need for longitudinal data and more theoretical underpinnings (e.g. Duff, 2004; Guney, 2009).

There are also unique limitations that apply to particular studies. For example, in Gammie *et al.* (2003), Type II errors may discourage students from inappropriately pursuing the honours route if the predictions are unfavourable. In Tickell & Smyrnios (2005), the particular hierarchy of independent variables is not explained. Also, in Bonaci *et al.* (2010), the data may be over-analysed, resulting in an over-fitted model.

20.5.2 Future directions

In an attempt to overcome the limitations of their studies and in response to their findings, several researchers and authors have suggested directions for future research. For example, they have suggested incorporating more theoretical constructs and underpinnings in future research. In this respect, Davidson (2002) has indicated that a deep SAL may not be sufficient to develop the skills and abilities needed to learn how to solve complex problems, or to think analytically or conceptually. There is a need, therefore, to consider the relationships between SAL and skills and abilities in future studies. He has also suggested including motivation, the relationship between the presentation of material to students and the examination of this material, and multiple graders to assure the validity of the performance measure in future studies.

Schleifer & Dull (2009) have expressed the need for future researchers and authors to examine the role of self-learning constructs (such as motivation, self-efficacy, personality, and attitude) as well as students' ability to monitor and evaluate their reading comprehension and memory. They also suggested including study-time allocations, meta-recognitive processing on problem-solving and the acquisition of problem-solving skills, and meta-recognitive training in a cooperative setting. On the dependent variable, Boncai *et al.* (2010) have urged future researchers and authors to investigate KSA (knowledge, skills and attitude) – derived from Bloom's taxonomy (Bloom, 1956; Anderson & Krathwohl, 2001: see also Needles, Chapter 2, and Kidwell & Lowensohn, Chapter 21 – both in this volume) in addition to academic performance.

Similar to the lack of a theoretical framework, several researchers and authors have viewed the incomplete specification of the research model as being a limitation, and have suggested that future research incorporate more potential determinants of students' academic performance in accounting programmes. Along this line, Duff (2004) has suggested considering the prevalence and pattern of effective and ineffective learners as well as replicating the study in other cultural environments and on other students (i.e. postgraduate, professional, and undergraduate students). Coate *et al.* (2005) suggested a variety of measures for cognitive ability and a broad array of skills as well as actual class assessments, and Byrne & Flood (2008) suggested replicating their study in other universities as well as exploring background variables such as SAL, study effort, part-time work commitments, and family circumstances. Al-Twaijry (2010) contributed teaching styles, course content, evaluation and examination structure, scheduling system, absenteeism, and students' capability as potential determinants for inclusion.

A few researchers and authors have asked that future studies go beyond cross-sectional data to longitudinal data (e.g. Al-Twaijry, 2010; Mo & Waples, 2011), and beyond quantitative analysis to a more qualitative approach (e.g. Lane & Porch, 2002; Byrne & Flood, 2008). It is deemed important that longitudinal studies be conducted to investigate changes over the years, and that qualitative research be employed to investigate the determinants of students' performance in accounting programmes. Cross-sectional analysis and longitudinal analysis as well as quantitative and qualitative research are not mutually exclusive. Instead, they complement and supplement one another.

Finally, there are some researchers and authors who suggest future directions that are specific to their area of study. For example, in the context of traditional and online learning, Potter & Johnston (2006) have suggested a future focus on the role of online technology in encouraging deep learning, a study of the effect of online learning on progression rates, and an examination of the impact of specific teaching strategies on students' learning outcomes in a range of contexts. Further, Keller *et al.* (2009) have suggested measuring students' preference for hybrid and traditional class formats, measuring motivation to learn, and systematically investigating what types of materials can be used in hybrid courses to increase learning relative to traditional courses. (For a discussion of the use of different types of teaching resources, see Stevenson *et al.*, Chapter 19 – this volume.)

20.5.3 Closing remarks

At the end of this chapter, one important question remains as to how future research on the determinants of students' performance in accounting programmes should proceed. It is unrealistic to expect that there can be a perfect study that will be based on a mega theory that can encompass all the potential determinants, and which will be tested on a sufficiently large sample that can lead to generalisable results across all universities, countries, and student populations. Academic research in this area will continue to be incremental and, hopefully, stronger in its academic rigour. However, the existing literature can give some guidance as to how future research can or should proceed.

First, future research should be based on a theoretical framework which considers the prior research to date. This will enable the formulation of research hypotheses, including the specification of the expected relationships. It will also be able to provide guidance on the research methodology/methods and facilitate the interpretation of results. A theoretical framework will put the study into a more macro- and higher-level context as well as contribute to theory construction that can lead to empirical testing. Any insignificant and unexpected findings should also be explored as a way to refine the theoretical framework.

Second, measurements of the variables should be clearly explained and justified. An effort should also be made to discuss any differences in the measurements of variables in a particular study vis-à-vis those of similar (if not the same) variables in other prior studies. This will help in the interpretation of the results as well as the understanding of the findings and limitations. It will also aid in understanding the differences across studies.

Third, sampling and contextual differences and particularities (arising, say, from differences in data sources from various countries, universities and student populations) should be explicitly discussed. This will facilitate the understanding of the findings as well as their implications. Very importantly, it will also explain the differences across studies and contribute towards fine-tuning the theoretical framework. In this respect, it will be very useful if researchers and authors can position their studies in the context of a broader theoretical framework, and in relation to other similar studies.

With the above suggestions implemented over time, it is expected that this body of knowledge can be made more substantial and more rigorous. Finally, it is hoped that this chapter can make a significant contribution to the literature on the determinants of students' performance in accounting programmes.

References

Accounting Education Change Commission (AECC) (1990) Objectives of education for accountants: position statement number one, *Issues in Accounting Education*, 5(2), 307–312.

Al-Twaijry, A.A. (2010) Student academic performance in undergraduate managerial-accounting courses, *Journal of Education for Business*, 85(6), 311–322.

Anderson, L.W. & Krathwohl, D.R. (2001) *A Taxonomy for Learning, Teaching and Assessing: A Revision of Bloom's Taxonomy of Educational Objectives*, New York: Longman.

Archer, J., Cantwell, R. & Bourke, S. (1999) Coping at university: an examination of achievement, motivation, self-regulation, confidence and method of entry, *Higher Education Research & Development*, 18(1), 31–54.

Biggs, J.B. (1985) The role of metalearning in study processes, *British Journal of Educational Psychology*, 55(2), 185–212.

Bloom, B.S. (1956) *Taxonomy of Educational Objectives*, Boston: Allyn and Bacon.

Bonaci, C.G., Mutiu, A. & Mustata, R.V. (2010) Influential factors of accounting students' academic performance: a Romanian case study, *Accounting and Management Information Systems*, 9(4), 558–580.

Byrne, M. & Flood, B. (2008) Examining the relationships among background variables and academic performance of first-year accounting students at an Irish university, *Journal of Accounting Education*, 26(4), 202–212.

Chen, C., Jones, K., & McIntyre, D.D. (2008) Analyzing the factors relevant to students' estimations of benefits and costs of pursuing an accounting career, *Accounting Education: an international journal*, 17(3), 313–326.

Coate, J.C., Lehman, A.H., & Stranak, J.H. (2005) Critical thinking and exam performance in a traditional managerial accounting principles course, *Journal of Accounting and Finance Research*, 13(5), 169–188.

Crawford, J., Dale, L. & Toney-McLin, P. (2003) Student performance factors in economics and accounting, *Proceedings of the Academy of Educational Leadership*, 8(2), 21–27.

Davidson, R.A. (2002) Relationship of study approach and exam performance, *Journal of Accounting Education*, 20(1), 29–44.

de Lange, P. & Mavondo, F. (2004) Gender and motivational differences in approaches to learning by a cohort of open learning students, *Accounting Education: an international journal*, 13(4), 431–448.

Duff, A. (2004) Understanding academic performance and progression of first-year accounting and business economics undergraduates: the role of approaches to learning and prior academic achievement, *Accounting Education: an international journal*, 13(4), 409–430.

Elias, R. (2005) Students' approaches to study in introductory accounting courses, *Journal of Education for Business*, 80(4), 194–198.

Fogarty, T.J. & Goldwater, P.M. (2010) Beyond just desserts: the gendered nature of the connection between effort and achievement for accounting students, *Journal of Accounting Education*, 28(1), 1–12.

Gammie, E., Jones, P.L., & Robertson-Millar, C. (2003) Accountancy undergraduate performance: a statistical model, *Accounting Education: an international journal*, 12(1), 63–78.

Gracia, L. & Jenkins, E. (2002) An exploration of student failure on an undergraduate accounting programme of study, *Accounting Education: an international journal*, 11(1), 93–107.

Guney, Y. (2009) Exogenous and endogenous factors influencing students' performance in undergraduate accounting modules, *Accounting Education: an international journal*, 18(1), 51–73.

Hartnett, R., Romcke, J., & Yap, C. (2004) Student performance in tertiary-level accounting: an international student focus, *Accounting and Finance*, 44(2), 163–185.

Huh, S., Jin, J., Lee, K.J., & Yoo, S. (2009) Differential effects of student characteristics on performance: online vis-à-vis offline accounting courses, *Academy of Educational Leadership Journal*, 13(2), 83–91.

Jonassen, D.H. & Grabowski, B.L. (1993) *Handbook of Individual Differences, Learning, and Instruction*, Hillsdale, NJ: Lawrence Erlbaum Associates.

Katsikas, E. & Panagiotidis, T. (2011) Student status and academic performance: accounting for the symptom of long duration of studies in Greece, *Studies in Educational Evaluation*, 37(2–3), 152–161.

Kealey, B.T., Holland, J., & Watson, M. (2005) Preliminary evidence on the association between critical thinking and performance in principles of accounting, *Issues in Accounting Education*, 20(1), 33–49.

Keller, J. H., Hassell, J.M., Webber, S.A., & Johnson, J.N. (2009) A comparison of academic performance in traditional and hybrid sections of introductory managerial accounting, *Journal of Accounting Education*, 27(3), 147–154.

Kirk, F.R. & Spector, C.A. (2006) Factors affecting student achievement in cost accounting, *Academy of Educational Leadership Journal*, 10, 191–104.

Koh, M.Y. & Koh, H.C. (1999) The determinants of performance in an accountancy degree programme, *Accounting Education: an international journal*, 8(1), 13–29.

Lane, A. & Porch, M. (2002) The impact of background factors on the performance of nonspecialist undergraduate students on accounting modules – a longitudinal study: a research note, *Accounting Education: an international journal*, 11(1), 109–118.

Lee, D.S.Y. (1999) Strength of high school accounting qualification and student performance in university-level introductory accounting courses in Hong Kong, *Journal of Education for Business*, 74(5), 301–306.

Mo, S. & Waples, E. (2011) Evidence on the association between major and performance in the introductory accounting course, *Academy of Educational Leadership Journal*, 15 Special Issue, 93–107.

Mustata, R.V., Bonaci, C.G., & Mutiu, A. (2010) Accounting students' academic performance: influential factors in review, *Review of Business Research*, 10(3), 184–190.

NAO (2002) *Improving Student Achievement in English Higher Education*, HC486, London: National Audit Office,

Pokorny, M. & Pokorny, H. (2005) Widening participation in higher education: student quantitative skills and independent learning as impediments to progression, *International Journal of Mathematical Education in Science and Technology*, 36(5), 445–467.

Potter, B.N. & Johnston, C.G. (2006) The effect of interactive on-line learning systems on student learning outcomes in accounting, *Journal of Accounting Education*, 24(1), 16–34.

Ramburuth, P. & Mladenovic, R. (2004) Exploring the relationship between students' orientations to learning, the structure of students' learning outcomes and subsequent academic performance, *Accounting Education: an international journal*, 13(4), 507–527.

Rankin, M., Silvester, M., Vallely, M. & Wyatt, A. (2003) An analysis of the implications of diversity for students' first level accounting performance, *Accounting and Finance*, 43(4), 365–393.

Rotenstein, A., Davis, H.Z., & Tatum, L. (2009) Early birds versus just-in-timers: the effect of procrastination on academic performance of accounting students, *Journal of Accounting Education*, 27(4), 223–232.

Schleifer, L.L. & Dull, R.B. (2009) Metarecognition and performance in the accounting classroom, *Issues in Accounting Education*, 24(3), 339–367.

Sizoo, S., Malhotra, N., & Bearson, J. (2003) A gender-based comparison of the learning strategies of adult business students, *College Student Journal*, 37(1), 103–110.

Sosa, E.R.C., Barrientos, L.G., Castro, P.E.G., & Garcia, J.H. (2010) Academic performance, school desertion and emotional paradigm in university students, *Contemporary Issues in Education Research*, 3(7), 25–35.

Svensson, L. (1977) On qualitative differences in learning: III – study skills and learning, *British Journal of Education Psychology*, 47(3), 233–243.

Tan, L.M. & Laswad, F. (2008) Impact of prior content and meta-cognitive knowledge on students' performance in an introductory accounting course, *Pacific Accounting Review*, 20(1), 63–74.

Tho, L.M. (1994) Some evidence on the determinants of student performance in the University of Malaya introductory accounting course, *Accounting Education: an international journal*, 3(4), 331–340.

Tickell, G. & Smyrnios, K.X. (2005) Predictors of tertiary accounting students' academic performance: a comparison of year 12-to-university students with TAFE-to-university students, *Journal of Higher Education Policy and Management*, 27(2), 239–259.

Wooten, T.C. (1998) Factors influencing student learning in introductory accounting classes: a comparison of traditional and non-traditional students, *Issues in Accounting Education*, 13(2), 357–373.

About the author

Hian Chye Koh is Assistant Provost and a Professor in the UniSIM College at SIM University, Singapore (hckoh@unisim.edu.sg). His current teaching, research and consulting interests are in business analytics, education and educational research, and statistical applications in accounting and business. He has served as a Senior Associate Editor of *Accounting Education: an international journal* (for which he received an *AE*/IAAER Distinguished Service Award).

21

Outcomes assessment in accounting education

Linda A. Kidwell* and Suzanne Lowensohn**

*UNIVERSITY OF WYOMING, U.S.A. **COLORADO STATE UNIVERSITY, U.S.A.

CONTENTS

Abstract

Outcomes assessment of learning, an important component of educational programmes, involves a systematic review of educational outcomes, aimed at evaluating and improving students' learning, development, and progression through an academic programme. It includes comparing students' learning with the intended learning outcomes or goals of an academic programme or curricular block of an academic programme. Once an occasional exercise performed in anticipation of accreditation or reaccreditation, assessment is now a continuous process that is intended to spread throughout an institution and elicit improvements over time (Rajkumar *et al.*, 2011). This chapter will provide an overview of outcomes assessment, including giving guidance for developing learning objectives and introducing the reader to assessment techniques.

Keywords

assessment, assurance of learning, learning goals, learning outcomes

21.1 Introduction

The main aims of this chapter are:

- to define outcomes assessment;
- to discuss the history of assessment in accounting education;
- to provide examples of learning goals and outcomes;
- to illustrate the assessment process; and
- to briefly critique methods adopted by accounting programmes.

Angelo and Cross (1993, p. 3) wrote: '*[L]earning can and often does take place without the benefit of teaching – and sometimes even in spite of it – but there is no such thing as effective teaching in the absence of learning.*' The subject of this chapter is assessment of that learning, which in turn should help improve the effectiveness of teaching. In Chapter 20 – this volume, Koh reviewed students' *inputs* and determinants of students' performance, and this chapter focusses on defining and measuring expected students' *outcomes*. Outcomes assessment of learning is a systematic process, which involves defining, constructing, and measuring learning goals within an academic programme.

This chapter explains outcomes assessment, discusses the history of assessment in accounting education, and describes options and considerations in assessment practices. It also offers suggestions, and critiques methods adopted by accounting programmes and published in the literature.

In the context of this chapter, assessment is the process of collecting information about students' learning and performance in order to improve education. Outcomes assessment is a term which denotes the comparison of students' learning with the intended learning outcomes or goals identified by an academic programme or curricular block of an academic programme. Learning goals are developed to reflect a university's mission, and assurance that such learning goals have been achieved is part of demonstrating accountability to stakeholders and assisting academic staff in improving their courses and teaching (AACSB, 2013c). In other words, outcomes assessment asks whether the services, activities, or experiences offered by an educational institution have the desired impact on students who partake in them. Emphasis on outcomes assessment in higher education has grown in recent years as '*Ministries of education along with critics of higher education institutions want real proof of student "learning outcomes" that can help justify large national investments in their colleges and universities*'(Olds, 2012).

21.2 History of assessment

21.2.1 History of assessment in higher education

In tracing the history of assessment of learning in accounting, one must first consider the history of assessment in the broader context of higher education. The early foundations of assessment lie in the educational and developmental psychology research of the 1930s and 1940s (Bresciani *et al.*, 2010). Researchers in this period aimed to understand how students learned, and what helped to improve their motivation to learn. Much of the history recounted below is from the U.S.A., reflecting both what is most familiar to the authors and the literature to which the authors have most access. However, one of the most influential entities in the assessment movement in business education, the Association to Advance Collegiate Schools of Business (AACSB) expanded its American focus to an international one in the mid-1990s, with current membership of 83 countries (AACSB, 2013a), leading to a common international experience in the rise of assessment in the last two decades. (Accreditation has its supporters and critics, as discussed by Apostolou and Gammie in Chapter 29 – this volume.)

From these beginnings, academic staff borrowed ideas from scientific management theory as developed in the early twentieth century by Frederick Taylor (e.g. Taylor, 1998). In the educational setting, scientific management theory considered sub-systems that provided inputs with which to generate outputs, with outcomes as the final product (Ewell, 2002). This led to the development of programme reviews and strategic planning in higher education in the 1960s and 1970s (Bresciani *et al.*, 2010). This programme evaluation approach led to the evolution of the assessment of outcomes approach, but not for several years.

Major momentum for the assessment movement in the U.S.A. came as a result of the publication of the National Commission on Excellence in Education's devastating report to the Secretary of Education, aptly entitled *A Nation at Risk: The Imperative for Educational Reform* (National Commission on Excellence in Education, 1983). Although this report mainly considered secondary school education, it also had implications for primary schools and universities. The report detailed the falling levels of performance in American schools, and the risk which such decline posed for economic vitality, responsible citizenship, and military readiness. In making recommendations, the committee developed what we today would call learning outcomes, such as: *'know our literary heritage and how it enhances imagination and ethical understanding, and how it relates to the customs, ideas, and values of today's life and culture'* (ibid., p. 22). However, the report was silent on matters of assessment of learning.

Initially, higher education relied on measures of process *'with little evidence it led to good outcomes'* (Massaro, 2010, p. 19). University quality and reputation were gauged through indirect measures, such as student retention, grants received, and educators' publications – that is to say, through input measures (Calderon *et al.*, 2003). National and international rankings, particularly in the popular media (e.g. *US News and World Report* rankings of universities and the *Financial Times* rankings of business programmes), continue to focus on inputs and process, measures which Massaro (2010, p. 19) maintains are taken as being surrogates for quality education because they are *'presentable in an apparently simple table'*.

In the 1990s, another management theory, total quality management (TQM), was imported into the education field. TQM introduced the idea of students as customers (Bresciani *et al.*, 2010). The paradigm for education shifted from providing instruction (inputs) to producing learning (outputs). Under the new paradigm, universities create opportunities for learning and measure outcomes, and academic staff use the feedback from assessment over time to learn how to facilitate learning more effectively. Furthermore, this shift in paradigm leads to increased institutional responsibility for students' learning outcomes. The higher education institution itself becomes a learning entity under this TQM approach (Barr & Tagg, 1995).

At about the same time that TQM was being implemented in higher education, public pressures for accountability of higher education institutions (HEIs) increased as educational resources became scarcer and more costly. Massaro (2010, p. 18) notes: '[A]s a system world-wide, higher education [had] not been sufficiently responsive to this growing unease about what it does and who it does it for.' Policy-makers began to demand accountability, not just for financial resources, but also for outcomes of education, through direct, documented evidence (Bresciani et al., 2010). Institutions facing increased accountability demands developed methods to demonstrate a commitment to the assessment of students' learning outcomes (Pusecker et al., 2011/2012). Initially, externally-derived instruments (such as standardized tests) were administered to large numbers of students to measure learning, assess curriculum strengths and weaknesses, and evaluate programme quality. These were largely top-down initiatives with little involvement on the part of academic staff, and the assessment process was tangential to the efforts of academic staff, if they were even aware such assessment was being done (Angelo and Cross, 1993).

By 1990, a large number of universities were under government mandates to participate in programme assessment. National government involvement in assessment became an international phenomenon, involving countries such as the U.S.A. (Angelo & Cross, 1993), England (Pepin & Moon, 1999; Boyle & Charles, 2010), Australia (Klenowski, 2011), and France and Germany (Pepin & Moon, 1999). By the mid-1990s in the U.S.A., however, regional accreditation agencies became the main external impetus for assessment at the institutional level, while national or international accrediting bodies drove assessment within certain disciplines, such as business, health sciences, and teacher education.

One of the challenges in implementing assessment was disagreement on whether assessment should focus on an institution, an academic unit or division, a course, or even on the specific technical or soft skills which a student should possess (Calderon et al., 2003). Regardless of approach, universities adopted TQM methods in part to maintain control of the assessment processes so that they would be able to avoid the type of standardized assessments which were prevalent in secondary schools (Bresciani et al., 2010). There may yet be increased pressure globally for universities to follow a standardized approach in the future, as the Organisation for Economic Co-operation and Development (OECD) is in the midst of developing an instrument, the Assessment of Higher Education Learning Outcomes (AHELO), that will 'test what students in higher education know and can do upon graduation . . . The test aims to be global and valid across diverse cultures, languages, and different types of institutions' (OECD, 2012: n.p.). As at the time of writing, the AHELO testing instruments had been developed and were being administered in participating institutions to determine whether they were scientifically and practically possible (ibid.).

Accreditation agencies can accredit programmes for quality, for access to accounting training, or for other purposes, as elaborated upon by Apostolou and Gammie in Chapter 29 – this volume. As assessment evolved in higher education into the twenty-first century, accreditors demanded a shift from the self-study of organizational management toward academic standards and curricular alignment (Bresciani et al., 2010). For example, the standards of the Association for the Advancement of Collegiate Schools of Business (AACSB) in the 1990s required assessment of whether educational goals aligned with the institution's mission, with documentation relying mainly on the measurement of inputs. This focus was primarily on assessment of programmes themselves, the subject which Calderon addresses in Chapter 22 – this volume. By the early 2000s, the AACSB standards had been revised to place more focus on the assessment of students' learning (Weldy & Turnipseed, 2010), with both formative and summative assessment becoming the norm. Formative assessment is used to capture the students' progress toward goals as they move through a programme, measuring their learning throughout their education, whereas summative assessment entails measuring their success in attaining desired learning outcomes by the end of their studies (Angelo & Cross, 1993).

One of the problems with externally-derived assessment demands is the potential for motivational conflict for academic staff. If assessment is intended for internal user groups (such as university personnel), then academic staff will develop assessment techniques to help improve their teaching, resulting in their willing participation in the assessment process. However, if the assessment is intended for external users (such as accreditors and government agencies), then assessment has the risk of becoming a process of ticking the box, and academic staff may merely go through the motions to meet external demands without developing or taking advantage of the feedback loop for their own improvement (Daigle *et al.*, 2007). They may also view assessment as being something to do more deliberately in the run-up to an accreditation visit, with a reduction in effort or reflection in the period immediately thereafter. Likewise, they may be concerned that assessment will be used to force them to accept a single, rigid model of accounting programmes with little room for localized focus (Accounting Education Change Commission, 1994). For assessment to be meaningful, university academic staff must be able to integrate the two user groups' needs. One method of identifying common expectations between groups may be to focus not on accrediting bodies solely, but also to build a set of desired outcomes based on professionally-identified competencies, such as those outlined in the International Education Standards (IES), the American Institute of Certified Public Accountants' (AICPA) Core Competency Framework, or the qualification specifications provided by the internationally-focussed Association of Chartered Certified Accountants (ACCA).

21.2.2 Assessment in business schools

While the terminology varies, central to all business school accreditation standards are the concepts of intended learning outcomes or goals and assessment of students' achievement of such ideals. Intended learning outcomes or goals (hereafter termed ILOs) flow from the mission of an HEI, and describe how degree programmes propose to achieve the mission. They should enumerate '*[the] desired educational accomplishments of the degree programs*' and '*translate the more general statement of the mission into the educational accomplishments of graduates*'(AACSB, 2012, p. 60). They communicate institutional objectives to academic staff, students, and other stakeholders, and designate how graduates will be '*different as a result of the completion of the program*' (ibid., p. 61).

In their accreditation standards, the European Quality Improvement System (EQUIS) distinguishes between programme objectives, which are general in nature, and ILOs, which relate to '*what students are expected to know, what they are expected to be able to do, and how they are expected to behave*'(EQUIS, 2013, p. 25).

Hence, according to the Association of MBAs (AMBA), ILOs describe ways in which an HEI '*recognises and assesses intellectual, analytical, personal and enterprise qualities as well as the specific knowledge developed by the programme*'(AMBA, 2012, p. 6). ILOs should be specified and evaluated for each degree programme (e.g. Bachelor of Science in Business Administration or Master of Science in Accounting). A thorough discussion of the development of programme goals and resulting assessment of programmes is more thoroughly addressed by Calderon in Chapter 22 – this volume. More detailed outcomes may be established at the discipline or course-level to help implement the broad programme-level outcomes, and this is where assessment of students' learning often takes place.

Academic staff who are trying to improve students' learning ask themselves what essential skills and knowledge they are trying to teach, how they can find out whether the students are learning, and how they can help them learn better (Angelo and Cross, 1993). Guidelines at the University of Glasgow in the U.K. provide the following questions to help in identifying ILOs (Mann, 2004, pp. 2–3):

1   What do you want students to know and be able to do by the end of this programme/ course?
2   How will students be able to use this learning? Doing what? In what contexts?
3   What level are you aiming for?
4   What will students need to do in order to demonstrate if and how well they have achieved these outcomes?
5   If someone were to ask the students what they have learnt in this programme/course, how would you like them to answer? This can give a good indication of what you are hoping they will learn.

ILOs are best stated in measurable terms so that success in meeting them can be assessed. In providing guidance on how best to develop ILOs and outcome assessment practices, the American Association for Higher Education (AAHE) described principles of good practice, listed below (AAHE Assessment Forum, 1992, pp. 2–3):

1   The assessment of students' learning begins with educational values.
2   Assessment is most effective when it reflects an understanding of learning as multi-dimensional, integrated, and revealed in performance over time.
3   Assessment works best when the programmes it seeks to improve have clear, explicitly-stated purposes.
4   Assessment requires attention to outcomes but also and equally to the experience that leads to those outcomes.
5   Assessment works best when it is ongoing, not episodic.
6   Assessment fosters wider improvement when representatives from across the educational community are involved.
7   Assessment makes a difference when it begins with issues of use and illuminates questions about which people really care.
8   Assessment is most likely to lead to improvement when it is part of a larger set of conditions that promote change.
9   Through assessment, educators meet responsibilities to students and to the public.

Academic staff are an integral part of the development and evaluation of ILOs. They must establish outcomes consistent with their institution's mission, and determine how the ILOs will be integrated into the curriculum (i.e., within specific courses, throughout the curriculum, or a combination strategy). Sample learning outcomes for accounting majors from the University of Wisconsin-River Falls in the U.S.A. (http://www.uwrf.edu/CBE/Programs/Accounting.cfm) are presented below:

1   Graduating accounting students will be able to use financial statements to make decisions.
2   Graduating accounting students will be able to help managers make decisions using internal and external information.
3   Graduating accounting students will be able to evaluate accounting systems.
4   Graduating accounting students will be able to file tax returns for individuals and businesses.
5   Graduating accounting students will be able to communicate verbally and in writing.

After formally identifying degree programme ILOs, academic staff should reflect upon each course which they regularly teach, and consider which learning experiences and outcomes are covered (or should be covered) within each course. For example, if an ILO pertains to technology, as described by Boritz and Stoner (in Chapter 16 – this volume), specific components of teaching with technology may be designated to particular courses, and learning may be assessed there. If one of the generic skills described by Watty (in Chapter 13 – this volume) is desired, academic staff in the programme need to agree on which educator in which course will be responsible for the assessment of a skill imparted across the curriculum. Academic staff then must consider potential teaching and assessment tools. This cycle is described in the next section.

21.3 Implementing outcomes assessment

21.3.1 The assessment cycle

An HEI's mission statement leads to the adoption of ILOs at the beginning of the assessment cycle, as depicted in Figure 21.1. After setting ILOs, academic staff design strategies to accomplish objectives, determine areas and methods of assessment, gather assessment data, use the assessment data to improve the programme, and repeat the continuous improvement cycle. This cycle addresses the following questions (MAA, 2007):

- What should our students learn?
- How well are they learning?
- What should we change so that future students will learn more and understand it better?

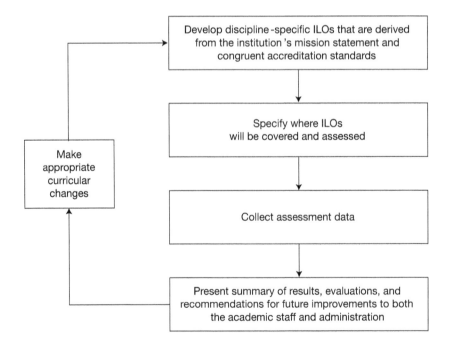

Figure 21.1 Sample assessment cycle and continuous improvement loop

21.3.2 Learning outcomes and assessment methods in accounting

In the top box of Figure 21.1, academic staff are asked to articulate the discipline-specific ILOs stemming from a degree programme's mission and the applicable accreditation standards. Programme-level outcomes are typically general in nature and may be similar across programmes. However, more ILOs are generally established at the discipline or course-level to help implement the broad programme-level ILOs. ILOs may be associated with particular classes or an entire degree programme, and may involve particular skills, values, attitudes, or areas of knowledge that students should exhibit after a learning experience. Herring & Izard (1992) identified three categories of outcomes:

- cognitive (including knowledge and skills);
- behavioural; and
- affective.

Broad examples include accounting knowledge, verbal, problem-solving, interpersonal skills, and independence. Several of the behavioural and affective outcomes could relate to the subject matter discussed by Watty (in Chapter 13 – this volume), whereas the cognitive outcomes may relate to critical thinking skills discussed by Cunningham (in Chapter 18 – this volume). The ILOs may be general (e.g. accounting programme graduates will be able to communicate effectively in professional situations), or specific (e.g. students will be able to prepare tax calculations for individuals or organizations).

Table 21.1 provides sample ILOs included in the International Education Standards (IESs) published by the International Accounting Education Standards Board (IAESB). These standards reflect the consensus of an international deliberative body affiliated with the IAESB, developed through due process, with input from almost every continent and from educators, standard setters, professional accounting bodies (PABs), and accounting professionals. The sample ILOs are categorized into:

- technical competencies;
- professional skills; and
- professional values, ethics and attitudes.

They span intermediate and advanced levels of proficiency. The IESs will be effective from July 2015.

Note that the ILOs proposed by the IAESB include minimum proficiency levels of foundation, intermediate, or advanced proficiency, which are described (though not defined) within the standards. For example, intermediate proficiency, the most common level required in the IESs, is described thus:

INTERMEDIATE: Learning outcomes focus on:
- Independently applying, comparing and analyzing underlying principles and theories from relevant areas of technical competence to complete work assignments and make decisions.
- Combining technical competence and professional skills to complete work assignments.
- Applying professional values, ethics, and attitudes to work assignments.
- Presenting information and explaining ideas in a clear manner, using oral and written communications, to accounting and non-accounting stakeholders.

Table 21.1 Sample ILOs from the proposed revisions of IESs

Competence area	Intended learning outcomes	Minimum level of proficiency
Technical Competence Examples (IES 2)		
Financial Accounting and Reporting	– Apply accounting principles to transactions and other events – Prepare primary financial statements, including consolidated financial statements, in accordance with IFRS, or other relevant standards – Evaluate the appropriateness of accounting policies used to prepare financial statements	Intermediate
Management Accounting	– Apply techniques to support management decision making, including product costing, variance analysis, inventory management, and budgeting and forecasting – Evaluate the performance of products and business segments	Intermediate
Taxation	– Prepare direct and indirect tax calculations for individuals and organizations – Analyze the taxation issues associated with non-complex international transactions	Intermediate
Audit and Assurance	– Assess the risks of material misstatement in the financial statements and consider the impact on audit strategy – Describe the objectives and strategies involved in performing an audit of financial statements	Intermediate
Professional Skills Examples (IES 3)		
Intellectual Skills	– Evaluate information from a variety of sources and perspectives through research, analysis and integration – Recommend solutions to unstructured, multifaceted problems	Intermediate
Personal Skills	– Set high personal standards of delivery and monitor personal performance, through feedback from others and through reflection	Intermediate
Interpersonal and Communication	– Display cooperation and teamwork when working towards organisational goals – Apply negotiation skills to reach appropriate solutions and agreements	Intermediate
Organizational	– Undertake assignments in accordance with established practices to meet prescribed deadlines – Apply people management skills to motivate and develop others	Intermediate

Table 21.1 Sample ILOs from the proposed revisions of IESs—*continued*

Competence area	Intended learning outcomes	Minimum level of proficiency
Professional Values, Ethics, and Attitudes (IES 4)		
Professional Scepticism and Professional Judgment	– Identify and evaluate reasonable alternatives to reach well-reasoned conclusions based on all relevant facts and circumstances	Intermediate
Ethical Principles	– Apply the fundamental ethical principles of integrity, objectivity, professional competence and due care, confidentiality, and professional behaviour to ethical dilemmas and determine appropriate approach – Explain the advantages and disadvantages of rules-based and principles-based approaches to ethics	Intermediate
Commitment to the Public Interest	– Explain the role of ethics within the profession and in relation to the concept of social responsibility – Analyze the consequences of unethical behaviour to the individual, to the profession, and to the public	Intermediate

Notes: Excerpted from Revised International Education Standards, as indicated.
IES 2: International Education Standard (IES) 2: Initial Professional Development – Technical Competence (Revised).
IES 3: International Education Standard (IES) 3: Initial Professional Development – Professional Skills (Revised).
IES 4: International Education Standard (IES) 4: Initial Professional Development – Professional Values, Ethics, and Attitudes (Revised).

> Learning outcomes at the intermediate level relate to work situations that are characterized by moderate levels of ambiguity, complexity and uncertainty
>
> (IAESB, 2014a, p. 12)

A more widely accepted approach to describing different levels of learning is Bloom's taxonomy (Bloom, 1956). (See also Needles, Chapter 2 – this volume.) As revised by Anderson & Krathwohl (2001), Bloom's taxonomy consists of six major classes of learning, representing a hierarchical order: remembering, understanding, applying, analyzing, evaluating, and creating. Academic staff in widely diverse fields have used Bloom's taxonomy as a foundation for developing ILOs. To elaborate, Bloom's first level, remembering, involves the basic knowledge of facts, rules, processes, and the like. Understanding is when a learner can make full use of the material, that is to say, interpret, summarize, compare, and explain information. Bloom's third level of learning is applying knowledge in specific situations or scenarios. This requires the learner to be able to apply his or her knowledge to unfamiliar situations, predict possible effects of changes in the underlying data, or recognize the appropriate knowledge and processes to bring to solving certain problems (Bloom, 1956; Anderson & Krathwohl, 2001).

The higher orders of learning explained in the taxonomy are analyzing, evaluating, and creating. When analyzing, a student must be able to break down problems into their components, distinguish between facts and assumptions or biases, and understand the relationships among the components of the problem. Evaluating requires learners to be able to make judgements about the relevance of information, to identify inconsistencies or illogical conclusions, and to compare against benchmarks. Finally, creating requires students to put diverse types of information together into a coherent whole, integrating them into a structure that can be understood, explained, and used (Bloom, 1956; Anderson & Krathwohl, 2001).

Bloom's taxonomy can help academic staff to consider more explicitly what level of learning they want students to obtain in various subject matter so that they can establish ILOs reflecting those levels. From there, appropriate assessment tools can be developed. In many cases, students are expected to gain fundamental knowledge in an introductory course, supplement the depth of knowledge to enhance understanding in a subsequent upper-level course, and apply the knowledge in analyzing a comprehensive business simulation. These would represent the first four of six levels of learning in Bloom's taxonomy. For example, undergraduate accounting majors would be expected to acquire fundamental financial accounting knowledge, such as the balance sheet equation, in an *Introductory Financial Accounting* course; enhance their level of understanding of more complex financial accounting theory and skills in an *Intermediate Accounting* course; and demonstrate mastery of financial accounting knowledge in an *Advanced Accounting* class or a capstone course requiring financial analysis of a business entity.

In addition to those listed in Table 21.1, excellent sources for identifying ILOs specific to the accounting discipline include, from the American perspective, the AICPA's *Core Competency Framework* (AICPA, 1999) and the Institute of Management Accountant's 1999 *Practice Analysis of Management Accounting* (Siegel & Sorensen, 1999), and from the international perspective, the syllabi for ACCA Fundamental Exams (ACCA, 2012), as well as previous academic articles which detail the development of assessment programmes in accounting (e.g. Herring & Izard, 1992; Demong *et al.*, 1994; Gainen & Locatelli, 1995; Akers *et al.*, 1997; Stivers *et al.*, 2000). Additional ILOs specifically relating to accounting ethics were developed by Kidwell *et al.* (2012). For example, the study guide for the ACCA examination on *International Financial Reporting* includes the following ILOs, which they term 'main capabilities':

- Discuss and apply conceptual framework for financial reporting; and
- Prepare and present financial statements which conform with International Financial Reporting Standards (ACCA, 2013, p. 4).

These can be used verbatim by academic staff in writing ILOs. The AICPA's *Core Competency Framework*, on the other hand, describes competencies in more detail than an educator would generally want to use as ILOs, but they can serve as guidance for that purpose. For example, the competency, Risk Analysis, is described by the AICPA as follows:

> *Risk analysis and control is fundamental to professional service delivery. The identification and management of audit risk (that is, the risk that the auditor will fail to detect a misstatement, caused by inadvertent error or fraud, that is, material to financial statements) is the basis for the conduct of a GAAS audit. The understanding of business risk (that is, the risk that an entity—either a client or the prospective accounting professional's employer—will fail to achieve its objectives) affects how business strategy is created and implemented.*
>
> (AICPA, 2005: Functional Competencies)

An educator could write a related ILO as: 'Students should be able to describe the audit risk model and its components and apply the model to facts presented.' HEIs applying for separate accounting accreditation from the AACSB must develop ILOs for specific learning experiences enumerated by the AACSB, including the following (AACSB, 2013c, p. 30):

- The roles accountants play in society to provide and ensure the integrity of financial, managerial, and other information.
- The ethical and regulatory environment for accountants.
- The critical thinking and analytical skills that support professional scepticism, assessment, and assurance of accounting information.
- Business processes and analysis.
- Internal controls and security.
- Risk assessment and assurance for financial and non-financial information.
- Recording, analysis, and interpretation of historical and prospective financial and non-financial information.
- Project and engagement management.
- The design of technology for accounting, as well as its application to financial and non-financial information.
- Tax policy, strategy, and compliance for individuals and enterprises.
- International accounting issues and practices, including roles and responsibilities played by accountants in a global context.

An overriding requirement of good assessment processes is that ILOs should be clearly communicated to all stakeholders – administration, academic staff, students, parents, employers, governments (where they demand accountability), and accrediting organizations. ILOs may relate to specific technical skills, such as those identified above from the proposed IESs and the AACSB standards. They may also relate as much to behavioural factors as to the acquisition of new knowledge, such as effective communication, leadership, and critical and reflective thinking skills.

After developing ILOs, academic staff should determine strategies to introduce and cover ILOs within their respective courses and select methods or instruments for gathering evidence to show whether students have achieved the ILOs. When identifying curriculum and instructional methods, they should take into account students' learning experiences and diverse learning styles (e.g. as discussed by Lucas & Mladenovic in Chapter 6, and by Duff in Chapter 8 – both in this volume), as well as research on how students learn. Assessment methods specify the areas of students' activities and accomplishments designed to measure students' progress toward completion of ILOs.

21.3.3 Assessment methods

While accrediting bodies do not mandate the adoption of specific assessment methods to measure attainment of ILOs, multiple measures of performance are recommended. Assessment can include *formative* classroom assessment, which involves students and their teachers in 'the continuous monitoring of students' learning' while in the classroom (Angelo & Cross, 1993, p. xiv), or *summative* assessment, generally involving assessment at the end of a course, programme, or even after graduation. The website of Kingston University in the U.K. (http://www.kingston.ac.uk/undergraduate-course/accounting-finance-2013/teaching-learning-assessment.html) explains that:

> *Assessment takes a variety of forms including portfolios of coursework, essays, business reports, case studies, presentations and last, but certainly not least, exams. Some of the assessment will be conducted in groups, while others will be individual.*

Although there are many approaches available, Angelo and Cross (1993, p. 31) caution individual educators: '*If a classroom assessment technique does not appeal to your intuition and professional judgment as a teacher, don't use it.*' As a case in point, Herring & Izard (1992) suggest that traditional paper and pencil tests are best suited to assessing accounting knowledge but are less effective for assessing skills such as listening, problem-solving, and ethical behaviour.

Attainment of students' learning is often assessed using 'direct' methods, such as course-embedded measurement and demonstration-through-performance. Direct evidence demonstrates students' learning directly, in an unfiltered way, and reveals what students know and can do in relation to ILOs. The AACSB standards (AACSB, 2013c, p. 68) provided the following accounting example:

Learning goal

Each student shall be able to evaluate the financial position of organizations through examination of balance sheets, cash flow statements, and budgets.

Demonstration of achievement

The school uses a course-embedded examination to assess performance on this learning goal. The final examination in the required Financial Accounting course includes a section specifically aimed at assessment of this goal at a level that has been determined by the accounting academic staff. Student results are collected across all students and summary results are used for curricula development and improvement. A student's performance on this section must satisfy the minimal level, or it must be retaken until it is passed. Students for whom the Financial Accounting course is waived by virtue of undergraduate accounting coursework, must satisfactorily pass an equivalent examination.

With course-embedded measurement, specified ILOs are covered in required coursework via assignments, examinations and quizzes, case-studies, research projects, or other means, as illustrated in Table 21.2. Under the demonstration-through-performance approach, students are required to illustrate attainment of skills as a requirement for graduation. Measurement may involve a senior project or thesis, a special departmental examination, or a presentation that demonstrates the required knowledge or skills. In the accounting discipline, we also have professional examinations – the certified public accountants' examination, the chartered accountants' examination, the certified management accountants' examination, and so on. The timing of assessment begins from students' admission dates, through coursework and graduation to, in the case of professional examinations or certifications, some years after graduation.

Direct measures are generally supplemented with indirect measures, whereby students or others report their perception of how well a given ILO has been achieved. As shown in Table 21.2, indirect measures include surveying alumni about their satisfaction with their degree programme and their level of preparedness to enter the job market, gathering job placement or graduate school admission data, or surveying employers about the strengths and weaknesses of graduates. While indirect evidence can provide some information about students' achievement, it is mediated by the person conducting the measurement and influenced by perceptions and experiences. Therefore, outcomes assessment is strongest with a combination of assessment

Table 21.2 Examples of direct and indirect measures of students' learning

Direct measures	Indirect measures
• Course and homework assignments • Examinations and quizzes • Standardized tests • Term papers and reports • Observations of field work, internship performance, service learning, clinical experiences • Research projects • Class discussion participation • Case-study analysis • Rubric scores for writing, oral presentations, and performances • Artistic performances and products • Grades based on explicit criteria related to clear ILOs • Capstone projects, senior theses, exhibits, or performances • Pass rates or scores on licensure, certification, or subject area tests • Students' publications or conference presentations • Employer and internship supervisor ratings of students' performance • Performance on tests of writing, critical thinking, or general knowledge • Rubric scores for class assignments in General Education, interdisciplinary core courses, or other courses required of all students • Performance on achievement tests • Explicit self-reflections on what students have learned related to institutional programmes such as service learning (e.g. asking students to name the three most important things they have learned in a programme)	• Course evaluations • Test blueprints (outlines of the concepts and skills covered on tests) • Percentage of class time spent in active learning • Grades that are not based on explicit criteria related to clear ILOs • Focus group interviews with students, academic staff, or employees • Registration or course enrolment information • Department or programme review data • Job placement • Employer or alumni surveys • Students' perception surveys • Proportion of upper-level courses compared to the same programme at other institutions • Graduate school placement rates • Locally developed, commercial, or national surveys of students' perceptions or self-report of activities (e.g. National Survey of Student Engagement) • Transcript studies that examine patterns and trends of course selection and grading • Annual reports including institutional benchmarks (e.g. graduation and retention rates, grade point averages of graduates, etc.)

Source: Adapted from Skidmore (2012). Available at: http://cms.skidmore.edu/assessment/Handbook/direct-v-indirect-assessment.cfm.

methods, and accrediting bodies do not allow indirect measures to replace direct measures. In Europe, for example, EQUIS accreditation criteria calls for '*rigorous assessment processes for monitoring the quality of students' work*' as well as '*feedback from students and other stakeholders*' (EQUIS, 2013, p. 15).

In their compendium of classroom assessment techniques, Angelo & Cross (1993) provide suggestions too numerous to recount here, and many of their suggestions are ill-fitted to accounting education. However, several that may be useful for accounting educators are described here. One generic skill which many students lack is time management. A formative assessment technique described for this skill is a productive study-time log, whereby students fill in a log of study time, rate the productivity of that study time, and provide weekly summaries of effective and ineffective study, what they discovered about their own study habits, and how they can improve them. A tool for assessing listening skill is to pause periodically during the delivery of a lecture and ask students to write a one-sentence summary of what they have learned, using those sentences to identify lapses in understanding, revisit topics of confusion, and guide students in how to attend to the material more effectively. Angelo & Cross also suggest several assessment tools for problem-solving, including:

- *problem recognition tasks*, where students receive descriptions of scenarios or data and have to identify what type of problem is at hand;
- *documented solutions*, where students provide a narrative description of their decision process in solving a problem;
- *applications cards*, where students write down on index cards how a concept they've just learned applies to a real-world situation; and
- *student-generated test questions*.

An accounting example of the applications card method might be to have students write about where materiality may apply to financial and non-financial decisions.

The assessments described above are formative, meaning that they can be used while a course is still underway, giving the educator feedback in order to make adjustments in the current semester. Many assessment techniques are summative, in that they are used to assess learning when a project, course, or programme is completed, with the aims of evaluating past performance and guiding future teaching and curricular changes. These include examinations, surveys, and rubrics. A common technique for assessing students' writing is a rubric, a narrative description of various levels of work quality on different dimensions. Excerpts from a rubric used by one of the authors is presented in Table 21.3. Rubrics can also be developed to assess oral communication, group work, and presentation skills. What the educator must do in developing a rubric is to identify characteristics of students' performance and write descriptions that capture varying levels of performance in those characteristics.

Once assessment methods are selected for ILOs, an assessment schedule, scheme, or systematic approach to measurement should be developed. Involved academic staff will not be required to assess attainment of each ILO for each student in all sections of a course every semester, but assessment data should be collected often enough to compare current assessments against past assessments to ensure that areas identified for improvement have been examined. Thus, assessment can be accomplished by periodically examining samples of students' work, or by collecting data from selected course sections. Also, a representative number of academic staff should be involved in the assessment process to ensure the integrity of assessment results and programme improvements throughout.

21.3.4 Closing the continuous improvement loop

Assessment data is gathered, summarized, and evaluated periodically. The process requires comparison of assessment results to stated goals as well as prior findings. It may reveal voids or inadequacies, requiring changes to either the outcomes or the curriculum. On both a departmental and individual educator level, academic staff are forced to examine the extent to which a topic that they think they cover well is actually addressed and evaluated. Fortunately, the process lends itself to improvements in subsequent course delivery.

Table 21.3 Written communication rubric

	Excellent	Good	Weak	Poor
Mechanics of format (e.g. margins, font, sub-headings)	The format is consistently correct and appropriate to the assignment and discipline.	The format is generally correct and appropriate, with minor exceptions.	The format is often incorrect or inappropriate. Several formatting issues and problems.	The format is incorrect or inappropriate.
Documentation	The writer employs citations and documentation styles appropriate to the disciplinary task. Significant research is done.	References are cited and documented, but may contain errors. Appropriate research is done.	References are not consistent. Documentation style is inappropriate. Insufficient research is done.	References are not cited. Inappropriate research is done.
Usage (grammar, syntax, punctuation, spelling)	Few errors in syntax, grammar, punctuation, and/or spelling, and these do not interfere with the reading and understanding of this text.	Some errors in syntax, grammar, punctuation, and/or spelling, which may disrupt the flow of reading.	Many errors in syntax, grammar, punctuation, and/or spelling, which interfere with communication and damage the writer's credibility.	Countless errors in syntax, grammar, punctuation, or spelling that impede communication. Reader has to reread parts of the essay in order to comprehend them.
Style/word choice	The writer has full command of complex sentence structure and uses effectively for the assignment. The writer successfully uses appropriate words from the discipline. Words are precise.	The writer uses sentence structure with some variance, which is mostly correct. Word choice is appropriate to the task. The writer generally uses appropriate words from the discipline.	The writer tends to use basic, choppy, and/or structurally- repetitive sentences. Many words are not precise or appropriate to the discipline.	The writer repeatedly uses basic, choppy, and/or structurally- repetitive. Word-choice errors are frequent. Discipline-specific language is lacking.
Thesis	The writer develops a specific thesis that controls the paper.	There is a consistent thesis, but it may not be developed fully.	The thesis may be unclear or implicit, and may change throughout the paper.	The thesis is unclear or difficult to identify.
Organization & logic	The organization is very clear and captures the designated purpose. There is a logical progression of ideas. The introduction is inviting and challenging, and appropriate to the topic or thesis. The conclusion is purposeful and perceptive.	The organization is generally clear and captures the purpose. For the most part, there is a logical progression of ideas. The introduction sets the stage for the rest of the paper. The conclusion provides satisfying closure to the argument.	The organization is somewhat unclear. The progression of ideas is often not logical. The introduction generally matches the topic and is somewhat effective. The conclusion summarizes previously stated information.	The organization is unclear and does not capture the purpose. The ideas are illogical. The introduction is overly general, missing, misleading, or ineffective. The conclusion is absent, incomplete, or unfocussed.

Assessment evidence should show what students have learned and what processes contributed to that learning. It should help determine whether:

- current learning strategies are effective;
- the assessment methods are measuring appropriately; and
- the ILOs are appropriate.

In this step, the objective is not simply a determination of whether ILOs have been met, but more broadly a consideration of whether the degree programme's content, delivery methods, and materials are relevant, up-to-date, and of high quality. Any systemic problems should be identified so that necessary changes can be made. The bottom box of Figure 21.1 notes 'Present summary of results, evaluations, and recommendations for future improvements to both the academic staff and administration.' However, HEIs should respond to convincing evidence at any point in the assessment cycle.

The continuous improvement loop is closed when changes are made to update ILOs, assessment methods, or the degree programme in terms of content, course delivery, or most importantly, students' learning. Formative assessment (i.e. assessment made mid-stream to determine whether ILOs have been achieved), also enables corrective action to be taken before a student graduates. HEIs are dynamic, hence programme changes occur over time as a result of societal changes, educator attrition, industry developments, and weakness noted through the outcomes assessment process.

21.4 Critiques of assessment methods

In choosing assessment methods, the pull of a standardized test is a strong one, especially among those external parties who want to be able to compare outcomes across universities of all types (Olds, 2012), and among administrators who want to demonstrate accountability to those who have little understanding of the educational process (Powell, 2011). One such standardized examination, the Collegiate Learning Assessment (CLA), focusses on critical thinking, analytic reasoning, written communication, and problem-solving (Douglass *et al.*, 2012). The CLA is becoming the 'gold standard' for assessment internationally (Olds, 2012). However, Olds (2012) notes that such tests seem '*[to] ignore how students actually learn and the variety of experiences among different sub-populations*'. Furthermore, the test captures learning that takes place through a full curriculum by only a small sample of students, thus using its feedback to improve teaching by any specific educator or within any individual programme is problematic.

Another test used at the end of the programme by several universities in the U.S.A., China, Brazil, and elsewhere is the Student Experience in the Research University Survey (SERU-S), which uses self-reports by students of their development in the same general and critical thinking skills. The results of this test generally show correlation between grade performance and students' perceptions of learning (Douglass *et al.*, 2012), but again, there is no tie back to individual academic staff who can use the results to improve teaching and learning outcomes.

As noted above, there are numerous assessment methods available to academic staff, so those who reject standardized tests have many options, some of which have been described in this chapter. Others, however, reject the whole process of outcomes assessment. Powell (2011, p. 2) points out that '*enormous amounts of work are going into efforts to implement and follow up on these [assessment] programs at universities*', when there has been no empirical research that outcomes-based education is an improvement over traditional education. Powell also posits that, where standardized tests are used, teachers teach to the test, taking time away from integrating information in the classroom. Among other criticisms, Powell (ibid., p. 15) also notes that academic staff, '*give grades, read papers, and give tests . . . these are assessments*', and '*these processes are well understood by all involved*'. Herring & Izard (1992) refer to this last criticism as the redundancy argument, to which they add the critique that job placement already provides achievement data for outcome assessment. However, they point out that undergraduate grades have little correlation with performance in graduate school, and that they have almost no relationship with long-term career success.

21.5 Conclusion

In closing, an important question to consider is 'Why is outcomes assessment done?' While some may mumble, 'The university administration, accrediting body, or governing board mandated it', the correct answer should be to improve courses, improve academic programmes, improve teaching, and enhance students' learning. When taken seriously, outcomes assessment can engage academic staff in serious dialogue about students' learning, increasing and enhancing student–teacher interaction, and providing academic staff with a stronger sense of responsibility for students' learning (MAA, 2007). Despite its critics, it appears that outcomes assessment is here to stay, and the charge to academic staff is to find the approaches that measure what they hope to achieve and use those results to make modifications as necessary. We have attempted to provide examples of ILOs and assessment techniques, but the development of good assessment tools is still in its early stages. Although some may prefer a one-size-fits-all approach to assessment, a real understanding of the process leads to the recognition that each programme, and perhaps even each educator, needs to tailor methods to measure ILOs. Given the diversity of subject matter, educational approach, accountability influences, and student bodies, the techniques available should continue to expand rather than contract into a simple testing mechanism.

References

AAHE Assessment Forum (1992) *Assessment Principles of Good Practice*, Washington, DC: American Association for Higher Education.

Accounting Education Change Commission (1994) *Assessment for the New Curriculum: A Guide for Professional Accounting Programs*, Sarasota, FL: American Accounting Association. Available at: http://aaahq.org/aecc/assessment/index.htm.

Akers, M.D., Giacomino, D.E., & Trebby, J.P. (1997) Designing and implementing an accounting assessment program, *Issues in Accounting Education*, 12(Fall), 259–281.

American Institute of Certified Public Accountants (AICPA) (1999) *AICPA Core Competency Framework for Entry into the Accounting Profession*. Available at: http://www.aicpa.org.

American Institute of Certified Public Accountants (AICPA) (2005) *Functional Competencies*. Available at: http://www.aicpa.org/INTERESTAREAS/AccountingEducation/Resources/DownloadableDocuments/Functional%20Competencies.doc.

Anderson, L.W. & Krathwohl, D.R. (eds), with Airasian, P.W., Cruikshank, K.A., Mayer, R.E., Pintrich, P.R., Raths, J., & Wittrock, M.C. (2001) *A Taxonomy for Learning, Teaching, and Assessing: A Revision of Bloom's Taxonomy of Educational Objectives*, New York: Longman.

Angelo, T.A. & Cross, K.P. (1993) *Classroom Assessment Techniques: A Handbook for College Teachers*, San Francisco, CA: John Wiley & Sons, Inc.

Association of Chartered Certified Accountants (ACCA) (2012) *ACCA Qualification Course Details*. Available at: http://www.accaglobal.com/en/qualifications/glance/acca/details.html.

Association of Chartered Certified Accountants (ACCA) (2013) *Financial Reporting (INT)(F7): June and December 2013 Study Guide*. Available at: http://www.accaglobal.com/content/dam/acca/global/PDF-students/acca/f7/studyguides/f7-int-sg-2013.pdf.

Association of MBAs (AMBA) (2012) *Criteria for the Accreditation of MBA Programmes*. Available at: http://www.mbaworld.com/accreditationcriteria.

Association to Advance Collegiate Schools of Business (AACSB) (2013a) *About AACSB.* 22 July 2013. St. Louis, MO: AACSB. Available at: http://aacsb.edu.

Association to Advance Collegiate Schools of Business (AACSB) (2013b) *Eligibility Procedures and Accreditation Standards for Accounting Accreditation.* 8 April 2013. St. Louis, MO: AACSB. Available at: http://aacsb. edu.

Association to Advance Collegiate Schools of Business (AACSB) (2013c) *Eligibility Procedures and Accreditation Standards for Business Accreditation.* 8 April 2013. St. Louis, MO: AACSB. Available at: http://aacsb.edu.

Association to Advance Collegiate Schools of Business (AACSB) (2012) *Eligibility Procedures and Accreditation Standards for Business Accreditation.* 31 January 2012. St. Louis, MO: AACSB. Available at: http:// aacsb.edu.

Barr, R.B. & Tagg, J. (1995) From teaching to learning: a new paradigm for undergraduate education, *Change,* 27, 12–25.

Bloom, B.S. (ed.), with Engelhart, M.D., Furst, E.J., Hill, W.H., & Krathwohl, D.R. (1956) *Taxonomy of Educational Objectives: The Classification of Educational Goals. Handbook 1: Cognitive Domain,* New York: David McKay.

Boyle, W.F. & Charles, M. (2010) Leading learning through assessment of learning, *School Leadership and Management,* 30(3), 285–300.

Bresciani, M.J., Gardner, M.M., & Hickmott, J. (2010) *Demonstrating Student Success: A Practical Guide to Outcomes-Based Assessment of Learning and Development in Student Affairs,* Sterling, VA: Stylus Publishing.

Calderon, T.G., Green, B.P., & Harkness, M.D. (2003) Program assessment: fundamental challenges and issues, in Calderon, T.G., Green, B.P., & Harkness, M.D. (eds) *Best Practices in Accounting Program Assessment,* Sarasota, FL: Teaching and Curriculum Section of the American Accounting Association.

Daigle, R.J., Hayes, D.C., & Hughes II, K.E. (2007) Assessing student learning outcomes in the introductory accounting information systems course using the AICPA Core Competency Framework, *Journal of Information Systems,* 21(1), 149–169.

Demong, R.F., Lindgreen Jr., J.H. & Perry, S.E. (1994) Designing an assessment program for accounting, *Issues in Accounting Education,* 9(Spring), 11–28.

Douglass, J.A., Thomson, G., & Zhao, C. (2012) The learning outcomes race: the value of self-reported gains in large research universities, *Higher Education,* 64, 317–335.

European Quality Improvement System (EQUIS) (2013) *EQUIS Standards and Criteria.* Available at: http://www.efmd.org/index.php/accreditation-main/equis/equis-guides.

Ewell, P.T. (2002) An emerging scholarship: a brief history of assessment, in Banta, T.W. (ed.) *Building a Scholarship for Assessment,* San Francisco: Jossey-Bass, pp. 3–25.

Gainen, J. & Locatelli, P. (1995) *Assessment for the New Curriculum: A Guide for Professional Accounting Programs* (American Accounting Association Accounting Education Series, no. 11). Available at: http://aaahq. org/AECC/assessment/index.htm.

Herring III, H.C. & Izard, C.D. (1992) Outcomes assessment of accounting majors, *Issues in Accounting Education,* 7(Spring), 1–17.

International Accounting Education Standards Board (2014a) *International Education Standard (IES) 2: Initial Professional Development – Technical Competence (Revised),* New York: International Federation of Accountants (IFAC).

International Accounting Education Standards Board (2014b) *International Education Standard (IES) 3: Initial Professional Development – Professional Skills (Revised).* New York: International Federation of Accountants (IFAC).

International Accounting Education Standards Board (2014c) *International Education Standard (IES) 4: Initial Professional Development – Professional Values, Ethics, and Attitudes (Revised),* New York: International Federation of Accountants (IFAC).

Kidwell, L.A., Fisher, D.G., Braun, R.L., & Swanson, D.L. (2012) Developing learning objectives for accounting ethics using Bloom's taxonomy, *Accounting Education: an international journal,* 22(1), 44–65.

Klenowski, V. (2011) Assessment for learning in the accountability era: Queensland, Australia, *Studies in Educational Evaluation,* 37(1), 78–83.

Mann, S.J. (2004) *Guidelines for Writing Aims and Intended Learning Outcomes at the Programme and Course level.* Available at: http://www.gla.ac.uk/media/media_105307_en.pdf.

Massaro, V. (2010) Cui bono? The relevance and impact of quality assurance, *Journal of Higher Education Policy and Management,* 32(1), 17–26.

Mathematical Association of America (MAA) (2007) *Assessment of Learning: What Is It, and Why Is It Important?* Available at: http://www.maa.org/saum/articles/assessmentppt/text6.htm.

National Commission on Excellence in Education (1983) *A Nation at Risk: The Imperative for Educational Reform*, Washington, DC: United States Department of Education. Available at: http://www.csus.edu/indiv/l/langd/Nation_at_Risk.pdf.

Olds, K. (2012) Searching for the Holy Grail of learning outcomes, *Inside Higher Ed*. Available at: http://www.insidehighered.com/blogs/globalhighered/searching-holy-grail-learning-outcomes#ixzz2RnSYfK3Q.

Organisation for Economic Co-operation and Development (OECD) (2012) *Testing Student and University Performance Globally: OECD's AHELO*. Paris: OECD. Available at: http://www.oecd.org/edu/ahelo.

Pepin, B. & Moon, B. (1999) *Curriculum, Cultural Traditions and Pedagogy: Understanding the Work of Teachers in England, France, and Germany*. Ebook: Education Resources Information Center (ERIC) ED437319.

Powell, J.W. (2011) Outcomes assessment: conceptual and other problems, *Journal of Academic Freedom*, (2), 1–25.

Pusecker, K.L., Torres, M.R., Crawford, I., Levia, D., Lehman, D., & Copic, G. (2011/2012). Increasing the validity of outcomes assessment, *Peer Review*, 13/14(4/1), 27–30.

Rajkumar, T. M., Anderson, P., & Benamati, J. (2011) Are student self-assessments a valid proxy for direct assessments in efforts to improve information systems courses and programs? An empirical study, *Communications of the Association for Information Systems*, 28(May), 537–548.

Siegel, G. & Sorensen, J.E. (1999) *Counting More, Counting Less, Transformations in the Management Accounting Profession* (The 1999 Practice Analysis of Management Accounting), Montvale, NJ: Institute of Management Accountants.

Skidmore College (2012) *Assessment at Skidmore College: Direct vs. Indirect Assessment Methods*. Available at: http://cms.skidmore.edu/assessment/Handbook/direct-v-indirect-assessment.cfm.

Stivers, B.P., Campbell, J.E., & Hermanson, H.H. (2000) An assessment program for accounting: design, implementation, and reflection, *Issues in Accounting Education*, 15(November), 553–581.

Taylor, F.W. (1998) *The Principles of Scientific Management*, Mineola, NY: Dover Publications.

Weldy, T.G. & Turnipseed, D.L. (2010) Assessing and improving learning in business schools: direct and indirect measures of learning, *Journal of Education for Business*, 85, 268–273.

About the authors

Linda A. Kidwell is an Associate Professor of Accounting at the University of Wyoming, U.S.A. (lkidwell@uwyo.edu) where she teaches auditing, financial accounting, and accounting ethics. She is also a member of the Executive Committee of the International Association for Accounting Education and Research (IAAER). Her primary research focus is accounting ethics.

Suzanne Lowensohn is an Associate Professor of Accounting at Colorado State University, U.S.A. (Suzanne.lowensohn@business.colostate.edu) where she chairs the undergraduate assurance of learning committee. Her primary research and teaching focus is on governmental accounting and auditing.

22

Evaluating accounting programmes

Thomas G. Calderon

UNIVERSITY OF AKRON, U.S.A.

CONTENTS

Abstract

This chapter, which complements Chapters 20, 21 and 29, discusses assessment from the perspective of a coherent Administrative Control System (ACS) and develops the foundation for a general framework to evaluate and promote the effectiveness of accounting programmes. A model of the ACS is presented as a normative framework for evaluating accounting programmes. The model, which was originally adapted from Kaplan & Norton's work on balanced scorecards and strategy maps (Kaplan & Norton, 1996, 2000), is holistic and incorporates the five major principles that guide the development of the ACS. The chapter also addresses input, process, and output control surrogates that are needed to facilitate operation of the ACS. Rooted in the discussion throughout this chapter is the assumption, adapted from Gates (2013) that, without measurement and reflection, change and improvement are 'doomed to be rare and erratic' (Rosen, 2012; Gates, 2013). Processes used to evaluate academic programmes at a sample of higher education institutions are surveyed. Implications and guidance for accounting programmes are presented and discussed.

Keywords

administrative control system, framework for programme evaluation, measurement surrogates, programme evaluation, programme review

22.1 Introduction

The main aims of this chapter are:

- to discuss programme evaluation from the perspective of a coherent administrative control system;
- to discuss the elements of the administrative control system as a general framework for evaluating accounting programmes;
- to present examples of an administrative control system and demonstrate the alignment that exists among the different elements;
- to reflect on the role of measurement and reporting in the administrative control system;
- to survey and discuss the processes which higher education institutions actually use to evaluate accounting programmes; and
- to discuss the implications of contemporary programme evaluation processes and offer guidelines for refining the processes used to evaluate accounting programmes.

Over the past three decades, stakeholders from all types of organizations, and across all continents, have proactively called for and supported greater transparency and accountability (Vedder, 2008). In particular, higher education institutions (HEIs) have been criticized for lack of transparency and accountability (McCormick, 2009; Dickeson, 2010). Politicians, leaders in the academy, and accreditation agencies have challenged HEIs to pay attention to and report on the effectiveness of their programmes. In addition to advocacy for greater accountability and transparency, stakeholders have also called for improvements in the quality of academic programmes (Ewell, 2008).

Many institutions have responded to calls for greater transparency and quality enhancements by requiring detailed reviews of academic programmes (Wergin & Swingen, 2000; Ewell, 2008; Dickeson, 2010). Reviews may be cyclical, triggered by financial or enrolment changes, government mandates, or even pressure from academic staff. The focus is often on demonstrating that programmes have clear goals and objectives, and that they are achieving their stated goals. Proponents of programme review believe that careful evaluation of academic programmes can lead to more desirable educational outcomes, quality enhancements, and greater effectiveness of higher education (Bresciani, 2006). The consequences of programme review and evaluation can be severe (Berrett, 2011). They can demonstrate that:

- programmes are being held accountable;
- their operations and activities are transparent;
- they are achieving their broad goals and objectives; and
- they are continuously improving.

On the other hand, programme review and evaluation can also uncover deficiencies in such areas as transparency, accountability, students' learning outcomes, students' success, research and professional development, and continuous improvement. Consequences can potentially include changes in leadership, personnel, curricula, and budgets.

The thesis of this chapter is that evaluation of accounting programmes should be designed and implemented as part of a coherent administrative control system (ACS). Controls in the context of this chapter refer to strategies, processes, and action that academic staff, administrators, and others who share in the governance of HEIs, use to foster goal-congruent behaviour in their respective programmes and educational units. Administrative control involves planning, programming, directing, and motivating behaviour toward organizational goals and specific objectives. Five core principles often guide the ACS of an HEI (Astin, 1993):

1 core educational values founded in the mission of the educational unit;
2 interests of stakeholders;
3 focus on outcomes as well as on input and processes that generate those outcomes;
4 coherent, well-articulated systems and processes, not *ad hoc* processes; and
5 academic leadership that fosters goal-congruent behaviour among participants in the system.

These principles are consistent with the ultimate objective of ACSs, i.e. to foster and achieve goal-directed behaviour among organizational participants. While the chapter calls for a coherent ACS, it must be noted that programme evaluation is most effective among institutions '*that give maximum flexibility to units to define for themselves the critical evaluation questions, identify the key stakeholders and sources of evidence, and determine the most appropriate analysis and interpretation procedures*' (Wergin & Swingen, 2000, p. 15).

A prerequisite for success of the ACS is a focus on process with a commitment to continuous improvement among the academic staff, rather than the mere production of a programme evaluation report (ibid.).

This chapter, which complements Chapters 20, 21, and 29 in this volume, discusses assessment from the perspective of a coherent ACS and develops the foundation for a general framework to evaluate and promote the effectiveness of accounting programmes. A model of the ACS is presented as a normative framework for evaluating accounting programmes. The model, which was originally adapted from Kaplan & Norton's work on balanced scorecards and strategy maps (Kaplan & Norton, 1996, 2000), is holistic and incorporates the five major principles that guide the development of the ACS. The chapter also addresses input, process, and output control surrogates that are needed to facilitate operation of the ACS. Rooted in the discussion throughout this chapter is the assumption, adapted from Gates (2013) that, without measurement and reflection, change and improvement are '*doomed to be rare and erratic*' (Rosen, 2012; Gates, 2013).

The chapter is organized into six sections beyond this Introduction. Section 22.2 defines the nature of programme review as presented in the chapter, and discusses the dimensions and scope of the ACS. The section highlights various examples from actual accounting programs. The focus in Section 22.3 is on measurement surrogates. The basic thesis is that measurement is often challenging, as several educational inputs, processes and outcomes may be nebulous and not physically observed. Much of this section comes from previous work which sought to develop a framework for encouraging effective teaching (Calderon *et al.*, 1996). In Section 22.4, the emphasis shifts to observations from the practice of programme review at various institutions. The section describes:

- the stated goals of programme review;
- scope, process, and ownership;
- review cycles and data management; and
- consequences of programme review and evaluation.

Actual programme review guidelines from 50 universities in the U.S.A., Canada, and Australia form the basis for that section. While most of these universities are in the U.S.A., the guidelines provide important insight that should be useful to administrators and educators in many different countries. Finally, the chapter ends with Section 22.5 which describes implications, and Section 22.6 which presents the conclusions.

Throughout the chapter, terms such as *programme review* and *programme evaluation* are used interchangeably. Similarly, the term *academic unit* is used in various sections of the chapter to refer to an area such as a department or a college within a university that has programmes which may be subject to review and evaluation. 'Credit hour', a widely used term in North American HEIs (Blumenstyk, 2010; Parry, 2013; Uitinen, 2013), is a measure of educational activity that takes place in a course during a week over one semester. Thus, a '3 credit hour course' would generally meet in a classroom for approximately three hours each week for one semester.

22.2 Evaluation of programmes

Academic staff and administrators do not always mean the same thing when they refer to evaluation of accounting programmes. It is important, therefore, to clarify the context in which this chapter is written. While some might think of programme evaluation from the narrow perspective of students' success in examinations, or demonstration of students' learning, this chapter defines programme evaluation as a systematic process used to assess attainment of desired goals and specific objectives that are aligned with the mission of an accounting programme. As such, it focusses on inputs and available resources, processes, and outcomes within the context of the stated mission, goals and objectives of an academic unit (e.g. an accounting department) or programme within an academic unit (e.g. the accounting programme). Programme evaluation is best organized as a collaborative (rather than adversarial) process that identifies opportunities for further development and improvement (Wergin & Swingen, 2000). This broad concept of programme evaluation is consistent with the core principles of ACS. It is also consistent with the view that programme evaluation needs to respect the diverse missions and foci of academic units and the programmes they offer (Wergin & Swingen, 2000; Bresciani, 2006).

The ACS in higher education serves the necessary function of integrating goals of numerous organizational participants and sub-entities into the ultimate goal of the organization. Effective leaders in the academy use the ACS to focus attention and motivate academic staff, students, and other stakeholders to accomplish university, college, departmental, and individual goals. Goal-directed behaviour is fostered through relevant programmes, guidelines, resources, and incentives that add value to the interests of stakeholders. Programme evaluation based on a coherent ACS, among other things, functions as a constant reminder of the links between the activities of the programme and its mission, goals and objectives.

A vital component of the evaluation process is comparison between observed performance and predetermined targets or performance norms. If actual performance is on target, the educational unit is presumed to be effective; otherwise, the unit may be viewed as being in need of development. In either case, the evaluation process will normally produce ideas and initiatives for nurturing success and fostering improvement. Effective leaders channel resources and motivate behaviour to develop and execute those ideas and initiatives. In general, a well-designed ACS will consist of both a technical and behavioural dimension (Ramanathan, 1982). Together, the two broad dimensions of the ACS define goals and motivate goal-directed behaviour. Both dimensions are discussed and illustrated below.

22.2.1 The technical dimension

The technical dimension of the ACS consists of an integrated set of components which defines and identifies what constitutes effectiveness. As implied by Figure 22.1, the technical dimension determines organizational effectiveness in the sense that its various components define mission, goals, and objectives as well as the specific outcomes or events that constitute goal attainment.

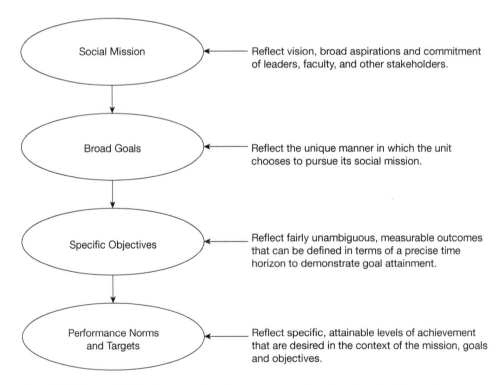

Figure 22.1 The administrative control system: components of the technical dimension

The social mission of the educational unit, the first component of the technical dimension, reflects the vision and commitment of its administrators, academic staff, and other stakeholders. The unit's mission determines its values and sets the stage for identifying, measuring, evaluating, and promoting desired outcomes (e.g. see Figure 22.2). The accounting department highlighted in Figure 22.2 pursues a mission of preparing students to become competent and responsible accounting and business professionals through bachelor's and master's degree programmes, which are driven by dedicated scholars and teachers who contribute to the profession, the discipline, and the community that they serve. This mission statement was developed through a collaborative process that involved the academic staff, administrative staff, the corporate community, alumni, and students. It aligns with the context of the broader institution in which the department operates, the environment in which the academic unit functions, and the specific values and interests of key internal and external stakeholders. Accreditation organizations and systems across the globe require a well-articulated mission as part of their criteria (e.g. the Association to Advance Collegiate Schools of Business (AACSB), the European Quality Improvement System (EQUIS), the Association of MBAs (AMBA), and the Accreditation Council for Business Schools and Programs (ACBSP)).

Broad goals represent the unique manner in which the unit chooses to pursue its social mission. They are both long-term and abstract in nature, and are designed to serve as continuing guidelines for directing activities and programmes. That is, they serve to define, in a fairly general manner, the primary ways in which the unit will pursue its mission (see Figure 22.2). In this example, the accounting department's mission implies that it will use scholars and teachers who contribute to the discipline and the profession. Thus, as a broad goal, it seeks to foster research and writing that contribute to excellence in the profession and the discipline. Identifying a series of specific objectives that define success further develops this and other broad goals. As a result, the accounting department outlines, as a specific objective, that its academic staff will conduct high quality research and publish research papers in aspirant professional and academic journals. It is implicit in this specific objective that the accounting programme has (or will) create a list of aspirant professional and academic journals. It also implies that the department will have a definition of 'high quality' in the context of its mission and the environment in which it operates.

In building a coherent ACS, broad goals are normally translated into specific objectives that organizational units will pursue. Normally, specific objectives are measurable events, items or outcomes that are associated with a precise time horizon (e.g. Figure 22.2). Since certain specific objectives for an educational unit may not be physically observed, and often contain nebulous concepts (e.g. *equip students with core knowledge, skills and abilities in business and accounting* as listed in Figure 22.2), measurement surrogates are frequently used to identify and assess the degree of achievement of specific objectives (Ramanathan, 1982; Green et al., 1998). It is through achievement of these specific objectives, measured directly or through a series of surrogates, that an educational unit demonstrates its effectiveness.

An educational unit with a mature ACS will normally develop and publicize (at least internally) performance norms and targets for each specific objective. Performance norms and targets are specific, attainable, and desirable. They emanate directly from the specific objectives of the unit and are, therefore, the signals that guide the behaviour of academic staff, administrative staff, and other stakeholders toward the goals of the entity. This is aptly illustrated in Figure 22.2 for an accounting department. Each performance norm/target is aligned with the specific objective of the department, and specific objectives are tightly linked to the broad goals of the unit.

A coherent and well-designed ACS can help the educational unit to fulfil its obligations to stakeholders by facilitating transparency and goal congruent behaviour. It also serves as a basis

MISSION

Prepare students to become competent and responsible accounting and business professionals through bachelor's and master's degree programs, which are driven by dedicated scholars and teachers who contribute to the profession, the discipline and the community that we serve.

BROAD GOALS

| Provide students with a relevant business and professional education to become dynamic players in a globally competitive economy. | Foster research and writing that contribute to excellence in the profession and the discipline. | Be an active participant in and a contributor to the business, professional, and civic communities |

SPECIFIC OBJECTIVES

| Equip students with core knowledge, skills and abilities in business and accounting. | Develop decision-making skills. | Develop relevant analytical, critical thinking, technology, oral and written communication skills. | Place graduates in desirable positions. | Conduct high quality research and publish research papers in aspirant professional and academic journals. | Conduct high quality seminars and work-shops for business and professional communities. | Participate in the leadership and governance of academic, professional and civic organizations. |

PERFORMANCE NORMS & TARGETS

Equip students with core knowledge	Decision-making skills	Critical thinking, analytical, technology and communication skills	Place graduates in desirable positions	Research and writing (yearly targets)	Seminars and work-shops (yearly targets)	Contribution to business, professional, academic and civic organizations (yearly targets)
– At least 80% of graduating students earn a score of 75% or better on in-house developed competency examination – At least 80% of students demonstrate satisfactory ability (based on faculty designed rubric) to apply their accounting and business knowledge, skills and abilities – At least a 80% pass rate on professional exams for eligible students.	– At least 80% of students demonstrate satisfactory skills (based on faculty designed rubric) in analyzing and presenting a comprehensive case analysis – At least satisfactory rating on all items included on an employer satisfaction survey.	– At least 80% of students demonstrate satisfactory skills (based on faculty designed rubric) in analyzing and presenting a comprehensive case analysis – At least satisfactory rating on all items included on an employer satisfaction survey. – Average of C or better on final examinations in selected classes in the curriculum designed to develop, nurture and evaluate these skills.	– Average at least 75% placement rate three months after graduation – 95% of students who receive employment within three-months after graduation are in high quality jobs – Compensation is at least at the level of the regional average for entry level professionals.	– Average of one article per year per faculty member per year in aspirant journals – Average one research seminar/workshop per semester.	– Average of one professional development seminar per academic year.	– Average of one leadership position in each type of organization per year (academic, professional, and civic) – Average of one service learning class with significant student participation per year.

Figure 22.2 Example of the technical dimension of an administrative control system

for programme evaluation and possibly resource allocation. These observations are reflected in Figure 22.2. As shown in Figure 2.22, the broad goals spell out, in general terms, how the unit will seek to pursue its mission. The specific objectives detail measurable outcomes that the unit will seek to achieve within a specified period. Finally, norms and targets are defined for each specific objective.

A glance at Figure 22.2 illustrates the values of the academic unit as well as the standards by which success (or failure) is assessed for purposes of programme evaluation. In that context, programme evaluation would require maintenance of information systems to ensure that relevant measures are captured, stored, compared with the stipulated norms and targets, and reported. Of course, it is assumed that appropriate leadership, programmes, and incentives are in place to promote goal-directed behaviour.

22.2.2 The behavioural dimension

Two major areas of emphasis in the behavioural dimension of the ACS are:

- acceptance by academic staff of the unit's performance norms and targets; and
- efforts to accomplish goal-directed behaviour.

It is widely believed that participation by academic staff and shared governance fosters acceptance of the technical dimension of the ACS, and fosters goal-directed behaviour among academic staff (AAUP, 1966; Stensaker, 2012). Nonetheless, acceptance by academic staff of the ACS, as well as their behaviour, is influenced by their expected intrinsic and extrinsic valences for organizational goals, and the specific programmes and tasks that are implemented to pursue those goals. For example, academic staff who expect to derive satisfaction from affiliation with and pursuance of a specific objective (e.g. ensuring that students are equipped to pass professional examinations) will perceive this objective positively. Similarly, academic staff who expect to be rewarded as a result of achieving the performance norm for this specific objective (e.g. a pass rate in professional examinations that is higher than last year's, and at least equal to the national average) will also have a favourable perception of that objective. If both situations prevail for all specific objectives, academic staff will not only accept the performance norms and targets of the unit, but will also direct their behaviour toward achieving the stated norms and targets.

Planning, programming, budgeting, reporting (feedback) and evaluation are overlapping activities in the behavioural dimension of the ACS which are geared toward influencing perceptions and motivating goal-directed behaviour. Together, these activities determine the nature of acceptance by the academic staff, their preferences and, ultimately, their contribution to the goals of the educational unit. Planning is concerned with goals, programming with specific objectives, and budgeting with short-term activities and events that will impact on performance norms and targets. Planning, programming, and budgeting are undertaken within the confines of the mission of the unit. Reporting and feedback provide information for understanding and monitoring progress toward goals and objectives. Further, reporting and feedback foster transparency, provide input for assessing an academic unit's effectiveness, and offer insight into the types of actions needed for alignment of performance with goals and objectives. Overall, activities in the behavioural dimension should enhance the tight, well-articulated link that exists in the technical dimension of the ACS, and should serve as the basis for motivating desired behaviour in the educational unit.

22.3 Measurement surrogates

There is no single indicator, such as earnings per share or stock market price, that serves as a gauge for assessing how well a non-profit institution or programme is performing (Ramanathan, 1982; Young & Anthony, 2008). Many goals and objectives in educational units are not physically observable and are often challenging to define. Thus, HEIs must carefully select indicators that most closely signal the extent to which they are attained. In that context, educational units use measurement surrogates to evaluate their programmes. Although not a perfectly precise gauge of a specific objective, measurement surrogates provide the most complete and reliable picture of the performance of an educational unit.

A well-designed ACS will include measurement surrogates for input, processes, and output. As implied in Chapters 20 and 21 of this volume, these types of surrogates inform educators and policy-makers, and assist with performance evaluation and decision-making. Each type of surrogate is discussed below.

22.3.1 Input surrogates

Input surrogates are needed to assess overall programme efficiency and the effectiveness of organizational units in securing required input. In situations where a process does not produce an observable, physically transformed output, input surrogates play the added role of demonstrating the incremental gains that are evident in the output (Ramanathan, 1982; Young & Anthony, 2008). In such situations, input surrogates are measured before and after they are processed by the system. The difference between the two measures represents an indicator of output generated by the process. For example, the impact of a programme on students' analytical skills and written communication skills is not assessable unless these skills are tested when students first enter the programme and then again when they leave. The programme is analogous to a treatment in an experiment, and it is presumed that differences between pre-treatment and post-treatment states are driven by the treatment (Yarbrough et al., 2011).

To produce or deliver desired outcomes, educational units must stipulate specific objectives and norms for all major inputs. These specific objectives and performance norms, which may be specified in terms of quality and quantity thresholds, then become the basis for assessing input (SUNY, 2012). The role of input assessment can be illustrated by focussing on a quality threshold. If it is known that all inputs enter the system with the specified quality threshold, and with little variation, then there is no need to assess input quality. On the other hand, if it is known that there is substantial variation in the quality of inputs, or if there is uncertainty about input quality, then a surrogate for input quality must be identified, measured, and assessed. An apt example of this latter situation is student quality in an accounting programme. Since there is usually a great deal of variation in the quality of students admitted to accounting and business programmes, it is essential that a surrogate for student quality be measured and assessed upon (or prior to) entry into the programme. Examples of quality surrogates that might be assessed are analytical skills, critical thinking skills, oral and written communication skills, and technology skills. These skills can then be measured and assessed at regular intervals (e.g. at the end of every academic year) to determine students' progress and the impact of the programme on these highly desirable skills. In fact, this process of measurement and remeasurement of skills can be the basis for assessing the success of quality management and continuous improvement efforts in the programme. Furthermore, while the initial goal of this process is to provide information on input quality, as the process continues over the academic cycle, it produces valuable output information.

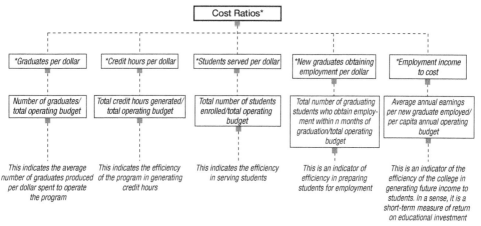

Figure 22.3 Cost ratios

Many resources consumed to produce output are valued in terms of cost. Costs confine the scope of activities and programmes and, therefore, limit the degree to which broad goals will be achieved. Costs also impact on the availability of rewards and incentives for academic staff and administrative staff who contribute to the attainment of programme goals. Thus, cost is an important surrogate for resources consumed to generate output. As a surrogate for input, cost is readily used to judge the efficiency of the educational unit in generating output. For example, ratios of output to costs provide valuable information about the efficiency of the system. Given that resource scarcity is often a major challenge in the academy, the assessment process should provide information on the efficiency of the organization in utilizing budget resources. Figure 22.3 provides some useful examples of output-to-cost ratios that shed light on the efficiency of an educational unit in its teaching efforts.

22.3.2 Process surrogates

Process surrogates are needed to gain better insight into the nature of the systems used to produce output and to provide a basis for assessing factors that contribute to success or failure. They also provide significant scope for nurturing and enhancing a system that currently produces desired outcomes. Process surrogates are essential in any programme that pursues total quality and continuous improvement. Teaching is the most fundamental process used in academia to transform input into output. Students enter the institution, learn from the instruction they receive from teachers, and develop skills through their interaction with the various participants in the teaching process. Thus, the effectiveness of the teaching process will have a direct bearing on the quality and characteristics of output. Teaching processes need to be measured, monitored, and evaluated to ensure that they yield desired outcomes. Similarly, processes used to encourage and support research must be carefully monitored and assessed to ensure that they yield the desired types of publications and other scholarly outcomes.

EFMD (2012) offers several examples of processes, which HEIs seeking EQUIS accreditation must pursue and monitor (see Figure 22.4). For example, these HEIs must demonstrate appropriate processes to develop a portfolio of programmes that is consistent with their mission

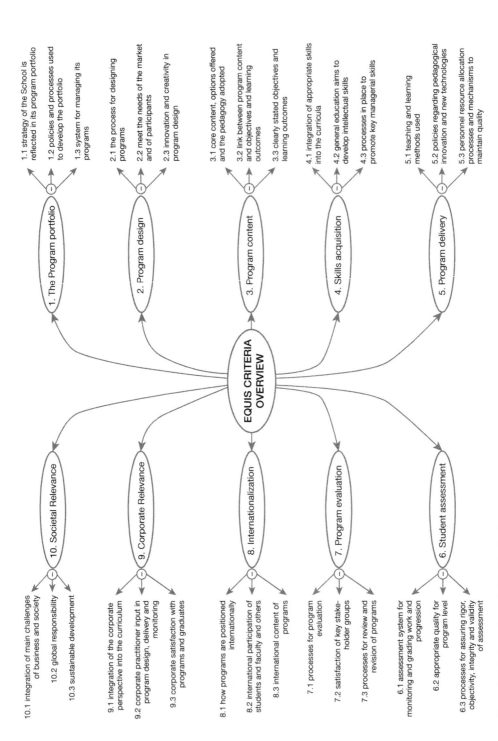

1.1 strategy of the School is reflected in its program portfolio
1.2 policies and processes used to develop the portfolio
1.3 system for managing its programs

2.1 the process for designing programs
2.2 meet the needs of the market and of participants
2.3 innovation and creativity in program design

3.1 core content, options offered and the pedagogy adopted
3.2 link between program content and objectives and learning outcomes
3.3 clearly stated objectives and learning outcomes

4.1 integration of appropriate skills into the curricula
4.2 general education aims to develop intellectual skills
4.3 processes in place to promote key managerial skills

5.1 teaching and learning methods used
5.2 policies regarding pedagogical innovation and new technologies
5.3 personnel resource allocation processes and mechanisms to maintain quality

1. The Program portfolio

2. Program design

3. Program content

4. Skills acquisition

5. Program delivery

EQUIS CRITERIA OVERVIEW

10. Societal Relevance

9. Corporate Relevance

8. Internationalization

7. Program evaluation

6. Student assessment

10.1 integration of main challenges of business and society
10.2 global responsibility
10.3 sustainable development

9.1 integration of the corporate perspective into the curriculum
9.2 corporate practitioner input in program design, delivery and monitoring
9.3 corporate satisfaction with programs and graduates

8.1 how programs are positioned internationally
8.2 international participation of students and faculty and others
8.3 international content of programs

7.1 processes for program evaluation
7.2 satisfaction of key stake-holder groups
7.3 processes for review and revision of programs

6.1 assessment system for monitoring and grading work and progression
6.2 appropriate quality for program level
6.3 processes for assuring rigor, objectivity, integrity and validity of assessment

Figure 22.4 Overview of EQUIS criteria

and strategy. Additionally, processes must be in place to design programmes that are relevant in the context of market and stakeholders' needs. Processes and mechanisms must exist to ensure effective delivery and quality of programmes, social and corporate relevance, internationalization, programme evaluation, and assessment of students. In that context, examples of process surrogates might include counts for such items as the number of times programmes are evaluated, students' and academic staff's satisfaction levels with programme delivery methods, extent of academic staff's satisfaction with and involvement in programme evaluation, and the number of classes that include coverage of global responsibility and sustainable development.

22.3.3 Output surrogates

Output surrogates may be classified into two broad categories: general outputs and outcome indicators. Outcome indicators are tied directly to specific objectives and serve to demonstrate overall effectiveness. They are the clearest signal that an educational unit is producing or delivering the results that its mission and broad goals dictate. General outputs, on the other hand, do not necessarily indicate achievement of a specific objective. They identify the results of processes and sub-processes, but may shed no direct light on the extent to which specific objectives are being achieved. For example, the number of students who graduate each semester from an accounting programme may shed very little light on the extent to which the programme is achieving its intended learning outcomes (ILOs). Yet, it provides a useful context for understanding the framework and perhaps the significance of achieving those ILOs. It is, therefore, a general output. Similarly, the total number of students registered in the accounting programme is not an outcome indicator. It is certainly an important indicator for assessing efficiency, but it does not reflect the effectiveness of the educational unit.

AACSB- and ACBSP-accredited accounting programmes generally use output surrogates that are related to such areas as branding and reputation, students' learning and students' success, research quality and productivity, and engagement with the business and professional community (AACSB, 2012; ACBSP, 2012). Similarly, institutions accredited by EQUIS use output surrogates related to students' learning and skills development, international positioning, relevance to the corporate community, and societal relevance (EFMD, 2012). These accreditation organizations require output surrogates to be tightly integrated with the mission, broad goals, and specific objectives of the educational unit or programme. For example, AACSB-accredited accounting programmes must demonstrate students' learning in such areas as:

- the roles played by accountants in society providing and ensuring the integrity of financial and other information;
- the ethical and regulatory environment for accountants;
- business processes and analysis;
- internal controls and security;
- risk assessment and assurance for financial and non-financial reporting;
- recording, analysis, and interpretation of historical and prospective financial and non-financial information;
- project and engagement management;
- design and application of technology to financial and non-financial information management;
- tax policy, strategy, and compliance for individuals and enterprises;
- international accounting issues and practices including roles and responsibilities played by accountants within a global context (AACSB, 2012).

To demonstrate learning in those broad educational areas, many AACSB-accredited accounting programmes use such measures as internally-developed examinations, simulations, and case studies and projects graded by using a rubric developed by the academic staff (Martell & Calderon, 2005; Weldy & Turnipseed, 2010; Apple *et al.*, 2012). An example of a written rubric can be seen in Table 21.3. These programmes measure the level of students' learning at the programme level by examining samples of the actual work produced by students and documenting the proportion of students who exceed a minimum threshold on these assessments. Because these approaches focus on the evaluation of actual work samples, assessment experts and accreditation organizations, such as the AACSB, refer to them as direct measures (Martell & Calderon, 2005; AACSB, 2007). Another approach used is to survey graduating students, alumni, and employers to determine their satisfaction with, or perceptions of the extent of learning, in the programme. Programmes also use meetings and focus group sessions with key stakeholders to solicit their views about the level of students' learning. Referred to as indirect measures of students' learning, surveys and focus group meetings can produce invaluable insight into the accomplishments, strengths and weaknesses of a programme (Ewell & Jones, 1993; Kelley *et al.*, 2010; Weldy & Turnipseed, 2010). However, various accreditation organizations, particularly those based in the U.S.A. (e.g. AACSB), have traditionally shown a preference for more direct measures (Martell & Calderon, 2005; AACSB, 2007; Kelley *et al.*, 2010). In Chapter 29 of this volume Apostolou and Gammie offer additional insight into business and accounting accreditation.

Although the above list of measures does not distinguish between outcome indicators and general output, it is generally observed that effective programme evaluation will consider the mission and goals of the academic unit (AACSB, 2012; ACBSP, 2012; EFMD, 2012). It is through the consideration of broad goals and specific objectives that output surrogates can be tailored to indicate outcomes and facilitate the design and implementation of effective programme reviews. The tailoring process normally requires the sequence of steps listed below.

1 Identify the broad goals that are linked to the mission of the programme.
2 Identify the specific objectives that detail how the broad goals are pursued.
3 Identify a broad set of measurable indicators that signal the achievement of specific objectives (achievement indicators).
4 Identify criteria for selecting among competing achievement indicators, e.g. cost, data availability, complexity, comprehension.
5 Evaluate competing achievement indicators relative to the selection criteria.
6 Select the best achievement indicators relative to the established criteria.
7 Establish acceptance of at least the face validity of the measures by academic staff and other stakeholders. The intent of this validation process is to have a shared understanding that outcome measures used to evaluate the programme can reasonably be employed for the purpose intended (Messick, 1990; Linn, 1993; IAESB, 2012).

Since HEIs, particularly in North America, generally link multiple specific objectives to each programme goal, it follows that the tailoring process described above will culminate in the eventual selection of multiple outcome indicators to evaluate each goal (see Figure 22.2). Indeed most AACSB-accredited accounting programmes use as many as three outcome indicators to evaluate the achievement of each of their goals and objectives (Calderon & Green, 1997; Martell & Calderon, 2005).

Although outcome indicators may represent the ultimate signals of achievement of an educational unit's goals and objectives, administrators will also measure and evaluate general input and process surrogates. Failure to measure and evaluate these surrogates inhibits attempts to assess the efficiency of activities and processes that contribute to the achievement of desired outcomes (Rosen, 2012; Gates, 2013). For example, achievement of ILOs, pass rates in professional examinations, post-graduation placement, and future career advancement might represent the decisive gauge of effective teaching for an accounting programme with a distinct professional orientation. However, failure to measure and evaluate input and process surrogates associated with teaching and learning processes could diminish the capacity to correct teaching deficiencies and foster continuous improvement (Rosen, 2012).

22.4 Observations from practice

This section describes observations from a survey of 50 universities (47 from the U.S.A., two from Australia, and one from Canada). The survey involved a review of the institutions' published programme review and evaluation processes, supplemented by telephone calls to officials at those institutions to verify items that needed clarification. A condition for inclusion in the survey was that the institution had to have a coherent programme review process that is published on its web page. The author and a graduate assistant searched each university's website using such key words as *program review, review of academic program, program evaluation, program assessment, course evaluation, degree evaluation, learning assessment,* and other related words. Fifty web pages were selected to conveniently assure a reasonably detailed understanding of documented and published programme review practices. The intent was not to select a random sample and make statistical inferences about programme review practices.

In addition, the web pages of several institutions with AACSB, EQUIS, and AMBA accreditation were surveyed, but it was observed that, in general, those institutions did not publicize their programme review processes on their public websites. No institution in the U.S.A. has all three types of accreditation, but 65 institutions from Africa (1), Asia (4), Australia (4), North America (Canada, 2/Mexico, 2), Europe (47), and South America (5) do have all three types of accreditation. It is possible that, for purposes of programme review, these institutions rely on the guidelines of international accreditation bodies (or, in some cases, their local authorities) rather than internally-developed guidelines.

Instead of focussing specifically on accounting programme evaluation, the survey examined the universities' broader processes and guidelines and identified situations where exceptions were made for programmes such as accounting and business with specialized accreditation. The foci include the goals of the programme review; the scope, process and ownership; the review cycles and data management; and the consequences of the programme review and evaluation. Each of these will now be discussed, but it should be noted that this section describes key observations rather than summative data.

22.4.1 Goals of programme review

There is a great deal of consensus on the goals of academic programme review and evaluation. Guidelines published by Butler University[1] (located in Indiana, U.S.A.) summarize what several universities publicize (implicitly or explicitly) as being the goals of an academic programme review:

- enhance the resources and quality of academic programmes by assessing programmes' strengths and challenges;
- align academic programmes' needs and campus priorities with the planning and budgeting processes; and

- ensure that programme priorities are consistent with the university's mission and strategic directions.

Butler University communicates a very explicit link between programme review, resource allocation and strategic planning. Virginia Tech's programme review process[2] includes similar language that draws a clear link between a programme's mission, strategic planning, performance and resource allocation, and other decision-making. While that link is implied in the guidelines published by many universities surveyed for this chapter, few communicate the link as explicitly as Butler or Virginia Tech. Several universities communicate the purpose of programme review and evaluation as a process that affords a department an opportunity to review its efforts, assess its achievements, and take proactive steps to improve quality and performance. In some cases (e.g. The University of Queensland in Australia), the university requires reviewers to employ a mandatory reporting template which includes a section that identifies areas for improvement as well as a proposed plan, and a timeline to strengthen the programme and address weak areas.

22.4.2 Scope, process ownership, and participants

Programme reviews and evaluations are generally prompted by state governments, the board of directors (or trustees) of an educational system, accreditation organizations, academic staff committees, or professional organizations. In some systems (e.g. the State University of New York), the faculty senate initiates and serves as a driver of programme review (SUNY, 2012). The SUNY Faculty Senate initially issued guidelines for academic programme review in 1983, and published revisions in 2001 and 2012. The SUNY system places primary responsibility for programme review on the academic staff, and defines their involvement as follows:

> *Effectively evaluating academic programs is a shared responsibility between faculty and other constituents of the institution. Because they are ultimately responsible for designing and implementing the academic program, faculty are central to the process. Assessment and program evaluation are important faculty responsibilities in program design, implementation and review.*

(SUNY, 2012, p.12)

The SUNY programme review and evaluation process requires, at a minimum '*an assessment of student learning, and an external review, which may involve specialized accreditation or campus selection of reviewers*' (ibid., p. 3). Additionally, each evaluation should meet or exceed regional accreditation standards as well as the standards established by specialized accreditation agencies (e.g. AACSB).

A self-study, conducted by the academic staff and administrative staff of an academic unit, is normally the centrepiece of the programme review process. It focusses on programmes offered by these units and examines the goals, objectives, and performance relative to goals and objectives. At least in the U.S.A., the scope of the evaluation normally cuts across the teaching, research, and service roles of the programme. It also addresses inputs (e.g. quality of students admitted), processes (e.g. processes in place to assure the integrity of examinations), and outcomes (e.g. students' attainment of ILOs). For example, at the University of Akron,[3] a large regional university in Ohio, mandatory programme review and evaluation require staff in academic departments to prepare a 10-page self-study report to be followed by reviews by the department chair, the Dean, and a university-wide committee made up of academic staff and administrators. The University of California at Berkeley[4] requires a comprehensive self-study report that expresses the programme's unique culture, assesses its strengths and deficiencies, and outlines a strategy that the unit will pursue to address challenges and opportunities. The unit must identify one to three areas it will study in depth, and the programme review leadership team may identify one to two additional areas for in depth study. At the University of Pittsburgh,[5] the evaluation process, which emphasizes programme improvement rather than accountability, is designed to provide '*an opportunity for faculty and administrators to obtain insights regarding the level of excellence of the programs*'. At that university, the Dean of an academic unit initiates programme review and evaluation. As a process driven by academic staff, the emphasis is on evaluation of the strengths and weaknesses of programmes. Normally, all programmes within a department are reviewed and evaluated simultaneously.

Georgia Southern University,[6] which has one of the most comprehensive programme review processes among the universities surveyed for this chapter, characterizes programme review as a thoughtful and thorough process driven by academic staff which uses data to determine how the quality of programmes can be improved. The process starts with a self-study that is completed by the academic staff in consultation with the department chair. It covers such areas as mission, goals and outcomes, curriculum, students, the teaching and scholarship of the academic staff, and resources. The academic staff as a whole, the department chair, and the Dean must each approve the self-study before it is sent to the university's chief academic officer (CAO). The department chair must include a one-page memorandum which makes a summative assessment that indicates whether each programme falls below expectations, meets expectations, or exceeds expectations. The Dean must also provide a similar summative assessment for each programme. Additionally, the process calls for a review of the self-study report by two external reviewers. The university exempts accredited programmes (e.g. accounting and business) from the external reviewer requirement and uses the latest accreditation report as a substitute. The CAO sends the department's self-study reports, along with the two summative assessments, to graduate and undergraduate committees for detailed evaluations. These committees make their own summative assessments (*falls below expectations, meets expectations,* or *exceeds expectations*),[7] and submit reports to the department as well as to the Faculty Senate. Georgia Southern University and Butler University are among a small number of universities which employ a comprehensive programme review rubric to guide the evaluation of programmes.

Programme reviews are commonplace in other countries besides the U.S.A. However, the degree of academic staff involvement and ownership of the review process is not as explicit. Furthermore, the scope of the review process tends to emphasize learning, teaching, and curricula aspects of the programme. On the other hand, the use of external reviewers in the programme review process outside the U.S.A. seems more explicit and commonplace. At the University of New South Wales[8] (UNSW) in Australia, for example, academic programme reviews are '*a primary means by which [academic units] engage the wider community in the process of reviewing and revising their programs and courses*'. The process focusses on curricula, teaching, students' learning outcomes, infrastructure, and programme viability. UNSW's programme review process is positioned largely as a teaching and learning initiative, and their guidelines do not include mention of research. This is also true for programme reviews conducted at The University of Queensland.[9] Interestingly, the programme review team at the University of Queensland may comprise up to three external members with nationally- or internationally-recognized expertise and knowledge. The university's senior leadership nominates other members of the committee (usually academic staff teaching in the programme being reviewed). The senior leadership, including the Dean of the academic unit, must also approve all members of the review team. The final programme review report is submitted to the university's senior leadership, including the Dean of the academic unit under review. The university expects academic staff, students, and other stakeholders to be involved in the process; however, ownership of the process appears to reside with the senior administration.

While programme reviews and evaluations will normally entail some level of academic staff involvement, certain British Commonwealth universities also work with external parties (e.g. an external examiner, professional association, or consultants) to design and conduct programme reviews. In one interesting case, a professional association engaged a review committee made up of two external consultants to assess whether a graduate accounting programme at a local university complied with International Education Standards (IAESB, 2012) published by the International Federation of Accountants. Although somewhat unusual, this type of review seeks to verify, through the lens of recognized experts, that learning, teaching, and the curriculum satisfy fairly objective standards that comply with the profession's expectations.

22.4.3 Programme review cycles and data management

There is a great deal of consensus among the universities surveyed on the length of review cycles. Five- to seven-year cycles are the norm, with most programme review processes making adjustments for specialized accreditation (e.g. AACSB) review cycles. However, it is not uncommon to see institutions with eight- to 10-year review cycles. It is noteworthy that most programme review processes do not absolve academic units with specialized accreditation from the programme review process. Rather, these units are generally permitted to use specialized accreditation reports as a substitute for external reviews in cases where such reviews are pre-scribed as part of the process. Universities with business accreditation also time their programme reviews to avoid duplication of effort and assure that reviews are conducted at a time that is convenient and non-disruptive for the academic unit. For example, the University of Central Florida[10] and Georgia Southern University permit academic units such as accounting and business to align the timing and use their accreditation reviews as a substitute for the universities' mandatory programme review.

At universities that specify a time line for executing programme reviews (e.g. Virginia Tech), the timeline from the start of the review to the department's submission of the final report to the university's senior academic leadership is about 12 months. This lead-time is longer if external reviewers must participate in the process.

Comprehensive programme review is highly data-intensive. Universities included in the survey require details about students (e.g. academic preparation for entrance, success on assessment activities, engagement in co-curriculum activities, progression through the programme, graduation rates, placement), teaching and learning (e.g. class size, number of students taught, assessment processes, learning outcomes), academic staff research and scholarship (e.g. publica-tions, working papers, presentations, editorial board participation), programme inventories, and budgets and resources to support programmes. Several (e.g. the University of Akron and Butler University) have developed searchable programme review databases that facilitate the data requirements of programme review. These databases are readily accessible to academic staff and others involved in the review process on the university's intranet for access by all academic staff, specialized applications which restrict access to those who need to use the data, or on the public Internet in full view of all stakeholders.

22.4.4 Consequences of programme evaluation

Programme review and evaluation can have important implications for academic units. Although it is often discussed in the context of accountability (Bresciani, 2006; McCormick, 2009;

Dickeson, 2010), practically every university surveyed in writing this chapter emphasizes improvement as a primary goal for their programme review and evaluation initiatives. Nonetheless, if done properly, programme review and evaluation processes will support both the accountability and improvement goals of stakeholders (Bresciani, 2006; Berrett, 2011; SUNY, 2012).

In general, the consequences of programme review may be mostly positive since the review process causes departments to take a thorough look at key aspects of their efforts and accomplishments within the context of their own mission, goals, specific objectives, and overall vision and strategy. This gives the department an opportunity to assess what works or does not work, and what is in need of improvement. Several of the universities surveyed document the specific benefits which they expect from programme review and evaluation.

The SUNY system expects programme review:

- to improve the academic experience of students;
- to contribute important information for planning across the university;
- to contribute to shared governance and certain accountability requirements at the state level; and
- to enhance the overall effectiveness of the programme, department, and institution.

Butler University expects programme review to help with:

- clarifying and assessing programme goals;
- reviewing programme resources;
- identifying needed changes; and
- justifying requests for programme enhancements.

Programme review at Butler is also seen as a process that assures programme alignment with planning, budgets and campus-wide priorities, and mission and strategic directions.

Some universities very explicitly emphasize the potential use of programme evaluation as part of their resource allocation and decision-making processes. For example, the programme review guidelines at the University of Akron state that, as part of the review process:

> [D]epartment chairs will make recommendations about enhancing, maintaining, or possible phasing out of the program or option(s)/track(s) of the program. The recommendations should also include estimated timeframes, costs, or associated cost savings information. In some situations, it might be advantageous to consider collaborating with a sister institution to create joint degree programs.

Similarly, guidelines from the University of Pittsburgh[11] state that:

> [I]n rare cases, as a result of the evaluation process, it may be determined that an existing degree program is no longer viable. In these cases, after such a recommendation is received, strategies may be employed to restructure or discontinue the program.

In a critical article about the consequences of programme review, Barrett (2011) mentions a fine arts programme at the University of Missouri which the programme review process identified as under-performing and was slated for elimination. The academic staff eventually reallocated resources within the department and salvaged the programme. The article also identified an engineering technology programme at the University of Central Florida that was eliminated after the programme evaluation process revealed it was performing below expectations relative to the university's mission, goals, and strategic direction. The programme emerged at a different institution with several of its original academic staff and about half its original student population. In addition to difficult resource allocation decisions that originate from programme review, it must be noted that the process itself requires academic staff to focus on tasks that are different from their traditional roles and responsibilities. Furthermore, it can be highly disruptive for students, as well as for academic staff, particularly when there is uncertainty about the performance of a programme or the extent of its alignment with the institution's strategic priorities.

22.5 Implications and guidance

The task of building an ACS, or preparing for academic programme review and evaluation is highly challenging. The universities surveyed for this chapter appear to focus on assuring responses to specific operational questions and issues rather than building and deploying a coherent ACS. Such an approach exposes programmes (and the academic units that house them) to significant risks:

- There seems to be little systematic attempt to clarify strategy and articulate links between planning, goal-setting, and performance norms and targets. Historically, academic staff seem to be more engaged in responding to the specific questions listed in the programme review template than in reflecting on matters related to the technical dimensions of the ACS (Wergin & Swingen, 2000). Interviews with accounting programme chairs for this chapter offer no evidence that the situation has changed.
- Programme review and evaluation cycles are long. Programmes that are not achieving expected performance norms and targets could have done so for protracted periods. By the time they are reviewed, it is possible that their challenges could become systematic, and perhaps resolvable only through severe intervention. Yet, leaders of academic programme review are traditionally reluctant to recommend drastic action (ibid.). It seems, therefore, that there are inherent conflicts in the goals of programme review and the manner in which they are designed and executed.
- As there may be no coherent ACS that helps to clarify vision and strategy and link them to academic efforts and initiatives, the task of identifying possible solutions might very well ignore the possibility of flawed strategies that constrain performance. A focus on outcomes in the context of a flawed strategy would diminish prospects for any degree of meaningful improvement. Finally, assuming that programme review is intended to satisfy stakeholders' quest for accountability and transparency, then it should be argued that a five- to 10-year programme review cycle is extraordinarily long. Shorter cycles seem more consistent with the spirit of accountability and transparency.

Programme review and evaluation are ultimately intended to support decision-making at universities (Stufflebeam, 1971; Kellaghan & Stufflebeam, 2003). Stufflebeam identifies four types of evaluation that support decision-making at universities: context, input, process, and product (CIPP) evaluation. According to Stufflebeam:

- context evaluation focusses on the total system;
- input evaluation focusses on strategies that might be used to achieve the stated objectives of an academic unit;
- process evaluation focusses on the implementation aspects of a strategy to address whether the strategy or its implementation needs strengthening; and

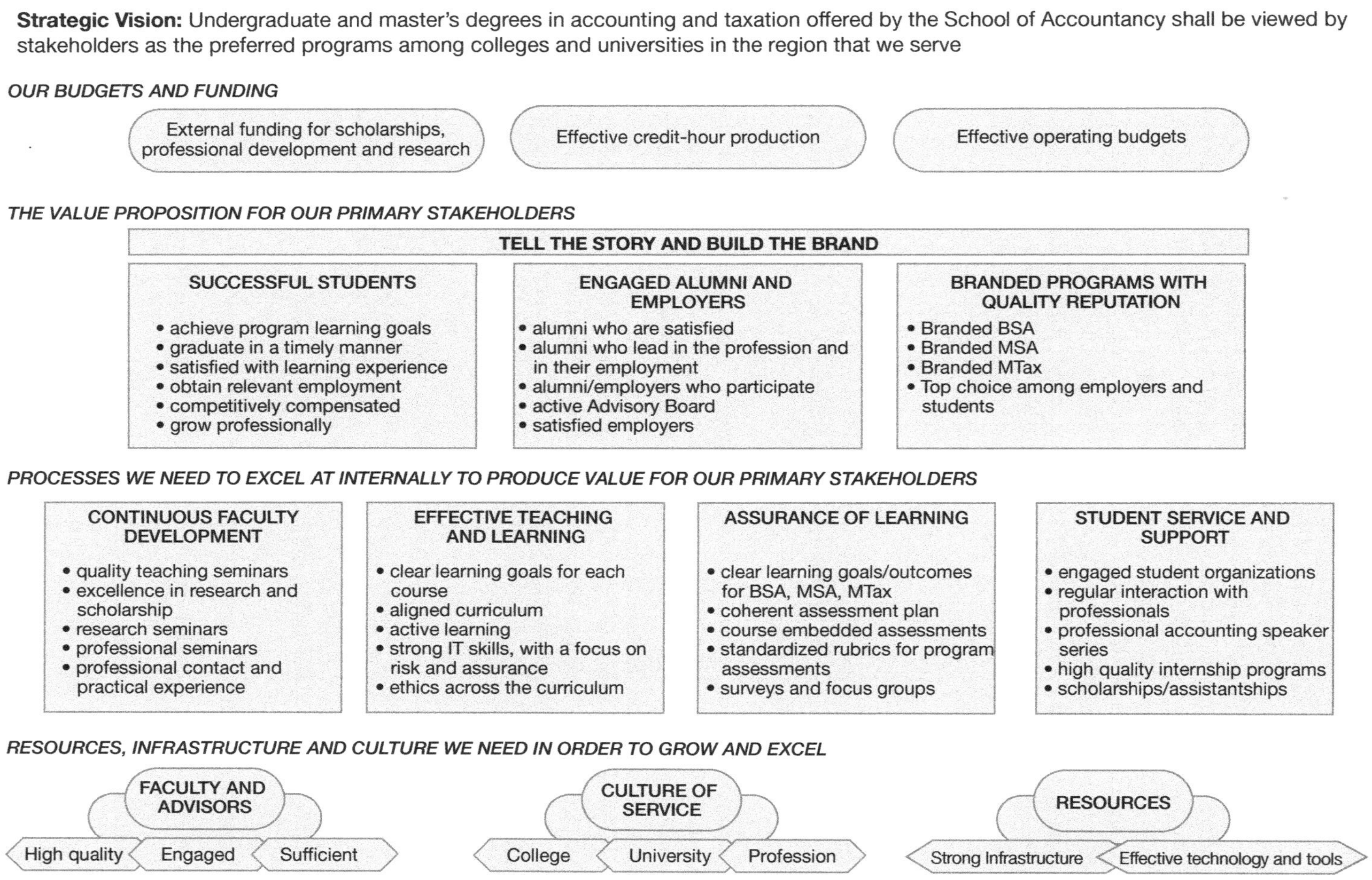

Strategic Vision: Undergraduate and master's degrees in accounting and taxation offered by the School of Accountancy shall be viewed by stakeholders as the preferred programs among colleges and universities in the region that we serve

OUR BUDGETS AND FUNDING

(External funding for scholarships, professional development and research)

(Effective credit-hour production)

(Effective operating budgets)

THE VALUE PROPOSITION FOR OUR PRIMARY STAKEHOLDERS

TELL THE STORY AND BUILD THE BRAND

SUCCESSFUL STUDENTS
- achieve program learning goals
- graduate in a timely manner
- satisfied with learning experience
- obtain relevant employment
- competitively compensated
- grow professionally

ENGAGED ALUMNI AND EMPLOYERS
- alumni who are satisfied
- alumni who lead in the profession and in their employment
- alumni/employers who participate
- active Advisory Board
- satisfied employers

BRANDED PROGRAMS WITH QUALITY REPUTATION
- Branded BSA
- Branded MSA
- Branded MTax
- Top choice among employers and students

PROCESSES WE NEED TO EXCEL AT INTERNALLY TO PRODUCE VALUE FOR OUR PRIMARY STAKEHOLDERS

CONTINUOUS FACULTY DEVELOPMENT
- quality teaching seminars
- excellence in research and scholarship
- research seminars
- professional seminars
- professional contact and practical experience

EFFECTIVE TEACHING AND LEARNING
- clear learning goals for each course
- aligned curriculum
- active learning
- strong IT skills, with a focus on risk and assurance
- ethics across the curriculum

ASSURANCE OF LEARNING
- clear learning goals/outcomes for BSA, MSA, MTax
- coherent assessment plan
- course embedded assessments
- standardized rubrics for program assessments
- surveys and focus groups

STUDENT SERVICE AND SUPPORT
- engaged student organizations
- regular interaction with professionals
- professional accounting speaker series
- high quality internship programs
- scholarships/assistantships

RESOURCES, INFRASTRUCTURE AND CULTURE WE NEED IN ORDER TO GROW AND EXCEL

FACULTY AND ADVISORS
High quality 〉 Engaged 〉 Sufficient

CULTURE OF SERVICE
College 〉 University 〉 Profession

RESOURCES
Strong Infrastructure 〉 Effective technology and tools

Figure 22.5 A strategic map

- product evaluation focusses on the achievement of specific objectives and whether the approaches used to achieve them are working.

This model, which Stufflebeam has offered as a comprehensive approach to addressing programme evaluation challenges for about five decades, is intriguing and can potentially address the types of challenges described in the previous paragraph. Nonetheless, the model may over-compartmentalize the programme review and evaluation process. The Kaplan–Norton strategy map/balanced scorecard methodology (Kaplan & Norton, 1996, 2000, 2001) could be readily adapted to address those challenges in a more integrated and holistic fashion. An example of a strategy map, which could be used to initiate this adaptation, appears in Figure 22.5. Based on this map, which clarifies the unit's strategy, academic staff and programme leaders in an accounting department could define performance measures, norms and targets, and initiatives that they will deploy to pursue their shared expectations. This approach could lead the way to a culture of evidence (Wergin & Swingen, 2000), continuous reporting, and much shorter programme review cycles.

22.6 Conclusion

The generalized administrative control model described in this chapter can be readily applied to accounting programmes. To be effective, the ACS used in an accounting department should have the following characteristics:

1 a clearly defined, fully articulated, internally consistent technical dimension which comprises a mission, broad goals, specific objectives, and performance norms and targets;
2 a behavioural dimension which complements the technical dimension and motivates academic staff to perform;
3 appropriate control surrogates for input, processes, and output;
4 acceptance of the system by academic staff and other stakeholders; and
5 a comprehensive information system to collect, store, process, retrieve, and report data and information.

Accounting departments offer multiple courses, employ several academic staff, and educate hundreds of students. Large volumes of data and information will result from any coherent attempt to enhance a department's ACS. Data and information management to support an ACS are critical. For success, a comprehensive information system must be developed to manage the large volumes of data that will result as a department works toward the high level of accountability that stakeholders demand.

Acknowledgements

Portions of the second and third sections of this chapter employ content that I originally wrote with Brian Patrick Green and Alex Gabbin (Calderon *et al.*, 1996). I wish to acknowledge my colleagues and thank them for permission to adapt from that material in writing this chapter.

Notes

1 See http://www.butler.edu/media/2553674/butler_program_review_guidelines.pdf.
2 See http://www.aap.vt.edu/APR/program_review.html.

3 See http://www.uakron.edu/ir/assessment-and-benchmarking/program-review.dot.
4 See http://vpapf chance berkeley.edu/apr/GUIDE_May2011.pdf. Note that, although Berkeley does not offer a major or minor in accounting, it offers a full set of courses that permit students to prepare for careers in accounting and sit the CPA examination.
5 See http://www.provost.pitt.edu/information-on/guidelines.html.
6 See http://academics.georgiasouthern.edu/provost/resources/comprehensivereview.
7 The university defines *Falls Below Expectations* as 'assessment of the academic program reveals that it is not consistently achieving its overall objectives'; *Meets Expectations* as 'assessment of the academic program reveals that it is accomplishing its overall objectives'; and *Exceed Expectations* as 'assessment of the academic program reveals that it is accomplishing its overall objectives and going beyond these objectives'.
8 See http://teaching.unsw.edu.au/academic-program-reviews.
9 See http://ppl.app.uq.edu.au/content/3.30.06-review-generalist-degree-programs.
10 See http://www.vpaa.ucf.edu/files/ProgramReviewWebsitedocs/UCF_APR_Process.pdf.
11 See http://www.pitt.edu/~provost/guidelines.pdf.

References

AACSB (2007) *AACSB Assurance of Learning Standards: An Interpretation*, AACSB White Paper No. 3. AACSB Accreditation Coordinating Committee and AACSB Accreditation Quality Committee. Tampa, FL: AACSB International. Available at: http://www.aacsb.edu/publications/whitepapers/ (accessed 20 January 2013).

AACSB (2012) *Eligibility Procedures and Accreditation Standards for Accounting Accreditation.* Tampa, FL: AACSB International. Available at: http://AACSB.edu/accreditation/accounting/standards (accessed 20 January 2013).

AAUP (1966) *1966 Statement on Government of Colleges and Universities*, Washington, DC: American Association of University Teachers.

ACBSP (2012) *ACBSP Standards and Criteria for Demonstrating Excellence in Baccalaureate/Graduate Degree Schools and Programs*, Overland Park, KS: Accreditation Council for Business Schools and Programs. Available at: http://www.acbsp.org/p/cm/ld/fid=81 (accessed 28 January 2013).

Apple, J.E., Gradisher, S., & Calderon, T.G. (2012) Enhancing functional and other competencies through role-playing, *Advances in Accounting Education*, 13, 237–275.

Astin, A.W. (1993) *Principles of Good Practice for Assessing Student Learning*, Leadership Abstracts, American Association for Higher Education Assessment Forum.

Berrett, D. (2011) Program Reviews can produce 'death spirals' or happy endings, *Chronicle of Higher Education*, 58, A1–A12.

Blumenstyk, G. (2010) New federal rule threatens practices and revenues at for-profit colleges, *Chronicle of Higher Education*, 57, A1–A19.

Bresciani, M.J. (2006) *Outcomes-Based Academic and Co-Curricular Program Review: A Compilation of Institutional Good Practices*, Sterling, VA: Stylus.

Calderon, T.G., Gabbin, A.L., & Green, B.P. (1996) *A Framework for Encouraging Effective Teaching*, Harrisonburg, VA: Center for Research in Accounting Education, James Madison University.

Calderon, T.G. & Green, B.P. (1997) Use of multiple information types in assessing accounting faculty teaching performance, *Journal of Accounting Education*, 15, 221–239.

Dickeson, R.C. (2010) *Prioritizing Academic Programs and Services: Reallocating Resources to Achieve Strategic Balance*, San Francisco, CA: Jossey-Bass.

EFMD (2012) *European Quality Improvement System: EQUIS Standards and Criteria.* European Foundation for Management Development (EFMD). Available at: http://www.efmd.org/index.php/accreditation-main/equis/equis-guides (accessed 20 January 2013).

Ewell, P.T. (2008) Assessment and accountability in America today: background and context, *New Directions for Institutional Research*, 2008, 7–17.

Ewell, P.T. & Jones, D.P. (1993) Actions matter: the case for indirect measures in assessing higher education's progress on the national education goals, *Journal of General Education*, 42, 123–148.

Gates, B. (2013) Bill Gates: my plan to fix the world's biggest problems – measure them! *Wall Street Journal*, 26 January, p .C1.

Green, B.P., Calderon, T.G., & Reider, B.P. (1998) A content analysis of teaching evaluation instruments used in accounting departments, *Issues in Accounting Education*, 13, 15–30.

IAESB (2012) *International Education Standard (IES) 6: Initial Professional Development – Assessment of Professional Competence (Revised)*, New York: International Accounting Education Standards Board/International Federation of Accountants. Available at: http://www.ifac.org/sites/default/files/publications/files/IES-6-(Revised).pdf. (accessed 20 January 2013).

Kaplan, R.S. & Norton, D.P. (1996) Using the balanced scorecard as a strategic management system, *Harvard Business Review*, 74, 75–85.

Kaplan, R.S. & Norton, D.P. (2000) Having trouble with your strategy? Then map it. *Harvard Business Review*, 78, 167–176.

Kaplan, R.S. & Norton, D.P. (2001) Transforming the balanced scorecard from performance measurement to strategic management: Part I, *Accounting Horizons*, 15, 87–104.

Kellaghan, T. & Stufflebeam, D.L. (2003) *International Handbook of Educational Evaluation*, Dordrecht: Kluwer Academic Publishers.

Kelley, C., Pingsheng, T., & Beom-Joon, C. (2010) A review of assessment of student learning programs at AACSB schools: a dean's perspective, *Journal of Education for Business*, 85, 299–306.

Linn, R.L. (1993) *Educational Measurement. Third Edition. American Council on Education Series on Higher Education*, Washington, DC: National Council on Measurement in Education /Washington, DC: American Council on Education.

Martell, K.D. & Calderon, T.G. (2005) *Assessment of Student Learning in Business Schools: Best Practices Each Step of the Way. Volume 1.1*, Tampa, FL: AACSB-International/Association for Institutional Research.

Mccormick, A.C. (2009) Toward reflective accountability: using NSSE for accountability and transparency, *New Directions for Institutional Research*, 85, 97–106.

Messick, S. (1990) *Validity of Test Interpretation and Use*, Princeton, NJ: Educational Testing Service.

Parry, M. (2013) Helping colleges move beyond the credit hour, *Chronicle of Higher Education*, 59, B7–B8.

Ramanathan, K.V. (1982) *Management Control in Nonprofit Organizations: Text and Cases*, New York: Wiley.

Rosen, W. (2012) *The Most Powerful Idea in the World: A Story of Steam, Industry, and Invention*, Chicago: University of Chicago Press.

Stensaker, B. (2012) Re-inventing shared governance: implications for culture and identity, keynote presented at the 34th EAIR Forum, University of Stavanger, Oslo, Norway, 5–8 September.

Stufflebeam, D.L. (1971) *The Relevance of the CIPP Evaluation Model for Educational Accountability*, Ohio State University, Columbus Evaluation Center. Paper originally presented at the Annual Meeting of the American Association of School Administrators, 24 February 1971. Available at: http://files.eric.ed.gov/fulltext/ED062385.pdf (accessed 16 August 2013).

SUNY (2012) *Guide for Evaluation of Undergraduate Programs*, Albany, NY: Faculty Senate, State University of New York.

Uitinen, A.M.Y. (2013) The curious birth and harmful legacy of the credit hour, *Chronicle of Higher Education*, 59, A23–A24.

Vedder, R. K. (2008) Colleges should go beyond the rhetoric of accountability, *Chronicle of Higher Education*, 54, A64.

Weldy, T.G. & Turnipseed, D.L. (2010) Assessing and improving learning in business schools: direct and indirect measures of learning, *Journal of Education for Business*, 85, 268–273.

Wergin, J.F. & Swingen, J.N. (2000) *Departmental Assessment: How Some Campuses Are Effectively Evaluating the Collective Work of Faculty*, Washington, DC: American Association for Higher Education.

Yarbrough, D.B., Shulha, L.M., Hopson, R.K., & Caruther, S.F.A. (2011) *The Program Evaluation Standards: A Guide for Evaluators and Evaluation Users*, Thousand Oaks, CA: SAGE.

Young, D.W. & Anthony, R.N. (2008) *Management Control in Nonprofit Organizations*, Cambridge, MA: Crimson Press.

About the author

Thomas Calderon is Professor of Accounting and Chair of the George W. Daverio School of Accountancy at the University of Akron, U.S.A. (tcalder@uakron.edu). He has written extensively on programme review and accounting programme assessment. He has also been an external reviewer for a number of universities in the U.S.A. and in other countries. Professor Calderon has served as President of the AAA's Teaching, Learning and Curriculum Section, and is an inductee of the Section's Hall of Honors.

Section F

Contextual considerations

Preface

David J.A. Alexander

UNIVERSITY OF BIRMINGHAM, U.K.

After the theory comes the application. And application does not happen in a vacuum. It requires a context. Now that the principles have been firmly established in the previous five sections, we turn in Section F to expositions of examples of contextual scenarios and applications. These are, of course, illustrative, and certainly not intended to be exhaustive. Uniqueness of place, and changes over time, will require readers to develop their own optimal operational scenarios. But this section presents four aspects which seem to be of particular importance at the present time, and which are likely to be so for some years to come.

The choice, and sequence, of these four chapters have been carefully made. *Financial Crises* (the focus of Chapter 23 by Ralph Adler, and note the plural) provide both a catalyst for the study of accounting education activities, and a wake-up call for their importance. Without doubt, there will be more such crises, different in detail, to come. *Ethics* (the theme of Chapter 24 by Gordon Boyce) surely links with the control and prevention of crises, but also pervades the reporting and accountability function in all its aspects.

In a slightly different dimension, the role of *Internships* is a major and permanent issue, and is considered by Beard & Humphrey in Chapter 25. There are pros and cons in the use of integrated internship (placement) periods in accounting (and other) educational courses, but they potentially provide real and realistic case study material for theory application, not least in terms of recent financial crises, and ethical consideration, and problems of applying theory to practice more generally.

Finally, and importantly, in Chapter 26, Calhoun & Karreman outline some implications of the global world, in terms of both the plethora of contemporary international influences on the student of today and the accounting practitioner of tomorrow, and of the variety of geographical and institutional contexts in which readers are likely to find themselves.

Both by illustration and example, and by its detailed content, this is an important section of this *Companion*.

23

The impact of financial crises on accounting education

Ralph W. Adler

UNIVERSITY OF OTAGO, NEW ZEALAND

CONTENTS

Abstract

This chapter discusses how such a salient, high profile, and highly topical event as the global financial crisis (GFC) can feature as a particularly effective pedagogical vehicle for enhancing students' learning and achievement. The chapter begins by providing a brief background and context to the GFC and what made it the perfect financial storm. As the perfect storm, the GFC begs the asking of such questions as 'What went wrong with the financial reporting supply chain?', 'What are the lessons for the practice of accounting?', and 'What are the lessons for the teaching and learning of accounting?' The chapter focusses primarily on the last of these three questions. It seeks to show how, beneath all the many negative outcomes with which the GFC is commonly associated, including the millions of people from around the world who lost jobs, homes, and life-savings, there is the potential for the development of a powerful extended parable that can serve as the framework for enhancing teaching and learning designs, as well as the benefits to students that flow from such improved designs. The theoretical and empirical works of relevant psychology and general education literatures are used to highlight why and how these benefits might be realised. The chapter proceeds to describe subjects/courses in which the GFC is well suited and can be readily integrated. Two case-in-point blueprints are provided: one featuring an *Intermediate Financial Accounting* course and the other an *Advanced Management Accounting* course. While these course blueprints come from university accounting educators teaching university courses, the blueprints evidence elements of generalisability that would make them applicable to comprising, or at least shaping, many of the continuing education programmes offered by professional accounting bodies.

Keywords

accounting education, course design, global financial crisis, pedagogy, students' learning

23.1 Introduction

The main aims of this chapter are:

- to discuss the education literature, both its empirical and theoretical work, to reveal how pedagogies that draw on financial crises can be useful for enhancing students' learning, performance, and motivation;
- to identify the accounting subjects/courses most likely to benefit from including pedagogies that highlight financial crises; and
- to provide pedagogical illustrations that draw on financial crises to motivate accounting students' learning and promote their understanding of how the accounting function forms one part of today's highly-complex and highly-integrated economic system.

The global financial crisis (GFC) has profoundly impacted on the international economy and created varying degrees of hardship, both economic and social, that have reverberated throughout the world. Tan (2011) offers some sobering facts to help put the GFC into context, including:

- On 13 September 2007, the U.K. experienced its first bank run since 1866.
- On 15 September 2008, Lehman Brothers became the largest bankruptcy filing in history.
- On 26 February 2009, the Royal Bank of Scotland reported a loss of £24 billion for 2008, which was the highest loss ever reported by a U.K. corporation.

These events, combined with such further headline-making news stories as the March 2008 collapse of Bear Sterns, and the September 2008 placing of Fannie Mae and Freddie Mac into U.S. government conservatorship, served as the backdrop which prompted Ben Bernake, the Federal Reserve Bank Chairman, to describe the GFC as being the '*worst financial crisis in global history including the Great Depression*' (FCIC, 2011, p. 354). While Mr. Bernake's comparison of the GFC to the Great Depression – with the latter's 25–30 per cent worldwide unemployment rates, its 50–70 per cent reduction in bilateral, inter-country trade, and its 30 per cent drop in wholesale prices – may be seen as being hyperbolic, it is fair to say that the absolute monetary scale of the GFC was unprecedented.

In many ways the GFC is but one financial crisis, albeit a very major one, in a long line of such crises (Galbraith, 1993). Whether it is the 1637 Dutch tulip 'mania', the 1720 collapse of the South Sea Company, the railway panic of 1893 in the U.S.A., the Florida land boom and bust of the 1920s, the Savings and Loan Crisis of the 1980s in the U.S.A., or the GFC, the one common characteristic they all shared was the initial growth and subsequent bursting of a speculative bubble, or what Kindleberger (2005, p. 16) describes as: '*an upward price movement over an extended range that then implodes*'. Many experts, both from industry and academia, have weighed in with their views about what caused the GFC. Some of the more commonly cited causes are:

- problems associated with the use of fair value accounting (Hellwig, 2009);
- a lack of transparency (Singleton-Green, 2012);
- decision-makers' silo-based approach to decision-making that misunderstood the systemic nature of the financial reporting supply chain (Bloom & Webinger, 2011a);
- regulatory arbitrage (Tett, 2009; Lanchester, 2010);
- the irrationality of banks and their customers (Barberis, 2010);
- the natural, periodic, and inevitable winnowing of organisational populations (Carnegie & West, 2011).

Perrow's (1999) Normal Accident Theory is consistent with the ideas comprising these six causes. Normal Accident Theory maintains that major accidents are inevitable in systems featuring both interactive complexity and tight coupling. In such environments, holistic management is often not practised due to the preponderance of specialised experts (i.e., those who are well-versed in small parts of the overall system), and the dearth of general experts (i.e., those who can see across and understand the entire system). As a consequence, poor understandings exist about the potential for small variations throughout the system to combine in unexpected, non-linear, and quickly cascading ways that lead to a complete system meltdown.

The GFC, as argued by Bloom & Webinger (2011a), goes well beyond the breakdown in the bond market. It represents the systemic breakdown in the financial reporting supply chain connecting preparers, auditors, regulators, and users (see Figure 23.1). Similar to most major disasters, whether it is the GFC or the Space Shuttle *Columbia* disaster, it is a string of many small and seemingly disconnected factors that combine to create the 'perfect storm'. Furthermore, it is often the case that disasters: '*incubate over long gestation periods during which errors and warning events accumulate*' (Choo, 2008, p. 32). In hindsight, the errors and warnings are quite evident; but in real time they are often ignored or marginalised because the decision-makers are only seeing a small part of the overall system. Unfortunately, the decision-makers' inattentiveness results in the building up and intensifying of problems which, in turn, cause the system to ultimately lapse into systemic failure.

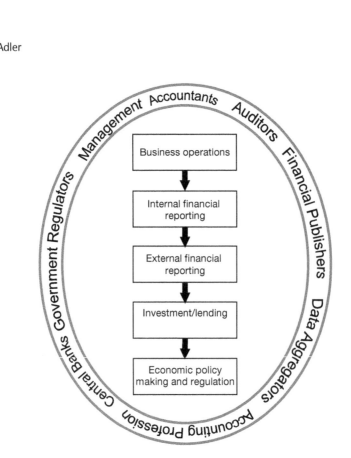

Figure 23.1 Financial reporting supply chain

Understanding the causes behind the GFC, while a highly interesting topic of study in itself, is not the main intent of the present chapter. Instead, the purpose is to discuss how financial crises, including the GFC, can provide a motivating context for the teaching of accounting. Accordingly, this chapter contributes to understanding how the incorporation of salient, high-profile, and highly topical events like the GFC can be used to support effective accounting education change (see Flood, Chapter 4 – this volume), including being a possible pedagogical agent for liberalising the accounting curriculum (see Amernic & Craig, Chapter 12 – this volume), and integrating the accounting curriculum (see Bloom, Chapter 14 – this volume).

While an appreciation of the 'perfect storm' origins that evolved into the GFC are likely to feature in most educators' uses of the GFC, the emphasis in this chapter is on exposing the theory and practice behind using such a salient event as the GFC, the U.S. Savings and Loan Crisis, or some other financial crisis to motivate students' learning. In addition, the chapter discusses the accounting courses[1] most amenable to using financial crises to stimulate students' learning. The chapter concludes with various examples of teaching and learning pedagogies that leverage financial crises.

23.2 Using the GFC to motivate teaching and learning

The benefits of using financial crises, especially the GFC, to motivate students' learning is an accepted axiom by many educators. Phillips, Johnstone, & Mackintosh (2011, p. 515), for example, refer to the expected students' learning benefits as being 'an intuitively agreeable proposition'. They go on to remark that embedding learning topics in 'engaging and meaningful' contexts is helpful for promoting 'desirable learning behaviours and outcomes' (ibid.). Meanwhile, empirical evidence to support the claim that enhanced teaching and learning benefits are associated with the use of highly topical and high profile historical events can be found in Knapp & Knapp's (2007) use of the fraud at Royal Ahold to engage students when teaching joint venture accounting, Bamber & Bamber's (2006) use of companies' 10-K reports to study managerial accounting topics, and Earley & Phillips' (2008) use of the toy industry to teach inventory valuation.

In addition to the intuitive and empirical support for the benefits associated with using high profile and highly topical issues to motivate students' learning, theoretical support exists as well. In particular, theory and research highlighting problem-based learning (Schmidt, 1983; Barrows, 1986; Boshuizen *et al.*, 1990; Patel *et al.*, 1991; Albanese & Mitchell, 1993; Sobral, 1995; Kaufman & Mann, 1996), learning environment enrichment (Adler *et al.*, 2001), and holistic learning (LeFevre, 1986; Palehonki, 1995; Armstrong & Larson, 1995) have demonstrated the positive effects which these three pedagogical approaches have on students' motivation. Problem-based learning is intended to stimulate students' learning by confronting students with learning situations that are characterised by real-world problems, requiring the students to take stock of relevant knowledge which they already possess and can usefully apply to the problem, as well as seeking out missing knowledge that is necessary to understanding and successfully resolving the problem (Barrows, 1986). (See also Hassall & Joyce, Chapter 17 – this volume.) Study and learning environment enrichment, which derives from the work of Hackman & Oldham (1980), has been successfully used to explain the motivational benefits to students that can be achieved through the enrichment of classroom/study settings (Adler *et al.*, 2001). Finally, holistic learning, which is characterised by students taking a richer and deeper approach to their learning, has been shown to promote students' understanding and enhance academic performance (Armstrong & Larson, 1995). The students' motivational benefits associated with each of these three pedagogical approaches are now discussed.

23.2.1 Problem-based learning

Problem-based learning (PBL) is a student-centred pedagogy in which students' learning is motivated by a real-world, multi-faceted problem that requires students to engage in an iterative problem-resolving process. Throughout the process, students must decide what information to collect and what new skills and knowledge they must master to successfully resolve the problem. PBL is viewed as being more consistent with the way in which cognitive psychologists suggest people recall, retain, and acquire knowledge (Norman & Schmidt, 1992). Furthermore, its use has been associated with significant learning benefits (Schmidt, 1983; Barrows, 1986; Boshuizen *et al.*, 1990; Patel *et al.*, 1991; Albanese & Mitchell, 1993; Sobral, 1995; Kaufman & Mann, 1996; Breton, 1999; Stanley & Marsden, 2012).

The first use of PBL is commonly attributed to the medical faculty at McMaster University in Canada who, during the 1960s, redesigned their undergraduate medical curriculum. One of the academic staff members, Howard Barrows, who co-authored the book *Problem-Based Learning: An Approach to Medical Education* with Robyn Tamblyn, is often viewed as being the originator of PBL (Stanley & Marsden, 2012). However, as Milne & McConnell (2001) suggest, PBL in substance, if not in name, can be traced to the earlier work of Dewey (1938).

The following seven characteristics comprise PBL (Barrows & Tamblyn, 1980):

1   Learning is student-centred.
2   Learning occurs in small groups.

3   Teachers serve as facilitators or guides, often being referred to as tutors.
4   A specific problem serves as the motivation and stimulus for learning.
5   Problems stimulate the development and use of problem-solving skills.
6   Students take stock of the relevant skills and knowledge they currently possess for resolving the problem.
7   Students engage in a process of self-directed learning to obtain missing knowledge relevant to the problem's resolution.

Using financial crises (and especially the GFC) within a PBL framework would appear to have strong potential for stimulating and motivating students' learning. The GFC holds significant prominence among today's students since it has affected and continues to affect nearly all, if not all, students. Whether it is job losses experienced by family and friends, reductions to the value of family homes and businesses, or the likelihood of reduced job prospects upon graduation, it is fair to say that the typical student possesses a good understanding and knowledge about the GFC (Bloom & Webinger, 2011b). Students can use this initial knowledge base as a platform from which further knowledge can be accessed and acquired (Howe & Berv, 2000), helping to create what PBL proponents commonly refer to as the *learning scaffolding* required for successful PBL task resolution.

Many accounting topics could be successfully taught using a PBL approach that incorporates financial crises like the GFC. As one example, the teaching of business ethics (see Boyce, Chapter 24 – this volume) might usefully feature a PBL approach which draws upon Goldman Sachs' practice of overtly promoting its clients' sub-prime collateral securities while simultaneously and covertly taking short positions on these very same contracts (United States Senate Reports, 2011). The PBL task might consist of examining and commenting on how Goldman Sachs' actions ran foul of any specific or general ethical standards.

When undertaking this particular PBL task, students, due to their familiarity with the GFC, could apply their initial understanding of and knowledge about the GFC to commence the PBL process. In particular, they would be capable of – by virtue of their knowledge about people who lost their jobs, had their houses repossessed, or saw their pension values plummet – applying some beginning understanding to such relevant ethical decision-making dimensions as the size, timing, and extent of the impact caused by Goldman Sachs' actions (see, for example, Rest, 1986). As students work through the problem, they could be asked to consider how their views might change if the Goldman Sachs' decision-makers were accountants and members of a professional accounting body (PAB). A more detailed discussion of how financial crises could be incorporated into teaching and learning, and in particular what courses are well suited for doing so, is discussed later in this chapter. Furthermore, when reading that later section, readers will likely find Chapter 24, which focusses on ethics and accounting education, a helpful companion.

23.2.2 Enrichment theory

Theories of situational motivation argue that some course designs are more motivating than others (Paris & Turner, 1994, p. 217). A student's inherent or base-line motivation will be enhanced or blunted by the motivating potential of the classroom setting. The challenge for educators is to design into their learning settings 'prototypical characteristics' that encourage student motivation (ibid., p. 221).

It is important to note that the construction of an engaging situational context is a necessary but insufficient vehicle for enhancing students' motivation (Hidi & Harackiewicz, 2000). Engaging situational contexts, for which financial crises like the GFC would qualify, may be a fine way of catching students' interest and perhaps even stimulating their affective and cognitive states. However, the achievement of sustained motivation on the part of students, and ultimately the ability to enhance their learning, requires the educator to create learning environments that encourage students both to apply their current stores of skills and knowledge (an idea that is conistent with the PBL literature) and to find high personal utility or meaningfulness in the learning task (Durik & Harackiewicz, 2007; Ainley, Hidi & Berndorff, 2002; Fitzpatrick, McConnell & Sasse, 2006; Brophy, 1999; Feather, 1988; Hidi & Harackiewicz, 2000; Krapp, 2002; Renninger, 2000; Wigfield & Eccles, 1992). Teaching and learning approaches that create strong motivating potential, whereby they include pedagogical designs that enable students to identify with and find meaningfulness in the teaching context, are associated with enhanced students' motivation (Meece *et al.*, 1988; Pintrich & DeGroot, 1990; Schiefele, 1991; Paris & Turner, 1994; Debnath *et al.*, 2007).

The education literature's situated motivation empirical findings can be readily understood using Hackman & Oldham's (1980) work enrichment theory, which is illustrated through their *job characteristics model*. In particular, the job characteristics model posits that work characterised by, among other things, high meaningfulness and significance will elicit higher motivation on the part of the person performing the work than will work which is associated with lower meaningfulness and less significance. The job characteristics model further states that the human personality trait 'growth need strength' (GNS) serves to moderate the relationship between enriched tasks and worker motivation. GNS captures the extent to which a person enjoys challenging tasks. High GNS workers are characterised by their enjoyment, even craving, of challenging tasks, especially in situations when the worker is given significant empowerment and job responsibility. People with low GNS dislike challenging tasks. They prefer work settings where someone else – generally their boss or, in an educational setting, their teacher – plans, assigns, monitors, and evaluates their work.

Adler *et al.* (2001), in a study of New Zealand final year accounting students, found relevant application of the job characteristics model to university teaching and learning. In particular, in their study of a sample of university accounting students in their final year of undergraduate studies, they observed:

1 The students on average displayed high levels of GNS.
2 The students exposed to relatively enriched learning environments displayed significantly higher levels of motivation than students exposed to relatively non-enriched learning environments.

Financial crises, as is inherent from the term 'crisis', embody the essence of 'meaningfulness' and 'significance' described in Hackman & Oldham's (1980) job characteristics model. The GFC, as an example, has had a very meaningful and significant impact on people, including students, even if this impact has been largely negative (lost jobs, diminished house values, and reduced pension values). Accordingly, teaching and learning pedagogies that incorporate the GFC should be capable of enhancing the significance and meaningfulness which students attach to their learning, thereby enhancing students' motivation and performance.

23.2.3 Holistic learning

As Adler (1999) notes, too often accounting topics are taught in isolation from one another. Educators adopt what Elliot (1992) refers to as the 'functional silo' approach. This teaching and learning approach promotes curriculum specialism, resulting in atomistic versus holistic perspectives of the world. (See also Bloom, Chapter 14 – this volume.)

The adoption of a silo-based learning approach typically results in students being pushed through an assembly line of highly-specialised accounting courses that often fail to encourage holistic thinking. Instead, students are trained to think about issues from a narrow, sub-discipline specific perspective, which produces sub-optimal learning outcomes. Failure to adopt a more integrated and interdisciplinary teaching and learning approach means that richer understandings by students of business phenomena are lost, learning synergies are missed, and overall students' learning is compromised. In addition, some scholars have suggested that narrowly-focussed and oversimplified teaching and learning approaches are at least partly to blame for the bad decision-making and unethical behaviour witnessed in the early 2000s surrounding Enron, Worldcom, Parmalat, and Waste Management (Ghoshal, 2005), as well as the more recent dysfunctional behaviours associated with the GFC (Marzo, 2011).

The problem with silo-based learning is that real-life business problems are seldom – if ever – discipline specific. Invariably these problems require decision-makers to think across functions and take a holistic or systemic view of their operations. As Brady (1989, p. 131) notes, educators should not be building barriers to what is a naturally holistic learning process.

Adler (1999) argues for a move away from a teaching and learning approach that is silo-based to one that is characterised by curriculum integration. He bases his argument on the education literature's demonstration of how integrated learning approaches enhance students' learning. In particular, LeFevre (1986), Palehonki (1995), and Armstrong & Larson (1995) have reported that higher levels of students' understanding and academic attainment occur when more holistic learning approaches are used. Palehonki (1995), as an example, showed how students who undertook to improve their spelling by adopting a more holistic approach – that is one that included tracing the word's origin, studying its context, as well as learning its spelling – outperformed those students who focussed solely on the spelling of words.

Financial crises, such as the GFC, are by definition drastic system failures. As previously discussed, financial crises result from many small and seemingly disconnected factors combining in complex and unexpected ways, leading to the system's ultimate failure. As a consequence, understanding, for example, how a failure in the global bond market contributed to the GFC requires, at a minimum, an understanding of the inter-coupling of the finance, banking, economics, and accounting sub-disciplines. In other words, the GFC is an ideal vehicle for encouraging holistic learning.

Returning to the findings of the Palehonki (1995) study just noted, teaching and learning approaches that draw upon the GFC should be associated with improved students' understanding of domain-specific knowledge. For example, studying fair value accounting through the lens of the GFC should improve accounting students' understandings of this accounting technique in the same way as the students observed by Palehonki used holistic learning to improve their spelling.

Using a GFC-based holistic learning approach to study such topics as financial reporting, auditing, and business ethics should provide teaching and learning benefits that extend beyond helping students in improving their understanding of a particular piece of the global economic system. More specifically, holistic learning approaches that leverage the GFC should help remedy what Bloom & Webinger (2011a) see as a lack of training and ability by decision-makers to see across today's highly-complex and highly-integrated economic system, a problem that led to the ignoring and marginalising of various system ailments until it was too late. A GFC-inspired pedagogy should directly contribute to the development of university graduates who – as the likely future leaders of industry, government, and key professional bodies – will be more capable of applying interdisciplinary and holistic perspectives to their decision-making. Trained and competent in seeing across the interacting components of the global financial system, such decision-makers should be in a better position to help minimise and avert future financial crises.

23.2.4 Summary of the benefits of teaching and learning approaches that draw on financial crises

Teaching and learning pedagogies that draw upon financial crises can enhance students' learning. Financial crises, such as the GFC, are fertile devices for instituting PBL, enriched learning environments, and holistic learning. Each of these three pedagogies has been associated with improved students' motivation and performance. It is further noted that the use of holistic learning may not merely enhance students' learning of discipline-specific knowledge, but it also has the potential for increasing the supply of professionals with interdisciplinary, holistic perspectives. Such professionals would be an important ingredient in helping reduce the frequency of financial crises.

Speaking of professional accountants, the benefits from using the GFC to motivate PBL, enriched learning, and holistic learning extends beyond the teaching and learning experiences associated with undergraduate or post-graduate programmes of study, and would also logically apply to PABs' continuing education programmes and, where appropriate, the pre-membership, extra-university, PAB-run educational programmes. An example of the latter is the New Zealand Institute of Chartered Accountants' (NZICA) professional accounting school (PAS) programme. PAS is a self-study programme that is supplemented by six two-day workshops. The programme is designed for recent university accounting graduates and seeks to ensure that aspiring NZICA members will have the appropriate range and level of competencies needed for professional success. These competencies include:

*   identify and solve business problems;
*   communicate effectively both verbally and in writing;
*   demonstrate ethical behaviour;
*   apply critical thinking;
*   access, analyse and synthesise information;
*   work effectively in a team and, when required, take a leadership role;
*   integrate knowledge across the accounting sub-disciplines and a range of other business disciplines; and
*   maintain currency of technical skills.

(See Watty, Chapter 13, and Cunningham, Chapter 18 – both in this volume, for a detailed discussion of these competencies.)

For the reasons previously noted in Sections 23.2.1, 23.2.2, and 23.2.3, the use of the GFC to motivate PBL-based, enriched learning-based, and holistic learning-based pedagogies would appear especially well suited to NZICA's professional accounting schools.

23.3 Courses likely to benefit from pedagogies that reference financial crises

There are several accounting courses that could benefit from using pedagogies that draw upon financial crises like the GFC. As previously noted, the GFC represents a breakdown in the financial reporting supply chain connecting preparers, auditors, regulators, and users. Since the typical curricula content of accounting courses feature at one or more points along this supply chain, it is fair to say that accounting educators could usefully incorporate a GFC-based approach in their teaching.

It is important to note that the term 'GFC-based approach' is used here to suggest that at least some pedagogical uses of the GFC can be successfully made in the typical accounting courses taught at university. Just how far and how much of a particular course's content is motivated by the GFC is a choice which each educator must make. And this choice will be predicated upon the other innovative pedagogies that the educator is already using or planning to implement. It is well understood that, prior to introducing any new teaching and learning innovation, whether it is the use of computer-assisted learning (CAL) or learning tasks that draw upon the GFC, the innovations must be assessed in relative terms. It is almost always the case that a teaching and learning innovation will have a positive impact on students' learning (Hattie, 2009). Since an educator does not have unlimited choice in innovation adoptions, possibly because the innovations are mutually exclusive (e.g. a seminar-based approach versus a highly-independent, self-directed approach, or the use of business case studies in a Harvard-style versus a student-led approach), or possibly because there are insufficient resources, it becomes the role of each educator to determine the pedagogies that comprise his/her course.

In the paragraphs below, some of the more obvious course candidates for GFC inclusion are discussed. It is expected that educators who are interested in motivating their teaching with reference to the GFC will heed this chapter's advice about the need to include pedagogies that do not merely catch students' interest, but which are also predicated on holistic learning, exhibit high meaningfulness, and/or enable students to apply their currently possessed skills and knowledge.

23.3.1 GFC and Financial Accounting courses

Financial Accounting represents one of the more obvious courses that could usefully incorporate a GFC-oriented teaching and learning approach. As a start, the study of the balance sheet accounts cash and receivables would readily benefit from leveraging the GFC. While cash and receivables are often considered to be the quintessential embodiment of a firm's liquidity, such an assumption was severely tested during the GFC. The 2008/2009 receivables of firms in the financial services industry were found to be a fraction of their 2007 reported values (Acharya & Schnabl, 2010). Lessons from the GFC can be used to caution students about the complexities and difficulties in measuring asset values.

Of course, cash and receivables are not the only balance sheet accounts that exhibit measurement problems. Inventories, investments and securities, and operating assets offer similar challenges. Furthermore, the application of measurement issues extends beyond the asset side of the balance sheet and touches on balance sheet liabilities and equities; for, at a minimum, the measurement and valuation of assets will directly affect the firm's reporting of its liabilities and equities. In a similar fashion, there are flow-on effects from the measurement and valuation of assets, liabilities, and equities to the measurement of income and analysis of a firm's profitability. In sum, the GFC provides a cornucopia of avenues into the teaching of *Financial Accounting*.

23.3.2 GFC and Auditing courses

The teaching of *Auditing* could also benefit from the use of pedagogies that draw upon financial crises like the GFC. Just how well the auditors acquitted themselves in upholding fundamentally important issues (such as firm accountability and governance) has been largely ignored, as various national and local government bodies' have chosen to peruse some of the more egregious GFC excesses. As an example, the New York Attorney General's office on 1 October 2012 filed under the auspices of the RMBS (*Residential Mortgage Backed Securities*) Working Group the first of its kind civil lawsuit against JP Morgan, charging the company with 'fraudulent and deceptive acts' allegedly committed by Bear Stearns, which JP Morgan purchased in 2008 (Eaglesham & Fitzpatrick, 2012).

Unlike the aftermath of the Enron scandal, when the auditing profession was placed squarely in the cross-hairs of the U.S. government's reform regulation, this time round the auditing profession has been rarely mentioned. It may be true that the auditors scrupulously adhered to accounting and auditing standards, but as Carnegie & West (2011) point out, this does not necessarily exonerate the auditors. These scholars note:

> *[A]ccounting is both defined and represented by an essentially incomplete set of accounting standards. It leaves the accounting professions with a ready-made scapegoat in instances of accounting failure: the tools that we are forced to work with are inadequate.*

> (2011, p. 501)

Auditors may not, at least at present, be feeling any external pressure for the role they played in the GFC. While they may not have committed any wrong, they may still be guilty by act of omission. In particular, educators and students might explore whether the Big Four accounting firms should have been more proactive in supporting accounting and auditing standards that work not just for large companies, but for society more generally.

23.3.3 GFC and Business Ethics courses

Ample scope exists for using financial crises to help teach *Business Ethics*. Financial crises, as previously mentioned, are characterised by the initial growth and subsequent bursting of a speculative bubble. Invariably, this bubble is fuelled by greed, which is a much truer name than the more euphemistic term some scholars like to use, such as *behaviour irrationality* (Barberis, 2010). There was nothing irrational in the actions of Goldman Sachs. This firm marketed toxic assets on behalf of their clients and, once sold, took an immediate short position on the asset (United States Senate Reports, 2011).

The President of the U.S.A., Barack Obama, has decried such common Wall Street practices, describing them as 'huge, reckless risks in pursuit of quick profits and massive bonuses' (Bowley, 2010). But as reckless and, it might be added, unethical, as these risks might be, it is certainly the case that Wall Street's investment bankers stand to profit handsomely. In 2007, in what might be described as the height of the underlying GFC turmoil, Goldman Sachs had total net earnings of $46 billion and paid compensation and bonuses of $20 billion to its employees. As described in the company's annual report, 'A substantial portion of our compensation expense represents discretionary bonuses' (Goldman Sachs 2007 Annual Report, p. 50). In other words, Goldman Sachs' profitability, and the employees' bonuses which it paid, were not hampered, and were probably helped by its questionable, if not unethical, behaviour.

Of course, the various investment banking firms were far from the only parties guilty of unethical behaviour. Rating agencies issued credit ratings despite the enormous conflict of interest under which they operated. In particular, they received remuneration from the very same firms, the securities in which they were asked to rate. The banks and their customers were also at fault: the former had no right lending and the latter had no right borrowing in the absence of sufficient collateral. In addition, regulators were negligent; and the accounting community and its auditors, as already mentioned, hid behind accounting and auditing standards to avoid blame over companies' failure to fully and completely disclose (Carnegie & West, 2011).

23.3.4 GFC and Management Accounting courses

Financial crises like the GFC may appear to be a *Financial Accounting & Reporting* issue, but links to *Management Accounting* exist as well. Management accountants are commonly responsible for establishing and overseeing the control of various organisational responsibility centres. The measurement and evaluation of these responsibility centres is an age-old problem. Trying to ensure employees' behaviour is congruent with the organisation's mission and strategy is a common endeavour of management accountants, and is referred to as the field of management control or performance management. (See Calderon's coverage of these activities in the context of programme review in Chapter 22 – this volume.)

Ensuring goal-congruent behaviour is a demanding task. Emmanuel, Otley & Merchant (1991), among others, have shown just how difficult this task can be. It is often the case that an organisation, in its hope of aligning employees' behaviour with its mission and strategy, produces a mix of desirable and undesirable/dysfunctional behaviour.

The GFC is replete with many examples illustrating behaviour that was highly dysfunctional (see Bloom & Webinger, 2011a). While the tactics pursued by the various parties (e.g. bankers, accountants, auditors, government regulators, and credit agency raters) were highly rational and consistent with the short-term aims of their respective organisations, these tactics were disastrous for their respective firm's long-term prospects and the wider economy. As management accountants who, among their other duties, are responsible for devising and overseeing employee incentive and reward programmes, there are many lessons to be learned from the GFC. Such lessons could readily be incorporated into the curricula of university courses in *Management Accounting*.

23.3.5 GFC and Accounting Theory courses

Courses in *Accounting Theory* are further logical candidates that could benefit from the inclusion of pedagogies that draw upon financial crises like the GFC. Connecting the study of accounting theory to the GFC provides a potential teaching and learning approach that throws into sharp relief the concepts of accounting substance and accounting form. The origins of the GFC are often traced to the U.S.A., which has some of the most, if not the most, detailed accounting rules of any country. That in the vast majority of cases companies and their auditors complied with the letter of the law is not in dispute. It is the spirit of the law that was often overlooked. As Carnegie & West (2011, p. 502) state: '*Achieving mere regulatory compliance with individual regulatory statements does not provide a lens through which well-informed assessments of liquidity, profitability, debt-paying capacity or other financial variables can be made.*'

The production of financial statements does not occur in a vacuum. A host of previously-decided accounting rules, principles, and professional judgements precede their preparation. Often compliance becomes an end in itself rather than a means to an end (Woods, 2011; West, 2003).

To avoid the situation where the forest (i.e., economic substance) is missed for the trees (i.e., statutory compliance), accounting students need to develop fuller, more thoughtful, and more critical understandings of accounting, both as a practice and as a profession. Accounting theory is a vital component to helping students achieve these improved understandings. Toward achieving this aim, students might be asked to ponder such questions as the following in relation to the GFC:

1　How are accounting rules decided?
2　Who determines what constitutes an adequate level of accounting disclosure?
3　Who are relevant stakeholders of the financial reporting process?
4　What are these stakeholders' needs?
5　What oversight processes exist for monitoring financial reporting quality?

This set of questions is, of course, a small subset of the various questions that could be used to promote in students a deeper and more critical understanding of accounting practice. Tying the study of these questions to such a salient event as the GFC is likely to reinforce just how important accounting's practice, including how it is conceived and shaped, is to society at large.

23.4 Pedagogical illustrations of accounting courses that leverage financial crises

The above paragraphs suggest some of the likely accounting courses that could usefully feature a GFC-infused component. In the paragraphs that follow, two more detailed examples are provided. One illustrates an *Intermediate Financial Accounting* course, and the other an *Advanced Management Accounting* course. The first example comes from Bloom & Webinger (2011a, 2011b), and is more fully described in *Accounting Education: an international journal*, Vol. 20, No. 5. The second example relates to a class which I have been teaching for more than 10 years.

23.4.1 GFC and Intermediate Financial Accounting

Bloom & Webinger (2011a, 2011b) present a description of an *Intermediate Financial Accounting* course incorporating concepts and issues from the GFC which they teach at a university in the U.S.A. Although the approach which they outline is envisioned for what they describe as the two-course sequencing of *Intermediate Accounting* at the typical North American university, it would likely transfer well to most other geographical/country settings too (Adler, 2011; Woods, 2011).

The course being advocated by Bloom & Webinger (2011a, 2011b) has two aims: (1) it seeks to contextualise the role of accounting in a highly salient, major financial crisis (the GFC); and (2) it promotes the integration of the *Financial Accounting* topic with other courses commonly taught in business schools. The first aim takes advantage of the high-impact value which the GFC has and, therefore, its ability to attract students' attention and motivate their learning. The second aim is intended to allow a more holistic understanding of the contribution that accounting, along with its allied business disciplines of economics, finance, and banking, makes to the study of real-world issues and problems.

Bloom & Webinger (2011a, 2011b) champion the design of an *Intermediate Financial Accounting* course that infuses elements of the GFC as a key part of the course's delivery, as opposed to a peripheral part to its purpose. They do so by bringing into the study of *Intermediate Financial Accounting* topics GFC-based mini-cases, vignettes, accounting journal entries, financial statements, disclosures, regulatory reports, news articles, and videos. For example, when studying the topic of 'environment of financial reporting,' Bloom & Webinger (2011a, pp. 472–473) thread into their presentation of the curriculum such questions as:

1　What role did the Bank of England play in this (GFC) crisis?
2　The IASB and FASB have been blamed for creating a crisis on valuation. What role did they play?

3   Is there compatibility between the financial accounting goal of transparency and the bank regulation goal of stability?

Bloom & Webinger (2011a, 2011b) provide a comprehensive discussion of how they infuse GFC practices and issues throughout such other *Financial Accounting* topics as statement of financial position, income statement, statement of cash flows, income measurement and profitability, various asset accounts (e.g. cash and receivables, inventories, investments, etc.), various liability accounts (e.g., leases, accruals for income taxes, accruals for pensions and employee benefits, etc.), and equity accounts (e.g. stock options, earnings per share, capital maintenance requirements, etc.). While the prescriptions of Bloom & Webinger (2011a, 2011b) can be readily followed, plenty of scope exists for an educator's tailoring of the course to meet his/her own particular needs.

Students who have studied the course reported enjoying '*the real world orientation of the course*' (Bloom & Webinger, 2011a, p. 484). The students awarded positive ratings to being able to learn and retain the accounting subject matter. Furthermore, and consistent with Bloom & Webinger's (2011a, 2011b) belief that infusing GFC practices and issues into an accounting course will enhance students' appreciation of the need to apply holistic and multi-disciplinary perspectives to the understanding and resolving of real-world business problems, Bloom & Webinger (2011a) found that, upon completion of the course, students reported a better understanding of the relationships among accounting, banking, and finance.

23.4.2 GFC and Advanced Management Accounting

Adler (2011) describes the success he has had with incorporating issues and events from various financial crises into an *Advanced Management Accounting* course which he teaches at a university in New Zealand. This is a fourth-year post-graduate level course, taught over two 13-week academic semesters. The course is taught as a seminar, with students and the teacher meeting once a week for three hours. Most students are either (undergraduate) honours students or master's students.

The course's curriculum includes ample reference and application to financial crises, including the GFC, to motivate discussions that connect to issues of ethics, leadership, organisational culture, and performance measurement. While most students understand the GFC in general terms, the typical student possesses only the most limited understanding of the crisis' details and its relative standing in history. To help students appreciate the magnitude of the problem, Adler assigns his students the preliminary task of charting a decade's worth of various national and international economic statistics. While the students are meant to choose their own measures of economic health, they generally collect and chart data about jobs, GDP, stock market indices, and house prices. The purpose behind this task is to get the students to see how abruptly and significantly these broad economic indicators changed with the emergence of the GFC.

Armed with this understanding of the GFC's significance, and hopefully with students' interest piqued, Adler asks his students to research various events occurring during the previous decade. He reminds his students that the GFC came only six years after Enron, one of the largest and most scandalous corporate failures in history. The Enron debacle, together with the corporate collapses of Parlamat, Worldcom, and Waste Management, plus the demise of the accounting firm Arthur Andersen, galvanised worldwide indignation and energised the U.S.A. to undertake a substantial overhaul of its financial reporting and auditing systems. This overhaul culminated with the U.S. government's introduction of a federal law known as the Sarbanes-Oxley Act 2002 (SOX). In spite of this major legislative and regulatory undertaking, the GFC arrived a scant six years later. Adler asks the students to ponder this thought as they connect the excessive risk-taking and greed that characterise much of this 10-year period to the course topics of ethics, leadership, organisational culture, and performance measurement.

To establish further that neither the GFC nor the era of corporate scandals that preceded it are aberrations, Adler asks his students to research the U.S. Savings and Loan Crisis of the 1980s. Here again, the students uncover repeating themes: the failure of regulators, accountants, lawyers, politicians, and companies' senior management. While the main purpose of Adler's use of financial crises is to incorporate non-trivial, high-impact historical events into the discussion of the course's topics, a second, albeit idealistic goal, is to help students learn from history.

23.5 Conclusion

This chapter sets out to explain why the use of salient and highly noteworthy events like financial crises can serve as a motivating catalyst of students' learning. As this chapter's discussion reveals, the education literature's empirical and theoretical work supports such a linkage. In particular, a substantial body of scholarly literature based on PBL, enriched learning environments, and holistic learning help to explain why the study of accounting topics in reference to a financial crisis like the GFC can have a positive effect on students' learning and achievement.

The chapter also highlights the types of accounting courses that are likely to benefit from incorporating financial crises into the courses' teaching and learning. The more obvious courses include *Financial Accounting & Reporting, Auditing, Business Ethics, Management Accounting*, and *Accounting Theory*. However, the actual list is probably much longer than this. If the GFC can be understood as the breakdown of the financial reporting supply chain, then there is really no accounting course that does not in some way contribute to this supply chain. As a consequence, all accounting courses, which would go beyond those offered by universities and include courses offered by various PABs from around the world, could conceivably benefit from incorporating financial crises like the GFC in their teaching.

The final part of the chapter highlighted two examples of university courses that make liberal use of the GFC to stimulate the study of their respective course topics. The first example is an *Intermediate Financial Accounting* course, taught in the U.S.A., and the second example is an *Advanced Management Accounting* course, taught in New Zealand. Both offer guidance on how other accounting educators might similarly motivate their courses.

Note

1   The term 'course' is being used here to signify the study of a particular topic within a wider subject area. Courses comprise the basic building blocks associated with any given university's major and qualification.

References

Acharya, V.V. & Schnabl, P. (2010) Do global banks spread global imbalances? Asset-backed commercial paper during the financial crisis of 2007–09, *IMF Economic Review*, 58(1), 37–73.

Adler, R.W. (2011) A commentary on 'Contextualizing the Intermediate Financial Accounting Courses in the Global Financial Crisis', *Accounting Education: an international journal*, 20 (5), 495–498.

Adler, R.W., Milne, M.J., & Stablein, R. (2001) Situated motivation: an empirical test in an accounting course, *Canadian Journal of Administrative Sciences*, 18 (3), 189–206.

Ainley, M., Hidi, S., and Berndorff, D. (2002) Interest, learning, and the psychological processes that mediate their relationship, *Journal of Educational Psychology*, *94* (3), pp. 545–561.

Albanese, M.A. & Mitchell, S. (1993) Problem-based learning: a review of the literature on its outcomes and implementation issues, *Academic Medicine*, 68 (1), 52–81.

Armstrong, B.E. & Larson, C.N. (1995) Students' use of part-whole and direct comparison strategies for comparing partitioned rectangles, *Journal for Research in Mathematics Education*, 26(1), 2–19.

Bamber, E.M. & Bamber, L.S. (2006) Using 10-K reports brings management accounting to life, *Issues in Accounting Education*, 21(3), 267–290.

Barberis, N. (2010) *Psychology and the Financial Crisis of 2007–2008*, Working Paper Series, New Haven, CT: Yale University.

Barrows, H.S. (1986) Problem-based learning in medicine and beyond: a brief overview, *New Directions for Teaching and Learning*, 68, (Winter), 3–14.

Barrows, H.S. & Tamblyn, R.M. (1980) *Problem-Based Learning: An Approach to Medical Education*, New York: Springer Publishing Company.

Bloom, R. & Webinger, M. (2011a) The Bloom and Webinger Forum: contextualizing the intermediate financial accounting courses in the Global Financial Crisis, *Accounting Education: an international journal*, 20(5), 469–494.

Bloom, R., & Webinger, M. (2011b) Rejoinder to commentaries on 'Contextualizing the Intermediate Financial Accounting Courses in the Global Financial Crisis', *Accounting Education: an international journal*, 20(5), 529–537.

Boshuizen, H.P.A., Schimdt, H.G., & Wassamer, I. (1990) Curriculum style and the integration of biomedical and clinical knowledge, paper presented at the 2nd International Symposium on Problem-based Learning, Yokyakarta, Indonesia.

Bowley, G. (2010) Strong year for Goldman, as it trims bonus pool, *The New York Times*, 21 January 2010. Available at: http://www.nytimes.com/2010/01/22/business/22goldman.html (accessed 1 October 2012).

Breton, G. (1999) Some empirical evidence on the superiority of the problem-based learning (PBL) method, Accounting Education, 8 (1), 1–12.

Brophy, J. (1999) Toward a model of value aspects of motivation in education: developing appreciation for particular learning domains and activities, *Educational Psychologist*, 34, 75–85.

Carnegie, G.D., & West, B. (2011) A commentary on 'Contextualizing the Intermediate Financial Accounting Courses in the Global Financial Crisis', *Accounting Education: an international journal*, 20(5), 499–503.

Choo, C.W. (2008) Organizational disasters: why they happen and how they may be prevented, *Management Decision*, 46(1), 32–45.

Debnath, S.C., Tandon, S., & Pointer, L.V. (2007) Designing business schools courses to promote student motivation: an application of the job characteristics model, *Journal of Management Education*, 31(6), 812–831.

Dewey, J. (1938) *Logic: The Theory of Inquiry*, New York: Holt & Co.

Durik, A.M. & Harackiewicz, J.M. (2007) Different strokes for different folks: how personal interest moderates the effects of situational factors on task interest, *Journal of Educational Psychology*, 99, 597–610.

Eaglesham, J. & Fitzpatrick, D. (2012) J.P. Morgan sued on mortgage bonds, *The Wall Street Journal*, 1 October 2012. Available at: http://online.wsj.com/article/SB10000872396390444413810457803090 3731665328.html (accessed 1 October 2012).

Earley, C.E. & Phillips, F. (2008) Assessing audit and business risk at Toy Central Corporation, *Issues in Accounting Education*, 23(2), 299–307.

Emmanuel, C., Otley, D., & Merchant, K. (1991) *Accounting for Management Control*, 2nd edn, London: Chapman & Hall.

FCIC (2011) *Financial Crisis Inquiry Report*. Available at: http://cybercemetery.unt.edu/archive/fcic/2011 0310173538/http://www.fcic.gov/report (accessed 28 September 2012).

Feather, N.T. (1988) Values, valences, and course enrollment: testing the role of personal values within an expectancy-value framework, *Journal of Educational Psychology*, 80, 381–391.

Fitzpatrick, L.E., McConnell, C.A., & Sasse, C. (2006) Motivating the reluctant, novice learner: principles of macroeconomics, *Journal of Economics and Economic Education Research*, 7(2), 23–45.

Galbraith, J.K. (1993) *A Short History of Financial Euphoria*, New York: Whittle Books.

Ghoshal, S. (2005) Bad management theories are destroying good management practices, *Academy of Management Learning and Education*, 4(1), 75–91.

Hackman, J. & Oldham, G. (1980) *Work Redesign*, Reading, MA: Addison-Wesley.

Hattie, J. (2009) *Visible Learning: A Synthesis of over 800 Meta-Analyses Relating to Achievement*, London: Routledge.

Hellwig, M. (2009) Systemic risk in the financial sector: an analysis of the subprime-mortgage financial crisis, *The Economist*, 157(2), 129–207.

Hidi, S. & Harackiewicz, J.M. (2000) Motivating the academically unmotivated: a critical issue for the 21st century, *Review of Educational Research*, 70, 151–179.

Howe, K. & Berv, J. (2000) Constructing constructivism, epistemological and pedagogical, in Phillips, D. (ed.) *Constructivism in Education: Ninety-Ninth Yearbook of the National Society for the Study of Education*, Chicago: National Society for the Study of Education, pp. 19–40.

Kaufman, D.M. & Mann, K.V. (1996) Comparing student attitudes in problem-based and conventional curricula, *Academic Medicine*, 71(10), 1096–1099.

Kindleberger, C.P. (2005) *Manias, Panics, and Crashers: A History of Financial Crises*, 5th edn, London: Macmillan.

Knapp, M.C. & Knapp, C.A. (2007) Europe's Enron: Royal Ahold, N.V., *Issues in Accounting Education*, 22(4), 641–660.

Krapp, A. (2002) An educational-psychological theory of interest and its relation to SDT, in Deci, E.L. & Ryan, R.M. (eds) *The Handbook of Self-Determination Research*, Rochester, NY: Rochester University Press, pp. 405–427.

Lanchester, J. (2010) *Whoops! Why Everyone Owes Everyone and No-One Can Pay*, London: Allen Lane.

LeFevre, P. (1986) *Exploring Fractions with Fourth Graders*, Washington, DC: ERIC Issue RIEAPR87.

Meece, J., Blumenfield, P., & Hoyle, R. (1988) Students' goal orientations and cognitive engagement in classroom activities, *Journal of Educational Psychology*, 80, 514–523.

Milne, M.J. & McConnell (2001) Problem-based learning: a pedagogy for using case material in accounting education, *Accounting Education: an international journal*, 10(1), 61–82.

Norman, G. and Schmidt, H. (1992) The psychological basis of problem-based learning: a review of the evidence, *Academic Medicine*, 67(9), 557–565.

Palehonki, A. (1995) *Improving Conventional Spelling through the Use of Words in Context Versus Words in Isolation*, ERIC Database No. ED380769.

Paris, S. & Turner, J. (1994) Situated motivation, in Pintrich, P., Brown, D. & Weinstein, C. (eds) *Student Motivation, Cognition, and Learning*, Hillsdale, NJ: Lawrence Erlbaum Associates.

Patel, V.L., Greon, G.J., & Norman, G.R. (1991) Effects of conventional and problem-based medical curricula on problem-solving, *Academic Medicine*, 66, 380–389.

Perrow, C. (1999) *Complex Organizations: A Critical Essay*, 3rd edn, New York: McGraw-Hill.

Phillips, F., Johnstone, N., & Mackintosh, B. (2011) A good story: a commentary on 'Contextualizing the Intermediate Financial Accounting Courses in the Global Financial Crisis', *Accounting Education: an international journal*, 20(5), 515–519.

Pintrich, P. & DeGroot, E. (1990) Motivational and self-regulated learning components of classroom academic performance, *Journal of Educational Psychology*, 82, 33–40.

Tan, R.G.K. (2011) A commentary on 'Contextualizing the Intermediate Financial Accounting Courses in the Global Financial Crisis', *Accounting Education: an international journal*, 20(5), 521–524.

Renninger, K.A. (2000) Individual interest and its implications for understanding intrinsic motivation, in Sansone, C. & Harackiewicz, J.M. (eds) *Intrinsic and Extrinsic Motivation: The Search for Optimal Motivation and Performance*, New York: Academic Press, pp. 373–404.

Rest, J. (1986) *Moral Development: Advances in Research and Theory*, New York: Praeger.

Schiefele, U. (1991) Interest, learning, and motivation, *Educational Psychologist*, 26, 299–323.

Schmidt, H.G. (1983) Problem-based learning rationale and description, *Medical Education*, 7, 11–16.

Singleton-Green, B. (2012) Commentary: financial reporting and financial stability: causes and effects, *Australian Accounting Review*, 22(1), 5–17.

Sobral, D.T. (1995) The problem-based learning approach as an enhancement factor of personal meaningfulness of learning, *Higher Education*, 29, 93–101.

Stanley, T. & Marsden, S. (2012) Problem-based learning: does accounting education need it?, *Journal of Accounting Education*, 30(3), 267–289.

Tett, G. (2009) *Fools Gold: How Unrestrained Greed Corrupted a Dream, Shattered Global Markets and Unleashed a Catastrophe*, London: Little Brown.

United States Senate Reports (2011) Wall Street and the financial crisis: anatomy of a financial collapse, Permanent Subcommittee on Investigations, April 13, Washington, DC.

Wigfield, A. & Eccles, J.S. (1992) The development of achievement task values: a theoretical analysis. *Development Review*, 12, 265–310.

Woods, M. (2011) A commentary on 'Contextualizing the Intermediate Financial Accounting Courses in the Global Financial Crisis', *Accounting Education: an international journal*, 20(5), 525–528.

About the author

Ralph W. Adler is Professor of Accounting at the University of Otago, New Zealand (ralph.adler@otago.ac.nz); a Senior Associate Editor of *Accounting Education: an international journal*; the Director of the Otago Centre for Organisational Performance Measurement and Management (COPMM); and the Convenor of the Performance Measurement Association of Australasia (PMAA). He has over 25 years' teaching experience at both undergraduate and postgraduate levels. His primary research interest in the field of accounting education, for which he has won a number of awards, is pedagogy – especially the use of active student learning, in which area he has published widely.

24

Ethics and accounting education

Gordon Boyce

LA TROBE UNIVERSITY, AUSTRALIA

CONTENTS

Abstract

This chapter canvasses the current state of ethics in accounting education, engaging with key contemporary debates, emerging themes and problems. Various perspectives are encompassed as the chapter examines key dimensions which affect the relevance of accounting ethics education to students, the accounting profession, and the wider community. Ethics in accounting education is considered from appropriate inter-disciplinary perspectives, and set within a changing global context. The chapter examines: the case for ethics education in accounting; curricular and pedagogical issues and approaches; and aspects of a future agenda for accounting ethics education.

Keywords

applied ethics, ethical theory, ethics education, moral exemplars, philosophical ethics, reform, social dimensions

24.1 Introduction

> [W]e, as individuals, become the resultant sum of each ethical confrontational event as experienced from the beginning of our careers.
>
> (Boisjoly, 1993, p. 59)

This chapter sets out to explain and further promote an agenda for ethics education within the accounting curriculum. The main aims of the chapter are:

- to examine the case for including ethics as a central element of accounting education;
- to explore a range of curricular and pedagogical issues related to ethics education; and
- to consider how the future agenda for accounting ethics education is likely to encompass contemporary developments in, and perspectives on, accounting.

The accounting and corporate scandals of the late twentieth and early twenty-first centuries serve as a reminder of the dramatic consequences of unethical business practices. There were numerous notable cases of accounting fraud, corporate governance failure, and deficient ethics and accountability in many countries including Australia, China, Germany, Greece, India, Italy, Japan, the Netherlands, Spain, Sweden, the U.K., and the U.S.A. (see Jones, 2011, for case examples from each of these countries). These events may be regarded as being emblematic of the significant socio-political influence of contemporary business activity, and of accounting as a means of representing and shaping that activity. Most prominently, in the U.S.A., the Enron/Arthur Andersen case ultimately saw the demise of both the corporation and the accounting firm implicated in the scandal, and the WorldCom scandal was the biggest accounting fraud in history (Cooper, 2008).

Accounting and business failures (such as those involving Enron and WorldCom) share a long lineage with a range of similar scandals and collapses that have occurred and recurred throughout the history of the corporation (see Sykes, 1998; Clarke *et al.*, 2003; Bakan, 2004; Merino, 2006; Jones, 2011). The questionable accounting practices that typify corporate scandals are not atypical business behaviours, despite the 'bad apple' characterisation that tends to focus on miscreant individual actors (see Ravenscroft & Williams, 2004; Cooper *et al.*, 2005). Staubus

(2005, p. 11) suggests that the ethics failures represented by these scandals are '*[a]lmost inevitable*', because of the conflict between the interests of those responsible for corporate financial reports (managers, accountants, auditors) and the ostensible beneficiaries, or users, of corporate financial statements. Multiple groups encompassing a large swathe of the accounting profession are implicated in these ethics failures: corporate accountants and managers, auditors, academic accountants, analysts, regulators, and accounting standard setters (see Jones, 2011).

Business schools are also implicated in the widespread public mistrust that has resulted from financial scandals and collapses, having '*produced ruthlessly talented graduates who have ambition in abundance but little sense for social responsibility or ethics*' (Beverungen *et al.*, 2013, p. 102). It has been observed that:

> [M]any of these [company] officers and, to a large extent, the cultures of these companies, felt comfortable with deceptions in the name of shareholder value because they were accomplishing what they were trained to do in business school.
>
> (Jennings, 2004, p. 14)

By '*propagating ideologically inspired amoral theories, business schools have actively freed their students from any sense of moral responsibility*' (Ghoshal, 2005, p. 76), and the longstanding '*history of sidestepping ethics*' has resulted in a crisis of legitimacy and confidence (Swanson, 2005, p. 247). Educators share some of the responsibility for ethical problems in the commercial world, due to their neglect of ethics in business and accounting curricula.

Enron, WorldCom, Arthur Andersen and other cases draw attention to the profound consequences of ethical failures within contemporary accounting and business – and accounting and business education (Owen, 2005).[1] Read differently, they may also point to the potential for greater ethical awareness and associated ethical action on the part of accountants and the accounting profession. Accounting failures, scandals, and crises present numerous 'teachable moments' of the type that the Global Financial Crisis (GFC) represented more broadly (see Adler, Chapter 23 – this volume).

The place of ethics in the accounting curriculum (and in business education more broadly) is the key concern for this chapter. The need to improve ethics education, sometimes associated with a more general need to broaden (or liberalise) the accounting curriculum as a whole, has been widely recognised for many years (see Amernic & Craig, Chapter 12 – this volume), but there has been insufficient action and progress to date, despite a number of initiatives. McPhail and Walters observe:

> There is a lot of discussion about professional ethics these days and lots of developments within the accounting profession . . . While these initiatives represent important developments within the profession, we wonder whether much of the discussion on the ethical challenges facing the profession nevertheless remain rather narrow in their focus and limited in their impact (sic).
>
> (2009, p. xi)

To help explain and further promote an ethics agenda for accounting education, and reflecting the aims outlined at the start of this section, the remainder of the chapter: outlines the case for accounting ethics education (Section 24.2); analyses a range of issues related to curriculum and pedagogy (Section 24.3); and, looking forward to a future agenda for accounting ethics education, discusses a number of relevant contemporary developments and perspectives (Section 24.4). For the purposes of the discussion and analysis in the chapter, it is accepted that, for practical purposes, accounting, business, and ethics are inseparable. Accounting ethics is regarded as being a part of business ethics, which is itself associated with organisational, personal, and societal ethics. Therefore, the chapter draws on a wide range of materials from within accounting and beyond.

24.2 Ethics in accounting education

Every business decision has ethical dimensions and, thus, ethics is an integral part of business decision-making.

(Felton & Sims, 1990, p. 390)

[I]t is professional accountants, those specialists who purport to have the public interest at heart . . . who have been the main contributors to the decline of ethical standards in business.

(McPhail, 1999, p. 835)

24.2.1 Ethics and business

Ethics may be broadly regarded as concerning *'the actions of people, in situations where these actions have effects on the welfare of both oneself and others'* (Gaa & Thorne, 2004, p. 1). In providing guidance for 'good' human conduct (and to help to judge the conduct of selves and others), ethics is about the pursuit of particular values in business, organisational, and social life. Ethical questions of right and wrong, propriety and impropriety, justice and injustice encompass individuals, groups, organisations, and society as a whole.

Accounting is at the forefront of many of the issues plaguing contemporary business and society, yet *'accounting remains off the ethical radar'* (McPhail & Walters, 2009, p. 3). This may be partly because it is culturally maligned and characterised by a range of negative and narrow cultural stereotypes (Friedman & Lyne, 2001; Dimnik & Felton, 2006) which perpetuate the image of an inaccessible technical, number-crunching, a-social domain. This produces a lack of substantive engagement with issues of ethics and social responsibility, even as a substantial body of research within the discipline attests to the ethicality and sociality of accounting (see Boyce *et al.*, 2012; Boyce & Greer, 2013).

24.2.2 Ethics education matters

Ethics education may be *'an important lever for changing business'* (Gentile & Samuelson, 2003, p. 2). This understanding contradicts some accounts which suggest that ethics education at university is unnecessary because, it is assumed, each individual's ethical values are (and should be) developed under the guidance and influence of parents, religious institutions, school teachers, and other influences (see, for example, Langenderfer & Rockness, 1989, on the 'Moral-Amoral Dilemma'; Hooker, 2004, on the 'moral development argument'). Although it is undoubtedly the case that students' ethical values are already formed to a certain degree by the time they reach university, there is ample evidence that education can and does influence ethical behaviour. Indeed, instilling particular values and influencing behaviour has been one of the basic social functions of education throughout history, and it is this that gives education much of its social significance (see Boyce, 2002).

Ethics education clearly has the potential to make a difference to students and societies but, as institutions, universities generally reflect dominant political and social values and tend to inculcate these values in a way that confirms and reinforces the status quo (ibid.). This generality applies no less to accounting education (see Merino, 2006; Boyce, 2008; Merino *et al.*, 2010). However, it is not totalising, for dominant hegemonies may be challenged (Boyce, 2002) while passivity reinforces the status quo.

Without definitive and determined action to change accounting education, students may be actively prevented from reaching higher levels of ethical maturity (McPhail, 1999)[2] and may be desensitised to moral dimensions of accounting (Mayper *et al.*, 2005). From a purely pragmatic perspective, a deficient ethics education will also leave students lacking in their capacity to address '*the kinds of values conflicts, crises, and trends that the press, the general public and our own faculty are concerned about*' (Gentile & Samuelson, 2003, p. 2).

24.2.3 Ethics education works

There is evidence that accountants in practice exhibit a lower level of moral reasoning than those in other professions (Armstrong, 1987; Ponemon, 1992; Eynon *et al.*, 1997), and are, at best, ethically '*average*' (Fleming, 1996). Nevertheless, the completion of a university business ethics course can improve ethical recognition and reasoning skills (Armstrong, 1993; Piper *et al.*, 1993; Ryan & Bisson, 1993; Geary & Sims, 1994; Eynon *et al.*, 1997; Gautschi & Jones, 1998). This can enhance the employability of graduates with broad and transferable ethical reasoning and associated generic skills (Graham, 2012; see also Watty, Chapter 13 – this volume). In this context, however, it is important to ensure that education targets a range of employment outcomes. Thus, it should not be assumed that an exclusive managerial focus within ethics education (e.g. focus on management decision-making) is appropriate (Geary & Sims, 1994, p. 6).

There is little doubt that, in many dimensions of their professional, business, social, and personal lives, accounting graduates will confront a range of significant ethical concerns. They will have to wrestle with dilemmas, justify their own conduct and/or the conduct of others, and excuse or condemn conduct (MacLagan & Campbell, 2011). In this context, it is necessary to recognise that the values and beliefs which students hold, and come to hold, may conflict with established values, beliefs, and practices in the business world. Therefore, a key aim of ethics education must be to help students:

> to understand their own values, the changing and dynamic environments in which they will make decisions, the often conflicting needs of stakeholders, the impact of managerial actions on the lives of others, and the need to give continuing attention throughout their careers to the development of ethical sensitivities and accountabilities.
>
> (Felton & Sims, 1990, p. 390)

Given the above, ethics education may work best if it is embedded within a broader and integrated liberal education framework (Ponemon & Glazer, 1990). Within the profession and beyond, such a framework for accounting education has long been acknowledged to be important for the development of a socially-relevant accounting and business education (Bedford *et al.*, 1986; Accounting Education Change Commission, 1990; Donaldson & Freeman, 1994; Fogarty, 2010; Sangster, 2010; Willits, 2011; Behn *et al.*, 2012; and see also Amernic & Craig, Chapter 12, and Bloom, Chapter 14 – both in this volume). Improving ethics education thus has the potential to advance the broader agenda for improving accounting education.

22.2.4 Unethical effects

Accounting education generates a tendency to engender a particular kind of identity within students which prioritises economic concerns and marginalises ethical ones (McPhail, 2001a; Ravenscroft & Williams, 2004). Consequently, the ethical development of students may actually be inhibited, in part, because students are indoctrinated into a narrow, profit-centred view of accounting that marginalises social, environmental, and ethical dimensions (Loeb, 1991; Gray et al., 1994).

Accounting students are '*taught that economically appropriate action is that which maximises company profits and . . . that morally good actions are concomitant with economically good actions*' (McPhail, 1999, p. 836). Similar findings apply to business students (McCabe et al., 1991); the priorities of students in business education shift towards the valorisation of shareholder value to the exclusion of other values (Gentile & Samuelson, 2003). It has been argued that this produces a situation in which accounting education serves to '*indoctrinate, pacify and cripple ethically our students*' (Tinker & Gray, 2003, p. 728). A paradoxical ethical effect of accounting education may be that it trains good people to do bad things (see Low et al., 2008).

22.2.5 Ethical neglect

Despite a generally broad acceptance that ethics education is needed, it has still not been given the prominence it merits in the accounting curriculum (Gaa & Thorne, 2004). Puxty, Sikka, & Willmott argue that accounting education was historically responsible for socialising '*successive generations*' (1994, p. 89) of accountants into an ostensibly amoral discipline without any meaningful reflection on the social obligations of the profession. There is '*a woeful lack of reflection*' (Ravenscroft & Williams, 2004, p. 8) in education and the wider profession on the fundamental premises of the discipline that has been so centrally involved in business scandals and corruption. In an examination of the North American academic response to contemporary accounting scandals, Cooper, Everett, & Neu found that, despite an ostensible '*ethics revival*' (2005, p. 374), it was characterised by appeals to moralistic and individualistic conceptions of ethics (where miscreants are deemed to be individual '*bad apples*'), portraying corporate and accounting misdeeds as being either isolated incidents or indicative of problems elsewhere in the financial system.

This style of response to pressures on accounting education continues a long-established pattern. In the mid-1980s, the Bedford Committee in the U.S.A. was asked '*to investigate and report on the future structure, content, and scope of accounting education, with the associated charge to recommend educational objectives and goals for adjusting university accounting education by the year 2000*' (Bedford & Shenkir, 1987, p. 86).

The Committee:

> examined developments in university accounting education programs over the . . . 1925–85 period. That review of required university courses, programs and teaching methods revealed that the substance of accounting education has remained essentially the same over the last 50 years . . . accounting education has not made significant efforts to improve its teaching methods over the last 60 years.
>
> (ibid., pp. 84–86)

The necessity of improved ethics education was clearly acknowledged, forming a key part of a recommended effort to ensure that students learnt both the technical professional accounting body of knowledge and acquired '*the ability to use that knowledge analytically, in creative and innovative ways in accordance with high standards of professional ethics*' (Bedford et al., 1986, p. 178). The Committee found that:

The scope and content of future accounting education should . . . extend well beyond technical skills . . . it must also instill the ethical standards and the commitment of a professional. The general effort to develop in students a concern for individual needs and for the overall advancement of society must be given more emphasis

(ibid., p. 179)

(See also St. Pierre & Rebele, Chapter 5 – this volume, for an alternative point of view.)

Before and since the Bedford Report, there have been numerous official calls for fundamental reconsideration and reorientation of accounting education in the U.S.A. (see Black, 2012, for a summary) and elsewhere, including major reviews by the Mathews Committee in Australia (Review Committee of the Accounting Discipline in Higher Education, 1990), and Solomons in the U.K. (Solomons, with Berridge, 1974). Reports such as those emanating from the U.S.A.'s Treadway Commission (Treadway *et al.*, 1987), Accounting Education Change Commission (AECC) (1990), and Albrecht & Sack (2000) have been globally influential, reflecting the broader influence of the U.S.A. in relation to the structure and content of accounting education (e.g. see Leung & Cooper, 1994; Mathews, 1994; Hancock *et al.*, 2009; Canarutto *et al.*, 2010). Demonstrated ethical failings over decades have made reform calls all the more significant, but to date they have produced little in the way of substantive change (Nelson, 1995; Merino, 2006). The promised and anticipated '*revolution in accounting education*' (Sundem *et al.*, 1990) has not eventuated and the level of ethics integration into courses continues to be low (Miller & Becker, 2011).

Although a range of institutional factors is undoubtedly at play in this apparent inertia, Langenderfer & Rockness (1989) discussed the historical reluctance on the part of *educators* to incorporate ethics into the accounting curriculum. They identified three key explanatory factors. First, the 'Legal-Ethical Dilemma' arises when educators are reluctant to clearly distinguish between law and ethics. In countering this position, Langenderfer & Rockness argued that:

we must recognize that the laws do not necessarily prescribe ethical behavior or reflect the ethical norms of society, and that universities have an obligation to discuss ethics and what is acceptable ethical behavior that transcends the law.

(1989, p. 60)

The 'Philosophical-Practical Dilemma' reflects the belief of some accounting educators that they are not equipped to teach in this area, thus advocating that ethics be taught from within a philosophy department. Langenderfer & Rockness counter this argument by noting that it prioritises philosophical over practical or applied ethics. They argue that '*if ethical education is to have a significant place in the accounting curriculum, it must be integrated into the accounting courses and taught by accounting faculty*' (ibid., p. 61) (see Section 24.3.1). There is evidence that accounting educators are actually willing to integrate ethics into the accounting curriculum (Cohen & Pant, 1989; Blanthorne *et al.*, 2007). Although some educators may have inadequate skills to teach accounting ethics, this general observation applies to any part of the curriculum. This alone is not an appropriate consideration for curricular design (beyond the short-term), since continuing and professional education and development can be designed to address any shortcomings.[3]

A 'Moral–Amoral Dilemma' reflects a more general reluctance on the part of accounting educators to present and discuss ethics issues in class. This may be based on a narrow (and unjustifiable) view that ethics education cannot affect students' moral values (see Section 24.2.2). Cohen & Pant (1989) identified a broader problem in that there is little incentive in academic work and reward structures for teachers to integrate ethics into their courses.

Although there are clearly a number of barriers and obstacles, there is also a clear case for including ethics in the curriculum as part of a broader change agenda for accounting education (see Flood, Chapter 4, and St. Pierre & Rebele, Chapter 5 – both in this volume).

24.3 Teaching ethics: curriculum and pedagogy

> *[T]he classroom is probably an effective place to start, particularly in terms of the ability to influence tomorrow's accounting professionals.*
>
> (Ravenscroft & Williams, 2005, p. 370)

24.3.1 Curriculum

Despite wide rhetorical support for accounting ethics education, the appropriate place of ethics within the curriculum continues to be debated, particularly the issue of whether ethics should be integrated across the curriculum or concentrated within a specialist subject or subjects. There is certainly a strong case for the adoption of an integrated approach but this does not necessarily obviate the case for one or more stand-alone or specialist ethics subjects within a degree programme. The key benefit of an integrated approach is that, if taught well, students come to realise that ethics is not an isolated issue which can be treated separately from other business and organisational concerns – a perspective that is fundamental to ethics in accounting (Loeb, 1988; Geary & Sims, 1994; Adler, 1999).

The Association to Advance Collegiate Schools of Business (AACSB)[4] has endorsed an integrated approach, but this decision generated considerable controversy. Critics felt that it represented lip-service to ethics education, and was a lost opportunity to make meaningful change in this important area (see Hartman & Hartman, 2004 for a detailed exposition, and Bloom, Chapter 14 – this volume, for a broader discussion of integration issues in the accounting curriculum). Although ethics can (and should) be successfully integrated into other subjects, a specialist and dedicated consideration of ethics is also necessary to facilitate depth of consideration and build an appropriate inter-disciplinary perspective (Swanson, 2005; Bean & Bernardi, 2007; Williams & Elson, 2010).[5] Ideally, stand-alone ethics subjects would be taught by accounting teachers with relevant skills, thus imparting contextual and domain-specific ethical knowledge, but combinations of accounting and ethics/philosophy staff are also possible (Hartman & Hartman, 2004; Abdolmohammadi, 2008).[6]

An obvious practical resolution of this issue is to take an integrated approach while also offering one or more specialist stand-alone ethics subjects that provide relevant and appropriate depth of understanding (see Armstrong, 1993). There seems little doubt that efforts to have accrediting bodies *require* at least one specialist ethics subject will continue, because history suggests that reliance on voluntarism in this domain is unlikely to produce needed change (Hartman & Hartman, 2004).

24.3.2 Philosophical or applied ethics

Ethics education in accounting has rather unreflectively tended to take a 'practical' or 'applied' approach to ethics by focussing on the ethical norms of the profession as expressed in codes of ethics and related pronouncements, and then applying them to cases and scenarios (further discussed in Section 24.3.5). By seeking to mimic 'real-world' decision-making contexts, this provides an avenue whereby educators may seek to engage students:

[B]usiness ethics education could be more effective and perhaps engender greater civic awareness and engagement among students . . . It is crucial that business ethics education engages with students in a way that attempts to address the disconnectedness that often comes from a purely academic approach to the subject.

(McPhail, 2006, p. 308)

Leaving aside, for the moment, the issue of whether such approaches can or do achieve the aim of being 'realistic', there is a more fundamental debate regarding the appropriate orientation of accounting ethics subjects. Rossouw (2008, p. 161) notes an 'unprecedented *growth and demand for Applied Ethics*', including business ethics, reflecting a desire (or preparedness) to address the ethical challenges which confront contemporary society. At the same time, Rossouw laments the turn away from philosophical ethics.

Philosophical ethics takes a more conceptual approach and gives attention to abstract moral concerns regarding the nature of ethical obligation, the formation and articulation of fundamental ethical principles, and meta-ethical principles that inquire into the nature of ethical reasoning and argumentation (see Fisher, 2011). This approach may be criticised as being inadequate for the practical concerns of professional ethics education but, as with the question of integration of stand-alone courses (see Section 24.3.1), the dichotomy drawn between philosophical and applied ethics is a false one. As Rossouw (2008) argues, applied ethics courses may engage meaningfully with ethical philosophy – and sometimes challenge it on the basis of insights that flow from attempts to *apply* ethical concepts and theories.

Even though educators may prefer to take a 'practical' and decision-oriented approach to ethics teaching, rather than a theoretical one (see Blanthorne *et al.*, 2007), pure practicality is elusive because practice models are themselves grounded in theory, and theorisation is an everyday part of practical thought (Maclagan & Campbell, 2011). 'Unapplied' ethics buttresses applied ethics! (Klonoski, 2003). Therefore, an adequate accounting ethics education must include both a rounded consideration of ethical theory and a considered application of theory to practice. This could include a theoretically-informed critique of practice models as expressed in codes of ethics.

By combining elements of both philosophical and applied ethics, students are likely to discover that seemingly contemporary ethical challenges have a long historical lineage. They should learn that ethical values and principles have a socio-cultural and historical character, and that particular approaches to ethical problems and problem-solving (including those expressed in professional codes) are mutable. In addition, the combination of philosophical and applied ethics can help in:

bringing to light the tension or contradiction between the particularity of given social regimes of value and the universal reasons offered as legitimations for those regimes. When this contradiction is brought to light, the application of philosophy to a problematic reality takes the form of a fundamental calling into question of the generally unquestioned limitations given social forms impose upon what counts as a solution to a given problem.

(Noonan, 2003, p. 37)

The ethical responsibility of teachers in this context is to develop students' intellectual capacities to grasp ethical philosophy *and* its practical application, while ensuring that ethics does not become '*subservient to the agenda of business*' (Rossouw, 2008, p. 166). By helping students to appreciate both historical and contemporary ways in which people and collectivities may decide what is

541

regarded as ethical, they should come to better understand the role of ethical values, reasoning, debate, discussion, decision-making, and action. Emphasis should be on informed debate and developing students' capacity for judgement (Maclagan & Campbell, 2011; Ponemon, 2011).

Several key ethical philosophies that are relevant to accounting education are outlined in Section 24.3.4. Section 24.4 includes discussion of a number of newer philosophies that underpin contemporary ethical thinking. The discussions in the remainder of Section 24.3 and in Section 24.4 also provide practical examples of the way in which philosophical and applied ethics may be combined.

24.3.3 Descriptive ethics

Descriptive approaches to ethics focus on two broad areas that may be treated independently or together:

1 The function, structure and content of professional codes of ethics, and modes of application and enforcement. This may include posited professional traits or characteristics, and examination of the profession's stated commitment to ethical behaviour and serving the public interest.
2 Identification and analysis of the moral and ethical beliefs that underlie decisions and actions in particular circumstances.

Although the particular circumstances of specific decisions and actions may be popularly or generally judged to have been ethical or unethical, descriptive ethics does not seek to make normative ethical judgements about individuals. It is, instead, an effort to understand *how and why* accountants act or acted in particular ways. Codes of professional ethics may be applied to assist in explaining the ethical behaviour and beliefs that (may) underlie particular actions.

An important aspect of descriptive ethics may be to explain how personal (such as age, gender, ethnicity, religion) and structural (such as culture, institutional arrangements) characteristics influence and shape ethical attitudes and actions (Yuthas & Dillard, 1999; Becker & Messner, 2005; McPhail *et al.*, 2005; Peace, 2006; Gammie & Gammie, 2009; Molisa, 2010).

24.3.4 Normative ethics

In contrast to the non-judgemental ethos of descriptive ethics, normative approaches bring an evaluative orientation based on particular sets of *norms* (i.e. expectations regarding appropriate behaviour). By prescribing what *ought* to be done in certain circumstances, normative approaches also permit judgements about what has been done against normative expectations: a prescriptive approach is applied at the ostensible point of making an ethical decision, while an evaluative approach is applied after a decision or action has been taken. Therefore, the former may include some anticipation of likely consequences of alternative decisions or actions, while the latter judgements can be made in light of known consequences.

Consequences themselves may or may not be regarded as being ethically relevant, depending on the ethical approach adopted. There are a number of ethical 'schools' that consider the appropriate principles to inform judgements about what is ethical (see Singer, 1994; MacIntyre, 2002). Although normative approaches are often divided into two broad categories – consequentialist and non-consequentialist approaches – for the purposes of the present review, three major schools of thought that inform accounting ethics education are considered: deontology, teleology, and virtue ethics.

1   *Deontological* (or deontic) ethics focusses on *duties* or obligations: the locus of analysis is the ethicality of particular acts or decisions in themselves. Duties may be formally expressed in rules. Likely or actual consequences of an act or decision are not an immediate concern – thus, deontological ethics are non-consequentialist. Underlying this approach is the view that ethical agents should only be judged on actions within their control, since the future cannot be controlled and the consequences of an action cannot be known, *ex ante*, with certainty.

2   *Consequences* are the realm of *teleological* (or teleic) ethics, which judges acts or decisions by analysing their (likely) outcomes or consequences. Consequentialist ethical philosophies focus normative judgements on the end-state or end-goal. Often this is expressed in the form of utilitarianism (i.e. that the ultimate consequence of concern is that the greatest good (utility) for the greatest number should be sought).

3   *Aretaic* ethics, also known as *virtue* ethics, focusses on the development of character or individual virtues. Under this approach, normative judgements are made with reference to the character of the moral agent rather than on the nature of the acts of the agent, or on the particular consequences of those acts. The focus is on the nature of the ethical 'being' rather than on the ethical 'doing'.

Although aretaic ethics has a long historical lineage to match the other major schools, present-day accounting ethics education: '*appears to have focussed on the choice dimension, and has not given equal attention to the values . . . and to the character traits . . . that help to drive the choices that accountants make in practice*' (Gaa & Thorne, 2004, p. 2). Virtue ethics has also received some significant recent attention and interest in this approach is likely to grow (e.g. Armstrong *et al.*, 2003; Jennings, 2004; Mintz, 2006; Everett, 2007). Mintz (1995) argues that there is a pressing need for greater attention to virtue in accounting because ultimately only virtues such as honesty, integrity, impartiality, open-mindedness, and trustworthiness enable individual accountants to resist client and commercial pressures to act unethically. Francis (1990, pp. 9–11) also argues that virtues fundamentally underlie accounting practice in many respects (see also Stewart, 1997).

On the other hand, it may be argued that, as applied to accounting-in-practice, virtue ethics is naïve, narrow, and idealistic, since it is implicitly based on a premise that '*if only account-ants (and others) were better people . . . they would make more ethical decisions*' (Boyce, 2008, p. 368). The significance of the ethical context within which people work may be ignored or marginalised.

There is considerable variety within all of the major ethical philosophies, and scope for much discussion and debate about appropriate rules or duties, *or* what constitutes the greatest good for the greatest number, *or* what characteristics should be regarded as being virtuous. A deeper understanding of the nature of codes of ethics may be derived from the critical interrogation of their underlying philosophical bases. For instance, codes of ethics often reflect a deontological approach, since their content is generally expressed in rules. However, the rules and requirements of codes may be based on an assessment of likely consequences (thus, rules may be designed to achieve particular outcomes), reflecting a consequentialist orientation. Further, some elements of codes may focus on the need for particular virtues, such as independence, reflecting an aretaic approach. To the extent that the differing philosophies which underlie ethical codes are recognised, there can also be an examination of their philosophical and practical integrity and consistency. The basis for practical ethical debates and arguments over the provisions of codes can be better understood.

24.3.5 Ethical decision-making

In 1990, the American Accounting Association (AAA) explicitly recognised the growing relevance of ethics to the education of future accountants through the publication of an important case book, *Ethics in the Accounting Curriculum: Cases and Readings* (May, 1990). May's seven-step decision-making model (see Table 24.1) for analysing ethical issues, particularly via the use of case studies, provided a convenient and accessible way for teachers of accounting to introduce and enliven classroom discussions of ethics (see also the similar 'Decision-Making Model for Evaluating Ethical Dilemmas', in Langenderfer & Rockness, 1989, p. 68).

The use of ethical decision-making models has significant currency in classroom settings (see Fulmer & Cargile, 1987; Armstrong *et al.*, 2003; O'Leary, 2009; Dellaportas *et al.*, 2011). This approach encourages students to '*develop a systematic approach to making decisions in any situation involving ethics issues*' (Langenderfer & Rockness, 1989, p. 66). Sometimes professional codes of ethics may be applied to 'solve' ethical problems.

However, this approach brings a number of significant potential shortcomings (Boyce, 2008). There is a danger that it may inculcate a narrow and rigidified understanding of professional responsibilities if it focusses significantly on applying professional codes. A focus on codes may reflect a banking model of education that disembeds students from their own personal context and isolates consciousness from the world (Freire, 1996; Beverungen *et al.*, 2013). Evidence suggests that mere knowledge of codes of ethics and how to apply their provisions do not change the actual or intended actions of students (Fulmer & Cargile, 1987). Therefore, it is wise to ensure that the analysis of practical ethical problems is not restricted to rule-bound application

Table 24.1 Ethical decision-making model

I.	Determine the facts *What? Who? Where? When? How?* *What do we know or need to know that will help define the problem?*
II.	Define the ethical issue *List the significant stakeholders.* *Define the ethical issues.*
III.	Identify the major principles, rules, and values *(For example, integrity, quality, respect for persons, profit)*
IV.	Specify the alternatives *List the major alternative courses of action, including those that represent some form of compromise or point between simply doing or not doing something.*
V.	Compare values and alternatives, see if there exists a clear decision *Determine if there is one principle or value, or combination, which is so compelling that the proper alternative is clear.*
VI.	Assess the consequences *Identify the short- and long-term, positive and negative consequences for the major alternatives. The common short-run focus on gain or loss needs to be measured against the long-run considerations. This step will often reveal an unanticipated result of major importance.*
VII.	Make your decision *Balance the consequences against your primary principles or values and select the alternative that best fits.*

Source: May (1990, pp. 1–2).

of codes of ethics. Broad ethical theories (such as those discussed in Section 24.3.4 above) may also be applied within ethical decision-making models, providing less for quasi-mechanistic application of rules and more for the exercise of broader values-based moral judgement (Felton & Sims, 1990; MacLagan, 2012).

Ethical problems are typically constructed as ethical dilemmas, which may reflect a situation where '*the rules are unclear, or there are conflicting principles, or conflicting interests of involved parties*' (Pettifor & Paquet, 2002, p. 262). However, if ethics cases are pre-coded and pre-interpreted as straightforward dilemmas in which 'decisions' must be made (see Stewart, 1997), deeper and more contextual analysis may be precluded.[7] Deeper analysis may discover ethical problems and issues where none were immediately apparent, revealing the complexity and socially-structured nature of ethical decision-making.

Care must be taken to ensure that ethical scenarios are not constructed to steer students towards an 'expected' answer. It may also be helpful to prompt students to question their own pre-existing assumptions about the context of ethical decision-making. Many business case scenarios may come to be seen as not necessarily involving *ethical* dilemmas at all, because one side of the problem may be economically rather than ethically unfavourable. Although this does not make the *business* decision any less complex, it is not immediately obvious that profit should be regarded as being morally equivalent to human rights or environmental protection, for example (see MacLagan, 2012, for a comparative perspective). In *ethical* decision-making, it may become 'necessary to deny the relevance of economic calculations when essentially ethical principles are at stake' (Harte *et al.*, 1991, p. 250).

If ethical decision-making is constructed as a kind of modular problem-solving, it is unlikely to encourage creative thinking or the development of a more expansive moral sensibility (McPhail, 1999, 2001b; Armstrong *et al.*, 2003). '*Representation of moral problems as multiple-choice or "decision problem" abstracts away from temporal unfolding and from expression and development of moral character*' (Whitbeck, 1992, p. 123). In addition, it is problematic when each decision and/or case is treated as being an individual and discrete unit of analysis disconnected from broader organisational and social-political contexts (Fogarty, 1995; Stewart, 1997; Yuthas & Dillard, 1999).

Classroom application of models and codes is necessarily abstracted from the complex and often contradictory realities of real-world decision-making. By prioritising set models or codes, this approach may not draw on or develop students' own individual (or collective) ethical value systems and capacities for action that flow from them. Further, the social context of ethical decision-making may be effaced, denying the collective dimension of ethics. Ethical decision-making should involve critical thinking as well as individual, collective, and professional reflection. (See Cunningham, Chapter 18 – this volume.)

24.3.6 Moral exemplars, and a case of whistle-blowing

The use of moral exemplars as a teaching tool may provide another means to interrogate actual ethical decisions (applied ethics), and to question the underlying ethical basis of such decisions (philosophical ethics). A number of authors have recommended this approach (Apostolou & Apostolou, 1997; Knapp *et al.*, 1998; Armstrong *et al.*, 2003). In general terms, moral exemplars may be a practical outworking of a virtue ethics approach, since moral exemplars are, *prima facie*, regarded as virtuous characters. However, the analysis of exemplary decisions or actions may also be undertaken using any of the normative (or descriptive) approaches. At the same time, caution is warranted when highlighting exemplar cases because '*the genius of morality, the saint, the moral hero, cannot serve as a yardstick for human goodness*' (Heller, cited in Wray-Bliss, 2013, p. 88).

Looking at contemporary ethical scandals (as discussed in the Introduction to this chapter) from a different perspective, the Enron and WorldCom cases produced two of *Time Magazine's* 2002 'Persons of the Year': Sherron Watkins, Enron's Vice-President of Corporate Development, and Cynthia Cooper, WorldCom's Vice-President of Internal Audit (Lacayo & Ripley, 2002). The actions of Watkins and Cooper, in blowing the whistle on unethical corporate accounting practices at Enron and WorldCom respectively, were regarded as being highly ethical. Cynthia Cooper was named as the AAA's Public Interest Section Exemplar Award winner for 2003, cited for '*notable contributions to professionalism and ethics in accounting education and/or practice*' (AAA's Public Interest Section, 2004).

It is worth asking what made Cynthia Cooper an exemplar of accounting ethics and professionalism. The ethically-valorised activity of whistle-blowing[8] brought Cooper, and Sherrin Watkins at Enron, to public attention, because they were seen to be prepared to take an ethical stand (Curtis & Taylor, 2009). But various explanations of their exemplary status are possible. Watkins and Cooper were described by *Time Magazine* as being:

> *of ordinary demeanor but exceptional guts and sense . . . heroes at the scene, anointed by circumstance. They were people who did right just by doing their jobs rightly—which means ferociously, with eyes open and with the bravery the rest of us always hope we have and may never know if we do.*
>
> (Lacayo & Ripley, 2002)

This extract, and the Cynthia Cooper story, illustrate how whistle-blowing may be interpreted as being an ethical act from a number of perspectives. For example, applying deontic ethics, whistle-blowing constitutes a form of truth-telling. From a consequentialist perspective, whistle-blowing may result in a better-informed market, or may result in wrongdoers being brought to account – consequences which could be regarded as being ethically worthwhile. From a virtue ethics perspective, whistle-blowing exhibits courage and forthrightness, often in the face of considerable pressure. On Cooper's own account (2008), it seems that her actions probably involved a combination of a number of these elements.

In an educational use of a case such as this, the rightness or goodness of a morally exemplary act like whistle-blowing may be held up against deontic, teleic, or aretaic norms as a basis for understanding and judging what was done. Competing ethical judgements which are informed by different perspectives will not always come up with identical conclusions, but classroom debate about the differences is likely to prove very fruitful.

24.3.7 Teaching tools

It is not the purpose of this chapter to detail the range of teaching tools that can be used to aid ethics instruction. Many are canvassed in the literature (Geary & Sims, 1994; Thomas, 2004; Leung *et al.*, 2006; Van Peursem & Julian, 2006; Cooper *et al.*, 2008; Dellaportas *et al.*, 2011). There is a strong argument for the use of ethics cases, which many educators believe are the most appropriate (Blanthorne *et al.*, 2007) and effective (Wilhelm, 2008) ethics teaching tool (Langenderfer and Rockness, 1989; May, 1990). Cases can be applied in varied ways to support different educational objectives (Boyce *et al.*, 2001).

Broadly, active rather than traditional didactic approaches are likely to be more effective (Pettifor & Paquet, 2002; Rockness & Rockness, 2010). The use of reflective learning techniques, including class discussion, quick papers, and reflective journals, can all help to develop new understandings of previously known or unknown situations (Mintz, 2006; McGuigan & Kern, 2009). Role-playing (Loeb, 1988) and game-playing (Haywood & Wygal, 2009) can enliven topics and foster reflective thinking. Drawing on literature (Lister, 2010), including seminal works (Jennings, 2004), works from other disciplines (Fetters *et al.*, 1989), and fiction (Young & Annisette, 2009) can all help to cultivate ethical imagination.

A mixture of teaching approaches is likely to nurture development across the four stages of the 'Ethics Education Continuum' recommended by the International Accounting Education Standards Board (IAESB) under the auspices of the International Federation of Accountants (IFAC): ethical knowledge, ethical sensitivity, ethical judgement, and ethical behaviour (see also Dellaportas *et al.*, 2011; Kidwell *et al.*, 2013; IAESB n.d., ¶ 14).[9]

24.4 Contemporary developments and perspectives

While the intended or expected role of accounting in organizations and society can be rationalized based on economic requirements, the actual use and form, as well as the information contained, are dependent on social values.

(Velayutham & Perera, 1996, p. 76).

24.4.1 Environmental, societal, cultural, and other dimensions

Broader ethics education can support a number of important emerging areas within the accounting curriculum (see Sangster, Chapter 15 – this volume). A number of writers have expressed particular concern at accounting educators' failure to adequately address the social and political context of accounting (e.g. Cooper *et al.*, 2005; Humphrey, 2005). To address this lacuna, analysis of ethical concerns must move beyond the accounting profession's self-expectations as expressed in codes of ethics, to explore social expectations of the profession. This must also extend beyond managerial perspectives on ethics and eschew the common assumption that internal organisational ethics is largely a matter of managerial prerogative (see Wray-Bliss, 2013).

In one of the few available textbooks on ethics in accounting – McPhail & Walters (2009) – both the traditional realm of the ethics of *accountants* and the ethics of *accounting* as a discipline are examined, effectively holding the discipline *itself* up to examination as a social and ethical practice. From this perspective, ethics education examines the ethical effects of accounting, including a range of environmental and social concerns. This draws on an understanding that: '*"Accounts", of whatever form . . . profoundly affect employees, communities, societies, planetary possibilities, the State and civil society itself*'(Gray, 2007, p. 170). By shifting the locus of concern from the ethics of individuals within the profession to the profession and the discipline itself, accounting can be seen to be an ethical discourse which privileges certain values over others (Puxty *et al.*, 1994; Williams, 2002, 2010).

An important goal of ethics education should be for students to be able to understand: '*the role the profession (collectively) plays in society, and their personal responsibility to take an active part in forming and revising professional policies*' (Armstrong, 1993, p. 81). McPhail & Walters (2009) aim to shift the discussion from relatively narrow and inward-looking codes of ethics to the larger social trends that are likely to be constitutive of future accounting problems and issues. This approach seeks to assist in developing an understanding of the way in which accounting itself structures and influences individual and societal responses to these issues.

Coming at this problem in a different way, Boyce (2008, p. 256) argued that:

[G]reater attention must be paid to the wider economic and social systems within which individual (un)ethical actions occur, and that systemic features of globalisation, in conjunction with events at local, regional and national levels, must be central to the analysis.

Similarly, Ravenscroft & Williams (2004, p. 19) argued:

> [E]thics in accounting is rather hopelessly mired in discussions of individuals facing dilemmas . . . we should look not only at individual behaviour and thinking but also more broadly at the structures that have been created and the power that has been granted to various groups. It is the morality of our institutions that should be of the greatest concern to us now.

These considerations make it particularly important to move beyond individual approaches to ethical issues and dilemmas to a critical examination of how ethics inheres in social structures, systems, and power (Boyce, 2008). This does not mean that the importance of the individual should be overlooked, but that ethics should not be reduced to individual decision-making. This perspective may also transcend the traditional privileging of the notion of ethical 'leadership' (see Wray-Bliss, 2013), engendering respect for difference in ethical standpoints. This could also include a consideration of how accounting *institutions* support – or could better support – ethical *practice* in accounting.

A range of other perspectives and considerations may also be embraced in order to support broader ethical considerations within accounting education. These include:

- existentialism, critical theory, and post-modernism (James, 2008; James & Walsh, 2011);
- the power and the practice of ethics as subordination and obedience to authority (McPhail, 2001b);
- feminist perspectives and ethics of care (Day, 1995; Reiter, 1997; McPhail, 2005);
- an ethic of accountability around social sustainability (Dillard, 2008);
- non-Western, non-white perspectives on ethics (Waldmann, 2000; Dunn, 2006; Boyce *et al.*, 2009);
- the nature of, and need for, ethical commitment to the Other (McPhail, 1999, 2001b; Shearer, 2002; Kosmala & McKernan, 2011).

24.4.2 Looking ahead: overcoming inertia

As noted in Section 24.2, the history of efforts to include ethics within the accounting curriculum, as with efforts at accounting education reform generally, is rather dismal. In 2012, yet another opportunity emerged from the U.S.A. offering the promise of meaningful change in accounting education. The Pathways Commission on Accounting Higher Education (Behn *et al.*, 2012, p. 9) represents the most recent attempt to consider 'the future structure of higher education for the accounting profession'. Outlining its approach and mission, the Commission stated that '[t]he educational preparation of accountants should rest on a comprehensive and well-articulated vision of the role of accounting in the wider society' (Behn *et al.*, 2012, p. 10). Perhaps surprisingly, the Commission did not mention ethics as part of its 'Value Proposition for a Broadly Defined Accounting Profession' (Ch. 2). In general, the Commission placed economic concerns in a social context but did so in a way that reflects a fairly traditional view of accounting. Ethics was included in the 'Foundational Body of Knowledge' (Ch. 7) as an element of 'Professional Integrity, Responsibility, and Commitment', but the accompanying narrative reflected orthodox rhetoric about professional characteristics and competencies. There was, however, a welcome advocacy that:

> [F]uture accountants must learn more than technical knowledge. To be successful, accountants should develop professional skills and the ability to act ethically in difficult situations. It is the integration of

knowledge, skills, and ethical action that form competency and fulfill the accounting profession's responsibility to society.

(Behn *et al.*, 2012, p. 134)

It is somewhat surprising that so little substantive emphasis was placed on ethics, other than in largely rhetorical flourishes about the importance of integrity to the profession and the social and economic purposes of accounting (such as the one above). There was not a clear sense or expression of the ethical values or philosophy underlying accounting; ethical practice in accounting was not portrayed as being related to fundamental values. The envisaged social function of accounting was tightly circumscribed:

The definition of any profession begins with a commitment to provide a benefit to the public . . . this commitment requires members of the profession to consistently provide accurate and reliable information to members of the public, which enables them to make sound investment decisions, and to managers to facilitate the efficient and productive use of resources.

(ibid., p. 21)

To some degree, the Commission's emphasis on the provision of reliable financial information is understandable in the post-Enron, post-WorldCom environment. However, the marginal-isation of ethics, other than in its capacity to undergird technical skills, reflected a largely instrumental approach to the maintenance of accounting's information-providing function in investment and capital market contexts. Thus, the Pathways Commission largely reflected traditional accounting practice and ideology, and presented little that is likely to challenge or change accounting education to infuse ethics.

Notwithstanding the above analysis, the inclusion of references to the social role of accounting and the recognition of the importance of ethics to the 'next generation of accountants' could be taken as an(other) opening for those who wish to take up the challenge of making accounting education more ethical. This endeavour could draw some support from the relevant pronouncements issued by the IAESB, in particular International Education Standard (IES) 4 *Professional Values, Ethics and Attitudes* (IAESB, 2005).[10] This Standard provides that:

The program of professional accounting education should provide potential professional accountants with a framework of professional values, ethics and attitudes for exercising professional judgment and for acting in an ethical manner that is in the best interest of society and the profession.

(ibid., ¶ 13)[11]

The coverage of values and attitudes in education programs for professional accountants should lead to a commitment to:

(a) the public interest and sensitivity to social responsibilities.

(ibid., ¶ 15)

Although the work of the IAESB and IFAC is potentially important in the endeavour to enhance ethics education in accounting, there is little evidence that these pronouncements have had much impact to date. The 'mandatory' nature of the Standards (Dellaportas *et al.*, 2006) applies in theory but, in practice, they may operate more at the level of guidance. Loeb (2007, pp. 6–7) describes these international education pronouncements as being '*crucial . . . provid[ing] strong positive support for accounting ethics education*', but goes on to note, more modestly, that they '*may be factors in increasing the demand for ethics education in accounting programs*' over time (2007,

p. 8). McPeak, Pincus, & Sundem (2012, p. 750) emphasise that IESs '*are influencing accounting education and training worldwide*'. They (and the IAESB) acknowledge, however, that the aim of '*convergence in educational outcomes and the competence of accounting professionals worldwide*' (ibid., p. 747) is tempered by differences in educational systems, professional programmes, and social systems including culture, language, and laws. Thus, a pragmatic consideration is that IESs must reflect '*common ground*' (McPeak *et al.*, 2012), which could produce a level of generality that could increase an awareness of ethics education while limiting practical impacts in terms of changing day-to-day educational practice. The outcomes and impacts – at least in Western developed countries – are yet to be seen, and the IAESB is '*little known among accounting educators unengaged in international discourse*' (Kidwell *et al.*, 2013, p. 7).[12]

There is little doubt that considerable and sustained effort will be required to overcome the ethical neglect which, on the whole, characterises outcomes to date. As a start, this will require recognition that questions of ethics are of fundamental significance and growing importance to accounting, and that significant change in educational programmes is required to grapple with the range of concerns in this realm. Ethics must come to be regarded as being central to the study of accounting and business.

24.5 Implications and conclusion

> *Neither the 'training' nor the 'education' of accounting students is satisfactory. This failure . . . has been consistently and persuasively linked with the behaviour of accountants in practice . . .*
>
> *Educational experience seems to be an important factor in both intellectual development and ethical maturity . . . and accounting education . . . provides the intellectual framework within which practice – and the dialogues of practice – operate . . . If there are ethical failures in accounting practice it is therefore probable that at least some of the responsibility must be laid at the door of the educators*
>
> (Gray *et al.*, 1994, p. 52)

It has been argued that corporations should be regarded as amoral entities because the legal and business environment in which they operate practically constrains their practical ability to practice ethics and corporate social responsibility (Hazelton & Cussen, 2005). This argument could be applied, by extension, to accounting but, in either case, the argument is unlikely to be widely accepted. There is an alternative (or perhaps complementary) view that corporations are pathological entities requiring fundamental reform in order to tackle the ethical and related problems that flow from the singular pursuit of profit, wealth, and power (Bakan, 2004). Underlying this perspective is a belief that ethical problems are likely to persist unless and until systemic social and economic factors are addressed. This underscores the urgency of the case for taking a broader perspective on accounting ethics education.

Accounting ethics education matters because it can make a difference. It works best when it takes a broad view of accounting, and of ethics within the discipline, incorporating an appreciation of both philosophical ethics and application to common – and unexpected – real-world problems. It may lead to problematisation of both ethics, and of accounting itself, in the light of its effects on the lives of people who are subject to it:

> *Accounting is saturated with moral implications. As a practice, it influences the quality of life for millions of people in subtle and often complex ways. Its vocabulary is one of values, of e-valuation, of welfare, of rights, of expectations, of obligations, of equity, of contracts, of punishments and rewards, of utility, satisfaction, responsibility and accountability. The moral force of accounting needs to be questioned in the light of the values that it promotes and the values that it impedes.*
>
> (Arrington & Francis, 1993, p. 105)

Ethics are fundamental to the practice and social functioning of accounting, and the challenges of integrating ethics into accounting education are likely to be a key continuing concern for accounting educators. Understanding the nature of ethics and its multi-faceted relationship with accounting is vital to activating the possibilities for making a difference through ethics education.

As accounting educators we *can* make a difference in our students' lives by critically and thoughtfully exposing them to multiple facets of ethical philosophy and its application. Such exposure can enhance students' abilities to think more critically when confronted by ethical issues, and to become '*thinking participants in the profession they will soon be entering*' (Armstrong, 1993, p. 90). If we are prepared to regard ethics as being a domain within which '*we wage our struggle to find the new and adequate ways of thinking of, about, and for the world we live in, and our lives within it*' (Bauman, 2009, p. 1, emphasis in original), we will truly be making a difference for accounting students, for society, for the future of the discipline, and for ourselves.

Notes

1 Ironically, Arthur Andersen had been regarded as a leader in developing ethics professional programmes for accountants. Its noted activities included developing '*educational materials relating to accounting ethics in addition to holding conferences that included discussions relating to business and accounting ethics education*' (Geary & Sims, 1994, p. 4).

2 Many researchers have adopted the work of Kohlberg (1981) and Rest (1986) which suggests students may go through several stages of cognitive moral development to reach ethical maturity, which progress from the 'preconventional' level where the focus is on the self (broadly, ethically egoist), through the 'conventional' level where the focus is on the group (broadly, sustaining social relationships), to the 'postconventional' level where the focus is on the inner self (broadly, autonomous and principle-based) (see Geary & Sims, 1994; Leung *et al.*, 2006, Ch. 2). Although this approach to understanding moral development and the process of ethical maturing has been widely used in ethics education research, it is problematic to the extent that it '*is devoid of a sense of collective fates and collective responsibilities*' within accounting (Fogarty, 1995, p. 106). Further, there are other conceptions of the '*ways through which human beings become moral agents*' (Furman, 1990, p. 33), suggesting that recognition of greater complexity may be appropriate. See Section 24.4.1 for some indications in this direction.

3 Similarly, some argue that accounting departments do not have sufficient resources to teach ethics (e.g. see Blanthorne *et al.,* 2007), but the resourcing argument is not specific to this area of the curriculum.

4 AACSB is a key business school accrediting body in the U.S.A., and, more recently, internationally. (See Calderon, Chapter 22, and Apostolou & Gammie, Chapter 29 – both in this volume, for a discussion of the role of accreditation in accounting education.)

5 There is some evidence that students prefer a stand-alone subject, where ethics is taught '*all in one place*' (Graham, 2012: 599, 609), but the practical effect of this students' preference may run counter to the aim for integrated and contextualised understanding.

6 Over time, specialist subjects will build specialist and dedicated in-house academic staff expertise (Hartman & Hartman, 2004).

7 Although common usage sometimes treats a dilemma as being simply a difficult situation, strictly speaking, there are *two* equally unfavourable choices in a *dilemma* (Macquarie Dictionary, 1991). Thus, in an *ethical* dilemma, there is no 'right' solution, as each available alternative is regarded as being likely to produce an ethically unfavourable outcome. As Whitbeck (1992, p. 127) points out, '*The only good responses to dilemmas are those that enable one to escape the dilemma, if this is possible.*'

8 Note that such valorisation was not evidenced in the business-focussed attitude which Cooper faced within WorldCom (Cooper, 2008).

9 These four stages can be related to the four components or aspects of ethical capacity as outlined by Rest (1986): moral sensitivity, moral reasoning, moral motivation, and moral character.

10 A revision of this Standard is expected to be completed by the end of 2013 (see IAESB, 2011). A supportive *Practice Statement* is also available (IAESB, n.d.).

11 This construction problematically assumes that the '*best interest*' of society and the profession are coincident (see Van Peursem & Julian, 2006: 14). In the draft revised standard still under consideration at the

time of writing (IAESB, 2011), this wording is proposed to be amended to: '*IFAC member bodies shall provide, through learning and development activities, a framework of professional values, ethics, and attitudes for aspiring professional accountants to exercise professional judgment in the public interest*' (IAESB, n.d., ¶ 7). Otherwise, the possibility of a disjunction between the interests of the profession, or of the requirements of professional codes, and the public interest, is not effectively dealt with.

12 In some senses, the key target of the convergence goal may be to influence and assist 'developing countries' as they introduce their own systems of professional education and recognition (see IAESB, 2009, p. 7; McPeak *et al.*, 2012, p. 747).

References

Abdolmohammadi, M. (2008) Who should teach ethics courses in business and accounting programs? *Research on Professional Responsibility and Ethics in Accounting*, 13, 113–134.

Accounting Education Change Commission (1990) Objectives of education for accountants: position statement number one, *Issues in Accounting Education*, 5(2), 307–312.

Adler, R. (1999) Five ideas designed to rile everyone who cares about accounting education, *Accounting Education: an international journal*, 8(3), 241–247.

Albrecht, W.S. & Sack, R.J. (2000) *Accounting Education: Charting the Course through a Perilous Future* (Accounting Education Series Vol. 16), Sarasota, FL: American Accounting Association.

American Accounting Association Public Interest Section (2004) Cynthia Cooper, 2003, Accounting Exemplar Award Recipient, *In the Public Interest*, 32(1). Available at: http://aaahq.org/Public Interest/docs/newsletters/spring04/spring04.htm.

Apostolou, B. & Apostolou, N. (1997) Heroes as a context for teaching ethics, *Journal of Education for Business*, 73(2), 121–125.

Armstrong, M.B. (1987) Moral development and accounting education, *Journal of Accounting Education*, 5(1), 27–43.

Armstrong, M.B. (1993) Ethics and professionalism in accounting education: a sample course, *Journal of Accounting Education*, 11(2), 77–92.

Armstrong, M.B., Ketz, J.E., & Owen, D. (2003) Ethics education in accounting: moving toward ethical motivation and ethical behavior, *Journal of Accounting Education*, 21(1), 1–16.

Arrington, C.E. & Francis, J.R. (1993) Accounting as a human practice: the appeal of other voices, *Accounting, Organizations and Society*, 18(2/3), 105–106.

Bakan, J. (2004) *The Corporation: The Pathological Pursuit of Profit and Power.* New York: Free Press.

Bauman, Z. (2009) *Does Ethics Have a Chance in a World of Consumers?* Cambridge, MA: Harvard University Press.

Bean, D.F. & Bernardi, R.A. (2007) A proposed structure for an accounting ethics course, *Journal of Business Ethics Education*, 4, 27–54.

Becker, A. & Messner, M. (2005) After the scandals: a German-speaking perspective on management accounting research and education, *European Accounting Review*, 14(2), 417–427.

Bedford, N., Bartholomew, E.E., Bowsher, C.A., Brown, A.L., Davidson, S., Horngren, C.T., Knortz, H.C., Piser, M.M., Shenkir, W.G., Simmons, J.K., Summers, E.L., & Wheeler, J.T. (1986) Future accounting education: Preparing for the expanding profession (The special report of the American Accounting Association Committee on the Future Structure, Content, and Scope of Accounting Education), *Issues in Accounting Education*, 1(1), 168–195.

Bedford, N.M. & Shenkir, W.G. (1987) Reorienting accounting education, *Journal of Accountancy*, 164(2), 84–91.

Behn, B.K., Ezzell, W.F., Murphy, L.A., Stith, M., Rayburn, J., & Strawser, J.R. (2012) *The Pathways Commission: Charting a National Strategy for the Next Generation of Accountants*, American Accounting Association and American Institute of CPAs.

Beverungen, A., Dunne, S., & Hoedemaekers, C. (2013) The financialisation of business ethics, *Business Ethics: A European Review*, 22(1), 102–117.

Black, W.H. (2012) The activities of the Pathways Commission and the historical context for changes in accounting education, *Issues in Accounting Education*, 27(3), 601–625.

Blanthorne, C., Kovar, S.E., & Fisher, D.G. (2007) Accounting educators' opinions about ethics in the curriculum: an extensive view, *Issues in Accounting Education*, 22(3), 355–390.

Boisjol, R.M. (1993) Personal integrity and accountability, *Accounting Horizons*, 7(1), 59–69.

Boyce, G. (2002) Now and then: revolutions in higher learning, *Critical Perspectives on Accounting*, 13(5/6), 575–601.

Boyce, G. (2008) The social relevance of ethics education in a global(ising) era: from individual dilemmas to system crises, *Critical Perspectives on Accounting*, 19(2), 255–290.

Boyce, G. & Greer, S. (2013) More than imagination: making social and critical accounting real, *Critical Perspectives on Accounting*, 24(2), 105–112.

Boyce, G., Greer, S., Blair, B., & Davids, C. (2012) Expanding the horizons of accounting education: incorporating social and critical perspectives, *Accounting Education: an international journal*, 21(1), 47–74.

Boyce, G., Prayukvong, W., & Puntasen, A. (2009) Social accounting for sufficiency: Buddhist principles and practices, and their application in Thailand, *Advances in Public Interest Accounting*, 14, 55–119.

Boyce, G., Williams, S., Kelly, A., & Yee, H. (2001) Fostering deep and elaborative learning and generic (soft) skill development: the strategic use of case studies in accounting education, *Accounting Education: an international journal*, 10(1), 37–60.

Canarutto, G., Smith, K.T., & Smith, L.M. (2010) Impact of an ethics presentation used in the USA and adapted for Italy, *Accounting Education: an international journal*, 19(3), 309–322.

Clarke, F.L., Dean, G.W., & Oliver, K.G. (2003) *Corporate Collapse: Regulatory, Accounting and Ethical Failure*, Cambridge: Cambridge University Press.

Cohen, J.R. & Pant, L.W. (1989) Accounting educators' perceptions of ethics in the curriculum, *Issues in Accounting Education*, 4(1), 70–81.

Cooper, B.J., Leung, P., Dellaportas, S., Jackling, B., & Wong, G. (2008) Ethics education for accounting students: a toolkit approach, *Accounting Education: an international journal*, 17(4), 405–430.

Cooper, C. (2008) *Extraordinary Circumstances: The Journey of a Corporate Whistleblower*, Hoboken, NJ: John Wiley & Sons.

Cooper, D., Everett, J., & Neu, D. (2005) Financial scandals, accounting change and the role of accounting academics: a perspective from North America, *European Accounting Review*, 14(2), 373–382.

Curtis, M.B. & Taylor, E.Z. (2009) Whistleblowing in public accounting: influence of identity disclosure, situational context, and personal characteristics, *Accounting and the Public Interest*, 9(1), 191–220.

Day, M.M. (1995) Ethics of teaching critical: feminism on the wings of desire, *Accounting, Auditing and Accountability Journal*, 8(3), 97–112.

Dellaportas, S., Jackling, B., Leung, P., & Cooper, B.J. (2011) Developing an ethics education framework for accounting, *Journal of Business Ethics Education*, 8, 63–82.

Dellaportas, S., Leung, P., Cooper, B.J., & Jackling, B. (2006) IES 4: Ethics education revisited, *Australian Accounting Review*, 16(38), 4–12.

Dillard, J. (2008) An ethic of accountability, *Research on Professional Responsibility and Ethics in Accounting*, 13, 1–18.

Dimnik, T. & Felton, S. (2006) Accountant stereotypes in movies distributed in North America in the twentieth century, *Accounting, Organizations and Society*, 31(2), 129–155.

Donaldson, T.J. & Freeman, R.E. (eds) (1994) *Business as a Humanity*, Ruffin Series in Business Ethics, New York: Oxford University Press.

Dunn, P. (2006) The role of culture and accounting education in resolving ethical business dilemmas by Chinese and Canadians, *Accounting and the Public Interest*, 6, 116–134.

Everett, J.S. (2007) Ethics education and the role of the symbolic market, *Journal of Business Ethics*, 76(3), 253–267.

Eynon, G., Hills, N.T., & Stevens, K.T. (1997) Factors that influence the moral reasoning abilities of accountants: implications for universities and the profession, *Journal of Business Ethics*, 16(12–13), 1297–1309.

Felton, E.L. & Sims, R.R. (1990) Teaching business ethics: targeted outputs, *Journal of Business Ethics*, 60(4), 377–391.

Fetters, M.L., Hoopes, J., & Tropp, M. (1989) Integrating concepts from accounting, American history and English literature: a cluster course approach, *Journal of Accounting Education*, 7(1), 69–82.

Fisher, A. (2011) *Metaethics: An Introduction*, Durham: Acumen.

Fleming, A.I.M. (1996) Ethics and accounting education in the UK: a professional approach? *Accounting Education: an international journal*, 5(3), 207–217.

Fogarty, T.J. (1995) Accountant ethics: a brief examination of neglected sociological dimensions, *Journal of Business Ethics*, 14(2), 103–115.

Fogarty, T.J. (2010) Revitalizing accounting education: a highly applied liberal arts approach, *Accounting Education: an international journal*, 19(4), 403–419.

Francis, J.R. (1990) After virtue? Accounting as a moral and discursive practice, *Accounting, Auditing and Accountability Journal*, 3(3), 5–17.

Freire, P. (1996) *Pedagogy of the Oppressed*, London, Penguin.

Friedman, A.L. & Lyne, S.R. (2001) The beancounter stereotype: towards a general model of stereotype generation, *Critical Perspectives on Accounting*, 12(4), 423–451.

Fulmer, W.E. & Cargile, B.R. (1987) Ethical perceptions of accounting students: does exposure to a Code of Professional Ethics help? *Issues in Accounting Education*, 2(2), 207–219.

Furman, F.K. (1990) Teaching business ethics: questioning the assumptions, seeking new directions, *Journal of Business Ethics*, 9(1), 31–38.

Gaa, J.C. & Thorne, L. (2004) An introduction to the special issue on professionalism and ethics in accounting education, *Issues in Accounting Education*, 19(1), 1–6.

Gammie, E. & Gammie, B. (2009) The moral awareness of future accounting and business professionals: the implications of a gender divide, *Pacific Accounting Review*, 21(1), 48–73.

Gautschi, F.H. & Jones, T.M. (1998) Enhancing the ability of business students to recognize ethical issues: an empirical assessment of the effectiveness of a course in business ethics, *Journal of Business Ethics*, 17(2), 205–216.

Geary, W.T. & Sims, R.R. (1994) Can ethics be learned? *Accounting Education: an international journal*, 3(1), 3–18.

Gentile, M.C. & Samuelson, J. (2003) *The State of Affairs for Management Education and Social Responsibility*, New York: Aspen Institute.

Ghoshal, S. (2005) Bad management theories are destroying good management practices, *Academy of Management Learning and Education*, 4(1), 75–91.

Graham, A. (2012) The teaching of ethics in undergraduate accounting programmes: the students' perspective, *Accounting Education: an international journal*, 21(6), 599–613.

Gray, R. (2007) Taking a long view on what we now know about social and environmental accountability and reporting, *Issues in Social and Environmental Accounting*, 1(2), 169–198.

Gray, R., Bebbington, J., & McPhail, K. (1994) Teaching ethics in accounting and the ethics of accounting teaching: educating for immorality and a possible case for social and environmental accounting education, *Accounting Education: an international journal*, 3(1), 51–75.

Hancock, P., Howieson, B., Kavanagh, M., Kent, J., Tempone, I., & Segal, N. (2009) *Accounting for the Future: More Than Numbers. Volume 1, Final Report*, Canberra, Australian Learning and Teaching Council.

Harte, G., Lewis, L., & Owen, D. (1991) Ethical investment and the corporate reporting function, *Critical Perspectives on Accounting*, 2(3), 227–253.

Hartman, L.P. & Hartman, E.M. (2004) How to teach ethics: assumptions and arguments, *Journal of Business Ethics Education*, 1(2), 165–212.

Haywood, M.E. & Wygal, D.E. (2009) Ethics and professionalism: bringing the topic to life in the classroom, *Journal of Accounting Education*, 27(2), 71–84.

Hazelton, J. & Cussen, K. (2005) The amorality of public corporations, *Essays in Philosophy* 6(2).

Hooker, J. (2004) The case against business ethics education: a study in bad arguments, *Journal of Business Ethics Education*, 1(1), 73–86.

Humphrey, C. (2005) 'In the aftermath of crisis: reflections on the principles, values and significance of academic inquiry in accounting': Introduction, *European Accounting Review*, 14(2), 341–351.

IAESB (2005) *International Education Standard IES 4: Professional Values, Ethics and Attitudes*, New York: International Federation of Accountants.

IAESB (2009) *Handbook of International Education Pronouncements*, New York: International Federation of Accountants.

IAESB (2011) *Proposed Revised International Education Standard IES 4: Professional Values, Ethics and Attitudes*, New York: International Federation of Accountants.

IAESB (n.d.) *International Education Practice Statement IEPS 1: Approaches to Developing and Maintaining Professional Values, Ethics and Attitudes*, New York: International Federation of Accountants.

James, K. (2008) A Critical Theory and postmodernist approach to the teaching of accounting theory, *Critical Perspectives on Accounting*, 19(5), 643–676.

James, K. & Walsh, R. (2011) 'What would Sartre say?' Using existentialism to inform teaching thought and practice in accounting and management, *Educational Research*, 2(8), 1317–1329.

Jennings, M.M. (2004) Incorporating ethics and professionalism into accounting education and research: a discussion of the voids and advocacy for training in seminal works in business ethics, *Issues in Accounting Education*, 19(1), 7–26.

Jones, M.J. (ed.) (2011) *Creative Accounting, Fraud and International Accounting Standards*, Chichester: John Wiley & Sons.

Kidwell, L.A., Fisher, D.G., Braun, R.L., & Swanson, D.L. (2013) Developing learning objectives for accounting ethics using Bloom's taxonomy, *Accounting Education: an international journal*, 22(1), 44–65.

Klonoski, R.J. (2003) Unapplied ethics: on the need for classical philosophy in professional ethics education, *Teaching Business Ethics*, 7(1), 21–35.

Knapp, M.C., Louwers, T.J., & Weber, C.K. (1998) Celebrating accounting heroes: an alternative approach to teaching ethics, *Advances in Accounting Education*, 1, 267–277.

Kohlberg, L. (1981) *The Philosophy of Moral Development: Moral Stages and the Idea of Justice*, San Francisco: Harper & Row.

Kosmala, K. & McKernan, J.F. (2011) From care of the self to care for the other: neglected aspects of Foucault's late work, *Accounting, Auditing and Accountability Journal*, 24(3), 377–402.

Lacayo, R. & Ripley, A. (2002) Persons of the Year 2002: the whistleblowers, *Time*, 30 December.

Langenderfer, H.Q. & Rockness, J.W. (1989) Integrating ethics into the accounting curriculum: issues, problems, and solutions, *Issues in Accounting Education*, 4(1), 58–69.

Leung, P. & Cooper, B.J. (1994) Ethics in accountancy: a classroom experience, *Accounting Education: an international journal*, 3(1), 19–33.

Leung, P., Cooper, B.J., Dellaportas, S., Jackling, B., & Leslie, H. (2006) *Approaches to the Development and Maintenance of Professional Values, Ethics and Attitudes in Accounting Education Programs*, Information Paper, New York: International Federation of Accountants.

Lister, R.J. (2010) A role for the compulsory study of literature in accounting education, *Accounting Education: an international journal*, 19(4), 329–343.

Loeb, S.E. (1988) Teaching students accounting ethics: some crucial issues, *Issues in Accounting Education*, 3(2), 316–329.

Loeb, S.E. (1991) The evaluation of 'outcomes' of accounting ethics education, *Journal of Business Ethics*, 10(2), 77–84.

Loeb, S.E. (2007) Issues relating to teaching accounting ethics: an 18-year retrospective, *Research on Professional Responsibility and Ethics in Accounting*, 11, 1–30.

Low, M., Davey, H., & Hooper, K. (2008) Accounting scandals, ethical dilemmas and educational challenges, *Critical Perspectives on Accounting*, 19(2), 222–254.

MacIntyre, A. (2002) *A Short History of Ethics: A History of Moral Philosophy from the Homeric Age to the Twentieth Century*, London, Routledge & Kegan Paul.

MacLagan, P. (2012) Conflicting obligations, moral dilemmas and the development of judgement through business ethics education, *Business Ethics: A European Review*, 21(2), 183–197.

MacLagan, P. & Campbell, T. (2011) Focussing on individuals' ethical judgement in corporate social responsibility curricula, *Business Ethics: A European Review*, 20(4), 392–404.

Macquarie Dictionary (1991) Sydney: The Macquarie Library.

Mathews, M.R. (1994) An examination of the work of the Accounting Education Change Commission 1989–1992, *Accounting Education: an international journal*, 3(3), 193–204.

May, W.W. (ed.) (1990) *Ethics in the Accounting Curriculum: Cases & Readings*. Sarasota, FL: American Accounting Association.

Mayper, A.G., Pavur, R.J., Merino, B.D., & Hoops, W. (2005) The impact of accounting education on ethical values: an institutional perspective, *Accounting and the Public Interest*, 5, 32–55.

McCabe, D.L., Dukerich, J.M., & Dutton, J.E. (1991) Context, values and moral dilemmas: comparing the choices of business and law school students, *Journal of Business Ethics*, 10(12), 951–960.

McGuigan, N.C. & Kern, T. (2009) The reflective accountant: changing student perceptions of traditional accounting through reflective educational practice, *International Journal of Learning*, 16(9), 49–68.

McPeak, D., Pincus, K.V., & Sundem, G.L. (2012) The International Accounting Education Standards Board: influencing global accounting education, *Issues in Accounting Education*, 27(3), 743–750.

McPhail, K. (1999) The threat of ethical accountants: an application of Foucault's concept of ethics to accounting education and some thoughts on ethically educating for the other, *Critical Perspectives on Accounting*, 10(6), 833–866.

McPhail, K. (2001a) The dialectic of accounting education: from role identity to ego identity, *Critical Perspectives on Accounting*, 12(4), 471–499.

McPhail, K. (2001b) The *Other* objective of ethics education: re-humanising the accounting profession – A study of ethics education in law, engineering, medicine and accountancy, *Journal of Business Ethics*, 34(3/4), 279–298.

McPhail, K. (2005) Care in the community: professional ethics and the paradox of pro bono, *Accounting Education: an international journal*, 14(2), 213–227.

McPhail, K. (2006) Going public: a brief note on civilising accounting ethics education, *Business Ethics: A European Review*, 15(3), 306–309.

McPhail, K., Gorringe, T., & Gray, R. (2005) Crossing the great divide: critiquing the sacred secular dichotomy in accounting research, *Accounting, Auditing and Accountability Journal*, 18(2), 185–188.

McPhail, K. & Walters, D. (2009) *Accounting and Business Ethics: An Introduction*, London: Routledge.

Merino, B. (2006) Financial scandals: another clarion call for educational reform – A historical perspective, *Issues in Accounting Education*, 21(4), 363–381.

Merino, B., Mayper, A.G., & Tolleson, T.D. (2010) Neoliberalism, deregulation and Sarbanes-Oxley: the legitimation of a failed corporate governance model, *Accounting, Auditing and Accountability Journal*, 23(6), 774–792.

Miller, W.F. & Becker, D.A.A. (2011) Ethics in the accounting curriculum: what is really being covered? *American Journal of Business Education*, 4(10), 1–9.

Mintz, S.M. (1995) Virtue ethics and accounting education, *Issues in Accounting Education*, 10(2), 246–267.

Mintz, S.M. (2006) Accounting ethics education: integrating reflective learning and virtue ethics, *Journal of Accounting Education*, 24(2–3), 97–117.

Molisa, P. (2010) White business education, *Critical Perspectives on Accounting*, 21(6), 526–528.

Nelson, I.T. (1995) What's new about accounting education change? An historical perspective on the change movement, *Accounting Horizons*, 9(4), 62–75.

Noonan, J. (2003) Can there be applied philosophy without philosophy?, *Interchange*, 34(1), 35–49.

O'Leary, C. (2009) An empirical analysis of the positive impact of ethics teaching on accounting students, *Accounting Education: An international journal*, 18(4&5), 505–520.

Owen, D. (2005) CSR after Enron: a role for the academic accounting profession?, *European Accounting Review*, 14(2), 395–404.

Peace, R. (2006) Accountants and a religious covenant with the public, *Critical Perspectives on Accounting*, 781–797(17), 6.

Pettifor, J.L. & Paquet, S. (2002) Preferred strategies for learning ethics in the practice of a discipline, *Canadian Psychology*, 43(4), 260–269.

Piper, T.R., Gentile, M.C., & Parks, S.D. (1993) *Can Ethics Be Taught? Perspectives, Challenges, and Approaches at Harvard Business School*, Boston: Harvard Business School.

Ponemon, L.A. (1992) Ethical reasoning and selection: socialization in accounting, *Accounting, Organizations and Society*, 17(3/4), 239–258.

Ponemon, L.A. (2011) Can ethics be taught in accounting?, *Journal of Accounting Education*, 11(2), 185–209.

Ponemon, L.A. & Glazer, A. (1990) Accounting education and ethical development: the influence of liberal learning on students and alumni in accounting practice, *Issues in Accounting Education*, 5(2), 195–208.

Puxty, A., Sikka, P., & Willmott, H. (1994) (Re)forming the circle: education, ethics and accountancy practices, *Accounting Education: An international journal*, 3(1), 77–92.

Ravenscroft, S. & Williams, P.F. (2004) Considering accounting education in the USA post-Enron, *Accounting Education: An international journal*, 13(Supplement 1), 7–23.

Ravenscroft, S. & Williams, P.F. (2005) Rules, rogues, and risk assessors: academic responses to Enron and other accounting scandals, *European Accounting Review*, 14(2), 363–372.

Reiter, S. (1997) The ethics of care and new paradigms for accounting practice, *Accounting, Auditing and Accountability Journal*, 10(3), 299–324.

Rest, J. (1986) *Moral Development: Advances in Research and Theory*, New York: Praeger.

Review Committee of the Accounting Discipline in Higher Education (1990) *Accounting in Higher Education: Report of the Review of the Accounting Discipline in Higher Education: Volume 1: Main Report and Recommendations*, Canberra, Australian Government Publishing Service.

Rockness, H.O. & Rockness, J.W. (2010) Navigating the complex maze of Ethics CPE, *Accounting and the Public Interest*, 10, 88–104.

Rossouw, D. (2008) Practising Applied Ethics with philosophical integrity: the case of Business Ethics, *Business Ethics: A European Review*, 17(2), 161–170.

Ryan, T.G. & Bisson, J. (1993) Can ethics be taught? *International Journal of Business and Social Science*, 2(12), 44–52.

Sangster, A. (2010) Liberalising the accounting curriculum, *Accounting Education: an international journal*, 19(4), 323–327.

Shearer, T. (2002) Ethics and accountability: from the for-itself to the for-the-other, *Accounting, Organizations and Society*, 27(6), 541–573.

Singer, P. (ed.) (1994) *Ethics*, Oxford Readers, Oxford: Oxford University Press.

Solomons, D., with Berridge, T.M. (1974) *Prospectus for a Profession: The Report of the Long-Range Enquiry into Education and Training for the Accountancy Profession*, London: Advisory Board of Accountancy Education.

Staubus, G.J. (2005) Ethics failures in corporate financial reporting, *Journal of Business Ethics*, 57(1), 5–15.

Stewart, I. (1997) Teaching accounting ethics: the power of narrative, *Accounting Education*, 2(2), 173–184.

Sundem, G.L., Williams, D.Z., & Chironna, J.F. (1990) The revolution in accounting education, *Management Accounting*, (December), 49–53.

Swanson, D.L. (2005) Business ethics education at bay: addressing a crisis of legitimacy, *Issues in Accounting Education*, 20(3), 248–253.

Sykes, T. (1998) *Two Centuries of Panic: A History of Corporate Collapses in Australia*, St Leonards, NSW: Allen & Unwin.

Thomas, W. (2004) An inventory of support materials for teaching ethics in the post-Enron era, *Issues in Accounting Education*, 19(1), 27–52.

Tinker, T. & Gray, R. (2003) Beyond a critique of pure reason: from policy to politics to praxis in environmental and social research, *Accounting, Auditing and Accountability Journal*, 16(5), 727–761.

Treadway, J.C., Batten, W.M., Kanaga, W.S., Marsh, H.L., Storrs, T.I., & Trautlein, D.H. (1987) *Report of the National Commission on Fraudulent Financial Reporting*, Washington, DC: National Commission on Fraudulent Financial Reporting.

Van Peursem, K.A. & Julian, A. (2006) Ethics research: an accounting educator's perspective, *Australian Accounting Review*, 16(1), 13–29.

Velayutham, S. & Perera, M.H.B. (1996) The influence of underlying metaphysical notions on our interpretation of accounting, *Accounting, Auditing and Accountability Journal*, 9(4), 65–85.

Waldmann, E. (2000) Teaching ethics in accounting: a discussion of cross-cultural factors with a focus on Confucian and Western philosophy, *Accounting Education: an international journal*, 9(1), 23–35.

Whitbeck, C. (1992) The trouble with dilemmas: rethinking applied ethics, *Professional Ethics* 1(1&2), 119–142.

Wilhelm, W.J. (2008) Integrating instruction in ethical reasoning into undergraduate business courses, *Journal of Business Ethics Education*, 5, 5–34.

Williams, J. & Elson, R.J. (2010) Improving ethical education in the accounting program: a conceptual course, *Academy of Educational Leadership Journal*, 14(4), 107–116.

Williams, P.F. (2002) Accounting and the moral order: justice, accounting, and legitimate moral authority, *Accounting and the Public Interest*, 2: 1–21.

Williams, P.F. (2010) The focus of professional ethics: ethical professionals or ethical profession? *Research on Professional Responsibility and Ethics in Accounting*, 14, 15–35.

Willits, S.D. (2011) Will more liberal arts courses fix the accounting curriculum? *Journal of Accounting Education*, 28(1), 1–42.

Wray-Bliss, E. (2013) A crisis of leadership: towards an anti-sovereign ethics of organisation, *Business Ethics: A European Review*, 22(1), 86–101.

Young, J.J. & Annisette, M. (2009) Cultivating imagination: ethics, education and literature, *Critical Perspectives on Accounting*, 20(1), 93–109.

Yuthas, K. & Dillard, J.F. (1999) Teaching ethical decision making: adding a structuration dimension, *Teaching Business Ethics*, 3(4), 339–361.

About the author

Gordon Boyce is Associate Professor in the Department of Accounting at La Trobe University, Melbourne, Australia (g.boyce@latrobe.edu.au), and an Associate Editor of *Accounting Education: an international journal*. His research (for which he has received many awards) primarily focusses on the connection between accounting and social, political, and environmental issues, and the associated role of technologies of accounting and accountability in public discourse.

25

Internships and accounting education

Deborah F. Beard and Roberta L. Humphrey

SOUTHEAST MISSOURI STATE UNIVERSITY, U.S.A.

CONTENTS

Abstract

In this chapter, we examine contextual considerations of internships in accounting education. Internships provide a unique opportunity to blend research, practice, and teaching that extends beyond the typical classroom. An overview of the research relating to the potential benefits to students, practitioners, and educators is provided. Internships can be important in career exploration and development, in the development and enhancement of students' competencies, and in curriculum development and assessment. Various suggestions and resources are provided in this chapter for consideration when developing, implementing, and assessing students' internship experiences. This chapter should be relevant to students, practitioners, and educators wishing to identify potential internships' benefits, and to understand how internships can be an important component of accounting education and the professional preparation of future accounting professionals.

Keywords

accounting education, career exploration, experiential learning, internships

25.1 Introduction

The aims of this chapter are:

- to provide an overview of research relating to internships in accounting education;
- to identify the benefits of internships to students, practitioners, and educators;
- to discuss issues and considerations in integrating internships into accounting curricula;
- to recognize that internships can be an integral part of assessment and programme improvement;
- to encourage the use of best practices in structuring and administrating internships.

Although the research and recommendations presented in this chapter are predominantly from the U.S.A., a framework for designing, implementing, and assessing internships globally is offered. Of course, cultural, economic, institutional, and other jurisdictional differences may require modifications. The authors make several normative assertions based on their experience with internships and their review of the literature that was available to them. These assertions should be validated by future research involving research design and statistical analyses to evaluate the benefits and efficacy of internships in accounting education. Such research should be undertaken globally and reported in publications that are readily available internationally.

25.1.1 Importance of accounting student internships

In earlier chapters, we have recognized the inevitability of change and the resultant need for change in accounting education. We have stressed the importance of developing an agenda for improving accounting education in a global and technology-rich environment. (See, for example, Flood, Chapter 4, St. Pierre & Rebele, Chapter 5, and Evans, Chapter 28 – all in this volume.) We have also stressed the importance of students' perceptions in the study of accounting, in gaining insight into the expectations for the accounting profession and in the workplace, and in developing and matching students' knowledge, skills, and attributes in career exploration and choice. (See Lucas & Mladenovic, Chapter 6; Duff, Chapter 8; and Jackling, Chapter 10 – all in this volume.) Various curricular, pedagogic, and assessment considerations have also been discussed.

In the previous two chapters, we have recognized the impact of financial crises on accounting education and the need to stress the importance of ethical behaviour to our accounting students. Chapter 25 is relevant to each of these considerations as well as to discussions relating to comparative accounting education and institutional considerations found in future chapters. (See Calhoun & Karreman, Chapter 26, and Chapters 27–30 in this volume.)

The importance of interaction and collaboration among practitioners, accounting educators, and administrators has become increasingly essential in identifying, developing, and assessing the desired competencies expected of accounting professionals. Knowledge of these competencies and assessments of students' performance are critical to improving accounting education and in preparing accounting students for professional success (see Watty, Chapter 13, and Kidwell & Lowensohn, Chapter 21 – both in this volume). Insights into the requisite knowledge, skills, and professional and ethical behaviour expected of entry-level accountants are vital when developing, implementing, and revising curricula and when selecting appropriate pedagogy (see Boyce, Chapter 24 – this volume). These insights can be gained from interactions among practitioners, accounting educators, and programme administrators.

A formalized student internship component of the accounting programme can provide an effective way to encourage meaningful discussions and assessments among these groups while offering accounting students valuable practical experience. (See Byrne & Willis, Chapter 7, and Hassall & Joyce, Chapter 17 – both in this volume.) These out-of-the-traditional classroom experiences can be used to enhance career development and placement, cognitive and soft skills, and perspectives of the workplace. Internships can provide unique opportunities to blend academic knowledge with workplace experience in preparing accounting graduates for successful entry into the accounting profession and for continued professional development.

Evidential support for the benefits of internships to students, practitioners, and academic programmes, insights into the current status of internships in accounting education, and suggested best practices in implementing and sustaining internship programmes is provided in this chapter. The impact of technology, sustainability, regulation, and future research relating to internships and accounting education are also considered.

Administrators, academic staff, students, and professional practitioners should find this chapter valuable because it identifies and summarizes published research and guidance relating to internships. This chapter highlights the benefits and best practices of internship programmes and provides resources that can be utilized in implementing, enhancing, and assessing internship programmes and interns' performance. The majority of the existing literature on accounting internships appears to be based on studies conducted and published in the U.S.A., with only a few exceptions. However, given little contrary evidence, the authors believe that the insights and suggestions published in studies from the U.S.A. should be considered when designing, implementing, and assessing accounting internship programmes in other jurisdictions as well as in the U.S.A.

The authors of this chapter have undertaken an international survey to solicit information concerning the status of internships worldwide but received few responses from educators at non-U.S. universities. The authors encourage accounting educators to conduct and publish additional research relating to internships in the preparation of accounting graduates globally. Of course, cultural, economic, institutional, and other differences may influence the integration of internships into curricula. Nevertheless, the discussion of the presented literatures should be appropriate to those seeking to improve accounting education and to promote important linkages between the academic setting and the practical workplace globally. The accounting internship expertise of the authors was obtained through their study and work in the U.S.A.

25.1.2 Relevance of internships to change in accounting education

A number of individuals and international organizations such as the International Accounting Education Standards Board (IAESB), the American Institute of Accountants (AIA), the American Accounting Association (AAA), the Association to Advance Collegiate Schools of Business (AACSB), the Accounting Education Change Commission (AECC), and the Pathways Commission have urged change in curricula and pedagogy in the education of future accounting professionals (AIA and AAA, 1955; Nelson *et al.*, 1988; AECC, 1990; Buck, 1992; Siegel & Sorensen, 1994; Dennis, 1996; Albrecht & Sack, 2001; Burnett, 2003; Bloom & Myring, 2008; IAESB, 2010; AACSB, 2011; Wally-Dima, 2011; the Pathways Commission, 2012).

In a project sponsored by the Institute of Management Accountants (IMA) and the Financial Executives Institute (FEI), Siegel & Sorensen (1994) expressed concern that entry-level account-ants were not meeting workplace expectations. Calls for changes in academic programmes and the learning environment have been considered vital to the future of the accounting profession by reducing the gap between traditional classroom learning and the demands of the profession on entry-level accountants. (For more information on the call to change accounting education see Flood, Chapter 4, and St. Pierre & Rebele, Chapter 5 – both in this volume.)

Through the years, accounting administrators, academic staff, and practitioners have been urged to work together to provide an environment conducive to professional interaction and provide relevant practical experience for accounting students. The AAA (1952) recognized decades ago the benefits to be derived from a period of practical experience being incorporated into the academic preparation of accountants. The AECC (1990) supported internships as a means for developing communication skills, intellectual skills, and interpersonal skills.

Klein & Levy (1993), Jeffords, Schneidt, & Thibadoux (2000), and Arlinghaus (2002) have recognized internships and practical work experiences as being valuable in the education of future accountants. Cerne & Zenzerovi (2011) called for academic and professional community cooperation in Croatia to meet their professional responsibilities in preparing accounting graduates for life-long learning, identifying practical experience as a way to improve accounting education, and to encourage on-going professional development and competency. Cord *et al.* (2010) analyzed students' reflections of their work-related learning experiences in the University of Wollongong Commerce Internship Programme in Australia. Students indicated in their reflections that they felt better prepared to transition from higher education to industry, and to manage their expectations in an ever-changing global workplace requiring life-long learning. Cord *et al.* (2011) viewed Australian internships as a means for developing generic workplace skills and urged educators and practitioners to work together to support and supervise students' development and transition to the workplace.

Ali, Heang, Mohammed, & Ojo (2008) recommended practical experiences, such as intern-ships, to expose students to professional issues and actual performance expectations. Albrecht & Sack (2001) and Burnett (2003) agreed that internships were the most preferred out-of-classroom learning activity. Other researchers (e.g. Brown-Liburd & Porco, 2011; Cook *et al.*, 2011) have found internships to be instrumental in strengthening cognitive, behavioural, and generic skills. Brown-Liburd & Porco (2011) reported that students completing an internship with public accounting firms displayed higher levels of cognitive moral development. Bloom & Myring (2008) supported a double internship model as being beneficial in skills development and student recruitment.

The IAESB (2010) has also recognized that practical experience is important in the education and training of competent professional accountants who continue to grow throughout their careers. The IAESB insists that the experience should focus on developing demonstrable competence and not just spending time in a work-related learning experience.

The AACSB (2011) has recognized experiential learning as being an important pedagogy for business school programmes to provide more effective learning than traditional classroom-based pedagogies, and to connect programmes and students to the business world. The AACSB (2011) has also stressed that experiential learning pedagogies can provide students with an appreciation for cultural, legal/regulatory, political, and economic differences across countries. The AACSB (2012) has offered a 'Curriculum Development Series' of seminars to help address major challenges in curriculum reform. Administrators, academic staff, and executives have been encouraged to participate and to recognize that internships and other experiential learning experiences provide unique opportunities for students to learn more effectively through practice than through traditional classroom-based pedagogy. One AACSB seminar focussed on methods for recruiting internship clients, supporting academic staff, and measuring outcomes of students' learning from internships and other experiential learning. The AACSB offers tools and templates to use in implementing effective teaching, promoting feedback and evaluation, the development of syllabi, and course materials. (For a broader discussion of experiential learning see Hassall & Joyce, Chapter 17 – this volume.)

In 2012, the Pathways Commission, jointly supported by the AAA and American Institute of Certified Public Accountants (AICPA), released its initial report on enhancing the accounting education process and the accounting profession. One of the seven recommendations of the Pathways Commission (2012, p. 11) called for building '*a learned profession for the future by purposeful integration of accounting research, education, and practice for students, accounting practitioners, and educators*'.

The Pathways Commission (ibid., p. 72) also stated their conclusion that '*a foundational clinical learning experience in which students integrate technical knowledge, professional skills, and understanding of the accounting profession's broad societal purposes and commitments should be required*'. The Commission believes these experiences '*must be jointly developed, implemented, overseen, and assessed by accounting educators and working accountants*'. (For more ideas on the integration of accounting research, education, and practice into the accounting curriculum, see Bloom, Chapter 14 – this volume.)

Internships have also been considered in the achievement of professional certifications in the U.S.A., such as the Certified Public Accountant (CPA) and Certified Internal Auditor (CIA). The U.S.A.-based National Association of State Boards of Accountancy (NASBA) does not require that candidates complete an internship, but NASBA (2011) does allow candidates to include internship credit as part of the required hours for sitting for the CPA examination. The U.S.A.-based Institute of Internal Auditors (IIA) requires an internship, cooperative educational experience, or case study as part of the Comprehensive Internal Audit Program certified by the IIA. The IIA requires that the duration of an internship be at least eight weeks, that students submit periodic reports and a final report, and that the internship provider gives feedback. Furthermore, the internship should ideally occur after (or at the end of) relevant course work. If taken for credit, the internship must be tracked, evaluated, and granted university credit.

CPA Australia has established its Internship CPA Passport Program to expose students to networking and mentoring opportunities, gain insight into the accounting industry, and assist students in assessing career fit and suitability. Mauldin *et al.* (2006) reported that completing an internship was a major factor in the hiring process. (For more discussion of the interface between accounting education and professional training, see Evans, Chapter 28 – this volume.)

Internships can play an important role in preparing accounting graduates not only for entry into the profession, but also in their professional development. Several professional organizations and individuals have stressed the benefits of internships to students, employing organizations, and academic programmes. In the next section, published research and professional publications will be examined to support the benefits of internships.

25.2 Internship benefits

The benefits of internships have been documented by numerous research studies. Unless otherwise indicated, the research was based on experiences in the U.S.A. In the next three sub-sections, the discussion of potential benefits to be derived by students, practitioners, and academic programmes and institutions is presented.

25.2.1 Benefits to students

Several individuals have compared the academic performance of accounting majors subsequent to completing an internship. Koehler (1974) reported improved grade point averages (GPAs). Knechel & Snowball (1987) found that, although interns performed better in auditing following an auditing internship, there was an insignificant difference in the GPAs (accounting or overall) of interns and non-interns. However, English & Koeppen (1993) found higher GPAs in accounting courses and overall for those students completing an internship. Ebied (2004) found that students at the United Arab Emirates University who completed an accounting internship performed significantly better in accounting courses and in overall GPA following their internships.

Chandra & Paperman (1983) supported internships as a means for students to learn about the accounting profession and to gain practical experience. McCombs & VanSycle (1994) concluded that internships help students clarify career goals and can provide students with meaningful work experience while students gain maturity. Lauber *et al.* (2004) supported internships for providing opportunities to apply what was learned in the traditional classroom. English & Koeppen (1993) advocated internships as a means of supplementing traditional courses with more relevant business applications and to improve job placements. Pasewark *et al.* (1989) determined that accounting majors completing an internship had a greater probability of receiving off-campus interviews. Cannon & Arnold (1998) determined that students view internships as a means for gaining a competitive edge in the employment process. The students believed that an increased sense of professionalism would be gained from the work experience. Hiltebeitel *et al.* (2000) found reduced 'reality shock' for entry-level accountants who had completed an internship. Siegel *et al.* (1992) reported better subsequent performance evaluations and advancement in regional accounting firms for those accounting students completing an internship. Siegel *et al.* (2011) reported that internal auditors who had completed an internship received higher performance evaluations and higher rates of promotion than those who had not completed an internship.

Beck & Halim (2008) explored what and how students in Singapore learned as a result of an eight-week internship, and believed that self-reflection of what was learned during the internship was key to students' learning. Accounting students reported that the internship led to significant improvements in personal and interpersonal skills, and believe that the internship had prepared them for their first job, had helped them make their career choice, and would support future professional development. Callanan & Benzing (2004) believed that completing an internship increased the probability of being hired. Mihail (2006) conducted face-to-face interviews to explore students' perceptions of the effects of a co-operative education programme that had recently been launched by the University of Macedonia in Greece. Students reported improvements in time management, communication, teamwork, task prioritization, and enhanced knowledge from their work experience. Mihail (2006) also concluded that internships are a means for linking theoretical knowledge and practice, enhancing employability after graduation.

Thorpe-Dulgarian (2008) surveyed students concerning the Pilot Internship Program at Bowie State University in Maryland, and reported that students believed that, as a result of their internships, they had gained a better appreciation of accounting and business, were more confident and motivated, and had an increased interest in accounting careers. Cord *et al.* (2011) encouraged educators and practitioners to get involved in the development of generic skills needed in the profession and in transitioning students to the workplace through internships and other collaborations.

Ali *et al.* (2008) reported a significant change in accounting students' perceptions of the audit expectation gap in Malaysia following an accounting internship. They supported using internships to complement auditing education to expose students to professional issues and as a means for gaining insight into the actual performance and duties of auditors. (For more discussion of accounting as a career choice, see Jackling, Chapter 10 – this volume.) By surveying accounting programme administrators throughout the U.S.A., Beard (1998) identified several benefits to students, firms involved in the internship programme, and accounting programmes offering internship programmes. The results support a win–win–win experience for students, practitioners, and programmes with the top reported benefit to each of these groups being associated with improvements in job/career placement opportunities for students and the recruitment of future employees.

Fesler & Caldwell (2001) determined that internships improved students' self-esteem, provided financial assistance, and were useful in assessing the compatibility of students' abilities with their chosen career paths. Henry (2002) noted that internships enable students to explore career options, to network, to acquire new skills, and to apply classroom knowledge. Ruh & Theuri (2002) reported that internships assist students in clarifying career choice, provide opportunities to strengthen oral, written, social, and interpersonal skills, and to gain insight into career expectations for professionalism and etiquette. Cook *et al.* (2011) believed that internships can have a beneficial impact on the emotional intelligence of accounting students and lead to improved performance in leadership, team building, client relations, and decision-making.

Hazelwood (2004) observed that internships have, in many cases, replaced on-campus recruiting for full-time positions, reporting a 50–60 per cent placement rate for students completing an internship. Green *et al.* (2011) reported improved career expectations and stronger interviewing skills for accounting majors completing an internship in comparison to non-internship students.

The research, therefore, provides evidential support that students who participate in internships have the opportunity to derive many benefits. These benefits include, among others, career exploration and development, improved academic performance subsequent to the internship, and enhanced interviewing and employer opportunities. The benefits to students from completing an internship are summarized in Table 25.1.

25.2.2 Benefits to accounting practitioners

Students are not the only potential winners from an internship. Many research studies indicate that practitioners benefit from participating in students' internship programmes. Unless otherwise indicated, the research flows from research and experiences in the U.S.A. Practitioner benefits include:

Table 25.1 Benefits to students from completing an internship

Benefits to students	Source (Location of study)
Connect academic coursework and workplace requirements	Henry, 2002 (U.S.A.) Lauber *et al.*, 2004 (U.S.A.) Mihail, 2006 (Greece)
Enhance communication, critical-thinking, problem-solving, interpersonal, and team skills	Henry, 2002 (U.S.A.) Ruh & Theuri, 2002 (U.S.A.) Mihail, 2006 (Greece) Beck & Halim, 2008 (Singapore) Cord & Clements *et al.*, 2010 (Australia) Cord *et al.*, 2010 (Australia) Cook *et al.*, 2011 (Canada, South Africa, U.S.A.)
Gain real-world experience and a business perspective	Chandra & Paperman, 1983 (U.S.A.) English & Koeppen, 1993 (U.S.A.) McCombs & VanSycle, 1994 (U.S.A.) Thorpe-Dulgarian, 2008 (U.S.A.)
Increase opportunity for full-time employment	Beard, 1998 (U.S.A.) Cannon & Arnold, 1998 (U.S.A.) Pasewark *et al.*, 1989 (U.S.A.) Callanan & Benzing, 2004 (U.S.A.) Hazelwood, 2004 (U.S.A.) Mauldin *et al.*, 2006 (U.S.A.) Green *et al.*, 2011 (U.S.A.)
Explore and confirm compatibility with career choice	McCombs & VanSycle, 1994 (U.S.A.) Fesler & Caldwell, 2001 (U.S.A.) Henry, 2002 (U.S.A.) Ruh & Theuri, 2002 (U.S.A.) Beck & Halim, 2008 (Singapore) Thorpe-Dulgarian, 2008 (U.S.A.) Cord *et al.*, 2010 (Australia)
Build confidence and self-esteem	Fesler & Caldwell, 2001 (U.S.A.) Beck & Halim, 2008 (Singapore)
Provide networking opportunities	Henry, 2002 (U.S.A.)
Enhance professional demeanour and etiquette	Ruh & Theuri, 2002 (U.S.A.)
Provide financial assistance	Fesler & Caldwell, 2001 (U.S.A.)
Improve interviewing skills	Green *et al.*, 2011 (U.S.A.)
Gain insight into expectations of accounting professional	Chandra & Paperman, 1983 (U.S.A.) Ali *et al.*, 2008 (Malaysia)
Enhance success as accounting professional	Siegel & Rigsby, 1988 (U.S.A.) Siegel *et al.*, 1992 (U.S.A.) Beck & Halim, 2008 (Singapore) Cook *et al.*, 2011(Canada, South Africa, U.S.A.)
Reduce transition shock when entering profession after graduation	Hiltebeitel *et al.*, 2000 (U.S.A.) Beck & Halim, 2008 (Singapore) Cord *et al.*, 2010 (Australia)
Increase academic focus and improved academic performance	English & Koeppen, 1993 (U.S.A.) Ebied, 2004 (United Arab Emirates)
Increase cognitive moral development	Brown-Liburd & Porco, 2011 (U.S.A.)

- improved recruitment of full-time employees;
- enhanced community visibility and professional image; and
- increased employees' performance, retention, and loyalty.

Lang (1979), Goodman (1982), Chandra & Paperman (1983), Kimmel & Kimmel (1988), McCombs & VanSycle (1994), Cannon & Arnold (1998), and Henry (2002) recognized that internships serve as a valuable tool in the recruitment of future full-time, well-qualified employees. McCombs & VanSycle (1994) also noted that exposure gained through internships make on-campus recruiting easier, and that internships provide opportunities to meet employment needs at lower costs and to assess internal training and supervision functions.

Internships can also affect the image of the sponsoring organization. Ricchiute (1980) stressed that interns can serve as goodwill ambassadors upon their return to campus. Chandra & Paperman (1983) not only perceived internships as assisting in the recruiting process, but also as a means for maintaining and improving relationships with universities. Schmutte (1986) encouraged practitioners in small firms to use internships in the recruitment of full-time employees, and in marketing themselves to other students and universities. Kimmel & Kimmel (1988) noted that internal auditing internships can enhance the reputation and visibility of firms within the college and the community, improve prospects of attracting top graduates as employees, and reduce personnel shortages. Talbott (1996) emphasized that positive perceptions by students of the potential employer is essential in recruiting employees, and that seeing the business from the inside during an internship can enhance the firm's image to the students.

Dennis (1996) noted that internships provide quality personnel while keeping costs to a minimum during the internship. Cannon & Arnold (1998) not only viewed internships as providing inexpensive help and a pool to draw upon for future employees, but also as a source of new ideas. DeFilippes (1982) encouraged the use of internships in small practices as a means of attracting and retaining employees. Crumley & Sumners (1998) recognized that participation in internships can enhance the employee selection process and relationships with universities while they demonstrate a commitment to the accounting profession. Lauber *et al.* (2004) stressed that internships yield financial and resource allocation benefits, strengthen alliances with the community and the university, and provide an edge in hiring the best and brightest graduates.

White & Fuller (2002) recognized benefits to practitioners from low-cost help, increased productivity, decreased hiring risk, enhanced value for the profession, and the opportunity for practitioners to learn as well as teach during the internship. Siegel *et al.* (2010) concluded that a structured internship can positively affect the performance evaluations, promotions, and retention of full-time employees who had completed an internship during their academic studies. Siegel *et al.* (2011) found higher performance evaluations and higher rates of promotion for internal auditors who had completed an academic internship. The benefits to accounting practitioners are summarized in Table 25.2.

25.2.3 Benefits to programmes and universities

Additionally, accounting programmes and their universities derive benefits from successful internships. When students and practitioners benefit from internship experiences, the accounting programmes and universities appear to benefit as well. Chandra & Paperman (1983) supported internships as a valuable link between universities and practitioners and beneficial in student recruitment. Coco (2000) pointed to endowments, support for research, and access to guest speakers and field trips as possible benefits from educators and practitioners working together in providing internships. Cook *et al.* (2004) emphasized that the university gains credibility and

Table 25.2 Benefits to practitioners from students' internships

Benefits to practitioners	Source (Location of study)
Increase pool of quality candidates for full-time employment	Lang, 1979 (U.S.A.)
	Goodman, 1982 (U.S.A.)
	DeFillippis, 1982 (U.S.A)
	Chandra & Paperman, 1983 (U.S.A.)
	Schmutte, 1986 (U.S.A.)
	Kimmel & Kimmel, 1988 (U.S.A.)
	McCombs & VanSycle, 1994 (U.S.A.)
	Talbott, 1996 (Switzerland, U.S.A.)
	Cannon & Arnold, 1998 (U.S.A.)
	Beard, 1998 (U.S.A.)
	Henry, 2002 (U.S.A.)
Increase opportunity to evaluate skills of potential employees	Crumley & Sumners, 1998 (U.S.A.)
	Lauber *et al.*, 2004 (U.S.A.)
Enhance community visibility and professional image	Ricchiute, 1980 (U.S.A.)
	Goodman, 1982 (U.S.A.)
	Chandra & Paperman, 1983 (U.S.A.)
	Schmutte, 1986 (U.S.A.)
	Talbott, 1996 (Switzerland, U.S.A.)
	Lauber *et al.*, 2004 (U.S.A.)
Increase loyalty and productivity of employees	White & Fuller, 2002 (U.S.A.)
	Siegel *et al.*, 2010 (U.S.A.)
Decrease costs for part-time employees	McCombs & VanSycle, 1994 (U.S.A.)
	Dennis, 1996 (U.S.A.)
	White & Fuller, 2002 (U.S.A.)
	Lauber *et al.*, 2004 (U.S.A.)
Decrease employee turnover rates	Kimmel & Kimmel, 1988 (U.S.A.)
	White & Fuller, 2002 (U.S.A.)
Demonstrate commitment to the future of the profession	Crumley & Sumners, 1998 (U.S.A.)
Reduce recruitment cost	McCombs & VanSycle, 1994 (U.S.A.)
New source for fresh ideas	Cannon & Arnold, 1998 (U.S.A.)
Increase employee performance	Siegel *et al.*, 2011 (U.S.A.)

important relationships between the university and business community. The connections made with practitioners and the results of students' self-assessments and supervisors' evaluations can provide valuable inputs to the curriculum and to students' development, student recruitment and placement, and programme assessment.

Beck & Halim (2008) identified several benefits of internships to universities. Internships allowed educators and administrators to gauge the relevance of curricula in a professional environment and, by assisting graduates in securing employment, increased university rankings for satisfaction and for graduate employability.

Beard (1998) asked undergraduate accounting programme administrators in the U.S.A. to rank seven benefits to the programme and university of accounting students' internships. The most highly ranked benefit was the increased placement upon graduation of students who had completed an internship. The second highest ranked benefit was that they believed the internship experience reinforced and enhanced the students' learning of classroom material. Out of the seven listed, the administrators ranked third the benefit of developing accounting professionals' support for their programme. Weible (2009) surveyed business deans in the U.S.A. Over 80 per cent of the respondents reported a greater connection to the community because of internships, and enhanced reputation as a result of internships. These and other benefits are noted in Table 25.3.

Table 25.3 Benefits to accounting programmes and universities from internship programmes

Benefits to accounting programmes/ universities	Source (Location of study)
Receive input provided by professionals into curriculum and student development	Beard, 1998 (U.S.A.) Cook *et al.*, 2004 (U.S.A.)
Improve student recruitment and career placement	Beard, 1998 (U.S.A.) Cannon & Arnold, 1998 (U.S.A.) Pasewark *et al.*, 1989 (U.S.A.) Callanan & Benzing, 2004 (U.S.A.) Hazelwood, 2004 (U.S.A.) Beck & Halim, 2008 (Singapore) Mauldin *et al.*, 2006 (U.S.A.) Green *et al.*, 2011 (U.S.A.)
Increase reinforcement and enhancement of classroom learning	Beard, 1998 (U.S.A.)
Increase access to professionals who serve as campus speakers	Coco, 2000 (U.S.A.)
Enhance access to valuable programmes and students' assessment information	Beck & Halim, 2008 (Singapore)
Receive validation of and enhancement ideas related to classroom learning	Beck & Halim, 2008 (Singapore)
Increase industry and community connections	Chandra & Paperman, 1983 (U.S.A.) Cook *et al.*, 2004 (U.S.A.) Weible, 2009 (U.S.A.)
Increase fund-raising contacts and partners	Coco, 2000 (U.S.A.)
Develop accounting professionals' support of the accounting programmes	Beard, 1998 (U.S.A.)
Enhance programme reputation	Weible, 2009 (U.S.A.)

25.3 Internship expectations and assessment

25.3.1 Students' expectations and assessments of students' performance in internships

Based on the authors' experience and their review of the literature focussing on internships, they suggest that the internship process should expect that students complete several activities before, during, and at the end of the internship. For example, Hergert (2009) stressed the importance of integrating the internship experience with career goals:

- Students should be expected to undertake career exploration to assess career opportunities and expectations, and identify internship sites consistent with their personal traits and career goals.
- Students should be aware of prerequisites for enrolling in an internship, and ensure that they stay on track to qualify for an internship.
- Students should prepare a professional résumé and covering letter, and should practise interviewing and business etiquette.

The authors also suggest that networking can be critical in identifying and in preparing for internships. Students should seek networking opportunities and participate in students' organizations and campus activities that bring accounting professionals and alumni to campus as guest speakers. Students should assume some responsibility for identifying internship sites consistent with their career goals, and explore publicly available information about organizations in order to learn about internship opportunities. These assertions are made based on the authors' experience and their review of publications promoting internships and providing suggestions to students desiring to complete an internship.

During the internship, students should demonstrate ethical behaviour and follow all policies and procedures of the organization. (An extended discussion of ethical behaviour is provided by Boyce, Chapter 24 – this volume.) Students' reflections on their learning during and at completion of the internship experience should be required. Student interns should reflect on what they have learned in the classroom and how it relates to the work experience through e-logs, journals, final papers, and self-assessment.

Cord *et al.* (2010) emphasized the importance of students' reflection through daily e-logging that not only encouraged the student to reflect on their personal and professional development, but also to provide a means for academic staff to monitor students' learning activities as a basis for offering support and feedback. Cord & Clements (2010) urged the integration of a reflective journal to use in evaluating soft skills. Beard (2007) suggested that students should submit a final report and an assessment of the internship experience at the end of the internship. She provided an example of possible components of an internship paper shown in Table 25.4.

At the end of their internship, students should complete a self-evaluation and programme evaluation. An example of such a form is provided in Figure 25.1.

25.3.2 Expectations for on-site supervisors

The expectations for on-site supervisors should be clearly delineated. White & Fuller (2002) and Cook *et al.* (2004) urged on-site supervisors to provide a positive, enriching, and rewarding learning experience for interns. Rothman (2007) reported that students suggested that employers wishing to improve internship experiences should ensure that tasks are clarified and that expectations for the completion of task be within a reasonable time period. Ongoing feedback, mentoring, exposure to other parts of the business, and respectful treatment were also among students' suggestions to employers. Beard (2007) suggested that employers' guidelines, such as those shown in Table 25.5, should clearly identify expectations of on-site supervisors. On-site supervisors should be expected to define the role of the intern at the entity, to provide a work environment orientation and training in the company's policies and procedures, and to provide professional work experiences and appropriate supervision for the student. Interns should be paid a salary commensurate with their job responsibilities.

Table 25.4 Internship paper components

Overview of the Professional Field

– Duties and Responsibilities
– Required Knowledge, Skills, and Attributes
– Salary Ranges
– Career Opportunities

Overview of the Company or Firm

– Brief History and Mission
– Overview of Products and/or Services Provided
– Organizational Chart
– Company Policies
– Expected Performance and Ethical Standards
– Description of Tasks Performed, Including Procedures and Responsibilities
– Computer Hardware and Software and Other Equipment Used
– Relevant Business Terminology Used
– Summary Time and Activities Log

Reaction to Internship

– Employment and Orientation Process
– Intern Evaluation Process
– Co-Worker Relationships
– Supervisor Relationships
– Benefits Gained Through Internship Experience

Evaluation of Internship and Traditional Classroom Components

– Discuss Coursework or Activities Most Valuable in Preparation for Internship
– Identify Coursework or Activities Wish Had Completed Before Internship Suggested Changes in
  Curriculum or Activities to Strengthen Overall Programme and Internship Programme

---

Source: D.F. Beard (2007) Assessment of Internship Experiences and Accounting Core Competencies, Accounting Education: an international journal, 16(2), 207–220, reprinted with permission of Taylor & Francis, Ltd, http://www.tandf.co.uk/journals.

On-site supervisors should also provide feedback to the intern during the internship and complete an assessment form that can be used to assess the performance of the student and reflect on the preparation of that student by the academic programme. Cook *et al.* (2011) encouraged practitioners to provide feedback to interns about their soft skills performance. The student's promptness, dependability, professional appearance, initiative, maturity, self-confidence, time management skills, oral and written communication skills, and the ability to work with others as a member of a team should be assessed by the on-site supervisor. Beard (2007) provided the sample internship supervisor evaluation form shown in Figure 25.2.

25.3.3 Expectations for university and programme personnel

Successful internship programmes should not operate on 'auto-pilot' and are not created overnight. Connections with the professional community and alumni should be cultivated. Academic advisors, educators, and administrators should know their students and have efficient means for communicating with them. Appropriate prerequisites, including grade requirements and prior course work, should be clearly communicated to potential candidates for internships.

Intern's Name_____

Intern Supervisor's Name _____

Name of Employing Company _____

Semester Internship Completed _____

Please indicate, using the scale below, your self-evaluation on the traits listed:

5 = Outstanding 4 = Above Average 3 = Average 2 = Below Average 1 = Poor

	5	4	3	2	1
Promptness					
Dependability					
Professional Appearance					
Initiative					
Maturity					
Self-Confidence					
Time Management					
Written Communication Skills					
Oral Communication Skills					
Ability to Work with Others					
Acceptance of Criticism					
Overall Performance					

Circle those traits above that you think improved significantly during the internship

Please answer the following questions and sign the self-assessment form:

1. What do you consider to be the most beneficial aspect(s) of your internship experience?

2. What do you consider to be the least beneficial aspect(s) of your internship experience?

3. What effect did this internship have on your future career goals?

4. Would you recommend this internship site to a future intern? Explain.

5. Do you have any suggestions for improving the internship programme?

Student's Signature _____

Figure 25.1 Student's Self-Evaluation and Programme Evaluation Form

Source: D.F. Beard (2007) Assessment of Internship Experiences and Accounting Core Competencies, Accounting Education: an international journal, 16(2), 207–220, reprinted with permission of the publisher Taylor & Francis, Ltd, http://www.tandf.co.uk/journals.

Table 25.5 Employer's guidelines for intern supervision

The supervision of an intern provides the opportunity to play a significant role in the learning experience of a future professional. You provide an important link between the student, the company, and the university. At a minimum, the supervisor at the employing company should assume responsibility for completing the following:

- Define the role of the intern and communicate this role to the intern and co-workers.
- Provide the intern with an appropriate orientation to the company, the work environment, and company policies and procedures. Suggested topics to include: company history, mission, and organization; overview of products and/or services; expected performance standards; office etiquette and attire; work hours; telephone manners; availability of supplies; confidentiality; and process for resolution of ethical dilemmas.
- Provide meaningful and challenging work experiences relating to the intern's academic and career goals, with adequate supervision and resources.
- If possible, schedule work activities that allow the intern to gain broad exposure to the professional field as well as develop proficiency in more narrow tasks.
- Schedule regular supervisory meetings with the intern to enable the student to ask questions, resolve problems, report on his/her progress, receive training and instructions, and receive advice related to his/her future career plans.
- At the end of the internship, an exit interview should be conducted with the intern to discuss the Supervisor's Evaluation Form. This form should be signed and mailed to the Department of Accounting Chairperson in the pre-addressed envelope.
- Notify the Department Chairperson immediately of any problems, or if you have questions or suggestions.

Source: D.F. Beard (2007) Assessment of Internship Experiences and Accounting Core Competencies, Accounting Education: an international journal, 16(2), 207–220, reprinted with permission of the publisher Taylor & Francis, Ltd, http://www.tandf.co.uk/journals.

In addition, an orientation focussing on professional dress, demeanour, and ethical behaviour should be provided to students. On-going communication should occur between the intern and on-campus supervisors.

Administrators should consider the impact of internships on educators, and should identify an internship programme director or coordinator who will assume primary responsibility for the internship programme. Contact information for that individual which is readily available to students, accounting professionals, educators, and alumni should be provided. Release time or additional compensation should be considered for the internship director or coordinator. Reward systems should include incentives for educators significantly involved in supporting the internship programme.

It should be recognized that preparing students for internships requires a team effort not only by accounting educators. Other university personnel (e.g. Student Services staff) should provide assistance in disseminating information about internships and in preparing students seeking internships. At Southeast Missouri State University, career exploration and preparation are integrated through the entire four-year undergraduate degree experience. The process begins in the student's freshman year and continues through to graduation as a vehicle for creating an awareness of careers available to students and the expectations for successful transitioning into the workplace. Students work with academic staff and Student Services professionals to create a career development plan, to make career assessments, and to search for internship opportunities. Career advising and various career events, seminars, and professional speaker presentations provide insights into the workplace expectations, including work ethic, ethical behaviour, and professional

Student's Name_____   Major_____

Employer_____   Location_____

Employer's Signature_____

INSTRUCTIONS: The immediate supervisor should evaluate the student objectively, comparing him/her with other students of comparable academic level, with other personnel assigned the same or similar positions, or with individual standards.

Attitude/Application to Work
_____ Enthusiastic
_____ Very interested and industrious
_____ Average in diligence and interest
_____ Somewhat indifferent
_____ Definitely not interested

Initiative
_____ Proceeds well on his/her own
_____ Frequently works well on own
_____ Does all assigned work
_____ Hesitates
_____ Must be pushed frequently

Dependability
_____ Completely dependable
_____ Above average in dependability
_____ Usually dependable
_____ Sometimes neglectful or careless
_____ Unreliable

Maturity, Poise
_____ Poised and confident
_____ Has good self-assurance
_____ Average maturity and poise
_____ Infrequent self-assertion
_____ Timid
_____ Brash

Judgment
_____ Exceptionally mature judgment
_____ Above average
_____ Usually makes right decision
_____ Often uses poor judgment
_____ Consistently uses bad judgment

Ability to Learn
_____ Learned tasks very well
_____ Learned work readily
_____ Average in understanding work
_____ Rather slow in learning
_____ Very slow to learn

Quality of Work
_____ Excellent
_____ Very good
_____ Average
_____ Below average
_____ Very poor

Relations with Others
_____ Exceptionally well-accepted
_____ Works well with others
_____ Gets along satisfactorily
_____ Difficulty working with others
_____ Works very poorly with others

Quantity of Work
_____ Unusually high output
_____ More than average
_____ Normal quantity
_____ Below average
_____ Low output and slow

Attendance
_____ Regular
_____ Irregular

Punctuality
_____ Regular
_____ Irregular

Overall Performance (Please Circle One)
OUTSTANDING   VERY GOOD   AVERAGE   MARGINAL   UNSATISFACTORY

List the student's outstanding personal qualities on a separate sheet.

List the personal qualities which the student should strive most to improve on a separate sheet.

Figure 25.2 Internship supervisor's evaluation

Source: D.F. Beard (2007) Assessment of Internship Experiences and Accounting Core Competencies, Accounting Education: an international journal, 16(2), 207–220, reprinted with permission of the publisher Taylor & Francis, Ltd, http://www.tandf.co.uk/journals.

demeanour, and etiquette. Résumé and covering letter preparation, mock interviews, and job search techniques should be integrated into co-curricular or extra-curricular activities.

As more accounting students and educators recognize the benefits of internships and more geographically diverse worksites are chosen, students may wish or need to complete other coursework while undertaking the internship. Accounting programme administrators should work with educators in considering flexibility in course offerings and means of delivery which allow students to complete an internship and still stay on track in completing their degree. For example, 8-week classes and on-line or hybrid courses might be considered. Certainly, technological advances are making these options more feasible: see Boritz & Stoner, Chapter 16 – this volume.

Internship sites and experiences should be evaluated on an on-going basis. Periodic visits to the internship site, where feasible, should be made by university personnel. And, as mentioned earlier, the internship process should be integrated into the accounting programme's assessment strategy. The results of those assessments should be analyzed, and appropriate action taken to improve the internship programme, the accounting programme, and students' preparation for the internship.

25.3.4 Internships and programme assessment

Internships can be an important component in programme assessment. From the accounting programme's viewpoint, programme assessment by students and internship employers (practitioners) is one of the benefits of integrating internships into the accounting programme. Internships can provide important relevant feedback about the programme's preparation of students for professional positions and can lead to programme improvement, increased student recruitment, and provide data for the assurance of the learning process.

When focussing on the assurance of learning, accounting educators should continue to seek and gain insight into what is expected by the accounting profession. From there, goals and objectives consistent with the mission can be identified, intended learning outcomes (ILOs) developed, pedagogy and instructional activities selected, measurement methods of students' learning established, and programme success judgement parameters solidified. The internship process can be valuable in identifying goals and objectives, providing an alternative and effective pedagogy, and in measures of students' learning and programme success. Feedback from internship supervisors and students completing internships can provide useful assessment data not only for the internship programme, but also for the accounting programme overall.

Several studies undertaken in the U.S.A. (e.g. Herring & Izard, 1992; Demong et al., 1994; Gainen & Locatelli, 1995; Akers et al., 1997; Lusher, 2010) have offered guidance in designing and implementing an Accounting Assessment Program. Others (Mason & Allaway, 1985; Hill et al., 1998; Cook et al., 2004; Beard, 2007; Beard et al., 2008; Beck & Halim, 2008; Verney et al., 2009; AICPA, 2011; Hogan et al., 2012; Elrod & Tiggeman, 2012) have indicated how internship assessments and surveys of accounting students can be used in programme assessment and educators' evaluations. Supervisors' evaluations, time and activity records, and students' reflection and self-assessment can provide cost-effective inputs into the assessment of learning and students' professional performance and demeanour. (More discussion on assessing an accounting programme can be found in Kidwell & Lowensohn, Chapter 21, and Calderon, Chapter 22 – both in this volume.)

In addition to requisite accounting and business knowledge, academicians have recognized that the professional workplace requires written and oral communication skills, critical thinking and problem-solving skills, and effective interpersonal and team skills. Internships can be an important component in developing and in assessing those skills. Beard, Schwieger, & Surendran (2008) revealed how internships can be integrated into the assessment of soft skills. They provided a model for assurance of learning and activities relating to assessment that are consistent with a programme's mission, accountability, and continuous improvement. Internship programme activities utilized at their institution included weekly e-mails, a student diary/journal, a final paper, an oral presentation, a self-assessment survey, a supervisor's evaluation, and a supervisors' survey. (Broader discussions of skills needed by accounting professionals can be found in Watty, Chapter 13, and Cunningham, Chapter 18 – both in this volume.)

25.4 Current status and considerations relating to internships

Strong support for offering internships to develop and expand competencies and to assist in a seamless transition to the professional workplace has come from many individuals, professional organizations, and institutions. Research has revealed that there are benefits to students, practitioners, and academic programmes and institutions. As a result, internships are becoming an integral part of an accounting education. Some universities (such as University of Texas – Austin, and Butler University, both in the U.S.A.) require an internship as part of their accounting degree. Other universities (such as the University of Missouri, the University of Mississippi, and Southeast Missouri State University, also in the U.S.A.) have modified their curricula or course delivery format to create a more conducive environment for non-local student internships. Cooperation between and among students, practitioners, and educators gives students more opportunities for a meaningful internship experience. Research indicates that students have more employment opportunities and success in their professional careers if they complete an internship during their college education (Beard, 1998; Cannon & Arnold, 1998; Siegel & Rigsby, 1988; Pasewark *et al.*, 1989; Siegel *et al.*, 1992; Callanan & Benzing, 2004; Hazelwood, 2004; Mauldin *et al.*, 2006; Beck & Halim, 2008; Cook *et al.*, 2011; Green *et al.*, 2011). Students want – and may soon demand – internships to enable them to better compete in the job market. Practitioners want the opportunity to preview the knowledge, skills, and professionalism of student interns prior to full-time employment offers. Universities want their accounting students to obtain meaningful accounting positions upon graduation. With all the positive benefits of internships and increased interest in using internship experiences in hiring decisions, the need for accounting internships should grow.

25.4.1 Current status of internships

Internships, as a part of experiential and work-related learning, continue to vary in availability, requirements, and structure. Beard (1998) surveyed accounting administrators in the U.S.A. and reported that most internship programmes were fairly young at that time, were for credit without a grade, occurred during the third year of education, were remunerated, and required that a written project be completed at the end of the internship. Nearly 80 per cent of the programmes only allowed students to earn six hours or less of academic credit for internships. Most programmes did not have full- or part-time coordinators, did not require on-site visits, and shared the responsibility for identifying internship sites with students and others. More recently, Thompson (2011) questioned accounting programme administrators in the U.S.A. to gain insight into the current status of internship programmes in accounting. Thompson reported that:

- 80 per cent of the respondents indicated that students were only eligible to participate in an internship in their third or fourth year of education.

- Over 90 per cent of internships were secured from students' initiatives, followed by those of the Accounting Department, and then those of the Placement Office.
- 86 per cent of the programmes offered credit for the internship.
- 92 per cent of the respondents reported that students had to write a paper at the end of the internship, but only 24 per cent maintained a daily log of work activities.
- 80 per cent of the respondents required that the sponsoring, on-site supervisors complete an evaluation of students' performance.

None of the respondents reported requiring students to complete a self-evaluation form (Thompson, 2011).

25.4.2 Components of successful internship programmes

Research and experience support the importance of structure for successful internship programmes. Hergert (2009) reported increased value from internships that were integrated into their academic programme, designed to meet students' career development needs, and had a specific structure. Beard (2007) suggested components of a structured internship. These components included employers' guidelines for intern supervision, internship programme requirements, and assessment instruments for the students and the on-site supervisors to be completed at the end of the internship. She also recommended that internship programmes should involve a process that includes the establishment of academic requirements for internship eligibility, an application process that includes a résumé and interview, and identification of goals and objectives of the internship. Assessments by the students and the on-site supervisors should be required.

In considering the components of successful internship programmes, several questions concerning expectations should be answered. These questions should explore the expectations of students' preparation, students' performance, on-site supervisors, and university/accounting programme administrators.

25.4.3 Considerations in adding an accounting internship programme to the curriculum

As programmes consider on-going curriculum design, a consideration of how and when to integrate experiential learning opportunities, especially internships, is warranted. The following are among several questions that should be asked, discussed, and answered:

1 Are suitable work sites available?
2 Will internships be required or optional?
3 Should academic credit be awarded for internships?
4 Will students receive a grade for the internship or only pass/fail?
5 What, if any, prerequisites (e.g. courses, GPA, and year of study) for the internship will be required?
6 What will be required of students during and at completion of the internship?
7 Should interns be remunerated by the sponsoring entity?
8 Who will be responsible for identifying, choosing, and evaluating workplace sites?
9 Will academic staff resources be allocated to coordinating and supervising interns?
10 Will on-site visits by academic staff be required or suggested?
11 Will trade-offs be required between internships and other courses being offered?

12   Do we accommodate students who are away from campus but want or need to complete additional courses during the period of the internship?

Academic staff and administrative staff will not all agree on the answers to the above questions, and will identify other issues and considerations for their institutions. However, by examining the research and other published works relating to internships, those involved in the design, implementation, and evaluation of an internship programme will have a starting point from which to work.

25.4.4 The impact of technology on internships

Technology impacts on internships in several ways. Technology has increased the visibility and accessibility to information concerning internships. Organizations with internships can provide job descriptions and contact information readily on their websites. Students, educators, practitioners, and administrators may utilize databases, e-mail, and social media to share information relating to internships. Many students seeking an internship now have greater access to internship opportunities. Students in remote areas or at universities with few or no campus visits by recruiters can have access to information concerning internship opportunities and the application procedures. Students can place their résumés online through professional organizations and professionally-focussed social media.

Accounting educators and administrators can connect with practitioners, especially alumni and other programme constituencies, using technology. Electronic communications allow on-campus personnel to stay in touch with on-site supervisors and to develop internship opportunities with other professionals.

Technology also enhances communication during internship experiences among students, educators, and practitioners. E-mail, forums, and other social media can be integrated into the internship process. During the internship, students, on-campus supervisors, and on-site supervisors can stay in touch and assess progress toward goals and objectives for the internship. Students can provide updates and reflections of their experiences and share their experiences with academic staff and other students. Depending on tools utilized, connections between interns can be developed where all share their experiences, knowledge gained, and challenges faced. Students and on-campus supervisors could offer ideas or suggestions on how to address each other's challenges. Of course, confidentiality should be maintained and client privacy should be protected.

Consequently, there can be several benefits from using technology in the administration of internships. Students' motivation should be increased and perception of an accounting career improved when students have greater access to information relating to accounting career paths, to accounting firms, and to internships. Students can more quickly receive information about the requirements of internship programmes, internship sites' availability, and contact information.

Students, academic staff, practitioners, and administrators have begun to recognize the opportunities and threats that result from these emerging technologies and tools. Today's students are accustomed to multi-tasking with the use of technology. Cell phones, iPads, Facebook, Twitter, and YouTube have changed the ways in which students communicate and complete tasks. Students should be advised as to the appropriateness of postings through Facebook, Twitter, and other social media. Prospective employers and internship site supervisors are increasingly utilizing this information in their decision process. Jobvite (2012) reported results from a global survey of human resource and recruiting professionals with over 1,000 respondents stating that 86 per cent of hiring firms look at prospective hires' social profiles and they negatively interpret references to drugs, sexual activities, profanity, spelling/grammar errors, and alcohol.

Opportunities for completing internships outside the summer months have increased as some institutions have expanded or replaced course offerings in the traditional, face-to-face classroom setting with online or hybrid course delivery. As students demand more internship opportunities, additional changes in course delivery may be needed. Students may wish to enrol in online courses while completing internships off campus. Demands for different course configurations, timing, and delivery of classes can provide challenges in staffing classes. Academic staff workloads, online course security issues, and trade-offs between internship hours allowed and traditional course requirements and electives must be considered.

Internships also provide opportunities to identify information technology (IT) competencies desired by the professional workplace. These IT competencies then, where feasible, can be built into the accounting and supporting disciplines and assessed during the internship. Internships can provide opportunities to use spreadsheets, databases, computer-assisted auditing techniques, tax software, and Internet-based tools. Internships can also provide opportunities to enhance the IT competencies of accounting students by their being exposed to emerging and cutting-edge technology in the professional workplace which may not be available to them on campus. Interns may have the opportunity to view and gain insights into accounting systems, social networks, and internal control frameworks. (See Boritz & Stoner, Chapter 16 – this volume.)

25.4.5 Internships' impact on the accounting profession's sustainability

Strategic planning and the implementation of accounting curricula, co-curricular activities, and processes for transitioning students from the classroom to the professional workplace are vital to sustaining accounting programmes that prepare students to enter a global business setting with extreme competition for professional opportunities. Accounting internships have been shown to improve one's success as an accounting professional, give real-world business experience, and help aspiring professionals more easily transition to full-time work (see list of students' benefits and citations in Table 25.1). Accounting programmes and educators should foster instructional strategies and activities that assure students' learning and prepare graduates for successful careers. Students completing accounting internships show enhanced communication, critical-thinking, problem-solving, interpersonal and team skills (see list of students' benefits and citations in Table 25.1) which are all necessary skills for success in the business world. Accounting educators and accounting practitioners should be urged to cultivate both formal and informal opportunities to network and to share their perceptions of the knowledge, skills, and professional attitudes required to sustain the profession and our accounting programmes. Accounting internships are one avenue of communication between educators and practitioners (Beard, 1998; Cook et al., 2004; Beck & Halim, 2008).

Attracting the best and brightest students with the aptitude and traits to succeed in our accounting programmes and in the accounting profession is of paramount importance to the accounting programme and the accounting profession's capability and sustainability. Recruiting students to our accounting programmes requires an accurate portrayal of the profession. Internships can be an effective way for students to gain insight into the accounting profession (Chandra & Paperman, 1983; Ali et al., 2008). Recruiting activities can use internship experiences to 'tell the story' and to demonstrate to stakeholders that we are connected to the profession and to support students' success. (See Laswad & Tan, Chapter 9, and Jackling, Chapter 10 – both in this volume, for discussions of factors influencing the choice of Accounting as a major, and the choice of Accounting as a career, respectively.)

Internships can provide opportunities for students to experience firsthand what accountants do. Turner (2006) recommended that internships be required to bring more practical experiences into the classroom. Kranacher (2006) suggested that internships be required to help meet public expectations with respect to competence and ethical behaviour.

Preparing a student for an internship can involve activities and discussions that are not only relevant to the internship, but also for successful entry to the profession and success in an accounting career. The internship process can provide an important pathway for transitioning accounting students from the classroom to the professional work-setting.

25.4.6 Regulatory and legal considerations

Swift & Russell (1999) identified several regulatory and legal areas that should be considered when participating in an internship programme in the U.S.A. These areas included compensation, workmen's compensation, unemployment insurance, Equal Employment Opportunity Commission (EEOC) guidelines, and general liability issues.

The United States Department of Labor (2012), and its U.K. counterpart, have been stepping up the regulation of unpaid internships for students. Most organizations are unaware that student interns are normally considered employees under the Fair Labor Standards Act, and are entitled to minimum wage and overtime pay, unless they meet certain criteria. Offering college credit does not necessarily mean that wage and hour regulations do not apply. There have been exceptions for individuals who perform voluntary services for a state or local government or for humanitarian, religious, charitable, and civic service for some non-profit organizations. An understanding of the Fair Labor Standards Act is important in the U.S.A. The regulations and laws of each country, territory, or state should be researched and communicated to internship participants.

The remaining chapters in this book all impact on the use of internships in accounting education. Various institutional considerations for improving accounting education and professional training are discussed by Sundem in Chapter 27, and by Apostolou & Gammie in Chapter 29. The interface between academic education and professional training in accounting is further examined by Evans in Chapter 28 and finally, in Chapter 30, Paisey & Paisey assess the state of professional accounting education and training.

25.5 Conclusion and implications for future research

Internships should be considered on the agenda for improving accounting education for many reasons. Internships involve students, practitioners, and educators in the educational process, and provide opportunities for interactions and collaborations between and among these groups. Internships can impact on students' perceptions of accounting careers, and assist students in evaluating their compatibility with those careers. Generic and cognitive skills can be enhanced and assessed during internship experiences. Internships can be integrated into accounting curricula, offer an alternative pedagogy, be a valuable component of programme assessment, and contribute to students' success in the classroom and in transitioning to the professional workplace. Internships can serve as an important interface between academic education and professional training in accounting.

Some implications for future research should be recognized. On-going research should be undertaken to identify changing expectations of the accounting profession, how these impact on accounting education, and what role internships play in gathering this information and in assessing success in meeting expectations. Students' perceptions of accounting careers prior to and after completing an internship should be collected and studied. Comparisons of performance in the academic setting and in the professional environment subsequent to graduation for students completing an internship with those not completing an internship should be studied. The relationships among students' completion of an accounting internship, students' satisfaction with the accounting programme, and placement rates should also be examined.

Research which identifies and shares best practices in designing, implementing, and assessing internship programmes and students' performance should continue. Additionally, research projects querying practitioners as to the value of internships and practitioners' preferences should be undertaken. This research should provide information concerning:

- the importance of internships in recruiting and transitioning accounting graduates to the profession;
- the preferred prerequisites for the internship;
- the timing and duration of internships; and
- the practitioners' perceptions of the benefits of internships to students, sponsoring entities, institutions of higher learning, and to the future of the accounting profession.

Research should provide valuable insights into internships and their potential impact on change in accounting education.

References

Accounting Education Change Commission (AECC) (1990) Objectives of education for accountants: position statement number one, *Issues in Accounting Education*, 5(2): 307–312.

Akers, M., Giacomino, D., & Trelsky, J. (1997) Designing and implementing an accounting assessment program, *Issues in Accounting Education*, 12(2), 259–280.

Albrecht, W. S. & Sack, R.J. (2001) The perilous future of accounting education, *The CPA Journal*, 71(3), 16–23.

Ali, A.M., Heang, L., Mohammed, R., & Ojo, M. (2008) Internship and audit expectation gap among undergraduate students in universiti utara Malaysia, *Journal of Financial Reporting and Accounting*, 6(1), 55–74.

American Accounting Association (AAA) (1952) Report of the Committee on Internship Programs, *The Accounting Review*, July, 316–323.

American Institute of Accountants (AIA) and American Accounting Association on Accounting (AAA) Personnel and Committee on Faculty Residency and Internship Programs (1955) Statement of standards and responsibilities under public accounting internship programs, *The Accounting Review*, 30(2), 206–210.

American Institute of Certified Public Accountants (AICPA) (2011) *Guidelines for Achieving AICPA Core Competencies Through Experiential Learning Programs*, available at: http://www.aicpa.org/interestareas/accountingeducation/resources/pages/internshipexperientiallearning.aspx (accessed 20 April 2013).

Arlinghaus, B. (2002) The environment for professional interaction and relevant practical experience in AACSB-accredited accounting programs, *Journal of Education for Business*, 78(1), 38–45.

Association to Advance Collegiate Schools of Business (AACSB) (2011) *Eligibility Procedures And Accreditation Standards for Business Accreditation*, AACSB International, The Association to Advance Collegiate Schools of Business, available at: http://www.aacsb.edu/accreditation/standards-2011-revised-jan2011-final.pdf (accessed October 2011).

Association to Advance Collegiate Schools of Business (AACSB) (2012) *AACSB Establishes a New Curriculum Series to Address Major Challenges of Curriculum Reform*, available at: http://www.aacsb.edu/publications/enewsline/curriculum_development (accessed 6 October 2012).

Beard, D.F. (1998) The status of internships/cooperative education experiences in accounting education, *Journal of Accounting Education*, 16(3), 507–516.

Beard, D.F. (2007) Assessment of internship experiences and accounting core competencies, *Accounting Education: an international journal*, 16(2), 207–220.

Beard, D., Schwieger, D., & Surendran, K. (2008) Integrating soft skills assessment through university, college, and programmatic efforts at an AACSB accredited institution, *Journal of Information Systems Education*, 19(2), 229–240.

Beck, J. & Halim, H. (2008) Undergraduate internships in accounting: what and how do Singapore interns learn from experience?, *Accounting Education: an international journal*, 17(2), 151–172.

Bloom, R. & Myring, M. (2008) Charting the future of the accounting profession, *The CPA Journal*, 78(6), 65–67.

Brown-Liburd, H. & Porco, B.M. (2011) It's what's outside that counts: do extracurricular experiences affect the cognitive moral development of undergraduate accounting students?, *Issues in Accounting Education*, 26(2), 439–454.

Buck, R. (1992) From academic to corporate, *Management Accounting*, 73(9), 52–53.

Burnett, S. (2003) The future of accounting education: a regional perspective, *Journal of Education for Business*, 78(3), 129–134.

Callanan, G. & Benzing, C. (2004) Assessing the role of internships in the career-oriented employment of graduating college students, *Journal: Education & Training*, 46(2) 82–89.

Cannon, J. & Arnold, M. (1998) Student expectations of collegiate internship programs in business: a 10-year update, *Journal of Education for Business*, 73(4), 202–205.

Cerne, K. & Zenzerovi, R. (2011) Academic and professional community cooperation in function of accountants' university education improvement, *Ekonomska Israzivanja*, 24(1), 213–226.

Chandra, G. & Paperman, J. (1983) Accounting internships and CPA firms, *The CPA Journal*, 53(9), 75–76.

Coco, M. (2000) Internships: a try before you buy arrangement, *S.A.M. Advanced Management Journal*, 65(2), 41–45.

Cook, G., Bay, D., Visser, B., Myburgh, J. & Njoroge, J. (2011) Emotional intelligence: the role of accounting education and work experience, *Issues in Accounting Education*, 26(2), 267–286.

Cook, S., Parker, R., & Pettijohn, C. (2004) The perceptions of interns: a longitudinal case study, *Journal of Education for Business*, 79(3), 179–185.

Cord, B., Bowrey, G., & Clements, M. (2010) Accounting students: reflection on a regional internship program, *Australian Accounting Business and Finance Journal*, 4(3), 47–64.

Cord, B. & Clements, M. (2010) Pathway for student self-development: a learning orientated internship approach, *Australian Journal of Adult Learning*, 50(2), 287–307.

Cord, B., Sykes, C., & Clements, M. (2011) Who cares wins: owning the learning transition, *Development and Learning in Organizations*, 25(4), 20–22.

CPA Australia, Get started in the industry, available at: http://www.cpaaustralia.com.au/cps/rde/xchg/cpa-site/hs.xsl/become-accounting-internships.htm. (accessed 12 March 2013).

Crumley, D. & Sumners, G. (1998) How businesses profit from internships, *The Internal Auditor*, 55(5), 54–58.

DeFilippes, R.A. (1982) Internship in small practice, *The CPA Journal*, January, 81–82.

Demong, R.F., Lindgreen, J.H., & Perry, S.E. (1994) Designing an assessment program for accounting, *Issues in Accounting Education*, 9(1), 11–27.

Dennis, A. (1996) The next generation, *Journal of Accountancy*, 182(6), 89–92.

Ebied, H. (2004) An empirical investigation of the impact of the student accounting internships on subsequent academic performance: the case of UAE university, *Journal of Economic and Administrative Sciences*, 20(2), 33–44.

Elrod, H. & Tiggeman, T. (2012) Using internship results as assessment of accounting outcomes, *Journal of Case Studies in Accreditation and Assessment*, 2, 1–11.

English, D.M. & Koeppen, D. R. (1993) The relationship of accounting internships and subsequent academic performance, *Issues in Accounting Education*, 8(2), 292–299.

Fesler, R.D. & Caldwell, C.W. (2001) The accounting internship: reasons and advice, *New Accountant*, 17(1), 9–11.

Gainen, J. & Locatelli, P. (1995) *Assessment for the New Curriculum: A Guide for Professional Accounting Programs*, Sarasota, FL: American Accounting Association and Accounting Education Change Commission.

Goodman, L. (1982) Internship programs: what CPA firms should know, *Journal of Accountancy*, 154(4), 112–114.

Green, B.P., Graybeal, P. & Madison, R. L. (2011) An exploratory study of the effect of professional internships on students' perception of the importance of employment traits, *Journal of Education for Business*, 86(2), 100–110.

Hazelwood, K. (2004) Internships: never more important, *Business Week Online*, February 3.

Henry, E.G. (2002) Setting up a student internship with a university, *National Public Accountant*, April/May, 23–24.

Hergert, M. (2009) Student perceptions of the value of internships in business education, *American Journal of Business Education*, 2(8), 9–13.

Herring, H.C. III & Izard, C.D. (1992) Outcomes assessment of accounting majors, *Issues in Accounting Education*, 7(1), 1–17.

Hill, N., Perry, S., & Stein, D. (1998) Using accounting student surveys in an outcomes assessment program, *Issues in Accounting Education*, 13(1), 65–78.

Hiltebeitel, K.M., Leauby, B.A., & Larkin, J.M. (2000) Job satisfaction among entry-level accountants, *The CPA Journal*, May, 76–78.

Hogan, E., Lusher, A., & Mondal, S. (2012) Development of an instrument for indirect assessment of college business programs, *Journal of Case Studies in Accreditation and Assessment*, 2:1–15.

Institute of Internal Auditors (IIA) (n.d.) *Global Model Internal Audit Curriculum*, available at: https://na.theiia.org/about-ia/Public%20Documents/Global _Model_IA_Curriculum.pdf (accessed 6 October 2011).

International Accounting Education Standards Board (IAESB) (2010) *Handbook of International Education Pronouncements, 2010 Edition*, New York: International Federation of Accountants (IFAC). Available at: http://www.ifac.org (accessed 20 April 2013).

Jeffords, R., Schneidt, M., & Thibadoux, G. (2000) Securing the future, *Journal of Accountancy*, February, 189(2), 49–53.

Jobvite (2012) *Social Recruiting Survey Results 2012*, available at: http://recruiting.jobvite.com/resources/social-recruiting-reports-and trends/ (accessed 24 July 2013).

Kimmel, D. & Kimmel, S. (1988) Internal auditing internships, *The Internal Auditor*, 45(4), 27.

Klein, L. & Levy, E. (1993) The CPA of the future: the role of higher education, *Journal of Education for Business*, March/April, 68, 227–230.

Knechel, W.R. & Snowball, D. (1987) Accounting internships and subsequent academic performance: an empirical study, *The Accounting Review*, 65(4), 799–807.

Koehler, R.W. (1974) The effect of internship programs on subsequent college performance, *The Accounting Review*, April, 382–384.

Kranacher, M. (2006) Regulating the accounting profession, *The CPA Journal*, 76(4), 80.

Lang, A.F. (1979) The value of interns to a regional or local firm, *The Ohio CPA*, 38(4), 162–163.

Lauber, C., Ruh, L., Theuri, P., & Woodlock, P. (2004) Road to the future, *Journal of Accountancy*, 198(1), 41–47.

Lusher, A. (2010) Assessment practices in undergraduate accounting programs, *Journal of Case Studies in Accreditation and Assessment*, 1, 1–20.

Mason, J. & Allaway, A. (1985) More than one way to evaluate a college professor's performance, *Marketing News*, 19(5), 14–16.

Mauldin, S., Morris, J.L., & Zachry, B. (2006) Does student work experience affect CPA firm recruiting decisions?, *The Accounting Educators' Journal*, 16, 41–51.

McCombs, G. & VanSycle, L. (1994) Accounting internships: a win–win arrangement, *National Public Accountant*, 39(5), 21–23.

Mihail, D. (2006) Internships at Greek universities: an exploratory study, *Journal of Workplace Learning*, 18(1/2), 28–41.

National Association of State Boards of Accountancy (NASBA) (2011) *Section 5 of Uniform Accountancy Act (UAA) Model Rules for Education, Revised July, 2011*, available at: http://www.nasba.org (accessed 20 April 2013).

Nelson, I., Bailey, J., & Nelson, A. (1988) Changing accounting education with purpose: market-based strategic planning for departments of accounting, *Issues in Accounting Education*, 13(2), 301–326.

Pasewark, W.R., Strawser, J., & Wilkerson, J. (1989) An empirical examination of the effect of previous internship on interviewing success, *Journal of Accounting Education*, 7(1), 25–40.

Pathways Commission (2012) *The Pathways Commission: Charting a National Strategy for the Next Generation of Accountants*, available at: http://commons.aaahq.org/files/0b14318188/Pathways_Commission_Final_Report_Complete.pdf (accessed 20 April 2013).

Ricchiute, D.N. (1980) Internships and the local practitioner, *Journal of Accountancy*, 150(1), 35–39.

Rothman, M. (2007) Lessons learned: advice to employers from interns, *Journal of Education for Business*, 82(3), 140–144.

Ruh, L. & Theuri, P. M. (2002) Enhancing students' accounting through co-ops with accountants, *National Public Accountant*, April/May, 21–22.

Schmutte, J. (1986) Student internships: a recruiting tool, *The CPA Journal*, 55, 83.

Siegel, G. & Sorensen, J. (1994) What corporate America wants in entry-level accountants, *Management Accounting*, 76(3), 26–31.

Siegel, P., Blackwood, B., & Landy, S. (2010) Tax professional internships and subsequent professional performance, *American Journal of Business Education*, 3(5), 51–59.

Siegel, P., Naser-Tavakolian, M., & O'Shaughnessy, J. (2011) An empirical comparison of internal auditors' performance with or without prior academic internship, *Internal Auditing*, 26(4), 25–31.

Siegel, P. & Rigsby, J. (1988) The relationship of accounting internships and subsequent professional performance, *Issues in Accounting Education*, 3(2), 423–432.

Siegel, P., Rigsby, J., & Shelton, M. (1992) Comparative career performance of accounting professionals in regional CPA firms, *Journal of Business and Entrepreneurship*, 4(1), 1–17.

Swift, C. & Russell, K. (1999) Business school internships: legal concerns, *Journal of Education for Business*, 75(1), 23–26.

Talbott, S.P. (1996) Boost your campus image to attract top grads, *Personnel Journal* (Supplement) 75(3), 6–8.

Thompson, J.H. (2011) A comparative empirical analysis of characteristics associated with accounting internships, *International Journal of Business, Humanities, and Technology*, 1(1), 54–68.

Thorpe-Dulgarian, T. (2008) The impact of internships on accounting students: a Bowie State study 2007, *The Business Review*, 10(1), 281–288.

Turner, L. (2006) In the public interest, *The CPA Journal*, 76(3), 32–37.

United States Department of Labor (2012) *Fact Sheet# 71: Internship Programs under the Fair Labor Standards Act*, available at: http://www.dol.gov/whd/regs/compliance/whdfs71.htm (accessed 20 April 2013).

Verney, T., Holoviak, S., & Winter, S. (2009) Enhancing the reliability of internship evaluations, *The Journal of Applied Business and Economics*, 9(1), 22–33.

Wally-Dima, L. (2011) Bridging the gap between accounting education and accounting practice: the case of the University of Botswana IUP, *Journal of Accounting Research and Audit Practices*, 10(4), 7–27.

Weible, R. (2009) Are universities reaping the available benefits internship programs offer?, *Journal of Education for Business*, 85(2), 59–63.

White, S.D. & Fuller, W.H. (2002) Managing a student internship, *Internal Auditor*, June, 36–41.

About the authors

Deborah F. Beard is Professor of Accounting in the Donald L. Harrison College of Business at Southeast Missouri State University in Cape Girardeau, U.S.A. (dfbeard@semo.edu). Her main research interests are experiential learning, assessment, and information literacy.

Roberta L. Humphrey is Assistant Professor of Accounting in the Donald L. Harrison College of Business at Southeast Missouri State University in Cape Girardeau, U.S.A. (rhumphrey @semo.edu). Her main research interests are the behavioural effects of financial reporting method, and learning methodologies in accounting.

26

Comparative accounting education

Charles H. Calhoun* and Gert H. Karreman**

*UNIVERSITY OF NORTH FLORIDA, U.S.A. **LEIDEN UNIVERSITY, THE NETHERLANDS
AND DEPAUL UNIVERSITY, U.S.A.

CONTENTS

Abstract

This chapter on comparative accounting education is divided into three sections. The focus of Section 26.1 is on general issues which are important for the comparison between countries of accounting education with its components of general and professional education, practical training and experience, and continuing professional development. The international comparability of professional qualifications is discussed in the context of the global financial infrastructure. A core model for accounting education is introduced for the comparison between countries with different characteristics. IFAC's International Education Standards provide benchmarks for the analysis of entry requirements for professional accountants and auditors. Attention is given to selection of countries, international mobility, and comparison of qualifications. Section 26.2 contains short descriptions of qualification requirements in 15 selected countries in five regions: Asia & Pacific, Europe, Latin America, North America, and Sub-Saharan Africa. The final section provides references to website details and printed sources.

Keywords

comparative accountancy education, comparative accounting education, global accountancy education, international education standards (IESs), qualifications of accountants, qualifications of auditors

26.1 General considerations

The main aims of this chapter are:

- to define comparative accounting education;
- to illustrate the relevance of comparative accounting education;
- to present a methodology for the comparison of accounting education in selected countries;
- to demonstrate the use of International Education Standards as benchmarks for international comparison; and
- to compare systems of accounting education in selected countries.

For the purposes of this chapter, comparative accounting education (CAE) is defined as '*the comparison of systems of accounting education between countries*'. Accounting education includes all elements that are necessary for the qualifications and ongoing expertise of professional accountants and auditors: general and professional education, practical training and experience, assessment, and continuing professional development (CPD).

The relevance of comparative accounting education is discussed in Section 26.1.1. The International Education Standards (IES) are introduced as benchmarks for the evaluation of accounting education at the country level. In Section 26.1.2 the contribution of comparative accounting education research to the international debate is discussed. A core model of accounting education that is described in Section 26.1.3 helps to identify all the factors that influence accounting education. The actual use of IESs as global benchmarks for accounting education is worked out in Section 26.1.4. To clarify differences between countries, a pillar structure for accounting education is presented in which a distinction is made between personal development, content of professional accounting education, professional development, and competence for audit professionals. The separate IES come back as milestones of the pillar structure. Approaches to competence and assessment are considered. Central to Section 26.1.5

are the selection of countries and international mobility. Section 26.1.6 compares qualifications from two perspectives: characteristics, and compliance with IES. This is followed by a Conclusion in Section 26.1.7.

Section 26.2 presents overviews of accounting education in 15 selected countries from five regions: Asia & Pacific, Europe, Latin America, North America, and Sub-Saharan Africa. The overviews illustrate for reasons of comparison the differences between countries in legal system, economic position, and educational structure.

26.1.1 Relevance of comparative accounting education

The Financial Crises Advisory Group (28 July, 2009, p. 1) recognizes that:

> *Financial reporting is of great importance to investors and other financial market participants in their resource allocation decisions and to regulators and other users. The confidence of all these users in the transparency and integrity of financial reporting is critically important to global financial stability and sound economic growth.*

Accountants and auditors play a crucial role in this process. Increasingly, international standards address their competence. A wide range of stakeholders (including regulators and standard setters, professional accounting bodies (PABs), and accounting firms, as well as issuers of financial reports and users of accounting services) depend on their professional expertise. Increasingly, providers of education and training are asked to provide programmes that comply with applicable international standards and regulation.

An understanding of accounting education in countries with different economic and legal backgrounds is an important condition for international cooperation and development. At present, mutual recognition of qualifications is relevant for the international mobility of individual accountants and auditors. However, in multinational accounting organizations, international mobility does not depend on recognition alone. Clarifying existing recognition systems will also promote mutual understanding as a basis for international cooperation. In this regard it is important to note that the International Standard on Auditing (ISA) 600[1] requires a group auditor to obtain an understanding of, *inter alia*, the component auditor's professional competence.

The International Federation of Accountants (IFAC)[2] addresses the requirements of the international standards in its *Statements of Membership Obligations* (SMO)[3] that are applicable to PABs (see Exhibit 26.1). All major international standards are covered except the OECD[4] *Principles of Corporate Governance*. According to IFAC, the SMOs provide benchmarks for ensuring high-quality performance by professional accountants. The expertise of accountants is covered in SMO 2 with reference to the IES that are issued by the International Accounting Education Standards Board (IAESB).[5] The IFAC *Handbook of International Education Pronouncements* (IFAC, 2010) covers the *Framework for the IES*, a *Glossary of Terms*, the *IESs 1–8*, and the *International Education Practice Statements* (IEPS) 1–3.

According to IFAC, the IESs establish the essential elements of the content and process of education and development at a level that is aimed at gaining international recognition, acceptance, and application. Recent accounting education research (Phelps, 2011; Karreman, 2013) has confirmed that the IESs can be a powerful tool for the evaluation of accounting education at the country level. As will be shown in this chapter, the IESs can be used as benchmarks for the comparison of accounting education in countries and regions around the world. (See also Sangster, Chapter 15, and Sundem, Chapter 27 – both in this volume.)

Exhibit 26.1 IFAC Statements of Membership Obligations

IFAC SMO 1, Quality Assurance: Quality assurance review programs for audit engagements of financial statements. It applies whether IFAC member bodies carry out such programs on their own behalf, on behalf of the profession, or on behalf of governments, regulators or other agencies, or whether the programs are carried out by another body.

IFAC SMO 2, International Education Standards for Professional Accountants: Obligations of member bodies of IFAC in relation to International Education Standards for Professional Accountants (IES) and related statements issued by the International Accounting Education Standards Board. It applies whether the member bodies issue such standards, or whether the standards are issued by another body.

IFAC SMO 3, International Standards for Quality Control, Audit and Assurance: Obligations of member bodies of IFAC in relation to standards on quality control, auditing and assurance issued by the International Auditing and Assurance Standards Board. It applies whether the member bodies issue such standards, or whether the standards are issued by another body.

IFAC SMO 4, Code of Ethics for Professional Accountants: Obligations of member bodies of IFAC in relation to the IFAC Code of Ethics for Professional Accountants and other pronouncements issued by the International Ethics Standards Board for Accountants. It applies whether the member bodies issue such standards, or whether the standards are issued by another body. Where government, regulators or other appointed bodies perform any of the functions covered by this SMO, member bodies should use their best endeavours to encourage those responsible for those functions to follow this SMO in implementing them.

IFAC SMO 5, International Public Sector Accounting Standards: Obligations of member bodies of IFAC in relation to International Public Sector Accounting Standards and other guidance issued by the International Public Sector Accounting Standards Board. It is to be applied by member bodies of IFAC to public sector accounting standards. Where government, regulators or other appointed bodies perform any of the functions covered by this SMO, member bodies should use their best endeavours to encourage those responsible for those functions to follow this SMO in implementing them.

IFAC SMO 6, Investigation and Discipline, Investigation and discipline of misconduct, including, but not limited to, breaches of professional standards and rules by their individual members (and, if local laws and practices permit, by their member firms). It applies whether the member bodies carry out such programs on their own behalf, on behalf of the profession, or on behalf of governments, regulators or other agencies, or whether the programs are carried out by another body.

IFAC SMO 7, International Financial Reporting Standards: Obligations of member bodies of IFAC in relation to International Financial Reporting Standards (IFRS) issued by the International Accounting Standards Board. Member bodies of IFAC should notify their members of every IFRS. In addition member bodies should use their best endeavours: (a) to incorporate the requirements of IFRSs in their national accounting requirements, or where the responsibility for the development of national accounting standards lies with third parties, to persuade those responsible for developing those requirements to comply with IFRSs.

The results described in this chapter are based on comparison with the current set of IESs. The IAESB is presently in the process of revising and redrafting the eight IESs.[6] As of November 2012, the IAESB has approved IES 1, IES 5, IES 6 and IES 7. The current work plan envisages that all IESs will have been revised and redrafted, or redrafted only, by the fourth quarter of 2013.

The IAESB has provisionally agreed that the revised IESs will be effective for implementation on or after July 2015. The potential influence of the revised IES on the professional qualifications of accountants and auditors is beyond the scope of this chapter.

26.1.2 Comparative accounting education research

Research into CAE as defined in this chapter is a rather small area of academic interest as can be illustrated by consideration of the work of the International Association for Accounting Education and Research (IAAER),[7] and the content of *Accounting Education: an international journal* (*AE*). The focus here on *AE* is due to the fact that the other specialist publications (i.e. *Accounting Educators' Journal*, *Advances in Accounting Education*, *Issues in Accounting Education*, and *Journal of Accounting Education*) are not including international coverage as part of their mission. Consequently, these other publications tend not to publish anything on CAE.

The IAAER administers three major research programmes to inform the following standard-setting bodies:

- International Accounting Standards Board (IASB);
- International Accounting Education Standards Board (IAESB); and
- International Auditing and Assurance Standards Board (IAASB).

The Association of Chartered Certified Accountants (ACCA) collaborates with the IAAER on the second of these programmes, and the research output informs the work of the IAESB. Topics that are addressed in the first round are:

- CPD in the Asia-Pacific Region;
- Ethics Education and Training;
- Non-Technical Skills; and
- IES 2, 3, and 4 Compliance.

In particular, the study of IES 2, 3, and 4 Compliance (Crawford *et al.*, 2010) is of interest for comparative accounting education. The research addresses the extent and impact of IES on university and professional associations' educational programmes for accountants in Australia, Brazil, China, Colombia, India, Italy, Mexico, Russia, Saudi Arabia, Uganda, the U.K., and the U.S.A. In the second round, one of the projects addressed a global model of accounting education and IES compliance in Australia, Japan, and Sri Lanka (Watty *et al.*, 2012).

AE is one of the two official journals of the IAAER. The major aims of the publication illustrate its international approach. They are to do the following:

1 enhance the educational base of accounting practice;
2 promote excellence in accounting education and training;
3 stimulate research in accounting education and training;
4 provide a means of highlighting the contributions of IT;
5 build links among those who teach, train, and employ accounting/finance students;

6   stimulate and develop the international (including comparative) dimensions of accounting education and training; and

7   assist in integrating the various elements of accounting education and training.

The criteria for the award of the British Accounting & Finance Association's Special Interest Group (BAFA-SIG) in Accounting Education Prize for the best paper published each year are:

* a focus on enhancing the educational base of accounting practice;
* a transferable message which goes beyond national or institutional practices; and
* empirical content. (See Wilson, 2013.)

Although the international dimensions of *AE* are specifically mentioned in aim (vi), and in the criteria for the BAFA-SIG prize, CAE research that considers either compliance with the IESs or accounting education in more than one country is rare, as is shown by the review below on this aspect of *AE* Volume 13 (2004), the year that the IES were published, to Volume 21 (2012). (It should be stressed that this review does not seek to be representative of *AE*'s content in general, or to question the journal's editorial stance.)

Some attention is given to the IESs in *AE Briefings* (Saville, 2007), and in two articles (Donovan, 2005; Berg, 2007). Up to and including Volume 21 (2012), no articles or briefings had been published in *AE* which addressed the objectives and content of the new set of draft IESs. However, some attention has been given to the work of the IAAER. The reason why comparative research on accounting education is not regularly published in *AE* is due to the very small number of submissions on this theme. In an earlier analysis of accounting education research in *AE* 13(1), CAE research was not included either (Paisey & Paisey, 2004).

* *AE* 13(3) is a themed issue *Accounting Education in Transitional Economies* (based on Anglo/American notions of accounting and education).
* *AE* 15(4) is a themed issue based on papers from the 2005 AFC/IAAER conference held in Bordeaux but, as a reflection of the papers presented there, none of the published articles addressed CAE.
* Professionalization claims and the state of professional accounting education in the U.K. are discussed in *AE* 16(1) with comments from experts in the U.K., Australia, and New Zealand.
* *AE* 16(2) is a themed issue on *Assessment*, with a briefing on IES 6.
* *AE* 16(4) is a themed issue on CPD with a briefing on IES 7.
* In an Editorial Essay in *AE* 17(2), the case for accounting education research is discussed by Wilson *et al.* (2008).
* The Supplement to *AE* Volume 17 contains a report on the Third IAAER Globalization Roundtable (Needles, 2008a) and a briefing on the code of ethics for accounting educators (Needles, 2008b).
* *AE* 18(4) is a themed issue on the interface between academic education and the professional training of accountants. (See also Evans *et al.*, 2012, and Evans, Chapter 28 – this volume.) Well worth noting in the context of this chapter is a contribution about the experience of the Institute of Chartered Accountants of Scotland (ICAS) with competence-based approaches to the assessment of professional accounting training (Gammie & Joyce, 2009).
* CAE is addressed in two articles in *AE* 19(3): one is about students' approaches to assessment in Australia, Singapore, and Hong Kong (Watty *et al.*, 2010); and the other is

about the role of cultural factors in learning style preferences of accounting students in Australia and Japan (Sugahara & Boland, 2010).

- In *AE* 19(6) there is a conference panel report about the impact of globalization on accounting education (Needles, 2010).

International financial developments depend largely on the expertise of accountants and auditors which, in most countries, is achieved in a combination of academic and professional settings. In a global economy, labour force mobility and the comparability of qualifications have become increasingly important over the last decade. Until now the academic community has hardly participated in this debate, leaving the decisions on professional qualifications to standard setters, regulators, and PABs. There is one field outside the scope of this chapter where the situation is different and in which much academic effort has been invested. This is the field of adoption and implementation of IFRS in which extensive research has been conducted. (See, for example, Wilson & Adler, 2012.)

26.1.3 Core model of accounting education

A core model for accounting education is used for the comparison of accounting education systems in various parts of the world. The model was developed during the first Global Accountancy Education (GAE) classification study (Karreman, 2002), and updated for the GAE 2012 research study (Karreman, 2013) to include all actors relevant to accounting education. The model includes country characteristics and international developments as key influences on the academic and professional elements of accounting education. The core elements of accounting education are placed in the centre of the model. (See Exhibit 26.2.) (Needles discusses modelling accounting education in Chapter 2 – this volume.)

In the model the content of accounting education is directly influenced by the accounting profession which is represented in the middle top row. The accounting profession itself is increasingly influenced by the demands of the global financial infrastructure and by the codification from standard setters and regulators represented at the left and right of the top row. The influence of standards, guidelines, and directives on accounting education is shown in the right middle row. Country characteristics can help to explain major differences between countries, not only in legal system and economic position, but also in the structure of higher education. The demands on accounting education and the roles of accountants and auditors vary greatly as a result of the national legal system and economic position. Moreover, universities and other higher education institutions (HEIs) in general cover a major component of accounting education as part of academic degree programmes. This is summarized in the left middle row.

Accounting education is the basis for accounting in the public interest. The design and delivery of accounting education take place in a complicated structure with stakeholders who may very well have conflicting interests. The stakeholder approach and the need for cooperation are mentioned in the left lower row. It has to be recognized that this cooperation has to take place in settings which have very different country characteristics. This is the core message in the middle lower row of the model. The statement that international networks play an important role in achieving comparability and progress is the final element in the right lower cell of the model.

The country characteristics of accounting education as included in the model can be used to identify differences between countries. The selection is based on an overview used by IFAC for its compliance programme for member bodies:[8]

Exhibit 26.2 Core model of accounting education

Global Financial Infrastructure	Accounting Profession	Standard Setters and Regulators
Professional expertise of accountants and auditors is a necessary condition for the functioning of the global financial infrastructure	IAESB International Education Standards for Qualifications of Professional Accountants and Auditors and IFAC Compliance Program for Professional Accounting Bodies	International, regional, and country standard setters are responsible for IFRS, ISAs and comparable standards that regulate the functioning of the global financial infrastructure
Country Characteristics	*Accounting Education*	*International Developments*
Differences between countries • Cultural background • Legal system • Economic position • Higher education Country characteristics define the regulatory environment and the structure of accounting education in a country	Core elements of accounting education • Professional qualification objective and standards • Final examination of professional competence • Professional education • Practical experience • General education	Codification based on international developments • Standards • Guidelines • Directives IAESB International Education Standards can be used as benchmarks for international comparability and recognition of qualifications
Accounting in the public interest	*Characteristics of accounting education*	*International cooperation*
Stakeholder approach to accounting education • Standard setters • Professional accounting and auditing bodies • Government agencies • Regulators • Donors • Educators • Investors Cooperation between stakeholders is a necessary condition for accounting education that is relevant on the country level and compliant with international standards	Certification requirements: professional accounting education, practical experience, final assessment, CPD Providers: professional accounting bodies, universities and education institutes, government Responsibility: government, government with the profession, professional accounting bodies, universities Licensing: academic study, practical experience, licensing examination, CPD and/or re-examination	Global and regional initiatives • IAAER academic and professional partnership • UNCTAD capacity building initiative • Regional academic associations • Global accounting firms and professional accounting bodies • Twinning International networks play an important role in achieving comparability and progress

Source: Extracts from Karreman, G. (2013) GAE 2012: Dynamics of Global Accountancy Education, published by Tilburg University, and used with permission.

- Certification Requirements: professional accounting education, practical experience, final assessment, CPD;
- Providers: PABs, HEIs, government;
- Responsibility: government, government with the accounting profession, PABs, HEIs;
- Licensing: academic study, practical experience, licensing examination, CPD and/or re-examination

Accounting education can be compared on five levels: regulation, final examination, professional education in combination with practical experience, general education, and life-long learning. In a competence-based approach to accounting education professional standards, important as they may be, cannot be effective without higher-level intended learning objectives (ILOs). (See Watty, Chapter 13 – this volume, and Watty *et al.*, 2012.) The combination of professional standards and ILOs leads to high demands on the resources needed for the initial qualification, education, and training of professional accountants and auditors (i.e. their initial professional development, or IPD), and their CPD.

26.1.4 Comparative accounting education benchmarks

In order to compare accounting education between countries, it is necessary to select and use benchmarks. The only global professional benchmarks are the IESs established by the IAESB. According to the IAESB, the IESs prescribe standards of generally accepted 'good practice' in the education and development of professional accountants. The IESs are intended to advance the profession of accounting by establishing benchmarks for the minimum learning requirements of qualified accountants, including education, practical experience, and CPD. (See Exhibit 26.3.) The IESs are mandatory standards for PABs and are recommended benchmarks for countries. The only set of regional standards is the European Union (EU) requirement for the qualification of audit professionals which is included in the national laws of EU member countries (EU, 1984). Although the requirements for auditors in the IES and according to the EU are comparable, there are two major differences:

1 the EU requires a final qualifying examination at university exit level (not specified), while the IESs do not have general level requirements; and
2 the IESs consider an auditor to be a specialized accountant, whereas the EU has stand-alone requirements for auditors.

For the comparison of countries and regions around the world, the GAE 2012 research study (Karreman, 2013) has developed a benchmarking methodology which uses the IESs as a global benchmark for comparison. The results of the study are an indication that IESs are widely-accepted as benchmarks for accounting education – even by providers who are not obliged to apply the IESs as mandatory standards. Out of a sample of 39 countries from the GAE 2012 study:

- 33 countries consider the IESs as benchmarks at least once in five years;
- in four countries the IESs are not considered in a systemic way; and
- in two (small) countries the IESs are not applicable as they do not have their own system of accounting education.

Another example of the global relevance of the IESs is the fact that the United Nations Conference on Trade and Development (UNCTAD)[9] uses the IESs as benchmarks on a country level for

---

Exhibit 26.3 IFAC International Education Standards

PRE-QUALIFICATION STANDARDS

Entry Requirements for Professional Accounting Education Programs (IES 1)

- IES 1 requires an entry level that is equivalent to that for admission in a recognized university degree program.

Content of Professional Accounting Education (IES 2, 3 and 4)

- IES 2, Content of Professional Accounting Education, is divided in Accounting, Finance & Related Knowledge, Organizational & Business Knowledge, and Information Technology.
- IES 3, Professional Skills and General Education, distinguishes five major areas: intellectual skills, technical and functional skills, personal skills, interpersonal and communication skills, organizational and business management skills.
- IES 4, Professional Values, Ethics and Attitudes, that are necessary to function as a professional accountant.

Practical Experience (IES 5)

- IES 5 requires a minimum period of three years for certification, one of which can be covered by theoretical education.

Assessment (IES 6)

- IES 6 requires a formal assessment before the qualification of professional accountant is awarded.

POST-QUALIFICATION STANDARDS

Continuing Professional Development (IES 7)

- IES 7 describes a CPD requirement as an integral component of a professional accountant's continued membership.

Specialization for Auditors (IES 8)

- IES 8, Competence Requirements for Audit Professionals, requires audit professionals to qualify as a professional accountant, to hold an undergraduate degree or its equivalent, and to satisfy specialization requirements for auditors.

Source: IFAC, (2010) *Handbook of International Education Pronouncements*, available at: www.ifac.org.

---

the evaluation of human capacity building for the global financial infrastructure (UNCTAD, 2010).

The IESs are professional standards with little attention paid to the academic contributions to the qualifications of accountants and auditors. Different approaches can be illustrated with examples from the EU and from the U.S.A. The two examples have in common the fact that attention is given to professional standards and to academic requirements which in the IESs are only mentioned in passing. The relevance of this observation is confirmed in the GAE 2012 research study. In general, the requirements of the IES were accepted as being relevant. However, there were doubts about the limited requirements of the IESs on the general level of education.

In the EU, the Common Content Initiative (CCI)[10] has established cooperation among, at the moment, leading PABs from six countries: France, Germany, Ireland, Italy, the Netherlands, and the U.K. One of its achievements is the agreement on common programme requirements. These should be based on the competence requirements of entry-level accountants and auditors and cover the following areas:

I   International Requirements
II Quality Assurance
III Learning Outcomes
IV Higher Level Skills
V   Academic Level

CCI, in its approach, considers both academic and professional requirements.

In the U.S.A., the National Association of State Boards of Accountancy (NASBA)[11] cooperates with the American Institute of Certified Public Accountants (AICPA)[12] in developing guidelines on the recognition of qualifications. For the comparison of qualifications from other countries, the principle of substantial equivalence with the CPA qualification in the U.S.A. is used for the following areas:

I   Cultural, Business, and Economic Environment
II Education Requirements
III Method and Scope of Professional Examinations and
IV Practical Experience

Once again, this shows a mixture of academic and professional requirements.

The issue of comparability of qualifications is also addressed by the Global Accounting Alliance (GAA).[13] According to its website, the GAA was established to promote quality services, share information, and collaborate on important international issues, while operating in the interest of a quality accounting profession and the public interest. One of its areas of interest is to strengthen the network of Reciprocal Membership and Mutual Recognition Agreements (MRAs). It is interesting to note the diversity in membership, with PABs from both common law and civil law countries, and from those with diverse systems for the qualification of accountants and auditors. Member bodies come from Australia, Canada, Germany, Hong Kong, Ireland, Japan, New Zealand, South Africa, the U.K., and the U.S.A.

For the comparison of accounting education between countries, it is necessary to be aware of the sometimes conflicting requirements at the global, regional, and country level. Moreover, there often are major differences in the relative priorities attached to the academic and professional components necessary for the qualifications of accountants and auditors. In order to bring some order to the comparison, use is made of the pillar structure for accounting education that was developed for the GAE 2012 research study (Karreman, 2013). Taken together, the pillars cover all IESs, as follows:

- Pillar 1: Personal Development (IES 1, 3, 4):

    — university entrance level and academic study
    — professional skills and general education
    — professional values, ethics, and attitudes

- Pillar 2: Professional Accounting Education (IES 2):

  — accounting, finance, and related knowledge
  — organizational and business knowledge
  — information technology

- Pillar 3: Professional Development (IES 5, 6, 7):

  — practical experience requirements
  — assessment of professional capabilities and competence
  — continuing professional development

- Pillar 4: Competence for Audit Professionals (IES 8).

Central to the IESs are the notions of competence and assessment. According to the *Framework for International Education Standards for Professional Accountants* (30 July, 2010, para 12, p. 13) competence is defined as '*the ability to perform a work role to a defined standard with reference to working environments*'. The paragraph goes on to say that candidates '*must possess the necessary (a) professional knowledge, (b) professional skills, and (c) professional values, ethics, and attitude*'.

The IESs follow from this definition. Although competence is defined in a working environment, assessment is not limited to that working environment. According to the Framework (para 30, p. 16): '*competence may be assessed by a variety of means, including workplace performance, workplace simulations, written and oral tests of various types, and self-assessment*'.

IES 6 stipulates (para 2, p. 65) that '*the assessment of professional capabilities and competence should require a significant proportion of candidates' responses to be in recorded form*'.

It is important to consider that different approaches can and do exist between countries. PABs from, for example, Australia, Canada, Hong Kong, South Africa, and the U.K. (Gammie & Joyce, 2009) have done extensive work on competencies and competence maps, and have included the results of these efforts in their testing and education. Other countries give more priority to the academic part of professional qualifications as can be illustrated by two examples:

- According to the Uniform Accounting Act in the U.S.A., an accounting degree is required with 150 academic credit hours.
- In The Netherlands, all *registeraccountants* are required to have a master's degree in Accounting.

Of interest from a research perspective are a critical review of competency-based education and assessment for the accounting profession (Boritz & Carnaghan, 2003), and a study on the usefulness of case studies (Weil *et al.*, 2002).

26.1.5 Selection of countries and international mobility

The selection of countries in this chapter is based on potential interest for the readers of this volume, and on access to available information. The IFAC compliance website has been used as a general source. More specific information is available in the GAE studies (Karreman, 2002, 2007, 2013), and the *Accountancy Development Index* (ADI) pilot project (Phelps, 2011). The characteristics of accounting education are considered for the following countries:

- Asia & Pacific: Australia, Hong Kong, India, Japan, and New Zealand
- Europe: Czech Republic, France, The Netherlands, the U.K. (all from the EU), and Turkey

- Latin America: Brazil and Mexico
- North America: Canada and the U.S.A.
- Sub-Saharan Africa: South Africa.

In the sample, countries have different legal systems, have different levels of economic development, and represent different geographic regions. Countries with middle and lower level economic development are under-represented. One reason is that, for countries with this background, CAE is usually less important than local development. The other reason is a lack of information.

In Section 26.1.6, an overview summarizes the different ways in which professional accountants and auditors are trained and educated in selected countries around the world. A distinction is made between university education and systems that use PABs to provide the accounting education. (See also Van Peursem *et al.*, 2012.)

In recent years, a number of PABs in various countries have taken actions to address the international mobility of professional accountants. One of the most important factors in the acceptance of other countries' professionals is the education which they have received in their 'home' country, especially in accounting and business subjects. When making the decision whether or not to accept professional credentials, most countries seek to determine that the education received in the 'home' country is substantially equivalent to their own. Only if that determination is positive, is it possible to adopt an MRA. As business and financial affairs have become more globalized, the mobility of accounting professionals has become an even more important issue.

In order to address recognition, the Canadian Institute of Chartered Accountants (CICA) formed an International Qualification Appraisal Board (IQAB) to study the 'underpinnings' of the credentialling of professional accountants from other countries, with a view toward granting 'practice rights' to accountants from (some) other countries to work in Canada. Initially, this practice was unilateral, but for several years now, it has been a mutual arrangement. In the early 1990s, with the advent of the North America Free Trade Agreement (NAFTA), the profession in the U.S.A. established its own IQAB, with six members representing NASBA and six representing the AICPA. The US-IQAB is tasked with considering and developing MRAs with the accounting professionals of other countries. No doubt similar bodies exist in countries other than Canada and the U.S.A., be they governmental agencies or PABs given such rights by the government.

The point to be made here is that the education of professional accountants plays a vital role in the international mobility of accounting professionals, and the concept of 'substantial equivalency' of the education of accounting professionals is of great relevance. The education standards pronounced by IFAC's IAESB, the UN's Model Curriculum, and similar pronouncements (if there are any) should provide guidance on the international accounting educational stage.

26.1.6 Comparison of qualifications

The qualifications of accountants and auditors can be compared from two perspectives: (1) by country characteristics; and (2) by compliance with IESs. The information in this chapter is based on the results of the GAE 2012 study (Karreman, 2013).

- Country characteristics: legal system (common law, civil law, mixed); economic position (based on the World Economic Forum (WEF)[14] classification: innovation-driven, efficiency-driven, factor-driven).

- Characteristics of accounting education: certification requirements; providers; responsibility; licensing (discussed in Section 26.1.3).

In the WEF Competitiveness Index, three stages of development are distinguished. These three stages are: factor-driven, efficiency-driven, and innovation-driven. The level of competitiveness increases as a country moves from factor-driven (low-skilled labour and natural resources) to efficiency-driven (more efficient production processes and increased product quality) to innovation-driven (new and different products, services, and processes). Naturally, as a country moves upwards in the WEF classification, the need for accounting services and qualified accountants and auditors will also increase.

Country characteristics are summarized in Table 26.1. Of 15 countries, six have a common law system, seven have a civil law system, and two have mixed legal systems. On the subject of economic development, 10 countries are innovation-driven, four are efficiency-driven, and one is factor-driven. Brazil, Mexico, and Turkey have intermediate positions, all in the process of transition from efficiency-driven to innovation-driven. In the last column of Table 26.1, data sources are mentioned. A distinction is made between previous GAE studies (Karreman, 2002, 2007, 2013), the ADI study (Phelps, 2011), and the World Bank's Report on the Observance of Standards and Codes (ROSC) reports. For each country, a description of the characteristics of accounting education is provided in Section 26.2.

An analysis of adoption and implementation of IESs in 40 countries and six regions is available in the GAE 2012 study. A detailed consideration is beyond the scope of this chapter. In general, a high level of compliance with the IES requirements has been found which, considering the differences between the countries in terms of legal system, economic position and, not least,

Table 26.1 Country characteristics

Country	Legal	Economic	Information
Asia & Pacific			
Australia	Common law	Innovation	GAE 2002, 2007, 2012; ADI
Hong Kong	Mixed	Innovation	GAE 2002, 2007, 2012; ADI
India	Common law	Factor	GAE 2002, 2007, 2012; ROSC 2004
Japan	Civil law	Innovation	GAE 2002, 2007, 2012
New Zealand	Common law	Innovation	GAE 2002, 2007, 2012
Europe			
Czech Republic (EU)	Civil law	Innovation	GAE 2002, 2007, 2012; ADI; ROSC 2003
France (EU)	Civil law	Innovation	GAE 2002, 2007, 2012; ADI
The Netherlands (EU)	Civil law	Innovation	GAE 2002, 2007, 2012; ADI
U.K. (EU)	Common law	Innovation	GAE 2002, 2007, 2012; ADI
Turkey	Civil law	Efficiency	GAE 2002, 2007, 2012; ADI; ROSC 2005
Latin America			
Brazil	Civil law	Efficiency	GAE 2012; ADI; ROSC 2005
Mexico	Civil law	Efficiency	GAE 2002, 2007, 2012; ADI; ROSC 2004
North America			
Canada	Common law	Innovation	GAE 2002, 2007, 2012
U.S.A.	Common law	Innovation	GAE 2002, 2007, 2012; ADI
Sub Saharan Africa			
South Africa	Mixed	Efficiency	GAE 2002, 2007, 2012; ADI; ROSC 2003

their educational systems, is rather surprising, and provides a good basis for further development of international comparison, recognition, and cooperation. The overall results are reproduced in Figure 26.1.

Separate IESs (or sections of IESs) are included in the framework as milestones:

- Professional accounting education: milestones programme components (from IES 2).
- Personal development: milestones (IES 1, IES 3, and IES 4).
- Auditors' competency: milestones programme components (from IES 8).
- Professional development: milestones (IES 5, IES 6, and IES 7).

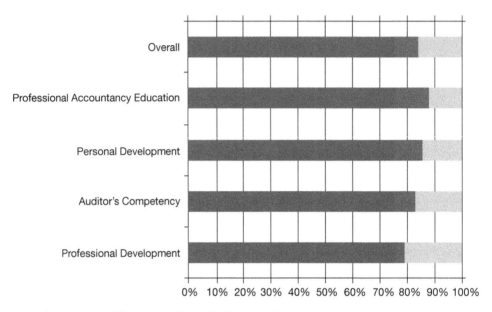

Figure 26.1 Accomplishments and gaps in 40 countries

26.1.7 Conclusion

The qualification of accountants and auditors in most, if not all, countries is based on a combination of academic education and professional education and training. Even for a relatively small sample of 15 countries, the results included in Section 26.2 show how great the differences between countries can be. However, as this chapter also shows, certainly over the last decade, important progress has been made with international comparability and recognition. The IESs were established by the IAESB. They codify good practice for the qualification of accountants and auditors. They are increasingly accepted as benchmarks on a country level.

The IESs concentrate on professional requirements and, in view of differences between countries, give little attention to academic requirements. Through the work of IFAC and others, much is known about the comparability of professional qualifications. Much less is known about the comparability of academic degrees which, increasingly, are the basis for the professional qualifications. Research tends to focus on specific subjects (such as *Financial Accounting* and *Management Accounting*). Building on general recognition systems between universities, it would be of interest to consider the comparability of accounting, auditing, and related business programmes.

This chapter on CAE is intended to show that, working with country characteristics, and by using the IESs as benchmarks, the qualifications of accountants and auditors can be compared to help understanding and promote globally compatible development.

26.2 Accounting education in 15 selected countries

This section provides an overview of accounting education in selected countries (as identified in Table 26.1). Attention is given to certification requirements, to education providers, to responsibility for qualification requirements, and to licensing requirements for auditors and accountants in public practice. Due to major differences between countries, the descriptions cannot be standardized and are not always easy to compare. The overviews are based on:

- consultation of IFAC Compliance Information;[15]
- country reviews which are included in the GAE 2007 and GAE 2012 studies (Karreman, 2007, 2013);
- information on the websites of PABs (if available in English); and
- information supplied by selected international experts.

As with any reference works on this theme (see, for example, Anyane-Ntow, 1992, and Fay, 1992), which can very rapidly become out of date, a similar problem can arise with other cited sources, so details of relevant websites are provided to facilitate easy access to up-to-date information. Most websites also are a source of more detailed descriptions of content and procedures.

26.2.1 Australia

In Australia, two qualifications are considered, the qualification of Certified Practising Accountant (CPA), and the qualification of Chartered Accountant (CA). CPA Australia[16] is responsible for the CPA qualification; the Institute of Chartered Accountants of Australia[17] (ICAA) is responsible for the CA qualification. The final examinations for the two qualifications are conducted separately by the two PABs. The educational requirements are comparable:

1 An accredited university undergraduate or master's degree in Accounting, and a professional programme offered by CPA Australia or the ICAA.
2 A university degree in another field supplemented by prescribed accounting and related courses and a professional programme offered by either CPA Australia or the ICAA.
3 Three years of supervised and mentored work experience in finance, accounting, or business.

Members of the two PABs have to meet ongoing requirements including CPD. There are no additional requirements for licensing. For both qualifications, MRAs with PABs in other countries address international recognition. (See Section 15.5.2 in Chapter 15 – this volume.)

26.2.2 Brazil

In Brazil, having a university degree of Bachelor of Science in Accounting is currently the sole requirement for candidates to access the profession and become members of the Conselho Federal de Contabilidade (CFC).[18] Membership in CFC is mandatory for accountants. CFC members acting as independent auditors are subject to an ongoing CPD requirement. The Ministry of Education regulates the content of professional accounting education at the universities.

For accountants to act as independent auditors in capital and financial markets, they need to pass a professional examination. Additionally, since 2002, independent auditors have been required to comply with a minimum CPD requirement. The time charged on these activities is converted into credits that are reported annually to the Securities and Exchange Commission. There is currently a project in Congress that will give to CFC the legal authority to require candidates to sit, in addition to university requirements, an examination in order to be registered as accountant at CFC. (See Section 15.6.2 in Chapter 15 – this volume.)

26.2.3 Canada

Admission requirements to become a CA in Canada include entrance requirements regarding academic study, prescribed programmes of professional education, a formal final examination of professional competence, and practical training. Membership in a Provincial Institute is mandatory in order to promote oneself as a Chartered Accountant. CPD is mandatory and is regulated by the Provincial Institutes. All CA candidates must sit the profession's Uniform Evaluation. The purpose of the examination is to assess whether candidates have acquired the competencies required of an entry-level CA. The professional education programme for a CA in Canada will vary between Canada's four regions, but each programme has the same objective: to prepare the candidates to be professional accountants, as defined nationally by the *CA Candidates' Competency Map*. An undergraduate degree from a Canadian university, or the equivalent from an out-of-country university, is required for admission to an Institute as a student. The compulsory university courses vary somewhat, Provincial Institute by Provincial Institute. All candidates must register with their Provincial Institute while completing practical experience. The Canadian Institute of Chartered Accountants (CICA) sets and marks the Uniform Evaluation on behalf of the Provincial Institutes. CICA[19] recognizes 14 international PABs, the members of which are recommended for exemption from the Uniform Evaluation. MRAs have been signed with two accounting bodies. (See Section 15.7.2 in Chapter 15 – this volume.)

26.2.4 Czech Republic

The Chamber of Auditors of the Czech Republic (CACR)[20] is the professional body of auditors. The title of auditor is protected by law. To obtain an auditor's certificate and be registered in the CACR register of auditors, one must pass examinations in subjects determined by the Act on Auditors Examination. Candidates must have obtained at least a bachelor's degree, and work for a minimum of three years as an audit assistant. The scope of the examination is determined by the Act on Auditors and details are specified by CACR. Preparatory courses for each examination are organized by the Audit Examination Committee of CACR which is an auxiliary body to the Executive Committee. All CACR members must complete 40 hours, or its equivalent, of CPD each year. Czech requirements for auditors comply with EU regulation; the auditor qualification is recognized in other EU countries.

26.2.5 France

The French accounting profession is organized through two separate professional bodies:

1   Ordre des Experts-Comptables (OEC),[21] under the jurisdiction of the Ministry of Economy and Finance, for the practising accountants; and
2   Compagnie Nationale des Commissaires aux Comptes (CNCC),[22] under the jurisdiction of the Ministry of Justice, for the statutory auditors.

Most of the professional accountants are members of the two Institutes. Candidates for OEC and CNCC memberships have to complete a professional accounting education programme delivered by universities and administered by the Ministry of Higher Education in cooperation with the OEC and CNCC, accomplish three years of practical training in an accounting/auditing firm, pass a final assessment, and obtain the French higher accounting degree, the Diplôme d'Expertise Comptable.

The Ministry of Higher Education has recently revised and redrafted the French accounting syllabus in collaboration with the OEC and the CNCC. The intermediary degrees (Diplôme de Comptabilité et de Gestion (DCG) and Diplôme Supérieur de Comptabilité et de Gestion) do not give access to the profession but are the first steps in this direction. The final diploma, Diplôme d'Expertise Comptable, is the only one giving access to the profession of *Expert-comptable* as well as the profession of *Commissaire aux comptes* if the training period includes a minimum of three years of practical training in an accounting/auditing firm. Requirements for statutory auditors comply with EU regulation and the auditor qualification is recognized in other EU countries. There are also MRAs with PABs in other French-speaking countries.

26.2.6 Hong Kong

The Hong Kong Institute of Certified Public Accountants (HKICPA)[23] is the statutory body responsible for registering CPAs in Hong Kong. HKICPA membership and a practising certificate are mandatory for practising public accounting in Hong Kong. Admission requirements as a member of HKICPA include completion of its Qualification Programme (QP), which comprises four technical modules with workshops and a formal final examination of professional competence, and supervised, structured, practical experience gained under an authorized employer/supervisor. The professional body is the provider of the QP, which is offered twice a year. For admission to the QP, a recognized degree in Accounting from any Hong Kong HEI, or an overseas degree or academic qualification accepted by the HKICPA as being of comparable standard, is required. Applicants for the issue of a practising certificate are required to have completed up to four years' full-time approved accounting experience, relevant Practising Certificate examinations in auditing, local law, and taxation, and CPD requirements. CPD is mandatory for members of the HKICPA for membership renewal. MRAs with PABs in other countries address international recognition and provide pathways for foreign qualified accountants from a recognized body to HKICPA membership and practising rights.

26.2.7 India

Admission requirements as a member of the Institute of Chartered Accountants of India (ICAI),[24] set up by an Act of Parliament, include a formal examination of professional competence, professional education, and practical training. A candidate can apply for membership of ICAI as a Chartered Accountant after completing prescribed practical training under an apprenticeship (i.e. articles) of at least three years' full-time work and six months of audit training, as applicable. A programme on general management and communication skills has to be completed prior to applying for membership. The professional examinations comprise three stages, starting with a Common Proficiency Test, followed by an Integrated Professional Competence Course (IPCC) consisting of two levels of seven subjects, and culminating in the Chartered Accountant Final Examination. The objectives of the Chartered Accountant Final Examination are to test: advanced knowledge; the ability to apply knowledge in various situations in actual practice; intellectual, interpersonal, and communication skills; as well as professional values. ICAI is the provider of the final examination and the IPCC.

The Board of Studies recognizes suitable institutions and grants accreditation for organizing classes. CPD is mandatory for members in the public practice of accounting. MRAs and memoranda of understanding (MOU) with PABs in other countries address mutual recognition and pathways to membership.

26.2.8 Japan

For membership of the Japanese Institute of Certified Public Accountants (JICPA),[25] the candidate must successfully pass the CPA examination. The administration and the requirements of the CPA examination are provided by the Certified Public Accountants Law. The examination is conducted by the Certified Public Accountants and Auditing Oversight Board, an advisory body to the Financial Services Agency. The examination is held annually, only in Japanese. It consists of a multiple-choice test and an essay. Successful candidates in the multiple-choice test are entitled to sit the essay part of the examination. Japan has no educational requirement to sit for the CPA examination. A candidate is required to have practical audit experience at an accounting firm, or specific training in industry, for a minimum of two years. Candidates may obtain practical experience either before taking the CPA examination or after passing the CPA examination. Successful candidates of the CPA examination are required to spend three years on the professional accounting education programme provided by the Japan Foundation for Accounting Education and Learning. The Foundation was established mainly by the CPA profession, with the cooperation of business and academic communities and other parties. Those who complete the professional accounting education programme are qualified to take the final assessment, which is conducted annually by JICPA. Those who pass the final assessment are eligible to register with JICPA. CPD is mandatory for Japanese CPAs. There is no international recognition of the Japanese CPA qualification. (See Section 15.4.2 in Chapter 15 – this volume.)

26.2.9 Mexico

A licence to practise public accounting, awarded by the Ministry of Education to holders of at least a Bachelor of Arts (BA) degree in Accounting, supported by recommendations from two members, is the only requirement to become a member of the Instituto Mexicana de Contadores Publicos (IMCP).[26] Membership in IMCP is voluntary and consists of certified and non-certified members. In 1999, IMCP introduced voluntary certification of public accountants (Contador Publico Certificado). Although this certification is voluntary, only CPCs can perform audits of registered public interest companies. Under the new arrangement, the IMCP organizes qualification examinations for those public accountants who intend to obtain the title of CPC – considered equivalent to the CPA in the U.S.A. The new arrangement is voluntary but it is comparable to other international licensing requirements; the Mexican licensee can practise accounting in most but not all jurisdictions of the U.S.A. and Canada, subject to passing examinations on national legislation and standards, in accordance with the provisions of the Professional MRA. All members of the IMCP must comply with the CPD requirements, with a minimum of 65 hours for Certified Public Accountant and of 45 hours for Public Accountants. CPD is monitored by IMCP. (See Section 15.7.1 in Chapter 15 – this volume.)

26.2.10 The Netherlands

Registeraccountants (RA) are required to have a master's degree. Education for statutory auditors is at postgraduate level. To become a member of Royal NIVRA[27] (NBA, Nederlandse Beroepsorganisatie van Accountants), *registeraccountants* are also required to complete three years mentored and supervised practical experience, at least one year of which must be in an audit environment. The final examination consists of a theoretical and a practical thesis. The government-appointed Commissie Eindtermen Accountantsopleiding (Committee for Learning Outcomes in Accounting and Auditing) is responsible for the intended learning outcomes (ILOs) of the full RA-syllabus (postgraduate accounting education); universities are free to design curricula based on the ILOs. Compliance is safeguarded through periodical reviews and accreditation by the CEA. Royal NIVRA (NBA) is responsible for the practical experience programme for aspiring *registeraccountants* and for CPD by *registeraccountants* (regulation, programme, and monitoring). Requirements for statutory auditors comply with EU regulations; the auditor qualification is recognized in other EU countries. There are also recognition agreements with some PABs in English-speaking countries outside the EU.

26.2.11 New Zealand

The New Zealand Institute of Chartered Accountants (NZICA)[28] is responsible for the CA qualification. A three-year accredited academic degree in Accounting and related subjects is required for entry to the professional Chartered Accountants programme which is offered by the Institute. Because the emphasis in the academic programme is on the essential theoretical and technical accounting knowledge and skills (as well as business and general education), the Professional Competence Programme concentrates on developing the higher-level professional skills. The programme includes technical modules and a final capstone module to integrate knowledge, skills, and competences. Three years of mentored and monitored practical experience is required to qualify as a Chartered Accountant. The professional body is the provider of the final examination. Members of NZICA have to meet ongoing requirements including CPD. There are no additional requirements for licensing. MRAs with PABs in other countries address international recognition. A new programme, jointly created by NZICA and the ICAA, began in February 2013. (See Section 15.5.3 in Chapter 15 – this volume.)

26.2.12 South Africa

The South African Chartered Accountant qualification, CA (SA) is regulated by the South African Institute of Chartered Accountants (SAICA).[29] Entrance requirements consist of a four-year academic programme, assessment of technical competence, a three-year professional training programme, and a final assessment of professional competence. The academic programme comprises a three-year undergraduate and a one-year postgraduate degree. The academic programme is taught by universities which offer specific programmes designed to meet the SAICA Competency Framework Requirements. Such programmes are also subject to formal accreditation and monitoring processes. The assessment of technical competence is administered by SAICA, with a focus on technical knowledge and skills appropriate for candidates without work experience. The formal training period of three years provides a prospective chartered accountant with the relevant practical experience and training to be able to apply the core technical skills. The professional training programme provides advanced education in conjunction with practical experience, which enables the final development of professional competence. The final examination assesses professional competence. SAICA is subject to review by the Independent Regulatory Board for Auditors (IRBA), which recognizes all elements of the qualification process in order to be recognized as a Registered Auditor. CPD is mandatory for chartered accountants. The CA (SA) qualification is recognized in several other English-speaking countries. SAICA is working closely with neighbouring countries in the Southern African region. (See Section 15.3.2 in Chapter 15 – this volume.)

26.2.13 Turkey

There are two recognized professional bodies in Turkey: the Expert Accountants Association of Turkey (EAAT),[30] and the Union of the Chambers of Certified Public Accountants of Turkey (TURMOB).[31] EAAT is a voluntary organization of professional accountants. TURMOB is the regulatory body in accounting. Candidates for TURMOB membership are required to hold a bachelor's degree in economics, law, or management. They have to complete a series of final examinations in order to obtain membership. The standards for the examination are set jointly by the government and TURMOB. For a practising licence, three years of practical experience are required. In addition, in order to maintain their membership, certified auditors have to satisfy CPD requirements. TURMOB distinguishes three levels in the qualification: independent accountant, CPA, and State Auditor. International recognition of the qualification has not been achieved.

(See Section 15.2.3 in Chapter 15 – this volume.)

26.2.14 The U.K.

This overview is limited to those three designations in the U.K. which comply with EU regulations for auditors, and which are the responsibility of PABs inside the U.K. ACCA is responsible for the qualification of Chartered Certified Accountant. The Institute of Chartered Accountants in England & Wales (ICAEW) uses the designations, dependent on experience, of Associate (ACA) and Fellow (FCA). Members of ICAS use the designation Chartered Accountant (CA). The three bodies are responsible for the qualifications of their members. Oversight of the Auditing requirements inherent in the respective qualifications is conducted by the Financial Reporting Council (FRC). Not considered in this analysis is the position of Chartered Accountants Ireland, which is the PAB having similar rights in Northern Ireland (which is part of the U.K.) and the Republic of Ireland (which is not).

- *ACCA:*[32] Admission requirements to become a member of the ACCA include a formal final examination of professional competence, and practical training. ACCA's membership qualification is divided into three parts. To register as a student of ACCA's professional scheme, a candidate must be at least 18 years of age and hold the minimum qualification for entry to a degree programme in the U.K. Holders of higher qualifications may attract exemptions from some of ACCA's examinations, but not from the final part. (See Apostolou & Gammie, Chapter 29 – this volume.)
- *ICAEW:*[33] Admission requirements to become a member of the ICAEW include Professional and Advanced Stage examinations (culminating in the Advanced Stage with three papers, including an integrated Advanced Case Study admitting examination), practical training, and work-based learning under the supervision of a qualified person within an authorized organization. Minimum admission requirements are the same as for university entrance in the U.K. but, in practice, most trainees have a university degree. Exemptions can be awarded based on the content and accreditation of the university degree.
- *ICAS:*[34] Admission requirements to become a member of ICAS include a formal final examination of professional competence, prescribed programmes of professional education, and practical training. A CA student will be eligible for admission to membership after completion of the prescribed period of approved service as a CA student, and passing all elements of the CA examinations. Prospective CA students will have a university degree and may be eligible for exemptions from the Competence level.

Members of the three PABs have to meet ongoing requirements including CPD. Registration as a Registered Auditor is required in order to perform audits of financial statements. European law requires examinations for those wishing to become registered auditors to be of at least degree standard. As noted above, the qualification of Chartered Accountants Ireland is recognized in both the U.K. and in the Republic of Ireland. MRAs with PABs in other countries address international recognition.

26.2.15 The U.S.A.

The education requirements for licensed professional accountants (i.e. CPAs) in the U.S.A. and its Territories are very similar. The U.S.A. has 50 states and four territories, comprising 54 jurisdictions, each of which licenses CPAs. Each of these jurisdictions has its own rules for licensure, but they are essentially the same. A non-binding Uniform Accountancy Act, jointly developed by NASBA[35] and the AICPA,[36] spells out specific educational requirements. In essence, these are possession of a university degree which includes:

- a specific number of 'semester hours'(courses) in accounting subjects (*Financial Accounting, Managerial Accounting, Taxation, Accounting Information Systems, Auditing*, etc.), and
- a specific number of general business courses (*Business Law, Finance, Management, Marketing, Information Technology*, etc.)

Almost all jurisdictions require one year of academic study beyond the four years normally required for a bachelor's degree. Most of that training is additional studies in accounting, and business towards the end. The AICPA, while it works closely with NASBA and the appropriate authorities in the 54 jurisdictions, does not license CPAs. Consequently, this PAB does not provide pre-qualification education, as is done in many other countries. Licensing for public practice is the responsibility of each State Board of Accounting. Normally at least one year's practical experience is required. Regular CPD is required following licensure. The US International Qualification Appraisal Board (US-IQAB) has negotiated several MRAs with PABs in other countries. Actual recognition is the responsibility of the State Boards of Accounting. (See Section 15.7.3 in Chapter 15 – this volume.)

Notes

1 IFAC, International Standards on Auditing 600: Special considerations audits of group financial statements (including the work of component auditors), paragraph 11.
2 IFAC, International Federation of Accountants, www.ifac.org.
3 IFAC, Membership & Compliance Program, www.ifac.org/about-ifac/membership.
4 OECD, Organisation for Economic Cooperation and Development, www.oecd.org.
5 IFAC, International Standard Setting Boards, Education, www.ifac.org.
6 IAESB, Update International Education Standards Revision Project, www.ifac.org/education.
7 IAAER, International Association for Accounting Education and Research, www.iaaer.org.
8 IFAC, Membership & Compliance Program, www.ifac.org/about-ifac/membership.
9 United Nations Conference on Trade and Development, www.unctad.org/isar.
10 Common Content Initiative, www.commoncontent.com.
11 National Association of State Boards of Accountancy, www.nasba.org.
12 American Institute of Certified Public Accountants, www.aicpa.org.
13 Global Accounting Alliance, www.globalaccountingalliance.com.
14 WEF, World Economic Forum Competitiveness Index.
15 IFAC, Membership & Compliance Program, www.ifac.org.
16 CPA Australia, www.cpaaustralia.com.au.

17 Institute of Chartered Accountants of Australia, www.charteredaccountants.com.au.
18 Conselho Federal de Contabilidade, www.cfc.org.br.
19 Canadian Institute of Chartered Accountants, www.cica.ca.
20 Chamber of Auditors of the Czech Republic, www.kacr.cz.
21 Ordre des Experts-Comptables, www.experts-comptables.fr.
22 Compagnie Nationale des Commissaires aux Comptes, www.cncc.fr.
23 Hong Kong Institute of Certified Public Accountants, www.hkicpa.org.hk.
24 Institute of Chartered Accountants of India, www.icai.org.
25 Japanese Institute of Certified Public Accountants, www.hp.jicpa.or.jp.
26 Instituto Mexicana de Contadores Publicos, www.imcp.org.mx.
27 Royal NIVRA, www.nivra.nl.
28 New Zealand Institute of Chartered Accountants, www.nzica.com.
29 South African Institute of Chartered Accountants, www.saica.co.za.
30 Expert Accountants Association of Turkey, www.tmud.org.tr.
31 Chambers of Certified Public Accountants of Turkey, www.turmob.org.tr.
32 Association of Chartered Certified Accountants, www.accaglobal.com.
33 Institute of Chartered Accountants in England and Wales, www.icaew.org.uk.
34 Institute of Chartered Accountants of Scotland, www.icas.org.uk.
35 National Association of State Boards of Accountancy, www.nasba.org.
36 American Institute of Certified Public Accountants, www.aicpa.org.

References

Anyane-Ntow, K. (ed.) (1992) *International Handbook of Accounting Education and Certification*, Oxford: Pergamon Press.

Berg, M.C. (2007) Continuing professional development: the IFAC position, *Accounting Education: an international journal*, 16(4), 319–327.

Boritz, J.E. & Carnaghan, C.A. (2003) Competency-based education and assessment for the accounting profession: a critical review, *Canadian Accounting Perspectives*, 2, 7–42.

Crawford, L., Helliar, C., Monk, E., Mina, M., Teodori, C., Veneziani, M., Wanyama, S., & Falgi, K. (2010) *IES Compliance and the Knowledge, Skills and Values of IES 2, 3 and 4*, IAAER/ACCA Research Project.

Donovan, C. (2005) The benefit of academic/practitioner collaboration, *Accounting Education: an international journal*, 14(4), 445–452.

EU (1984) *Eight Council Directive of 10 April 1984*, Brussels: European Union.

Evans, E., Juchau, R., & Wilson, R.M.S. (eds) (2012) *The Interface of Accounting Education and Professional Training*, Abingdon: Routledge.

Fay, J.R. (1992) *Accounting Certification, Educational, & Reciprocity Requirements: An International Guide*, Westport, CT: Quorum Books.

Gammie, E. & Joyce, Y. (2009) Competence-based approaches to the assessment of professional accountancy training work experience requirements: the ICAS experience, *Accounting Education: an international journal*, 18(4), 443–466.

IFAC (2010) *Handbook of International Education Pronouncements*, available at: www.ifac.org.

Karreman, G.H. (2002) *Impact of Globalisation on Accountancy Education*, London: International Accounting Standards Committee Foundation.

Karreman, G.H. (2007) *Trends in Global Accounting Education*, Amsterdam: Royal NIVRA.

Karreman, G.H. (2013) *Dynamics of Accountancy Education*, Tilburg: University of Tilburg.

Needles, B.E. (2008a) International Education Standards: Issues of Implementation – A Report on the Third IAAER Globalization Roundtable, *Accounting Education: an international journal*, 17(Supplement), S69–S79.

Needles, B.E. (2008b) The International Association for Accounting Education and Research: The Code of Ethics for Accounting Educators, *Accounting Education: an international journal*, 17(Supplement), S81–S86.

Needles, B.E. (2010) Accounting education: the impact of globalization, *Accounting Education: an international journal*, 19(6), 601–605.

Paisey, C. & Paisey, N.J. (2004) An analysis of accounting education research in *Accounting Education: an international journal*, 1992–2001, *Accounting Education: an international journal*, 13(1), 69–100.

Phelps, R.W. (2011) *Measuring Country-Level Accountancy Performance and Achievement*, CARANA Corporation.

Sangster, A. & Wilson, R.M.S. (eds) (2013) *Liberalising the Accounting Curriculum in University Education*, Abingdon: Routledge.

Saville, H. (2007) International Education Standards for professional accountants, *Accounting Education*, 16(1), 107–113.

Sugahara, S. & Boland, G. (2010) The role of cultural factors in the learning style preferences of accounting students: a comparative study between Japan and Australia, *Accounting Education: an international journal*, 19(3), 235–255.

UNCTAD (1998) Global Curriculum for the Professional Education of Professional Accountants, available at: www.unctad.org/isar.

UNCTAD (2010) *Capacity-building Framework for High-quality Corporate Reporting*. Available at: www.unctad.org/isar.

Van Peursem, K.A., Monk, E.A., Wilson, R.M.S., & Adler, R.W. (eds) (2012) *Audit Education*, Abingdon: Routledge.

Watty, K., Jackling, B., & Wilson, R.M.S. (eds) (2012) *Personal Transferable Skills in Accounting Education*, Abingdon: Routledge.

Watty, K., Jackson, M., & Yu, X. (2010) Students' approaches to assessment in accounting education: the unique student perspective, *Accounting Education: an international journal*, 19(3), 219–234.

Watty, K., Sugahara, S., Abayadeera, N., Perera, L., & McKay, J. (2012) *Developing a Global Model of Accounting Education and Examining IES Compliance in Australia, Japan and Sri Lanka*, IAAER/ACCA Research Project.

Weil, S., Oyelere, P., & Rainsbury, E. (2002) The usefulness of case studies in developing core competencies in a professional accounting programme: a New Zealand study. Available at: www.nzica.com.

Wilson, R.M.S. (ed.) (2013) *Accounting Education Research: Prize-Winning Contributions*, Abingdon: Routledge.

Wilson, R.M.S. & Adler, R.W. (eds) (2012) *Teaching IFRS*, Abingdon: Routledge.

Wilson, R.M.S., Ravenscroft, S.P., Rebele, J.E., & St. Pierre, K. (2008) The case for accounting education research, *Accounting Education: an international journal*, 17(2), 103–111.

Websites

ACCA, Association of Chartered Certified Accountants, www.accaglobal.com
AICPA, American Institute of Certified Public Accountants, www.aicpa.org
CACR, Chamber of Auditors of the Czech Republic, www.kacr.cz
CCI, Common Content Initiative, www.commoncontent.com
CFC, Conselho Federal de Contabilidade, www.cfc.org.br
CICA, Canadian Institute of Chartered Accountants, www.cica.ca
CNCC, Compagnie National des Commissaires aux Comptes, www.cncc.fr
CPA Australia, www.cpaaustralia.com.au
EAAT, Expert Accountants Association of Turkey, www.tmud.org.tr
GAA, Global Accounting Alliance, www.globalaccountingalliance.com
HKICPA, Hong Kong Institute of Certified Public Accountants, www.hkicpa.org.hk
IAAER, International Association for Accounting Education and Research, www.iaaer.org
ICAA, Institute of Chartered Accountants of Australia, www.charteredaccountants.com.au
ICAEW, Institute of Chartered Accountants in England and Wales, www.icaew.org.uk
ICAI, Institute of Chartered Accountants of India, www.icai.org
ICAS, Institute of Chartered Accountants of Scotland, www.icas.org.uk
IFAC, International Federation of Accountants, www.ifac.org
IFAC, International Standard Setting Boards, Education, www.ifac.org
IFAC, Membership & Compliance Program, www.ifac.org/about-ifac/membership
IMCP, Instituto Mexicana de Contadores Publicos, www.imcp.org.mx
JICPA, Japanese Institute of Certified Public Accountants, www.hp.jicpa.or.jp
NASBA, National Association of State Boards of Accountancy, www.nasba.org
NZICA, New Zealand Institute of Chartered Accountants, www.nzica.com
OEC, Ordre des Experts-Comptables, www.experts-comptables.fr

OECD, Organisation for Economic Co-operation and Development, www.oecd.org
Royal NIVRA, www.nivra.nl
SAICA, South African Institute of Chartered Accountants, www.saica.co.za
TURMOB, Union of the Chambers of Certified Public Accountants of Turkey, www.turmob.org.tr
UNCTAD, United Nations Conference on Trade and Development, www.unctad.org/isar

About the authors

Charles H. Calhoun is Professor of Accounting at the University of North Florida, U.S.A. (ccalhoun@unf.edu). He served for six years as Chair of the Consultative Advisory Group of the IAESB, several years on NASBA's International Qualification Appraisal Board, and 10 years on the Florida State Board of Accountancy.

Gert H. Karreman is Visiting Professor at DePaul University, U.S.A. (g.karreman @inter.nl.net). His primary interest is international research into the global development of accountancy education. Results from this programme of work were published in 2002, 2005, 2007, and 2013.

Section G

Institutional considerations

Preface

Aileen Pierce

UNIVERSITY COLLEGE DUBLIN, IRELAND

Institutions, whether academic accounting associations, professional accounting bodies (PABs), accreditation bodies, universities, accounting firms, or standard-setters have influenced the structure of, approach to, and curriculum content within accounting education for a considerable period of time. Initially, education and training in accounting were the preserve of PABs and firms of accountants. Subsequently, and particularly over the past 50 years, other institutional stakeholders have responded to perceived limitations in the extant educational models in accounting by engaging in constructive criticism or progressive challenge. Much of this criticism and challenge has impacted positively on accounting education practices. Critical reflection, broadening of curricula, and innovation in teaching and learning are now accepted as being normal components of accounting education programmes.

Nonetheless, substantial change in the environment within which accountants operate continues to drive high-level critiques of the educational underpinnings of the profession, the range and details of qualification or certification pathways and, indeed, whether or not accounting is a profession or an industry.

Tensions within the institutional infrastructure around accounting have also emerged over the years. There are tensions between the concepts of education and training, between accounting academics and practising accountants, and between research-led proposals for change and politics, all of which continue to exist in discourse and policy-making around accounting education. Potential benefits of collaboration among stakeholders are sometimes counter-balanced by competition between institutions.

In the context of a multi-faceted profession with a complex web of interacting institutional stakeholders, the chapters in Section G provide wide-ranging, informative, and thought-provoking insights into the significant aspects of *Institutional Considerations* as they relate to accounting education.

27

Fifty years of change in accounting education

The influence of institutions

Gary L. Sundem

UNIVERSITY OF WASHINGTON, U.S.A.

CONTENTS

Gary L. Sundem

Abstract

The last 50 years have seen much change in accounting education, and much of this change has been motivated by various institutions. From the Carnegie and Ford Foundation reports in the U.S.A. in 1959, through the developing research emphasis in universities in the following decades, to the American Accounting Association's Bedford Committee Report, the Big 8 White Paper, and the Accounting Education Change Commission (AECC) in the late 1980s, the Albrecht & Sack monograph in 2000, and finally to the Pathways Commission report in 2012, accounting education in the U.S.A. had reacted to many institutional pressures. Similar reports from academic and professional bodies in the U.K., Australia, and New Zealand have affected accounting education in those countries. This chapter traces the influence of various institutional studies and reports to show how accounting education has reached its current state. The chapter concludes with an assessment of today's accounting education environment and the challenges and constraints it faces in preparing accounting students to meet the needs of the accounting profession of the future.

Keywords

accounting change, accounting education history, accounting institutions

27.1 Introduction

Accounting education has changed significantly in the last five decades. These changes have been influenced by studies supported by a variety of institutions, including government bodies, professional accounting bodies (PABs), academic associations, and foundations. As we have now passed the 50th anniversary of two major foundation-sponsored studies that brought about major changes in business and accounting education in the U.S.A. and, eventually, globally, it is instructive to examine the nature of accounting education over these 50 years, how it has evolved in response to various institutional pressures, and what it portends for the future.

The main goals of this chapter are:

- to identify many of the major institutional studies that have influenced accounting education in the last 50 years;
- to place these studies in context and examine their impact; and
- to assess the current state of accounting education with an emphasis on the influence of institutions.

I will focus primarily on the evolution of accounting education in the U.S.A. because that is what I know best. Furthermore, many of the institutional calls for change came first in the U.S.A. and subsequently influenced accounting education in other parts of the world. However, I will also make some references to similar influences of institutions in other countries.[1]

27.2 The rise of academic accounting, 1959–1986

27.2.1 The Ford and Carnegie Reports

In 1959, the Ford Foundation and Carnegie Commission issued critical reports on business education in the U.S.A. (Gordon & Howell, 1959, and Pierson, 1959). Among their criticisms were:

- poor quality of student admissions,
- the over emphasis on vocationalism,
- the narrowness of the curriculum,
- the low level and quality of academic research,
- the heavy reliance on part-time academic staff,
- the lack of enough doctorally-qualified educators, and
- the minimal coverage of liberal arts subject matter.

The reports also recommended that business and accounting educators develop a conceptual basis for business topics based on disciplines such as economics, mathematics, psychology, and sociology. (See also Fogarty, Chapter 1, Amernic & Craig, Chapter 12, Bloom, Chapter 14 – all in this volume, and Sangster & Wilson, 2013.) Business schools in the U.S.A., and accounting programmes in particular, spent much of the next 25 years addressing the issues that they raised, and accounting programmes in Europe, Asia, and other parts of the world eventually adopted many of the same changes.

Prior to 1960, most business and accounting education in the U.S.A. focussed on teaching what is done in practice and researching topics that had direct application in practice. A recent article in *The Economist* (2009) that looked back on the Gordon & Howell report stated: '*Business faculty tended to teach from field experience rather than theory—thus, business education was considered akin to learning a trade, rather than a true academic discipline.*'

Although conceptual underpinnings were not completely ignored, they were secondary to learning the methods currently in practice. The emphasis was on 'How?' and not on 'Why?' But, in the early 1960s, business schools responded to the challenge to develop and teach a framework that would explain not only what practitioners do but why they do it. Robert Trueblood, a future President of the American Institute of Certified Public Accountants (AICPA), reinforced the recommendations of these reports within accounting, and also emphasized that accounting should be learned within the context of other business functions, stating that accounting should be differentiated from general business education 'only to the extent of a thorough understanding of the basic principles of the accounting discipline' (1963: 90). He also argued against 'excessive educational differentiation for industrial and public accountants'. In addition, he challenged accounting educators to develop a curriculum focussed on the 'basic principles of the accounting discipline' and to undertake research that would lead to a better understanding of conceptual underpinnings of accounting so that accounting graduates could adapt to a changing environment throughout their careers.

27.2.2 The American Accounting Association leads change

Progress in research came first in the U.S.A., with the American Accounting Association (AAA) leading the way to a more research-oriented academy.[2] Building on financial support from the Ford Foundation for doctoral education in business, PhD programmes expanded their emphasis on developing accounting educators' research capabilities, especially the ability to carry out basic research. Universities began seeking to hire academic staff capable of basic – as opposed to only applied – research, and began rewarding research-productive staff with promotions, salary increases, and endowed professorships. The progress of this research emphasis in a single decade is illustrated in two AAA publications: *A Statement of Basic Accounting Theory*, or ASOBAT (Committee to Prepare a Statement of Basic Accounting Theory, 1966) and *Statement on Accounting Theory and Theory Acceptance*, or SATTA (Committee on Concepts and Standards for

External Financial Reports, 1977). ASOBAT is an insightful overview of accounting theory, but it is based on careful reasoning by accounting scholars rather than on rigorous research. There were no references to the accounting research literature. SATTA was supposed to be '*a statement that would provide the same type of survey and distillation of current thinking on accounting theory as [ASOBAT] provided in an earlier decade*'. It was substantially different to ASOBAT with extensive citation of the research literature. It included a reference list of 200 citations, including 60 from the non-accounting literature (mainly economics, psychology, mathematics, and statistics). By 1977, the discipline of accounting was very different to what it was in 1966 and, as accounting educators focussed more resources on research and changed the nature of that research, there was a spill-over effect on accounting teaching.

The Carnegie and Ford Foundation reports also had a direct effect on the teaching of accounting. Business schools and accounting departments in the U.S.A. focussed on making their programmes more academic and attractive to more and better students.[3] In the early 1960s, nearly twice as many freshman students saw their university experience as a way to 'develop a meaningful philosophy of life' rather than a way to become 'very well off financially'. By 1980, more freshmen subscribed to the latter than the former. The percentage of university students majoring in business in the U.S.A., which was barely over 10 per cent in 1960, reached 20 per cent by 1980, just short of its current level of 22 percent (U.S. Department of Education, 2012). Meanwhile, every year the number of accounting degrees granted increased by more than five-fold between 1961 and 1985, from about 11,000 to nearly 58,000. Clearly something was making business, and especially accounting, more appealing to university students.

What did accounting programmes do to increase the appeal of accounting education and accounting careers? One thing was to open the doors to an increasing number of female accounting students. In 1960, only about 5 per cent of accounting majors were women. By 1985, women had become the majority of undergraduate accounting majors. (See Laswad & Tan, Chapter 9, on choosing to major in the accounting discipline, and Jackling, Chapter 10, on choosing an accounting career – both in this volume.)

Another step was to increase the qualifications and commitment of academic staff. In the early 1960s, nearly 90 per cent of full-time-equivalent (FTE) accounting educators in the U.S.A. were part-time academics. By 1986, this had dropped to 40 per cent. Less than 30 per cent of accounting educators in the early 1960s had doctorates; in 1986, this was 60 per cent and climbing. The demand for PhDs was driven partly by what is now called the Association to Advance Collegiate Schools of Business (AACSB) which, in 1969, passed a requirement that accredited business schools need a minimum number of academic staff with doctorates. This influence was felt first in the U.S.A. because the AACSB accredited only universities in the U.S.A., but now it has worldwide influence because AACSB has accredited universities in 50 countries and territories.[4] Its influence on accounting education grew in the early 1980s when the AACSB started separately accrediting accounting programmes, imposing doctoral degree requirements (as well as other requirements) at the accounting department level.[5]

Despite the growing number of PhDs among the academic staff, more than 70 per cent of accounting educators in the late 1970s continued to be certified public accountants (CPAs), which shows that the professional dimension of accounting remained strong even as the academic dimension increased. Nevertheless, research assumed a much larger role in academic staff performance evaluations, and staff were devoting more time to scholarly activities – nearly 30 per cent of their time by the mid-1980s in doctoral-granting universities. Teaching loads, measured by both contact hours per week and number of preparations, fell. By 1986, 67 per cent of accounting educators spent fewer than 10 contact hours in class per week. Demand for accounting staff with doctorates remained high. During the late 1970s and into the early 1980s, an average of five positions were available for every accounting doctoral graduate.

27.2.3 The golden age of accounting education

I would call the 1970s the golden age of accounting education in the U.S.A., especially for educators but also for students. Significant research contributions in areas such as capital market research, information economics, analytical modelling, and behavioural accounting made for an intellectually-stimulating environment. The Financial Accounting Standards Board (FASB) was developing and publishing its conceptual framework,[6] and accounting education increasingly included coverage of the conceptual underpinnings of accounting. And demand for accounting classes seemed limitless.

The focus on concepts in accounting education was not limited to the U.S.A. In 1974, the Solomons Report (Solomons, with Berridge, 1974) in the U.K. distinguished between theoretical and practical education and recommended that theoretical education in accounting precede practical education.

27.2.4 Problems in the 1980s

However, by 1980, some dark clouds were already on the horizon. The success rate for accounting educators seeking tenure started falling in the late 1960s and dropped to under 40 per cent in the 1980s. The number of publications required for promotion shot up. At the same time, critics were calling much of accounting research irrelevant. A gap between accounting academics and accounting practitioners, first identified in the 1970s, became a chasm in the 1980s. (See Bloom *et al.*, 1994.) Public accounting firms in the U.S.A. were feeling unprecedented competition. This competition was fuelled to a great extent by the 1976 and 1977 reports from U.S. Congressional Committees (U.S. House of Representatives, 1976, and U.S. Senate, 1977). The reports addressed independence but focussed mostly on fostering competition among public accounting firms. A further influence was a U.S. Supreme Court ruling in 1977 that opened the door to advertising by public accounting firms. Practising accountants, many of whom previously interacted with academics and contributed to the understanding of broad conceptual issues in accounting, needed to devote more of their time to the business aspects of their firms. Meanwhile, academic accountants, many of whom interacted with and contributed to the issues faced by practitioners, began to focus more on 'academic' research to justify their existence within universities. As a result, accounting academic staff became more isolated from practitioners, and this impact began to be felt in accounting classrooms.

The accounting curriculum also faced challenges in the 1980s. Accounting classes became bogged down in techniques, rules, and regulations. In 1960, the U.S. generally accepted accounting principles (GAAP) consisted of 43 *Accounting Research Bulletins* (ARBs) comprising 412 paragraphs. By the early 1980s this had grown to more than 5,000 paragraphs in 51 ARBs, 31 *Accounting Principles Board Opinions*, and more than 50 FASB Standards (soon to be 90 by the mid-1980s). Similar increases occurred in SEC pronouncements, auditing standards, and tax regulations. Memorization of the technical literature was replacing the conceptual components of the curriculum, and even then a smaller and smaller proportion of the technical literature was being covered. Just as the accounting profession was facing a changed regulatory environment, growing litigation threats, expanding scope and complexity of accounting services, and rapid advances in technology that were revolutionizing (and threatening) the profession, accounting education was narrowing and turning out graduates who did not easily adapt to such changes. In addition, the number of accounting students was declining and their average ability (as evidenced by university entrance examination scores) was falling. By the mid-1980s, accounting had quickly gone from the golden age to a profession in trouble. Much of the blame was placed on academic accounting programmes. The golden age of accounting education was over.

27.3 The Bedford Committee report and the Big 8 White Paper

Both the accounting profession and the academic community were aware of the rising tide of discontent with the state of the profession and the academic preparation of accountants. In 1984, the AAA appointed a Blue Ribbon committee to study the future of accounting education. The composition of what came to be called the Bedford Committee was five prominent accounting practitioners representing industry, government, and public accounting, along with seven distinguished academic accountants. The committee's report (AAA *Committee on the Future Structure, Content, and Scope of Accounting Education,* 1986, p. 172) concluded '*extensive changes and expansions must occur in the accounting professional education program by the year 2000*'.

The report also stated (ibid., p. 179) that changes should include: '*1) a revised, expanded curriculum, 2) a more effective education delivery process, and 3) a better articulated structure for the institutional units through which the programs will be offered*'.

Three AAA committees in 1986-87, and one in 1987–88, followed up on the recommendations of the Bedford Committee. These committee reports are published in Schultz (1989). This led to much discussion but little action. By 1989 the then Big 8 accounting firms in the U.S.A. were anxious to drive real change in accounting education. They issued a White Paper (*Perspectives on Education,* 1989) which outlined '[the] *partnership of faculty and practitioners necessary to quickly bring about the needed changes in accounting education*'.The White Paper had two main aims:

- First, it set out the capabilities, the skills and knowledge, needed by accountants entering the profession. It placed much emphasis on skills, specifically intellectual skills, communication skills, and interpersonal skills. It also described the general knowledge and organizational and business knowledge as well as the accounting and auditing knowledge required. The summary statement under accounting and auditing knowledge is: '*Passing the CPA examination should not be the goal of accounting education. The focus should be on developing analytical and conceptual thinking versus memorizing rapidly expanding professional standards.*'

   A phrase that summarizes this is *creative, adaptive life-long learners.* Accounting education should set a base, a solid conceptual understanding of accounting and its role in society, which allows accountants to adapt their knowledge and skills through continual learning as the world around them changes.

- Second, it proposed a process and promised resources to support an AAA effort to implement the needed changes in universities in the U.S.A. This led to the creation of the Accounting Education Change Commission (AECC). The objective of the AECC was '*[to] foster changes in the academic preparation of accountants consistent with the goal of improving their capabilities for successful professional careers in practice*' (see Sundem 1999, Chapter 2), or essentially to implement the recommendations of the White Paper and the Bedford Committee. The combined force of the eight largest public accounting firms in the U.S.A. and the AAA created action where earlier reports, regardless of how prestigious the source, had failed.

27.4 The Accounting Education Change Commission (AECC)

From 1989 to 1996, the Accounting Education Change Commission (AECC) promoted change efforts at universities in the U.S.A. Their influence was also felt worldwide as AECC members spoke at international venues, the Commission's written materials were disseminated world-wide, and the International Association for Accounting Education and Research (IAAER) sponsored tours of universities in the U.S.A. that were implementing changes for international accounting educators. The seven years of AECC's activity focussed on two areas:

- funding change projects at specific universities; and
- promoting change widely across universities.

For more details about the activities and impacts of the AECC, see my overview of the commission in Sundem (1999), and for information about the grant projects, see Flaherty (1998).

The AECC grant programme received the most attention. The AECC granted $3 million to 12 projects for the actual implementation of change, not simply planning for or designing changes. Nearly every project led to significant changes at the university receiving the grant. However, only a small number of the projects were successfully transferred to other universities. Textbooks used elsewhere were produced from two projects, but the most successful in exporting its changes was Project Discovery, a joint project at the University of Illinois and Notre Dame University which eventually included Nanyang Technological University in Singapore. Although the grant programme had its successes, it failed to produce models of improved accounting education that could be transported to many other universities, and thus its impact was not as widespread as the AECC had anticipated. (On modelling accounting education, see Needles, Chapter 2 – this volume.)

The AECC's success in promoting change in other universities was similarly mixed. In the Commission's first four years, commission members made more than 300 presentations and published 20 papers about accounting education change. The Commission also published six issue statements and two position statements. The most quoted line from the AECC is from the first position statement (Accounting Education Change Commission 1990, p. 1): '*Accounting programs should prepare students to **become** professional accountants, not to be professional accountants at the time of entry to the profession*' (emphasis in the original).

All of this activity led to much discussion and some action. Many universities instituted changes advocated by the Commission, but most dealt with the easy initiatives and avoided the hard ones. Among the successes was large-scale expansion of emphasis on written and oral communications, and working in teams in accounting programmes. There was also some increase in the use of cases and other unstructured problem-solving exercises. (See Hassall & Joyce, Chapter 17 – this volume.) Whether this would have occurred in the absence of the AECC is hard to tell. However, few universities tackled the major issue of changing the basic approach to accounting education. While the AECC advocated emphasis on understanding concepts, using professional literature simply as examples and not the objective of the education (similar to how law schools teach the law), most universities stayed focussed on a comprehensive knowledge of techniques, rules, and regulations. For an argument favouring a strong technical focus, see St. Pierre & Rebele, Chapter 5, and for an argument favouring 'soft skills' see Watty, Chapter 13 – both in this volume, and Watty *et al.*, 2012.)

27.5 Non-U.S. influences

Concern with accounting education in the late 1980s and 1990s was not confined to the U.S.A. At about the same time as the Bedford Committee report came out in the U.S.A., Burgess (1986) edited a U.K. volume that criticized the accounting education system for placing emphasis on the understanding of facts as opposed to decision-making, organizing information, and problem-solving. In Australia, the Matthews Committee report (Matthews *et al.*, 1990) focussed primarily on the underfunding of accounting education. Finally, a movement toward competency-based accounting education (see Birkett, 1993; Johns, 1995; and the special issue of *Accounting Education: an international journal*, 3(1), March 1995) addressed some of the issues troubling accounting educators in the U.K., Australia, and New Zealand, as well as in the U.S.A.

27.6 The Albrecht & Sack monograph

While the activities of the 1990s led to improvements in accounting education, problems remained. In the preface to my monograph summarizing the AECC (Sundem 1999, p. ii), I wrote: 'There is one overriding measure of success: *that another similar commission is not needed.*' If that was the goal, the appearance of the Albrecht & Sack monograph (Albrecht & Sack, 2000) was evidence that the AECC and the other change efforts of the 1990s were not completely successful. The AAA, sponsor of Albrecht & Sack, again tackled the task of trying to change accounting education. Although Albrecht & Sack focussed mainly on different issues to those addressed by the AECC, it indicated that something was still 'broken' in accounting education, specifically the following:

- the number and quality of accounting students continued to decline;
- the basic model of accounting education, with its continued focus on professional pronouncements, was deemed outmoded by many practitioners; and
- a large number of accounting practitioners indicated that they would choose another profession if they had to do it over again.

Albrecht & Sack (2000, p. 4) recognize some progress but not enough:

> [S]ome accounting programs, schools, and academic staff have made significant and meaningful changes in recent years. We applaud those efforts. However, the evidence is clear that, while there have been significant changes by some, the changes have not been significant or pervasive enough.

What do Albrecht & Sack recommend? I would summarize their recommendation in a simple phrase: accounting educators must look ahead not backwards. They recognize that the 'one-size-fits-all' model of accounting education so prevalent in the past is not likely to succeed in the future. Each university's accounting educators, every PAB's education division, indeed the accounting profession itself, must develop a strategic-planning process to anticipate the future needs of the accounting professional and adapt education and training programmes accordingly. The strategy must set goals that anticipate environmental changes, it must focus on both curriculum and pedagogy, it must recognize and seek the resources needed to develop programmes to meet the strategy, and it must provide for assessment of attainment of the stated goals.

As universities go forward and adapt their accounting programmes to a changing environment, it is important to remember an important observation of Albrecht & Sack (2000: 59):

[W]hether accounting programs survive as currently structured probably is not all that important. What matters is that we determine how to add high value to our students as they prepare for careers in a fast-changing business world.

The investment that academic accounting staff, administrators, and PABs have in the current institutional structure of accounting education and training should not keep them from seeing what is best for accounting students – those who will determine the future of the accounting profession.

27.7 The last 10 years

27.7.1 Globalization and IFRS

Two major trends in accounting education have emerged in the last decade and will likely continue into the next. The first is the increasing globalization of accounting education (see Karreman, 2002). International accounting was a small niche in accounting academe until recently. In most countries, the educational focus was on national rather than global issues. But, responding to the global interests of the accounting profession, universities have put increasing emphasis on the ability of graduates to function in a global environment. Evidence of this is the growing international focus of academic accounting associations. Regional associations (such as the European Accounting Association and the Asian Academic Accounting Association) have led to sharing of best practices across national borders. The AAA, with nearly one-third of its membership international, has placed added emphasis on its global outreach. The IAAER has greatly expanded its influence, especially its contributions to international accounting and auditing standard setting. Finally, the International Accounting Education Standards Board (IAESB) has issued eight International Accounting Education Standards (IESs) that are influencing accounting education, especially in developing economies.[7] I will elaborate on the role of the IAAER and IAESB later in this chapter.

The second trend is related – the growing influence of International Financial Reporting Standards (IFRS). Because IFRS are principles-based, they require a more conceptual approach to accounting education. Education for IFRS begins with the objectives of financial reporting, from which it develops concepts, principles, and finally rules. (See Wilson & Adler, 2012.) Curricula that traditionally regarded accounting theory as a capstone course are being revised to include theory early in one's accounting education. However, this trend is really just starting to gain momentum because much of the last decade had been devoted to reacting to two major economic crises.

27.7.2 The 2000s: good news and bad news

Charles Dickens might have been referring to the accounting profession in the 2000s when he began *A Tale of Two Cities* with '*It was the best of times; it was the worst of times*'. The decade began with a stock market implosion that led to exposure of a series of accounting scandals, surfacing first in the U.S.A. but then expanding worldwide. It ended with the Global Financial Crisis (GFC), precipitated by a worldwide credit crisis that some blamed on accounting, especially fair-value accounting. However, few accountants were among the perpetrators of the scandals, and there is little evidence that fair-value accounting played a role in the credit crisis. (See Adler, Chapter 23 – this volume.)

The larger problem, especially in the early-decade scandals, was that many accountants ignored their 'watchdog' role and passively accepted actions which they knew were wrong. On the positive side, a majority of the 'whistle-blowers,' those risking their careers to point out wrongdoings, were accountants. Nevertheless, the accounting profession's reputation was sullied by the scandals. It seemed like the worst of times.

As a quick response, the U.S. Congress passed the Sarbanes-Oxley (SOX) Act, or what I call the 'Accountants Employment Act of 2002', Despite criticisms of the accounting profession, SOX relied heavily on accountants to clean up the mess. Increased oversight of companies' financial matters, including attesting to the adequacy of internal controls, created a tremendous demand for more accountants. The effect was felt worldwide, not only in the U.S.A., as many countries tightened their regulations and asked accountants to attest to compliance. For accountants, it seemed to be the best of times. (See Van Peursem *et al.*, 2012.)

How did this affect accounting education? From an accounting educator's view it was a boon. First, more and better students were attracted to accounting. Part of this was the disappearance of many high-tech jobs as the technology bubble burst about the same time as the scandals were occurring. But the scandals also had an unexpected positive effect. Accounting had traditionally had a reputation, especially among students, as being a highly ethical but boring career. After the scandals, the integrity of accountants might be questionable, but it was suddenly exciting. Accountants were getting headlines – some good and some bad – but headlines nonetheless. This was illustrated well in a *New Yorker* cartoon where two young men were in a bar. One was obviously trying to impress a young woman. The other man whispered to him: 'Don't just say you are in finance, tell her you are an accountant!'

The second effect was the opening of tremendous job opportunities for accountants. Accounting graduates had multiple job offers, and some were even receiving signing bonuses. The professional scepticism built into accounting education became valuable throughout organizations, and no one could hire enough accountants. Of course, this also increased the number of students wanting to enter accounting.

Unfortunately, this positive situation had a dark side. It allowed accounting educators to ignore some of the warnings of the AECC and Albrecht & Sack. Instead of focussing on changing curricula and pedagogy, accounting administrators turned their attention to hiring enough academic staff to service the increase in demand for accounting classes. Some accounting education programmes continued to change and improve, but the urgency was gone, especially the dire enrolment predictions of Albrecht & Sack. In my view, the main curricular change since 2000 has been an increased emphasis on ethics. Partly as a response to the accounting scandals, and partly due to concern about what was attracting some of the new entrants into accounting careers, instilling integrity in accounting graduates became a priority in many accounting programmes. It has always been clear that, for accountants to provide value, their reports and interpretations must be credible, and credibility requires integrity. However, many accounting educators had maintained that integrity is not teachable. Recently this argument has faded, and the teaching of ethics and integrity has generally been accepted as being an important part of accounting programmes. (See Boyce, Chapter 24 – this volume.)

27.8 Recent educational initiatives

Three recent analyses by Australian institutions and one in the U.S.A. continue the institutional influence on accounting education. The Australian reports are by Hancock *et al.* (2009), Capellatto (2010), and Evans *et al.* (2010). The latter two were summarized and discussed by De Lange and Watty (2011). The report by Hancock *et al.* investigated the changing skills set (technical and non-technical) deemed necessary for accounting graduates over the next 10 years and the strategies for embedding such skills in accounting programmes. The research team found that non-technical skills were viewed by employers as being very important in recruitment, training, and workplace skills development, whereas employers generally had modest expectations regarding new graduates' technical skills and accepted that these would need to be developed in the workplace. A set of 18 strategies was offered to provide a variety of approaches to help accounting educators embed non-technical skills in accounting programmes at Australian universities. (Compare this with the views of St. Pierre & Rebele, Chapter 5 in this volume.)

The Evans *et al.* (2010) report, produced by the Institute of Chartered Accountants of Australia (ICAA) and the Centre for Accounting, Governance and Sustainability at the University of South Australia, is a collection of contributions by 12 different authors and covers a variety of issues. The main purpose of the report was to promote an open discussion on the issues raised. The Capallatto (2010) Report, commissioned jointly by CPA Australia, ICAA, and the Institute of Public Accountants, focussed more on identifying and illustrating the problems facing accounting education in Australia. As with the Matthews (1990) Report of more than 20 years ago, both of the current reports deal first and foremost with the under-funding of accounting education. Several other themes were common to the two reports, most of them stemming from the under-funding, especially:

- large class sizes;
- a growing number of international students (who pay full tuition fees);
- unmet demand for accounting graduates; and
- an inability on the part of universities to deliver a quality accounting education, especially an inability to provide graduates with sufficient communication skills.

The reports also address the ageing of academic accounting staff and the relationship between academic accounting staff and the accounting profession.

A major effort in the U.S.A. was focussed on providing a path for accounting education into the next decade. In 2008, the U.S. Treasury Department issued the report of its Advisory Committee on the Auditing Profession (ACAP) (U.S. Department of the Treasury, 2008). Section VI of this far-ranging report was on Human Capital and focussed on '*[the]auditing profession's ability to cultivate, attract, and retain the human capital necessary to meet developments in the business and financial reporting environment and ensure audit quality for investors.*' Among the recommendations of this section was one that the AICPA and AAA form a joint commission '*[to] provide a timely study of the possible future structure of higher education for the accounting profession*'.

In response to the ACAP report, the AICPA and AAA formed the Pathway Commission, which published its report on the future paths of higher education for the accounting profession in July 2012 (Pathways Commission, 2012).[8] The Commission's charge was (2012, p. 9):

> to study the future structure of higher education for the accounting profession and develop recommendations for educational pathways to engage and retain the strongest possible community of students, academics, practitioners, and other knowledgeable leaders in the practice and study of accounting.

The Commission identified seven recommendations for change and eight impediments that need to be addressed for change to actually happen. The Commission focussed on establishing '*an ongoing process to implement these or future recommendations and putting in place the structures and relationships needed to overcome the limitations of periodic efforts to sustain the vitality of accounting education and practice*' (ibid., p. 10). Like the AECC in the 1990s, this was an attempt to do more than just prepare a report – it sought to directly influence accounting education so that it better meets the needs of the accounting profession.

27.9 Accounting education today

This brings us to the current state of accounting education. First, let me make a distinction between education and training.[9] I see education and training as being quite different. Education, derived from the Latin *educare*, to draw out, means developing one's capabilities. While it may include transfer of knowledge, it is much more than that. It is often process-oriented, focussed on developing and exercising innate abilities to reason, communicate, and solve problems. Training is more limited in scope, though no less important. It focusses on instructing someone on a particular job or task so as to make them proficient at it.

Much learning, especially that related to a profession, is a combination of education and training, and accounting is no exception. The key is to provide the right combination of education and training at the right times to create the capabilities needed. Universities and other educational institutions are often the best sources of education. At the same time they provide some training, but it is simply an adjunct to the basic goal of education. Professional programmes and on-the-job experience usually provide the best training, although training programmes inevitably provide some education as well. Because both education and training are essential for developing entry-level as well as long-term career capabilities, it is important for universities and the profession to work together to provide potential accountants with an effective and efficient path to gaining the required capabilities.

What capabilities do candidates need to be accounting professionals? How should they gain the necessary capabilities? Many institutions have weighed in on these questions. I will pick and choose from these institutional views to present my thoughts on accounting education in the next decade. The main challenge to today's accounting educators is to equip students with an ever-expanding set of capabilities using a limited (and often shrinking) set of resources. (See Watty, Chapter 13, Cunningham, Chapter 18, and Stevenson *et al.*, Chapter 19 – all in this volume.)

27.10 Knowledge, skills, and attitudes for success in accounting

27.10.1 AECC knowledge, skills, and attitudes

In the last 40 years there have been at least 20 different statements in the U.S.A. (and many more worldwide), from a variety of educational and professional institutions, formalizing the expectations of knowledge, skills, and attitudes[10] (KSAs) for accounting university graduates. I will focus on the KSAs proposed by the AECC (1990) based on the recommendations of the Bedford Committee and presented in Exhibit 27.1. I may be partial to this AECC list because I helped develop it. Nevertheless, despite being more than 20 years old, it represents well my view of the capabilities needed by accounting professionals today.

Of the eight categories listed in Exhibit 27.1, only two are unique to accounting.[11] The other areas may be partially covered in accounting curricula, but they can also be learned outside of accounting programmes. Even if the KSAs are learned outside the accounting curriculum, accounting courses need to reinforce them by showing their applicability in accounting. Further, this list and most of the similar lists ignore an important aspect of competencies – the depth of knowledge required in each area. That depth is *de facto* defined by the Uniform CPA examination

Exhibit 27.1 Composite profile of capabilities needed by accounting graduates

1 **General knowledge**
- An understanding of the flow of ideas and events in history and the different cultures in today's world.
- Basic knowledge of psychology, economics, mathematics through calculus, and statistics.
- A sense of the breadth of ideas, issues, and contrasting economic, political, and social forces in the world.
- An awareness of personal and social values and of the process of inquiry and judgment.
- An appreciation of art, literature, and science.

2 **Intellectual skills**
- Capacities for inquiry, abstract logical thinking, inductive and deductive reasoning, and critical analysis.
- Ability to identify and solve unstructured problems in unfamiliar settings and to apply problem-solving skills in a consultative process.
- Ability to identify ethical issues and apply a value-based reasoning system to ethical questions.
- Ability to understand the determining forces in a given situation and to predict their effects.
- Ability to manage sources of stress by selecting and assigning priorities within restricted resources and to organize work to meet tight deadlines.

3 **Interpersonal skills**
- Ability to work with others, particularly in groups, to influence them, to lead them, to organize and delegate tasks, to motivate and develop people, and to withstand and resolve conflict.
- Ability to interact with culturally and intellectually diverse people.

4 **Communication skills**
- Ability to present, discuss, and defend views effectively through formal and informal, written and spoken language.
- Ability to listen effectively.
- Ability to locate, obtain, organize, report, and use information from human, print, and electronic sources.

5 **Organizational and business knowledge**
- A knowledge of the activities of business, government, and non-profit organizations, and of the environments in which they operate, including the major economic, legal, political, social, and cultural forces and their influences.
- A basic knowledge of finance, including financial statement analysis, financial instruments, and capital markets, both domestic and international.
- An understanding of interpersonal and group dynamics in business.
- An understanding of the methods for creating and managing change in organizations.
- An understanding of the basic internal workings of organizations and the application of this knowledge to specific examples.

Exhibit 27.1 continued

6 Accounting knowledge

- History of the accounting profession and accounting thought.
- Content, concepts, structure and meaning of reporting for organizational operations, both for internal and external use, including the information needs of financial decision-makers and the role of accounting information in satisfying those needs.
- Policy issues, environmental factors, and the regulation of accounting.
- Ethical and professional responsibilities of an accountant.
- The process of identifying, gathering, measuring, summarizing, and analyzing financial data in business organizations, including:
  - the role of information systems;
  - the concepts and principles of information system design and use;
  - the methods and processes of information system design and use;
  - the current and future roles of computer-based information technology.
- The concepts, methods, and processes of control that provide for the accuracy and integrity of financial data and safeguarding of business assets.
- The nature of attest services and the conceptual and procedural bases for performing them.
- Taxation and its impact on financial and managerial decisions.
- In-depth knowledge in one or more specialized areas, such as financial accounting, management accounting, taxation, information systems, auditing, non-profit, government, and international accounting.

7 Accounting skills

- Ability to apply accounting knowledge to solve real-world problems.

8 Personal capacities and attitudes

- Creative thinking
- Integrity
- Energy
- Motivation
- Persistence
- Empathy
- Leadership
- Sensitivity to social responsibilities
- A commitment to life-long learning

Source: This Exhibit is a reproduction of Appendix B from AECC (1990, pp. 7–8).

in the U.S.A. and by similar examinations in most parts of the world. This creates a problem. The CPA examination has dual purposes in:

- ensuring a minimum level of expertise on which the market can rely when hiring an accountant; and
- providing statutory authority to attest to publicly-issued financial statements.

Because the second of these is the legal basis of most accounting certifications, it tends to dominate the content of the examination. Most certification examinations focus on knowledge (and, to a lesser extent, skills) specific to accounting and attestation. These are the components of items 6 and 7 in Exhibit 27.1. Although other areas in this exhibit may periodically appear in certification examinations, they are tested less often and in less depth. Thus, the examinations may reliably identify those with the knowledge to attest to financial statements, they do not ensure competence across the broad array of KSAs required to provide valuable accounting services. Thus, an education based on simply passing a certification examination is likely to be deficient in many crucial KSAs. This is made clear from the definition of competence promulgated by the International Accounting Education Standards Board (IAESB), which views competence in terms of being able to perform work-related roles to an acceptable standard with reference to real working environments.

The conflict between the content of certification examinations and the KSAs required for success as a professional accountant has created a dilemma for many universities. Some have elected to focus on training students to pass the examination, others have opted to focus on educating students for long-term careers as accounting professionals, and most have tried to do some combination of both. This has led to some accounting graduates who are well-educated but under-trained, and some who are well-trained but under-educated. Of course, some also graduate with a good balance of education and training. This dilemma is not unique to the U.S.A. Although the relationship between accounting programmes at universities and programmes provided by PABs varies across countries, the tension between broad education and technical accounting training inevitably exists. (See Calhoun & Karreman, Chapter 26 in this volume.)

The variety of approaches taken by universities leaves the profession, and especially the PABs, to fill an assortment of holes in the capabilities of candidates for certification. On-the-job training and formal training programmes offered by PABs do an excellent job at filling the training holes left by universities, but they often are less effective if the holes are educational. Why? Practising members of the profession have great practical knowledge and experience in accounting – essential elements in training novice accountants. In contrast, most academic accounting staff in universities focus on a broad understanding of the underlying concepts of accounting and the complementary knowledge and skills needed by a competent professional. The advantage of accounting professionals flows from their expertise in accounting practice – thus, training for specific accounting-related functions is effective and efficient. Universities, on the other hand, rely on their expertise in building a base for life-long learning, giving accounting students a solid foundation for tomorrow's world, not just today's practices. (See Flood, Chapter 4, and Paisey & Paisey, Chapter 30 – both in this volume.)

27.10.2 Development of accounting KSAs

The area in which there is most diversity world-wide, and for which both universities and PABs can claim some advantages, is the development of *accounting* KSAs (items 6 and 7 in Exhibit 27.1). In the U.S.A. this has generally been the domain of universities but, in other parts of the world, the profession and PABs have played a larger role. From my potentially biased view as a university educator, I think the need for students to build a solid conceptual understanding of accounting to allow adaptability as the world changes gives universities an advantage. This is especially true as more of the world adopts IFRSs. The change in focus of university business and accounting programmes in the last half-century has led to educators having a deeper understanding of the role of accounting – essentially the information services that accounting provides to organizations and the economy. As technology, globalization, and other forces change the specifics of how that information is gathered, analyzed, and reported, accounting information continues to serve the same function (i.e. informing economic decision-makers). By educating students in the function of accounting, and asking them to reason through various ways of satisfying that function, universities can produce graduates who are better able to adapt to changes in the environment of accounting. (See Wilson *et al.*, Chapter 3, and Boritz & Stoner, Chapter 16 – both in this volume.)

This does not mean that PABs could not hire the educational expertise and develop accounting education programmes that could compete with those of universities. It just means that such programmes already exist at universities, and it may not be efficient to duplicate them within PABs. More important, to the extent that the PABs provide accounting education (as opposed to training), it is incumbent on them to offer prospective accountants the conceptual understanding and skills development needed to establish a base for life-long professional careers, not just short-term certification. This is especially true as the world moves to the more principles-based IFRS.

At the same time, academic accounting staff in universities have less and less ability to offer the practical training needed by the profession because of the demands for research output. Many of these research demands are generated internally by universities, but increasingly they are exacerbated by governments that allocate resources to universities based on research rankings. (This is well-established in the U.K. where most universities are dependent upon state funding.) These rankings usually ignore the professional contributions of accounting educators and simply add up publications in approved journals. This creates a greater need for professional accounting programmes to provide the needed practical knowledge and training.

27.11 Standards of the IAESB

I mentioned earlier a relatively new player in determining educational standards for accounting education and certification – the International Accounting Education Standards Board (IAESB), a part of the International Federation of Accountants (IFAC). The IAESB issues International Education Standards (IESs), the first of which was published in October 2003. Will these standards help establish preferred methods for achieving accounting education and training throughout the world? I think it is still too early to definitively answer this question, but their influence is increasing, especially in countries where the quality of accounting education has been lagging.[12]

So far the IAESB has issued eight standards:[13]

IES 1:   Entry Requirements to a Program of Professional Accounting Education
IES 2:   Content of Professional Accounting Education Programs
IES 3:   Professional Skills
IES 4:   Professional Values Ethics and Attitudes
IES 5:   Practical Experience Requirements
IES 6:   Assessment of Professional Capabilities and Competence
IES 7:   Continuing Professional Development: A Program of Lifelong Learning and Continuing Development of Professional Competence
IES 8:   Competence Requirements for Audit Professionals

These standards are quite general and most are not likely to be binding for the majority of developed countries. They will not provide a blueprint for accounting education and training. However, on the positive side, they demonstrate the breadth of capabilities required of accountants throughout the world and establish a framework for addressing issues of accounting education and training.

As these IESs evolve, they may provide more guidance. The IAESB still seems to be struggling with the purpose of the standards. Are they to be minimum acceptable standards so that any jurisdiction that falls short in any way is judged to be certifying under-qualified accountants? Or are they 'best-practices', or at least 'good-practices', providing goals to be achieved? The latter implies that there is an expectation that all of the standards may not be met, but movement toward meeting them is sufficient. This is the current view of the IAESB. Because of legal and cultural differences, setting minimal acceptable standards may result in IESs that are so watered down as to be meaningless. However, with the IAESB setting targets of best-practices, it may indeed lead to a useful framework for accounting education and training.

27.12 The emergence of the IAAER

Another institution mentioned earlier that has achieved increased prominence in the last decade is the International Association for Accounting Education and Research (IAAER). Although founded in 1984, the IAAER has become a more important global player in accounting education in the last decade. Its mission, which is on IAAER's web site home page (http://www.iaaer.org/), is '*to promote excellence in accounting education and research on a worldwide basis and to maximize the contribution of accounting academics to the development and maintenance of high quality, globally recognized standards of accounting practice*'. Its main impact is to bring together accounting practitioners and academics to address important issues of the profession. Its conferences, most of which are jointly sponsored with local or national academic accounting associations, foster international sharing of best practices in teaching and research. It has been instrumental in developing educators' expertise in teaching IFRS. It has also focussed on the contributions that academic research can make to practice. The main emphasis of this has been supporting academic research that directly informs accounting standard setters such as the IASB, the IAESB, and the International Auditing and Assurance Standards Board (IAASB). Especially pertinent to this chapter is the series of IAAER/ACCA research projects to inform the IAESB. Reports from all six projects in the series can be found on the IAAER's website (http://www.iaaer.org/research_grants/index.htm). Finally, the IAAER holds advisory positions where an academic voice is needed but where political or other considerations require an international rather than national or regional representative.

27.13 The problem of resources

Before concluding, I want to address one issue that will potentially affect the future delivery of accounting education and training worldwide – the declining public financial support of universities. Although such declining public support is not universal, it affects many countries. Academics in Australia have been especially vocal about the underfunding of accounting education. In the U.S.A., the result to date is mainly shifting the cost of education from the public to students. The quality of accounting education in the U.S.A. has not been severely affected, though it may be in the future. In other countries, where it is more difficult to pass on the costs of education to students, there has been a need to significantly change educational delivery systems to conserve resources. This has created two main pressures:

- adaptation of university accounting programmes so that they consume fewer resources; and
- pressure for alternatives to university education in accounting.

Consider first the response of universities to budget cuts. The most common reaction has been to increase class sizes. Without a restructuring of the delivery system within the classes, this leads to a decrease in quality. To further exacerbate the problem, the largest classes are usually at the introductory level, the class that is most important in attracting good students to accounting. (See Laswad & Tan, Chapter 9, Jackling, Chapter 10, and Wygal, Chapter 11 – all in this volume.) And finally, an increasing number of classes are being taught by non-tenure track staff, many of them teaching on a part-time basis.

Some universities have recognized the need to restructure their delivery systems and have sought technology solutions. Traditional education is labour-intensive, and thus economies have been hard to achieve. Whereas many industries have achieved economies by replacing employees with technology-based processes, universities that have tried to do the same have been only partially successful. To the extent that knowledge transfer is the goal, technology-based education (such as distance-learning) works well. Thus, there is part of the accounting curriculum that can benefit from technology. However, technology solutions require much investment upfront to achieve savings later, and often resources for such investment are not available. Further, without one-on-one interactions with educators, students' motivation may be a problem. Finally, developing critical thinking and problem-solving, improving skills such as oral and written communications and teamwork, and instilling integrity and professionalism are much more difficult in a technology-driven curriculum. (See Boritz & Stoner, Chapter 16, Hassall & Joyce, Chapter 17, and Cunningham, Chapter 18 – all in this volume.)

A better solution is to use academic staff as 'coaches'. They would design learning environments, using technology solutions for knowledge transfer and creating various techniques for developing skills. They would form 'learning contracts' where each student takes charge of his or her own learning. The academic staff are the motivators, provide a structure for learning, and give feedback and help when needed. They become facilitators of learning, not the fount of all knowledge. When resources are scarce, it is a shame to waste educators' time by having them lecturing on material that is available elsewhere. There is much more value created when they are interacting with students and helping each achieve his/her individual potential.

Now let's consider the reaction of the profession, and especially PABs. There is a large incentive for the accounting profession to protect itself from unqualified practitioners, the actions of whom can taint the entire profession. If the universities are not adequately preparing students to enter the accounting profession, someone must step in. A first step, as we saw with the AECC and the Pathways Commission in the U.S.A., is to supply resources to universities, both expertise and financial resources, to help them achieve the needed quality of accounting education. But that volunteer effort is not a viable long-run solution. Thus, it is not surprising to see growing educational divisions within accounting firms and PABs. Even if universities are the most efficient and effective organizations to provide accounting education, if they cannot get the resources to do it right, it leaves an opening for others to step in. This is a challenge to university accounting programmes to fight for the needed resources and to design programmes that make the best use of those resources. If universities succeed, it will be better for both the universities and the accounting profession.

27.14 Conclusion

Accounting education has come a long way in the last 50 years. The basic trajectory has been a steady improvement, but there have been ups and downs along the way. While we continue to hear complaints about the preparation of students for the accounting profession, those voices would be much louder if accounting education had not progressed from what it was in the 1950s and 1960s. Still, huge challenges remain. In today's 'information economy' there are tremendous opportunities for accountants. But the knowledge and skills necessary to take advantage of these opportunities continually grow. Only through cooperation among universities, practising accountants, and PABs can we have a system of education and training of accountants that ensures that those entering the profession can be life-long contributors to the profession as well as upholding its public interest obligations.

Notes

1 To examine an alternative analysis of the evolution of accounting education, one that goes back more than 50 years, see Black (2012).
2 The influence of academic accounting associations started later in the U.K. than in the U.S.A. According to Parker (1997), the British equivalent of the AAA, the Association of University Teachers of Accounting (now the British Accounting & Finance Association), nearly 'flickered out of existence' in the early 1960s. Its influence on accounting education started to increase in 1966 and was solidified by a successful conference at the University of Kent in 1971. The first BAFA Special Interest Group (SIG) was set up in 1991 by Richard M. S. Wilson, focussing on accounting education, and this became the exemplar for subsequent BAFA SIGs.
3 Most of the statistics in this and the following paragraphs are from Schultz (1989, pp. 31–139).
4 See the AACSB Web site, at www. aacsb.edu.
5 Current AACSB Accounting Accreditation Standards may be found at: http://www.aacsb.edu/ accreditation/accounting/standards/2013/. There are nine specific accounting standards in four areas: Strategic Management and Innovation Standards, Participants Standards, Learning and Teaching Standards, and Academic and Professional Engagement Standards. For a further coverage of the evaluation of accounting programmes, see Calderon, Chapter 22 and, for a more general discussion of accreditation in accounting, see Apostolou & Gammie, Chapter 29 – both in this volume.
6 The conceptual framework project was started in 1973 and resulted in the publication of six Statements of Financial Accounting Concepts between 1978 and 1985. In 1989, the International Accounting Standards Committee (now the International Accounting Standards Board) published a framework with many similarities.
7 For more information about the IAESB, see McPeak et al. (2012). The Standards, as of 2013, can be found in the *Handbook of International Education Pronouncements: 2010* Edition (http://www.ifac. org/sites/default/files/publications/files/handbook-of-international-e-2.pdf). However, a revision of the standards is nearing completion, and the up-to-date information on the standards can be found on the IAESB website at http://www.ifac.org/education.
8 For an executive summary of the Pathways Commission report, see Behn (2012).
9 Most dictionaries do not make this distinction, using education and training as synonyms. However, I find this distinction useful in assessing how accountants can most effectively and efficiently gain their competencies. For more on education and training of accountants, see Evans, Chapter 28 – this volume; and Evans et al. (2012).
10 Some people refer to KSAs as knowledge, skills, and abilities. In Position Statement No. 1, the AECC (1990) refers to 'professional orientation' instead of attitudes or abilities.
11 For more on the generic skills required by accountants, see Watty, Chapter 13 – this volume, and Watty et al. (2012).
12 Calhoun & Karreman use these standards as a framework for their analysis of entry requirements for professional accountants and auditors: see Chapter 26 – this volume.
13 From the IAESB website: http://www.ifac.org/Education.

References

Accounting Education Change Commission (1990) *Objectives of Education for Accountants*, Position statement no. 1, Sarasota, FL: American Accounting Association. Included in Accounting Education Change Commission (1996) *Position and Issues Statements of the Accounting Education Change Commission*, (AAA Education Series, Vol. 13), Sarasota, FL: American Accounting Association. Available at: http://aaahq.org/ AECC/PositionsandIssues/cover.htm.

Albrecht, W.S. & Sack, R.J. (2000) *Accounting Education: Charting the Course through a Perilous Future* (Accounting Education Series, Vol. 16), Sarasota, FL: American Accounting Association. Available at: http://aaahq.org/pubs/AESv16/toc.htm.

American Accounting Association Committee on the Future Structure, Content, and Scope of Accounting Education (The Bedford Committee) (1986) Future accounting education: preparing for the expanding profession, *Issues in Accounting Education* 1(1), 168–195.

Behn, B.K., Ezzell, W.F., Murphy, L.A., Rayburn, J.D., & Strawser, J.R. (2012) The Pathways Commission on accounting higher education: charting a national strategy for the next generation of accountants, *Issues in Accounting Education* 27(3), 595–560.

Big 8 (1989) *Perspectives on Education: Capabilities for Success in the Accounting Profession* (The White Paper), New York: Arthur Andersen & Co., Arthur Young, Coopers & Lybrand, Deloitte Haskins & Sells, Ernst & Whinney, Peat Marwick Main & Co., Price Waterhouse, and Touche Ross. In Sundem, G. L. (1999) available at: http://aaahq.org/AECC/history/cover.htm.

Birkett, W.P. (1993) *Competency Based Standards for Professional Accountants in Australia and New Zealand*, Sydney: CPA Australia, ICAA, NZICA.

Black, W.H. (2012) The activities of the Pathways Commission and the historical context for changes in accounting education. *Issues in Accounting Education*, 27(3), 601–625.

Bloom, R., Heymann, H.G., Fuglister, J., & Collins, M. (1994) *The Schism in Accounting*, Westport, CT: Quorum Books.

Burgess, T. (ed.) (1986) *Education for Capability*, London: NFER-Nelson.

Capellatto, G. (2010) *Challenges Facing Accounting Education in Australia*, Melbourne: AFAANZ. Available at: http.//afaanz.org/.

Committee on Concepts and Standards for External Financial Reports (1977) *Statement on Accounting Theory and Theory Acceptance*, Sarasota, FL: American Accounting Association.

Committee to Prepare a Statement of Basic Accounting Theory (1966) *A Statement of Basic Accounting Theory*, Chicago: American Accounting Association.

De Lange, P. & Watty, K. (2011) Accounting education at a crossroad in 2010 and challenges facing accounting education in Australia, *Accounting Education: an international journal*, 20(6), 625–630.

Evans, E., Burritt, R., & Guthrie, J. (eds) (2010) *Accounting Education at a Crossroad in 2010*, Sydney: Centre for Accounting, Governance and Sustainability, University of South Australia and Institute of Chartered Accountants in Australia. Available at: http://www.charteredaccountants.com.au/Students/Academics-teachers-and-career-advisors/News-and-updates/News/New-publication-Accounting-Education-at-a-Crossroad-in-2010.aspx.

Evans, E., Juchau, R., & Wilson, R.M.S. (eds) (2012) *The Interface of Accounting Education and Professional Training*, Abingdon: Routledge.

Flaherty, R. (ed.) (1998), *The Accounting Education Change Commission Grant Experience: A Summary* (Accounting Education Series, Vol. 14), Sarasota, FL: American Accounting Association. Available at: http://aaahq.org/AECC/changegrant/cover.htm.

Gordon, R.A. & Howell, J.E. (1959) *Higher Education for Business*, New York: Columbia University Press.

Hancock, P., Howieson, B., Kavanagh, M., Kent, J., Tempone, I., & Segal, N. (2009) *Accounting for the Future: More Than Numbers*, Vol. 1: *Final Report*, Vol. 2: *Strategies for Embedding Non-Technical Skills into the Accounting Curricula*, Sydney: Australian Learning & Teaching Council. Available at: www.altc.edu.au.

Johns, A. (1995) Competency standards for professional accountants in Australia and New Zealand, *Accounting Education: an international journal*, 4(1), 37–42.

Karreman, G.H. (2002) *The Impact of Globalisation on Accountancy Education*, London: International Accounting Standards Committee Foundation.

Matthews, R., Jackson, M., & Brown, P. (1990) *Accounting in Higher Education: Report of the Review of the Accounting Discipline in Higher Education*, Canberra: Department of Employment, Education, and Training, Commonwealth of Australia.

McPeak, D., Pincus, K.V., & Sundem, G.L. (2012) The International Accounting Education Standards Board: influencing global accounting education, *Issues in Accounting Education* 27(3), 743–750.

Parker, R.H. (1997) Flickering at the margin of existence: The Association of University Teachers of Accounting, 1960–1971, *British Accounting Review*, 29(1–2), 41–61.

Pathways Commission (2012) *Charting a National Strategy for the Next Generation of Accountants*, AAA and AICPA. Available at: http://commons.aaahq.org/files/0b14318188/Pathways_Commission_Final_Report_Complete.pdf.

Pierson, F.C. (1959) *The Education of American Businessmen*, New York: McGraw-Hill Book Company.

Sangster, A. & Wilson, R.M.S. (eds) (2013) *Liberalising the Accounting Curriculum*, Abingdon: Routledge.

Schultz, J.J., Jr. (1989) *Reorienting Accounting Education: Reports on the Environment, Professoriate, and Curriculum of Accounting* (Accounting Education Series, Vol. 10), Sarasota, FL: The American Accounting Association.

Solomons, D., with T.M. Berridge (1974) *Prospectus for a Profession*, London: ABAE.

Sundem, G.L. (1999) *The Accounting Education Change Commission: Its History and Impact* (Accounting Education Series, Vol. 15), Sarasota, FL: American Accounting Association. Available at: http://aaahq.org/AECC/history/cover.htm.

The Economist (2009) The Gordon-Howell Report of 1959: the more things change . . . a seminal critique of American business education, five decades on (4 June). Available at: http://www.economist.com/node/12762453.

Trueblood, R.M. (1963) Education for a changing profession, *Journal of Accounting Research*, 1(1); 86–94.

U.S. Department of Education, National Center for Education Statistics (2012) *Digest of Education Statistics, 2011*. NCES 2012-001, Chapter 3. Available at: nces.ed.gov/FastFacts/display.asp?id=75 - 24k.

U.S. Department of the Treasury (2008) *Final Report of the Advisory Committee on the Auditing Profession*. Washington, DC: U.S. Government Printing Office. Available at: http://www.treasury.gov/about/organizational-structure/offices/Documents/final-report.pdf.

U.S. House of Representatives, Subcommittee of Oversight and Investigations of the Committee on Interstate and Foreign Commerce (Moss Committee) (1976) *Federal Regulation and Regulatory Reform*, Washington, DC: U.S. Government Printing Office.

U.S. Senate, Subcommittee on Reports, Accounting and Management of the Committee on Governmental Affairs (Metcalf Committee) (1977) *The Accounting Establishment*, Washington, DC: U.S. Government Printing Office.

Van Peursem, K.A., Monk, E.A., Wilson, R.M.S., & Adler, R.W. (eds) (2012) *Audit Education*, Abingdon: Routledge.

Watty, K., Jackling, B., & Wilson, R.M.S. (eds) (2012) *Personal Transferable Skills in Accounting Education*, Abingdon: Routledge.

Wilson, R.M.S. & Adler, R.W. (eds) (2012) *Teaching IFRS*, Abingdon: Routledge.

About the author

Gary L. Sundem is Emeritus Professor of Accounting at the Foster School of Business, University of Washington, Seattle, Washington, U.S.A. (glsundem@uw.edu). He is a former president of both the American Accounting Association (AAA) and the International Association for Accounting Education and Research (IAAER), a former editor of *The Accounting Review*, and was Executive Director of the Accounting Education Change Commission (AECC).

28

The interface between academic education and professional training in accounting

Elaine Evans

MACQUARIE UNIVERSITY, SYDNEY, AUSTRALIA

CONTENTS

Abstract

The interface between *academic education* and *professional training* in accounting has been a contentious issue over many decades. The debate has been particularly active in Australia, the U.K., and the U.S.A. where institutional arrangements for the preparation of professional accountants differ significantly.

What are these 'contentious' issues and why have there been diverse views posited by accounting academics, professional accounting bodies, and accounting practitioners over such a long period of time? Using three analytical themes, this chapter will review the evolution of the debate in time and space, in order to understand the current state of the debate and the reasons why the issues remain contentious.

The final section of the chapter presents a number of suggestions about how accounting academics, the professional accounting bodies, and accounting practitioners can work together in a collaborative manner to forge a more positive *interface* based on mutual understandings and cooperative relations.

Keywords

academic education, accounting academics, accounting education, accounting practitioners, interface, professional accounting bodies, professional training

28.1 Introduction

The main aims of this chapter are:

- to review the current state of the debate through the extant literature and through examples of the interface between providers of accounting education and professional training (academics, practitioners, and the professional accounting bodies (PABs));
- to trace the debate about the place of accounting as a discipline in a university;

- to critique the role of academic research and professional practice in the generation and regeneration of accounting knowledge and practice; and
- to synthesize the literature on various approaches to preparing students for professional practice through work-experience programmes.

The aims of the chapter align with three analytical themes which reflect the current institutional arrangements for the education and training of professional accounting practitioners. However, agreement on the individual role of each of these institutions (the academy, the profession, and the workplace) is problematic. This chapter will analyse the more contentious aspects of the interface among these institutions under the following themes:

- the role of universities in educating professional accountants;
- the generation and regeneration of the accounting profession's knowledge-base through academic research; and
- the integration of conceptual knowledge (which is research-based) and vocational skills (which are workplace-based) through programme-based work experience.

This chapter provides a comprehensive and authoritative (but not exhaustive) source of reference for accounting academics and practitioners and the PABs in the domain of accounting education and professional training, not as competing institutions but as collaborators in the formation of effective accounting practitioners and educated professionals. It covers current debates and issues which are relevant to the academy, the profession and the workplace. In addition, the chapter includes contemporary trends such as alternate pathways in Australia and the U.K., and the Pathways Commission in the U.S.A., in addition to work-integrated learning schemes which require cooperative arrangements between accounting academics, PABs, and accounting practitioners. The purpose of these inclusions is to inform current and future debates about such vexed questions as the appropriate roles of various institutions in the preparation of the next generation of business and accounting professionals.

In the final section there are suggestions for future strategies and action items which will enhance cooperative arrangements between the accounting academy, PABs, and accounting practitioners.

28.2 The nature of the interface

28.2.1 Introduction

The interface between academic education and professional training in accounting has been a contentious issue globally and hotly debated in the academic literature over many decades (for example, see Geddes, 1995; Elliott & Jacobsen, 2002; Paisey & Paisey, 2006; Annisette & Kirkham, 2007; Gammie & Kirkham, 2008; King & Davidson, 2009; Wilson et al., 2009; Kaplan, 2011). Currently, the strength of links between accounting academics, accounting practitioners, and the PABs is being tested because of pressure from students and employers to move professional accounting preparation to a more efficient, economic, and practical basis (for an example of the tension in Australia, see Poullaos & Evans, 2008). The changing expectations of academics, students, employers and the PABs struggle for alignment as the current university and professional employment environment generates new demands for changing the academic and professional pathways to membership of PABs and professional accounting practice (for example, see Gammie et al., 2002; Hassall et al., 2005; Jackling & De Lange, 2009; Pan & Perera, 2012).

28.2.2 Shifts in the interface

Recently, Evans *et al.* (2012) suggest that there are unresolved issues which contribute to a perceived or real tension between accounting academics, PABs, and accounting practitioners. Burritt *et al.* (2010, p. 14) discuss the challenges facing accounting education in Australia and posit that '*the way forward is an alliance between the academy and the profession that seeks . . . to co-operatively develop accounting education in the academy, in the profession and in the workplace*'.

Wilson *et al.* (2009) debate whether, in fact, there is interdependency between accounting educators in the university sector and accounting educators or trainers within the profession: or are their roles mutually exclusive? In earlier research, Poullaos & Evans (2008) argue that the formation of professional accountants is a shared role which requires mutual understanding and cooperation.

In the extant literature, there is general agreement that the academy, PABs, and accounting practitioners all have roles to play in the formation of the professional accountant (for example, see Geddes, 1995; Wilson *et al.*, 2009; Wilkerson, Jr, 2010). However, other literature has argued that accounting education in universities is under the control of the PABs, and consequently the potential to produce reflective professionals is compromised (for example, see Craig & Amernic, 2002; Sikka & Wilmott, 2002; Sikka *et al.*, 2007). Work by Annisette & Kirkham (2007), Gammie & Kirkham (2008), and King & Davidson (2009) describes the academy interface in the U.K. as 'separateness' and 'parallel existence': a state which appears to suit both parties. Annisette & Kirkham (2007) describe the profession's relationship with the university as a whole as one where the Institute of Chartered Accountants in England & Wales (ICAEW) attaches a low value to university education. These authors concede that it is the vocational nature of the accounting curriculum which contributes to accounting's struggle to maintain its place in the university system in the U.K. According to Gammie & Kirkham (2008, p. 361), the Institute of Chartered Accountants of Scotland (ICAS) disregards '*university provisioned education*', thus casting doubt on the ability of university education to contribute to the formation of a professional accountant.

King & Davidson (2009, p. 270) make two observations about the U.K. scene:

- the '*accountancy profession in the U.K. enjoys sufficient standing of its own making and has no pressing need for legitimation from academia*'; and,
- universities do receive benefits from an academy–profession link but the benefits '*do not appear central to the legitimacy of accounting as an academic subject in the U.K.*'.

Recent moves by the Institute of Chartered Accountants Australia (ICAA) and CPA Australia to create alternate pathways for non-accounting graduates and school leavers (Evans & Poullaos, 2012) signal shifts in the academy–profession interface in Australia in line with the situation in the U.K.

28.2.3 Externalities impacting on the interface

Clearly, maintaining educational preparation for the accounting profession in three separate silos of academy, profession, and workplace is not desirable. A productive interface between academic education and professional training necessarily requires creative alliances between accounting academics, accounting practitioners, and PABs in an increasingly complex context where a range of factors impact on aspects of that interface, including:

- the broadening of accounting work to encompass aspects of corporate social reporting, corporate governance, sustainability, and risk management;
- international accounting and auditing standards;
- technology and overseas outsourcing of routine, technical accounting tasks;
- competing and globalizing PABs;
- over-representation of international students in business schools and accounting departments, and increasing university dependence on the revenue which these students bring in; and
- a perception that academic accounting research is only relevant to other accounting academics and does not address real-world issues.

(See also Flood, Chapter 4 – this volume.)

28.3 Importance of the interface

28.3.1 Three key events

In the past few years, the importance of the interface between accounting academics, the accounting profession, and accounting practitioners has been more positive and is highlighted in three different events. The relative importance and impact of these three events provide strong motivations for the writing of this chapter:

- the Accounting Education Symposium (AES) held during the 2009 Annual Congress of the European Accounting Association (EAA) in Finland;
- the Centre for Accounting, Governance and Sustainability (CAGS) at the University of South Australia and the ICAA's 3rd Annual Thought Leadership Forum held in Adelaide in February in 2011;
- finally, the publication in the U.S.A. of the 2012 report of the Pathways Commission on Accounting Higher Education: *Charting a National Strategy for the Next Generation of Accountants*. The Commission was created by the American Accounting Association (AAA) and the American Institute of Certified Public Accountants (AICPA) 'to study the future structure of higher education for the accounting profession' (AAA AICPA, 2012, p. 9).

28.3.2 The Accounting Education Symposium, 2009

In reporting the focus of the AES, Wilson *et al.* (2009) raise a number of suggestions in relation to the interface:

- research findings to be used as inputs for PABs and professional firms to inform practice and policy-making; and
- improvements in the interaction and alignment between accounting education research and education and training policy which will lead to the development of a more effective accounting practitioner.

One of the concluding comments was that academe and (the practice of) accounting are inextricably linked.

28.3.3 The CAGS ICAA 3rd Annual Thought Leadership Forum, 2011

The findings of the CAGS ICAA 3rd Annual Thought Leadership Forum are reported in a book entitled *Bridging the Gap between Academic Accounting Research and Professional Practice*, published in 2011 (Evans *et al.*, 2011). Guthrie *et al.* (2011) summarize the challenges to the academic/professional interface as being:

- the need for more communication and coordination between accounting practitioners, accounting policy-makers, and academic accounting researchers;
- the perception that academic research findings have little relevance for policy and practice; and
- the need for accounting education in university programmes to emphasize the value of academic research.

28.3.4 The Pathways Commission Report, 2012

Finally, one of the recommendations of the Pathways Commission, created by the AAA and the AICPA, was for '*[the] purposeful integration of accounting research, education and practice for students, accounting practitioners, and educators*' (AAA AICPA, 2012, p. 11). The Commission also recognized that there was a lack of collaboration between accounting educators and practitioners; that accounting practitioners were not readers of accounting research; and that accounting education in universities did not require students to read and understand academic research.

28.3.5 Three themes of accounting

Clearly the issue of the interface between education and professional training in accounting is very much alive and the three events described above are clear evidence of this. Section 28.4 explores this interface based on three themes which capture important elements of the interface: (1) university education (the role of universities); (2) academic accounting research (generation of knowledge through academic research); and (3) professional accounting practice (work experience programmes).

According to Laughlin (2011, p. 21), accounting research, policy, and practice need to work together yet not dilute their respective contributions. The literature reviewed mainly emanates from experiences in Australia, the U.K., and the U.S.A. where the debate has been most prominent over many decades. Currently in Australia and the U.S.A., an accounting undergraduate or post-graduate degree is the preferred pathway for entrants to the professional examinations of the dominant national bodies such as the AICPA, CPA Australia and ICAA (Evans & Poullaos, 2012; Pincus, 2012). In the U.K., the majority of entrants to the professional examinations of the ICAEW and ICAS have obtained non-relevant degrees (i.e. the graduates have not majored in accounting). A number of authors have argued that this arrangement suits the PABs and employers because the PABs are in a better position to prepare graduates (both with and without an accounting degree) for the accounting profession through professional examinations which are formulated through close alignment with accounting practice (for example, see Annisette & Kirkham, 2007; Sikka *et al.*, 2007; Gammie & Kirkham, 2008; King & Davidson, 2009).

28.4 Exploring the interface: the role of universities

28.4.1 Introduction

This section of the chapter will trace the debate about the place of accounting as a discipline in a university. Important to this debate is the notion of accounting as both a profession and a research-based practice However, accounting education within a university context is not a universal experience, and international differences will be canvassed. (See Calhoun & Karreman, Chapter 26 – this volume.)

Historically and globally, a university has been characterized as being '*[a] seat of learning . . . insulated from pragmatic and economic exigencies*' (Symes, 1999, p. 242). However, the university as an 'ideal type' of liberal institution maintaining the values of Western culture is now an anachronism (ibid., p. 243). (See Amernic & Craig, Chapter 12 – this volume, and Sangster & Wilson, 2012.) Universally, government policies are making university education economically relevant as a response to the labour market demands for 'work-ready' graduates. (On related competences, see also Watty, Chapter 13, Boritz & Stoner, Chapter 16, and Cunningham, Chapter 18 – all in this volume.) Global imperatives now require graduates to be trained for modern industry, commerce, and the professions. Many of these professions (such as medicine, law, and engineering) have a long history of fitting well into a university environment because of their scientific and theoretical underpinnings, and their credentialing and legitimising capabilities. Alas for accounting, this has not been the case – at least not in Australia, the U.K., and the U.S.A.

28.4.2 Experience in Australia

In Australia, accounting as an academic discipline only really consolidated its place in the 1980s when Federal Government education policy dissolved a tier of higher education which predominantly catered for part-time students who were usually employed in industry or the professions (Evans & Juchau, 2009). These previously vocationally-oriented institutions, which were devoted to the application of practical knowledge, and closely aligned to the needs of industry and business, were often amalgamated with other vocational institutions to form a 'university'. As a result, they were expected to be transformed into institutions with a research orientation. The teachers in these previously vocational institutions generally had been employed on a part-time basis and came from practice. Certainly very few of the full-time academic staff had PhDs or were active in academic research, although generally they were very active in the PABs.

28.4.3 Experience in the U.S.A.

In the U.S.A., accounting education in universities began in 1893 (Chu & Man, 2012). To ensure the status of the profession, the early professionals wanted the educational model to be similar to the recognized professions of medicine and law. Comprehensive histories of accounting and accounting education in the U.S.A. include Flesher *et al.* (1996), Langenderfer (1987), Previts & Merino (1998), and Van Wyhe (1994, 2007a, 2007b). All the authors agree that, over many decades, there has been (and still is) an over-emphasis on technical skills and preparation for the CPA examination, as well as the production of narrowly-trained graduates. This was not the intent of the founding fathers. Evidence of this is seen in an article in *Accounting Horizons*, by Demski *et al.* (2002) who report on a panel discussion at the 2001 Carnegie Mellon University

Accounting Mini-Conference. The theme of the conference was 'Intellectual Foundations of Accounting'. Interestingly, the authors refer to an article by Henry Rand Hatfield published in the *Journal of Accountancy* in 1924. They speculate that Hatfield was motivated: '*by the perceived meagre status of accounting as a legitimate scientific discipline both outside and inside the profession*' (Demski et al., 2002, p. 157).

There is further evidence from *The Accounting Review* which reveals a variety of views about the status of accounting as a profession and the role of universities in the U.S.A. in professional formation. This historical perspective is important for an understanding of the unresolved issues between accounting academics, accounting practitioners, and the accounting profession. For example, Belser (1927, p. 38), who worked for Price, Waterhouse and Company, argued that: '*the successful accountant must be well grounded in theory . . . the application of the theory is as important as the theory itself*'.

Further, Belser (ibid., p. 40) recommended more theory and a sounder education. Stevenson (1931) reflects the uncertainty about the professional status of accounting in the early 1930s and recounts that it was the accounting profession in the U.S.A. which requested the introduction of accounting courses in universities. Yet Stevenson comments, even back then, that the collegiate schools of business and the profession had not cooperated well in developing accounting courses. Bevis (1958) argues for '*training at an academic level*' within a five-year programme, that is, more time in a '*scholastic program*'.

A few years later, the debate in *The Accounting Review* had shifted to 'The Objectives of Accounting Education'. Swick (1961) seems to indicate that there was little debate about the issue and no apparent agreement. He distinguishes the primary objective of preparation of students to be able '*[to] evaluate conditions and situations . . . in which monetary or economic considerations are paramount, yet with a full awareness, on the part of the evaluator, of the moral and ethical considerations involved*' (ibid., p. 627). Swick sees this as being separate and distinct from vocational training. Lynn (1964) was the Director of Education of the AICPA when he wrote an article in *The Accounting Review*. Along with his predecessors writing on the topic, he states strongly that accounting is a profession with a common body of knowledge imparted through formal educational processes leading to a bachelor's degree. For these early writers, there was no question that accounting was a profession worthy of a degree within its own right. Interestingly, while professional identity was very important to the early accounting academics and practitioners, contemporary academics such as Baker (2001) question the proposition that there is an '*accounting profession*' which requires an appropriate level of education, as is the case with other professions such as medicine and law. Earlier Zeff (2003a, 2003b) had identified the troubled state of the accounting profession in the U.S.A. which he blamed on a gradual degeneration of professional values.

28.4.4 Experience in the U.K.

In *The Accounting Review* in 1938, an article appeared noting that '*few universities [in England] offering accounting courses . . . stress the development of a general intellectual background which may be drawn upon when future problems are presented*' (Murphy, 1938, p. 404). In fact, Murphy commented that the universities were in no way connected with training for the profession. Anderson-Gough (2008, p. 309) explores the history of accounting education in England and Scotland, and notes that '*this education not taking place in a university did not prevent accountants creating a professional identity and a market for their services*'.

Little has changed in the U.K. as noted in a very recent paper in *Critical Perspectives on Accounting* (Hopper, 2013). Hopper's claims are very relevant to this chapter as he links this theme to the second theme of research by stating that '*unlike other professions, that of accounting does not see universities as the reservoir and developer of its knowledge base*' (2013, p. 131).

In the U.K., professional accounting education is technical, vocational, and there are few explicit links to the conduct and outcomes of research. It is no wonder that practising accountants think that academic research is not relevant, a theme pursued in the next section.

As noted by Annisette & Kirkham (2007), Gammie & Kirkham (2008), and King & Davidson (2009), there are many professional accountants in the U.K. without a university degree in accounting (or in anything else). Hunt (2007) observes that the majority of accounting students in the U.K. are from non-relevant degree backgrounds, while Baker (2001) observes that a similar trend is emerging in the U.S.A. where employers are seeking students who have not studied accounting. In Australia, Poullaos & Evans (2008) interviewed senior members of Big 4 firms in Australia who also confirmed this trend.

28.4.5 The contested role of universities

The role of the universities in the education of professional accountants is contestable, and the debate in Australia, the U.K., and the U.S.A. can be traced back at least to the early 1930s. Most recently, Wilson (2011) contends that rigorous liberal academic preparation for accounting practice is the foundation for the preparation of effective practitioners. By way of contrast, other accounting education researchers (such as Jackling & De Lange (2009), Ballantine & Larres (2009), Wells *et al.* (2009) and Gammie & Joyce (2009)) have all argued that the role of university education is to meet the needs of employers for work-ready graduates. It can be argued that, if the academy resists or ignores this role, it may be difficult for accounting departments/business schools to recruit students to undertake an accounting degree in a university, because there are now alternate pathways which meet the educational requirements of PABs.

Within the last decade different opinions about the role of the university in accounting education still remain. For example, Hatherly (2007, p. 33) clearly articulates a role for accounting education in universities as '*understanding the bigger picture of how accounting relates to wealth creation, financial activity, social control and wealth distribution*'.

At another level, Craig & Amernic (2002) discuss the accountability of university accounting educators. They position the teaching of accounting within a university to be focussed more on social critique rather than on technical menus. (But see St. Pierre & Rebele, Chapter 5 – this volume, for an alternative perspective.) Clearly there are mixed views about the nature of accounting as an academic discipline and its role within a university.

Is accounting worthy of a degree? This debate has raged for decades and we are no closer to an agreed position than we were 70 years ago. In the U.K. context, Hopper (2013, p. 135) forcefully states that '*if the curricula and pedagogy of universities transpire to imitate professional [accounting] courses, then what is the point of having accounting taught in universities?*'

Research is the key and this leads to the theme of knowledge generation and regeneration through accounting research.

28.5 Exploring the interface: generation of knowledge through academic research

28.5.1 Introduction

If accounting education is placed within a university setting, then, as an academic discipline, accounting educators must engage in research. However, over many years there has been a debate that academic accounting research has become too far removed from the interests of the profession and practitioners and is, in fact, irrelevant to both. In response, accounting academics consider that many practical issues of concern to practising accountants and the PABs do not warrant the attention of researchers. This section of the chapter will analyse the current state of play in this debate, giving particular attention to future possibilities for improving aspects of the interface so that the generation and regeneration of accounting knowledge through research can be a shared experience and not just the domain of one party.

While the purpose of university education has changed during the past few decades, the recent *Review of Australian Higher Education* (DEEWR, 2008) recognizes the nexus between liberal and utilitarian views of education by recommending that universities should be required to:

> carry out research in the field in which they teach so that they can contribute fully to the knowledge economy and produce graduates who embody the distinctive value of teaching that is informed by research.
>
> (Recommendation 19, p. xx)

The Pathways Commission on Accounting Higher Education in the U.S.A. recommends the purposeful integration of accounting research, education, and practice for students, accounting practitioners, and educators (AAA AICPA, 2012, Recommendation 1). The associated objectives include the focussing of more academic research on relevant practice issues, and the integration of accounting research into accounting courses and programmes.

28.5.2 The research-practice and policy gap

In the light of decades of debate about the limited contribution of contemporary scholarly accounting research to accounting practice, these dictums sound simplistic at best and naïve at worst. Rutherford (2011) uses words such as '*schism*' and '*substantiative gap*' when he reviews the literature (particularly from Australia, the U.K. and the U.S.A.) on the disconnect between accounting academia and the world of practice. Additional commentary on this gap is cited below.

Writing a final article as editors of *Accounting Horizons*, Burton & Sack summarize the reasons why they believe that accounting research '*seems to have so little value*' (1991, p. 144). They cite the 1958 experience of the Accounting Principles Board created by the AICPA. The research division of AICPA, with both practitioners and academics, was charged with the responsibility of developing an accounting framework and studies of specific topics. The AICPA expected that adequate research '*would make solutions to accounting problems obvious*' (ibid., p. 144). This endeavour failed and then again, in 1973, the AICPA created the Financial Accounting Standards Board (FASB), supported by a Director of Research and Technical Activities, and a staff of approximately 50 professionals. It had the responsibility of developing a conceptual framework through research: and, once again, the result was an apparent failure. FASB encouraged research but their pronouncements are mainly a result of a political bargaining process. Burton & Sack (1991) encouraged different parts of the profession to talk to each other, but came to the discouraging conclusion that researchers suggest that practice problems are mundane or provincial, while practitioners suggest that researchers are impractical or inexperienced.

Bloom (2011) cites Sandy Burton as an example of an academic who bridged the gap between accounting in the academy and accounting in practice. According to Bloom, in 1991, Burton accused academics of being more concerned about applying sophisticated methodologies to unimportant questions. He bemoaned the state of accounting practice, research, and education. In the 1990s, Burton & Sack, who were still co-editors of *Accounting Horizons* at the time, accused the academy of insularity. They set three challenges:

- solve problems that society cares about;
- research a broad range of business topics; and
- talk to the accounting profession and accounting practitioners.

For them, a clear imperative was '*[to] overtly build bridges between practitioners and researchers so that misplaced perceptions [of irrelevance] do not grievously damage both parts of the profession*' (1991, p. 145).

In the same vein, Granof & Zeff (2008) state that accounting educators have contributed little to the establishment of new practices, have failed to perform a needed role as a watchdog of the profession, and have created a disconnect between their teaching and their research. This criticism comes from 'inside the camp'!

Singleton-Green (2010) argues that it is an open question how far accounting research has influenced accounting developments. At the time of writing, he was employed by the ICAEW. Although he was writing about the influence of research on standard setting, nevertheless he claims that there is a '*gap between accounting academics and the rest of the world*'. He lists deterrents to effective communication between academics and accounting practitioners and policy-makers including:

- volume and dispersion of research;
- research methodology, which is often incomprehensible;
- disagreement between 'experts', leaving the layperson confused;
- research is becoming more remote and irrelevant to practice and practitioners, and the problem is exacerbated because there are few, if any, rewards, for academics to publish their research in professional magazines and other more accessible media;
- academics need to know that their work has influence; and
- there is a need for an intermediary to connect the two worlds of accounting practice and accounting research.

28.5.3 Bridging the gap

A contemporary view of the gap is captured in *Bridging the Gap between Academic Accounting Research and Professional Practice* (Evans *et al.*, 2011), in which Kevin Stevenson, the Chairman and CEO of the Australian Accounting Standards Board (AASB), and a member of the Australian Financial Reporting Council (FRC), wrote:

> *[E]ven if the research ticks all the right boxes in terms of intent and methodology, are its findings communicated in a manner that people can, on a timely basis, see the mosaic or picture being pieced together, or are they confined to staring for long periods at an unrecognisable and isolated pixel?*
>
> (Stevenson, 2011, p. 104)

Further, Lee White, the CEO of ICAA, commented:

> *I'm just casting my mind back to when I've looked at different pieces of research, the ones which are pretty highly mechanized, statistical approach, I must admit, leave me generally pretty cold. And that's even as a – previously as a practitioner who used to do all sorts of models in terms of altered evidence and all this sort of stuff. I find it pretty hard to read.*
>
> (Leung *et al.*, 2011, p. 90)

These views were expressed by a practitioner/policy-maker and a representative from a PAB. Further commentary on the relationship between accounting research and practice is expressed by academics, in particular, Tilt (2010), who questions the impact of academic accounting research on professional practice, and Carlin (2011), who suggests there is an endemic lack of engagement between accounting scholars and practitioners. Although these articles were produced in an Australian context, they cite international research papers which echo the same theme: the accounting profession's knowledge and practice base is not being generated and regenerated through academic research because of a perceived or real gap/schism among accounting academics, PABs, and accounting practitioners, which has been written about and debated for decades. (See, for example, Bloom *et al.*, 1994.)

After years of debate, it is time to find a way forward, and this may be through accounting education. The final theme explores how the workplace may become a way of strengthening the links between accounting academics, accounting practitioners, and the PABs. Placing students in the workplace, as part of their academic programme, requires negotiations between the three groups, and has the possibility of promoting understanding and appreciation of each other's perspective.

28.6 Exploring the interface: work-experience programmes

28.6.1 Introduction and definition

Accounting is a profession based on professional practice of the highest quality. The formation of professional accountants requires an academic approach to education which emphasizes the importance of a grasp of theory and general principles, underpinned by research and the inculcation of professional knowledge, skills and capabilities (including critical and analytical skills), which are appropriate for the workplace. The concepts of work-integrated learning, internships, and work placements are important ways of balancing academic education and professional training. This section of the chapter will synthesize the literature on various approaches to preparing students for professional practice through work-experience programmes.

Work-integrated learning can be defined as '*educational programs which combine and integrate learning and its workplace application, regardless of whether this integration occurs in industry or whether it is real or simulated*' (Atchison *et al.*, 2002, p. 3). Internships can differ in the fact that they may not necessarily be part of an educational programme but may be undertaken on a private basis outside of the requirements of a programme, over a summer vacation, for example.

There is evidence that the relationship between universities and workplaces has been evolving over the past few decades, including the introduction of work-based degrees and the growth of 'work integrated learning' systems (McIntyre & Solomon, 2000; Atchison *et al.*, 2002). Work-integrated-learning, work placements, cooperative learning, and internships are all models of integration of academic knowledge, practical knowledge, and professional practice. Pressure for integration to produce 'work-ready' graduates comes from the PABs which accredit courses and devise professional examinations for graduates wishing to gain membership of those bodies, and employers who want graduates with technical competence, communication skills, social skills, and workplace competence on entry to employment. (See Watty, Chapter 13, and Apostolou & Gammie, Chapter 29 – both in this volume.) The physical location of a university is separate from the workplace and connections come through the involvement of accounting academics and students with the PABs and with employers. Academics are increasingly growing out of touch with accounting practice because they have never been in practice and were recruited because of their PhDs and publications (Grumet, 2001). Therefore, they should not have the sole responsibility for preparing students for professional accounting practice.

28.6.2 Internships in the U.S.A.

An early view about internships comes from Bevis (1958) who, at the time, was a partner with Touche, Niven, Bailey and Smart in the U.S.A. He argues that internships should be an integral part of a university programme and that the internship should be for six months. At that time, his view was out of step with those of 'teachers of accounting' who did not believe that such an internship 'should constitute a requirement for either a bachelor or master degree' (Smith, 1964, p. 1025). Despite the early polarization of views, work-integrated-learning, work placements, cooperative learning, and internships are accepted models of education for students wishing to enter the accounting profession. A recent article in *Journal of Accounting Education* (Dombrowski *et al.*, 2013) describes an in-house auditing internship contemporary model in the U.S.A. which is organized and conducted as an actual accounting practice. 'The Firm', as it is known, has an Executive Partner who is the auditing instructor and is staffed by accounting undergraduate students. It provides real audit and accounting services to clients. (See also Beard & Humphrey, Chapter 25 – this volume; and Van Peursem *et al.*, 2012.)

28.6.3 Work placements in the U.K.

The experience of placements in the U.K. is reported by Surridge (2009) where he details the arrangements for work experience of periods from six weeks, three months, six months, and sometimes a one-year placement. These placements normally take place before the final year of study, they are supervised by academic staff, and require the student to produce an assessable report. Hopper (2013) describes an elite form of internship in the U.K. where the PABs have developed four-year degrees (which includes a year of professional training) for sponsored students, while other universities have negotiated arrangements with particular accounting firms for students to complete both their undergraduate degree and their professional certification within six years.

28.6.4 Work-integrated learning in Australia

In the Australian context, Freudenberg *et al.* (2010) outline a professional degree that involves students studying full-time for their first year and then moving to part-time in the second and third years while, at the same time, undertaking a two-year paid internship. Freudenberg *et al.* state that the success of the programme depends on the creation of a meaningful link between the university and the profession, and that the involvement of industry in the design and delivery of the programme is critical.

28.6.5 Benefits of work-experience programmes

Importantly, they are seen as being of benefit to the students in terms of academic performance and professional performance (for example, see Koehler, 1974; Knechel & Snowball, 1987; Siegel & Rigsby, 1988; Pasewark *et al.*, 1989; English & Koeppen, 1993; Myring *et al.*, 2005; Surridge, 2009).

One of the advantages of internships and their equivalents is the opportunity for accounting practitioners to build relationships and understandings with accounting academics (Violette *et al.*, 2013). A further advantage is the interaction between students, accounting practitioners, and accounting academics (Beard, 2007). In addition, internships allow students to understand the skill set that is required of a graduate, and to help them understand how well they are prepared for future employment (Yu *et al.*, 2013), and the importance of employment traits (Green *et al.*, 2011).

Work-experience programmes such as internships, placements, etc., allow students to integrate the conceptual knowledge of accounting gained through their university studies with practical skills that are required in the workplace. Research shows that students benefit in terms of their academic and professional performance. Further, the benefit for the academy is that links are forged with industry and the profession, thus creating a more positive interface based on mutual understandings and cooperative relations.

On other aspects of work experience, see also Byrne & Willis, Chapter 7, and Hassall & Joyce, Chapter 17 – both in this volume.

28.7 Future directions for a more productive interface

28.7.1 Specific action items

In pursuit of a more cooperative and collaborative interface, there have been calls for specific action. Bloom & Myring (2008) suggest more active involvement from industry and commerce leaders on university advisory boards. This involvement may have benefits for both the academy and practitioners. The academic members of the board can have:

- access to real-life case studies and projects;
- greater possibilities of access to data;
- possibilities for internships for students; and
- more access to funding from industry for innovations in accounting education.

Practitioners can meet accounting academics and be aware of the implications of research for current practice and policy-making.

Guthrie *et al.* (2011) note that PABs include academic work in their professional publications; research funding is available through the PABs; academic researchers have been commissioned by the PABs to undertake studies (for example, see Unerman & O'Dwyer, 2010, commissioned by ACCA; Gammie *et al.*, 2007, commissioned by ICAS; and the ICAS and the FRC research project: 'The skill and competency requirements of auditors', available at http://icas.org.uk/technical-research/research-centre/joint-research-projects/FRC/).

28.7.2 Liberalizing the accounting curriculum

Some commentators suggest that the future of accounting education in universities will be a combination of a liberal arts learning philosophy, which focusses on underlying knowledge, and a broad range of skills, competencies, and values but with only some specific technical knowledge. For example, Diamond (2005) sees that many subjects will be taught outside accounting departments and business schools, and that students will not necessarily be prepared for professional examinations. Fogarty (2010, p. 412) advocates a '*deep application of the liberal arts to improve accounting education*' which will require embedding it in a professional context and integrating the approach with the accounting curriculum. A liberal arts learning philosophy has the possibility of revealing the social role of accounting and reconnecting accounting education with ethical and moral dimensions of accounting practice (Chabrak & Craig, 2013). (See also Amernic & Craig, Chapter 12 – this volume.)

Interestingly in 2010, *Accounting Education: an international journal* devoted a themed edition to the subject of *Liberalising the Accounting Curriculum*. Sangster (2010) describes this approach as developing students' general capabilities as well as their ability to be lifelong learners.

The themed edition takes the form of a thought-provoking paper by Lister (2010), 11 commentaries by authors based in eight different countries, and a rejoinder by Lister. (See also Sangster & Wilson, 2012.) Reference is made to the themed edition in this concluding section because the notion of liberalising the accounting curriculum through literature has possibilities for enhancing the academic/profession/practitioner interface. Through the development of soft skills (for example, creative writing, reading a wide range of literature, and exposure to a world view which is much wider than a narrow vocational and technical curriculum), students are able to acquire a broad set of graduate capabilities which the PABs and employers have been demanding from accounting departments and business schools.

While not all the commentators agree with some of Lister's specific suggestions about literature, there are some like Evans & Fraser (2010, p. 353), who state that *'perhaps there is potentially a wider argument here for the incorporation of a (perhaps preliminary?) liberal arts element in the university education of those whose intention is to train for the professions'*.

Jelly (2010, p. 362), then Director of Education at the Chartered Institute of Management Accountants (CIMA), sees some merit in Lister's proposition and acknowledges that:

> *[E]mployers to date want graduates who are both competent in their chosen specialized area of study and who are broadly educated individuals who can think critically, evaluate, analyse, synthesize and in general acknowledge that there is a world 'out of their (accounting) box' which they should access in solving problems and finding solutions. The novel (classical or modern) and poetry can assist in this objective to broaden learning.*

IFAC, in its International Education Standards, also recognizes that a broad *'general education'* is a requirement to become a Professional Accountant.

28.7.3 Recommendations of the Pathways Commission

The Pathways Commission (AAA AICPA, 2012) makes a number of important observations and recommendations for the future of accounting education, and for the accounting profession, all of which have possibilities for a productive interface. The majority of these have been discussed already in this chapter (and elsewhere in this volume):

- accounting practitioners do not read academic accounting research;
- accounting education focusses too much on technical material;
- accounting students are not given sufficient exposure to accounting research; and
- there are gaps in the links between research and practice, practice and education, and education and research.

The recommendations give future objectives, such as: focus more academic research on relevant practice and business issues (1.2); enhance the value of exchanges between accounting academics and practitioners (1.3); and integrate accounting research into accounting courses and programs (1.4).

Action items to achieve these goals can include:

- dialogue between academics and PABs over emerging areas of research – such as sustainability and audit quality;
- representatives from the PABs and practitioners can give guest lectures, speak at graduation ceremonies, and be invited to meetings of students' associations;

- PABs can act as industry partners in funding applications;
- accreditation requirements can include embedding research into the curriculum;
- academics can chair sessions and/or speak about their research at industry and professional conferences;
- retired practitioners can become Adjunct Professors or Executives-in-Residence; and
- the necessity for academics to make arrangements for work-experience programmes can create valuable exchanges between academics and practitioners.

(See also Sundem, Chapter 27 – this volume.)

28.8 Conclusion

This chapter sees a future for academic accounting education and professional training in the interface of three models of accounting education. (See Needles, Chapter 2 – this volume.)

First, within the university where a student becomes capable of being an accountant (in the broadest sense of the word) – *the intellectualization of accounting*. While this may not be the experience within the U.K. where entrants to the profession mainly come through non-relevant degrees, nevertheless accounting academics in business schools, in which accounting is taught, can ensure that their students are exposed to academic accounting research and its benefits for knowledge creation and renewal, critical analysis of accounting practice and relevance for the sustainability of the profession. In addition, liberalizing the accounting curriculum has the potential to ensure a framework for students to know how to think critically, question, challenge, and communicate.

Second, within the workplace where employees are made ready to be accountants – *the vocationalization of accounting*. This distinction is not meant to dilute the contributions of the academy and the workplace in the formation of an effective practitioner. It is meant to meaningfully engage academics and practitioners so that they do not discount or ignore each other's roles. It is probably most effective through a work-experience programme where students can integrate conceptual knowledge of accounting with vocational skills.

Finally, within the PABs, their examination and continuing professional development (CPD) processes which enable a graduate/employee/academic to be professional in their work – *the professionalization of accounting*. Already there are many examples of academics on Education Boards which set professional examinations. Academics can be invited to speak about their research at industry conferences and CPD events.

These models of interface will not necessarily be linear and static but rather circular, dynamic, and interactive.

In concluding, it is apt to quote from an article written by A. C. Littleton (1942) in *The Accounting Review* over 70 years ago. The position he takes is as relevant today as it was then: '*Preparation for a professional career is not all, or even mostly, a matter of acquiring tools and skill. A profession should rest upon wide knowledge rather than narrow training*' (1942, p. 220).

References

AAA AICPA (2012) *The Pathways Commission: Charting a National Strategy for the Next Generation of Accountants*, Sarasota, FL: AAA, and New York: AICPA.

Anderson-Gough, F. (2008) Education, in Edwards, J.R. & Walker, S.P. (eds) *The Routledge Companion to Accounting History*, London: Routledge.

Annisette, M. & Kirkham, L. (2007) The advantages of separateness explaining the unusual profession-university link in the English chartered accountancy, *Critical Perspectives on Accounting*, 18(1), 1–30.

Atchison, M., Pollock, S., Reeders, E., & Rizzetti, J. (2002) Work integrated learning paper, *RMIT University–Morgan & Banks Career Management Project*, Melbourne: RMIT.

Baker, C.R. (2001) Whether there is an accounting profession? A commentary on "Whither (or wither) accounting education in the new millennium" by M. R. Mathews, *Accounting Forum*, 25(4), 402–404.

Ballantine, J. & Larres, P. M. (2009) Accounting undergraduates' perceptions of cooperative learning as a model for enhancing model interpersonal and communication skills to interface successfully with professional accountancy education and training, *Accounting Education: an international journal*, 18(4–5), 387–402.

Beard, D.F. (2007) Assessment of internship experiences and accounting core competencies, *Accounting Education: an international journal*, 16(2), 207–220.

Belser, F.C. (1927) How the universities can aid the accounting profession, *The Accounting Review*, 2(1), 37–42.

Bevis, D.J. (1958) Professional education for public accounting, *The Accounting Review*, 33(3), 445–449.

Bloom, R. (2011) Sandy Burton's accounting legacy: regulation and education, *Accounting Education: an international journal*, 20(1), 97–106.

Bloom, R., Heymann, H.G., Fuglister, J., & Collins, M. (1994) *The Schism in Accounting*, Westport, CT: Quorum Books.

Bloom, R. & Myring, M. (2008) Charting the future of the accounting profession, *The CPA Journal*. Available at: http://www.nysscpa.org/cpajournal/2008/608/essentials/p65.htm.

Burritt, R., Evans, E., & Guthrie, J. (2010) Challenges for accounting education at a crossroad in 2010, in Evans, E., Burritt, R., & Guthrie, J. (eds) *Accounting Education at a Crossroad in 2010*, Sydney: CAGS and ICAA.

Burton, J.C. & Sack, R.J. (1991) Editorial: accounting research: a new direction, *Accounting Forum*, 5(4), 142–146.

Carlin, T. (2012) Leveraging academic research to improve financial reporting, in Evans, E., Burritt, R., & Guthrie, J. (eds) *Bridging the Gap between Academic Accounting Research and Professional Practice*, Sydney: CAGS and ICAA.

Chabrak, N. & Craig, R. (2013) Student imaginings, cognitive dissonance and critical thinking, *Critical Perspectives on Accounting*, 24, 91–104.

Chu, S. & Man, H. (2012) History of accounting education, *Journal of Higher Education Theory and Practice*, 12(1), 119–128.

Craig, R. & Amernic, J. (2002) Accountability of accounting educators and the rhythm of the university: resistance strategies for postmodern blues, *Accounting Education: an international journal*, 11(2), 121–171.

Demski, J.S., Fellingham, J.C., Ijiri, Y., & Sunder, S. (2002) Some thoughts on the intellectual foundations of accounting, *Accounting Horizons*, 16(2), 157–168.

Department of Education, Employment and Workplace Relations (DEEWR) (2008) *Review of Australian Higher Education* (The Bradley Report), Canberra: DEEWR.

Diamond, M. (2005) Accounting education, research and practice: after Enron, where to go? *European Accounting Review*, 14(2), 353–362.

Dombrowski, R.F., Smith, K.J., & Wood, B.G. (2013) Bridging the education–practice gap: The Salisbury University auditing internship program, *Journal of Accounting Education*, 31, 84–106.

Elliott, R.K. & Jacobson, P.D. (2002) The evolution of the knowledge professional, *Accounting Horizons*, 16(1), 69–80.

English, D.M. & Koeppen, D.R. (1993) The relationship of accounting internships and subsequent academic performance, *Issues in Accounting Education*, 8(2), 2902–2909.

Evans, E. & Juchau, R. (2009) *Colleges of Advanced Education in Australia: A Lasting Legacy*, Berlin: VDM Verlag Publishing.

Evans, E., Juchau, R., & Wilson, R.M.S. (2012) The relationship between academic accounting education and professional training: an overview, in Evans, E., Juchau, R., & Wilson, R.M.S. (eds) *The Interface of Accounting Education and Professional Training*, London: Routledge.

Evans, E. & Poullaos, C. (2012) A brief history of the various pathways to the accounting profession in Australia, in Evans, E., Burritt, R., & Guthrie, J. (eds) *Emerging Pathways for the Next Generation of Accountants*, Sydney: CAGS and ICAA.

Evans, L. & Fraser, I. (2010) A commentary on 'A Role for the Compulsory Study of Literature in Accounting Education', *Accounting Education: an international journal*, 19(4), 351–354.

Flesher, D., Miranti, P., & Previts, G. (1996) The first century of the CPA, *Journal of Accountancy*, 182(4), 51–56.

Fogarty, T.J. (2010) Revitalizing accounting education: a highly applied liberal arts approach, *Accounting Education: an international journal*, 19(4), 403–419.

Freudenberg, B., Brimble, M., & Cameron, C. (2010) Where there is a WIL there is a way, *Higher Education Research and Development*, 29(5), 575–588.

Gammie, B., Gammie, E., & Cargill, E. (2002) Personal skills development in the accounting curriculum, *Accounting Education: an international journal*, 11(1), 63–78.

Gammie, E., Gammie, B., Matson, M., & Duncan, F. (2007) *Women of ICAS Reaching the Top: The Demise of the Glass Ceiling*, Edinburgh: ICAS.

Gammie, E. & Joyce, Y. (2009) Competence-based approaches to the assessment of professional accountancy training work experience requirements: the ICAS experience, *Accounting Education: an international journal*, 18(4–5), 443–466.

Gammie, E. & Kirkham, L.M. (2008) Breaking the link with a university education in the creation of the chartered accountant: the ICAS story, *British Accounting Review*, 40(4), 356–375.

Geddes, B. (1995) The development of accountancy education training and research in England: a study of the relationship between professional education and training, academic education and research, and professional practice in English chartered accountancy, unpublished PhD thesis, University of Manchester.

Granof, M.H. & Zeff, S.A. (2008) Research on accounting should learn from the past, *The Chronicle of Higher Education*, 54, 28.

Green, B.P., Graybeal, P., & Madison, R.L. (2011) An exploratory study of the effect of professional internships on students' perception of the importance of employment traits, *Journal of Education for Business*, 86, 100–110.

Grumet, L. (2001) Bridging the education gap, *The CPA Journal*, 71(8), 9.

Guthrie, J., Burritt, R., & Evans, E. (2011) The relationship between academic accounting research and professional practice, in Evans, E., Burritt, R., & Guthrie, J. (eds) *Bridging the Gap between Academic Accounting Research and Professional Practice*, Sydney: CAGS and ICAA.

Hassall, T., Joyce, J., Montanto, J., & Anes, J. (2005) Priorities for the development of vocational skills in management accountants: a European perspective, *Accounting Forum*, 25(4), 398–401.

Hatherly, D. (2007) A commentary on 'Professionalizing Claims and the State of UK Professional Accounting Education: Some Evidence', *Accounting Education: an international journal*, 16(1), 31–34.

Hopper, T. (2013) Making accounting degrees fit for a university, *Critical Perspectives on Accounting*, 24, 127–135.

Hunt, D.M. (2007) A commentary on 'Professionalizing Claims and the State of UK Professional Accounting Education: Some Evidence', *Accounting Education: an international journal*, 16(1), 35–38.

Jackling, B. & De Lange, P. (2009) Do accounting graduates' skills meet the expectations of employers? A matter of convergence or divergence, *Accounting Education: an international journal*, 18(4–5), 369–385.

Jelly, R. (2010) A commentary on 'A Role for the Compulsory Study of Literature in Accounting Education', *Accounting Education: an international journal*, 19(4), 361–363.

Kaplan, R.S. (2011) Accounting scholarship that advances professional knowledge and practice, *The Accounting Review*, 86(2), 367–383.

King, R. & Davidson, I. (2009) University accounting programmes and professional accountancy training: can UK pragmatism inform the Australian debate? *Australian Accounting Review*, 50(3), 261–273.

Knechel, W.R. & Snowball, D. (1987) Accounting internships and subsequent academic performance: an empirical study, *The Accounting Review*, 54(4), 799–807.

Koehler, R.W. (1974) The effect of internship programs on subsequent college performance, *The Accounting Review*, 49(2), 382–384.

Langenderfer, H. (1987) Accounting education's history: a 100-year search for identity, *Journal of Accountancy*, 163(5), 302–331.

Laughlin, R. (2011) Accounting research, policy and practice: worlds together or worlds apart? In Evans, E., Burritt, R., & Guthrie, J. (eds) *Bridging the Gap between Academic Accounting Research and Professional Practice*, Sydney: CAGS and ICAA.

Leung, P., White, L., & Cooper, B. (2011) Audit research and practice: a dialogue on 'relevance', in Evans, E., Burritt, R., & Guthrie, J. (eds) *Bridging the Gap between Academic Accounting Research and Professional Practice*, Sydney: CAGS and ICAA.

Lister, R.J. (2010) A role for the compulsory study of literature in accounting education, *Accounting Education: an international journal*, 19(4), 329–343.

Littleton, A.C. (1942) The meaning of accounting education, *The Accounting Review*, 17(3), 215–221.

Lynn, E. S. (1964) Education for the profession, *The Accounting Review*, 39(2), 371–376.

McIntyre, J. & Solomon, N. (2000) The policy environment of work-based learning: globalisation, institutions and workplaces, in Symes, C. & McIntyre, J. (eds) *Working Knowledge: The New Vocationalism and Higher Education*, Maidenhead: SRHE and Open University Press.

Murphy, M. E. (1938) Education and training of English accountants, *The Accounting Review*, 13(4), 404–410.

Myring, M., Bloom, R., & Shortridge, R.T. (2005) The effect of an accounting internship on sequent academic performance, *Journal of Accounting & Finance Research*, 13(1), 169–175.

Paisey, C. & Paisey, N. J. (2006) Cutting to the core? A reflection upon the recent education policy debates within the Institute of Chartered Accountants in England and Wales, *British Accounting Review*, 38(1), 31–61.

Pan, P. & Perera, H. (2012) Market relevance of university accounting programs: evidence from Australia, *Accounting Forum*, 36(2), 91–108.

Pasewark, W.R., Stawser, J., & Wilkerson, Jr., J. (1989) An empirical examination of the effect of previous internship on interviewing success, *Journal of Accounting Education*, 150(1), 35–39.

Pincus, K. (2012) The US Pathways Commission: origin, structure, initial report and prospects, in Evans, E., Burritt, R., & Guthrie, J. (eds) *Emerging Pathways for the Next Generation of Accountants*, Sydney: CAGS and ICAA.

Poullaos, C. & Evans, E. (2008) The ICAA pathways project: identifying the issues, paper presented to a meeting of the University of Sydney Pacioli Society, 27 November, Sydney Australia. Available at: http://www.econ.usyd.edu.au/staff/chrisp.

Previts, G.J. & Merino, B. (1998) *A History of Accountancy in the United States: The Cultural Significance of Accounting*, Columbus, OH: Ohio State University.

Rutherford, B.A. (2011) Accounting research and accounting policy: what kind of gap? *Accounting in Europe*, 8(2), 141–154.

Sangster, A. (2010) Editorial; liberalising the accounting curriculum, *Accounting Education: an international journal*, 19(4), 323–327.

Sangster, A. & Wilson, R.M.S. (eds) (2012) *Liberalising the Accounting Curriculum in University Education*, Abingdon: Routledge.

Siegel, P.H. & Rigsby, J.T. (1988) The relationship of accounting internships and subsequent professional performance, *Issues in Accounting Education*, 3(2), 423–432.

Sikka, P., Haslam, C., Kyriacou, O., & Agrizzi, D. (2007) Professionalising claims and the state of UK professional accounting education: some evidence, *Accounting Education: an international journal*, 16(1), 3–21.

Sikka, P. & Willmott, H. (2002) Commentary on 'Accountability of accounting educators and the rhythm of the university: resistance strategies for postmodern blues', *Accounting Education: an international journal*, 11(2), 191–197.

Singleton-Green, B. (2010) The communication gap: why doesn't accounting research make a greater contribution to debates on accounting policy? *Accounting in Europe*, 7(2), 129–145.

Smith, C.A. (1964) The internship in accounting education, *The Accounting Review*, 39(4), 1024–1027.

Stevenson, K. (2011) Leveraging academic research to improve financial reporting: a standard-setter's view, in Evans, E., Burritt, R., & Guthrie, J. (eds) *Bridging the Gap between Academic Accounting Research and Professional Practice*, Sydney: CAGS and ICAA.

Stevenson, R.A. (1931) Avenues of entry to the profession, *The Accounting Review*, 6(2), 140–141.

Surridge, I. (2009) Accounting and finance degrees: is the academic performance of placement students better?, *Accounting Education: an international journal*, 18(4–5), 471–485.

Swick, R.D. (1961) Objectives of accounting education, *The Accounting Review*, 36(4), 626–630.

Symes, C. (1999) 'Working for our future': the rise of the vocationalised university, *Australian Journal of Education*, 43(3), 241–256.

Tilt, C.A. (2010) The impact of academic accounting research on professional practice, in Evans, E., Burritt, R., & Guthrie, J. (eds) *Accounting Education at a Crossroad in 2010*, Sydney: CAGS and ICAA.

Unerman, J. & O'Dwyer, B. (2010) *The Relevance and Utility of Leading Accounting Research*, London: ACCA.

Van Peursem, K.A., Monk, E.A., Wilson, R.M.S., & Adler, R.W. (2012) *Audit Education*, Abingdon: Routledge.

Van Wyhe, G. (1994) *The Struggle for Status*, New York: Garland Publishing.

Van Wyhe, G. (2007a) A history of US higher education in accounting, Part I: Situating accounting within the academy, *Issues in Accounting Education*, 22(2), 165–181.

Van Wyhe, G. (2007b) A history of US Higher Education in Accounting, Part II: Reforming accounting within the academy, *Issues in Accounting Education*, 22(3), 481–501.

Violette, G., Violette, J., & Hendrix R. (2013) Hiring academically inexperienced accounting interns, *The CPA Journal*, January, 11–12.

Wells, P., Gerbic, P., Kranenburg, I., & Bygrave, J. (2009) Professional skills and capabilities of accounting graduates: the New Zealand expectation gap? *Accounting Education: an international journal*, 18(4–5), 403–420.

Wilkerson, Jr. J.E. (2010) Accounting educators as the accounting profession's trustees: lessons from a study of peer professions, *Issues in Accounting Education*, 25(1), 1–13.

Wilson, R.M.S. (2011) Alignment in accounting education and training, *Accounting Education: an international journal*, 20(1), 3–16.

Wilson, R.M.S., Pierce, A., Allison, M., Hoogendoorn, M., Kral, B., & Watty, K. (2009) Accountancy and academic/professional inter-dependency (or mutual exclusivity?), *Accounting in Europe*, 6(2), 149–166.

Yu, S., Churyk, N.T., & Chang, A. (2013) Are students ready for their future accounting careers? Insights from observed perception gaps among employers, interns, and alumni, *Global Perspectives on Accounting Education*, 10, 1–15.

Zeff, S. (2003a) How the US accounting profession got where it is today: Part I, *Accounting Horizons*, 17(3), 189–205.

Zeff, S. (2003b) How the US accounting profession got where it is today: Part II, *Accounting Horizons*, 17(4), 267–286.

About the author

Elaine Evans is an Associate Professor in the Department of Accounting and Corporate Governance at Macquarie University, Australia (Elaine.evans@mq.edu.au). Her research interests include the interface between academic education and professional training for accountants, and the integration of graduate attributes in the accounting curriculum. She is on the editorial review boards of *Accounting Education: an international journal*, *Issues in Accounting Education*, and *Journal of Accounting Education*.

29

The role of accreditation in accounting education and training

Barbara Apostolou and *Elizabeth Gammie***

*WEST VIRGINIA UNIVERSITY, U.S.A. **THE ROBERT GORDON UNIVERSITY, U.K.

CONTENTS

Abstract

Accreditation can be defined as the certification of competence in a specified subject area such as accounting, and of the integrity of an agency, firm, group or person, such as a university department or accounting degree, awarded by a duly recognized and respected accrediting organization, such as a professional accounting body. This chapter considers the role of accreditation in the context of accounting programmes through a global lens by presenting and discussing the three overarching purposes of accreditation. First, we outline the role of compulsory and voluntary accreditation as a quality benchmark. The benefits and costs of seeking voluntary accreditation within this sphere are subsequently explored. Second, we consider the role of accreditation as a means to access the accounting profession. Third, we demonstrate how accreditation can serve as a means of exemption from certain professional examinations. The chapter concludes by airing criticisms about the access and exemption roles of accreditation as a mechanism to encourage further dialogue and research in this area.

Keywords

accreditation, certification, curriculum, quality, voluntary

29.1 Introduction

The main aims of this chapter are:

- to describe accreditation of business and accounting programmes;
- to consider how accreditation and curriculum are interconnected;
- to identify benefits of accreditation; and
- to report criticisms of the existing mission-based accreditation process.

This chapter provides an overview of current global accreditation practices, providing an account of historical development as appropriate. The context for the discourse begins by defining accreditation and outlining what it seeks to achieve. Owing to the many abbreviations used to designate organizations involved in accreditation, we refer the reader to the Schedule of Abbreviations at the beginning of this volume for definitions of the abbreviations used throughout. Different types of accreditation will be outlined as follows:

1 accreditation used as a quality benchmark as evidenced, for example, by the Association to Advance Collegiate Schools of Business (AACSB International);
2 accreditation used to gain access to professional accounting training as evidenced, for example, by the South African Institute of Chartered Accountants (SAICA); and
3 accreditation used to exempt students from the early stages of professional accounting examinations, as evidenced by bodies such as the Institute of Chartered Accountants of Scotland (ICAS) and the Institute of Chartered Accountants in England & Wales (ICAEW).

Within each of these three areas, examples from around the world will be given to illustrate the historical development of accreditation, and similarities and differences within the global professional community will be highlighted. Costs and benefits of accreditation will be articulated with particular reference to the criticisms levelled at accreditation from a variety of different stakeholders, such as academic staff, university administrators, professional accounting bodies (PABs), and employers of graduates.

29.2 The definition of accreditation

Accreditation is defined as '*[the] certification of competence in a specified subject area or areas of expertise, and of the integrity of an agency, firm, group or person awarded by a duly recognised and respected accrediting organisation*' (http://www.businessdictionary.com/definition/accreditation.html). Thus, in the context of accounting programmes, there are three overarching purposes of accreditation:

- to explicitly act as a quality benchmark of the educational programme, which implicitly improves the quality of the educational experience;
- to certify an underpinning programme in the discipline, thus providing access to further study;
- to certify knowledge and understanding of students in a specific area as a means to exempt from particular aspects of a further qualification.

While it is acknowledged that none of these purposes are mutually exclusive, the chapter will discuss each of these purposes in turn.

29.3 Accreditation as a quality benchmark

The first purpose of accreditation of relevance to accounting programmes and departments is recognition by an outside agency which acts as a benchmark of quality. Recognition may be of a compulsory nature, the absence of which would prevent the degree being offered to students. This higher-education concept of accreditation was initially derived by the trend away from a fixed to elective collegiate curriculum, which subsequently resulted in a diversity of degrees that prepared students for a range of careers (Altbach *et al.*, 2011). Recognition may also be voluntary. This type of voluntary recognition may promote higher education institutions (HEIs) that have been awarded such status into the upper echelons of the quality spectrum, or at least the perceived quality spectrum.

Two concepts are essential to the role of accreditation as a quality benchmark in higher education:

- accountability, and
- autonomy (ibid.).

Universities originally served an elite segment of society and functioned autonomously with respect to the construction of courses and curricula, and the means of delivery. Demand for accountability regarding outcomes evolved as access to universities increased over time, and financial support from governments and private funding increased (both in terms of budget support and government research grants). Thus there existed a tension between the university's desire for autonomy and the demand for accountability by constituencies (e.g. funding sources, professional licensing organizations, and students). *Ceteris paribus*, the primary role of accreditation is to serve as a mediator between the HEI's desire for autonomy and the external pressures for accountability. Government entities therefore exist to monitor and accredit educational processes across disciplines in every country, which in the U.S.A. is undertaken by one of six approved regional accrediting bodies (as summarized in Table 29.1). These bodies accredit at the university level to ensure that general education requirements are appropriate across disciplines. Regular maintenance of accreditation reviews address resources and measurable learning outcomes.

However, business schools and accounting programmes have tended to supplement this primary mandatory accreditation by voluntarily seeking secondary recognition from other accrediting bodies such as AACSB. This accreditation certifies HEIs or programmes which achieve minimum standards of excellence and, therefore, distinguishes between high-quality HEIs that meet the requirements to function as universities from those that do not achieve the quality

Table 29.1 Six regional accreditation bodies for universities and colleges in the U.S.A.

Origin	Name	Jurisdictions covered
1885	New England Association of Schools and Colleges (NEASC) http://www.neasc.org	Connecticut, Maine, Massachusetts, New Hampshire, Rhode Island, and American/international schools in more than 60 nations worldwide
1887	Middle States Commission on Higher Education (MSCHE) www.msche.org	Delaware, the District of Columbia, Maryland, New Jersey, New York, Pennsylvania, Puerto Rico, the U.S. Virgin Islands, and several locations internationally
1895	Southern Association of Colleges and Schools Commission on Colleges (SACS) http://sacscoc.org	Alabama, Florida, Georgia, Kentucky, Louisiana, Mississippi, North Carolina, South Carolina, Tennessee, Texas, Virginia, and Latin America
1895	North Central Association of Colleges and Schools (NCACS) www.northcentralassociation.org	Arkansas, Colorado, Illinois, Indiana, Iowa, Kansas, Michigan, Minnesota, Missouri, Nebraska, New Mexico, North Dakota, Ohio, Oklahoma, South Dakota, West Virginia, Wisconsin, and Wyoming
1917	Northwest Commission on Colleges and Universities (NWCCU) www.nwccu.org	Alaska, Idaho, Montana, Nevada, Oregon, Utah, and Washington
1923	Western Association of Schools and Colleges Accrediting Commission for Senior Colleges and Universities (WASC) www.wascweb.org	California and Hawaii, the territories of Guam, American Samoa, Federated States of Micronesia, Republic of Palau, Commonwealth of the Northern Marianas Islands, the Pacific Basin, East Asia, and areas of the Pacific and East Asia where American/International schools or colleges may apply.

threshold set by the accrediting body (MacKenzie, 1964). It is therefore argued that these voluntary accreditation bodies promote quality education as HEIs 'up their game' to achieve the standards set (ibid.).

There are currently five global voluntary accreditation bodies that consider business education. The three major ones are the AACSB, the Association of MBAs (AMBA), and the European Quality Improvement System (EQUIS). There are two other accreditation entities based in the U.S.A. which also accredit business programmes globally, namely, the Accreditation Council for Business Schools and Programs (ACBSP), and the International Assembly for Collegiate Business Education (IACBE). Each of these bodies is discussed below.

The first voluntary accreditation body concerned with business education, in which accounting education is a constituent, was the AACSB, originally established as the American Association of Collegiate Schools of Business in 1916 when there were only 30 Schools of Business in the U.S.A. The first accreditations were made in 1919. The AACSB required, as a condition for accreditation, that accounting, business law, finance, marketing, and statistics courses be offered, starting in 1925. By 1966, the AACSB had 106 member institutions, all accredited, and by 2006, it recognized 506 accredited institutions. In 2003, the AACSB revised its standards to apply to international business programmes and, at the time of writing, lists 681 member institutions that hold accreditation, representing nearly 50 countries and territories. Of those accredited business schools, 179 are separately accredited in accounting. Up-to-date listings are available at www.aacsb.edu.

The AACSB (2013a) lists as key factors in the assessment of business school quality:

- the qualifications, development, and involvement of the academic staff;
- the design and effectiveness of the curriculum;
- the nature and effectiveness and resources needed and used for instructional and learning purposes;
- the academic preparation and capabilities of entering students;
- the processes in place to plan, assess, and assure quality; and
- the intellectual contributions of the academic staff.

The relative importance of each factor depends upon the academic unit's mission and each programme's enunciated educational objectives.

The ACBSP was founded in 1988 for the specific purpose of accrediting business schools and programmes that emphasized teaching and learning, in contrast to the AACSB's emphasis at that time on research productivity. ACBSP is a global, middle-tier accreditation body, though most of the approximately 800 member institutions are in the U.S.A. A member institution can be accredited, a member in candidacy, or a member only. Separate accreditation for accounting programmes was authorized in 2006, and is available as an option when the companion business unit has, or is simultaneously seeking, ACBSP accreditation. The focus is on classroom excellence and the encouragement of scholarly research. The criteria for accreditation emphasize intended learning outcomes (ILOs) as they are linked to the institution's mission.

The IACBE has offered accreditation for business degrees since 1997, with more than 800 currently holding the designation in at least 20 countries. Its focus is on teaching and learning, with an emphasis on ILOs. Accreditation is available for programmes that offer associate, bachelor's, master's, and doctoral degrees in business, although the institution must offer at least a bachelor's degree to be a candidate.

Another business-related body is AMBA, the origins of which can be traced to 1967 when eight holders of Master of Business Administration (MBA) degrees from the U.S.A., and two from London Business School's first graduating class, founded the Business Graduates Association (BGA) in London. The purpose of this association was to improve public perceptions of the value of the MBA in Europe. The subsequently-derived AMBA now provides the global standard for MBA, Doctor of Business Administration (DBA), and Master of Business Management (MBM) degrees, and accredits business schools the degrees of which meet their standards. The organization has grown significantly, and continues to add members and to accredit programmes against a rigorous set of criteria. Its current membership boasts accredited programmes at 189 business schools in over 70 countries.

The complement of global business accrediting bodies is completed by the European Foundation for Management Development (EFMD), which was founded in 1977. This is a European-based international organization, recognized globally as a body that plays a central role in shaping an international approach to management education which includes operating an accreditation service for institutions (Business Schools) under the auspices of EQUIS, and individual business school programmes under the auspices of the European Foundation for Management Development (EFMD) Programme Accreditation System (EPAS). EFMD has over 750 member organizations in 81 countries.

The aim of EQUIS is to raise the standard of management education worldwide, and its scope extends to the entire suite of business programmes offered by an institution. EQUIS looks for a balance between high academic quality and the professional relevance provided by close interaction with the corporate world. A strong interface with the world of business is, therefore, as much a requirement as is strong research potential. EQUIS attaches particular importance to the creation of an effective learning environment that favours the development of students' managerial and entrepreneurial skills, and which fosters their sense of global responsibility. It also looks for innovation in all respects, including programme design and pedagogy. As a consequence, while institutions must demonstrate high quality in all the dimensions as articulated above, an additional requirement is to demonstrate a degree of internationalization (EQUIS, 2013). This desire for internationalization is not restricted to the syllabi, but extends to the requirement for international students and international exchanges (ibid.).

Rather than going for full institutional status through EQUIS, it is also possible through EPAS to seek recognition for an individual programme. The aim of EPAS is to evaluate and accredit, where appropriate, the quality of any business and or management programme that has an international perspective. The EPAS standards and criteria cover all facets of programme provision:

* the institutional, national, and international environment;
* programme design;
* programme delivery;
* programme outcomes; and
* quality assurance.

They particularly emphasize achievements in the areas of academic rigour, practical relevance, and internationalization. While the majority of programmes granted accreditation via this route are more general in nature, there is evidence of finance-related master's (such as the MSc in Finance from the ALBA Graduate Business School, Greece, and an MSc in Banking and Financial Services Management from the Boston University Metropolitan College, U.S.A.) being awarded such status.

Unravelling the differences in accreditation purposes can be daunting. In summary, AACSB has the broadest scope by accrediting business and accounting programmes at the institutional level. AMBA accredits the portfolio of MBA offerings, which includes full-time, part-time, executive, and online programmes. EQUIS requires the curriculum to have a strong international emphasis, and accredits the business school rather than specific programmes. ACBSP accredits business programmes, with separate accounting accreditation for bachelor's and graduate programmes. IACBE covers business and business-related programmes without separate accounting accreditation.

While these global accrediting bodies are not specifically targeted at accounting and finance-related programmes, given that they accredit Business Schools (AACSB, EQUIS) or business programmes (AMBA, EPAS, ACBSP, IACBE), a more recent development has been the introduction of more specialized accreditation of accounting departments and programmes by the AACSB in 1982 and ACBSP in 2009. Despite the fact that the accounting programme may be able to free-ride on an institution's general business accreditation without investing the additional effort for an additional layer of accreditation (Kren et al., 1993), this specialized accreditation is available to member institutions which offer undergraduate and/or graduate degree(s) in accounting. However, in order to be eligible for the accounting accreditation, an institution must hold the AACSB Business Accreditation, or be simultaneously applying for both accreditations. ACBSP similarly commenced separate accreditation for accounting degree programmes in 2009.

Discourse about the need for specific accounting accreditation (as opposed to a more generic accreditation that covered a variety of business programmes) can be traced to the 1960s (MacKenzie, 1964; Stettler, 1965), when academicians and professional groups spoke in its favour as a means to ensure the following:

- Academic programmes would maintain pace with the dynamic changes occurring in the profession.
- Accounting programmes would maintain their professional status alongside the professions of medicine and law, both of which had established accreditation models in place.

However, this was not a universal view as the AACSB saw separate accounting accreditation as being both unnecessary and undesirable (Anderson & Previts, 1984; Langenderfer, 1987). Nevertheless, the AACSB was motivated to develop criteria for separate accounting accreditation to pre-empt an effort by the American Institute of Certified Public Accountants (AICPA) and the American Accounting Association (AAA) to create their own accounting accreditation agency. Accordingly, AACSB set its first standards for accounting accreditation in 1980 with counsel from representatives of the AICPA, AAA, the Institute of Management Accountants (IMA), the Financial Executives Institute (FEI), the Federation of Schools of Accountancy (FSA), the Government Accountability Office (GAO), and national public accounting firms (Pastore, 1989). The first accounting accreditations were awarded by the AACSB in 1982 to 18 institutions, and this has subsequently been extended to 179 institutions across 43 countries.

The original AACSB accounting standards developed in 1980 were subsequently replaced by new standards and a peer-review process in 1991 in response to objections that the original standards had the unintended effects of stunting innovation, experimentation, and the development of new accounting programmes (Bailey & Bentz, 1991). The subsequently revised AACSB standards for accounting accreditation simply required institutions to show they were fulfilling their mission, thus they recognized programme diversity, and allowed for flexibility (Kren et al., 1993).

A peculiarity of the specialist accreditation by AASCB and ACBSP is that separate accreditation for accounting can only occur if the institution is already accredited in business (or applying concurrently for accreditation in business). There is, therefore, no scope for an exceptional accounting department to be awarded the appropriate quality badge if the accounting unit is not connected to a commensurate quality business school. Bitter et al. (1999) observe that separate accounting accreditation may be more challenging to achieve than general business accreditation because the scope of the review is concentrated on one academic unit.

Institutions that achieve recognition from three of the bodies (AASCB, supplemented as appropriate by the specialist accounting accreditation, AMBA, and EQUIS) are referred to as Triple Accreditation or Triple Crown institutions, and these are commonly regarded as gold-standard institutions. Very few institutions have achieved this status, with the School of Accounting and Commercial Law at Victoria University of Wellington in New Zealand being only the 58th Business School to achieve Triple Accreditation, a distinction accomplished in December 2011. This also included separate accreditation of its accounting programmes.

The availability for voluntary accreditation as a quality benchmark has clearly proliferated since the introduction of the AACSB in 1916. This raises the question of what benefits accrue to an institution which seeks, and is subsequently granted, accredited status?

29.3.1 The benefits of voluntary accreditation

Gaharan *et al.* (2007) surveyed administrators of accounting programmes which had earned or were in candidacy for separate AACSB accounting accreditation. The survey results revealed the following perceived benefits of separate accounting accreditation:

* the curriculum has improved;
* better-qualified students and academic staff are attracted to the programme; and
* improved placement for students.

Hence, accredited institutions use their status as a marketing tool to attract the brightest and the best students. This is evidenced, for example, by the opening overview of a triple rated Business School in a website promoting top degree programmes abroad: '*University of Strathclyde holds the *Triple Crown accreditation: AACSB, EQUIS and AMBA. Only 51 out of 3,900 university business schools worldwide have that distinction*' (emphasis in original).

The resulting ability to attract the best students subsequently results in students from accredited institutions having improved job opportunities upon graduation when compared to students of non-accredited institutions. Starting salaries tend to be higher for accounting graduates of AACSB-accredited programmes because the employer has assurance that educational requirements have been met. Accreditation, and triple-rated accreditation in particular, also facilitate the ability of institutions to charge premium rates for their courses, which subsequently results in the ability of the institution to pay premium rates for their academic staff. Hence, while accreditation raises the general standard of the education provision through its intensive peer-review process, once an institution has gained membership to the 'elite' club, the status that this membership affords allows the institution to continuously enhance quality, and hence widen the gap even further between the 'elite' and the non-accredited institutions.

Voluntary accreditation has particular resonance in the U.S.A. since it brings significant benefits to students planning to take the Certified Public Accountant (CPA) examination. As background, there are currently 50 states and five jurisdictions subject to a variety of curricular requirements to take the CPA examination. Most of these 55 jurisdictions require, or are moving to require, 150 hours of post-secondary education from a regionally accredited institution to be eligible to take the CPA examination. This typically equates to obtaining a bachelor's degree in accounting (typically at least 120 semester hours) as well as a master's degree in accounting or taxation (typically at least 30 semester hours). However, the form of the 150 hours depends upon the rules of each separate State Board of Accountancy (which grants CPA licences within its own jurisdiction). Thus the student has the burden of identifying the specific curricular requirements in the jurisdiction in which licensure is sought. However, when courses are taken at an accredited institution, the acceptance of the educational requirement is more automatic than when they are not. Subsequently, a State Board of Accountancy may require additional hours to be undertaken at an accredited institution when the original transcript is from an institution that has no accreditation status.

29.3.2 The costs of voluntary accreditation

There are, however, considerable costs associated with accreditation, and these build up through the four stages of the accreditation process:

* the internal evaluation of whether or not the institution meets the set formal standards and criteria, and the resulting changes that may be put in place in an attempt to meet the formal requirements;

- the external evaluation undertaken by competent authorities which judge an institution's adherence to the standards and criteria;
- the internal activities undertaken to address any shortfalls in successfully meeting the standards prior to accreditation being granted; and
- the external periodic review of the accredited institution and programmes to make sure they still meet the standards and criteria (Allyn, 1966).

Accreditation has developed into a mini-industry, and the accrediting bodies are funded by the relevant institutions through the levying of fees, initially through the staged application process, and thereafter through the periodic review. For example, as at the time of writing, EQUIS charges an application fee of €9,150, a review fee of €15,250, and a re-accreditation fee of €9,150 or €15,250 depending on whether a three-year or five-year accreditation period is granted. A vast amount of academic staff time is also devoted to preparing the relevant documentation, networking with representatives from the appropriate accreditation body, hosting accreditation visits, and engaging in accreditation-related events.

Much of the focus across the accreditation bodies is similar and this results in a duplication of effort as institutions are tasked with providing similar information but it must be individually tailored to meet the documentation needs of each accrediting body (see, for example, the *Eligibility Procedures and Accreditation Standards for Business Accreditation*, AACSB (2012), and the EQUIS (2013) *Standards and Criteria*). There is, however, also evidence of disparity, which may not necessarily be in the best interests of the particular department. For example, prior to the new 2013 accreditation standards being issued, following the deliberations of the Blue Ribbon Committee on accreditation quality (AACSB, 2013b), the AACSB set a benchmark for the qualifications of academic staff which required at least 90 per cent of those staff to be 'academically-qualified (AQ)' or 'professionally-qualified (PQ)', and a minimum of 50 per cent of academic staff to be AQ if only undergraduate programmes were offered. This minimum threshold of 50 per cent needed to increase with the offering of graduate and doctoral programmes (AACSB, 2012). While the AACSB gave guidelines as to the definition of AQ and PQ, it was the responsibility of the institution under examination to develop their own criteria for defining the AQ and PQ status of the academic staff (AACSB, 2011). Departments primarily resourced by professionally-qualified accountants may not have met this threshold, which may have excluded those departments from the opportunity for separate accreditation. The new AACSB standard on academic staff quality and engagement should help in this regard as academic staff are now to be categorized as scholarly practitioners, scholarly academics, instructional practitioners, or practice academics (AACSB, 2013b). With the expectation that only 40 per cent of academic staff will need to be classified as scholarly academics with an underpinning doctoral qualification (ibid.), there is more scope for departments resourced by professionally-qualified accountants who would be classified as scholarly practitioners to gain accreditation.

In contrast, EQUIS simply indicates that the key requirement for academic staff is the existence of a permanent core, with a minimum size of 25 members of academic staff. In addition, an institution needs to be able to demonstrate that the size, composition, and qualifications of the academic staff are in accordance with the strategic objectives of the institution and can adequately service the institution's programmes (EQUIS, 2013). The test, therefore, is more akin to a 'fit for purpose' test.

Other criticisms levelled at accreditation highlight that the accreditation body has an undue influence on the role of the academic staff in curriculum design (see the chapters making up Section C of this volume) and delivery (see the chapters making up Section D of this volume).

The primary reason which administrators of unaccredited accounting programmes have provided for not seeking accreditation is that the cost, the time of the academic staff and that of administrative time, are not offset by the increased standing amongst their peers which accreditation might bring. However, the presence of alternatives to AACSB (notably ACBSP and IACBE in the U.S.A.) offer a prestige cost to the unaccredited programme, hence there is ostensibly no reason not to be accredited if an accessible option exists. Mission-linked standards have been criticized as being too inclusive, thereby reducing the distinction of AACSB (Jantzen, 2000). Others argue that the AACSB's mission-linked approach harms curricula because it does not prescribe a body of knowledge as long as the institution defends its course offerings with respect to its own mission (Lowrie & Willmott, 2009). Another criticism is that the AACSB hinders dynamic strategic planning because the emphasis on documentation of the past for the review teams slows the forward progress of the institution (Julian & Ofori-Dankwa, 2006).

However, in the increasingly competitive market place of university education, where institutions from around the world are competing for the highest quality of domestic student and the full fee-generating overseas student, the benefits of voluntary accreditation exceed the costs and issues associated with seeking the accreditation status. Significant numbers of quality institutions, therefore, seek at least one of the accreditation badges, which results in a tiered global stratification of universities into those which have accreditation and those which have not.

29.4 Accreditation as the certification of the underpinning programme as a means to access

The route to becoming a professionally-qualified accountant varies quite significantly depending on institution and country (FEE, 2002; Karreman, 2002, 2007). (See also Calhoun & Karreman, Chapter 26, and Evans, Chapter 28 – both in this volume.) Pre-admission requirements for professional accounting training often (but by no means universally) commence, however, with the necessity to hold an appropriately accredited accounting degree regulated by the respective professional accounting body (PAB). Global examples include:

- The Institute of Chartered Accountants in Australia (ICAA) and CPA Australia, two Australian-based bodies which have collaborated on accreditation and which require students to successfully complete an accredited programme before they can gain entry into either of the bodies' chartered accountancy programmes (ICAA & CPA, 2009).
- The South African Institute of Chartered Accountants (SAICA), which accredits certain programmes which are specifically designed to allow access to Part 1 of their Qualifying Examination.
- The AICPA which requires that candidates earn required accounting educational credits, though it does not stipulate that a CPA candidate should earn these credits or a degree from an accredited accounting programme. However, the acceptance of credit hours to meet the educational requirements can be challenged by State Boards of Accountancy if they were not earned at an accredited institution.

One of the roles of accreditation in these circumstances is to govern the coverage of compulsory topics such as *Financial Accounting, Management Accounting, Auditing,* and *Taxation,* though this can be extended to demand coverage of liberal topics as evidenced by the requirement of the New Zealand Institute of Chartered Accountants (NZICA) to include a minimum of 15 per cent of liberal or general study in the four-year degree programme. (See Amernic & Craig,

Chapter 12 – this volume, and Sangster & Wilson, 2012.) There is, however, evidence that PABs are moving away from the heavily-prescribed input-based system of technical coverage to a competency-based output system (see Paisey & Paisey, Chapter 30 – this volume). An example of this is SAICA which has developed a competency framework (SAICA, 2010) which identifies the competencies that should be acquired by students during their educational programme at university. (Care is needed, however, in the light of the International Accounting Education Standards Board's definition of competence since this involves being able to perform a work role to a defined standard, with reference to real working environments, which suggests that competence cannot be assessed in the classroom.) Rather than prescribe what should be taught, and how, SAICA has now tasked universities with designing courses that enable the acquisition of knowledge at the stipulated proficiency level of the competencies identified. While SAICA still expects coverage of the four core disciplines, it will no longer be prescribing syllabi for 'supportive' courses. NZICA has followed suit by providing universities with more academic freedom as it is reducing the requirement for prescriptive topics from 2013, and there will no longer be a requirement to teach in an applied manner. Thus, PABs are introducing an element of flexibility into their requirements, which should '*provide an opportunity for innovation in course and curriculum design*' (SAICA, 2010, p. 15).

In the U.S.A., the AICPA Pre-Certification Education Executive Committee (PcEEC) exists to assist educators to incorporate its skills-based core competencies into curricula. The AICPA is not linked to an accreditation body. Instead, it advises academia about how to develop a curriculum to best prepare students for entry into the accounting profession. Academic staff determine the manner in which the guidance is implemented, accreditation teams then consider whether the implementation and outcomes are consistent with the institutional mission. The AICPA's Core Competency Framework identifies functional, personal, and broad business perspectives competencies. Hence, the Framework focusses on skills (see Watty, Chapter 13 – this volume) and is not structured around traditional subject/content areas, or accounting services. This skills-based approach is advocated, because the body of knowledge and the accounting profession are changing so rapidly (see Flood, Chapter 4 – this volume). Therefore, while the knowledge requirements of an accountant will change with time, the core set of competencies identified by the Framework should have long-term value and will thus support a variety of career opportunities for the future CPA. PcEEC has mapped the core competencies to the skills tested on the Uniform CPA examination, including analysis, judgement, communication, research, and understanding. Progressive accounting programmes should therefore consider adapting the PcEEC Framework; however, unlike some of the PABs which mandate compliance, the AICPA only 'recommends' but does not require institutions to do so.

The AICPA and the National Association of State Boards of Accountancy (NASBA) developed a model called the Uniform Accountancy Act to motivate uniformity and standardization of educational requirements for admission to the accounting profession in the 55 jurisdictions of the U.S.A. While not authoritative in itself, a State Board of Accountancy may adopt it, which increases mobility for CPAs who move from the original licensing jurisdiction. Thus academic staff are responsible for the following:

- creating a curriculum acceptable to the broadest number of jurisdictions;
- developing courses that satisfy entry requirements to the profession (e.g. technical and core competencies); and
- satisfying the metrics studied by the accrediting body for propriety of inputs, processes, and outcomes.

29.5 The certification of competence as a means to exemption

Interestingly, the PABs in the U.K. do not follow the common global requirement for an accounting degree (see Evans, Chapter 28, and Paisey & Paisey, Chapter 30 – both in this volume) as a precursor to further professional accounting studies, and not all entrants into professional training actually hold a degree (Gammie & Kirkham, 2008; FRC, 2011). Graduates who enter professional accounting training from an accounting background, however, can be exempt from the initial layer of PABs' examinations after successful accreditation of their undergraduate programmes. Accreditation is therefore sought with each individual PAB in order to gain the appropriate exemptions which leads universities to apply for accreditation with more than one PAB. Accreditation of university courses by the U.K.-based PABs (i.e. the Association of Chartered Certified Accountants (ACCA), the Chartered Institute of Management Accountants (CIMA), the Chartered Institute of Public Finance and Accountancy (CIPFA), the Chartered Accountants Ireland, ICAEW, and ICAS) therefore provides exemption from certain professional examinations as opposed to providing a gateway for further study. Universities that run accounting programmes use the level of exemptions awarded as a marketing tool to attract undergraduates, as evidenced by the following quotation from a university website: '*The BAcc at Dundee is fully accredited and recognised for exemption purposes by all the leading accountancy bodies in the UK and Ireland.*' Indeed, there is evidence that demand for exemptions from the examinations of PABs by accounting students drives universities to maximize the exemptions sought via accreditation (Duff & Marriott, 2012). As a result, universities seek recognition from multiple PABs. This is resource-intensive both on the part of the university seeking the accreditation and on the part of the PAB granting the exemption.

Previous attempts had been made by the U.K.-based PABs to try and collaborate on accreditation. However, despite joining together into one umbrella accreditation board, this board was subsequently disbanded. In order to understand the current accreditation position in the U.K., with the apparent duplication of effort by both PABs and higher education HEIs, it is important to articulate the creation and demise of this collaborative board.

ICAEW set the ball rolling by setting up the Board of Accreditation of Educational Courses (BAEC) in 1973, other PABs were invited to join and, by 1988, all six member bodies of the Consultative Committee of Accountancy Bodies (CCAB), with the exception of Chartered Accountants Ireland which stopped short of full participation but retained observer status, joined the BAEC to act collaboratively for accreditation purposes (BAAEC, 2000). In 1995, however, the ACCA withdrew from the joint accreditation process and set up its own desk-top review which looked primarily at the technical content of the syllabus covered by each university. The BAEC was subsequently reconstituted as the Board of Accreditation of Accountancy Educational Courses (BAAEC) (BAAEC, 2000).

The main role of the BAAEC was to review and approve, as appropriate, academic courses on behalf of the participating CCAB bodies. The primary objective of the BAAEC was '*[to] establish a measure of credit for the study of accounting at university/college in relation to the examination requirements of professional bodies*' (ibid.).

The advantage of having a joint accreditation body was that HEIs had to deal with only one body as opposed to seeking accreditation from a variety of different PABs. The advantage for the participating PABs was that the scheme prevented duplication of effort. While each PAB had its own distinctive requirements for membership, they shared sufficient identifiable common ground on educational coverage to give scope for collaboration. The BAAEC also maintained that, by encouraging partnership in the process of professional education, it supported and developed a stronger academic base for professional activity and standards (ibid.).

The BAAEC aimed to visit all accredited institutions at the time of initial application and, thereafter, at approximately five-year intervals. The broad thrust of the review undertaken at these visits was to consider:

- the institutional element (in other words, whether the institution had the ability and resources to deliver an accounting-related programme effectively), and
- the technical subject content element, which concentrated on the direct matching of syllabi for exemption purposes (ibid.).

In addition, annual updates provided by institutions, which ran to several hundred pages and included the completion of self-assessment grids (RGU, 1998), were monitored by the BAAEC and these could also trigger a visit outside the normal visit cycle if any problematic issues were identified. HEIs seeking accreditation paid an annual levy which varied dependent on the level of accreditation sought, but the levy for full accreditation was set at around £700 per institution (ICAS, 2001a).

In 1997, a risk-matrix approach was developed by the BAAEC in an attempt to minimize costs and the time-consuming nature of accreditation, and reviews were then based on this risk approach (ibid.). Where an institution clearly demonstrated a commitment to a high-quality approach, with clearly defined ILOs and an insight into professional expectations, reviewers could quickly move to consider the detailed matching of requirements in terms of content and assessment. The overall risk score determined the following:

- the extent of checking for new applications and re-submissions;
- the frequency and intensity of annual monitoring; and
- the timing and character of the visit.

HEIs seeking the highest level of accreditation, but which were rated as low-risk, were subsequently visited every five years, and were required to provide detailed commentary on two random institutional areas each year. High-risk institutions were unlikely to be considered for the highest level of accreditation but, if this was granted, they were visited every three years and were required to provide detailed commentaries on the problem areas identified (BAAEC, 2000).

When educational developments at ICAEW resulted in the withdrawal of exemptions from core syllabus subjects (such as *Financial Accounting*), the decision was taken at a meeting of CCAB in April 2001 to close the BAAEC (ICAS, 2001a). HEIs were then once more faced with the prospect of dealing with the multiple individual PABs in order for their degree programmes to be accredited and gain exemptions. PABs were also tasked with introducing their own accreditation systems and dealing with transitional arrangements from BAAEC to in-house (ICAS letter, 15 May 2001).

ICAS responded to the demise of BAAEC by inviting all of the Heads of Department from Scottish universities to a meeting on 7 June 2001, at which there was a unanimous view by the academic community that accreditation should continue, but that it should also give value (ICAS, 2001b). The view was also expressed that the BAAEC scheme was costly and that it had become progressively cumbersome, particularly as much of the institutional material was already being assessed by the four-year Quality Assurance Agency for Higher Education (QAA) visits, which regulated the provision of all degree programmes in the U.K. The academics therefore believed that the demise of the BAAEC provided HEIs and PABs with the opportunity to forge more effective and direct relationships. Interestingly, when the ICAS had undertaken a survey into accreditation in 1998, only 25 per cent of Scottish universities were supportive of the BAAEC system, with 58 per cent preferring that ICAS take over responsibility for awarding exemptions from their examinations (ICAS, survey results, 29 May 1998). Thus there was clearly unrest within the academic community in this local setting regarding the process.

Dealing with all the different PABs on an individual basis, however, was also not welcomed by HEIs, and there was an appeal to the CCAB by some HEIs requesting that PABs should standardize the information which they demanded in respect of accreditation and exemptions. CCAB responded to this by publishing an accreditation guidance document (CCAB, 2006).

Table 29.2 Standard information requested

	ACCA	CIMA	ICAEW	CAI	ICAS	Standard information
Type of review						
Desk top	Yes	Yes	Yes	Yes		
Desk top and visit					Yes	
Length of accreditation	5 yrs	5 yrs	*	3 yrs	3 yrs	
Annual updates required	Yes	Yes	*	Yes	Yes	
Information requested						
Accreditation application form	Yes		Yes			
Programme validation document		Yes		Yes	Yes	Yes
QAA reports		**		Yes	Yes	
Pass/progression rates		Yes			Yes	
Module descriptors	Yes	Yes	Yes	Yes	Yes	Yes
Examination papers for relevant modules	Yes	Yes	Yes	Yes	Yes	Yes
External Examiners' reports		Yes		Yes	Yes	Yes
Information on assessment strategy		Yes	Yes	Yes	Yes	Yes
Information on staff development		Yes				
Mapping of route/pathway including options	Yes	Yes	Yes	Yes	Yes	Yes
Programme regulations	Yes	***				
Franchise, articulation or validation agreements, and quality assurance arrangements	Yes					
Course handbook	Yes			Yes	Yes	Yes
Course entry standards and maximum student numbers		***		Yes		
Information on other university activities				Yes		
Outline of staff development activity		Yes				
Annual programme review					Yes	
CVs of teaching staff				Yes		
Research methodology training				Yes		
Information technology facilities and access				Yes		

Notes: * While the CCAB document did not disclose the length of the accreditation nor whether any annual updates were required, the accreditation is usually awarded for a five-year period with annual updates required in the intervening period. ** QAA reports are accessed directly from QAA. *** If not included in validation documentation.

The document set out the accreditation process for each of the CCAB bodies, and also detailed what information was required to be submitted by each HEI to enable an application for accreditation to be processed. To assist the HEIs a table summarizing the standard information requested was produced and appears in Table 29.2.

29.6 Criticisms levelled at accreditation as a means of access or exemption

Accreditation – when used either to grant access to professional accounting training, or to provide exemption from certain examinations of PABs, like the voluntary accreditation discussed above – goes beyond any governmental quality-assurance requirements. However, this accreditation has been put in place to ensure that the resources (human and material), programme orientation (syllabus), and teaching and assessment processes are appropriate in terms of the learning required to underpin further professional study. Thus the remit of accreditation by PABs at this level is wide-ranging. PABs are not just interested in the programme structure, individual course content, and assessment mechanisms, but the accreditation remit can include:

- the mission and objectives established by the HEI provider in relation to its accounting programmes;
- demonstrated coherence between the stated mission and objectives of accounting programmes and the resources and curriculum activities committed to achieving them;
- the resource base, comprising the academic and support staff, physical facilities, and the financial provision available for these and to other needs;
- educational qualifications, status and duties, level of appointment, and relevant educational and professional experience of academic staff;
- programme entry requirements;
- effectiveness of interaction between students and academic staff in the teaching process;
- extent to which teaching methodologies facilitate development of both technical and generic skills;
- extent, nature, and standard of the on-going scholarly activities of academic staff;
- nature and effectiveness of quality assurance processes as they relate to accredited accounting programmes.

The extent of this type of review would therefore appear to encroach on the quality assurance mechanisms already in place at university and government levels which authorize the host institution to run degree programmes and subsequently validate and monitor the degree programmes on an individual basis. For example, in the U.K. (as depicted in Table 29.3), an accounting programme is likely to be exposed to the following scrutiny: first, at institutional level, which percolates down to subject level via periodic reviews (e.g. Research Assessment Exercises (RAE) in the past, and the Research Excellence Framework (REF) with effect from 2013), which in turn percolates down to individual degree programmes.

While it may be argued that PABs, which accredit certain degrees as the access programmes to their final qualification, have a role to play as the gatekeepers of quality, this argument holds less sway with PABs which are simply granting exemption from certain subjects. In this regard, the focus should surely simply be concerned with syllabus coverage, the level of the assessment, together with the related validity and reliability of results.

Interestingly, this validity and reliability have been questioned in the U.K. by employers of accounting graduates who have received exemptions from the initial stages of the professional

Table 29.3 Quality control mechanisms in the U.K.

	University level	Subject level	Degree level
Enhancement-led institutional review	*		
Research assessment exercise, such as the 2008 RAE and the 2013 REF		*	
Validation of degree, which ensures compliance with the QAA generic benchmarking statements for all accounting-related degrees in the U.K. (QAA, 2007).			*
External examiners' feedback			*
Annual course appraisal			*
Five-year subject review		*	*

qualification. This is because pass rates from an accredited student have been lower than those recorded for graduates from non-accounting backgrounds (see Koh, Chapter 20 – this volume). For example, in relation to ICAS, the average pass rate (between 2008 and 2011) for graduates from non-accounting backgrounds was higher than that for accounting graduates in all four subjects at the Test of Professional Skills (TPS) stage of the ICAS qualification (personal communication from ICAS). While this could be due to a myriad of reasons, this weaker performance has led some employers to ignore the exemption awarded by ICAS and require the student to sit the TPC examinations irrespective of any exemption granted (Douglas, ongoing).

The sub-agenda here is that PABs can then exert pressure on HEIs to 'up their game', which may mean further aligning their later years' education with the PABs' syllabi, with an inappropriate concentration on the technical preparation required to ensure candidates' chances of success in their subsequent professional examinations. For example, ICAS, as part of its professional accreditation, has recently provided individual universities with their comparative pass rates for each of the TPS level of examinations. The provided analysis highlights how graduates from a particular university compare to:

- graduates from all disciplines, and
- graduates from fully-accredited degree programmes only.

Accounting educators have been highly critical of the influence that accreditation has on the content and assessment of modules in undergraduate accounting programmes, highlighting the constraints on academic freedom both in terms of curriculum content (see the chapters in Section C on curriculum considerations) and patterns of assessment (see the chapters in Section E on assessment considerations) (AECC, 1990; Sundem, 1999; Marino, 2006; Reckers, 2006; Wilson, 2011). The Accounting Education Change Commission (1990), for example, argued that the role of the university is to prepare students to *become* accountants, whereas the role of professional training is to prepare trainees to *be* accountants (see also Sundem, Chapter 27, and Evans, Chapter 28 – both in this volume). Thus university education should provide the foundation upon which life-long learning can be built, and students should be taught how to learn (ibid.). University education and PAB training should therefore be distinctive, albeit complementary (Wilson, 2011).

However, students undertaking professionally-oriented courses tend to study modules in which the content is focussed on how to undertake technical tasks (such as the preparation of a consolidated set of accounts, or performing a tax computation). This is often at the expense of the acquisition of intellectual skills such as recognizing and managing complexity and uncertainty (Griffiths, 2004). (See also Cunningham, Chapter 18 – this volume.) Professionally-focussed university degrees are also criticized for encouraging students to rote-learn (Sikka & Willmott, 2002) and surface-learn (e.g. Beattie *et al.*, 1997; Booth *et al.*, 1999; Byrne *et al.*, 2002) as these approaches can secure success in professional-style examinations (Power, 1991) without a rigorous understanding of the underlying concepts.

The focus on technical techniques, rules, and regulations can also lead to a 'technical and instrumental view of accounting' (Sikka *et al.*, 2007, p. 3) at the expense of the critical perspective (but see St. Pierre & Rebele, Chapter 5 – this volume, for an alternative perspective). This issue is exacerbated by the fact that many texts used in university accounting courses are professionally-orientated (Ferguson *et al.*, 2005). (See also Stevenson *et al.*, Chapter 19 – this volume.) It follows that accounting students are not exposed to critical enquiry. Linked to this criticism is the argument that liberal education is a necessary element in any vocational preparation (Dewey, 1916; Paisey & Paisey, 2000; Gray *et al.*, 2001; Sangster, 2010; Sangster & Wilson, 2012). However, in a packed curriculum dictated to by PABs, academic staff in HEIs find themselves with little space in which to include this type of education (see the chapters in Section C on curriculum considerations).

In terms of assessment, an exemption from a U.K.-based PAB examination paper will only be granted if at least 70 per cent of any module contributing towards the assessment leading to the exemption is assessed via a formal examination. This restricts the ability of the university to use more innovative assessment tools (such as group work, student presentations, or extended critical enquiry reports, as a means to develop other relevant skills such as those of a non-technical nature (Gammie *et al.* 2010). (See also Hassall & Joyce, Chapter 17 – this volume.) Considering the 'backwash' effect of assessment (ibid.) (see Kidwell & Lowensohn, Chapter 21 – this volume), if accounting courses are curtailed in their assessment methodology, this will also curtail the ability of the institution to develop appropriate skills in students such as critical analysis, research and communication skills (see Watty, Chapter 13, and Cunningham, Chapter 18 – both in this volume). Indeed, Wilson (2011) suggested that, if the possession of a degree in accounting is subsequently allowed to permit exemptions from professional accounting examinations, then the overall outcome of the combined educational and training programme is likely to be devalued and diminished. The professional qualification erodes what an accounting degree with no restrictions can achieve. Duff & Marriott concluded that the majority of accounting academics '*saw accreditation as a restrictive force and was something that discouraged lecturing staff from developing their own curriculum based on their interests, motivations and skills*' (2012, p. 43).

Accreditation throws further challenges for institutions seeking exemptions in terms of academic staff, as there has been a decline in the proportion of professionally-qualified academic staff (Brown *et al.*, 2007) and a further decline is predicted (Beattie & Smith, 2012). As academic staff quality standards are set by the accreditation requirements of individual PABs, which are keen to acknowledge the necessity of professionally-qualified academic staff (ibid.), some HEIs have voluntarily given up their exemptions as they do not have professionally-qualified staff available to teach the technically-orientated courses (ibid.). HEIs can also face conflicting demands. AACSB, for example, in its role of providing a benchmark for quality, is looking for the majority of academic staff to be academically-qualified. PABs, on the other hand, such as ICAS and ICAEW, which are awarding exemptions, demand professionally-qualified academic staff.

However, the ultimate choice, in terms of exemption, rests with the HEIs, which have the freedom to choose whether to try and maximize exemptions at the expense of providing a more liberal and critical education. In the current education and economic climate, HEIs which do not offer 'two-for-the-price-of-one', or 'buy-one-get-one-free' (Wilson, 2011, p. 5) are unlikely to attract students onto their programmes (see Evans, Chapter 28 – this volume). HEIs therefore may feel pressurized into offering value for money, and their role in the creation of accountants may be compromised.

29.7 Conclusion

This chapter has offered an overview of the accreditation of accounting programmes with a global focus. Accreditation was defined and its evolution to extant practices described. Examples from around the world were provided to illustrate both similarities and differences in the global professional community. Criticisms levelled at accreditation from a variety of different stakeholders, such as academic staff, university administrators, PABs, and employers of graduates, were articulated. The elite Triple Crown accreditation (AACSB, EQUIS, and AMBA) was described.

Accreditation is a quality signal about the curriculum and academic staff, including a commitment to continuous improvement. Academic administrators and academic staff have a duty to create an infrastructure that facilitates the required on-going reflective review of curriculum and ILOs (Apostolou, 1999; Sinning & Dykxhoorn, 2001). Accreditation, therefore, is a process '*that, at its heart, consists of guided self-evaluation and self-improvement and serves as a centre-piece to the little understood, informal, but elaborate "system" of self-regulation*' (Young et al., 1983, p. x).

The value of accreditation as a quality benchmark is therefore to be found in the process itself. Subsequently, accreditation should be judged by its effectiveness in encouraging and assisting HEIs to evaluate and improve their educational offerings (ibid.).

Despite the hassle and ongoing costs associated with voluntary accreditation, particularly when used as a quality benchmark, considerable benefits accrue to an HEI which achieves the recognition. Students and academic staff are attracted to highly-rated HEIs which enable the institution to be selective with their admissions and recruitment decisions, charge premium fees, and hence pay premium salaries. The benefits therefore of accreditation as a quality benchmark outweigh the costs, and HEIs which do not consider accreditation run the risk that they will be categorized as the underlings of the higher education sector.

Despite the fact that many accounting graduates will choose their degree programme on the basis of what their course offers in terms of access or accelerated access to a professional accounting qualification, there is much criticism levelled at these types of accreditation. (See Laswad & Tan, Chapter 9, and Jackling, Chapter 10 – both in this volume.) Not only does accreditation as a means of access and as a means of exemption cause the same issues in terms of cost and hassle, but there is considerable discontent from academic staff about the impact which this type of accreditation has on the quality of the educational process. Academic staff bemoan the restrictive curriculum which is too technically-focussed, and the restrictive assessment which stifles innovation and the development of more generic skills sought after by employers. However, this type of accreditation is entered into through choice by the HEI. It is perfectly feasible for an HEI to enhance its standards through accreditation as a quality benchmark without trying to accommodate access to further professional study or chase exemptions from future PABs' examinations.

HEIs therefore need to carefully consider down which pathway they wish to proceed. If they are of the view that access or exemption accreditation detracts or devalues the educational programme on offer, then they do not have to seek this type of recognition. An HEI choosing to 'opt out' of this voluntary process would then need to 'make the case' to applicants and employers of prospective graduates to show how their course provision is superior to the 'buy-one-get-one-free' model criticized above (Wilson, 2011). In the light of the poor performance by accounting graduates vis-à-vis their non-accounting graduate counterparts in professional accounting examinations, this challenge may not be too difficult to overcome.

References

Accounting Education Change Commission (AECC) (1990) *Objectives of Education for Accountants, Position Statement Number One*. Available at: http://aaahq.org/AECC/pdf/position/pos1.pdf (accessed 6 March 2013).

Allyn, R.G. (1966) Accreditation of accounting curriculums, *The Accounting Review*, 41(2), 363–370.

Altbach, P.G., Gumport, P.J., & Berdahl, R.O. (2011) *American Higher Education in the Twenty-First Century: Social, Political, and Economic Challenges*, 3rd edn, Baltimore, MD: Johns Hopkins University Press.

Anderson, W.T. & Previts, G. J. (1984) Accounting accreditation and schools of accountancy in the United States, *Advances in Accounting*, 1, 89–104.

Apostolou, B. (1999) Outcomes assessment, *Issues in Accounting Education*, 14(1), 177–197.

Association to Advance Collegiate Schools of Business (AACSB) (2011) *Deploying Academically Qualified Faculty: An Interpretation of AACSB Standards*. Available at: http://www.aacsb.edu/publications/white papers/Deploying_AQ_Faculty.pdf (accessed 6 March 2013).

Association to Advance Collegiate Schools of Business (AACSB) (2012) *Eligibility Procedures and Accreditation Standards for Business Accreditation*. Available at: http://www.aacsb.edu/accreditation/standards-busn-jan2012.pdf (accessed 7 March 2013).

Association to Advance Collegiate Schools of Business (AACSB) (2013a) Accredited institutions. Available at: http://www.aacsb.edu/accreditation/accreditedmembers.asp (accessed 6 March 2013).

Association to Advance Collegiate Schools of Business (AACSB) (2013b) 2013 Business Accreditation Standards. Available at: http://www.aacsb.edu/accreditation/business/standards/2013/academic-and-Professional-eng (accessed 31 July 2013).

Bailey, A.R. & Bentz, W.F. (1991) Accounting accreditation: change and transition, *Issues in Accounting Education*, 6(2), 168–177.

Beattie, V., Collins, B., & McInnes, B. (1997) Deep and surface learning: a simple or simplistic dichotomy? *Accounting Education: an international journal*, 6(1), 1–12.

Beattie, V. & Smith, S.J. (2012) *Today's PhD Students: Is There a Future Generation of Accounting Academics or Are They a Dying Breed? A UK Perspective*. Project Report, Edinburgh: Institute of Chartered Accountants of Scotland.

Bitter, M.E., Stryker, J.P., & Jens, W.G. (1999) A preliminary investigation of the choice to obtain AACSB accounting accreditation, *The Accounting Educators' Journal*, 11, 1–15.

Board of Accreditation of Accountancy Educational Courses (BAAEC) (2000) *Members' Information Booklet*, Central Milton Keynes: BAECC.

Booth, P., Luckett, P., & Mladenovic, R. (1999) The quality of learning in accounting education: the impact of approaches to learning on academic performance, *Accounting Education: an international journal*, 8(4), 277–300.

Brown, R., Jones, M., & Steele, T. (2007) Still flickering at the margins of existence? Publishing patterns and themes in accounting and finance research over the last two decades, *British Accounting Review*, 39, 125–151.

Byrne, M., Flood, B., & Willis, P. (2002) The relationship between learning approaches and learning outcomes: a study of Irish accounting students, *Accounting Education: an international journal*, 11(1), 27–42.

Consultative Committee of Accountancy Bodies (CCAB) (2006) *CCAB Accreditation Guidance Document*. Available at: http://www.ccab.org.uk/PDFs/App%20C%20accreditation%20booklet%20-%20September.pdf (accessed 6 March 2013).

Dewey, J.R. (1916) *Democracy and Education*, New York: Macmillan.

Douglas, S. (ongoing) PhD thesis, Robert Gordon University.

Duff, A. & Marriott, N. (2012) *Teaching and Research: Partners or Competitors?* Edinburgh: Institute of Chartered Accountants of Scotland.

European Quality Improvement System (EQUIS) (2013) *EQUIS Standards & Criteria*. Available at: http://www.efmd.org/images/stories/efmd/EQUIS/EQUIS_Standards_and_Criteria_2013.pdf (accessed 7 March 2013).

Fédération des Experts-comptables Européens (FEE) (2002) *Admissions to the Professions of Accounting and Auditing*, Brussels: Federation des Experts-comptables Europeens.

Ferguson, J., Collison, D., Power, D., & Stevenson, L. (2007) What are recommended accounting textbooks teaching students about corporate stakeholders? *The British Accounting Review*, 37(1), 23–46.

Financial Reporting Council (FRC) (2011) *Key facts and Trends in the Accountancy Profession*, London: Financial Reporting Council. Available at: https://frc.org.uk/Our-Work/Publications/POB/Key-Facts-and-Trends-in-the-Accountancy-Profession.aspx (accessed 6 March 2013).

Gaharan, C., Chiasson, M.A., Foust, K.M., & Mauldin, S. (2007) AACSB International accounting accreditation: benefits and challenges, *The Accounting Educators' Journal*, 17, 13–29.

Gammie, E., Hamilton, S., & Cargill, E. (2010) *Searching for Good Practice in the Development and Assessment of Non-Technical Skills in Accounting Trainees: A Global Study (IAAER)*, Aberdeen: Robert Gordon University.

Gammie, E. & Kirkham, L. (2008) Breaking the link with a university education in the creation of a chartered accountant: the ICAS story, *The British Accounting Review*, 40(4), 356–375.

Gray, R., Collison, D., French, J., McPhail, K., & Stevenson, L. (2001) *The Professional Accountancy Bodies and the Provision of Education and Training in Relation to Environmental Issues*, Edinburgh: ICAS.

Griffiths, R. (2004) Knowledge production and the research-teaching nexus: the case of the built environment disciplines, *Studies in Higher Education*, 29 (6), 709–726.

Institute of Chartered Accountants in Australia and CPA Australia (ICAA and CPA) (2009) *Professional Accreditation Guidelines for Higher Education Programs*. Available at: http://www.cpaaustralia.com.au/cps/rde/xbcr/cpa-site/Professional_accreditation_guidelines_for_higher_education_programs.pdf (accessed 6 March 2013).

Institute of Chartered Accountants of Scotland (ICAS) (2001a) *Student Education Minutes*, 6 June 2001. Contact the authors.

Institute of Chartered Accountants of Scotland (ICAS) (2001b) *Notes of Meeting*, June 2001. Contact the authors.

Jantzen, R.H. (2000) AACSB mission-linked standards: effects on the accreditation process, *Journal of Education for Business* (Jul/Aug), 343–347.

Julian, S.D. & Ofori-Dankwa, J.C. (2006) Is accreditation good for the strategic decision making of traditional business schools? *Academy of Management Learning & Education*, 5(2), 225–233.

Karreman, G.H. (2002) *The Impact of Globalisation on Accountancy Education*. IAAER Task Force Report, Brussels: European Institute for Advanced Studies in Management (EIASM).

Karreman, G.H. (2007) *Trends in Global Accounting Education*. Available at: http://media.leidenuniv.nl/legacy/gae-2007-trends-global-accounting-education.eng.pdf (accessed 6 March 2013) (Amsterdam: Royal NIVRA).

Kren, L., Tatum, K.W., & Phillips, L.C. (1993) Separate accreditation of accounting programs: an empirical investigation, *Issues in Accounting Education*, 8(2), 260–272.

Langenderfer, H.Q. (1987) Accounting education's history: a 100-year search for identity, *Journal of Accountancy*, May, 302–331.

Lowrie, A. & Willmott, H. (2009) Accreditation sickness in the consumption of business education: the vacuum in AACSB standard setting. *Management Learning*, 40(4), 411–420.

MacKenzie, O. (1964) Accreditation of accounting curricula, *The Accounting Review*, 39(2), 363–370.

Marino, B.D. (2006) Financial scandals: another clarion call for educational reform – a historical perspective, *Issues in Accounting Education*, 21(4), 363–381.

Paisey, C. & Paisey, N.J. (2000) *A Comparative Study of Undergraduate and Professional Education in the Professions of Accountancy, Medicine, Law and Architecture*, Edinburgh: Institute of Chartered Accountants of Scotland.

Pastore, Jr., J.M. (1989) Developing an academic accreditation process relevant to the accounting profession, *The CPA Journal*, May, 18–26.

Power, M. K. (1991) Educating accountants: towards a critical ethnography, *Accounting, Organizations and Society*, 16(4), 333–353.

Quality Assurance Agency (QAA) (2007) *Subject Benchmark Statement: Accounting*, February, Gloucester: Quality Assurance Agency.

Reckers, P.M.J. (2006) Perspectives on the proposal for a generally-accepted accounting curriculum: a wakeup call for academics, *Issues in Accounting Education*, 21(1), 31–43.

Robert Gordon University (RGU) (1998) Annual accreditation update, November, Aberdeen, Scotland: RGU. Contact the authors.

Sangster, A. (ed.) (2010) Liberalising the accounting curriculum, *Accounting education: an international journal*, 19(4), 323–438.

Sangster, A. & Wilson, R.M.S. (eds) (2012) *Liberalising the Accounting Curriculum in University Education*, Abingdon: Routledge.

Sikka, P., Haslam, C., Kyriacou, O., & Agrizzi, D. (2007) Professionalizing claims and the state of UK professional accounting education: some evidence, *Accounting Education: an international journal*, 16(1), 3–21.

Sikka, P. & Willmott, H. (2002) Commentary on 'accountability of accounting educators and the rhythm of the university: resistance strategies for post-modern blues', *Accounting Education: an international journal*, 11(2), 191–197.

Sinning, K.E. & Dykxhoorn, H.J. (2001) Processes implemented for AACSB accounting accreditation and the degree of faculty involvement, *Issues in Accounting Education*, 16(2), 181–204.

South African Institute of Chartered Accountants (SAICA) (2010) *Competency Framework Detailed Guidance for Academic Programmes*. Johannesburg, South Africa: South African Institute of Chartered Accountants.

Stettler, H.F. (1965) Accreditation of collegiate accounting programs, *The Accounting Review*, 40(4), 723–730.

Sundem, G.L. (1999) *The Accounting Education Change Commission: Its History and Impact* (Accounting Education Series Vol. 15), Sarasota, FL: American Accounting Association.

Wilson, R.M.S. (2011) Alignment in accounting education and training, *Accounting education: an international journal*, 20(1), 3–16.

Young, K.E., Chambers, C.M., Kells, H.R., & Associates (1983) *Understanding Accreditation: Contemporary Perspectives on Issues and Practices in Evaluating Educational Quality*, London: Jossey-Bass Publishers.

About the authors

Barbara Apostolou is Professor of Accounting at West Virginia University, U.S.A. (Barbara.Apostolou@mail.wvu.edu). Her primary interests in the education realm are curriculum and instruction. She provides service on editorial boards of two accounting education journals. Her body of work includes many publications on accounting education topics, and discipline-specific issues related to auditing and financial accounting.

Elizabeth Gammie is Professor of Accounting and Head of the Department of Accounting and Finance, Aberdeen Business School, The Robert Gordon University, Scotland, U.K. (e.gammie@rgu.ac.uk). Her primary research interests in the education realm are assessment, predictive models of performance, development of competencies and non-technical skills. She has undertaken several funded educational research projects on behalf of the ACCA, CIMA, IAESB, ICAS, and FRC, and represents academia on several professional body boards including the ICAS Council.

30

The state of professional accounting education and training

Catriona Paisey and Nicholas J. Paisey**

*UNIVERSITY OF GLASGOW, U.K. **HERIOT-WATT UNIVERSITY, U.K.

CONTENTS

Abstract

This chapter begins by examining the nature and purpose of professional accounting education and training, locating the discussion within a review of the nature of professions and professional knowledge. The chapter also distinguishes between education and training. This provides the context for the subsequent discussion of the two stages of professional education and training – initial professional development (IPD), and continuing professional development (CPD). The picture that emerges is of a variety of models being used, though there are some broad themes common to most. At the IPD stage, these include the assessment of competence, the incorporation of work experience and syllabi developments in such areas as sustainability and ethics. At the CPD stage, there is a broad distinction between the more prevalent input-based approaches and the rarer output-based ones. There is some early evidence of increased co-operation between professional accounting bodies (PABs) and of increasing diversification to offer additional qualifications.

Keywords

continuing professional development, initial professional development, input-based, knowledge, output-based, professional accounting education, professions, training

30.1 Introduction

The main aims of this chapter are:

- to discuss the nature and purpose of professional accounting education and training;
- to describe and discuss professional accounting education and training leading to initial qualification; and
- to describe and discuss professional accounting education and training in relation to continuing professional development.

The chapter begins by discussing the nature and purpose of professional accounting education and training. This discussion is located within a review of the nature of professions and knowledge, and the distinction between education and training. A distinction is also drawn between initial professional development (IPD) and continuing professional development (CPD). Then the chapter reviews models of professional accounting education and training (including models relating to both IPD and CPD), highlighting main features, developments and key issues. Many of the examples given in this chapter reflect the authors' U.K. context, but the chapter does review both IPD and CPD practices from a number of other jurisdictions around the world, and its content has applicability more widely.

30.2 The nature of professional accounting education and training

30.2.1 Professions

Professions typically regard their education systems as a fundamental part of their being, serving as both an important part of their professional claim and a distinguishing characteristic (Paisey & Paisey, 2000). While there is considerable debate concerning the definition of a profession (Larson, 1977; Roslender, 1992), a commonly used approach is to specify a range of characteristics associated with professional status (see, for example, Wilensky, 1964; Perks, 1993), such as ethical codes, a public interest perspective, and the development of education systems (including rigorous examinations).

There are three broad approaches to the sociology of professions, termed the functionalist, interactionist, and critical approaches (Willmott, 1986):

- The *functionalist approach* focusses on the skilled tasks that professionals perform, exemplified by Hughes (1963) in his comment that what professionals do is to profess to know better than others the nature of certain matters. Abbott (1988) elaborated, suggesting that the act of professing involves a complex process whereby the professional must acquire specialised knowledge, be able to refer to it appropriately, reflect upon it, judge it, and select from it in order to provide professional advice.
- The *interactionist approach* sees professions as interest groups which refer to themselves as professions and which are recognised by others as being professions (Torstendahl, 1990; Geddes, 1995). By this definition, accounting is a profession because the professional bodies have referred to themselves as professions for a long time (Carr-Saunders & Wilson, 1933).
- The *critical approach* focusses instead on the level of control which a profession exercises over its tasks, sometimes referred to as jurisdiction, defined by Abbott (1988) as a state governed by the regulatory framework within which the profession operates. Professions evidence such control via their regulations covering professional entry and examinations, both as a means of upholding standards and in order to limit access to their professional grouping. Critical theorists argue that this mechanism maintains the market for the professional's services and, by restricting competition, protects the professional's status and livelihood (Abel, 1988).

Although these sociological approaches view professions from different perspectives, they are united in their underlying belief in the importance of professional knowledge in order that clients can have confidence that the professionals are competent. This confidence is in large part attributable to the rigour associated with professional examinations. Hence, key components of the professionalisation process are the acquisition and maintenance of professional knowledge, and the development of an examination system (Larson, 1977; Abbott, 1988).

30.2.2 Knowledge

Definitions of professions frequently refer to the importance of the knowledge base in the conferment of professional status (Hoskin & Macve, 1986), with the knowledge base being regarded as more crucial to the professional claim than skills and attributes (Watts, 2000). Jarvis (1983) distinguished between knowledge and understanding. Facts can be known without being understood, especially where they have been rote-learned, and so it is important that knowledge is internalised by the professional, reflected upon and assimilated rather than merely being regurgitated (Paisey & Paisey, 2000). (See also Flood, Chapter 4, Lucas & Mladenovic, Chapter 6, and Duff, Chapter 8 – all in this volume.)

A distinction is drawn in the educational literature between propositional (or declarative) knowledge, and procedural knowledge. Propositional, or declarative, knowledge is based on facts and information (Billett, 1996). Much accounting knowledge, based on legislation, accounting standards, and official guidance, is of this type. Propositional or declarative knowledge has long been associated with accounting. The oldest professional accounting body (PAB), the Institute of Chartered Accountants of Scotland (ICAS), emerged in 1951 as a result of a merger between three professional associations which had been founded in Edinburgh and Glasgow (both in 1853) and Aberdeen (1866). From 1893, they offered joint examinations which were an important element in their professionalisation process (Lee, 1995). Shackleton (1992) listed the earliest examination requirements. These covered general education, bookkeeping, law, actuarial science, economics, preparation of balance sheets and profit and loss accounts, audit, trust accounts, schemes of division, bankruptcy and liquidation, references, remits, and proofs. Taxation was introduced at a later date. Today's professional examinations, focussing on areas such as law, economics, bookkeeping, financial reporting, and auditing, are not dissimilar, showing that these propositional areas have been regarded as being key topics for over a century.

Procedural knowledge combines knowledge with techniques and skills (Anderson, 1982). Earlier literature nicely encapsulated this as *knowledge that* and *knowledge how* (Ryle, 1949). In the light of concerns about ever-expanding professional curricula, such a classification is important because it calls into question the extent to which learners need to know specific facts and information (i.e. the propositional or declarative knowledge). It also focusses attention on the value inherent in learners being equipped with procedural knowledge, such as knowing how to update their knowledge and research new areas as a basis for lifelong learning (Paisey & Paisey, 2007). Further discussion of accounting skills can be found in Watty, Chapter 13 and Sundem, Chapter 27 – both in this volume, and the influence of institutions in this regard is also discussed in Chapter 27. The seminal reports by two of these institutions, the American Accounting Association's (AAA) Bedford Committee (AAA, 1986), distinguishing between initial and life-long learning, and the Accounting Education Change Commission's (AECC) (1990) Position Statement Number One, *Objectives of Education for Accountants* (AECC, 1990), which specifies the desirable characteristics of accountants, both show that there is a recognition that accounting education should encompass both propositional/declarative knowledge in the form of general, organisational and accounting knowledge, and procedural knowledge in the form of communication, intellectual, and interpersonal skills.

The most recent work on the nature of professions continues this focus on knowledge.

Saks (2012, p. 1) argues that the nature of professions rests on the epistemic dimension, in relation to knowledge and expertise. Cruess *et al.* (2000, p. 156) summarise the characteristics of a modern profession, in their case, the medical profession, but their view seems equally applicable to accounting (emphasis added):

> *First, as professions hold specialised knowledge not easily understood by the average citizen, they are given a monopoly over its use and are responsible for its teaching. Second, this knowledge is used in the service of individual patients and society in an altruistic fashion. Third, the inaccessible nature of the knowledge and the commitment to altruism are the justification for the profession's autonomy to establish and maintain standards of practice and self-regulation to assure quality. Fourth, professionals are responsible for the integrity of their knowledge base, its expansion through research, and for ensuring the highest standards for its use.*

This brief review has shown the importance of education systems to professions, both to secure and maintain professional status and to ensure that members of the profession are equipped to act competently and in the public interest. It has also shown the importance of knowledge within the education system. The precise nature of the education system will now be examined, with a distinction being drawn between education and training.

30.2.3 Education and training

Education is often associated with schools (primary and secondary education) and universities (tertiary education). At one end of the educational spectrum lies liberal education, with its roots in the ancient Greek idea of a *'civilised'* person (Rothblatt, 1990). This conception of liberal education assumes that knowledge is an end in itself, focussed on intellectual curiosity and learning for its own sake (Newman, 1907). Entwistle (1988, p. 226) views education as being *'a preparation for life'*. Barnett (1990, p. 150) distinguishes education by *'the student's ability to understand what is learned or what is done, to conceptualise it, to grasp it under different aspects, and to take up critical stances in relation to it'*.

Characteristics associated with a liberal approach to education include intellectual, moral, and personal development (Barnett, 1988; Duke, 1990); understanding, freedom, impartiality, tolerance, and respect for persons (Bagnall, 1991); self-knowledge (Wegener, 1978); and educational breadth (Dean, 1988). At the other end of the educational spectrum lies vocational education, with an emphasis on preparing people for employment (Stokes, 1989). (See also St. Pierre & Rebele, Chapter 5, and Amernic & Craig, Chapter 12 – both in this volume, and Sangster & Wilson, 2012.)

Education, however defined, is considered to be broader than training. Training focusses on preparation for specific tasks and the development of skills (Feinberg & Horowitz, 1990). In particular, training stresses the importance of learning from experience (Eraut, 1997; Eraut et al., 2001). Thus, while education is about preparation for life, training is more focussed, preparing the trainee for work or for some specific task. This distinction is evident in the quality assurance processes adopted at professional level, which have parallels with, but tend to be more rigorous than, those within higher education (McChlery & Paisey, 2003).

The complementarity of education and training is recognised by Eraut (1994) who argues that knowledge is situated in the context where it is acquired and requires further learning for its transfer. Eraut states (1994, p. 25) that *'learning knowledge and using knowledge are not separate processes but the same process. The process of using knowledge transforms that knowledge so that it is no longer the same knowledge.'*

Wilson (2011, p. 5) presents a model for the creation of the effective accounting practitioner. His model distinguishes between education and training, with the school and university stages focussing on the former and the professional stage emphasising the latter, but with both being essential to the creation of an effective accounting practitioner (Figure 30.1).

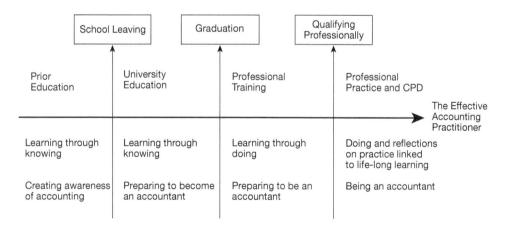

Figure 30.1 Alignment in accounting education and training

Source: Reprinted with permission of Taylor & Francis Ltd., from R.M.S. Wilson (2011) 'Alignment in Accounting Education and Training', Accounting Education: an international journal, 20(1), 5. See www.tandfonline.com

As this model shows, both education and training focus on knowledge but in different ways, beginning with 'learning through knowing' to 'learning through doing' to 'doing and reflection'. It also shows the central role played by both education and training in the creation of an effective accounting practitioner. Further discussion of this model can be found in Section 30.4.1.

Barnett (1990) argues that, for an experience to meet the requirements of education, it should promote:

- a deep understanding of some knowledge claims (similar to a deep approach to learning);
- a radical critique of these knowledge claims;
- a developing competence to conduct that critique in the company of others;
- some form of independent enquiry;
- the student's engagement in that enquiry in a process of open dialogue and co-operation; and
- self-reflection by students.

He sees this as having emancipatory potential, given that knowledge is combined with broader objectives. To illustrate, a student studying an accounting standard at university might learn about the historical background to the standard, why it was required, the alternatives that were considered, and how the standard works in practice. This knowledge and understanding could be enhanced by argument and debate, and with engagement with research literature. If that same standard was being taught at a professional level, the emphasis would be more likely to be placed on the specific requirements of the standard and its application in practice. In this respect, the nature of education and training cannot be considered fully unless the purpose of the process is also considered.

30.3 Purpose of professional education and training

Professional accounting education and training can be separated into two distinct phases. The International Federation of Accountants (IFAC) refers to these stages as initial professional development (IPD) and continuing professional development (CPD). This is consistent with the Accounting Education Change Commission's Position Statement Number One, *Objectives of Education for Accountants* (AECC, 1990, p. 307) which, as noted in several other chapters in this volume, states '*accounting programs should prepare students to **become** professional accountants, not to be professional accountants*' (emphasis in original).

30.3.1 Initial professional development (IPD)

IPD focusses on the testing of professional knowledge leading to certification through examination success (Hines, 1989). IPD sometimes incorporates competence-based assessment (CBA), which is a form of assessment that is derived from the specification of a set of outcomes – both general and specific – that assessors, students, and other interested parties can use to make reasonably objective judgements with respect to students' achievement and non-achievement in relation to these outcomes. CBA was originally used in the U.K. for vocational education. While noting the benefits of precision, concern has been raised that CBA can be indicative of lower status qualifications, reducing learning to predetermined outcomes rather than taking a broader view (see, for example, Wolf, 1995; Hussey & Smith, 2002; Mulder *et al.*, 2007). Notwithstanding, within accounting, CBA gained prominence in the U.K. when it became part of government policy following the publication of a White Paper, *Working Together: Education and Training*

(HMSO, 1986), for all occupations, including the professions, to be competence-based, a policy that was later abandoned. In the U.S.A., too, CBA gained prominence when the AECC issued its list of 55 competencies in 1990 (see Exhibit 27.1), and has had more recent impetus with the issue of the American Institute of Certified Public Accountants' (AICPA) *Core Competency Framework*. Underpinning the idea of CBA is the belief that it is important that a competent person can do some task rather than simply displaying some knowledge of it. Competence-based assessment is considered further in Section 30.4.2.

IPD also instils a professional ideology and critical awareness, equipping newly-qualified professionals so that they can exercise the judgement that distinguishes professions from other occupations (Jarvis, 1983). The exercise of judgement, of course, requires knowledge, but heated debates can take place regarding the content of this stage. One example of this was reported in Paisey & Paisey (2006). This paper discussed events at the Institute of Chartered Accountants in England & Wales (ICAEW) as this PAB debated whether to adopt a core and options (electives) model for its IPD. Proposals were put forward to address concerns about the ever-increasing curriculum as the range of legislative and professional pronouncements increased, and questions were asked about what a newly-qualified accountant should be expected to know – the core – and what could be tailored to individual preferences and career plans – the options or electives. Supporters of a move to a core and options model argued that such a model would allow a broader curriculum to be offered by freeing up space for a wider range of electives, and also allow space for the development of a wider range of soft skills (see Watty, Chapter 13 – this volume). Such calls had also been made in other countries including Australia (Mathews, 1990) and the U.S.A. (Albrecht & Sack, 2000) where it had been argued that PABs should move away from the idea of having to teach everything in order to address the practicalities of equipping trainees with the skills to enable them to continually update their knowledge and skills throughout their professional lives. However, the proposals were vigorously opposed by a group of members of ICAEW who felt that all chartered accountants should undergo the same training as this was 'a tie that binds'. In other words, they wished to see the preservation of the generalist professional.

Underlying the various arguments was the question of the knowledge base of professionals. Accounting education suffers from many of the problems identified by educators in medicine and law (Paisey & Paisey, 2010), including an ever-increasing knowledge base. Proponents of a core and options approach did not see knowledge as being an end in itself. Rather, they were willing to see some curricular areas reduced or deleted if the consequence was that space could be used more effectively. The fact that a small but vociferous group of ICAEW's members could block such a move shows that the environment within which educational decisions are taken in PABs is complex, extending beyond educational matters into a more overtly political arena, and striking at the heart of the purpose of IPD. For the opponents of the proposed changes, IPD was an important first stage in the making of a professional accountant who was generalist in approach and whose knowledge was – notionally, at least – unbounded.

Even now, there is still a tendency towards the retention of quite traditional educational models by PABs. There appears to be a reluctance to introduce options or electives although the current education programmes of Chartered Accountants Ireland and The Association of Chartered Certified Accountants (ACCA) do include electives in *Advanced Taxation, Advanced Performance Management,* and *Advanced Audit and Assurance,* while ACCA offers a fourth elective in *Advanced Financial Management.* These are situated at the final examination level, with earlier levels being completely core for all candidates. Therefore, although there is some limited movement towards the recognition of a different way of developing a professional accountant via a more tailored qualification, the retention of the typical multi-stage, all compulsory subject model for professional examinations by most PABs ensures that most accountants continue to be educated in much the same way. Indeed, the ICAEW case shows that some members felt that this uniform tie was important not simply for education, but also for social reasons (i.e. a commonality among all chartered accountants of the same rite of passage into the ICAEW).

In other ways, too, IPD in accounting incorporates a socialisation process (Power, 1991; Roslender, 1992; Anderson-Gough et al., 1998, 2001, 2002, 2005). Anderson-Gough et al. (1998), in a study of the organisational and professional socialisation of ICAEW trainees, argue that the making of a professional accountant combines the schooling and examination process with work experience, thus socialising the aspiring chartered accountant into the organisational culture and professional norms of the employing firm. They found that the trainees were primarily concerned with acquiring a qualification that would act as a passport to career success. Trainees therefore viewed examinations as being an obstacle to be cleared, and cared little for the actual syllabus content. All that really mattered was securing a pass. Beyond that, doing especially well in the examinations was not particularly valued (Anderson-Gough et al., 2002). The trainees therefore thought simply in terms of getting through examinations rather than of wider learning. The paucity of such an approach is clear, on both curricular and social grounds, and also in terms of future professional effectiveness.

30.3.2 Continuing professional development (CPD)

IPD provides a passport into the world of the qualified accountant. The certification is a licence to practise (Jarvis, 1983). However, the accounting environment is changing constantly and so the competent accountant requires some means of keeping up-to-date, hence IFAC's distinction between IPD and CPD. The CPD stage begins on initial qualification and continues throughout the remainder of the professional accountant's working life, and sometimes beyond that too into retirement if the accountant continues to undertake accounting-related work, even of a voluntary nature.

Friedman et al. (1999) noted that, among professionals generally, CPD has historically been regarded mainly as the responsibility of individuals, not their professional associations. Within accounting, CPD (or CPE – continuing professional education – as it is sometimes called) was not originally regarded as being a compulsory activity. Rather it was viewed as being implicit in a professional accountant's ethical responsibility to carry out his or her work with due skill and care (Paisey & Paisey, 1996). Essentially, the idea was that a professional accountant should maintain competence and knowledge of current developments in order to be able to act with due skill and care. Therefore, while not explicitly required, some form of CPD was assumed by the PABs. However, this view of the updating of knowledge and the continued ability to exercise judgement depended upon the willingness of the individual accountant to engage in appropriate activities, one of which could be CPD as defined by PABs. From a PAB's perspective, ensuring that members maintained their ability to offer a quality service was important in helping to assure clients and the wider public that accounting professionals were competent and capable of being relied upon to provide good quality advice. CPD is one means whereby that ability can be evidenced, and the PABs have increased their regulation of this area since the 1980s (Paisey et al., 2007).

While CPD could be said to have been expected of all professional accountants if they were to maintain their competence, it was initially only compulsory for certain categories of members. In the U.K., for example, CPD became compulsory for auditors and insolvency practitioners under legislation introduced in the 1980s (Paisey et al., 2007). International Education Standard (IES) 7, *Continuing Professional Development*, effective from January 2006 (IFAC, 2004), fundamentally altered the nature of CPD by requiring all accountants to undertake CPD irrespective of their area of work. The underlying premise of IES 7 is stated as being that:

> *all professional accountants have an obligation to develop and maintain their professional competence, relevant to the nature of their work and professional responsibilities. This obligation applies to all professional accountants, irrespective of whether they are involved in traditional accounting fields or other areas.*
>
> (IFAC, 2012, para. 14)

CPD itself is defined in paragraph 5 as *'learning and development that develops and maintains capabilities to enable professional accountants to perform their roles competently'*.

In 2012, IFAC issued a redrafted version of IES 7, *Continuing Professional Development (Redrafted)* which became effective from 1 January 2014. This revision has maintained the compulsory nature of CPD, and reiterates that the purpose of CPD is to develop and maintain professional competence to enable professional accountants to continue to perform their roles competently. It continues (ibid., para. 4) that:

> *CPD provides continuing development of the (a) professional knowledge, (b) professional skills, (c) professional values, ethics, and attitudes, and (d) competence achieved during IPD, refined appropriately for the professional activities and responsibilities of the professional accountant. In addition, professional accountants may take on new roles during their careers that require new competences. In such cases, CPD that includes many of the same elements as IPD may be necessary for roles that require additional breadth or depth of knowledge, skills, and values.*

IES 7, in both its original and revised forms, stresses that CPD is intended to enable professional accountants to continue to be able to perform their roles effectively. Therefore, this is a narrower purpose than that envisaged by IPD because IPD is designed to meet the needs of accountants generally, rather than to meet the specific needs of a particular role.

30.4 Professional accounting education and training leading to initial qualification

30.4.1 Models of initial professional development

Some professions have a very structured and uniform pathway to qualification. Medicine, for example, requires a medical degree followed by a period of work experience. The precise details vary from country to country, and the length of degree programmes may differ, with some countries now permitting graduates of related disciplines to enter for medical degrees as second degrees. Nonetheless, there is a fairly typical route towards qualification with a higher education stage being followed by a post-graduation phase. The accounting profession permits a much greater variety of routes to qualification. The entry qualifications of trainees, and their experiences of higher education (if any), vary considerably. Professional education also differs in terms of length of training, coverage of syllabus content and skills, whether full- or part-time and whether incorporating work experience provision. (See Beard & Humphrey, Chapter 25 – this volume.) Professional accountants throughout the world are therefore made in many different ways. Chapter 2 (Needles), Chapter 26 (Calhoun & Karreman), Chapter 28 (Evans), and Chapter 29 (Apostolou & Gammie) compare accounting education in a range of countries and show that the education models vary a great deal. This section aims to investigate further some of this variety and to assess some underlying implications.

Wilson's (2011) model for the creation of the effective accounting practitioner (see Figure 30.1) shows four stages – school, university, IPD, and CPD. Evans, in Chapter 28 – this volume, deals with the interface between academic education and professional training. Points of relevance here are, first, that not all professionally-qualified accountants have studied accounting in their prior education, for example, at school (McPhail et al., 2010). (See also Byrne & Willis, Chapter 7 – this volume.) Second, a degree in accounting is not universally required for entry to the accounting profession. Data is not available on a worldwide basis, but the Professional Oversight Board for Accountancy (FRC, 2012) publishes data annually about the U.K.'s PABs. This shows that ICAS comes closest in the U.K. to all-graduate entry, with approximately 98 per cent of its students possessing degrees. Next comes Chartered Accountants Ireland, with approximately 93 per cent, and the ICAEW, with just over 80 per cent. ACCA and The Chartered Institute of Management Accountants (CIMA), with both bodies having sizeable numbers of overseas trainees and members, each have 40–50 per cent of their trainees in possession of a degree. Almost 80 per cent of Chartered Accountants Ireland's trainees possess a relevant degree (i.e. with a major in Accounting). However, the percentages of relevant degree holders are considerably smaller in respect of the other PABs (just over 40 per cent for ACCA, around 30 per cent for ICAS and around 20 per cent for CIMA). Therefore, in the U.K., while increasing numbers of accounting trainees possess degrees, the accounting profession in the U.K. falls far short of being an all-graduate profession. The numbers possessing a relevant accounting degree, or one with a substantial accounting component, are fewer still. Therefore, despite the accreditation processes reviewed by Apostolou & Gammie, Chapter 29 – this volume, many entrants will not receive exemptions from the examinations of PABs. Other countries have similar requirements. For example, an accounting degree is not required for entry to the Japanese Institute of Certified Public Accountants (JICPA, 2008. See also Noguchi, Section 15.4.2, Chapter 15).

The features of Wilson's ideal model at prior education and university education stages, therefore, are not universally present. The consequence is that accounting training at the professional stage must have mechanisms to accommodate trainees who possess no prior knowledge of accounting. Thus, there are various entry routes into membership of PABs, with graduates frequently receiving some – often minimal – advanced entry (i.e. with some exemptions from PABs' examinations), and relevant graduates entering at a slightly higher level again. Typically, however, the U.K.'s PABs insist that even relevant graduates should undertake and pass their more advanced examination stages.

This review impacts upon the making of the professional accountant since not all professional entrants will be graduates, despite such an attribute becoming associated increasingly with professional status (Gammie & Kirkham, 2008). Furthermore, not all accountants undergo academic education in accounting. This means that the professional training stage is crucial since it is the first stage that all aspiring accountants go through.

An interesting development in the U.K. is the fusion of the university and professional stages in a number of new combined degrees that incorporate professional qualifications. For example:

- ICAS, Ernst and Young, and the University of Lancaster have combined to offer an integrated four-year degree that meets the university's requirements for a degree and also provides exemptions from all but the final stage of ICAS's examinations.
- PricewaterhouseCooper and ICAEW have similar combined programmes with the University of Newcastle and Henley Business School.
- KPMG has recently launched a six-year programme with ICAS and the Universities of Bristol, Durham, and Exeter, whereby school-leavers can gain a full ICAS qualification

and degree in a scheme that incorporates academic education, professional training, and work experience in a fully-integrated programme. This is an alternative route to qualification which avoids the necessity of students having to fund their university studies since they receive a salary throughout this period.

This review has shown the range of models within the U.K. A striking feature of professional education in accounting is the amount of variation in different countries and even, in the case of the U.S.A., variation between states. In the U.S.A., candidates wishing to become members of the AICPA must sit the Uniform Certified Public Accountant's (CPA) Examination. This examination comprises 14 hours of examinations in *Financial Accounting and Reporting; Auditing and Attestation; Regulation*; and *Business Environment and Concepts*. The examination is prepared nationally, but each State Board of Accountancy in the U.S.A. specifies the educational requirements within its jurisdiction for eligibility to sit the examination, along with the work experience requirement (where applicable) to become licensed as a CPA. During the 1990s, most states required candidates to have undertaken a minimum of 150 hours of college education (equivalent to five years of tertiary education) in order to sit. However, in 2009, only 22 of the 54 jurisdictions administering the Uniform CPA Examination required a minimum of 150 credit hours, with the remaining jurisdictions requiring only 120 credit hours (equivalent to four years of tertiary education) (Briggs & He, 2012).

In order to show the extent of differences in IPD, the routes to qualification in different PABs are now compared. The following examples are drawn from PABs which are members of the recently formed Chartered Accountants Worldwide,[1] which self-styles itself as comprising the leading PABs from around the world. First, the education schemes of two PABS that require students to have studied for a relevant degree which gives exemptions via accreditation, as discussed by Apostolou & Gammie in Chapter 29 – this volume, are considered. The IPD models of the South African Institute of Chartered Accountants (SAICA) and the recently-launched joint model of the Institute of Chartered Accountants in Australia (ICAA) and the New Zealand Institute of Chartered Accountants (NZICA) fall into this category.

The SAICA scheme requires a B.Com degree or equivalent accounting qualification, after which trainees enter into a three- to five-year training progamme either within or outside of professional practice, during which they sit professional examinations. The professional examinations comprise an Assessment of Core Technical Knowledge, followed by specialist examinations in Financial Management and Audit (SAICA, 2013).

ICAA and NZICA previously had separate education systems, but launched their combined programme in 2013. In order to be eligible for the programme, students must have studied for an accredited undergraduate or master's degree that includes the following range of subjects at an approved tertiary institution provider:

- Financial Accounting
- Management Accounting
- Auditing and Assurance
- Taxation
- Finance
- Commercial & Corporate Law
- Accounting Information Systems
- Economics
- Organisational Management
- Quantitative Methods.

There then follows three years of approved full-time (or equivalent) mentored practical experience. During this period, trainees study four subjects:

- Audit and Assurance
- Financial Accounting and Reporting
- Management Accounting and Applied Finance
- Taxation.

These are studied via a mix of online learning and virtual classrooms over a period of 12 weeks for each subject. They are assessed by three online assessments, comprising 20 per cent of the final grade, and a final examination, comprising the remaining 80 per cent. The final, capstone, stage involves 14 weeks of online learning focussing on case-studies, with three face-to-face workshops (40 per cent) and a final examination (60 per cent).

To summarise, in the SAICA and ICAA/NZICA models, the IPD stage combines examinations with practical experience. These models therefore include the university, IPD, and CPD parts of the Wilson (2011) model.

In contrast, the ICAEW and ICAS models show more flexible entry routes, including:

- school leaver entry;
- membership of the Association of Accounting Technicians (which is a junior body);
- accredited degree with exemptions from the first stage of examinations;
- non-relevant degree that may offer some exemptions from parts of the first stage of examinations (e.g. economics or law);
- non-relevant degree that offers no exemptions;
- routes that combine university study with professional qualification.

For these routes, the IPD and CPD stages of Wilson's (2011) model are common to all, but the university stage is not.

One aspect of the IPD process which has not received sufficient attention is access in countries that are less affluent and which have less developed PABs. One exception is Uche's (2007) study of accounting education in Nigeria, Ghana, and Sierra Leone. This shows that the development of education systems is particularly challenging in countries that have only recently begun to professionalise accounting. ACCA has addressed this issue with its joint examination scheme that permits students to study for ACCA examinations and thereby to gain joint membership of ACCA and their local PAB. Currently, this scheme links ACCA with PABs in Belize, Botswana, Cambodia, Cyprus, Greece, Guyana, Jamaica, Lesotho, Malawi, Malta, Sierra Leone, Swaziland, Thailand, Trinidad, and Vietnam. The ACCA partnership therefore brings membership of an internationally-recognised PAB within the reach of trainees in countries in which their own PABs would not have the resources to mount full education programmes of their own.

30.4.2 Work experience and competence

Sitting alongside formal examinations, the Wilson (2011) alignment model shows that work experience is incorporated into the professional stage in order for accountants to learn by doing. However, work experience requirements vary in rigour. For some bodies, such as ICAEW and ICAS, three years of relevant work experience is required. For others, such as AICPA, one year is recommended but some State Boards of Accountancy in the U.S.A. either have no work experience requirement within their specific jurisdiction, or permit experience to be gained in a wide range of settings, such as teaching in academia (which would not meet the requirements of ICAS or the ICAEW).

As discussed briefly earlier, work experience requirements are often couched in terms of competence. By its very nature, competence needs to be assessed in the workplace. The International Accounting Education Standards Board (IFAC, 2003) distinguished between capability and competence, with capability comprising the attributes held by individuals, which enable them to perform their roles, whereas competence reflects an individual's ability to perform a work role to a defined standard within a real-world (rather than a classroom-based) environment.

Competence-based learning and qualifications have been developed and progressively introduced into vocational and professional education and training since the 1990s (Thomson, 1995), with the U.K.'s Association of Accounting Technicians (AAT) being an early adopter (Langley, 1995). However, the argument has been put that competence is a somewhat limiting term, with Brown & McCartney (1995) preferring the term 'meta-competence'. In practice, the specification of competence can be difficult (Hardern, 1995), and competence-based assessment may be perceived differently depending upon the gender and language of the trainee (Weil *et al.*, 2004).

In 1998, AICPA released the *Core Competency Framework for Entry into the Accounting Profession* as an educational component of its CPA Vision Project (Bolt-Lee & Foster, 2003). ICAS was one of the first professional bodies in the U.K. to introduce a competence-based approach in 1999 (Gammie & Joyce, 2009). A typical current example is the Canadian Institute of Chartered Accountants' (CICA) requirement that entrants should hold a four-year, 120-credit hour university degree, have passed professional examinations, and undergone a minimum of three years of work experience that shows progression in terms of responsibility and appropriate supervision. Competence expectations are specified in six broad areas:

- performance measurement and reporting
- governance strategy and risk management
- taxation
- assurance
- management decision-making, and
- finance.

The competence-based approach appears to have been widely adopted and to have achieved success within audit education in particular (Chaffrey *et al.*, 2011; Marriott *et al.*, 2011). Specific examples of evidence of competence are the requirements of Chartered Accountants Ireland for trainees to complete an online diary, and the ICAS log book that must be completed by all trainees.

30.4.3 Syllabus coverage

The Wilson (2011) model shows that a combination of learning and skills development is assumed in order to develop the effective accounting practitioner. Actual subject coverage varies depending upon the orientation of the PAB in question. For example, CIMA, specialising in management accounting, has more course requirements within the area of management accounting, management, and decision-making, while some other PABs (such as ICAEW and ICAS) focus more on financial reporting. Debates continue about the syllabus and, in particular, whether it should all be core or whether a greater range of subjects should be provided by splitting subjects into core and optional ones. One subject area that has been downsized in recent years is taxation. Some PABs based in the U.K. have reduced the emphasis placed on tax in their syllabi. For example, CIMA only includes taxation as a minor (20 per cent) component in its *Financial Reporting and Tax Principles* paper, whereas previous CIMA syllabi devoted a whole paper to the subject. ICAS has removed taxation altogether as a requirement for gaining exemptions from subsequent professional examinations.

Other syllabus changes and developments often reflect the concerns of the time. Early volumes of *Accounting Education: an international journal*, for example, contained a wide range of papers discussing the incorporation of information technology (IT) into the curriculum, but these tended to discuss the incorporation of IT into university rather than professional curricula. Recent years have seen a shift in focus from the teaching of aspects of IT to using IT in examinations. (See Boritz & Stoner, Chapter 16 – this volume.) Some PABs use computerised examinations for earlier stage papers, especially multiple-choice examinations (for example, CIMA) on grounds of efficiency and in order to be able to provide an instantaneous result. The final stage examinations of ICAS and CICA involve students working on a case study and preparing their

Table 30.1 References to sustainability and ethics in the syllabi of four professional accounting bodies in the U.K.

PAB	Sustainability	Ethics
ACCA	Specifically included in the syllabus for eight papers: • Accounting in Business • Advanced Audit and Assurance • Advanced Financial Management • Advanced Performance Management • Business Analysis • Corporate Reporting • Financial Reporting • Professional Accountant	The ACCA qualification includes a full examination paper on Governance, Risk and Ethics
CIMA	Specifically included in the syllabus for one paper: • Enterprise Operations	Specifically included in the syllabus for six papers: • Enterprise Management • Enterprise Operations • Enterprise Strategy • Financial Management • Financial Operations • Performance Strategy
ICAEW	Specifically included in the syllabus for three papers: • Assurance • Business and Finance • Business Strategy	ICAEW requires trainees to undertake its web-based structured training in ethics teaching and assessment
ICAS	Specifically included in the syllabus for two papers: • Advanced Finance • Financial Reporting	ICAS trainees must attend two days of specialist ethics coverage and complete an ethics assignment before admission

report under examination conditions using a computer in order to replicate, as far as possible, the business environment. Even where computers are not used, case studies increasingly feature at the final stage (for example, both CIMA and ICAEW use case studies to examine material in a more integrated way).

Two areas that have gained increased prominence in recent syllabi are sustainability and ethics. Sustainability features as an item in many syllabi, but tends not to feature as a stand-alone subject, whereas ethics is increasingly being examined separately. In order to show the variety of approaches to subject coverage, Table 30.1 compares these two areas in the syllabi of four of the major PABs in the U.K. (Further discussion of ethics is provided by Boyce in Chapter 24 – this volume.)

Of course, the inclusion of a topic in a syllabus does not indicate how that topic is taught or examined, nor does its exclusion mean that sustainability or ethical issues are not covered. Nonetheless, the syllabus content does give some public indication of the importance attached to topics by each professional body. Table 30.1 shows clearly that there is some agreement as to which new areas should be incorporated into syllabi, but that the precise nature and extent of coverage can vary considerably.

This review has shown that the making of the professional accountant may begin in pre-university education or at university, but that not all trainees possess this background. The IPD stage is therefore the first one that is common to all trainees, although even here many trainees will be eligible for exemptions from some parts of IPD due to their pre-IPD education. The only stage, therefore, that is truly required by all accountants in its entirety is the CPD stage, which will now be considered.

30.5 Approaches to continuing professional development

30.5.1 Models of continuing professional development

The International Accounting Education Standards Board's (IAESB) International Education Standard (IES) 7 outlines three broad approaches to CPD, input, output and combination approaches.

- *Input-based approaches* establish a set amount of learning activity that is considered to be appropriate to develop and maintain competence, typically by specifying the number of hours or learning units of CPD that should be undertaken in a given period. IES 7 further specifies that member bodies operating an input-based approach should require the professional accountant to complete at least 120 hours or equivalent learning units of relevant professional development activity in each rolling three-year period, of which 60 hours or equivalent learning units should be verifiable, with at least 20 hours or equivalent learning units in each year.
- *Output-based approaches* require professional accountants to demonstrate, by way of outcomes, that they develop and maintain professional competence.
- *Combination approaches* combine elements of the input- and output-based approaches, setting the amount of learning activity required, and measuring the outcomes achieved.

In practice, different PABs have adopted a variety of policies that are either input- or output-based. A summary of the approaches adopted by a variety of PABs is included in Table 30.2. Selected examples are now reviewed in greater detail.

Table 30.2 Types of CPD schemes

	Input	Output	Combination
Chartered Accountants Worldwide			
Chartered Accountants Ireland	*	*	*
Institute of Chartered Accountants in Australia	*		
Institute of Chartered Accountants in England & Wales		*	
Institute of Chartered Accountants of Scotland		*	
New Zealand Institute of Chartered Accountants	*		
South African Institute of Chartered Accountants		*	
Other bodies			
American Institute of Certified Public Accountants	*		
Association of Chartered Certified Accountants	*		
Certified General Accountants Association of Canada	*		
Chartered Institute of Management Accountants		*	
Chartered Institute of Public Finance and Accountancy	*		
Chartered Professional Accountants of Canada	*		
CPA Australia	*		
Hong Kong Institute of Certified Public Accountants	*		
Institute of Certified Public Accountants in Ireland	*		
Institute of Chartered Accountants of India	*		
The Institute of Chartered Accountants of Pakistan	*		
South African institute of Professional Accountants	*		

Some input-based CPD schemes essentially adopt the IES 7 guidance in its entirety. The schemes operated by the Hong Kong Institute of Certified Public Accountants and CPA Australia require all members, except those exempt from complying with the CPD requirements to do the following:

(a) complete at least 120 hours of relevant CPD activities in each rolling three-year period;
(b) complete at least 20 of these hours each year; and
(c) track and measure learning activities to meet the above requirements.

The Institute of Chartered Accountants of Pakistan specifies 40 hours per year.

Another example of an input-based approach is that operated by ACCA. Members following their unit-based route plan and organise their own CPD, being required to complete 40 relevant units of CPD each year, where one unit is equal to one hour of development. Twenty-one units must be verifiable; the other 19 can be non-verifiable. In order for the CPD activity to meet the ACCA's criteria for verifiability, it should be relevant to the member's career, the member must be able to explain how he/she will apply the learning in the workplace, and should be able to provide evidence that he/she actually undertook the learning activity. Non-verifiable CPD is general learning that is not related to a specific outcome, such as general reading and research.

The scheme operated by the ICAA is similar, defining acceptable activities broadly to include 'soft' skills (such as software training and management training) where needed in order to facilitate members in their role(s). Members are required to undertake a minimum of 120 hours of Training and Development over a three-year period (triennium). Of these, a maximum of 30 hours may comprise technical reading.

The above examples show a high degree of uniformity among input-based schemes, with most staying close to the wording and intent of IES 7. The AIPCA also has an input-based scheme, requiring members to measure CPE in credits. However, AICPA stresses that the objective of its scheme must always be maintenance/enhancement of professional competence, not attainment of credits. AICPA requires members to select learning activities through a thoughtful, reflective process addressing the individual CPA's current and future professional plans, current knowledge and skills level, and desired or needed additional competence to meet future opportunities and/or professional responsibilities. In 2012, the AICPA issued new CPE standards, effective from 2014. While maintaining an input-based approach, these revised standards '*will provide flexibility for innovation in learning techniques and allow for future considerations around outcome-based learning. Significant revisions are in the areas of group internet-based learning and self-study programs*' (AICPA, 2012). This wording has much in common with the output-based approaches which will be reviewed next. Hence, although essentially an input-based scheme, it seems that the AICPA is, in some respects, paving the way for a possible change in approach at a future date.

ICAS has adopted an output-based approach. Its rules require each member to engage in four steps:

1   defining their current and future role(s);
2   deciding on the skills and knowledge levels needed to meet the expectations identified in their current and future roles in order to enable effective performance and to decide on further training and development needs;
3   developing or undertaking a personal development programme and recording each CPD activity; and
4   reflecting on the learning outcome of CPD activities during the year concerned.

Each year, members are required to certify that they have complied with their CPD requirements, and should be able to produce their CPD record on request.

CIMA has a broadly similar, but slightly more defined, model specifying six steps. CIMA locates CPD within its professional development cycle. Its members are required to work through this cycle annually and to record their development activities, stating that members will be compliant with the CPD policy if they address each stage of the cycle, as follows:

- Step 1 is to define what is expected of the member in his/her role, and future goals.
- Step 2 is to assess development needs and outcomes, comparing what is expected in the current, or a future role, against the member's current capabilities.
- Step 3 is to design and document a programme around activities that the member believes are relevant to the current role.
- Step 4 is to undertake the development activities as planned.
- Step 5 is to reflect on the development activities, consider what has been learned, how that can be applied, and consider the changes that the member would make next time.
- Step 6 is to evaluate actual development against development needs and outcomes, carrying forward any outstanding development to the next cycle.

Likewise, ICAEW has adopted an output-based approach, specifying instead that members simply need to complete as much development activity as they feel is required in order to remain competent in their role(s). This policy stresses that attendance at training courses is not necessary to maintain CPD compliance, and that people learn in different ways, through several different channels. Examples of suggested CPD activities include:

- reading ICAEW email alerts that contains updates and news items;
- attending a workshop, conference, seminar, or webinar;
- reading a book or journal, participating in the ICAEW community; and
- arranging an informal training session with a colleague.

SAICA previously had an input-based approach but changed to an output-based approach in 2013. Chartered Accountants Ireland amended its policy in 2012 to permit input, output, or combination approaches. Therefore, there is some evidence that there is the beginning of a shift from input-based approaches to ones that recognise outputs.

The above examples show that output-based approaches may be expressed in different terms but, essentially, all ask that members identify and act upon their own development needs. This exemplifies the fundamental difference between IPD and CPD whereby CPD is much more closely attuned to an actual working role rather than to the IPD curriculum.

This emphasis on the role performed by members of PABs is further illustrated by the fact that some bodies have now accredited employers whereby members who have engaged in an employer's development and appraisal process are automatically deemed to have satisfied their PAB's requirements too. Such schemes are operated by several U.K.-based bodies, including ACCA, CIMA, ICAEW, and ICAS. Employers can apply for accreditation for their companies' professional development schemes. If a member of a PAB works for an accredited/approved employer, that member may achieve CPD by participating in the organisation's employee development programme. Most of the large firms of chartered accountants, and many large companies, have achieved accredited status.

CPD schemes in practice, then, fall mainly into two broad categories: the more prevalent input-based, and much rarer output-based, with little adoption of combination approaches.

30.5.2 Issues in continuing professional development

While research into higher education in accounting is widespread, and there is some work being done in relation to IPD, very little research has been undertaken into CPD. Reflection is an aspect that is generally regarded as being crucial to CPD (Schön, 1983, 1987), and is a concept that is mentioned in several of the CPD policies of PABs surveyed earlier in this section. Early papers discussed reflective aspects of CPD and analysed the nature of CPD respectively (Velayutham & Perera, 1993; Paisey & Paisey, 1995, 1996). These papers showed that CPD in the accounting profession did not incorporate reflection in the same way as was evident in best practice in other professions, and that it was characterised by differential requirements for different types of accountants which were difficult to justify on educational grounds. This latter aspect has, of course, been addressed by the revised IES 7.

There is only limited research on the actual CPD activities undertaken by accountants, but a themed issue of *Accounting Education: an international journal* (Volume 16, number 4, 2007) sought to focus attention on this important topic. The following review summarises the papers in that issue:

- Wessels (2007) examined accountants' perceptions of the effectiveness of CPE in North Carolina, U.S.A., where CPAs have had a mandatory CPE requirement since 1985. She found that the focus of many CPE requirements was on compliance rather than with whether the experience has been effective. Her findings indicate that the North Carolina CPAs did regard their CPD as being effective in relation to maintenance of the image of the profession, but they were less certain about its impact on their personal effectiveness.

- Paisey *et al.* (2007) analysed the CPD activities actually undertaken by accountants in public practice in the U.K. in the period immediately before the introduction of IES 7. Their findings gave cause for concern since only approximately 80 per cent of accountants in public practice, whether required or only recommended to engage in CPD, undertook levels of CPD that satisfied their PABs' CPD requirements at that time. The most frequently reported CPD activity was technical reading. Members also attended a range of courses, such as those currently offered by the PABs and other providers. There was a body of members in public practice who engaged in little or no CPD under the former policies. For example, a substantial minority of such members did not engage in technical reading to any great extent. Since this is the most readily accessible form of CPD, not encumbered by impediments of cost and location, it was of particular concern that it was not more widely performed. Paisey *et al.* (2007) also found that opportunities for reflection continued to be lacking in CPD courses offered by PABs.
- Zajkowski *et al.* (2007) examined the CPD activities of accounting academics in Australia and New Zealand, many of whom were also professional accountants and so were subject to the new mandatory CPD requirements. This study found that most academic respondents had a professional accounting CPD requirement but not a university one. However, despite not requiring CPD, most universities did fund attendance at courses and conferences that could count towards CPD. This paper raises the issue of the nature of CPD where an accountant's current role differs from that typically envisaged by IPD.
- Wessels (2007) and Paisey *et al.* (2007) both examined the main barriers to participation in CPD. Wessels found that the most significant barriers were course quality, relevance of material, course length, value relative to course costs, and lack of information to potential participants of prior participants' ratings of courses, or of how the course would benefit them professionally. She found that distance, the level of the course, and course timing were not found to be determinants whereas Paisey *et al.* found that the main barriers in the U.K. were cost, time, and location of CPD activities.
- Jackling *et al.*'s (2007) paper examined the CPD intentions of graduates at two Australian universities, and specifically their intentions to undertake further studies as a measure of their commitment to lifelong learning, thus emphasising the continuum between university education, IPD, and CPD.
- Fisher *et al.*'s (2007) research examined the ethical responsibility of accountants to maintain competence, and lamented the fact that ethics forms only a small part of the CPD offering of PABs.

Rahman & Velayutham's (1998) paper on instructional approaches and the nature of obsolescence in CPD in accounting is also informative.

30.6 Developments

The preceding sections have referred to a number of recent developments, including:

- the new combined degree/professional qualification routes to entry being developed by PABs, professional firms, and universities in the U.K. (Section 30.4.1);

- increasingly flexible entry routes, such as school-leaver entry (Section 30.4.1);
- the coverage of new syllabus areas, such as sustainability and ethics (Section 30.4.3);
- the still limited but increasing use of output-based models of CPD (Section 30.5.1);
- the establishment of Chartered Accountants Worldwide (Section 30.5.1).

There is also evidence of increasing international collaborations. The new chartered accountant qualification jointly developed by ICAA and NZICA was illustrated in Section 30.4.1. Another development is the collaboration between the AICPA and CIMA, with the launch of their joint Chartered Global Management Accountant designation in 2012. This provoked considerable controversy among members of the Institute of Management Accountants in the U.S.A. (Cohn, 2012).

PABs have also launched new qualifications. For example, ICAS now offers an ICAS Tax Professional Qualification, an IFRS Diploma, and an Investment Accounting Diploma. ICAEW offers a range of specialist qualifications in corporate finance, charity accounting, forensic accounting, insolvency, sustainability, IFRS, and treasury. CIMA has started to offer certificates and a diploma in Islamic Finance 'to provide the skills and knowledge needed to exploit the global shortage of qualified Islamic finance professionals'. (See *Financial Management*, December 2012: 40.) While these developments do not impact on IPD and CPD, but instead offer additional qualifications, they do indicate that some PABs are adopting a more commercial approach that may not necessarily sit easily with professional ideals.

30.7 Conclusion

When compared with university education in accounting, research on the IPD and CPD stages is much more limited. This is regrettable because, as this chapter has shown, there are important philosophical and practical issues that need to be addressed in relation to IPD and CPD. The nature and purpose of IPD and CPD differ from that of higher education in accounting, being more vocational and training-orientated, as opposed to the more liberal, educational approach which is typically associated with higher education.

IPD has developed in line with topical trends, embracing the use of technology and competence-based assessment, and incorporating the teaching of issues such as sustainability and ethics. It is still a surprisingly varied stage, however, and debates continue over such issues as core and options models, and the relative importance of training versus practical experience. CPD also shows variability with input- and output-based models, and debates continue about what constitutes appropriate CPD activities.

CPD is the one stage that applies to all accountants in equal measure. As people continue to work for longer, the CPD stage can easily stretch for over 40 years, yet little is known about the effectiveness of CPD, the best means of promoting it, or what it should cover. Taken together, IPD and CPD are crucial stages in the making of the professional accountant as they set professional accountants off on the road to a professional career, and keep them on that path.

In relation to IPD, research could be undertaken into new routes to qualification and to new syllabus areas, including ethics. In relation to CPD, further research needs to be undertaken to see what CPD is actually undertaken by professionally-qualified accountants, and with what effect. Research could also be conducted to ascertain the types of CPD that are available, and to assess whether CPD in practice is the enabling and reflective process that many PABs claim it should be. Finally, recent years have seen a range of new developments. While it is too early to evaluate these, they give a strong indication that PABs are beginning to become more proactive in seeking collaborations and in developing new qualifications, while also refreshing their core professional accounting offerings. In short, this is a time of great change for the worldwide accounting profession but, amid these changes, the PABs need to be mindful of the nature and purpose of their profession and educational provision.

Notes

1 Chartered Accountants Worldwide comprises Chartered Accountants Ireland, ICAA, ICAEW, ICAS, NZICA, and SAICA.

References

Abbott, A. (1988) *The System of Professions*, Chicago: University of Chicago Press.

Abel, R.L. (1988) *The Legal Profession in England and Wales*, Oxford: Basil Blackwell.

AECC (1990) Objectives of Education for Accountants: Position Statement Number One, *Issues in Accounting Education*, 5(2), 307–312.

AICPA (2012) NASBA and AICPA give final approval to revisions to continuing professional education (CPE) provider standards. Press release. Available at: http://www.aicpa.org/press/pressreleases/2012/pages/nasba-and-aicpa-revisions-to-cpe.aspx (accessed 25 April 2013).

Albrecht, W.S. & Sack, R.J. (2000) *Accounting Education: Charting the Course of a Perilous Future* (Accounting Education Series 16), Sarasota, FL: American Accounting Association.

Anderson, J.R. (1982) Acquisition of cognitive skill, *Psychological Review*, 89, 369–406.

Anderson-Gough, F., Grey, C., & Robson, K. (1998) *Making Up Accountants. The Organizational and Professional Socialization of Trainee Chartered Accountants*, Aldershot: Ashgate/ICAEW.

Anderson-Gough, F., Grey, C., & Robson, K. (2001) Tests of time: organizational time-reckoning and the making of accountants in two multi-national accounting firms, *Accounting, Organizations and Society*, 26(1), 99–122.

Anderson-Gough, F., Grey, C., & Robson, K. (2002) Accounting professionals and the accounting profession: linking conduct and context, *Accounting and Business Research*, 32(1), 41–56.

Anderson-Gough, F., Grey, C., & Robson, K. (2005) Helping them to forget . . . : the organizational embedding of gender relations in two large audit firms, *Accounting, Organizations and Society*, 30(5), 469–490.

Bagnall, R.G. (1991) Relativism, objectivity, liberal adult education and multiculturalism, *Studies in the Education of Adults*, 23(1), 61–84.

Barnett, R. (1988) Does higher education have aims? *Journal of Philosophy of Education*, 22(2), 239–250.

Barnett, R. (1990) *The Idea of Higher Education*, Buckingham: The Society for Research into Higher Education/OUP.

Billett, S. (1996) Constructing vocational knowledge: history, communities and ontogeny, *Journal of Vocational Education and Training*, 48(2), 141–154.

Bolt-Lee, C. & Foster, S.D. (2003) The core competency framework: a new element in the continuing call for accounting education change in the United States, *Accounting Education: an international journal*, 12(1), 33–47.

Briggs, G.P. & He, L. (2012) The 150 credit-hour requirement and CPA examination pass rates: A four year study, *Accounting Education: an international journal*, 21(1), 97–108.

Brown, R. & McCartney, S. (1995) Competence is not enough: meta-competence and accounting education, *Accounting Education: an international journal*, 4(1), 43–53.

Carr-Saunders, A.M. & Wilson, P.A. (1933) *The Professions*, Oxford: Oxford University Press.

Chaffey, J., Van Peursem, K.A., & Low, M. (2011) Audit education for future professionals: perceptions of New Zealand auditors, *Accounting Education: an international journal*, 20(2), 153–185.

Cohn, M. (2012) AICPA and CIMA launch CGMA management accounting designation, *Accounting Today*, 31 January 2012. Available at: http://www.accountingtoday.com/news/AICPA-CIMA-Launch-CGMA-Management-Accounting-Designation-61566-1.html.

Cruess, R.L., Cruess, S.R., & Johnston, S.E. (2000) Professionalism: an ideal to be sustained, *The Lancet*, 356, July, 156–159.

Dean, P. (1988) Policy on higher education, *Liberal Education and General Educator*, 59, Spring, 35–38.

Duke, C. (1990) Liberal adult education: a note from the epicentre, *Adults Learning*, 1(9), 241–242.

Entwistle, N. (1988) *Styles of Learning and Teaching*, London: David Fulton Publishers.

Eraut, M. (1994) *Developing Professional Knowledge and Competence*, London: Routledge.

Eraut, M. (1997) Perspectives on defining 'The Learning Society', *Journal of Educational Policy*, 12(6), 551–558.

Eraut, M., Alderon, J., Cole, G., & Senker, P. (2001) Development of knowledge and skills at work, in Coffield, F. (ed.) *Differing Visions of a Learning Society*, Vol. 1, Bristol: Policy Press, pp. 231–262.

Feinberg, W. & Horowitz, B. (1990) Vocational education and equality of opportunity, *Journal of Curriculum Studies*, 22(2), 188–192.

Fisher, D.G., Swanson, D.L., & Schmidt, J.J. (2007) Accounting education lags CPE ethics requirements: implications for the profession and a call to action, *Accounting Education: an international journal*, 16(4), 345–363.

FRC (2012) *Key Facts and Trends in the Accountancy Profession*, London: Financial Reporting Council.

Friedman, A., Hurran, N., & Durkin, C. (1999) Good practice in CPD among UK professional associations, *Continuing Professional Development*, 2, 52–68.

Gammie, E. & Joyce, Y. (2009) Competence-based approaches to the assessment of professional accountancy training work experience requirements: the ICAS experience, *Accounting Education: an international journal*, 18(4–5), 443–446.

Gammie, E. & Kirkham, L. (2008) Breaking the link with a university education in the creation of a chartered accountant: the ICAS story, *British Accounting Review*, 40, 356–375.

Geddes, S.B. (1995) The development of accountancy education, training and research in England: a study of the relationships between professional education and training, academic education and research, and professional practice in English Chartered Accountancy, unpublished PhD thesis, University of Manchester.

Hardern, G. (1995) The development of standards of competence in accounting, *Accounting Education: an international journal*, 4(1), 17–27.

Hines, R.D. (1989) Financial accounting knowledge, conceptual framework projects and the social construction of the accounting profession, *Accounting, Auditing and Accountability Journal*, 2(2), 72–92.

HMSO (1986) *Working Together: Education and Training*, Cmnd 9823, London: Her Majesty's Stationery Office.

Hoskin, K.W. & Macve, R.H. (1986) Accounting and the examination: a genealogy of disciplinary power, *Accounting, Organisations and Society*, 11(2), 105–136.

Hughes, E. (1963) Professions, *Daedalus*, 92(Fall), 655–668.

Hussey, T. & Smith, P. (2002) The trouble with learning outcomes, *Active Learning in Higher Education*, 3(3), 220.

IFAC (2003) *Framework for International Accounting Education*, New York: The International Federation of Accountants.

IFAC (2004) *International Education Standard for Professional Accountants, Continuing Professional Development: A Programme of Lifelong Learning and Continuing Development of Professional Competence*, New York: The International Federation of Accountants.

IFAC (2012) *International Education Standard 7, Continuing Professional Development (Redrafted)*, New York: The International Federation of Accountants.

Jackling, B., De Lange, P., & Ravon, J. (2007) Accounting graduate employment destinations and commitment to CPD: a study from two Australian universities, *Accounting Education: an international journal*, 16(4), 329–343.

Jarvis, P. (1983) *Professional Education*, Beckenham: Croom Helm Ltd.

JICPA (2008) *The CPA Profession in Japan*, Tokyo: The Japanese Institute of Certified Public Accountants.

Langley, F. (1995) The application of competences to an accounting qualification (the experience of the UK Association of Accounting Technicians (AAT)). *Accounting Education: an international journal*, 4(1), 29–36.

Larson, M.S.L. (1977) *The Rise of Professionalism: A Sociological Analysis*, Berkeley, CA: University of California Press.

Lee, T. (1995) The professionalization of accountancy: a history of protecting the public interest in a self-interested way, *Acccounting, Auditing and Accountability Journal*, 8(4), 48–69.

Marriott, N., Telford, B., Davies, M., & Evans, J. (2011) Students' perceptions of work-based training and examination-based learning relating to the professional competence of auditors and the impact of regulatory changes on audit training in the UK, *Accounting Education: an international journal*, 20(2), 133–151.

Mathews, R. (1990) *Accounting in Higher Education: Report of the Accounting Discipline in Higher Education*, Canberra: AGPS.

McChlery, S. & Paisey, C. (2003) Quality in professional accounting education provision in the UK: the CIMA experience, *Accounting Education: an international journal*, 12(2), 197–225.

McPhail, K., Paisey, C., & Paisey, N. (2010) Class, social deprivation and accounting education in Scottish schools: implications for the reproduction of the accounting profession and practice, *Critical Perspectives on Accounting*, 21(1), 31–50.

Mulder, M., Weigel, T., & Collins, K. (2007) The concept of competence in the development of vocational education and training in selected EU member states: a critical analysis, *Journal of Vocational Education and Training*, 59(1), 67–88.

Newman, J.H. (1907) *The Idea of the University*. Available at: www.newmanreader.org/works/idea/ (accessed 16 March 2010).

NZICA (2013) CA Pathway. Available at: http://www.nzica.com/CApathway.aspx (accessed 21 August 2013).

Paisey, C. & Paisey, N.J. (1995) Developments in the education of accountants: objectives, objections and implications for higher education, *Capability*, 1(3), 18–30.

Paisey, C. & Paisey, N.J. (1996) Continuing professional education: pause for reflection? *Critical Perspectives on Accounting*, 7(1), 103–126.

Paisey, C. & Paisey, N.J. (2000) *A Comparative Study of Undergraduate and Professional Education in the Professions of Accountancy, Medicine, Law and Architecture*, Edinburgh: The Institute of Chartered Accountants of Scotland.

Paisey, C. & Paisey, N.J. (2006) Cutting to the core? A reflection upon recent education policy debates within The Institute of Chartered Accountants in England and Wales, *British Accounting Review*, 38(1), 31–61.

Paisey, C. & Paisey, N.J. (2007) Balancing the vocational and academic dimensions of accounting education: the case for a core curriculum, *Journal of Vocational Education and Training*, 59(1), 87–103.

Paisey, C. & Paisey, N.J. (2010) Comparative research: an opportunity for accounting researchers to learn from other professions, *Journal of Accounting and Organizational Change*, 6(2), 180–199.

Paisey, C., Paisey, N.J., & Tarbert, H. (2007) Continuing professional development activities of UK accountants in public practice, *Accounting Education: an international journal*, 16(4), 379–404.

Perks, R.W. (1993) *Accounting and Society*, London: Chapman and Hall.

Power, M.K. (1991) Educating accountants, towards a critical ethnography, *Accounting, Organizations and Society*, 16(4), 333–353.

Rahman, A.R. & Velayutham, S.K. (1998) Instructional approaches and the nature of obsolescence in continuing professional education (CPE), *Accounting Education: an international journal*, 7(4), 287–303.

Roslender, R. (1992) *Sociological Perspectives on Modern Accountancy*, London: Routledge.

Rothblatt, S. (1990) The carriers of civilisation, *Higher Education Policy*, 3(1), 9–12.

Ryle, G. (1949) *The Concept of Mind*, London: Hutchinson University Library.

SAICA (2013) Career in Accounting Diagram, available at: https://www.saica.co.za/Portals/0/Learners Students/documents/Diag_CareerInAccounting.pdf (accessed 21 August 2013).

Saks, M. (2012) Defining a profession: the role of knowledge and expertise, *Professions & Professionalism*, 2(1), 1–10.

Sangster, A. & Wilson, R.M.S. (eds) (2012) *Liberalising the Accounting Curriculum in University Education*, Abingdon: Routledge.

Schön, D. (1983) *The Reflective Practitioner. How Professionals Think in Action*, New York: Basic Books.

Schön, D. (1987) *Educating the Professional Practitioner: Towards a New Design for Teaching and Learning in the Professions*, San Francisco: Jossey-Bass.

Shackleton, K. (1992) The evolution of education policy within the Institute of Chartered Accountants of Scotland, in Anyane-Ntow, K. (ed.) *International Handbook of Accounting Education and Certification*, Oxford: Pergamon Press, pp. 417–444.

Stokes, P. (1989) Vocationalising education: perspectives, processes and problems, *Welsh Journal of Education*, 1(1), 31–38.

Thompson, P.J. (1995) Competence-based learning and qualifications in the UK, *Accounting Education: an international journal*, 4(1), 5–15.

Torstendahl, R. (1990) Essential properties, strategic aims and historical development: three approaches to professionalism, in Burrage, M. & Torstendahl, R. (eds) *Professions in Theory and History*, London: Sage Publications, pp. 44–61.

Uche, C. (2007) *The Accounting Profession in British West Africa*, Edinburgh: The Institute of Chartered Accountants of Scotland.

Velayutham, S. & Perera, H. (1993) The reflective accountant: towards a new model for professional development, *Accounting Education: an international journal* 2(4), 287–301.

Watts, C. (2000) Issues of professionalism in higher education, in Bourner, T., Katz, T., & Watson, D. (eds) *New Directions in Professional Higher Education*, Buckingham: The Society for Research in Higher Education/Open University Press, pp. 11–18.

Wegener, C. (1978) *Liberal Education and the Modern University*, Chicago: University of Chicago Press.

Weil, S., Oyelere, P., & Rainsbury, E. (2004) The usefulness of case studies in developing core competencies in a professional accounting programme: a New Zealand study, *Accounting Education: an international journal*, 13(2), 139–169.

Wessels, S.B. (2007) Accountants' perceptions of the effectiveness of mandatory continuing professional education, *Accounting Education: an international journal*, 16(4), 365–378.

Wilensky, H. (1964) The professionalization of everyone? *American Journal of Sociology*, 70, September, 174–158.

Willmott, H. (1986) Organizing the profession: a theoretical and historical examination of the development of the major accountancy bodies in the UK, *Accounting, Organizations and Society*, 11(6), 555–80.

Wilson, R.M.S. (2011) Alignment in accounting education and training, *Accounting Education: an international journal*, 20(1), 3–16.

Wolf, A. (1995) *Competence-based Assessment*, Buckingham: Open University Press.

Zajkowski, M., Sampson, V., & Davis, D. (2007) Continuing professional development: perceptions from New Zealand and Australian accounting academics, *Accounting Education: an international journal*, 16(4), 405–420.

About the authors

Catriona Paisey is Professor of Accounting at the University of Glasgow, U.K. (catriona.paisey@glasgow.ac.uk). Her research focusses on the accountancy profession and accounting history. She is researching the making of the professional accountant from school, through university, to the initial professional development stages. She currently serves on the ICAS Ethics Committee, having previously been a member of its Qualification Board, and is a former Associate Editor of *Accounting Education: an international journal*.

Nicholas J. Paisey is Professor of Accounting at Heriot-Watt University, Edinburgh, U.K. (n.paisey@hw.ac.uk). His primary research interest is the accountancy profession, including education, and accounting history. His current research focusses mainly on accounting at school and continuing professional development. He serves on the ICAS CPD Committee, having previously been a member of its Student Education Committee.

William Threipland Baxter

A tribute to his teaching

Michael Bromwich and Richard Macve[1]

LONDON SCHOOL OF ECONOMICS & POLITICAL SCIENCE, U.K.

But I don't think the School yet catered for the students as well as it does now. I don't think there were many, if any, classes of small groups of students so that they tended to organise the classes for themselves. I remember going to a Polish student's residence and being led through an elementary description of averages with a group of other students. Then on Saturday morning we all played badminton down in the gymnasium and the Director came too, Beveridge, and bounded about with us. It was all very good fun.

Will Baxter describing his year registered as an 'occasional' student at the London School of Economics & Political Science (LSE) in 1934 after spending two years in the U.S.A. on a Commonwealth Fund Fellowship visiting the University of Pennsylvania (the Wharton School) and then Harvard Business School; and before taking up a lectureship at Edinburgh University and then a Chair in Cape Town.[2]

Looking back on it all, I feel that with what I've picked up in the course of the years, and particularly since I retired, I could have been a much better teacher if I'd been starting afresh. But it's been a happy life, and it's been very good fun.

Will Baxter's summary of his teaching career in his concluding remarks in his interview with Professor Geoffrey Whittington (2005).[3]

Introduction

Reinforcing academic discipline with fun, some games, and sometimes pointed irony was the hallmark of Will as a researcher and a teacher. He was born on 27 July 1906 in Grimsby and died on 8 June 2006 in London. We were both fortunate to be his students at LSE – Bromwich as a BSc (Econ) student in 1962–1965, and Macve as a part-time MSc Accounting & Finance student in 1974–1976 – and were later both colleagues of Will at LSE.

Early days

To understand someone's skills as a teacher it is sometimes helpful to know their earlier background and the influences of their colleagues and of their academic environment. Will went to a good school in Scotland and qualified as member of the Institute of Chartered Accountants of Scotland (ICAS) in a small office whilst exceptionally also obtaining a BCom degree at the University of Edinburgh. He was well aware that the teaching was poor and scrappy but was drawn to teaching, albeit part-time.

On qualifying in 1930 he moved to a larger firm, where one of the partners was Professor Annan, his professor at Edinburgh, who helped set him on an academic career by suggesting that he apply – successfully – for a two year scholarship to attend the University of Pennsylvania and Harvard University.[4] At the latter, in an effort to begin to understand differences between theory and practice – a lifetime interest – he undertook historical research studying the accounting records of a Boston business, again a continuing interest.[5]

He continued this work in London on his return to Britain in 1934 where he first came in contact with LSE and was amazed how well-trained and facile in economics were the students of business administration under Sir Arnold Plant. They seemed to him to behave as professors. When he returned to Edinburgh University as a lecturer in 1934, he maintained his connection with LSE, absorbing the work of Coase, Edwards, and Fowler, who were each in their own way revolutionising aspects of accounting for decision-making, cost structures, and accounting income (Buchanan & Thirlby, 1973). This gave him a strong economic perspective on accounting and suggested one of his most used and useful teaching tools – a focus on opportunity cost and, more basically, always ask: what difference will it make?

In 1937, at the early age of 31, he took the Chair of Accounting at the University of Cape Town, South Africa, on the suggestion of Plant where he developed further his ideas on accounting theory and maintained his interest in economics as applied to accounting. He also discovered Bonbright's book *The Valuation of Property*, which helped to generate the concept of 'deprival value' that he applied in accounting and which figured very strongly – and still does – in LSE teaching and research.

Professor at LSE

Will joined LSE in 1947 as the first full-time professor of accounting, again at the suggestion of Plant. His colleagues were David Solomons, who had graduated from LSE and joined LSE after World War II;[6] and fellow scholar and teacher, Harold Edey (who had started his own career as a Chartered Accountant in practice and then become a financial analyst).[7] Together they formed the 'LSE triumvirate' who shaped the pattern for U.K. academic accounting after World War II as well as having a major influence on accounting standard setting on both sides of the Atlantic (see especially Napier, 2011; also Whittington, 1994; Zeff, 1997; Parker *et al.*, 2012). They sought to make accounting into a recognised academic discipline.[8]

'Research-led teaching' and a broad-based curriculum were (and remain) the basis of LSE accounting teaching. Will and his colleagues required undergraduate students to take some of the specialist economics courses as it was an economic lens through which they focussed on accounting. Other courses included law, mathematics, and statistics. Accounting courses never dominated the study programme. Much of the content of the accounting courses was relatively conventional at that early time, containing a very good introduction to double-entry bookkeeping (as is still the case at LSE now), and dealing with the proper treatment of transactions as practised at the time. The novel aspects introduced over time were:

- the economics-based approach to accounting information for decision-making and for performance measurement, utilising opportunity costs and decision analysis based on what difference a decision option makes;
- discounted cash flow investment appraisal;
- economic models of income ('Hicksian income') and wealth and of depreciation; and, of course,
- deprival value and fully stabilised current value accounting.

Much of this material was elementary: for example, fairly comprehensive courses in modern finance were not taught until the late 1960s, although these subjects were central to the MSc in Accounting and Finance introduced in 1964 which trained many of the next generation of the U.K.'s accounting professors and researchers in the 1960s and 1970s.

Will responded to what he saw as being the lack of innovation in the accounting literature by editing his pioneering collection *Studies in Accounting* (Baxter, 1950). This includes studies of accounting history, suggestions as to how to deal with contemporary accounting problems – including accounting for price level changes, and a section entitled 'accounting theory' which provides a number of perspectives on what is wrong with conventional accounting and which was aimed at providing his students and others with access to refreshingly insightful perspectives on the theory and practice of accounting. Over the next three decades it ran through two further editions (in 1962 and 1977) in collaboration with Sidney Davidson of the University of Chicago (Baxter & Davidson, 1977). The papers challenged (and still challenge) the conventional wisdom. Generations of students, both at LSE and beyond, have been brought up on the triumvirate's economics-based approach to accounting within an overall framework which sees management accounting and financial accounting as being two sides of the same coin, while regarding an understanding of accounting's history and development as also crucial in understanding its present and its possible futures.

Will's healthily sceptical views on the role of accounting standards, both financial and management, still remain the basis for repeated pleas by researchers for independence of mind in the face of the demands for ever-increasing convergence towards a unique 'global' set of international accounting standards (e.g. Sunder, 2007). Generations of students across the U.K. have been exposed to all these ideas as, for example, some 40 per cent of the accounting professors in posts in the U.K. in 1971 were trained at LSE (Parker, 1997). Many overseas students and visitors at LSE and at other universities have disseminated these ideas in many parts of the world.

Will was happy to venture outside the educational mainstream. In order to build up academic accounting from almost nothing, Will and his LSE colleagues looked out for bright young professional accountants without relevant undergraduate degrees, or without any degrees at all, and provided them with the necessary academic induction, primarily through a 'preparatory year' of economics and quantitative methods, followed by the MSc in Accounting and Finance. As was widespread at LSE at the time, much of the teaching was arranged for the evenings so that students could enrol part-time while continuing their existing employments, including teaching accounting at other universities and (then) polytechnics. Many of the U.K.'s leading accounting academics started that way. Unconventional as always, Will also enthusiastically supported the foundation in the 1970s of the independent University of Buckingham, where two of his LSE students (Peter Watson and David Pendrill) became professors (and, in Watson's case, deputy/acting Vice-Chancellor). Will was awarded an honorary Doctorate there in 1980.

Will Baxter as a teacher

Will was a very clear teacher who took great pains to explain things carefully at a time when teaching was often poor. He was a gentleman and always courteous. He could seem a little intimidating as, in a dark suit, he looked a little like a rather dignified, middle-aged schoolmaster – a persona which he maintained throughout his life. But this was misleading as he cared deeply for students and welcomed joining them on Departmental weekend schools, and inviting them to his home. In staff seminars and other meetings with his peers, he was the master of the cordial understated comment which could conceal a sharp barb.

For teaching, Will adopted, and maybe pioneered, 'tricks of the trade' that have become part of the repertoire of modern educational practice. He had trained himself to be able to deliver a well-structured lecture or public talk so that it appeared to be given spontaneously (while his memory was actually being jogged by counting off the headings and sub-headings on his fingers, with his hands hidden behind his back). Having been brought up in largely pre-microphone days, he remained able to project his voice clearly and distinctly *'to the back row of the lecture hall'*. Both these presentational skills he retained into his nineties. In class, students were asked to mark the work of their classmates and then justify their gradings; and among examination questions that looked deceptively simple (and sometimes were) were those that could turn out to challenge the most intellectually accomplished. Consider this example from a final year examination:

Think of a question about Accounting. Now answer it.

Other innocuous-seeming questions asked: how do you depreciate a haircut, or value the left leg of a pair of trousers? Or, further to test understanding of decision relevance, deprival value and opportunity cost: 'Write a short essay on the cost logic of these two quotations: Hostess – "Now do have a little more fish – it won't keep", and Youth – "Mabel darling, you've simply got to marry me, after all the money I've spent on dating you."'

Of course, teaching was different then. Staff, when examining, had time to follow Will's instructions to reconcile each incorrect student's answer with the solution, as in the late 1960s, the Department still only had an annual total of under 90 undergraduate accounting specialists and some 25 on the MSc programme. The teachers knew all the students for good or ill, and vice versa. It was, perhaps, much easier to concentrate attention on the really bright students.

While many of his pupils went on to become professionally-qualified accountants, Will's own teaching (like that of the others in the triumvirate) was highly critical of the traditional nostrums of much professional education. But even if his ideas were often too much to swallow, the profession, after some difficult early relationships, nevertheless came to accord him great respect.[9]

Who is best placed to provide an appreciation of Will as a teacher? The affection, respect, and sometimes awe in which he was held is demonstrated by his former pupils and his academic colleagues having given him the rare honour of two *Festschriften* (Edey & Yamey, 1974, and Lapsley, 1996), the former on his 'retirement' and the latter on the occasion of his 90th birthday. To these we can do no better than add a small proportion of the more than 100 tributes paid to him at the symposium at LSE held shortly after his death (taken from Bromwich & Macve, 2006).

Selected reminiscences

In our Foreword to Bromwich & Macve (2006), we said:

> *Will Baxter was a much loved colleague and friend to many staff and former students at LSE. His sense of fairness, kindness and sharp humour were qualities that made him a respected teacher and mentor to many. His lectures and his generosity in mentoring his students and younger academic colleagues ensured that his tradition of scholarly thought in accounting was passed on to future generations of accounting practitioners and scholars . . . The reminiscences [here] are personal recollections . . . of those who knew him in a number of capacities throughout his long and distinguished career – former students who have gone on to successful careers in accounting practice, academe and industry; colleagues who have worked with and learned from Will; and individuals who have come to know Will and his work in various other ways.*

A necessarily small selection from these tributes is marshalled here[10] by the decades when the contributors were Will's students or colleagues (as the latter also learned much from him). Many were originally composed in anticipation of celebrating his 100th birthday (as was Bromwich *et al.* 2006) but, unfortunately, Will died a few weeks before, on 8 June 2006, and instead the event which was held at LSE on 15 July 2006 became a celebratory memorial symposium (Weetman, 2007).

1930s

> *Will began teaching at the University of Cape Town in March 1937. He soon showed that he was an unusual teacher of accounting. Within a few months he had referred to Luca Pacioli and all that . . ., as well as to the kinds of issues concerning accounting for decision-taking which were being explored at the LSE by the three Ronnies: Coase, Edwards and Fowler. He also introduced local touches, such as explaining the annuity method of depreciation in the context of the breeding habits of the rabbit population on Robben Island. Though several of my fellow students didn't quite know what to make of it all, virtually all of us came to appreciate Will as an unusually inspiring, effective and considerate teacher who, besides knowing what seemed to be rather esoteric stuff, also knew all about double-entry, cost or market, and the consolidation of accounts . . . . Our short period together as colleagues at the UCT made me an even greater debtor to Will than I had been before.*
>
> (Basil S. Yamey, Emeritus Professor of Economics at LSE,
> Student (1937–1938) and faculty member (1946–1947)
> at the University of Cape Town)

1940s

> *Professor Baxter's* Studies in Accounting *has a prominent place on my book shelves to remind me of the debt I owe him for introducing me in a friendly and stimulating way to the wider implications of accounting in economic life.*
>
> (John Hammond, student and part-time lecturer
> (1948–1951) and (1952–1953))

> *Professor Baxter, typically at the start of a lecture, summarised the topic in a few words. It was usually a light-hearted introduction. I remember the few words to introduce the General Ledger – 'A Thing of Monstrous Beauty Like the Hindquarters of an Elephant'.*

701

I remember him as a kindly man. I think he may have played a part in my obtaining of Articles that paid a small monthly amount. In those days it was usual for articled clerks to pay for Articles. I am sure I will not have been the only student beneficiary.

(Alfred William Girling, student (1949–1952))

1950s

Accounting for inflation – oh dear!

(G. J. Osborn, student (1950–1953))

There can be few members of the Athenaeum who at 75 can still meet his favourite college tutor as an active fellow member. Will Baxter's influence on me was immense. Steering me into a Harkness Fellowship of which he was a past holder and greatly influencing my work on Accounting Standards, as holder of the Chair of the Committee 1982–1984. His work on current value is especially important.

(Ian Hay Davison. He was my LSE tutor (1950–1953).
Later I taught part-time in his Department.)

Professor Baxter was without equal in his ability to explain complex issues in simple terms.

(George Thomas, student (1952–1955))

I guess there are many but particularly I recall:

- *His kind way of being gently and 'shyfully' interested in one's welfare as one of his students: making learning with him a joy.*
- *His help in this way when in a significant (personal) crisis.*
- *His occasional walks with students on e.g. Hampstead Heath and down at Dorking, and his interest in one's fitness generally.*
- *His unusual 'spatial-physical' approach to evaluating students' relative performances in exams and projects! I well recall these as an external!*
- *I guess I particularly benefited from his healthy, critical, scepticism of the profession and its attitude towards its practice(s). And recognised his courage and concern about this.*

(Tony Lowe, undergraduate student (1954–1957),
External Examiner (1958–1967))

The best I can do is quote a line from Jean Genet's play, The Balcony: *'The world is full of whores. What it needs is a good accountant'. And Will was a very good accountant indeed.*

(Kenneth Minogue, Emeritus Professor of Political Science,
LSE. Colleague and neighbour of the Accounting
Department (1956–1995))

More than any other faculty member, I felt Professor Baxter took a real interest in me as a person and not just an enthusiastic member of his class. I felt an empathy and an encouragement of my broader development. Of course, we all took our turn in receiving his presents – often copies of public company accounts garnered from an obscure source, which we were expected to critically assess (although we weren't tested). That was in the good old days when it only needed 26 pages to provide shareholders with all they needed to know! . . .

Gentle, soft-spoken and far from dominating, I felt that Professor Baxter brought out the best in his students (including a great sense of loyalty). And he gave one a valuable head start in getting behind the obscurities of accounting to the core principles and the overriding 'true and fair' precept that for me still serve as the solid foundation which our profession needs to preserve at all costs. . .

(Derek Stevens, took the Accounting elective with
him for B.Sc (Econ.) (1957–1960))

I remember his Accounting lectures as being very clear and precise. I was delighted to have him as my tutor in the final year of the B.Sc.(Econ.). He was a great source of encouragement when he reviewed my work, and asked me to critique an article he was writing. His greatest impact was his suggestion that I apply for a Harkness Fellowship of the Commonwealth Fund for 1960-62, which laid the foundation of my later academic career. I will remember him as very gracious, very methodical, and a great advisor.

(Roger B. Upson (1957–1960): he was my tutor in 1959–1960)

Having been among the first students from Mauritius to follow the B.Sc. (Econ.) course before signing articles (as they were then called), I had the chance to be lectured by Professor Baxter. Besides being a charming and soft-spoken person, he was a distinguished scholar, who obviously knew what he was teaching. After graduating, as I was starting my professional training, I realized how advanced he was in his thinking and his proposals, so as to try and free the accounting world from the straitjacket of the historical cost convention. Although current cost accounting has not survived the onslaught of fair value and IFRS, he must be remembered for having dared, as an academic, to challenge the dominant thinking of his time.

(Pierre Dinan, undergraduate, reading for the B.Sc. Economics
degree, with specialisation in Accounting (1958–1961))

W. T. told me off for being too thin and weak. He directed me to swim regularly. I built up muscles and increased body weight.

(Premchand D. F. Shah, undergraduate student (1959–1962))

1960s

Will, you were successful in confirming my interest in accounting as a career and in assisting me in deciding to join a then almost unknown firm. You did fail to persuade me to stay on to become an academic. I now know that two out of three is good for an accountant. . .

(Brian Smith, student (1960–1963))

I and two other post-graduate students attended Professor Baxter's third year undergraduate lectures on income theory, and I have to say that they were easily the best lectures on accounting I have ever attended. A complex subject area was made to seem straightforward, and it is not an exaggeration to say that he set a teaching standard that any accounting academic should strive to achieve. On a more light-hearted note, as part of the MSc programme, we three post-graduate students had to present papers to staff at a series of seminars. It soon became clear to us that there was a friendly rivalry between two 'camps' of staff within the department. On the one hand there were the 'Baxterites' (including, as I recall, Peter Bird, John Flower and Bob Parker); and on the other the 'Edeyites' (mainly, it seemed, Bryan Carsberg and Mike Bromwich). As the gladiators shaped up to each other, a series of lively debates ensued – which taught us as students a great deal. . .

(Richard Morris, M.Sc. student (1965–1966))

I remember Will Baxter's classes as being a wonderful combination of calm and excitement. The presentation was calm but the ideas were exciting.

(Richard Lewis, student (1968–1971))

I have many fond memories of Will of which I will mention two.

First, I was one of a small group of young faculty who Will invited, one evening a week, to work through the drafts of his manuscript on Depreciation. *This enormous privilege taught me much about the way a top-class academic brain worked. As each evening ended with a dinner at Will's expense, it also kept me fed!*

Second, I recall seeing him (from a higher office on the other side of the building) on many days taking a 15 minute nap after lunch – long before the concept of 'power-napping' entered the management arena. Hopefully this was one factor that contributed to his impressive longevity.

Will was an outstanding academic and a lovely man – a great pioneer in academic accountancy. He will be sorely missed.

(John Arnold, as a very junior colleague at LSE (1965–1967) and
subsequently as a member of the academic accountancy community
that he played such a large part in developing)

Professor Baxter was one of my favourite professors: always courteous; always friendly; always explaining in understandable language the most obtuse accounting obscurities; and with an extraordinary memory and a gleam in his eye – altogether a gentle, caring and lovable person. This is how he remains in my memory.

(Pauline Graham, evening student (1960–1965))

1970s

As a tribute to the enormous influence Professor Baxter had on my career three episodes stand out. First, as a day-release student at Glasgow College of Commerce in 1969 I became aware that accounting had a theoretical dimension when I discovered a copy of Baxter & Davidson's Studies in Accounting Theory *in their library. Second, Professor Baxter interviewed me in 1970 for admission as a mature student to study economics at LSE and thirdly, his lectures on Accounting Theory in the MSc programme in 1973–74 kindled a life-long interest in the theory and practice of income measurement and I became interested in pursuing a career as an accounting academic.*

Since my time at LSE I have taught accounting at universities in Edinburgh, Bristol and Belfast, and have continued to develop and communicate my understanding of the accounting issues that were central to Professor Baxter's contribution to the subject.

In my experience Professor Baxter was always the perfect gentleman and his intellectual integrity serves as a beacon to us all.

(John Forker, past student (1970–1974))

From your MSc classes at LSE I learnt as much about the art of teaching as about the art of accounting.

(David Citron, MSc Accounting & Finance
student (1970–1971))

Will taught me the skill of presenting complex issues simply and not the other way around, which is what many seem to do.

(Duncan Paterson, MSc student (1976–1978);
lecturer at LSE (1976–1980))

1980s

I was a part-time MSc student at LSE from 1980 to 1982 and was very privileged to have been taught by Professor Baxter. He was always kind and considerate and took immense interest in his students. He was a man of great intellect and a great teacher. He inspired us all to think outside the box and not to easily run with the crowd. The advancing years did not diminish his sharpness or concerns to make this world a better place. A couple of years ago I met him at a BAA conference and he was as friendly, gentle, kind and sharp as ever. He maintained his disdain for modern rules bound accounting.

It had indeed been my good fortune to have met a colossus like Professor Baxter. He was an example to us all and will live in hearts and minds forever.

(Prem Sikka, MSc student (1980–1982))

Other reminiscences

The work of Professor Baxter, and that of his pupils, has had a profound effect on my thinking during the last 15 years working on accounting standards at ASB. I have also learned from his work how complex and powerful ideas can be explained elegantly and simply.

(Andrew Lennard, Accounting Standards Board)

So, although Will himself did not really get directly involved in professional, business or regulatory activities outside LSE, among his pupils (and not only those represented here) have not only been many who became leading accounting academics (alongside whom were also leading academics in economics and finance), but also those who reached the heights of the accounting profession and of financial and general management in many spheres. Others became leading regulators of competition policy or accounting standards setters. All acknowledge his profound and lasting influence over their thinking. Will is one of those teachers for whom this epitaph is particularly suitable (adapted from the famous line for Sir Christopher Wren inscribed in St Paul's cathedral):

Lector, si monumentum requiris, videte discipulos (Reader, if you seek his monument, look at his pupils).

In conclusion . . .

As 'official' tributes to the impact of his life-long devotion to research and teaching, Will was honoured with the BAA's Lifetime Achievement Award (in 2004) and by induction into the American Accounting Hall of Fame (in 2005). Newton famously said: '*If I have seen further it is by standing on the shoulders of giants*'.[11] In developing his own thinking, Will had drawn heavily on the work of earlier LSE 'giants' such as R.S. Edwards and Ronald Coase, just as he was later to find inspiration in the work of outstanding Americans such as Bonbright and Edwards & Bell. But he also was fascinated by pioneering work in other spheres, such as by Kenneth Boulding, the economist who, with others, advanced General Systems Theory, and with whom he had shared a room in his early days at Edinburgh – they remained life-long friends. Or by Geoffrey de Ste. Croix, a student of ancient economic and political history, whom he persuaded – during his temporary appointment at LSE – to write what became the classic paper on ancient Greek and Roman accounting (see e.g. Macve, 2002). Again they remained life-long friends and shared the notable characteristic of having published much of their significant work after retirement – Will's last publication appeared in his 99th year (Baxter, 2005). Until the late 1980s Geoffrey was invited back to LSE from Oxford each year by Will to give a lecture based on his paper to the third year Accounting and Finance specialist undergraduates in order to 'widen their horizons'.[12]

Now Will has himself become one of the giants and we, like his other pupils and colleagues, have climbed on his shoulders. Which leaves the troubling question: how in the modern era can academics – driven by the relentless pressures of the U.K.'s Research Excellence Framework and similar publication treadmills – find time to be the accessible teachers and mentors of Will's generation, whose pupils will remember them for the rest of their lives and will further transmit their memories and values to their own pupils and colleagues? Academic publication is important: but inspiring teaching surely remains even more so.

Notes

1 Corresponding author: Professor R. Macve, Department of Accounting, LSE, London WC2A 2AE, U.K. R.Macve@lse.ac.uk
2 From an interview with Theo Barker 17 March 1994 reproduced in Bromwich and Macve (2006).
3 Published (together with a biographical note by Geoffrey Whittington, Will's former pupil) in Walker (ed.) (2005).
4 Will valued this early experience so much that, supported by the generosity of the Baxter family and of some of Will's former pupils, the Accounting Department at LSE now offers in his memory an annual travel scholarship to visit North America to a graduate returning to LSE for further study: http://www.lse.ac.uk/accounting/news/WilliamTBaxterTravelScholarship.aspx
5 This work was published in 1945 as *The House of Hancock—Business in Boston, 1724-75*.
6 David Solomons left LSE for a chair at Bristol in1955 and then at the University of Pennsylvania. See Parker *et al.* (2012) pp. 118-126.
7 Harold Edey's reminiscences are to be found both in Bailey, 2009 (see Zeff, 2009) and in an interview in Matthews & Pirie (2000).
8 In addition to Will's own reminiscences in the interviews with Theo Barker (reproduced in Bromwich & Macve, 2006), and with Geoffrey Whittington (in Walker, 2005), there is also an obituary in *Accounting and Business Research* (2006) 37(3): 135-6.
9 Alongside LSE and the British Accounting Association (now BAFA), the symposium held in his honour at LSE on 15 July 2006 was also generously sponsored by the Institute of Chartered Accountants in England & Wales (ICAEW) and the Institute of Chartered Accountants of Scotland (ICAS).
10 Some of the selected tributes we have shortened and, for this publication, we have also removed the 'birthday greetings' contained in many of the originals. The full text of the tributes is available in Bromwich & Macve (2006) at http://www.lse.ac.uk/accounting/news/AF-Conf-Rem-inside-2.pdf
11 The quotation is inscribed round the edge of an issue of the British £2 coin and is the motto of Google Scholar. Newton was himself here standing on the shoulders of Bernard of Chartres who referred to himself and his fellow 'modern' scholars in the 12th century AD as 'dwarfs standing on the shoulders of giants' (McGarry, 1962, p. 167).
12 The School has now formally adopted this objective in the recently introduced interdisciplinary course 'LSE 100: *The LSE Course—Understanding the Causes of Things*' which all undergraduates across the School now take in their first year: http://www2.lse.ac.uk/intranet/students/LSE100/Home.aspx

References

Bailey, N. (ed.) (2009) *Harold Cecil Edey: 20th Century Accounting Reformer. An Autobiography* (private publication by Nerys Bailey: donbaileyis@gmail.com).
Baxter, W.T. (1950) *Studies in Accounting*, London: Sweet & Maxwell.
Baxter, W.T. (2005) Direct versus absorption costing: a comment. *Accounting, Business and Financial History*, 15(1): 89–91.
Baxter, W.T. & Davidson, S. (eds) (1977) *Studies in Accounting*, 3rd edn, London: ICAEW.
Bonbright, J.C. (1937) *The Valuation of Property*, New York: McGraw-Hill.

Bromwich, M. & Macve, R. (2006) *Professor W.T. Baxter, 1906–2006: Reminiscences* (presented to Mrs Leena Baxter at a Symposium celebrating the work of Professor W.T. Baxter, at The London School of Economics and Political Science, 15 July 2006). LSE Department of Accounting and ICAS. Available at: http://www.lse.ac.uk/accounting/news/AF-Conf-Rem-inside-2.pdf.

Bromwich, M., Macve, R., & Ranger, D. (2006) Will Baxter: 100 years young, *British Accounting Review,* 38(2), 221–223.

Buchanan, J.M. & Thirlby, G.F. (1973) *L.S.E. Essays on Cost*, London: London School of Economics and Political Science.

Edey, H. & Yamey, B.S (eds) (1974) *Debits, Credits, Finance and Profits*, London: Sweet & Maxwell.

Lapsley, I. (ed.) (1996) *Essays in Accounting Thought: A Tribute to W T Baxter*, Edinburgh: ICAS.

Macve, R. (2002) Insights to be gained from the study of ancient accounting history: some reflections on the new edition of Finley's *The Ancient Economy, European Accounting Review*, 11(2), 453–471.

Matthews, D. & Pirie, J. (2000) *The Auditors Talk: An Oral History of a Profession from the 1920s to the Present Day*, New York: Garland Publishing.

McGarry, D. (trans.) (1962) *The Metalogicon of John of Salisbury*, Berkeley, CA: University of California Press.

Napier, C. (2011) Accounting at the London School of Economics: opportunity lost? *Accounting History*, 16(2): 185–205.

Parker, R.H. (1997) Flickering at the margin of existence: The Association of University Teachers of Accounting, 1960–1971, *British Accounting Review*, 29 (Special Issue): 41–61.

Parker, R.H., Zeff, S.A., & Anderson, M. (2012) *Major Contributors to the British Accountancy Profession: A Biographical Sourcebook*, Edinburgh: ICAS.

Sunder, S. (2007) Not by Will: Baxter and the rise of authoritative accounting standards, in Weetman (2007), 236–237.

Walker, S. (ed.) (2005) *Giving an Account: Life Histories of Four CAs*. Edinburgh: ICAS.

Weetman, P. (ed.) (2007) Comments on deprival value and standard setting in measurement: from a symposium to celebrate the work of Professor William T. Baxter, *Accounting and Business Research* 37(3): 233–242.

Whittington, G. (1994) The LSE Triumvirate and its contribution to price change accounting, in Edwards, J.R. (ed.) *Twentieth-Century Accounting Thinkers*, London: Routledge, Chapter 14.

Zeff, S.A. (1997) The early years of the Association of University Teachers of Accounting: 1947–1959, *The British Accounting Review*, 29 (Special Issue): 3–39.

Zeff, S.A. (2009) Capsule commentary on Bailey (2009) *The Accounting Review*, 84(4) (July): 1316.

About the authors

Michael Bromwich is the CIMA Professor of Accounting and Financial Management (Emeritus) at the London School of Economics. He is a Past President of CIMA (1987/88), sometime chairman of the U.K. accounting profession's Joint Accreditation Board for Accounting Degrees, and the founding editor (1989) of *Management Accounting Research*.

Richard Macve is Professor of Accounting (Emeritus) at the London School of Economics. He has chaired the ICAEW's Student Education Advisory Group, been Academic Advisor to ICAEW's Research Advisory Board, and is a member of the FRC's Accounting Academic Panel. He holds honorary appointments in the PRC at both the University of International Business & Economics, Beijing, and Zhongnan University of Economics & Law, Wuhan.

Raymond J. Chambers

A personal reflection

Michael Gaffikin

THE UNIVERSITY OF WOLLONGONG, AUSTRALIA

I was working in a (then) fairly insignificant accounting department of what was at the time a small university in New Zealand when I was charged with the responsibility of accompanying Ray Chambers and his wife Margaret to dinner. He had accepted an invitation to the University from its Accounting Student Society and for us it was a great occasion – to have such a distinguished, internationally-acclaimed visitor. During a wide-ranging conversation that evening, Ray suggested I consider joining his Department at the University of Sydney as he thought I would find it (intellectually) stimulating. I took up his suggestion and did not live to regret it. The Department was indeed an intellectually energetic place and working with Chambers was a stimulating experience: I learned a lot from him – most especially the need to aspire to intellectual rigour in my work. In this, Chambers certainly led by example and, over the years, while many people did not accept the conclusions in the theory he developed, I believe it is generally agreed by those who are familiar with his work and the context in which it was written that he demonstrated the highest standards of scholarship in developing and promoting his ideas. It has been internationally acknowledged that he was truly one of accounting's greatest scholars. For example, Staubus (2003) has referred to him as '*an intellectual giant*'; Moonitz (1982) as an '*accounting pioneer*'. There is also evidence of his recognition in the large number of awards, citations and other prestigious forms of recognition he received.

As such an eminent scholar, there has been much written about Chambers, and he himself has given several accounts of what he was trying to achieve in his work. A Festschrift issue of Abacus published in 2000 (v 36, no. 3), a year after his death, is a good example – it contains papers by those who had been associated with him and it covers different aspects of his achievements as well as previously unpublished papers by Chambers, which appear to be drafts of what he might have intended to have been part of an autobiography.[1] In addition, recently, as part of the celebration of the 50th anniversary of what was originally the Department of Accounting at the University of Sydney, a monograph prepared by some of his apostles[2] (Clarke, Dean and Wells, 2010) provides an account of his achievements. These authors have had access to Chambers' private and professional papers, most of which survived destruction after his death largely due to the efforts and foresight of his one-time Research Assistant (now Professor) Graeme

Dean. The bulk of these are now housed and accessible at the University of Sydney in an archive called The R. J. Chambers Collection (see Dean, Clarke and Wolnizer, 2006).

This paper is presented as a tribute to Chambers. As its title suggests, it is a personal reflection through the eyes of someone who worked closely with him over a period of 10 years during a latter part of his career, and who completed a doctoral thesis with aspects of the work of Chambers as its subject. During this time I was fortunate to have many discussions, debates and academic arguments with him again over a wide range of topics. Despite my obvious admiration for him, I believe that his achievements and contributions to accounting knowledge qualify him as a scholar fully worthy of a tribute as a significant figure in the history of the discipline.

Brief background sketch

Raymond Chambers was born in Newcastle, Australia, where he undertook his early education under what we would now consider '*difficult circumstances*' (see Chambers, 2000a). To his educators he showed promise and enthusiasm and was encouraged to further his studies. He earned a university place which enabled him to undertake a university education at the University of Sydney where he studied for an economics degree. His father's small business, like so many others during the Depression of the 1930s, had suffered badly (Chambers, 2000b, p. 321). Thus, for economic reasons, Chambers was unable to attend university full-time and had to study part-time (economics and accounting rather than his possibly preferred engineering, architecture or medicine). This involved attending evening classes while working during the day. He was first employed in the accounting office of the Department of the Attorney-General and of Justice, part of what was then referred to as the New South Wales Public Service. From there he moved to employment in the petroleum industry where he worked as an inventory control officer, and then to a similar position with the Electricity Meter and Allied Industries. From 1943 to 1945 he was engaged as an investigation officer with the Australian Prices Commission. It was in this last position that he felt he became more actively engaged with accounting, and he was amazed at the diverse manner in which organisations determined prices and calculated profits. Without subscribing to simple cause and effect claims, it seems that the observations he made with the Prices Commission, together with his experiences while being involved with the 'accounting' of his father's business, greatly influenced his later work. He felt that through these experiences he was made aware of the *ad hoc* and confusing way in which account-ing rules and practices were developed – dogma rather than rigorous analysis and thought (cf., Chambers, 2000a).

In 1945 he was appointed to his first academic position – lecturer in the Department of Industrial Management in the Sydney Technical College (a second tier tertiary educational institution). His responsibilities were not in accounting as we now know it but for 'costing and cost control', which were part of the requirements for a more general management education'. However, Chambers felt there was an urgent need for education in the financial dimensions of management. Consequently, he developed a subject(s) in what he termed financial management. That was the title of his first book produced in 1947, which went through several re-writings (rather than mere revisions) and was hailed as a seminal work. It placed accounting within the framework of financial management. On first seeing this book I was intrigued by a quotation in the frontispiece (of the second edition; 1953), viz.:

> *Bad production management and bad sales management have slain their thousands, but bad faulty finance has slain its tens of thousands.*

(Colin Brooks)

While employed by the Sydney Technical College he also published several research papers and presented many invited research lectures.

In 1953 Chambers was appointed to the first full-time academic position – senior lecturer – in accounting at the University of Sydney. Two years later he was promoted to Associate Professor and subsequently, after five years, to the Foundation Chair in Accounting at that university, a position he held until his retirement in 1982, at which time he was made an Emeritus Professor. With his appointment in 1953, the University of Sydney introduced an accounting major in its Bachelor of Economics programme and, on his appointment to Professor in 1960, the University established the Department of Accounting. As part of its economics and business educational programmes, the University of Sydney had taught individual accounting subjects since 1907. Initially the teachers were drawn from those in business and professional accounting practice rather than full-time academics.

Recognition

During his life Chambers received very many awards and had several honours conferred upon him. These include the award of a Gold Medal by the American Institute of Certified Public Accountants for the contribution to accounting of his book *Accounting, Evaluation and Economic Behavior* (Chambers, 1966) (AEEB); election by the American Accounting Association (AAA) as its inaugural Distinguished International Lecturer in 1976; the AAA's Outstanding Accounting Educator Award in 1991; the Kappa Psi Foundation Award for distinguished service and accomplishment in accounting; election to the Accounting Hall of Fame at the Ohio State University, in 1991; and election to the Australian Accounting Hall of Fame at the University of Melbourne, in 2010. In 1978 he received a civic award, being named an Officer of the Order of Australia for service to commerce and education. These are but a few examples and he was awarded other national and international honours in recognition of his being a distinguished and highly-respected international accounting scholar. He was very often invited by many institutions around the world to serve as a distinguished visiting fellow/scholar/professor. He received honorary Doctor of Science degrees and other academic accolades from several universities.

A leader in ideas

Chambers published a dozen sole-authored books (some of which went through many revised editions), several edited books, well over 200 journal articles, and hundreds (if not thousands) of lesser published and unpublished pieces (cf., Chambers and Dean, 2000). This would suggest that he was not short of ideas! What were some of these ideas?

On entering an academic career Chambers said (2000b, p. 321), on the basis of his experiences, he had learned two things:

- Accounting universally claimed to be related to the growth of business and finance.
- Its rules and products were not the outcome of disciplined reasoning – as in mathematics and physical and biological sciences – but of traditional rules of thumb and the dogma of its elders such as initial cost.

As stated above, without subscribing to simplistic cause and effect explanations, it seems that Chambers' ideas were greatly influenced by his experiences (and observations). His time at the Prices Commission had led him to the second of the conclusions above – the haphazard way in which accounting proceeded. He held that:

Accounting is about financial affairs, about the financial consequences of engagements and transactions of one person, business firm or other organisation, with all other such parties (in a nutshell, with the rest of the world).

(Chambers, 2000a, p. 314)

Financial affairs refers to those everyday activities in which we all engage that have to do with money, money's worth and claims to money. Accounting then is:

. . . in principle, a systematic process of recording successively, and summarizing occasionally, the effects of events and exchanges on the property holdings and wealth of an identified party.

(Chambers, 2000a, p. 314)

The summarised record becomes the basis on which decisions could be made. This forms the 'core' idea of the theory he developed for resolving the problems with which accounting was so spectacularly (and unsuccessfully) grappling – the failure of extant accounting practice to provide 'useful' (in his terms '*truthful*') information to users of financial statements in times of variable price levels.

To Chambers there were universal accounting truths that should be established. That is, he believed accounting should have principles which existed at all levels, from accounting for households to accounting for large corporations. The difference lay in the increased complexity of corporate financial affairs but, like individuals, managers needed to know what resources were at their command to make effective decisions about future courses of action.

The conduct of household and business affairs alike proceeds by the recurrent inflow and outflow of identified quantities of goods and services and money, and the holding, between times, of identifiable stocks of goods and money.

(Chambers, 2000a, p. 313)

The capacity to engage in actions would depend on the stock (quantity) of goods and money at a particular point in time. The difference between the record of this stock from one time to another would represent income (or profit).

The summarised record up to a given date would 'provide reliable grounds' for decision-making. However, discrepancies between the record and the observed quantity of goods and money would be the result of deliberate deceit, inadvertent gains or losses, or errors in recording. In the recording of the stocks of goods and resources the common denominator is money. That is, underlying this information were the measures of money (or money equivalents). This, in turn, led to an emphasis on the principles and theories of measurement.

In developing his ideas Chambers clearly thought 'outside the box'. He looked beyond the conventional technical conventions. In developing his courses in financial management at the Sydney Technical College he had concluded that accounting was inextricably bound up with financial management (hence the first of his conclusions alluded to above). Thus, unlike the conventional approaches, to him accounting was not a technical exercise in its own right, but was to serve the needs of those managing their financial affairs – for individuals or large organisations. In all cases money was a sensible, common and widely understood (and necessary) element. Hence, his theory of continuously contemporary accounting (CoCoA) was based on current cash equivalents (CCE) – up to date (current and not past) measures of money.

An innovator in accounting education

Chambers' first task at the Sydney Technical College was to develop courses in costing and cost controls. He found most textbooks treated these subjects as standalone specialisms with their 'own more or less isolated, rationale', and at first he followed this approach. However, he soon concluded how wrong this was.

Very early in his academic career Chambers distinguished accounting training from accounting education. In an early article on the subject, he stated that:

> Education may be considered as a process by which the innate qualities of the student are drawn out and developed, and by which the student's mind is enriched both because of the experience suffered and because of the knowledge gained. Teaching to be really educational should, therefore, aim to provide such stimuli for the student that he (sic) goes forward seeking an understanding of the principles of his subject rather than sitting back smug in the knowledge that he "swatted" the correct material for his examination.
>
> ('The training of accountants', Chambers, 1948, p. 322; quoted in Wolnizer and Dean, 2000, p. 248)

These notions continued to guide his actions throughout his academic career. At the University of Sydney, accounting education 'was to have firmer, more rigorous intellectual underpinnings than the conventional kind' (Wolnizer and Dean, 2000, p. 250). In addition, as Chambers himself was to say:

> We developed the teaching program from being a hand-me-down bunch of rote recipes to a course of study worthy to be included with other courses leading to masters and Ph.D. degrees.
>
> (Chambers, 2000b, p. 322)

There is little doubt that the educational programmes which Chambers developed at Sydney were unique and revolutionary in their approach (cf., Chambers, 1991). Maintaining the intellectual rigour he insisted on was difficult for his colleagues, but it is interesting to note that almost all rose to and willingly accepted the challenge. As one of these colleagues I concurred with his demands for developing courses that were directed to education and not training; to encourage students to think for themselves and not simply regurgitate past practices. It was certainly a far cry from many programmes today where lecturers adopt a textbook so long as the publishers include all the 'extras' in order to help them avoid having to think about course design and development. For example, we could never simply take examination questions from some past (or even current) text but had to tailor questions that attempted to determine how much the students had really learned. As Clarke, Dean and Wells mention:

> Unbeknown to students, preparations of examination papers under Chambers was likely as much an ordeal for staff setting the examination papers, as it was for the students sitting them . . . Examination time was a thoroughly testing time for both staff as well as for students.
>
> (Clarke, Dean and Wells, 2010, p. 85, emphasis in the original)

For Chambers, the aim 'was to discover whether students understood the propositions put to them in the lectures and the evidence for them, rather than merely what the conventional texts presented to be the case . . .' (Clarke, Dean and Wells, 2010, p. 85).

As Head of Department, he 'went through every examination paper with its authors, asking what answers were expected' (Clarke, Dean and Wells, 2010, p. 85).

The curricula designed by Chambers at both undergraduate and postgraduate levels were highly innovative. At the undergraduate level subjects were taught as full year subjects. The first year (Stage I) subject was entitled *Introduction to Accounting* and comprised two (integrated) 'parts', the first referred to as 'Technique', the second as 'Theory'. The overall subject was described as involving investigation of:

> *The social and business functions of accounting. Accounting as a system of communications, and as a means of representing business sets and processes formally. Decision-making in business; the function of knowledge; accounting as a means of accumulating and storing knowledge. Some consequences of the formal nature of accounting.*

The description of 'Theory' included expressions such as the *'general content of a theory of accounting. Pure theory. Normative and positive propositions'*.[3]

Teaching large numbers of first year students without a regular (conventional?) textbook placed demands on our resourcefulness. Chambers felt that the available accounting textbooks were generally woeful and totally inadequate in inculcating a spirit of genuine intellectual enquiry into and understanding of the discipline. Therefore, it was necessary to have recourse to a wide range of sources from many other, related disciplines. Demands on academic staff were considerable in the interests of establishing a rigorous and effective accounting education designed to service adequately (a well-used Chambers expression) the discipline and the business community. Nevertheless, complying with such rigour had its (speaking for myself, at least) long-term rewards. However, I do not think I am alone in this. Many past colleagues and students of Chambers have taken up appointments at other institutions and his influence can be seen in the educational programs which they have developed. An example is in the rigour of the extensive educational research on competency standards for accounting professionals undertaken by the late Bill Birkett (for example, see Birkett, 1992a; b). There are also many other senior academics in Australia and overseas who would acknowledge his influence. Private conversations with many of his students who have entered practice have often revealed an appreciation of the strenuous demands Chambers placed on them in class which have later served them well. Through this they feel that they learned the capacity to think about issues that arise rather than seek, for the sake of it, well-trodden formulae.

Strong academic leadership

From his date of appointment as an academic Chambers led by example – he demonstrated the skills of an academic exemplar. When he arrived he found a discipline with little respect for cerebral endeavour, content to continue to be at the beck and call of strong business interests rather than develop a 'real' academic discipline worthy of a place in a university. He found the challenge 'exhilarating' and has referred to it as 'living on the fringe'. Such *'[l]iving on the fringe is always demanding, sometimes exhilarating, always adventurous . . . Some get their kicks out of doing what's not been done before, some from outdoing rivals, some from public applause – some from simply pursuing goals of their choice which others have held to be unattainable'* (Chambers, 2000b, p. 322). In the university environment he suffered the fate that many older accounting academics would remember that they had to face on disclosing their discipline – the constant challenge of 'What's bookkeeping doing in a university?' With the record at that time of the so-called profession, it was a charge that often lent one to cringe – corporate collapses, financial scandals, economic disasters. So what's new? These days I guess, others have become used to having us around and besides we bring in a lot of funds to our institutions. However, to Chambers it was a challenge to make accounting worthy of its university place. On arriving at Sydney, I was pleasantly surprised to find acceptance of my being an academic accountant and I soon realised that this was largely due to the respect which Chambers had earned through his intellectual approach to the subject.

Such respect had been earned from the nature of his publications and the rigour of the academic programmes. However, Chambers also sought to establish an academic accounting research journal. For him this was a journey fraught by constant frustration, disappointment and sometimes betrayal. Yet he doggedly persisted and *Abacus* was successfully launched (see Wells, 2000). From my position of political naivety, it is difficult for me to conceive of reasons why so many senior members of the discipline – academics, practitioners and professional body representatives – placed so many obstacles in front of Chambers' endeavours to launch the journal. For example, Chambers, as a matter of courtesy and professional respect, had enquired of the Institute of Chartered Accountants in England and Wales (ICAEW) whether he could use the term *accounting research* as part of the journal title as the ICAEW had sponsored a journal by that title but which had ceased publication some years earlier. The ICAEW responded they would certainly object even though there was at the time very little accounting research (as it is now understood) being undertaken in either England or Wales. Similar lack of encouragement was received from the international academic community and the matter is detailed by Wells (2000).

Chambers was universally recognised as an academic leader and was constantly invited to present lectures at universities around the world. For example, 10 of the most prestigious universities in the U.S.A. in 1966; 15 universities in North America (Mexico to Canada) in 1970; the four most important universities in Japan in 1971; 11 universities in the U.S.A. and four in the U.K. in 1976 (and of course New Zealand).

In Australia he had been one of the instigators of the Association of University Teachers of Accounting in Australia and served as its inaugural chairman. This body was later to become AAANZ (Accounting Association of Australia and New Zealand) and subsequently AFAANZ, (Accounting and Finance Association of Australia and New Zealand), the body that supposedly represents the interests of accounting and finance academics in tertiary educational institutions in Australia and New Zealand.

An unacknowledged leader of professional practice

Early in his career Chambers had published learned papers in the professional body journals – when they published such things as there were no academic research journals. He was invited to present research lectures many times at such occasions as their annual congresses. He served as examiner for many subjects for both Australian professional accounting bodies – the Institute of Chartered Accountants in Australia (ICAA) and the then Australian Society of Accountants (ASA) (now CPA Australia). Nevertheless, despite his having a *'research record of no mean dimension'* (Chambers, 2000b, p. 323), he was not asked to serve on the Australian Accounting Research Foundation (AARF) on its establishment (jointly sponsored by the two bodies) in 1965. He was urged to seek nomination to Council of the ASA but failed to win election each time. However, some time later he was asked to fill a casual vacancy and later served as New South Wales State president and then the National President of the Society (ASA).

He worked extremely hard for the Society as a Councillor then its President, yet his ideas were continually ignored or summarily dismissed (see Chambers, 2000b). He made countless submissions to the ARF and other regulatory bodies in Australia as well as in the U.S.A., the U.K. and Canada, yet they too were ignored. It may possibly be another manifestation of my political naivety but some of the political machinations (by practitioner and academics!) that were engaged in to prevent Chambers having input into any accounting regulations have to be read to be believed. The actions of many senior members of the profession were obstructive, disingenuous and deliberatively designed and manipulated to avoid allowing his input – attempts were made to marginalise or, even better, silence him (see Clarke, Dean and Wells, 2010, chapter 2, for the details of many of these incidents).

There are at least two aspects of this opposition to Chambers which are worth noting. First, it highlights the deep conservatism of the profession. Chambers wanted to change the way accounting is practised because he saw anomalies (in the Kuhnian sense) in extant practices. This was clearly apparent in the persistence with historical cost despite the strong evidence against it as an appropriate form of measurement. This is especially so if accounting is viewed as providing information which users can use as the basis for making decisions. To him this was incredible, but it seems the profession was loathe to want to change despite the rhetoric suggesting otherwise.

He notes that:

> An international professional conference in Sydney in 1972 saw speaker after speaker denounce conventional accounting – the dogs were barking it: the days of cost-based valuations in balance sheets were over! But no sooner had they all gone home than the standards committees brought forth standards for the valuation of commodities, inventories especially, on the basis of historical costs!
>
> (Chambers, 2000b, p. 324)

And, later, he was to suggest:

> In no field do practitioners want to believe that what they are paid handsomely to do is logically fallacious and practically pernicious.
>
> (Chambers, 1994, p. 2)

Thus, it seems that Chambers was viewed as a change agent which would take many out of their comfort zones. He was advocating moving from historical costs to CCE, ironically something close to fair values to which the profession some 30 to 40 years later has turned (or at least is attempting to).

The second aspect worth noting about the opposition to Chambers is the extent to which the profession was prepared to go to preclude him from any role in policy formulation. The conclusion to be drawn from this is that many felt threatened by his presence which would suggest that they were recognising his ability to present a strong case for changing the status quo: his ability to demonstrate the irrationality of the practices in which they had a stake. This was a sort of 'back-handed compliment'.

Surprisingly, Chambers did not resort to cynicism and despair. Not only did he creatively devise ways of circumventing these Machiavellian obstructions, he retained a belief that one test would see the survival of his ideas and work – history. His apparent stubborn persistence in the face of such opposition can be attributed to (at least) two factors. First, an intellectual belief in the superiority of his suggested solution to the problems of accounting measurement. This 'solution' was not an *ad hoc*, opportunistic response to the issues, but something in which he had made a deep intellectual commitment, the first seeds of which had appeared in the 1950s (Chambers, 1955a; b) and had been systematically developed and empirically evaluated. Second, was what he perceived as the unethical behaviour of accountants in presenting information which was clearly, in his eyes, untruthful. This had led to countless corporate failures and economic and social hardship to many of those caught up in these disasters.

Chambers was a very private person and kept his personal life separate from his professional activities. However, this behaviour suggests something about him as an individual; namely, he was someone with considerably high ethical standards and who sought to practice these ideals. To reiterate, to him, presenting false information to users who relied on it was unacceptable social behaviour. Corporate failures were a strong interest of his and he developed a large database of such instances. Part of this appeared in his book *Securities and Obscurities* (Chambers, 1973) but he also developed a course in corporate failures (entitled Corporate Dilemmas, Difficulties and Disasters) which formed an integral part of his postgraduate programmes (the master's degrees).

An intellectual legacy

Chambers' commitment to furthering the intellectual foundations of accounting was tremendous. Unfortunately, given the way accounting (and probably many disciplines) operates, this contribution has all too often been overlooked. In 1955 he challenged the complacency of the established thinking in accounting with a call for increased rigour and the use of a scientific approach to developing an accounting theory. The ideas in this seminal paper also laid down the foundations of his own approach to developing accounting theory; many other papers followed, each consciously building on those that had preceded them. He remained consistent with the understanding of theory construction which he had developed from his wide reading and the experiences and observations described above. He was always loathe to point to any direct individual sources for his ideas as his reading had been the leading works in many disciplines – philosophy of science, economics, science, psychology, history, engineering, law and others. His early papers ushered in a period of extensive methodological debate in accounting (see Gaffikin, 2008, chapter 3).

I have previously stated that, in developing his theory, Chambers followed a conventional methodological approach – essentially hypothetico-deductivism (HD) – although its use in accounting was quite radical at the time (Gaffikin, 1988; 2000).[4] While I still believe this to be true in respect of his earlier work, I now think that, while it remained as the basic belief, in his later work this is not quite as explicit. The term *modernism* has a variety of meanings but in the philosophical sense it is usually used to refer to a belief in the central tenets of the Enlightenment – the centrality of the method of science for establishing meaningful knowledge.[5] This method is HD (although it sometimes has other names) and it has been the focus of attention of philosophers of science for the last 400 years and has come to dominate Western methodological thinking. Essentially it involves starting with a hypothesis and a set of conditions and then deducing what facts follow from them. The facts (deduced conclusions) must then be empirically tested to determine the truth or falsity of the hypotheses.

It is little wonder that, with his broad reading and intellectual commitment, Chambers believed that the rigour necessary for accounting theory would be derived from accepted principles in the philosophy of science. He set these out in his paper 'Blueprint for a theory of accounting' (Chambers, 1955a) which was soon followed by another paper entitled 'A scientific pattern for accounting theory' (Chambers, 1955b). His theory development (AEEB) was completely faithful to this; carefully setting up linked propositions from which he could deduce consequences. His work subsequent to this was designed to refine and continually seek empirical and theoretical evidence to support the main thrust of the theory – CoCoA. To me, no other theory in accounting has been so carefully constructed and presented yet it failed to win general acceptance and he (his ideas) was constantly assaulted – invariably on grounds other than intellectual. To me there are multiple reasons for this lack of acceptance. He failed to recognise (or accept) many of these reasons as they were usually on grounds he had held were beyond the boundaries of the discipline, or at least what the theory (or any theory) represented.[6] In many of my discussions with him I argued for the importance of the sociology of knowledge but he constantly argued that such considerations were outside the parameters of the discipline. For example, he argued that suggestions as to what was accounting theory popularised by Watts and Zimmerman were not a theory of accounting but of the behaviour of accountants (cf., Chambers, 1993). Despite his arguments being intellectually sound, they were going to fall on deaf or closed ears. For example, the absurdly false distinction made between positive and normative theorising to which he drew attention (1993, pp. 8–11) has not prevented countless accounting theory texts (as well as many more articles) still devoting chapters to distinguishing between what they refer to as normative theories and positive theories – the former being of little value as the latter was the only real path to true knowledge! The reference earlier (above) to the curriculum he had designed (for first year accounting study) had demonstrated the folly of such misguided thinking many years earlier.

One of the most persistent pieces of positive propaganda has been the misuse of the term *empirical*. It represents a form of dogma (and ignorance) which Chambers felt had unfortunately permeated accounting thinking when he entered the academic world. Empiricism means that meaningful knowledge can only be established on the basis of direct sensory experience. This belief has a noble heritage in the history of English philosophy (let alone threads going back to the Ancient Greek scholars) and was the dominant tenet in the works of Bacon, Boyle, Locke, Hume, Mill and many others (especially in the 20th century analytical philosophy that so dominated the Anglo-American world). However, in accounting writing of the last 40 years, it has usually been used to refer to knowledge derived from (large-scale) data bases which could be subjected to several tests of statistical significance. Chambers (and probably most of those theorists dismissed as non-empirical or normative or a priori or with other pejorative terms) was always concerned with determining the basis of his assumptions and propositions from the world of practice: he constantly referred to *observation* as the source of ideas. Some positive theorists, in a world where large scale data bases and computers had become available, argued that it was only 'systematic observations' that could be considered empirical, thus making a normative decision as to what evidence was admissible and what not.

Empiricism has been a central element of scientific methodology since the time of Galileo to whom knowledge was to be gained through observation and experiment. The method of science was refined in the Enlightenment and empiricism was the critical element. It has remained this way, with minor modifications, right into the twenty-first century; it is fundamental to the scientific method whether it be called modernism or positivism (or one of its variants). Thus, it was a central part of Chambers' methodology (see, for example, Chambers, 1955a; b). Belief in empiricism means a belief in the possibility of an observable truth – facts. Chambers never lost a belief in this possibility of establishing certain truths through observation:

> The substance of a statement of fact may be shown to be true or false – to be or not to be the case – by appeal to evidence accessible to but independent of its utterer.

(Chambers, 1999, p. 134)

This implies observation as the source of evidence but also reinforces the Platonic concept of objectivity through the distinction between the observer and the observed. Objectivity has remained the cornerstone for meaningful – scientific – knowledge, and it is derived through empiricism.

A matter of style

Despite such a categorically positivist statement as the above, there are signs that Chambers entertained alternative approaches to knowledge. Understandably he did not like to be boxed or labelled although, as claimed above, his early work especially suggested he was very much that of a methodological conventionalist – a positivist who saw HD as the appropriate approach to theorising (although HD is associated with its two most famous exponents Hempel and Popper).[7] As stated above, its 'origins' as *the* method of science is usually traced back to the beginnings of modern science and became the standard for Enlightenment methodological thought. It has been the subject of much debate over the centuries but its basic form has remained the same. From the various comments in his writings it is obvious that Chambers was well read in these debates, especially those in the English 'tradition'. In fact his writing often reflected the style of argument used by earlier scholars sometimes resulting in what can be called a rather turgid text for a modern reader. There is no doubting his scholarship (of this tradition) but I would suggest that herein lay a problem. The Anglo-American world has long been suspicious of intellectuals, perhaps no more so than in accounting – a discipline which is not only unintellectual but, worse, anti-intellectual.[8] I believe Chambers was perceived by much of the accounting community to be an intellectual, which resulted in his being viewed with suspicion (in English-speaking countries – not so in countries such as Japan and Italy). I also believe that Chambers greatly admired intellectual pursuits[9] but, despite the expressed admiration of Dean *et al.* (2006, p. 76) for his commitment to Newman's dictum, few in the accounting community would have even heard of Newman let alone aspired to his ideals.

In has later works Chambers lay great emphasis on practice. He was vitally concerned with the advancement of the practical everyday affairs of accounting. To him, it was imperative that any theory have the potential for advancing practice:

Clearly then there is little or no merit in the view that scientific inquiry may or can dissociate itself from practical matters.

(Chambers, 2000c, p. 331)

Taken at face value this would suggest a commitment to pragmatism as it would seem consistent with that great twentieth century American philosophical movement. There are other 'indications': to Peirce and James, two of the foremost of the pragmatists, the concept of truth was crucial. They believed in the importance of commonsense and the facts of experience, a phrase very similar to that which Chambers continually referred to as being essential (in accounting). They held to the belief in the importance of the method of science. However, the similarities are, in the main, only superficial: despite the similarities there are deeper differences and Chambers could not be considered to be a pragmatist. It is likely that Chambers would reject the pragmatists' (especially Dewey's) instrumentalism.[10] To him, unlike the pragmatists (especially James), truth and certainty *could be* established through theory development – he remained committed to the Cartesian certainty to which positivists hold so dear; pragmatists tended to be anti-Cartesian and an essential or foundational universal truth was a casualty of that position – truth changes over time. However, in his work there are indications of *eclecticism*. There is a commitment to the certainty of positivism mixed with the possibility of the solution of everyday problems through the use of language as championed by the pragmatists.

The reason for discussing the possibility of Chambers' pragmatic thinking is that it leads to two other important features of Chambers' work. His seminal methodological papers (1955a; b; and particularly 1956) brought him into conflict with a doyen of U.S. accounting academe – Littleton. Littleton adhered to pragmatist philosophy, most especially as it was championed in the work of John Dewey. On the surface, the disagreement concerned two different opinions on accounting in a period of price changes. Littleton was a strong supporter of retaining historical cost accounting which Chambers perceived as representing the failure of accounting to deal with a crisis of meaning in financial statements. However, on deeper reflection, the difference concerned two very different opinions as to the function of accounting. To Littleton, accounting should remain separate from economics and retain its primary function of stewardship reporting. Accordingly, historical costs were quite an appropriate basis for financial reporting. Chambers had been caught up in the post-Canning (1929) move to make accounting more economically relevant. Thus, historical costs were fairly meaningless for providing the basis of economic decisions. Accounting became the hand-servant of economics. This has remained the dominant perspective since that time, most especially, of course, in the view of positive accounting theorists with their belief in the omnipotence of the market and the associated myths of efficient markets and the capital asset pricing model. What the work of Chambers ushered in was the era of decision usefulness accounting. Accordingly, valuation and measurement become critical features in generating financial information. Measurement was an essential element (if not the most important) of his thought and work. It is also central to many other accounting authors: for example, Christensen and Demski (2003, p. 4) claim that *accounting is a formal measurement system*. What then, makes an information content approach so different from a decision usefulness approach? This is not the place to debate this (or related) matter(s)!

A second consideration concerns the implications of a belief in market values, most especially current cash equivalents. The period of late capitalism (consumer capitalism or whatever other name is used) has been marked by attempts to measure all aspects of our existence in economic terms – what some have referred to as the cash nexus (ignoring the book of that title by Thatcherite economic historian Niall Ferguson). I have no doubt that Chambers was only intending to refer to economic (business) matters, but there are implications arising from how 'economic' is defined in this age of global ecological crises and lack of eco justice. Nevertheless, Chambers was committed to a belief in the importance of the market place as an independent arbiter to the same extent as later accounting writers (such as the positive accounting theorists). However, despite this common underlying belief I think that there can be little doubt that he did not see the need for a total reliance on the market as do later writers. For him the reliance on a neutral market removed the possibility of financial information manipulation. He believed that the use of market information had significant ethical considerations. Once again, this is not the place to debate this, but it is certainly worth noting. Chambers did partially address this matter in his book, *Foundations of Accounting*, chapter 9 'Axiological foundations' (Chambers, 1991).

Throughout his life Chambers was constantly criticised for his ideas. Very often the critics resorted to personal, *ad hominem* argument. However, Chambers *never* resorted to such tactics. He was content to attack people's ideas and arguments and he often did so with great zeal. In a world of sensitive egos, obviously some took such criticism to heart and responded in ways which their limited intellectual skills allowed them to. As alluded to above, when this failed, some resorted to more Machiavellian responses.

Noblesse oblige

As stated in its title, this paper has been a personal reflection. My major interest has always been intellectual history – the development of ideas. Chambers recognised this and this formed the basis of the many long, stimulating and enjoyable discussions he and I had and for which I was, am and will be ever grateful. This was Chambers the teacher. His approach was basically Socratic and involved lengthy debates and arguments. I was required to critically examine the issues in question and justify my position. This was also his approach to his research students. They were required to encapsulate their research questions succinctly and then justify their conclusions.

As with his own work, he approached these sessions with considerable rigour and it sometimes left students in despair. However, there was little doubt that if they could convince him then they would not be troubled by convincing examiners, such was his rigour. The approach also generated students' confidence in their capacity to address issues critically. He was also interested in students' capacities for original thinking – a new slant to resolving an issue was encouraged.

Chambers adopted a similar approach to his classroom teaching. Students were subjected to demonstrating their critical understanding of issues. In addition, he had the capacity to express fundamental issues in simple metaphors and everyday language. A favourite example of a colleague is his statement:

> *I have always thought an asset was something I could buy a hamburger with. The wisdom of the standards boards, however, is that an asset is a future economic benefit.*
>
> (Chambers, 1994, p. 4)

A question that has remained in my mind is how someone so obviously capable of making a tremendous intellectual contribution to the development of accounting knowledge could be so dismissed in the everyday world of practical accounting and overlooked by so many academic accountants.

However, there are some who believe they have kept the 'light burning' by continuing to constantly reiterate many of his arguments. I consider it more appropriate to salute his great contribution and practice what he taught me. As indicated above, the essential tenet of his ideas of education was to inculcate the ability to think critically and independently rather than learn (and regurgitate) 'rote recipes'. I interpret this as taking on board what he taught and extending it through rigorous thought and research – situations and circumstances change over time and I would rather try and critically reflect on and extend his work rather than see it set in stone. I enjoy and greatly admire the music of Schubert, but that does not mean I should not listen and enjoy the music of later, often radically different, composers such as Bartok, Stravinsky, Steve Reich or John Cage. Not only do his apostles repeat his conclusions, but they appear not to question or reflect on his outmoded modernist methodological approach. Chambers would be the first to agree that greatness does come from rubbing shoulders with great people. Rather, it is necessary to engage critically with what makes them great (cf., Gaffikin, 2010). With some pretension I could quote Kant

> *As regards those who wish to pursue a scientific method, they have now the choice of following either the dogmatical or the sceptical, while they are bound never to desert the systematic mode of procedure . . . The critical path alone is still open. If my reader has been kind and patient enough to accompany me on this hitherto untravelled route, he can now judge whether, if he and others will contribute their exertions towards making the narrow foot-path a high road of thought . . .*
>
> (Kant, 2003, p. 480; emphasis in original)

It has been claimed by some that Chambers is the '*father of fair value accounting*' (e.g. Clarke *et al.*, 2010, p. 11). While there is little doubt that exit prices formed a key to his theory of accounting, I believe recourse to history would make this a contestable claim. Such 'criticism' does not diminish the enormity of his contribution to accounting thought. While, I believe he produced a convincing argument for the use of exit prices as the basis of accounting measures, I think his contributions go well beyond that. For example, consider his massive *Accounting Thesaurus* (Chambers, 1995) which contains over 6000 fully-referenced quotations about accounting matters and which are catalogued and cross-referenced, thus providing a very useful database for researchers.

There have been several people at the frontiers of accounting knowledge to whom we should pay tribute. To me Chambers is a shining beacon in these several and deserves full acknowledgment of this as this brief tribute clearly indicates.

Notes

1 This issue also reprints the paper, 'Aide-Memoire' which is a full listing of all his publications as well as his letters to the general and professional press, submissions to public and professional bodies, lectures, addresses and seminars and other presentations – Chambers and Dean (2000).
2 Whereas disciples are followers, apostles are those who believe they have to spread the 'good word'.
3 The full subject descriptions (undergraduate and postgraduate) are reprinted in Clarke, Dean and Wells (2010), Appendix II (from which the above have been reproduced).
4 For those not familiar with HD it has been, with minor variations, the commonly perceived method of modern science from its earliest days; from Galileo (1564–1642), Bacon (1561–1626), Newton (1642–1727) to being championed by Karl Popper and Carl Hempel in the twentieth century. Its description has dominated research methodology texts to the present day. Despite this widespread acceptance, it had not been very evident in the accounting literature until the 1950s when Chambers advocated its use as necessary to provide intellectual rigour to accounting thought (Chambers, 1955a; 1955b).
5 See, for example, Giddens (1990) for a general discussion of modernity. Interestingly, given Chambers' claims about the intellectual state of accounting thinking, in a religious context, historically, the term is used to refer the opposition to (religious) dogma.
6 Thus overlooking Plato's advice in his Republic, that any theory of man (sic), implicit or explicit, will be reflected in a theory of the state (Rist, 2002, pp. 228–229).
7 Although named by the nineteenth-century polymath William Whewell (according to The Stanford Encyclopedia of Philosophy: http://plato.stanford.edu/archives/win2009/entries/whewell accessed 7 July 2011).
8 There will be some (even many) who will take exception to my comments. However, I am more than prepared to defend them. The history of analytical philosophy, established by intellectuals, espoused anti-intellectual tendencies (for example, the development of ordinary language philosophy). Pragmatism shared 'the anti-intellectualist tendency' of empiricism (James, 1907, p. 27, emphasis in original). The pejorative connotations to the term ivory tower. My experiences in countries such as Australia, where bright students are discouraged by practitioners from undertaking postgraduate study; in New Zealand and South Africa where the professional bodies appear to show little or no purpose to research in accounting and insist on educational programs which stress the technical (e.g. details of IFRS); and my perception of the extremely limited 'acceptable' approaches to research espoused and practised in the U.S.A. and supported by the AAA 'decision-makers'.
9 The last section of AEEB is entitled 'A Copernican Revolution', an allusion to the title of a work by Thomas Kuhn, but it could also allude to the work of Kant who, it is popularly believed, also described his work as having revolutionised our understanding of knowledge!
10 Seemingly popular with exponents of positive accounting adherents. A theory is seen as an 'instrument' for explaining phenomena. Consequently truth is of lesser importance. For example, the well-quoted claim by Milton Friedman that the reality of the assumptions of a theory is irrelevant, what is relevant is whether the theory is successful (see Friedman, 1953).

References

Birkett, W.P. (1992a) Competency standards for the profession: aspirations and issues, *Charter*, 63(10), pp. 64–65.
Birkett, W.P. (1992b) Competency standards for the profession: competency and education, *Charter*, 63(11), pp. 70–71.
Canning, J.B. (1929) *The Economics of Accounting*, New York: Ronald Press
Chambers, R.J. (1953) *Financial Management – A Study of the Bases of Financial Decisions in Business*, 2nd edn, Sydney: The Law Book Co of Australia Pty Ltd.
Chambers, R.J. (1955a) Blueprint for a theory of accounting, *Accounting Research*, 6(1), pp. 17–25.

Chambers, R.J. (1955b) A scientific pattern for a theory of accounting, *The Australian Accountant*, October, pp. 428–434.

Chambers, R.J. (1956) Some observations on Structure of Accounting Theory (by A.C. Littleton), *The Accounting Review*, 31(4), pp. 584–592.

Chambers, R.J. (1966) *Accounting, Evaluation, and Economic Behavior*, Englewood Cliffs: Prentice-Hall.

Chambers, R.J. (1973) *Securities and Obscurities: A Case for Reform of the Law of Company Accounts*, Melbourne: Gower Press). Reprinted in 1982 as *Accounting in Disarray*, New York: Garland.

Chambers, R.J. (1991) *Foundations of Accounting*, Geelong: Deakin University Press.

Chambers, R.J. (1993) Positive accounting theory and the PA cult, *Abacus*, 29(1), pp. 1–26.

Chambers, R.J. (1994) Opening Address: Research! – but what of practice? *AAANZ Conference 1994 – Pacioli 500 Years On*, Wollongong: Accounting Association of Australia & New Zealand.

Chambers, R.J. (1995) *An Accounting Thesaurus – 500 Years of Accounting*, Oxford: Elsevier Science.

Chambers, R.J. (1999) The case for simplicity in accounting, *Abacus*, 35(2), pp. 121–137.

Chambers, R.J. (2000a) Early beginnings: introduction to Wisdom of Accounting, *Abacus*, 36(3), pp. 313–320.

Chambers, R.J. (2000b) Life on the fringe – an accounting odyssey, *Abacus*, 36(3), pp. 321–326.

Chambers, R.J. (2000c) Common sense, technology and science, *Abacus*, 36(3), pp. 327–333.

Chambers, R.J. & Dean, G.W. (2000) Aide memoire, *Abacus*, 36(3), pp. 334–386.

Christensen, J.A. & Demski, J.A. (2003) *Accounting Theory, an Information Content Perspective*, New York: McGraw-Hill Higher Education.

Clarke, F.L., Dean, G.W., & Wells, M.C. (2010) *The Sydney School of Accounting – The Chambers Years*, Sydney: The University of Sydney.

Dean, G.W., Clarke, F.L., & Wolnizer, P.W. (2006) The R. J. Chambers collection: an archivist's revelations of 20th century accounting thought and practice, *The Accounting Historians Journal*, 33(2), pp. 145–166.

Friedman, M. (ed.) (1953) The methodology of positive economics, *Essays in Positive Economics*, pp. 3–49, Chicago: University of Chicago Press.

Gaffikin, M.J.R. (1988) *Accounting Methodology and the Work of R. J. Chambers*, New York: Garland Publishing Inc.

Gaffikin, M.J.R. (2000) Chambers on methods of inquiry, *Abacus*, 36(3), pp. 285–297.

Gaffikin, M.J.R. (2008) *Accounting Theory: Research, Regulation and Accounting Practice*, Sydney: Pearson Publishing.

Gaffikin, M.J. (2010) Being critical in accounting, *International Review of Business Research Papers*, 6(5), pp. 33–45.

Giddens, A. (1990) *The Consequences of Modernity*, Stanford: Stanford University Press.

James, W. (1907) *Pragmatism*, New York: Barnes and Noble.

Kant, I. (2003) *Critique of Pure Reason*, (first published 1781), New York: Dover Publications Inc.

Moonitz, M. (1982) Chambers at the American Institute of Certified Public Accountants, *Abacus*, 18(2), pp. 106–111.

Rist, J. (2002) *Real Ethics – Rethinking the Foundations of Morality*, Cambridge: Cambridge University Press.

Staubus, G. (2003) An accountant's education, *Accounting Historians Journal*, 30(1), pp. 155–196.

Wells, M.C. (2000) Founding Abacus: frustration to fulfilment, *Abacus*, 36(3), pp. 255–266.

Wolnizer, P.W. & Dean, G.W. (2000) Chambers as educator and mentor, *Abacus*, 36(3), pp. 243–254.

A tribute to Professor Stephen A. Zeff

Thomas R. Dyckman and Will C. Uecker

CORNELL UNIVERSITY, U.S.A., RICE UNIVERSITY, HOUSTON, U.S.A.

Introduction

This tribute will address Professor Stephen A. Zeff's scholarship and educational contributions to our profession. We begin with a brief history of how he came to select accounting as his field of interest, his early introduction to the field, and his professional contributions. The discussion then turns to his research, which typically reflects an historical approach to viewing the field. The last main section examines Professor Zeff's work as a teacher, often as seen through his students' reflections.

A brief career history

Stephen Zeff's college education began at the University of Colorado from which he received his BS degree in Accounting with honors in 1955 and his MS in management (with a minor in accounting) in 1957. Steve's interest in accounting was stimulated by Wilton Anderson and his interest in a teaching career by the urging of Robert Wasley. After graduation, Steve remained at Colorado for two years as an instructor while pursuing an MS degree. The experience as an instructor in accounting convinced him to pursue a teaching/research career. He enrolled in the Doctoral Program at the University of Michigan, receiving an MBA in 1960 and PhD in 1962. While at Michigan, Steve was significantly influenced by Professors William Paton and William Schlatter. The latter was his thesis advisor. During this time, he also assisted with the revisions of Finney and Miller's intermediate and advanced accounting text books.

University professorial appointments followed with an initial appointment at Tulane University in 1961. In 1978, Steve was named the W. R. Irby Professor of Accounting at Tulane. After a visiting position at Harvard University, he was lured to Rice University in 1978 by Robert Sterling, becoming the Herbert S. Autrey Professor of Accounting in 1979, a position he continues to hold. Steve has not confined his presence to his current home university. Over the years he has held visiting professor appointments at 15 different leading universities, of which nine have been outside the U.S.A. In addition, Steve has traveled the world lecturing and presenting his work in over 50 countries on more than 600 occasions. Sixteen of these were invited lectureships at renowned universities. Over half were again international. His career membership in professional societies, numbers over 25, again including many located outside the U.S.A. To this impressive total, we should add a series of 30 lectures given by Steve in eight countries when he was the AAA Distinguished Visiting Lecturer to Latin America in 1977. These lectures were all given in Spanish.

Professional contributions – U.S.A.

Despite this ambitious schedule, Steve has found time to serve on over 25 American Accounting Association Committees, chairing many of them. In 1961, he was nominated to be book review editor for the *Accounting Review* by Professor Samuel Hepworth of the University of Michigan, a position he held from 1962 to 1966, returned to in 2006, and still holds. The availability of serious book reviews, in addition to his meticulous editorship, is a highly notable contribution to the academy. Anyone who has worked with Steve, or had him commission a review, will testify as to the rigorous care with which he dissects their work, both as to substance and accuracy. In a typical example pointed out to one of the present authors, Steve discovered an error in the footnote of a text he was reviewing. The year of the citation to an FASB pronouncement was misstated by one year. The author had inadvertently cited the date of the pronouncement rather than the year when the document was actually published.

Steve has applied his editorial skills on 42 editorial boards during his career; the majority of which are international, and currently remains active on 26 of those boards. Steve headed the committee in charge of organizing the 1974 annual meeting of the American Accounting Association; was on the distinguished faculty in numerous AAA Doctoral Consortia (1975; 1978; 1979; 1981; 1984; and 1987), participated as a faculty member in many European Doctoral Consortia (1985 and annually from 1985 to 2000), and served as a faculty member at the 2007 AAA/Deloitte Doctoral Consortium. Steve was a member of the AAA Committee appointed by President Doyle Williams and chaired by Harold Langenderfer, which led to the founding of *Accounting Horizons* in 1986, under the editorship of Robert K. Mautz – a publication designed to foster communication between educators and practicing accountants, but which unfortunately never achieved its goal as the journal became instead another outlet for refereed academic research.

Steve was the first AAA Director of Education (1969–1971), and he served as Editor of *The Accounting Review* for three terms (1977–1982), the longest of any editor since the 1950s. During his editorship, a $25 submission fee was begun, a notes section was introduced, and a financial reporting section was added. Steve served as President of the American Accounting Association for the year 1985–1986. An important event in his tenure was the establishment of the Seminal Contributions to Accounting Literature Award to recognize a single research effort at most once every three years, for a contribution published at least 15 years earlier that has significantly influenced the future of the profession.

International contributions

While AAA President, Steve – relying on a proposal by a committee headed by Professor Yuji Ijiri – reached out to eight international academic accounting associations, inviting them to become AAA Associate Members. By the end of his presidency six had accepted and one more was expected and ultimately joined. The Zeff Presidency was the first to see several international faculty selected as plenary speakers. By these actions, Steve substantially extended the international inclusion efforts initiated by presidents S. Paul Garner and David Solomons before him. Steve followed up by inaugurating the practice of inviting delegates of these associations to attend the president's reception. He initiated a program to distribute the association's publications to libraries in third-world countries. Steve also inaugurated the initial international conference of accounting standard setters in the summer of 1986 and selected David Solomons to organize the event. A significant number of the invited international participants from the over 20 countries represented remained afterward for the annual AAA meeting at which several international scholars gave plenary talks. The number of international associate members and international exchanges has markedly increased since these actions were taken.

Steve's commitment to diversity and inclusiveness on the international scene is also reflected in his views on accounting research. Twenty years ago Steve warned that the increased use of formal empiricism and mathematical model building combined with increased emphasis on doctoral programs to prepare teachers would lead to methods-driven as opposed to problem-driven accounting research and would severely limit the diversity of methods and approaches in accounting research (see Zeff, 1989a). Consistent with his views, Steve has tried to increase the diversity of approaches in accounting research through his own research and by encouraging other research approaches. For example, Steve managed to induce the Touche Ross Foundation to sponsor the very first Symposium on Behavioral Science Research in Accounting. Asked for his views on accounting research today, Steve says that he is not opposed to formal empiricism and mathematical model building.

> I just don't like to see it the only research that is rewarded in the best universities and that is to be expected of doctoral students . . . It's not just a United States phenomenon; it's being picked up in Europe, it's being picked up in Asia, and it was picked up in Australia many years ago. And I'm worried that we'll lose this wonderful diversity of approaches to research that we've seen around the world, that we used to have in the United States, and for the most part we don't have much of that anymore. That worries me.

(Steve Zeff interview, 15 July 2010)

Professional recognition

The list of professional recognitions garnered by Steve is extensive, consisting of some 30 in number including the following: Hourglass Awards (1973; 2001) for 'meritorious contribution to literature on accounting history'; election to the Accounting Researchers International Association (1975); the AAA's Outstanding Accounting Educator Award (1988); and election to the Accounting Hall of Fame as the 70th member (2002).

Steve's recognition on the international scene is also formidable. His selection as the AAA's Outstanding International Accounting Educator in 1999 is one testament to his legacy. Steve was responsible in 1968 for founding *Bolet ın Interamericano de Contabilidad*, a publication devoted to interchange among Spanish-speaking accounting professionals. He also received an honorary degree of Doctor of Economics in 1990 from the Turku School of Economics and Business Administration, Finland, and an honorary degree of Doctor of Letters from the University of Waterloo, Canada, in 2010, the Diploma de Honor al Merito of the Asociacion Interamericana de Contabilidad (1997), the AAA's Outstanding International Educator Award (1999), and was recipient of the inaugural Anthony G. Hopwood Award for Academic Leadership (2009), presented by the European Accounting Association. All of these honors recognized Steve's international contributions. The esteem with which Steve is held overseas is testified to by his international service since 1990 on seven advisory committees, five advisory councils including his memberships on the Academic Panel of the Accounting Standards Board (U.K.), and

12 editorial boards including *The British Accounting Review, Accounting and Business Research, The International Journal of Accounting*, and *Accounting Education: an international journal*. Indeed, it has been alleged that Steve once proposed that the AAA should be renamed the III (perhaps, we are told, standing for the International Information Institute). Steve, however, claims no knowledge of this proposal. His international credentials are further bolstered by his addiction to the game of squash and that he is perhaps the only American accounting professor who actually understands, let alone appreciates, the sport of cricket.

Research contributions

Steve's scholarly writings, which number over 200, cannot easily be categorized because his eclectic interests span a wide swathe of the accounting discipline. However, they can be conveniently viewed, as several others have noted, through an historical lens. Thus, for example, Steve's extensive concern with international accounting matters is typically captured within an historic context. The same observation applies to his history of the Harvard Business School's development of Managerial Control titled 'Contribution of the Harvard Business School to Management Control' (see Zeff, 2008c). This review at best tries to capture some of the major thrusts of Steve's contributions.

Early writings

The genesis of Steve's interest in history was evident early in his undergraduate honors thesis, 'Collective Bargaining vs. the Conspiracy Doctrine and the Injunction in the United States: Until 1932.' His Michigan doctoral thesis, 'A Critical Examination of the Orientation Postulate in Accounting, with Particular Attention to Its Historical Development,' and his article, 'Replacement Cost: Member of the Family, Welcome Guest, or Intruder?' (published in *The Accounting Review*, 37(4), October 1962) continued this historical trend. The latter paper was Steve's first publication in a major accounting journal and heralded his interest in alternative ways of addressing price changes in accounting reports. Believing there was a good deal of confusion in the literature of the time, Steve set out to explain the contending views of past scholars on the matter with particular attention to the treatment of unrealized gains and losses and whether they should be considered income or taken directly to stockholders' equity.

Encouragement in 1963 from Professor Maurice Moonitz, of the University of California at Berkeley, led Steve to review the works of Henry Rand Hatfield, the first full-time accounting academic with a professorial title. This research culminated 37 years later in Steve's first of several books and articles on the contributions of early twentieth-century scholars to the field. His research approach relied heavily on interviews, correspondence, and Hatfield's published writings. The effort, representing his decision to integrate a combination of research approaches, was not only unusual but a process Steve honed which has served him faithfully throughout his career.

Biographical histories

Steve is justifiably proud of *Henry Rand Hatfield: Humanist, Scholar, and Accounting Educator* published by JAI Press Inc./Elsevier in 2000. This effort led to his second Hourglass Award. Publication of the works on MacNeal (*Accounting Review*, July 1982); Canning (*Abacus*, February 2000); Mathews, Gynther, and Chambers (*Accounting and Business Research*, Summer, 2001); Limperg (*Twentieth-Century Accounting Thinkers*, Routledge, 1994); Solomons (*Accounting and*

Business Research, Autumn, 1995); Paton (*International Encyclopedia of Business and Management,* 1996); Storey and Kircher (both in *Accounting Education News,* Autumn, 1999); Davidson and Sprouse (*Accounting Education News,* Autumn, 2007 and Winter, 2008, respectively); and Moonitz (*Accounting Education News,* Autumn, 2009) continued this stream of his research to the present, as do publications in progress profiling the early years of New Zealand accounting departments and a biographical work on British accountants.

Standard setting

Steve's historical perspective provides a window to a rich landscape of accounting thought that emphasizes several themes. The first involves his work on the historical development of the standard-setting process; a second reflects the evolution of accounting thought; while the third captures the maturing of the profession and the practice of auditing. These three streams of work intermingle over a sustained time period beginning in the early 1960s and continue today. Indeed, Steve's writing invariably reflects combinations of these basic themes.

The research approach adopted by Steve is often unusual if not unique. He has amassed a rich collection of interviews from scholars laboring in the twentieth century. To this material, Steve has added extensive research involving materials in the archives of major accounting firms, the SEC, and other private bodies. Fortunately, this accumulation of source data has been preserved and organized. The collection currently resides in his library-like office and Rice University's Fondren Library. This material provides the foundation for Steve's extensive contributions to the literature. Professor Dennis Beresford of the University of Georgia, a past chairman of the FASB, characterizes Steve's singular insight as 'a unique understanding of the people and situations involved that make his analysis much more true to the fact, based on my understanding of what happened in many of these cases. I would describe Steve as a good investigative reporter with a reasonably skeptical attitude but not predetermined biases'.

In the late 1960s, Steve began his research on how the norms of practice became embodied in official pronouncements. The impetus for this effort came from Professor Edward Stamp who invited Steve to be the 1970 annual Arthur Andersen Lecturer at the University of Edinburgh. This invitation resulted in a major effort to cover the historical evolution of approaches to standard setting and led to his tour-de-force publication in 1972 titled *Forging Accounting Principles in Five Countries [Canada, England, Mexico, Scotland and the United States]: A History and an Analysis of Trends.* Overcoming the secrecy surrounding the communications of the early standard setting bodies Committee on Accounting Procedure (CAP) and the Accounting Principles Board (APB) was a major hurdle in determining the dynamics underlying the decision-making process. Fortunately, Arthur Andersen & Co. provided access to CAP and APB files from its subject file microfilm, and to records in other countries. (The Andersen files also served as source material for several additional historical papers authored by Steve.) In addition, the Securities and Exchange Commission (SEC) also provided considerable documentation of relevance to this effort, including letters addressed to the SEC, research studies, and exposure drafts. Additional critical input was obtained from numerous interviews with the principal actors in all of the countries. This research was the basis for Steve's first Hourglass Award.

Fortunately, Steve continued his series on forging accounting principles to include Australia in 1973 and New Zealand in 1979. In addition, two relatively new books address the international setting of accounting standards. The first, with F. van der Wel and K. Camfferman, is titled *Company Financial Reporting: A Historical and Comparative Study of the Dutch Regulatory Process* (North-Holland, 1992) and the second, also with K. Camfferman, is titled *Financial Reporting and Global Capital Markets: A History of the International Accounting Standards Committee* 1973–2000 (Oxford University Press, 2007).

Steve's research into the historic development of accounting also can be found in several pieces published in the 1970s including '1926 to 1971 Chronology of Significant Developments in the Establishment of Accounting Principles in the United States' in '*Corporate Financial Reporting: The Issues, the Objectives and Some New Proposals*' (Commerce Clearing House, Inc., 1972), *The American Accounting Association – Its First Fifty Years* (AAA, 1966 and reprinted in 1991), and 'Some Junctures in the Evolution of the Process of Establishing Accounting Principles in the U.S.A.: 1917–1972' in the *Accounting Review* (1984) – in which Steve notes that the major changes in the structure of the standard setting process reflected a resistance to government intervention by proposing the implementation of better solutions. Several other of Steve's recent writings also relate to the historical development of accounting standards, including 'How the U.S. Accounting Profession Got Where It Is Today' (Parts I and II in *Accounting Horizons*, 2003) and 'The Evolution of U.S. GAAP: The Political Forces Behind Professional Standards' (*CPA Journal*, January and February 2005). This latter article, covering the period 1930 to 2005 and published in two successive issues, was based on notes he used to structure a lecture given to the International Symposium of Accounting Standards organized by the Chinese Ministry of Finance and held in July 2004 at the National Accounting Institute in Beijing, China.

Observations on the accounting profession

Even a cursory reading of these histories will reveal that Steve developed over time a feeling of unease concerning, as he put it, the 'very troubled state' of the U.S. accounting profession. The reader will also get the sense that the trouble, which began in the mid-1960s, gathered steam over the period 1980 to 2000. Steve attributes the decline in professionalism in part to the incentives faced by CEOs in attempting to justify their compensation by acceding 'to accounting practices arguably beyond the realm of acceptability'. The perverse incentives of the CEOs were mirrored by incentives for the audit firms to keep their clients content. (The WorldCom and Enron situations may come to mind, although Steve did not identify any specific situation. In both of these cases the auditor was Arthur Andersen & Co. Steve observes, in his paper 'Arthur Andersen & Co. and the Two-Part Opinion in the Auditor's Report 1946–1962' published in the Spring 1992 issue of *Contemporary Accounting Research*, that the firm rephrased its opinion to read 'present fairly and were prepared in conformity with GAAP' rather than to 'present fairly in conformity with GAAP'. The difference is significant and relevant to Andersen's auditing during this period.) Steve also notes the additional pressures on the audit firms related to their practice of providing consulting services to their audited firms. Many changes have occurred in the auditing world since Steve's last update. One of these changes relates to the periodic changing of auditing firms. Steve again reminds us that historically the Du Pont Company followed a policy of annual auditor changes from 1910 to 1954. (See Zeff, 2003a.)

Steve's concern about the decline in professionalism in accounting was not only reflected in his writings but also in his public commentary, and it remains a concern to this day. In a talk given at the invitation of the Texas State Board of Accountancy at the inauguration ceremony for new CPAs in 1986, Steve voiced his concerns about the accounting profession by questioning whether the CPA belonged to a profession. He later published his concerns as an article in *Accounting Horizons* (June 1987). Commenting on the talk in an interview, he said '*Nobody seemed to care that this question was being raised, which led me to believe that the leaders of the profession themselves didn't care whether they were part of a profession or not*'. (Steve Zeff interview, 15 July 2010.) Another symptom of the decline in professionalism was noted by Steve in his article, 'Big Eight Firms and the Accounting Literature: The Falloff in Advocacy Writing,' *Journal of Accounting, Auditing, and Finance*, (Spring 1986), in which he reported the decrease in articles and speeches by CPA firm partners on controversial accounting standards. Asked about his view of accounting professionalism today, Steve observed,

> *I don't think it's any different. It was very bad then. It got worse in the 90's which I think led to some of the crises at the end of the 1990's. The profession lost its way. And you already could see it in the 1980's. That was a clarion call I sent out; nobody paid any attention to it.*
>
> (Steve Zeff interview, 15 July 2010)

There are also several extensive books which Steve has edited on the development of accounting standards, including *Accounting Principles Through the Years: The Views of Professional and Academic Leaders, 1938–1954* (Garland Publishing, 1982), *The Accounting Postulates and Principles Controversy of the 1960's* (Garland Publishing, 1982), and *Financial Reporting and Global Capital Markets: A History of the International Accounting Standards Committee 1973–2000*, with K. Camfferman, (Oxford University Press, 2007). This latter piece reflects Steve's to-be-expected interest in the setting of international accounting standards, which is reflected in his writings since 1990. These papers include 'The Coming Confrontation on International Accounting Standards', (*The Irish Accounting Review*, Autumn, 1998) in which he speculates on what the SEC's reaction to the new international standards will be. The setting of international accounting standards continues in several recent papers – often combining a historic flavor and an auditing perspective – including 'Some Obstacles to Global Financial Reporting Comparability and Convergence at a High Level of Quality' (*The British Accounting Review*, December 2007); 'IFRS Developments in the USA and EU, and Some Implications for Australia' (*Australian Accounting Review*, December 2008); and 'Auditors' Affirmations of Company Compliance with IFRS and around the World: An Exploratory Study,' with C. Nobes (*Accounting Perspectives*, 7(4), 2008).

Steve has also relied on an historical prism along with a keen intellect when he elected to address unique problems facing standard setters. In Steve's words, '*My aim has been to try to understand this dynamic [of the standard-setting process] through historical research*'. Several of the issues addressed in depth include his extensively cited 1978 paper in *The Accounting Review*, 'The Rise of Economic Consequences' in which Steve advises accounting standard setters not to ignore the unintended future consequences potentially associated with a specific standard. What, Steve notes, '*is abundantly clear is that we have entered an era in which economic and social consequences may no longer be ignored as a substantive issue in the setting of accounting standards*'. This article, his most often cited paper, relating a series of interventions into the standard-setting process, was originally given as an invited lecture at Stanford University in 1978 and it has been extensively reprinted.

A later piece relates several serious attempts by influential parties affected by the standard-setting process to squash a proposed standard contrary to their own self interest (*Accounting Horizons*, March 2002). We also see Steve's concern with the intrusion of politics into the standard setting process in several other papers, including 'The Politics of Accounting Standards', *Economia Aziendale* (August, 1993) and '"Political" Lobbying on Proposed Standards: A Challenge to the IASB' (*Accounting Horizons*, March 2002).

Steve's most recent contribution to this stream of thought is 'The SEC Rules Historical Cost Accounting: 1934 to the 1970s' (*Accounting and Business Research*, 2007). In this paper, Steve focusses on the role the SEC played in not allowing firms to revalue property and plant above historical cost. This work – and several others noted below – is directly relevant today to an understanding of the fair-value reporting controversy. In addition, the research should remind us of the degree to which those who feel their particular interests are in jeopardy, whether preparers, users, regulators or auditors, will go to influence a particular standard.

> *Steve also wrote several pieces analyzing the multiple approaches to reflecting the impact of price-level changes relative to an historical-cost approach, including his initial article in the October 1962 Accounting Review. The 1962 paper was followed shortly thereafter with 'Episodes in the Progression of Price-Level Accounting in the United States', The Accountants' Magazine (April, 1964). This article provides another example of his application of a historical rendering of a current topic. Steve's more broadly based earlier historical treatise was his 'Paton on the Effects of Changing Prices on Accounting, 1916–55'.*

> > (Essays in Honor of William A. Paton: Pioneer
> > Accounting Theorist, 1979)

Steve's continuing interest in historical research has motivated him to launch a personal campaign to preserve the institutional history of accounting. In recent years he has successfully persuaded a number of accounting bodies and standard setters to have their histories recorded. The Canadian Academic Accounting Association, the Financial Accounting Standards Board, the International Federation of Accountants, and the Institute of Chartered Accountants in England and Wales have all initiated or completed institutional histories so that their historical development is preserved in our literature. Steve has contributed to these institutional histories by writing the history of the American Accounting Association (*The American Accounting Association – Its First Fifty Years*, American Accounting Association, 1966) and he is currently writing the early history of the International Accounting Standards Board. He has also persuaded the Publications Committee of the AAA to authorize 'intellectual obituaries' or memorials for recently deceased major figures in Accounting.

A quotation from a letter from Professor Michael Granof of Texas captures, we believe, the essence of Steve's scholarship:

> *Steve's greatest contribution is in making us aware that the issues with which the accounting profession grapples today did not just arise today. They invariably arose over time and any effort[s] to resolve them without placing them in their historical context are likely to be of limited value.*

Award-winning teacher and mentor

In addition to his prodigious scholarship, Steve has continued to teach throughout his career. At Tulane and Rice Universities together he has received 21 teaching-related awards. Steve's awards reflect not only his superior teaching but also his support of students outside the classroom. For example, at Rice University Steve received the Mentor Recognition Award and, for 10 consecutive years, he received the Outstanding Associate Award for his work as faculty associate at one of Rice's residential colleges. Steve's concern for students is not limited to those interested in careers in accounting. Much of his teaching at Rice has been to undergraduate and MBA students who do not intend to pursue careers in accounting. Comments from former students, which are taken from letters written between 2002 and 2004 in support of Steve's nomination for a teaching award, show Steve to be not only a rigorous and demanding teacher (his undergraduate Principles of Accounting course typically experiences a 30% dropout rate) but also a caring human being.

When asked why he has been so successful in the classroom, Steve replied: '*I think that most of the awards I've gotten are not for teaching as much as advising students, which I have done actively ever since I started teaching. I ask students to come in, I talk about what their plans are academically and in terms of career, give them advice, and write letters of recommendation for them'.* Steve describes his teaching as

> *... I'm always very well organized. I stick to my schedule. The students know from the beginning exactly what their obligations are during the semester. I return the exams the very next class period fully graded. When I give term papers I write memos to the students on the computer and send them to the students together with their paper grade so they get feedback on their papers ... I don't use PowerPoint, I don't give out notes ... I provide some of the historical background, how things came about.*
>
> (Steve Zeff interview, 15 July 2010)

A student commenting on Steve's mastery of the subject matter provides an interesting confirmation and contrast:

> *As would be expected, there was good structure around the material he wanted to convey to us, and he followed that structure until a student question or a current event in the business world took us in another direction ... He would bring in examples (some of which were 50 years old, and others that had happened the week before) that would reinforce a point ... I never saw Dr Zeff fail to have a viewpoint on an issue, and I never saw him fail to have an example supporting that viewpoint.*
>
> (Partner, Ernst & Young)

Comments from other students below provide further insights into Steve's teaching and mentoring.

> *Dr Zeff was a challenging professor who expected a lot of his students, but at the same time consistently developed personal relationships with his students and provided a truly open door policy and wise counsel on any topics a student wanted to discuss.*
>
> (Partner, Deloitte, Touche, Tohmatsu)

> *There were no "teacher's pets"; and to do well throughout a course, students had to constantly be on their toes and earn their stripes day after day.*
>
> (Chief Financial Officer, International MATEX Tank Terminals)

> *Mentoring from Dr Zeff started my sophomore year with a run-in at the accounting library that began with, "What's that you are studying?" [Intro to Accounting] "What do you want to do when you graduate?" [Law School] "Do you have good grades? Why don't you show them to me after this semester?" The following summer, I received a letter from Dr Zeff with a challenge, "Your grades are a full point below your potential, and you know it." He offered to meet weekly to discuss how to improve them. Dr Zeff and I met every Friday to discuss the commitment and whether the long-term payoff was worth the short-term sacrifices. The commitment continued and 14 weeks later, the grades came back ...*
>
> (VP, Sales and Marketing, Daimler Chrysler Motors Corporation)

> *Dr Zeff was the single greatest contributor to my intellectual and personal growth while I attended Rice ... The most important thing Dr Zeff taught me was to never compare myself to my peers. He emphasized that the real accomplishment was in maximizing your own potential and reaching your own goals and not to settle for relative success.*
>
> (Executive Vice President, Countrywide Home Loans)

. . . Dr Zeff was more effective at teaching than anyone I had at Rice. I say he was more effective for three specific reasons: First, command of the material being taught . . . Secondly, he had a passion for what he taught . . . Finally, and perhaps most importantly, was his commitment to the student.

(Partner, Ernst & Young)

I didn't take a class from Dr Zeff nor have I heard him lecture . . . I entered Rice University in 1982 on an athletic scholarship . . . Soon I began focussing more on athletics and less on academics. Before long I was academically suspended and gladly prepared to leave wondering if I would ever receive a degree. I vividly remember loading up my car and walking across the campus feeling solemn, angry, and embarrassed. By pure chance, Dr Zeff strolled by and struck up a conversation. I mentioned that I had just been suspended and was leaving. He asked me if I would make the time to have a simple conversation with him the next day. I agreed. During that conversation, Dr Zeff listened to my concerns and we exchanged ideas. We talked as friends. Immediately he made me feel like an intelligent student, and not a failure . . . At the end of this first meeting he challenged me with a question. Did you give it your all? If you did, you can walk away without a concern, but if you didn't you owe it to yourself to try again . . . Eight months later I returned to Rice still unsure if I could make it. Even though Dr Zeff had a full teaching schedule and a collection of assigned students to advise, he made time for me. Each week he gave me an hour . . . He kept me realistic, focussed, and encouraged. It worked.

(Silicon Valley Entrepreneur)

Dr Zeff taught principles in the real sense that his students learned the theory and economic reasons behind accounting practices. He held students to high academic standards, using course materials and assigning papers that demanded thought, independent research, and careful evaluation of available literature. Then his students were required to return their own observations and conclusions to him in coherent form, backed up by logic and evidence of study of the subject . . . Dr Zeff's knowledge of and interest in his students extends beyond the university experience. He keeps up with his former students, in my case almost 40 years.

(Founder, AV Communications)

Comments from his students demonstrate that Steve is an exceptionally dedicated teacher who cares deeply about the welfare of his students. In reflecting on what he tries to accomplish, Steve summarized,

I've tended to believe that we ought to prepare accounting thinkers and not just accounting doers. And that's what I've tried to dedicate my life to in some ways to help prepare accounting thinkers and to encourage people out there to think and not just do.

(Steve Zeff interview, 15 July 2010)

Steve's success in the classroom is a reminder that in this age of technology and social media, which Steve largely eschews, old-fashioned rigor is still appreciated by today's students.

Books for classroom use

In addition to being an award winning teacher, Steve also published materials for classroom use. He has co-edited six books of readings on financial accounting. The first, *Financial Accounting Theory: Issues and Controversies*, with Tom Keller, was published in 1964 by McGraw-Hill. Keller was also co-editor of *Financial Accounting Theory II: Issues and Controversies*,

(McGraw-Hill, 1969) and editions two and three of *Financial Accounting Theory: Issues and Controversies*, published in 1973 and 1985, respectively. The fourth and fifth editions, published in 1994 and 1997, were co-edited with Bala Dharan. The motivation for the first edition, as stated in the preface, was 'to stimulate critical thinking, to help develop analytical reasoning, and to inform the budding accountant that his chosen field is not serenely free of debate and disagreement' (p. v). The intended use was as a supplement to an intermediate textbook, but also as a basis for class discussion in advanced undergraduate or graduate courses. The first edition began with a general guide to the accounting literature by Steve. Each part of the book was introduced with a description of the general nature of the issues and controversies being addressed. The motivation, general format, and intended audience were maintained throughout the series although the selected articles changed, (e.g. the third edition included none of the articles from the previous two editions). The fifth edition also included an *Instructor's Manual*. The motivation to stimulate critical thinking and to broaden the perspective of accounting education that these books reflected were also manifest in Steve's views on the content of accounting courses and the CPA examination.

Accounting course content and the CPA examination

In an editorial in *The Accounting Review* (July 1979), Steve expressed his concern about the content of the traditional Intermediate Financial Accounting course, which he believed was being transformed from a mixture of theory and practice to a legalistic study of the pronouncements of authoritative accounting bodies. He questioned whether the focus on current practice in the intermediate course would adequately prepare students for long-term careers in accounting. He noted that the CPA Examination's emphasis on testing candidates' understanding of current accounting practices and pronouncements was a major factor in the trend toward a legalistic focus in the Intermediate Accounting course. Acknowledging that 'legal accounting' had a place in the accounting curriculum, he maintained that it should not be allowed to drive out instruction in theory and that theory needed to be taught early in the curriculum, not just at the end. Theory, he argued, '. . . should provide a framework within which students might endeavor to rationalize (if they can) and assess extant practice, and it should help them to be informed critics and interpreters of exposure drafts and pronouncements yet to come – and for other kinds of change' (p. 83). Asked his view of financial accounting textbooks and courses today, Steve replied,

> *It's no better and if anything it's worse because the standards are even more voluminous; they're more detailed especially when you bring in financial instruments, which are incredibly complex as is the accounting for financial instruments. So I think it's even worse than it was in the 1980s.*
>
> (Steve Zeff interview, 15 July 2010)

Consistent with his position on the importance of theory in Intermediate Accounting courses was Steve's view on the importance of recognizing in intermediate and advanced accounting courses the role that '*economic consequences*' played in the setting of accounting standards. In an editorial in *The Accounting Review* (October 1980), Steve examined several intermediate and advanced accounting textbooks and found that they were largely silent on the role that economic consequences played in the establishment of extant accounting practices. He identified possible reasons for the failure of textbooks to incorporate economic consequences and argued that the omission deprived students of an indispensable element in explaining how change in accounting practice actually occurs and why contradictory accounting practices exist. Eight years later, Steve again reviewed the extent to which intermediate accounting textbooks included economic consequences in their explanation for extant accounting practices and found that only in half of the issues examined did the explanation of economic consequences meet a minimum standard of reporting the occurrence of self-interested lobbying and the underlying motivation (*Issues in Accounting Education*, Autumn 1988, pp. 433–444). Asked if he thought that economic consequences received greater attention in financial accounting textbooks and courses today, Steve replied, '*my impression is they are no better. They may not be any worse. They couldn't be much worse than they were in the late 1980's, which I think was the last time I did that study*' (Steve Zeff interview, 15 July 2010.) To address the void in describing the role of economic consequences in standard setting, Steve has written a chapter on political lobbying on accounting standards, which has been included in recent editions of *Comparative International Accounting* by Christopher Nobes and Robert Parker.

Steve's emphasis on developing critical thinking and analytical reasoning skills in the education of accountants is reflected in his leadership as President of the American Accounting Association (AAA) in adopting two resolutions on the CPA Examination. The resolutions called for a broadening of the content of the CPA examination, retaining essay questions in the examination, and scheduling the examination outside the academic year. In discussing the resolutions, Steve emphasized the importance of expanding the scope of the examination to include subjects, such as economics, finance, and information technology. He cautioned that the exclusive reliance on objective questions on the CPA examination would result in an emphasis on rote memorization rather than the development of professional judgment in applying technical standards. Scheduling the CPA examination, with its emphasis on current practice, outside the academic year would reduce the incentive to 'teach the exam' and would not be a distraction to students completing their accounting degree work. (*Accounting Education News*, June 1986.)

Looking back, Steve reflected that the AAA's Executive Committee was successful in retaining some essay questions in the CPA examination, but not because of the resolutions passed by the committee. The AAA had no authority or lobbying influence over the CPA examination, so what Steve did was to write letters, on behalf of the AAA Executive Committee, to each of the State Boards of Accountancy and State Societies of CPAs making the case for retaining essay questions in the CPA examination. Enough state boards and societies were persuaded by the letters to voice concern about eliminating essay questions that the movement to make all CPA examination questions objective was stopped. (Steve Zeff interview, 15 July 2010.)

Conclusion

The *Centennial Issue of the Journal of Accountancy* (May 1987) featured 15 articles including the second article titled 'Leaders of the Accounting Profession: 14 Who Made a Difference' authored by Steve. He limited his selection to the members of the accounting profession who, in his opinion, 'have made especially important contributions to the betterment of the profession'. Steve further restricted eligibility to those for whom 'the preponderance of their achievements occurred before the 1970s'. The restriction was made to allow time to permit reflection on the impact of each individual's accomplishments.

Consider now the year 2030. The time would be ripe to repeat the exercise. The choice set will be much expanded and the required research to justify a similar sized group substantially more complex. Yet regardless of the task, Steve would be a strong candidate for inclusion. The selectees for the 1987 list were all directly involved in the practice of accounting and nearly three quarters of them taught accounting at the university level. Today, the connections of the leaders in both practice and university service are not nearly as close. Relatively few of the distinguished academic writers are engaged actively in the practice of accounting and vice versa. Steve emerges from the crowd as one who effectively bridges this gap. We know and honor him for his historical perspective pointing the way to improved standard-setting processes, the international perspective of his career, a commitment to his students, and for contributions to the development and understanding of current accounting issues and auditing practice. Perhaps this is what one – or even two as Steve would say – would expect of someone who clearly loves what he does.

While few would likely encourage doctoral students or young faculty to emulate Steve's research orientation or even his teaching style today, it would be a difficult, if not an impossible, task to identify an individual who has contributed more to the academy, the American Accounting Association, and to the internationalization of our profession. Equally daunting would be the search for one whose knowledge of its history surpasses that of Steve Zeff.[1]

Note

1 This tribute has drawn from the following additional sources beyond the publications noted in the body of this essay: Résumé of Stephen A. Zeff; Preface and Introduction to 'History of the First Ten Years of the International Accounting Standards Board, 2001–2011,' with Kees Camfferman (in the research stage 2010); Introduction by Stephen Zeff and Preface by Professor John R. Edwards, Cardiff University, to *Insights from Accounting History: Selected Writings of Stephen Zeff* (Routledge, 2010); Accounting Hall of Fame, Induction 2002; Dale L. Flesher, *The Third Quarter Century of the American Accounting Association 1966–1991*, The American Accounting Association, 1991; letters from former students; a personal interview with Zeff by Wil Uecker on 15 July 2010; and correspondence with Professor Dennis Beresford (University of Georgia), Michael H. Granof (University of Texas), and Stephen A. Zeff.

References

Camfferman, K. & Zeff, S.A. (1994) The Contributions of Theodore Limperg Jr (1879–1961) to Dutch Accounting and Auditing, in J. Edwards (ed.) *Twentieth-Century Accounting Thinkers*, pp. 121–141, London: Routledge.

Camfferman, K. & Zeff, S.A. (2007) *Financial Reporting and Global Capital Markets: A History of the International Accounting Standards Committee 1973–2000*, Oxford: Oxford University Press.

Edwards, J.R. (2010) *Insights from Accounting History: Selected Writings of Stephen Zeff*, London: Routledge.

Flesher, D.L. (1991) *The Third Quarter Century of the American Accounting Association 1966–1991*, Sarasota: The American Accounting Association.

Nobes, C.W. & Parker, R.H. (2008) *Comparative International Accounting*, Upper Saddle River, NJ: Prentice Hall.

Nobes, C.W. & Zeff, S.A. (2008) Auditors' affirmations of company compliance with IFRS around the world: an exploratory study, *Accounting Perspectives*, 7(4), pp. 279–292.

Uecker, W. (2010) Personal Interview with Stephen A. Zeff, 15 July 2010.

Whittington, G. & Zeff, S.A. (2001) Mathews, Gynther and Chambers: three pioneering Australian theorists, *Accounting and Business Research*, 31(3), pp. 203–233.

Zeff, S.A. (1962) Replacement cost: member of the family, welcome guest, or intruder? *The Accounting Review*, 37(4), pp. 611–625.

Zeff, S.A. & Keller, T.F. (eds) (1964a) *Financial Accounting Theory: Issues and Controversies*, New York: McGraw-Hill Book Company.

Zeff, S.A. (1964b) Episodes in the progression of price-level accounting in the United States, *The Accountants' Magazine*, 68(October), pp. 285–304.

Zeff, S.A. (1966) *The American Accounting Association – Its First Fifty Years*, Sarasota: American Accounting Association.

Zeff, S.A. & Keller, T.F. (eds) (1969) *Financial Accounting Theory II: Issues and Controversies*, New York: McGraw-Hill Book Company.

Zeff, S.A. (1972a) *Forging Accounting Principles in Five Countries: A History and an Analysis of Trends*, Champaign: Stipes Publishing Co.

Zeff, S.A. (1972b) 1926 to 1971 Chronology of significant developments in the establishment of accounting principles in the United States, *Journal of Accounting Research*, 10(1), pp. 217–227.

Zeff, S.A. (1973a) Forging Accounting Principles in Australia, Melbourne: Australian Society of Accountants.

Zeff, S.A. & Keller, T.F. (eds) (1973b) *Financial Accounting Theory I: Issues and Controversies*, second edition, New York: McGraw-Hill Book Company.

Zeff, S.A. (1978) The rise of 'economic consequences', *Journal of Accountancy*, 146(6), pp. 56–63.

Zeff, S.A. (1979a) *Forging Accounting Principles in New Zealand*, Wellington: Victoria University Press.

Zeff, S.A. (1979b) Paton on the effects of changing prices on accounting, 1916–55, in S. Zeff, J. Demski & N. Dopuch (eds) *Essays in Honor of William A. Paton: Pioneer Accounting Theorist*, Division of Research, Graduate School of Business Administration, the University of Michigan.

Zeff, S.A. (1979c) Theory and 'intermediate' accounting, Editorial, *The Accounting Review*, 54(2), pp. 592–594.

Zeff, S.A. (1980) 'Intermediate' and 'advanced' accounting: the role of 'economic consequences, Editorial, *The Accounting Review*, 55(4), pp. 658–663.

Zeff, S.A. (ed.) (1982a) *Accounting Principles Through the Years: The Views of Professional and Academic Leaders, 1938–1954*, New York: Garland Publishing.

Zeff, S.A. (ed.) (1982b) *The Accounting Postulates and Principles Controversy of the 1960s*, New York: Garland Publishing.

Zeff, S.A. (1982c) Truth in accounting: the ordeal of Kenneth MacNeal, *The Accounting Review*, 57(3), pp. 528–553.

Zeff, S.A. (1984) Some junctures in the evolution of the process of establishing accounting principles in the U.S.A.: 1917–1972, *Accounting Review*, LIX(3), pp. 131–154.

Zeff, S.A. & Keller, T.F. (eds) (1985) *Financial Accounting Theory: Issues and Controversies*, 3rd edn, New York: McGraw-Hill Book Company.

Zeff, S.A. (1986) Big eight firms and the accounting literature: the falloff in advocacy writing, *Journal of Accounting, Auditing & Finance*, 1(2), pp. 131–154.

Zeff, S.A. (1986) President's message, *Accounting Education News*, 14 (June), pp. 1–3.

Zeff, S.A. (1987a) Does the CPA belong to a profession? *Accounting Horizons*, 1(2), pp. 65–68.

Zeff, S.A. (1987b) Leaders of the accounting profession: 14 who made a difference, *Journal of Accountancy*, 163(5), pp. 46–71.

Zeff, S.A. (1988) Economic consequences in intermediate textbooks: a review after eight years, *Issues in Accounting Education*, Autumn, Vol. 3 (Fall), pp. 433–444.

Zeff, S.A. (1989a) Recent trends in accounting education and research in the USA: some implications for UK academics, *The British Accounting Review*, 21(2), pp. 159–176.

Zeff, S.A. (1989b) Does accounting belong in the University curriculum? *Issues in Accounting Education*, 4(3), pp. 203–210.

Zeff, S.A., van der Wel, F., & Camfferman, K. (1992a) *Company Financial Reporting: A Historical and Comparative Study of the Dutch Regulatory Process*, New York: North-Holland.

Zeff, S.A. (1992b) Arthur Andersen & Co. and the two-part opinion in the auditor's report: 1946–1962, *Contemporary Accounting Research*, 8(2), pp. 443–467.

Zeff, S.A. (1993) The politics of accounting standards, *Economia Aziendale*, (August), pp. 123–142.

Zeff, S.A. (1994) Limperg, *Twentieth-Century Accounting Thinkers*, New York: Routledge.

Zeff, S.A. & Dharan, B.G. (1994) *Readings and Notes on Financial Accounting: Issues and Controversies*, fourth edition, New York: McGraw-Hill Book Company.

Zeff, S.A. (1995) David Solomons (1912–1995) – an appreciation, *Accounting and Business Research*, 25(5), pp. 315–319.

Zeff, S.A. (1996) Paton, William Andrew (1889–1991), in M. Warner (ed.) *International Encyclopedia of Business and Management*, pp. 3998–4003, London: Routledge.

Zeff, S.A. & Dharan, B.G. (1997) *Readings & Notes on Financial Accounting: Issues and Controversies*, 5th edn, New York: The McGraw-Hill Companies.

Zeff, S.A. (1998) The coming confrontation on international accounting standards, *The Irish Accounting Review*, 5(2), pp. 89–117.

Zeff, S.A. (1999a) Reed Karl Storey (1926–1999), *Accounting Education News*, 27(5), p. 3.

Zeff, S.A. (1999b) Paul Kircher (1915–1999), *Accounting Education News*, 27(5).

Zeff, S.A. (2000a) *Henry Rand Hatfield: Humanist, Scholar, and Accounting Educator*, New York: JAI Press Inc./Elsevier.

Zeff, S.A. (2000b) John B. Canning: a view of his academic career, *Abacus*, 36(1), pp. 4–39.

Zeff, S.A. (2002) 'Political' lobbying on proposed standards: a challenge to the IASB, *Accounting Horizons*, 16(1), pp. 43–54.

Zeff, S.A. (2003a) Du Pont's early policy on the rotation of audit firms, *Journal of Accounting and Public Policy*, 22(1), pp. 1–18.

Zeff, S.A. (2003b) How the U.S. accounting profession got where it is today: part I, *Accounting Horizons*, 17(3), pp. 189–206.

Zeff, S.A. (2003c) How the U.S. accounting profession got where it is today: part II, *Accounting Horizons*, 17(4), pp. 267–287.

Zeff, S.A. (2005) The evolution of U.S. GAAP: the political forces behind professional standards, *The CPA Journal*, 75(1–2), pp. 18–27; 29.

Zeff, S.A. (2006) Political lobbying on accounting standards – national and international experience, in C. Nobes & R.H. Parker (eds) *Comparative International Accounting*, ninth edition, pp. 189–218, Harlow, UK: FT Prentice Hall.

Zeff, S.A. (2007a) The SEC rules historical cost accounting: 1934 to the 1970s, *Accounting and Business Research, International Accounting Policy Forum Issue*, 37(3), pp. 48–62.

Zeff, S.A. (2007b) Some obstacles to global financial reporting comparability and convergence at a high level of quality, *The British Accounting Review*, 39(4), pp. 290–302.

Zeff, S.A. (2007c) Sid Davidson (in memoriam), *Accounting Education News*, 35(4), pp. 17.

Zeff, S.A. (2008a) Robert Thomas Sprouse 1922–2007, *Accounting Education News*, 36(1), pp. 8.

Zeff, S.A. (2008b) IFRS developments in the USA and EU, and some implications for Australia, *Australian Accounting Review*, 18(4), pp. 275–282.

Zeff, S.A. (2008c) The contribution of the Harvard Business School to management control, 1908–1980, *Journal of Management Accounting Research*, 20(Special Issue), pp. 175–208.

Zeff, S.A. (2009) Maurice Moonitz, *Accounting Education News*, 37(4), pp. 23.

Zeff, S.A. & Camfferman, K. (2010) History of the first ten years of the international accounting standards board, 2001–2011, manuscript in process.

Zeff, S.A. (2010) Introduction *Insights from Accounting History: Selected Writings of Stephen Zeff*, New York: Routledge.

Author index

Note: Page numbers in **bold** type refer to **figures**. Page numbers in *italic* type refer to *tables*. Page numbers followed by 'n' refer to notes

Subject index

Note: Page numbers in **bold** type refer to **figures**. Page numbers in *italic* type refer to *tables*. Page numbers followed by 'n' refer to notes